APPEALS FROM ARBITRATION AWARDS

LLOYD'S COMMERCIAL LAW LIBRARY

Interests in Goods
by Norman Palmer and
Ewan McKendrick
(1993)

The Law of Insurance Contracts
second edition
by Malcolm A. Clarke
(1994)

EC Banking Law
second edition
by Marc Dassesse, Stuart Isaacs QC
and Graham Penn
(1994)

Appeals from Arbitration Awards
by D. Rhidian Thomas
(1994)

THE LAW AND PRACTICE RELATING TO

APPEALS FROM ARBITRATION AWARDS

A THEMATIC ANALYSIS OF THE ARBITRATION ACT 1979

BY

D. RHIDIAN THOMAS

M.A., LL.B., A.C.I. Arb.

Professor of Law at the University of East Anglia

|L|L|P|

LONDON   NEW YORK   HAMBURG   HONG KONG
LLOYD'S OF LONDON PRESS LTD
1994

Lloyd's of London Press Ltd.
Legal Publishing Division
27 Swinton Street
London WC1X 9NW

USA AND CANADA
Lloyd's of London Pres Inc.
Suite 308, 611 Broadway
New York NY 10012 USA

GERMANY
Lloyd's of London Press GmbH
59 Ehrenbergstrasse
2000 Hamburg 50, Germany

SOUTH EAST ASIA
Lloyd's of London Press (Far East) Ltd.
Room 1101, Hollywood Centre
233 Hollywood Road
Hong Kong

©

D. Rhidian Thomas
1994

First published in Great Britain, 1994

British Library Cataloguing in Publication Data
A catalogue record for this book is
available from the British Library

ISBN 1–85044–505–2

Text set in 10/12 pt Linotron 202 Times by
Interactive Sciences, Gloucester
Printed in Great Britain by
Hartnolls Ltd, Bodmin, Cornwall

Cyflwynir y llyfr hwn
er cof am fy nhad
y
Parchedig R. O. Thomas

PREFACE

Hopefully it will be generally agreed that sufficient time has passed by to justify a reflective analysis of the Arbitration Act 1979. The 1979 Act has come to occupy a dominant position in the contemporary law and practice of arbitration, not simply because of its precise area of concern, but, more widely, because of its impact on the entire jurisprudential landscape of arbitration. Looked at narrowly the 1979 Act realigns the relationship between the courts and the arbitral process with regard to questions of law, and most significantly introduces a new and constrained appellate procedure in relation to questions of law arising out of arbitral awards. But the significance of the 1979 Act has travelled substantially beyond its domestic boundaries and it may be doubted whether any aspect of the total relationship between the courts and arbitration is wholly free of its ubiquitous influence, constantly nudging the jurisprudence of arbitration law to the greater acceptance of the finality of arbitral awards and the autonomy of the arbitral process. Although the 1979 Act was alchemised to cure a localised ailment, the cup in which it was served has been drunk of deeply and the medicine has revealed itself to possess wider curative properties.

A primary purpose of the text is to expound and analyse the precise provisions of the 1979 Act. The focus is on the new appellate link in relation to questions of law that the Act establishes, together with the associated incidents of the linkage, namely, reasoned awards, exclusion agreements and the determination of preliminary questions of law. But even in this regard the task is not perceived wholly in terms of narrative and statutory interpretation. As the sub-title to the text proclaims, the endeavour is made to pursue a thematic approach to the subject, with the components of the new legislation scrutinised not in isolation, but in the context of historical themes with which they may be associated. The solutions which the 1979 Act provides may be new, but the issues which the Act addresses are far from new. To differing degrees each has its place in the historical evolution of the modern law of arbitration. Each has its rich vein of intellectual debate, public policy issues and unresolved questions. The dynamism of arbitration law has not been arrested by the 1979 Act. To the contrary, the Act is merely an aspect of a constantly unfolding jurisprudence and the text attempts to respond to this reality by examining the provisions of the legislation in terms of dynamical issues with a life and interest beyond the confines of the 1979 Act.

There can be no doubting that the Arbitration Act 1979 stands as a significant milestone in the history of English arbitration law. It may nonetheless be doubted whether those who participated in and influenced the debates out of which the legislation emerged fully appreciated the significance which the advocated reforms were to have. This is not surprising, for on the available evidence it is doubtful whether the more signal and wider effects of the new legislation were strategically planned in advance. Rather it would seem that the new legislation offered an opportunity to place a hand on the tiller and redirect the course of the law, and this opportunity the judiciary, after early indecision, grasped decisively. The irony of the situation may not be lost on posterity, and history may well record, rightly, that the impact of the 1979 Act owes more to judicial interpretation and the judicial willingness to carry the policy associated with the legislation to the wider reaches of arbitration law than to any other influence. But whatever the precise derivative forces, the fare served up has proved digestible, both nationally and internationally. The model of the 1979 legislation has been followed in many foreign jurisdictions within the common law tradition and the philosophy of the legislation has permeated more broadly and contributed to contemporary perceptions of international public policy.

I am deeply indebted to The Hon. Mr Justice Colman for consenting to the adoption of precedents which appear in his acclaimed monograph *The Practice and Procedure of the Commercial Court*. Mr David Bird of the Admiralty and Commercial Court Registry generously agreed to scrutinise parts of the text concerned with practice and procedure. His assistance proved invaluable and was greatly appreciated. The errors and shortcomings which may remain are, of course, wholly my own responsibility. A very substantial debt of gratitude is also owed to the publishers who have throughout shown limitless patience and a consummate dexterity in bringing order to an unwieldy manuscript.

The text makes every effort to state the law as on 31 January 1994.

School of Law   D. RHIDIAN THOMAS
Earlham Hall
University of East Anglia

CONTENTS

CONTENTS

CONTENTS

12 DETERMINATION OF PRELIMINARY POINTS OF LAW BY THE HIGH COURT AND ON-APPEALS THEREFROM

13 EXCLUSION AGREEMENTS

TABLE OF CASES

All references are to paragraph numbers or appendices

TABLE OF LEGISLATION AND INTERNATIONAL CONVENTIONS, ETC.

All references are to paragraph numbers or appendices
References in bold type indicate where the provision is reproduced in full

PART I

THE ARBITRATION ACT 1979 IN THE GENERAL SCHEME OF THINGS

CHAPTER 1

THE EMERGENCE AND IMPACT OF THE ARBITRATION ACT 1979

1.1 INTRODUCTION

1.1.1 The modern law of arbitration functions within the context of the total legal corpus.[1] To understand the concept and dynamic of arbitration it is necessary to adopt a broad perspective and to embrace many established institutions of law, such as legislation, contract, *vires* and natural justice. Equally when addressing the question of the delicate balance between the arbitral process and the courts it is necessary not only to be aware of the specific supervisory powers conferred on the courts by the arbitration legislation but also the more general jurisdiction to give injunctive and declaratory relief. To the forefront of the myriad legal components which make up what may be described as arbitration law there exists the arbitration statutes, principally the Arbitration Acts 1950, 1975, 1979, supplemented by a miscellany of other statutory provisions.[2] No great claim can be made for the comprehensiveness and coherence of this body of statutory arbitration law.[3] Deriving from the Arbitration Act 1698 it has evolved pragmatically and without theoretical design, concerned primarily with reactive cures and questions of functional efficacy.[4] In general terms the broad effect of the arbitration legislation is to give recognition to the legal validity of arbitration agreements and to the arbitral process; to facilitate and aid the arbitral process and the enforcement of arbitration awards; to subject arbitrators, the arbitral process and awards to judicial supervision and review; and to give effect to the international obligations of the United Kingdom government assumed in relation to the international arbitral process.[5]

1.1.2 The Arbitration Act 1979 (hereafter the 1979 Act) contributes to the jurisdiction vested in the courts to review awards and to a lesser extent to assist the arbitral process. The judicial reviewing powers over awards in their generality are founded on considerations of substantive validity, jurisdiction, procedure, public policy and the application of prevailing law. The latter in particular emphasises the position of arbi-

---

1. See generally Mustill and Boyd, *Commercial Arbitration* (2nd edn.); *Russell on Arbitration* (20th edn.), ed. Walton and Vitoria; Merkin, *Arbitration Law*; Redfern and Hunter, *International Commercial Arbitration* (2nd edn.).
2. The legislation is set out in Appendices D to F.
3. See Mustill, "Transnational Arbitration in English Law" in *International Commercial and Maritime Arbitration*, ed. Rose, p. 18, where the statutory arbitration law is described as "incoherent and fragmentary".
4. *Ibid.*, p. 16.
5. See generally Kerr, "The English Courts and Arbitration" in *International Commercial Arbitration* (vol. 1), ed. Schmitthoff.

tration as a fragment of the administration of civil justice[6] and the obligation of arbitrators to apply themselves to the resolution of disputes within legal terms of reference.[7] An arbitrator is obliged to adopt and apply the settled principles of prevailing law and an arbitrator who goes wrong in law has long been at risk of seeing his award become the subject of judicial review.[8] At common law the reviewing jurisdiction arose whenever an error of law could be shown on the face of an award.[9] By statute there was introduced a special case procedure whereby a question of law arising out of an award might be stated for the opinion of the court.[10] Both these processes are repealed by the 1979 Act and replaced by an orthodox but limited appeal procedure from reasoned awards based on party consent or with leave of the High Court.[11] Under the former law the special case procedure was also adopted so as to assist the arbitral process by rendering it possible for a question of law arising in the course of a reference to be put before a judge of the High Court for his opinion.[12] The so-called consultative case is perpetuated by the 1979 Act but with procedural changes.[13]

1.1.3 The real significance of the 1979 Act is not solely the fact that it restructures and rationalises the advisory and appellate links between arbitrators and arbitration awards and the courts with regard to questions of law but further the way it has expressly and indirectly redefined these relationships and in so doing has significantly moved the jurisprudence of the subject towards the acceptance of greater finality of arbitral decision-making in relation to questions of law.[14] It achieves this shift expressly by rendering valid exclusion agreements by virtue of which the risk of applications to the courts and appeals from awards on questions of law may be excluded.[15] This without more represents a major change in public policy.[16] Less directly the shift has been made possible by rendering appeals without consent subject to the giving of leave by the High Court. This in turn provided a platform for the guiding hand of judicial discretion which the judiciary readily grasped as providing the opportunity to direct the law towards the greater recognition of the finality of arbitration awards.[17] In the result, following the 1979 Act the appealability of an award for error of law is a much reduced prospect.[18] The same jurisprudential redirectioning is witnessed in the

6. See generally Mann, "Private Arbitration and Public Policy" (1985) 4 C.J.Q. 257; *Czarnikow* v. *Roth, Schmidt & Co.* [1922] 2 K.B. 478 (C.A.).
7. This principle and its precise force in the contemporary law is considered *infra*, para. 1.2.2.2.
8. See generally Thomas, "Commercial Arbitration—Justice According to Law" (1983) 2 C.J.Q. 166.
9. Considered *infra*, para. 1.4.
10. *Ibid.*
11. Section 1. The new appeal process is elaborated in Part II of the text.
12. Considered *infra*, para. 1.4.2.
13. Section 2. The new consultative case procedure is elaborated in Chapter 12.
14. *Bank Mellat* v. *Helleniki Techniki S.A.* [1984] Q.B. 291, 301, per Kerr L.J., "our courts exercise a measure of control over the awards of arbitrators on questions of law, although this aspect has been deliberately and significantly curtailed by the Arbitration Act 1979".
15. See Chapter 13. Also Mustill, "Transnational Arbitration in English Law", pp. 15–35, 17, in *International Commercial and Maritime Arbitration*, ed. Rose; Staughton, "Arbitration Act 1979—A Pragmatic Compromise" [1979] N.L.J. 920.
16. Cf. Mann, "Private Arbitration and Public Policy" (1985) 4 C.J.Q. 257. See also *infra*, para 1.5.
17. See Part II of the text. Also *Home and Overseas Insurance Co. Ltd.* v. *Mentor Insurance Co. (U.K.) Ltd.* [1989] 1 Lloyd's Rep. 473, 479, per Hirst J.
18. See Part II of the text. See also Schmitthoff, "Commercial Arbitration and the Commercial Court" in *Commercial Law in a Changing Economic Climate* (2nd edn.).

reformulated consultative case procedure although here the drift is towards the greater recognition of the finality of the choice of forum.[19]

1.1.4 The interrelationship between arbitral autonomy and judicial review of the arbitral process is a question and issue that has been present throughout the modern phase of arbitration law.[20] The historical characterisation of English arbitration law is one of growing judicial interventionism, and this also came, not without justification, to be the foreign perception of London arbitration.[21] The English position compared sharply with many foreign systems of arbitration law where the judicial role was more reserved and with greater emphasis given to arbitral autonomy.[22] English law subscribed to the maxim "arbitration for better or worse"[23] but it proved to be a maxim more revered in the breach than the adherence.[24] In addressing the debate there probably exists broad agreement that the issue is truly one of balancing the competing considerations rather than choosing between them.[25] To concede to arbitration an absolute autonomy is to contemplate the unthinkable.[26] To render arbitration wholly and without restriction subject to judicial review is to undermine the logic of arbitration as an alternative or extra-judicial dispute-resolving mechanism aimed at achieving the speedy and final resolution of disputes. But where precisely the balance is to be struck between arbitral autonomy on the one hand and judicial review on the other is an issue capable of provoking legitimate debate and firm differences of opinion.[27] It is an issue on which national laws may and do differ[28] and in relation to which international initiatives such as the UNCITRAL Model Law attempt to promote international uniformity.[29]

1.1.5 The historic and traditional posture of English law has been to lean towards the accommodation of judicial intervention. The significance of the Arbitration Act 1979 is that it represents a reassessment of established orthodoxy and relocates the fulcrum so as to tilt the balance substantially in favour of the finality of awards and the autonomy of the arbitral process.[30] The finality of awards with regard to questions of fact has long been firmly established.[31] The 1979 Act is far from making the arbitration tribunal also the final voice on questions of law, but it does materially reduce

---

19. See Chapter 12.
20. See Diplock, "The Case Stated—its Use and Abuse" (1978) 44 *Arbitration* 107.
21. See Hacking, "A new competition—Rivals for centres of arbitration" [1979] L.M.C.L.Q. 435.
22. Cf. Kerr, "Arbitration and the Courts—The UNCITRAL Model Law (1984) 50 *Arbitration* 4; (1985) 34 I.C.L.Q. 1.
23. *Phillips* v. *Evans* (1843) 12 M. & W. 309, per Baron Alderson; *In re Montgomery Jones & Co. and Liebenthal* (1898) 78 L.T. 406, 408, per Smith L.J.; *In re Keighley Maxted & Co. and Bryan Durant & Co.* [1893] 1 Q.B. 405, 409, 410, per Lord Esher M.R. *African & Eastern (Malaya) Ltd.* v. *White, Palmer & Co. Ltd.* (1930) 36 Ll.L.Rep. 113, 114, per Scrutton L.J.
24. Cf. *Hutchinson* v. *Shepperton* (1849) 13 Q.B. 955, 958, per Lord Denman C.J.
25. See Kerr, "Arbitration and the Courts—The UNCITRAL Model Law" (1984) 50 *Arbitration* 4; (1985) 34 I.C.L.Q. 1.
26. Cf. *The Derby* [1985] 2 Lloyd's Rep. 325, 333, per Kerr L.J. Also Kerr, "Arbitration and the Courts—The UNCITRAL Model Law", *ibid.*, where the writer perceives judicial review to be a "bulwark against corruption, arbitrariness, bias, improper conduct and—where necessary—sheer incompetence".
27. See Park, "The Lex Loci Arbitri and International Commercial Arbitration" (1983) 32 I.C.L.Q. 21.
28. See Staughton, "Arbitration Act 1979—A Pragmatic Compromise" [1979] N.L.J. 920.
29. See Kerr, "Arbitration and the Courts—The UNCITRAL Model Law" (1984) 50 *Arbitration* 4; (1985) 34 I.C.L.Q. 1.
30. See *infra*, para. 1.5.
31. See *infra* para. 1.2.2.1.

the opportunities open to the parties to appeal an award on the basis of an alleged error of law or to raise for the opinion of the court a question of law arising in the course of a reference.[32] To the extent that the strategy of the 1979 Act is to nudge English jurisprudence towards accepting a more autonomous arbitral process, but at the same time retaining much of the historical ethos, albeit in a diluted form and embraced by new processes, it has rightly resulted in the new legislation being characterised as a compromise.[33] Of course the new strategy has its potential costs in terms of disputed and inconsistent arbitral decision-making, but these are costs which the parties are now taken to have voluntarily assumed.[34]

1.1.6 In its express terms the 1979 Act is confined to questions of law arising in the course of a reference or out of an award, but the impact of the legislation is much wider. The new policy associated with the 1979 Act has permeated into the wider jurisprudence of arbitration law and in consequence it is unlikely that any aspect of the interrelationship between arbitration and the courts will be untouched by its influence.[35] It is the combination of its particular provisions and its wider influence on the development of English arbitration law that renders the 1979 Act such an important milestone.[36]

1.1.7 At first glance the 1979 Act comes forth as a relatively straightforward statutory measure. A closer and more considered scrutiny readily reveals the beguiling deceptiveness of this first impression, for behind the ostensible simple façade is concealed myriad complexities and intricacies. The 1979 Act is yet another statute that gives force to the far from novel adage that "there is more learning required to explain a law made, than went to the making of it". The purpose of this text is to attempt a comprehensive statement of the place of the 1979 Act in the historical evolution of English arbitration law and to develop an elaboration of the substance and technicality of the statute.

1.2 SYNOPSIS OF THE PRINCIPAL FEATURES OF THE 1979 ACT

The 1979 Act introduces into the contemporary law much which is new and even radical. But it also gives a renewed emphasis to much which is established and long familiar. In identifying and summarising the principal features of the 1979 Act a broad division may be drawn between those features that derive directly or indirectly from the express language of the statute and those features of the established law that are implicitly endorsed or highlighted by the statute.

---

32. See *infra*, para. 1.2. Also Part II of the text and Chapter 12.
33. See, Staughton, "Arbitration Act 1979—A Pragmatic Compromise" [1979] N.L.J. 920; Kerr, "The Arbitration Act 1979" (1980) 43 M.L.R. 45; Kerr, "Commercial Dispute Resolution," pp.111–130, in *Liber Amicorum for Lord Wilberforce*, ed. Bos and Brownlie.
34. Cf. *The Chrysalis* [1983] 1 Lloyd's Rep. 503, 508, per Mustill J.
35. See *infra*, para. 1.6.
36. See Mann, "Private Arbitration and Public Policy" (1985) 4 C.J.Q. 257, 259, "the Act of 1979, by abandoning much that was believed to be required by public policy, has radically changed the subjection of arbitration to control by the State, perhaps more radically than the text of the law seems to suggest". See also *Bremer Vulkan Schiffbau und Maschinenfabrik* v. *South India Shipping Corpn. Ltd.* [1981] A.C. 909, 996, 997, per Lord Scarman.

1.2.1 The salient express features of the 1979 Act

1.2.1.1 The judicial review of awards with regard to questions of law restructured[1]

1.2.1.1.1 The first principal feature of the 1979 Act is that it establishes a wholly new process for the judicial review of awards with regard to questions of law. Under the former law an alleged error of law in an award could be brought forward for review by the court in one of two distinct ways: at common law for error of law on the face of the award and by statute under what became commonly referred to as the special case procedure. Each of these procedures is given further consideration later in this chapter,[2] albeit that their practical significance is now spent, for some familiarity with the pre-1979 legal regime continues to be necessary for an informed appreciation of the emergence of the 1979 Act and of the unfolding judicial response to its proper interpretation. By section 1 of the 1979 Act both these review procedures are abrogated,[3] except for transitional purposes,[4] and replaced by a unitary appeal procedure based on reasoned awards and the constraint of judicial discretion.

1.2.1.1.2 The statutory basis of the new appeal procedure is set out in section 1(2), (3), (4) and (8). Appeals are confined to questions of law[5] and the appeal procedure is not available to arbitrating parties as of right. An appeal may only be brought with leave of the High Court except where *all* the parties to the reference consent to the bringing of an appeal.[6] The determination of an application for leave to appeal falls to be decided in the discretion of the High Court. Herein lies the critical factor, for in the exercise of the discretion conferred by the statute the court has the power to control the flow of appeals coming before the court and thereby define and superintend the quantitive and qualitative balance between arbitration and the courts on questions of law. On the face of the 1979 Act the discretion is unfettered but the courts have divined the policy of the 1979 Act to be supportive of the greater finality of awards in matters of law and have fashioned the exercise of the discretion accordingly.[7] But leave to appeal may not be granted unless the question of law in issue is regarded as one that could in the circumstances of the case substantially affect the rights of one or more of the parties to the arbitration agreement,[8] and in granting leave the court may attach any conditions it considers appropriate.[9]

1.2.1.1.3 From the foregoing commentary it will be clear that the new appeal procedure has two distinct stages, which are equally distinct in the practice developed about section 1(2) appeals. The first is the application for leave to appeal[10] and the second the substantive appeal.[11] It is necessarily the case that the second stage of the process only comes into operation if the initial judicial discretion is exercised in favour of granting leave to appeal. If leave is refused the matter comes to a close, subject to a

---

1. See Part II of the text for a detailed consideration of this topic.
2. *Infra*, para. 1.4.
3. Section 1(1).
4. *Infra*, para. 1.7.1.
5. Section 1(2). See further Chapter 3, para. 3.2.
6. Section 1(3). See further Chapter 4.
7. See *infra*, para. 1.5. Also Chapters 5 and 6.
8. Section 1(4). See also Chapter 4, para. 4.3.3.
9. Section 1(4). See also Chapter 4, para. 4.3.4.
10. See Chapter 7.
11. See Chapter 9.

very limited right of appeal,[12] and the award is final as to the question of law in issue. Whereas the first stage is summary in nature, the second follows the orthodox appeal procedure, with full legal argument in open court.

To institute and advance an appeal an arbitrating party must be able to allege and establish an error of law in the award itself, and this in turn necessarily requires not only a formal award but also a documentary statement of the reasons of the arbitrator. Without such an overt documentary record there is nothing to scrutinise and it is consequently impossible to expose any error of law. In the result the new system of judicial review is based on the concept of appeals from reasoned awards and in support thereof subsections (5) and (6) of section 1 of the 1979 Act set out ancillary powers whereby the making of adequately reasoned awards may be ordered. These powers are outlined in the following section of the text.

1.2.1.1.4 In determining an appeal the court may confirm, vary or set aside the award in question.[13] Alternatively the court may remit the award to the arbitrator so that it may be reconsidered in the light of the court's opinion on the question of law raised on appeal.[14] When the court chooses to vary the award on appeal the award as varied takes effect as if it were the award of the arbitrator.[15] When the award is remitted the arbitrator must, unless the order otherwise directs, make his award within three months after the date of the order.[16]

1.2.1.2 *Reasoned awards*

1.2.1.2.1 The new appeal procedure introduced by section 1 of the 1979 Act is implicitly based on appeals from reasoned awards. The necessity for reasons to render possible the review of an award and the revelation of legal error has already been commented upon.[1] As a natural and necessary adjunct to the new appeal procedure the 1979 Act also establishes a new discretionary judicial power to direct an arbitrator to give reasons where none have been made or to give further reasons where reasons have been given but are shown to be insufficient or inadequate. The jurisdiction is exercisable only on the instigation of a party to the reference. The court cannot intervene and make an order of its own volition.

The statutory jurisdiction is set out in section 1(5) and (6).[2] Again the legislation does not establish an entitlement to an order for reasons once the absence, insufficiency or inadequacy of reasons is established. The making of an order under section 1(5) is subject to the discretion of the court, and where the complaint is the total absence of reasons the jurisdiction of the court is preconditioned by the criteria specified in section 1(6). The court must be satisfied that before the award was made one of the parties to the reference gave notice to the arbitrator or umpire concerned that a reasoned award was required or otherwise that there exists some special reason why such a notice was not given.[2a]

---

12. Section 1(6A), considered in Chapter 10.
13. Section 1(2). For a full discussion of the appeal powers, see Chapter 8.
14. *Ibid*.
15. Section 1(8).
16. Section 1(2).
1. *Supra*, para. 1.2.1.1.3.
2. See Chapter 11 for a detailed examination of reasoned awards under the Act.
2a. See Chapter 11, para, 11.7.3.

Except where all the parties to the reference consent to an application, an application for an order for reasons or further reasons may only be made with leave of the court.[3] There is under section 1(5) a two staged procedure similar to that applicable to appeals from awards: the application for leave to apply and the substantive application. But in contrast to the appeal process, the practice developed about section 1(5) has resulted in the total merger of the two stages.[4]

1.2.1.2.2 An application for an order for reasons or further reasons will in its nature frequently represent the first step taken by a party to the reference who is contemplating an appeal from the award on a question of law. In practice an order for further reasons may also be sought concurrently with an application for leave to appeal under section 1(3). Where the court grants an application for reasons the court's jurisdiction is restricted to an order directing the arbitrator or umpire concerned to state the reasons for his award in sufficient detail to enable the court, should an appeal be brought under section 1(2), to consider any question of law arising out of the award.[5] Where an application is refused this will in the great majority of cases baulk or render exceptionally difficult any attempt to raise an appeal. This will certainly be the case when the grievance concerns the total absence of reasons and will often be the case when the grievance is directed to the insufficiency of reasons. But the making of an order for reasons or further reasons does not of itself secure the institution of an appeal. The court retains its discretion under section 1(3): notwithstanding that the court is prepared to make an order for reasons under section 1(5) it may nonetheless validly refuse leave to appeal under section 1(3).[6] Further, the revealed reasons may serve only to endorse the correctness in law of the arbitrator's decision or the question of law to be one in relation to which the court is unlikely to grant leave to appeal and so cause the party to cease to contemplate the viability of the appeal.

1.2.1.2.3 Beyond the above outline the 1979 Act does not establish a general statutory obligation to make a reasoned award.[7] Under the English common law an unreasoned award is perfectly valid, for reasons have never been perceived as a necessary prerequisite to the substantive validity of an award. This represents a point of contrast between the English and many foreign systems of law where only "speaking" or "motivated" awards are valid. The 1979 Act does not impinge on the general common law, nor does it detract from the right of parties to regulate the issue of reasons by express provision in their arbitration agreements. It does, however, materially change the prevailing psychology to one that encourages the giving of reasons. This is achieved in an indirect manner by the abolition of the jurisdiction under the common law to review awards for error of law on the face of the award[8] and by the establishment of the new power under section 1(5) to direct the giving of reasons or further reasons. The terms of section 1(6) may also suggest that there exists a quasi-statutory duty to give reasons when at least one of the parties to the reference requests before the award is made that reasons be given.[9]

---

3. Section 1(5).
4. See Chapter 11, para. 11.12.2.1.
5. Section 1(5).
6. See Chapter 6, para. 6.2.4.
7. See Chapter 11, para. 11.4.1.
8. *Infra*, para. 1.4.1.
9. See Chapter 11, para. 11.7.3.1.8.

The cumulative effect of the 1979 Act is widely perceived as changing the direction of English arbitration law in relation to arbitral reasons and to effect a turning of the tide in favour of the making of reasoned awards. But the new environment continues to be servile to the sovereignty of the parties who continue to be entitled to contract for unreasoned awards if that is their wish.[10]

1.2.1.3 *Consultative case*

1.2.1.3.1 Alongside the appeal procedure established under section 1, which relates to questions of law arising out of awards, there is established by section 2 of the 1979 Act an associated procedure whereunder a disputed question of law arising in the course of a reference, and therefore prior to the making of an award, may be brought forward for determination by the High Court. This is the consultative case procedure which has long been present in English law[1] and which may be considered a natural adjunct to the arbitrator's duty to decide disputes and differences according to the settled principles of law.[2] The opinion of the court is expressed in the manner of a declaratory judgment and the utility of the procedure is that it enables disputed questions of law to be resolved at an early stage in the arbitral process, so permitting the subsequent stages to move with speedy certainty and increasing the likelihood that the ultimate award will enjoy the advantage of finality.

1.2.1.3.2 An application under section 2 for a consultative case may be brought by any of the parties to the reference with the consent of the arbitrator or umpire who has entered on the reference or with the consent of all the other parties.[3] In the absence of such an application the High Court has no jurisdiction to intervene on its own initiative and direct the institution of a consultative case. But even when either of the requisite consents is present there does not exist a right to a judicial determination of the question in law in issue. The court has a discretion whether or not to entertain the application and this discretion survives even when the application is made with the consent of all the other parties to the reference.[4] There is again witnessed in section 2 two levels of judicial involvement: the initial decision whether or not to entertain the application; and in the event of the discretion being exercised in favour of permitting the application to proceed, the substantive determination of the question of law in issue. But in sharp contrast to appeals under section 1 of the 1979 Act, the two stages indicated on the face of section 2 have become fused and consequently in practice the procedure under section 2 assumes the form of a single application.[5]

1.2.1.3.3 There is one significant constraint on the jurisdiction of the High Court under section 2. Where an application is made with the consent only of the arbitrator or umpire who has entered on the reference, the High Court has no jurisdiction to entertain the application unless it is satisfied that the determination of the application might produce substantial savings in costs to the parties and the question of law is one in respect

---

10. See Chapter 11, para. 11.8.1.9.
1. See Chapter 12 for a detailed examination of the consultative case procedure.
2. See *infra*, para. 1.2.2.2.
3. Section 2(1).
4. See Chapter 12, para. 12.6.1.
5. See Chapter 12, para. 12.10.4.

of which leave to appeal would be likely to be given under section 1(3)(b) of the 1979 Act.[6]

1.2.1.4 *Greater arbitral autonomy with regard to questions of law and related matters*

Beyond realigning the structural relationship between arbitration and the courts with regard to questions of law, the 1979 Act also moves the law significantly towards the greater acceptance of the finality of awards and the choice of arbitral fora in matters of law. This development is not expressed on the face of the statute but it is a product of the perceived legislative policy underlying the 1979 Act and it has exerted a critical influence on the interpretation of the statute.[1] In particular it has had a profound impact on the judicial attitude towards the discretionary powers conferred by the legislation, especially the discretionary power to give or refuse leave to appeal with regard to a question of law arising out of an award under section 1(3)(b).[2]

The impact of this policy is that appeals and applications relating to questions of law and reasoned awards under the 1979 Act will be closely scrutinised and only entertained when it can be established that there exists good and compelling reason to detract from the finality of the award or to impinge on the choice of arbitral forum. In relative terms it is clear that appeals will be permitted less frequently than was the case with regard to non-appellate review under the pre-1979 Act legal regime and that other applications will be responded to with judicious disinclination. In enlarging arbitral autonomy the Act has taken a significant step towards establishing the arbitrator or umpire as the final adjudicator not only of fact but also of law, and in so doing has correspondingly diminished the reviewing jurisdiction of the courts. But it remains the case that no true parallel can be drawn between fact and law. In matters of law a reviewing jurisdiction continues to exist and is expressly preserved by the 1979 Act, albeit in reduced terms. The significance of the new legislation is that it has rendered this reviewing jurisdiction exceptional.

The whole issue of the policy underlying the 1979 Act and its impact on appeals and applications under the Act is considered in greater detail later in this chapter[3] and elsewhere in the text.[4]

1.2.1.5 *Exclusion agreements*

1.2.1.5.1 The most radical express feature of the 1979 Act is provided by sections 3 and 4 which have the effect, subject to the terms of the statutory provisions, of validating exclusion agreements affecting all or any of the rights of application arising under sections 1 and 2.[1] The validification applies only to consensual arbitration and does not extend to statutory arbitration.[2] Under an exclusion agreement the parties

---

6. Section 2(2).

1. See *infra*, para. 1.5. See also *Everglade Maritime Inc.* v. *Schiffahrtsgesellschaft Detlef von Appen m.b.H.* (*The Maria*) [1993] 2 Lloyd's Rep. 167, 173, Sir Thomas Bingham M.R.

2. See Chapters 5 and 6 where the criteria governing the exercise of the discretion to give or refuse leave to appeal under s. 1(3)(b) are considered.

3. *Infra*, para 1.5.

4. See Chapters 5, 6, 11, 12.

1. For a detailed discussion of exclusion agreements see Chapter 13.

2. Section 3(5).

may by contract exclude the right to apply for leave to appeal with respect to a question of law arising out of an award under section 1(2) and (3); and the right to seek leave to apply for an order for reasons or further reasons under section 1(5) and (6); and/or the right to apply that the court determine a preliminary question of law arising in the course of a reference under section 2.[3] An exclusion agreement has the effect of severing the relationship established by the 1979 Act between arbitration and the courts on questions of law and the related issue of reasoned awards, with the ultimate effect that the arbitral process is ascribed an absolute autonomy and with the arbitrator becoming the final voice on questions of law as well as fact. Exclusion agreements represent the ultimate step in the movement towards the finality of awards and the autonomy of the arbitral process discernible in the Act as a whole and commented upon in the preceding section. The power to enter into an exclusion agreement is however variously and materially constrained and this fact again reveals the compromise which the 1979 Act is seen to represent.[4]

1.2.1.5.2 An exclusion agreement must be in writing[5] and whether an agreement which the parties to a reference have entered into amounts to an exclusion agreement within the meaning of the 1979 Act will in each case be a question of construction.[6] As also will be the answer to any question addressed to the precise scope of any valid exclusion agreement.[7] An exclusion agreement applicable to an award made on a reference under a non-domestic arbitration agreement and raising a dispute whether a party has been guilty of fraud extends, unless the exclusion agreement provides otherwise, to exclude the jurisdiction of the High Court under section 24(2) of the Arbitration Act 1950, whereby the court may remove the dispute from arbitration and determine the issue itself.[8] But otherwise an exclusion agreement cannot have any wider impact than to affect all or any of the qualified rights arising under sections 1 and 2. The reviewing powers of the courts that arise under other statutory provisions or the common law are not and cannot be affected by an exclusion agreement.[9]

1.2.1.5.3 To the general recognition which the 1979 Act gives to the validity of exclusion agreements there exist two significant qualifications. First, where an award is made on or a question of law arising in the course of a reference arises under a domestic arbitration agreement, an exclusion agreement is of no effect unless entered into after the commencement of the arbitration in which the award is made or the question of law arises.[10] The concept of a domestic arbitration agreement is defined by section 3(7). Secondly, where an award or question of law arising in the course of a reference relates, in whole or in part, to a special category dispute, which in general terms relates to claims and questions within the Admiralty jurisdiction and disputes arising under insurance and commodity contracts,[11] an exclusion agreement is of no effect

---

3. Section 3(1).
4. Cf. Staughton, "Arbitration Act 1979—A pragmatic compromise" [1979] N.L.J. 920.
5. Section 3(1).
6. Cf. section 3(4).
7. Section 3(2).
8. Section 3(3). Commented upon in Thomas, "The Judicial Supervision of Arbitral References Involving an Allegation of Fraud" (1990) 9 C.J.Q. 381, 398.
9. Cf. *Czarnikow* v. *Roth, Schmidt & Co.* [1922] 2 K.B. 478 (C.A.).
10. Section 3(6).
11. Section 4(1) and (2).

unless either (i) the exclusion agreement is entered into after the commencement of the arbitration in which the award is made or in which the question of law arises, or (ii) the award or question of law relates to a contract which is expressly governed by a system of law other than the law of England and Wales.[12]

1.2.1.5.4 An exclusion agreement is valid in all instances when it is entered into after the commencement of the arbitration in which the award is made or the question of law arises. For the purposes of the Act the question as to when an arbitration is deemed to commence is governed by the Arbitration Act 1950, section 29(2) and (3).[12a] It is only with regard to pre-commencement exclusion agreements that the legislation imposes additional protective criteria but these are not of universal application. The statute declares a pre-commencement exclusion agreement to be of no effect only in relation to "domestic arbitration agreements"[13] and "special category disputes", not being contractual disputes governed by a law other than the law of England and Wales.[14] In all other cases pre-commencement exclusion agreements are valid. They are in consequence valid with regard to all international arbitrations not involving a special category dispute.

1.2.1.5.5 The recognition of the validity of exclusion agreements by the 1979 Act is a radical departure from the former governing public policy. In *Czarnikow* v. *Roth, Schmidt & Co.*[15] the attempt in a standard form trade contract to exclude the right to apply for the statement of an award as a special case was held by the Court of Appeal to be void as being contrary to public policy. The precise reach of this authority was never subsequently tested but it was widely regarded as rendering invalid any attempt to exclude the special case procedure.[16] The effect of the 1979 Act is to overturn the decision in *Czarnikow* although some of the policy considerations that found favour with the Court of Appeal continue to influence the substance of the contemporary law under the 1979 Act, in particular the special rules applicable to "domestic arbitration agreements" and "special category disputes".[17]

1.2.1.6 *Restriction on on-appeals*

1.2.1.6.1 The 1979 Act establishes a restricted and controlled relationship between arbitration and the High Court, as a first tier appellate court, with regard to questions of law. As previously emphasised the policy underlying the 1979 Act weighs heavily in favour of arbitral autonomy and the finality of awards, and in consequence the divide between arbitration and the High Court is not readily bridged.[1] But it is equally the policy of the legislation that when access to the judicature is achieved any issue taken by the High Court, whether in the nature of a preliminary application or a substantive appeal or question, shall predominantly be finally determined by the High Court and

---

12. Section 4(1).
12a. Section 7(2).
13. Section 3(6).
14. Section 4(1).
15. [1922] 2 K.B. 478 (C.A.).
16. See *infra*, para. 1.4.3.
17. See generally Chapter 13, paras. 13.4.3 and 13.4.4.
1. *Infra*, para. 1.5; also Chapters 5 and 6.

only in rare circumstances will an on-appeal to the Court of Appeal be permitted.[2] By virtue of the 1979 Act appeals and applications from arbitration to the High Court on questions of law and related issues will be rare, and on-appeals from the High Court to the Court of Appeal will be still rarer.[3] The policy of restricting on-appeals is achieved by expressly qualifying the right of appeal, and the terms of the various qualifications are set out in subsections (6A) and (7) of section 1[4] and subsections (2A) and (3) of section 2.[5]

1.2.1.6.2 Under sections 1 and 2 of the 1979 Act the High Court is vested with two general categories of decision-making. The first relates to preliminary applications, namely applications for leave to appeal[6] or to apply for an order for reasons or further reasons,[7] or to agree to entertain an application to determine a preliminary point of law.[8] From the decision of the High Court on any of these preliminary matters no appeal lies to the Court of Appeal unless the High Court gives leave.[9] The second category of decision-making relates to substantive determinations, namely the decision whether or not to make an order for reasons or further reasons[10]; the determination of a question of law appealed from an award[11] and the opinion expressed on a preliminary question of law.[12] In relation to the making of an order for reasons or further reasons no appeal lies without leave of the High Court.[13] With regard to the determination of an appealed or preliminary question of law no appeal lies to the Court of Appeal unless (i) the High Court or the Court of Appeal gives leave, and (ii) it is certified by the High Court that the question of law to which its decision relates either is one of general public importance or is one which for some other special reason should be considered by the Court of Appeal.[14]

Appeals to the House of Lords from the Court of Appeal are not governed by the 1979 Act but by the legislation and practice relating to the appellate jurisdiction of the House of Lords.[15]

2. See Chapters 10, 11 and 12.

3. See Kerr, "The Arbitration Act 1979" (1980) 48 M.L.R. 45, 52. The policy reflects the opinion of Lord Wilberforce in *Compagnie d'Armement Maritime S.A.* v. *Compagnie Tunisienne de Navigation S.A.* [1971] A.C. 572, 600, "If, for uniformity or otherwise, supervision of the courts is something required, I cannot but think that, otherwise than in exceptional cases by leave, decision by commercial judge should end the matter." There was also judicial concern about special cases ascending the hierarchy of courts; see *K. C. Sethia (1944) Ltd.* v. *Partabmull Rameshwar* [1950] 1 All E.R. 51, 58, per Singleton L.J.; *Macpherson Train & Co. Ltd.* v. *J. Milhem & Sons* [1955] 2 Lloyd's Rep. 59, 64, per Singleton L.J.; *J. H. Vantol Ltd.* v. *Fairclough Dodd & Jones* [1955] 1 W.L.R. 642, 648, per McNair J.; *Bremer Handelsgesellschaft m.b.H.* v. *Raiffeisen Hauptgenossenschaft E.G.* [1982] 1 Lloyd's Rep. 210, 211, where Lloyd J. comments on the special cases provoked by the soya bean embargo imposed by the U.S. government in June 1973, and the degree to which they subsequently progressed upward on appeal. See also Diplock, "The Case Stated—its Use and Abuse" (1978) 44 *Arbitration* 107, 110–111.

4. Considered in detail in Chapters 10 and 11.

5. Considered in detail in Chapter 12.

6. Section 1(3).

7. Section 1(5).

8. Section 2(1).

9. Section 1(6A) and s. 2(2A).

10. Section 1(5).

11. Section 1(2).

12. Section 2(1).

13. Section 1(6A).

14. Section 1(7) and s. 2(3).

15. Appellate Jurisdiction Act 1876, and the Administration of Justice (Appeals) Act 1934, s. 1. As to matters of practice, see *Supreme Court Practice* (1993), Part 16.

1.2.1.7 *Miscellaneous provisions*

Beyond the foregoing the 1979 legislation also enacts other provisions not relating to the relationship between arbitration and the courts with regard to questions of law. As such they are outside the province of the text, but for the sake of completeness these further provisions are considered in outline.

1.2.1.7.1 DEFAULT POWERS

The default powers of arbitrators and umpires is an incompletely developed and uncertain area of arbitration law. It is in consequence an aspect of arbitral practice where arbitrators display a cautious diffidence. The default powers of judges are various and well appreciated, although the exercise of the associated discretion is frequently the subject of appellate review. But the extent to which an arbitrator or umpire may make a peremptory and coercive interlocutory order and in the face of a refusal or failure to comply thereafter visit upon the party in default the threatened penalty is substantially less well understood.

No default jurisdiction arises as a necessary incident of the status of arbitrators[1]; and none is directly conferred by the arbitration legislation.[2] Any default jurisdiction which does in any particular instance exist can only derive from the express or implied terms of the contractual arbitral mandate.[3] In practice it is rare for express contractual default powers to be conferred and when such powers do exist it is invariably as a result of the incorporation of formal arbitral Rules into arbitration agreements, but even then the default powers are likely to be limited to particular situations and uncoordinated.[4]

1.2.1.7.2 In most cases, therefore, the real question will be whether an implied default jurisdiction has been conferred on the arbitrator. Although this is a question of law the answer to the question will depend very heavily on the facts of individual cases. But beyond the factual enquiry, section 12(1) of the Arbitration Act 1950 also assumes a crucial significance. The effect of the subsection is to imply into every written arbitration agreement, subject to a contrary intention, a term conferring specific procedural powers on the appointed arbitrator or umpire and a general power to "do all other things which during the proceedings on the reference the arbitrator or umpire may require". These words have been construed to empower arbitrators to make any order which is necessarily incidental to the determination of the dispute or difference in question.[5] No default powers are expressly conferred by section 12(1), but to the extent that the arbitrator enjoys a jurisdiction by virtue of section 12(1) to make an interlocutory order, it would also seem by necessary implication that the arbitrator also enjoys a discretionary power to make the order an "unless" order. There is no authority which gives direct support to this view of the law, but it is suggested that the

---

1. *Bremer Vulkan Schiffbau und Maschinenfabrik* v. *South India Shipping Corpn. Ltd.* [1981] A.C. 909.
2. Contrast the UNCITRAL Model Law on International Commercial Arbitration, Art. 25.
3. *Supra*, note 1.
4. This will be the case, for example, when Art. 25 of the Model Law (*supra*, note 2) is given contractual effect. See also The London Maritime Arbitrators' Association Terms (1987), first schedule, (A) Jurisdiction.
5. *Re Unione Stearinerie Lanza and Wiener* [1917] 2 K.B. 558; *Kursell* v. *Timber Operators and Contractors Ltd.* [1923] 2 K.B. 202. See also *Kirkawa Corpn.* v. *Gatoil Overseas Inc.* (*The Peter Kirk*) [1990] 1 Lloyd's Rep. 154.

approach takes substantial indirect support from the decision and reasoning of the House of Lords in *Bremer Vulkan Schiffbau und Maschinenfabrik* v. *South India Shipping Corpn. Ltd.*[6]

1.2.1.7.3 Section 5 of the 1979 Act introduces an entirely new dimension to the topic and makes provision for the making of "extension orders" by the High Court. Where a party to a reference under an arbitration agreement fails within the time specified in an order or, if no time is specified, within a reasonable time to comply with an order made by the arbitrator or umpire, then on the application of the arbitrator or umpire, or of any party to the reference, the High Court may make an order empowering the arbitrator or umpire to continue with the reference and respond to the default in like manner as a judge of the High Court might respond to a failure to comply with an order of the High Court or a requirement of rules of court. An "extension order" is discretionary and its scope may be limited by the express terms of the order and also made subject to conditions. The default powers of a judge of the High Court are many and various, including a power to make default judgments. It is widely considered that a principal purpose underlying the enactment of section 5 is to introduce a means by which arbitrators and umpires can make default awards analogous to a default judgment made in the course of a High Court action.

The hallmark of section 5 is that a default jurisdiction is conferred on arbitrators and umpires by an order of the High Court. The section establishes an interplay between the High Court and arbitral fora, with the High Court being the source of the default jurisdiction but with the power actually exercised by the arbitral forum. This represents a quite novel and unprecedented mode of procedure where the overriding purpose is to equip the judiciary to assist the efficient functioning of the arbitral process.[7]

1.2.1.7.4 THE ARBITRAL TRIBUNAL

Section 6 of the 1979 Act makes several amendments to the Arbitration Act 1950, in relation to matters touching on the arbitral tribunal.

1.2.1.7.4.1 *Two-arbitrator tribunals and the appointment of umpires.* In its original form section 8(1) of the 1950 Act incorporated an implied term into every arbitration agreement to the effect that where a reference was to two arbitrators, the two arbitrators were obliged to appoint an umpire immediately following their own appointment. In keeping with general principle the statutory implied term was capable of being displaced by an express term to the contrary. In this format the notorious deficiency of the statutory implied term was that it required the immediate appointment of an umpire in all circumstances with the consequence that the appointment would be redundant and wasteful should the two arbitrators be in agreement. This prospect is now avoided by the amendment made to section 8(1) of the 1950 Act by section 6(1) of the 1979 Act and as a consequence of which the two arbitrators are only obliged to appoint an umpire if they cannot agree, in which case

---

6. [1981] A.C. 909, in particular the speech of Lord Diplock. For a contrary opinion see the comments of Lord Frazer at p. 989.
7. See *Waverley S.F. Ltd.* v. *Carnaud Metalbox Engineering plc* [1994] 1 Lloyd's Rep. 38; *Sumitomo Heavy Industries Ltd.* v. *Oil and Natural Gas Commission* [1994] 1 Lloyd's Rep. 45.

they must appoint forthwith. Prior to a failure to agree they are vested with a discretionary power to appoint an umpire.

1.2.1.7.4.2 *Three-arbitrator tribunals.* Section 9(1) of the 1950 Act, prior to its replacement, established either a legal rule or an implied term, it was uncertain which, in favour of umpirage where in the case of a three-arbitrator tribunal the third arbitrator was appointed by two arbitrators, one of whom had in turn been appointed by each of the parties. This had the effect of converting the third arbitrator into an umpire which did not necessarily correspond with the intention of the parties. Where the third arbitrator was appointed otherwise than as described above no similar rule operated and a true three-arbitrator tribunal was established. Section 6(2) of the 1979 Act substitutes a new section 9 to the 1950 Act with the effect that the former bias in favour of umpirage is erased. If parties desire a three-arbitrator tribunal their intentions will be satisfied whatever procedure is adopted for the appointment of the third arbitrator. The new section 9 simply provides that in the absence of a contrary intention, in any case of a reference to three arbitrators, the award of any two of the arbitrators shall be binding.

1.2.1.7.4.3 *Appointment of arbitrators by the High Court.* The powers of the court to appoint an arbitrator or umpire in the event of incapacity or default are specified in section 10 of the 1950 Act. The 1979 Act makes two amendments to the section. First, section 6(3) of the 1979 Act amends section 10(c) of the 1950 Act so as to extend the power of the court to appoint a third arbitrator to include a situation where there is a default on the part of the parties who are under the arbitration agreement required to appoint the third arbitrator. Section 6(4) of the 1979 Act introduces a new subsection (2) to section 10 under which the court is given a new power to appoint an arbitrator or umpire where there is default on the part of a third party, that is a person who is neither one of the parties nor an existing arbitrator.

1.2.2 Features of the general arbitration law endorsed by the 1979 Act

1.2.2.1 *Fact–law dichotomy*

1.2.2.1.1 The distinction between fact and law is one present and of significance throughout the modern history of arbitration law[1] and the distinction is both perpetuated and accentuated by the 1979 Act.[2] The traditional view is that the arbitrator is the tribunal of fact and over the factual findings and conclusions of arbitrators the courts have resolutely refused to assume a supervisory jurisdiction.[3] The same is not true of questions of law with regard to which the courts have assumed a significant

---

1. See *infra*, para. 1.4.
2. See in particular, Chapter 3, para. 3.2.
3. *Royal Greek Government* v. *Minister of Transport* (1950) 83 Ll.L.Rep. 228, 238, per Devlin J., "All conclusions of fact—that is, fact and inference from fact . . . , are for the arbitrator." *Kaffeehandelsgesellschaft K.G.* v. *Plagefim Commercial S.A.* [1981] 2 Lloyd's Rep. 190, 193, per Mustill J., "It may be . . . that the applicants have a genuine grievance and that the award of the arbitrators was wrong in fact, but that is of course not a matter of which the Court can take any note at all." *Bremer Handelsgesellschaft m.b.H.* v. *Raiffeisen Hauptgenossenschaft E.G.* [1982] 1 Lloyd's Rep. 599, 603, per Kerr L.J., "An arbitral tribunal has the final word on all questions of fact." *Bulk Oil (Zug) A.G.* v. *Sun International Ltd. and Sun Oil Trading Co. (No. 2)* [1984] 1 Lloyd's Rep. 531, 533 per Bingham J., "The findings of fact of an arbitrator are binding on the Court and the Court cannot go behind these findings so far as they are questions of fact." See also Lord Parker of Waddington, "The Development of Commercial Arbitration" [1959] J.B.L. 213.

degree of control.[4] The special case procedure apropos awards was firmly confined to questions of law notwithstanding that it was not so expressly framed by the legislation.[5] In contrast the special case procedure with regard to questions arising in the course of a reference left nothing to chance and was expressly restricted to questions of law by the legislation.[6] So also the common law reviewing jurisdiction based on error on the face of the award functioned exclusively about errors of law.[7] As already observed the reviewing jurisdiction under the 1979 Act is unambiguously confined to questions of law.[8] Although in many regards an imperfect and dangerous analogy, the relationship between the courts and arbitration with regard to questions of fact and law is somewhat akin to the relationship which subsists between judge and jury in relation to such matters. Whereas questions of law are for the judge, questions of fact are for the jury. But whatever the expositional benefits of the analogy it is nonetheless the case that arbitration is a very different kind of institution from that of the civil jury, and disputed questions of law are frequently referred to the decision of arbitrators.[9] But it is only in relation to questions of fact that the findings and conclusions of arbitrators are conclusive and awards final. Pearson L.J. has expressed the view that the preservation of the independence of an arbitrator in respect of his findings of fact to be an important general principle of arbitration law.[10]

1.2.2.1.2 That arbitration awards should be final as to matters of fact is abundantly supportable. It is in keeping with general principle and if it were otherwise the potential expedition and economy of arbitration would be seriously undermined. In each case there would be the risk that transcripts of the evidence and bundles of documentary evidence would be regimented a second time before the courts for their scrutiny. It is the arbitrator who sees, observes and hears the parties and witnesses, and it is the arbitrator who therefore is best positioned to assess the credibility and reliability of the parties and the witnesses called, and to judge the cogency to be accorded to the evidence.[11] On questions of fact there is no reason to think otherwise than that the arbitrator is as competent as any court to determine the issues; indeed the arbitrator may often be better positioned and equipped than a court to discharge the task by virtue of his special qualifications and experience. It is the duty of the arbitrator not solely to recite the evidence but to assess it and make his primary and secondary findings of fact, and to arrive at his conclusions of fact. To the extent he may err he is not

4. *Infra*, para. 1.4.
5. *Infra*, para. 1.4.2.
6. *Ibid.*
7. *Infra*, para. 1.4.1.
8. Section 1(2). The point is further developed in Chapter 3, para. 3.2.
9. Even when this may not be the prudent course: see *Rowe Bros.* v. *Crossley Bros.* (1913) 108 L.T. 11 (C.A.), 14, per Lord Cozens-Hardy M.R., "there cannot be anything more absurd than to refer to a civil engineer difficult questions arising under the law of contract." For the view that arbitrators have taken the place of juries in the dynamic of the evolution of commercial law, see *Tsakiroglou & Co. Ltd.* v. *Noblee Thorl G.m.b.H* [1962] A.C. 93, 124, Lord Radcliffe.
10. *Tersons Ltd.* v. *Stevenage Development Corporation* [1965] 1 Q.B. 37, 55.
11. Cf. *Voest Alpine Intertrading G.m.b.H.* v. *Chevron International Oil Co. Ltd.* [1987] 2 Lloyd's Rep. 547, 558, per Hirst J., "In making my findings of primary fact, I take into account both the inherent probabilities, and also the assessment I have made of the witnesses whom I saw in the witness box, with ample opportunity to judge their reliability." And also in relation to litigation, see *Nocton* v. *Lord Ashburton* [1914] A.C. 932, 957, Viscount Haldane L.C.: "it is only in exceptional circumstances that judges of appeal, who have not seen the witness in the box, ought to differ from the finding of fact of the judge who tried the case as to the state of mind of the witness."

guilty of misconduct,[12] nor is the error subject to review.[13] But in determining fact the arbitrator must act *intra vires*[14] and discharge his procedural obligation to act fairly.[15]

1.2.2.1.3 To the general rule that an award is final as to questions of fact there exist a small number of exceptions. A clerical mistake or error arising from an accidental slip or omission may be corrected by the arbitrator under a power established by the Arbitration Act 1950, section 17, unless a contrary intention is expressed in the arbitration agreement.[16] Such a correcting power may also be expressly conferred by the parties.[17] Where the arbitrator admits an error of fact and invites that the award be returned to him for correction the court enjoys a power to remit under the Arbitration Act 1950, section 22.[18] There is also an indication in authority that an inadvertent factual mistake in an award which can be shown to be the product of gross carelessness may amount to misconduct[19]; but this jurisdiction, if indeed it was ever capable of being established, has probably been overtaken by the two statutory developments considered above. Also, if an arbitrator is moved to summarise the evidence which he accepts, it appears to be misconduct if he summarises it inaccurately or in a manner which is a misrepresentation of the evidence, or if it can be shown that the evidence accepted is incredible, in the sense that a reasonable person could not accept the evidence as truth.[20] But the existence or sufficiency of evidence to support a finding of fact is a question of law, albeit that it is a form of pleading disliked and not encouraged, for it is a rule that tends to cloud the distinction between fact and law.[21]

1.2.2.1.4 The 1979 Act continues to draw the vital distinction between fact and law. The new system of judicial review it establishes relates only to questions of law. An appeal under section 1(2) is confined to questions of law arising out of an award made on an arbitration agreement.[22] A consultative case under section 2(1) is restricted to questions of law arising in the course of the reference.[23] Even the court's power to direct the giving of reasons or further reasons under section 1(5) is tied to putative

12. *Gillespie Bros. Ltd.* v. *Thompson* (1922) 13 Ll.L.Rep. 519, 524, per Atkin L.J.; *Oversea Buyers Ltd.* v. *Granadex S.A.* [1980] 2 Lloyd's Rep. 608, 613, per Mustill J; *Bremer Handelsgesellschaft m.b.H* v. *Raiffeisen Hauptgenossenschaft E.G.* [1982] 1 Lloyd's Rep. 599, 603, per Kerr L.J.; *Moran* v. *Lloyd's* [1983] 1 Lloyd's Rep. 51, 59, per Lloyd J.; *Mutual Shipping Corp.* v. *Bayshore Shipping Co.* (*The Montan*) [1985] 1 Lloyd's Rep. 189 (C.A.).

13. *Ibid.* and further *Bulk Oil (Zug) A.G.* v. *Sun International Ltd. and Sun Oil Trading Co. (No. 2)* [1984] 1 Lloyd's Rep. 531, 533; *Interbulk Ltd.* v. *Aiden Shipping Co. Ltd. etc. (The Vimeira)* [1983] 2 Lloyd's Rep. 424, 431; *Geogas S.A.* v. *Trammo Gas Ltd.* (*The Baleares*) [1993] 1 Lloyd's Rep. 215, 228, Steyn L.J.

14. Cf. *Armada Lines Continent-Mediterranean Service Ltd.* v. *Naviera Murueta S.A. (The Elexalde)* [1985] 2 Lloyd's Rep. 485.

15. *Faghirzadeh* v. *Rudolf Wolff (S.A.) Pty. Ltd.* [1977] 1 Lloyd's Rep. 630, 639, per Mocatta J.; *Fox and Others* v. *P. G. Wellfair Ltd.* [1981] 2 Lloyd's Rep. 514, 529, per Dunn L.J.; *Edible Oil Products (Malaysia) B.H.D.* v. *Jayant Oil Mills Private Ltd. and Others* [1982] 2 Lloyd's Rep. 95, 97–98, per Staughton J.

16. See Thomas, "The power of arbitrators to cure accidental errors" [1985] L.M.C.L.Q. 263, where the section and authorities are discussed. See also Chapter 11, para. 11.3.3.1.

17. See, for example, LMAA Terms (1994), The First Schedule, (A) Jurisdiction, Rule 5.

18. *Mutual Shipping Corpn.* v. *Bayshore Shipping Co. (The Montan)* [1985] 1 Lloyd's Rep. 189 (C.A.); *Atlantic Lines and Navigation Co. Inc.* v. *Italmare S.p.A. (The Apollon)* [1985] 1 Lloyd's Rep. 597. See also Chapter 11, para. 11.3.3.2.

19. *In re Hall and Hinds* (1841) 2 Man. & G. 847.

20. *Tersons Ltd.* v. *Stevenage Development Corporation* [1965] 1 Q.B. 37, 41, per Willmer L.J. and p. 52 per Upjohn L.J.

21. See Chapter 3, para. 3.2.4 and Chapter 6, para. 6.2.11.

22. See Chapter 3, para. 3.1.

23. See Chapter 12.

appeals on questions of law arising out of awards.[24] Exclusion agreements cannot extend beyond the rights arising under sections 1 and 2 of the 1979 Act.[25] The 1979 Act makes no provision for appeals on questions of fact nor for the stating of preliminary questions of fact for determination by the court.

1.2.2.1.5 The Act by its overt emphasis on questions of law strongly suggests by necessary implication the finality of awards on questions of fact. But the Act goes even further and by its express terms polarises the fact–law divide. Section 1(1) provides in part: "the High Court shall not have jurisdiction to set aside or remit an award on an arbitration agreement on the ground of errors of fact or law on the face of the award." The Act therefore makes it clear that not only is there no appeal on a question of fact but that otherwise an award may not be set aside or remitted for error of fact on the face of the award. The subsection is nonetheless troublesome and raises several difficulties. In its entirety its central purpose is to abrogate the former statutory and common law jurisdictions enabling questions of law arising out of arbitration awards to be reviewed. But in erasing the common law jurisdiction by its express language it extends its reach to errors of law *and* fact. This implicitly suggests that at common law an award might be set aside or remitted for error of fact on its face and in cases subsequent to the introduction of the 1979 Act Sir John Donaldson M.R. (as he then was) appears *obiter dictum* to accept the existence of this jurisdiction.[26] The Commercial Court Committee in its *Report on Arbitration* also assumes the existence of the jurisdiction.[27] But the position is far from clear and the existence of such a jurisdiction is not free from doubt. A case may even be made out that no such jurisdiction existed. There appears to be no readily identifiable authority which supports the jurisdiction. The existence of such a jurisdiction is also contrary to the general statements of principle emanating from the courts even in the pre-1979 phase.[28] The only clear occasions when the courts were prepared to intervene was when an arbitrator admitted an error of fact or where the error of fact amounted to misconduct or resulted ultimately in an error of law.[29] The latter two situations would appear to be quite distinct for the judicial intervention is explained by virtue of that which is produced by the error of fact and not by the bare factual error itself. Only the first situation is a true example of judicial review for error of fact, but even this situation must be assessed in context and may be perceived as a special head of jurisdiction developed under the statutory jurisdiction to remit.[30] It is not further a basis for setting aside an award. But it is a jurisdiction which depends on the arbitrator admitting the error of fact[31]; and also invariably inviting the return of the award so that the error may be corrected, although it would seem that this is not an absolute precondition to the invocation of the discretionary jurisdiction.[32]

24. See Chapter 11.
25. Section 3(1) and see Chapter 13.
26. *Moran* v. *Lloyd's* [1983] 1 Lloyd's Rep. 472, 475; *Mutual Shipping Corpn.* v. *Bayshore Shipping Co. (The Montan)* [1985] 1 Lloyd's Rep. 189, 191; *Aden Refinery Co. Ltd.* v. *Ugland Management Co. Ltd.* (*The Ugland Obo One*) [1987] 1 Q.B. 650, 655. [1986] 3 All E.R. 737, 739.
27. (1978) Cmnd. 7284, para. 5. The Report is considered *infra* and is set out in Appendix A.
28. *Supra* n. 3. See also *Gillespie Bros. & Co.* v. *Thompson Bros. & Co.* (1922) 13 Ll.L.Rep. 519; *Oleificio Zucchi S.p.A.* v. *Northern Sales Ltd.* [1965] 2 Lloyd's Rep. 496.
29. *Supra*, para. 1.2.2.1.3.
30. *Supra* n. 18.
31. *Atlantic Lines and Navigation Co. Inc.* v. *Italmare S.p.A.* (*The Apollon*) [1985] 1 Lloyd's Rep. 597.
32. *Ibid.*

1.2.2.1.6 A further uncertainty concerns the precise impact of section 1(1). Beyond its central purpose, considered above, the question arises whether it further abrogates the jurisdiction to set aside or remit awards under sections 22 and 23(1) of the Arbitration Act 1950, to the extent that this jurisdiction may be associated with errors of fact; and in particular whether the jurisdiction to remit for admitted errors of fact is abrogated. It does not do so specifically but the statutory words are drafted in such general terms that they quite clearly could have this effect. But to give section 1(1) this wider interpretation might well be considered as extending the ambit of the subsection beyond its central purpose and to give the legislation an unintended consequence. Although the issue remains open to argument there is much to be said against adopting any wider interpretation than is necessary to achieve the precise purpose of the subsection, and thereby safeguarding the supervisory jurisdiction to remit for admitted mistake of fact.[33]

1.2.2.1.7 It is also to be noted that section 1(1) applies to an award made "on an arbitration agreement", which is defined by the 1979 Act as a written agreement to arbitrate.[34] In consequence the subsection has no application to an award made on a parol arbitration agreement and with regard to such informal arbitration agreements the common law jurisdiction to set aside awards for error of fact (such as it may be) or law would appear to survive. The jurisdiction to remit awards is wholly statutory in source[35] and would appear to be confined to arbitration agreements in writing notwithstanding the general terms in which section 22 of the Arbitration Act 1950 is expressed.[36] Judicial statements to the effect that following the enactment of section 1(1) of the 1979 Act there exists no surviving jurisdiction to set aside or remit an award for error of fact or law on the face of the award are, it is suggested, to be understood in the context of the preceding observation.[37]

Although the finality of awards on questions of fact has been firmly emphasised throughout the modern era of arbitration law, following the enactment of the 1979 Act it is a principle impressed by the judiciary with yet greater force and confidence.[38]

1.2.2.2 *Duty of arbitrators to apply the law*

1.2.2.2.1 The 1979 Act gives unambiguous implicit recognition to the general rule of English law that arbitrators must decide disputes and differences referred according to the prevailing principles of law. Lord Goddard C.J. entertained no doubt "that *prima facie* the duty of an arbitrator is to act in accordance with the law of the land".[1] "Law" in this context carries the widest connotation and alludes to legislation, common law,

---

33. *Supra* n. 18.
34. See Chapter 3, para. 3.4.
35. Deriving originally from the Common Law Procedure Act 1854, s. 8; and subsequently re-enacted in the Arbitration Act 1889, s. 10. For a recent judicial consideration of the jurisdiction see *King* v. *Thomas McKenna Ltd*. [1991] 1 All E.R. 653 (C.A.).
36. *Supra* n. 34.
37. See, for example, *Bulk Oil (Zug) A.G.* v. *Sun International Ltd. and Sun Oil Trading Co. (No. 2)* [1984] 1 Lloyd's Rep. 531, 533.
38. *Kaffehandelsgesellschaft K.G.* v. *Plagefim Commercial S.A.* [1981] 2 Lloyd's Rep. 190, 191, Mustill J.; *Geogas S.A.* v. *Trammo Gas Ltd. (The Baleares)* [1993] 1 Lloyd's Rep. 215, 228, Steyn L.J. (C.A.).
1. *Podar Trading Co.* v. *Tagher* [1949] 2 K.B. 277, 288. See also *Hooper & Co.* v. *Balfour, Williamson & Co.* (1890) 62 L.T. 646; *Mitchell Gill* v. *Buchan*, 1921 S.C. 390; *N.V. Vulcaan* v. *Mowinckels Rederi A/S* [1938] 2 All E.R. 152; *David Taylor & Son Ltd.* v. *Barnett Trading Co.* [1953] 1 W.L.R. 562; *Tehno-Impex* v. *Gebr. van Weelde Scheepvaartkantoor B.V.* [1981] 2 All E.R. 669.

equity, Admiralty,[2] and in appropriate circumstances E.E.C. law[3] and the principles of public international law.[4] The general rule derives from a firmly implanted public policy[5] and does not yield to an express agreement to the contrary.[6] In a wholly domestic context the applicable law will be English municipal law. Where the dispute sports a foreign element the governing law may be wholly or in part a foreign system of law, or a regional or international system of law.[7]

1.2.2.2.2 The duty of arbitrators to decide according to law is firmly supported by authority and the general principle probably derives from the turn of the nineteenth century when the common law jurisdiction to set aside awards for error of law on their face was being established.[8] The underlying policy probably emanates from the fact that arbitration, albeit predominantly consensual and voluntary, is nonetheless perceived as a fragment of the administration of civil justice and in common with all its other component parts must function in accordance with legal principles. The adoption of this principle ensures that arbitrations can be effectively supervised; that the total arbitral decision-making process functions with at least a substantial degree of consistency; and that a fair balance is maintained between arbitrating parties.[9] As Denning L.J. (as he then was) curtly explained, "There is not one law for arbitrators and another for the court. There is one law for all."[10]

1.2.2.2.3 The necessary implication of the general rule is that English law does not recognise arbitral decisions *extra legem*. Arbitrators do not have the capacity to act as *amiables compositeurs*; nor to determine disputes *ex aequo et bono*, and this remains the case even when the parties attempt to confer an express jurisdiction to this effect. Megaw J. (as he then was) summarised the position in English law in the following terms[11]:

. . . it is the policy of the law in this country that, in the conduct of arbitrations, arbitrators must in general apply a fixed and recognisable system of law, which primarily and normally

---

2. *Vulcaan (N.V. etc.)* v. *Mowinckels Rederi A/S* [1938] 2 All E.R. 152.
3. Cf. *Bulk Oil (Zug) A.G.* v. *Sun International Ltd. and Sun Oil Trading Co.* [1983] 1 Lloyd's Rep. 655; [1984] 1 Lloyd's Rep. 531.
4. *Vulcaan (N.V. etc.)* v. *Mowinckels Rederi A/S* [1938] 2 All E.R. 152; *Orion Cia. Espanola de Seguros* v. *Belfort Maats. etc.* [1962] 2 Lloyd's Rep. 257.
5. See generally Mustill and Boyd, *Commercial Arbitration* (2nd edn.), Chapter 4; Thomas, "Commercial Arbitration—Justice According to Law" (1983) 2 C.J.Q. 166–183: also *Czarnikow* v. *Roth, Schmidt & Co.* [1922] 2 K.B. 478 (C.A.).
6. *Maritime Insurance Co. Ltd.* v. *Assecuranz-Union von 1865* (1935) 52 Ll.L.Rep. 16; *Orion Cia. Espanola de Seguros* v. *Belfort Maats. etc.* [1962] 2 Lloyd's Rep. 257. Contrast *Jager* v. *Tolme and Runge and The London Produce Clearing House Ltd.* [1916] 1 K.B. 939 (C.A.); *Norske Atlas Insurance Co. Ltd.* v. *London General Insurance Co. Ltd.* (1927) 28 Ll.L.Rep. 104.
7. Such questions will be governed by the principles appertaining to the conflict of laws process which is a branch of English municipal law.
8. *Aubert* v. *Maze* (1801) 2 Bos. & Pul. 371, 375, *per* Chambre J., "There is no doubt that an arbitrator is bound by the rules of law like every other Judge, and if it appears on the face of the record that the arbitrator has acted contrary to law, his award may be set aside." See also *Morgan* v. *Mather* (1792) 2 Ves. Jun. 15; *Kent* v. *Estob* (1802) 3 East 18; *Blennerhasset* v. *Day* (1811) 2 Ball & B. 104; *Hodgkinson* v. *Fernie* (1857) 3 C.B. (N.S.) 189; and *infra*, para. 1.4.1.
9. *Czarnikow* v. *Roth, Schmidt & Co.* [1922] 2 K.B. 478 (C.A.); *Orion Cia. Espanola de Seguros* v. *Belfort Maats. etc.* [1962] 2 Lloyd's Rep. 257.
10. *David Taylor & Son Ltd.* v. *Barnett Trading Co.* [1958] 1 W.L.R. 562, 570.
11. *Orion Cia. Espanola de Seguros* v. *Belfort Maats. etc.* [1962] 2 Lloyd's Rep. 257, 264. See also *Maritime Insurance Co.* v. *Assekuranz-Union von 1869* (1935) 52 Ll.L.Rep. 16; *Home and Overseas Insurance Co. Ltd.* v. *Mentor Insurance Co. (U.K.) Ltd.* [1989] 1 Lloyd's Rep. 473 (C.A.).

would be the law of England, and they cannot be allowed to apply some different criterion such as the view of the individual arbitrator or umpire on abstract justice or equitable principles, which, of course, does not mean "equity" in the legal sense of the word at all.

This feature of English law highlights a major point of contrast between English law (together with some of its derivatives) and many foreign jurisdictions which accommodate *extra legem* arbitral decision-making, although in many foreign jurisdictions the power is confined to instances when the parties establish an express mandate to decide *extra legem*.[12]

1.2.2.2.4 As for the source of the obligation to decide according to law the arbitration legislation is silent on the point and it is rare for arbitration agreements to contain an express provision requiring arbitrators to decide according to law, except in an international context when a particular system of law may be identified as the proper or governing law. In the absence of express provision the obligation may arise either as a rule of law under the common law or as an implied term of the arbitration agreement. The distinction is probably of greater theoretical interest than of practical consequence and this in all likelihood accounts for the absence of any serious judicial discussion of the point. There is some judicial comment that supports the implied term thesis[13] and this may be in keeping with the discernible drift in the contemporary law to define duties and rights in the context of arbitration as arising expressly or impliedly from the arbitration agreement.[14] But even if the implied term thesis prevails nonetheless it would seem that it is a species of implied term that cannot be displaced by a contrary or inconsistent express term.[15]

1.2.2.2.5 To the general rule there are certain qualifications. It does not extend so as to require arbitrators to adhere to rules of practice that have been developed and adopted by the courts.[16] Between a rule of practice and a rule of law there is a clear theoretical difference but it is nonetheless a distinction that is often difficult to draw.[17] In the context of arbitration it also appears that rules of evidence, which are equally rules of law, may be relaxed if the parties expressly or impliedly agree.[18] English law also sanctions "equity arbitration agreements" whereunder with regard to disputes relating to the proper construction of an agreement or document an arbitrator may be expressly or impliedly mandated to depart from a strict legal construction and adopt a more equitable, commercial and lenient approach. Such an agreement was upheld by

---

12. For a statement of what may be presumed to represent international public policy on the question see the UNCITRAL Model Law on International Commercial Arbitration, Art. 28(3) and (4).

13. *Chandris* v. *Isbrandtsen Moller Co. Inc.* [1951] 1 K.B. 240; *Tehno-Impex* v. *Gebr. van Weelde Scheepvaarkantoor B.V.* [1981] 2 All E.R. 669. See also *Re Astley and Tyldesley Coal and Salt Co. and Tyldesley Coal Co.* (1899) 68 L.J.Q.B. 252; *Board of Trade* v. *Cayzor, Irvine & Co.* [1927] A.C. 610; *Ram Dutt Ramkissendas* v. *Sassoon & Co.* (1929) 98 L.J.P.C. 58; *Vulcaan (N.V. etc.)* v. *Mowinckels Rederi* [1938] 2 All E.R. 152; *Racecourse Betting Control Board* v. *Secretary for Air* [1944] Ch. 114.

14. See, for example, *Bremer Vulkan Schiffbau und Maschinenfabrik* v. *South India Shipping Corp. Ltd.* [1981] A.C. 909, particularly the speech of Lord Diplock.

15. *Maritime Insurance Co. Ltd.* v. *Assecuranz-Union von 1865* (1935) 52 Ll.L.Rep. 16; *Orion Cia. Espanola de Seguros* v. *Belfort Maats. etc.* [1962] 2 Lloyd's Rep. 257.

16. *Re Badger* (1819) 2 B. & Ald. 691; *The Kosara* [1973] 2 Lloyd's Rep. 1, [1976] Q.B. 292; *Tehno-Impex* v. *Gebr. van Weelde Scheepvaartkantoor B.V.* [1981] 2 All E.R. 669.

17. For judicial comment on the distinction, see *Carne and Another* v. *Debono*, The Times, 28 June 1988.

18. *Macpherson Train & Co. Ltd.* v. *J. Milhem & Sons* [1955] 2 Lloyd's Rep. 59 (C.A.); *Henry Bath & Son Ltd.* v. *Birgby Products* [1962] 1 Lloyd's Rep. 389.

the Court of Appeal in *Eagle Star Insurance Co. Ltd.* v. *Yuval Insurance Co. Ltd.*[19] and although the case does not go so far as to sanction an express agreement mandating an arbitrator to act *extra legem*, it does appear to represent a half-way house by drawing a distinction between acting according to law and acting according to the strictness of the law. An equity arbitration agreement justifies a departure from the latter, but not the former. This general line of approach appears to have been endorsed by the Court of Appeal in *Home and Overseas Insurance Co. Ltd.* v. *Mentor Insurance Co. (U.K.) Ltd.*,[20] where on the facts an arbitration clause in a reinsurance contract mandated arbitrators to "make their award with a view to effecting the general purpose of this Reinsurance in a reasonable manner rather than in accordance with a literal interpretation of the language". In the judgment of the court these words did not entitle the arbitrators to disregard the law and decide according to their own notions of fairness, but they did permit the arbitrators to depart from the ordinary or literal meaning of the language of the reinsurance contract and adopt a contextual approach. In the result it would seem that the express mandate achieved little, for it did no more than indicate a mode of approach to the question of construction which the arbitrators in any event could or may have been obliged to adopt under the general law. In the case of international arbitration a more generous approach may be also possible, as is suggested by the decision of the Court of Appeal in *D.S.T.* v. *Rakoil*.[21] The court refused to declare as unenforceable on grounds of public policy a convention award made on a non-domestic arbitration agreement that enabled the arbitrator to determine the substantive obligations of the parties according to "internationally accepted principles of law governing contractual relations". This is of course a decision made in a different context to the present discussion, but it is a decision marked for its tolerance and accommodation of *extra-legem* arbitration. It may therefore represent some manner of indicator as to the future attitude of the English judiciary.

1.2.2.2.6 The 1979 Act does not in any way affect the historical and prevailing bond between arbitration and the law. It in fact impliedly underpins the general principle of legality. The effect of the 1979 Act is purely procedural. It restructures the mode of judicial review of questions of law. Nor does the fact that the 1979 Act for the first time admits the validity of exclusion agreements, whereby the structural link between arbitration and the courts with regard to questions of law may be severed, in any way impinge on the principle of legality. A valid exclusion agreement is not a licence to decide disputes *extra legem*.[22] The execution of a valid exclusion agreement merely has the effect that if an arbitrator comes bona fide to his task but nonetheless falters and gets the law wrong there is no remedy by way of appeal to the High Court. In this circumstance the finality of the award is elevated above considerations of legal accuracy. But an arbitrator who wilfully ignores or rejects the rules of law is probably

---

19. [1978] 1 Lloyd's Rep. 357. Commented upon in *Didymi Corpn.* v. *Atlantic Lines and Navigation Co. Inc.* [1987] 2 Lloyd's Rep. 166, 170. Contrast *Maritime Insurance Co. Ltd.* v. *Assecuranz-Union von 1865* (1935) 52 Ll.L.Rep. 16; *Orion Cia. Espanola de Seguros* v. *Belfort Maats. etc.* [1962] 2 Lloyd's Rep. 257.

20. [1989] 1 Lloyd's Rep. 473 (C.A.).

21. *Deutsche Schachtbau-und-Tiefbohrgesellschaft m.b.H.* v. *Ras Al Khaimah National Oil Co. and Shell International Petroleum Co. Ltd.* [1987] 2 Lloyd's Rep. 246 (C.A.).

22. Contrast Mann, "Private Arbitration and Public Policy" (1985) 4 C.J.Q. 257.

guilty of misconduct[23] and any resulting award may be in addition to appellate relief remitted or set aside under sections 22 and 23(2) of the Arbitration Act 1950; or at an earlier stage steps may be taken to prevent the continuation of the reference by the grant of an injunction or even to seek the removal of the arbitrator under section 23(1) of the 1950 Act.

1.2.2.3 *Error of law and enforcement of awards*

On an action to enforce an award at common law no defence is admissible other than one which seeks to establish that the award is void, as distinct from voidable. This is the so-called *Rule in Thorburn* v. *Barnes*.[1] Its principal effect is to assert that misconduct on the part of an arbitrator not amounting to fraud must be taken on a motion to set aside or remit an award, and if this action is not taken within the stipulated time limit the parties are assumed to have waived the irregularity and cannot thereafter raise the misconduct as a defence to an action on the award.[2]

For an arbitrator to err in fact or law is not misconduct.[3] Nor is an award void for error of fact or law. An error of law may be cured by the appeal procedure established under the 1979 Act, but if this procedure is not pursued the error of law cannot later be resurrected as a defence to an action on the award.[4] Consistent with this principle, in *Cohen* v. *Baram*[5] it was held that the propriety of an award of costs could not be raised as a defence to the enforcement of a domestic award. Since the enactment of the 1979 Act costs are subject to appellate review under section 1(2)[6]; and no application for leave to appeal having been made the defendant was precluded from raising the matter by way of defence and the award stood as an unassailable award.

1.2.2.4 *Detraction from the finality of awards*

1.2.2.4.1 One of the necessary substantive ingredients of a valid award is that it be final and binding. An arbitration agreement may make an express declaration to this effect, although such a declaration is rare in practice. When the arbitration agreement is silent on the point then, subject to a contrary intention, an implied term to the same effect is incorporated into every arbitration agreement by virtue of the Arbitration Act 1950, section 16.[1]

The binding character of an award lies at the root of the arbitration process, for in

---

23. Cf. *Darlington Waggon Co.* v. *Harding* [1891] 1 Q.B. 245; *Kelantan* v. *Duff Development Co. Ltd.* [1923] A.C. 395; *David Taylor & Son Ltd.* v. *Barnett Trading Co.* [1958] 1 W.L.R. 562.

1. (1867) L.R. & C.P. 384. For the defences available to the enforcement of a Convention award, see Arbitration Act 1975, section 5.

2. *Ibid.*; see also *Bache* v. *Billingham* [1894] 1 Q.B. 107; *Oppenheim & Co.* v. *Mahomed Haneef* [1922] 1 A.C. 482; *Scrimaglio* v. *Thornett & Fehr* (1923) 18 Ll.L.Rep. 148; *Birtley & District Co-operative Society Ltd.* v. *Windy Nook and District Industrial Co-operative Society Ltd.* [1959] 1 W.L.R. 142.

3. *Supra*, para. 1.2.2.1; also *Geogas S.A.* v. *Trammo Gas Ltd. (The Baleares)* [1993] 1 Lloyd's Rep. 215, 228, per Steyn L.J.

4. Cf. *Middlemiss & Gould (A Firm)* v. *Hartlepool Corpn.* [1972] 1 W.L.R. 1643.

5. *The Times*, 16 December 1993.

6. See Chapter 6, para. 6.2.14.1.

1. The section provides: "Unless a contrary intention is expressed therein, every arbitration agreement shall, where such a provision is applicable to the reference, be deemed to contain a provision that the award to be made by the arbitrator or umpire shall be final and binding on the parties and the persons claiming under them respectively."

the last resort it represents the contractual basis for the enforcement of an unperformed award. In entering into an arbitration agreement each party impliedly undertakes to perform or discharge the award ultimately made.[2] Although the form of action is customarily described as an action on the award, this is a misleading way of describing the legal process, for the action derives from an implied contract emanating not from the award but the agreement to arbitrate.[3] By section 26 of the Arbitration Act 1950 there also exists a summary mode of procedure for the enforcement of awards, which avoids the trappings of a full trial associated with the common law action.[4] The statutory procedure however is only available where the validity of an award is beyond doubt or reasonably clear.[5]

1.2.2.4.2 The concept of finality is less certain in its meaning. It has probably not one but several meanings or nuances. In part it manifests the commitment of the parties to the decision of the arbitral tribunal of their choice and to the exclusion of all other dispute-resolving institutions and procedures. In agreeing to arbitrate each party undertakes not only to be bound by the award in the sense considered above but also that the award shall be a final determination of their dispute or difference. But the agreement of the parties is that they shall be bound by the final decision of the arbitrator, by which is meant the ultimate and decisive determination of the arbitrator, as distinct from a provisional determination or a preliminary statement of the thinking of the arbitrator, and by virtue of which the arbitrator is rendered *functus officio*.[6] On occasions the term finality is also used to describe the need for completeness in an award. The arbitrator must decide all the issues referred by the parties and if he fails in this duty and makes an incomplete award the award is void.[7] The significance of this aspect of the law has however been materially diminished with the introduction of an implied authority to make interim awards.[8]

1.2.2.4.3 The requirement of and the emphasis on the finality of awards, together with the maxims that have evolved in association with this perspective, such as "arbitration for better or worse" and "arbitration with all faults", does nonetheless tend to

---

2. *Purslow* v. *Baily* (1704) 2 Ld. Raym. 1039, 1040 per Holt C.J., "The submission is an actual mutual promise to perform the award of the arbitrators." For an action on a foreign award see *Norske Atlas Insurance Co. Ltd.* v. *London General Insurance Co. Ltd.* (1927) 28 Ll.L.Rep. 104.

3. *Bremer Oeltransport G.m.b.H* v. *Drewry* [1933] 1 K.B. 753; *The Saint Anna* [1983] 1 Lloyd's Rep. 637.

4. Section 26 provides:

"(1) An award on an arbitration agreement may, by leave of the High Court or a judge thereof, be enforced in the same manner as a judgment or order to the same effect, and where leave is so given, judgment may be entered in terms of the award.

(2) If a county court so orders, the amount sought to be recovered shall be recoverable (by execution issued from the county court or otherwise) as if payable under an order of that court and shall not be enforceable under subsection (1) above.

(3) An application to the High Court under this section shall preclude an application to a county court, and an application to a county court under this section shall preclude an application to the High Court."

5. *Ex parte Caucasian Trading Corp. Ltd.* [1896] 1 Q.B. 368; *In re Boks & Co. and Peters, Rushton & Co. Ltd.* [1919] 1 K.B. 491; *Margulies Bros. Ltd.* v. *Dafnis Thomaides & Co. (U.K.) Ltd.* [1958] 1 W.L.R. 398; *Middlemiss & Gould (A Firm)* v. *Hartlepool Corpn.* [1972] 1 W.L.R. 1643; *Jugoslavenska Oceanska Plovidba* v. *Castle Investment Co. Inc.* [1974] Q.B. 292; *Dalmia Dairy Industries* v. *National Bank of Pakistan* [1978] 2 Lloyd's Rep. 223; *Ex Comm Ltd.* v. *Ahmed Abdul-Qawi Bamaodah (The St. Raphael)* [1985] 1 Lloyd's Rep. 403.

6. Cf. *Hiscox* v. *Outhwaite (No. 1)* [1992] 1 A.C. 562.

7. *Wilkinson* v. *Page* (1842) 1 Hare 276; *Re O'Conor and Whitlaws Arbitration* (1919) 88 L.J.K.B. 1242.

8. The power may exist by express agreement or by a term implied by virtue of the Arbitration Act 1950, s. 14.

misrepresent arbitration jurisprudence in so far as it suggests an arbitral autonomy that does not in fact exist. In English law the arbitral process and awards are subject to judicial review under statutory and common law powers and these judicial inroads have meant that the concept of the finality of awards and the associated maxims have to be understood not in an absolute sense but as indicative of a leaning in the law. English law has never in its contemporary history subscribed to the concept of absolute arbitral autonomy and finality of awards. It has throughout been a question of balance, and it is in striking the balance that the concept of the finality of awards has played its part, providing to hand a counterweight to claims based on public policy in support of judicial review of awards. The finality of awards may be a delusion, but the historical tradition of thought associated with the concept has contributed to the present-day sensitivity towards the relationship between arbitration awards and the courts, to the jealous scrutiny of all claims to judicial review of awards and to the determination to define the relationship, such as it may be at any moment in time, with precision.

1.2.2.4.4 The 1979 Act continues the ambivalent tradition of English law to the question of the finality of awards. It both subscribes to and detracts from the finality of awards. In matters of fact it endorses the finality of awards.[9] With regard to questions of law it assumes the opposite posture, for in providing an appeal process based on reasoned awards it establishes a significant system of judicial review.[10] But even in so doing the tug of finality has proved itself to be a significant force and has influenced the operation of the appellate process to favour finality as against judicial review. This it achieves by greatly restricting the right of appeal by the cautious exercise of the discretion associated with the power to give or refuse leave to appeal, with the consequence that fewer appeals are permitted under the 1979 Act than under the former special case procedure.[11] Also the new legislation admits the validity of exclusion agreements whereunder parties may be contractually precluded from invoking the appeal procedure.[12] Where there is in existence a valid exclusion agreement the award is in effect rendered final as to matters of law and fact. The 1979 Act reassesses the striking of the balance and leans the law towards the greater acceptance of the finality of awards in the true sense of that term, but without committing the law to the undiluted acceptance of the concept. The 1979 Act does nothing to disturb the established rule that an error of law does not preclude an award from being final and binding.[13]

1.2.2.5 *Restrictive character of judicial review*

1.2.2.5.1 The 1979 Act confers on the courts a jurisdiction to review questions of law arising in the course of a reference and out of awards. As such it extends on the supervisory jurisdiction conferred by other provisions of the arbitration legislation, principally sections 22 and 23 of the Arbitration Act 1950, and by the general jurisdiction

9. *Supra*, para. 1.2.2.1.
10. *Supra*, para. 1.2.1.1 and Part II of the text.
11. *Supra*, para 1.2.1.4 and Chapter 5.
12. *Supra*, para. 1.2.1.5 and Chapter 13.
13. *Middlemiss & Gould (A Firm)* v. *Hartlepool Corpn.* [1972] 1 W.L.R. 1643.

vested in the courts to give injunctive and declaratory relief. The question has arisen whether the reviewing jurisdiction of the courts is confined to these defined sources or whether the courts enjoy a more broadranging and inherent jurisdiction to intervene in the arbitral process whenever the interests of justice demand.

1.2.2.5.2 Historically a restrictive view of the ambit of the reviewing jurisdiction held sway and an example of its acceptance is found in the dictum of Willmer L.J. asserting that, "[t]he degree of control exercised by the court over an arbitrator is strictly limited by statute."[1] However, in *The Angelic Grace*,[2] Lord Denning M.R. for the first time asserted that beyond its statutory jurisdiction the court also enjoyed an inherent jurisdiction to supervise the conduct of arbitrators and in consequence the court was able to provide an appropriate remedy whenever it was in the interests of justice to intervene. The notion of a perambulating and untrammelled inherent jurisdiction was not expressly accepted by the other member of the Court of Appeal, Waller L.J.,[3] but the opinion enunciated by Lord Denning M.R. began to take root and influenced the approach of many judges at first instance.[4]

1.2.2.5.3 The particular issue came before the House of Lords in *Bremer Vulkan Schiffbau und Maschinenfabrik* v. *South India Shipping Corp.*,[5] where the opinion enunciated by Lord Denning M.R. was denounced and the historical and restrictive doctrine reasserted. Lord Diplock proclaimed as a general principle that the courts have no wider jurisdiction to supervise arbitration than that conferred by legislation that expressly addresses the arbitral process or which otherwise arises under the general jurisdiction to give injunctive and declaratory relief. Apart from authority, Lord Diplock also considered the assertion of an open-ended power of intervention to be contrary to prevailing policy for it would discourage resort to London arbitration under international contracts between foreign parties who have no connection with the United Kingdom other than the desire to utilise London arbitration.[6]

1.2.2.5.4 The 1979 Act is wholly consistent with the restrictive and particularist view of the judicial supervisory jurisdiction. It does nothing to disturb the decision in *Bremer Vulkan* nor does it in its express terms confer a roving jurisdiction to supervise the arbitral process. It confers on the courts specific powers to entertain appeals and applications in relation to questions of law and gives a precise definition to these powers. The purpose of the legislation is to lay down an exclusive definition of the province of the supervisory jurisdiction in matters of law, and the extent of this jurisdiction will turn on the proper interpretation of the legislation.[7]

---

1. *Tersons Ltd.* v. *Stevenage Development Corporation* [1965] 1 Q.B. 37, 48. See also *Exormisis Shipping S.A.* v. *Oonsoo, the Democratic People's Republic of Korea and the Korean Foreign Transportation Corporation* [1975] 1 Lloyd's Rep. 432.
2. *Japan Line Ltd.* v. *Aggeliki Charis Compania Maritima S.A. and Davies and Potter (The Angelic Grace)* [1980] 1 Lloyd's Rep. 288, 292.
3. It was a two-judge Court of Appeal.
4. See *The Anna Maria* [1980] 1 Lloyd's Rep. 192; *The Splendid Sun* [1980] 1 Lloyd's Rep. 333; *Sanko Steamship Co. Ltd.* v. *Shipping Corpn. of India and Selwyn and Clark (The Jhansi Ki Rani* [1980] 2 Lloyd's Rep. 569; *The Estia* [1981] 1 Lloyd's Rep. 541. Contrast *Exormisis Shipping S.A.* v. *Oonsoo, etc.* [1975] 1 Lloyd's Rep. 432; *Crawford* v. *Prowting Ltd.* [1973] 1 Q.B. 1.
5. [1981] A.C. 909. See also *Channel Tunnel Group Ltd.* v. *Balfour Beatty Constitution Ltd.* [1993] 1 All E.R. 664, 688, per Lord Mustill.
6. *Ibid.* p. 979.
7. *Michael I. Warde* v. *Feedex International Inc.* [1985] 2 Lloyd's Rep. 289, 300 per Bingham J.

1.2.2.6 *Lifting the veil of privacy*

1.2.2.6.1 The potential advantages of arbitration are many although not guaranteed. Economy, expedition and expertise are frequently cited. Privacy is yet another. Unlike the judicial process the public and media have no right of access to the arbitral process and the awards of arbitrators are not published in the same manner as law reports.[1] Unless the parties determine otherwise the arbitration process is private and this probably is the feature which the consumers of arbitration find particularly attractive. But privacy does not without more amount to confidentiality and therefore, for example, documents produced in the course of a private arbitration may be subject to an order for discovery in subsequent public litigation.[2] The privacy of the arbitral process is probably underpinned by an implied term in the arbitration agreement prohibiting the publication of the award, although it appears that the implied term may give way in the face of special circumstances, as when an arbitrating party can show that it is necessary to disclose the award to a third party in order to establish or protect a legal right against the third party.[2a] It is also the case that an arbitrator may in appropriate circumstances be called as a witness to give evidence in open court of matters which have occurred during the course of the reference before him.[3]

1.2.2.6.2 To admit judicial review renders the arbitral process less advantageous for there is introduced delay and additional cost. It also removes the veil of privacy, for the arbitral dispute is brought into the public arena. An appeal or application under the 1979 Act also has this effect.[4] Although in practice many preliminary applications such as leave to appeal or liberty to apply are taken in chambers, even in these situations the parties often agree to judgment being given in open court when an important point of principle is in issue. Substantive appeals and applications are made in open court with the potential attendant publicity and with the judgment frequently reported.

It has long been recognised that the advantage of privacy is lost whenever the arbitral process falls subject to some mode of judicial review, and this is equally the case when the supervisory jurisdiction established by the 1979 Act is invoked.[5] With regard to the province of the 1979 Act privacy can only be guaranteed by a valid exclusion agreement.[6]

1.2.2.7 *Contemporary confidence in the arbitration process*

1.2.2.7.1 The 1979 Act represents yet further affirmation of the contemporary acceptance of the arbitration institution and of the confidence that now reposes in

1. Many awards emanating from institutional and *ad hoc* arbitration are published, although this is only possible with the consent of the parties and with the identity of the arbitrating parties often concealed. See generally Hunter, "Publication of Arbitrating Awards" [1987] 3 L.M.C.L.Q. 139; Samuel "The Unauthorized Publication of Arbitration Awards" [1989] 2 L.M.C.L.Q. 158.

2. *Shearson Lehman Hutton Inc. and Another* v. *Maclaine Watson & Co. Ltd. and Others* [1989] 1 All E.R. 1056.

2a. *Hassneh Insurance Co. of Israel and Others* v. *Steuart J. Mew* [1993] 2 Lloyd's Rep. 243.

3. *Duke of Buccleuch and Queensberry* v. *Metropolitan Board of Works* (1872) L.R. 5 H.L. 418.

4. See, for example, *Oxford Shipping Co. Ltd.* v. *Nippon Yusen Kaisha (The Eastern Saga)* [1984] 2 Lloyd's Rep. 373.

5. *Hassneh Insurance Co. of Israel and Others* v. *Steuart J. Mew, supra*, p. 247.

6. *Marine Contractors Inc.* v. *Shell Petroleum Co. of Nigeria Ltd.* [1984] 2 Lloyd's Rep. 77, 82, Ackner L.J.

arbitrators and the arbitral process. Long gone are the days of indiscriminating hostility, resentment and distrust. The arbitration institution exists as an important aspect of the administration of civil justice and stands in partnership with the courts and other tribunals. Both arbitration and the courts have important and often complementary roles to play. Arbitrators, particularly professional and trade arbitrators who operate in association with institutional arbitration, enjoy the respect and confidence of the judiciary, with the judiciary hesitant to assume their superintendence of the arbitral process unless wholly unavoidable in the circumstances of the case.[1] The courts are particularly reluctant to interfere with the exercise of discretion by or the award of an experienced and expert arbitrator.

1.2.2.7.2 The arbitration tribunal has always been regarded as the final tribunal of fact. Following the enactment of the 1979 Act it is also increasingly the final tribunal of law. It gives to arbitrators a greater responsibility because this is perceived to be the wish of the arbitrating parties and also because there now prevails a general acceptance that arbitrators have the competence to comprehend and apply the relevant principles and rules of law when they arise in the context of a dispute.[2]

1.2.2.7.3 The 1979 Act represents the most recent expression of public confidence in arbitrators. Beyond their established position as masters of fact, the legislation extends to arbitrators a new and substantial responsibility in relation to questions of law arising in association with referred disputes. Where the parties enter into an exclusion agreement they effectively make their arbitrators the final arbiters of law and fact. But even in the absence of an exclusion agreement arbitrators generally, and particularly professional, trade and other specialist arbitrators, are entrusted with greater responsibility for the determination and application of any legal questions and principles in issue, with the courts hesitant to intervene except when compelling cause can be established.

1.3 EMERGENCE OF THE 1979 ACT AND FORCES FOR REFORM

1.3.1 The Arbitration Act 1979 derives directly from and gives legislative effect to certain, but not all, of the recommendations of the Commercial Court Committee[1] made in its *Report on Arbitration*, published as a government document in July 1978.[2] The anxieties that weighed on the deliberations of the Committee concerning the judicial review of awards on question of law were at the time quite widespread in the legal-commercial community. The Commercial Judges made known their concerns

1. Cf. *K/S A/S Bill Biakh and K/S A/S Bill Biali* v. *Hyundai Corporation* [1988] 1 Lloyd's Rep. 187, 189, Steyn J.; *Exmar B V* v. *National Iranian Tanker Co. (The Trade Fortitude)* [1992] 1 Lloyd's Rep. 169, 175, Judge Diamond, Q.C.
2. *Everglade Maritime Inc.* v. *Schiffahrtsgesellschaft Detlef von Appen m.b.H. (The Maria)* [1993] 3 All E.R. 748, 754, Sir Thomas Bingham M.R.: "It is generally accepted that those who entrust decisions to arbitrators do so because they wish to rely on the judgment, skill and fairness of those arbitrators. If a decision of the courts was what the parties had wanted they would not have chosen to arbitrate. While, therefore, a power in the courts to review arbitral awards on grounds of legal error is preserved, it is, as the authorities show, a power to be exercised with the utmost caution."
1. The Commercial Court Committee is a forum established by the Lord Chancellor in 1977 with the purpose of establishing a direct link between the Commercial Court and users of the court: see Colman, *The Practice and Procedure of the Commercial Court* (3rd ed.), Chapter 2.
2. Cmnd. 7284. The relevant parts of the Report are set out in Appendix A.

about the defects in the prevailing law and how they might be corrected in both their judicial[3] and extra-judicial capacities.[4] Of particular force was the 1978 Alexander Lecture delivered by Lord Diplock and tellingly titled "The Case Stated—Its Use and Abuse".[5] Outside the judicial arena the London Arbitration Group[6] and a Joint Committee of the London Court of Arbitration,[7] the Institute of Arbitrators[8] and the London Maritime Arbitrators Association[9] also addressed the same issues and advocated reform. Parliamentary debate was initiated in the House of Lords by Lord Hacking,[10] an active and prominent reformer,[11] and there following the *Report on Arbitration* was published as a Command paper.[12] The government was quickly satisfied of the merits of the reformist case and a government bill was brought forward in the House of Lords which in its later progress sped through the parliamentary stages with all-party support and so avoided being lost by the pending dissolution of Parliament.[13] The Royal Assent was received on 14 April 1979 and the Act came into force on 1 August of the same year.[14]

1.3.2 In the first part of its *Report on Arbitration* (hereafter the Report) the Commercial Court Committee (hereafter the Committee) subsumed its deliberations and recommendations under the title "Judicial Supervision and Review of Arbitration Proceedings". The title is far too broad, for in reality the Committee attempted nothing so sweeping but focused more particularly on the review of arbitration awards for error of law and on the entrenchment of that review process. Its overwhelming concern was the functioning of the special case procedure as established by the Arbitration Act 1950, section 21,[15] and on the way in practice the procedure could be readily misused and abused by arbitrating parties. The Committee commented that at the time there existed "without doubt considerable and justified dissatisfaction at the

---

3. See, for example, *Provimi Hellas A.E.* v. *Warinco A.G.* [1978] 1 Lloyd's Rep. 67, 80, per Mocatta J.; *Eagle Star Insurance Co. Ltd.* v. *Yuval Insurance Co. Ltd.* [1978] 1 Lloyd's Rep. 357, 362, per Lord Denning M.R. *Tramountana Armadora S.A.* v. *Atlantic Shipping Co. S.A.* [1978] 1 Lloyd's Rep. 391, 394. See also *Tradax Export S.A.* v. *Andre & Cie S.A.* [1978] 1 Lloyd's Rep. 639, 642–643, where Donaldson J. incorporates into his judgment a statement of the way the law could be reformed.

4. See the letter by Donaldson J. (as he then was) published in *The Times*, 3 March 1978.

5. (1978) 44 *Arbitration* 107–116. The lecture was delivered by Lord Diplock in his capacity as President of the Institute of Arbitrators (as it then was).

6. An association of concerned British and American lawyers under the chairmanship of Mr Mark Littman Q.C. See further Littman, "England Reconsiders 'The Stated Case'" (1979) 13 *The International Lawyer*, 253–259.

7. Now the London Court of International Arbitration.

8. Now the Chartered Institute of Arbitrators.

9. Under the chairmanship of Mr Clifford Clark.

10. Debate on arbitration in the House of Lords raised by Lord Hacking, 15 May 1978 (392 *Hansard* c. 89–117).

11. See, Hacking, "A new competition—Rivals for centres of arbitration" [1979] 4 L.M.C.L.Q. 435; Hacking, "International Commercial Arbitrations—Recent Developments in London, Paris and Stockholm" (Text of Address to Society of Maritime Arbitrators, New York, 2 February 1979). Hacking, "What the Act has Achieved", in *The Arbitration Act 1979 and its Effect on Commercial Disputes*, Lloyd's of London Press (1980).

12. *Supra* n. 2.

13. The urgency was caused by the decision of the then Prime Minister Mr James Callaghan (now Lord Callaghan) to dissolve Parliament on 7 April 1979 and call a general election. See Marshall, "The Arbitration Act 1979" [1979] J.B.L. 241.

14. See *infra*, para. 1.7. For a full legislative history see "Arbitration Act 1979", 1979 *Commercial Laws of Europe* 304, 309.

15. See *infra*, para. 1.4.2.

abuse of the existing special case procedure".[16] Arbitrators were being requested or the court invited to direct arbitrators to state awards as special cases when there existed no genuine grievance that the arbitrator had erred in law but in order to engineer delay and a postponement of a party's obligation to pay compensation under the terms of an award.[17] Once instituted a special case entailed a full hearing before the court and a deferral of the finality of the award until the court answered the question(s) raised in the special case. This manner of malpractice was a relatively new phenomenon and was closely related to and tacitly encouraged by the economic and fiscal climate which prevailed from the early 1970s and onwards for a number of years, the signal features of which were high inflation and erratic exchange rates. In this economic environment arbitral delay had the potential to ease cash flow difficulties and to materially alter the financial benefit and burden of an award. Although aware of these developments the courts were often helpless to intervene and discourage or resist the practice. This was in substantial part due to inherent defects in the special case procedure,[18] and in particular to the way the Court of Appeal in *The Lysland*[19] had structured the judicial discretion under section 21 of the Arbitration Act 1950. With regard to the latter the Committee was of the view that "case law has or is widely thought to have established that if any real point of law arises the arbitrator should adopt the special case procedure even if there is no great sum in dispute, no point of general importance is involved or the answer is reasonably clear".[20] In the upshot the finality of a London arbitration award was being grievously eroded and the sanctions of costs and interest awards were not necessarily effective deterrents to unmeritorious applications given the benefits that could otherwise be reaped from delay.[21]

1.3.3 The Committee's response to the prevailing problem and discontent was to recommend the abolition of the special case procedure and its replacement by an appeal process based on reasoned awards and confined to questions of law.[22] This was perceived as an alternative means of achieving the same object as underlay the special case procedure, namely the review and correction of awards for legal error, but with fewer disadvantages.[23] An obvious and immediate obstacle confronting this suggested new approach was the common law reviewing jurisdiction based on error of law on the face of an award, which co-existed with the statutory special case procedure, and which actively discouraged the making of reasoned awards but encouraged the prac-

---

16. Para. 49. See also Lord Diplock, "The Case Stated—its Use and Abuse", *supra*; Kerr, "The English Courts and Arbitration" in *International Commercial Arbitration* ed. Schmitthoff (Vol. 1); Littman "England Reconsiders 'The Stated Case'", *supra*; Schmitthoff, "Commercial Arbitration and the Commercial Court" in *Commercial Law in a Changing Economic Climate* (2nd edn.).

17. Cf. *Provimi Hellas A.E.* v. *Warinco A.G.* [1978] 1 Lloyd's Rep. 67, 80, per Mocatta J, "it would be to blind one's eyes to realities if one did not recognise that requests for special cases are sometimes made by unsuccessful parties at arbitration primarily for purposes of delay".

18. See *infra*, para. 1.4.2.

19. *Halfdan, Greig & Co. A.S.* v. *Sterling Coal and Navigation Corp. (The Lysland)* [1973] Q.B. 843. The case is considered in greater detail *infra*, para. 1.4.2.8 *et seq*.

20. Para. 12.

21. See paras. 19–24 for the Committee's assessment of the misuse and defects in the special case procedure. But compare *Granvias Oceanica Armadora S.A.* v. *Jibsen Trading Co. (The Kavo Peiratis)* [1977] 2 Lloyd's Rep. 344, 349–350, 353, per Kerr J.

22. Some commentators favoured reform based on a reshaping of the special case procedure, see Schmitthoff, "The Reform of the English Law of Arbitration" [1977] J.B.L. 305.

23. Para. 19.

tice of giving extra-award reasons.[24] The Committee recommended the removal of the obstacle by the abolition of the common law jurisdiction. This would leave arbitrators free to give reasons and at the same time also have the desirable effect of accentuating the rationality of the arbitral process. By bringing English practice on reasoned awards closer to that prevailing in the vast majority of foreign jurisdictions the proposed change might also have the effect of making English awards more acceptable and therefore also more readily enforceable abroad. The existence of a reasoned award would also provide access to the facts found by the arbitrator and so enable the court to determine whether a question of law actually arose for decision. For the proposed new appeal procedure to be effective it was further necessary for a party to a reference to have the power to ask for a reasoned award and when confronted with a refusal for the court in appropriate cases to be able to order the giving of reasons.[25]

1.3.4 The proposed new appeal procedure based on reasoned awards was not, however, viewed in terms of an absolute right. An appeal would only be capable of being initiated with the agreement of all parties or with leave of the High Court.[26] The Committee considered that leave to appeal should only be given if the High Court was satisfied "that the question of law in issue might be determined on appeal in a way which would affect the rights of the parties under the award",[27] and in giving leave the court should also have the power to attach conditions.[28] From the decision of the High Court there would be a further right of appeal to the Court of Appeal but this appellate link should be strictly limited and only available following the giving of a certificate by the High Court judge and the grant of leave by the High Court or the Court of Appeal.[29] The Committee considered that these reforms would provide English law with,

a modern and efficient system of judicial review which would meet the legitimate needs of those who submit their disputes to arbitration. Successful parties would be able to obtain speedy enforcement of awards. Unsuccessful parties would be able to obtain relief in the comparatively rare cases in which an arbitrator misapplied the law in a material respect, but would be deprived of the opportunity of avoiding their commitments by procedural devices.[30]

1.3.5 Embodied within the special case procedure established by section 21 of the Arbitration Act 1950 there also existed the so-called consultative case procedure whereby a question of law arising in the course of a reference could be placed before the High Court for its opinion.[31] The consultative case procedure received only brief comment in the Report, although it is clear that the Committee supported its retention.[32] The Committee, however, appears to have contemplated quite a different form of procedure for it recommended that the High Court should possess a power "to

24. See Chapter 11 for a full discussion of reasoned awards.
25. Paras. 25–31. See also Chapter 11.
26. Para. 35.
27. Para. 35. See *infra*, para. 1.5 and Chapter 5 for the manner in which the judiciary has perceived and developed the discretionary power to give or refuse leave to appeal under the 1979 Act, and which has resulted in a much more restricted appellate link between arbitration awards and the High Court than the Committee in its Report anticipated.
28. Para. 35. The conditions contemplated by the Committee were the payment of the minimum sum due to the successful party or the securing of the sum in dispute. See further Chapter 4, para. 4.3.4.
29. Para. 37. See further Chapter 10.
30. Para. 38. See also para. 31.
31. See *infra*, para. 1.4.2 and Chapter 12.
32. Para. 36.

require arbitrators to make a reasoned interim award" which it saw as an equivalent procedure to the pre-existing consultative case.[33] This particular recommendation has not been adopted although the Committee's suggested precondition to the making of an order for a reasoned interim award has; namely, if "the Court was satisfied that a question of law had arisen in the course of the reference a decision on which might produce substantial savings in costs to the parties and that it was one in respect of which leave to appeal might be given".[34]

1.3.6 A major feature of the special case procedure was its entrenched character. It could not be displaced even by the express will of the parties. Following the decision of the Court of Appeal in *Czarnikow* v. *Roth, Schmidt and Co.*[35] it was widely considered that any attempt to exclude by contract the right to apply under the statutory special case procedure was void as being contrary to public policy. As summarised by the Committee, the perceived considerations of public policy were "that there should, in principle, be no sphere of national activity in which the King's writ did not run, that there should be but one system of law and that those who were commercially weak should be protected by law from those who were commercially strong".[36] The special case procedure as formulated contributed to the certainty of English commercial law and also provided an institutional framework for its sensitive evolution.[37] There was nonetheless a cost in consequence of the detraction from the finality of awards, the delay in the arbitral process and discouragement to the expansion of London arbitration to meet the demands emanating from the new and growing areas of international commercial practice.[38] With the passage of time these impediments loomed ever larger and generated a growing sensitivity of their potential impact on the growth of London arbitration.[39]

1.3.7 Ironically when a procedure analogous to the special case was first and belatedly introduced in Scotland by the Administration of Justice (Scotland) Act 1972 it was also provided that the parties could exclude the new statutory procedure by express agreement.[40] The Committee while continuing to be impressed by the public policy considerations enunciated in *Czarnikow*[41] nonetheless considered that the English position should move some way towards the Scottish. In its most radical proposal it recommended that it ought to be open to arbitrating parties to contract out of the new judicial review by way of appeals from reasoned awards it was proposing.[42] In so recommending the Committee took a restrictive view of the continuing relevance of the public policy considerations associated with *Czarnikow*,[43] and also had a keen eye on the national interest, for the effect of its recommendation was potentially to make

---

33. Para. 36.
34. Para. 36 and see further in Chapter 12.
35. [1922] 2 K.B. 478 (C.A.).
36. Para. 13. See *infra*, para. 1.4.3.
37. The benefits of the special case procedure were also stressed by Lord Diplock, "The Case Stated—its Use and Abuse", *supra*.
38. Paras. 16–18.
39. Staughton, "Arbitration Act 1979—A Pragmatic Compromise" (1979) N.L.J. 920, 921. Note also the speech of the Lord Chancellor in introducing the Second Reading of the Bill in the House of Lords, 397 *Hansard* c. 434–464.
40. Section 3. See generally, Hunter, *The Law of Arbitration in Scotland*.
41. *Supra*, n. 36.
42. Paras. 39–52.
43. Para. 42.

London a substantially more attractive arbitration venue, particularly for the arbitration of disputes arising out of the so-called supranational contracts which hitherto had been directed to foreign arbitration centres.[44] But in making this recommendation the Committee was not prepared to contemplate an unfettered right to contract out and so lose all sight of the public policy considerations advanced in *Czarnikow*. In particular there had to be provided a measure of protection for the commercially weak,[45] and the continued development of English commercial law had also to be in some way safeguarded.[46] In the result its recommendations relating to the validity of contracting out agreements were complex and heavily qualified, with special protective provisions made for domestic arbitration agreements and the arbitration of what were coined special category disputes. The issue of validity was to turn variously on the moment a contracting out agreement was concluded, whether before or after a dispute had arisen and been referred to arbitration; the nature of the arbitration agreement, whether it was a domestic or non-domestic agreement; the governing law of the substantive dispute, whether the governing law was that of a constituent part of the United Kingdom or a foreign system of law; and the character of the dispute referred, in particular whether it was a "special category dispute", alluding to maritime, insurance and commodity trading contract disputes.

1.3.8 In general terms the Committee adopted a contracting out rather than a contracting in rule. In other words a right to judicial review was to prevail unless there was in existence a valid contracting out agreement, eventually styled an exclusion agreement in the 1979 Act.[47] The one exception related to the arbitration of a dispute arising out of a contract, the proper law of which was expressly stated to be a system of law other than that of the United Kingdom or any part thereof.[48] In English law a question of foreign law is one of fact and therefore any basis for review would be most unusual but not wholly impossible. The Committee considered that English law might assume a relevance as being the *lex fori* or by virtue of the doctrine of *renvoi*.[49] In this kind of circumstance the Committee recommended that there should be no right of review unless the parties expressly agreed that such a right should exist; in other words the parties had contracted in to judicial review.[50] The substance of this recommendation can be traced into the 1979 Act, although the format in which it appears is very different from that contemplated in the Report of the Committee.[51]

1.3.9 The Committee also drew a crucial distinction between contracting out agreements concluded before and after a dispute had arisen and been referred to arbitration. In the latter circumstance the Committee recommended that in all cases the parties should be free to exclude any right to judicial review.[52] It was reasoned that after a dispute had arisen and been referred to arbitration the parties were in a position to determine whether speed and finality of decision were of such importance that they were prepared to accept the risk that the arbitrator's decision might be wrong in

---

44. Paras. 18 and 45.
45. Para. 47.
46. Para. 48.
47. See Chapter 13.
48. Para. 41.
49. Para. 9.
50. Paras. 44 and 52(a).
51. See Chapter 13.
52. Paras. 43 and 52(b).

law. Further, once a dispute had been referred the relative position of the parties was more greatly equalised and the concern to protect weaker parties need not be so greatly emphasised. A contracting out agreement entered into after the reference of the dispute was also likely to be a truly voluntary agreement and therefore only likely to be agreed to when it was in the interests of all parties.[53]

1.3.10 The Committee also considered that parties should be free to conclude contracting out agreements prior to a dispute arising and being referred to arbitration but subject to two very significant qualifications. The first related to domestic arbitration agreements,[54] which in essence are arbitration agreements which provide for arbitration in the U.K. and with the parties thereto nationals of and habitually resident in the U.K., or companies incorporated in and having their central management and control in the U.K.[55] With regard to this category of arbitration agreement the Committee considered that the public policy considerations set out in *Czarnikow* should continue to hold sway and therefore that the right to judicial review should be entrenched. It was also considered that in relation to disputes within the province of domestic arbitration agreements a protective element was justified, for the parties to such agreements often stood in positions of unequal bargaining power and an entrenched right of judicial review offered the weaker party necessary protection.[56] In the result the Committee took the position that in relation to a dispute arising under a domestic arbitration agreement a contracting out agreement was to be valid only if entered into after the dispute had been referred to arbitrators.

1.3.11 The second qualification related to "special category disputes", alluding to the types of commercial disputes traditionally resolved in London institutional arbitration and arising out of maritime matters, insurance and commodity contracts.[57] The major public policy consideration with regard to this broad category was that the historical entrenched right of review over such arbitrations had provided the vehicle for the development of English commercial law and its establishment as the first choice system of law in international commerce.[58] Within the individual spheres of the category there was also no evidence of any widespread desire to contract out. Further, no issue of protective jurisprudence arose and such arbitrations were invariably non-domestic in character, involving at least one and often two foreign parties.[59] The Committee implicitly considered that arbitrations relating to "special category disputes" should follow the rule with regard to non-domestic arbitrations, with the parties free to contract out even before a dispute had arisen and been referred to arbitration.[60] But it equally believed that once the superiority of the new system of judicial review it was recommending was fully established, few would wish to contract out. The Committee also feared that given the prevailing discontent with the special case procedure, there was a danger that if no restriction on the right to contract out

---

53. Para. 43.
54. Paras. 40, 47 and 52(b)(i).
55. Para. 47 and see further Chapter 13, para. 13.4.3.
56. Para. 47.
57. Paras. 41, 48–50, 52(c)(ii).
58. This line of thought has attracted unrestrained criticism from certain commentators, see Mann, "Private Arbitration and Public Policy" (1985) 4 C.J.Q. 257; Goode, "The Adaptation of English Law to International Commercial Arbitration" (1992) 8 Arb. Int. 1.
59. Paras. 16 and 48.
60. Para. 49.

was imposed there would arise an immediate and extraordinary exodus from judicial review and with the environment even ripe for contracting out agreements to become normal trading terms. If this were to occur the new system would not be given a fair test. The Committee therefore recommended that with regard to "special category disputes" the right of review should be entrenched for a period of two to three years, but that any legislation implementing its Report should contain a power to vary the recommendation in the light of the then prevailing circumstances. Such a variation could permit contracting out prior to the reference of a dispute, although in this regard the Committee contemplated that the contracting out agreement should be in writing and separate from the arbitration agreement, and that it should be formally registered with the High Court.[61] The concluded view of the Committee, therefore, was that at least in the short term a contracting out agreement entered into in relation to a special category dispute should not be valid unless entered into after the dispute had arisen and been referred to arbitration.

1.3.12 In all other cases the parties were to be free to contract out of judicial review prior to the emergence and reference of a dispute. This alluded to non-domestic or international arbitration agreements (other than those under which special category disputes arose) and in particular included arbitrations arising under the so-called supranational development contracts.[62] As a class these contracts were at the time a fairly new phenomenon relating to such matters as mineral exploration; construction of new plant, airports, harbours, towns, power stations, etc.; long-term supply contracts; management and consultancy arrangements; joint ventures and other similar commercial, industrial and financial agreements. Although the subject matter of these agreements might vary materially they nonetheless frequently displayed a number of common features which moulded them into a loosely distinct category. They often involved foreign governments or the organs of foreign governments and multinational companies; phenomenally large sums of money were involved with complex financial arrangements incorporated into the agreement; they were not concluded on the basis of standard form contracts but were "tailor-made" agreements with the parties negotiating at arms length with the benefit of professional and other expert advice; the parties eschewed the municipal courts of any country and sought a neutral and competent international arbitration as a means of producing a final resolution of any dispute that might arise.[63] The Committee was of the opinion that the desire to avoid judicial embroilment under any State jurisdiction on the part of parties arbitrating disputes arising under supranational development contracts was understandable and reasonable. It also felt that the entrenched right of judicial review had hitherto discouraged these arbitrations from coming to London, notwithstanding that the parties might otherwise be happy to use London arbitration and its professional arbitrators, and also to adopt English law as the proper law of their contracts. This had resulted in loss to the national economy and it was undoubtedly in the national interest that the deterrent be removed. To permit contracting out prior to the emergence of a dispute arising

---

61. Paras. 49 and 50. See further Chapter 13.
62. Paras. 18, 41, 45 and 52(c)(iii).
63. See further Littman, "England Reconsiders 'The Stated Case'" (1979) 13 *The International Lawyer* 253; Kerr, "Commercial Dispute Resolution" in *Liber Amicorum for Lord Wilberforce* ed. Bos. and Brownlie.

out of a supranational contract also involved no intolerable sacrifice of policy for the parties were invariably fully advised by experts and needed no protection; and further the disputes were not usually of a nature which would contribute to the development of English commercial law.[64] In the upshot the Committee recommended a legal regime whereunder parties to supranational development contracts who wish to arbitrate their dispute in London may do so on terms which enable them to freely contract out of the right to judicial review, either before or after a dispute has arisen, and thereby preclude any risk of judicial entanglement with regard to questions of law.[65]

1.3.13 The *Report on Arbitration* of the Commercial Court Committee represents the most significant development in the modern history of arbitration law. In addressing and reconsidering one of the central issues of the subject, namely the judicial review of arbitration awards on questions of law, it came forward with recommendations influenced by new considerations of policy and aimed at giving English law a new direction. The Committee deliberated within an environment which manifested a real concern for the surviving reputation of London arbitration and for its capacity to accommodate the new demands of international commercial practice. It responded by recommending new and improved procedures and by casting the law in a more consumer friendly mould. The exercise is also a witness to the economic realities of contemporary commercial law and its institutions, and to the heightened political sensitivity to these realities. Had it not been for the threat to the national economic interest which the then state of the law represented it is doubtful whether Parliament could have been imposed upon to act so expeditiously. The Committee and the legislature were motivated principally by a concern that the existing and indissoluble relationship between the courts and arbitration in English arbitral jurisprudence, and the abuses which the relationship readily lent itself to, were deterring parties to international commercial agreements and their advisers from adopting London arbitration. It was feared that international arbitrations were being increasingly referred to other world arbitral fora where, in the view of at least certain sections of the international mercantile community, the domestic legal regimes were by virtue of a more limited judicial supervisory jurisdiction more favourable, less open to abuse, and more conducive to the demand that arbitration be swift and final. The motivation for urging the reform which was so quickly responded to in the shape of the Arbitration Act 1979 is therefore clear. It was to secure the position of London as an international arbitral centre and to remove an obstacle to its further growth.[66] The Committee itself concluded with the following unambiguous message:

In the view of the Committee the need for these simple, but far-reaching, reforms is extremely urgent. This country can retain its position as the international leader in commercial law and arbitration only so long as it provides the service which its customers need. The existing customers, many of whom are of long standing, need an appeals system which is speedy and efficient, yet cannot be abused. Our future customers, the parties to supranational contracts, need to be able to contract out of the appeals system if so advised. Only when this becomes possible will they consider England as a possible venue for arbitration. Time is short, for if they

---

64. Paras. 18 and 45.
65. Para. 52(c)(iii).
66. See Schmitthoff, "Commercial Arbitration and the Commercial Court" in *Commercial Law in a Changing Economic Climate* (2nd edn.); Kerr, "Commercial Dispute Resolution" in *Liber Amicorum for Lord Wilberforce, supra.*

once establish arbitral links with other countries, it will become very much more difficult to attract them to this country.[67]

1.3.14 In the second part of its Report the Committee made a number of miscellaneous recommendations for the improvement of arbitration law. Only a minority of these were acted upon and incorporated into the 1979 Act. These related to matters appertaining to the establishment of an arbitration tribunal[68] and the creation of a jurisdiction vested in the High Court to confer a default power on arbitrators.[69] Other recommendations relating to the establishment of an Arbitration Rules Committee,[70] the consolidation of arbitrations,[71] certain matters appertaining to costs,[72] and the discontinuance of the term misconduct for procedural breach of duty, not involving dishonesty,[73] were not pursued but remain lively areas of debate.

1.4 THE DISPLACED REGIME OF JUDICIAL REVIEW

Although by any measure the 1979 Act is a radical provision, it is nonetheless important to bear in mind that the Act does not itself establish for the first time the link between arbitration and the courts with regard to questions of law. This relationship had been developed over the two centuries preceding the enactment.[1] The significance of the 1979 Act is that it rationalises and restructures the relationship. It also introduces a significant filter mechanism by which the flow of legal questions and appeals coming forth from arbitration for decision by the courts may be regulated[2]; and in giving recognition to exclusion agreements it also makes it possible for parties to exclude the possibility of judicial entanglement with regard to questions of law.[3] But to fully understand the impact of the 1979 Act some knowledge of the preceding law and its development is essential.

At common law an award could be reviewed for error of law on the face of the award and by statute a special case procedure was introduced which was again confined to questions of law.[4] Both procedures are abolished by section 1(1) of the 1979 Act and survived only for transitional purposes. Nonetheless the transitional phase proved to be surprisingly resilient and awards stated as special cases continued to be reported until very recent times.[5] But the former regime may now be presumed to be

---

67. Para. 53.
68. Paras. 58 and 59. See *supra*, para. 1.2.1.7.4.
69. Para. 57. See *supra*, para. 1.2.1.7.1.
70. Para. 55.
71. Para. 56.
72. Paras. 60–66.
73. Para. 67.
1. Considered *infra*.
2. See Chapters 5 and 12 in particular.
3. See Chapter 13.
4. Both procedures are discussed *infra*. For an example of these procedures operating concurrently see *Glatki Shipping Co. S.A.* v. *Pinius Shipping Co. No. 1 (The Maira) (No. 2)* [1984] 1 Lloyd's Rep. 660; [1985] 1 Lloyd's Rep. 300 (C.A.).
5. The attempt to identify the precise historical moment the last special case came forward for consideration before the courts proved to be something of a judicial parlour game: see the comments in *Bremer Handelsgesellschaft m.b.H.* v. *Westzucker G.m.b.H. (No. 3)* [1989] 1 Lloyd's Rep. 198; [1989] 1 Lloyd's Rep. 582 (C.A.). Without suggesting that it is the last, the honour may come to be claimed by *Antclizo Shipping Corporation* v. *Food Corporation of India (The Antclizo) (No. 2)* [1991] 2 Lloyd's Rep. 485; [1992] 1 Lloyd's Rep. 558 (C.A.).

moribund. The precise extent of the abrogation achieved by section 1(1) is however uncertain and may not be as great as may have been originally intended. Whereas the special case procedure is unambiguously and comprehensively repealed the common law jurisdiction is abrogated only with regard to awards made "on an arbitration agreement". Under the 1979 Act an arbitration agreement is defined as a written arbitration agreement.[6] This leaves open at least the possibility that the common law jurisdiction survives with regard to awards made on a parol arbitration agreement.[7] Whereas, of necessity, the common law jurisdiction required a written award, it does not appear further to have been confined to written arbitration agreements. But even if the point here made is legitimate, it will nonetheless not be of material concern for informal arbitration agreements are exceptionally rare in practice.

1.4.1 Error of law on the face of an award

1.4.1.1 In point of time the common law jurisdiction based on error of law on the face of an award was the first to be established. Its emergence at the turn of the nineteenth century was in all probability closely associated with the recognition during the same historical phase of an arbitrator's duty to decide disputes and differences referred according to legal criteria. Prior to this development the supervisory jurisdiction of the courts over awards tended to be restricted to that permitted by the express language of the Arbitration Act 1698,[1] under which the courts had jurisdiction to set aside awards procured by corruption or undue means.[2] The conjunction of the duty to determine disputes according to law and the emergent common law supervisory jurisdiction was succinctly expressed by Chambre J. in *Aubert* v. *Maze*[3]: "There is no doubt that an arbitrator is bound by the rules of law like every other Judge, and if it appears on the face of the record that the arbitrator has acted contrary to law his award may be set aside." The newly materialised common law jurisdiction was endorsed in *Kent* v. *Estob*,[4] and other authorities of the period.[5] There following there was set in train a strand of judicial supervisory jurisdiction which survived until its abrogation by the 1979 Act.[6] There was, however, never total judicial satisfaction with the jurisdiction, and the history of the subject is sprinkled with expressions of

---

6. See *infra*, para, 1.7.5.
7. See also *supra*, para. 1.2.2.1.7.
1. 9 & 10 Wm. 3, c. 15. See also *Morgan* v. *Mather* (1792) 2 Ves. Jun. 15, 18.
2. See generally Lord Parker C.J., "The History and Development of Commercial Arbitration" (The Hebrew University of Jerusalem Lionel Cohen Lectures, Fifth Series, January 1959). The lecture is partially republished under the title "The Development of Commercial Arbitration" [1959] J.B.L. 213. Note also Schmitthoff, "Commercial Arbitration and the Commercial Court" in *Commercial Law in a Changing Economic Climate* (2nd edn.), where the emergence of the common law regime is seen as a clear expression of the suspicion, if not outright hostility, which the judiciary felt historically towards arbitration.
3. (1801) 2 Bos. & Pul. 371; 126 E.R. 1333. Contrast *Morgan* v. *Mather* (1792) 2 Ves. Jun. 15, 18, where such a jurisdiction was doubted.
4. (1802) 3 East 18.
5. See, for example, *Blennerhasset* v. *Day* (1811) 2 Ball & B. 104, *Steff* v. *Andrews* (1816) 2 Mad. 6; *Ames* v. *Milward* (1818) 8 Taunt. 637; *Stimpson* v. *Emmerson* (1847) 9 L.T. (O.S.) 199.
6. In addition to cases cited, *infra*, see, *British Westinghouse Co.* v. *Underground Electric Ry. Co.* [1912] A.C. 673; *The Attorney-General for the Province of Manitoba* v. *Thomas Kelly Ltd.* [1922] 1 A.C. 268 (P.C.); *Racecourse Betting Control Board* v. *Secretary for Air* [1944] Ch. 114.

judicial reservation and regret.[7] In more recent years Lord Diplock castigated the jurisdiction as "confessedly anomalous".[8] The unease contributed to a judicial determination to keep the jurisdiction within tight boundaries and not to accommodate applications too readily; even to discourage applications.[9]

1.4.1.2 The common law jurisdiction was wholly divorced from considerations of procedure. It was confined to the review of awards emanating from the arbitral process,[10] and based on the establishment of a demonstrable error of law on the face of the award.[10a] This necessarily connoted a written award, with the concept of "the face of an award" including the award *per se* and any document expressly or impliedly incorporated into the award.[11] Whereas an express incorporation could give rise to questions of construction, the assertion of an implied incorporation frequently gave rise to deeper difficulties for the issue turned on the intention of the arbitrator, which of necessity was to be decided on the facts and circumstances of individual cases.[12] If the award, as so defined, revealed no error of law then the common law jurisdiction was of no avail; as equally was the case if the error of law was revealed elsewhere than on the face of the award. Lord Dunedin summarised the common law jurisdiction in the following terms[13]:

An error in law on the face of the award means . . . that you can find in the award or a document actually incorporated thereto, as for instance a note appended by the arbitrator stating the reasons for his judgment, some legal proposition which is the basis of the award and which you can then say is erroneous.

It was for the party challenging the award to demonstrate on a balance of probabilities the existence of a clear error of law derivable from the face of the award itself.[14] To establish the mere possibility of error was not enough nor was silence on a particular point or issue normally sufficient to establish a basis for detecting a demonstrable

---

7. See, for example, *Hodgkinson* v. *Fernie* (1857) 3 C.B. (N.S.) 189, at pp. 202, 205 per Williams and Willes JJ.; *Champsey Bhara & Co.* v. *Jivraj Balloo Spinning and Weaving Co.* [1923] A.C. 480, 487 per Lord Dunedin; *R.* v. *Northumberland Compensation Appeal Tribunal* [1951] 1 K.B. 711, 721, per Lord Goddard C.J.; *Eagle Star Insurance Co. Ltd.* v. *Yuval Insurance Co. Ltd.* [1978] 1 Lloyd's Rep. 357, 362, per Lord Denning M.R.

8. *Bremer Vulkan Schiffbau und Maschinenfabrik* v. *South India Shipping Corp. Ltd.* [1981] A.C. 909, 978.

9. *Gunter Henck* v. *Andre & Cie S.A.* [1970] 1 Lloyd's Rep. 235; *Kruse* v. *Ralli Maclaine (formerly Ralli Merrill Lynch Int. Ltd.)* [1982] 1 Lloyds's Rep. 162; *Glafki Shipping Co. S.A.* v. *Pinios Shipping Co. No. 1 (The Maira) (No. 2)* [1984] 1 Lloyd's Rep. 660.

10. *Bremer Vulkan Schiffbau und Maschinenfabrik* v. *South India Shipping Corp. Ltd.*, *supra*. p. 978.

10a. There was no jurisdiction to intervene if the error did not appear on the face of the award: see, *Hagger* v. *Baker* (1845) 14 M. & W. 9, per Baron Pollock, "The general rule is, that if an arbitrator makes a mistake which is not apparent on the face of his award, the party injured has no redress; and there is no difference between a mistake in the law of evidence and in other matters."

11. *Kent* v. *Elstob* (1802) 3 East 18, *Sharman* v. *Bell* (1816) M. & S. 504; *Hodgkinson* v. *Fernie* (1857) 3 C.B. (N.S.) 189; *Champsey Bhara & Co.* v. *Jivraj Balloo Spinning and Weaving Co.* [1923] A.C. 480 (P.C.); *Giacomo Costa fu Andrea* v. *British Italian Trading Co. Ltd.* [1961] 2 Lloyd's Rep. 392 (first instance); *Aktiebolaget Legis* v. *V. Berg & Sons Ltd.* [1964] 1 Lloyd's Rep. 203.

12. *Ibid.* See also *Andrea* v. *British Italian Trading* [1962] 1 Lloyd's Rep. 151 (C.A.); *Pearl Marin Shipping A/B* v. *Pietro Cingolani S.A.S. (The General Valdes)* [1981] 1 Lloyd's Rep. 170 (first instance).

13. *Champsey Bhara & Co.* v. *Jivraj Balloo Spinning and Weaving Co.* [1923] A.C. 480, 487 (P.C.).

14. *Gunter Henck* v. *Andre & Cie S.A.* [1970] 1 Lloyd's Rep. 235; *Pagnan & F.Lli* v. *Coprosol S.A.* [1981] 1 Lloyd's Rep. 283; *Kruse* v. *Ralli Maclaine (formerly Ralli Merrill Lynch Int. Ltd.)* [1982] 1 Lloyd's Rep. 162; *Glafki Shipping Co. S.A.* v. *Pinios Shipping Co. No. 1 The Maira (No. 2)* [1984] 1 Lloyd's Rep. 660.

error of law.[15] The award was to be construed in a fair and reasonable manner.[16] It was not for the court to act as a detective and investigate beyond or below the surface of the award,[17] and therefore it was not competent for the court to examine extrinsic evidence,[18] although a document specified in the award and which lay at the foundation of the legal proposition on which the award proceeded could be examined.[19] The error of law had to be shown to exist in the substance of the award, which included the reasons of the arbitrator,[20] but not the recitals and narrative.[21] The posture adopted by the court meant that it was highly unlikely that the court could be persuaded to exercise the general jurisdiction to remit if the effect of the remission was to increase the exposure of the award to judicial review.

1.4.1.3 At common law there existed a jurisdiction to set aside awards only.[22] There was no power to correct errors or to remit awards. It was by statute that the court came to enjoy an enlarged jurisdiction to remit awards.[23] There following the judicial position was substantially more flexible and it became possible to remit an award as an alternative to setting it aside; or to set aside an award to the extent to which it was erroneous in law and to remit the residue of the award for reconsideration by the arbitrator.[24]

The establishment of an error of law on the face of the award did not without more create a right to a remedy. There was an element of discretion and in each case it was for the court to consider whether it was just that the award be set aside or remitted.[25] Although there was a reluctance to set aside awards,[26] nonetheless once a material error of law that substantially affected the position of one of the arbitrating parties was demonstrated it was difficult for the court to do otherwise than intervene and set aside the award.[27] The jurisdiction to remit was however in appropriate circumstances

---

15. *The Maira (No. 2)*, *ibid*.

16. *Diestal* v. *Stephenson* [1906] 2 K.B. 345, 351; *Kruse* v. *Ralli Maclaine (formerly Ralli Merrill Lynch Int. Ltd.)*, *supra*.

17. *Kruse* v. *Ralli Maclaine (formerly Ralli Merrill Lynch Int. Ltd.)*, *supra*.

18. *Kelantan Government* v. *Duff Development Co.* [1923] A.C. 395, 417, per Lord Parmoor.

19. *Landauer* v. *Asser* [1905] 2 K.B. 186, considered in *Champsey Bhara & Co.* v. *Jivraj Balloo Spinning and Weaving Co.* [1923] A.C. 480 (P.C.). Contrast *Blaiber & Co. Ltd.* v. *Leopold Newborne (London) Ltd.* [1953] 2 Lloyd's Rep. 427; *Aktiebolaget Legis* v. *V. Berg & Sons Ltd.* [1964] 1 Lloyd's Rep. 203.

20. *Pearl Marin Shipping A/B* v. *Pietro Cingolani S.A.S. (The General Valdes)* [1982] 1 Lloyd's Rep. 17. (C.A.).

21. *Champsey Bhara & Co.* v. *Jivraj Balloo Spinning and Weaving Co.* [1923] A.C. 480 (P.C.).

22. *Ex parte Cuerton* (1826) 7 Dow & Ry K.B. 774; *Re Keighley Maxted & Co. and Durant & Co.* [1893] 1 Q.B. 405, 409; *Simpson* v. *IRC* [1914] 2 K.B. 842; *Potato Marketing Board* v. *Merricks* [1958] 2 Q.B. 316; *Meyer* v. *Leanse* [1958] 2 Q.B. 371.

23. The statutory power was first introduced by s. 8 of the Common Law Procedure Act 1854 and thereafter re-enacted in s. 10 of the Arbitration Act 1889 and s. 22 of the Arbitration Act 1950, which is the extant statutory provision. Apart from statute there did exist modes by which an award might be remitted, deriving from the nature of a reference and procedural mechanisms conjured up by the judiciary, but these are now solely of historical interest: see generally *King* v. *Thomas McKenna Ltd.* [1991] 1 All E.R. 653 where Lord Donaldson M.R. alludes to and explains the "Richard's" clause.

24. See, for example, *Syros Shipping Co. S.A.* v. *Claghill Trading Co. (The Proodos C)* [1980] 2 Lloyd's Rep. 390; *Pearl Marin Shipping A/B* v. *Pietro Cingolani S.A.S. (The General Valdes)* [1982] 1 Lloyd's Rep. 17. Contrast *Re Montgomery, Jones & Co. and Liebenthal Co.'s Arbitration* (1898) 78 L.T. 406 (C.A.).

25. *Glafki Shipping Co. S.A.* v. *Pinios Shipping Co. No. 1 (The Maira) (No. 2)* [1984] 1 Lloyd's Rep. 660, 671, per Hobhouse J.

26. See cases cited in n. 9, *supra*.

27. *Glafki Shipping Co. S.A.* v. *Pinios Shipping Co. No. 1 (The Maira) (No. 2)* [1984] 1 Lloyd's Rep. 660.

a useful remedy by which to hold the balance between judicial intervention and the finality of awards.

1.4.1.4 There emerged one particular situation when notwithstanding the existence of a demonstrable error of law the courts refused to intervene. This position arose when the parties submitted a specific question of law to the decision of the arbitrator. In this situation the parties were taken to have chosen their tribunal and were compelled to accept the arbitral determination as final. The parties could not thereafter question the award and seek to have it set aside or remitted. The principle was summarised by Channell J. in *In re King and Duveen*[28] in the following terms:

It is no doubt a well-established principle of law that if a mistake of law appears on the face of the award of an arbitrator, that makes the award bad, and it can be set aside . . . but it is equally clear that if a specific question of law is submitted to an arbitrator for his decision, and he does decide it, the fact that the decision is erroneous does not make the award bad on its face so as to permit of its being set aside. Otherwise it would be futile ever to submit a question of law to an arbitrator.

Although the question does not appear to have arisen, the principle was probably one based on discretion rather than jurisdiction. But whatever its basis, the principle was endorsed by the House of Lords in *Kelantan Government* v. *Duff Development Co.*[29] On the facts of the case a question concerning the construction of a deed had been referred to the decision of an arbitrator. Viscount Cave L.C. observed,[30] "But where a question of construction is the very thing referred for arbitration, then the decision of the arbitrator upon that point cannot be set aside by the court only because the court would itself have come to a different conclusion." It has to be emphasised that the principle only applied when a *specific* question of law had been referred to the decision of an arbitrator.[31] Whether a question of law had been so specifically submitted fell in each case to be determined on a construction of the terms of the particular submission.[32] In particular a distinction had to be drawn between the reference of a specific question of law and the reference of a question of law material to the resolution of the dispute or difference. In *The Maira (No. 2)*[33] Hobhouse J. rejected the application of the *Kelantan* principle because the "question of law merely arose in the course of the reference as and when various facts were proved or contentions advanced. It could not . . . have been said at the time of the submission to arbitration what actual questions of law were going to arise."[34]

1.4.1.5 The common law jurisdiction never developed so as to assume a dominant position, primarily because the fundamental nature of the jurisdiction also contained the means for its own effective circumvention. The common law never insisted that reasons were a substantive precondition to a valid award. A bare award with brief for-

28. [1913] 2 K.B. 33, 35–36.
29. [1923] A.C. 395. See also *Holmes Oil Co.* v. *Pumpherstone Oil Co.* (1891) 18 R.(H.L.) 52; *Adams* v. *Great North of Scotland Ry.* [1891] A.C. 31, 39; *British Westinghouse Co.* v. *Underground Electric Rys. Co.* [1912] A.C. 673; *Absalom (F.R.)* v. *Great Western (London) Garden Village* [1933] A.C. 592.
30. *Ibid.*, p. 409.
31. *Attorney-General for Manitoba* v. *Kelly* [1922] 1 A.C. 268 (P.C.).
32. *Kelantan Government* v. *Duff Development Co.* [1923] A.C. 395, 418 per Lord Parmoor. See also *Absalom (F.R.)* v. *Great Western (London) Garden Village* [1933] A.C. 592.
33. *Glafki Shipping Co. S.A.* v. *Pinios Shipping Co. No. 1 (The Maira) (No. 2)* [1984] 1 Lloyd's Rep. 660.
34. *Ibid.* p. 671. The dictum is unaffected by the decision of the Court of Appeal in *Glafki Shipping Co. S.A.* v. *Pinios Shipping Co. No. 1 (The Maira) (No. 2)* [1985] 1 Lloyd's Rep. 30.

mal recitals and a succinct statement of the arbitrator's decision is at common law as valid as an award following the pattern of a contemporary judgment of a judge of the High Court. At the same time the *sine qua non* of the common law jurisdiction was a written award. It followed that an effective and valid stratagem for avoiding the risk of the common law jurisdiction being activated and the finality of the award challenged was to keep the face of the award as bare as possible, and in particular to keep the reasons of the arbitrator off the face of the award. This was simply achieved by making a purely formal award which contained so little, if any, relevant information that it was effectively immune from challenge. It was most clearly impossible to demonstrate any error of law on the face of such an award. This practice became widespread and operated to diminish the significance of the common law jurisdiction. The disadvantage of the practice was that it kept the parties ill-informed, but in time even this disadvantage was countered by the development of the practice of giving the parties a separate documentary statement of the arbitrator's reasons accompanied by an express statement that the reasons provided were not part of the award. The practice of giving extra-award reasons accompanied by express disclaimers continues, notwithstanding the abolition of the common law jurisdiction by the 1979 Act. Under prevailing practice it is also customary for the reasons to be declared to be confidential, in the sense that they are intended not to be capable of being alluded to in any proceeding on or in connection with the award.[35]

1.4.1.6 There also exists the notion that the common law jurisdiction extended to errors of fact on the face of the award. It is, however, difficult to reconcile this view of the extent of the jurisdiction with the fundamental principle and it must therefore be of doubtful validity. This particular debate has been addressed earlier in the text and what was there said is of equal application to the present context.[36]

1.4.2 The special case procedure

1.4.2.1 The special case procedure with regard to awards, as distinct from the consultative case procedure applicable to questions of law arising in the course of the reference,[1] was first introduced by the Common law Procedure Act 1854, section 5,[2] and subsequently re-enacted in the Arbitration Act 1889, section 7(b).[3] Under both enactments the power to state an award in the form of a special case was vested in the arbitrator or umpire. The power was of a discretionary nature and made subject to a contrary intention expressed in the submission. Section 19 of the 1889 Act extended the special case procedure and for the first time enabled the statement of a consulta-

35. See Chapter 11, para. 11.2.7. Also Commercial Court Committee, *Report on Arbitration*, *supra*, para. 6.
36. *Supra*, para 1.2.2.1.5.
1. See Chapter 12 for an elaboration of the consultative case procedure in its present format.
2. The section provided: "It shall be lawful for the arbitrator upon any compulsory reference under this Act, or upon any reference by consent of the parties where the submission is or may be made a rule or order of the superior courts of law or equity at Westminster, if he shall think fit, and if it is not provided to the contrary, to state his award, as to the whole or any part thereof, in the form of a special case for the opinion of the Court, and when an action is referred, judgment, if so ordered, may be entered according to the opinion of the Court."
3. The section provided: "The arbitrators or umpire acting under a submission shall, unless the submission expresses a contrary intention, have power— . . . (b) to state an award as to the whole or part thereof in the form of a special case for the opinion of the Court."

tive case on the lines described above. It was not until the Arbitration Act 1934, section 9, that the special case and consultative case procedures were consolidated in their statutory formulation, and that it also became possible for the court to order the statement of an award in the form of a special case.[4] A further feature of the 1934 Act was that the ostensible subordination of the jurisdiction to a contrary intention expressed in the submission was also abandoned. Section 9 of the 1934 Act was reproduced in substantially identical terms in the Arbitration Act 1950, section 21,[5] which is now repealed by the 1979 Act,[6] save for transitional purposes,[7] which period is now probably spent.

1.4.2.2 Section 21 of the Arbitration Act 1950 provides:

(1) An arbitrator or umpire may, and shall if so directed by the High Court, state—
    (a) any question of law arising in the course of the reference; or
    (b) an award or any part of an award,
in the form of a special case for the decision of the High Court.

(2) A special case with respect to an interim award or with respect to a question of law arising in the course of a reference may be stated, or may be directed by the High Court to be stated, notwithstanding that proceedings under the reference are still pending.

(3) A decision of the High Court under this section shall be deemed to be a judgment of the Court within the meaning of section twenty-seven of the Supreme Court of Judicature (Consolidation) Act 1925 (which relates to the jurisdiction of the Court of Appeal to hear and determine appeals from any judgment of the High Court), but no appeal shall lie from the decision of the High Court on any case stated under paragraph (a) of subsection (1) of this section without the leave of the High Court or of the Court of Appeal.

The special case procedure introduced into the realm of arbitration law in 1854 was modelled on the practice that by the middle of the nineteenth century had been developed by the Courts of Quarter Sessions, whereby orders might be made in the form of a special case setting out a question(s) of law arising on the facts stated for the opinion of the Court of Queen's Bench. Only after the directions of the Queen's Bench had been given, remitted to and acted upon by the Court of Quarter Sessions would its order come into force.[8] Quarter Sessions have long ceased to exist[9] but the special case procedure continues to survive as an important means of ensuring the legal correctness of the decisions of inferior courts[10] and tribunals.[11] The advantage of adopting the special case procedure in the arbitral process was that it allowed a point of law to be judicially determined without putting the entire arbitral process in jeopardy.

1.4.2.3 The statutory special case procedure as applied to arbitration operated in

---

4. This erased an anomaly in the law for although under the Arbitration Act 1889, s. 19, the court or a judge could direct an arbitrator or umpire to state a consultative case, there existed no corresponding jurisdiction with regard to the stating of awards as special cases under s. 7(b) of the 1889 Act.

5. The only difference between the two sections was that s. 9 of the 1934 Act made reference to "Court" whereas s. 21 of the 1950 Act referred to "High Court".

6. Section 8(3)(b).

7. See *infra*, para. 1.7.

8. See Diplock, "The Case Stated—its Use and Abuse" (1978) 44 *Arbitration* 107–116, 108. See also *The Overseers of the Poor of Walsall and the Mayor of Walsall* v. *The Directors etc. of the London & N.W. Ry. Co.* (1878–79) 4 A.C. 30.

9. Quarter Sessions and Assize Courts were abolished by the Courts Act 1971 and replaced by Crown Courts.

10. See, for example, Magistrates' Courts Act 1980, section 111; County Courts Act 1984, section 77(6).

11. See, for example, Employment Protection (Consolidation) Act 1978, section 136(4).

the same general manner as its historical analogue. It was neither a review of the award, as was the common law jurisdiction for error of law on the face of an award, nor an appeal from the arbitrator.[12] It was in its pure form a procedure for bringing a question(s) of law in issue in an arbitration award before the court for its opinion. The arbitrator continued to make the findings of fact and in consultation with the parties formulated the question of law; but it was the court which expressed an opinion as to the correct answer to the question of law posed.[13] The effect of the procedure was to remove the question of law from the arbitration process and assign it to a judge. But the arbitrator remained the final judge of all questions of fact.[14] Indeed, an award in the form of a special case which left questions of fact for the court was invalid.[15] The distinction between fact and law was therefore of crucial importance and the problem of distinguishing the one from the other was a difficulty endemic to the procedure.[16]

1.4.2.4 An award in the form of a special case was a provisional and not a final award. Under the special case procedure in its purest form the award did not become final until the opinion of the court was communicated to the arbitrator and the arbitrator proceeded to make his decision with the aid of the expressed opinion.[17] But such a remission was often unnecessary for in practice the procedure was invariably streamlined in the interest of speed and economy. Although not in strictness obliged to do so the arbitrator would invariably arrive at his own decision on the question of law and express his special case award to be final "subject to the decision of the court on the question of law".[18] The advantage of this procedure was that in the event of the court agreeing with the decision of the arbitrator and affirming his award the special case award could take immediate effect as a final award. Only in the contrary circumstance would the award be remitted. But to counter the possibility that the court might take a different view of the law, the practice was also developed of making alternative awards. The arbitrator anticipated two or more answers the court might give to the question of law posed and framed the award in the manner of alternative awards to take account of the various possible answers. In this event even if the court disagreed with the favoured decision of the arbitrator on the question of law, it was nonetheless in a position to affirm and render final the award provided there was contained in the

---

12. *GKN Centrax Gears Ltd.* v. *Matbro Ltd.* [1976] 2 Lloyd's Rep. 555, 575, per Lord Denning M.R.; *Compagnie General Maritime* v. *Diakan Spirit S.A. (The Ymnos)* [1982] 2 Lloyd's Rep. 574, 587, per Robert Goff J.

13. *Suzuki & Co.* v. *Benyon & Co.* (1926) 31 Com. Cas. 183, 197, per Lord Sumner.

14. *Nicobah Shipping Co.* v. *Alam Maritime Ltd. (The Evdokia)* [1980] 2 Lloyd's Rep. 107, 115, per Donaldson J., "it has been established for very many years that it is the duty of the court on a special case to consider questions of law and not to act as an appellate court on questions of fact". *Overseas Buyers Ltd.* v. *Granadex S.A.* [1980] 2 Lloyd's Rep. 608, 613, per Mustill J., "It is the arbitrators, not the court, who find the facts . . . nor has the court the power to substitute its own findings or to send the findings back for reconsideration, even if it were to feel on the material facts before it (which is not necessarily all the material available to the arbitrators) it would itself have arrived at a different view."

15. *N. & S.W. Junction Ry.* v. *Brentford Union* (1888) 13 App. Cas. 592.

16. Cf. *Bremer Handelsgesellschaft m.b.H.* v. *Deutsche Conti-Handelsgesellschaft m.b.H.* [1984] 1 Lloyd's Rep. 397. The split of law and fact between the courts and arbitrators respectively was frequently viewed as a disadvantage of the special case procedure: see, *Bremer Handelsgesellschaft m.b.H.* v. *Raiffeisen Hauptgenossenschaft, E.G.* [1982] 1 Lloyd's Rep. 599, 602, Kerr L.J. (C.A.).

17. *Ficom S.A.* v. *Sociedad Cadex Limitada* [1980] 2 Lloyd's Rep. 118; *Tropwood A.G. of ZUG* v.*Jade Enterprises Ltd. (The Tropwind)* [1981] 1 Lloyd's Rep. 45, 54.

18. When this practice was adopted the precise weight to be given to the opinion of the arbitrator remained a question of conjecture.

award an alternative decision that corresponded with the opinion of the court.[19] Alternative awards came to be standard practice and were rendered necessary because the court could not of its own volition correct, amend or make anew an award to correspond with its answer to the question(s) of law. Without an alternative award the court had no choice but to remit the award for the reconsideration of the arbitrator.[20] But the practice had its limitations. In its nature the practice was complex and intricate, and the degree of complexity and intricacy increased measurably as the number of legal questions multiplied and the range of possible answers to the various questions of law increased. In this kind of situation there was often no alternative but to return to fundamentals and for the court, whether invited to or not, to remit the award together with a statement of its opinion on the law.[21]

1.4.2.5 In stating an award in the form of a special case there was also the danger that it would not thereafter be set down for hearing by the court or having been set down it would subsequently be withdrawn. To counter this danger it became the practice to state in the award that in the event of the award not being set down within six weeks of its publication, or being so set down it was thereafter withdrawn, the award "will stand as a final award".[22]

1.4.2.6 There was however no right to a special case. It had never been the case that when a question of law arose in arbitration proceedings the arbitrator or the court was obliged, when requested, to state a special case. The power of both the arbitrator and court was discretionary.[23] Although not expressly required by the legislation, as a matter of practice the application for a special case was in the first instance to the arbitrator. The arbitrator was unlikely to state an award as a special case on his own volition, although in strictness he was empowered to do so.[24] If both or all the parties supported the application, only in exceptional circumstances would the arbitrator be justified in rejecting the application, as when he was satisfied no question of law arose. Where the application was opposed the arbitrator was obliged to consider carefully the criteria governing the exercise of his discretion, which are discussed later. If the arbitrator rejected the application then recourse could be had to the court; although a refusal was not a necessary condition to the right of a party to apply to the court.[25] If

---

19. Commercial Court Committee, *Report on Arbitration, supra*, para. 10. See also *Andre & Cie S.A.* v. *Tradax Export S.A.* [1981] 2 Lloyd's Rep. 355, 366; *Société Italo-Belge Pour Le Commerce et L'Industrie* v. *Palm and Vegetable Oils (Malaysia) Sdn. Bhd. (The Post Chaser)* [1981] 2 Lloyd's Rep. 695, 702; *Tradax Export S.A.* v. *European Grain & Shipping Ltd.* [1983] 2 Lloyd's Rep. 100, 108; *Tradax Export S.A.* v. *Italgrani Di Francesco Ambrosio* [1986] 1 Lloyd's Rep. 112 (C.A.).

20. See *Damon Compania Naviera S.A.* v. *Hapag-Lloyd International S.A. (The Bankenstein) etc.* [1983] 2 Lloyd's Rep. 522; *Pagnan & Fratelli* v. *Finagrain Compagnie Commerciale Agricole et Financière S.A. (The Adolf Leonhardt)* [1986] 2 Lloyd's Rep. 395.

21. *Government of Ceylon* v. *Chandris* [1963] 2 Q.B. 327. See also *N.V. Stoom Maats de Maas* v. *Nippon Yusen Kaisha (The Pendrecht)* [1980] 2 Lloyd's Rep. 56, 67; *Satef Huttenes Albertus S.p.A.* v. *Paloma Tercera Shipping Co. S.A. (The Pegase)* [1981] 1 Lloyd's Rep. 175, 186; *Transamerican Steamship Corporation* v. *Tradax Export S.A. (The Oriental Envoy)* [1982] 2 Lloyd's Rep. 266, 272.

22. See, *Pagnan & Fratelli* v. *Tradax Overseas S.A.* [1980] 1 Lloyd's Rep. 665, 670; *Fratelli Moretti S.p.A.* v. *Nidera Handelscompagnie B.V.* [1980] 1 Lloyd's Rep. 534, 541; *Compagnie General Maritime* v. *Diakan Spirit S.A. (The Ymnos)* [1982] 2 Lloyd's Rep. 574, 587.

23. *Baguley* v. *Markwick* (1861) 30 L.J.C.P. 342; *Holloway* v. *Francis* (1861) 9 C.B. (N.S.) 559; *In re Nuttall and Lynton and Barnstaple Rly Co.* (1899) 82 L.T. 17; *Union-Castle Mail Steamship Co. Ltd.* v. *Horston Line (London) Ltd.* (1936) 55 Ll.L.Rep. 136; *Orion Compania Espanola de Seguros* v. *Belfort Maatschappij voor Algemene Verzekgringeen* [1962] 2 Lloyd's Rep. 257.

24. *Middlemiss & Gould (A Firm)* v. *Hartlepool Corpn.* [1972] 1 W.L.R. 1643; [1973] 1 All E.R. 172.

25. *Glafki Shipping Co. S.A.* v. *Pinios Shipping Co. No. 1 The Maira* [1982] 1 Lloyd's Rep. 257, 261.

the arbitrator refused the application, he was obliged in all but the most exceptional circumstances to allow the party a reasonable period of time to make an application to the court before making his award. Failure to do so amounted to misconduct.[26] Confronted by such misconduct the court had powers to set aside the award and remove the arbitrator but only rarely was it likely that the court could be persuaded to make such a harsh response.[27] The more likely response was a remission of the award with a direction to state a special case.[28] In relation to the application the court again had a discretion whether or not to direct the arbitrator to state a special case.[29] In considering the application it examined the issue afresh and not as an appeal from the refusal of the arbitrator. The relationship between the arbitrator and court can be characterised by saying that the arbitrator enjoyed a primary discretion and the court a residuary or controlling discretion.

1.4.2.7 In stating or directing the statement of a special case both the arbitrator and the court enjoyed a jurisdiction to attach conditions. The jurisdiction of the court arose under section 28 of the Arbitration Act 1950 and that of the arbitrator under the express or implied terms of his mandate.[30] The implication was somewhat readily made and in consequence the power to impose conditions became closely associated with the arbitral appointment.[31] To impose an unreasonable or unfair condition would probably have amounted to misconduct and might even have been construed as an effective refusal to state a special case. The fact that the arbitrator agreed to state a case subject to conditions did not preclude the jurisdiction of the court; an application could still be made to the court in the hope it might exercise its discretion unconditionally or subject to less burdensome conditions.[32]

1.4.2.8 Not until the decision of the Court of Appeal in *The Lysland*[33] did there emerge a clear and comprehensive statement of general principle regarding the basis on which the discretion under section 21 of the 1950 Act was to be exercised, applicable to both the court and arbitrators.[34] In so doing the Court of Appeal did not see

---

26. *In re Palmer & Co. and Hosken & Co.* [1898] 1 Q.B. 131; *In re Fischel & Co. and Mann & Cook* [1919] 2 K.B. 431; *General Rubber Co. Ltd.* v. *Hessa Rubber Maatschappij* (1927) 28 Ll.L.Rep. 362; *Giacomo Costa Fu Andrea* v. *British Trading Co.* [1962] 2 All E.R. 53; *Czarnikow* v. *Roth, Schmidt & Co.* [1922] 2 K.B. 478 (C.A.); *Exormisis* v. *Oonsoo* [1975] 1 Lloyd's Rep. 432; *The Food Corporation of India* v. *Carras (Hellas) Ltd. (The Dione)* [1980] 2 Lloyd's Rep. 577.

27. *In re Fischel & Co. and Mann & Cook* [1919] 2 K.B. 431; *G. W. Potts Ltd.* v. *MacPherson Train & Co.* (1927) 27 Ll.L.Rep. 445; *Miller's Timber Trust Co. Ltd.* v. *Plywood Factory Julius Potempa Ltd.* (1939) 63 Ll.L.Rep. 184.

28. Where it could be shown that had the application been made to the court within time it would have refused to direct a special case, then notwithstanding the misconduct of the arbitrator the court would neither set aside nor remit the award for in such a circumstance there was no injustice: see *The Food Corporation of India* v. *Carras (Hellas) Ltd. (The Dione)* [1980] 2 Lloyd's Rep. 577.

29. *Federal Commerce & Navigation Ltd.* v. *Suisse-Atlantique Société D'Armement S.A. (The Cruzeiro Do Sul)* [1982] 2 Lloyd's Rep. 110 (C.A.).

30. *Provimi Hellas A.E.* v. *Warinco A.G.* [1978] 1 Lloyd's Rep. 67, 79–80; [1978] 1 Lloyd's Rep. 373, 375 (C.A.); *Antco Shipping Ltd.* v. *Seabridge Shipping Ltd.* [1979] 2 Lloyd's Rep. 267, 269.

31. *Antco Shipping Ltd.* v. *Seabridge Shipping Ltd. (The Furness Bridge)* [1979] 2 Lloyd's Rep. 267; *Japan Line Ltd.* v. *Aggeliki Charis Compania Maritima S.A. (The Angelic Grace)* [1980] 1 Lloyd's Rep. 288; *Glafki Shipping Co. S.A.* v. *Pinios Shipping Co. No. 1 (The Maira)* [1982] 1 Lloyd's Rep. 257.

32. *Glafki Shipping Co. S.A.* v. *Pinios Shipping Co. No. 1 (The Maira), ibid.*, p. 261.

33. *Halfdan, Greig & Co. A/S* v. *Sterling Coal and Navigation Corp. and Another (The Lysland)* [1973] 1 Q.B. 843 C.A.; [1973] 1 Lloyd's Rep. 296 (C.A.).

34. *GKN Centrax Gears Ltd.* v. *Matbro Ltd.* [1976] 2 Lloyd's Rep. 555.

itself as doing anything beyond confirming the established practice of the courts. When an application was made to the court it was invariably the case that the application was opposed by the other arbitrating party and the court was in consequence compelled to hold the balance between the opposing parties on the one hand and the relationship between arbitration and the courts with regard to questions of law on the other. On its face the discretion under section 21 was unqualified and unfettered but it had never been so openly construed by the judiciary. In *The Lysland* Lord Denning M.R. identified the criteria to be taken into account and weighed in the exercise of the discretion in the following terms[35]:

When one party asks an arbitrator or umpire to state his award in the form of a special case, it is a matter for his discretion. If the issues are on matters of fact and not of law, he should refuse to state a case. If they raise a point of law, it depends on what the point of law is. He should agree to state a case whenever the facts, as proved or admitted before him, give rise to a point of law which fulfils these requisites:

The point of law should be real and substantial and such as to be open to serious argument and appropriate for decision by a court of law[36]—as distinct from a point which is dependent on the special expertise of the arbitrator or umpire.[37]

The point of law should be clear cut and capable of being accurately stated as a point of law— as distinct from the dressing up of a matter of fact as if it were a point of law.

The point of law should be of such importance that the resolution of it is necessary for the proper determination of the case—as distinct from a side issue of little importance.

If those three requisites are satisfied, the arbitrator or umpire should state a case. He should not be deterred from doing so by such suggestions as these: it may be suggested that a special case should be reserved for cases which are of general application (such as the construction of a standard form) or which would elucidate or add to the general principles of law (such as the doctrine of frustration or repudiation). I would not so limit the stating of a special case. In most cases the parties themselves are concerned, not with general principles, but with their particular dispute. If the case does involve a point of law which satisfies the requisites which I have mentioned, either of the parties should be enabled to have it decided by a judge of the High Court. When the parties agree to arbitrate, it is, by our law, on the assumption that a point of law can, in a proper case, be referred to the courts.

It may be suggested that if the point of law is only as to the construction of a particular document or of the words in it—as applied to the proved facts—then it should be left to the arbitrator or umpire. I do not agree. Most of the special cases are stated on points of construction. No one hitherto has thought that they should be refused on that ground.

It may be suggested that, if the point of law is only as to the proper inference, or the appropriate implication—to be drawn from the proved facts—then it should be left to the arbitrator or umpire. Again, I do not agree. Some of the most important awards have been of that kind.[38]

It may be suggested that if only a small sum is in dispute, a special case should be refused. Sometimes a small sum can involve big issues of much importance for the parties. In those cases a special case should be stated. But, when the sum is so small as not to justify further time or money being spent on it, it should be refused.

1.4.2.9 The other members of the court did not expressly endorse this statement; nor did they attempt as comprehensive a statement. They did, however, clearly agree with the central thrust of the approach. Megaw L.J. was of the view that the court,

---

35. *Supra*, p. 862.
36. Citing *In re Nuttall and Lynton and Barnstaple Railway Co.* (1899) 82 L.T. 17.
37. Citing *Orion Compania Espanola de Seguros* v. *Belfort Maatschappij voor Algemene Verzekgringeen* [1962] 2 Lloyd's Rep. 257.
38. Citing *In re Comptoir Commercial Anversois and Power, Son and Co.* [1920] 1 K.B. 868, 898.

subject to special factors that may exist in any particular case, should direct the statement of a special case when the question of law in issue was "a clear cut question of law which is seriously arguable, substantial in the sense of being important for the resolution of the dispute and to the parties, and which is raised bona fide and not merely for the purpose of delay".[39] Scarman L.J. expressed the opinion that the power to direct a special case should not be exercised "unless there has arisen a point of law real, substantial, relevant and such as ought to be decided by the High Court".[40]

1.4.2.10 In retrospect, the decision in *The Lysland* lends itself to three observations.[41] In the first place the enunciated criteria were unrestrictive and with the consequence that special cases were readily acceded to or directed by both arbitrators and the courts. Provided there was a genuine, definable, real, substantial and arguable question of law the award was readily stated in the form of a special case.[42] In the result the special case procedure had *de facto* translated itself into a general right of appeal.[43] This generous approach was probably in keeping with the expectation that arbitrating parties harboured by virtue of section 21 and which was articulated by Scarman L.J. in the following language[44]: "the statute makes plain that our law offers to those who refer their disputes to arbitration the opportunity of seeking a decision of the court on a point of law, the decision of which is necessary for the proper determination of their dispute." Secondly, the Court of Appeal was not consciously seeking to refashion the relationship between the courts and arbitration or to restrict or diminish the flow of special cases from arbitration to the courts.[45] It saw itself as enunciating criteria or factors consistent with the historical practice of the courts. Whereas the decision clarified the general principles underlying the exercise of the statutory discretion, it did not otherwise seek to alter the balance between arbitration and the courts.[46] Thirdly, the decision recognised that in a particular case there may exist special factors that justified a departure from or at least not too firm an adherence to the enunciated principles.[47] Such special factors might arise when the question of law was closely related to trade practice, usage or custom, or involved the construction of commercial terminology, or related to an issue of which the arbitrator had special

---

39. *Supra*, p. 865, citing from the judgment of Kerr J. at first instance.
40. *Supra*, p. 868.
41. For subsequent authorities endorsing the principles enunciated in *The Lysland*, see *GKN Centrax Gears Ltd.* v. *Matbro Ltd.* [1976] 2 Lloyd's Rep. 555; *Cerealmangimi S.p.A.* v. *Toepfer (The Eurometal)* [1979] 2 Lloyd's Rep. 72; *Peter Lind & Co. Ltd.* v. *Constable Hart & Co. Ltd.* [1979] 2 Lloyd's Rep. 248; *Food Corpn. of India* v. *Carras (Hellas) Ltd. (The Dione)* [1980] 2 Lloyd's Rep. 577.
42. Cf. *Gale & Co.* v. *Marshall and French* (1921) 9 Ll.L.Rep. 19. But the process was not wholly automatic, see *Food Corpn. of India* v. *Carras (Hellas) Ltd. (The Dione), supra; Michalos* v. *The Food Corpn. of India (The Apollon)* [1983] 1 Lloyd's Rep. 409, 416.
43. *Ismail* v. *Polish Ocean Lines (The Ciechocinek)* [1976] 1 Lloyd's Rep. 489, 497, per Ormrod L.J. See also Kerr "Commercial Dispute Resolution—The changing Scene", pp. 111, 123 in *Liber Amicorum for Lord Wilberforce* ed. Bos and Brownlie.
44. *Supra*, p. 868.
45. At first instance Kerr J., at p. 855, emphasised that his decision "should not be taken as any indication . . . that special cases should be stated less frequently in the future than in the past". The fact that his decision inclined to this result formed one of reasons that caused the Court of Appeal to allow the appeal from his judgment.
46. *Supra*, p. 863 per Lord Denning M.R.
47. *Ibid*.

knowledge. In this kind of circumstance the arbitration tribunal might well be in a better position to determine the question than any court of law.[48] Another special factor might arise when the question of law related to the existence or sufficiency of evidence to support a finding or conclusion of fact. Such questions of law rarely arose[49] and when they did the judiciary firmly discouraged any attempt to bring them before the court for determination.[50] The courts had long been on their guard to protect against the risk of this head of jurisdiction being used as a ploy to review the arbitrator's findings of primary and secondary facts.[51]

1.4.2.11 A particular problem with regard to the exercise of discretion arose when the procedural rules under which the arbitration was being conducted provided for an appeal to an arbitration appeal tribunal. Although in such a circumstance there was nothing to preclude the first tier award being stated as a special case,[52] nonetheless, in the absence of special considerations, the instinct of the court was to wait and allow the arbitral appellate process to be pursued first.[53]

1.4.2.12 Beyond the crucial question of discretion there emerged a number of difficulties and indeed deficiencies in the way the special case procedure functioned in practice. An award in the form of a special case became a very formal and stylistic document which arbitrators were not always happy drafting and therefore frequently sought professional assistance.[54] This in itself produced delay and additional expense. In its typical form a special case award recited the circumstances in which the arbitration had arisen, the issues involved and the contentions of the parties, the question of law on which the opinion of the court was sought, the relevant findings of fact and formal award.[55]

Further, the outwardly simple notion of bringing forward a question of law for the opinion of the court concealed a number of difficulties. In its Report of 1962 the Commercial Court Users' Conference exhorted that a point(s) of law it was desired to state as a special case should be formulated in a concise form and protested against the practice of stating "vague or indeterminate points of law".[56] Although there were degrees of vagueness which the courts would not tolerate,[57] they were nonetheless prepared to accept general legal questions, such as "whether on the facts

---

48. See *Re Gray, Laurier & Co. and Boustead & Co.* (1892) 8 T.L.R. 703; *Re Nuttall and Lynton and Barnstaple Rly. Co.* (1899) 82 L.T. 17; *Bornholm (Owners)* v. *Exportchleb, Moscow* (1937) 58 Ll.L.Rep. 59; *Orion Compania etc. Belfort Maatschappij etc.* [1962] 2 Lloyd's Rep. 257. Note also the observations of Lord Denning M.R. in *Sterling Coal & Navigation Corp. of New York* v. *Halfdan Grieg & Co. A/S* [1976] 1 Lloyd's Rep. 427, 439.

49. *Zim Israel Navigation Co. Ltd.* v. *Effy Shipping Corpn. (The Effy)* [1972] 1 Lloyd's Rep. 18, 33–34 per Mocatta J.

50. *Granvias Oceanicas Armadora S.A.* v. *Jibsen Trading Co. (The Kavo Peiratis)* [1977] 2 Lloyd's Rep. 344, 352; *GKN Centrax Gears Ltd.* v. *Matbro Ltd.* [1976] 2 Lloyd's Rep. 555, 584. See also Chapter 6, para. 6.2.11.

51. *Tersons Ltd.* v. *Stevenage Development Corpn.* [1965] 1 Q.B. 37, 55–56; *Pagnan & Fratelli* v. *Corbisa Industrial Agropacuaria Ltd.* [1969] 2 Lloyd's Rep. 129.

52. *In re Fischel & Co. and Cook and Mann* [1919] 2 K.B. 431.

53. Cf. *Provimi Hellas A.E.* v. *Warinco A.G.* [1978] 1 Lloyd's Rep. 67.

54. See Chapter 11, para. 11.6.3.3.

55. For an example of a typical special case award see *Finagrain S.A. Geneva* v. *P. Kruse Hamburg* [1976] 2 Lloyd's Rep. 508.

56. Cmnd. 1616, paras. 30 and 31.

57. *Hudson's Bay Co.* v. *Domingo Mumbru Sociedad Anonima* (1922) 10 Ll.L.Rep. 476 (C.A.); *Williams* v. *Manisselian Frères* (1923) 17 Ll.L.Rep. 72 (C.A.).

found and the proper construction of the contract A was liable to B".[58] So also the formulation of the question of law so as to reflect the precise issue to be decided was not always the easiest of exercises, but the difficulty was ameliorated by the willingness of the court to amend or even to reframe the question of law or to add a new question of law when the circumstances made it necessary.[59] In the absence of the agreement of the parties the arbitrator had no such power and ultimately was compelled to state the question of law as defined by the party seeking a special case or as otherwise agreed between the parties.[60]

1.4.2.13 A far greater problem derived from the fact that of necessity the arbitrator was asked to state a special case before he had made his award and therefore before he had arrived at his findings and conclusions of fact.[61] There was in such a situation no guarantee that the question of law the arbitrator had been invited to state would continue to be relevant or appropriately fit the facts when found. More fundamentally it was often difficult to determine whether and, if so, what substantial question of law arose for decision.[62] The first kind of problem could be saved by a reformulation of the question of law but this was possible only if all the parties agreed.[63]

The findings and conclusions of fact were of crucial importance to the court for they were in the great majority of cases essential to providing an answer to the question of law.[63a] But the findings of fact were in the sole province of the arbitrator and it was

58. See, for example, *S.S. Matheos (Owners)* v. *Louis Dreyfus & Co.* [1925] A.C. 654; *Minister of Food* v. *Reardon Smith Line Ltd.* [1951] 2 Lloyd's Rep. 265; *Soproma S.p.A.* v. *Marine and Animal By-Products Corpn.* [1966] 1 Lloyd's Rep. 367; *Awilco* v. *Fulvia S.p.A. di Navigazione (The Chikuma)* [1979] 1 Lloyd's Rep. 367; *D'Amico Societa Di Navigazione* v. *Promoteca S.A. (The Cesare D'Amico)* [1982] 1 Lloyd's Rep. 493; *A/S Brovigtank and I/S Brovig* v. *Transcredit and Oil Tradeanstalt (The Gunda Brovig)* [1982] 2 Lloyd's Rep. 39 (C.A.); *Lakeport Navigation Company Panama S.A.* v. *Anonima Petroli Italiana S.p.A. (The Olympic Brilliance)* [1982] 2 Lloyd's Rep. 205 (C.A.). Note also *Cobec Brazilian Trading and Warehousing Corporation* v. *Alfred C. Toepfer* [1982] 1 Lloyd's Rep. 528, 530, where the question of law was framed in the following terms—"whether on the facts found and on the true constitution of the Contract the Buyers are liable in damages to the Sellers and, if so, in what sum". A party could take any question of law which was open on the facts found and required no further facts for its determination, provided it was within the general point of law raised, see *D'Amico Societa di Navigazione* v. *Promoteca S.A. (The Cesare D'Amico)* [1982] 1 Lloyd's Rep. 493; *Tradax Export S.A.* v. *Cook Industries Inc.* [1982] 1 Lloyd's Rep. 385, 392 (C.A.); *Hudson Bay Co.* v. *Domingo Mumbru S.A.* (1922) 10 Ll.L.Rep. 476, 478–479.

59. *Ismail* v. *Polish Ocean Lines (The Ciechocinek)* [1976] Q.B. 893; [1976] 1 Lloyd's Rep. 489; *Finagrain S.A. Geneva* v. *P. Kruse Hamburg* [1976] 2 Lloyd's Rep. 508; *Port Sudan Cotton Co.* v. *Govindaswamy Chettiar & Sons* [1977] 1 Lloyd's Rep. 166; *Toepfer* v. *Warrinco A.G.* [1978] 2 Lloyd's Rep. 573. *Glafki Shipping Co. S.A.* v. *Pinios Shipping Co. No. 1 (The Maira) (No. 2)* [1984] 1 Lloyd's Rep. 660.

60. *Ismail* v. *Polish Ocean Lines (The Ciechocinek)* [1976] 1 Lloyd's Rep. 489; *Faghirzadeh* v. *Rudolf Woolf (S.A.) Pty. Ltd.* [1977] 1 Lloyd's Rep. 630.

61. Once the award was made the arbitrator was *functus officio* and had no power to state the award as a special case unless the court could be persuaded to remit the award and thereby renew the authority of the arbitrator to consider the application for a special case. See *Re Montgomery, Jones & Co. and Liebenthal & Co.* (1898) 78 L.T. 406; *Re Palmer & Co. and Hosken & Co.* [1898] 1 Q.B. 131; *Lobitos Oilfields Ltd.* v. *Admiralty Comrs.* (1917) 33 TLR 472; *Ismail* v. *Polish Ocean Lines (The Ciechocinek)* [1976] 1 Lloyd's Rep. 489; *Intermare Transport G.m.b.H.* v. *International Copra Export Corp. (The Ross Isle and Ariel)* [1982] 2 Lloyd's Rep. 589, 590.

62. See *Ismail* v. *Polish Ocean Lines (The Ciechocinek), supra*; *Tradax Export S.A.* v. *Andre & Cie S.A.* [1978] 1 Lloyd's Rep. 639.

63. *Bunge S.A.* v. *Compagnie Européene de Céréales* [1982] 1 Lloyd's Rep. 306, 311. The court would only allow a new question of law to be introduced in very limited circumstances; see *Ismail* v. *Polish Ocean Lines (The Ciechocinek), supra*.

63a. The court could have regard to the facts expressly found and also to the inferences capable of being drawn from the express facts: see *Blackgold Trading Ltd. of Monrovia* v. *Almare S.p.A. di Navigazione Genoa (The Almare Seconda etc.)* [1981] 2 Lloyd's Rep. 433; *Bremer Handelsgesellschaft m.b.H.* v. *Westzucker G.m.b.H. (No. 3)* [1989] 1 Lloyd's Rep. 582 (C.A.).

often the case that the factual findings were too ambiguous or inadequate to enable the court to perform its task. When this was the case the court possessed a discretion to remit the special case award so that it might be elucidated or further relevant facts found.[64] The arbitrator was not obliged to set out *in extenso* a narrative of the evidence, nor annex the documentary evidence, nor record comprehensively the reasoning that led him to his conclusions except for the rare occasions when the question of law in issue related to the sufficiency of the evidence to support findings of fact, but even on these occasions it was open to the arbitrator to be selective and highlight the relevant evidence and summarise its effect on his mind.[65] It was nonetheless the duty of the arbitrator to make all the necessary findings of fact to enable the court to determine the special case. To assist in the discharge of that duty the practice developed of inviting the parties to present a list of all the questions of fact they required to be answered. This again proved a time-consuming and costly practice, for the parties frequently demanded the arbitrator to make factual findings unrelated to the proper determination of the question(s) of law in issue.[66]

1.4.2.14 The judicial perception of the place of the special case process in the general scheme of English arbitral law, the identified criteria governing the exercise of the associated discretion, the delicate balance between law and fact which the special case procedure highlighted, and the developed practice and procedure all contributed to an environment wherein the limitations of the special case procedure became readily visible and made possible the manner of abuse which has been described elsewhere in the text. The inability of arbitrators and the courts to prevent the misuse and abuse of the special case procedure placed under threat the speedy finality of awards and became a serious problem. The malpractice of some arbitrating parties was well appreciated[67] and in *The Lysland*[68] the Court of Appeal exhorted watchfulness and encouraged the rejection of applications not raised bona fide but with some ulterior

64. *Ben Line Steamers Ltd.* v. *Compagnie Optorg of Saigon* (1937) 57 Ll.L.Rep. 194; *Universal Cargo Carriers Corp.* v. *Citati* [1957] 2 Lloyd's Rep. 191 (C.A.); *Messers Ltd.* v. *Heidner & Co.* [1960] 1 Lloyd's Rep. 500; *Vardinoyannis* v. *Egyptian General Petroleum Corpn. (The Evaggelos TH)* [1971] 2 Lloyd's Rep. 200; *Intertradex S.A.* v. *Lesieur Tourteaux S.A.R.L.* [1978] 2 Lloyd's Rep. 509; *Compania Financiera Soleada S.A.* v. *Hamoor Tanker Corpn. Inc. (The Borag)* [1980] 1 Lloyd's Rep. 111; *Bremer Handelsgesellschaft m.b.H.* v. *Raiffeisen Hauptgehossenschaft E.G.* [1982] 1 Lloyd's Rep. 599 (C.A.). *Bremer Handelsgesellschaft m.b.H.* v. *Continental Grain Co.* [1983] 1 Lloyd's Rep. 269; *Interbulk Ltd.* v. *Aiden Shipping Co. Ltd. (The Vimeira) (No. 1)* [1985] 2 Lloyd's Rep. 410 (C.A.) (Note). The point is elaborated further in Chapter 11, para. 11.3.2.

65. *Nello Simoni* v. *A/S M/S Straum* (1949) 83 Ll.L.Rep. 157; *Macpherson Train & Co. Ltd.* v. *J. Milhelm & Sons* [1955] 2 Lloyd's Rep. 59 (C.A.); *Universal Cargo Carriers Corpn.* v. *Citati* [1957] 2 Q.B. 401; *East Yorkshire Motor Services* v. *Clayton* [1961] 1 W.L.R. 1454; *Tersons Ltd.* v. *Stevenage Development Corpn.* [1965] 1 Q.B. 37; *Compania Financiera Soleada S.A.* v. *Hamoor Tanker Corpn. Inc. (The Borag)* [1980] 1 Lloyd's Rep. 111.

66. The practice is alluded to in *The Evaggelos TH* [1971] 2 Lloyd's Rep. 200, 206; *Schiffahrtsagentur Hamburg Middle East Line G.m.b.H.* v. *Virtue Shipping Corporation Monrovia (The Oinoussian Virtue)* [1981] 1 Lloyd's Rep. 533, 539; *Glafki Shipping Co. S.A.* v. *Pinios Shipping Co. No. 1 (The Maira) (No. 2)* [1984] 1 Lloyd's Rep. 660, 662 (first instance). See also the critical comments in *Vinava Shipping Co. Ltd.* v. *Finelvet P.G. (The Chrysalis)* [1983] 1 Lloyd's Rep. 503, 507–508, per Mustill J.; *Bremer Handelsgesellschaft m.b.H.* v. *Westzucker G.m.b.H. (No. 2)* [1981] 2 Lloyd's Rep. 130, 132–133, per Donaldson L.J.; *The Mozart* [1985] 1 Lloyd's Rep. 239, 244.

67. *Provimi Hellas A.E.* v. *Warinco A.G.* [1978] 1 Lloyd's Rep. 67, 80, per Mocatta J., "it would be to blind one's eyes to realities if one did not recognise that requests for special cases are sometimes made by unsuccessful parties at arbitrations primarily for purposes of delay".

68. *Supra.*

motive in mind.[69] To establish *mala fides* or abuse of process was, however, not always easy; nor was the situation assisted by the general tenor of the decision in *The Lysland* which leaned in favour of granting applications and giving the benefit of the doubt in borderline cases. Indeed following the decision of the Court of Appeal arbitrators were of the general opinion that they had little choice but to grant applications for special cases.[70] But although the problems were substantial the special case procedure fell short of transmuting itself into an unqualified right. There were distant limitations which saw some applications founder.[71]

Once a special case was permitted it was not restricted to a consideration by the High Court, but might further proceed upward to the Court of Appeal and thence to the House of Lords.[72] Such an entanglement with the judicature placed under great strain the advantages customarily advocated of arbitration.[73] The position was even further exacerbated when the special case followed on from a contractual appeal within the arbitral process.[74]

1.4.3 Entrenchment of judicial review

1.4.3.1 The extent to which it was possible to contract out of the common law jurisdiction based on error of law on the face of an award or the statutory special case procedure proved to be a difficult and controversial question and brought into close focus important issues of public policy.[1]

The common law jurisdiction could as a matter of practice be quite easily circumvented by keeping reasons off the face of the award.[2] But beyond this simple stratagem it was uncertain whether the parties could also validly enter into an agreement under which they surrendered the right to challenge the award on this basis. In *Sinai Mining Co. Ltd.* v. *Compania Naviera Sota y Azhar*[3] an agreement to this effect was extracted from correspondence the parties had entered into and upheld as valid. The

---

69. *Supra*, p. 863, per Lord Denning M.R., "A party may seek to raise a point of law which is too plain for serious argument. Or he may seek to use it as a means of delaying the day when a final award is made against him. In all cases where the arbitrator or umpire is of the opinion that the application is not raised bona fide, but for some ulterior motive, he should, of course, refuse it."

70. Note the observations of Lord Diplock in *Pioneer Shipping Ltd. and Others* v. *B.T.P. Tioxide Ltd.* (*The Nema*) [1982] A.C. 724, 740.

71. See, for example, *Federal Commerce & Navigation Ltd.* v. *Suisse-Atlantique Société D'Armement S.A. (The Cruzeiro Do Sul)* [1982] 2 Lloyd's Rep. 110.

72. See, for example, *André et Cie* v. *Cook Industries Inc.* [1987] 2 Lloyd's Rep. 463 (C.A.); *Glafki Shipping Co. S.A.* v. *Pinios Shipping Co. No. 1 (The Maira) (No. 2)* [1986] 2 Lloyd's Rep. 12 (H.L.); *La Pintada Compania Navegacion S.A.* v. *The President of India (The La Pintada)* [1984] 2 Lloyd's Rep. 9 (H.L.); *Gill & Duffus S.A.* v. *Berger & Co. Inc.* [1984] 1 Lloyd's Rep. 227 (H.L.); *Nereide S.p.A. di Navigazione* v. *Bulk Oil International Ltd. (The Laura Prima)* [1982] 1 Lloyd's Rep. 1 (H.L.); *Bunge Corporation* v. *Tradax Export S.A.* [1981] 2 Lloyd's Rep. 1 (H.L.); *A/S Awilco* v. *Fulvia S.p.A. di Navigazione* [1981] 1 Lloyd's Rep. 371 (H.L.).

73. It was also opposed to certain strands of judicial thought: see *Compagnie Tunisienne de Navigation S.A.* v. *Compagnie D'Armement Maritime S.A.* [1971] A.C. 573, 600, per Lord Wilberforce, "It is surely regrettable that, after a choice of English arbitrators, these foreign parties should have been subjected to litigation in three courts on top of the arbitration and that on a preliminary point."

74. The judgment of Lord Sterndale M.R. in *Gillespie Bros. & Co.* v. *Thompson Bros. & Co.* (1923) 13 Ll.L.Rep. 519, 520–521, provides a sobering reminder of the problem. Note also *Cook Industries Inc.* v. *Tradax Export S.A.* [1985] 2 Lloyd's Rep. 454, 455–456, per Kerr L.J.

1. See generally Schmitthoff "Commercial Arbitration and the Commercial Court" in *Commercial Law in a Changing Economic Climate* (2nd edn.).

2. *Supra*, para. 1.4.1.5.

3. (1927) 28 Ll.L.Rep. 364.

sole arbitrator was unaware of the agreement and gave reasons, thereby implicitly inviting scrutiny of his award for error of law. Nonetheless it was held that neither party had the competence to challenge the award and the parties had to abide by the decision, whether the arbitrator was right or wrong in law. Lord Diplock, speaking extra-judicially, was of an opposing opinion and denied the validity of an agreement which purported to exclude the common law jurisdiction.[4] In retrospect, given that the jurisdiction could be so readily circumvented by indirect means, it is difficult to see why any objection should be taken to its direct exclusion. Moreover, the attitude of the courts to the similar question in relation to the special case procedure is not necessarily conclusive of the position which would have prevailed in relation to the common law jurisdiction.[5]

1.4.3.2 The effect of an agreement excluding the statutory special case procedure was initially uncertain,[6] but following the important decision of a unanimous and strong Court of Appeal in *Czarnikow* v. *Roth, Schmidt & Co.*[7] the invalidity of such agreements came to be widely assumed, although the case had never subsequently been closely and discriminatingly considered, and doubts survive as to the precise scope of the decision.[8] Nonetheless, in the context of the facts that prevailed in the case there can be no ambiguity that an agreement to oust the court of its statutory jurisdiction to direct the statement of a special case for the opinion of the court was contrary to public policy and void.

The facts in *Czarnikow* related to a contract for the sale of sugar on a standard form of the Refined Sugar Association which expressly incorporated the Rules of the Refined Sugar Association. The Rules embodied a *Scott* v. *Avery* arbitration agreement and further provided:

Neither buyer, seller, trustee in bankruptcy, nor any other person as aforesaid, shall require, nor shall they apply to the court to require any arbitrators to state in the form of a special case for the opinion of the court, any question of law arising in the course of the reference, but such question of law shall be determined by arbitration in manner herein directed.

On a dispute arising between sellers and buyers, the buyers asked the arbitrators to state a case under section 19 of the Arbitration Act 1889 or alternatively under section 7 of the same Act, or to postpone making an award until the buyers had an opportunity of applying to the court under section 19 of the 1889 Act. All the applications were refused and the arbitrators proceeded to make their award, believing the exclusion agreement in the Rules to be valid and to prevent the parties from making such applications. The buyers sought and succeeded in having the award set aside on the ground that the exclusion agreement in the Rules was invalid and that the arbitrators

---

4. Diplock, "The case stated—its Use and Abuse" (1978) 44 *Arbitration* 107, 108.
5. But note *Czarnikow* v. *Roth, Schmidt & Co.*, *infra*, p. 491, per Atkin L.J.
6. In *Re Hansloh and Others and Reinhold, Pinner and Co.* (1895) 1 Com. Cas. 215 an agreement excluding the procedure provided for by the Arbitration Act 1889, s. 19, was held to be ineffectual and did not preclude the jurisdiction of the court to direct a special case. In *Re Montgomery and Liebenthal* (1898) 78 L.T. 406, Collins L.J. left the question open. In *Lobitos Oilfields (Limited)* v. *Lords Commissioners of the Admiralty* (1917) 33 T.L.R. 472 Avory J. appears to accept that the section 19 procedure was capable of being excluded by express agreement; but merely to express an award to be final and binding did not achieve this result. Bray J. does not seem to have been of the same mind.
7. [1922] 2 K.B. 478 (C.A.). The point had been left open by the Divisional Court below.
8. Considered *infra*, para 1.4.3.5.

had misconducted themselves in refusing to defer making their award until the buyers had had a reasonable opportunity to make their application to the court.[9]

1.4.3.3 The Court of Appeal struck down the exclusion provision in the Rules on the basis that it was a species of agreement ousting the jurisdiction of the courts and consequently was against public policy and void. The pronouncements of the individual members of the Court of Appeal have historically been so intrinsically important and have had such a bearing on the relationship between the courts and arbitration in relation to questions of law that the opinions of the individual judges deserve to be communicated in the language of their original expression. Bankes L.J. observed[10]:

> The ground of objection to the rule is that as an agreement it ousts the jurisdiction of the courts of law, and is consequently against public policy and void. The importance of maintaining in its integrity the rule of law in reference to public policy is in my opinion a matter of considerable importance at the present time. Powerful trade organisations are encouraging, if not compelling, their members and persons who enter into contracts with their members to agree, as far as they can lawfully do so, to, abstain from submitting their disputes to the decision of a Court of law. The present case is a case in point. There have been others before the Courts. Among commercial men what are commonly called commercial arbitrations are undoubtedly and deservedly popular. That they will continue their present popularity I entertain no doubt, so long as the law retains sufficient hold over them to prevent and redress any injustice on the part of the arbitrator, and to secure that the law that is administered by an arbitrator is in substance the law of the land and not some home-made law of the particular arbitrator or the particular association. To release real and effective control over commercial arbitrations is to allow the arbitrator, or the Arbitration Tribunal, to be a law unto himself, or themselves, to give him or them a free hand to decide according to law or not according to law as he or they think fit, in other words to be outside the law. At present no individual or association is, so far as I am aware, outside the law except a trade union. To put such associations as the Refined Sugar Association in a similar position would in my opinion be against public policy. Unlimited power does not conduce to reasonableness of view or conduct. It is however with the purely legal position that we have to deal. No one has ever attempted a definition of what constitutes an ouster of jurisdiction. Each case must depend on its own circumstances. Each agreement needs to be separately considered. In the present case the parties have expressly agreed, by r. 17, that questions of law as well as questions of fact must be submitted to arbitration. If therefore the agreement that neither party shall apply to the Court to require the arbitrator to state a special case is to stand, the only hold which the Court can have over the proceedings is, (1) if the Arbitration Tribunal itself states a case for the opinion of the Court, or states its award in the form of a special case, or (2) if either party applies to set aside the award for misconduct on the part of the Arbitration Tribunal or upon the ground of error on the face of the award. To hold that under these circumstances the agreement not to apply for a special case is not to oust the jurisdiction of the Court within the meaning of the rule of law as I interpret it is in effect to decide that the Appeal Tribunal is entitled to be a law unto itself, and free to administer any law, or no law, as it pleases. I cannot but think that this is against public policy. I therefore hold that so much of r. 19 as provides that neither party shall apply for a special case, when incorporated into an agreement, is unenforceable and void.

Scrutton L.J. observed[11]:

> I am of opinion that r. 19 of the rules of the Refined Sugar Association in so far as it purports to prevent a party to an arbitration before the Association from exercising his right under the Arbitration Act to ask for a special case for the opinion of the Court on a question of law is contrary to public policy and so unenforceable. . . .
> Arbitrators, unless expressly otherwise authorised, have to apply the laws of England. When

---

9. Following *In re Palmer & Co. and Hosken & Co.* [1898] 1 Q.B. 131.
10. *Supra*, pp. 484–486.
11. *Supra*, pp. 487–489.

they are persons untrained in law, and especially when as in this case they allow persons trained in law to address them on legal points, there is every probability of their going wrong, and for that reason Parliament has provided in the Arbitration Act that, not only may they ask the Courts for guidance and the solution of their legal problems in special cases stated at their own instance, but that the Courts may require them, even if unwilling, to state cases for the opinion of the Court on the application of a party to the arbitration if the Courts think it proper. This is done in order that the Courts may insure the proper administration of the law by inferior tribunals. In my view to allow English citizens to agree to exclude this safeguard for the administration of the law is contrary to public policy. There must be no Alsatia[12] in England where the King's writ does not run. . . .

Without attempting precisely to define the limits within which an agreement not to take proceedings in the King's Courts is unenforceable, I think an agreement to shut out the power of the King's Courts to guide the proceedings of inferior tribunals without legal training in matters of law before them is calculated to lead to erroneous administration of law, and therefore injustice, and should therefore not be recognised by the Courts. I am ready to go very far in ignoring technicalities and irregularities on the part of arbitrators, unless there is some real substance of error behind them, but I think commercial men will be making a great mistake if they ignore the importance of administering settled principles of law in commercial disputes, and trust to the judgment of business men, however experienced in business, based only on the facts of each particular case, and with no knowledge of or guidance in the principles of law which must control the facts and which arbitrators must administer.

Atkin L.J. observed[13]:

The jurisdiction that is ousted in this case is not the common law jurisdiction of the Courts to give a remedy for breaches of contract, but the special statutory jurisdiction of the Court to intervene to compel arbitrators to submit a point of law for determination by the Courts. This appears to me to be a provision of paramount importance in the interests of the public. If it did not exist arbitration clauses making an award a condition precedent would leave lay arbitrators at liberty to adopt any principles of law they pleased. In the case of powerful associations such as the present, able to impose their own arbitration clauses upon their members, and, by their uniform contract, conditions upon all non-members contracting with members, the result might be that in time codes of law would come to be administered in various trades differing substantially from the English mercantile law. The policy of the law has given to the High Court large powers over inferior Courts for the very purpose of maintaining a uniform standard of justice and one uniform system of law. Analogous powers have been possessed by the Court over arbitrators, and have been extended by the provisions of s. 19. If an agreement to oust the common law jurisdiction of the Court is invalid every reason appears to me to exist for holding that an agreement to oust the Court of this statutory jurisdiction is invalid.

1.4.3.4 Taking a global view of the judgments there appears to emerge several clear and paramount considerations of policy, the relevance of which have not all dimmed with the passage of time. Arbitration was perceived as a component part of the administration of civil justice generally. It, as with the other parts, was required to function within legal terms of reference. The whole is a unified system wherein common legal principles and rules are applied. The special case procedure, in both its forms, provided a supervisory mechanism to secure that arbitrators not only applied the law but applied it correctly and thereby also prevented any drift towards *extra legem* modes of dispute resolution. Beyond legalism and uniformity the statutory procedures also guaranteed the continuous evolution of English commercial law as a comprehensive, relevant and certain code. Alongside these central themes the Court of Appeal also

---

12. For an explanation of "Alsatia" see Kerr, "Commercial Dispute Resolution", pp. 111–130, 123, in *Liber Amicorum for Lord Wilberforce*, ed. Bos and Brownlie.
13. *Supra*, p. 491.

identified features of arbitral practice that potentially compounded matters and made more probable that which the Court of Appeal viewed as most undesirable, namely arbitrators resolving disputes *extra legem*. The first was the dominance of trade organisations and the imposition of their power and influence on members and contracting non-members through standard form contracts and arbitration rules. If exclusion agreements were recognised as valid and adopted by trade organisations they would prevail in the absence of what might be considered true consent and encourage the emergence within the fields of influence of individual trade organisations of distinct codes of rules different from the law of the land. The second was the practice of referring questions of law to non-legally qualified arbitrators. Such arbitrators confronted by lawyers arguing points of law in the context of an adversarial system were in real danger of taking a wrong view of the relevant law.

1.4.3.5 The precise and ostensibly qualified manner in which the individual members of the Court of Appeal expressed themselves on the question of the then prevailing public policy provokes many questions as to the precise ambit of the decision in *Czarnikow*. Would a different approach have been adopted had the exclusion clause been embodied in an arbitration agreement in a one-off contract negotiated at arms length and with professional advice? Would it have made any difference if the ouster agreement had been entered into after the dispute had arisen and been referred to arbitration? In both these situations the "involuntariness" associated with standard forms and the rules of trade organisations is absent and it has been suggested that had the facts been so, the Court of Appeal might have taken a different approach.[14] Again, would it have made any difference if the arbitrators had not been trade arbitrators but legally qualified or professional arbitrators, or at least chaired by such a qualified person? All these questions are now of course academic but if it is an accurate analysis of the case to deduce a paramount policy consideration based on "maintaining a uniform standard of justice and one uniform system of law"[15] it is very doubtful that, had any of the factual variations contemplated above been present in the facts of the case, the Court of Appeal in *Czarnikow* would have arrived at a different conclusion, notwithstanding that the voluntariness of ouster clauses and the qualification of arbitrators are factors integrated into the reasoning of the court. It would seem that these particular arguments were introduced to emphasise what were foreseen by the Court of Appeal as undesirable features of arbitral practice that would derive from or at least be accentuated by a fracturing of the link between arbitration and the courts established by the special case procedure. Following the decision of the Court of Appeal in *Czarnikow* it was widely assumed that any ouster agreement was void and it seems highly likely that the assumption also reflected the true legal position.[16]

1.4.3.6 The decision of the Court of Appeal in *Czarnikow* is also capable of taking implicit support from the manner in which the statutory law was cast at the time of the decision, although this particular point was not taken by the Court of Appeal. The

14. Diplock, "The Case Stated—its Use and Abuse" (1978) 44 Arb. 107, 109, 112–113; Commercial Court Committee, *Report on Arbitration* 1978, *supra*, para. 42.

15. *Supra*, p. 491, per Atkin L.J.

16. See for example, Commercial Court Users' Conference Report 1962, para. 30, Cmnd. 1616; Kerr, "The English Courts and Arbitration", in *International Commercial Arbitration* (Part I) ed. Schmitthoff. The policy did not prevail in Scotland, for with the enactment of the Administration of Justice (Scotland) Act 1972, s. 3, parties were permitted to contract out of the case stated procedure.

principal statute then prevailing was the Arbitration Act 1889, with the statement of an award as a special case governed by section 7(b) and the statement as a special case of any question of law arising in the course of the reference governed by section 19. It was the latter section that was before the Court of Appeal, for at the time it was only under section 19 that the court had jurisdiction to direct the statement of a special case. No such jurisdiction existed under section 7(b). Further, and of particular interest, whereas the jurisdiction conferred on arbitrators under section 7(b) was subject to the qualification "unless the submission expresses a contrary intention", no similar qualification existed to the jurisdiction of arbitrators and the court under section 19. Given the close alliance between the two sections it was at least open to argument that the difference in drafting manifested a legislative intention that the statutory jurisdiction conferred under section 19 was not to be capable of being ousted by the agreement of the parties.[17]

1.4.4 Relationship between "error of law" and "special case" procedures

1.4.4.1 The common law and special case review procedures were quite distinct processes beyond the fact of their different legal sources.[1] Under the common law it was for the applicant to establish an error of law on the face of the award, on the basis of the award as it stood at that moment with its findings, conclusions and incorporations.[2] In contrast, under the special case procedure a question(s) of law was put before the court for determination. This process demanded that the court be informed of sufficient facts to enable it to provide an answer to the question(s) presented. If crucial findings of fact had not been made this could prove fatal to the pursuer of the special case. The court however had a discretionary power to remit the award for further or better findings of fact, although the jurisdiction was cautiously and restrictively developed.[3] The risk of the award not containing critical factual findings was also minimised by the practice of the parties being given the opportunity to request particular findings of fact in connection with a special case.[4]

1.4.4.2 The issue of the precise relationship between error of law on the face of an award and the special case did not come forward for judicial consideration until fairly recent times. The precise question that arose was whether they existed as strictly alternative procedures or could they be invoked concurrently? There was nothing in the substantive framework of either that asserted mutual exclusivity, but in practice it would generally be sufficient for a party to adopt one or other of the two procedures.[5] However, this might not always be the case and when this was so the question arose whether an award in the form of a special case could also be challenged for error of law on its face. In strict principle there appeared no reason to prohibit this possibility,[6]

---

17. There can be no optimism that this argument would have prevailed for the phrase in question, which appeared in both s. 5 of the Common Law Procedure Act 1854 and s. 7(b) of the Arbitration Act 1889, appears to have been effectively ignored by the judiciary.
1. *Glafki Shipping Co. S.A.* v. *Pinios Shipping Co. No. 1 (The Maira) (No. 2)* [1984] 1 Lloyd's Rep. 660, 672.
2. *Gunter Henck* v. *André & Cie S.A.* [1970] 1 Lloyd's Rep. 235, 239.
3. *Supra*, para. 1.4.2.13.
4. *Glafki Shipping Co. S.A.* v. *Pinios Shipping Co. No. 1 (The Maira) (No. 2)*, *supra*, p. 662.
5. See, for example, *Pearl Marin Shipping A/B* v. *Pietro Cingolani S.A.S. (The General Valdes)* [1982] 1 Lloyd's Rep. 17.
6. *Bjorn-Jensen & Co.* v. *Lysaght (Australia) Ltd. (The Gamma)* [1979] 1 Lloyd's Rep. 494.

but it must be recalled that the common law jurisdiction was discretionary and it would have been futile for it to have been activated if the alleged error of law corresponded with the question of law submitted to the court under the special case procedure. It was also unlikely to be exercised if the question of law was otherwise of a kind that it could and should reasonably be incorporated into the special case procedure. This was the approach adopted *obiter dictum* by Donaldson J. in *Port Sudan Cotton Co.* v. *Govindoswamy Chettiar & Sons*[7]:

I deplore any attempt to rely upon error of law on the face of the award as a ground for remission or setting aside where the award concerned is in the form of a special case. If the alleged error goes to a question submitted for the opinion of the Court, it is irrelevant. If it goes to any other question, it should have been the subject matter of a request for a question to be submitted to the Court. It is only if it arises without prior opportunity for the parties to make submissions about it and is not covered by the questions submitted to the Court, that it may perhaps be relied upon in the context of a special case.

On the facts of the case all the complaints were matters which fell within the scope of the questions submitted to the court under the special case procedure.

1.4.4.3 The dictum contemplated that in rare and special circumstances the error of law procedure could be utilised with regard to a special case award. In a later case, *The Maira (No. 2)*,[8] Hobhouse J. rationalised the dictum in the following terms, "In essence what [Mr Justice Donaldson] is saying is that where a special case is stated on one question, it will not normally be just to allow other questions of law to be raised as well."[9] The question of what might be just was to be decided on the facts and circumstances of each case. On the facts in *The Maira (No. 2)* the common law error of law on the face of the award jurisdiction was entertained in relation to an award in the form of a special case principally because the experienced arbitrator involved had voluntarily incorporated his reasons in the award without the customary disclaimer. This led to the inference that the arbitrator was inviting the parties to consider invoking the error of law jurisdiction with regard to any alleged errors on the face of the award.[10] The court was also satisfied that, had the further question of law been raised at the same time as the initial questions of law relating to the application that the award be stated as a special case, it would not have affected the judicial response to that application.

1.5 POLICY OF THE NEW LEGISLATION

1.5.1 Although the 1979 Act derives directly from the *Report on Arbitration* (1978) of the Commercial Court Committee,[1] the policy underpinning the legislation owes

---

7. [1977] 1 Lloyd's Rep. 166, 179.
8. *Glafki Shipping Co. S.A.* v. *Pinios Shipping Co. No. 1 (The Maira) (No. 2)*, *supra*.
9. *Ibid.*, p. 672.
10. Following *Pearl Marin Shipping A/B* v. *Pietro Cingolani S.A.S. (The General Valdes)*, *supra*, pp. 20–21, where the arbitrator, as in *The Maira (No. 2)*, chose to make a reasoned award and which decision Lord Denning M.R. interpreted in the following terms: "There being no disclaimer here stated by Sir Gordon Willmer—himself most experienced in arbitration—it seems to me that the proper inference is that, when issuing his award with the reasons attached to it, he was virtually saying (as Mr Justice Le Blanc said over 100 years ago [In *Kent* v. *Elstob* (1802) 3 East 18, 21]) that he was inviting the parties, if they wished the points of law to be considered by the Court, to take it up and suggest to the Court that there was an error on the face of the award, and the Court could consider it accordingly."
1. *Supra*, para. 1.3.

more to the influence of the House of Lords[2] than to the analysis of the Commercial Court Committee.[3]

The Act came quickly before the House of Lords for consideration; first in *The Nema*[4] and later in *The Antaios*.[5] The early consideration of the legislation by the highest appellate court was in substantial part due to the very conservative approach taken to the interpretation of the 1979 Act by Robert Goff J., then a judge of the Commercial Court,[6] who refused to read into the statute any consideration of policy not overtly expressed in the language of the statute; and who also considered that, to the extent it was desirable to impose any check on the relationship between the courts and arbitration established by the Act, this could be adequately achieved by the judicious exercise of the court's power to impose conditions on the grant of leave to appeal under section 1(4).[7] The difficulty with this line of reasoning was that it represented the new law in the same liberal image associated with the former legal regime and did not necessarily secure the eradication of the abuses that plagued the displaced regime and so troubled the Commercial Court Committee.[8] The House of Lords rejected the approach and saw in the unwritten depths of the Act a legislative intention to move this aspect of arbitral jurisprudence towards a favouring of the finality of awards and away from demanding strict legal accuracy. In the result the 1979 Act is not solely about redesigning and rationalising the procedures by which questions of law that arise in arbitration can be brought forward for review before the court. It also changes the balance between the courts and arbitration with regard to questions of law and renders the prospect of judicial review more restrictive.[9] The House of Lords deduced its comprehension of the associated parliamentary intention from the proper interpretation of the first four sections of the statute and was in consequence intent on taking a very different view of the basis on which the court's discretion to grant or refuse leave to appeal under section 1(3)(b) was to be exercised from that adopted by the Court of Appeal in *The Lysland*[10] in relation to the discretion associated with the special case procedure.[11] Appeals under the new appellate procedure would, even in the absence of an exclusion agreement, be far less frequently granted than were orders under the former law directing arbitrators to state special cases; and the same would also be true of on-appeals. The overriding impact of the 1979 Act is to give greater autonomy to the arbitral process and a greater finality to awards and this is achieved by keeping in firm check the judicial powers of intervention.

1.5.2 The approach of the House of Lords to the interpretation of the 1979 Act has been of central importance. It has also been mildly controversial and has raised some debate whether it was in fact an exercise in interpretation or an independent act of

---

2. *Infra.*
3. *Infra.*
4. *Pioneer Shipping Ltd. and Others* v. *B.T.P. Tioxide Ltd. (The Nema)* [1982] A.C. 724.
5. *Antaios Compania Naviera S.A.* v. *Salen Rederierna A.B. (The Antaios)* [1985] 1 A.C. 191.
6. Now Lord Goff of Chieveley, Lord of Appeal in Ordinary in the Judicial Committee of the House of Lords.
7. See Chapter 4, para. 4.3.4.
8. *Pioneer Shipping Ltd. and Others* v. *B.T.P. Tioxide Ltd. (The Nema)*, *supra*, pp. 745–746, per Lord Roskill.
9. See Chapters 4, 5 and 6.
10. *Halfdan, Greig & Co. A/S* v. *Sterling Coal and Navigation Corp. and Another (The Lysland)* [1973] 1 Q.B. 843 (C.A.).
11. See *supra*, para. 1.4.2.8.

judicial law-making whereby a veneer of judicial policy has overlaid the substance of the legislation. As eminent a jurist as Kerr L.J. has queried whether the policy of the 1979 Act was *interpreted* or *laid down* by the House of Lords.[12] The policy grasped upon by the House of Lords does not obviously emanate from the *Report on Arbitration* of the Commercial Court Committee; nor does it inevitably derive from the express language of the statute, which is open to various interpretations. But it is equally clear that it represents a valid and supportable approach, particularly when it is assessed against the historical backdrop of the review of awards on questions of law. In taking the impact of the 1979 Act beyond the eradication of procedural abuse and according greater autonomy and finality to arbitration and awards the House of Lords has tuned the legislation to the contemporary mood, both domestically and internationally, and also probably made a significant contribution to the attractiveness of London arbitration.[13]

1.5.3 The decisions of the House of Lords in *The Nema* and *The Antaios* set out the policy framework within which the judiciary are to operate with regard to the 1979 Act.[14] The decisions are of such paramount and crucial importance that lengthy citations are justifiable. No judicial observation and analysis is of greater moment than the judgment of Lord Diplock in *The Nema*, which articulates the unanimous opinion of the House of Lords, and which is the keystone of this branch of arbitral jurisprudence. Lord Diplock observed[15]:

The judicial discretion conferred by subsection (3)(b) to refuse leave to appeal from an arbitrator's award in the face of an objection by any of the parties to the reference is in terms unfettered; but it must be exercised judicially; and this, in the case of a dispute that parties have agreed to submit to arbitration, involves deciding between the rival merits of assured finality on the one hand and upon the other the resolution of doubts as to the accuracy of the legal reasoning followed by the arbitrator in the course of arriving at his award, having regard in that assessment to the nature and circumstances of the particular dispute.

My Lords, in weighing the rival merits of finality and meticulous legal accuracy there are, in my view, several indications in the Act itself of a parliamentary intention to give effect to the turn of the tide in favour of finality in arbitral awards (particularly in non-domestic arbitrations of which the instant case is one), at any rate where this does not involve exposing arbitrators to a temptation to depart from "settled principles in law." Thus section 1(1) removes a former threat to finality by abolishing judicial review (formerly certiorari) for error of law on the face of the award. Section 1(3) withdraws the previous power of an arbitrator to accede to a request to state his award in the form of a special case if such request was made by any party to the reference. It is notorious, particularly after the decision of the Court of Appeal in *Halfdan Grieg & Co. A/S* v. *Sterling Coal & Navigation Corporation (The Lysland)* [1973] Q.B. 843, that, if such request were made it was virtually impracticable for an arbitrator to refuse it.

---

12. *Universal Petroleum Co. Ltd.* v. *Handels- und Transport Gesellschaft m.b.H.* [1987] 1 Lloyd's Rep. 517, 529. Note also the aside of Sir Thomas Bingham M.R. in *Everglade Maritime Inc.* v. *Schiffahrtsgesellschaft Detlef von Appen m.b.H. (The Maria)* [1993] 2 Lloyd's Rep. 168, 173.

13. See Kerr, "Commercial Dispute Resolution: The Changing Scene", pp. 111, 125–126, in *Liber Amicorum for Lord Wilberforce*, ed. Bos and Brownlie, where Kerr L.J. speaks of the purposive approach to the interpretation of the 1979 Act as rescuing the legislation.

14. For significant restatements of the policy in the lower courts, see *Universal Petroleum Co. Ltd.* v. *Handels- und Transport Gesellschaft m.b.H.* [1987] 1 W.L.R. 1178 (C.A.); *Aden Refinery Co. Ltd.* v. *Ugland Management Co. (The Ugland Obo One)* [1987] Q.B. 650 (C.A.); *Seaworld Ocean Line Co. S.A.* v. *Catseye Maritime Co. Ltd. (The Kelaniya)* [1989] 1 Lloyd's Rep. 30 (C.A.); *Ipswich Borough Council* v. *Fisons plc* [1989] 2 All E.R. 737; *Geogas S.A.* v. *Trammo Gas Ltd. (The Baleares)* [1991] 2 All E.R. 110 (C.A.).

15. *Supra* pp. 739–742.

Except when all parties to the reference consent, the first part of section 1(4) places an absolute bar upon the grant of leave to appeal unless the determination of the disputed point of law would substantially affect the rights of one or more parties to the reference; and this, be it noted, even though the point might have arisen under a standard form contract and be of outstanding importance to the trade generally. I find it impossible to infer from the inclusion of a power to impose conditions in the latter part of the same subsection a parliamentary intention that whenever that absolute bar did not operate leave to appeal *should* be granted albeit that it might be made subject to conditions.

Section 1(7) is another provision in favour of reaching finality as soon as possible; the stringent conditions imposed upon a further appeal from the judge to the Court of Appeal are clearly adapted from the provisions of the Criminal Appeal Act 1968 relating to appeals to the House of Lords in criminal matters—another field of law in which speedy finality is much to be desired. The subsection also draws a significant distinction between a question of law which arises in connection with a "one-off" case and a question of law of general importance to a substantial section of the commercial community, such as may arise under standard term contracts. I add parenthetically that it is one of the ironies of the instant case that if the judge's initial error in granting leave to appeal to the High Court had not been compounded by his also giving a certificate and leave to appeal to the Court of Appeal under this subsection (which a fortiori in such a "one-off" case he never should have done), the owners would have been left with a decision against them which, although it is not one of general public importance both the Court of Appeal and this House have unanimously held to be wrong.

Section 3 gives effect to a reversal of public policy in relation to arbitration as it had been expounded more than half a century before in *Czarnikow* v. *Roth, Schmidt & Co.* [1922] 2 K.B. 478. Exclusion agreements, which oust the statutory jurisdiction of the High Court to supervise the way in which arbitrators apply the law in reaching their decisions in individual cases, are recognised as being no longer contrary to public policy. In principle they are enforceable, subject only to the special limitations imposed, for the time being, by section 4 in the case of awards made in respect of certain limited classes of contracts which important as they are to the role of London as a forum for international arbitrations, represent what is numerically only a small fraction of the total arbitrations, large and small, that take place in England.

The classes of contracts listed in section 4 in respect of which the right to make exclusion agreements is not unfettered but is subjected to some qualifications, are those in which (i) the use of standard forms of contract, in the vast majority of transactions, is a commercial necessity; (ii) English law is very widely chosen as the "proper law" of the contract, even though the parties are foreign nationals and no part of the transaction is to take place in England, and (iii) provision is very frequently made for London arbitration. I have already drawn attention to the fact that decisions of the English courts on cases stated by arbitrators under the previous system had made an important contribution in giving to English commercial law the comprehensiveness and certainty that makes it a favoured choice as the "proper law" of contracts in the classes listed, and London arbitration as the favoured curial law for the resolution of disputes arising under them. Even in respect of contracts falling within these classes, however, exclusion agreement may be made and will be enforceable if entered into after the dispute arose. What is not enforceable is an exclusion agreement covering possible future disputes under the contract before they have arisen. Nevertheless, when a dispute under the contract has arisen and the award of an arbitrator made, an appeal to the High Court on a point of law arising out of it is not as of right; it is still subject to the discretion of the judge under section 1(3)(b).

My Lords, it seems to me quite evident that the parliamentary intention evinced by section 4 in maintaining for the time being a prohibition on pre-dispute exclusion agreements only was to facilitate the continued performance by the courts of their useful function of preserving, in the light of changes in technology and commercial practices adopted in various trades, the comprehensiveness and certainty of English law as to the legal obligations assumed by the parties to commercial contracts of the classes listed, and particularly those expressed in standard terms; it was not Parliament's intention to encourage appeals from arbitrators' awards even under those classes of contracts where such appeals would not fulfil this purpose. That Parliament was alert to the possibility of such abuse in the case of any or all of the listed classes of contracts appears to me to follow from the provision in subsection (3) that the Secretary of State may at any time *remove* the ban upon pre-dispute exclusion agreements in respect of all or any of the classes of contracts included in the list but he has no power to *add* any other class of contract to them.

My Lords, I can deal much more briefly with the terms in which the right of appeal to the High Court is conferred by section 1(2). The power to require an arbitrator to state an award in the form of a special case for the opinion of the High Court under the previous Arbitration Acts from 1889 to 1950 was not conferred in terms that restricted it expressly to cases in which questions stated for the opinion of the High Court were confined exclusively to points of law. Parliament had been content to allow any such restriction to be implied from its use of the phrase "special case for the opinion of the . . . court" which, by 1889, had become a term of legal art; and many and varied (and, if I may be forgiven for saying so, at times confusing) were the authorities as to findings of arbitrators in particular cases that could or could not be upset by the High Court in the exercise of this power. The right of appeal to the High Court, on the other hand, under the substituted procedure for challenging an arbitrator's award which is provided by section 1(2), viz. "an appeal . . . to the High Court on any question of law arising out of" an award, is given in terms which expressly confine the appeal to questions of law.

My Lords, in view of the cumulative effect of all these indications of Parliament's intention to promote greater finality to arbitral awards than was being achieved under the previous procedure as it was applied in practice, it would, in my view, defeat the main purpose of the first four sections of the Act if judges when determining whether a case was one in which the new discretion to grant leave to appeal should be exercised in favour of an applicant against objection by any other party to the reference, did not apply much stricter criteria than those stated in *The Lysland* [1973] Q.B. 843 which used to be applied in exercising the former discretion to require an arbitrator to state a special case for the opinion of the court.

1.5.4 The House of Lords reaffirmed its perception of the policy underlying the 1979 Act and also the new philosophical outlook it evoked in *The Antaios*. Lord Diplock again made the leading speech, in which the other members of the House concurred, and commented[16]:

My Lords, the course followed in the proceedings in the Supreme Court, illustrates the difficulty of preventing counsel instructed in commercial arbitrations of the kinds to which section 4 of the Arbitration Act 1979 applies, from indulging (no doubt in the supposed commercial interests of their clients) in delaying tactics, so as to attain a similar result to that which it had been possible to achieve before the passing of the Act of 1979 by using the procedure of demanding that an award be stated in the form of a special case whenever the contract sued upon raised a question of construction that was arguable, however faint the prospects of success.

Unless judges are prepared to be vigilant in the exercise of the discretion conferred upon them by sections 1 and 2 of the Arbitration Act 1979, including in Section 1 the new subsection (6A) that was added by section 148(2) of the Supreme Court Act 1981, they will allow to be frustrated the intention of Parliament, as plainly manifested by changes in procedure that these statutes introduced, to promote speedy finality in arbitral awards rather than that insistence upon meticulous semantic and syntactical analysis of the words in which business men happen to have chosen to express the bargain made between them, the meaning of which is technically, though hardly commonsensically, classified in English jurisprudence as a pure question of law.

That such was Parliament's intention this House was at pains to indicate in the analysis of the provisions of the Arbitration Act 1979 made in my own speech in *Pioneer Shipping Ltd.* v. *B.T.P. Tioxide Ltd. (The Nema)* [1982] A.C. 724 in which the other members of the House who were present at the hearing concurred. At that time the way in which the parliamentary intention was being thwarted was by parties to arbitrations applying for leave to appeal from any award that involved a question that was even remotely arguable as to the construction of the relevant contract, and by some, though not all, commercial judges following a policy of granting leave in virtually all such cases, albeit upon conditions as to provision of security for, or pay-

16. *Supra* pp. 199–200.

ment into court of, the whole or a substantial part of the amount of the award. Accordingly, although the Court of Appeal's judgment in the *The Nema* [1982] A.C. 724, reversing that of Robert Goff J. [1980] 2 Lloyd's Rep. 83 granting leave to appeal from an arbitral award, appeared prima facie to an Appeal Committee of this House to be right, leave to appeal from that judgment was granted by this House in order to afford it an opportunity of laying down guidelines as to the circumstances in which the statutory discretion to grant leave to appeal from arbitral awards by section 1(3)(b) ought to be exercised.

Lord Roskill indorsed these observations and commented further[17]:

One purpose of arbitration, especially in commercial disputes, is the avoidance of delays, traditionally if often unfairly associated with the judicial process. The award of an arbitral tribunal can, it is supposed, be obtained swiftly and simply and without elaboration. Unhappily, the former virtually unrestricted right to demand a special case from arbitral tribunals made these admirable objectives almost impossible of attainment. The arbitral process became even more protracted than the judicial, with one or sometimes, as in commodity trade arbitrations, two extra tiers of tribunal added below the High Court, the Court of Appeal and your Lordships' House. The resultant abuse was notorious. Hence the demand for the abolition of the special case successfully accomplished in 1979. But if the restricted appellate system substituted for the special case and the equally outdated motion to set aside an award for error of law on its face, is to be operated in such a way as to make appeals to the High Court, and even beyond the High Court, readily available, not only are the worst features of the system now abolished restored but the additional, albeit not unrestricted autonomy, of arbitral tribunals which the Act of 1979 was designed to establish, seriously hampered.

1.5.5 In examining and analysing the various perceptions of the policy of the 1979 Act there is an ostensible and interesting want of juxtaposition between the approach of the House of Lords and that of the Commercial Court Committee. The primary objectives of the Committee were to establish a rational and efficient appeal procedure which would be attractive to the commercial community and also rid the law of the abuses associated with the special case procedure. In recommending the validity of exclusion agreements the Committee was concerned to give London arbitration a greater competitiveness in the face of growing overseas competition. In making its recommendations the Committee did not see itself, at least overtly, as materially changing the direction of English arbitration jurisprudence and in particular as restricting the relationship between the courts and arbitration on questions of law. Even the recommended recognition of exclusion agreements was founded on expediency and heavily qualified.[18] But notwithstanding that the legislature saw itself as giving legislative effect to the Report of the Commercial Court Committee, the House of Lords has proceeded a step further and interpreted the legislative language as manifesting an intention to ascribe to arbitration a greater autonomy and finality on questions of law than previously existed.[19] Few would now criticise this development for it represents a rational advance[20] and is supportable by reference to both domestic and international public policy. In bringing English arbitral law more in tune with the

---

17. *Supra* pp. 208–209.
18. *Supra*, para. 1.3.
19. See argument of counsel and the observations of Lord Denning M.R. in *Italmare Shipping Co.* v. *Ocean Tanker Co. Inc. (The Rio Sun)* [1982] 1 W.L.R. 158.
20. For an example of the contrary argument see Wallace, "Control by the Courts: A Plea for More, Not Less" (1990) 6 Arb. Int. 253. The article is responded to by Mayer, "Seeking the Middle Ground of Court Control: A Reply to I. N. Duncan Wallace" (1991) 7 Arb. Int. 311.

tenets of the latter, the 1979 Act has strengthened the international status of English arbitration.[21]

1.6 WIDER IMPACT OF 1979 ACT

1.6.1 One of the significant and remarkable features of the 1979 Act is that its impact has extended much wider than its particular provisions. The policy of the 1979 Act has been adopted as the prevailing policy relevant to the generality of arbitration law and practice. The Act is in consequence a signal and historic milestone in the evolution of arbitration jurisprudence for it has created a judicial mood significantly more greatly committed to a hands-off style of judicial supervisory management. The finality of awards and the autonomy of the arbitral process, although to some degree ever present in the modern law, have in the result become values more firmly implanted in the philosophical bedrock of the law. In short the policy of the 1979 Act has also become the policy of the contemporary law.[1] Bingham J. has observed that "the very strong trend of current judicial opinion is in favour of restricting rather than protracting challenges to arbitral awards".[2] The alignment between the policy of the Act and the general policy of the law has been even more openly acknowledged by Hirst J. in a dictum that recognised that, "the policy of the law, as laid down in the Arbitration Act 1979, and in numerous cases of the highest authority decided since, has strongly reflected the especial importance in arbitration proceedings of the general principle that litigation should be quickly and finally concluded."[3] It is possible to identify many trends in the post-1979 law which provide evidence of the penetrative influence of the 1979 Act.

1.6.2 Following the definition of the policy underlying the new legislation the courts have showed a determination to protect the restrictive provisions of the 1979

---

21. *Kansa General Insurance Co. Ltd.* v. *Bishopsgate Insurance plc* [1988] 1 Lloyd's Rep. 503, 513, per Hirst J. "the central policy of the 1979 Act [is] to strengthen the international status of English arbitration by discouraging Court interference with awards". See also *Universal Petroleum Co. Ltd.* v. *Handels- und Transport Gesellschaft m.b.H.* [1987] 1 Lloyd's Rep. 517, 529, per Kerr L.J., "The 1979 Act was designed to attract more international arbitrations to this country by overcoming, or at least mitigating, the constant criticism from foreign arbitral organisations, lawyers and their clients that our system permits too much interference by the Courts with the finality of arbitral awards. Such criticism has often come from persons who otherwise have the highest regard for this country as a forum for the resolution of international disputes and who would in principle like to arbitrate here. Fortunately this criticism appears to have greatly abated in recent years, as participants in international conferences and seminars on arbitration will have noticed with satisfaction."

1. It is now only of historical interest to note that the policy of the 1979 Act also influenced the final years of the old law during the transitional phase from the old to the new. With regard to arbitrations commenced before the 1979 Act came into force and which were subject to the special case procedure the courts were disinclined to allow the differences between the old and new processes to survive and applied to the special case procedure the same discretionary criteria as were being developed in association with the new appeal procedure: see *Compagnie Général Maritime* v. *Diakan Spirit S.A. (The Ymnos)* [1982] 2 Lloyd's Rep. 574, 587; *Cobec Brazilian Trading and Warehousing Corpn.* v. *Alfred C. Toepfer* [1983] 2 Lloyd's Rep. 386, 390; *Glafki Shipping Co. S.A.* v. *Pinios Shipping Co. No. 1 (The Maira) (No. 2)* [1985] 1 Lloyd's Rep. 300, 302; *Cook Industries Inc.* v. *Tradax Export S.A.* [1985] 2 Lloyd's Rep. 454, 460.

2. *Saleh Farid* v. *Mackinnon Mackenzie & Co. Ltd. (The Sheba and Shamsan)* [1983] 2 Lloyd's Rep. 500, 508. See also *Atlantic Lines and Navigation Co. Inc.* v. *Italmare S.p.A. (The Apollon)* [1985] 1 Lloyd's Rep. 597, 610.

3. *Aiden Shipping Co. Ltd.* v. *Interbulk Ltd. (The Vimeira) (No. 2)* [1985] 2 Lloyd's Rep. 377, 399 (first instance).

Act by refusing to exercise the supervisory jurisdiction arising elsewhere under the arbitration legislation in a manner that would effectively counter the 1979 Act and defeat its policy. This has been particularly evident in connection with the jurisdiction to set aside and remit awards under sections 22 and 23 of the Arbitration Act 1950,[4] but extends more widely. The courts have been cautious not to permit the enlargement of the concept of misconduct under section 23[5] nor to allow the general jurisdiction to remit under section 22 to be utilised as stratagems for circumventing the restrictive philosophy of the 1979 Act.[6] Sir John Donaldson M.R. was quick to "make it clear to all who are concerned in and with arbitration that neither section 22 nor section 23 is available as a backdoor method of circumventing the restrictions upon the Court's power to intervene in arbitral proceedings which have been created by the 1979 Act".[7] In a subsequent case Steyn J. was equally firm and gave the approach an even wider horizon. The learned judge observed: "The courts will not allow the policy of judicial restraint which was enshrined in the 1979 Act to be subverted by a misuse of the concepts of misconduct or excess of authority, or a strained interpretation of section 12 of the 1950 Act."[8] In keeping with this approach there has been a trenchant rejection of argument seeking to translate error of law or fact into a question of *vires*,[9] and a growing judicial reluctance to intervene in the arbitral process.[10] The non-interventionist policy has also contributed to the shaping of law reform proposals[11] which in recent years have witnessed the abrogation of the statutory judicial power in relation to references to order discovery of documents and interrogatories[12]; and with the new statutory power to dismiss claims in arbitration for want of prosecution conferred on arbitrators and umpires, and not the High Court.[13]

4. *Saleh Farid* v. *Mackinnon Mackenzie & Co. Ltd. (The Sheba and Shamsan)* [1983] 2 Lloyd's Rep. 500, 501.

5. *Evmar Shipping Corpn.* v. *Japan Line Ltd. (The Evmar)* [1984] 2 Lloyd's Rep. 581, 583, per Leggatt J., "I can see an argument that the availability of the new procedure for review and the practice governing it might have or tend to have a restrictive effect upon what the Court is prepared to regard as misconduct. It would be quite wrong for there to grow up a practice of seeking to characterise an arbitrator's conduct as misconduct for the sole purpose of circumventing the procedure under s. 1 of the 1979 Act in circumstances where an applicant was unable to comply with the requirements of that section." See also *Moran* v. *The Committee of Lloyd's, infra*; *Mabanaft G.m.b.H.* v. *Consentino Shipping Co. S.A. (The Achillet)* [1984] 2 Lloyd's Rep. 191, 192.

6. *L'Office National du The et du Sucre* v. *Philippine Sugar Trading (London) Ltd.* [1983] 1 Lloyd's Rep. 89, 91–92. *Bulk Oil (Zug) A.G.* v. *Sun International Ltd. and Sun Oil Trading Co. (No. 2)* [1984] 1 Lloyd's Rep. 531, 533; *Italmare S.p.A.* v. *Stellar Chartering & Brokerage Inc. (The Marina Di Cassano)* [1984] 2 Lloyd's Rep. 577, 579; *Atlantic Lines and Navigation Co. Inc.* v. *Italmare S.p.A. (The Apollon)* [1985] 1 Lloyd's Rep. 597, 610. Contrast *King* v. *Thomas McKenna Ltd.* [1991] 1 All E.R. 653.

7. *Moran* v. *The Committee of Lloyd's* [1983] 1 Lloyd's Rep. 472, 475. See also *Interbulk Ltd.* v. *Aiden Shipping Co. Ltd. (The Vimeira)* [1983] 2 Lloyd's Rep. 424; *Bulk Oil (Zug) A.G.* v. *Sun International Ltd. and Sun Oil Trading Co. (No. 2)* [1984] 1 Lloyd's Rep. 531, 533.

8. *K/S A/S Bill Biakh and K/S A/S Bill Biali* v. *Hyundai Corporation* [1988] 1 Lloyd's Rep. 187, 190–191.

9. *K/S A/S Bill Biakh and K/S A/S Bill Biali* v. *Hyundai Corporation, ibid*; *Bank Mellat* v. *GAA Development and Construction Co.* [1988] 2 Lloyd's Rep. 44, 53; *Geogas S.A.* v. *Trammo Gas Ltd. (The Baleares)* [1993] 1 Lloyd's Rep. 215, 228 (C.A.).

10. *Comdel Commodities Ltd.* v. *Siporex Trade S.A.* [1987] 1 Lloyd's Rep. 325, 329 (decision otherwise reversed on appeal); *K/S A/S Bill Biakh and K/S A/S Bill Biali* v. *Hyundai Corporation, supra*.

11. See the Report on Delay: Striking out Claims in Arbitration, of the Departmental Advisory Committee on Arbitration Law, published in (1988) 4 Arb. Int. 160.

12. Courts and Legal Services Act 1990, s. 103, repealing s. 12(6)(b) of the Arbitration Act 1950.

13. Courts and Legal Services Act 1990, s. 102 inserting a new s. 13A into the Arbitration Act 1950. For a criticism of this development see Thomas, "Arbitral Delay and the Recommendation of the Departmental Advisory Committee" [1990] J.B.L. 110.

1.6.3 In tandem with the judicial determination to prevent the wider arbitral law from being developed in a manner that would betray the policy of the 1979 Act there has developed a policy of avoiding or at least minimising the possibility of overlapping jurisdictions. A specific jurisdiction established under the 1979 Act is generally viewed as exhaustive and to preclude the possibility of a concurrent jurisdiction being recognised by reference to the wider arbitration legislation. The prime and possibly only example of this principle is the developed relationship between section 1(5) of the 1979 Act which empowers the court to order the giving of reasons or further reasons for an award in aid of the appellate process,[14] and the general remitting jurisdiction established by section 22 of the 1950 Act. The precise scope of the latter jurisdiction has been the subject of persistent uncertainty,[15] but it was utilised in relation to the former special case procedure to achieve a purpose roughly analogous to that now served by section 1(5) in relation to the new appeal procedure.[16] Section 22 could quite clearly be utilised to serve the same function as section 1(5), and had there been no section 1(5) it may well have been so utilised. But the reality is that section 1(5) and section 22 co-exist and in response the courts have been reluctant to allow them to occupy a common ground and so be capable of interchangeable use.[17] Section 1(5) is the primary provision and to the extent of its provisions section 22 is displaced. The developed relationship is probably one based on discretion rather than strict jurisdictional criteria. This leaves open a potential for section 22, which may be resorted to as a supplementary jurisdiction when the interests of justice demand.[18]

1.6.4 A further but possibly less direct illustration of the judicial mood against overlapping jurisdictions is the rationalisation of the review of awards of costs which has taken place following the 1979 Act, and which portends a similar development in relation to the review of awards of interest. Under the preceding law the judicial review of awards of costs was firmly based on the concept of misconduct, with the powers to set aside or remit deriving from sections 23(2) and 22 of the 1950 Act. With the benefit of hindsight this now appears a little curious, but the history of this branch of the law has been displaced and the matter placed on a wholly new footing by the 1979 Act. The underlying principles governing the award of costs and interest are as much principles of law as are many of the questions relating to substantive disputes between arbitrating parties, and this view of the subject has been adopted in the post-1979 Act law, with the consequence that the review of awards of costs and interest has been brought within the appellate regime established by the 1979 Act. The historical non-appellate review jurisdiction has been expunged and there would seem to be no question of it continuing to be available, even as a concurrent jurisdiction, when the only allegation is arbitral error. The principle that error of fact or law does not amount to misconduct now extends into the realm of awards of costs and interest.[19]

---

14. See Chapter 11.
15. The uncertainty has been added to by the decision of the Court of Appeal in *King* v. *Thomas McKenna Ltd*. [1991] All E.R. 653.
16. The remitting power exercised in relation to the special case procedure was however viewed as being a jurisdiction based on distinct criteria and separate from the general considerations applicable to s. 22; see *Universal Cargo Carriers Corporation* v. *Pedro Citati* [1957] 2 Lloyd's Rep. 191. See further Chapter 11, para. 11.3.1.
17. See Chapter 11, para. 11.11.
18. *Ibid*.
19. This topic is discussed in some detail in Chapter 6, paras. 6.2.14.1 and 6.2.14.2.

1.6.5 The new approach adopted to the review of awards of costs also indicates a judicial determination to channel all questions relating to the review of the arbitral process with regard to questions of law into the province of the 1979 Act. It is unambiguously established that error of law does not amount to misconduct,[20] so precluding the possibility of non-appellate review. It is also highly unlikely that the courts would in present times revoke the authority of an arbitrator who is falling into legal error,[21] given the existence of the consultative case procedure and other possible remedies.[22] But if this suggested trend represents an accurate analysis an interesting question arises in relation to the future application of section 4(1) of the 1950 Act. Section 4(1) confers a discretion to stay litigation brought in disregard of a domestic arbitration agreement. In the judicial development of the discretion there emerged the understanding that certain questions of law arising out of a dispute between parties to an arbitration agreement might be inappropriate to be decided by the arbitrator and that where this was the case it would justify a refusal to order a stay.[23] The question now arises whether this position survives the 1979 Act.[24] If the procedures established under the 1979 Act now monopolise arbitral review on questions of law the natural consequence is that the discretionary power under section 4(1) is lost. The argument would run that a question of law referred to an arbitrator is to be disposed of by the agreed procedure subject to an appeal or consultative case under the 1979 Act. Conversely it is arguable that section 4(1) addresses a distinct and separate kind of situation and in deciding whether a dispute should be determined by arbitration or litigation the courts may have regard to the nature, importance and difficulty of the question of law in issue. If the question of law is of such significance to the resolution of the dispute that the question of an appeal is likely to be to the forefront of the mind of the losing party and if the question of law is also of a kind that the court might be persuaded to give leave to appeal, there exists at least some justification for the refusal of a stay. Such a stay anticipates the prospect of future judicial intervention and may even expedite the resolution of the dispute. So even if the discretionary power under section 4(1) survives, which arguably it does, it is likely to be refashioned in the image of the discretion arising under section 1(3)(b) of the 1979 Act.[25]

1.6.6 Another broad influence of the 1979 Act is that it appears to have changed attitudes towards reasoned awards and encouraged the gratuitous giving of reasoned awards.[26] To this extent the Act has heightened the judicious rationality of English arbitration law. The historical position of English law in relation to reasoned awards and the explanation for the reluctance on the part of arbitrators to give reasons are developed elsewhere in the text.[27] The pre-1979 Act practice also highlighted a significant point of contrast between English law and many foreign systems of law, particu-

---

20. See *supra*, para. 1.2.2.3.
21. The power to revoke the authority of an arbitrator arises under s. 1 of the Arbitration Act 1950. See also *East & West India Dock* v. *Kirk* (1887) 12 App.Cas. 938.
22. See Chapter 12.
23. *Rowe Bros. & Co. Ltd.* v. *Crossley Bros. Ltd.* (1912) 108 L.T. 11 (C.A.); *Bristol Corpn.* v. *John Aird & Co.* [1913] A.C. 241; *Heyman* v. *Darwins Ltd.* [1942] A.C. 356, 391, per Lord Wright. See also *Radford* v. *Hair and Others* [1971] Ch. 758.
24. Cf. Mann, "Private Arbitration and Public Policy" (1985) 4 C.J.Q. 257, 261.
25. See Chapter 5.
26. *Pearl Marin Shipping A/B* v. *Pietro Cingolani S.A.S. (The General Valdes)* [1982] 1 Lloyd's Rep. 17, 21 per Ackner L.J.
27. *Supra*, para. 1.4.1.5 and Chapter 11.

larly continental codes where "speaking" or "motivated" awards were not only common in practice but frequently required by law.[28] The Act does not expressly oblige arbitrators to give reasoned awards, but by virtue of its restructuring and rationalisation of the judicial review process with regard to questions of law there is now much less to be feared from the making of a reasoned award and to a corresponding degree the Act indirectly encourages the practice of making reasoned awards.[29]

1.6.7 An aspect of the policy associated with the 1979 Act is concerned to render London arbitration more attractive to the international community and thereby enhance London's competitiveness as an international arbitral forum.[30] Here again the policy of the legislation has assumed a force beyond the boundaries of the 1979 Act. In any case with an international dimension it is highly probable that the court will be sensitive to the impact of its decision on the reputation and appeal of London arbitration. To the extent that there may exist an international public policy of arbitration, the English courts have probably become more sensitive to its tenets following the 1979 Act. An example of the trend is provided by the case of *Shearson Lehman Bros. Inc.* v. *Maclaine Watson & Co. Ltd. (No. 3)*[31] where Webster J. held that documents produced in the course of a private arbitration were not confidential and could be directed to be disclosed in litigation on the application of a party who was not a party in the arbitration. Of particular interest to the present discussion, in coming to that conclusion Webster J. took into account that the courts would not wish to do anything to cause foreign litigants to fear using English arbitration proceedings. A further example is possibly provided by *Channel Tunnel Group Ltd.* v. *Balfour Beatty Construction Ltd.*[32] where the House of Lords refused to grant interim relief in aid of a foreign arbitration on grounds which included the reason that to accede to the application would be to act contrarily to "the spirit of international arbitration".[33]

1.6.8 The impact of the 1979 Act has not been confined to national public policy. It appears to have set in train a major international reconsideration of the relationship between courts and arbitration in relation to questions of law. Many common law countries have followed the design but not necessarily the detail of the new appellate process introduced by the 1979 Act.[34] But even more widely the 1979 Act has evoked, or at least contributed to the debate as to the degree of autonomy and finality the arbitral process should enjoy, and the extent to which the public policy touching on international arbitration has different claims from the public policy of domestic arbitration.[35] The policy associated with the 1979 Act is however in conflict with the philosophy of the UNCITRAL Model Law on International Commercial Arbitration[36] where no right of appeal on questions of law is recognised.[37]

---

28. Commercial Court Committee, *Report on Arbitration, supra* paras. 6 and 7.
29. See Chapter 11 for a detailed consideration of reasoned awards.
30. *Supra*, paras 1.3.13 and 1.5.5.
31. [1988] 1 W.L.R. 946.
32. [1993] A.C. 334.
33. *Ibid*, p. 368 per Lord Mustill.
34. See, for example, Commercial Arbitration Act (British Columbia) 1986, ss. 31–34; Arbitration Ordinance Chap. 341 (Hong Kong) 1982, ss. 23–23B.
35. See generally, Mustill, "Contemporary Problems in International Commercial Arbitration: A Response" 1989 Int. Bus. Lawy. 161.
36. Adopted by UNCITRAL on 21 June 1985: see UN document A/40/17. For a commentary on the Model Law see Redfern and Hunter, *International Commercial Arbitration* (2nd edn.), Chapter 9.
37. See Kerr, "Arbitration and the Courts: The UNCITRAL Model Law" (1985) 34 I.C.L.Q. 1.

1.7 TECHNICAL ASPECTS OF THE 1979 ACT

1.7.1 Commencement of the Act and arbitrations to which the Act applies

The 1979 Act came into force on 1 August 1979 (the appointed day) and applies to all arbitrations within the contemplation of the Act[1] commenced on or after the appointed date.[2]

The 1979 Act is not applicable to arbitrations commenced before 1 August 1979[3] unless all the parties to the reference agree in writing that the Act shall apply to the arbitration. When such an agreement is entered into the Act applies from the appointed day or the date of the agreement whichever is the later.[4] In the absence of such an agreement arbitrations commenced before the coming into operation of the 1979 Act are governed by the former law and rules of practice.[5]

By section 7(2) of the 1979 Act the "commencement" of an arbitration is defined in the same terms as specified in section 29(2) and (3) of the Arbitration Act 1950,[6] which provide:

(2) . . . an arbitration shall be deemed to be commenced when one party to the arbitration agreement serves on the other party or parties a notice requiring him or them to appoint or concur in appointing an arbitrator,[7] or, where the arbitration agreement provides that the reference shall be to a person named or designated in the agreement, requiring him or them to submit the dispute to the person so named or designated.

(3) Any such notice as is mentioned in subsection (2) of this section may be served either—
  (a) by delivering it to the person on whom it is to be served; or
  (b) by leaving it at the usual or last known place of abode in England of that person; or
  (c) by sending it by post in a registered letter addressed to that person at his usual or last known place of abode in England;
as well as in any other manner provided in the arbitration agreement; and where a notice is sent by post in manner prescribed by paragraph (c) of this subsection, service thereof shall, unless the contrary is proved, be deemed to have been effected at the time at which the letter would have been delivered in the ordinary course of post.

These provisions are in substance identical with the provisions set out in the Limitation Act 1980, section 34(3) and (4), with the consequence that the 1979 Act adopts the same meaning to the phrase "the commencement of an arbitration" as is adopted

---

1. See *infra*.
2. Section 8(2) and The Arbitration Act 1979 (Commencement) Order 1979 (S.I. 1979 No. 750) Art. 2. See also *Coral Navigation Inc.* v. *Avin Chartering S.A. (The Kwai)* [1981] 2 Lloyd's Rep. 563; *Peter Cremer G.m.b.H. & Co.* v. *Sugat Food Industries Ltd. (The Rimon)* [1981] 2 Lloyd's Rep. 640; *Greenwich Marine Inc.* v. *Federal Commerce & Navigation Co. Ltd. (The Mavro Vetranic)* [1985] 1 Lloyd's Rep. 580.
3. Cf. *Food Corporation of India* v. *Marastro Cia Naviera S.A. (The Trade Fortitude)* [1985] 2 Lloyd's Rep. 579.
4. The Arbitration Act 1979 (Commencement) Order 1979 (S.I. 1979 No. 750) Arts. 2 and 3. See also *Mondial Trading Co. G.m.b.H.* v. *Gill & Duffus Zuckerhandelsgesellschaft m.b.H.* [1980] 2 Lloyd's Rep. 376, 377; *Filikos Shipping Corpn. of Monrovia* v. *Shipmair B.V. (The Filikos)* [1981] 2 Lloyd's Rep. 555, [1983] 1 Lloyd's Rep. 9 (C.A.); *B.V.S. and Another* v. *Kerman Shipping Co. S.A. (The Kerman)* [1982] 1 W.L.R. 166, 174.
5. See, for example, *Compania Maritima Zorroza S.A.* v. *Maritime Bulk Carriers Corporation (The Marques de Bolarque)* [1980] 2 Lloyd's Rep. 186; *Greenwich Marine Inc.* v. *Federal Commercie & Navigation Co. Ltd. (The Mavro Vetranic)* [1985] 1 Lloyd's Rep. 580.
6. Re-enacting s. 16(3)–(5) of the Arbitration Act 1934. See further Chapter 13, para. 13.4.2.2.
7. Considered in *N.V. Stoomv Maats de Maas* v. *Nippon Yusen Kaisha (The Pendrecht)* [1980] 2 Lloyd's Rep. 56, 64 *et seq*.

for the purpose of statutory time limits under the Limitation Act 1980 or any other limitation enactment.

1.7.2 Territorial reach

The 1979 Act forms part of the law of England and Wales only.[1] It does not apply in Scotland[2] and Northern Ireland.[3]

1.7.3 Crown

The 1979 Act, together with Part I of the Arbitration Act 1950, binds the Crown.[1]

1.7.4 Statutory arbitrations

The 1979 Act applies to statutory arbitrations, in addition to consensual arbitrations, except in so far as the 1979 Act is inconsistent with the Act establishing the statutory arbitration or with any rules or procedure authorised or recognised by that Act.[1]

An arbitration conducted under section 64 of the County Courts Act 1984[2] is not a statutory arbitration for this purpose and therefore neither the 1979 Act nor Part I of the Arbitration Act 1950 apply to such arbitrations.[3]

1.7.5 Arbitration agreements

With the exception of section 2, the various provisions of the 1979 Act are expressly concerned with awards made "on an arbitration agreement",[1] or to references "under an arbitration agreement",[2] or quite simply "arbitration agreements".[3] But even with regard to section 2 it is probable that the section will be interpreted so that the allusion therein to "a reference" will be understood to mean "a reference arising out of an arbitration agreement".[4]

The definition of an arbitration agreement provided by section 32 of the Arbitration Act 1950, and applicable to Part I of that Act, is also made applicable to the 1979 Act.[5] Unless the context otherwise requires section 32 defines an arbitration agreement to mean "a written agreement to submit present or future differences to arbitration, whether an arbitrator is named therein or not".[6] The definition embraces

---

1. Section 8(4). See also Arbitration Act 1950 s. 34. In contrast, the Arbitration Act 1950, Part II and the Arbitration Act 1975 apply to the UK in its entirety.
2. For the relevant Scottish Law see Administration of Justice (Scotland) Act 1972 (c. 59), section 3; Law Reform (Miscellaneous Provisions) (Scotland) Act 1990 (c. 40), section 66 and Schedule 7.
3. For the relevant law of Northern Ireland, see, Arbitration Act (Northern Ireland) 1937.
1. Section 7(1)(c), which makes s. 30 of the Arbitration Act 1950 applicable to the 1979 Act. In contrast Part II of the Arbitration Act 1950 and the Arbitration Act 1975 do not bind the Crown.
1. Section 7(1)(d) which makes s. 31 of the Arbitration Act 1950 applicable to the 1979 Act. See also *Moran* v. *Lloyd's* [1983] 1 Lloyd's Rep. 51; [1983] 1 Lloyd's Rep. 472 (C.A.).
2. And County Court Rules, Ord. 19.
3. Section 7(3).
1. Section 1(2).
2. Section 5(1).
3. Sections 3(3), 5(5) and 6.
4. Cf. *Imperial Metal Industries (Kynoch) Ltd.* v. *Amalgamated Union of Engineering Workers* [1979] 1 All E.R. 847, 858 per Roskill L.J.
5. Section 7(1)(e).
6. Compare the definition of an "arbitration agreement" provided by the Arbitration Act 1975, s. 7(1).

submissions of existing disputes and references of future disputes, and it is immaterial whether or not the arbitrator or tribunal is specified in the agreement. In strictness the definition is not unyielding for by the express language of section 32 it is to prevail "unless the context otherwise requires". This qualifying phrase has however assumed little or no force and may even be redundant.

The definition also carries a formal element: the arbitration agreement must be a "written agreement", and it is this aspect of the definition which has attracted the greatest attention. The formal requirement of the definition and the circumstances when it is satisfied are considered in detail in Chapter 3.[7] For present purposes it is sufficient to comment that the 1979 Act aligns itself with the arbitration legislation at large in confining its application to formal arbitration agreements and in not extending to parol arbitration agreements, which are otherwise valid at common law.[8] The requirement of writing is not strictly construed and includes not only arbitration agreements reduced into writing but also arbitration agreements evidenced or acknowledged by writing.[9]

1.7.6 Relationship between the 1979 Act and the arbitration legislation

Beyond providing that for certain purposes the sections of the 1979 Act take effect as if they were included in Part I of the Arbitration Act 1950,[1] there is no express statutory statement of the relationship that exists between the 1979 Act and the arbitration legislation.[2] Nonetheless the 1979 Act would appear a component of the legislative scheme established by Part I of the 1950 Act and to be *in pari materia*[3] with that Part of the 1950 Act. If this is the case then for the purposes of statutory interpretation the entirety of Part I of the 1950 Act represents an aspect of the context of the 1979 Act.

1.7.7 Interpretation of the 1979 Act

1.7.7.1 The 1979 Act, as are the other components of the arbitration legislation, is what is termed a "technical statute", with the consequence that in applying the Act its precise language must be carefully observed.[1] But as the present text reveals a careful scrutiny of its provisions will often have the effect of disclosing uncertainty and ambiguity. When the provisions of the 1979 Act are unclear the question arises as to the proper approach to their interpretation and the aids the courts may take into consideration in endeavouring to determine the intention of the legislature.

1.7.7.2 The interpretation of the 1979 Act must of course follow the general prin-

---

7. Para. 3.4.
8. *Westminster Chemicals and Produce Ltd.* v. *Eichholz and Loeser* [1954] 1 Lloyd's Rep. 99, 104–105, per Devlin J.
9. *Supra*, n. 7.
1. Section 7(1). See also *Michael I. Warde* v. *Feedex International Inc.* [1984] 1 Lloyd's Rep. 310, 316.
2. Ignoring the amendments made to the 1950 Act by s. 6 of the 1979 Act.
3. For an elaboration of this concept see *R.* v. *Loxdale* (1758) 1 Burr 445, 447; *Phillips* v. *Parnaby* [1934] 2 K.B. 299; *Attorney General* v. *Prince Ernest Augustus of Hanover* [1957] A.C. 436, 461.
1. *Re Franklin and Swathling's Arbitration* [1929] 1 Ch. 238, 241; *Ministry of Food Government of Bangladesh* v. *Bengal Liner Ltd. (The Bengal Pride)* [1986] 1 Lloyd's Rep. 167, 170. Contrast *Kiril Mischeff Ltd.* v. *British Doughnut Co. Ltd.* [1954] 1 Lloyd's Rep. 237, 246 where a less technical and more liberal approach is advocated by Singleton L.J.

ciples applicable to the interpretation of statutes.[2] But given the close association between the 1979 Act and the *Report on Arbitration* of the Commercial Court Committee the obvious and particular question that arises is whether the court may take the aid of the Report when interpreting the language of the Act. The major tradition in English law has been to reject such extrinsic aids but there are strong indications that judicial attitudes are changing. The House of Lords has recently relaxed the historical rule prohibiting the courts from referring to parliamentary material, particularly Hansard, as an aid to statutory interpretation.[3] It is now well established that in the face of uncertainty a statute implementing an international convention may be construed with the aid of the convention, whether annexed to the legislation or not, and also the *travaux préparatoires*.[4] It is also acknowledged that where a statute has been preceded by and gives effect to the recommendations of a Law Commission Report, the courts may refer to the Report to determine the proper interpretation of the statute.[5] The same principle prevails when legislation follows on from a governmental White Paper.[6] These examples may be more than individual and exceptional developments, and may represent a broad and growing trend on the part of the courts to take as an aid to statutory interpretation the reports produced by expert bodies and on which legislation is based.[7] The precise status of the Commercial Court Committee has not been judicially considered but it has claim to be considered a public or official body, having been established by the Lord Chancellor in 1977,[8] and its Report was directly responsible for the 1979 Act, although the Committee did not go so far as to append a draft Bill to its Report. On this view of the status of the Committee it is at least arguable that it would be legitimate for courts to have regard to the Report in interpreting the 1979 Act; but the sparse judicial consideration of the question to date may suggest a contrary conclusion. Of particular significance the House of Lords in *The Nema*[9] refused an invitation to examine the Report when addressing the proper interpretation of the legislation. In contrast, the Court of Appeal in *The Rio Sun*[10] allowed and responded to argument which sought to impress a particular interpretation of the legislation when read in the light of the Report. When the question came before Staughton J. at first instance the learned judge was uncertain whether he was allowed to know anything of the parliamentary history of the 1979 Act.[11] The utility of the Report as an aid to interpretation is further diminished when it is recalled that the

---

2. See generally Cross, *Statutory Interpretation* (2nd edn.); also *Kansa General Insurance Co. Ltd.* v. *Bishopsgate Insurance plc* [1988] 1 Lloyd's Rep. 503, 507, where Hirst J. considered that sections of the Act were to be construed in the context of related sections, and subsections in the context of the entire section within which they are embodied.

3. *Pepper (Inspector of Taxes)* v. *Hart* [1993] A.C. 593.

4. *Fothergill* v. *Monarch Airlines Ltd.* [1981] A.C. 251; *Salomon* v. *Commissioners of Customs and Excise* [1967] 2 Q.B. 116 (C.A.); *Datacard Corporation* v. *Air Express International* [1983] 2 Lloyd's Rep. 81; *Gatoil International Inc.* v. *Arkwright-Boston Manufacturers Mutual Insurance Co. (The Sandrina)* [1985] 1 Lloyd's Rep. 181 (H.L.); *The Estate of the Deceased Shipowner Anders Jahre* v. *The Government of the State of Norway* [1986] 1 Lloyd's Rep. 496 (C.A.).

5. *R.* v. *Shirpuri* [1986] 2 W.L.R. 988, 1000; *Aswan Engineering Establishment Co.* v. *Lupdine Ltd. and Another (Thurga Bolle Ltd., third party)* [1987] 1 All E.R. 135, 147 (C.A.).

6. *Attorney General's Reference (No. 1 of 1988)* [1989] 2 All E.R. 1.

7. Cf. *Black Clawson International Ltd.* v. *Papierwerke Waldhof-Aschaffenburg A.G.* [1975] A.C. 591; *Davis* v. *Johnson* [1978] 1 All E.R. 1132. See also Roskill, 1981 *Statute Law Review* 177.

8. See generally Colman, *The Practice and Procedure of the Commercial Court* (3rd edn.), Chapter 2.

9. *Pioneer Shipping Ltd. and Others* v. *B.T.P. Tioxide Ltd. (The Nema)* [1982] A.C. 724, 730.

10. *Italmare Shipping Co.* v. *Ocean Tanker Co. Inc. (The Rio Sun)* [1982] 1 W.L.R. 158, 168.

11. *Michael I. Warde* v. *Feedex International Inc.* [1984] 1 Lloyd's Rep. 310, 317.

1979 Act does not in matters of detail follow the precise recommendations made in the Report.[12]

1.7.8 Conflict of laws

1.7.8.1 The provisions of the 1979 Act form a part of the English curial law.[1] They apply to all arbitrations which have their seat in England and Wales.[2] The allusion in the 1979 Act to awards and references connote as a matter of statutory interpretation awards and references made in or taking place in England and Wales.[3] The 1979 Act has no application to foreign references and awards[3a]; nor does it confer jurisdiction on foreign courts.[4]

There is a strong and almost irresistible presumption that the curial law of an arbitration is the law of the seat of the arbitration, also variously labelled the *lex loci arbitri* or *lex fori*.[5] In most cases it will not be necessary to progress beyond this presumption, but in principle it is now also accepted that the curial law of arbitration may be as much the object of the express or implied choice of the parties as the proper law of the dispute or of the arbitration agreement.[6] In consequence it is open to the parties to abandon the historical and natural association between the curial law of arbitration and the *lex loci arbitri*. To translate principle into fact, it is accepted that a London arbitration may be conducted by reference to a foreign curial law and a foreign arbitration may be conducted by reference to English curial law.[7]

1.7.8.2 The development of the curial law in the manner indicated raises some fundamental questions concerning the operation of the 1979 Act in the sphere of international arbitration. In the first place it may be enquired whether the 1979 Act is displaced in the event of a London arbitration being conducted in accordance with a foreign curial law. If the principle the courts have embraced in recent times is given an unqualified application it would seem that this result follows. The consequence can only be resisted if the 1979 Act is interpreted as being an overreaching statute,[8] or by reference to public policy, or by giving the principle of party choice a restricted ambit so as to exclude that aspect of procedure relating to the relationship between arbi-

---

12. *Supra*, para. 1.3.
1. By the term curial law is meant the procedural law of the arbitration, including the internal rules of procedure, rules of evidence, remedies and the relationship between the arbitral process and the courts.
2. In English law every arbitration must have a seat. English law does not recognise delocalised arbitration: see *Bank Mellat* v. *Helleniki Techniki S.A.* [1984] Q.B. 291, 301 (C.A.).
3. Cf. *Channel Tunnel Group* v. *Balfour Beatty Construction Ltd.* [1993] A.C. 334. But even in relation to a foreign reference or award the parties may be estopped from asserting the foreign element: see *Hiscox* v. *Outhwaite* [1992] 1 A.C. 562.
3a. Cf. *Black Clawson International Ltd.* v. *Papierwerke Waldhof-Aschaffenburg A.G.* [1981] 2 Lloyd's Rep. 446, 453, Mustill J.
4. Cf. *Spurrier* v. *La Cloche* [1902] A.C. 446.
5. *Channel Tunnel Group* v. *Balfour Beatty Construction Ltd.*, *supra*, p. 662, per Lord Mustill. See also *Naviera Amazonica Peruana S.A.* v. *Compania Internacional de Seguros del Peru* [1988] 1 Lloyd's Rep. 116, 119; *Everglade Maritime Inc.* v. *Schiffartsgesellschaft Detlef von Appen m.b.H. (The Maria)* [1992] 2 Lloyd's Rep. 167, 171.
6. *Channel Tunnel Group* v. *Balfour Beatty Construction Ltd.*, *supra*; *Naviera Amazonica Peruana S.A.* v. *Compania Internacional de Seguros del Peru*, *supra*, p. 120, per Kerr L.J. see also *James Miller & Partners Ltd.* v. *Whitworth Street Estates (Manchester) Ltd.* [1970] A.C. 583; *Black Clawson International Ltd.* v. *Papierwerke Waldhof-Aschaffenburg A.G.* [1981] 2 Lloyd's Rep. 446.
7. *Naviera Amazonica Peruana S.A.* v. *Compania Internacional de Seguros del Peru*, *supra*.
8. Cf. *The Hollandia* [1983] 1 A.C. 565.

tration and the courts.[9] A natural consequence of recognising the unqualified right of the parties to choose the curial law is that the parties would be compelled to approach the courts of the chosen curial law to seek judicial assistance or review. Why parties should wish to establish such a legal regime is hard to contemplate, but given the increasing fluidity in both the practice and jurisprudence of international arbitration it may be within the spirit of things that in principle, and subject to considerations of public policy, the parties should be able to achieve this result. To the extent that English law has developed in this realm, it appears to support this conclusion although conscious of the practical problems that may be created.[10]

1.7.8.3 The particular question here raised has not to date been directly addressed by the courts, although Saville J.[11] in an *obiter dictum* has rejected the possibility that the review jurisdiction of the English courts may be effectively removed by the choice of a foreign curial law. In the opinion of the learned judge the right of parties to English arbitration to choose a foreign curial law is limited to this extent and with the consequence that where such a choice of foreign curial law is made the English arbitration will be governed by two curial laws, the contractual curial law elected by the parties and English curial law, which will be confined to matters of judicial supervision.[12] It is easy to appreciate the practical convenience of this position but no explanation is given for the existence of the limitation beyond the statement that the supervisory jurisdiction of the English courts can only be excluded by the same legislation that establishes the supervisory jurisdiction.[13] This in turn may imply that the learned judge viewed the arbitration legislation as overreaching. In relation to appeals (as distinct from non-appellate review) it would seem more difficult to justify the limitation by reference to public policy, for the 1979 Act itself reveals the right of appeal is not an entrenched right.

1.7.8.4 The converse issue is where a foreign arbitration is conducted according to English curial law. On these facts the question arises whether the 1979 Act applies to the foreign arbitration. This question is more problematical than the first because it further involves the extraterritorial application of legislation. Clearly there are territorial limitations on the reach of the 1979 Act and it does not apply to foreign arbitrations.[14] Parties to a foreign arbitration subject to English curial law who wish to avail themselves of the 1979 Act must therefore act so as to give the English High Court personal jurisdiction over themselves and a jurisdiction over the reference or award. Personal jurisdiction may be achieved by a submission to jurisdiction, and it could even be that the choice of English curial law might be construed as such a submission. To establish jurisdiction over the reference or award is more problematical and it is difficult to see where the solution is to be found, if indeed a solution exists.

9. A possible hint of this approach may be provided by the definition of the curial law enunciated by Lord Mustill in *Channel Tunnel Group* v. *Balfour Beatty Construction Ltd.*, *supra*, p. 662: "the national law which the parties have expressly or by implication selected to govern the relationship between themselves and the arbitrator in the conduct of the arbitration."

10. *Naviera Amazonica Peruana S.A.* v. *Compania Internacional de Seguros del Peru, supra*, p. 120, per Kerr L.J.

11. *Union of India* v. *McDonnell Douglas Corporation* [1993] 2 Lloyd's Rep. 48.

12. *Ibid.* p. 51.

13. *Ibid.*

14. *Black Clawson International Ltd.* v. *Papierwerke Waldhof-Aschaffenburg, supra*; *Navieria Amazonica Peruana S.A.* v. *Compania Internacional de Seguros del Peru, supra*, p. 120; *Channel Tunnel Group* v. *Balfour Beatty Construction Ltd.*, *supra*, pp. 681–684, per Lord Mustill.

There might be a solution in recognising a deemed or assumed jurisdiction, or it might even be that the parties will be compelled to relocate the seat of the arbitration in order to take the benefit of all the implications arising from their choice of curial law. There would appear to be no difficulty of principle in the relocation of the seat of an arbitration, although it may be questionable whether parties can change the seat of an arbitration retroactively, that is after a final award had been made.

PART II

APPEALS FROM ARBITRATION AWARDS TO THE HIGH COURT ON QUESTIONS OF LAW AND ON-APPEALS

CHAPTER 2

AN INTRODUCTION TO THE APPEAL AND ON-APPEAL PROCESSES

2.1 THE APPELLATE PROCESSES

2.1.1 The central feature of the 1979 Act is that it restructures in both an organic and jurisprudential sense the interrelationship between arbitration awards and the courts on questions of law. The organic restructuring is achieved by the express language of section 1; the jurisprudential restructuring as a consequence of the judicial interpretation given the legislation in pursuance of the perceived legislative policy underlying the Act.[1] But although radical the legislation remains within the evolutionary tradition of English arbitration law and in particular continues to give firm recognition to the notion that arbitrations are an integral part of the administration of civil justice,[1a] with arbitrators and umpires under a legal obligation to apply the settled principles of law.[2]

2.1.2 The 1979 Act by section 1(1) expunges the former modes of judicial review of arbitration awards on questions of law, namely at common law for error of law on the face of an award and the special case procedure, most recently provided for by the Arbitration Act 1950, section 21(1)(b).[3] In their place there is established by section 1(2), (3) and (4) of the 1979 Act a single, unified, but restricted system of appeal with regard to any question of law arising out of an award made on an arbitration agreement. The appellate process is by section 1(3) preconditioned upon the consent of all the other parties to the reference or the giving of leave to appeal by the High Court, in practice predominantly the Commercial Court. The question of leave to appeal may be justifiably viewed as the crucial and central concept in the new appeal procedure for it represents the control mechanism, frequently alluded to as a sieve, by which the flow of appeals on questions of law from arbitration awards to the courts is regulated and the conflicting claims of the finality of awards and meticulous legal reasoning in the arbitral decision-making process adjusted.[3a] The judicial stance that has emerged is that the discretionary power to grant leave to appeal must be exercised in a manner consistent with the policy of the 1979 Act and this has resulted in the establishment of a firmly structured and restrictive discretion.[4] No leave to appeal may be granted, by virtue of sec-

1. See Chapter 1, para. 1.5 and Chapter 5.
1a. Cf. *Czarnikow* v. *Roth, Schmidt & Co.* [1922] 2 K.B. 478 (C.A.); *Exormisis Shipping S.A.* v. *Oonsoo, Democratic People's Republic of Korea and Korean Foreign Transportation Corporation (No. 1)* [1975] 1 Lloyd's Rep. 432.
2. See Chapter 1, para. 1.2.2.2.
3. See Chapter 1, para. 1.4.
3a. See Chapter 4, para. 4.3.
4. See Chapters 5 and 6.

tion 1(4), unless the question of law in issue merits the description "substantial",[5] and the same subsection also empowers the court to attach conditions to the granting of leave.[6]

2.1.3 When leave to appeal is granted the appeal is in the first place to the High Court and with a further, but very restricted, right of appeal to the Court of Appeal.[7] In relation to the appellate process the High Court has therefore a dual role. The first, where the consent of all the other parties to the reference is absent, to determine the application for leave to appeal; and the second, when leave to appeal is given, to determine the full substantive appeal. On the substantive appeal the powers of the High Court are set forth in section 1(2), wherein it is provided the High Court may confirm, vary, set aside or remit the award which is the subject of the appeal.[8] Where an award is varied it takes effect as the award of the arbitrator or umpire.[9] Confronted by a remission the arbitrator or umpire must make his reconsidered award within three months of the date of the order, unless the order otherwise directs.[10] By section 1(6A) a restricted right of appeal is established to the Court of Appeal from a decision of the High Court granting or refusing leave to appeal.[11]

2.1.4 The appeal process established under section 1 is clearly premised on the notion of reasoned awards. Without a reasoned award it will be impossible to ascertain in the first place whether a question of law is involved and, if so, whether the arbitrator has fallen into error with regard to a question of law in issue. But the 1979 Act does not impose a positive statutory duty on arbitrators and umpires to give reasons. There is, however, established by section 1(5) and (6) a discretionary and circumscribed judicial power to order the remission of an award which is unreasoned or which is shown to be insufficiently reasoned. In each case the judicial power is limited to a power to order the arbitrator or umpire concerned to state the reasons for his award in sufficient detail to enable the court, should an appeal be brought under section 1, to consider any question of law arising out of the award.[11a] The entire subject of reasoned awards is considered in detail in a later chapter.[12] The question of arbitral reasons also arises in association with the giving or refusal of leave to appeal, although this aspect of the topic is not addressed by the 1979 legislation and has come to be regulated by judicial practice.[13]

2.1.5 The basis of the new appeal procedure to the High Court with regard to questions of law arising out of arbitration awards is established by subsections (2), (3), (4) and (8) of section 1 of the 1979 Act, which are to following effect:

(2) Subject to subsection (3) below, an appeal shall lie to the High Court on any question of law arising out of an award made on an arbitration agreement; and on the determination of such an appeal the High Court may by order—
  (a) confirm, vary or set aside the award; or
  (b) remit the award to the reconsideration of the arbitrator or umpire together with the court's opinion on the question of law which was the subject of the appeal;

5. Considered in Chapter 4, para. 4.3.3.
6. Considered in Chapter 4, para. 4.3.4.
7. Section 1(7). Considered in Chapter 10, para. 10.3.
8. Section 1(2). Considered in Chapter 8, para. 8.7.
9. Section 1(8).
10. Section 1(2).
11. Considered in Chapter 10, para. 10.2.
11a. Section 1(5).
12. Chapter 11.
13. Considered in Chapter 7, para. 7.3.3.

and where the award is remitted under paragraph (b) above the arbitrator or umpire shall, unless the order otherwise directs, make his award within three months after the date of the order.

(3) An appeal under this section may be brought by any of the parties to the reference—
    (a) with the consent of all the other parties to the reference; or
    (b) subject to section 3 below, with the leave of the court.

(4) The High Court shall not grant leave under subsection (3)(b) above unless it considers that, having regard to all the circumstances, the determination of the question of law concerned could substantially affect the rights of one or more of the parties to the arbitration agreement; and the court may make any leave which it gives conditional upon the applicant complying with such conditions as it considers appropriate.

(8) Where the award of an arbitrator or umpire is varied on appeal, the award as varied shall have effect (except for the purposes of this section) as if it were the award of the arbitrator or umpire.

2.1.6 Where the parties to a reference so desire they may by agreement contract out of the right to apply to the High Court for leave to appeal under section 1(3)(b) and in effect render the arbitration award final on any question of law that arises in connection with the dispute. Such agreements are termed exclusion agreements under the 1979 Act and the subject of exclusion agreements, as provided for by sections 3 and 4 of the 1979 Act, is separately considered in a later chapter.[14]

2.1.7 On-appeals from the Court of Appeal to the House of Lords are not overtly within the province of the 1979 Act and continue to be governed primarily by the specific legislation and procedural rules regulating appeals to the House of Lords.[15] This is especially true of substantive appeals. But there is a qualification to be made with regard to the question of leave to appeal to the Court of Appeal, for on this matter the Court of Appeal is the final forum with no further right of appeal to the House of Lords. This consequence results from the language of section 1(7)(a) and the interpretation given to such legislative language. In the upshot, if the Court of Appeal refuses leave to appeal that represents a final determination of the matter, with the House of Lords not enjoying any jurisdiction to entertain an appeal from the refusal.[16]

2.2 WHO MAY INSTITUTE AN APPEAL

2.2.1 By section 1(3) an appeal under section 1(2) may be brought by "any of the parties to the reference". In contrast to the former special case procedure apropos awards there is no involvement of the court in the institution of an appeal.[1] The court cannot direct that an appeal be instituted. Nor is the consent of the arbitrator or umpire a necessary precondition to an appeal, as is the case with regard to an application for leave to apply under section 2(1)(a).[2] The matter rests wholly with the parties to a reference. All, any or one of the arbitrating parties may institute an appeal, subject to the other requirements of section 1(3).[3]

2.2.2 The concept of "a party to the reference" is one that recurs, with one excep-

14. Chapter 13.
15. See Chapter 1, para. 1.2.1.6.3.
16. The whole topic is considered further in Chapter 10, para. 10.2.
1. See Chapter 1, para. 1.4.2.
2. See Chapter 12 for the jurisdiction of the High Court to determine as a preliminary issue questions of law arising in the course of a reference.
3. See Chapters 3 and 4.

tion, throughout the 1979 Act[4] and it is highly probable that the phrase bears a common meaning throughout the legislation. The phrase therefore merits more than a passing consideration.

2.2.3 In the first place it would seem that the phrase in a general sense alludes to a person who is a party to the process of arbitrating a dispute and who has agreed to be bound by any arbitration award made, but does not include the arbitrator, arbitration tribunal or umpire appointed to resolve the dispute. Although the arbitrator or umpire is an integral part of the arbitration machinery and process, neither is a party to the reference in the sense that phrase is used in the 1979 Act. Although this is a conclusion that may be arrived at from an interpretation of the statute in isolation, it is a conclusion that is readily endorsed when the legislative drafting of section 1(3) of the 1979 Act is contrasted with that of the proactively repealed section 21 of the Arbitration Act 1950,[5] and with the language of section 2(1) of the 1979 Act.[6] This interpretation also appears to be indirectly accepted in *The Nema*[7] where Lord Diplock considered the effect of section 1(3) to be to withdraw the previous power of an arbitrator under the Arbitration Act 1950, section 21, to accede to state his award in the form of a special case if such request was made by any party to the reference.

2.2.4 It must be carefully noted that the statutory phrase alludes to a "party to the reference" and not to a "party to the arbitration agreement". When the entire body of arbitration legislation is viewed at large it will be seen that the two forms of phrase are used variously. As commented upon previously, in the 1979 Act the phrase "party to a reference" prevails, subject to one exception.[8] In the Arbitration Act 1975 the contrary is the case, with the phrase "party to an arbitration agreement" adopted.[9] Under the terms of the Arbitration Act 1950 both phrases are variously adopted.[10] There is probably a difference of meaning between the two phrases notwithstanding that in the vast majority of instances a party to a reference will also be a party to the arbitration agreement out of which the reference arises. An arbitration agreement establishes the obligation to arbitrate; and is also the contractual basis of the arbitrator's jurisdiction and of the entire arbitral process. The phrase "the reference" on the other hand is one customarily adopted to describe the arbitration process set in train when a dispute within the compass of an arbitration agreement is referred to arbitration.

2.2.5 A reference therefore presupposes a valid arbitration agreement and is the procedural product of its legal effect and terms. But even adopting this approach there arises a question of scope. Does a reference encompass the whole arbitral process following on from an arbitration agreement or only some part of the consequential process? There is early authority which offers some support for the argument that "the reference" is confined to the actual hearing or other equivalent occasion when the

---

4. See sections 1(3); 2(1); 3(1) and 5(1). The exception is found in s. 1(4) where the phrase "parties to the arbitration agreement" is adopted.
5. See Chapter 1, para. 1.4.2.
6. See Chapter 12, para. 12.2.1.
7. *Pioneer Shipping Ltd.* v. *B.T.P. Tioxide Ltd.* (*The Nema*) [1982] A.C. 724, 740.
8. *Supra* n. 4.
9. Sections 1(1) and 5(2)(a).
10. The phrase, "party to an arbitration agreement" is adopted in ss. 3(2): 4, 7 (implicitly), 10 (implicitly), 24 (implicitly) and 25(2). The phrase "party to a reference" is used in ss. 8(3), 12(1) and (4), 13(3), 18(4) and 19(2).

referred dispute or difference is determined.[11] It is suggested that this represents a far too restrictive approach. To the contrary it is suggested that "the reference" attracts a broad interpretation and alludes to the arbitral process in its totality. As such it embraces both the pre-hearing and hearing phases of the arbitral process, from the commencement of the arbitral process to the making of the final award. The only difficulty associated with the broader interpretation is to determine precisely when a reference commences. There are various possibilities. A reference may commence when the parties decide to refer a dispute; when the arbitrator or tribunal consents to act; or when the arbitrator who has consented to act initiates or takes some step in the process. The second and third propositions appear to represent fairly safe circumstances when it may be said that a reference is in being. Once an arbitrator or a full tribunal has consented to act there can be little doubt that a reference in pursuance of an arbitration agreement has been established and it is thereafter logical to speak of an arbitrator entering on a reference when he takes a step in the discharge of his mandate.[12] But it is at least arguable that a reference is in being even at an earlier point in time, when a party or the parties resolve to activate the arbitral process and take some necessary step to refer the dispute. An analogy might be drawn with the language of section 34(3) of the Limitation Act 1980, which defines when an arbitration is commenced for the purpose of the 1980 Act and other limitation enactments. The general effect of section 34(3) is to define the commencement of an arbitration by reference to a step taken to establish an arbitral tribunal or in the case of a tribunal nominated or designated in the arbitration agreement, by reference to a step taken to submit the dispute to the tribunal.[13] The legislation gives clear recognition to the possibility of an arbitration commencing in accordance with the first proposition considered above and there is at least the chance that a court asked to pronounce on the moment a reference is initiated might provide a parallel answer. Adopting this line of reasoning it is at least arguable that a reference comes into being once the arbitral process is commenced.

2.2.6 In the context of section 1(3) it is unlikely that the theoretical niceties associated with the precise meaning of the phrase "the reference" will come forward for consideration often. The phrase "parties to the reference" would appear to be used in acknowledgement of the fact that parties other than those who are party to the *original* arbitration agreement may become parties to the subsequent arbitral process (the reference) and agree to be bound by any award that may be made. The 1979 Act protects their rights of appeal, as well as those who are parties to the original arbitration agreement. The phenomenon here described may arise in various circumstances.

2.2.7 Where the dispute is contractual a joint contractor may agree to be a party to a reference notwithstanding that he was not a party to the arbitration agreement entered into by his co-contractor. Where the respondent in an arbitration has an indemnity or right of recourse against a third party, the third party may agree to be joined to the arbitration proceedings, notwithstanding that he was a stranger to the original arbitration agreement, and with the arbitrator therefore having no jurisdiction to order third party proceedings. Another example might also arise when parties agree to consolidate two or more separate arbitrations which share a common factual platform and within which arise synonymous legal issues. These then are the kinds of

11. *Baker* v. *Stephens* (1867) L.R. 2 Q.B. 523.
12. See the language used in section 2(1)(a). See also Chapter 12, para. 12.4.3.1.3.
13. See Chapter 1, para. 1.7.1.

circumstances which seem to be in the contemplation of the legislation and which illustrate situations of a party attaching himself to an arbitral process and agreeing to be bound by the resulting award, but without being a party to the original arbitration agreement.

2.2.8 But there is a certain artificiality in the analysis developed so far, deriving from the distinction drawn between a party to the reference and a party to the *original* arbitration agreement. Although the distinction is a legitimate one to make and is of utility in explaining the object of the legislation, it is nonetheless a little unreal for a party who agrees to be a party to a reference and to be bound by the resulting award will inevitably exist in some manner of contractual association with the other parties, albeit not a party to the original arbitration agreement. There will in other words exist a new and subsequent arbitration agreement whereunder the third party submits his personal liability, and therefore rarely, if ever, will it be possible to conceive of a party to a reference who is not also a party to some manner of arbitration agreement, although not necessarily the original arbitration agreement. The subsequent arbitration agreement may be express, but is otherwise capable of being implied from the conduct of the parties. The agreement, unless the opportunity is taken to make amendments or introduce new terms, as might be necessary when a third party indemnity or recourse claim is added, will *prima facie* be on the same basis as the original arbitration agreement and have the effect of enlarging the number of parties bound by it. The fact that the new agreement may be informal and not reduced to writing or otherwise evidenced by writing will not necessarily result in it ceasing to be an arbitration agreement within the meaning of the 1979 Act. For this purpose it may be sufficient if the original arbitration agreement alone satisfies the statutory requirements as to form.[14]

14. See Chapter 3, para. 3.4.9.

CHAPTER 3

PARAMETERS OF THE SUBSTANTIVE APPEAL PROCESS TO THE HIGH COURT

3.1 FRAMEWORK OF THE INITIAL APPEAL

By section 1(2) it is expressly stipulated that the substantive appeal process to the High Court is confined to "any question of law arising out of an award made on an arbitration agreement". This phrase is of particular importance for it provides a definition of the basic parameters of the new appeal process.[1] It incorporates three interlinked concepts, namely (i) a question of law (ii) arising out of an award made (iii) on an arbitration agreement. It is now proposed to consider separately each of these concepts.

3.2 QUESTIONS OF LAW

3.2.1 The 1979 Act draws a fundamental distinction between questions of law and fact. The appeal procedure established by section 1(2) is expressly confined to questions of law and by necessary implication no appeal lies on a question of fact.[1] All questions of fact are for the decision of the arbitrator alone.[2] In section 1(2) the phrase "question of law" is framed in the singular, but it is clearly the case that the statute is to be interpreted such that the singular includes the plural.[3] An appeal may be instituted in relation to more than one question of law arising out of the same

---

1. *Geogas S.A.* v. *Trammo Gas Ltd.* (*The Baleares*) [1993] 1 Lloyd's Rep. 215, 227–228, Steyn L.J.
1. *Moran* v. *Lloyd's* [1983] 1 Lloyd's Rep. 51, 56 per Lloyd J. (first instance), "At the outset it should be emphasised that the Court has no discretion at all to correct errors of fact. The Court is concerned exclusively with errors of law." See also *S.L. Sethia Liners Ltd.* v. *Naviagro Maritime Corporation* (*The Kostas Melas*) [1981] 1 Lloyd's Rep. 18, 30; *Interbulk Ltd.* v. *Aiden Shipping Co. Ltd.* (*The Vimeira*) [1983] 2 Lloyd's Rep. 424, 431; *Saleh Farid* v. *Mackinnon Mackenzie & Co. Ltd.* (*The Sheba and Shamsan*) [1983] 2 Lloyd's Rep. 500, 501; *Bulk Oil (Zug) A.G.* v. *Sun International Ltd. and Sun Oil Trading Co. (No. 2)* [1984] 1 Lloyd's Rep. 531, 533; *Heinrich Hanno & Co. B.V.* v. *Fairlight Shipping Co. Ltd. etc.* (*The Kostas K*) [1985] 1 Lloyd's Rep. 231, 236; *The President of India* v. *Lips Maritime Corporation* (*The Lips*) [1985] 2 Lloyd's Rep. 180, 182.
2. *Uni-Ocean Lines Pte. Ltd.* v. *C-Trade S.A.* (*The Lucille*) [1983] 1 Lloyd's Rep. 387, 393. See also Chapter 1, para. 1.2.2.1; *Gillespie Bros. & Co.* v. *Thompson Bros. & Co.* (1922) 13 Ll. L. Rep 519; *Oleificio Zucchi S.p.A.* v. *Northern Sales Ltd.* [1965] 2 Lloyd's Rep. 496; *Oversea Buyers Ltd.* v. *Granadex S.A.* [1980] 2 Lloyd's Rep. 608; *Geogas S.A.* v. *Trammo Gas Ltd.* (*The Baleares*) [1993] 1 Lloyd's Rep. 215, 227–228, Steyn L.J.
3. Interpretation Act 1978, s. 6(c).

award and with the multiple questions of law capable of being wholly independent of each other or otherwise interdependent.[4]

3.2.2 The distinction between law and fact is far from novel in the jurisprudence of arbitration[5] or that indeed of the general law wherein substantive and procedural rights often revolve about the distinction.[6] In particular, appeals from and the stating of special cases by the lower courts and inferior tribunals are often confined to questions of law.[7] Even when an appeal on fact is possible, as from the High Court to the Court of Appeal,[8] the general attitude of appeal courts is not to interfere unless satisfied that the findings of fact by the trial judge are plainly wrong. It is not sufficient that the appeal court would have reached a different view on the same evidence.[9] But although the distinction between fact and law is familiar the basis on which the distinction is made is often elusive, perplexing and troublesome, except on the rare occasions when the distinction is expressly made by statute.[10]

3.2.3 The 1979 Act does not provide a definition of what is a question of law; nor does it treat the issue as a residuary concept by providing a definition of a question of fact. In the result the distinction falls to be determined by reference to general principle, if such a phenomenon exists, and the not insignificant quantum of authority that has accumulated about the distinction. But authority is not always helpful for it is often incoherent, irreconcilable and without uniformity.[11] Moreover streams of authority developed outside the framework of arbitration law are probably to be approached with caution. The basis on which the distinction between fact and law is made may vary as between different legal fields and it follows that criteria adopted in other areas of the law may be largely irrelevant to arbitration law.[11a] In examining authority greatest weight must therefore be given to that developed within the context of the relationship between arbitration and the courts. This caution and particularity

---

4. As in *Pioneer Shipping Ltd.* v. *B.T.P. Tioxide Ltd. (The Nema)* [1982] A.C. 724, where the character of the contract, as being either an entire or divisible contract, was a necessary initial question of law to address before proceeding to a consideration of the central legal question, whether the contract had been frustrated.

5. See Chapter 1, para. 1.4.

6. See Stein, *Historical Development of Legal Institutions*, Chapter 4; Milsom, "Law, Fact and Legal Development", in *Studies in the History of the Common Law*; Wilson, "A Note on Fact and Law" (1963) 26 M.L.R. 609; de Smith's *Judicial Review of Administrative Action* (4th edn.), Evans, Chapter 3.

7. For example, the special case procedure from magistrates' courts to the Divisional Court is confined to questions of law, Magistrates' Courts Act 1980, s. 111. Appeals from industrial tribunals to the Employment Appeal Tribunal and thence to the Court of Appeal are confined to questions of law, Employment Protection (Consolidation) Act 1978, s. 136. An appeal from official referees to the Court of Appeal is again confined to questions of law, R.S.C. (1965) Ord. 58, rule 4, except where a charge of fraud or breach of professional duty is in issue.

8. Supreme Court Act 1981, s. 16. Under the County Courts Act 1984, s. 77, there is an appeal on fact to the Court of Appeal; and under the Magistrates' Courts Act 1980, s. 108, an appeal on fact from magistrates to the Crown Court.

9. See generally Goodhart, "Appeals on Questions of Fact" (1955) 71 L.Q.R. 402; also *Pao On* v. *Lau Yiu Long* [1980] A.C. 614 (P.C.); *Grace Shipping* v. *Sharp* [1987] 1 Lloyd's Rep. 207 (P.C.).

10. See, for example, Bills of Exchange Act 1882, s. 20; Marine Insurance Act 1906, ss. 18(4), 20(7) and 88; Sale of Goods Act 1979, ss. 8(3) and 29(5). On occasions statute may change a characterisation. Thus the Sale of Goods Act 1979, s. 29(5) makes the issue of what is a "reasonable hour" a question of fact. Under the common law the question was one of law, see *Startup* v. *Macdonald* (1843) 6 M. & G. 593 Ex. Ch. See also *Kansa General Insurance Co. Ltd.* v. *Bishopsgate Insurance plc* [1988] 1 Lloyd's Rep. 503, 512.

11. Cf. de Smith's, *Judicial Review of Administrative Action* (4th edn.), Evans, Chapter 3.

11a. *Geogas S.A.* v. *Trammo Gas Ltd. (The Baleares)* [1993] 1 Lloyd's Rep. 215, 231, Steyn L.J., "what is a question of law in a judicial review case may not necessarily be a question of law in the field of consensual arbitration".

of approach gives further recognition to the widely held belief that the distinction between fact and law is an area of the law which lacks a clear conceptual basis and where the attributes of the law are anything but scientific. The law in this regard would appear to be impregnated with liberal portions of historical considerations, pragmatism and policy.[12] In the result it is probably as relevant to enquire after the reason why the distinction is made as it is to seek to establish criteria on the basis of which to make the distinction.[13] In the context of the 1979 Act the distinction between fact and law is made so as to identify those decisions of an arbitration tribunal the High Court may encroach upon and, if necessary, substitute its own view of the right answer for that of the arbitration tribunal. The underlying rationale appears to be that there exist certain kinds of legal issues and questions with regard to which the High Court is more likely to provide the right or at least a better decision; and a decision, where the issue or question is of wide interest, which is likely to provide a more reliable guide for the community at large or interested sections of the community: but constantly bearing in mind that to admit judicial encroachment has a counterbalancing cost. It undermines the finality of awards and erodes the potential advantages associated with the arbitral process, particularly expedition and privacy.

3.2.4 It might quite reasonably be supposed on first addressing the subject and without any awareness of its troublesome history that the distinction between law and fact offers no difficulty. In part it does not. The perception of the senses quite clearly raises a question of fact; as does a phenomenon that is governed by non-legal rules or laws, such as the height or weight of a person. On the other hand a legal proposition in the abstract is unambiguously a question of law, as also is a question of legal liability between persons or the effect in law of an event or combination of events. But in equal part the distinction can be an arcane and troublesome issue and with the path of the law often difficult to comprehend and expound. The difficulties arise because of the absence of conceptual orderliness and also because of the close association that may on occasions exist between law and fact. A factual issue may arise not in a pure form but against the backdrop of a legal proposition and with the fundamental object of the enquiry at hand being to determine whether the material terms of the legal proposition are satisfied by the facts found.[14] In other situations law and fact may be inextricably intertwined so that it is impossible to give an answer to a question raised except after an accurate statement of the appropriate legal principle or rule in issue and a careful and related scrutiny of the facts, and with the factual scrutiny often calling for the making of a judgment. In this kind of instance there is no identifiable pure question of law or fact, but a greater or lesser relationship of fact and law, and such questions are usually characterised as being questions of mixed fact and law or as

---

12. See, for example, the observations of Lord Diplock in *The Nema*, *supra*, p. 736, discussing the characterisation of the construction of a contract as a question of law.

13. Cf. *British Launderers' Research Association* v. *Borough of Hendon Rating Authority* [1949] 1 K.B. 462, 471 per Denning L.J. The case is further considered *infra*, para. 3.2.9. Also, *Geogas S.A.* v. *Trammo Gas Ltd.* (*The Baleares*) [1993] 1 Lloyd's Rep. 215, 231, Steyn L.J.: "It is often difficult to decide what is a question of law, or a question of mixed law and fact, rather than a pure question of fact. In law the context is always of critical importance. The enquiry: 'Is it a question of law?' must therefore always be answered by the counter-enquiry 'For what purpose?' What is a question of law in a judicial review case may not necessarily be a question of law in the field of consensual arbitration. In short the closest attention must always be paid to the context in order to decide whether a question of law arises."

14. Considered further, *infra*.

raising conclusions of law.[15] The cause of clarity is further muddled by the rule which although recognising the arbitration tribunal to be the primary finder of fact nonetheless characterises any question directed to the existence or sufficiency of evidence to support a finding of fact as one of law.[16] Further, even a conclusion of fact may be converted to a question of law where on the facts found the conclusion is such that no person acting judicially and properly instructed as to the relevant law could have come to the conclusion in question.[17]

3.2.5 In many regards the foregoing represents a necessary introduction to any attempt to begin to understand the distinction between questions of fact and law. It is now proposed to examine the distinction or at least the approach to the distinction more closely, always bearing in mind that any definition can be nothing more than tentative and equally recognising that it is unlikely that any proffered explanation will succeed in being wholly free of deficiency. A *pure* question of fact may be viewed as one that in itself does not raise a legal proposition or the operation or application of a legal doctrine, principle or rule. It is a question which may be answered wholly independently of legal criteria. But even the concept of pure fact is not uniform for it is possible to identify many variant forms. There are primary facts which allude to specific facts perceived by the senses—what was said or done, or more generally what happened or what were the prevailing conditions.[18] The state of the elements, such as the swell of the sea, are ready and elementary examples. Then there are secondary facts which are deductions or inferences drawn from the proved or admitted primary facts.[19] If a man arrives at a hostelry dripping wet it may be fairly deduced that it is raining outside. Further, there are conclusions of fact, which are factual determinations arrived at following an assessment and evaluation of the primary and secondary facts.[20] There is in practice a tendency to compound into one category secondary facts and conclusions of fact[21] and although it is possible to comprehend the reason for this, each having an inferential dimension, the two categories are nonetheless in strictness quite distinct. An inference is what arises necessarily from the primary facts, whereas a conclusion pinpoints the effect of the total findings of fact, both primary and secondary (if any). Whether a person is guilty of wilful default would appear to be a question answered by arriving at a conclusion of fact.[22] A further category of factual question is customarily characterised as being one of fact and degree. This manner of appellation is applied to questions of fact which also give rise to the exercise of a judgement on the part of the fact-finder and with regard to which different fact-finders might reasonably arrive at

---

15. Considered further, *infra*.
16. Considered further, *infra*. See also Chapter 6, para. 6.2.11.
17. *Edwards* v. *Bairstow* [1956] A.C. 14; *Torbell Investments Ltd.* v. *Williams (Inspector of Taxes)* (1986) 59 T.C. 357.
18. See *British Launderers' Research Association* v. *Borough of Hendon Rating Authority*, *infra*. Also *Voest Alpine Intertrading G.m.b.H.* v. *Chevron International Oil Co. Ltd.* [1987] 2 Lloyd's Rep. 547, 558 *et seq.*
19. See Wilson, "A Note on Fact and Law" (1963) 26 M.L.R. 609.
20. Cf. *Cobec Brazilian Trading and Warehousing Corporation* v. *Alfred C. Toepfer* [1983] 2 Lloyd's Rep. 386, 390, Kerr L.J.
21. See, for example, *British Launderers' Research Association* v. *Borough of Hendon Rating Authority*, *infra*.
22. *Pleasants* v. *Atkinson (Inspector of Taxes)* (1990) 60 T.C. 228. Where the question in issue was whether professional accountants employed by a taxpayer were guilty of wilful default in acting on his behalf notwithstanding an express finding by the general commissioners that the taxpayer himself was unaware of any misleading information being included in his tax returns.

different determinations on the same facts.[23] Questions directed to "ordinary residence"[24] and "exclusive possession"[25] would appear to fall within this category. Finally, questions that fall to be answered by reference to the laws of the natural and physical sciences again raise issues of fact. The cubic capacity of a ship or the amount of cargo loaded into a ship's hold raise questions of fact,[26] as do the state of a man's digestion or his mind.[27]

3.2.6 A question may, however, remain one of fact notwithstanding that it arises in the context of legal criteria and therefore cannot in strictness be described as one of pure fact. Such questions arise when what is in issue is the application of evaluated facts to an abstract legal proposition. What is a partnership is a question of law with the legal concept defined by the Partnership Act 1890, section 1.[28] But whether a particular relationship amounts to a partnership is characterised as a question of fact.[29] The same is true of analogous questions raised in the context of contract. To ask what is a contract is to raise a legal question for a contract is a legal concept defined by the common law[30]: but whether, in any particular instance, a contract exists is a question of fact.[31] In each of these situations the question of fact is not one at large, in the sense that it arises wholly independently of legal criteria, but to the contrary it arises in the specific context of a legal concept and with the overt purpose of determining whether the facts as found satisfy the criteria expounded by the legal concept. The foregoing reveals that merely because a line of enquiry is embarked upon by first examining a legal proposition, which itself raises a question of law, does not render all questions that thereafter necessarily fall to be determined equally questions of law. This general approach to the question of characterisation was forcefully underlined by Mustill J. in *Overseas Buyers Ltd.* v. *Granadex S.A.*[32] where the learned judge refused to characterise the question whether a seller c.i.f. had used his best endeavours to obtain the necessary export licence as a question of mixed fact and law, notwithstanding that the first step in the enquiry was the construction of the relevant terms of the contract. The issue was in the opinion of Mustill J. a conclusion of fact[33]:

. . . the buyers contend that the finding is one of mixed fact and law, which is open to review by the court . . . I do not agree. It is true that in order to arrive at their conclusion, the arbitrators

23. See generally, Wilson, "Questions of Degree" (1969) 32 M.L.R. 361.

24. *Lysaght* v. *I.R.C.* [1928] A.C. 234; *R* v. *Barnet L.B.C. ex parte Shah* [1983] A.C. 309; *Reed (Insp. of Taxes)* v. *Clark* [1985] S.T.C. 323.

25. *Brooker Settled Estates Ltd.* v. *Ayers* [1987] 1 E.G.L.R. 50 (C.A.).

26. Cf. *Portunus Navigation Co. Inc.* v. *Avin Chartering S.A. (The World Prestige)* [1982] 1 Lloyd's Rep. 60.

27. Cf. *Edgington* v. *Fitzmaurice* (1885) 29 Ch. D. 459, 483, per Bowen L.J. Also *Angus* v. *Clifford* [1891] 2 Ch. 449, 470.

28. Wherein a partnership is defined: "Partnership is the relationship which subsists between persons carrying on business in common with a view of profit."

29. Cf. *Blackpool Marton Rotary Club* v. *Martin (Insp. of Taxes)* [1988] S.T.C. 823.

30. There exists no universally agreed definition but a multitude of judicial offerings and textbook definitions.

31. *Brandt & Co.* v. *Liverpool, Brazil and River Plate Steam Navigation Company Ltd.* [1924] 1 K.B. 575; *Paal Wilson & Co. A/S* v. *Partenreederei Hannah Blumenthal (The Hannah Blumenthal)* [1983] 1 Lloyd's Rep. 103, 116–117, per Lord Diplock; *Ilyssia Compania Naviera S.A.* v. *Ahmed Abdul-Qawi Bamaodah (The Elli 2)* [1985] 1 Lloyd's Rep. 107; *Kaukomarkkinat O/Y* v. *"Elbe" Transport-Union G.m.b.H. (The Kelo)* [1985] 2 Lloyd's Rep. 85; *Carl Aune Ageneia Maritima Afretamentos Ltda* v. *Engenharia E. Maquinas S.A. and others* [1986] 1 Lloyd's Rep. 544.

32. [1980] 2 Lloyd's Rep. 608.

33. *Ibid.* pp. 612–613.

had to start with a premise as to the relevant law. But the law applicable to a dispute such as the present was not in issue at the arbitration, and is not in issue here. When arbitrators reach a conclusion on the evidence before them, in the light of an undisputed principle of law, they are engaged in making findings of fact, not of mixed fact and law. A question of fact cannot be dressed up as a question of law, appropriate for an appeal to the High Court, merely by showing that the investigation took a proposition of law as its starting point.

But as will be seen later in the text, there is a difficulty in identifying the precise circumstances when this particular approach will be adopted.

3.2.7 As to what amounts to a question of law, beyond the observations already made, it may in the broadest of terms be asserted that the greater the answer to any question turns on the enunciation or application of a legal criterion or criteria the more likely it is that the question will be characterised as a question of law. There are a few uncontentious illustrations that may be given. Any question that raises in the abstract a statement or examination of a legal rule, principle or doctrine is clearly a question of law and is further a pure question of law. A question that addresses the admissibility of evidence by a tribunal obliged to observe the rules of evidence is again a question of law.[34] The interpretation of a statute[35] or the construction of a contract[36] raises a question of law. So also does any question aimed at the sufficiency of the evidence to support a finding of fact of whatever character.[37] Beyond these particular illustrations it may more generally be opined that any question that can only be answered by applying legal criteria to the facts and circumstances of individual cases *may* be characterised as one of law and the greater it is also perceived that the ques-

---

34. *East and West Dock Co.* v. *Kirk and Randall* (1887) 12 App.Cas. 738.

35. *Cozens* v. *Brutus* [1973] A.C. 854; *Re Energy Conversion Devices Inc.* [1983] R.P.C. 231 (H.L.); *Mirror Group Newspapers Ltd.* v. *Gunning* [1986] 1 W.L.R. 546 (C.A.); *Commonwealth Smelting Ltd. and Another* v. *Guardian Royal Exchange Assurance Ltd.* [1986] 1 Lloyd's Rep. 121; *The Derbyshire* [1986] 1 Lloyd's Rep. 418; *L'Office Cherifien des Phosphates and Unitramp S.A.* v. *Yamashita-Shinnihon Steamship Co. Ltd.* (*The Boucraa*) [1993] 2 Lloyd's Rep. 149 (C.A.); [1994] 1 Lloyd's Rep. 251 (H.L.).

36. *Edwards* v. *Bairstow* [1956] A.C. 14; *Halfdan Greig & Co. A/S* v. *Sterling Coal and Navigation Corpn. and AC Neleman's Handel- en Transportondernerming (The Lysland)* [1973] 1 Q.B. 843; *Pilgrim Shipping Co. Ltd.* v. *State Trading Corpn. of India Ltd.* (*The Hadjitsakos*) [1975] 1 Lloyd's Rep. 356 (C.A.); *Bunge Corporation* v. *Tradax Export S.A.* [1980] 1 Lloyd's Rep. 294 (C.A.); *Mondial Trading Co. G.m.b.H.* v. *Gill & Duffus Zuckerhandelsgesellschaft m.b.H.* [1980] 2 Lloyd's Rep. 376; *Schiffahrtsagentur Hamburg Middle East Line G.m.b.H. Hamburg* v. *Virtue Shipping Corporation Monrovia (The Oinoussian Virtue)* [1981] 1 Lloyd's Rep. 533; *Portaria Shipping Co.* v. *Gulf Pacific Navigation Co. Ltd. (The Selene G.)* [1981] 2 Lloyd's Rep. 180; *International Sea Tankers Inc.* v. *Hemisphere Shipping Co. Ltd. (The Wenjiang)* [1981] 2 Lloyd's Rep. 308; *Marrealeza Compania Naviera S.A.* v. *Tradax Export S.A. (The Nichos A)* [1982] 1 Lloyd's Rep. 52. *B.V.S. and The Khuztestan Water and Power Authority* v. *Kerman Shipping Co. etc. (The Kerman)* [1982] 1 Lloyd's Rep. 62, [1982] 1 W.L.R. 166; *Astro Valiente Compania Naviera S.A.* v. *The Government of Pakistan Ministry of Food and Agriculture (The Emmanuel Colocotronis) (No. 1)* [1982] 1 Lloyd's Rep. 297; *Phoenix Shipping Co.* v. *Apex Shipping Corpn. (The Apex)* [1982] 2 Lloyd's Rep. 407; *Blue Anchor Line Ltd.* v. *Alfred C. Toepfer International G.m.b.H. (The Union Amsterdam)* [1982] 2 Lloyd's Rep. 432; *D/S A/S Idaho* v. *Colossus Maritime S.A. (The Concordia Fjord)* [1984] 1 Lloyd's Rep. 385; *Glafki Shipping Co. S.A.* v. *Pinios Shipping Co. No. 1 (The Maira) (No. 2)* [1985] 1 Lloyd's Rep. 300, 302; *Commonwealth Smelting Ltd. and Another* v. *Guardian Royal Exchange Assurance Ltd.* [1986] 1 Lloyd's Rep. 121; *Reardon Smith Line Ltd.* v. *Sanko Steamship Co. Ltd. (The Sanko Honour)* [1985] 1 Lloyd's Rep. 418, 422.

37. *Nello Simoni* v. *A/S M/S Straum* (1949) 83 Ll.L.Rep. 157; *Edwards* v. *Bairstow* [1956] A.C. 14; *Citland Ltd.* v. *Kanchan Oil Industries Put. Ltd.* [1980] 2 Lloyd's Rep. 274; *Mondial Trading Co. G.m.b.H.* v. *Gill & Duffus Zuckerhandelsgesellschaft m.b.H.* [1980] 2 Lloyd's Rep. 376; *Mediolanum Shipping Co.* v. *Japan Lines Ltd. (The Mediolanum)* [1982] 1 Lloyd's Rep. 47; *Compagnie Générale Maritime* v. *Diakan Spirit S.A. (The Ymnos)* [1982] 2 Lloyd's Rep. 574; *Athens Cape Naviera S.A.* v. *Deutsche Dampfschiffahrtsgesellschaft "Hansa" Aktiengesellschaft and Another (The Barenbels)* [1985] 1 Lloyd's Rep. 528, 532. See further, Chapter 6, para. 6.2.11.

tion properly belongs to the province of a judge or court the more likely it is that the question *will* be categorised as one of law. But as with questions of fact, so also questions of law may come in different varieties, and with the variety of forms so also does the distinction between fact and law tend to become more opaque. Beyond pure questions of law, where any question involves a close intermingling of fact and law it is customary to characterise the question as one of mixed fact and law; and further, where a question is perceived as bringing into issue a legal consequence of facts, that question is often characterised as raising a conclusion of law. Frustration is an example of the former[38] and waiver a possible example of the latter.[39] The precise distinction between these latter characterisations is notoriously difficult to enunciate, assuming there to be a real distinction, which is far from clear, and practice tends to reveal a degree of arbitrariness. They are nonetheless very important characterisations for they arise frequently in practice.

3.2.8 The application of legal propositions to the facts of individual situations can therefore raise questions of law. Robert Goff J. has expressed the view that it does not follow that "simply because there is no dispute as to the general law, the application of the law to the facts cannot itself raise a question of law".[40] The advocation of this principle raises a difficulty of reconciliation with that expounded by Mustill J. in *Oversea Buyers Ltd*. v. *Granadex S.A.*[41] The entire subject is just too fluid and precarious to suggest that the two approaches are in conflict. But even assuming that they are capable of independent existence, they nonetheless raise the threshold difficulty of selection. The problem remains of knowing which to adopt and in what circumstances. In support of his proposition Robert Goff J. took as an example the question whether a contract is repudiated, which he considered to fall into the same category as questions of waiver and promissory estoppel, and went on to observe[40]:

. . . if one takes for example, a question of repudiation, one could state very easily and very simply the general principle of law as to what constitutes a repudiation of the contract. Then a question could arise whether or not, on the primary facts found by the arbitrator (which very often, as we know full well, in modern days consists of telex messages) there was in law a repudiation. It is perfectly possible that what is necessary in law to constitute a repudiation might not be in dispute between the parties; nonetheless the question might arise as to whether certain communications did amount to a repudiation. That could well give rise to a question of law which could be the subject matter of an appeal under the Arbitration Act 1979; though on the hearing of the appeal weight would of course be given to the view formed by the arbitrators. But

---

38. *Universal Cargo Carriers Corp.* v. *Citati* [1957] 2 Q.B. 401; *Tsakiroglou & Co.* v. *Noblee Thorl G.m.b.H.* [1962] A.C. 93; *Kodros Shipping Corp.* v. *Empresa Cubana de Fletes (The Evia)* [1981] 2 Lloyd's Rep. 613, [1982] 1 Lloyd's Rep. 334 (C.A.), [1982] 2 Lloyd's Rep. 307 (H.L.); *B.T.P. Tioxide Ltd.* v. *Pioneer Shipping Ltd. and Armada Marine S.A. (The Nema)* [1980] 1 Lloyd's Rep. 519; [1980] 2 Lloyd's Rep. 83; [1980] 1 Q.B. 547 (C.A.); [1982] A.C. 724 (H.L.); *International Sea Tankers Inc.* v. *Hemisphere Shipping Co. Ltd. (The Wenjiang)* [1981] 2 Lloyd's Rep. 308; [1982] 1 Lloyd's Rep. 128 (C.A.); *(No. 2)* [1983] 1 Lloyd's Rep. 400; *Uni-Ocean Lines Pte. Ltd.* v. *C-Trade S.A. (The Lucille)* [1984] 1 Lloyd's Rep. 244, 246 (C.A.). Although it has also been characterised as a legal inference, see *Trade and Transport Inc.* v. *Ino Kaiun Kaisha Ltd. (The Angelia)* [1973] 1 W.L.R. 210, 221 per Kerr J.; and a conclusion of law, see *Pioneer Shipping Ltd. and others* v. *B.T.P. Tioxide Ltd. (The Nema)* [1982] A.C. 724, 738, per Lord Diplock.
39. *Fidelitas Shipping Co. Ltd.* v. *V/O Exportchleb* [1966] 1 Q.B. 630, 649 per Diplock L.J., "Waiver is not a fact but a legal consequence of facts."
40. *Italmare Shipping Co.* v. *Ocean Tanker Co. Inc. (The Rio Sun)* [1981] 2 Lloyd's Rep. 489, 492 (first instance).
41. *Supra*, n. 32.

one cannot say that, because the applicable principles are not in dispute, therefore the application of those principles to the facts raises a question of fact.

3.2.9 In drawing a distinction between fact and law judges have often been more given to arbitrary characterisations than reasoned explanations. A significant exception is the much cited dictum of Denning L.J. (as he then was) in *British Launderers' Research Association* v. *Borough of Hendon Rating Authority*.[42]

Primary facts are facts which are observed by witnesses and proved by oral testimony or facts proved by the production of a thing itself, such as original documents. Their determination is essentially a question of fact for the tribunal of fact, and the only question of law that can arise on them is whether there was any evidence to support the finding. The conclusions from primary facts are, however, inferences deduced by a process of reasoning from them. If, and in so far as, those conclusions can as well be drawn by a layman (properly instructed on the law) as by a lawyer, they are conclusions of fact for the tribunal of fact: and the only questions of law which can arise on them are whether there was a proper direction in point of law; and whether the conclusion is one which could reasonably be drawn from the primary facts: see *Bracegirdle* v. *Oxley* [1947] K.B. 349 at p. 358. If, and in so far, however, as the correct conclusion to be drawn from primary facts requires, for its correctness, determination by a trained lawyer—as, for instance, because it involves the interpretation of documents or because the law and the facts cannot be separated, or because the law on the point cannot properly be understood or applied except by a trained lawyer—the conclusion is a conclusion of law on which an appellate tribunal is as competent to form an opinion as the tribunal of first instance.

The dictum is useful as a general guideline but it is not comprehensive nor is it free of ambiguity. It does, however, emphasise the pragmatic character of the exercise and the policy considerations which permeate this particular branch of the law.

3.2.10 At this stage it may be of benefit to pause and illustrate by reference to decided authorities the way in which the numerous questions that may arise about a single topic may be variously characterised as questions of fact or law or some variant of each. To take contract as an example.

What is a contract is a question of law but whether a contract exists is a question of fact.[43] The categorisation of a contract, including the question whether a contract is entire or divisible, raises a question of law.[44] The capacity of a person to enter into a contract is a question of law, but the ability of a person to enter into a contract raises a question of fact.[45] What was said during the contractual negotiations raises a question of fact,[46] but what are the contractual terms (express and implied) and documents, and what are mere representations raise questions of law.[47] The characterisation of contractual terms as conditions, warranties and intermediate terms raise questions of

---

42. [1949] 1 K.B. 462, 471. Cited in *Compagnie Générale Maritime* v. *Diakon Spirit S.A. (The Ymnos)* [1982] 2 Lloyd's Rep. 574.

43. *Supra* nn. 29 and 30.

44. *Dominion Coal Co. Ltd.* v. *Roberts* (1920) 4 Ll.L.Rep. 434; *Larrinaga & Co. Ltd.* v. *Société Franco-Américaine des Phosphates de Medulla, Paris* (1922) 28 Com.Cas. 1; (1923) 29 Com.Cas. 1; *Pioneer Shipping Ltd.* v. *B.T.P. Tioxide Ltd. (The Nema)* [1982] A.C. 724.

45. *James* v. *Smith* [1931] 2 K.B. 317n, 322 per Atkin L.J. See also Murdoch, *The Law of Estate Agency and Auctions*, p. 228 *et seq*.

46. *Showa Oil Tanker Co. Ltd. of Japan* v. *Maravan S.A. of Caracas (The Larissa)* [1983] 2 Lloyd's Rep. 325, 330.

47. *Oscar Chess Ltd.* v. *Williams* [1957] 1 W.L.R. 370; *Universal Petroleum Co. Ltd.* v. *Handels- und Transport Gesellschaft* [1987] 1 Lloyd's Rep. 517, 526; *Orient Overseas Management and Finance Ltd.* v. *File Shipping Co. Ltd. (The Energy Progress)* [1993] 1 Lloyd's Rep. 355.

law.[48] The construction of a contract is a question of law,[49] but the ordinary meaning of an English word is a question of fact[50]; as also is the context of the factual matrix within which the contract has come into existence, including the business purpose for the introduction of a contract or clause, which it is legitimate to allude to in construing an ambiguous contract.[51] Whether a contract is voidable is a question of law, but the existence of grounds rendering a contract voidable is a question of fact.[52] Questions addressing issues such as frustration,[53] repudiation,[54] waiver[55] and estoppel[56] are in the nature of questions of mixed fact and law or conclusions of law. How a contracting party has conducted himself is a question of fact, but whether that conduct is in breach of contract is a conclusion of law[57]; but to enquire further whether the breach is fundamental is a question of fact.[58] The principles on which damages are assessed raise questions of law,[59] with causation a question of mixed fact and law.[60] But the quantification of damages,[61] and where relevant the existence of an available market[62] raise questions of fact; as also does the question whether a contractor has acted reasonably

48. *Michael I. Warde* v. *Feedex International Inc.* [1984] 1 Lloyd's Rep. 310; [1985] 2 Lloyd's Rep. 289; *Gill & Duffus S.A.* v. *Société pour l'Exportation des Sucres S.A.* [1985] 1 Lloyd's Rep. 621; [1986] 1 Lloyd's Rep. 322 (C.A.).

49. *Supra* n. 36.

50. *Cozens* v. *Brutus* [1973] A.C. 854; *Belgravia Navigation Company S.A.* v. *Cannor Shipping Ltd.* (*The Troll Park*), [1988] 1 Lloyd's Rep. 55, 2 Lloyd's Rep. 423 (C.A.).

51. *Bunge Corpn.* v. *Tradax Export S.A.* [1980] 1 Lloyd's Rep. 294, 303 per Megaw L.J.

52. *Pao On* v. *Lau Yiu Long* [1980] A.C. 614 (P.C.).

53. *Universal Cargo Carriers Corpn.* v. *Citati* [1957] 2 Q.B. 401, 435; *Kodros Shipping Corpn.* v. *Empresa Cubana de Fletes (The Evia)* [1981] 2 Lloyd's Rep. 627; [1982] 1 Lloyd's Rep. 334 (C.A.); [1982] 2 Lloyd's Rep. 307 (H.L.).

54. *Italmare Shipping Co.* v. *Ocean Tanker Co. Inc. (The Rio Sun)* [1981] 2 Lloyd's Rep. 489 (first instance).

55. *Fidelitas Shipping Co. Ltd.* v. *V/O Exportchleb* [1966] 1 Q.B. 630; *Kodros Shipping Corporation* v. *Empresa Cubana de Fletes (The Evia)* [1981] 2 Lloyd's Rep. 627; *Italmare Shipping Co.* v. *Ocean Tanker Co. Inc. (The Rio Sun)* [1982] 1 W.L.R. 158; [1981] 2 Lloyd's Rep. 489; *Bunge S.A.* v. *Compagnie Européenne de Céréales* [1982] 1 Lloyd's Rep. 306; *The Antaios* [1984] 3 W.L.R. 592.

56. *Brown* v. *Westminster Bank Ltd.* [1964] 2 Lloyd's Rep. 187, 200; *Woodhouse A.C. Israel Cocoa Ltd. S.A.* v. *Nigerian Produce Marketing Co. Ltd.* [1972] A.C. 741.

57. *President of India* v. *Diamantis Pateras (Hellas) Marine Enterprises Ltd. (The Nestor)* [1987] 2 Lloyd's Rep. 649.

58. *Cook Industries Inc.* v. *Tradax Export S.A.* [1985] 2 Lloyd's Rep. 454.

59. *H. Parsons (Livestock) Ltd.* v. *Uttley Ingham & Co. Ltd.* [1978] 1 All E.R. 521 (C.A.); *Kodros Shipping Corpn.* v. *Empresa Cubana de Fletes (The Evia)* [1981] 2 Lloyd's Rep. 627; *Retla Steamship Co.* v. *Gryphon Shipping Co. S.A. etc. (The Evimeria)* [1982] 1 Lloyd's Rep. 55; *B.V.S. and The Khuzestan Water and Power Authority* v. *Kerman Shipping Co. (The Kerman)* [1982] 1 Lloyd's Rep. 62; [1982] 1 W.L.R. 166; *Uni-Ocean Lines Pte. Ltd.* v. *C-Trade S.A. (The Lucille)* [1984] 1 Lloyd's Rep. 244. *Rheinoel G.m.b.H.* v. *Huron Liberian Co. (The Concordia C)* [1985] 2 Lloyd's Rep. 55; *The President of India* v. *Lips Maritime Corpn. (The Lips)* [1985] 2 Lloyd's Rep. 180. *Transworld Oil Ltd.* v. *North Bay Shipping Corpn. (The Rio Claro)* [1987] 2 Lloyd's Rep. 173; *Sealace Shipping Co. Ltd.* v. *Oceanvoice Ltd. (The Alecos M)* [1991] 1 Lloyd's Rep. 120 (C.A.).

60. *Royal Greek Government* v. *Minister of Transport* (1949) 83 Ll.L.Rep. 228; *Vardinoyannis* v. *Egyptian General Petroleum Corpn. (The Evaggelos TH)* [1971] 2 Lloyd's Rep. 200; *Federal Commerce & Navigation Ltd.* v. *Suisse-Atlantique Société D'Armement S.A. (The Cruzeiro do Sul)* [1982] 2 Lloyd's Rep. 110; *Uni-Ocean Lines Pte. Ltd.* v. *C-Trade S.A. (The Lucille)* [1984] 1 Lloyd's Rep. 244. *Paros Shipping Corpn.* v. *NAFTA (GB) Ltd. (The Paros)* [1987] 2 Lloyd's Rep. 269, 275; *Batis Maritime Corpn.* v. *Petroleos del Mediterraneo S.A. (The Batis)* [1990] 1 Lloyd's Rep. 345.

61. *British Westinghouse Electric & Manufacturing Co. Ltd.* v. *Underground Electric Rly. Co. of London Ltd.* [1912] A.C. 673, 688–689 per Viscount Haldane L.C.; *Bulk Oil (Zug) A.G.* v. *Sun International Ltd. and Sun Oil Trading Co. (No. 2)* [1984] 1 Lloyd's Rep. 531, 543.

62. *Koch Marine Inc.* v. *D'Amico Societa Di Navigazione A.R.L. (The Elena D'Amico)* [1980] 1 Lloyd's Rep. 75.

in mitigation of loss suffered from a breach of contract.[63] The proper law of a contract raises a question of law.[63a]

3.2.11 The distinction between fact and law is of central importance in relation to the appellate process established under the 1979 Act. Yet there is continuing uncertainty concerning the distinction and the criteria to be taken into account in addressing the distinction.[64] Any attempt at an articulation of the correct approach tends to be overlaid with defensive caution. Precedent will of course introduce certainty and it is probably the case that the great majority of the typical disputes referred to arbitration, predominantly contractual, will by now have had the benefit of previous judicial consideration and characterisation. Only in relation to unconsidered questions will the problem of underlying principle arise. The vagueness of the law on this crucial distinction does however represent a danger to the policy of the 1979 Act and judges will have to be ever vigilant to protect against the risk of questions of fact being dressed up as questions of law with a view to attempting to initiate an appeal from an arbitration award.[65] It has been suggested that in the light of the vagueness of the distinction between fact and law, and also the policy of the 1979 Act, that judges may be more inclined to characterise questions raised on appeal as questions of fact and thereby subscribe to the increasing finality of awards,[66] but there is little evidence to support the emergence of such a trend. What is more likely is that a firm judicial eye will be kept on the question of characterisation and with any attempt to expand the concept of a question of law in the context of arbitration resisted.[67]

3.3 ARISING OUT OF AN AWARD MADE

3.3.1 The question of law must be one arising out of an award made. Section 1 establishes an appeal from the award of an arbitrator or umpire and is in contrast to section 2 which is concerned with the determination of points of law that arise in the course of a reference and therefore of necessity before an award is made.[1] The review jurisdictions established under sections 1 and 2 do not overlap but are complementary. Prior to the making of an award section 2 prevails. Once an award is made section 1 is solely applicable.[2]

A question of law arises out of an award most clearly when it relates to the merits of

---

63. *Payzu Ltd.* v. *Saunders* [1919] 2 K.B. 581; *Tor Line A.B.* v. *Alltrans Group of Canada Ltd. (The TFL Prosperity)* [1982] 1 Lloyd's Rep. 617; [1983] 2 Lloyd's Rep. 18 (C.A.); *Rudolf A. Oetker* v. *IFA Internationale Frachtagentur A.G. (The Almak)* [1985] 1 Lloyd's Rep. 557.

63a. *Compagnie d'Armement Maritime S.A.* v. *Compagnie Tunisienne de Navigation S.A.* [1971] A.C. 572, 600, Lord Wilberforce.

64. Cf. Staughton (1979) N.L.J. 920.

65. Diplock (1978) 44 Arb. 107, 109, "I have never ceased to wonder at what an ingenious advocate can dress up as constituting an arguable point of law." See also *Overseas Buyers Ltd.* v. *Granadex S.A.* [1980] 2 Lloyd's Rep. 608; *Italmare Shipping Co.* v. *Ocean Tanker Co. Inc. (The Rio Sun)* [1981] 2 Lloyd's Rep. 489.

66. Schmitthoff, "Commercial Arbitration and the Commercial Court" in *Commercial Law in a Changing Economic Climate* (2nd edn.).

67. *Geogas S.A.* v. *Trammo Gas Ltd. (The Baleares)* [1993] 1 Lloyd's Rep. 215, 231, Steyn L.J.: "Given the fact that the resolution of this preliminary issue determines whether the Court has jurisdiction to substitute its view for the view of the tribunal, freely chosen by parties of full contractual capacity, there is in my view no sensible reason for adopting an enlarged view of what constitutes a question of law."

1. See Chapter 12.

2. *Ibid.* para. 12.2.2.

the dispute or difference referred to the arbitrator or umpire. The primary object underlying section 1(2) is to establish an appeal in relation to the substantive issues(s) put before an arbitration tribunal and in particular to provide a mode of recourse in relation to the legal determinations made in an award with regard to the substantive issue(s) referred. A question of law arises out of an award when it is inextricably associated with the resolution of the substantive dispute referred and it is overtly addressed in the award made by the tribunal. The vast majority of appeals arising under the 1979 Act fall into this particular category.[3]

3.3.2 Cases which fall outside this self-evident category are capable of posing difficulties. A particularly interesting question arises in connection with orders for costs and interest. If an arbitrator falls into legal error in making an order for costs and/or interest, how is a remedy to be effected? Historically the error was perceived as misconduct and the award was liable to be set aside or remitted under the jurisdiction conferred by sections 22 and 23(2) of the Arbitration Act 1950.[4] But following the enactment of the 1979 Act, does this kind of case not now amount to an error of law arising out of an award made, with the remedy to be effected by an appeal under the 1979 Act? After some early uncertainty[5] it has been judicially determined that the position has been radically changed by the 1979 Act and that alleged errors of law associated with awards of costs are primarily reviewable under the appellate machinery established by the 1979 Act.[6] This development would appear to apply equally to awards of interest. Subject to the terms of his mandate, an arbitrator is obliged to dispose of costs and interest. His decision on such matters is as much part of the award as is his decision on the merits of the substantive dispute referred.[7] It is wholly logical to insist that any allegation that the arbitrator has gone wrong in law in making his award of costs and/or interest is to be tested solely by an appeal under the 1979 Act. An error of law associated with an order for costs and/or interest is therefore characterisable as an error of law arising out of an award made.

3.3.3 The language of section 1(2) is restrictive and the precise statutory phrase "arising out of an award made" has to be weighed cautiously. It would appear to bear a meaning quite different from phrases such as "in relation to" or "with regard to" or "in connection with" an award. The form of wording used in section 1(2) would appear to bear a meaning synonymous with "arising out of a decision of an arbitrator or umpire on the merits of the dispute referred and any associated order with regard

3. As is witnessed by the vast majority of the authorities cited in this Part of the text.

4. See generally, Thomas, "Costs, discretion and issues of technical misconduct" [1982] 2 L.M.C.L.Q. 288. Also *Heaven & Kesterton Ltd.* v. *Sven Widaeus A/B* [1958] 1 W.L.R. 248; *Tramountana Armadora S.A.* v. *Atlantic Shipping Co. S.A.* [1978] 1 Lloyd's Rep. 391; *Smeaton Hanscomb & Co. Ltd.* v. *Sassoon I. Setty, Son & Co. (No. 2)* [1953] 1 W.L.R. 1481; *Lewis* v. *Haverfordwest R.D.C.* [1953] 1 W.L.R. 1486; *L. Figueiredo Navegacas S.A.* v. *Reederei Richard Schroeder K.G. (The Eric Schroeder)* [1974] 1 Lloyd's Rep. 192.

5. *Evmar Shipping Corporation* v. *Japan Line Ltd. (The Evmar)* [1984] 2 Lloyd's Rep. 581, 582–583. See also *Tharros Shipping Co. Ltd.* v. *Mitsubishi Corpn.* [1981] 1 Lloyd's Rep. 166.

6. *Blexen Ltd.* v. *G. Percy Trentham Ltd.* (1990) 42 E.G. 133 (C.A.); *King* v. *Thomas McKenna Ltd.* [1991] 1 All E.R. 653, 663–664, per Lord Donaldson M.R. See also *Salen Rederierna A.B.* v. *Antaios Compania Naviera S.A. (The Antaios)* [1981] 2 Lloyd's Rep. 284, 298 *et seq*; *Islamic Republic of Iran Shipping Lines* v. *P. & O. Bulk Shipping Ltd.* [1985] 2 Lloyd's Rep. 494 (C.A.). Note. See further Chapter 6, para. 6.2.14.

7. Under the pre-1979 law arbitral determinations as to costs and interest were viewed as distinct and separate aspects of the awards. It is also possible for an arbitrator to deal with questions of costs and interest in a separate final award, having made his determination on the merits of the substantive dispute in an earlier interim final award.

to costs and/or interest, or other procedural issue". In the result it is suggested that questions of law that may arise in connection with an award but which are unrelated to the decision of the arbitrator on the merits of the dispute and any associated order are outside the scope of an appeal under section 1(2). An allegation that the award is *ultra vires*; or is defective in substance or form; or has been improperly procured; or is otherwise voidable because of misconduct cannot be a basis of an appeal under the 1979 Act but continues to be reviewable under the jurisdiction conferred by the Arbitration Act 1950, sections 22 and 23; or at common law; or under the jurisdiction to give declaratory and/or injunctive relief. Such allegations may give rise to questions of law but they are not questions of law "arising out of an award" in the sense intended by section 1(2). Some support for this view may be derived from the preliminary application in *The Antaios (No. 2)*[8] where Staughton J. doubted, *obiter dictum*, whether an allegation asserting illogicality in an award (substantive defect) could be considered a ground for giving leave to appeal under section 1(3)(b). So also in *The Vasso*[9] Lloyd J. said of questions of law touching on the jurisdiction of an arbitrator to make interlocutory orders that it was "difficult to envisage them as questions of law on the award at all". In subsequent authorities it has been emphasised more generally that the question of law must arise out of the award in question and not out of the arbitration.[10] But this distinction will not always be easy to make and may give rise to difficult situations.[11] The circumstances relating to the award of costs may provide an example. It has already been asserted that an error of law with regard to the award of costs is an error of law arising out of the award for the purpose of section 1(2). But if the grievance arises out of the failure to dispose of costs, representing a breach of duty on the part of the arbitrator, then it would seem that there is no question of law arising out of the award, but a question of law arising out of the arbitration.

3.3.4 In the final analysis what matters is not the nature or character of the question of law, or the precise relationship of the question of law to the arbitral process, but whether the question of law arises on the face of an award. Provided this test is satisfied, the question of law is subject to the appellate process defined by section 1(2), whatever be its nature. It follows that a question of law relating to a purely procedural matter, and therefore unrelated to the substantive dispute, is equally subject to a section 1 appeal, provided the procedural decision is embodied in an award.[12]

3.3.5 But a purely procedural decision taken in the course of a reference is not within section 1(2) unless the decision has been made in the form of an award. In turn this raises the potentially difficult question as to when a procedural decision may amount to an award. The answer is governed by the intention of the arbitral tribunal, which is necessarily a question of fact to be determined on the facts and circumstances of individual cases. When the decision is given in writing and described as an award,

8. *Antaios Compania Naviera S.A.* v. *Salen Rederierna A.B. (The Antaios) (No. 2)* [1983] 2 Lloyd's Rep. 473, 476.

9. [1983] 2 Lloyd's Rep. 346, 348.

10. *Universal Petroleum Co. Ltd.* v. *Handels- und Transport Gesellschaft m.b.H.* [1987] 1 Lloyd's Rep. 517, 524, per Kerr L.J.; *Kansa General Insurance Co. Ltd.* v. *Bishopsgate Insurance plc* [1988] 1 Lloyd's Rep. 503, 511, per Hirst J.

11. Cf. *Montedipe S.p.A. and Another* v. *JTP-Ro Jugotanker (The Jordan Nicolov)* [1990] 2 Lloyd's Rep. 11.

12. *Leif Hoegh & Co. A/S* v. *Petrolsea Inc. (The World Era) (No. 2)* [1993] 1 Lloyd's Rep. 363; *L'Office Cherifien des Phosphates and Unitramp S.A.* v. *Yamashita-Shinnihon Steamship Co. Ltd. (The Boucraa)* [1993] 2 Lloyd's Rep. 149 (C.A.); [1994] 1 All E.R. 20 (H.L.).

or some variant of an award, this will be compelling evidence of an intention to embody the decision in an award. The evidence will be more compelling still if reasons are also given. But where the decision is communicated orally or by correspondence during the course of or at the termination of the reference, and without more, this will be evidence strongly indicating that no award was intended. In addressing the distinction between a procedural decision and an award, it is highly likely that the court will again be influenced by the policy of the 1979 Act and consequently be reluctant to convert a procedural decision into an award, for the effect of such a recognition will be to open up the reference to judicial review by way of appeal.[13]

3.3.6 Apart from the obvious precondition that the award be a valid award[14] and also that it must be the award in issue between the parties and not any award, the concept of an award is otherwise very broadly interpreted. The term "award" includes an interim, interim final and final award; the award of a sole arbitrator, umpire, first tier arbitration tribunal or appeal tribunal; a money payment or declaratory award.[15]

3.3.7 Where there is constituted a tribunal of two or more arbitrators the award of the tribunal alludes to whatever constitutes in the context of the particular arbitration a valid award. *Prima facie* this is the unanimous award of the tribunal,[16] but frequently in practice provision is made that in the event of disagreement the award of the majority shall prevail or, when such a majority cannot be established, for the award of the tribunal to be the decision of a particular member of the tribunal, such as its chairman or president.[17] In this kind of circumstance any dissenting opinion is not part of the award for the purpose of section 1(2).[18]

3.3.8 Although it is not expressly stipulated, the 1979 Act is premised on the assumption of formal awards reduced into writing as distinct from informal parole awards.[19] In practice parole awards are exceptionally rare. The award includes not only the award itself but also all extraneous documents that are expressly or impliedly incorporated into the award.[20]

3.3.9 A further requirement is that the award must be "made". The making of an award is a technical concept and in English law an award is considered to have been made when the arbitrator has "declared his final mind" and is thereafter *functus officio*.[21] In contemporary practice the making of an award is closely allied with the signing of an award, whether or not the signature is also witnessed, but ultimately the

---

13. *Exmar B. V.* v. *National Iranian Tanker Co.* (*The Trade Fortitude*) [1992] 1 Lloyd's Rep. 169.

14. If the award is a nullity there is nothing to appeal from, see *Baytur S.A.* v. *Finagro Holding S.A.* [1991] 4 All E.R. 129, 134.

15. It seems unnecessary to support this part of the text by citing authority. The authorities in their generality abound with examples of the different categories of awards enumerated in the text and with no attempt made in them to restrict the interpretation of an "award" for the purpose of the 1979 Act.

16. *United Kingdom Mutual S.S. Assurance Association* v. *Houston* [1896] 1 Q.B. 567.

17. See, for example, Rules of London Court of International Arbitration (1985), Art. 16.3; International Chamber of Commerce Rules of Conciliation and Arbitration (1988), Art. 19; UNCITRAL Arbitration Rules (1976), Art. 31.

18. Cf. *Orient Overseas Management and Finance Ltd.* v. *File Shipping Co. Ltd.* (*The Energy Progress*) [1993] 1 Lloyd's Rep. 355.

19. See Chapter 11.

20. *Andrea* v. *British Italian Trading Company Ltd.* [1962] 1 Lloyd's Rep. 151; D.S. *Blaiber & Co. Ltd.* v. *Leopold Newborne (London) Ltd.* [1953] 2 Lloyd's Rep. 427; *Orion Compania Espanola de Seguros* v. *Belfort Maatschappij voor Algemene Verzekeringeen* [1962] 2 Lloyd's Rep. 257. See also Chapter 8, para. 8.4.1.

21. *Hiscox* v. *Outhwaite (No. 1)* [1992] 1 A.C. 562, 594, Lord Oliver.

precise moment an award is made would seem to be a question of fact, to be decided on the facts and circumstances of each individual case. The making of an award cannot therefore be inseparably associated with the act of signing.

3.4 ON AN ARBITRATION AGREEMENT

3.4.1 The final requirement is that the question of law must arise out of an award made "on an arbitration agreement".

An arbitration agreement is in essence a special category of contract and in consequence the preconditions of a valid arbitration "agreement" are governed by the general law of contract. The only issue which will be pursued in the text is the requirement as to form, which in the context of the arbitration legislation as a whole is a question of substantial importance and uncertainty. At common law there is no formal requirement,[1] but the arbitration legislation has consistently taken a different approach.

3.4.2 By virtue of section 7(1)(e) of the 1979 Act an "arbitration agreement" within the Act has the same meaning as that specified in section 32 of the Arbitration Act 1950,[2] which is to the following effect:

In this Part of this Act, unless the context otherwise requires, the expression "arbitration agreement" means a written agreement to submit present or future differences to arbitration, whether an arbitrator is named therein or not.

This definition is closely followed by the definition of an arbitration agreement proffered by the Arbitration Act 1975. Section 7(1) of the 1975 Act defines an arbitration agreement as meaning "an agreement in writing (including an agreement contained in an exchange of letters or telegrams) to submit to arbitration present or future differences capable of settlement by arbitration;". The drafting is different from the definition in section 32 of the 1950 Act, but in relation to the requirement as to form it is doubtful that there exists any substantive difference between the two definitions.

3.4.3 In the result for an arbitration agreement to be within the meaning of the phrase "on an arbitration agreement", as it appears in section 1(2) of the 1979 Act, it must be a "written agreement". There is no appeal under section 1 from an error of law arising out of an award made on a parole arbitration agreement, even when the error is manifest in a written award and the parole arbitration agreement is capable of being established with certainty. In the event of such an unlikely situation, the error of law can only be reviewed under the common law jurisdiction for error of law on the face of an award, which it would seem survives for this purpose.[3]

3.4.4 An arbitration agreement embodied in and emanating from a consensus manifested in writing, as where the parties enter into a formal written arbitration agreement or into a formal written contract with an arbitration clause, is clearly within the statutory perception of a "written agreement". Writing in this context probably

1. *Westminster Chemicals & Produce Ltd.* v. *Eichholz & Loeser* [1954] 1 Lloyd's Rep. 99.
2. Re-enacting section 21(2) of the Arbitration Act 1934. In the Arbitration Act 1889 the term "submission" was adopted for what is now referred to as an "arbitration agreement" and was defined by section 27 in the following terms, "unless the contrary intention appears—'Submission' means a written agreement to submit present or future differences to arbitration, whether an arbitrator is named therein or not".
3. See Chapter 1, para. 1.4.

bears an extended meaning and includes any permanent form of communication or record such as printing, typography, computerised print-outs and longhand. But even when there does not exist a formally executed written contract in the traditional sense, but the creative elements of a contract, namely the offer and acceptance, are in writing and embody an obligation to arbitrate, then again the formal requirements of section 32 are satisfied.[4]

3.4.5 It also must be emphasised that it is the arbitration agreement alone that must be in writing. Any contract to which the arbitration agreement relates need not be in writing.[5] So also section 32 is satisfied if a written arbitration agreement is expressly and directly incorporated by reference into a contract, or an extraneous document containing an arbitration clause is so incorporated. The incorporation of the arbitration agreement is effective independently of the knowledge of the parties provided that on its proper construction the incorporation clause extends to the arbitration clause.[6] This principle would appear to prevail even when the incorporating contract is parole. In *Zambia Steel and Building Supplies Ltd.* v. *James Clark and Eaton Ltd.*[7] a parole agreement was concluded on the terms of a quotation sent by sellers to buyers and containing an arbitration clause. The Court of Appeal held that the buyers by their conduct had assented to the quotation terms, including the arbitration clause, and that there was in existence an arbitration agreement in writing for the purpose of section 7(1) of the Arbitration Act 1975. That the same approach would be adopted under the 1979 Act has been cast in some doubt by the dictum of Bingham L.J. in *E. Turner and Sons Ltd.* v. *Mathind Ltd.*,[8] where the learned judge declared that "the fact that written terms were incorporated by oral reference does not make it a written agreement". This dictum appears to run counter to the acknowledged fact that an entire contract may be in part written and in part parole and would appear to be irreconcilable with the approach adopted in *Zambia Steel*, which it is suggested cannot be distinguished by virtue of it being a decision relating to the proper interpretation of section 7(1) of the Arbitration Act 1975, and which it is submitted represents the more desirable approach.

3.4.6 Beyond the requirement of writing, the legislation makes no further express requirement and therefore there would appear to be no justification for demanding the signature of the parties or any further formality such as attestation. But although a literal and practical interpretation of the statute suggests this to be the case, doubt has been cast upon it by the interpretation given by Lord Greene M.R. in *Frank Fehr & Co.* v. *Kassam Jivraj & Co. Ltd.*[9] to section 27 of the Arbitration Act 1889, which sets out a definition of a "submission" in substantially similar terms to that of an "arbitration agreement" in section 32 of the 1950 Act. Lord Greene M.R. observed[10]:

I am quite content to proceed on what I am bound to say, *prima facie*, I should have thought, was the right construction of the Act. Where the Act speaks about a written agreement, it is

---

4. Cf. *E. Turner and Sons Ltd.* v. *Mathind Ltd.* (1989) 5 Const.L.J. 273, 279; Arbitration Act 1975, s. 7(1).
5. *Excomm Ltd.* v. *Ahmed Abdul-Qawi Bamaodah (The St. Raphael)* [1985] 1 Lloyd's Rep. 403 (C.A.).
6. *Golodetz* v. *Schrier* (1947) 80 Ll.L.Rep. 647, explaining *McConnell and Read* v. *Smith*, 1911 S.C. 635. See also *Tracomin S.A.* v. *Sudan Oil Seeds Co. Ltd.* [1983] 1 Lloyd's Rep. 560 (first instance).
7. [1986] 2 Lloyd's Rep. 225. Noted by Mann, 3 Arb.Int. 171.
8. (1989) 5 Const.L.J. 273, 279.
9. (1949) 82 Ll.L.Rep. 673 (C.A.).
10. *Ibid* p. 676.

contemplating not only an agreement which is in writing but an agreement which is signed by both parties. I do not find it necessary to decide that question, but I am prepared to accept that view and I base my judgment on it.

3.4.7 Argument to the same effect was, however, expressly rejected by Lord Coleridge in *Baker* v. *Yorkshire Fire and Life Assurance Co.*[11] and there are other authorities which give support to this as representing the better and correct approach.[12] To demand the signature of the parties is also to introduce an unnecessary fetter to the free flow of commercial activity and to disregard many facets of current commercial practice where the validity of arbitration agreements is accepted notwithstanding the absence of signature.[13] The issue has now probably been finally resolved and settled by the decision of the Court of Appeal in *The St. Raphael*[14] where on the weight of authority and the proper interpretation of the express language of section 32 of the 1950 Act the court was of the opinion that an arbitration agreement was within the legislative definition even if not signed provided it was otherwise in writing.[15]

3.4.8 The requirement of writing has, however, been widely construed so as to include not only written agreements in the strict sense of the term but also agreements that are evidenced or acknowledged by writing. The statutory definition is in consequence capable of being satisfied if a pre-existing parole arbitration agreement is subsequently verified or acknowledged in a later document or documents (or other form of permanent record). Omitting the allusion to the need for signature, the observations of Lord Greene M.R. in the *Frank Fehr*[16] case have otherwise been generally accepted as representing the proper approach to the interpretation of section 32[17]:

. . . the section, to my mind, is quite clearly satisfied if there is produced a document or documents . . . which records a pre-existing agreement or authenticates or recognises the existence of an agreement to submit. That, to my mind, is sufficient to satisfy the statute, [counsel] emphasised the distinction, which, of course, is well known, between an agreement and a note or memorandum of an agreement. That appears to me to be an irrelevant distinction in this case. What we have to look at is to see whether or not there is a written . . . document recognising, incorporating, or confirming the existence of an agreement to submit.

This interpretation was adopted by the Court of Appeal in *The St. Raphael*[18] where Lloyd L.J. observed[19]:

I would hold that an arbitration agreement need not be signed and that the definition in s. 32 of the Act is satisfied provided there is a document or documents in writing which, to use the

---

11. [1892] 1 Q.B. 144, 146.

12. *Hickman* v. *Kent and Romney Marsh Sheep-Breeders' Association* [1915] 1 Ch. 881; *Anglo-Newfoundland Development Co.* v. *R* [1920] 2 K.B. 214; *Bankers' and Shippers' Insurance Co. of New York* v. *Liverpool Marine and General Insurance Co. Ltd.* (1925) 21 Ll.L.Rep. 86.

13. A large number of contracts are concluded by the exchange of documents transmitted by correspondence, telex or fax; or in association with the transfer of a document of title such as a bill of lading. The absence of a signature(s) does not affect the establishment of a contract in any of these situations; nor has it been doubted that an incorporated arbitration agreement is any less valid by virtue of the absence of the signature of the contracting parties.

14. *Excomm Ltd.* v. *Ahmed Abdul-Qawi Bamaodah (The St. Raphael)* [1985] 1 Lloyd's Rep. 403 (C.A.).

15. *Ibid* p. 409 per Lloyd L.J. and p. 412 per Sir John Donaldson M.R. See also *Arab African Energy Corp. Ltd.* v. *Olieprodukten Nederland B.V.* [1983] 2 Lloyd's Rep. 419.

16. *Supra*.

17. *Supra* at pp. 676–677.

18. *Supra*.

19. *Supra* at p. 409. See also *Arab African Energy Corp. Ltd.* v. *Olieprodukten Nederland B.V. supra* at p. 421.

language of Lord Greene, " . . . recognize, incorporate or confirm the existence of an agreement to submit".

3.4.9 A written arbitration agreement may of course be varied, amended or enlarged by a subsequent agreement. Where the subsequent agreement is also in writing or otherwise acknowledged by writing there exists no difficulty. But where it assumes the form of an informal parole agreement there arises the question whether the subsequent agreement continues to be within the statutory definition. The likelihood of such a question arising is far from being fanciful for in the course of a reference the parties may orally agree to extend, vary or amend the terms of the original arbitration agreement, as where the parties agree that the arbitrator be given a jurisdiction or power not conferred by the original arbitration agreement. In such a situation, the arbitration agreement is in part in writing and in part parole and it would be highly unsatisfactory if the law was to closely discriminate between the written and informal parts and hold the arbitration legislation to be applicable to the former but not the latter. Authority offers no decisive answer, but there is authority which at least leans in favour of a solution, which also represents the commonsense solution, to the effect that the statutory definition of an arbitration agreement extends so as to include not only a wholly written agreement, in the wide sense considered above, but also written arbitration agreements that are subsequently orally varied by the parties.[20] The parole variation might be considered as merging into the original written arbitration agreement.[21]

20. *Westminster Chemicals and Produce Ltd.* v. *Eichholz and Loeser* [1954] 1 Lloyd's Rep. 99; *A/B Legis* v. *V. Berg & Sons Ltd.* [1964] 1 Lloyd's Rep. 203; *Luanda Exportadora S.A.R.L.* v. *Wahbe Tamari & Sons Ltd. and Jaffa Trading Co.* [1967] 2 Lloyd's Rep. 353.
21. For recent deliberation of the general question, see the Final Report of the Sub-Committee on Arbitration Law of the Commercial Court Committee, 22 October 1985.

CHAPTER 4

PRELIMINARIES TO AN APPEAL TO THE HIGH COURT

4.1 INTRODUCTION

4.1.1 An appeal on a question of law cannot be brought as of right but is preconditioned upon either the consent of all the other parties to the reference or the giving of leave by the High Court. Section 1(3) provides:

An appeal under this section may be brought by any of the parties to the reference—
    (a) with the consent of all the other parties to the reference; or
    (b) subject to section 3 below, with the leave of the court.

Both requirements are regulators, although otherwise quite distinct in nature, which operate to control the flow of appeals from arbitration awards to the High Court. The requirement of leave in particular has provided a focus to the development of an early statement of the policy underlying the 1979 Act and of the criteria to guide the exercise of judicial discretion when considering applications for leave.[1] Where, however, an appeal is brought with consent, the particular policy considerations that touch on the exercise of judicial discretion on an application for leave to appeal are of no consequence, for they are superseded by the will of the parties.[2]

4.1.2 The two requirements set out in section 1(3) are quite distinct and unrelated. The disjunctive "or" appears to make this plain. An appeal may be advanced either with consent *or* with leave. In strictness, therefore, it would appear unnecessary to show on an application for leave that the consent of all the other parties to the reference has been first sought and refused. But in practice this is the likely approach, for if the consent of the other parties can be obtained it will save the expense and delay necessarily associated with an application for leave, which may of course be resisted. There is presently little evidence to suggest that the failure first to seek the consent of the other parties is a factor which the court takes into account in considering an application for leave. Consent is nonetheless rarely likely to be present,[3] and therefore the vast majority of appeals will be dependent on the granting of leave. In giving leave to appeal the court may attach such conditions as it considers appropriate.[4]

4.1.3 The jurisdiction of the court to give leave to appeal is dependent on the requirement set out in section 1(4) that the question of law in issue is of a kind that its determination could substantially affect the rights of one or more of the

---

1. See *infra*, para. 4.3.2.
2. See *infra*, para. 4.2.
3. See *infra*, para. 4.2.
4. Section 1(4). Considered further *infra*, para. 4.3.4.

parties to the arbitration agreement being satisfied,[5] and also on the absence of a valid and applicable exclusion agreement. Paragraph (b) of section 1(3) is expressed to be "subject to Section 3 below", which is the section dealing with exclusion agreements and which are considered fully in a later chapter.[6] No similar provision is found in paragraph (a). In the result, even when a valid and applicable exclusion agreement exists, the subsequent consent of all the parties to the reference to the bringing of an appeal will operate as a waiver or as an agreement suspending the operation of the exclusion agreement. The exclusion agreement is not, without more, abandoned but simply ceases to be of effect with regard to the appeal in question.[7]

4.2 APPEALS WITH CONSENT

4.2.1 By virtue of section 1(3)(a) an appeal may be initiated with the consent of all the other parties to the reference, with potential saving of both time and costs. But notwithstanding the potential advantages it is probable that only rarely will such consent be forthcoming.[1] An appeal is substantially in the sole interest of the loser in the arbitration and the victor will not wish to do or to encourage the doing of any act that places at risk the finality of the award given in his favour. Nonetheless appeals brought with consent are not unknown.[2]

4.2.2 Where both parties wish to appeal it may be to their mutual convenience for each party to consent to the appeal of the other.[3] Where a central question of law lies to the heart of a dispute and is placed as a preliminary issue before the arbitrator for decision in an interim award, this may represent the kind of circumstance more likely to attract universal consent to an appeal than the case of a final award on the merits.[4] So also where a legal question in issue is of wide relevance, for example, to a body of traders accustomed to trading on common terms, it may be that the parties to the reference will consent to an appeal, but on terms that the appeal shall not prejudice the initial award so far as the immediate parties to the reference are concerned.[5]

4.2.3 The consent must be that of *all* the other parties to the reference and nothing less will satisfy the statute. The phrase "other parties" alludes to those parties to the reference who are not party to the bringing of the proposed appeal and it must be borne in mind that as a matter of procedure an appeal may be brought jointly by two

5. See *infra*, para. 4.3.3.
6. Chapter 13.
7. *Ibid*.
1. *Stinnes Interoil G.m.b.H.* v. *A. Halcoussis & Co. (The Yanxilas) (No. 2)* [1984] 1 Lloyd's Rep. 676, 685 per Bingham J.
2. *Ibid*; *Filikos Shipping Corporation of Monrovia* v. *Shipmair B.V. (The Filikos)* [1981] 2 Lloyd's Rep. 555; *Athens Cape Naviera S.A.* v. *Deutsche Dampfschiffahrtsgesellschaft "Hansa" Aktiengesellschaft and Another (The Barenbels)* [1984] 2 Lloyd's Rep. 388; *MSC Mediterranean Shipping Co. S.A.* v. *Alianca Bay Shipping Co. Ltd. (The Argonaut)* [1985] 2 Lloyd's Rep. 216; *Torvald Klaveness A/S* v. *Arni Maritime Corporation (The Gregos)* [1992] 2 Lloyd's Rep. 40.
3. See, for example, *Superfos Chartering A/S* v. *N.B.R. (London) Ltd. (The Saturnia)* [1984] 2 Lloyd's Rep. 366 (upheld on appeal [1987] 2 Lloyd's Rep. 366); *Société Anonyme Marocaine de L'Industrie du Raffinage* v. *Notos Maritime Corporation (The Notos)* [1985] 1 Lloyd's Rep. 149.
4. See, for example, *Atkins International H.A.* v. *Islamic Republic of Iran Shipping Lines, (The A.P.J. Priti)* [1987] 2 Lloyd's Rep. 37 (C.A.).
5. *Pioneer Shipping Ltd. and Others* v. *B.T.P. Tioxide Ltd. (The Nema)* [1982] A.C. 724, 744 per Lord Diplock, and where Lord Diplock also contemplates the prospect of an appeal being brought by consent of all the parties as a test case under section 1(3)(a).

or more parties to a reference. The word "party" as used in the plural in section 1(3) is probably not to be construed as synonymous with the notion of "claimant" and "respondent" in an arbitration, at least when used as collective terms. It probably alludes to all the individual parties, human and juristic, involved in the arbitration proceedings. Where in consequence the "claimant" and "respondent" are constituted by more than a single human and juristic person, each is to be considered a party to the reference for the purposes of section 1(3).

The notion as to who is a party to a reference, as distinct from an arbitration agreement, has previously been considered in the context of the question who may bring an appeal from an award on a question of law, and that elaboration is of equal application to the present discussion.[6]

4.2.4 Consent is a question of fact and must in each case be clearly established.[7] The subsection makes no requirement as to form and therefore it may be assumed that subject to adequate proof consent may be parole or expressed in writing; but as a matter of practice it is clearly desirable that the consent should be in writing. In principle the consent may be express or implied from conduct. But silence *per se* cannot amount to consent; nor is consent to be implied from a failure to challenge a notice of motion that wrongly implies that an appeal was being brought with consent.[8] Consent is probably more than a state of mind and there is in consequence no valid consent until it is communicated to the party wishing to appeal, either directly or through an authorised or reliable intermediary. Although there is no formal requirement in the terms of section 1(3)(a) with regard to the question of consent, nonetheless by the R.S.C. Order 73, rule 5(5), it is at least contemplated that the consent will be in writing. The question of consent is an interlocutory procedural requirement, and it seems to be the case that any oral consent initially given must at a subsequent stage be translated into writing.[9]

4.2.5 It is probable that the consent must prevail at the time the appeal is instituted, which probably takes place when the notice of motion is served and entered. This in turn suggests that, unless otherwise precluded, a consent given may be revoked at any time prior to the institution of an appeal. But this is so only if the consent is revocable. It may cease to be so by contract or estoppel. In *The Emmanuel Colocotronis (No. 1)* it appears to have been accepted by Staughton J. that a party may bind himself by contract to consent to the bringing of an appeal.[10] But apart from contract, if a party relies on a consent given and proceeds to prepare the appeal on the basis that it will be an

---

6. *Supra*, Chapter 2, para. 2.2.
7. *Bulk Oil (Zug) A.G.* v. *Sun International Ltd. and Sun Oil Trading Co.* [1983] 1 Lloyd's Rep. 655, 659, per Bingham J., "Despite a submission to the contrary, I am of the opinion that this is not a case falling within s. 1(3)(a) of the Arbitration Act, 1979, in which both parties consent to the decision of the arbitrator being subject to appeal. It appears that both sides, before the arbitrator, showed a firm intention to seek to appeal against a decision which was adverse to them, but I do not understand either party to have consented, or to have given the impression that it would consent, to an appeal by the other party if the decision was in its own favour. The matter must therefore be approached as falling under s. 1(3)(b) of the Act."
8. *Astro Valiente Compania Naviera S.A.* v. *The Government of Pakistan Ministry of Food and Agriculture (The Emmanuel Colocotronis) (No. 1)* [1982] 1 Lloyd's Rep. 297, 298–299.
9. See Appendix G where R.S.C., Ord. 73, is set out.
10. *Supra* pp. 298–299. See also *Vinava Shipping Co. Ltd.* v. *Finelvet A.G. (The Chrysalis)* [1983] 1 Lloyd's Rep. 503, where the parties agreed in advance of the publishing of the award that each should have a right of appeal.

appeal with consent, it is arguable that the party who has given consent is thereafter estopped from subsequently withdrawing that consent. But the position is obviously otherwise when the consent is given on the express or implied understanding that it is revocable at any time prior to the issue of the notice of motion.

4.2.6 A consent is not necessarily a blanket provision applicable to all the points of law capable of arising out of an award. Where there is more than one point of law in issue a party may give his consent to an appeal with regard to a single or specified points, leaving the others subject to an application for leave.[11] It also seems that it is open to a party to give a conditional consent, for example, by making his consent subject to a condition that the party wishing to appeal give security for the amount of the award.[12]

Where there is consent there is an absolute right of appeal.[13] The court has no discretion in the matter and the question of leave does not arise. Equally section 1(4) has no application.[14] In this regard there exists an important difference between the consent of all the parties to the reference under section 1(3)(a) and such consent given under section 2(1)(b).[15] But apart from their mode of institution, there is otherwise no difference between an appeal brought with consent and an appeal with leave. The substantive basis of the appeal and the position of the first tier appellate judge is the same for all appeals, whatever the underlying procedure.[16]

4.3 APPEALS WITH LEAVE OF THE HIGH COURT

4.3.1 Introduction

4.3.1.1 Where the consent of all the other parties to the reference is absent, an appeal may be brought only with leave of the High Court.[1] For reasons previously considered, this will be the mode of progressing in the vast preponderance of appeals. If leave is refused, the award of the arbitrator is final,[2] although there does exist a limited right of appeal to the Court of Appeal from the decision of a first tier judge giving or refusing leave to appeal.[3] Leave is of course a question of discretion, but a precondition to the granting of leave is that the court must be satisfied that the ques-

---

11. *Stinnes Interoil G.m.b.H.* v. *A. Halcoussis & Co. (The Yanxilas) (No. 2)* [1984] 1 Lloyd's Rep. 676, 685.

12. *Portunus Navigation Co. Inc.* v. *Avin Chartering S.A. (The World Prestige)* [1982] 1 Lloyd's Rep. 60. On the facts of the case shipowners indicated to charterers that they were prepared to consent to an appeal from an award made in their favour provided the charterers gave security for the amount payable under the award. In the event no security was provided and although Parker J. did not consider the validity of the shipowners' conditional consent, the learned judge did not expressly disapprove of the practice.

13. *Babanaft International Co. S.A.* v. *Avant Petroleum Inc. (The Oltenia)* [1982] 2 Lloyd's Rep. 99, 106, per Donaldson L.J.

14. Considered *infra*, para. 4.3.3.

15. Considered in Chapter 12.

16. *Vinava Shipping Co. Ltd.* v. *Finelvet A.G. (The Chrysalis)* [1983] 1 Lloyd's Rep. 503, 507, per Mustill J.

1. Section 1(3)(b).

2. *B.T.P. Tioxide Ltd.* v. *Pioneer Shipping Ltd. and Armada Marine S.A. (The Nema)* [1980] 2 Lloyd's Rep. 339, 344, per Lord Denning M.R. (C.A.).

3. Section 1(6A), considered in Chapter 10, para. 10.2.

tion of law in issue is "substantial".[4] Where leave is granted it may be made conditional.[5]

The fact that leave is first required means that the appeal procedure established under section 1 of the 1979 Act has two facets, which are in most instances quite distinct in practice. The first is the application for leave to appeal; and where leave is granted, the second is the full substantive appeal hearing.[6]

4.3.1.2 Section 1(3)(b) is the crucial provision in the new appellate procedure established under the 1979 Act; it is the linchpin of the entire statute. It may be so perceived for it represents a metaphorical confluence where the express and laconic language of the 1979 Act and the judicial perception of the legislative policy underlying the Act flow into one another. It represents yet another illustration of policy adorning express statutory language, and to such a degree that a reader of the statute without knowledge of the associated developing judicial law is provided with little or no information of the precise legal position.[7]

4.3.2 Leave a question of discretion

4.3.2.1 It is patently clear that under section 1(3)(b) the court has a discretion to grant or refuse leave.[1] The discretion is that of the judge at first instance who hears the application; and the judge is not bound by, although he may take into account, any observations that may have been volunteered by other judges at first instance who have heard interlocutory applications relating to the same arbitration.[2] On the face of the statute the discretion is without fetter, apart from that which is necessarily implicit and to the effect that the discretion must be exercised judicially, for there is no express indication given as to how the discretion is to be exercised, nor of the criteria to be taken into account. But what is absent in the legislation has been introduced by the judges under the guiding hand of the judicial perception of the underlying legislative policy.[3] The policy behind the 1979 Act has previously been considered and will be returned to again later. For the present it is sufficient to recall that the 1979 Act is seen as a measure aimed at moving English jurisprudence towards the greater recognition of the finality of arbitration awards and away from the requirement that awards display meticulous legal accuracy.[4] The recognition of this policy has influenced the judicial interpretation of section 1(3)(b); and also operated to structure the discretion and give direction to the judicial role in considering applications for leave.

4.3.2.2 In the result the discretion has become circumscribed with judges not over-ready to grant leave.[5] It is clear that the establishment of a substantial error of

---

4. Section 1(4), considered *infra*, para. 4.3.3.
5. Section 1(4), considered *infra*, para. 4.3.4.
6. See Chapters 7 and 9.
7. This point is developed in some detail in Chapters 5 and 6.
1. *Pioneer Shipping Ltd. and Others* v. *B.T.P. Tioxide Ltd. (The Nema)* [1982] A.C. 724, 739, per Lord Diplock. The criteria governing the exercise of the discretion are considered in Chapters 5 and 6.
2. *Pioneer Shipping Ltd. and Armada Marine S.A.* v. *B.T.P. Tioxide Ltd. (The Nema)* [1980] 1 Lloyd's Rep. 519, 522 per Robert Goff J. (first instance).
3. Considered in Chapters 5 and 6. See also Kerr, "Arbitration and the Courts—The UNCITRAL Model Law" (1985) 34 I.C.L.Q. 1.
4. See Chapter 1, para. 1.5.
5. See Chapters 5 and 6.

law in an award will not of itself necessarily secure the grant of leave to appeal. In the context of section 1(3)(b), the traditional obligation of the judiciary to exercise discretionary powers judicially has come to mean in accordance with the established general principles developed in the authorities and in relation to the facts of individual cases.[6] Of course this formula will not produce an inevitable and predictable outcome. Different judges all acting judicially may come to different yet reasonable decisions in the eyes of the law. This is an inevitable incident of any discretionary jurisdiction.[7]

The discretionary jurisdiction, as it has been developed, functions in the manner of a filter, allowing certain questions of law to pass forward for judicial consideration and rejecting others. The way the court selects and chooses between the various questions of law is the key issue in this area of the 1979 Act and will be considered later.[8]

4.3.3 Substantial question of law

4.3.3.1 By virtue of section 1(4) no leave to appeal shall be given unless the High Court considers "that, having regard to all the circumstances, the determination of the question of law concerned could substantially affect the rights of one or more of the parties to the arbitration agreement". This requirement gives effect to a recommendation embodied in the *Report on Arbitration* of the Commercial Court Committee that, "Leave to appeal should only be given if the High Court is satisfied that the question of law in issue might be determined on appeal in a way which would affect the rights of the parties under the award".[1] The statute adopts a different form of words and probably establishes a more demanding precondition. Section 1(4) does not require that the determination of the question of law *will* substantially affect the rights of one or more of the parties, it is sufficient if it *could* have this result. It is also not sufficient to show that the rights of one or more of the parties could be affected, for the statute expressly demands that the determination must be such that it could "substantially" affect the rights of any of the parties. Further, the legislation is satisfied if the defined potential impact befalls at least one of the parties. Section 1(4) is also distinct from the other provisions of the 1979 Act for it alone alludes to "the parties to the arbitration agreement" as opposed to "the parties to the reference."[2] It is doubtful if the changed phraseology assumes a significance for it is unlikely that the chosen words will be construed so as to confine the subsection to the original parties to the arbitration agreement. It is suggested that the phrase extends to embrace both the original parties to the arbitration agreement and any party who subsequently agrees to participate in the reference on the terms of the original arbitration agreement, with or without amendment.

The concept of a "question of law" as adopted in section 1(4) has the same meaning

---

6. Cf. *Scherer* v. *Counting Instruments Ltd.* [1986] 1 W.L.R. 615, 618 *et seq.* per Buckley L.J.

7. *Antaios Comparia Naviera S.A.* v. *Salen Rederierna A.B., (The Antaios)* [1985] A.C. 191, 204, per Lord Diplock; *Aden Refinery Co. Ltd.* v. *Ugland Management Co. Ltd.* (*The Ugland Obo One*) [1987] 1 Q.B. 650, 668, per Mustill L.J.

8. See Chapters 5 and 6.

1. *Supra*, para. 35.

2. See Chapter 2, para. 2.2.

as in the phrase "any question of law arising out of an award made on an arbitration agreement" used in section 1(2).[3]

4.3.3.2 Section 1(4) only applies when leave to appeal is sought. It has no relevance where an appeal is consented to by all the parties to the reference.[4] Where leave to appeal is sought the issue of substantiality is the first question the judge must address.[5] If the test is not satisfied the court has no jurisdiction to grant leave to appeal. The substantialness of a question of law raises a question of jurisdiction and not of discretion.[6] It is an issue which may be raised by the court itself, and whenever the substantialness of a question of law is challenged the burden of proof falls on the party seeking leave to appeal to establish on a balance of probabilities that a substantial question of law is in issue. But although it is for the applicant to establish that a substantial question of law is in issue, it would seem that the applicant will not bear the full burden of proof unless the issue is challenged. The test of substantiality must be applied to every question of law with regard to which leave to appeal is sought.

4.3.3.3 The purpose underlying section 1(4) is to ensure that leave to appeal is given only with regard to material and live issues of law, the resolution of which will or could have a significant bearing on the resolution of the dispute referred to arbitration and the question of liability between the parties. The object is to exclude appeals which may be regarded as academic, hypothetical, insignificant, frivolous, trivial or flimsy.[7] Sir John Donaldson M.R. has commented, "This subsection is, as is apparent, intended to prevent appeals on academic questions of law, which were a feature of the old special case procedure."[8] Lord Denning M.R. has observed, "In short, it must be a point of practical importance—not an academic point—nor a minor point."[9] The materiality and significance of a question of law is be to be measured wholly in the context of the dispute between the parties. There is in this regard no wider dimension, and the fact that the question of law may be of general importance is an irrelevant consideration.[10] It will in each case be a question of fact and degree whether any particular question of law satisfies the text of substantiality.

4.3.3.4 In the main it would appear that the text of substantiality will be fairly

---

3. *Universal Petroleum Co. Ltd.* v. *Handels- und Transport Gesellschaft m.b.H.* [1987] 1 Lloyd's Rep. 517, 524 per Kerr L.J.
4. The opening words in section 1(4) state, "The High Court shall not grant leave under subsection (3)(b) . . .".
5. *Bulk Oil (Zug) A.G.* v. *Sun International Ltd. and Sun Oil Trading Co.* [1983] 1 Lloyd's Rep. 655, 659, per Bingham J.
6. *Moran* v. *Lloyd's* [1983] 1 Lloyd's Rep. 51, 57 per Lloyd J. (first instance).
7. For an example of a hypothetical question of law arising under the former special case procedure, see *The Ion* [1971] 1 Lloyd's Rep. 541, 545, per Brandon J.
8. *Aden Refinery Co. Ltd.* v. *Ugland Management Co. Ltd. (The Ugland Obo One)* [1987] 1 Q.B. 650, 656 (C.A.).
9. *B.T.P. Tioxide Ltd.* v. *Pioneer Shipping Ltd. and Armada Marine S.A. (The Nema)* [1980] 2 Lloyd's Rep. 339, 344 (C.A.).
10. *Seaworld Ocean Line Co. S.A.* v. *Catseye Maritime Co. Ltd. (The Kelaniya)* [1989] 1 Lloyd's Rep. 30, 31, per Lord Donaldson M.R. "It was included in the Act (i.e. section 1(4)) in order to stop people debating academic points, [which] although of great interest to the commercial fraternity, did not actually affect the parties to the dispute." *Pioneer Shipping Ltd. and Others* v. *B.T.P. Tioxide Ltd. (The Nema)* [1982] A.C. 724, 740, per Lord Diplock, "Except when all parties to the reference consent, the first part of section 1(4) places an absolute bar upon the grant of leave to appeal unless the determination of the disputed point of law would substantially affect the rights of one or more parties to the reference; and this, be it noted, even though the point might have arisen under a standard form contract and be of outstanding importance to the trade generally."

readily satisfied. It is difficult to see how any question of law touching on a material liability of a party can be anything other than substantial.[11] If according to the answer given to a question of law the incidence of legal liability as between claimant and respondent depends on the kind and/or degree of remedial relief one party may demand against another, it would appear quite clear that the question of law is substantial for the purpose of section 1(4). To look at the issue from a slightly different perspective: a question of law will be perceived as substantial if the argument presented about it by the applicant for leave, if accepted by the court, would lead the court to set aside, vary or remit the award.[12] There may be occasions when the significance of a question of law will be accentuated by its financial significance to the parties.[13] On the other hand a question of law will be insubstantial if its determination by the court would have no or no material impact on the distribution of liabilities or the effective result arrived at by the arbitrator in his award[14]; or would otherwise result in such a marginal adjustment as not to justify the institution of the appellate process established by the 1979 Act. The latter will often give rise to difficult questions of judgment, but this is an unavoidable consequence of the adoption of the adverb "substantially" in section 1(4).

4.3.3.5 The appellation "insubstantial" is particularly likely to be admitted in the relative context of several questions of law. In this manner of circumstance a particular question of law, when analysed alongside the other questions of law, may be viewed as an incidental and minor question of law; and this approach may be even more readily adopted when the sum in issue in association with the particular question of law is also relatively very small.[15] In the relative context of two or more questions of law, the importance of any one question of law may also fluctuate with the view taken of any other. This is to recognise an element of conditionality. In this way a question of law, although of potential material significance if it existed in isolation, may by virtue of the view taken of another question of law, assume little or no significance in the full context of the application for leave to appeal.[16]

To establish a question of law as substantial, in the sense expounded above, does not mean that leave to appeal will be granted automatically. It is a first step and a necessary prerequisite. If it is not established there can be no appeal, for the court has

---

11. *Bulk Oil (Zug) A.G.* v. *Sun International and Sun Oil Trading Co.*, *supra* p. 657. See also *Kansa General Insurance Co. Ltd.* v. *Bishopsgate Insurance plc* [1988] 1 Lloyd's Rep. 503, 513.

12. Cf. *B.T.P. Tioxide Ltd.* v. *Pioneer Shipping Ltd. etc. (The Nema)* [1980] 2 Lloyd's Rep. 339, 344, per Lord Denning M.R. See also *Seaworld Ocean Line Co. S.A.* v. *Catseye Maritime Co. Ltd. (The Kelaniya)*, *supra*, p. 31.

13. *Portaria Shipping Co.* v. *Gulf Pacific Navigation Co. Ltd. (The Selene G)* [1981] 2 Lloyd's Rep. 180. See also *Aden Refinery Co. Ltd.* v. *Ugland Management Co. Ltd. (The Ugland Obo One)* [1987] 1 Q.B. 650, 656, per Sir John Donaldson M.R., "It is not suggested that the subsection had any application in the circumstances of the instant case. If the charterers were right in their contentions, their rights would be affected to the tune of U.S. \$70,000, not to mention further sums in respect of interest and costs."

14. *Exmar BV* v. *National Iranian Tanker Co. (The Trade Fortitude)* [1992] 1 Lloyd's Rep. 169, 178.

15. See further Chapter 6, para. 6.2.22.

16. *B.V.S. S.A. and Another* v. *Kerman Shipping Co. S.A. (The Kerman)* [1982] 1 W.L.R. 166, 168, per Parker J., "Both these matters clearly raise questions of law. The determination of the first question could, plainly, substantially affect the rights of the parties. The determination of the second question could only do so if the arbitrator's decision of the first question was reversed. If, however, that decision stands, the determination of the second question would be entirely without effect as between the parties." See also *Universal Petroleum Co. Ltd.* v. *Handels- und Transport Gesellschaft m.b.H.* [1987] 1 Lloyd's Rep. 517, 526, Kerr L.J.

no jurisdiction to give leave to appeal. But even if substantiality is established there continues to exist a discretion under section 1(3)(b) to give or refuse leave to appeal.

4.3.4 Conditional leave

4.3.4.1 Under the jurisdiction conferred by section 1(4) it is open to a judge to make any leave granted conditional on the applicant complying with such conditions as are considered appropriate. The power to attach conditions is not to be perceived as the primary mechanism by which to regulate the flow of appeals on questions of law from arbitration awards to the High Court.[1] It is a useful power which may be used by a judge who is minded to give leave to appeal so as to secure that justice continues to be done between the parties. Nonetheless, a judge who suspects that leave to appeal is being sought to engineer delay would be justified in using the power to attach conditions so as to defeat the ulterior purpose of the applicant.[2] Speaking in the House of Lords on the Bill Lord Diplock anticipated that the power would be exercised "robustly" when there were grounds for suspecting that the appellate process was being abused.[3]

4.3.4.2 The legislation does not specify the conditions that may be attached. This is left at large and within the discretion of the judge. The only constraint is that which arises by implication and which requires the judge to act judiciously. The possible conditions are many and various. The whole or a part of the sum in dispute may be ordered to be paid into court[4] or into a joint account[5] or otherwise secured.[6] The applicant may be directed to pay the minimum sum unquestionably due to the successful party.[7] A condition may be made with regard to the costs[8] or requiring security for costs.[9] Leave may be granted subject to the applicant satisfying a procedural or evidentiary condition, such as making available documents identified in the award for examination during the full appeal hearing.[10]

1. See Chapter 5, para. 5.1.1.
2. Cf. *Coastal States Trading (UK) Ltd.* v. *Mebro Mineraloel-Handelsgesellschaft G.m.b.H.* [1986] 1 Lloyd's Rep. 465, 468.
3. H.L.Deb. Vol. 398, col. 1475. See also Kerr, "The Arbitration Act 1979" 43 M.L.R. 45, 49; *Mondial Trading Co. G.m.b.H.* v. *Gill Duffus Zuckerhandelsgesellschaft m.b.H.* [1980] 2 Lloyd's Rep. 376, 382. Cf. *Coastal States Trading (UK) Ltd.* v. *Mebro Mineraloel-Handelsgesellschaft G.m.b.H.* [1986] 1 Lloyd's Rep. 465, 468.
4. *Pioneer Shipping Ltd.* v. *B.T.P. Tioxide Ltd. (The Nema)* [1982] A.C. 724, 739, per Lord Diplock; *Antaios Compania Naviera S.A.* v. *Salen Rederierna A.B. (The Antaios)* [1985] 1 A.C. 191, 199, per Lord Diplock; cf. *Anteo Shipping Ltd* v. *Seabridge Shipping Ltd.* [1979] 1 W.L.R. 1103. See also *Glafki Shipping Co. S.A.* v. *Pinios Shipping Co. (The Maira) (No. 1)* [1982] 1 Lloyd's Rep. 257.
5. Cf. *Compania Commercial y Naviera San Martin S.A.* v. *China National Foreign Trade Transportation Corpn. (The Constanza M)* [1980] 1 Lloyd's Rep. 505. Also, *Antco Shipping Ltd.* v. *Seabridge Shipping Ltd. (The Furness Bridge) (No. 2)* [1979] 2 Lloyd's Rep. 267 (C.A.).
6. See, generally, *Report on Arbitration, supra,* para. 35; *Antaios Compania Naviera S.A.* v. *Salen Rederierna A.B. (The Antaios)* [1985] 1 A.C. 191, 199; *Procter & Gamble Philippine Manufacturing Corpn.* v. *Kurt A. Becher G.m.b.H. & Co. K.G.* [1988] 2 Lloyd's Rep. 21, 27. See also *Japan Line Ltd.* v. *Aggeliki Charis Compania Maritima S.A. (The Angelic Grace)* [1980] 1 Lloyd's Rep. 288 (C.A.).
7. *Ibid.* Cf. *Uni-Ocean Lines Pte. Ltd.* v. *C Trade S.A. (The Lucille)* [1984] 1 Lloyd's Rep. 244, 246. See also *Congimex S.A.R.L. (Lisbon)* v. *Continental Grain Export Corporation (New York) and Others* [1979] 2 Lloyd's Rep. 346; *Texaco Ltd.* v. *The Eurogulf Shipping Co. Ltd.* [1987] 2 Lloyd's Rep. 541.
8. Cf. *D/S A/S Idaho* v. *Peninsular and Oriental Steam Navigation Co. (The Strathnewton)* [1982] 2 Lloyd's Rep. 296, 303.
9. See Staughton, "Arbitration Act 1919—A Pragmatic Compromise" [1979] N.L.J. 920, 922.
10. *Transgrain Shipping B.V.* v. *Global Transporte Oceanico S.A. (The Mexico I)* [1988] 2 Lloyd's Rep. 149, 157.

4.3.4.3 Although the jurisdiction to attach conditions may be very useful, nonetheless the fact must not be lost sight of that the result of imposing a condition may be to prevent an appeal from progressing. If this is wholly at the election of the applicant for leave there can be no concern. But there may be concern if it results from the nature of the condition imposed and the inability of the applicant to meet the terms of the condition. Laying down conditions, particularly of a financial nature, which it is impossible for the applicant to fulfil may render the exercise of the discretion injudicious and the condition void.[11]

11. Cf. *M.V. Yorke Motors* v. *Edwards* [1982] 1 W.L.R. 444, where the House of Lords held that under Ord. 14 it was a wrong exercise of discretion to impose on the defendant as a condition of granting leave to defend a financial condition that it would be impossible to fulfil. See also *Watts* v. *Moore*, *The Times*, 3 June 1988.

CHAPTER 5

EXERCISING THE JUDICIAL DISCRETION TO GIVE LEAVE TO APPEAL

5.1 THE FUNDAMENTAL APPROACH

5.1.1 The principles that are to govern the exercise of the discretion arising under section 1(3)(b) came into immediate question following the enactment of the 1979 legislation. The issue provoked disagreement between judges in the Commercial Court[1]; and between Robert Goff J. (as he then was) and the Court of Appeal.[2] Particularly controversial was the approach adopted by Robert Goff J. to the interpretation of the new legislation. In the view of the learned judge there was nothing in the express language of the statute to suggest that a restrictive approach was to be taken to the exercise of the discretion conferred by section 1(3)(b), with the consequence that the court should give leave in the case of certain categories of questions of law but decline to give leave in the case of other categories. The reasoning of Robert Goff J. was that whereas the court had to be satisfied that a substantial question of law was involved, as required by section 1(4),[2a] once it was so satisfied the only proper exercise of the discretion arising under section 1(3)(b) was to grant leave to appeal, unless there were special considerations. Under section 1(4) the court also had power to impose conditions when giving leave to appeal,[3] and if the court had reservations about the argument advanced to it alleging that the arbitrator had erred in law, for example, if the court considered it flimsy or doubted the motives of the applicant, it was open to the court to utilise this power by, for example, requiring the payment of the whole or part of the award into court or the provision of a security.[4]

---

1. *Pioneer Shipping Ltd. and Others* v. *B.T.P. Tioxide Ltd. (The Nema)* [1982] A.C. 724, 735, where Lord Diplock recounts the history of the early interlocutory applications associated with the case.
2. See *Schiffahrtsagentur Hamburg Middle East Line G.m.b.H. Hamburg* v. *Virtue Shipping Corporation Monrovia (The Oinoussian Virtue)* [1981] 1 Lloyd's Rep. 533, where Robert Goff J. criticised and refused to follow the guidelines laid down by the Court of Appeal in *B.T.P. Tioxide Ltd.* v. *Pioneer Shipping Ltd. and Armada Marine S.A. (The Nema)* [1980] Q.B. 547, [1980] 2 Lloyd's Rep. 339.
2a. Considered in Chapter 4, para. 4.3.3.
3. Considered in Chapter 4, para. 4.3.4.
4. A full statement of the approach of Robert Goff J. may be extracted from *Pioneer Shipping Ltd. and Armada Marine S.A.* v. *B.T.P. Tioxide Ltd. (The Nema)* [1980] 1 Lloyd's Rep. 519; *Schiffahrtsagentur Hamburg Middle East Line G.m.b.H. Hamburg* v. *Virtue Shipping Corporation Monrovia (The Oinoussian Virtue)* [1981] 1 Lloyd's Rep. 533; *Mondial Trading Co. G.m.b.H* v. *Gill & Duffus Zuckerhandelsgesellschaft m.b.H.* [1980] 2 Lloyd's Rep. 376; *International Sea Tankers Inc.* v. *Hemisphere Shipping Co. Ltd. (The Wenjiang)* [1981] 2 Lloyd's Rep. 308; *Portaria Shipping Co.* v. *Gulf Pacific Navigation Co. Ltd. (The Selene G)* [1981] 2 Lloyd's Rep. 180. A summary of the approach of Robert Goff J. is also included in the speech of Lord Diplock in *Pioneer Shipping Ltd. and Others* v. *B.T.P. Tioxide Ltd. (The Nema)* [1982] A.C. 724, 739.

5.1.2 The House of Lords in *The Nema*[4a] was of one voice in rejecting this approach. It erroneously focused on section 1(4) and failed to pay sufficient regard to the general discretion arising under section 1(3)(b), by virtue of which it is open to the court to refuse leave absolutely.[5] An implied and central purpose of the 1979 Act was to promote greater finality in arbitral awards than hitherto had been the case and this required the adoption of much stricter criteria than those previously applied in relation to the special case procedure and which were enunciated in *The Lysland*.[6] Further, the approach of Robert Goff J. did nothing to avoid the procedural manipulation which had been notorious in the era of the special case procedure and which had produced such unsatisfactory results.[7]

5.1.3 In *The Nema* the central emphasis in the speech of Lord Diplock was on the discretion inherent in section 1(3)(b) and the policy of the legislature, divinable from the first four sections of the Act, which was perceived as moving the law towards the greater recognition of the finality of awards in matters of legal determination and away from meticulous legal accuracy. Lord Diplock defined the fundamental position of a judge exercising the discretion under section 1(3)(b) in the following terms[8]:

The judicial discretion conferred by sub-s. (3)(b) to refuse leave to appeal from an arbitrator's award in the face of an objection by any of the parties to the reference is in terms unfettered; but it must be exercised judicially; and this, in the case of a dispute that parties have agreed to submit to arbitration, involves deciding between the rival merits of assured finality on the one hand and upon the other the resolution of doubts as to the accuracy of the legal reasoning followed by the arbitrator in the course of arriving at his award, having regard in that assessment to the nature and circumstances of the particular dispute.

5.1.4 The function of the judge in holding the balance between arbitral finality and meticulous legal accuracy is not in itself a wholly new theme. The significance of the 1979 Act is that it tilts the jurisprudential balance towards finality and to a corresponding degree sacrifices legal accuracy. The judge therefore comes initially to his task against the backdrop of the new statutory posture, wherein the finality of awards, even with regard to questions of law, is promoted; where the exercise of the associated discretion is based on much more restrictive criteria than those adopted in the pre-1979 Act era; and where by necessary implication a substantial standard of proof is imposed upon applicants who seek to persuade the court that it should give leave to appeal. Lord Diplock developed the fundamental approach, its implications and evidentiary basis in the following terms[9]:

In weighing the rival merits of finality and meticulous legal accuracy there are, in my view, several indications in the Act itself of a parliamentary intention to give effect to the turn of the tide in favour of finality in arbitral awards (particularly in non-domestic arbitrations of which the instant case is one), at any rate where this does not involve exposing arbitrators to a temptation to depart from "settled principles of law".

4a. *Pioneer Shipping Ltd.* v. *B.T.P. Tioxide Ltd. (The Nema)* [1982] A.C. 724.
5. *Ibid.* p. 739.
6. *Ibid.* p. 742. For a statement of the criteria enunciated in *Halfdan Greig & Co. A/S* v. *Sterling Coal & Navigation Corporation (The Lysland)* [1973] Q.B. 843 (C.A.), see Chapter 1, para. 1.4.2.8.
7. *Ibid.* pp. 745–746 per Lord Roskill.
8. *Ibid.* p. 739.
9. *Ibid.* pp. 739–740.

And later[10]:

In view of the cumulative effect of all these indications of Parliament's intention to promote greater finality in arbitral awards than was being achieved under the previous procedure as it was applied in practice, it would, in my view, defeat the main purpose of the first four sections of the Act if Judges when determining whether a case was one in which the new discretion to grant leave to appeal should be exercised in favour of an applicant against objection by any other party to the reference, did not apply much stricter criteria than those stated in *The Lysland* which used to be applied in exercising the former discretion to require an arbitrator to state a special case for the opinion of the Court.

5.1.5 In *The Antaios* Lord Diplock perpetuated the same theme and in the context of a dispute of law concerning the construction of a contract perceived the legislative intention underlying the 1979 Act[11]:

. . . to promote speedy finality in arbitral awards rather than that insistence upon meticulous semantic and syntactical analysis of the words which businessmen happen to have chosen to express the bargain made between them, the meaning of which is technically, though hardly commonsensically, classified in English jurisprudence as a pure question of law.

5.1.6 Although the upshot of this approach is greatly to restrict the possibility of appeals from awards on questions of law, particularly when compared with the pre-1979 Act law, it obviously does not take the law to the opposite extreme of barring appeals completely. To the contrary it recognises that there will arise cases where it will be appropriate to maintain a measure of control over the legal decisions of arbitral tribunals.[12] It is the balance which has been adjusted by the 1979 Act and in weighing the competing claims of finality and legal accuracy Lord Diplock in *The Nema* indicated that a judge must have regard to "the nature and circumstances of the particular dispute",[13] which are now to be assessed in the context of the new ambience established by the 1979 Act. The kind of considerations that may assume a significance under this prescription have been substantially developed by the House of Lords in *The Nema* and later endorsed and in part further elaborated in *The Antaios*, and thereafter further developed by the decisions of lower courts.[14] The emergent criteria have become widely identified as *The Nema/Antaios* guidelines, and are considered in detail later in the text.[15] The guidelines are a manifestation of the fundamental approach as here defined, for they reveal how that approach may operate in particular circumstances often encountered in practice. They are consequently of subordinate importance and care is necessary to avoid ascribing to the guidelines an elevation and prominence such as to result in the fundamental approach established in connection with the general discretion to give or refuse leave to appeal being displaced or lost sight of.[16]

5.1.7 It is a necessary incident of what is here identified as the fundamental approach that the finality of an award will be protected and leave refused where the

10. *Ibid.* p. 742. See also *Retla Steamship Co.* v. *Gryphon Shipping Co. S.A. etc. (The Evimeria)* [1982] 1 Lloyd's Rep. 55, 57, 58, per Staughton J.
11. *Antaios Compania Naviera S.A.* v. *Salen Rederierna A.B. (The Antaios)* [1985] 1 A.C. 191, 199.
12. *Alfred C. Toepfer Schiffahrtsgesellschaft G.m.b.H* v. *Tossa Marine Co. Ltd. (The Derby)* [1985] 2 Lloyd's Rep. 325, 333, per Kerr L.J.
13. *Supra*, p. 739.
14. See *infra* and Chapter 6.
15. *Infra*, para. 5.2.
16. *Aden Refinery Co. Ltd.* v. *Ugland Management Co. Ltd. (The Ugland Obo One)* [1987] 1 Q.B. 650, 667–668, per Mustill L.J. See also *infra*, para. 5.3.

bona fides of an applicant is justifiably doubted, as where the court is satisfied that the appeal process is being used to manufacture delay or otherwise misused.

The approach which has been adopted towards the exercise of the discretion arising under section 1(3)(b) has the consequence of rendering the judiciary reluctant to give leave to appeal, with such leave granted only in a relatively limited number of cases.[17] Judges consider applications with the "utmost caution",[18] and Lord Jauncy has summarised the position in the following terms: "section 1 of the 1979 Act contemplates that judicial review of arbitration awards shall take place only in limited circumstances."[19]

5.2 THE NEMA/ANTAIOS GUIDELINES

5.2.1 Introduction

5.2.1.1 The observations that derive from the two House of Lords decisions in *The Nema*[1] and *The Antaios*[2] relating to the manner a judge of the High Court ought to approach the exercise of his discretion on an application for leave to appeal under section 1(3)(b) have come to be universally referred to as *The Nema/Antaios* guidelines. The guidelines are in effect an enunciation of the kinds of factors and prevailing circumstances that may be taken into account and weighed upon in deciding whether the discretion to grant or refuse leave to appeal should be exercised in favour of or against the applicant. They recognise and apply to identified categories of situations the kinds of relevant considerations which derive from the fundamental tenet of policy developed by Lord Diplock in *The Nema*, wherein the general policy of finality is entwined with the nature and circumstances of particular disputes.[2a] The guidelines, however, are not comprehensive and many situations arise which are outside their compass.[2b] Their status as guidelines, distinct from firm and immutable rules, must also not be forgotten. Nor is their relationship to the perceived fundamental policy associated with the 1979 Act and the central test it evokes to be lost sight of.[3] The guidelines are evocations of fundamental policy: they do not replace it. Although the two decisions of the House of Lords in *The Nema* and *The Antaios* are of supreme importance, an appreciation of the global legal position also demands an elaboration of the way the Court of Appeal and the judges at first instance have perceived, construed, developed and applied *The Nema/Antaios* guidelines. Of particular note is the judgment of Parker J. in *The Kerman*.[4]

5.2.1.2 In their substance and in general terms *The Nema/Antaios* guidelines

---

17. *Uni-Ocean Lines Pte. Ltd.* v. *C-Trade S.A. (The Lucille)* [1984] 1 Lloyd's Rep. 244, 245 (C.A.); *C.A. Venezolana de Navegacion* v. *Bank Line Ltd. (The Roachbank)* [1988] 2 Lloyd's Rep. 337, 341 (C.A.); *Seaworld Ocean Line Co. S.A.* v. *Catseye Maritime Co. Ltd. (The Kelaniya)* [1989] 1 Lloyd's Rep. 30, 32 (C.A.).

18. *Everglade Maritime Inc.* v. *Schiffahrtsgesellschaft Detlef von Appen m.b.H. (The Maria)* [1993] 3 All E.R. 748, 754, Sir Thomas Bingham M.R.

19. *Geogas S.A.* v. *Trammo Gas Ltd. (The Baleares)* [1991] 2 Lloyd's Rep. 318, 321 (H.L.).

1. *Supra.*

2. *Supra.*

2a. *Supra*, para. 5.1.6.

2b. See Chapter 6.

3. See, in particular, *infra*, para. 5.3.

4. *B.V.S. S.A. and Another* v. *Kerman Shipping Co. S.A. (The Kerman)* [1982] 1 W.L.R. 166.

emphasise the significance of the circumstances in which an arbitration has arisen; the provisional assessment by the judge of the correctness or otherwise of the decision of the arbitrator[5]; the nature of the question of law in issue and whether its significance is confined to the arbitrating parties or is of wider interest; the distinction between pure questions of law and questions of mixed fact and law and lastly the factual circumstances in which a question of law has arisen for determination.

In the result it may be necessary for a judge to pose to himself different tests as may be appropriate to the different types of cases out of which an application for leave to appeal may arise.[6] Although the guidelines focus materially on the question of law in issue, the emphasis is not wholly in this direction. Special circumstances extraneous to the merits of the point of law in issue may assume a significance.[7] The guidelines make no pretence to be exhaustive and within them there is an ever attendant allowance that on the facts and circumstances of individual cases there may exist special considerations.[8]

The Nema/Antaios guidelines would appear to lend themselves to the following categorisation.

5.2.2 Circumstances appertaining to the reference to arbitration

5.2.2.1 In determining whether or not to grant leave to appeal the court may have regard to the general circumstances surrounding the reference of the dispute to arbitration, and in particular the expectation the parties held out for the arbitration.

In *The Nema*[1] the particular circumstance of material relevance was that the parties to the dispute that had arisen in the context of a consecutive voyage charterparty wished and sought from the reference of the dispute to arbitration a speedy decision so that they might know what were their contractual rights and obligations for the remainder of a particular phase of the contract. To facilitate this process the original arbitration agreement was amended so as to permit the dispute to be referred to a single and experienced London maritime arbitrator. The House of Lords considered that this in itself represented, independently of the other considerations in the case, an overwhelming reason why leave should not have been granted. Lord Diplock made the point in the following terms[2]:

The dispute submitted to the arbitration of a London maritime arbitrator of great experience arose between charterers and owners under a consecutive voyage charter-party . . .

It is sufficient for my purpose to mention that the reason why the parties submitted the dispute to speedy arbitration was that they wanted to know, not later than the end of September 1979, how they then stood as respects the employment of the chartered vessel, the *Nema*, during the remainder of the 1979 Saint Lawrence River open water season at the loading port under the charter, Sorel, in the Province of Quebec. Was she, as the charterers claimed, bound to proceed forthwith from Spain, where she then lay, to Sorel and wait there at the owners' expense

---

5. *Italmare Shipping Co.* v. *Ocean Tanker Co. Inc. (The Rio Sun)* [1982] 1 W.L.R. 158, 165, per Lord Denning M.R., "When we have before us an application for leave to appeal, we often take a provisional view as to the correctness of the decision below. It is one of the factors for consideration." See also *Bunge A.G.* v. *Sesotrad S.A. (The Alkeos C)* [1984] 1 Lloyd's Rep. 687, 689.

6. *Antaios Compania Naviera S.A.* v. *Salen Rederierna A.B. (The Antaios)* [1985] A.C. 191, 206.

7. *B.V.S. S.A. and Another* v. *Kerman Shipping Co. S.A. (The Kerman), supra,* p. 171.

8. See *infra*, para. 5.2.7.

1. *Supra.*

2. *Supra*, pp. 734–735. For a subsequent application of the principle see *National Rumour Compania S.A.* v. *Lloyd-Libra Navegacao S.A.* [1982] 1 Lloyd's Rep. 472, 474.

until either the strike at Sorel ended and she could be loaded, or the end of the open water season had made loading impossible, whichever should first occur? Or, as the owners claimed, had their contractual obligation to perform any further voyages in the 1979 open water season been dissolved by frustration?

. . . the particular circumstances in which the parties wanted a quick decision as to where they stood as respects the future employment of the *Nema* are, no doubt, exceptional. In my view, they are in themselves sufficient to make a grant of leave to appeal from the arbitrator's award under section 1 of the Arbitration Act 1979 an unjudicial exercise of the discretion conferred upon the judge by that section.

5.2.2.2 The same view had been held by the three judges at first instance, including two of the then most experienced commercial judges, who had heard three contested interlocutory applications in the matter before application for leave to appeal had been sought.[3] In the Court of Appeal Lord Denning M.R., after reflection, also appears to have come to hold the same opinion and further to consider that where parties in the prevailing context have made it plain that they desire speedy arbitration, leave to appeal should normally be refused even though both parties had also requested a reasoned award.[4]

5.2.2.3 In *The Kerman*[5] Parker J. in following the prescribed guideline also emphasised that the circumstances surrounding a reference to arbitration may function not only to suggest the refusal of leave to appeal, but to the converse also that leave ought to be granted. The learned judge observed[6]:

It is plain that where the parties have sought and obtained a quick decision by arbitration in order to determine their future conduct, as opposed to seeking relief in respect of events long past, that fact alone will normally result in leave being refused: [citing *The Nema, supra*]. Thus, when considering an application for leave to appeal, it is clear that the court can and should consider not merely the reasoned award itself but the circumstances leading up to it. In [*The Nema*] case such circumstances were regarded as requiring, of themselves, a refusal of leave. But, clearly, such circumstances may also point the other way. In [*The Rio Sun, infra*] for example, the majority took the view that the circumstances in which the arbitrator had come to make a reasoned award were significantly in favour of granting leave.

5.2.2.4 The dictum helps to illuminate the meaning of "circumstance" in the present context and appears to render it clear that the concept is not inseverably associated with speedy arbitration. Any circumstances surrounding the reference of a dispute and the making of an award which is capable of providing evidence of the state of mind and desire of the parties, as to the finality or otherwise of the award may assume a relevance.[7] In *The Rio Sun*[8] a request for a reasoned award was in the cir-

3. Mocatta J., Donaldson J. and Mars-Jones J. For a survey of the early contested interlocutory application see *The Nema, supra*, p. 735 per Lord Diplock and p. 748 per Lord Roskill. Lord Diplock there states that Mocatta J. was of the opinion "that in the circumstances in which the arbitration had arisen the way in which any judge would exercise his discretion would be to refuse leave to appeal from the arbitrator's award when his reasons had been given, even though the judge might have doubts as to the correctness of the arbitrator's reasons for his conclusions on any question of law involved". On the application for leave to appeal Robert Goff J. took an opposing view, see [1980] 1 Lloyd's Rep. 519.

4. *B.T.P. Tioxide Ltd.* v. *Pioneer Shipping Ltd. and Armada Marine S.A.* (*The Nema*) [1980] 2 Lloyd's Rep. 339, 343–344 (C.A.).

5. *B.V.S. S.A. and Another* v. *Kerman Shipping Co. S.A.* (*The Kerman*) [1982] 1 W.L.R. 166.

6. *Ibid.* pp. 169–170.

7. Cf. *Astro Valiente Compania Naviera S.A.* v. *The Government of Pakistan Ministry of Food and Agriculture* (*The Emmanuel Colocotronis*) (*No. 1*) [1982] 1 Lloyd's Rep. 297, 300.

8. *Italmare Shipping Co.* v. *Ocean Tanker Co. Inc.* (*The Rio Sun*) [1982] 1 W.L.R. 158, 162, per Lord Denning M.R.

cumstances of the case interpreted as a denial of the finality of the award and a recognition of the prospect of an appeal. As such it was a circumstance suggesting that leave to appeal ought to be granted. Lord Denning M.R. commented,[9] "Seeing that the owners asked for a reasoned award, it is plain that they wanted to have recourse to the courts, if the award went against them." On the other hand, in *The Kerman*[10] action by the parties changing the composition and character of the arbitration tribunal from that of a trade arbitration tribunal to a tribunal composed of an experienced and eminent Queen's Counsel acting as a sole arbitrator was viewed as being indicative of an intention that the award should be final.[11] The change had been effected in pursuance of the recognition by the parties that the points in dispute were pure legal issues which required no special commercial expertise or knowledge. The arbitration in the case antedated the introduction of the 1979 Act but the parties nonetheless agreed, as they were entitled, that the new legislation should apply.[12] This resulted in the abandonment of a request that the award be stated as a special case and a request was made for a reasoned award. In total this was interpreted as indicating that the claimants were content to accept the arbitrator's award as final.[13]

5.2.2.5 The extent to which the request or absence of any request for a reasoned award may be meaningfully interpreted as illuminating of the intention of the parties as to the finality or potential appealability of an award must be open to serious doubt. It has already been seen that in *The Rio Sun*[14] the request for reasons was grasped upon and interpreted by Lord Denning M.R. as indicating a denial of finality.[15] On the facts of the case this might well appear a bold inference. But, this point apart, it would certainly be dangerous to utilise the case to support any general principle or even *prima facie* presumption. Reasons have always been a question of contract or practice; but following the enactment of the 1979 Act a reasoned award may be secured by judicial order; and following a unilateral request for reasons it is the *prima facie* duty of the arbitrator to respond positively. Moreover the 1979 Act has changed the whole mood of the law and the making of reasoned awards is now greatly encouraged. Nor are reasons to be associated inseverably with appeals, for reasons also serve the purpose of explaining to the parties why they won or lost.[16] It has also been earlier observed that a request for a reasoned award does not necessarily detract from the implication of finality where the parties manifest an intention to participate in speedy arbitration.[17] Accordingly it would seem to be against the policy of the 1979 Act to create a situation wherein a party can only obtain a reasoned award at the cost of placing at risk the finality of the award. It may therefore be best to treat the request or failure to request a reasoned award as a neutral circumstance, unless there are present

---

9. *Ibid.* p. 162.
10. *Supra.*
11. *Supra*, p. 174 per Parker J.
12. See Chapter 1, para. 1.7.1.
13. *Supra*, p. 174 per Parker J. On the facts of the case this appears a bold inference. With equal cogency an inference to the contrary might also have been made, with the parties revealing no more than a contentment to replace the old special case procedure with the new appellate procedure under the 1979 Act.
14. *Supra.*
15. See also *Astro Valiente Compania Naviera S.A.* v. *The Government of Pakistan Ministry of Food and Agriculture (The Emmanuel Colocotronis) (No. 1)* [1982] 1 Lloyd's Rep. 297, 300.
16. The various points here made are discussed further in Chapter 11.
17. *Supra*, n. 4.

other circumstances which in association and additionally are capable of manifesting a particular intention.

5.2.2.6 Given the fact that a court may take into account the circumstances surrounding a reference to arbitration and the making of an award in determining an application for leave to appeal, it would seem to follow that as a matter of good practice arbitrators should give careful consideration to including in their awards factual information indicating the circumstances in which the dispute arose and was referred to arbitration. But at the same time there is no suggestion that evidence of surrounding circumstances is deducible solely from the award; it may be established by extraneous evidence.

5.2.3 Construction of "one-off" contracts and contractual clauses

5.2.3.1 In commerce and in many other spheres a vast number of questions of law arise in connection with the construction of contracts and contractual terms. When this is the case and a question of leave to appeal comes into issue the judicial discretion may be exercised differently according to whether in the first place[1] the question of construction arises in the context of a "one-off" contract or clause, or that of a standard form contract or clause.

Where what is in issue is the construction of a "one-off" contract or clause it would appear that the discretion is to be strictly applied and leave to appeal normally refused unless the judge is satisfied that the construction given by the arbitrator is obviously wrong. In *The Nema*[2] the charterparty contract was viewed by the House of Lords as a clear illustration of a "one-off" contract and therefore the question whether the charterparty was an entire or divisible contract, which was a question of law that turned on the proper construction of the contract, would have fallen within the instant category had any question of leave to appeal been before the court. Lord Diplock explained the approach to be adopted with regard to a question of law involving a question of "one-off" construction in the following terms[3]:

Where, as in the instant case, a question of law involved in the construction of a "one-off" clause the application of which to the particular facts of the case is an issue in the arbitration, leave should not normally be given unless it is apparent to the judge upon a mere perusal of the reasoned award itself without the benefit of adversarial argument, that the meaning ascribed to the clause by the arbitrator is obviously wrong. But if on such perusal it appears to the judge that it is possible that argument might persuade him, despite first impression to the contrary, that the arbitrator might be right, he should not grant leave; the parties should be left to accept, for better or for worse, the decision of the tribunal that they had chosen to decide the matter in the first instance. The instant case was clearly one in which there was more than one possible view as to the meaning of the "one-off" clause as it affected the issue of divisibility. It is in my view typical of the sort of case in which leave to appeal on a question of construction ought not to be granted.

5.2.3.2 The key phrase in the context of the instant category is "obviously wrong", for *prima facie* only when a judge so concludes should he give leave to appeal.[4] Other

---

1. See *infra* for other relevant considerations which may be taken into account.
2. *Pioneer Shipping Ltd. and Others* v. *B.T.P. Tioxide Ltd. (The Nema)* [1982] A.C. 724.
3. *Ibid* pp. 742–743.
4. *Kansa General Insurance Co. Ltd.* v. *Bishopsgate Insurance plc* [1988] 1 Lloyd's Rep. 503, 511, Hirst J. (first instance): *Geogas S.A.* v. *Trammo Gas Ltd. (The Baleares)* [1991] 2 All E.R. 110, 116, Dillon L.J. (C.A.).

judges have used such phrases as "clearly wrong"[5] or "it does not look right to me",[6] or "plainly wrong".[7] If on the other hand a judge is satisfied that the view taken by the arbitrator is obviously or clearly right, or is probably right, or is likely to be right or might or may be right, or there is a fifty-fifty chance that the arbitrator is right,[8] then *prima facie* the application for leave to appeal should be refused. Sir John Donaldson M.R. has indicated that "[u]nder *The Nema* guidelines in the case of a 'one-off' contractual clause, judges are advised to refuse leave to appeal if they consider that the arbitrator might have been right".[9] In *The Antaios*[10] Lord Diplock rephrased the *prima facie* test and presented it in the following terms, "whether the arbitrator was in the judge's view so obviously wrong as to preclude the possibility that he might be right".

5.2.3.3 But it is quite clearly not the case with regard to the construction of a "one-off" contract or clause that leave to appeal should *never* be given unless the judge is satisfied that the arbitrator is obviously wrong. The rule enunciated is to the effect that leave should not *normally* be given.[11] In consequence recognition is given to the possible existence of exceptional circumstances that may justify a departure from the *prima facie* rule.[12] But equally any such departure is likely to be very rare and conceded only in exceptional circumstances. Where an arbitral award decides a dispute as to the proper construction of one-off contractual words, it would appear that the arbitral decision will be virtually unassailable in the absence of evidence of patent error.[13]

5.2.3.4 The rationale underlying the instant categorisation and the associated judicial attitude to the question of discretion was further explained by Lord Diplock in *The Nema* in the following language[14]:

In the case of a "one-off contract" where the exact combination of words and phrases that fall to be construed has not only never been used before and so did not possess an already established meaning of which each party was entitled to assume the other knew when he entered into the contract, but is also unlikely to be used in future by any other parties, it is not self-evident that an arbitrator or arbitral tribunal chosen by the parties for his or their experience and knowledge of the commercial background and usages of the trade in which the dispute arises, is less competent to ascertain the mutual intentions of the parties than a judge of the Commercial Court, a Court of Appeal of three Lords Justices or even an Appellate Committee of five Lords of Appeal in Ordinary. A lawyer nurtured in a jurisdiction that did not owe its origin to the common law of England would not regard it as a question of law at all. This, I believe, was all that

---

5. *Reardon Smith Line Ltd.* v. *Sanko Steamship Co. Ltd. (The Sanko Honour)* [1985] 1 Lloyd's Rep. 418, 421–422, per Hobhouse J.

6. *Italmare Shipping Co.* v. *Ocean Tanker Co. Inc. (The Rio Sun)* [1982] 1 W.L.R. 158, 165, per Griffiths L.J.

7. *Seaworld Ocean Line Co. S.A.* v. *Catseye Maritime Co. Ltd. (The Kelaniya)* [1989] 1 Lloyd's Rep. 30, 32, per Lord Donaldson M.R.

8. See, for example, *Marrealeza Compania Naviera S.A.* v. *Tradax Export S.A. (The Nichos A.)* [1982] 1 Lloyd's Rep. 52, 54.

9. *Aden Refinery Co. Ltd.* v. *Ugland Management Co. Ltd. (The Ugland Obo One)* [1987] 1 Q.B. 650, 659.

10. *Antaios Compania Naviera S.A.* v. *Salen Rederierna A.B.* [1985] A.C. 191, 206.

11. See *infra*, para. 5.2.7.

12. See *infra*, paras. 5.2.7 and 5.3.

13. *Tropwood A.G. of Zug* v. *Jade Enterprises Ltd. (The Tropwind)* [1982] 1 Lloyd's Rep. 232, 239, per Dunn L.J., "under the 1979 Act, this being a 'one-off' clause, their finding would be virtually conclusive".

14. *Supra*, p. 736. See also *Seaworld Ocean Line Co. S.A.* v. *Catseye Maritime Co. Ltd. (The Kelaniya)* [1989] 1 Lloyd's Rep. 30, 32, per Lord Donaldson M.R.

Lord Denning M.R. meant to convey by his vivid, if somewhat less than tactful, phrase: "On such a clause, the arbitrator is just as likely to be right as the judge—probably more likely".[15]

To this it may be added that to bring the question of construction before the court would in all probability make no contribution to the development, comprehensiveness and certainty of English commercial law. Furthermore, "one-off" contracts will often belong to those categories of contracts with regard to which pre-dispute or pre-arbitral commencement exclusion agreements may be validly executed.[16]

5.2.3.5 In summary, applying the present guideline to the facts in *The Nema* it would appear that the following reasoning would have prevailed had other considerations not been present. The question of the divisibility of the contract was an issue that turned on the construction of the contract and in particular on certain of the contractual clauses. Further, the question arose in the context of "one-off" clauses in a "one-off" contract and in consequence the determination of the question of construction was independent of precedent and would make no contribution to the future conduct of commercial relations or the development of English commercial law. The question of construction was reasonably open to more than one possible solution and that adopted by the arbitrator could not be said to be "obviously wrong". In these circumstances the appointed arbitral tribunal was as competent as any grade of judge to determine the proper construction of the contract and therefore the case was not a suitable one for giving leave to appeal.

5.2.3.6 In *The Kerman*[17] Parker J., whilst adopting and applying the guideline, also considered it necessary to refine the adopted linguistic formulation so as to recognise the realities of practice and judicial predilection. In the first place Lord Diplock had contemplated that the question of leave would be determined "upon a mere perusal of the reasoned award itself without the benefit of adversarial argument",[18] whereas in practice an application for leave is by originating motion to a judge in chambers and the situation is therefore necessarily one in which the judge will reach his conclusion after argument, albeit brief. The provisional determination of the judge is in consequence arrived at following a perusal of the reasoned award and the hearing of argument; and if after that the judge reaches the provisional view that the arbitrator is clearly wrong he should not refuse leave to appeal merely because he had not formed that view prior to argument.[19] Lord Diplock also contemplated that whatever the first impression of the judge, if he nonetheless regarded it as possible that he might be persuaded by argument that the arbitrator might be right he should not grant leave to appeal. Of this Parker J. considered that "[i]t must be rarely, if ever, that a judge can exclude the possibility that he might be persuaded that an arbitrator might be right. It may be that he considers it unlikely, but it appears to me that such a possibility must nearly always exist. On this basis, no one would ever get leave in a 'one-off' case in the absence of special circumstances, and I cannot think that this is what the House of Lords intended".[20] Where, therefore, the judge after hearing argument forms the pro-

---

15. *Pioneer Shipping Ltd. and Another* v. *B.T.P. Tioxide Ltd. (The Nema)* [1980] 1 Q.B. 547, 564 (C.A.).
16. Considered in Chapter 13.
17. *B.V.S. S.A. and Another* v. *Kerman Shipping Co. S.A. (The Kerman)* [1982] 1 W.L.R. 166.
18. *Supra*, n. 3.
19. *Supra*, p. 170.
20. *Supra*, pp. 170–171.

visional view that the arbitrator was wrong, leave to appeal should not be refused merely because the judge thinks it possible that he might be persuaded by further argument that the arbitrator might be right. These necessary qualifications, which were endorsed by the House of Lords in *The Antaios*,[21] together with the approach taken by the Court of Appeal in *The Rio Sun*,[22] led Parker J. to reformulate the effect of the guideline in the following terms[23]:

(a) that in a "one-off" case, in the absence of special circumstances, leave should not be given unless on the conclusion of argument on the application for leave the court has formed the provisional view that the arbitrator was wrong and considers that it would need a great deal of convincing that he was right, (b) that if the court does form such a view then, again in the absence of special circumstances, leave should be granted.

5.2.3.7 A difficulty with the present guideline, and it is a problem associated with *The Nema/Antaios* guidelines as a whole, is the question of characterisation. What precisely is meant by a "one-off" contract or contractual clause and how are the boundaries of the "one-off" concept to be delineated? Is the category to be understood as something very precise, with clearly identifiable parameters; or is it to be comprehended as a more amorphous phenomenon? The essential contrast is with a standard form contract and it is therefore natural that much of the energy exerted in endeavouring to come to an understanding should focus on the central differences between the two general forms of contract.

5.2.3.8 In its purest form a "one-off" contract is one negotiated, drafted and agreed to *de novo* to accommodate the personal positions of the parties in the circumstance of the particular transaction they have entered into. As such it is tailor-made and unique. It has no wider application beyond the particular parties and their respective positions. This appears to be the approach adopted by Lord Diplock in *The Nema*,[24] where the learned judge perceived a "one-off contract" to be one "where the exact combination of words and phrases that fall to be construed has not only never been used before and so did not possess an already established meaning of which each party was entitled to assume the other knew when he entered into the contract, but is also unlikely to be used in future by any other parties . . . ". Lord Diplock further said of the charterparty before the House of Lords that "the terms of the charter-party and its addenda that are relevant to the disputed issue of frustration are unique; it is almost inconceivable that they will be found again in any other charter".[25]

5.2.3.9 But the facts and speeches in *The Nema* also illustrate that to fall within the characterisation of a "one-off contract" a contract need not be wholly novel and original in its conception, design and drafting. A contract may be "one-off" notwithstanding that its basis is a standard form contract, if it has received substantial amendments and/or additions to meet the particular needs and expectations of the parties.[26] The

---

21. *Supra*.
22. *Italmare Shipping Co.* v. *Ocean Tanker Co. Inc. (The Rio Sun)* [1982] 1 W.L.R. 158.
23. *Ibid*. p. 171. See also *Jamil Line for Trading and Shipping Ltd.* v. *Atlanta Handelsgesellschaft Harder & Co. (The Marko Polo)* [1982] 1 Lloyd's Rep. 481.
24. *Supra*, p. 736.
25. *Supra*, p. 735.
26. Cf. *Petroleo Brasileiro S/A etc.* v. *Elounda Shipping Co. (The Evanthia M)* [1985] 2 Lloyd's Rep. 154, 157.

practice of modifying standard form contracts is widespread in commerce and it is notorious that the exercise is often carelessly done, and in consequence produces difficult and on occasions almost impossible questions of construction. But it is equally clear that not every amendment, qualification, deletion or addition is capable of converting a standard form contract into a "one-off contract".[27] It is ultimately a question of degree, and where the line is to be drawn may on occasions give rise to difficult questions. In the final analysis all will turn on the facts and circumstances of individual cases. A general test may be to ask whether the amendments, additions and the like have had the effect of materially altering the character and function of the standard form contract, so that any wider interest in the contract and its judicial construction ceases to exist.[28] This was plainly the case in *The Nema*. The parties had used as the basis of their agreement a standard form, C (Ore) 7, a form designed for use for a single voyage, and then made substantial amendments and additions so as to render it applicable to a multi-voyage engagement. Lord Roskill considered the amendments and additions to be sufficiently substantial that the finished product well justified the characterisation "one-off".[29]

5.2.3.10 Nor will it necessarily be the case that a contract will be incapable of being characterised as "one-off" by virtue of the fact that it incorporates what may be described as some standard contractual terms. Although again in each case it will be a question of degree, the mere existence of some standard clauses will not result in what is primarily a "one-off contract" losing its dominant identity. The charterparty contract in *The Nema* probably retained some of the standard clauses of the otherwise amended standard form contract which formed the basis of the agreement between the owners and charterers.

5.2.3.11 A further problem is to define the precise basis of this particular guideline. In his speech Lord Diplock variously refers to "one-off" *contracts* and *clauses*. On the facts in *The Nema* this does not offer any difficulty, for the charterparty was treated as a "one-off" contract with "one-off" clauses. But they are nonetheless distinct concepts and their interchangeable use does produce uncertainty. In its purest form a "one-off" contract will contain "one-off" clauses. But there does not exist an inevitable association between the characterisation of a contract as an entire whole and that of its individual parts. To characterise a contract as "one-off" or as a "standard form contract" does not have the automatic consequence that all of its component terms will be similarly characterised. A "one-off contract" may contain standard contractual clauses and contrariwise a "standard form contract" may contain "one-off" clauses. In the latter case the mere existence of a "one-off" clause or clauses will not necessarily operate to change the basic characterisation of the wider contract. There is nothing unprincipled in describing a contract as a standard form with some "one-off" clauses. But where this is the case and the construction of a "one-off" clause is in

---

27. Cf. *Seaworld Ocean Line Co. S.A.* v. *Catseye Maritime Co. Ltd. (The Kelaniya)* [1989] 1 Lloyd's Rep. 30.

28. *Ibid.*

29. *Supra*, p. 746 per Lord Roskill, "The parties used a standard form, C (Ore) 7, as the basis of their agreement but since that form is designed for use for a single voyage it naturally required, and indeed received, substantial amendment and addition; so much so that the finished product well justifies the application of . . . Lord Diplock's word, 'one-off'."

issue, it is submitted that the instant guideline prevails.[30] In other words it is suggested that the "one-off" characterisation applies both to entire contracts and to contractual terms.[31] Each is a "one-off case", which is another phrase used by Lord Diplock in *The Nema*.[32] What falls to be characterised in each case is the part or parts of the contract relevant to the disputed issue or issues of construction.

5.2.3.12 Although there is a generally understood difference between a "one-off" and a standard form contract, it is a difference which is not always a simple matter to apply to the facts of particular situations; nor in practice is it invariably a choice between two distinct alternatives. Rather than representing an either/or question, the position may assume more the circumstance of a spectrum with contracts and contractual clauses being characterised not on the basis that they fall clearly into either extreme alternative, but by virtue that they incline more greatly in one direction than the other.[33] So also the uniqueness of a "one-off" contractual provision will not necessarily preclude a generic interest. A clause which by virtue of its drafting clearly falls to be characterised as "one-off", may nonetheless represent a variant of a class of clause frequently incorporated into contracts generally or in relation to specific kinds of contracts, and with the consequence that the response of the courts to the particular clause may be by analogy with the wider interest.[34]

5.2.3.13 Confronted with an awkward question of characterisation it is submitted that the more beneficial and rewarding approach is not to embark on the exercise by first attempting an all-embracing definition of a one-off contract or contractual term, but by emphasising the underlying rationale associated with the characterisation. The essence of the one-off concept in relation to contracts and contractual terms is that it raises an issue of concern which is confined to the particular contracting parties and "in which the general market and the commercial fraternity has no interest".[35] It is a "question of a singular character unlikely to recur".[36] It is this associated philosophy which calls for initial emphasis, so that the threshold question comes to be framed not in terms seeking a meaning of the phrase "one-off" when used in relation to contracts, but as an enquiry into the degree of interest in the resolution of the contractual dispute in issue.

---

30. Cf. *Jamil Line for Trading and Shipping Ltd.* v. *Atlanta Handelsgesellschaft Harder & Co. (The Marko Polo)* [1982] 1 Lloyd's Rep. 481. See also *International Sea Tankers Inc.* v. *Hemisphere Shipping Co. Ltd. (The Wenjiang)* [1982] 1 Lloyd's Rep. 128, 131, per Lord Denning M.R., "The Judge should look to see if it is a 'one-off' case. It may be 'one-off' . . . because it is a point of construction of a clause singular to this case which is not likely to be repeated."

31. *Phoenix Shipping Corporation* v. *Apex Shipping Corporation (The Apex)* [1982] 1 Lloyd's Rep. 476, 479, per Bingham J., "the issue turns on a clause designed by the parties to the contract to suit their own special circumstances, being a clause unlikely to be used by any other parties".

32. *Supra*, p. 735. See also *infra*, para. 5.2.6.

33. *Phoenix Shipping Corporation* v. *Apex Shipping Corporation (The Apex)*, *supra*. See also *Astro Valiente Compania Naviera S.A.* v. *The Government of Pakistan Ministry of Food and Agriculture (The Emmanuel Colocotronis) (No. 1)* [1982] 1 Lloyd's Rep. 297, 300; *Marrealeza Compania Naviera S.A.* v. *Tradax Export S.A. (The Nichos A)* [1982] 1 Lloyd's Rep. 52, 54.

34. Cf. *Babanaft International Co. S.A.* v. *Avant Petroleum Inc. (The Oltenia)* [1982] 1 Lloyd's Rep. 448; [1982] 2 Lloyd's Rep. 99 (C.A.), where at p. 107 Sir John Donaldson M.R. treats the clause in question as "one-off" and proceeds to comment, "It was a one-off clause even if there are other clauses in circulation bearing a family relationship."

35. *Seaworld Ocean Line Co. S.A.* v. *Catseye Maritime Co. Ltd. (The Kelaniya)* [1989] 1 Lloyd's Rep. 30, 32, Lord Donaldson of Lymington M.R.

36. *Stinnes Interoil G.m.b.H.* v. *A. Halcoussis & Co. (The Yanxilas)* [1982] 2 Lloyd's Rep. 445, 447, per Bingham J.

5.2.3.14 To summarise: when a disputed question of law assumes the character of a question of construction of a one-off contract or contractual term and the parties are content to refer the question of law to the decision of an arbitrator, there is a strong presumption that the decision of the arbitrator shall be final and immune from judicial intervention. The court will not lightly substitute its own determination for that given by the appointed arbitrator. In this circumstance the maxim that referring parties take their arbitrator for better or for worse assumes a more literal truth than it generally enjoys in arbitral law, and there is a near parallel as between questions of fact and law. But at the same moment the arbitrator is not elevated to the position of the ultimate arbiter. There are limits, and although hesitant to intervene the court will protect against patent error, and also support the demands of justice when warranted by exceptional circumstances.

5.2.4 Construction of standard form contracts and standard contractual clauses

5.2.4.1 When a question of law relates to the construction of a standard form contract or a standard contractual clause different and less stringent considerations apply to the exercise of judicial discretion. Such contractual provisions have by virtue of their convenience and efficiency an established place in commercial practice and in adopting standard terms the parties expect that they will receive a consistent construction by both the courts and arbitrators.[1] Any question of construction is not therefore of sole interest to the immediate contracting parties. By virtue of their wide relevance and usage there arises a general or sectional interest in the construction given to standard forms or terms. Uniformity of construction contributes also to the certainty of commercial relations and as a beneficial incident of their regular consideration by the judiciary there often develops a comprehensive and certain body of commercial law about the principal standard forms. The question of their construction therefore is not one to be left to arbitrators, even experienced and specialist arbitrators, without at least some cautious reserve, and the courts are therefore more ready to entertain a question of law relating to the construction of a standard form contract or term than a "one-off" contract or term, notwithstanding the initial reference to arbitration.

Lord Diplock in *The Nema* explained the approach to be adopted in the exercise of the section 1(3)(b) discretion when the relevant question of law appertained to the construction of a standard form contract or standard contractual term in the following terms[2]:

. . . rather less strict criteria are in my view appropriate where questions of construction of contracts in standard terms are concerned. That there should be as high a degree of legal certainty as it is practicable to obtain as to how such terms apply upon the occurrence of events of a

---

1. See, *The Annefield* [1971] P. 168, 183, per Lord Denning M.R., "Once a court has put a construction on commercial documents in standard form, commercial men act upon it. It should be followed in all subsequent cases." *Skips A/S Nordheim and Others* v. *Syrian Petroleum Co. Ltd. and Petrofina S.A. (The Varenna)* [1983] 2 Lloyd's Rep. 592, 597, per Oliver L.J., "What does seem to me important is that documents in use and containing familiar expressions which have a well-established meaning among commercial lawyers should be consistently construed and that a well-established meaning, particularly as regards something like an arbitration agreement where clarity and certainty are important to both parties, should not be departed from in the absence of compulsive surrounding circumstances or a context which is strongly suggestive of some other meaning." See also *Federal Bulk Carriers Inc.* v. *C. Itoh & Co. Ltd. and Others, (The Federal Bulker)* [1989] 1 Lloyd's Rep. 103 (C.A.).
2. *Pioneer Shipping Ltd. and Others* v. *B.T.P. Tioxide Ltd. (The Nema)* [1982] A.C. 724, 743.

kind that it is not unlikely may reproduce themselves in similar transactions between other parties engaged in the same trade, is a public interest that is recognised by the Act particularly in section 4. So, if the decision of the question of construction in the circumstances of the particular case would add significantly to the clarity and certainty of English commercial law it would be proper to give leave in a case sufficiently substantial to escape the ban imposed by the first part of section 1(4) bearing in mind always that a superabundance of citable judicial decisions arising out of slightly different facts is calculated to hinder rather than to promote clarity in settled principles of commercial law. But leave should not be given even in such a case, unless the judge considered that a strong prima facie case had been made out that the arbitrator had been wrong in his construction; . . .

5.2.4.2 The broader rationalisation underlying the guideline was expressed by Lord Diplock in the following terms[3]:

. . . when contracts are entered into which incorporate standard terms it is in the interests alike of justice and of the conduct of commercial transactions that those standard terms should be construed and treated by arbitrators as giving rise to similar legal rights and obligations in all arbitrations in which the events have given rise to the dispute do not differ from one another in some relevant respect. It is only if parties to commercial contracts can rely upon a uniform construction being given to standard terms that they can prudently incorporate them in their contracts without the need for detailed negotiation or discussion. Such uniform construction of standard terms had been progressively established up to 1979, largely through decisions of the courts upon special cases stated by arbitrators. In the result English commercial law has achieved a degree of comprehensiveness and certainty that has made it acceptable for adoption as the appropriate proper law to be applied to commercial contracts wherever made by parties of whatever nationality. So, in relation to disputes involving standard terms in commercial contracts an authoritative ruling of the court as to their construction which is binding also upon all arbitrators under the sanction of an appeal from an award of an arbitrator that has resulted from his departing from that ruling performs a useful function that is lacking in that performed by the court in substituting for the opinion of an experienced commercial arbitrator its own opinion as to the application of a "one-off" clause to the particular facts of a particular case.

5.2.4.3 The guideline was affirmed by the House of Lords in *The Antaios*.[4] In the upshot a less guarded approach is adopted in relation to standard form contracts and terms than is the case in relation to "one-off" contracts and terms; and with the courts more ready to substitute their own determination for that of the appointed arbitrator.[5] Distilled to its essence the instant guideline would appear to demand that the judge be satisfied as to two cumulative considerations before being prepared to consider giving leave to appeal. First, the judge must be satisfied that the resolution of the question of construction would add significantly to the clarity, certainty and comprehensiveness of English commercial law; and secondly,[6] when so satisfied, that there is

---

3. *Ibid.* pp. 737–738.
4. *Antaios Compania Naviera S.A.* v. *Salen Rederierna A.B.* [1985] A.C. 191, 203, per Lord Diplock. See also *Home and Overseas Insurance Co. Ltd.* v. *Mentor Insurance Co. (UK) Ltd.* [1989] 1 Lloyd's Rep. 473, 486, per Parker L.J. (C.A.); *Geogas S.A.* v. *Trammo Gas Ltd. (The Baleares)* [1991] 2 All E.R. 110, 116, per Dillon L.J.
5. *Kansa General Insurance Co. Ltd.* v. *Bishopsgate Insurance plc* [1988] 1 Lloyd's Rep. 503, 511, per Hirst J., "It is well settled as a result of the decision of the House of Lords in *The Nema* . . . that, where the case turns on the construction of a standard term, leave should not be given unless the Judge considers a strong *prima facie* case has been made out that the arbitrator was wrong in his construction, and that in one-off cases the much higher burden of showing that the arbitrators were obviously wrong is applicable." See also *Kodros Shipping Corp.* v. *Empresa Cubana De Fletas (The Evia) (No. 2)* [1982] 2 Lloyd's Rep. 307; *Charles E. Ford Ltd.* v. *AFEC Inc.* [1986] 2 Lloyd's Rep. 307; *Oriental Maritime Pte. Ltd.* v. *Ministry of Food Government of the People's Republic of Bangladesh (The Silva Plana)* [1989] 2 Lloyd's Rep. 371.
6. The two elements of the test are cumulative, see *Marrealeza Compania Naviera S.A.* v. *Tradax Export S.A. (The Nichos A)* [1982] 1 Lloyd's Rep. 52, 53–54.

strong *prima facie* evidence that the arbitrator has gone wrong in his construction.[7] When the first requirement is not satisfied, the guideline appropriate to "one-off" contracts and clauses would appear *prima facie* to apply.[8] The guideline is again one which is normally to apply and in consequence may be displaced in the face of special circumstances.[9]

5.2.4.4 This two-step approach would seem to be endorsed by the way in which the guideline has been judicially formulated in subsequent authorities. In *The Kerman* Parker J. phrased the guideline in the following words[10]:

. . . even if the decision on the question of construction in the circumstances of the particular case would add significantly to the clarity and certainty of English commercial law, leave should not be given unless the judge considers that a strong prima facie case that the arbitrator was wrong has been made out.

In *The Ugland Obo One* Sir John Donaldson M.R. expressed his understanding of the guideline in the following terms[11]:

In the case of standard terms . . . [Judges] are advised to apply rather less strict criteria, taking account of whether or not a decision on the question or questions of law would add significantly to the clarity and certainty of English commercial law. But even then the advice is that leave to appeal should be refused, unless the Judge considers that a strong *prima facie* case has been made out that the arbitrator has been wrong in his construction.

5.2.4.5 The potential contribution that the resolution of a question of law by the court may make to the comprehensiveness, completeness and certainty of English commercial law will in each case be a question of judgment for the judge taking the application for leave. Where a widely used but judicially little considered standard contract or term comes forward to be construed it may be thought that the question will be readily satisfied. But new and novel questions of construction may continue to arise even with regard to those standard form contracts with which the judiciary have become familiar by virtue of the regularity with which they come before the courts and again in such cases a ready affirmative answer may be anticipated to the question.[12] The potential contribution of a judicial pronouncement may be heightened when the void left by the absence of authority is accompanied by a difference of view in the mar-

---

7. *Tor Line A.B.* v. *Alltrans Group of Canada Ltd. (The TFL Prosperity)* [1982] 1 Lloyd's Rep. 617, 626, per Bingham J., "The question arises on a standard clause in a form that has been in use for a long time and which is much used. The clause has been considered by the Courts on a number of occasions, but never with reference to precisely the present point. The importance of the answer to the question goes well beyond the immediate interests of these parties and is of general importance to the shipping community. It is not in the public interest that there should be doubt on the point, and it is the sort of point on which the authoritative ruling of the Courts is desirable if the comprehensiveness and certainty of English commercial law are to be maintained. In such a situation it is incumbent upon the owners to make out a strong *prima facie* case that the umpire was wrong in his conclusion. I am satisfied that they have done so. Accordingly I give leave to appeal." See also *Portunus Navigation Co. Inc.* v. *Avin Chartering S.A. (The World Prestige)* [1982] 1 Lloyd's Rep. 60; *Clea Shipping Corporation* v. *Bulk Oil International Ltd. (The Alaskan Trader)* [1983] 1 Lloyd's Rep. 315.
8. *Marrealeza Compania Naviera S.A.* v. *Tradax Export S.A. (The Nichos A)*, *supra*, p. 54.
9. See *infra*, para. 5.2.7.
10. *B.V.S. S.A. and Another* v. *Kerman Shipping Co. S.A. (The Kerman)* [1982] 1 W.L.R. 166, 171.
11. *Aden Refinery Co. Ltd.* v. *Ugland Management Co. Ltd. (The Ugland Obo One)* [1987] 1 Q.B. 650, 659.
12. See, for example, *Belcore Maritime Corporation* v. *F. Lli. Moretti Cereali S.p.A. (The Mastro Giorgis)* [1983] 2 Lloyd's Rep. 66.

ket as to the effect of a contract or certain of its clauses.[13] The opposite conclusion may have its claim when the question of construction is already decided by authority, or the decision of the arbitrator conforms with the understanding and expectation of the commercial community or when the standard form in question has only a very restricted or limited use and operates at the periphery of commerce or any other field of activity. But in evaluating the potential benefit of a new precedent, regard must also be had to Lord Diplock's admonition that a superabundance of authority established on a platform of similar facts may hinder rather than promote the clear evolution of English commercial law.[13a]

5.2.4.6 As for the assessment of the correctness of the decision of an arbitrator, the vital test is that leave should not be given unless the judge is satisfied that a strong *prima facie* case has been made out that the arbitrator is wrong in the construction he has adopted.[14] If to the contrary the judge is satisfied that the arbitrator is right or is probably right or at the very least there is a strong *prima facie* case that the arbitrator is right then normally leave ought to be refused,[15] notwithstanding that an appeal to the court might otherwise contribute beneficially to the development of English commercial law. The evaluative test is clearly less strict than that applicable to "one-off" contracts and clauses[16] but otherwise raises difficulties as to its precise meaning. What precisely is meant by a strong *prima facie* case? In the present context any attempt at a precise abstract definition would in all probability be both inappropriate and unrewarding.

The essential gist of the adopted test would appear to be that the applicant must satisfy the judge that there exists a real possibility that the arbitrator has gone wrong in his construction of the standard form contract or term. Given the policy of the 1979 Act, it would appear that the test must be more restrictive than that enunciated in *The Lysland* in relation to the former special case procedure[17]; and it is therefore not satisfied merely by establishing that the question of law is open to serious argument.[18] In terms of pitch the test seems to aim at a position somewhere between that adopted under the preceding law and that adopted under the new law in relation to "one-off" contracts and terms. Any assessment of the correctness of the arbitral decision must of necessity be provisional and arrived at following a perusal of the reasoned award and the hearing of brief argument.[19]

5.2.4.7 The two considerations inherent in the guideline under consideration are, however, not necessarily mutually exclusive. Factors may at the same moment touch both on the clarity and certainty of English commercial law and influence the task of arriving at a provisional assessment of the correctness of the arbitrator's decision. An uncertain legal background to the relevant question of law, such as conflicting judicial decisions or dicta would appear to provide an illustration. The existence of such a

---

13. Cf. *Linnett Bay Shipping Co. Ltd.* v. *Patraicos Gulf Shipping Co. S.A. (The Al Tawfiq)* [1984] 2 Lloyd's Rep. 598, 599 per Lloyd J.

13a. *Supra*, n. 2.

14. *Supra*, para. 5.2.4.3.

15. *Aden Refinery Co. Ltd.* v. *Ugland Management Co. Ltd. (The Ugland Obo One)*, *supra*, p. 656, per Sir John Donaldson M.R., reproducing the reasons of Leggatt J. in refusing the original application for leave. See also *Coral Navigation Inc.* v. *Avin Chartering J.A. (The Kwai)* [1981] 2 Lloyd's Rep. 563.

16. *B.V.S. S.A. and Another* v. *Kerman Shipping Co. S.A. (The Kerman)*, *supra*, p. 172.

17. See Chapter 1, para. 1.4.2.8.

18. *B.V.S. S.A. and Another* v. *Kerman Shipping Co. S.A. (The Kerman)*, *supra*, p. 172.

19. *Ibid.*

legal matrix may well operate to introduce uncertainty into the law and also make the task of the judge in arriving at a provisional assessment of the decision of the arbitrator particularly more difficult, if not impossible. The approach that is to prevail when standard form contracts or standard terms fall to be construed against the backdrop of a conflictive legal matrix was elaborated upon by Lord Diplock in *The Antaios* and in whose speech a very precise distinction is made between conflicting judicial decisions and dicta[20]:

> I think that your Lordships should take this opportunity of affirming that the guideline given in *The Nema* [1982] A.C. 724, 743 that even in a case that turns on the construction of a standard term, "leave should not be given . . . unless the judge considered that a strong prima facie case had been made out that the arbitrator had been wrong in his construction," applies even though there may be dicta in other reported cases at first instance which suggest that upon some question of the construction of that standard term there may among commercial judges be two schools of thought. I am confining myself to conflicting dicta not decisions. If there are conflicting decisions, the judge should give leave to appeal to the High Court, and whatever judge hears the appeal should in accordance with the decision that he favours give leave to appeal from his decision to the Court of Appeal with the appropriate certificate under section 1(7) as to the general public importance of the question to which it relates; for only thus can be attained that desirable degree of certainty in English commercial law which section 1(4) of the Act of 1979 was designed to preserve.
>
> Decisions are one thing; dicta are quite another. In the first place they are persuasive only, their persuasive strength depending upon the professional reputation of the judge who voiced them. In the second place, the fact that there can only be found in dicta but no conflicting decisions on the meaning of particular words or phrases appearing in the language used in a standard term in a commercial contract, especially if, like the N.Y.P.E. withdrawal clause, it has been in common use for very many years, suggests either that a choice between the rival meanings of those particular words or phrases that are espoused by the conflicting dicta is not one which has been found in practice to have consequences of sufficient commercial importance to justify the cost of litigating the matter; or that business men who enter into contracts containing that standard term share a common understanding as to what those particular words and phrases were intended by them to mean.
>
> . . . I do not agree with Sir John Donaldson M.R. [1983] 1 W.L.R. 1362, 1369H–1370B where in the instant case he says that leave should be given under section 1(3)(*b*) to appeal to the High Court on a question of construction of a standard term upon which it can be shown that there are two schools of thought among puisne judges where the conflict of judicial opinion appears in the dicta only. This would not normally provide a reason for departing from *The Nema* guideline [1982] A.C. 724 which I have repeated earlier in this speech.

Reduced to its essence, Lord Diplock is asserting that where a question of law relating to the construction of a standard contract or term arises against the background of conflicting judicial decisions, the judge should give leave to appeal. However, where the context reveals nothing beyond conflicting judicial dicta, the established guideline applies without any special qualification. But again the approach is not presented in absolute terms. The existence of conflicting judicial dicta will not *normally* provide a reason for departing from the principal guideline[21]: but in the special circumstances of any particular case it may.

5.2.4.8 The reassertion of the applicability of the principal guideline notwithstanding the existence of conflicting judicial dicta was subsequently followed by the Court of Appeal in *The Ugland Obo One*, and where Sir John Donaldson M.R. formulated

---

20. *Antaios Compania Naviera S.A.* v. *Salen Rederierna A.B. (The Antaios)* [1985] A.C. 191, 203–204.
21. *Ibid*. p. 204.

the principle which was to apply where there existed conflicting judicial decisions in the following terms[22]:

Where there are conflicting decisions at first instance, a judge should give favourable consideration, in an appropriate case, to giving leave to appeal if, but only if, he is of the view that it was a proper case for the High Court not only to add another judicial decision, but, having done so, to grant a certificate and leave to appeal to this Court [i.e. the Court of Appeal] under s. 1(7) of the 1979 Act. It is not in the interests of arbitrators or the commercial community that a situation should be allowed to continue in which there are conflicting decisions, each of which binds all commercial arbitrators.

5.2.4.9 The Master of the Rolls was further of the opinion that the same principle applied when there exist conflicting arbitral decisions[23]:

What was not considered in *The Antaios* was a situation in which there are no judicial decisions at first instance, but there are conflicting decisions by arbitrators. Since no arbitrator's decision binds any other arbitrator, the same reasoning would apply mutatis mutandis and in my judgment a Judge should in such a case give favourable consideration to granting leave to appeal to the High Court, but not necessarily beyond that Court, in order that there might be a decision binding all arbitrators and producing uniformity of decisions by all arbitrators.

It would seem that direct evidence of conflicting arbitral awards need not be brought before the court, a requirement which might be difficult to fulfil in practice and which might also challenge the traditional privacy of the arbitral process. The Master of the Rolls considered that it would be sufficient if arbitrators in their award (or possibly otherwise) indicated that the award raised a question on which it is well known that there was a division of view between arbitrators operating in a particular field of commerce or otherwise, coupled with a plea that the matter be resolved by the court. In this kind of circumstance it was open to the court to infer the existence of conflicting arbitral decisions.[24]

5.2.4.10 The approach pursued by Lord Diplock makes much of the distinction between judicial decisions and dicta. The distinction and its effect are well understood but the reasons advanced for its introduction into the guidelines governing the exercise of the discretion under section 1(3)(b) are unconvincing. The point is excessively technical and even unreal, particularly in the context of commercial arbitration. Also judicial dicta cannot be dismissed with too ready an alacrity, for they have in the history of the law been the basis for many important strands of legal development. Indeed *The Nema* guidelines when first formulated by the House of Lords were themselves in strictness dicta but this was never perceived as a ground for undermining their authority or circumventing their effect.[25] But on a more pragmatic plane it is difficult to accept that conflicting dicta are less productive of uncertainty than conflicting decisions. Each in its own way may generate uncertainty. What differs is the manner in which a judge or arbitrator will assess and relate technically to the sources of the uncertainty. But in the ultimate what would appear to be of overriding importance is the determination that uncertainty exists by virtue of the attributes of the prevailing legal matrix, whatever the technical nature of the attributes.[26]

---

22. *Aden Refinery Co. Ltd.* v. *Ugland Management Co. Ltd. (The Ugland Obo One)*, *supra*, p. 661.
23. *Ibid.* p. 341.
24. *Ibid.* p. 341.
25. See *infra*, para. 5.3.
26. See Thomas, "*The Antaios—The Nema* Guidelines Reconsidered", [1985] J.B.L. 200.

5.2.4.11 It is important not to lose sight of the reason why the distinction between decisions and dicta is made. In itself it is not the determinant for giving or refusing leave to appeal. More precisely it governs the approach to the question. Where there are conflicting dicta the principal guideline applies without qualification. In other words the judge must be satisfied that a strong *prima facie* case has been established that the arbitrator was wrong and that to give leave would result in a decision which would make a significant contribution to the clarity and certainty of English law. The latter consideration in the circumstances would appear to be readily satisfied but the former still allows the judge to make a provisional assessment of the correctness of the arbitral decision and to refuse leave if he considers, notwithstanding the background of the case, that the arbitrator is probably right. But where there exist conflicting decisions the judge must more readily give leave to appeal although the precise situation is uncertain. In *The Antaios* Lord Diplock was of the opinion that if there are conflicting decisions "the judge should give leave to appeal".[27] The "should" of a Law Lord can readily become the "must" of first tier judges and with the discretion effectively overridden. Alternatively it may be that the existence of conflicting decisions in itself provides evidence that satisfies the criteria of the principal guideline, and the role of the judge is in consequence effectively usurped by the facts that confront him. In contrast, Sir John Donaldson M.R. in *The Ugland Obo One* used less peremptory language, albeit dicta, and appears to preserve to the judge some degree of discretion. Where there exist conflicting decisions the Master of the Rolls considered the judge "should give favourable consideration, in an appropriate case, to giving leave to appeal"[28] and then only if the judge was also satisfied that it was a proper case not only for the High Court but also the Court of Appeal to consider. If this represents the right approach and the judge retains some discretion then it would seem that the reason for drawing the distinction between decisions and dicta is substantially diluted. But it may be doubted if the language of the Master of the Rolls accurately echoes the much firmer and uncompromising proposition enunciated by Lord Diplock.

5.2.4.12 The enunciation of Lord Diplock is probably to be construed in the context of his speech in *The Nema* as a whole and with the consequence, it is suggested, that it is to be understood as being to the effect that a judge "should *normally* give leave to appeal", thus creating a firm pointer to the appropriate judicial response, but preserving a discretion to decide otherwise in special circumstances.

5.2.4.13 The question and problem of characterisation again arises with regard to the present guideline. What is meant by a standard form contract in the context of the guideline? There is also the associated question whether the guideline extends beyond the clear case of a standard form with standard terms to include standard contractual terms in isolation and so equally apply to the construction of standard terms incorporated into a "one-off" contract or any other form of contract not capable of being characterised as a standard form.

The traditional understanding of a standard form contract is that of a pre-prepared contract, invariably in printed form, which the parties adopt either directly by signing (whether in person or through agents) or indirectly by incorporation by reference or

---

27. *Supra*, p. 204.
28. *Supra*, p. 341.

some other mode of adoption. They are often prepared and published by professional and trading organisations as part of a service provided either generally or to specific groups with the object of facilitating commercial and other forms of exchange and activity. Such standard form contracts will often possess a significant mutual character, for they will have been settled after consultation with all potential interested users of the form. Standard form contracts are also prepared and used by major suppliers of goods and services out of personal convenience and to give a clear definition to their own contractual position, which is to a substantial degree incapable of renegotiation. These contracts are strongly unilateral and frequently operate as contracts of adhesion, for the other contracting party is provided with no real opportunity to contribute to the contracting process and effectively has no alternative but to contract on the terms proffered or to go without. In contemplating standard form contracts in *The Nema* Lord Diplock appears to have had the former category primarily in mind[29]:

The great majority of international maritime and commercial contracts which contain a London arbitration clause, and typically those falling within the categories of disputes in respect of which it is, at least for the time being, forbidden by section 4 of the Arbitration Act 1979 to enter into an "exclusion agreement" covering disputes that have not already arisen, are made on standard printed forms on which the particulars appropriate to the contract between the actual parties are inserted, and any amendments needed for reasons special to the particular contract are either made to the printed clauses or dealt with in added clauses, which sometimes may themselves be classified as standard. Business on the Baltic, the insurance market and the commodity markets would be impracticable without the use of standard terms to deal with what are to be the legal rights and obligations of the parties upon the happening of a whole variety of events which experience has shown are liable to occur, even though it be only rarely, in the course of the performance of contracts of those kinds.

5.2.4.14 It must be doubtful that the distinction between mutual and unilateral standard forms will assume a material significance for present purposes.[30] It would seem that each category will be within the aegis of the instant guideline, although in practice most standard forms that come forward to be construed by the Commercial Court will reflect the prevailing prevalence of arbitration in those areas of commerce where mutual standard forms prevail. What would appear to be important is not the precise characterisation of the standard form contract but its currency and popularity, for such considerations will be of crucial significance in determining the wider interest in any judicial pronouncement on the proper construction of the standard form and the extent the pronouncement will contribute to the clarity and certainty of English law.[31] But even in this regard a distinction may be possible between commercial and non-commercial matters, for it is English commercial law that is perceived principally as the commodity vying for acceptance within the international commercial community. Of course, viewed strictly, the question of characterisation is not directly associated with matters of currency, usage and popularity. A standard form contract is no less standard merely because it has fallen into disuse or is little used. But these very

---

29. *Supra*, pp. 736–737.
30. For an elaboration of the two general categories of standard form contracts, see *Schroder Music Publishing Co. Ltd.* v. *Macaulay* [1974] 3 All E.R. 616, 624, Lord Diplock.
31. *Phoenix Shipping Corporation* v. *Apex Shipping Corporation (The Apex)* [1982] 1 Lloyd's Rep. 476, 479, per Bingham J., "it is clear that a case is not to be regarded as 'one-off' if it is dealing with a standard clause in a contract because then the proper construction of that clause is a question of interest to all users".

same factors are crucial in determining the wider interest in the judicial construction of the contract and the potential contribution any decision may make to the development of English commercial law, and in consequence may justify the adoption of the more stringent test applied to "one-off" contractual provisions.[32]

5.2.4.15 Again there is every reason for believing that the instant guideline applies both to standard forms and to standard contractual terms. In many instances the distinction will be immaterial for the standard form will incorporate standard terms.[33] But terms may be added to a standard form and as Lord Diplock recognised in his speech in *The Nema*, these also may be regarded as standard terms.[34] For a clause to fall within the characterisation "standard" it is not essential that it appear in every contract in the precise same language and format. It is sufficient if the clause belongs to a type which frequently appears in certain kinds of contracts, albeit that the precise language adopted may vary, although not with any substantial consequence when determining the intention of the contracting parties.[35] But added clauses do not automatically assume the characterisation of the wider contract and such clauses may equally be "one-off" in character.[36] All will turn on the substance of the added clause, its history and association with the wider contract. Equally it is possible for a printed standard form contract or term to change its characterisation to a "one-off" contract or term by virtue of its amendment by the parties. It will in each case be a question of degree whether a particular amendment or cluster of amendments effect a change in characterisation of the contract as a whole or any contractual term. Contrariwise it would appear possible for standard terms incorporated into a "one-off" contract to retain their character as standard contractual terms provided they are capable of existing independently and their construction is not coloured by the new contractual environment.

5.2.4.16 In determining whether a question of construction falls within or outside the instant guideline, it is again suggested that the emphasis should not focus on an attempt to establish a technical definition of a standard contract or contractual provision, but should be directed to the philosophy underlying the guideline. To ponder the attributes of an acceptable definition may well be both vexing and unrewarding; but the same is not true of an enquiry into the potential significance of the issue of con-

---

32. *Marrealeza Compania Naviera S.A.* v. *Tradax Export S.A. (The Nichos A)* [1982] 1 Lloyd's Rep. 52, 54.

33. As in *Aden Refinery Co. Ltd.* v. *Ugland Management Co. Ltd. (The Ugland Obo One)*, *supra*, where the construction of a printed clause in the Asbantankvoy form was in issue.

34. *Supra* p. 737. See also *Italmare Shipping Co.* v. *Ocean Tanker Co. Inc. (The Rio Sun)* [1982] 1 W.L.R. 158 where an anti-technicality clause typed as an additional clause to the printed clauses of the New York Produce Exchange time charterparty was treated as a standard term clause: *D/S A/S Idaho* v. *Colossus Maritime S.A. (The Concordia Fjord)* [1984] 1 Lloyd's Rep. 385, 386, per Bingham J., "I approach this matter on the basis that although a typewritten clause, and in that sense strictly one-off, this is, nonetheless, a clause of a kind which, with one variant or another, is to be found in very many charter-parties and therefore I do not think that it would be right to approach the matter as if it were of no interest other than to the particular parties to this dispute."

35. *Phoenix Shipping Co.* v. *Apex Shipping Corpn. (The Apex)* [1982] 2 Lloyd's Rep. 407.

36. See, for example, *Lakeport Navigation Co. Panama S.A.* v. *Anonima Petroli Italiana S.p.A. (The Olympic Brilliance)* [1981] 2 Lloyd's Rep. 176, 178, where Parker J. comments with regard to a typed clause incorporated into a charterparty, "In the present case the special clause, which is a typed clause, and was clearly introduced for the purpose of this particular venture, changes the position of the parties, at least to some extent, from that which would have prevailed had there been no such clause."

struction in question. The more beneficial approach appears to be to pose the question whether the question of construction is of interest to the contracting parties alone or whether the potential interest extends beyond the immediate contracting parties to the community at large or to a determinable section of the community.[37]

5.2.4.17 To summarise: where the question of law relates to the construction of a standard form contract or standard contractual clause, leave to appeal will not normally be given unless a strong *prima facie* case can be established showing that the arbitrator has fallen into error. The discretion is less stringently applied than is the case in relation to "one-off" questions of contractual construction and with the court more ready to intervene and substitute its own determination. The lower standard is justified by reference to the wider interest in the issue of law in question and by the opportunity it offers to establish a new precedent contributing to the comprehensiveness, clarity and efficacy of English commercial law. The lower test is therefore preconditioned not simply by reference to a standard case of contractual construction, but also on the court being satisfied as to the contributive potential of the decision it is being called upon to make. Where the latter quality is absent, the same test applies as in the case of one-off issues of contractual construction. If the question of construction arises against the backdrop of conflicting judicial decisions, then the desirability of promoting certainty in the English system of commercial law means that leave to appeal will invariably be given.

5.2.5 Questions of mixed fact and law and analogous legal questions

5.2.5.1 Questions of construction, whether of standard form or one-off contracts and contractual clauses, raise pure questions of law. However, many of the important questions of law that frequently arise in practice do not share this pure quality but further possess a substantial interrelated factual element, and with the exercise of a judgment by the decision-maker also frequently called into existence. Such questions of law are variously characterised as questions of mixed fact and law and as conclusions of law. The basis and features of these particular characterisations have been discussed earlier in the text and questions of frustration, waiver, estoppel, causation and remoteness provide classical illustrations of the kinds of questions of law that fall within the characterisation.[1]

5.2.5.2 In *The Nema*[2] the particular question of mixed fact and law in issue was whether a divisible part of a consecutive voyage charterparty had been frustrated by the delay and changed circumstance brought about by a strike at the loading port. Confronted with an application for leave to appeal from the decision of an arbitrator

---

37. See for example, *Tor Line A.B.* v. *Alltrans Group of Canada Ltd. (The TFL Prosperity)* [1982] 1 Lloyd's Rep. 617, 626, per Bingham J., "the question goes well beyond the immediate interests of these parties and is of general interest to the shipping community". *Stinnes Interoil G.m.b.H.* v. *Halcoussis & Co. (The Yanxilas)* [1982] 2 Lloyd's Rep. 445, 457, per Bingham J., "The next question I must consider is whether I should consider these grounds as raising questions of general commercial significance or as questions of a singular character unlikely to recur." See also *Phoenix Shipping Co.* v. *Apex Shipping Corpn. (The Apex)* [1982] 2 Lloyd's Rep. 407.
1. Chapter 3, para. 3.2.4.
2. *Pioneer Shipping Ltd. and Others* v. *B.T.P. Tioxide Ltd. (The Nema)* [1982] A.C. 724.

with regard to such a question of law, Lord Diplock laid down the following guide-line[3]:

> In deciding how to exercise his discretion whether to give leave to appeal under section 1(2) what the judge should normally ask himself in this type of arbitration, particularly where the events relied upon are "one-off" events, is not whether he agrees with the decision reached by the arbitrator, but: does it appear upon perusal of the award either that the arbitrator misdirected himself in law or that his decision was such that no reasonable arbitrator could reach?

The same approach had been adopted by Lord Denning M.R. in the Court of Appeal.[4]

5.2.5.3 In *The Rio Sun*[5] the issue concerned the waiver of a right under an anti-technicality clause in a time charterparty to 48 hours notice before the owner could withdraw the vessel for non-payment of hire. The circumstances surrounding the alleged waiver were not perceived as being "one-off", but even if they were assumed to be so, Griffiths L.J. nonetheless considered that leave to appeal would still have been given. The learned judge commented *obiter dictum*[6]:

> . . . even treating this as a "one-off" case, my immediate reaction to the finding of waiver is one of very considerable surprise. It is undesirable at this stage that I should say more than that I should take a very great deal of persuading that the facts of this case justified a finding of waiver. At the moment it does not look right to me; and that, as I understand *The Nema*, is itself a sufficient reason for giving leave even in a "one-off" case.

5.2.5.4 The dictum of Lord Diplock in *The Nema* again requires refinement to correspond with procedural realities. The provisional view of the judge is arrived at not solely following a perusal of the award, but also after the benefit of brief argument. Further, the guideline enunciated has been interpreted as being applicable only to "one-off" cases.[7] This led Parker J. in *The Kerman*[8] to conclude that the test which operates within the guideline must be the same as in "one-off" contract construction cases. The learned judge expressed the opinion[9]:

> Leave should not be given unless the court, on the conclusion of argument, (a) reaches a provisional view that the arbitrator has applied the wrong test or, if no test is disclosed, that no reasonable arbitrator applying the right test could have reached such a conclusion and (b) is of the opinion that it would take a great deal of convincing to the contrary. If the court does reach such a firm provisional view then leave should be given.

Where the question of law arises in the context of a standard case, then the operative test is adjusted to correspond with standard form contract construction cases.[10]

5.2.5.5 This particular guideline follows the general principle laid down by the House of Lords in *Edwards* v. *Bairstow*[11] governing the approach of reviewing and appellate courts when the decisions of tribunals and lower courts are challenged for

---

3. *Ibid*. p. 744.
4. [1980] Q.B. 547, 566.
5. *Italmare Shipping Co.* v. *Ocean Tanker Co. Inc. (The Rio Sun)* [1982] 1 W.L.R. 158.
6. *Ibid*. p. 165.
7. See *infra*, para. 5.2.6.
8. *B.V.S. S.A. and Another* v. *Kerman Shipping Co. S.A. (The Kerman)* [1982] 1 W.L.R. 166.
9. *Ibid*. p. 172.
10. See *infra*, para. 5.2.6.
11. [1956] A.C. 14, 36 per Lord Radcliffe. See also *Uni-Ocean Lines Pte. Ltd.* v. *C-Trade S.A. (The Lucille)* [1984] 1 Lloyd's Rep. 244, 246–247, per Kerr L.J. Also Chapter 8, para. 8.6.

error of law.[12] The rationality of the guideline is that with such issues as contractual frustration, although they raise questions of law the evidentiary basis of the doctrine turns on questions of fact and degree, commercial usage and the understandings of commercial men.[13] It is these latter characteristics that so often renders the doctrine of frustration exceptionally difficult to apply in practice. Whether changed and unforeseen circumstances render performance or further performance of a contract radically or fundamentally different from that contemplated when the contract was entered into is in itself often a question of innate difficulty, to be determined ultimately by reference to the construction of the contract in question and on the facts and circumstances of individual cases. With regard to this and like questions different opinions may not unreasonably be held by different decision-makers.[14] It follows that where law and fact are closely intertwined an arbitration tribunal is as competent as any other to confront and determine the issues, and may even be better positioned where the parties have appointed a specialist tribunal, with expertise and experience in the realm of the dispute referred. In these circumstances a court will be very reluctant to substitute its own decision for that of the tribunal appointed by the parties,[15] and will only do so in exceptional circumstances.[16] Provided the arbitration tribunal has directed itself properly on the relevant law, its decision on the assessment and effect of the facts will normally be accepted unless perverse or otherwise wholly unsupportable.[17]

5.2.5.6 The instant guideline has emerged and been developed substantially in the context of the doctrine of contractual frustration but the approach embodied in the guideline is equally applicable to all questions of law that may be characterised as questions of mixed fact and law or conclusions of law; and also to analogous questions of law, however characterised. In *The Nema* Lord Diplock considered the guideline to be equally applicable to the question whether a party to a commercial contract is entitled to treat a breach as a repudiation of the contract.[18] To this example may be added others, such as legal questions and issues relating to waiver,[19] estoppel,[20]

12. In this regard in *Pioneer Shipping Ltd. and Another* v. *B.T.P. Tioxide Ltd. (The Nema)* [1980] 1 Q.B. 547, 567, Lord Denning M.R. considered "[a]n arbitrator in the City of London is a specialist tribunal".
13. *Tsakiroglou & Co. Ltd.* v. *Noblee Thorl G.m.b.H.* [1962] A.C. 93, 124, per Lord Radcliffe. *The Nema, supra,* p. 752, per Lord Roskill. See also *Congimex Compania Geral De Comercio Importadora E Exportadora S.A.R.L.* v. *Tradax Export S.A.* [1981] 2 Lloyd's Rep. 687.
14. *The Nema, supra,* p. 752, per Lord Roskill.
15. *International Sea Tankers Inc.* v. *Hemisphere Shipping Co. Ltd. (The Wenjiang) (No. 2)* [1983] 1 Lloyd's Rep. 400, 402; *Cobec Brazilian Trading and Warehousing Corpn.* v. *Alfred C. Toepfer* [1983] 2 Lloyd's Rep. 386, 390; *Uni-Ocean Lines Pte. Ltd.* v. *C-Trade S.A. (The Lucille)* [1984] 1 Lloyd's Rep. 244, 246.
16. *Federal Commerce & Navigation Ltd.* v. *Suisse-Atlantique Société D'Armement S.A. (The Cruzeiro do Sul)* [1982] 2 Lloyd's Rep. 110, 111, per Kerr L.J.
17. *Kodros Shipping Corpn.* v. *Empresa Cubana de Fletes (The Evia) (No. 2)* [1981] 1 Lloyd's Rep. 613; [1982] 1 Lloyd's Rep. 334 (C.A.); [1982] 2 Lloyd's Rep. 307 (H.L.); *International Sea Tankers Inc.* v. *Hemisphere Shipping Co. Ltd. (The Wenjiang) (No. 2)* [1981] 2 Lloyd's Rep. 308; [1982] 1 Lloyd's Rep. 128 (C.A.); [1983] 1 Lloyd's Rep. 400 (H.L.); *André & Cie S.A.* v. *Tradax Export S.A.* [1983] 1 Lloyd's Rep. 254 (C.A.); *Vinava Shipping Co. Ltd.* v. *Finelvet A.G. (The Chrysalis)* [1983] 1 Lloyd's Rep. 503; *Uni-Ocean Lines Pte. Ltd.* v. *C-Trade S.A. (The Lucille)* [1984] 1 Lloyd's Rep. 244 (C.A.); *Glafki Shipping Co. S.A.* v. *Pinios Shipping Co. No. 1 (The Maira) (No. 2)* [1985] 1 Lloyd's Rep. 300, 311 (C.A.).
18. *Supra* pp. 743–744. See also *Compagnie General Maritime* v. *Diakan Spirit S.A. (The Ymnos)* [1982] 2 Lloyd's Rep. 574, 586–587.
19. Cf. *Bunge S.A.* v. *Compagnie Européene de Céréales* [1982] 1 Lloyd's Rep. 306; *Bremer Handelsgesellschaft m.b.H.* v. *Deutsche Conti-Handelsgesellschaft m.b.H.* [1983] 1 Lloyd's Rep. 689.
20. Cf. *Motor Oil Hellas (Corinth) Refineries S.A.* v. *Shipping Corporation of India (The Kanchenjunga)* [1990] 1 Lloyd's Rep. 391.

causation,[21] remoteness,[22] the concept of a safe port in relation to contracts of affreightment,[23] whether reliance on a contractual term is reasonable under the terms of the Unfair Contract Terms Act 1977,[24] and the characterisation of contractual terms.[25]

5.2.5.7 To summarise: there appears to exist a parallel between the manner in which the court determines questions of leave to appeal under the 1979 Act in relation to questions of mixed fact and law and conclusions of law, and the way in which the court reviews substantive appeals relating to such legal questions when leave to appeal is granted,[26] and also with the wider principles underpinning appellate and non-appellate review in relation to such questions of law.[27] The category well exemplifies the way in which the new legislation accords greater respect to the decisions of arbitrators and imposes restraint upon judicial intervention.[28] The preconditions to intervention are of a kind that only in exceptional circumstances will it be possible to persuade the court to intervene and give leave to appeal, the logical consequence of which may result in the court substituting its own decision for that of the chosen arbitrator.[29] Rarely will the court be prepared to differ from the conclusion or judgment of the arbitrator,[30] particularly bearing in mind that the correctness of a conclusion or judgment is not a simple matter of right or wrong, but raises the question whether the conclusion of the arbitrator falls within the range of acceptable and unchallengeable decisions.[31] The mere fact that the reviewing judge after hearing the evidence might have arrived at a different conclusion or judgment does not condemn the arbitrator as being wrong, nor does it justify intervention if the conclusion or judgment of both judge and arbitrator are within the permissible range.[32]

5.2.6 One-off events and events of wider significance

5.2.6.1 In the discussion of the preceding guidelines, apart from the first, it has been seen that the approach of a judge to the question of leave to appeal is governed in substantial part by the significance of the question of law in issue. Much weight is attached

---

21. *Federal Commerce & Navigation Ltd.* v. *Suisse-Atlantique Société D'Armement S.A. (The Cruzeiro do Sul)* [1982] 2 Lloyd's Rep. 110; *Uni-Ocean Lines Pte. Ltd.* v. *C-Trade S.A. (The Lucille)* [1984] 1 Lloyd's Rep. 244, 246–247; *New A Line* v. *Erechthion Shipping Co. S.A. (The Erechthion)* [1987] 2 Lloyd's Rep. 180, 185–189.

22. *Tor Line A.B.* v. *Alltrans Group of Canada Ltd. (The TFL Prosperity)* [1982] 1 Lloyd's Rep. 617; *Uni-Ocean Lines Pte. Ltd.* v. *C-Trade S.A. (The Lucille)*, ibid.

23. *Kodros Shipping Corpn.* v. *Empresa Cubana de Fletes (The Evia) (No. 2)*, supra.

24. *George Mitchell (Chesterhall) Ltd.* v. *Finney Lock Seeds Ltd.* [1983] 2 All E.R. 737, 743, per Lord Bridge.

25. *State Trading Corporation of India Ltd.* v. *M. Golodetz Ltd. (Now Transcontinental Affiliates Ltd.)* [1989] 2 Lloyd's Rep. 277, 284. See also *Hong Kong Fir Shipping Co. Ltd.* v. *Kawasaki Kisen Kaisha Ltd.* [1962] Q.B. 26.

26. See Chapter 8.

27. *Edwards* v. *Bairstow, supra*; see also *Hiscox* v. *Outhwaite (No. 3)* [1991] 2 Lloyd's Rep. 524, 533.

28. *State Trading Corporation of India Ltd.* v. *M. Golodetz Ltd.* [1989] 2 Lloyd's Rep. 277, 284, Kerr L.J. (C.A.).

29. *Federal Commerce & Navigation Ltd.* v. *Suisse-Atlantique Société D'Armement S.A. (The Cruzeiro do Sul)* [1982] 2 Lloyd's Rep. 110, 111 (C.A.); *International Sea Tankers Inc.* v. *Hemisphere Shipping Co. Ltd. (The Wenjiang) (No. 2)* [1983] 1 Lloyd's Rep. 400, 402 (first instance); *Atisa S.A.* v. *Aztec A.G.* [1983] 2 Lloyd's Rep. 579.

30. *Uni-Ocean Lines Pte. Ltd.* v. *C-Trade S.A. (The Lucille)* [1984] 1 Lloyd's Rep. 244, 246 (C.A.).

31. See *infra*.

32. Cf. *Transworld Oil Ltd.* v. *North Bay Shipping Corporation (The Rio Claro)* [1987] 2 Lloyd's Rep. 173, 177, per Staughton J. See also *infra*.

to the distinction between questions of law of interest to the contracting parties alone and questions of law of wider interest. The same manner of distinction is further made with regard to the factual milieu in which questions of law arise and to which they are to apply; and with the further characterisation of factual circumstances into "one-off" and those of wider interest again capable of exerting a powerful influence on the exercise of judicial discretion.

This particular phenomenon has already been anticipated in the discussion of the immediately preceding guideline, but its potential relevance goes much wider. The impact which the factual environment is capable of exerting on the way *The Nema/Antaios* guidelines function is also enlightening, for it serves to emphasise that the fundamental rationale of the guidelines is to distinguish between one-off and standard "cases",[1] and not any narrower and particular ingredient.

5.2.6.2 A question of contractual breach will always arise in the context of an event or events that have actually occurred or, more rarely, that are anticipated may occur. Such an event or events may be particular, even unique, to the position of the contracting parties and therefore highly unlikely to recur. When this is the case the surrounding circumstances may be characterised as "one-off".[2] On the other hand, the prevailing or anticipated factual environment may lack this particular and personalised quality, with the event or events that arise closely associated with the entire working environment of the contract in question. As such the materialised or contemplated event or events will be anticipated and accommodated by the terms of the contract. This kind of situation is capable of being regarded as the classical feature of standard from contracts and it is clear that the manner in which the standard form is construed to deal with the anticipated and therefore unexceptional factual situation will be of interest not only to the particular contractors in dispute but to all who contract on the basis of the standard form. But even the most carefully considered and drafted standard form contract will not always succeed in anticipating all the possible factual circumstances in which it will be required to function and thereby reconcile the conflicting interests of the contracting parties. There is always the danger of the draftsman overlooking some possibilities and also of the factual environment subsequently giving forth new and exceptional factual dimensions. Unanticipated factual circumstances may impose a substantial strain on a standard form contract and raise questions of law of enormous difficulty. Moreover they will not of necessity be one-off in character but may represent an event or events of wide interest and also with the potential to recur.

5.2.6.3 The surrounding factual environment may further assume a wider significance and interest by virtue of the fact that it impacts not only upon a particular class of contract but upon a range of other similar and/or associated classes of contract adopted by members of the commercial community engaged in the same or connected trades. Examples of events in recent history which have had such a wide and deeply injurious impact on the course of trade are the closure of the Suez Canal in 1956, the U.S. soya bean embargo in 1973, and most recently the conflict between Iran and Iraq with its entrapment of shipping in the Shatt al Arab waterway and its effect on shipping in the Persian Gulf. The legal analysis of the effect of these events on trading

---

1. The phrase "one-off case" is adopted by Lord Diplock in *The Nema, supra*, p. 735.
2. Cf. *Retla Steamship Co.* v. *Gryphon Shipping Co. S.A. (The Evimeria)* [1982] 1 Lloyd's Rep. 55, 58, per Staughton J.

contracts may be of interest not only to that branch of the commercial community which has adopted the particular class of standard form directly in question, but also to other sections of the commercial community who have been caught up in the same event or events while engaged in similar or associated commercial transactions but on the basis of different classes of standard form contracts.

5.2.6.4 In *The Nema* Lord Diplock tied the exercise of judicial discretion under section 1(3)(b) to the characterisation of the event or events in the context of which a question of law arises. In normal circumstances the more "one-off" an event or events, the more strictly the discretion is to be exercised; the wider the likely significance of an event or events, the more liberal may be the exercise of the discretion. This dimension was developed by Lord Diplock with regard to both questions of contractual construction and the doctrine of frustration of contracts; and the underlying policy is in common with that developed in relation to the guidelines previously considered, except for the first. The effect of highlighting the relevance of the factual milieu is that it may qualify the approach of the court to the threshold issue of characterisation, which is such a central feature of *The Nema/Antaios* guidelines, and produce a different answer from that which might otherwise prevail. In particular, it may signally affect the approach of the court to the characterisation of questions of law relating to the construction of standard form contracts and clauses, and also to questions of mixed fact and law.

5.2.6.5 Where a question of law concerns the construction of a standard form contract or clause, the rule that is to apply normally with regard to the question of leave, is that leave should not be given unless the judge considers that a strong *prima facie* case has been made out that the arbitrator is wrong in his construction[3]; and to this guideline now may be added the emphasis that its suggestive force is even greater when the surrounding factual environment renders the situation a standard event, as when the factual circumstances are frequently encountered or capable of being anticipated.[4] But where the event or events in relation to which the question of construction arises are "one-off" in character, the test to be applied is much stricter and leave should normally not be given unless the judge is satisfied that the arbitrator is "obviously wrong". In other words the *prima facie* rule changes and coincides with the test applicable to the construction of "one-off" contracts or clauses. Lord Diplock made the point in the following terms[5]:

. . . and when the events to which the standard clause fell to be applied in the particular arbitration were themselves "one-off" events, stricter criteria should be applied on the same lines as those that I have suggested as appropriate to "one-off" clauses.

5.2.6.6 In *The Kerman* Parker J. phrased the guiding principle in the following manner[6]:

. . . if the question of law concerns the application of a standard clause to "one-off" events, the criteria to be applied are similar to those prevailing in cases involving the construction of "one-off" clauses.

---

3. *Supra*, para. 5.2.4.3.
4. *Marc Rich & Co. Ltd.* v. *Tourlotti Compania Naviera S.A. (The Kalliopi A)* [1987] 2 Lloyd's Rep. 263; 268 (Note); [1988] 2 Lloyd's Rep. 101 (C.A.).
5. *The Nema, supra*, p. 743.
6. *B.V.S. S.A. and Another* v. *Kerman Shipping Co. S.A. (The Kerman)* [1982] 1 W.L.R. 166, 171.

Parker J. considered the facts in *The Kerman* to represent a classic "one-off" case. The question of law in issue was whether owners of cargo loaded on deck were obliged to insure the cargo. The bill of lading created such an obligation when cargo was loaded on deck pursuant to an authorisation or faculty given under a clause in the bill of lading. In the instant case there existed an antecedent agreement between the parties that the cargo should be loaded on deck and it was this antecedent agreement and not the bill of lading which provided the authorisation or faculty for the deck carriage. In the result no obligation to insure arose. Further, the antecedent agreement had not been superseded by the bill of lading, notwithstanding that a clause in the bill of lading attempted to achieve this result. These facts amounted to a "one-off" event for the purpose of the exercise of judicial discretion under section 1(3)(b). In reviewing the decision of the arbitrator, which rested wholly on the proper construction of the two contracts, Parker J. observed, "Far from forming a provisional view that he was wrong, I have formed the provisional view that he was right, and that I should need a great deal of convincing that he was wrong. If I am right that this is a 'one-off' case, leave must, therefore, in the absence of special circumstances, be refused."[7]

The contrary position also applies with equal force. The more a *prima facie* "one-off" category of legal question arises in the context of an event or events of wide and potentially recurring application and interest, the more that legal question shifts towards being characterised and considered in the same way as a standard case.[8]

5.2.6.7 Where the question of law in issue addresses the question whether or not a contract has been frustrated the appropriate judicial approach has already been indicated. In brief the normal rule is that leave should only be given if the arbitrator has misdirected himself as to the relevant law or has arrived at an unreasonable conclusion.[9] Lord Diplock emphasised that this guideline should normally apply "particularly where the events relied upon are 'one-off' events".[10] Where, however, the alleged frustrating event is of a wider character, affecting not only the particular contractual relationship before the court but also a range of other similar or associated contractual relationships between other parties engaged in the same or related commercial activity, a more generous approach may be adopted to the application for leave. In such circumstances a judicial decision would not solely resolve the immediate dispute before the court but would also provide guidance to arbitrators and the relevant sections of the commercial community. It would have the benefit of creating certainty and thereby also encourage settlements.[11] But even when circumstances of wide relevance prevail, Lord Diplock considered that the merit of the arbitral decision

---

7. *Ibid* p. 174. See also *Industriebeteiligungs & Handelsgesellschaft* v. *Malaysian International Shipping Corpn. Berhad (The Bunga Melawis)* [1991] 2 Lloyd's Rep. 271.

8. *Phoenix Shipping Corp.* v. *Apex Shipping Corp. (The Apex)* [1982] 1 Lloyd's Rep. 476, 479, Bingham J., "a case may take itself out of the 'one-off' category, at any rate to some extent, if it is a factual situation which involves many people in a commercial context. The closure of the Suez Canal is one example; the war between India and Pakistan is another; the war between Iran and Iraq is another, and one could multiply examples".

9. *Supra*, para. 5.2.5.2.

10. *The Nema*, *supra*, p. 744.

11. In *Italmare Shipping Co.* v. *Ocean Tanker Co. Inc. of Monrovia (The Rio Sun)* [1981] 2 Lloyd's Rep. 489, 495, Lord Denning M.R., in the context of a dispute as to the existence of a waiver by a charterer of rights under an anti-technicality clause, said, "This is not a one-off case. These withdrawal clauses—and the anti-technicality clause—are in common use. The waiver argument repeatedly occurs. It is of the first importance that the Commercial Courts should know the commercial laws with regard to them."

under scrutiny should not be ignored and that in the result leave should only be given if the judge is satisfied that the arbitrator's conclusion is "not right", albeit it might otherwise be a conclusion which it was open to the arbitrator reasonably to arrive at. Lord Diplock developed the guideline and its rationale in the following language[12]:

> . . . there may be cases where the events relied upon as amounting to frustration are not "one-off" events affecting only the transaction between the particular parties to the arbitration, but events of a general character that affect similar transactions between many other persons engaged in the same kind of commercial activity, the closing of the Suez Canal, the United States soya bean embargo, the war between Iraq and Iran, are instances within the last two decades that spring to mind. Where such is the case it is in the interests of legal certainty that there should be some uniformity in the decisions of arbitrators as to the effect, frustrating or otherwise, of such an event upon similar transactions, in order that other traders may be sufficiently certain where they stand as to be able to close their own transactions without recourse to arbitration. In such a case, unless there were prospects of an appeal being brought by consent of all the parties as a test case under section 1(3)(a) it might be a proper exercise of the judge's discretion to give leave to appeal in order to express a conclusion as to the frustrating effect of the event that would afford guidance binding upon the arbitrators in other arbitrations arising out of the same event, if the judge thought that in the particular case in which leave to appeal was sought the conclusion reached by the arbitrator, although not deserving to be stigmatised as one which no reasonable person could have reached, was, in the judge's view, not right.

On the facts of *The Nema* the qualification did not operate, for the event that preceded and led up to the dispute between the parties, namely the strike at the loading port, was unique to the particular contractual relationship before the court and had no relevance to any other charterparties. It was a clear "one-off" event.[13]

5.2.6.8 In *The Kerman*[14] Parker J. again introduced refinements to the original enunciation of Lord Diplock. The opinion of the judge must of necessity be a provisional view arrived at following a perusal of the award and after hearing brief argument. In the context of a standard event the test which is appropriate to assessing the correctness of the award is analogous to that adopted with regard to standard contracts and standard contractual terms, and consequently the judge must be satisfied that a strong *prima facie* case has been made out that the arbitrator was "not right". The precise words of Parker J. again merit citation[15]:

> Lord Diplock deals with the situation where the frustrating events relied upon are of a general character likely to affect very many commercial transactions, such as, for example, the closing of the Suez Canal. Here it is said that it might be proper to give leave in the interests of legal certainty if the judge thought that "the conclusion reached by the arbitrator, although not deserving to be stigmatised as one which no reasonable person could have reached, was, in the judge's view, not right."
>
> "In the judge's view" must, in the context of an application for leave, be taken to mean "the judge's provisional view." The test is clearly intended to be less strict than in the "one-off" cases and more strict than the test in *The Lysland* [1973] Q.B. 843. Although Lord Diplock used different language, I am myself unable to ascertain any middle position other than that applicable in the case of standard terms. I conclude, therefore, that in cases of the type in question what is normally required for leave is that the judge should form the provisional view that a strong prima facie case that the arbitrator was "not right" (or wrong) has been made out.

Although the discussion of principle has taken place predominantly in relation to the

---

12. *The Nema, supra*, p. 744.
13. *The Nema, supra*, pp. 735 and 743.
14. *Supra.*
15. *Supra*, pp. 172–173.

doctrine of frustration of contracts, the same approach applies to all questions of law characterised as conclusions of law or as questions of mixed fact and law.[16]

5.2.7 Exceptional cases

5.2.7.1 In enunciating the initial guidelines in *The Nema* Lord Diplock emphasised that they represented criteria that are to apply "normally".[1] A close examination of Lord Diplock's judgment reveals that this qualification is only used expressly in the context of "one-off" cases but there is no reason to suppose that the qualification is confined to this particular category of case. The general tenor of the subsequent judicial development of the guidelines has been to view this innate qualification as one of general application.

5.2.7.2 The guidelines in consequence are not to be understood as absolute criteria but as *prima facie* rules that are to apply "in all ordinary cases",[2] by which is meant cases within the ambit of the guidelines and not manifesting any exceptional circumstances.[3] In the face of exceptional or special circumstances the guidelines possess an inherent flexibility so enabling the judge to tailor the exercise of his discretion to meet the particular circumstances of the case. This presumably may result in *The Nema/ Antaios* guidelines either being ignored wholly or being applied in a qualified manner. In *The Kerman* Parker J. summarised this inherent quality in the following terms[4]:

I should perhaps stress that Lord Diplock repeatedly used the word "normally" when setting out the guidelines, thus recognising that each case must as Lord Denning M.R. said in *Italmare Shipping Co.* v. *Ocean Tanker Co. Inc.*[5] . . . ultimately depend upon its own circumstances.

5.2.7.3 The dictum is marginally dangerous in that on its face it tends to suggest that the discretion is more open-textured than may truly be the case. The true underlying intention is probably best divined by placing the emphasis on the word "ultimately", thus underscoring the point that the exercise of discretion is at large only where there exist prevailing circumstances or considerations that justify a displacement or qualified application of the *prima facie* guidelines. But even when exceptional circumstances appertain, the discretion must continue to be exercised with due regard to the fundamental policy associated with the 1979 Act.[6]

5.3 REFLECTIONS ON THE NEMA/ANTAIOS GUIDELINES

5.3.1 The House of Lords was quick to take the opportunity to lay down guidelines to give direction to the exercise of judicial discretion under section 1(3)(b) with the object of fulfilling the perceived legislative policy underlying the 1979 Act, and with the consequential effect of erasing the uncertainty initially associated with the sub-

---

16. See Chapter 3, para. 3.2.7.
1. *Pioneer Shipping Ltd. and Others* v. *B.T.P. Tioxide Ltd. (The Nema)* [1982] A.C. 724, 742 and 744.
2. *Moran* v. *Lloyds* [1983] 1 Lloyd's Rep. 51, 56 per Lloyd J. (first instance).
3. *Pioneer Shipping Ltd. and Others* v. *B.T.P. Tioxide Ltd. (The Nema), supra*, p. 738 per Lord Diplock.
4. *B.V.S. S.A. and Another* v. *Kerman Shipping Co. S.A. (The Kerman)* [1982] 1 W.L.R. 166, 173. See also the further comments of Parker J. at pp. 171 and 173.
5. [1982] 1 W.L.R. 158, 162.
6. *Supra*, para. 5.1.

section. Although their initial enunciation in *The Nema*[1] was in strictness *obiter dicta*, this technicality never tempted the judiciary into any form of action other than to work within the guidelines laid down. Griffiths L.J. considered that not to follow the guidelines "would make a mockery of our system of judicial precedent" and would be "an act of judicial anarchy".[2] Following the adoption of the guidelines by the Court of Appeal in *The Rio Sun*[3] and their affirmation and refinement by the House of Lords in *The Antaios*[4] there can be no further technical argument raised as to the status of the guidelines.

5.3.2 The guidelines are nonetheless a very limited and restricted code. They relate only to certain categories of legal questions, albeit questions that are very prevalent in practice and of significant importance. They also contemplate legal questions arising in the context of what may be described as London institutional commercial and maritime arbitration. There will in consequence be many questions of law which fall outside the express scope of *The Nema/Antaios* guidelines[5]; and also many classes of arbitration, such as construction and civil engineering arbitration, tenancy and rent review arbitration, consumer arbitration and a miscellany of *ad hoc* arbitrations, not within their direct contemplation.[6] But to say of the guidelines that they fail to be all-embracing is not to be construed as a criticism. This is a feature of all or at least most guidelines, for it is beyond the bounds of reasonableness to embrace and legislate for all possibilities.[7] Indeed, in *The Antaios* Lord Diplock declared that when the guidelines were first promulgated in *The Nema* they were not intended to be all-embracing[8] and also proceeded to describe them as "general" guidelines.[9] As for cases falling outside the scope of the guidelines a judge must be guided by the underlying philosophy and spirit of the guidelines.[10]

5.3.3 Nor are the guidelines to be perceived as a rigid and immutable code. At any given moment in time they have within themselves the potential for "refinement to meet problems of kinds that were not foreseen".[11] Equally over time the guidelines have the capacity to evolve in response to changes in their operational environment. As with the law itself, commercial practice and the expectations and aspirations of the commercial community are susceptible not only to constant and disciplined evolutionary development, but also to more spasmodic and erratic states of flux. To

1. *Pioneer Shipping Ltd. and Others* v. *B.T.P. Tioxide Ltd. (The Nema)* [1982] A.C. 724.
2. *Italmare Shipping Co.* v. *Ocean Tanker Co. Inc. (The Rio Sun)* [1982] 1 W.L.R. 158, 165. See also *B.V.S. S.A. and Another* v. *Kerman Shipping Co. S.A. (The Kerman)* [1982] 1 W.L.R. 166, 169.
3. *Ibid.*
4. *Antaios Compania Naviera S.A.* v. *Salen Rederierna A.B. (The Antaios)* [1985] A.C. 191.
5. *B.V.S. S.A. and Another* v. *Kerman Shipping Co. S.A. (The Kerman)* [1982] 1 W.L.R. 166, 173, per Parker J.; *Bulk Oil (Zug) A.G.* v. *Sun International Ltd. and Sun Oil Trading Co.* [1983] 1 Lloyd's Rep. 655, 659, per Bingham J., [1983] 2 Lloyd's Rep. 587, 589, per Ackner L.J. (C.A.). See also Chapter 6.
6. Cf. *Moran* v. *Lloyd's* [1983] 1 Lloyd's Rep. 51. [1983] 1 Lloyd's Rep. 472 (C.A.); *Merton London Borough* v. *Stanley* (1985) 32 B.L.R. 51; *Lucas Industries plc* v. *Welsh Development Agency* [1986] 2 All E.R. 858, 860, per Sir Nicolas Browne-Wilkinson V.C. See Chapter 6; and also the observations of Staughton J. made in another context in *Kurkjian (Commodity Brokers) Ltd.* v. *Marketing Exchange For Africa Ltd. (No. 2)* [1986] 2 Lloyd's Rep. 618, 625.
7. Cf. *Aden Refinery Co. Ltd.* v. *Ugland Management Co. Ltd. (The Ugland Obo One)* [1987] 1 Q.B. 650, 667–669, per Mustill L.J.
8. *Supra*, p. 200.
9. *Supra*, p. 200.
10. See *infra* and Chapter 6.
11. *Antaios Compania Naviera S.A.* v. *Salen Rederierna A.B. (The Antaios)*, *supra*, p. 200 per Lord Diplock. See also *Lucas Industries plc* v. *Welsh Development Agency*, *supra*, p. 860.

maintain their relevance and serve prevailing policy over time the guidelines must be able to respond to change. What may be described as the contextual dynamic of the guidelines was asserted in *The Antaios* by Lord Diplock[12]:

From the general guidelines stated in the *The Nema* I see, as yet, no reason for departing. Like all guidelines as to how judicial discretion should be exercised they are not intended to be all-embracing or immutable, but subject to adaptation to match changes in practices when these occur or to refinement to meet problems of kinds that were not foreseen, and are not covered by, what was said by this House in the *The Nema*.

To facilitate such reconsideration as may become necessary, the discretion governing the question whether leave to appeal to the Court of Appeal should be given by a judge under section 1(6A), from his decision to grant or refuse leave to appeal from the award of an arbitrator to the High Court under section 1(3)(b), has been fashioned so that a judge should only give leave if satisfied that the extant guidelines require some amplification, elucidation or adaptation to changing practices.[13]

5.3.4 The question also arises as to the precise force of the guidelines with regard to questions of law or circumstances *prima facie* within their scope. The practice of appellate courts laying down guidelines for the guidance of lower courts and tribunals is long familiar in English law; and it is also appreciated that the impact of guidelines may vary greatly from those which operate with the force of legislation to those which are purely advisory. In short there are guidelines and guidelines. It is well appreciated that *The Nema/Antaios* guidelines are not legislative but judicial; and also that they are not absolute in character. They apply in normal circumstances and yield to special considerations. But in the absence of special considerations what is their force and authority? Do they represent a sacrosanct and peremptory blueprint or are they merely advisory? Are they a distinct and independent creed or are they subordinate to the consideration of fundamental policy out of which they were spawned? In their enunciation and confirmation by the House of Lords there is detectable a firmness of application. Subject to what has been described as the contextual dynamic of the guidelines and the accommodation of special circumstances, the guidelines are otherwise to represent the framework of reference of a first tier judge in considering whether to give or refuse leave to appeal. This approach appears to have been consistently followed by first tier judges, although not without the occasional broadside, such as the dictum of Staughton J., that, "after all, it is a question of discretion and discretion can never be fettered by rules".[14] The Court of Appeal however has on occasions ostensibly adopted a less firm approach and deflected the emphasis away from the guidelines to the general nature of judicial discretion and to the fundamental policy which the enunciated guidelines serve. The first indication of this is found in the judgment of Lord Denning M.R. in *The Rio Sun*, where the Master of the Rolls observed[15]:

. . . I feel that we must go by the guidelines set out by the House of Lords. Subject to remembering this—they are only guidelines. Ultimately the question is one for the discretion of the judge of the Commercial Court. The only fetter strictly imposed by the statute is that leave is

---

12. *Supra* p. 200.
13. See Chapter 10, para. 10.2.1.3.
14. *Retla Steamship Co.* v. *Gryphon Shipping Co. S.A. (The Evimeria)* [1982] 1 Lloyd's Rep. 55, 58.
15. *Italmare Shipping Co.* v. *Ocean Tanker Co. Inc. (The Rio Sun)* [1982] 1 W.L.R. 158, 162. The dictum is also cited in *Retla Steamship Co.* v. *Gryphon Shipping Co. S.A. (The Evimeria)*, *ibid*, pp. 58–59.

not to be given *unless* it is a point of law which substantially affects the rights of the parties. Apart from that fetter, the judge has in law a complete discretion. Useful as guidelines often are, nevertheless it must be remembered that they are only guidelines. They are not barriers. You can step over guidelines without causing any harm. You can move them, if need be, to suit the occasion. So let each case depend on its own circumstances.

5.3.5 This approach has been followed on occasions at first instance[16] but it does appear to represent a particularly unstructured and unrestrained approach to the question of judicial discretion under section 1(3)(b), and it is difficult to reconcile the dictum of Lord Denning even with the limited and dynamic view of the guidelines adopted by the House of Lords in *The Antaios*. Nonetheless, Sir John Donaldson M.R. in *The Ugland Obo One*[17] said of the decision in *The Antaios*, "If there was ever any doubt about the purely advisory, limited and mutable status of these guidelines, it was removed by Lord Diplock's speech in *The Antaios*." Whilst there can be no doubting the limited and mutable character of the guidelines, to further characterise them as advisory would appear an unjustified dilution of their intended and actual influence. In the same case Mustill L.J. emphasised that in his view the guidelines are subordinate to the fundamental principle recognised by the House of Lords, and that the promulgation of guidelines did not absolve a first tier judge from exercising his discretion taking into account the entire facts and circumstances before him and applying himself to them in the spirit of the enunciated fundamental principle. The analysis of Mustill L.J. is of substantial importance and utility, and merits an extended citation[18]:

> Although the general tenor of the legislation was clear, there was for a time some uncertainty as to the principles on which the new discretion should be exercised. These were largely laid to rest by *The Nema* [1982] A.C. 724, where the House of Lords emphasised (*per* Lord Diplock, at pp. 739–740):
>
> > "a parliamentary intention to give effect to the turn of the tide in favour of finality in arbitral awards (particularly in non-domestic arbitrations . . .), at any rate where this does not involve exposing arbitrators to a temptation to depart from 'settled principles of law'."
>
> Similarly, *The Antaios* [1985] A.C. 191, Lord Diplock spoke of the parliamentary intention, at p. 199,
>
> > "to promote speedy finality in arbitral awards rather than that insistence upon meticulous semantic and syntactical analysis of the words in which businessmen happen to have chosen to express the bargain made between them, the meaning of which is technically, though hardly commonsensically, classified in English jurisprudence as a pure question of law."
>
> In my judgment a distinction is to be drawn between, on the one hand, these and similar passages from the speeches in the two leading cases and, on the other, the "guidelines" which are contained in those speeches. The former contain authoritative pronouncements on the spirit in which the judge should approach the exercise of his discretion under section 3(1)(*b*). They set the tone for the appeal procedure. The judge must honour them, and there is no reason to doubt that all judges do honour them. The status of the guidelines is different. They were, as it seems to me, intended simply to guide the judge by furnishing him with illustrations of the way in which the spirit of the legislation can be given practical effect in certain situations commonly encountered.

---

16. See, for example, *Astro Valiente Compania Naviera S.A.* v. *The Government of Pakistan Ministry of Food and Agriculture (The Emmanuel Colocotronis) (No. 1)* [1982] 1 Lloyd's Rep. 297, 300, Staughton J.; *Lucas Industries plc* v. *Welsh Development Agency* [1986] 2 All E.R. 858, 860, per Sir Nicolas Browne-Wilkinson V.C.

17. *Aden Refinery Co. Ltd.* v. *Ugland Management Co. Ltd. (The Ugland Obo One)* [1987] 1 Q.B. 650, 659.

18. *Ibid*. pp. 667–669.

I believe that the distinction between these two aspects of *The Nema* and *The Antaios* is sometimes overlooked, and that the guidelines are from time to time treated as if they constituted a complete and immutable code, converting the exercise of the discretion conferred on the judge by statute into a mechanical process yielding an answer which follows inexorably, once a dispute and the resulting award have been assigned to one of various categories. To employ the guidelines in this way would in my opinion be a mistake. It is understandable that counsel should wish to latch on to any words in the speeches which appear to favour the grant or refusal of leave in the individual case, and it is natural that the judges also should pay close regard to the precise wording of the guidelines: for, after all, their Lordships' House has twice had occasion to correct misapprehensions as to the correct use of the discretion, and no judge would care to seem indifferent to what is said in the speeches, the more so after the stern rebuke delivered in *The Antaios* to Bench and Bar alike. Understandable or not, however, I believe that this is not the way to use the help which the guidelines have provided.

In my judgment the discretion conferred by section 1(3)(*b*) remains a discretion. The tension between the conflicting factors to which I have referred persists, although the weight to be given to each of them has been authoritatively prescribed by the House of Lords. The speeches could not legislate for every situation which the judge might face. Disputes vary infinitely in complexity and intellectual difficulty; in the prominence which issues of law play in the overall resolution of the dispute; in their size, and in their significance for the commercial futures of the parties. Questions of law vary from those which are of general importance to the community at large; those which are important to the international trading community; those which are important to the members of a particular trade; those which are important to some members of that trade, faced with similar problems; down to those which are of no importance to anyone except the parties. The answer to the question of law may be obvious or delicately balanced. Awards may be long or short, lucid or opaque. They may reveal unanimity of opinion, or sharp divisions. Every application for leave to appeal is different. No judicial pronouncement, however elaborate, could legislate for them all. It seems to me plain that in stating the guidelines their Lordships did not set out to do so. It involves no disrespect at all to note that experience has cast up problems which the guidelines (as distinct from the statements of general principle) do not cover, and practical difficulties which in some instances make it impossible to put into effect the procedures which they envisage. This situation is precisely what was foreseen when the guidelines were pronounced: see *per* Lord Diplock in *The Antaios* [1985] A.C. 191, 200B.

Thus, if Leggatt J. had taken the view that the guidelines formally bound him to arrive at a particular conclusion, without regard to the individual circumstances of the application before him, he would in my judgment have misunderstood the law. If he had left out of account the importance of appeals on questions of general significance to the continued development of English commercial law, or if he had ignored the service which the courts can perform to mediate where conflicting arbitral decisions are in circulation at the same time, he would have exercised the discretion on an unsound basis; and if the *Scherer* principle had been applicable in this field, there would have been grounds for an appellate court to intervene. In fact, however, I can draw no such inference. The argument of [counsel] is founded on the word "accordingly" in the terse account of the judge's reasons which Sir John Donaldson M.R. has already quoted. For my part, I do not understand this word as an indication that, having matched the facts against the guidelines, the judge proceeded directly to a decision, without exercising an independent judgment about whether this was a suitable case for an appeal. The judge's finding of a strong prima facie case that the majority were right was plainly an important element which the judge evidently treated as tipping the scale. But it does not follow that he regarded it as conclusive in itself, and neglected all the other relevant factors. No doubt there are judges who would have reached a different conclusion, in the light of the arbitrators' own expressed opinion on the value of a ruling from the High Court. But the discretion was for the judge, not the arbitrators, to exercise, and it is in the nature of a discretion that judges may differ in their opinion.

5.3.6 This dictum brings into sharp relief the whole debate as to the precise status of the guidelines. Its thrust is to perceive the guidelines as emanations of, but ultimately also as being subordinate to, the fundamental principle underlying the section 1(3)(b) discretion. The guidelines do no more than reveal the application of fundamental principle in defined circumstances, and are not to be understood as mechanical agents capable of providing clear conclusions. The guidelines, albeit important and powerful, are not necessarily exclusive. In determining an application for leave to appeal a judge must in appropriate circumstances be prepared to peer beyond the narrow tenets of the appropriate guideline to the broader tenets of fundamental principle.[19] There is in this approach a clear intellectual attraction and legitimacy. It would also appear to be consistent with the jurisprudence of the House of Lords and to represent an elaboration of the qualifications introduced by the House of Lords in presenting the guidelines as aids which will "normally" apply in given situations and to be subject to exceptional circumstances. The one reservation the dictum elicits is that it fails to acknowledge the limited prospect for circumstances outside the parameters of a defined guideline being introduced and influencing the exercise of discretion and thereby also tends to understate the true influence of the guidelines on the exercise of discretion. It is also uncertain whether all the wider factors itemised by way of illustration by Mustill L.J. are capable of being taken into account by a judge in the exercise of his discretion.[19a] If one makes a broad examination of the way the discretion has been exercised by the judiciary since the initial elaboration of *The Nema/Antaios* guidelines there is a recognition of the forceful influence the guidelines have come to assume. They do often tend to be applied mechanically and with little evidence of the qualifying pull of the wider fundamental principle. The reason for this appears to be due to a reluctance to admit criteria outside the parameters of the guidelines as capable of influencing the exercise of the discretion so as to open up awards; and as for such criteria as are admitted, to the rarity of such accommodation. In the result the practice of the law does not always suggest the theoretical analysis advanced by Mustill L.J. with its view of the subordination of the guidelines.

5.3.7 Within the philosophical undergrowth of the guidelines there are many strands of policy which have been identified in the preceding elaboration of the individual guidelines. There is however one strand of policy which merits particular attention in this retrospective. This is the emphasis given to the wider interest and benefit of having a particular question of law considered on an appeal to the courts, in contradistinction to the innate importance of the question of law or its importance to the parties in dispute, or even the correctness of the arbitral decision with regard to the question of law. This facet of policy surfaces most clearly where an application falls to be characterised as a standard case, with regard to which a less rigorous test is applied and with the court more ready to undermine the finality of an award. The policy does not prevail wholly independently of any assessment of the correctness of the original arbitral determination, but nonetheless it represents a powerful influence. In the result, in deciding whether or not to grant leave to appeal, the concern is not confined to considerations of justice as between the immediate parties in dispute but extends to accommodate the wider interest and benefit in obtaining a judicial pronouncement on the question of law in issue.[20] A decision of wide significance will inevitably contribute to the comprehensiveness, certainty, and efficiency of the relevant area of English law in question, predominantly English commercial law, which is a powerful consideration

---

19. Cf. *Geogas S.A.* v. *Trammo Gas Ltd. (The Baleares)* [1991] 2 All E.R. 110, 119, Dillon L.J.
19a. See Chapter 6.
20. Cf. *Phoenix Shipping Corporation* v. *Apex Shipping Corporation (The Apex)* [1982] 1 Lloyd's Rep. 476, 479, per Bingham J.

of policy underpinning the guidelines. The deflection of concern away from the parties in dispute to the wider interest in maintaining the active development of English (commercial) law produces the graphic image of arbitrating parties funding the evolution of English law, by providing beneficial precedents. This aspect of the prevailing policy has attracted criticism,[21] but it is far from novel. It is frequently a relevant factor within the court system whenever appeals are not a matter of right but of discretion.[22] And although it is impossible to be insensitive to the criticisms, nonetheless the adopted policy is justifiable, for it is legitimate in developing the discretion about an appellate process to have regard to the broader benefits that may emanate from allowing an appeal to proceed.

5.3.8 Beyond the issues and difficulties associated with the substance and status of the guidelines, the guidelines have also created an incidental difficulty of characterisation. The preceding discussion will have made it clear that the guidelines have been fashioned to operate in different kinds of circumstances. In consequence an initial and unavoidable issue facing a judge, to whom application for leave to appeal is made, is to determine precisely which category of circumstance the application falls within. This is the initial question of characterisation. It is a question of significant importance and, as has been seen in the discussion of the individual guidelines, it is often also frequently one of difficulty. The defining criteria and boundaries of the various categories are not necessarily clearly identifiable and the slotting of individual applications into the appropriate guideline category may cause considerable difficulty. It may be assumed that this is an unintended consequence of the judicial development of the guidelines, but it does have the undesirable result that on occasions a substantial amount of intellectual energy, with the attendant penalties of cost and delay, is spent debating the threshold question of characterisation, before progressing to address the central and real issue of whether or not leave to appeal should be granted.[23] The result of developing the exercise of judicial discretion around a system of guidelines is that on occasions the focus of concern is diverted from the central issue and concentrates on the technicalities of the techniques adopted in aid of the central issue. This is wasteful and unproductive.

---

21. See for example Goode, "The Adaptation of English Law to International Commercial Arbitration" (1992) 8 Arb.Int. 1.

22. It may also be a relevant consideration in relation to the discretion exercisable by the Court of Appeal under s. 1(7) of the 1979 Act, with regard to on-appeals: see *Geogas S.A.* v. *Trammo Gas Ltd. (The Baleares)*, *supra*, p. 127, per Leggatt L.J.

23. For a recent example see *Kansa General Insurance Co. Ltd.* v. *Bishopsgate Insurance plc* [1988] 1 Lloyd's Rep. 503.

EXERCISING THE DISCRETION— CATEGORIES OF CASES OUTSIDE THE EXPRESS CONTEMPLATION OF THE NEMA/ ANTAIOS GUIDELINES

6.1 GENERAL APPROACH

6.1.1 It has already been emphasised that *The Nema/Antaios* guidelines are a limited code. It follows that questions of law and prevailing circumstances may arise that are outside the express contemplation of the guidelines and with regard to which there exists no direct guiding authority.[1] In any such situation the judge is obliged to exercise his discretion by drawing on general principle or proceeding by analogy. The basic premise governing the exercise of discretion under section 1(3)(b) is the recognition that the intention underlying the 1979 Act is to "turn . . . the tide in favour of finality in arbitral awards"[2] and "to promote speedy finality in arbitral awards".[3] These enunciations of the legislative intention in turn define "the spirit in which the judge should approach the exercise of his discretion under [section 1(3)(b)]. They set the tone for the appeal procedure. The judge must honour them."[4] This is the jurisprudence that governs the first judicial step in responding to an application for leave to appeal, and it is a jurisprudence which applies to all applications, whether they fall within or are outside the ambit of the guidelines.[5]

6.1.2 But although the judge is to be guided primarily by general principle, it cannot be the case that the enunciated guidelines, notwithstanding their limitations, are wholly devoid of significance. Just as the guidelines are borne of the spirit of fundamental principle, so also they themselves may offer spiritual assistance to the judge endeavouring to navigate uncharted waters with the guidance only of general principle. The guidelines represent concrete examples of the application of fundamental policy, and as such have the capacity to offer direct and practical assistance in near parallel and analogous situations. Evidence of a judicial willingness to tap the inherent message of the guidelines in situations outside their express scope is provided by the

---

1. *Moran* v. *Lloyd's* [1983] 1 Lloyd's Rep. 51, 56 per Lloyd J. (first instance); *Bulk Oil (Zug) A.G.* v. *Sun International Ltd. and Sun Oil Trading Co.* [1983] 1 Lloyd's Rep. 655, 659; [1983] 2 Lloyd's Rep. 587, 589 (C.A.).
2. *Pioneer Shipping Ltd.* v. *B.T.P. Tioxide Ltd. (The Nema)* [1982] A.C. 724, 739, per Lord Diplock.
3. *Antaios Compania Naviera S.A.* v. *Salen Rederierna A.B. (The Antaios)* [1985] A.C. 191, 199, per Lord Diplock.
4. *Aden Refinery Co. Ltd.* v. *Ugland Management Co. Ltd. (The Ugland Obo One)* [1987] 1 Q.B. 650, 667, per Mustill L.J.
5. *Ibid.* pp. 667–669.

judgment of Parker J. in *The Kerman*[6]:

What then of other cases which do not directly fall within the categories specifically dealt with? It is, in my judgment, clear that in all cases more is normally required than the criteria in *The Lysland* [1973] Q.B. 843 unless there are special circumstances. It is also clear that the more far reaching the effects of the determination of the point of law involved, the less strict the criteria should be. It therefore appears to me that, if the point is one which will affect not only persons within a particular trade but persons in other trades as well, and, indeed, persons not in commerce or trade at all, it would be proper to grant leave on the basis of very little more than a demonstration that the point was capable of serious argument. Furthermore, if the point was, in addition, an entirely new one on which there was no authority, I would regard this as a special circumstance making it proper to grant leave on no more than *The Lysland* criteria on the ground that it was of importance that authoritative guidance be given at the earliest possible moment.

This dictum looks outward beyond the express ambit of *The Nema/Antaios* guidelines, but with a flavour that clearly reflects identifiable themes associated with the guidelines.

6.2 PARTICULAR CATEGORIES OF CASES OUTSIDE THE NEMA/ ANTAIOS GUIDELINES

There have been many occasions when the court has exercised its discretion under section 1(3)(b) with regard to questions of law and prevailing circumstances not expressly provided for in *The Nema/Antaios* guidelines. Equally, there have been fewer occasions when the court has, in entertaining an application for leave to appeal with regard to a question of law or circumstance within *The Nema/Antaios* guidelines, proceeded to impress a consideration not expressly expounded in the guidelines. The object of this section of the text is to attempt an analysis of these circumstances and to isolate the criteria identified by the court as pertinent to the exercise of the discretion in the various circumstances. The analysis on occasions goes further than that presently suggested by authority and also attempts to identify situations that may assume a relevance in the future development of the law or which are of an uncertain or controversial character. There is in consequence to be found in the text much which is conjectural, undetermined by authority or the uncertain substance of a continuing debate, the answers to which are ultimately in the hands of the judiciary. It is in the nature of judicial law that traditional interpretations and emphasis may be reassessed over the passage of time and as between different generations of judges.

6.2.1 Circumstances relating to the application for leave to appeal

6.2.1.1 *The Nema/Antaios* guidelines recognise that circumstances relating to the reference to arbitration may assume a relevant consideration in the exercise of the judicial discretion.[1] The decision of the Court of Appeal in *The Ugland Obo One*[2] sug-

---

6. *B.V.S. S.A. and Another* v. *Kerman Shipping Co. S.A. (The Kerman)* [1982] 1 W.L.R. 166, 173. Cited with approval in *Bulk Oil (Zug) A.G.* v. *Sun International Ltd. and Sun Oil Trading Co.* [1983] 1 Lloyd's Rep. 655, 659, per Bingham J., [1983] 2 Lloyd's Rep. 587, 590, per Ackner L.J. (C.A.). See also *Kansa General Insurance Co. Ltd.* v. *Bishopsgate Ins. plc* [1988] 1 Lloyd's Rep. 503, 511–513 per Hirst J.
1. Chapter 5, para. 5.2.2.
2. *Aden Refinery Co. Ltd.* v. *Ugland Management Co. Ltd. (The Ugland Obo One)* [1987] 1 Q.B. 650.

gests that circumstances relating to the environment in which an application for leave
to appeal is made may equally assume a relevance. The disputed question of law
before the Court of Appeal concerned the construction of a standard form voyage
charterparty on the Asbantankvoy form and concerning which there existed a division
of opinion among London maritime arbitrators. This division of opinion was expressly
recognised by the arbitrators in their award, and they also expressed an opinion on the
desirability of a judicial decision to resolve the prevailing difference. The relevant part
of the award provided[3]:

That issue is one of considerable practical importance and it raises a question upon which it is
well known that there is a division of view between London maritime arbitrators—a division
which has manifested itself in the instant case. It is highly desirable that the question should be
submitted to judicial decision and this dispute would appear to offer an ideal opportunity for the
position to be resolved by such decision.

With this encouragement, the charterers applied for leave to appeal but the application was rejected. The Court of Appeal considered that it had no jurisdiction to
interfere with the exercise of discretion by the first tier judge, and even if it had, it
would not in the circumstances have interfered notwithstanding that it might have
decided the application differently.[4] Nonetheless, the two members of the Court of
Appeal proceeded to indicate *obiter dicta,* that had they individually been charged
with determining the original application for leave they would have given much
greater weight to the plea of the arbitrators for judicial intervention. Sir John Donaldson M.R. indicated that on the facts of the case he would himself have granted leave
"because I firmly believe that the Commercial Court exists to serve the interests of its
customers, *as those customers see them*, and I should have been extremely reluctant to
reject a plea from so well informed a source as these three arbitrators".[5] Mustill L.J.
commented in a less personalised way, "No doubt there are judges who would have
reached a different conclusion, in the light of the arbitrators' own expressed opinion
on the value of a ruling from the High Court".[6]

6.2.1.2 A similar approach is discernible in the judgment of Lord Denning M.R. in
the Court of Appeal in *The Nema*.[7] The Master of the Rolls considered that in relation
to a question of law concerning the construction of a "one-off" clause in a "one-off"
contract, in the ordinary way leave to appeal should not be given in the absence of
some special reason, and then proceeded to express the opinion that a special reason
would arise "if the arbitrator intimated that he would welcome an appeal".[8]

6.2.1.3 Of course, the pleading of an arbitrator or tribunal can only be of significance if in its substance it is justified and relevant. When these criteria are satisfied, its
particular relevance is that it brings to the attention of the court the assessment of the
arbitrator or tribunal of the desirability of a judicial decision and of the potential
benefit that will derive from that decision. But although the expression by arbitrators
of the desirability and benefit of a judicial decision on appeal communicates a significant message to the courts, it is improbable that in itself it will conclude the question

3. *Ibid.* p. 656.
4. See Chapter 10, para. 10.2.
5. *Ibid.* p. 661.
6. *Ibid.* p. 669.
7. *Pioneer Shipping Ltd. and Another* v. *B.T.P. Tioxide Ltd. (The Nema)* [1980] 1 Q.B. 547 (C.A.).
8. *Ibid.* p. 565.

of discretion in favour of allowing an appeal. The views of arbitrators in this regard will be of great weight, but they are nonetheless only one criterion in the equation and ultimately the question of leave is to be determined having regard to all the facts of the case. In a finely balanced case the fact that the arbitrator has actively canvassed for an appeal could well tip the balance in favour of giving leave to appeal.

6.2.1.4 Although express exhortation by an arbitral tribunal for judicial intervention may be of particular weight, equally it may not be absolutely necessary for the exhortation to be express, if the circumstances which would justify such an urging are otherwise present. In *The Nema*[9] the sole arbitrator in his award expressed a concern, which was shared among London maritime arbitrators, that the courts in applying the doctrine of frustration of contracts were adopting too strict a test and that commercial justice required a slightly more liberal approach.[10] This statement was at least capable of being construed as an implied plea for reconsideration by the courts, but even in the absence of such a construction, it was evidence of disharmony between the prevailing commercial law and the expectations of the commercial community, sufficient to encourage the court of its own volition to at least give serious consideration to take the opportunity offered to reappraise the question.[11]

6.2.1.5 The pleadings of arbitrators do not exhaust all the possible relevant factors. The conduct of the parties may represent yet a further illustration of a potential circumstance capable of falling within the present category of case. Where all the parties consent to an appeal, a party may have his appeal under section 1(3)(a).[12] But in the absence of consent, the manner in which the other party or parties respond to an application for leave to appeal may have a bearing on the exercise of discretion under section 1(3)(b). *The Nema/Antaios* guidelines appear to have been constructed on the assumption that the application will be resisted by the other party or parties. This doubtlessly represents the customary position. But it is open to a party not to take any step to resist an application for leave to appeal and yet not give express or implied consent to the appeal. It may be assumed that without more mere failure to resist an application does not amount to implied consent.[13] When this kind of situation prevails the conduct of the other party or parties would appear to be a factor which the court may take into account in determining an application for leave to appeal.[14]

6.2.2 Conduct of parties during the course of the reference

It is probably the case that a judge may take into account in the exercise of his discretion the conduct of the parties during the course of the reference which reveals

9. *B.T.P. Tioxide Ltd.* v. *Pioneer Shipping Ltd. and Armada Marine S.A. (The Nema)* [1980] 2 Lloyd's Rep. 83, 93.

10. The statement reads: "There are some in the City of London, and other maritime centres, who think that commercial justice is sometimes sacrificed upon the altar of certainty, and that a slightly more liberal approach, in the application of frustration principles, to supervening events, would be more appropriate to the pace of modern commercial life." See *The Nema* [1980] 1 Q.B. 547, 568.

11. *B.T.P. Tioxide Ltd.* v. *Pioneer Shipping Ltd. and Armada Marine S.A. (The Nema)* [1980] 2 Lloyd's Rep. 83, 93, per Robert Goff J.; [1980] 1 Q.B. 547, 568, per Lord Denning M.R.

12. See Chapter 4, para. 4.2.

13. See Chapter 4, para. 4.2.5.

14. See *Uni-Ocean Lines Pte. Ltd.* v. *C-Trade S.A. (The Lucille)* [1984] 1 Lloyd's Rep. 244, 245, where it is commented on an application for leave to appeal by shipowners in relation to a charterparty dispute that the charterers did not oppose the application. But it must be noted that the charterers were themselves seeking leave to appeal on other legal points.

either an intention that there should exist the possibility of a future appeal or that the award should be final. Such conduct may neither amount to effective consent within the meaning of section 1(3)(a),[1] nor to an exclusion agreement within the meaning of section 3(1), most particularly for want of form[2]; but it may nonetheless influence the exercise of discretion under section 1(3)(b) and sway the judge towards a decision in keeping with the ostensible intention of the parties. The relevance of party conduct indicating an attitude to the finality or otherwise of any future award does not appear to have attracted any direct judicial comment; but in an extra-judicial capacity Lord Donaldson M.R. has commented on the position when both parties indicate to the arbitrator that they will accept his award as final, and said of it that it represents "a powerful, and possibly decisive, matter if and when either party subsequently seeks leave to appeal".[3]

6.2.3 Request for reasons made to the arbitrator

6.2.3.1 There is a strong relationship between reasoned awards and the appeal process established by the 1979 Act.[1] As an incident of this relationship the question arises whether the request or failure to request reasons may assume a relevance in any future application for leave to appeal. The question presumes the intentions of the parties to be a potential material consideration in the exercise of the section 1(3)(b) discretion, and that the conduct of the parties in requesting or failing to request reasons may be a tacit evidentiary indication of their intentions *vis-à-vis* the finality or otherwise of the award. The request for reasons is capable, at least to some degree, of being construed as an indication that the parties do not intend the award to be final, but to be open to review by appeal[2]; and the failure to ask for reasons, or a decision not to be provided with reasons, as possibly indicating an intention that the award is to be final and unappealable. Nonetheless, it has to be admitted that to put the proposition in this way is deceptively simple, for it ignores the gamut of factual variations that may arise in individual cases. Clearly the possible analyses and implications may differ markedly with factual variations and bearing this in mind the ensuing discussion focuses on the more readily identifiable and likely factual circumstances.

6.2.3.2 Where both parties request a reasoned award, which the arbitrator is obliged to provide, it is highly improbable that without more this can be translated into a firm intention that the award is to be appealable. It is at highest a neutral consideration or no stronger than a factor to be taken into account in the exercise of the section 1(3)(b) discretion and with the precise weight it carries capable of varying with

1. See Chapter 4, para. 4.2.
2. See Chapter 13.
3. Donaldson, "Commercial Arbitration—1979 and After", pp. 1–13, 8, in *International Commercial and Maritime Arbitration*, ed. Rose.
1. See Chapter 11.
2. Under the pre-1979 Act law, to make a reasoned award was on occasions open to the construction that it amounted to an invitation to judicial review: see *Re Hansloh and others and Reinhold, Pinner, and Co.* (1895) 1 Com. Cas. 215.The same thinking survives in the contemporary law: see *Exmar BV* v. *National Iranian Tanker Co.* (*The Trade Fortitude*) [1992] 1 Lloyd's Rep. 169, 175, Judge Diamond, Q.C., "[the arbitrators] have given detailed reasons with a view, presumably, to the possibility of an appeal under the 1979 Act".

the wider facts and circumstances of individual cases.[3] The requesting of reasons is not inseverably associated with appeals and the making of reasoned awards is also actively encouraged by the 1979 Act.[4] To develop some equation between mutually requested reasons and the appealability of awards would be to flout the policy of the 1979 Act. It is not even the case that an order made under section 1(5) will automatically result in leave to appeal being granted in any subsequent application.[5] In the absence of special circumstances, it would appear that mutually requested reasons represent an equivocal consideration and with it likely that the courts will resist drawing an implication contrary to the policy of the legislation. The same reasoning would appear to apply when the requirement of a reasoned award is incorporated into an arbitrator's contractual mandate.

6.2.3.3 An arbitrator, by virtue of section 1(5), is also under an implied or quasi-duty to give reasons when requested to do so by only one of the parties, even if the other party protests.[6] Notwithstanding the significant factual variation, it is unlikely that this position differs from that when both or all the parties request reasons. The same considerations would appear to apply and if anything the absence of mutuality hardens the argument suggesting neutrality or variable weighting according to the wider circumstances, which in the kind of case under consideration will include the very relevant fact that at least one of the parties does not overtly support the request for reasons and may even have resisted the request. Confronted with this kind of situation in *The Rio Sun*[7] Lord Denning M.R. considered there to exist an agreement that the award of the arbitrator was not to be final and subject to an appeal. The existence of an intra-arbitral agreement in such circumstances is difficult to comprehend, but also in other regards the implication would appear to be substantially too strong. The analysis was however not necessary to support the decision of the court and clearly *obiter dictum*.

6.2.3.4 Where reasons are given voluntarily, as when there exists no contractual mandate to make a reasoned award and neither party requests reasons, the position assumes a greater difficulty for there exists the possible implication that the parties would have been content with an unreasoned award and willing to accept the implications of that circumstance under the 1979 Act.[8] In the absence of a prohibitory mandate, an arbitrator who volunteers reasons is not guilty of misconduct and the policy of the 1979 Act is again to encourage the practice.[9] The impact of voluntary reasons on the discretion associated with section 1(3)(b) has received a degree of judicial attention and also provoked a judicial debate. In *The Oinoussian Virtue*[10] Robert Goff J. rejected a submission to the effect that if neither party has requested a reasoned award the court should not ordinarily give leave to appeal. In other words the failure to specifically request reasons was not by implication to be construed as a mutual

3. *Trave Schiffahrtsgesellschaft m.b.H. & Co. K.G.* v. *Ninemia Maritime Corporation (The Niedersachsen)* [1986] 1 Q.B. 802. The case is considered in greater detail *infra*, para. 6.2.3.4.
4. See Chapter 11.
5. See *infra*, para. 6.2.4.
6. See Chapter 11, para. 11.7.3.1.8.
7. *Italmare Shipping Co.* v. *Ocean Tanker Co. Inc. (The Rio Sun)* [1982] 1 W.L.R. 158, 162.
8. See the limitations imposed by section 1(6), considered in Chapter 11, para. 11.7.3.
9. See Chapter 11.
10. *Schiffahrtsgentur Hamburg Middle East Line G.m.b.H.* v. *Virtue Shipping Corpn. (The Oinoussian Virtue)* [1981] 2 All E.R. 887, 891–892.

intention that the award be final and unappealable. In contrast, in the development of the discretion under section 1(5), in determining whether or not to make an order for further reasons, the courts have taken into account the conduct of the parties, and in particular whether reasons were or were not requested.[11] In the course of the development of the criteria relevant to the section 1(5) discretion, in *Warde* v. *Feedex International Inc.*[12] Staughton J. expressed his disagreement with the observation of Robert Goff J. and later in *The Niedersachsen*[13] viewed the difference of approach as being one of principle meriting consideration by the Court of Appeal. On appeal the approach of Staughton J. was favoured and Sir John Donaldson M.R. observed[14] "that in exercising the court's discretion whether or not to grant leave to appeal, it can take account of whether the parties asked for a reasoned award or, for special reasons, were excused from so doing". The primary concern of the Court of Appeal was to protect the finality of voluntarily reasoned awards and not to discourage the practice of giving voluntarily reasons, and this could be achieved by allowing the judge hearing an application for leave to appeal to take into account the fact that the parties had not requested reasons. To adopt again the words of Sir John Donaldson M.R.,[15] "it would be unfortunate if arbitrators were to come to regard the making of reasoned awards, in the absence of a request so to do, as giving hostages to fortune". The precise weight to be given to the absence of a request for reasons will vary with the circumstances; and if there were special reasons why no request was made, within the meaning of section 1(6), then the absence of a request would presumably assume no significance. The observations of the Court of Appeal are patently *obiter dictum* and are not necessarily in conflict with the opinion of Robert Goff J. which was directed at the extreme proposition that when unrequested reasons are given leave to appeal should not normally be given. The proposition supported by the Court of Appeal is much milder and to the effect that the fact that no reasons were requested may be taken into account in the exercise of the section 1(3)(b) discretion and with the precise weight accorded to the failure to request reasons capable of varying with the wider circumstances of each case. This appears a reasonable and supportable proposition, but on a more general point it would not appear helpful to compound into one common framework the discretionary powers arising under the 1979 Act. In particular section 1(3)(b) and section 1(5) serve very different purposes and the criteria underpinning the discretionary powers associated with each subsection may legitimately differ.

6.2.3.5 The position would appear to be very different when the parties contractually mandate for or otherwise request an unreasoned award, or stipulate that extra-award reasons be given, which is much the same thing, but the arbitrator nonetheless proceeds to give reasons. According to the circumstances, an arbitrator who so conducts himself may be in breach of contract or guilty of misconduct.[16] In this kind of situation the parties appear to be making it abundantly clear that they intend the award to be final, with the possibility of an appeal excluded, and it may be presumed

11. See Chapter 11, para. 11.8.1.6.
12. [1984] 1 Lloyd's Rep. 310, 314. See also *Vermala Shipping Enterprises Ltd.* v. *Minerals and Metals Trading Corporation of India Ltd. (The Gay Fidelity)* [1982] 1 Lloyd's Rep. 469, 470.
13. *Trave Schiffahrtsgesellschaft m.b.H. & Co. K.G.* v. *Ninemia Maritime Corporation (The Niedersachsen)* [1986] 1 Q.B. 802, 807 (C.A.).
14. *Ibid*. p. 808.
15. *Ibid*. p. 808.
16. See Chapter 11, para. 11.8.1.9.

that the court would require a great deal of convincing before it would exercise its discretion otherwise than by refusing any application for leave to appeal.

6.2.4 Order made under section 1(5)

A request for reasons or further reasons may be formalised by an application made under section 1(5).[1] It is well appreciated that an order under section 1(5) may be sought in order to lay the foundation for a possible application for leave to appeal.[2] But notwithstanding this strategic association the two processes are quite distinct and the discretion about each has essentially been developed independently. In the result the fact that the court is prepared to make an order under section 1(5) assumes little or no significance in the exercise of the section 1(3)(b) discretion in any subsequent application for leave to appeal. Leave to appeal does not follow automatically from the making of an earlier section 1(5) order; the application for leave to appeal is to be decided on its own merits according to the established criteria.[3]

6.2.5 Backdrop of disparate arbitral awards

6.2.5.1 It has been observed that within *The Nema/Antaios* guidelines special considerations are capable of applying when a question of law (particularly a question of law relating to the construction of a standard form contractual provision) arises against the background of conflicting judicial decisions, and in exceptional circumstances possibly even conflicting judicial dicta.[1] There are grounds for suggesting that an analogous approach prevails when a question of law comes into issue against the background of conflicting arbitral decisions.[2] Conflicting arbitral awards may be the product of any of the contemporary forms of institutional arbitration and are most likely to arise when an event of wide import impacts on the functioning of a number of similar or related contracts. The existence of conflict will be rendered all the more visible when the awards are also published or otherwise brought into the public domain. In such circumstances the existence of different legal analyses and conclusions developed and arrived at by separate tribunals may be viewed as innately unsatisfactory and to be productive of uncertainty and confusion. The ultimate justification for giving leave to appeal in such a circumstance is that it would establish a judicial precedent which would bring certainty and harmony into an area of the law in which there was a sectional interest. Confronted with a backdrop of conflicting awards, the arbitrator might also be inclined to invite judicial intervention by way of appeal[3] and the correctness of the immediate award may also be more difficult to assess.

    6.2.5.2 The approach to be adopted when there are conflicting awards was not considered by the House of Lords in *The Antaios*,[4] but in *The Ugland Obo One*[5] Sir John

---

    1. See Chapter 11, para 11.4.
    2. *Universal Petroleum Co. Ltd. (in liquidation)* v. *Handels- und Transport Gesellschaft m.b.H.* [1987] 2 All E.R. 737, 748, Kerr L.J.
    3. *Warde* v. *Feedex International Inc.* [1984] 1 Lloyd's Rep. 310, 312, Staughton J. See further Chapter 11, para. 11.8.3.
    1. *Supra*, para. 5.2.4.9.
    2. See cases considered *infra*, and Chapter 5, para. 5.2.4.11.
    3. *Supra*, para. 6.2.1.
    4. *Antaios Compania Naviera S.A.* v. *Salen Rederierna A.B. (The Antaios)* [1985] A.C. 191.
    5. *Aden Refinery Co. Ltd.* v. *Ugland Management Co. Ltd. (The Ugland Obo One)* [1987] 1 Q.B. 650.

Donaldson M.R. considered *obiter dictum* that the approach to be adopted in the face of conflicting arbitral decisions (as distinct from comment) should mirror that adopted by the courts where there exist conflicting judicial decisions and "a judge should in such a case give favourable consideration to granting leave to appeal to the High Court, but not necessarily beyond that court, in order that there might be a decision binding all arbitrators and producing uniformity of decisions by all arbitrators".[6] On the facts in *The Ugland Obo One* it was unclear whether there existed a background of conflicting arbitral decisions, although the arbitrators had indicated in their award that the award raised a question which it was well known had given rise to a division of professional opinion between London maritime arbitrators, and this, together with the other facts of the case, was construed as an implied indication of conflicting awards. Mustill L.J. also emphasised the significance of conflicting arbitration awards to the exercise of the judicial discretion and in a powerful *obiter dictum* was of the opinion that "had [the judge] ignored the service which the courts can perform to mediate where conflicting arbitral decisions are in circulation at the same time, he would have exercised the discretion on an unsound basis".[7] Both Sir John Donaldson M.R. and Mustill L.J. appear to make it clear that on the facts of the case had the application been made to either of them they each would have been inclined to grant leave to appeal, although the judge to whom application was made had refused leave, and in so deciding the Court of Appeal was satisfied that the judge had acted judiciously.

6.2.5.3 Where conflicting arbitral awards accompany other facts and circumstances which incline matters towards giving leave to appeal, the significance of the background of conflicting awards as contributing to the general weight of the case in favour of permitting an appeal must be quite uncontentious. The position is more difficult when the case for an appeal is confined to the existence of conflicting awards and where the judge has no reason to believe that the arbitrator has gone wrong in law. In such a case all turns on the desirability of achieving certainty through a binding legal decision. The preceding discussion has shown that the claims of certainty are very powerful and argument based wholly on this consideration will carry great weight, such as to justify the giving of leave to appeal, even when the judge is satisfied that the arbitrator is right in law.[8] The position as it now appears to stand gives approval to the approach adopted by Robert Goff J. in *The Wenjiang (No. 1)*,[9] a case concerning *inter alia* the frustration of a time charterparty following the entrapment of the chartered vessel in the River Shatt during the Iran–Iraq conflict. The application for leave to appeal took place against a background of conflicting maritime arbitral decisions arising from a consideration of similar disputed legal questions in relation to other chartered vessels caught up in the conflict in similar circumstances, with arbitrators coming to different conclusions as to the precise date of the contractual frustration. Notwithstanding that Robert Goff J. was not prepared to hold that the arbitrator had misdirected himself in law or that he had arrived at a conclusion which no reasonable arbitrator could have arrived at, the learned judge nonetheless considered it right to give leave to appeal in order to establish uniformity in the application of the relevant

6. *Ibid*. p. 661.
7. *Ibid*. p. 669.
8. *Ibid*.
9. *International Sea Tankers Inc.* v. *Hemisphere Shipping Co. Ltd.* *(The Wenjiang)* [1981] 2 Lloyd's Rep. 308. See also [1982] 1 Lloyd's Rep. 128 (C.A.); *(The Wenjiang) (No. 2)* [1983] 1 Lloyd's Rep. 400.

law.[10] Beyond the particular policies associated with the individual guidelines, Robert Goff J. was prepared to identify a wider policy underlying the judicial review of arbitration awards on questions of law, which was "to prevent the injustice which would arise if the law was not consistently applied in arbitrations".[11]

6.2.5.4 The fact that different arbitrators arrive at different conclusions does not necessarily establish the existence of conflicting awards. Where questions of mixed fact and law and conclusions of law are in issue, raising issues of factual degree and judgment, there is no necessarily right answer but a range of possible right answers.[12] Provided each arbitrator is within the range, it cannot be said that any particular arbitrator has gone wrong. The result is differential arbitral decision-making, but of the acceptable kind. In this regard there is profit in recalling the dictum of Lord Roskill in *The Nema*,[13] "Where questions of degree are involved, opinions may, and often do, legitimately differ."

6.2.6 Character of the arbitration tribunal

6.2.6.1 Trade and maritime arbitration

6.2.6.1.1 Many arbitration tribunals are composed of professional arbitrators who are experienced and expert in the matters referred to their decision. This is particularly the case with regard to the commodity and maritime arbitrations conducted in London, which occupy such a central position in relation to appeals under the 1979 Act, but it is equally true of construction, civil engineering and building arbitrations and many others. The courts have long espoused a high regard for the deliberations and awards of these specialist tribunals and a reluctance to intervene in their processes.[1]

The fact that an award emanates from a specialist maritime or trade arbitration tribunal is clearly not an absolute ground for refusing leave to appeal; nor is it otherwise a serious obstacle to giving leave to appeal if the facts and circumstances otherwise incline to that conclusion. The accumulating caselaw is unambiguous on the point. But the character of the tribunal is probably a factor to be taken into account, particularly in cases where the expertise and experience of the arbitration tribunal is highlighted, as where the commercial context of a contract or a question of construction is in question or where a question of law is commingled with matters of commercial practice and usage, or where a question of commercial or professional judgment or discretion is in question, or where technical issues or matters of professional practice are otherwise involved.[2]

10. *Ibid.* pp. 311–315.
11. *Ibid.* p. 314.
12. *Supra*, para. 5.2.5.
13. *Pioneer Shipping Ltd* v. *B.T.P. Tioxide Ltd.* (*The Nema*) [1982] A.C. 724, 752. See also *Kodros Shipping Corpn.* v. *Empresa Cubana de Fletes* (*The Evia*) (*No. 2*) [1982] 2 Lloyd's Rep. 307, 322, per Lord Roskill.
1. See, for example, *Colonial Bank* v. *European Grain & Shipping Ltd.* (*The Dominique*) [1987] 1 Lloyd's Rep. 239, 243–244; *Tradax Export S.A.* v. *Italgrani di Francesco Ambrosio* [1986] 1 Lloyd's Rep. 112, 119 (C.A.); *State Trading Corporation of India Ltd.* v. *M. Golodetz Ltd.* (*Now Transcontinental Affiliates Ltd.*) [1989] 2 Lloyd's Rep. 277, 284 (C.A.); *Everglade Maritime Inc.* v. *Schiffahrtsgesellschaft Detlef von Appen m.b.H.* (*The Maria*) [1993] 3 All E.R. 748, 765, Evans L.J.
2. Cf. *A/S Awilco* v. *Fulvia S.p.A. Di Navigazione* (*The Chikuma*) [1980] 2 Lloyd's Rep. 409; *Henry Ltd.* v. *Wilhelm G. Clasen* [1973] 1 Lloyd's Rep. 159 (C.A.); *Sterling Coal and Navigation Corporation of New York* v. *Halfdan Grieg & Co. A/S* (*The Lysland*) [1976] 1 Lloyd's Rep. 427 (C.A.).

6.2.6.1.2 The influence of a specialist maritime or trade tribunal on the exercise of discretion will therefore depend primarily on the precise nature of the legal question in respect of which leave to appeal is sought, and the circumstances in which the legal question arises. But it is in all regards likely to be an influence not only difficult to articulate but also to quantify in terms of real results. The influence is probably substantially less than might at first glance be suggested by the language used by the judiciary to express their respect for specialist arbitrators. It may be that the influence is predominantly psychological, to instil in the judiciary a greater confidence when asserting the central tenet of the legislation favouring the greater recognition of the finality of awards. Thus where the construction of a "one-off" contract adopted by parties within a particular trade is referred to an arbitrator or tribunal with knowledge and experience of the commercial context and usages of the trade, it may be that the judge hearing the application for leave to appeal will find himself able to apply the appropriate guideline with greater confidence and vigour.[3] A similar position may prevail when the proper construction of a standard form contract is referred to an arbitrator or tribunal experienced in the use of the contract and the commercial expectations surrounding it.[4] But even in this regard the understandings and expectations of the relevant commercial community cannot supersede the language of the contract or the impact of precedent. Nonetheless, apart from those questions of law with a substantial factual or judgmental ingredient, or which otherwise are particularly appropriate to be decided by an expert tribunal, there seems little reason for assuming that a maritime or trade tribunal is more likely to be right in law than any other kind of tribunal and in consequence there appears little justification for developing a more demanding test of error than applies generally within the guidelines.

6.2.6.2 *Lease, tenancy and rent review arbitration*

6.2.6.2.1 *The Nema/Antaios* guidelines were promulgated in the context of international maritime and commercial arbitration, which represents what may be described as the leading edge of London arbitration. The question arises whether the guidelines and the philosophy they manifest are confined to these modes of arbitration or whether they reach out more broadly and apply equally to the great variety of other forms of arbitration, such as building and civil engineering arbitration; lease, tenancy and rent review arbitration; consumer arbitration and the varieties of *ad hoc* arbitrations which take place. It would seem plain that the context and legal basis of disputes, the kinds of questions and issues which arise, the potential wider significance of arbitral decisions, may vary greatly between the various identifiable categories of

---

3. *B.V.S. S.A. and Another* v. *Kerman Shipping Co. S.A. (The Kerman)* [1982] 1 W.L.R. 166, 170 per Parker J., "the circumstances, if they exist, that the dispute is one concerning the construction of a 'one-off' contract relating to a particular trade, and that the parties have selected an arbitrator or arbitrators for their experience and knowledge of the commercial background and usages of the trade, constitute a factor which is proper to be taken into account and to put into the balance of circumstances on the side of the refusal of leave".

4. In *A/S Awilco* v. *Fulvia S.p.A. di Navigazione (The Chikuma)* [1980] 2 Lloyd's Rep. 409, 413, Lord Denning said in the context of the former special case procedure, "in a case of this kind [construction of New York Produce Exchange time charterparty] where the parties have agreed in the standard form to arbitration, and they have agreed upon a commercial man in the City of London, and have agreed that his decision should be final, prima facie his finding should be regarded as correct unless it is shown plainly to be erroneous in point of law".

arbitrations which take place. In turn this could give rise to different considerations in defining the relationship between each category and the courts, and therefore also to the way the discretion associated with section 1(3)(b) may be perceived and exercised. The possibility of a variable application of the section 1(3)(b) discretion according to the category of arbitration in issue was not addressed by the House of Lords in either *The Nema*[1] or *The Antaios*.[2] The question was left to subsequent judicial deliberation, the result of which in general terms has been to insist that the fundamental policy supporting the finality of awards is of universal application, but the manner in which the fundamental policy and associated guidelines are applied may be sensitive to the factual and legal context of different categories of arbitration.

6.2.6.2.2 The most significant discussion concerning the wider application of *The Nema/Antaios* guidelines has taken place in the context of tenancy and rent review arbitration. In *Lucas Industries plc* v. *Welsh Development Agency*,[3] Sir Nicolas Browne-Wilkinson V.-C., considered that *The Nema/Antaios* guidelines had no application to arbitrations on rent review clauses, particularly when the award also governed the outcome of future periodical rent reviews. In the view of the Vice-Chancellor the different circumstances demanded a lower standard than a strong *prima facie* case of error, and accordingly it was held that the granting of leave to appeal was appropriate if the judge was left in real doubt as to the correctness in law of the award. The Vice-Chancellor adopted the same test in *Ipswich B.C.* v. *Fisons plc*,[4] a case concerned with a dispute over the terms of a new lease, but was overruled by the Court of Appeal.[5] Lord Donaldson M.R.[6] considered the instant and preceding case to have fallen within the standard terms category and therefore a judge should not give leave to appeal unless there was a strong *prima facie* case for thinking that the arbitrator had fallen into error. In arriving at its decision the Court of Appeal appears to have asserted that the fundamental policy associated with the discretion arising under section 1(3)(b), creating a presumption in favour of finality, applies in all cases when leave to appeal from an award is sought; but the presumption is not of constant weight and the manner in which it is capable of being rebutted may differ as between the various categories of arbitration which take place in practice.

6.2.6.3 *Lawyers appointed as arbitrators*

There appears to be no suggestion that the exercise of the discretion is modified when an experienced lawyer is appointed as an arbitrator, umpire or as chairman of an arbitral tribunal. Quite frequently an eminent Queen's Counsel[1] or a retired judge[2] is appointed as a sole arbitrator or as an umpire. When a three arbitrator tribunal is established, the third arbitrator is often an experienced lawyer, who also acts as chair-

1. *Supra*.
2. *Supra*.
3. [1986] Ch. 500. See also *Warrington and Runcorn Development Corp.* v. *Greggs plc* [1989] 1 E.G.L.R. 9.
4. [1989] 3 W.L.R. 818.
5. [1990] 1 All E.R. 730.
6. Woolf and Beldam L.JJ. agreeing.
1. See, for example, *Actis Co. Ltd.* v. *The Sanko Steamship Co. Ltd. (The Aquacharm)* [1980] 2 Lloyd's Rep. 237; *Vinava Shipping Co. Ltd.* v. *Finelvet A.G. (The Chrysalis)* [1983] 1 Lloyd's Rep. 503.
2. See, for example, *Mosvolds Rederi A.S.* v. *Food Corporation of India (The Arras and Hoegh Rover)* [1989] 1 Lloyd's Rep. 131.

man of the tribunal. The practice of appointing lawyers is usually followed when a significant and difficult question of law lies at the root of the dispute and represents yet another illustration of the flexibility of the arbitral institution. But notwithstanding the presence of a significant legal expertise, there would appear to exist no receptive and compensating acknowledgement in the exercise of the section 1(3)(b) discretion. There is no concession of a greater probability of correctness: nor is there any adjustment of the appropriate test of correctness.[3]

6.2.6.4 *Judge-arbitrators and judge-umpires*

6.2.6.4.1 By virtue of section 4 of the Administration of Justice Act 1970, a judge of the Commercial Court may accept appointment as a sole arbitrator or umpire.[1] When acting in such a capacity the judge is styled a judge-arbitrator or judge-umpire.[2] Such an appointment can only be made if provided for by or by virtue of an arbitration agreement within the meaning of the Arbitration Act 1950, and is confined to disputes of a commercial character.[3] Further, an appointment may only be accepted if the Lord Chief Justice confirms the availability of the judge.[4] But even when all these conditions are satisfied the judge of the Commercial Court retains a discretion whether or not to accept appointment. A judge may, if in all the circumstances he thinks fit, accept appointment.[5] When an appointment is accepted the judge-arbitrator or judge-umpire enjoys no special status or additional powers by virtue of his judicial status. His jurisdiction and powers derive from the express and implied terms of the arbitration agreement and from the legislation in aid of arbitration.[6] So also the forum is an ordinary consensual arbitration tribunal and not a court of law.

6.2.6.4.2 The 1970 Act is silent on the question when the facility of judicial arbitration should be adopted. This is left to the discretion of the Commercial judges. Judicial arbitration is in its nature an exceptional and special mode of arbitral process and is only likely to be adopted in the case of arbitrations which are for one reason or another outside the normal run of cases. Cases might be considered suitable because they involve a question of principle, or otherwise involve an important or difficult question of law, or a question of law in which there is a general interest, or because a large sum of money is in issue.[7] But whatever the potential of this specialised mode of arbitration, it is little used in practice.[8]

---

3. It is instructive to note *Koch Marine Inc.* v. *D'Amico Societa di Navigazione A.R.L. (The Elena D'Amico)* [1980] 1 Lloyd's Rep. 75 where Christopher Staughton Q.C. (now Lord Justice Staughton) in considering an application to state a special case directed himself without qualification on the basis of the principles set out in *The Lysland*.

1. See, generally, Mustill and Boyd, *Commercial Arbitration* (2nd edn.) Chapter 20; Thomas, "Judge-Arbitrators" [1983] L.M.C.L.Q. 120.

2. Administration of Justice Act 1970, Sch. 3, cl. 1(c).

3. Section 4(1).

4. Section 4(2).

5. Section 4(1).

6. The one exception exists with regard to the default jurisdiction under s. 5 of the Arbitration Act 1979; see s. 5(3) and (4).

7. See, for example, *The Bamburi* [1982] 1 Lloyd's Rep. 312.

8. It would appear that on average there have never been more than two or three judicial arbitrations each year, with judges of the Commercial Court rarely holding at any moment in time more than one appointment as a judge-arbitrator or judge-umpire. The ever increasing popularity and demands on the Commercial Court will probably have the inevitable effect of diminishing the facility still further, with even the danger that as a question of practice it will cease to be available altogether; see n. 1 *supra*.

With the appointment of a judge-arbitrator or judge-umpire the reviewing jurisdiction over arbitration vested in the High Court is substantially transferred to the Court of Appeal.[9] This is particularly the case with regard to any jurisdiction exercisable by the High Court in relation to arbitrators and umpires "otherwise than under the Arbitration Act 1950".[10] The effect of this provision is that an application for leave to appeal from the award of a judge-arbitrator or judge-umpire is to the Court of Appeal, and any substantive appeal which may follow is also to the Court of Appeal.[11]

6.2.6.4.3 Bearing in mind the circumstance in which judicial arbitration is likely to arise, and also the fact that the parties have voluntarily chosen to appoint an experienced and expert Commercial judge to resolve the dispute referred, this might cumulatively be regarded as a powerful reason for supporting the finality of an award arising out of judicial arbitration even more strongly than is generally the case. The fact of judicial arbitration strongly suggests that the parties want a definitive and final award. By virtue of its authorship the award has claim to be considered as a quasi-judgment of the Commercial Court, although it is in truth very different from such a judgment. The upshot of this line of reasoning is to anticipate that appeals from judicial arbitration will be permitted only in exceptional circumstances but the reality appears to be very different. On the only occasion an application for leave to appeal from the award of a judge-arbitrator has been made to the Court of Appeal an orthodox and unexceptional approach was adopted. In *The Kelaniya*,[12] where the question of law was a standard case, Lord Donaldson M.R., applied the ordinary *Nema/Antaios* guideline (strong *prima facie* case of error), without any qualification for the fact that the arbitration was in the nature of judicial arbitration. Any anticipation of the motives of the parties did not reach out beyond the recognition of a presumption that the parties appointed a Commercial judge "because he was likely to get the law right".[13] The Master of the Rolls further considered that had the parties really wanted an authoritative decision they should have waived the arbitration agreement and put the issue before the Commercial Court,[14] where the question might have been decided by the same person who had acted as judge-arbitrator. This approach seems a little surprising. It ignores the reasonable implication that in appointing a judicial arbitrator the parties may also be seeking finality and also appears to ignore the policy surrounding section 4 of the Administration of Justice Act 1970. It is far from clear that this policy is wholly superseded by the 1979 Act, as distinct from coming into some balanced alignment with it, and with the consequence that an applicant for leave to appeal from the award of a judge-arbitrator should quite reasonably be under a more burdensome standard of proof.

6.2.7 Disciplinary proceedings in the form of arbitration

6.2.7.1 That the arbitral process may be adopted in unusual and surprising circumstances is well illustrated in *Moran* v. *Lloyd's*.[1] On the facts of the case, part of a disci-

---

9. Administration of Justice Act 1970, s. 4(4) and Sch. 3.
10. *Ibid.*, s. 4(5).
11. The same was the case under the former special case procedure: see, for example, *Terkol Rederierne* v. *Petroleo Brasileiro S.A. and Frota Nacional de Petroleiros (The Badagry)* [1985] 1 Lloyd's Rep. 395.
12. *Seaworld Ocean Line Co. S.A.* v. *Catseye Maritime Co. Ltd. (The Kelaniya)* [1989] 1 Lloyd's Rep. 30.
13. *Ibid* p. 32.
14. *Ibid.*
1. [1983] 1 Lloyd's Rep. 51; [1983] 1 Lloyd's Rep. 472 (C.A.).

plinary process brought by Lloyd's against an underwriting member was referred to arbitration under the provision of the Lloyd's Act 1871, section 20 (as subsequently amended). The purpose of the arbitration was to determine the factual validity of the wrongs alleged.[2] As such the arbitration was statutory in source and played a vital role in the disciplinary process of a professional organisation associated with a particular insurance market.

6.2.7.2 For the purpose of determining whether to give leave to appeal with regard to alleged errors of law arising out of an award, the circumstances prevailing in *Moran* v. *Lloyd's* are anything but ordinary. It is highly improbable that Parliament had this kind of case in mind when enacting the 1979 legislation, notwithstanding that the Act is expressly made applicable to statutory arbitrations,[3] and equally improbable that the House of Lords contemplated such a case when initially enunciating *The Nema* guidelines. The facts also introduce a new dimension. Although the quest for speedy finality may continue to be relevant to disciplinary arbitral proceedings, it must be counterbalanced by the recognition that disciplinary proceedings necessarily place at risk the professional reputation and livelihood of the person concerned. This latter consideration might in turn suggest that the courts should take a generous or at least a relatively more generous approach to the matter of appeals and accede to an application for leave to appeal when there is shown to exist the possibility of legal error or at least an arguable case.

6.2.7.3 At first instance in *Moran* v. *Lloyd's* Lloyd J. considered that in the novel circumstances of the case the right approach to adopt lay somewhere between speedy finality and ready assent. The learned judge observed[4]:

Each case must, of course, depend on its own circumstances. I would accept that in disciplinary proceedings, it is in general desirable that the process should be left, so far as possible, in the hands of the trade or profession concerned with the minimum of interference by the courts. But I would myself be willing to grant leave to appeal in this case if I could find a clear-cut question of law which could substantially affect [the applicant's] rights—for, without that precondition, the jurisdiction to grant leave to appeal does not arise—and on which he can make out a prima facie case that the umpire was wrong.

No such *prima facie* case having been made out, the application for leave to appeal was refused. The question of the proper exercise of the discretion in these unusual circumstances did not come before the Court of Appeal[5] for consideration when the case went on appeal, but no comment of an adverse nature was made suggesting the approach of Lloyd J. to be erroneous in principle.

---

2. The effect of s. 20, as amended, was to render a member of Lloyd's liable to exclusion by the votes of four-fifths of the members of the Society present at a meeting specially convened for the purpose, if the member had violated any of the fundamental rules of the Society or been guilty of an act or default discreditable to him as an underwriter or otherwise in connection with the business of insurance. But the power of exclusion could only be exercised if the fact that the member had been guilty of any such conduct or default had first been determined by arbitral award, and in making an award the arbitrators and umpire were to take into account all the circumstances of the case, both moral and legal.
3. See Chapter 1, para. 1.7.4.
4. *Supra*, pp. 56 and 57.
5. *Supra*, n. 1.

6.2.8 Relative importance of the question of law

6.2.8.1 One of the more puzzling and troublesome aspects of the new appellate process is untangling the precise relationship between leave to appeal and the existence of a question of law of supreme significance and importance arising out of an award; a question of law not merely of importance to the parties or to a section of the public; something beyond a question of law of general public importance, but a question of law of profound proportions by virtue of the fact that it drives to the root of legal doctrine and principle. As with the philosopher's elephant such questions of law may be more readily recognised than defined in the abstract, for the concept will never be free of considerations of judgment and degree. Examples drawn from recent legal developments would probably include the question whether the doctrine of frustration applied to leases[1]; whether an entitlement to salvage arose from beneficial services rendered in non-tidal waters[2]; and whether a claimant could recover direct from a Protection and Indemnity Association under the Third Parties (Rights Against Insurers) Act 1930, where the Rules of the Association contained a "pay to be paid" rule.[3] The intuitive judicial response when confronting questions of law of such magnitude and importance might well be to see the need for an immediate definitive and binding precedent and without more to give leave to appeal, in the knowledge that the question of law would also satisfy the "general public importance" test in section 1(7) and therefore in all probability climb further up the hierarchy of courts.[4] This kind of situation however is not directly addressed in *The Nema/Antaios* guidelines, nor directly in any subsequent judicial development, and therefore the extent to which the importance of the question of law in issue may override other factors more obviously associated with the philosophy of the guidelines remains a troublesome issue.

6.2.8.2 The central problem derives from the predominant emphasis in the guidelines on some manner of assessment of the correctness of the arbitral decision. The rebuttal of the presumption of finality, in the words of Lord Donaldson M.R.,[5] "must always be based on at least a suspicion that the arbitrator has gone wrong". Yet confronted with a question of law of the magnitude, importance and complexity here contemplated the judge may find it impossible to come to any manner of rational assessment beyond a reaffirmation of the profoundness of the question and the issues involved. At the end of the day the arbitrator may well be right, but equally he may be wrong, and to engage in any deliberation of degrees of rightness and wrongness may be wholly unreal, fanciful and even disingenuous. The question demands a higher plane of consideration. Even if the judge inclined to favouring the opinion of the arbitrator, his judicial disposition would probably excite extreme caution and a consciousness of the inappropriateness of entertaining even tentative views at this stage of the

---

1. *National Carriers Ltd.* v. *Panalpina (Northern) Ltd.* [1981] A.C. 675.
2. *The Goring* [1988] A.C. 831; [1988] 1 Lloyd's Rep. 397.
3. *Firma C-Trade S.A.* v. *Newcastle Protection and Indemnity Association (The Fanti)* [1987] 2 Lloyd's Rep. 299, 301, where Staughton J. comments on the importance and perplexity of the question. See also *Socony Mobil Oil Co. Inc. and Others* v. *West of England Ship Owners Mutual Insurance Association Ltd. (The Padre Island) (No. 2)* [1987] 2 Lloyd's Rep. 529. For the combined appeal of the two cases to the House of Lords, see [1991] 2 A.C. 1.
4. See Chapter 10, para. 10.3.
5. *Ipswich Borough Council* v. *Fisons plc* [1990] 1 All E.R. 730, 734. See also *Industriebeteiligungs & Handelsgesellschaft* v. *Malayan International Shipping Corporation Berhad (The Bunga Melawis)* [1991] 2 Lloyd's Rep. 271.

process. In these circumstances any emphasis on an initial assessment of the correctness of the arbitral decision appears to demand either the impossible or the infelicitous. The question therefore arises whether the sheer importance of the question of law in issue may itself be sufficient to displace the presumption of finality, without regard to any assessment of the correctness of the arbitral decision, so that leave to appeal may be granted even if the judge was not convinced that the arbitrator had fallen into error.

6.2.8.3 That a modified position may be adopted in these circumstances is at least capable of being supported by a variety of judicial dicta. Robert Goff J.[6] has given recognition to a "wider policy" beyond the guidelines, with the granting of leave to appeal justified to achieve consistency in arbitral decision-making. The particular facts of the case do not necessarily exhaust the potential of this wider policy. The approach adopted by Bingham J. to the question of law confronting him in *The Alaskan Trader*[7] may also be of particular significance. The precise question in issue was whether an owner was free to decline to accept the repudiation of a time charterparty by the charterer. Although the question of law arose in the context of charterparties, it raised a profoundly important question of contract law generally, with regard to which the authorities were inconclusive. In giving leave to appeal the learned judge observed,[8] "The case does, I think, raise a fundamental question of contract law and not merely a question arising on a standard clause in a charterparty or other commercial form. It is a question which has agitated legal writers and practitioners and it is an important question in this particular field." On the facts of the case this consideration represented only one of the reasons why leave to appeal was granted, but Bingham J. was further of a mind to observe that by virtue of the significance of the question of law it was strongly arguable that a lesser test was applicable for leave to appeal.[9] The important judgment of Mustill L.J. in *The Ugland Obo One*[10] offers further support. Although not appearing to give express recognition to the point here under discussion, Mustill L.J. nonetheless acknowledged the variety of forms in which questions of law came forward for consideration and the need for the judge hearing an application for leave to appeal to exercise, beyond the established guidelines, "an independent judgment about whether [the case before him] was a suitable case for an appeal".[11]

6.2.8.4 Although direct authority is absent, there are strong reasons for suggesting that where the question of law arising out of an award is of fundamental and profound importance, this fact itself should entitle the judge to conclude that the case is suitable for an appeal, even if of a mind that the arbitrator has probably come to the correct legal conclusion. The huge benefit of obtaining an authoritative and binding decision outweighs the claim of finality and an authoritative judgment is significantly more desirable than whatever may be made of an award in respect of which leave to appeal has been refused. Alternatively, it is arguable that the judge should be entitled to apply a lesser test than might otherwise be suggested by the guidelines and grant leave

6. *International Sea Tankers Inc.* v. *Hemisphere Shipping Co. Ltd. (The Wenjiang)* [1981] 2 Lloyd's Rep. 308, 314.
7. *Clea Shipping Corpn.* v. *Bulk Oil International Ltd. (The Alaskan Trader)* [1983] 1 Lloyd's Rep. 315.
8. *Ibid.* p. 318.
9. *Ibid.*
10. *Aden Refinery Co. Ltd.* v. *Ugland Management Co. Ltd. (The Ugland Obo One)* [1987] 1 Q.B. 650.
11. *Ibid.* pp. 667–669.

to appeal if satisfied that the question of law is open to serious argument, which is the test that operated in the pre-1979 Act law.[12]

6.2.8.5 At the other end of the scale the position is more clear. The relative unimportance of a question of law is a factor which the court may take into account and in the absence of other considerations is a factor that weighs against granting leave to appeal. A question of law, although "substantial" within the meaning of section 1(4),[12a] may nonetheless, within the global context of the dispute referred to arbitration, be of such relative unimportance to justify refusing leave to appeal. This appears to be the principle adopted by Staughton J. in *The Evimeria*.[13] A final hire statement dispute under a time charterparty was referred to arbitration. There were eight items in dispute but application for leave to appeal was sought with regard to only one item which raised the question whether a payment by an innocent contractor to an unconnected third party could be recovered as a head of damages against a contract breaker. The sum in question was $20,000 which represented only a small part of a wider dispute involving the sum of $164,000. The issue raised a question of mixed fact and law and it arose in the context of a one-off event. As such *The Nema/Antaios* guidelines suggested that leave should not be given unless the arbitrator had misdirected himself in law or otherwise had arrived at a decision which no arbitrator could reach, and the court in coming to its provisional view would take a great deal of convincing to the contrary.[14] On the facts of the case Staughton J. expressed "considerable doubt" whether the arbitrator had correctly applied himself in law and also that he "had doubts" about the correctness of the conclusions of the arbitrator.[15] Nonetheless the learned judge refused to give leave to appeal because the point of law in issue was "a side issue of little importance"[16], and went on to elaborate[17]:

. . . the particular issue here concerns only $20,000. In the arbitration it was either a minor issue or one of a large number of equal issues. It is certainly not a major issue of importance to this dispute.

. . . it would be a wrong exercise of discretion, in my view, to grant leave to appeal in such a case where the arbitrator has decided seven issues and a greater part of the eighth without encountering any complaints from the parties, and it is only as to a small part that his award encounters criticism. Even then, if there was plainly an error of law one might perhaps grant leave because, after all, it is a question of discretion and discretion can never be fettered by rules. In my judgment this is not a proper case to grant leave.

6.2.8.6 Staughton J. reasoned that *The Nema/Antaios* guidelines had to be read in the context of a case where the dispute was of major proportions and central to the whole arbitration, and where the question of law in issue went to the very heart of the dispute. The guidelines were consequently not the only and exclusive test and did not necessarily apply to a relatively minor issue in the context of a reference. Further, it was doubtful whether a relatively unimportant issue such as the present would have

---

12. *Halfdan Greig & Co. A/S* v. *Sterling Coal and Navigation Corpn. (The Lysland)* [1973] 1 Lloyd's Rep. 296, 306, per Lord Denning M.R.
12a. See Chapter 4, para. 4.2.3.
13. *Retla Steamship Co.* v. *Gryphon Shipping Co. S.A. (The Evimeria)* [1982] 1 Lloyd's Rep. 55.
14. *Supra*, Chapter 5, para. 5.2.5.
15. *Supra,* pp. 57 and 59.
16. Borrowing the phrase of Lord Denning M.R. in *The Lysland*, *infra*, n. 18.
17. *Supra*, p. 58.

been within the criteria specified in *The Lysland*,[18] had they still been in vogue; and on the basis that stricter criteria were now to be applied under the 1979 Act, this represented yet another argument for refusing leave to appeal.

6.2.9 Question of law specifically referred

6.2.9.1 Most questions of law arise as a necessary incident to the resolution of a dispute referred to arbitration. It is, however, open to the parties to expressly refer a specific question of law to the decision of an arbitrator. Where this was done prior to the 1979 Act the courts refused to intervene under the common law jurisdiction to set aside awards for error of law on their face, even though the arbitrator could be shown to have fallen into error.[1] It is unlikely that the refusal went to the question of jurisdiction, but in all probability it was associated with the exercise of discretion. The parties having chosen an arbitral tribunal to decide a specific question of law, they were precluded from thereafter seeking judicial intervention.[2] Whether the same consideration also influenced the exercise of judicial discretion in association with the special case procedure does not appear to have been considered and is therefore uncertain. But it would have been surprising had a different approach been adopted under the statutory procedure, for the considerations of policy and principle appear to be the same. The policy appears to have a yet wider ambit for courts will normally grant a stay in the exercise of the discretion under section 4(1) of the Arbitration Act 1950, when it can be shown that a specific question of law has been referred to the decision of an arbitrator.[3]

6.2.9.2 Although the question is undetermined by authority, there is a clear logic to the position adopted in the pre-1979 law being carried forward into the exercise of the discretion under section 1(3)(b). The taking into account of the fact that the question of law in issue had been specifically referred to the decision of the arbitrator and the perception of this fact as reinforcing the presumption of finality would appear wholly consistent with the general philosophy associated with the 1979 Act. The presumption in favour of finality might be even greater when the parties had also appointed a legally qualified arbitrator or a judge-arbitrator or judge-umpire to determine the question of law. It must also be borne in mind that a general object associated with the 1979 Act is to reduce the occasions when the courts may intervene in the arbitral process, compared with the pre-1979 position, and the adoption of a position contrary to that suggested in the text would have the very opposite effect.[4]

6.2.10 Question of European Community law

6.2.10.1 Following the enactment of the European Communities Act 1972 (and subsequent legislation) the law of the European Union has become an integral part of

---

18. *Halfdan Greig & Co. A/S* v. *Sterling Coal and Navigation Corpn. (The Lysland)* [1973] Q.B. 843, 862, where Lord Denning M.R. said, "The point of law should be of such importance that the resolution of it is necessary for the proper determination of the case—as distinct from a side issue of little importance."
1. See Chapter 1, para. 1.4.1.5.
2. *Ibid.*
3. *Absalom Ltd.* v. *Great Western Garden Village Society Ltd.* [1933] A.C. 592, 607–608.
4. See also the discussion by Mann, "Private Arbitration and Public Policy" (1985) 4 C.J.Q. 257.

English law.[1] To this extent the general duty of an arbitrator to determine disputes according to the prevailing principles of law has become correspondingly enlarged.[2] Under article 177 of the Treaty of Rome a court of a member state may refer a question of European law to the Court of Justice of the European Communities for its authoritative ruling.[3] No similar mode of reference is possible from arbitration directly. Under the legal regime of the European Union the control of arbitration proceedings is the domain of national systems of law. In consequence the responsibility for securing the observance of European law in arbitration proceedings is borne by the national courts of member states and is effectively discharged through their supervisory jurisdiction over arbitration.[4] Where a question of European law arises in the course of the arbitration process it cannot be referred under article 177 unless it is first brought before a court, and this, in the absence of consent is only possible if the High Court gives leave to appeal under the 1979 Act. Once leave to appeal is given, the court may entertain and grant an application for a reference under article 177.[5]

6.2.10.2 In *Bulk Oil (Zug) A.G.* v. *Sun International Ltd.*[6] Bingham J. considered it to be established that *The Nema* guidelines did not apply to all cases and that where a question of E.E.C. law was in issue, as compared with a purely domestic question of law, some difference of approach was capable of being justified.[7] On the facts of the case the validity of U.K. governmental export policy came into issue in the context of E.E.C. law. A contract for the sale of North Sea crude oil contained a clause which read: "Destination Free but always in line with exporting country's Government policy. United Kingdom Government policy at present does not allow delivery to South Africa." The buyers nominated a vessel for delivery of crude oil to Israel. The sellers refused to load the cargo claiming that the export of crude oil to Israel was contrary to the policy of the government of the United Kingdom. This refusal led to claims and counterclaims which were referred to arbitration. The arbitrator held the refusal to load was justified and the buyers to be in breach of contract. In so concluding the arbitrator held that the export of crude oil to Israel was contrary to United Kingdom government policy and that that policy did not offend against E.E.C. law, as argued by the buyers. Clearly, the reference in the contract to U.K. government policy was to be construed as a reference to valid and lawful governmental policy; and if it could be shown that the adopted policy of the U.K. government was invalid and unlawful, for whatever reason, the liabilities of the parties in dispute would be reversed, with the sellers in breach of contract. In affirming the validity of U.K. governmental policy the arbitrator arrived at two crucial conclusions of law. The first was an express conclusion that U.K. governmental policy was not contrary to an Agreement between the E.E.C. and Israel made on 11 May 1975 and enacted into law

---

1. Section 2.
2. See Chapter 1, para. 1.2.2.2.
3. For the advantages enjoyed by the Court of Justice of the European Communities when deciding questions of Community law, see *Customs and Excise* v. *A.P. Samex (Hamil) Synthetic Fibre Industrial Co. Ltd.*, *Third Party* [1983] 1 All E.R. 1042, 1050.
4. *Broekmeulen*, Case 246/80 [1981] E.C.R. 2311; *Nordsee Deutsche*, Case 102/81 (1982).
5. *Bulk Oil (Zug) A.G.* v. *Sun International Ltd. and Sun Oil Trading Co. (No. 2)* [1984] 1 Lloyd's Rep. 531, 553–554.
6. *Bulk Oil (Zug) A.G.* v. *Sun International Ltd. and Sun Oil Trading Co.* [1983] 1 Lloyd's Rep. 655.
7. *Ibid.* pp. 659–660.

by Council Regulation 1274/75.[8] The second, an inferential conclusion, was to the effect that although the Community had assumed to regulate commercial relations between the Community and the member states on the one hand and third countries on the other, and had enacted various regulations governing relations with Israel, the U.K. was not thereby precluded from implementing national measures without first notifying and consulting the Commission and seeking its approval.

6.2.10.3 On both conclusions Bingham J. was not tentatively of the view that the arbitrator was plainly wrong, nor that a strong *prima facie* case had been made out that he was wrong. To the contrary, the learned judge was, on the basis of the materials presented, of the opinion that the arbitrator was right, and would himself have decided the two points in the same way as the arbitrator.[9] The fundamental view of Bingham J. appears to have been that the case fell to be considered outside *The Nema* guidelines, but to the extent it was appropriate and necessary to compress the facts into the framework presented by *The Nema* guidelines, the less demanding test of the "standard form case" and "general events" was the more appropriate. Bingham J. explained his justification for this conclusion on the question of characterisation in the following terms[10]:

There has been some discussion before me as to whether this case should be treated as a one-off question affecting these parties only or as a more general question affecting a wider section of the commercial community. On the one hand, it is apparently the case that the clause in question is not a printed clause to be found in any standard form. On the other hand, I am told that it is a clause which is to be found in North Sea oil contracts, either in this form or in a very similar form. It also appears to me that any British prohibition on the export of crude oil to Israel is likely to affect traders other than Bulk and, given the importance of oil to the economy of any country, it is a question of potentially very great importance to the state of Israel. It is not, moreover, Israel alone which is the subject of the British prohibition, but it extends to any country not falling within the group formed by the International Energy Agency, the member states of the Community and, as I understand, Finland. It therefore appears to me that any doubt about the legality of the British policy is an important matter far transcending the interests of the particular parties to this litigation. If either of the "Nema" tests (see [1981] 2 Lloyd's Rep. 239) is appropriate, it would therefore seem to me that the lower of those tests is what Bulk must satisfy.

6.2.10.4 Bingham J. further considered that notwithstanding his assessment of the correctness of the arbitrator's conclusions, these broader considerations justified a departure from *The Nema* guidelines, and that the additional presence of a question of E.E.C. law was a still further reason for so departing. The judge explained[11]:

But there is an additional reason for not directly following what the House of Lords has laid down as the ordinary rules. On a point of English law, an English Judge can reasonably be expected to take a view, on reading an award and hearing summary argument, whether he considers an arbitrator's award to be right or wrong. He may in the event prove to be incorrect in his decision, but it is a task which nonetheless he can reasonably be expected to undertake. It is a very much harder task for him to undertake on a point of Community law and harder still for him to do with any confidence of being correct. The cases show that even where English Judges have been confident that a point of Community law should be decided in one way, the Court of Justice of the European Communities has not infrequently decided it in the other.

8. For the general principles guiding the construction of the Treaty, Regulations and Directives, see, *R* v. *Henn* [1981] A.C. 850, 904, per Lord Diplock.
9. *Ibid*. pp. 658–659.
10. *Ibid*. p. 659.
11. *Ibid*. pp. 659–660.

6.2.10.5 The analysis and decision of Bingham J. to give leave to appeal was upheld by the Court of Appeal.[12] Ackner L.J. in summarising the factors on which the decision to grant leave was based included the point,[13] "It involved a question of Community law of complexity upon which the view which both he [the judge] and the arbitrator had formed could well be wrong." The Court of Appeal, however, made it clear that it did not follow that whenever a question of Community law arises leave to appeal must be given. All must turn on the circumstances of individual cases. In particular, Ackner L.J. indicated that the question of Community law must be capable of serious argument and not admit of only one possible answer or be covered by a Community authority precisely in point.[14]

6.2.11 Sufficiency of evidence to support findings and conclusions of fact

6.2.11.1 It is well established that a question directed to the existence or adequacy of evidence to support a finding or conclusion of fact raises a question of law.[1] The characterisation has, however, always been regarded as somewhat exceptional and the logical implications of the characterisation in terms of judicial review entertained only with extreme caution. The reason for the cautious reception is because any question directed to the existence or sufficiency of evidence to support the factual findings and conclusions of arbitrators lies at the very precipice of the distinction between fact and law, and further tends to subvert the traditional perception of an arbitration tribunal as a tribunal of fact and with the arbitrator the sole judge of fact.[2] In the result, although a question directed to the existence or sufficiency of evidence to support findings and conclusions of fact may be raised on an appeal under the 1979 Act, it is probable that such applications will be rigorously scrutinised and leave given exceptionally sparingly.

6.2.11.2 The general approach of the judiciary to this special kind of question of law was firmly established under the former special case procedure. In *The Effy* Mocatta J. defined the judicial perspective in the following language[3]:

There is no doubt that an umpire or arbitrator may state as a question of law whether there is any evidence on which he could come to a particular finding of fact since this itself is a question of law . . . the jurisdiction to order a special case to be stated on a question of law of this character is one that should be exercised sparingly, since there is a danger that in so ordering the distinction between the functions of the arbitrator as sole judge of fact and those of the court to determine questions of law is blurred.

---

12. [1983] 2 Lloyd's Rep. 587 (C.A.).
13. *Ibid*. p. 591.
14. *Ibid*. p. 591.
1. *Gillespie Bros. & Co.* v. *Thompson Bros. & Co.* (1922) 13 Ll.L.Rep. 519; *Nello Simoni* v. *A/S M/S Straun* (1950) 83 Ll.L.Rep. 157, 161, per Devlin J.; *Tersons Ltd.* v. *Stevenage Development Corporation* [1965] 1 Q.B. 37; *Zim Israel Navigation Co. Ltd.* v. *Effy Shipping Corporation (The Effy)* [1972] 1 Lloyd's Rep. 18; *Exormisis Shipping S.A.* v. *Oonsoo, Democratic People's Republic of Korea and Korean Foreign Transportation Corporation (The Aristides Xilas)* [1975] 2 Lloyd's Rep. 402; *Mitsubishi International G.m.b.H.* v. *Bremer Handelsgesellschaft m.b.H.* [1981] 1 Lloyd's Rep. 106; *Blue Anchor Line Ltd.* v. *Alfred C. Toepfer International G.m.b.H. (The Union Amsterdam)* [1982] 2 Lloyd's Rep. 432.
2. See Chapter 1, para. 1.2.2.1.
3. *Zim Israel Navigation Co. Ltd.* v. *Effy Shipping Corpn. (The Effy)* [1972] 1 Lloyd's Rep. 18, 33–34.

This general approach was subsequently reaffirmed by Mustill J. in the following terms[4]:

It is . . . a question of law whether there was sufficient evidence to justify a particular finding of fact. Such a question of law can properly be raised for decision by the High Court through the medium of an award in the form of a special case. The procedure should, however, be used very sparingly, for unless strictly controlled it tends to undermine the rule that the arbitrator is the sole judge of fact.

6.2.11.3 The reluctance of the courts under the special case procedure to entertain the kind of legal question here under consideration is carried forward into the new appeal procedure under the 1979 Act. *The Nema/Antaios* guidelines do not expressly address the question of evidentiary sufficiency, but there is nothing that has occurred in association with the enactment and development of the 1979 Act to displace the established policy. To the contrary, the 1979 Act reinforces and entrenches the historical analysis. In *The Barenbels*[5] the Court of Appeal accepted that the question whether there is any evidence to support a finding of fact raised a question of law and Robert Goff L.J. went on to comment[6]: "It is conceivable that an appeal on such a question may lie under section 1 of the 1979 Act: though appeals of this kind will be at least as much discouraged under that Act, as were special cases on similar points under the old procedure." In *Universal Petroleum*[7] Kerr L.J. was of the same view and while again admitting the jurisdiction nonetheless considered that the "courts will be likely to stifle such appeals at the stage of the application for leave, on the grounds that they are out of accord both with the general principle that the arbitrator is master of the facts, and with the specific commercial aims of the new system".

6.2.11.4 The restrictive approach adopted by the courts means that only in exceptional circumstances will leave to appeal be given in relation to a question of law relating to the existence or sufficiency of evidence to support a finding of fact. So rare is the likelihood that in *The Baleares*[8] Steyn L.J. was moved to a more rigorous line of thought, for the "concept of a jurisdiction which ought never to be exercised is not attractive".[9] In the opinion of Steyn L.J. the historical jurisdiction to review questions of law relating to the existence or sufficiency of evidence to support factual findings was inconsistent with the new appellate regime introduced by the 1979 Act and had been displaced by it. Steyn L.J. observed[10]:

The power to review a finding of fact of a tribunal on the ground that there is no evidence to support it, and that there is therefore an error of law, is a useful one in certain areas of the law,

---

4. *Mitsubishi International G.m.b.H.* v. *Bremer Handelsgesellschaft m.b.H.* [1981] 1 Lloyd's Rep. 106, 108; see also *The Kavo Peiratis* [1977] 2 Lloyd's Rep. 344, 352, per Kerr J.; *Mondial Trading Co. G.m.b.H.* v. *Gill & Duffus Zuckerhandelsgesellschaft m.b.H.* [1980] 2 Lloyd's Rep. 376, 379 per Robert Goff J.; *Hayn Roman & Co. S.A.* v. *Cominter (UK) Ltd.* [1982] 2 Lloyd's Rep. 458, 462, per Robert Goff J.; *Interbulk Ltd.* v. *Aiden Shipping Co. Ltd.* etc. *The Vimeira* [1983] 2 Lloyd's Rep. 424, 429, per Lloyd J.; *Bulk Oil (Zug) A.G.* v. *Sun International Ltd.* [1984] 1 Lloyd's Rep. 531, 533, per Bingham J.
5. *Athens Cape Naviera S.A.* v. *Deutsche Dampfschiffahrtsgesellschaft "Hansa" Aktiengesellschaft and Another (The Barenbels)* [1985] 1 Lloyd's Rep. 528 (C.A.).
6. *Ibid.* p. 532. See also *Mondial Trading Co. G.m.b.H.* v. *Gill & Duffus Zuckerhandelsgesellschaft m.b.H.* [1980] 2 Lloyd's Rep. 376, 379 per Robert Goff J.
7. *Universal Petroleum Co. Ltd.* v. *Handels- und Transport Gesellschaft m.b.H.* [1987] 1 Lloyd's Rep. 517, 525 (C.A.).
8. *Geogas S.A.* v. *Trammo Gas Ltd.* (*The Baleares*) [1993] 1 Lloyd's Rep. 215
9. *Ibid.* p. 232.
10. *Ibid.*

notably in the administrative law field. But in the [limited] appellate jurisdiction of the court under s. 1 of the Arbitration Act 1979 this concept has no useful role to play. It is inconsistent with the filtering system for the granting of leave to appeal which was created by the Arbitration Act 1979. In my judgment it has not survived the changes introduced by the reforming measure of 1979.

These comments are in strictness *obiter dictum* and were not expressly endorsed by the other members of the Court of Appeal.[11] In essence they suggest that leave to appeal should never be given in relation to the kind of question of law here in issue, as distinct from the established position, that leave to appeal will only be given very rarely and only in exceptional circumstances. As a matter of practice there may be little difference between the two positions. To exclude the discretion in its entirety may be pressing the point too hard and to retain a residue of discretion always allows for the interests of justice to be accommodated. It cannot further be the case that the 1979 Act has changed the characterisation, so that a question of evidentiary sufficiency is no longer a question of law.

6.2.12 Question of law previously considered on a consultative case

6.2.12.1 Where the parties have sought the opinion of the High Court on a consultative case under section 2 of the 1979 Act[1] and the arbitrator subsequently adopts and incorporates the judicial opinion into his award, the fact of the prior judicial involvement does not preclude the allegation that the arbitrator has erred in law and an appeal can be instituted under section 1(2). This is so because a judicial opinion expressed under the consultative case procedure is not *res judicata*. This was the analysis of the legal effect of an opinion given under the consultative case procedure as it existed in the pre-1979 Act law, and it is unlikely that the remoulded procedure under section 2 of the 1979 Act has changed the analysis.[2]

But although an appeal is possible, it is no doubt to be rigidly scrutinised, with the applicant for leave to appeal bearing an exceptional burden. To permit the appeal results in a question of law arising in an arbitration visiting the High Court on two distinct occasions and is in effect an appeal to a judge of the High Court from an opinion expressed by another judge of the High Court.[3] Nothing could be more patently contrary to the policy of the 1979 Act. The burden assumed by an applicant for leave to appeal will probably assume an even mightier dimension when the prior consultative case ascended the appellate hierarchy of courts.

6.2.12.2 The relationship between the section 2 consultative case procedure and the discretion arising under section 1(3)(b) has to date not been squarely considered by the courts. But that a cautious and restrictive approach is likely to prevail is suggested by an *obiter dictum* of Donaldson L.J. in *The Oltenia*[4]:

---

11. *Ibid.* p. 227, where Neil L.J. felt unable without the benefit of further argument of reaching a final conclusion on the point, but nonetheless expressed himself to be "impressed by the argument" advanced by Steyn L.J.

1. Considered in Chapter 12.

2. See Chapter 12, para. 12.7.2.

3. It would seem highly undesirable that the judge who gave the opinion on the consultative case should be involved in the subsequent appeal procedure, whether on the application for leave to appeal or the full appeal.

4. *Babanaft International Co. S.A.* v. *Avant Petroleum Inc. (The Oltenia)* [1982] 2 Lloyd's Rep. 99, 107.

[Counsel] rightly pointed out that in an application for leave to appeal under s.1 on a question of law which had already been decided by the Court in the same arbitration under s.2. the applicant would undertake a considerable burden. This is correct. He would have to satisfy the Judge that the question was fit for consideration by a Court having power to declare the s.2 decision to have been wrong and, with this in mind, the Judge would normally want to be satisfied that if he gave leave to appeal to the High Court, he would be likely also to certify the question under s.1(7)(b) with a view to giving the Court of Appeal jurisdiction to entertain a further appeal.

The reference to section 1(7)(b)[5] seems to indicate that beyond the criteria inherent in *The Nema/Antaios* guidelines, the question of law in issue must also be of a nature that its proper resolution is a matter of general public importance or that there exists some other special reason why it should be considered by the court and also possibly a subsequent appellate court with power to finally determine the question of law in issue.

6.2.13 Question of law not raised in the arbitration

6.2.13.1 A problem endemic to any system of appeals tied to questions of law is the extent to which an appellate tribunal may entertain questions of law not raised and argued before a first tier tribunal. That question has prevailed and proved troublesome within both the judicial and arbitral systems. As for the judicature, the appellate courts retain a discretion in the matter. There is a discretion to admit or to refuse to entertain the new question of law; but the general prevailing position appears to be that a new question of law will only be admitted if the other party has had an opportunity to meet it; that he has not acted to his detriment on the faith of the earlier omission to raise it; and that he can be adequately protected in costs.[1] A roughly parallel position applied under the former special case procedure in arbitration, with the court enjoying a discretion to entertain or reject a fresh question of law. But in the exercise of its discretion the court appears to have adopted a particularly firm stance, the effect of which was that a fresh question of law would only be entertained if it fell within the parameters of the specific question of law stated in the award and that it was capable of being determined on the facts found in the award. If it was necessary to ascertain further facts which the arbitrator might reasonably have been invited to find in his award, so making a remission a necessary precondition to future progress, this was invariably fatal to any attempt to invite the court to consider the fresh question of law.[2] Considerations of justice also prevailed, with the court not willing to permit the introduction of a new question of law if, in the circumstances of the case, that would be unfair to the other party or if the applicant by his conduct was precluded from raising the new question of law.[2a]

---

5. See Chapter 10, para. 10.3.
1. *Ex parte Firth (The Cowburn)* (1882) 19 Ch.D. 419, 427, per Sir George Jessel M.R. See also *MacDougall* v. *Knight* (1889) 14 A.C. 194; *The Tasmania* (1890) 15 A.C. 223; *Pittalis* v. *Grant* [1989] 2 All E.R. 622.
2. *Kates* v. *Jeffery* [1914] 3 K.B. 160; *Hudson's Bay Company* v. *Domingo Mumbru Sociedad Anonima* (1922) 10 Ll.L.Rep. 476; *Sinason-Teicher* v. *Oilcake and Oilseeds Trading Co. Ltd.* [1954] 1 Lloyd's Rep. 376; *Soproma S.p.A.* v. *Marine & Animal By-Products Corporation* [1966] 1 Lloyd's Rep. 367; *Yamashita Shinnihon Steamship Co. Ltd.* v. *Elios S.p.A. (The Lily Prima)* [1976] 2 Lloyd's Rep. 487; *D'Amico Societa di Navigazione* v. *Promoteca S.A. (The Cesare D'Amico)* [1982] 1 Lloyd's Rep. 493.
2a. *Ismail* v. *Polish Ocean Lines* [1976] Q.B. 893; *Bunge S.A.* v. *Kruse* [1980] 2 Lloyd's Rep. 142; *Tradax Export S.A.* v. *Cook Industries Inc.* [1982] 1 Lloyd's Rep. 385.

6.2.13.2 The ethos of the preceding law permeates the approach adopted under the 1979 Act. There is no prohibition imposed by the legislation upon the court considering and giving leave to appeal in relation to a question of law not before the arbitrator, but it is in each case a question of discretion. In *Petraco (Bermuda) Ltd.* v. *Petromed International S.A.*[3] Staughton L.J. set down the framework within which the discretion is to be exercised in the following terms[4]:

Next I turn to the question of how a judge should regard the introduction of a new point of law when exercising his discretion under s 1(3) of the Arbitration Act 1979 to grant or refuse leave to appeal. I would suggest an additional guideline (and it is accepted that an additional guideline is called for, because this point is not covered by previous authority) as follows. First, the fact that the point which it is proposed to argue was not argued before the arbitrator is not an absolute bar to the grant of leave to appeal. Both sides accept this in the present case. Second, it is, however, to be taken into account in the exercise of the general discretion provided by s 1(3). Both sides accept that. Third, where the failure to argue the point below has had the result that all the necessary facts are not found, this will be a powerful factor against granting leave. Fourth, even in such a case it may in very special circumstances be right to remit the award for further facts to be found with a view to granting leave. One cannot entirely exclude the exercise of the discretion in that way in what would probably be a very unusual case. Fifth, if all the necessary facts have been found, the judge should give such weight as he thinks fit to the failure to argue the point before the arbitrator. In particular, he should have regard to whether the new point is similar to points that were argued, perhaps a variant of one of those points or a different way of putting it on the one hand, or whether it is a totally new and different point on the other.

On the facts of the case the fresh question of law was no more than a nuance of a question of law argued in the arbitration and this together with the other facts of the case made it, in the opinion of the Court of Appeal, an appropriate case to grant leave to appeal.

6.2.13.3 In *The Padre Island (No. 2)*[5] leave was granted on the substantive appeal to introduce a new point of law that had not been before either the arbitrator or the judge on the application for leave to appeal; and this was justified by the emergence of a subsequent judicial decision of material significance to the dispute between the parties.[6] An applicant for leave to appeal a fresh point of law may assist his cause by expressing a willingness to abide with the facts as found in the award and thereby take the risk of the award not containing the findings of fact necessary to sustain his legal argument.[7]

6.2.14 Costs and interest

6.2.14.1 Costs

6.2.14.1.1 In the pre-1979 Act law awards of costs were subject to review under the jurisdiction of the court to set aside and remit awards established by sections 22 and 23(1) of the Arbitrations Act 1950.[1] An arbitrator who fell into legal error in making

---

3. [1988] 2 Lloyd's Rep. 357.
4. Pp. 359–360. Sir Roualeyn Cumming-Bruce and Purchas L.J. agreeing.
5. *Socony Mobil Oil Co. Inc. and Others* v. *West of England Ship Owners Mutual Insurance Association Ltd. (The Padre Island) (No. 2)* [1987] 2 Lloyd's Rep. 529, 531–532.
6. Namely *Firma C-Trade S.A.* v. *Newcastle Protection and Indemnity Association (The Fanti)* [1987] 2 Lloyd's Rep. 299.
7. *Novorossisk Shipping Co.* v. *Neopetro Co. Ltd. (The Ulyanovsk)* [1990] 1 Lloyd's Rep. 425, 427.
1. *Heaven and Kesterton* v. *Sven Widaeus A/B* [1958] 1 W.L.R. 248, 255–256, Diplock J.

an order of costs was guilty of misconduct, and it was this concept which lay at the root of the reviewing jurisdiction.[2] Following the 1979 Act the position has been radically changed and in the present law the only mode by which an award of costs may be reviewed is by an appeal to the High Court under section 1(2) of the 1979 Act. Although the award of costs depends to a substantial degree on the facts of individual cases and the exercise of discretion, nonetheless the process is underpinned by legal principles and where an arbitrator falls into error in identifying and applying these principles no distinction is now made between legal error in relation to costs and any other kind of legal error.[3] Notwithstanding the change of procedure the substantive basis of review remains the same.[4] The natural implications of the change in procedure are that the obtaining of leave to appeal (in the absence of consent) will be a necessary precondition to an appeal[5] and that in relation to the award of costs an order for reasons or further reasons may be made under section 1(5).[6]

6.2.14.1.2 The grounds on which an award of costs may be challenged are various. It may be alleged that the arbitrator has gone wrong in principle; that he has taken into account an illegitimate criterion or that he has failed to take into account a relevant and material criterion[7]; or that he has applied a relevant criterion in an erroneous manner, such as the effect on the exercise of discretion of a sealed offer supplied by the respondent to the arbitral tribunal.[8] Alternatively the grievance may be directed not to the criteria adopted and applied but to the ultimate order made, alleging it to be an order that no arbitrator or tribunal acting reasonably could have arrived at.[9] But whatever the basis of challenge, in each case leave to appeal will be a necessary first step (in the absence of consent) and the question arises how the associated discretion is to be approached. The review of awards of costs would seem analogous to the review of questions of mixed fact and law[10] and it would seem to follow that a common approach is to be taken to the question of leave to appeal.[11] In the result leave to appeal will not be given unless the applicant can clearly and unambiguously satisfy the judge that the arbitrator has addressed the matter of costs erroneously or that the arbitrator, notwithstanding that he has addressed the matter of

---

2. See, generally, Thomas, "Costs, discretion and issues of technical misconduct" [1982] 2 L.M.C.L.Q. 288; Wetter and Priem, "Costs and their Allocation in International Commercial Arbitrations" (1991) 2 The Am. Rev. of Int. Arb. 249.

3. *Blexen Ltd.* v. *G. Percy Trentham Ltd.* (1990) 42 E.G. 133 (C.A.); *King* v. *Thomas McKenna Ltd.* [1991] 2 W.L.R. 1234; *President of India* v. *Jadranska Slobodna Plovidba* [1992] 2 Lloyd's Rep. 274; *Everglade Maritime Inc.* v. *Schiffahrtsgesellschaft Detlef von Appen m.b.H.* (*The Maria*) [1993] 2 Lloyd's Rep. 167 (C.A.). Note also *Warinco A.G.* v. *Andre & Cie S.A.* [1979] 2 Lloyd's Rep. 298, 299; *Evmar Shipping Corpn.* v. *Japan Line Ltd.* (*The Evmar*) [1984] 2 Lloyd's Rep. 581, 582–583. See also *Cohen and Others* v. *Baram*, *The Times*, 16 December 1993.

4. Considered *infra*.

5. Considered *infra*.

6. See Chapter 11, para. 11.8.1.12.

7. Cf. *Lewis* v. *Haverfordwest R.D.C.* [1953] 1 W.L.R. 1486; *Matheson & Co. Ltd.* v. *A. Tabah & Sons* [1963] 2 Lloyd's Rep. 270; *L. Figueiredo Navegacas S.A.* v. *Reederei Richard Schroeder K.G.* (*The Erich Schroeder*) [1974] 1 Lloyd's Rep. 192.

8. Cf. *Everglade Maritime Inc.* v. *Schiffahrtsgesellschaft Detlef von Appen m.b.H.* (*The Maria*), *supra*. Also *Tramountana Armadora S.A.* v. *Atlantic Shipping Co. S.A.* [1978] 1 Lloyd's Rep. 391; Commercial Court Committee, Report on Arbiration (1978), paras. 62–66. For the corresponding position in litigation see R.S.C., Ord. 22, rule 3(4); Ord. 62, rules 5(4), 9(1)(b) and (d).

9. Cf. Chapter 5, para. 5.2.5.

10. *President of India* v. *Jadranska Slobodna Plovidba*, *supra*, p. 281, Hobhouse J.

11. See Chapter 5, para. 5.2.5.

costs correctly, has made an order which in the circumstances of the case is unreasonable, in the sense that it is an order which no reasonable arbitrator could have made. The test the applicant must satisfy is very stringent and will not be readily discharged. Hobhouse J. has articulated the applicant's position in the following terms[12]: "a party will normally have to be prepared to satisfy the highest category of test in *The Nema* which is tantamount to persuading the Court that the appeal will almost certainly be successful." This particular approach to the exercise of discretion is apt when the question of costs turns on the facts and circumstances of the particular case, as will more often than not be the case, and which will therefore in the context of arbitral appeals attract the characterisation "one-off".[13] But where the basis of challenge raises a question of principle, so that there is raised a question of wide relevance and significance, it may be anticipated that the applicant will be confronted by the less demanding test associated with "standard cases", and consequently will be obliged to establish a strong *prima facie* case of error or unreasonableness.[14]

6.2.14.1.3 Without clear justification the court will be reluctant to interfere with the exercise of arbitral discretion in disposing of costs.[15] Provided the award of costs is otherwise valid, the court will not give leave to appeal merely because, had the matter to be decided by the court, it would have exercised the discretion differently and therefore made a different award of costs.[16]

6.2.14.2 Interest

6.2.14.2.1 The award of interest bears a marked procedural similarity to costs in the arbitral process, although the two concepts are patently distinct and serve different purposes. Notwithstanding that the award of interest is in the discretion of the arbitrator and influenced by the facts of individual cases, the subject has an underlay of legal principles. If the arbitrator misdirects himself as to any of the legal principles or otherwise comes to an unreasonable determination, the arbitrator is guilty of technical misconduct. In turn the latter concept established the basis for the judicial review of interest awards and with the court having a jurisdiction to set aside or remit by virtue of sections 23(1) and 22 of the Arbitration Act 1950.[1]

6.2.14.2.2 Although not yet decided, it seems very probable that the post-1979 Act developments in relation to costs will be mirrored by interest awards.[2] Error of law rather than misconduct is likely to become the basis of judicial review, with the appellate process established by the 1979 Act replacing the non-appellate review jurisdic-

---

12. *President of India* v. *Jadranska Slobodna Plovidba, supra*, p. 281.
13. See Chapter 5, paras 5.2.3 and 5.2.6.
14. See Chapter 5, paras 5.2.4 and 5.2.6.
15. Cf. *Ritter* v. *Godfrey* [1920] 2 K.B. 47, 52, Lord Sterndale; *Donald Campbell & Co. Ltd.* v. *Pollak* [1927] A.C. 732, 811, Viscount Cave.
16. *Taramountana Armadora S.A.* v. *Atlantic Shipping Co. S.A.* [1978] 1 Lloyd's Rep. 391, 396, Donaldson J. See also *Pitkin* v. *Saunders & Forster Ltd.* (1923) 128 L.T. 789; *Rosen* v. *Dowley and Selby* [1943] 2 All E.R. 172; *Perry* v. *Stopher* [1959] 1 W.L.R. 415; *Dineen* v. *Walpole* [1969] 1 Lloyd's Rep. 261; *Blue Horizon Shipping Co. S.A.* v. *E.D. & F. Man Ltd.* (*The Aghios Nicolaos*) [1980] 1 Lloyd's Rep. 17 (C.A.).
1. *Panchaud Freres S.A.* v. *Pagnan and Fratelli* [1974] 1 Lloyd's Rep. 394; *P. J. Van Der Zijden Wildhandel NV* v. *Tucker and Cross Ltd.* [1976] 1 Lloyd's Rep. 341; *Thos. P. Gonzalez Corpn.* v. *F. R. Waring* (*International*) (*Pty.*) *Ltd.* [1978] 1 Lloyd's Rep. 494; *Warinco A.G.* v. *Andre & Cie S.A.* [1979] 2 Lloyd's Rep. 298.
2. *Supra*, para. 6.2.14.1.1.

tion to set aside or remit awards. If this proves an accurate prediction then, in the absence of consent, leave to appeal will be a necessary precondition to judicial review.

6.2.14.2.3 In considering an application for leave to appeal it seems likely that the court will take the same approach as it does in relation to an award of costs.[3] Leave to appeal will normally not be given unless the applicant can clearly and unambiguously show that the arbitrator has acted injudiciously in making or failing to make an award of interest. The test is demanding and must be satisfied by reference to an examination of the award alone. In the vocabulary of *The Nema/Antaios* guidelines the phrase "obviously wrong" possibly communicates the standard of proof confronting the applicant for leave to appeal; save that a less demanding test may be applied when a principle of general interest is in question, in which case the applicant may be obliged to establish a strong *prima facie* case of legal error.

6.2.14.2.4 Provided the arbitrator has exercised the discretion in a way reasonably open to him, leave to appeal is unlikely to be given if the sole grievance is with the way the arbitrator has exercised the discretion. It is in the character of discretion that it may be exercised differently in relation to a common set of facts, and the fact that the judge hearing the application for leave to appeal would have exercised the discretion differently is of no consequence, provided the discretion could be exercised in the way the arbitrator chose to exercise it.

6.2.15 Legal matrix in a state of flux

6.2.15.1 The common law is to some degree in a state of perpetual evolution, bringing with it judicial reconsideration, affirmation, amendment, refinement, and at times radical change. The process is predominantly disciplined and orderly, but there are occasions when it is intense, frenetic and rapid. In consequence the daily practice of legal decision-making takes place against a constantly shifting jurisprudential backdrop, with the pace of change fluctuating from the constant to the rapid, and often regulated by the occurrence of external events. The legal context of arbitration is therefore a dynamic phenomenon, with it always possible for the arbitral process to become embroiled in significant shifts and developments in the legal matrix. The present enquiry addresses the impact this kind of circumstance may have on appeals from arbitration awards.

6.2.15.2 There is always the possibility that a substantive change in the law may take place subsequent to the commencement of an arbitration, but prior to the application for leave. When a change in the law takes place during the course of a reference, it may be readily taken into account (provided the parties are aware of it) in the argument and evidence of the parties.[1] When a change occurs after the conclusion of a reference but before publication of an award, that is during the period the arbitral tribunal is considering its award, an application may be made for the reference to be

---

3. *Supra*, para. 6.2.14.1.2.
1. Cf. *L'Office Cherifien des Phosphates and Unitramp S.A.* v. *Yamashita Shinnihon Steamship Co. Ltd.* (*The Boucraa*) [1993] 2 Lloyd's Rep. 149 (C.A.), where it is observed that many arbitrations were held in abeyance awaiting the outcome of the proper interpretation to be given to the Arbitration Act 1950, section 13A (power to dismiss a claim for want of prosecution). For the appeal to the House of Lords, see [1994] 1 Lloyd's Rep. 251; [1994] 1 All E.R. 20.

reconvened and the new development considered.[2] Although the decision to recon-
vene is to be decided in the discretion of the arbitral tribunal, it should be slow to
refuse the parties the opportunity to respond to the new legal development.[3] The
major question arises when the law is changed or refashioned by judicial decision following the publication of an award, when the arbitral tribunal is *functus officio*, and
prior to the application for leave to appeal to the court.[3a] In the result the law is different at the time of the application for leave to appeal from that which it was considered
to be at the time of the publication of the award. An award which when made may
have been considered legally unimpeachable is suddenly rendered vulnerable at the
time of the application for leave by virtue of the post-award legal developments. To
what extent can and should a legal development of this nature be taken into account in
the exercise of the discretion under section 1(3)(b)?

6.2.15.3 In principle it is clear that the court must consider an application for leave
to appeal on the basis of the law as it then stands. The court cannot confine itself to the
historical position at the date of the publication of an award. Equally, it must be the
case on an application for leave that the party making or resisting the application cannot be precluded from adopting and relying on post-award legal developments. Either
party may invite the court to come to a provisional view of the correctness of the
award on the basis of the law then prevailing, unless a party is precluded by his conduct from doing so.[3b] This being the case, it is difficult to see that the court will be
tempted to develop any firm rule restricting the giving of leave in cases of post-award
legal developments or even to adopt more rigorous *prima facie* tests than those laid
down in *The Nema/Antaios* guidelines. But the wide discretion that exists under section 1(3)(b) provides the court with the necessary flexibility to respond to the claims of
justice on the facts of any particular case.

6.2.15.4 A difficulty confronting a party wishing to take advantage of a post-award
legal development is that findings of fact necessary to sustain the new point of law may
not be incorporated in the award. The new law not being to mind at the time of the
reference, necessary factual points may not have been considered or investigated.
Without these findings of fact the party seeking leave to appeal may not be able to
bring himself within the new legal position and this in turn may engender frustration
and create a sense of injustice. The potential solution is an order under section 1(5),
or less probably under section 22 of the Arbitration Act 1950.[4] But it is far from certain that the court will be prepared to make such an order, at least as a matter of
course. Under the former special case procedure the courts on occasions refused to
remit awards for the finding of further facts on the so-called "changes in the law"
ground resulting from judicial decisions construing the GAFTA 100 standard form
contract in the context of the problems created by the embargo imposed by the U.S.

---

2. *Société Commerciale de Reassurance* v. *Eras International Ltd.* (*The Eras Eil Actions*) [1992] 1 Lloyd's
Rep. 570, 600, Mustill L.J.
3. Cf. *Yamashita Shinnihon Steamship Co. Ltd.* v. *Elios S.p.A. (The Lily Prima)* [1976] 2 Lloyd's Rep.
487, 500–501, per Kerr J.
3a. See, for example, *Bunge S.A.* v. *Compagnie Européene de Céréales* [1982] 1 Lloyd's Rep. 306, 311;
Pancommerce S.A. v. *Veecheema B.V.* [1982] 1 Lloyd's Rep. 645, 646. See also *Arnold* v. *National Westminster Bank plc* [1991] 3 All E.R. 41.
3b. Cf. *Tradax Export S.A.* v. *Cook Industries Inc.* [1982] 1 Lloyd's Rep. 385, 394, per Kerr L.J.
4. See Chapter 11, particularly para. 11.11. See also, *Bremer Handelsgesellschaft m.b.H.* v. *Westzucker
G.m.b.H. (No. 2)* [1981] 1 Lloyd's Rep. 214, 221–222.

government in June 1973 on the export of soya bean.[5] In so deciding the courts were influenced by the risk of a flood of similar applications; a due regard for settlements on the basis of the law as it was then understood to be; the unfairness that may arise in remitting awards after the passage of a considerable period of time and the overriding need to uphold the finality of awards.[6] The spate of special cases relating to the proper construction of the GAFTA 100 contract in the face of the U.S. embargo was in many regards a very special circumstance, but the judicial sentiments then expressed may well carry forward into the contemporary law. But in circumstances where the potential ramifications of a remission are of less consequence, it is at least open to the court to adopt a more generous approach. There is a discernible justice in allowing a party to attempt to complete the necessary findings of fact, so as to advance a point of law open to him, particularly where the failure of the initial award to address the factual point(s) is not attributable to the fault of the party in question. The justice of the case is the other way if the necessary facts could and reasonably should have been determined in the initial award, or where the party had indicated by his conduct, express or implied, that the facts were not in issue.[7]

6.2.15.5 Beyond post-award changes in the law, a variant, but associated, circumstance arises when a point of law in issue in an arbitration comes under active reconsideration by the courts and begins to ascend the hierarchy of appellate courts. Although the final outcome has yet to be determined, the flurry of judicial activity may well be a harbinger of change, and at the very least creates uncertainty. The judicial reconsideration in the first half of the last decade of the proper construction of the safe port warranty in a charterparty probably provides an example of the kind of situation here contemplated.[8] In such an unsettled legal environment it is difficult and possibly imprudent to come to any provisional assessment of the correctness of an arbitral award. Where the question of law in issue is also one of substantial importance and wide relevance, the prevailing situation may readily justify an adjournment of the hearing of the application for leave, or alternatively the giving of leave to appeal but with the full appeal deferred, until the legal issue is finally determined. So to proceed will ensure certainty and consistency.[9]

6.2.16 Discretionary procedural arbitral powers

Where the question of law arising out of an award relates to the exercise of discretionary procedural arbitral powers the court is likely to display a particular reluctance to

5. *Tradax Export S.A.* v. *Cook Industries Inc.* [1982] 1 Lloyd's Rep. 385, 394–395 (C.A.); *Bremer Handelsgesellschaft m.b.H.* v. *Raiffeisen Hauptgenossenschaft E.G.* [1982] 1 Lloyd's Rep. 599, 602, per Kerr L.J.
6. *Ibid.* See also *Tradax Export S.A.* v. *Cook Industries Inc.* [1981] 1 Lloyd's Rep. 236, 247–248 per Robert Goff J. (judgment subsequently overruled on other grounds).
7. Cf. *Cook Industries Inc.* v. *Meunerie Liegeois S.A.* [1981] 1 Lloyd's Rep. 359: *Bremer Handelsgesellschaft m.b.H.* v. *Westzucker G.m.b.H.* [1981] 2 Lloyd's Rep. 130 (C.A.).
8. See, for example, *Uni-Ocean Lines Pte. Ltd.* v. *C-Trade S.A. (The Lucille)* [1984] 1 Lloyd's Rep. 244; *Kodros Shipping Corpn.* v. *Empresa Cubana de Fletes (The Evia) (No. 2)* [1983] 1 A.C. 736.
9. Cf. *Oriental Maritime Pte. Ltd.* v. *Ministry of Food Government of the People's Republic of Bangladesh (The Silva Plana)* [1989] 2 Lloyd's Rep. 371, 375: arbitrators had decided a question relating to the computation of laytime on the basis of a particular decision which had since been reversed on appeal, but in respect of which a further appeal to the House of Lords was pending. It was argued that the appropriate course was to allow the appeal, with the contingency of the possible reversal of the Court of Appeal's decision capable of being covered by an appropriate provision in the minute of order.

intervene and allow the discretionary power to be reviewed on appeal.[1] The approach that will prevail may be analogous to that adopted in relation to conclusions of law and questions of mixed fact and law.[2] Provided the arbitrator has addressed himself correctly in principle and exercised the power reasonably, the court will not intervene, even though on the facts of the case the court would have been inclined to exercise the discretion differently.[3]

An arbitrator may be required to make many and various procedural decisions during the course of the pre-hearing and hearing phases of an arbitral process. A particular example arises when an arbitrator having decided that the claimants were out of time under the prevailing arbitration rules, thereupon also refuses to exercise, in favour of the claimants, a discretion given by the rules to grant an extension of time. Both issues raise questions of law but nonetheless they represent distinct categories of legal questions for the purposes of the section 1(3)(b) discretion. In relation to the second the court is likely to be very hesitant to intervene save in the exceptional circumstances considered above.[4]

6.2.17 Interim awards embodying interlocutory orders

6.2.17.1 Although the validity of an interlocutory order made in the ordinary course of a reference will not usually be capable of being challenged by an appeal because the issue will not be a question of law "arising out of an award",[1] it is nonetheless possible for an interlocutory order to be embodied in an interim award and when this practice is followed the validity of the order may legitimately give rise to a question of law arising out of the interim award. The use of the jurisdiction to make interim awards in this way represents an alternative to the consultative case procedure under section 2 of the 1979 Act and also has several advantages over that procedure.[2]

An interim award made in the manner here described may call for special consideration for it is distinct from a final or interim award determining the whole or part of the merits of a dispute referred to arbitration. Also such an interim award does not readily fall within the terms of *The Nema/Antaios* guidelines. It can, however, be addressed in the context of the spirit of the guidelines, taking into account an initial assessment of the correctness of the interim award and the general importance of the question of law in issue.

6.2.17.2 In law an arbitral interlocutory order may be challenged on the basis of jurisdiction or with regard to the exercise of the associated discretion to make or

---

1. Cf. *K/S A/S Bill Biakh and K/S A/S Bill Biali* v. *Hyundai Corporation* [1988] 1 Lloyd's Rep. 187, 189, Steyn J.: "A judicial power to correct during the course of the reference procedural rulings of an arbitrator which are within his jurisdiction is unknown in advanced arbitration systems . . . and the creation of such a power by judicial precedent in this case would constitute a most serious reproach to the ability of our system of arbitration to serve the needs of users of the arbitral process." See also *Ulysses Compania Naviera S.A.* v. *Huntingdon Petroleum Services Ltd.* (*The Ermoupolis*) [1990] 1 Lloyd's Rep. 160, 165, Steyn J.; *Exmar BV* v. *National Iranian Tanker Co.* (*The Trade Fortitude*) [1992] 1 Lloyd's Rep. 169, 175, Judge Diamond Q.C.
2. See Chapter 5, para. 5.2.5.
3. Cf. *Exmar BV* v. *National Iranian Tanker Co.* (*The Trade Fortitude*), *supra*, n. 1, at p. 175.
4. See, for example *Comdel Commodities Ltd.* v. *Siporex Trade S.A.* (*No. 2*) [1989] 2 Lloyd's Rep. 13, 17.
1. See Chapter 3, para. 3.3.
2. See Chapter 12, para. 12.11.1.

refuse the order or the terms on which an order is made.[3] The question of jurisdiction will invariably be governed by the proper interpretation of a statute or the construction of an arbitration agreement or may involve an examination of the common law; and the closeness with which the court on an application for leave to appeal will choose to scrutinise the correctness of the arbitrator's determination may vary with the importance and general interest in the question of law in issue. The greater the general interest and importance, the more likely it is that leave will only be given if a strong *prima facie* case has been made out that the arbitrator came to a wrong determination.[4] The more rarefied and particular the issue, the stricter may be the test, with the court unlikely to give leave to appeal unless satisfied that the arbitrator is obviously wrong.[5]

Where the alleged error of law is directed not to the question of jurisdiction but to the exercise of discretion it is unlikely that the court may be persuaded to give leave to appeal unless satisfied that the arbitrator had misdirected himself as to the criteria to be taken into account in the exercise of the discretion or to have exercised the discretion in a manner no reasonable arbitrator would have. The mere fact that an arbitrator, who has otherwise properly directed himself, has exercised the discretion differently from the way the court would have exercised the discretion in the same circumstances, is not in itself a reason for giving leave to appeal.[6]

6.2.18 Domestic and international arbitration

6.2.18.1 In contrast to many foreign systems of law, there is in English law no jurisprudential schism between domestic and international arbitration, in the sense that each is subject to a separate regimen of law based on different considerations of public policy.[1] Nonetheless the distinction has a limited presence in English arbitration law, both in the arbitration legislation[2] and in the manner in which the judicial supporting discretionary jurisdiction is exercised.[3] These qualifications to the general premise, although restricted and fragmented, are nevertheless significant for they show a partial and selective acceptance of the claim of the international arbitral process to enjoy a greater degree of autonomy than that ordinarily conceded to the domestic process. To this limited extent English law is in harmony with what may be described as the evolving international public policy of arbitration.[4] It would appear highly likely that appeals under the 1979 Act will represent yet a further illustration of this harmony.

---

3. Cf. *The Vasso* [1983] 2 Lloyd's Rep. 346; *Ulysses Compania Naviera S.A.* v. *Huntingdon Petroleum Services Ltd.* (*The Ermoupolis*) [1990] 1 Lloyd's Rep. 160.
4. See Chapter 5, para. 5.2.4.
5. See Chapter 5, para. 5.2.3.
6. See Chapter 5, para. 5.2.5.
1. *Bank Mellat* v. *Helleniki Techniki S.A.* [1984] Q.B. 291; *Deutsche Schachtbau- und Tiefbohrgesellschaft m.b.H.* v. *Ras Al Khaimah National Oil Co.* [1987] 3 W.L.R. 1023 (C.A.). See generally Mustill, "Transnational Arbitration in English Law", in *International Commercial and Maritime Arbitration*, ed. Rose.
2. See, for example Arbitration Act 1950, Part II; Arbitration (International Investment Disputes) Act 1966, and Arbitration Act 1975.
3. *Mavani* v. *Ralli Bros. Ltd.* [1973] 1 W.L.R. 468; *K/S A/S Bani and K/S A/S Havbulk 1* v. *Korea Shipbuilding and Engineering Corporation* [1987] 2 Lloyd's Rep. 445 (C.A.).
4. As suggested in part by the UNCITRAL Model Law of International Commercial Arbitration. See also Goode, "The Adaptation of English Law to International Commercial Arbitration" (1992) 8 Arb. Int. 1.

6.2.18.2 Although the point has not to date attracted express judicial consideration, it is suggested that the concession of greater autonomy to international arbitration is likely to permeate the appellate regime established by the 1979 Act and render the presumption of finality even more difficult to rebut in the case of an award made in international arbitration. Beyond the tenets of international public policy, support for the proposition also derives from the manner in which the 1979 legislation establishes a less restrictive regime for exclusion agreements in relation to awards arising out of the international arbitration process, as compared with domestic arbitration.[5] The liberality with which the legislation relates to the international arbitration process in this regard, in turn suggests that leave to appeal from an award arising out of international arbitration may be significantly more difficult to obtain than in the case of a domestic award. This reasoning and the policy it suggests is nonetheless confined to what in the context of the 1979 Act may be described as residual international arbitrations. It does not extend to the special category disputes, which are caught up in a distinct policy of their own, and which would not support the adoption of a more rigorous test where they are also international in character.[6] Further support for the proposition here advanced also derives from the speech of Lord Diplock in *The Nema*[7] where he considered the legislative policy in favour of the finality of awards to be of *particular* application in the case of non-domestic arbitrations.

6.2.18.3 For purposes associated with the section 1(3)(b) discretion, it would seem that the notion of what is "international" need not necessarily follow the definition of an international arbitration agreement derivable from section 1(4) of the Arbitration Act 1975.[8] It may in each case be a question of fact and degree.

6.2.19 Unexercised arbitral appeal

6.2.19.1 In the Rules of institutional arbitration provision is sometimes made for a right or qualified right of appeal to an arbitration appeal tribunal.[1] Where such a right exists, but is not exercised, an interesting question arises whether the failure to first utilise the contractual appeal may be taken into account in considering an application for leave to appeal, and, if so, what weight is to be given to it. The question does not appear to have been considered in relation to the 1979 Act, but it is not a novel question in the context of the wider arbitration law. Under the former special case procedure it appears that a first tier award could be stated as a special case notwithstanding the existence of an unexercised right of appeal.[2] Where the wider supervisory jurisdiction of the courts is sought to be invoked, the existence of an unex-

---

5. Ss. 3 and 4 of the 1979 Act which are considered in greater detail in Chapter 13.
6. See the discussion of "special category disputes" in Chapter 13, para. 13.4.4.
7. *Pioneer Shipping Ltd.* v. *B.T.P. Tioxide Ltd. (The Nema)* [1982] A.C. 724, 739–740.
8. Considered in Chapter 13, para. 13.4.3.1.
1. This is typically the case with the various institutional commodity arbitrations centred on London. See generally, Johnson, *International Commodity Arbitration* (Lloyd's of London Press Ltd., 1991). The Lloyd's salvage arbitration established under the Lloyd's Open Form also provides for an appeal arbitrator. See generally Darling and Smith, *LOF 90 and the New Salvage Convention* (Lloyd's of London Press Ltd., 1991). For a consideration of some of the legal issues which may arise in connection with arbitral rules providing for an appeal, see *Provimi Hellas A.E.* v. *Warinco A.G.* [1978] 1 Lloyd's Rep. 67; *Cargill SRL Milan (formerly Cargill S.p.A.)* v. *P. Kadinopoulos S.A.* [1992] 1 Lloyd's Rep. 1 (H.L.).
2. *Re Fischel & Co. and Cook and Mann* [1919] 2 K.B. 431; *Provimi Hellas A.E.* v. *Warinco A.G., supra* p. 80. For a contrary opinion see *Amalgamated Metal Corpn.* v. *Khoon Seng Co. Ltd.* [1976] 2 Lloyd's Rep. 646, 648, per Lord Denning M.R. See also Chapter 1, para. 1.4.2.

ercised right of appeal appears to represent a consideration the courts may take into account in the exercise of their discretionary powers.[3] In other areas of the law, such as judicial review in public law, the courts are conspicuously reluctant to order judicial review when the applicant has an alternative remedy, and will only do so in exceptional circumstances.[4]

6.2.19.2 The fact that an applicant has available an alternative mode of remedy by which an alleged error of law may be corrected, namely a contractual right of appeal within the arbitration process, does appear to represent in principle a factor which the court ought to be able to take into account in the exercise of its discretion. It could quite convincingly, in the light of the policy of the 1979 legislation, be viewed as the first avenue of redress for an aggrieved party. But bearing in mind the position that appears to have prevailed under the former special case procedure,[5] and taking into account the development of analogous issues in other areas of arbitration law,[6] it is unlikely that the courts will firmly close the door to the possibility of an appeal until the internal remedial arbitral procedures are first exhausted. It will in each case probably be a question of discretion and the precise weight to be given to the availability of an alternative remedy will depend on the facts and circumstances of individual cases. But where the parties have agreed an alternative contractual appellate process, leave to appeal, it is suggested, should not readily be granted; and it is arguable that leave should not be granted save in exceptional circumstances, as when it would work injustice to the applicant to compel a first resort to the alternative contractual remedy.[7]

6.2.20 Defective exclusion agreement

6.2.20.1 The 1979 Act, by sections 3 and 4, makes it possible for parties to enter into what are styled exclusion agreements, the effect of which is to exclude the possibility of an appeal.[1] An exclusion agreement will of course only have this effect if it is legally valid and there will undoubtedly be occasions when a purported exclusion agreement will falter by virtue of a factual or legal defect, such as want of consensus, defect of form, the moment entered into or inadequate drafting.[2] An intended but defective exclusion agreement is clearly ineffective and incapable of achieving its purpose of excluding the possibility of an appeal.

6.2.20.2 But this does not mean that a defective agreement is wholly without effect, for it is at least arguable that it may be taken into account by the court in determining an application for leave to appeal. Even a defective exclusion agreement has the capacity to reveal the underlying intentions of the parties and their determination that

---

3. *Montrose Canned Foods Ltd.* v. *Eric Wells (Merchants) Ltd.* [1965] 1 Lloyd's Rep. 597, 602.
4. *R* v. *Chief Constable of the Merseyside Police, ex parte Calveley* [1986] Q.B. 424; *R* v. *Secretary of State for the Home Department, ex parte Swati* [1986] 1 W.L.R. 477; *R* v. *Civil Service Appeal Board, ex parte Bruce (Attorney-General intervening)* [1989] 2 All E.R. 907; *R.* v. *Leeds City Council, ex p. Hendry, The Times,* 20 January 1994. See generally Lewis, "The Exhaustion of Alternative Remedies in Administrative Law" (1992) 51 Camb. L.J. 138.
5. *Supra,* n. 2.
6. See, for example, *Comdel Commodities Ltd.* v. *Siporex Trade S.A. (No. 2)* [1990] 2 Lloyd's Rep. 207, where the House of Lords held that the jurisdiction to extend a contractual time stipulation for the commencing of an arbitration, under the Arbitration Act 1950, s. 27, continued to be available notwithstanding that the arbitrator had been conferred with a contractual dispensing power.
7. Cf. *R* v. *Panel on Take-overs and Mergers, ex parte Guinness plc* [1989] 1 All E.R. 509 (C.A.).
1. See Chapter 13.
2. *Ibid.*

the dispute referred shall be resolved wholly and finally within the arbitral process. What is here contemplated is capable of assuming a particular importance in relation to standard form maritime, insurance and commodity contracts (the so-called special categories[3]) which attempt to associate an exclusion agreement with the arbitration clause, and where the exclusion agreement is consequently defective by virtue of it pre-dating the commencement of any future arbitration. If the point made in the text is valid it would mean that a judge in exercising the section 1(3)(b) discretion may take into account the defective exclusion agreement as evidence of the intention of the parties that the award be final. Argument to the contrary would presumably be based on the notion that a defective agreement is no agreement at all and therefore can have no impact on the exercise of discretion. This is of course theoretically correct but possibly unrealistic: the conduct of the parties and what they have attempted to do remains. A more serious objection might be based on argument that to take such evidence into account would run counter to the policy of the 1979 Act. The policy that renders the exclusion agreement invalid in the first place may also exclude the possibility of a defective exclusion agreement from assuming any evidentiary relevance.

6.2.20.3 The existence of a valid exclusion agreement will preclude an appeal, but it would be far too bold a proposition to attempt to assert that the absence of an exclusion agreement was evidence that the parties did not view the award as final.

6.2.21 Rules of evidence

6.2.21.1 In strictness an arbitrator is obliged to apply the rules of evidence[1] unless the parties expressly or impliedly decide to the contrary[1a]; and in the pre-1979 Act law an award was liable to be set aside if it could be shown that the arbitrator had admitted inadmissible evidence.[2] Rules of evidence being matters of law, they may equally give rise to an appeal under the 1979 Act if it can be established in the award that the arbitrator has erred.[3]

6.2.21.2 Notwithstanding the strict legal position, there has long existed an ambiguity concerning the relationship between rules of evidence and the arbitration process, an ambiguity which is also capable of being felt with regard to specialist commercial courts. Technical objections to the admissibility of evidence would not be seen by all as conduct consistent with the spirit expected to prevail in the workings of a contemporary specialist commercial court. The same imprecise feelings extend into arbitration and it is probably the case that the courts have extended a degree of lati-

---

3. See s. 4(1), which is considered in Chapter 13, para. 13.4.4.

1. Civil Evidence Act 1968, s. 18; *A.G.* v. *Davison* (1825) M'cle. & Y. 160; *East and West India Dock Co.* v. *Kirk and Randall* (1887) 12 App. Cas. 738, H.L.; *Re Enoch and Zaretzky, Bock & Co.* [1910] 1 K.B. 327, C.A.

1a. *Macpherson Train & Co. Ltd.* v. *J. Milhelm & Sons* [1955] 2 Lloyd's Rep. 59 (C.A.); *Henry Bath & Sons Ltd.* v. *Birgby Products* [1962] 1 Lloyd's Rep. 389.

2. *"Agro-export" Entreprise D'Etat pour le Commerce Exterieur* v. *N.V. Goorden Import Cy. S.A.* [1956] 1 Lloyd's Rep. 319; *Verheijdens Veevoeder Commissehandel B.V.* v. *I. S. Joseph Co. Inc.* [1981] 1 Lloyd's Rep. 102.

3. *K/S A/S Bill Biakh and K/S A/S Bill Brali* v. *Hyundai Corpn.* [1988] 1 Lloyd's Rep. 187, 189, per Steyn J., "the admission of, for example, utterly irrelevant evidence and reliance on it in the reasons for the award might . . . afford evidential material for a broader attack on the award itself". See also *Citland Ltd.* v. *Kanchan Oil Industries Pvt. Ltd.* [1980] Lloyd's Rep. 274, 277, Mustill J.

tude to the arbitral process with regard to the rules of evidence, but without abandoning the fundamental position.[4]

6.2.21.3 The historical and contemporary ambiguity tempts the suggestion that the courts may place questions of law relating to matters of evidence into a discrete category and apply to them different considerations from those adopted in relation to questions of law touching on the substantive dispute. The suggestion carries the implication that the courts may display an even greater reluctance to grant leave to appeal when the question of law concerns a rule of evidence. Under the pre-1979 Act law the courts hesitated to intervene unless the wrongful admission of evidence could be shown to have had a material and clear impact on the ultimate resolution of the dispute.[5] The position under the 1979 Act must be at least as demanding.

6.2.22 Amount in dispute

6.2.22.1 The amount in dispute has no necessary relationship with the complexity or importance of a question of law, but it can be relevant to the substantialness of a question of law as between the arbitrating parties.[1] Under the former special case procedure quantum could be a relevant consideration[2] and it is also a factor which a judge may take into account in exercising the section 1(3)(b) discretion.[3]

Although quantum may be taken into account in exercising the discretion to give or to refuse leave to appeal, when it is taken into account the precise weight to be attached to it may vary considerably with the wider facts and circumstances. When the sum in issue is large this may provide comforting reinforcement for the view taken from the other facts of the case that leave to appeal should be given, and in more evenly balanced situations it may help to tip the balance in favour of giving leave to appeal.[4] But it is improbable that the monetary scale of a dispute will alone turn round a case where it is otherwise wholly inappropriate to give leave to appeal.

6.2.22.2 The smallness of the sum in issue will not automatically render an award unappealable. The related question of law may nonetheless be one of importance and general interest, and for these reasons it may be appropriate to give leave to appeal.[5] But in a less clear case, the smallness of the sum in dispute may raise a serious question whether the expense and delay of an appeal is justified.[6] Smallness in the present context is often a relative measurement, being assessed against the total amount in

---

4. *Re Enoch and Zaretzky, Bock & Co., supra*, p. 336, per Farwell L.J.

5. *Re M'Clean & Co. and Marcus* (1890) 6 T.L.R. 355; *Re Enoch and Zaretzky, Bock & Co., supra*; *Grand Trunk Rly Co. of Canada* v. *R.* [1923] A.C. 150; *British Metal Corpn. Ltd.* v. *Ludlow Bros. (1913) Ltd.* (1938) 61 Ll.L.Rep. 351.

1. See, Chapter 4, para. 4.3.3; also *Stinnes Interoil G.m.b.H.* v. *A. Halcoussis & Co. (The Yanxilas)* [1982] 2 Lloyd's Rep. 445, 456–457, per Bingham J.

2. *Halfdan Greig & Co. A/S* v. *Sterling Coal and Navigation Corporation etc. (The Lysland)* [1973] 1 Lloyd's Rep. 296, 307, per Lord Denning M.R., "It may be suggested that if only a small sum is in dispute, a special case should be refused. Sometimes a small sum can involve big issues of much importance for the parties. In those cases a special case should be stated. But, where the sum is so small as not to justify further time or money being spent on it, it should be refused." See also *The Food Corporation of India* v. *Carras (Hellas) Ltd. (The Dione)* [1980] 2 Lloyd's Rep. 577, 580, per Lloyd J.

3. See cases cited *infra*.

4. Cf. *International Sea Tankers Inc.* v. *Hemisphere Shipping Co. Ltd. (The Wenjiang)* [1981] 2 Lloyd's Rep. 308, 312.

5. Cf. *A/S Brovigtank and I/S Brovig* v. *Transcredit and Oil Tradeanstalt (The Gunda Brovig)* [1982] 1 Lloyd's Rep. 43.

6. *The Lysland, supra*.

issue in the controversy between the parties. When the question of law in relation to which leave to appeal is sought bears in terms of quantum little significance in relation to the total amount in issue, there appears to exist a marked judicial reluctance to give leave to appeal.[7] But where the court is of a mind to give leave to appeal with regard to another or other questions of law, the fact that a particular question of law is of little consequence in monetary terms will be of substantially less significance than if that question of law had stood in isolation, and the particular question may be allowed to progress to appeal, together with the other questions of law. Having been prepared to open the judicial door to the big fish there is little harm in allowing the odd minnow to follow.

6.2.23 Defective curial law agreement

6.2.23.1 The concept of the curial law of arbitration and the difficulties surrounding the concept have been briefly addressed elsewhere in the text.[1] That discussion however suggests that the arbitration legislation, to the extent it relates to the relationship between the courts and arbitration, applies to all arbitrations with their seat within England and Wales, and that this position cannot be affected by any agreement of the parties to the contrary. To this extent any choice of a foreign curial law by the agreement of the parties is void, and any such agreement does not therefore displace the appellate regime established by the 1979 Act. The finality of an award cannot be achieved by the choice of a foreign curial law.

6.2.23.2 But although a foreign curial law agreement is ineffective, it may nonetheless provide evidence of the intentions of the parties, and in particular show the parties to have been attempting to establish final arbitration without the risk of judicial intervention. To the extent that the appellate relationship between the courts and arbitration is founded on judicial discretion, the court may be prepared to take account of the frustrated intentions of the parties in the exercise of its discretion, and "it might well be slow to interfere with the arbitral process".[2]

---

7. *Retla Steamship Co.* v. *Gryphon Shipping Co. S.A. etc. (The Evimeria)* [1982] 1 Lloyd's Rep. 55, 58, per Staughton J.; *Clea Shipping Corpn.* v. *Bulk Oil International Ltd. (The Alaskan Trader)* [1983] 1 Lloyd's Rep. 315, 319, per Bingham J.
1. Chapter 1, para. 1.7.8.
2. *Union of India* v. *McDonnell Douglas Corporation* [1993] 2 Lloyd's Rep. 48, 51, Saville J.

CHAPTER 7

PROCEDURE AND PRACTICE APPERTAINING TO APPLICATIONS FOR LEAVE TO APPEAL

7.1 INTRODUCTION

7.1.1 R.S.C. Order 73: an introductory note

Court proceedings relating to arbitration, including proceedings arising under the Arbitration Act 1979, are governed generally by R.S.C. Order 73.[1] The introduction of the new appeal process by section 1 of the 1979 Act, and the related developments associated with the legislation, necessarily required the Rules of the Supreme Court to be amended so as to establish a procedural framework to facilitate the applications contemplated by the Act. The attempt at drafting new Rules has a chequered history and it took several amendments to the original new Rules drafted in direct response to the new legislation to finally settle an apposite and unambiguous procedural framework.[2] The practice to be followed by judges in hearing and considering applications for leave to appeal, which exists alongside but without being formally integrated into the R.S.C., also took time to consolidate.[3] Aspects of the contemporary practice are described in the *Guide to Commercial Court Practice*, Part VII.[4]

From the first the Rules of Court have drawn a clear distinction between applications for leave to appeal and full appeals, and subsequent amendments to the Rules have served to emphasise the distinction. The application for leave to appeal is nearly always a distinct and separate proceeding from the hearing of the full appeal.[5]

7.1.2 Evidentiary burden

It is for the applicant seeking leave to appeal to satisfy the judge on a balance of probabilities that the case is one in respect of which it is appropriate for leave to appeal to be granted. The criteria to be taken into account in determining an application for leave to appeal have been considered previously.[1]

---

1. Rules of the Supreme Court 1965 (as amended), made under the Supreme Court Act 1981, s. 84. For the proper approach to the interpretation of Rules of Court, see *Société Libanaise pour L'Industrie du Bois "Libanbois" S.A.L. and Another* v. *Fama Shipping Ltd.* [1992] 1 Lloyd's Rep. 197, 199, Steyn J.
2. *Mebro Oil S.A.* v. *Gatoil International Inc.* [1985] 2 Lloyd's Rep. 234, 236–237, where Bingham J. gives an account of the procedural history.
3. Considered *infra*, para. 7.3.
4. Appendix I.
5. *Infra*, para. 7.3 and Chapter 9, para. 9.2.
1. See Chapters 5 and 6.

7.2 PROCEDURE ON AN APPLICATION FOR LEAVE TO APPEAL

7.2.1 Application to judge in chambers

Order 73, rule 3(2) provides: "Any application (a) for leave to appeal under s. 1(2) of the Arbitration Act 1979 . . . shall be made to a judge in chambers." Each party wishing to appeal must obtain leave to appeal (in the absence of consent[1]), and leave must be obtained in relation to every question of law which a party wishes to take on appeal. There is nothing to preclude both (or all) parties to a reference being given leave to appeal.[2]

The fact that an application has been made does not preclude a further application for leave to appeal in relation to a new question of law not considered on the occasion of the previous application, provided the application remains within the Rules of Court.[3]

7.2.1.1 Judge

Judge alludes to a Commercial judge, unless any such judge otherwise directs.[1] This express provision in the R.S.C. does not however prevent the powers of a Commercial judge from being exercised by any judge of the High Court,[2] as may become necessary during a vacation period or where an appointed Commercial judge is not available or it is otherwise impracticable for the application to be heard by a Commercial judge.[3]

The R.S.C. implicitly recognise that arbitration is substantially a commercial phenomenon. This is unquestionably the case, with most of the court applications arising in connection with arbitration relating to arbitrations conducted under the aegis of the many institutionalised forms of arbitration centred in London. It is therefore both natural and desirable that applications under the 1979 Act should primarily be determined by a Commercial judge. But arbitration is not synonymous with commerce and it is a patent fact that the practice of arbitration extends significantly beyond the boundaries of commercial activity, especially if commercial activity is defined in the same terms as that adopted in the R.S.C. to delineate the jurisdiction of the Commercial Court.[4] It is neither natural nor necessarily desirable that a Commercial judge should determine applications arising out of or in connection with what may be described non-commercial arbitrations. Confronted with such a circumstance a Commercial judge may, by virtue of Order 73, rule 6(1), direct the application for leave to be heard by another and more appropriately experienced judge of the High Court. Where, for example, leave to appeal is sought from an award determining the rent payable under a rent review clause in a lease it has become the customary practice to

---

1. See Chapter 4, para. 4.2.
2. See, for example, *International Sea Tankers Inc.* v. *Hemisphere Shipping Co. Ltd. (The Wenjiang)* [1981] 2 Lloyd's Rep. 308 (first instance); *Uni-Ocean Lines Pte. Ltd.* v. *C-Trade S.A. (The Lucille)* [1983] 1 Lloyd's Rep. 387 (first instance).
3. Cf. *Novorossisk Shipping Co.* v. *Neopetro Co. Ltd. (The Ulyanovsk)* [1990] 1 Lloyd's Rep. 425, 427.
1. R.S.C. Order 73, rule 6(1). See, for example, *Novorossisk Shipping Co.* v. *Neopetro Co. Ltd. (The Ulyanovsk)* [1990] 1 Lloyd's Rep. 425, 427.
2. R.S.C. Order 73, rule 6(2).
3. See the note to R.S.C. Order 73, rule 2(1) in *The Supreme Court Practice 1993*.
4. R.S.C. Order 72, rule 1(2).

refer the application for determination by a judge of the Chancery Division.[5] So also where the award relates to a construction or building dispute, it is the practice to refer any application for leave to appeal to an official referee.[6] But even if a Commercial judge retains to himself consideration of an application for leave to appeal from an award made in non-commercial arbitration and gives leave to appeal, it is thereafter possible for a direction to be made that the substantive appeal be heard by a judge other than a Commercial judge.[7]

7.2.1.2 Chambers

Subject to the specific provisions in R.S.C. Order 73, the jurisdiction of the High Court under the Arbitration Act 1979 may be exercised by a judge in chambers, a master or the Admiralty Registrar.[1] However, under R.S.C. Order 73, rule 3(2) an application for leave to appeal must be to a judge in chambers, which represents a change to the former and original procedure, whereunder application was to a single judge in court.[2] The amended procedure is clearly more in keeping with the philosophy of the 1979 Act and the practice developed about it.[3]

A practice statement by Parker J., given on 15 March 1982, addressed the practice that is to appertain in a chambers application, and introduced a notice which in its current version reads as follows[4]:

It is the responsibility of all parties to an application to a Commercial Judge in Chambers to ensure that copies (**not originals**) of the relevant documents are lodged in the Commercial Court Listing Office **Room E201** by **NOON 2 DAYS BEFORE** the date fixed for the hearing. These should include the main pleadings, affidavits and exhibits, which should all be bound in a convenient loose-leaf file or files.

Where the summons is a summons for directions (not being a formal summons in third party proceedings) a completed information sheet in the form appended to the Guide to Commercial Court Practice (Order 72 Rule A29) must be lodged **TWO CLEAR DAYS** before the date fixed for the hearing.

Failure to comply with these directions will normally result in the application not being heard on the date fixed at the expense of the party in default.

On the first occasion when any inter-parties application is heard the parties should be prepared, if necessary, to justify the retention of the case in the Commercial Court.

A copy of this notice, together with a copy of the form of information sheet (where relevant) should be attached to the copy application served on the other parties.

PLEASE NOTE
The time shown on the summons is a general indication only it is therefore advisable for parties to telephone the Commercial Court Listing Office after 3.00PM on the day before the date fixed for the hearing in order to clarify the listing (071 936 6826).

---

5. *Lucas Industries plc* v. *Welsh Development Agency* [1986] 2 All E.R. 858, 859, per Sir Nicolas Browne-Wilkinson V.C., "As is now usual in such cases, the application for leave to appeal has been referred by a judge of the Commercial Court for determination by a judge of the Chancery Division."
6. *Tate and Lyle Industries Ltd.* v. *Davy McKee (London) Ltd.* [1990] 1 Lloyd's Rep. 116 (C.A.).
7. *F. G. Whitley & Sons Co. Ltd.* v. *Clwyd County Council* (1982) 22 B.L.R. 48, 63, per Donaldson L.J.
1. Order 73, rule 3(1).
2. The procedural change was introduced by R.S.C. (Amendment No. 2) 1983 (S.I. 1983 No. 1181). For the original practice see *B.V.S. and The Khuzestan Water and Power Authority* v. *Kerman Shipping Co. (The Kerman)* [1982] 1 Lloyd's Rep. 62, 65.
3. Considered *infra*, para. 7.3.
4. See Appendix H(4).

Copies of the notice are available from the Commercial Court Office and it is the responsibility of the applicant to attach a copy to the summons served on the opposite party.[5]

7.2.2 Form of application

An application for leave to appeal must, where an action is pending, be made by summons in the action, and in any other case by an originating summons which must be in Form No. 10 in Appendix A to the R.S.C.[1] In either case the summonses are issued in the Admiralty and Commercial Court Registry. By virtue of the fact that the appeal and application for leave to appeal are brought concurrently, and the effect of initiating an appeal is to establish a pending action, an application for leave to appeal will invariably amount to a summons in the action. It follows that the summons is issued under the relevant notice of motion,[2] with the latter being required to conform with the terms of a Practice Direction dated 3 May 1985.[3]

The court enjoys a discretion to sanction an amendment to the notice of motion.[4]

7.2.3 Respondent's notice

A respondent to an application for leave who desires to contend that the award should be upheld on grounds not expressed or not fully expressed in the award and reasons, must not less than two clear days before the hearing of the application lodge with the court and serve on the applicant a notice specifying the grounds of his contention.[1]

The form and content of the respondent's notice is governed by a Practice Direction dated 3 May 1985, which is considered later in the text in relation to full appeals.[2] Subject to the discretion of the court, a respondent will be confined to the points made in the respondent's notice.[3]

7.2.4 Time limit

7.2.4.1 The summons for leave to appeal must be served within 21 days after the award has been made and published to the parties: provided that, where reasons material to the appeal are given on a date subsequent to the publication of the award, the period of 21 days shall run from the date on which the reasons are given. This is the effect of Order 73, rule 5(2).[1] The stipulated time limit is consistent with the policy

---

5. *Ibid.*
1. R.S.C. Order 73, rule 3(3). See Appendix J(1) for a model precedent.
2. R.S.C. Order 73, rule 2(2).
3. See Chapter 9, para. 9.6 and Appendix H(5).
4. R.S.C. Order 20, rule 7.
1. R.S.C. Order 73, rule 5(9). See, for example, *Socony Mobil Oil Co. Inc. and Others* v. *West of England Ship Owners Mutual Insurance Association Ltd. (The Padre Island) (No. 2)* [1987] 2 Lloyd's Rep. 529, 531; *Procter & Gamble Philippine Manufacturing Corpn.* v. *Kurt A. Becher G.m.b.H. & Co. K.G.* [1988] 2 Lloyd's Rep. 21, 27.
2. Chapter 9, para. 9.8. See also Appendix H(5).
3. *Pagnan S.p.A.* v. *Tradax Ocean Transportation S.A.* [1987] 2 Lloyd's Rep. 342, 353.
1. This has the laudable result of resolving an unfortunate ambiguity arising from the omission to make any express time stipulation in the preceding Rules of Court: see the observations in *Mebro Oil S.A.* v. *Gatoil International Inc.* [1985] 2 Lloyd's Rep. 234, 236–238. The amendment was introduced by R.S.C. (Amendment) 1986 (S.I. 1986 No. 632 (L.2)).

of the 1979 Act which is that appeals from arbitration awards must be speedily pursued, with the same time limit applied to the summons for leave to appeal as is applied to the originating motion of appeal.[2]

7.2.4.2 An award is made when the arbitrator declares his final mind and is thereafter *functus officio*[2a]; and the award is published to the parties when the arbitrator gives notice to the parties that it is ready to be collected,[3] usually against payment of any outstanding charges.[4] Time runs from the moment of the notice and not from the moment any one of the parties takes up the award. Parties who delay in taking up an award must in consequence assume the risk of their inaction.

7.2.4.3 With regard to the proviso, the question arises as to when reasons are "given" by the arbitral tribunal. It is to be noted that the proviso does not speak of the reasons being given to the parties. There can be no question about reasons having been "given" when they are delivered to the parties; but it is possible to speak of reasons having been given at an earlier moment in time, particularly bearing in mind that what is in issue is a time limit in the context of the policy of the 1979 Act. It would seem arguable that reasons are "given" once the arbitration tribunal indicates to the parties that its reasons have been finalised and are ready for collection. But it might be rare for a tribunal actually to follow this practice, for where post-award reasons are given it is highly probable that the tribunal has already received its remuneration. In this circumstance it is likely that the tribunal will be happy to deliver its reasons to the parties once they are finalised. It is also possible for the giving of post-award reasons to be governed by the agreement of the parties.

7.2.4.4 The court enjoys a discretion to permit an application for leave to appeal out of time.[5] The discretion will not be exercised as a matter of course, but only on the establishment of an acceptable explanation for the delay and also a good arguable case on the merits.[6] The application for extension of time should be made at the same time as the application for leave to appeal and asked for in the summons for leave.

7.2.5 Service out of jurisdiction

7.2.5.1 Where the respondent is not within the jurisdiction, it is necessary to obtain leave to serve the summons outside jurisdiction.[1] The procedure is the same as

---

2. See Chapter 9, para. 9.5.

2a. *Hiscox* v. *Outhwaite* [1992] 1 A.C. 562, 594–595, Lord Oliver. See also *Brooke* v. *Mitchell* (1840) 6 M. & W. 473, 151 E.R. 498.

3. See *Brooke* v. *Mitchell* (1840) 6 M. & W. 473, 151 E.R. 498; *Bulk Transport Corpn.* v. *Sissy Steamship Co. Ltd.* (*The Archipelagos*) [1979] 2 Lloyd's Rep. 289; *Selous Street Properties Ltd.* v. *Oronal Fabrics Ltd.* (1984) 270 E.G. 643.

4. Cf. *Hiscox* v. *Outhwaite, supra.*

5. R.S.C. Order 3, rule 5. See, for example, *Astro Valiente Compania Naviera S.A.* v. *The Government of Pakistan Ministry for Food and Agriculture* (*The Emmanuel Colocotronis*) (*No. 1*) [1982] 1 Lloyd's Rep. 297, 301; *President of India* v. *Taygetos Shipping Co. S.A.* (*The Agenor*) [1985] 1 Lloyd's Rep. 155, 160; *Procter & Gamble Philippine Manufacturing Corpn.* v. *Kurt A. Becher G.m.b.H. & Co. K.G.* [1988] 2 Lloyd's Rep. 21, 27.

6. *Everglade Maritime Inc.* v. *Schiffahrtsgesellschaft Detlef Von Appen m.b.H.* (*The Maria*) [1992] 2 Lloyd's Rep. 167, 177–178; cf. *Industria de Oleos Pacaebu S.A.* v. *N. V. Bunge* [1982] 1 Lloyd's Rep. 490.

1. R.S.C. Order 73, rule 7.

that applicable to R.S.C. Order 11, except that it is unnecessary for the applicant to depose to facts showing the claim to be within the categories specified in Order 11. The essential precondition is that the applicant be able to establish in his supporting affidavit that the arbitration to which the application relates is governed by English law or that it has been, is being, or is to be held, within the jurisdiction of the English courts.[2] In each case, whether service out of jurisdiction will be permitted, is a matter to be decided in the discretion of the court.[3] No leave will be granted unless the court is satisfied that the case is a proper one for service out of the jurisdiction.[4]

7.2.5.2 Bingham L.J. has observed on the similarities and differences between Orders 11 and 73, rule 7, in the following instructive terms[5]:

The second procedural point is this. The defendants say that the plaintiff's application should have been under O. 73, r. 7(1), and not under O. 11, r. 1. That submission seems to me to be correct, the latter rule being very much more specific and therefore more apt. The procedures have much in common. Order 11, r. 4(2), provides that no leave shall be granted unless it shall be made sufficiently to appear to the Court that the case is a proper one for service out of the jurisdiction under the order, and language to substantially the same effect appears in O. 73, r. 7(2). It is also plain that under each rule the Court has a discretion to order service out or not to do so. There is, however, one difference in the language of the rules. Order 11, r. 4(1), requires an affidavit stating that inter alia in the deponent's belief that plaintiff has a good cause of action. Order 73, r. 7(2), requires an affidavit stating some of the other matters required in O. 11, r. 4(1), but not any statement of belief concerning the cause of action. Also, as it seems to me, a necessary difference in the Court's approach to the exercise of discretion arises. In the ordinary case of Court proceedings under O. 11, the Court is exercising an exorbitant jurisdiction, reaching out to assert jurisdiction over a party not resident here. Authority shows that this is a jurisdiction to be exercised with caution, and that a foreign party will not be put to the expense and inconvenience of defending himself here unless the plaintiff shows a good arguable case. If the Court is not satisfied that there is a good arguable case or chooses not to exercise its discretion, the plaintiff can always sue the defendant wherever abroad he may be found. Under O. 73, r. 7, the position is rather different. No doubt the plaintiff must show a good arguable case that there is an arbitration agreement between the parties and that differences have arisen falling within it. But the Court must bear in mind, in exercising its jurisdiction under O. 73, r. 7 as also under s. 10(3), that the plaintiff has ex hypothesi bound himself to refer differences to arbitration and cannot therefore pursue his substantive claim against the defendant in legal proceedings abroad. He may also be bound to pursue the arbitration reference here, this being one of the cases covered by O. 73, r. 7(1). If, therefore, the Court exercises discretion so as to prevent the plaintiff achieving a properly constituted arbitration tribunal, it may leave him with no means of pursuing his claim anywhere, this being a notable distinction with the position under O. 11.

7.2.5.3 The right to serve out of the jurisdiction where the Civil Jurisdiction and Judgments Act 1982 is applicable[6] does not apply where the subject-matter relates to arbitration.[7]

---

2. *Ibid.* See also *Sumitomo Heavy Industries Ltd.* v. *Oil and Natural Gas Commission* [1994] 1 Lloyd's Rep. 45, 55 *et seq.*, per Potter J.
3. Cf. *Marc Rich & Co. A.G.* v. *Società Italiana Impianti p.A. (The Atlantic Emperor)* [1989] 1 Lloyd's Rep. 548.
4. R.S.C. Order 73, rule 7(2).
5. *Mayer Newman and Co. Ltd.* v. *Al Ferro Commodities Corporation S.A. (The John C. Helmsing)* [1990] 2 Lloyd's Rep. 290, 293. For recent consideration of Order 11, see *Seaconsar Far East Ltd.* v. *Bank Markazi Jomhouri Islami Iran* [1993] 3 W.L.R. 756; [1993] 4 All E.R. 456 (H.L.).
6. R.S.C. Order 11, rules 2 and 9.
7. R.S.C. Order 11, rule 9; Order 73, rule 7(1).

7.2.6 Remitting for further reasons

On an application for leave to appeal the court has jurisdiction to remit an award for further reasons, if this is necessary for the proper disposal of an application. A remission is likely to be considered when the arbitral reasons are unclear or incomplete, or in the face of special circumstances; and when an order is made with a view to assisting the determination of an application for leave to appeal it will invariably be accompanied by an adjournment of the application, until the further reasons are made.[1]

The jurisdiction to remit arises principally under section 1(5) and the making of an order is in the discretion of the court.[2] But where it can be shown to be necessary in the interests of justice, it is probable that the general discretionary jurisdiction to remit under section 22 of the Arbitration Act 1950 may also be resorted to.[3] The discretion is again exercised with close regard to the policy of the 1979 Act and with due regard to the general rule that it is the responsibility of the applicant for leave to appeal to ensure that the necessary findings of fact are made in an award.[4]

7.2.7 Order giving leave to appeal

7.2.7.1 When leave to appeal is given it is the established practice of the court to specify the question or questions of law to which the order of the court relates.[1] In turn it follows that the order giving leave tailors the future appeal by establishing its parameters.[2] It is not the practice of the court in giving leave to appeal to open up the award to an all-embracing and indiscriminatory legal attack,[3] although a question of law may be formulated in very broad terms.[4] It is difficult to reconcile the latter practice with the policy of the 1979 Act. The practice was frowned upon in the context of the former special case procedure[5] and it would seem even more inappropriate and unacceptable in relation to the new appeal procedure.[6]

7.2.7.2 The question of leave to appeal appertains to each individual question of law highlighted by the applicant and it is open to the court to respond differently to

1. *Stinnes Interoil G.m.b.H.* v. *A. Halcoussis & Co. (The Yanxilas)* [1982] 2 Lloyd's Rep. 445; *The Yanxilas (No. 2)* [1984] 1 Lloyd's Rep. 676.
2. *Ibid*. See Chapter 11.
3. See Chapter 11, para, 11.11.
4. *Athens Cape Naviera S.A.* v. *Deutsche Dampfschiffahrtsgesellschaft "Hansa" Aktiengesellschaft etc. (The Barenbels)* [1985] 1 Lloyd's Rep. 528, 532.
1. See, for example, *Stinnes Interoil G.m.b.H.* v. *A. Halcoussis & Co. (The Yanxilas) (No. 1)* [1982] 2 Lloyd's Rep. 445; *Heinrich Hanno & Co. B.V.* v. *Fairlight Shipping Co. Ltd. (The Kostas K)* [1985] 1 Lloyd's Rep. 231, 236–237.
2. See Chapter 8, para. 8.1.
3. *Stinnes Interoil G.m.b.H.* v. *A. Halcoussis & Co. (The Yanxilas) (No. 2)* [1984] 1 Lloyd's Rep. 676, 685. For examples of leave to appeal being given in relation to specific and clearly defined questions of law, see *Torvald Klaveness A/S* v. *Arni Maritime Corporation (The Gregos)* [1992] 2 Lloyd's Rep. 40; *Niobe Maritime Corporation* v. *Tradax Ocean Transportation S.A. (The Niobe)* [1993] 2 Lloyd's Rep. 52.
4. See, for example, *Geogas S.A.* v. *Trammo Gas Ltd. (The Baleares)* [1990] 2 Lloyd's Rep. 130, [1993] 1 Lloyd's Rep. 215 (C.A.), where Saville J. formulated the question of law in the following terms: "Whether on the facts found, the charterers are entitled to recover from the owners the damages awarded by the arbitrators."
5. See Chapter 1, para. 1.4.2.12.
6. For examples of desirable practice see *Torvald Klaveness A/S* v. *Arni Maritime Corporation (The Gregos)* [1992] 2 Lloyd's Rep. 40; *Niobe Maritime Corporation* v. *Tradax Ocean Transportation S.A. (The Niobe)* [1993] 2 Lloyd's Rep. 52.

each question of law, giving leave in the case of some and refusing it in the case of others.[7] Where the judge gives leave to appeal generally, this will be construed in the context of the application and held to relate to each question of law advanced.[8] It has been suggested *obiter dictum* that it is open to an applicant to argue the issue of the sufficiency of the evidence to support the findings of the arbitrator whenever leave is given in relation to a discrete question of law.[9] The notion of leave being given by implication has not attracted much discussion, and possibly for good reason, for the idea would seem to stand in opposition to the policy of the 1979 Act. Moreover the question of the sufficiency of evidence would seem in all instances to be a distinct question of law and separate from any specific question of law in respect of which leave to appeal is given.

7.2.8 Stay of execution

In giving leave to appeal the court also enjoys a discretion to stay any proceedings at common law or under the Arbitration Act 1950, section 26, aimed at enforcing the award. A stay may be necessary to protect the interests of the appellant, for if the appeal succeeds there is a danger that the appellant will have paid under an award which has subsequently been set aside on appeal, and there is no absolute guarantee that the appellant will be able to recover back the monies paid. The court will exercise its discretion in favour of granting a stay whenever it is fair and reasonable to do so, but giving full and proper weight to the starting principle that there has to be a good reason for depriving the successful party from obtaining the fruits of an award.[1] An alternative strategy is to allow the award to be enforced but subject to the giving of a satisfactory security.[2]

7.2.9 Consolidated and concurrent applications

Two or more applications for leave to appeal from different awards may be consolidated and heard together where, for example, the legal and factual issues are common to all, as may be the case with arbitrations arising out of back-to-back or otherwise associated contracts.[1]

There is also nothing to preclude an application for leave to appeal being made concurrently with other applications seeking non-appellate relief, such as applications that the award be set aside or remitted,[2] or that the arbitrator be removed for misconduct,[3] or that the period for commencing an arbitration be extended.[4] But where this

---

7. *President of India* v. *Taygetos Shipping Co. S.A. (The Agenor)* [1985] 1 Lloyd's Rep. 155, 156.
8. *Novorossisk Shipping Co.* v. *Neopetro Co. Ltd. (The Ulyanovsk)* [1990] 1 Lloyd's Rep. 425, 427.
9. *Geogas S.A.* v. *Trammo Gas Ltd. (The Baleares)* [1993] 1 Lloyd's Rep. 215, 272, Steyn L.J.
1. *Winchester Cigarette Machinery Ltd.* v. *Payne and Another (No. 2)*, *The Times*, 15 December 1993.
2. Cf. *Exmar BV* v. *National Iranian Tanker Co. (The Trade Fortitude)* [1992] 1 Lloyd's Rep. 169, 177.
1. See, for example, *International Sea Tankers Inc.* v. *Hemisphere Shipping Co. Ltd. (The Wenjiang)* [1981] 2 Lloyd's Rep. 308, 315 (first instance); *Clea Shipping Corpn.* v. *Bulk Oil International Ltd. (The Alaskan Trader)* [1983] 1 Lloyd's Rep. 315, 316.
2. Arbitration Act 1950, ss. 23(2) and 22.
3. Arbitration Act 1950, s. 23(1).
4. Arbitration Act 1950, s. 27.

is the case the court may direct that one application be heard before the other or, where appropriate, that they be heard together.[5]

7.3 PRACTICE OF THE COMMERCIAL COURT

7.3.1 Under prevailing practice the application for leave to appeal and the full substantive appeal are predominantly distinct and separate procedures governed by different considerations.[1] In contrast, under the initial practice adopted following the enactment of the 1979 Act the application for leave and the substantive appeal were effectively determined conjointly.[2] In the result the question of leave tended to follow the substantive assessment and its outcome. If the court was of a mind to allow an appeal on the question of law raised, it would of necessity be required to give leave to appeal in satisfaction of what had by that time turned into a technicality. If on the other hand it was unsympathetic to the legal argument of the appellant, the court would be more likely to refuse leave to appeal, rather than go through the meaningless motions of giving leave and then dismissing appeal. The disadvantage of the practice was that the court heard full argument on every application for leave, and under the R.S.C. as originally drafted this was to a judge in open court. The result was a practice diametrically opposed to the policy of the 1979 Act. The practice also militated against the good management of Commercial Court business, because reserved time might not be used.[3] But where leave to appeal was granted the practice was able to secure a speedy and possibly less expensive disposal of the appeal.[4] Subsequent developments have made the necessary procedural corrections, with applications now made to a judge in chambers[5] and the application for leave divorced from the substantive appeal, except for cases where it can be shown that there exist overwhelming reasons for conjoining the two processes, as in cases of urgency or where the question of law is very short and clear and can be disposed of quickly.[6] In a Practice Direction by Parker J. given on 9 November 1981 a motion for leave to appeal is considered an urgent matter which should be dealt with swiftly by the Commercial Court.[7]

7.3.2 On an application for leave to appeal the sole question before the court is whether to give or refuse leave.[8] It is not for the court at this stage to determine the question(s) of law in issue. The application is to be determined having regard to the

---

5. See Appendix I, para. 7.4.

1. See Chapter 9, para. 9.2. Also *Tor Line A.B.* v. *Alltrans Group of Canada Ltd. (The TFL Prosperity)* [1982] 1 Lloyd's Rep. 617, 626–627, per Bingham J., "The Court will in general strongly discourage attempts to convert applications for leave into full hearings."

2. See *Portaria Shipping Co.* v. *Gulf Pacific Navigation Co. Ltd. (The Selene G)* [1981] 2 Lloyd's Rep. 180; *International Sea Tankers Inc.* v. *Hemisphere Shipping Co. Ltd. (The Wenjiang)* [1981] 2 Lloyd's Rep. 308, 313; *Tor Line A.B.* v. *Alltrans Group of Canada Ltd. (The TFL Prosperity)* [1982] 1 Lloyd's Rep. 617, 626; *River Plate Products Netherlands B.V.* v. *Etablissement Coargrain* [1982] 1 Lloyd's Rep. 628.

3. *Bunge A.G.* v. *Sesotrad S.A. (The Alkeos C)* [1984] 1 Lloyd's Rep. 687, 691.

4. *International Sea Tankers Inc.* v. *Hemisphere Shipping Co. Ltd. (The Wenjiang)* [1981] 2 Lloyd's Rep. 308, 313.

5. *Supra*, para. 7.2.1.

6. See Chapter 9, para. 9.2.

7. See Appendix H(3) and [1982] 1 Lloyd's Rep. 115.

8. See generally *Vinava Shipping Co. Ltd.* v. *Finelvet A.G. (The Chrysalis)* [1983] 1 Lloyd's Rep. 503, 506.

policy of the 1979 Act and the guidelines laid down in the judicial authorities.[9] It is in its nature a preliminary issue to be disposed of speedily, simply and informally. The application for leave is not the occasion for full, lengthy and time consuming argument.[10] Beyond a perusal of the award, oral argument should be brief and restricted. As for the assessment of the correctness and significance of the question of law, this must of necessity be summary and all that is necessary is for the judge to come to a provisional assessment. A final and considered determination will follow on the full appeal hearing. In the *Guide to Commercial Court Practice* it is observed that the hearing is not expected to last more than half an hour.[10a]

The application is *inter partes*,[11] with the judge arriving at his provisional determination on the basis of a perusal of the award and brief oral argument. Where the respondent fails to appear, the application will proceed in his absence, but with counsel for the applicant under a professional duty to bring all the relevant points before the court, including those that speak against the application.[12]

7.3.3 Nor is it necessary for a judge in granting or refusing leave to appeal to give reasons for his decision.[13] All that is normally required is for the judge to say that he gives or refuses leave to appeal. To give reasons, when leave to appeal is given, would only serve to create unnecessary conflict between the judge giving leave and the judge hearing the appeal or to otherwise embarrass the latter.[14] This rule of practice is one that is to prevail normally and so on the facts of particular cases exceptions may be justified.[15] There is, however, one clearly identified exception to the normal rule and this applies where a judge in giving or refusing leave is also of a mind to give leave to appeal to the Court of Appeal from his own decision under section 1(6A). In this circumstance reasons are necessary so as to inform the Court of Appeal of the precise reasons why the judge at first instance considers the case suitable for consideration by the Court of Appeal.[16]

7.3.4 The above commentary derives substantially from the decision of the House of Lords in *The Antaios*, wherein is set out a blueprint of the practice to be followed

---

9. See Chapters 5 and 6.

10. *Retla Steamship Co.* v. *Gryphon Shipping Co. S.A. (The Evimeria)* [1982] 1 Lloyd's Rep. 55, 59; *International Sea Tankers Inc.* v. *Hemisphere Shipping Co. Ltd. (The Wenjiang)* [1982] 1 Lloyd's Rep. 128, 130; *National Rumour Compania S.A.* v. *Lloyd-Libra Navegacao S.A.* [1982] 1 Lloyd's Rep. 472, 476; *Tor Line A.B.* v. *Alltrans Group of Canada Ltd (The TFL Prosperity)* [1982] 1 Lloyd's Rep. 617, 626–627; *Bulk Oil (Zug) A.G.* v. *Sun International Ltd. and Sun Oil Trading Co.* [1983] 1 Lloyd's Rep. 655, 658.

10a. See Appendix I, para. 7.3.

11. Cf. Boyd, "Innovation and Reform in the Law of Arbitration" (1988) 2 C.J.Q. 148, 162–163, where the suggestion is made that an application for leave should be made *ex parte* in the first instance, either orally or in writing, and so avoid the necessity of a formal hearing *inter partes*.

12. *River Plate Products Netherlands B.V.* v. *Etablissement Coargrain* [1982] 1 Lloyd's Rep. 628, 629; cf *Canadian Pacific (Bermuda) Ltd.* v. *Lagon Maritime Overseas (The Fort Kipp)* [1985] 2 Lloyd's Rep. 168, 169.

13. *Antaios Compania Naviera S.A.* v. *Salen Rederierna A.B. (The Antaios)* [1985] 1 A.C. 191, 205–206, per Lord Diplock; *Petraco (Bermuda) Ltd.* v. *Petromed International S.A. and Beverli S.A.* [1988] 2 Lloyd's Rep. 357, 358–359. For an indication of the early practice see *Bunge A.G.* v. *Sesostrad S.A. (The Alkeos C)* [1984] 1 Lloyd's Rep. 687, 689; *Marine Contractors Inc.* v. *Shell Petroleum Co. of Nigeria Ltd.* [1984] 2 Lloyd's Rep. 77, 81. For reservations expressed extra-judicially with regard to present practice see Bingham, "Reasons and Reasons for Reasons: Differences between a Court Judgment and an Arbitration Award" (1988) 4 Arb. Int. 141, 142.

14. *Bunge A.G.* v. *Sesostrad S.A. (The Alkeos C)* [1984] 1 Lloyd's Rep. 687, 689; *Lucas Industries plc* v. *Welsh Development Agency* [1986] 2 All E.R. 858, 861.

15. *Supra* n. 13.

16. *Supra* n. 13 and Chapter 10, para. 10.2.2.

by the court in considering applications for leave to appeal. The relevant part of the leading speech of Lord Diplock merits an unabridged citation[17]:

However, save in the exceptional case in which he does give leave to appeal to the Court of Appeal under section 1(6)(A) . . . a judge ought not normally to give reasons for a grant or refusal under section 1(3)(b) of leave to appeal to the High Court from an arbitral award. He should follow the practice that has been adopted in your Lordships' House ever since a would-be appellant from a judgment of the Court of Appeal was required to petition this House for leave to appeal to it when leave to do so had not been granted by the Court of Appeal itself. It has been the practice of this House at the close of the short oral argument on the petition, to say no more than that the petition is allowed or refused as the case may be.

Save in very exceptional circumstances which I find myself unable at present to foresee, I can see no good reason why a commercial judge in disposing of an application under section 1(3)(b) should do more than that, and several good reasons why he should not. In the first place, he is not himself deciding at this stage the question of law arising out of the award which usually involves a question of construction of a commercial contract. He is simply deciding whether the case is of a kind that is recognised, under the current guidelines laid down by appellate courts, as suitable to be admitted to appeal. In the second place, it adds to the already excessive volume of reported judicial semantic and syntactical analysis of particular words and phrases appearing in commercial contracts which judges are inveigled to indulge in by the detailed oral arguments which it appears to be current practice to allow on applications under section 1(3)(b) whereas all that the judge has to decide on the application is: first, is this dispute, on the one hand, about a one-off clause or event, or, on the other hand, about a standard term or an event which is a common occurrence in the trade or commercial activity concerned? If it is the former, he must then consider: whether the arbitrator was in the judge's view so obviously wrong as to preclude the possibility that he might be right; if it is the latter, he must then consider whether a strong prima facie case has been made out that the arbitrator was wrong? Unless the answer he would give to the question appropriate to the type of case to which the application with which he is concerned is: "Yes," he should refuse leave to appeal.

The proliferation of reported judicial statements made in applications under section 1(3)(b) which are refused, that become available for subsequent citation in argument in cases where the actual question of law that arose in the arbitration does fall to be decided by the court itself, may have been mitigated since the date of Parker J.'s judgment in *The Kerman* [1982] 1 W.L.R. 166 by the change in practice in the hearing of applications under section 1(3)(b), from hearings on motion in open court to hearings in chambers; but your Lordships have been informed that this has not prevented judges from allowing to have inflicted on them on such applications pro-tracted arguments by counsel which frequently extend over two or three days.

My Lords, to permit such prolonged and therefore costly arguments on applications for leave to appeal to the High Court under section 1(3)(b), assists in frustrating the policy of Parliament in enacting the Act of 1979. As respects the extent to which detailed argument should be toler-ated on such applications, too, it is appropriate that the practice of this House in dealing with petitions for leave to appeal from judgments of the Court of Appeal in civil actions should be followed. In the first instance, a three-member Appeal Committee of the House peruses the judgment delivered in the courts below and the grounds set out in the written petition for leave to appeal that are relied upon by the petitioner as making the case one in which leave ought to be granted. Upon this material the members of the Appeal Committee, if they are all three of opinion that the petition could not possibly succeed, may dismiss it ex parte without requiring or permitting any oral argument; but this is exceptional; generally a brief oral hearing inter partes is permitted of which the average duration is ten to fifteen minutes; the parties are not allowed to use the hearing as an opportunity to argue the appeal that is the subject of the petition. The only question to be determined is whether the case in which leave to appeal is sought is of such a nature that it ought to be re-argued in this House instead of leaving the judgment appealed from as the final judgment in the case. If argument of this length is found to be adequate by the House of Lords to enable it to decide a question whether leave to appeal ought to be given, it

17. [1985] 1 A.C. 191, 205–207.

should be good enough for commercial judges who have to make up their minds upon a similar question where the criteria as to whether to grant leave or not are, under *The Nema* guidelines [1983] A.C. 724, less complex than those applicable to the grant of leave to appeal to this House from judgments of the Court of Appeal.

In *The Kerman* [1982] 1 W.L.R. 166, Parker J. pointed out that the passage in *The Nema* guidelines dealing with cases concerned with the construction of a "one-off" clause it appeared to be contemplated by this House that applications in such cases would normally be dealt with on the papers alone. It is correct that it was contemplated that a painstaking perusal of the award and the reason set out in the application as constituting the grounds why leave to appeal should be granted, would play the major part in the decision-making process of the commercial judge; but not so as to preclude subsequent brief oral argument limited to the question whether the grant of leave would fall within *The Nema* guidelines to the exclusion of any anticipatory argument directed to the merits of the appeal if leave should be granted.

My Lords, it may be, as your Lordships have found in the course of exercising the analogous jurisdiction of an Appeal Committee of this House, that there are occasionally applications for leave to appeal under section 1(3)(b) that are so hopeless that they can be properly disposed of by a refusal made ex parte on the papers alone without incurring the delay and expense of an oral hearing. The introduction of any such procedure to deal with obviously hopeless applications would be a matter for the Rules Committee rather than your Lordships so I limit myself to the suggestion that it may be worthy of consideration by that committee.

7.4 COSTS

The question of costs in relation to an application for leave to appeal will in each case fall to be determined in the discretion of the court.[1]

When leave to appeal is given the most likely approach is for the application for leave to be treated as an interlocutory matter, with costs to follow the final outcome. In short, the costs of the application will be costs in the appeal.[2] Only in exceptional circumstances will an independent order for costs in favour of the applicant be made.

When leave to appeal is refused the costs of the application are likely to be disposed of forthwith and in normal circumstances the respondent will recover costs from the applicant for leave.[3]

1. Supreme Court Act 1981, section 51(1). For the purpose of this section it is highly probable that an application for leave to appeal is a "proceeding" in the High Court: note *Rozhon and Another* v. *Secretary of State for Wales*, *The Times*, 29 April 1993.

2. *Schiffahrtsguntur Hamburg Middle East Line G.m.b.H* v. *Virtue Shipping Corporation* (The *Oinoussian Virtue*) [1981] 1 Lloyd's Rep. 533, 540; *Bunge A.G.* v. *Sesostrad S.A. (The Alkeos C)* [1984] 1 Lloyd's Rep. 687, 689.

3. Cf. *Retla Steamship Co.* v. *Gryphon Shipping Co. S.A. (The Evimeria)* [1982] 1 Lloyd's Rep. 55, 59; *Rozhon and Another* v. *Secretary of State for Wales, supra.*

CHAPTER 8

SUBSTANTIVE APPEALS AND APPELLATE POWERS

8.1 INTRODUCTION

Once leave to appeal has been granted the full substantive appeal may be pursued, subject to the provisions of the Rules of Court.[1] The full appeal is necessarily confined to the question or questions of law in relation to which leave has been given and the appellate review conducted by the High Court is restricted to an examination of the award, external documents incorporated into the award and argument presented on appeal.[2] If there are insufficient findings of fact to enable the appeal to be properly determined a potential cure may be an order for reasons or further reasons under section 1(5) or a utilisation of section 22 of the 1950 Act.[3] The powers enjoyed by a first tier judge on appeal are set out in section 1(2).[4] The role of the High Court on a substantive appeal is very different from that on an application for leave to appeal under section 1(3)(b).[5] On a substantive appeal the sole issue is the correctness in law of the decision of the arbitration tribunal.[6]

Where an appeal is from the award of a judge-arbitrator or judge-umpire, the appeal is to the Court of Appeal.[7]

8.2 BURDEN AND STANDARD OF PROOF

It is in each case for the appellant to establish on a balance of probabilities that the award contains an error of law.[1]

---

1. See Chapter 9.
2. See *infra*, para. 8.4.
3. See *infra*, para. 8.5.
4. These are considered in detail, *infra*, para. 8.7.
5. See Chapter 9, para. 9.2.
6. *Vinava Shipping Co. Ltd.* v. *Finelvet A.G. (The Chrysalis)* [1983] 1 Lloyd's Rep. 503, 506–507, per Mustill J.
7. Administration of Justice Act 1970, s. 4(5).
1. *The President of India* v. *Lips Maritime Corporation. (The Lips)* [1985] 2 Lloyd's Rep. 180, 182, per Lloyd J., "It is for the appellant to show that the award is wrong in law. If the award could be right in law, then the appeal must fail." Cf. *Pagnan & F.LLi* v. *Coprosol S.A.* [1981] 1 Lloyd's Rep. 283; *Kruse* v. *Ralli Maclaine Ltd. (Formerly Ralli Merrill Lynch Int. Ltd.)* [1982] 1 Lloyd's Rep. 162; *Glafki Shipping Co. S.A.* v. *Pinios Shipping Co. No. 1 (The Maira) (No. 2)* [1984] 1 Lloyd's Rep. 660; *Vargas Pena Apezteguia Y Cia SAIC* v. *Peter Cremer G.m.b.H.* [1987] 1 Lloyd's Rep. 394.

8.3 GENERAL JUDICIAL APPROACH TO THE REVIEW OF AWARDS

8.3.1 The courts have long adopted a generous and liberal approach to the scrutiny and proper understanding of awards.[1] Arbitration awards are frequently drafted by non-specialists, without legal or other professional assistance; and in consequence the intention underlying an award is on occasions clumsily or inappropriately or confusingly expressed. The established judicial attitude has been to give such awards a tolerant and sympathetic consideration, and this is particularly so when the award derives from a specialist arbitration process, such as trade arbitration.[2] A consequence of this broad approach results in the court, when such a strategy is open to it, weighing up the general purport of an award rather than focusing closely on the technicalities, structure and presentation of language.[3] This way of addressing awards manifests a historical bias in favour of the *prima facie* binding validity of awards, a policy significantly accentuated following the enactment of the 1979 Act.

8.3.2 The established historical approach to the scrutiny of awards survives into the appellate review process established by the 1979 Act.[4] In the face of challenge the court will scrutinise the award sensibly,[5] avoiding the assumption of an excessively critical or pedantic approach.[6] In particular it is emphasised that the scrutinisation of an award in connection with the determination of an appeal is a very different exercise from the interpretation of legislation.[7] The process by which an Act of Parliament and an arbitral award come into existence are so materially different that it is not only appropriate but necessary to adopt wholly different postures when attempting to divine their respective intent and meaning. In the case of awards a more liberal approach may be adopted, but at the same time the precise terms of the award in question cannot be lost sight of. The adoption of a liberal perspective does not extend so as to permit imaginative reconstruction.[8]

Under the 1979 Act the awards of specialist tribunals continue to enjoy a high respect, particularly when conclusions of law or questions of mixed fact and law or other questions involving the making of a commercial judgment are in issue.[9] But high respect does not translate into a *de facto* immunity from effective challenge. Whereas the judicial deference may in a borderline situation tip the balance in favour of affirming the award, nonetheless where there is clear error the court is bound to intervene,

---

1. *Eardley* v. *Steer* (1835) 4 L.J. (Ex.) 293; *Diestal* v. *Stephenson* [1906] 2 K.B. 345, 351.
2. *Andrea* v. *British Italian Trading Co. Ltd.* [1962] 1 Lloyd's Rep. 151, 161; [1963] 1 Q.B. 201, 208.
3. *Pagnan & F. LLi* v. *Coprosol S.A.* [1981] 1 Lloyd's Rep. 283, 285–286.
4. *Indian Oil Corpn. Ltd.* v. *Greenstone Shipping S.A. (The Ypatianna)* [1987] 2 Lloyd's Rep. 286, 291.
5. Cf. *Mediolanum Shipping Co.* v. *Japan Lines Ltd., The Mediolanum* [1982] 1 Lloyd's Rep. 47, 50; *F.R. Waring (U.K.) Ltd.* v. *Administraçao Geral do Acucar e do Alcool E.P.* [1983] 1 Lloyd's Rep. 45, 50.
6. *J.H. Rayner (Mincing Lane) Ltd.* v. *Shaher Trading Co.* [1982] 1 Lloyd's Rep. 632, 636; also *Industriebeteiligungs & Handelsgesellschaft* v. *Malaysian International Shipping Corpn. Berhad (The Bunga Melawis)* [1991] 2 Lloyd's Rep. 271, 277, where Webster J. speaks of "reading the award with common sense and without undue legality".
7. *Supra* n. 4.
8. *Leif Hoegh & Co. A/S* v. *Maritime Mineral Carriers Ltd. The Marques de Bolarque* [1983] 1 Lloyd's Rep. 660, 665.
9. *André et Cie* v. *Cook Industries Inc.* [1986] 2 Lloyd's Rep. 200, 204; *State Trading Corpn. of India Ltd.* v. *M. Golodetz Ltd. (Now Transcontinental Affiliates Ltd.)* [1989] 2 Lloyd's Rep. 277, 284.

whatever the character of the tribunal or the characterisation of the question of law in issue.[10]

8.4 THE EVIDENTIARY BASIS OF APPEALS

8.4.1 The appellate process established under the 1979 Act is confined to questions of law arising out of awards made on arbitration agreements.[1] It follows that the error of law must be manifested in the award itself and be capable of being established by reference to the information embodied in the award.[2] The evidentiary basis to support an appeal must therefore derive from the face of the award; its express and implied reasoning[3] (in the broad sense); extraneous documents expressly or impliedly incorporated into the award,[4] or otherwise expressly identified in the reasoning of the award.[5] Without incorporation or reference, all materials outside the four corners of an award are extraneous and inadmissible.[6] Affidavit evidence is therefore inadmissible, as is any other manner of statement by counsel or solicitors.[7] Problems which might arise from a strict application of what may be coined the four corner rule are in practice often tempered by the agreement of the parties.[8] Where reasons and documents are expressly declared not to form part of an award, there can be little doubting their extraneous character.[9]

8.4.2 Where the award challenged is a valid but not unanimous award, it would appear that the reasons of any dissenting arbitrator may be alluded to in argument and

10. *Compagnie Commerciale Sucres et Denrées* v. *C. Czarnikow Ltd. (The Naxos)* [1989] 2 Lloyd's Rep. 462, 475 (C.A.).

1. Section 1(2); considered in Chapter 3.

2. *Comdel Commodities Ltd.* v. *Siporex Trade S.A. (No. 2)* [1988] 2 Lloyd's Rep. 590, 591, per Steyn J., "The facts pertinent to an appeal under s. 1 of the Arbitration Act 1979 are to be gathered only from the reasons of the award."

3. Cf. *Reinante Transoceanic Navegacion S.A.* v. *The President of India (The Apiliotis)* [1985] 1 Lloyd's Rep. 255. Note also *Geogas S.A.* v. *Trammo Gas Ltd. (The Baleares)* [1993] 1 Lloyd's Rep. 215, 233, Steyn L.J., "a court hearing an appeal under s.1 of the Arbitration Act 1979 may not speculate about the facts".

4. *Athens Cape Naviera S.A.* v. *Deutsche Dampfschiffahrtsgessellschaft "Hansa" Aktiengesellschaft and Another (The Barenbels)* [1985] 1 Lloyd's Rep. 528, 532 (C.A.); *Universal Petroleum Co. Ltd.* v. *Handels- und Transport Gesellschaft m.b.H.* [1987] 1 Lloyd's Rep. 517, 528 (C.A.). See also *Portunus Navigation Co. Inc.* v. *Avin Chartering S.A. (The World Prestige)* [1982] 1 Lloyd's Rep. 60 (reasons annexed to the award).

5. *Transgrain Shipping B.V.* v. *Global Transporte Oceanico S.A. (The Mexico I)* [1988] 2 Lloyd's Rep. 149, 157.

6. *S.L. Sethia Liners Ltd.* v. *Naviagro Maritime Corporation (The Kostas Melas)* [1981] 1 Lloyd's Rep. 18, 30. In *International Sea Tankers Inc.* v. *Hemisphere Shipping Co. Ltd. (The Wenjiang) (No. 2)* [1983] 1 Lloyd's Rep. 400, 401–402, Bingham J. considered it an incontrovertible proposition that "[w]hen reviewing the decision of an arbitrator as to when frustration of a given contract occurred it is not permissible for a court to pay attention to the decisions of other arbitrators in different references arising out of the same facts with a view to achieving uniformity between them". See also *Athens Cape Naviera S.A.* v. *Deutsche Dampfschiffahrtsgesellschaft "Hansa" Aktiengesellschaft and Another (The Barenbels)* [1985] 1 Lloyd's Rep. 528, 532 (C.A.); *Michael I. Warde* v. *Feedex International Inc.* [1985] 2 Lloyd's Rep. 289, 299–300 (first instance).

7. *Universal Petroleum Co. Ltd. (in liquidation)* v. *Handels- und Transport Gesellschaft m.b.H.* [1987] 1 Lloyd's Rep. 517, 521 (C.A.).

8. *Heinrich Hanno & Co. B.V.* v. *Fairlight Shipping Co. Ltd. (The Kostas K)* [1985] 1 Lloyd's Rep. 231, 234.

9. See Chapter 11, para. 11.2.6.

taken into account in the deliberations of the appellate judge. The propriety of this practice does not appear to have been expressly questioned, but it is a practice so widely followed that it must be seriously doubted that any objection to it would now be entertained.[10] There is nonetheless a certain difficulty. It may be assumed that the reference to an award in section 1(2) alludes to a valid award of an arbitrator or tribunal. Where the arbitration agreement provides for a majority award (or even some other manner of non-unanimous award) it equally defines what amounts to a valid award for the purpose of section 1(2). It is the majority or otherwise defined decision which represents the valid and binding award of the tribunal, and it is arguable that the reasons of a dissenting arbitrator are not properly to be considered part of the award.[11] Only by adopting a less strict analytical approach and viewing the concept of an award in the same general way that might be adopted by the parties themselves is it possible to incorporate dissenting reasons into the award. Although this may be a vulnerable analysis and likely to give rise to inconsistencies, it is nonetheless defensible on pragmatic grounds. Dissenting reasons have a clear significance in the appeal process and may play a significant part in the detection of error and the determination of appropriate remedies. Dissenting judgments have often assisted the functioning of the court appeal system, and it would materially disadvantage the appeal judge under the 1979 Act if he was denied knowledge of any arbitral dissenting point of view.[12]

8.4.3 Where an appeal is provided for within the contractual arbitral process, it is the award of the appeal tribunal which comes into issue and not the award of the first tier tribunal, which is superseded by the appellate award.[13] The evidentiary basis of an appeal must in consequence be mounted on the basis of the reasons embodied in the appellate award, with the first tier award extraneous. But although this may be strictly the case, it is doubtful whether the courts will be content to deny themselves access to the first tier award, and may seek to draw a parallel between a first tier award and the reasons of a dissenting arbitrator. A first tier arbitral award overruled on an arbitral appeal may be just as useful an aid to the deliberations of an appellate judge as the reasoning of a dissenting arbitrator.

In the ultimate it is for the party contemplating the possibility of a future appeal to ensure that the reasoning contained in the award is sufficiently comprehensive to enable an appeal to be mounted.[14]

---

10. See, for example, *Rudolph A. Oetker* v. *IFA Internationale Frachagentur A.G. (The Almak)* [1985] 1 Lloyd's Rep. 557; *Summit Investment Inc.* v. *British Steel Corporation (The Sounion)* [1986] 2 Lloyd's Rep. 593; [1987] 1 Lloyd's Rep. 230 (C.A.); *Lips Maritime Corpn.* v. *National Maritime Agencies Co. (The Star of Kuwait)* [1986] 2 Lloyd's Rep. 641; *New A Line* v. *Erechthion Shipping Co. S.A. (The Erechthion)* [1987] 2 Lloyd's Rep. 180; *Palm Shipping Inc.* v. *Kuwait Petroleum Corporation (The Sea Queen)* [1988] 1 Lloyd's Rep. 500; *Kansa General Insurance Co. Ltd.* v. *Bishopsgate Insurance plc* [1988] 1 Lloyd's Rep. 503, 510–511; *General Feeds Inc.* v. *Burnham Shipping Corporation (The Amphion)* [1991] 2 Lloyd's Rep. 101.

11. In *Exmar B.V.* v. *National Iranian Tanker Co. (The Trade Fortitude)* [1992] 1 Lloyd's Rep. 169, the reasons of the majority and a dissenting arbitrator were incorporated in separate documents and attached to the award. In determining the appeal Judge Diamond, Q.C., confined his scrutiny to the reasons of the majority.

12. For examples of contemporary practice see *Exmar B.V.* v. *National Iranian Tanker Co. (The Trade Fortitude)* [1992] 1 Lloyd's Rep. 169, 172; *Dolphin Hellas Shipping S.A.* v. *Itemslot Ltd. (The Aegean Dolphin)* [1992] 2 Lloyd's Rep. 178, 181–182.

13. *Comdel Commodities Ltd.* v. *Siporex Trade S.A. (No. 2)* [1988] 2 Lloyd's Rep. 590, 592.

14. *Athens Cape Naviera S.A.* v. *Deutsche Dampfschiffahrtsgesellschaft "Hansa" Aktiengesellschaft and Another (The Barenbels), supra,* p. 532 per Robert Goff L.J.

8.5 REMEDY FOR INADEQUATE EVIDENTIARY BASIS

8.5.1 Where an award provides an inadequate evidentiary basis to determine whether or not there has been an error of law, the court enjoys a discretion to remit the award to the arbitrator for the further elaboration of fact and law. The primary remedy is an order for further reasons under section 1(5).[1] This remedy is discretionary and it is open for an order to be made even during the hearing of the substantive appeal. The court, however, cannot make an order of its own volition, and no doubt the precise time an application is made and its impact on the expeditious disposal of an appeal, will be taken into account in the exercise of the judicial discretion.

8.5.2 Although it is stressed that applications for further reasons should ordinarily be made under section 1(5), this emphasis does not wholly put out of reach the general remitting power conferred by section 22 of the Arbitration Act 1950.[2] The latter section has the advantage of enabling the court to remit an award of its own motion without overt jurisdictional constraint as opposed to discretionary constraints.[2a] It appears to have been acknowledged that in appropriate circumstances the appellate judge may utilise the section 22 jurisdiction in aid of the appeal process.[3] The court will however be reluctant to remit when neither party desires a remission and on occasions it may be possible to avoid such a course by making findings of implicit fact,[4] or by the parties agreeing facts for the purposes of the appeal,[5] or by the parties agreeing to the introduction of relevant documents.[6]

8.5.3 An appeal under section 1 of the 1979 Act is closer to the philosophy of the former common law jurisdiction to set aside awards for error of law on their face than to the special case procedure. The object underlying an appeal is to determine whether the award contains an error of law and not to place a question of law before the court for its determination. It would seem to follow that it is for the appellant to ensure that the award contains the necessary information for the purpose of an appeal and with the court correspondingly and centrally concerned to evaluate the legal accuracy of the award at the moment of the appeal. Remission, it would therefore appear, is not a remedy which the appellant should think of in terms of a right. The court is likely to exercise the jurisdiction cautiously and restrictively, and to give a remedy only when the justice of the case is unambiguous.

1. See Chapter 11.
2. See Chapter 11, para. 11.11. Also *Athens Cape Naviera S.A.* v. *Deutsche Dampfschiffahrtsgesellschaft "Hansa" Aktiengesellschaft and Another (The Barenbels)* [1985] 1 Lloyd's Rep. 528 (C.A.).
2a. *King* v. *Thomas McKenna Ltd.* [1991] 1 All E.R. 653 (C.A.).
3. *Eurico S.p.A.* v. *Philipp Bros. (The Epaphus)* [1986] 2 Lloyd's Rep. 387, 394 (Staughton J. decided against remission because of the smallness of the sum of money in issue). Cf. *Kaffeehandelsgesellschaft K.G.* v. *Plagefim Commercial S.A.* [1981] 2 Lloyd's Rep. 190, 192–193; *President of India* v. *Taygetos Shipping Co. S.A. (The Agenor)* [1985] 1 Lloyd's Rep. 155, 160. *Heinrich Hanno & Co. B.V.* v. *Fairlight Shipping Co. Ltd. (The Kostas K)* [1985] 1 Lloyd's Rep. 231, 234; *Indian Oil Corporation Ltd.* v. *Greenstone Shipping S.A. (The Ypatianna)* [1987] 2 Lloyd's Rep. 286, 299; *Transgrain Shipping B.V.* v. *Global Transporte Oceanico S.A. (The Mexico I)* [1988] 2 Lloyd's Rep. 149, 157.
4. *Athenian Tankers Management S.A.* v. *Pyrena Shipping Inc. (The Arianna)* [1987] 2 Lloyd's Rep. 376; Cf. *Reinante Transoceanic Navegacion S.A.* v. *The President of India (The Apiliotis)* [1985] 1 Lloyd's Rep. 255 (special case procedure).
5. Cf. *Comdel Commodities Ltd.* v. *Siporex Trade S.A. (No. 2)* [1988] 2 Lloyd's Rep. 590, 591.
6. *Heinrich Hanno & Co. B.V.* v. *Fairlight Shipping Co. Ltd. (The Kostas K)* [1985] 1 Lloyd's Rep. 231, 234.

8.6 ESTABLISHING LEGAL ERROR

8.6.1 In reviewing the correctness in law of an award or part of an award the court adopts the same approach as that long established by the courts in reviewing the determinations on questions of law of tribunals which are not themselves courts of law.[1] In other words an error of law may be ascertained from an express revelation on the face of an award or by necessary implication from the express provisions of an award[2]; or may be deduced from the unreasonableness of a determination arrived at by an arbitrator or tribunal. In *The Nema*[3] the House of Lords endorsed the classic passage of Lord Radcliffe in *Edwards* v. *Bairstow*[4] as signposting the correct approach to be adopted:

If the case contains anything ex facie which is bad law and which bears upon the determination, it is, obviously, erroneous in point of law. But, without any such misconception appearing ex facie, it may be that the facts found are such that no person acting judicially and properly instructed as to the relevant law could have come to the determination under appeal. In those circumstances, too, the court must intervene. It has no option but to assume that there has been some misconception of the law and that this has been responsible for the determination. So there, too, there has been error in point of law.

8.6.2 Thus, by way of example, where the question of law in dispute relates to the alleged frustration of a contract, the first tier appellate judge must address himself to two separate questions. First, did the arbitrator misdirect himself in law? Secondly, did the arbitrator arrive at a decision that no reasonable arbitrator could reach? If the arbitrator misdirected himself then the error of law is manifest and it is unnecessary to proceed further. But even if the arbitrator did direct himself correctly, there is nonetheless an error of law if it can be shown that the arbitrator then proceeded to arrive at a conclusion which no reasonable arbitrator could reach.[5] In the latter instance the presumption of legal error derives from the unreasonableness of the ultimate determination. But if the arbitrator did arrive at a decision which a reasonable arbitrator might have arrived at, it matters not that the reviewing court, if left to its own devices, would have arrived at a different decision.

8.6.3 The broader basis of review established on the notion of reasonableness is of course only of relevance when law and fact are inextricably interwoven or questions of judgment or value are in issue, as in the case of questions characterised as conclusions

---

1. *Pioneer Shipping Ltd. and Others* v. *B.T.P. Tioxide Ltd. (The Nema)* [1982] A.C. 724, 742, per Lord Diplock. See also *Athenian Tankers Management S.A.* v. *Pyrena Shipping Inc. (The Arianna)* [1987] 2 Lloyd's Rep. 376, 383–385.
2. *Société Anonyme des Minerais* v. *Grant Trading Inc. (The Ert Stephanie)* [1987] 2 Lloyd's Rep. 371, 375. But contrast *Geogas S.A.* v. *Trammo Gas Ltd. (The Baleares)* [1993] 1 Lloyd's Rep. 215, 228, Steyn L.J.
3. *Supra*, p. 742
4. [1956] A.C. 14, 36. See also *C. Maurice & Co. Ltd.* v. *Minister of Labour* [1969] 2 A.C. 346; *International Sea Tankers* v. *Hemisphere Shipping Co. Ltd. (The Wenjiang) (No. 2)* [1983] 1 Lloyd's Rep. 400, 402, per Bingham J., "Since an appeal to the High Court against the decision of an arbitrator lies only on questions of law, a successful appellant must now establish one or other of the grounds defined in *Edwards* v. *Bairstow* [1956] A.C. 14. He must either show from the reason given by the arbitrator that he misdirected himself in law, or he must persuade the Court that on the findings made by the arbitrator no reasonable arbitrator properly directing himself in law could have reached the decision in question;" *Athenian Tankers Management S.A.* v. *Pyrena Shipping Inc. (The Arianna)*, *supra*; *Société Anonyme des Minerais* v. *Grant Trading Inc. (The Ert Stephanie)*, *supra*.
5. *Pioneer Shipping Ltd. and Another* v. *B.T.P. Tioxide Ltd. (The Nema)* [1980] 1 Q.B. 547, 566–567 per Lord Denning M.R. (C.A.); [1982] A.C. 724, 542 per Lord Diplock, pp. 253–254, per Lord Roskill (H.L.).

of law or as questions of mixed fact and law.[6] In contrast, where prevailing issue raises nothing beyond a pure question of law there is but a single question which arises and that is whether the arbitrator has properly directed himself on the specific question of law. The answer to that question is to be found in the express reasons and necessary implications of the award.[7] There is however a further intermediate situation which must be considered and that is when following the application of the relevant law to the facts there is but one possible conclusion, for it arises automatically and inevitably from the marrying of the law to the facts. In this kind of circumstance the narrower basis of review applies, and this continues to be the case even if the arbitrator has initially stated the law correctly, for in the circumstances the court is driven to assume that the arbitrator did not properly understand the law.[8] The broader basis of review founded on reasonableness only assumes a relevance when there are two or more possible conclusions.[9]

8.6.4 There are therefore contemplated within the *Edwards* v. *Bairstow* principle two broad categories of legal error and correspondingly two spheres of judicial review. The one is *ex facie* and raises a blunt issue of right or wrong; the other appertains to the reasonableness of arbitral conclusions and is more judgmental. Each also represents legal error arising at different stages in the typical arbitral decision-making process. After ascertaining the facts and determining disputed factual issues, an arbitrator proceeds to ascertain the relevant law, drawing on all the appropriate sources. If the arbitrator falls into error at this stage it will be *ex facie*, for the legal error will be capable of being demonstrated from an examination of the express terms of the award and, if necessary, with the aid of necessary inferences. At this stage the judicial review process reduces itself to a straightforward question of right or wrong. But even if the arbitrator ascertains and enunciates the law accurately, there may be error in the next stage of the arbitral decision-making process, which represents the ultimate decision(s) of the arbitrator, arrived at by marrying fact to law or by the exercise of a judgment. Error at this stage is assessed by reference either to an absolute standard of right and wrong or to the concept of reasonableness, according to the circumstances. Where only a single and inevitable conclusion is possible but the arbitrator has arrived at another, then the arbitrator is considered to have fallen into error notwithstanding that he may have ascertained the law accurately.

8.6.5 In this circumstance an absolute standard of right and wrong operates and the error derives from the failure to comprehend and apply the principles of law correctly identified. Where there is no single conclusion that follows automatically, but a range of possible conclusions from which the arbitrator may choose, then it is the notion of reasonableness which lies at the foundation of the judicial review process. In this manner of situation the arbitrator is called upon to exercise a judgment; he must weigh the consequences of marrying fact and law, and with it impossible to assert that there exists any uniquely correct conclusion. To the contrary, there often exists a range of possible conclusions that the arbitrator may arrive at, all supportable, and none of

---

6. *Alfred C. Toepfer Schiffahrtsgesellschaft G.m.b.H.* v. *Tossa Marine Co. Ltd.* [1984] 1 Lloyd's Rep. 635; [1985] 2 Lloyd's Rep. 325 (C.A.); *Athenian Tanker Management S.A.* v. *Pyrena Shipping Inc. (The Arianna)*, *supra*.
7. *Société Anonyme des Minerais* v. *Grant Trading Inc. (The Ert Stephanie)*, *supra*.
8. *Vinava Shipping Co. Ltd.* v. *Finelvet A.G. (The Chrysalis)* [1983] 1 Lloyd's Rep. 503, 507.
9. *Ibid*.

which are capable of being dismissed as unquestionably wrong. This range in turn provides the basis and parameters of the concept of reasonableness. Provided the arbitrator remains within the range it cannot be said that he has fallen into error and consequently the reviewing court will not intervene, notwithstanding that the court itself might have been inclined to come to a different conclusion within the range, had the decision been for it to make. It is only when the arbitrator arrives at a conclusion outside the permitted range that the conclusion is unreasonable and consequently wrong in law. The unreasonableness of the conclusion is in itself evidence of incomprehension and misunderstanding of the relevant law, notwithstanding that the arbitrator may have outwardly enunciated the law accurately.[10]

8.6.6 Where the disputed question of law relates to the existence or sufficiency of evidence to support a finding or conclusion of fact[11] the role of the first tier appellate judge is not to determine whether the court itself would have made the same findings of fact or come to similar conclusions of fact; the sole issue is whether there was sufficient evidence to justify the findings and/or conclusions of the arbitrator. The test is objective and is customarily framed by asking the question whether on the evidence a reasonable arbitrator could have made that finding or arrived at that conclusion of fact.[12] Further, the court is concerned only with the particular question whether there existed any or sufficient evidence to support the particular finding or conclusion in issue. It is not concerned with the wider issue whether the decision of the arbitrator was against the weight of evidence as a whole.[13]

8.6.7 In the exercise of its reviewing function the court is primarily concerned with the decision of the arbitrator and not the reasoning underpinning the decision. Provided that the ultimate decision is right in law, it matters not that the reasoning is erroneous, or at least that the judge is of a mind to come to the same decision as the arbitrator but for different reasons[14]: and conversely, an erroneous decision cannot be saved by unimpeachable reasoning. It is unexceptional for an appellate court to affirm the decision of a lower court, but for reasons different from those adopted by the lower tribunal.[15] But although for the purposes of review the arbitral decision and reasoning must be kept distinct, it will nonetheless frequently be the case that erroneous reasoning will result in an erroneous decision.

8.6.8 The arbitrator must apply himself to the dispute referred by applying the relevant rules and principles of law. The appellate process and the basis of review established by the 1979 Act affirm the generally held view that an arbitrator must decide according to law and not *extra legem*.[16] But an arbitral award is not a legal precedent and it follows that neither an arbitral tribunal nor a reviewing court is obliged to have regard to other arbitral decisions, even when the other awards arise out of similar dis-

---

10. *Ibid*. See also *Alfred C. Toepfer International G.m.b.H.* v. *Itex Itagrani Export S.A.* [1993] 1 Lloyd's Rep. 360 (where the legal question in issue related to an alleged wrongful repudiation of contract).
11. See, generally, Chapter 6, para. 6.2.11.
12. *Mitsubishi International G.m.b.H.* v. *Bremer Handelsgesellschaft m.b.H.* [1981] 1 Lloyd's Rep. 106.
13. *Ibid*.
14. Cf. *Uni-Ocean Lines Pte. Ltd.* v. *C-Trade S.A. (The Lucille)* [1983] 1 Lloyd's Rep. 387 (first instance).
15. Cf. *Fercometal S.A.R.L.* v. *MSC Mediterranean Shipping Co. S.A. (The Simona)* [1987] 2 Lloyd's Rep. 236 (C.A.); [1988] 2 Lloyd's Rep. 199 (H.L.).
16. See Chapter 1, para. 1.2.2.2.

putes raising similar questions of law, and when much could be said in favour of achieving uniformity of approach.[17]

8.7 POWERS OF FIRST TIER JUDGE ON APPEAL

8.7.1 The powers of a first tier judge in determining an appeal on a question of law arising out of an arbitration award are specified in section 1(2) of the 1979 Act. The High Court may by order:

    (a) confirm, vary or set aside the award; or

    (b) remit the award to the reconsideration of the arbitrator or umpire together with the court's opinion on the question of law which was the subject of the appeal;

and where the award is remitted under paragraph (b) above the arbitrator or umpire shall, unless the order otherwise directs, make his award within three months after the date of the order.

The particular novelty of section 1(2) is that it introduces a power to vary an award without the need to first return the award to the arbitrator,[1] and where an award is varied on appeal it takes effect as if it were the award of the arbitrator or umpire who made the original award.[2] Otherwise the powers to confirm, set aside and remit awards have long been associated with the non-appellate reviewing jurisdiction vested in the courts by the common law and under sections 22 and 23 of the Arbitration Act 1950, although the power to remit did not exist at common law and is a wholly statutory development.[3]

8.7.2 The jurisdiction to vary awards established by section 1(2) has of course no wider application than section 1 of the 1979 Act. But although the statutory power to vary is new and limited, it is nonetheless more generally established that such a power may be conferred on the court by the agreement of the parties,[4] or by contract on an arbitration appeal tribunal.[5] When so conferred the proper application and extent of the power is a question of construction. In judicial proceedings it is also open to the parties to agree that a judge should have the power to vary an award so as to give effect to a conclusion the judge has arrived at.[6] The potential advantage of such an agreement is that it saves the delay and expense of a remission which would in the absence of such an agreement be ordered.

---

17. *International Sea Tankers Inc.* v. *Hemisphere Shipping Co. Ltd. (The Wenjiang) (No. 2)* [1983] 1 Lloyd's Rep. 400, 401. See also *Kodros Shipping Corpn.* v. *Empresa Cubana de Fletes. (The Evia) (No. 2)* [1982] 2 Lloyd's Rep. 307, 332; *The Nema* [1982] A.C. 724, 745 *et seq.*, per Lord Roskill.

1. At common law there existed no power to alter or amend an award, see *Hall* v. *Alderson* (1825) 2 Bing. 476; *Moore* v. *Butlin* (1837) 7 A. & E. 595. See also *Report on Arbitration* (1978) para. 5; set out in Appendix A.

2. s. 1(8).

3. The power to remit was first introduced by s. 8 of the Common Law Procedure Act 1854. For comment on the early history and development of the jurisdiction, see *King* v. *Thomas McKenna Ltd.* [1991] 1 All E.R. 653.

4. See, for example, *Warinco A.G.* v. *Andre & Cie S.A.* [1979] 2 Lloyd's Rep. 298, 300; *P.J. Van der Zijden Wildhandel N.V.* v. *Tucker & Cross Ltd.* [1976] 1 Lloyd's Rep. 341, 343; *Armada Lines Continent-Mediterranean Service Ltd.* v. *Naviera Murueta S.A. (The Elexalde)* [1985] 2 Lloyd's Rep. 485, 489.

5. *Montrose Canned Foods Ltd.* v. *Eric Wells (Merchants) Ltd.* [1965] 1 Lloyd's Rep. 597; *Bremer Handelsgesellschaft m.b.H.* v. *Bunge Corporation* [1982] 1 Lloyd's Rep. 108, 111.

6. This sometimes occurs on an application for remission under s. 22 of the Arbitration Act 1950.

8.7.3 The specified appellate powers may be separately applied to each award, where more than one award is under appeal.[7] Moreover in relation to a particular award the powers are not restricted to the award as a global entity, but may be directed to individual points of appeal raised in relation to any part of the award. Notwithstanding that section 1(2) appears to suggest the contrary by alluding to *the* award, it nonetheless has become widely assumed that any of the appellate powers may be exercised in relation to the award as a whole or any severable part of the award.[8]

8.7.4 The powers specified in section 1(2) are not mutually exclusive. Where appropriate they may be combined or expressed in the alternative in order to produce the result desired by the court.[9] To a certain degree there appears to prevail the impression that an award must be first set aside before it may be varied or remitted.[10] It may be doubted if this is the case. An order of variation would appear by necessary implication to set aside that which is varied; and an order of remission empowers the arbitrator to reconsider, and again by necessary implication conveys the power to set aside any determination which on reconsideration is found to be erroneous. This approach to the question appears to have been endorsed and advanced still further by Lord Donaldson M.R. in *Hiscox* v. *Outhwaite (No. 1)*,[11] where the Master of the Rolls observed, "A variation involves a partial setting aside. A remission involves a total setting aside, because the award remitted has no validity unless and until it is confirmed by the arbitrator at a later date and so becomes to that extent a different award. In most cases he will make a new award in different terms."[12] The Master of the Rolls further considered that a remission under section 22 of the 1950 Act was to the same effect.[13]

8.7.5 When an appeal is allowed the precise remedial power to be applied will fall to be decided in the discretion of the court. To date there has been no determined judicial attempt to map out with the aid of guidelines the circumstances in which it is appropriate to use the various appellate powers. It would nonetheless appear that the exercise of the discretion will depend primarily on the nature of the question of law in issue and the sufficiency of the associated factual findings in the award.[14] In exercising its discretion the court will also invariably seek out the views of the parties as to the most appropriate remedy. The appellant will often set out the remedy sought in the

---

7. *Heinrich Hanno & Co. B.V.* v. *Fairlight Shipping Co. Ltd.* (*The Kostas K*) [1985] 1 Lloyd's Rep. 231.

8. See, for example, *President of India* v. *Jebsens (UK) Ltd. and Others (The General Capinpin)* [1987] 2 Lloyd's Rep. 354.

9. See, for example, *Damon Compania Naviera* v. *E.A.L. Europe Afrika Line G.m.b.H. (The Nicki R.)* [1984] 2 Lloyd's Rep. 186, 190 (part of an award varied and part remitted); *Rashtriya Chemicals and Fertilizers Ltd.* v. *Huddart Parker Industries Ltd (The Boral Gas)* [1988] 1 Lloyd's Rep. 342, 351; *Vagres Compania Maritima S.A.* v. *Nissho-Iwai American Corporation (The Karin Vatis)* [1988] 2 Lloyd's Rep. 330, 337 (C.A.); *Islamic Republic of Iran Shipping Lines* v. *Zannis Compania Naviera S.A. (The Tzelepi)* [1991] 2 Lloyd's Rep. 265.

10. See, for example, *Showa Oil Tanker Co. Ltd. of Japan* v. *Maravan S.A. of Caracas (The Larissa)* [1983] 2 Lloyd's Rep. 325, 332; *Etablissements Soules et Cie* v. *Intertradex S.A.* [1991] 1 Lloyd's Rep. 378, 383. Traces of the same mode of thinking can be found in the law outside the 1979 Act; see *Rooke, Sons & Co.* v. *Piper & May* (1927) 28 Ll.L.Rep. 49; *F.E. Hookway & Co. Ltd.* v. *Alfred Isaacs & Sons* [1954] 1 Lloyd's Rep. 491.

11. [1991] 2 All ER 124, 133.

12. This aspect of the dictum should be read subject to the possibility that only a part of an award may be remitted when it is that part alone which is set aside and not the total award.

13. *Ibid.*

14. The various remedial powers are discussed *infra.*

notice of motion or in the course of argument. When an appeal is allowed counsel may be invited to address the question as to which remedy the court should give, without of course in any way tying the hands of the court.[15] Following a successful appeal the parties may agree the remedy that should follow, and except in very special circumstances the court is likely to be ready to affirm such agreement. Given that the question of remedy following a successful appeal is a matter of discretion, it is theoretically possible for an appeal to be allowed and for the court to refuse any remedy, although this kind of situation is only likely to arise in the most exceptional of circumstances, as when the conduct of the appellant attracts serious censure. In the exercise of its appellate powers it is unlikely that the court will divorce itself from the established position of doing all that is reasonable to support rather than unnecessarily striking down arbitral awards, and in consequence it may be anticipated that there will exist antipathy towards too ready an adoption of the power to set aside awards.[16]

Although not expressly provided for in section 1(2), an order under the subsection may be made conditional on the occurrence of a specified event.[17] An appeal may be brought concurrently with other applications and it necessarily follows that when all the applications succeed some further kind of legal remedy, such as declaratory relief, may be sought and granted alongside the statutory appellate remedies provided for in section 1(2).[18]

8.8 CONFIRMATION

8.8.1 Where an appeal is dismissed in its entirety, the automatic effect is that the arbitral award is left undisturbed and with the judicial confirmation thereafter made effective by an express order to that effect[1] or by necessary implication from the judicial determination.[2] An order of confirmation substantiates the operational part of an award and not necessarily the reasons or reasoning of the arbitrator. It is possible for

15. See, for example, *Heinrich Hanno & Co. B.V.* v. *Fairlight Shipping Co. Ltd. (The Kostas K)* [1985] 1 Lloyd's Rep. 231, 237; *Paros Shipping Corporation* v. *Nafta (GB) Ltd. (The Paros)* [1987] 2 Lloyd's Rep. 269, 271; *Colonial Bank* v. *European Grain & Shipping Ltd. (The Dominique)* [1987] 1 Lloyd's Rep. 239, 258; *Procter & Gamble Philippine Manufacturing Corpn.* v. *Kurt A. Becher G.m.b.H. & Co. K.G.* [1988] 1 Lloyd's Rep. 88, 91. *Kurt A. Becher G.m.b.H. & Co.* v. *Voest Alpine Intertrading G.m.b.H. (The Rio Apa)* [1992] 2 Lloyd's Rep. 586, 592. Counsel may also be invited to draft an appropriate order following judgment, see *Stinnes Interoil G.m.b.H.* v. *A. Halcoussis & Co. (The Yanxilas) (No. 2)* [1984] 1 Lloyd's Rep. 676.

16. This point is considered further *infra*, para. 8.11.

17. *Indian Oil Corpn. Ltd.* v. *Greenstone Shipping S.A. (The Ypatianna)* [1987] 2 Lloyd's Rep. 286, 289–290; *Vagres Compania Maritima S.A.* v. *Nissho-Iwai American Corporation (The Karin Vatis)* [1988] 2 Lloyd's Rep. 330, 337 (C.A).

18. See, for example, *The Transcontinental Underwriting Agency S.R.L.* v. *Grand Union Insurance Co. Ltd. and P.T. Reasuransi Umum Indonesia* [1987] 2 Lloyd's Rep. 409, 415.

1. See, for example, *Richco International Ltd.* v. *Alfred C. Toepfer International G.m.b.H. (The Bonde)* [1991] 1 Lloyd's Rep. 136.

2. The reported cases do not always record the making of an express order following the dismissal of an appeal. Of course, this does not mean that an order is not subsequently drawn up. But even in the absence of an express order, it may be that an implied confirmation will follow from the dismissal of an appeal. For examples of appeals being dismissed and with no indication in the reports of any order being made, see *C. Czarnikow Ltd.* v. *Bunge & Co. Ltd.* [1987] 1 Lloyd's Rep. 202; *Islamic Republic of Iran Shipping Lines* v. *The Royal Bank of Scotland plc (The Anna Ch.)* [1987] 1 Lloyd's Rep. 266; *Naviera Mogor S.A.* v. *Société Métallurgique de Normandie (The Nogar Marin)* [1987] 1 Lloyd's Rep. 456.

an appellate judge to confirm the operational part of the award, but for reasons different from or more expansive than those of the arbitrator.[3]

8.8.2 The practice developed about the appellate powers makes it clear that the power to confirm is not restricted to the award in its entirety, so that the only decision facing a judge is whether or not to confirm the whole award. A part or parts of an award may be confirmed, with the remaining unconfirmed parts set aside, varied or remitted in the discretion of the judge.[4] The reference to an award in paragraphs (a) and (b) of section 1(2) would appear to include a reference to a part of an award. Any contrary approach would be unreasonably restrictive and inflexible.

8.8.3 With confirmation there is removed a possible obstacle to the award assuming its full legal significance. The award thereafter is *res judicata* and may be enforced by an action on the award or by summary procedure under section 26 of the Arbitration Act 1950. The order of confirmation does not however of itself guarantee the legal effect and enforceability of the award, nor is it a necessary condition precedent. It is quite simply the case that while an appeal is pending the precise status and effect of the award may represent an awkward issue unless, for example, leave to appeal was granted on the condition that no step would be taken to enforce the award pending the outcome of the appeal, or the court otherwise directed a stay of execution.[4a]

8.9 VARIATION

8.9.1 The power to vary an award on appeal raises a surprising number of difficulties, both conceptual and procedural. Nevertheless it is clearly an advantageous and desirable power in the itinerary of an appellate judge. But it is a power that is likely to be cautiously perceived and adopted only in unambiguously appropriate circumstances.

The conceptual difficulty derives from the fact that a variation witnesses a judicial infiltration into the arbitral process, with the consequence that the decision-making power is, at least to some degree, removed from the appointed arbitrator and assumed by the appellate judge. To the extent of the variation there has taken place a judicial usurpation, which it is not wholly impossible to perceive as being diametrically opposed to the intention of the parties who have agreed to be bound by the decision of the appointed arbitrator. In such a circumstance the ultimate award is represented by the original decision of the chosen arbitrator as subsequently varied by a non-contractual appellate judge. On the other hand, the significant advantage of the power is that it makes available the means of correcting legal error and yet at the same time ensuring that an immediate and valid award emerges from the arbitral process, avoiding the costs and delay associated with the alternative remedial powers to set aside or remit awards. The presence of the power is also consistent with the overriding policy of finality which is so intimately associated with the 1979 Act, for its availability expedites the finality of awards. Its availability also aids the movement away from the practice associated with the former special case procedure, for it renders it unneces-

---

3. See, for example, *Portaria Shipping Co.* v. *Gulf Pacific Navigation Co. Ltd. (The Selene G)* [1981] 2 Lloyd's Rep. 180, 186; *Tradax Export S.A.* v. *Italgrani di Francesco Ambrosio etc.* [1983] 2 Lloyd's Rep. 109, 115; *Empresa Cubana de Fletes* v. *Kissavos Shipping Co. S.A. (The Agathon) (No. 2)* [1984] 1 Lloyd's Rep. 183, 192.
4. Considered *infra*.
4a. See Chapter 7, para. 7.2.8.

sary for an award to be made subject to the determination of the court, or for the decision of the arbitrator to be expressed in the form of alternative awards.

8.9.2 In deciding when to use the remedy, the judiciary may determine to adopt an approach which represents a balance between the two possible opposed responses to the appellate power, choosing to use the power to vary when it secures the incidental advantages associated with the remedy but without effectively removing the central decision-making power from the appointed arbitrator. In other words, in circumstances when the variation is an undisputable consequence flowing from the revelation of legal error and without any further contribution reasonably capable of being made by the arbitrator. Before the power to order a variation is exercised it may be anticipated that in general two preconditions must be satisfied. First, all the facts relevant to the determination of the question of law in issue must have been found by the arbitrator. Secondly, following the identification of the legal error, the correct legal answer must be self-evident and capable of being incorporated into the award without the need for the arbitrator to make any further finding of fact, or elaborate further the facts found, or exercise any judgment or discretion. Where, to the contrary, some further role remains capable of being performed by the arbitrator, the more appropriate remedy is to remit the award for his reconsideration.[1]

8.9.3 The appellate power to order a variation has been most frequently adopted when the revealed legal error relates to the proper basis for the computation of damages,[2] demurrage[3] or *quantum meruit*[4]; or to contractual payment entitlements[5] or when a set-off is wrongly admitted.[6] But it is not to be assumed from this that the power is confined to computation cases. Provided the essential preconditions are satisfied the power may be adopted generally. In *The Paros*[7] an award was varied on a question of causation so as to reflect what the judge considered to be the only possible correct conclusion in law on the facts found and assumed. In *The Ert Stefanie*[8] an

---

1. *River Plate Products Netherlands B.V.* v. *Etablissement Coargrain* [1982] 1 Lloyd's Rep. 628.

2. *Shipping Corporation of India Ltd.* v. *NSB Niederelbe Schiffahrtsgesellschaft m.b.H. & Co. (The Black Falcon)* [1991] 1 Lloyd's Rep. 77, 81; *Sealace Shipping Co. Ltd.* v. *Oceanvoice Ltd. (The Alecos M)* [1990] 1 Lloyd's Rep. 82, 85 (actual decision reversed on appeal [1991] 1 Lloyd's Rep. 120); *Procter & Gamble Philippine Manufacturing Corpn.* v. *Kurt A. Becher G.m.b.H. & Co. K.G.* [1988] 1 Lloyd's Rep. 88; [1988] 2 Lloyd's Rep. 21 (C.A.); *President of India* v. *Lips Maritime Corporation (The Lips)* [1985] 2 Lloyd's Rep. 180; [1987] 1 Lloyd's Rep. 131 (C.A.); [1987] 2 Lloyd's Rep. 311 (H.L.).

3. *Etablissements Soules et Cie* v. *Intertradex S.A.* [1991] 1 Lloyd's Rep. 378, 383; *Marc Rich & Co. Ltd.* v. *Tourlotti Compania Naviera S.A. (The Kalliopi A)* [1987] 2 Lloyd's Rep. 263 (reversed on appeal [1988] 2 Lloyd's Rep. 101) *K/S Arnt J. Moerland* v. *Kuwait Petroleum Corporation (The Fjordaas)* [1988] 1 Lloyd's Rep. 336; *Superfos Chartering A/S* v. *N.B.R. (London) Ltd. (The Saturnia)* [1984] 2 Lloyd's Rep. 366; affirmed [1987] 2 Lloyd's Rep. 43 (C.A.); *Société Anonyme Marocaine de L'Industrie du Raffinage* v. *Notos Maritime Corporation (The Notos)* [1985] 1 Lloyd's Rep. 149; [1985] 2 Lloyd's Rep. 334 (C.A.); *Rheinoel G.m.b.H.* v. *Huron Liberian Co. (The Concordia C)* [1985] 2 Lloyd's Rep. 55, 58; *Cargill Inc.* v. *Marpro Ltd. (The Aegis Progress)* [1983] 2 Lloyd's Rep. 570, 577.

4. *Batis Maritime Corporation* v. *Petroleos del Mediterraneo S.A. (The Batis)* [1990] 1 Lloyd's Rep. 345, 353.

5. *Vagres Compania Maritima S.A.* v. *Nissho-Iwai American Corporation (The Karin Vatis)* [1988] 2 Lloyd's Rep. 330 (C.A.); *Vargas Pena Apezteguia y Cia SAIC* v. *Peter Cremer G.m.b.H.* [1987] 1 Lloyd's Rep. 394; *President of India* v. *Olympia Sauna Shipping Co. S.A. (The Ypatia Halcoussi)* [1984] 2 Lloyd's Rep. 455, 459; *Islamic Republic of Iran Shipping Lines* v. *P&O Bulk Shipping Ltd. (The Discaria)* [1985] 2 Lloyd's Rep. 489; *Greenmast Shipping Co. S.A.* v. *Jean Lion et Cie S.A. (The Saronikos)* [1986] 2 Lloyd's Rep. 277.

6. *Colonial Bank (Now Bank of Boston Connecticut)* v. *European Grain & Shipping Ltd. (The Dominique)* [1987] 1 Lloyd's Rep. 239; [1988] 1 Lloyd's Rep. 215 (C.A.); [1989] 1 Lloyd's Rep. 431 (H.L.).

7. *Paros Shipping Corporation* v. *Nafta (GB) Ltd. (The Paros)* [1987] 2 Lloyd's Rep. 269.

8. *Société Anonyme des Minerais* v. *Grant Trading Inc. (The Ert Stefanie)* [1987] 2 Lloyd's Rep. 371.

award was varied because on the facts the only conclusion sustainable in law was that the liability of the shipowner was a product of his actual fault and in consequence the shipowner was not entitled to limit his liability.

8.9.4 The power to vary is therefore likely to enjoy a limited and special area of application and to be confined to those circumstances when the appellate judge can make the necessary legal adjustment within the framework of fact already established by the arbitrator. This is most likely to be possible when the court agrees with the determination of liability, but not with the arbitral perception of the consequences of that liability. It is equally a likelihood when a question of law is determined in an interim award, in the nature of declaratory relief. In *The Aegean Dolphin*[9] an interim award declared a contractual breach to be repudiatory. On appeal, the court came to the opposite conclusion and the interim award was varied accordingly. But more generally, an order of variation will always be a possibility when an arbitration tribunal has erred in not recognising the full legal rights of the appellant, and it is open to the court to rectify the error on the basis of the wider legal and factual findings made in the award. In *The Tzelepi*[10] the tribunal fell into legal error by failing to recognise the entire indemnity entitlement of agent claimant. On the facts of case the full legal entitlement of the agent was clear, and in allowing the appeal the court varied the award to reflect the agent's full indemnity entitlement. Where a tribunal has gone wrong in law but has anticipated the possibility by making alternative awards, this may be perceived as a tacit invitation to correct the error by an order of variation.[11]

The power to vary extends to the variation of an order for costs and interest, to the extent such a variation may be necessary following the variation of the substantive legal basis of an award.[12] Of course, when it is the legal basis of the order of costs or interest which is directly in issue, then the variation order will operate directly in relation to the order of costs or interest and not as a consequence of some other variation made to the award.[13]

8.9.5 Section 1(8) provides that where an award is varied, the award as varied shall have effect as if it were the award of the arbitrator or umpire. The natural meaning of the subsection suggests that following the making of an order no further procedural step is contemplated whereby the variation is incorporated into the original award, either by the arbitral tribunal or the court. The award continues to stand as made, but must thereafter be read in association with the order made on the appeal. Although this approach to the matter secures a speedy conclusion to the appellate process, it may be doubtful if it creates a wholly happy solution. Beyond the straightforward problem associated with handling two documents rather than one, more weightily the present practice clouds the distinction between awards and judgments, and an unwanted product of this ambiguity may be difficulty in obtaining the enforcement

---

9. *Dolphin Hellas Shipping S.A.* v. *Itemslot Ltd.* (*The Aegean Dolphin*) [1992] 2 Lloyd's Rep. 178.

10. *Islamic Republic of Iran Shipping Lines* v. *Zannis Compania Naviera S.A.* (*The Tzelepi*) [1991] 2 Lloyd's Rep. 265.

11. Cf. *Everglade Maritime Inc.* v. *Schiffahrtsgesellschaft Detlef von Appen m.b.H* (*The Maria*) [1992] 2 Lloyd's Rep. 167, [1993] 2 Lloyd's Rep. 168 (C.A.).

12. *Etablissements Soules et Cie* v. *Intertradex S.A.* [1991] 1 Lloyd's Rep. 378, 383; *Shipping Corporation of India Ltd.* v. *NSB Niederelbe Schiffahrtsgesellschaft m.b.H & Co.* (*The Black Falcon*) [1991] 1 Lloyd's Rep. 77, 81; *Pera Shipping Corporation* v. *Petroship S.A.* (*The Pera*) [1984] 2 Lloyd's Rep. 363, 366; *Cargill Inc.* v. *Marpro Ltd.* (*The Aegis Progress*) [1983] 2 Lloyd's Rep. 570, 579.

13. Cf. *Kaines (UK) Ltd.* v. *Osterreichische etc. Austrowaren Gesellschaft m.b.H.* [1993] 2 Lloyd's Rep. 1, 13 (C.A.).

and recognition of varied awards abroad. A desirable solution, keeping close to the spirit of section 1(8), would be to introduce into the Rules of the Supreme Court a procedure by which the award itself may be varied in accord with the order of the court.

8.9.6 A court frequently works a variation by first setting aside the erroneous part of an award and thereafter substituting its own solution to the question of law.[14] It may be doubted whether this two-step strategy is absolutely necessary. An order varying an award would appear also to have the necessary impact of setting aside that which is varied in the original award.[15] Further, it goes without saying that the variation order must give effect to the judgment of the court given on the appeal.[16]

8.9.7 A variation involves the court substituting its own views of the law for that of the arbitral tribunal. But where the appeal is from the award of an arbitration appeal tribunal, the variation may in substance be founded on the preference of the appellate judge for the award of the first tier tribunal or arbitrator to that of the arbitral appeal tribunal.[17] Although outwardly this appears as a decision as to which of the two differing arbitral opinions is correct, it is nonetheless in strictness a variation of the appeal award effected by and through the order of the court.

The power to vary will not however be extended to its extremes and used as a mode of correcting an award whenever an arbitrator has fallen into legal error. Where the particular conditions justifying a variation are absent, there may be no alternative but to set aside or remit the award.

8.10 REMISSION

8.10.1 An award may be remitted to the reconsideration of the arbitrator together with the court's opinion on the question of law in issue in the appeal. Given the logic of the appellate power, the remission can only be to the arbitrator whose award has been appealed.[1] The essence of the power is reconsideration and not a fresh consideration by a new arbitrator. Where an award is remitted the reconsidered award must be made within three months after the date of the order, unless the order expressly directs otherwise.[2]

A remission has the advantage of keeping the award alive, but it otherwise produces delay and additional expense, which may nonetheless be acceptable if the only alternative is to set aside the award.

---

14. See, for example, *Showa Oil Tanker Co. Ltd. of Japan* v. *Maravan S.A. of Caracas (The Larissa)* [1983] 2 Lloyd's Rep. 325, 332; *Establissements Soules et Cie* v. *Intertradex S.A.* [1991] 1 Lloyd's Rep. 378, 383.

15. *Supra*, para. 8.7.4.

16. The order of the court need not be drawn up immediately following judgment. It may be deferred for a specified period of time with the parties given liberty to apply to the judge in chambers within the specified time on matters relating to the substance of the order.

17. See, for example, *Ch. Daudruy Van Cauwenberghe & Fils S.A.* v. *Tropical Products Sales S.A.* [1986] 1 Lloyd's Rep. 535 (where an appeal from the Board of Appeal of FOSFA was allowed and the award of the umpire reinstated).

1. In contrast to a remission under s. 22 of the Arbitration Act 1950, which it appears in certain circumstances may be to a different arbitrator, see Chapter 11, para. 11.11. This interpretation of the scope of s. 22 is nonetheless controversial and cannot be considered beyond further argument. In a different context note also *Mallozzi* v. *Carapelli S.p.A.* [1981] 1 Lloyd's Rep. 552.

2. s. 1(2).

8.10.2 As a general principle it may be surmised that remission is likely to be ordered when following the establishment of legal error in an award and the substitution by the court of the correct legal rule, principle or test, the dispute nonetheless continues to be incapable of final resolution without the application of the correct legal rule, principle or test to the facts already established by the arbitrator or such further facts as it may be necessary for the arbitrator to determine in the light of the law correctly substituted on appeal, or the exercise of a judgment or discretion by the arbitrator. In these circumstances it would in principle be unacceptable for the court itself to apply the law to the facts or to exercise any judgment in weighing fact and law, or to attempt to make any further findings of fact that might be necessary. The final legal determination properly remains that of the appointed arbitrator. But where these conditions do not prevail, the court will not order a remission merely to give an arbitrator a further bite at the cherry.

8.10.3 A dictum of Hobhouse J. in *The Tzelepi*[3] appears to come closest to providing a judicial statement of principle. Hobhouse J. expressed the opinion that[4] "there is no basis for remitting a matter to the arbitrator unless there is something further for the arbitrator to consider and upon which he should exercise his own judgment afresh". The learned judge further considered that it would be improper to order a remission purely as a speculation, so as to provide a party with an opportunity to collect fresh evidence and advance new contentions before the arbitrator.[5] On the facts in *The Tzelepi* the judge refused to order a remission because the right of indemnity of the agent, which was one of the issues in contention, was unambiguously established and there was no additional material for the arbitrator to consider. In the circumstances the judge directed a variation of the award, to reflect the legal entitlement of the agent.[5a]

8.10.4 Subsequent authorities would also appear to be in harmony with the general approach advocated by Hobhouse J. In *The Energy Progress*[6] arbitrators fell into legal error in refusing to imply a term into a contract. With the establishment of the implied term on the appeal, the contractors admitted that they were in breach of contract. But by virtue of the approach adopted by the arbitrators, there had been no factual enquiry or findings as to the loss suffered by the innocent contractor, nor as to the issue of mitigation. The court held on these facts that the appropriate order was to remit the award to the arbitrators.[7]

In *The Niobe*[8] arbitrators went wrong in law in their construction of a clause in a contract. In consequence they had not made any factual enquiry determining whether there had been a breach of the contract, applying the correct construction. The court

---

3. *Islamic Republic of Iran Shipping Lines* v. *Zannis Compania Naviera S.A. (The Tzelepi)* [1991] 2 Lloyd's Rep. 265.
4. *Ibid.* p. 269. See also *Motor Oil Hellas (Corinth) Refineries S.A.* v. *Shipping Corporation of India (The Kanchenjunga)* [1987] 2 Lloyd's Rep. 509, 518, Hobhouse J.
5. *Ibid.* p. 270. 5a. *Supra*, para. 8.9.4.
6. *Orient Overseas Management and Finance Ltd.* v. *File Shipping Co. Ltd. (The Energy Progress)* [1993] 1 Lloyd's Rep. 355.
7. The court came to this conclusion notwithstanding that the arbitrators had expressed provisional views in the award as to what their perceptions were of the outstanding questions of fact. Nonetheless the court was influenced by the fact that the arbitrators were not of one accord and had made a majority award, and there were other reasons which made it necessary for the tribunal to reassemble.
8. *Niobe Maritime Corporation* v. *Tradax Ocean Transportation S.A. (The Niobe)* [1993] 2 Lloyd's Rep. 52.

considered it appropriate to remit the award so that the tribunal could address the relevant questions of fact.

8.10.5 Questions of law relating to costs and interest tend to turn materially on the facts and to be very judgmental. In the face of legal error they therefore represent the kinds of circumstance where the court will incline towards an order of remission; and this will be the case whether an order of costs or interest is directly in issue in an appeal, or whether the terms of an order require to be reconsidered as a consequence of the substantive appeal being successful, either in whole or part.[9] Only when the appropriate order as to costs or interest is so compellingly clear that the position speaks for itself, or when the tribunal has also fully considered the alternative possibility, is the court likely to dispose of the matter itself and order a variation of an award.[10] As a matter of practice it is likely that a remission of an award of costs or interest will be conditional on the parties failing to settle the matter by agreement.[11]

8.11 SETTING ASIDE

8.11.1 When an appeal is allowed the gravest response open to the court is to set aside the award. The practical effect of a setting aside is to render the arbitral reference wholly ineffectual and wasteful, for the arbitration will have failed to produce a valid and binding award. For this reason it may be anticipated that the court will exercise the power cautiously and only in appropriate circumstances. Such a cautious approach would also be consistent with established jurisprudence and the general policy of the 1979 Act to protect the finality of awards. An award is therefore only likely to be set aside when legal error has been revealed and in the circumstances of the case it would be inappropriate for the court to correct the error by an order of variation or to remit the award to the reconsideration of the arbitrator. The remedy is essentially a remedy of last resort and to be used only when there does not exist any realistic alternative course. The same caution will not always be appropriate in the case of an interim award, which may be set aside without necessarily inflicting a mortal blow to the reference.[1] In this kind of circumstance and in the absence of agreement between the parties it will be for the arbitrator in the exercise of his discretion to decide how to take the reference forward following the setting aside of the interim award.[2]

8.11.2 The precise effect in law of a setting aside order is surprisingly a matter about which there continues to exist much uncertainty. Certain matters are however clear. The order deprives an award of all legal and factual effect. The order vacates the award: accordingly there is no award and no award ever existed, for it is difficult to

9. *Vagres Compania Maritima S.A.* v. *Nissho-Iwai-American Corpn. (The Karin Vatis)* [1988] 2 Lloyd's Rep. 330, 337. See also *Panchaud Frères S.A.* v. *Pagnan & Fratelli* [1974] 1 Lloyd's Rep. 394 (C.A.).

10. Cf. *Everglade Maritima Inc.* v. *Schiffahrtsgesellschaft Detlef von Appen m.b.H. (The Maria)* [1993] 2 Lloyd's Rep. 168 (C.A.).

11. Cf. *Vagres Compania Maritima S.A.* v. *Nissho-Iwai American Corpn. (The Karin Vatis), supra,* note 9.

1. Cf. *Leon Corporation* v. *Atlantic Lines and Navigation Co. Inc. (The Leon)* [1985] 2 Lloyd's Rep. 470; *The Transcontinental Underwriting Agency S.R.L.* v. *Grand Union Insurance Co. Ltd. and P.T. Reasuransi Umum Indonesia* [1987] 2 Lloyd's Rep. 409.

2. *Leon Corporation* v. *Atlantic Lines and Navigation Co. Inc. (The Leon), ibid.*, p. 476. See also *Japan Line Ltd.* v. *Aggeliki Charis Compania Maritima S.A. and others (The Angelic Grace)* [1980] 1 Lloyd's Rep. 288; *S.L. Sethia Liners Ltd.* v. *Naviagro Maritime Corporation (The Kostas Melas)* [1981] 1 Lloyd's Rep. 18.

apprehend that the order operates otherwise than retroactively. Consequently there is neither *res judicata* nor the possibility of issue estoppel; nor is there anything capable of being enforced. The same continues to be the case when an award is severable and a severable part is set aside, although the remainder of the award continues to exist as a final and binding award.[3]

8.11.3 There is however uncertainty as to the precise effect of a setting aside order on the reference. In point of principle it is arguable that the effect of setting aside an award is to revive the jurisdiction of the arbitrator and in consequence, if the parties so desire, the dispute may be returned to the arbitrator for resolution, in the light of the judgment of the court. Following the judicial order it cannot be said that there has been a final decision, and it is equally difficult to suggest that the arbitrator is *functus officio*. To suggest that the order terminates the arbitration agreement by operation of law would also appear to be an unsustainable argument.[4] To the contrary the arbitration agreement and the obligations arising thereunder appear to continue unaffected. In the upshot it is arguable that the impact of a setting aside order is to return the reference to the state that existed up to the moment immediately preceding the making of the award. If this is the case it follows that the arbitrator remains in his appointment with a surviving jurisdiction to determine the dispute referred.

8.11.4 That principle and authority may not be in harmony is suggested by the way a setting aside order appears to be understood in the context of the statutory and common law jurisdiction to review awards. In this sphere of non-appellate review a setting aside order appears to have the effect of not only annulling the award but also of removing the arbitrator from his superintendence of the reference.[5] The jurisdiction of the arbitrator can only be protected if the award is also remitted to his reconsideration. Otherwise, if the parties remain intent on arbitrating the dispute, the dispute must be revived before a new arbitrator or tribunal.[5a] Notwithstanding the setting aside order, the arbitration agreement continues to bind the parties. But in the context of the non-appellate reviewing jurisdiction it must be borne in mind that an award is most likely to be set aside in circumstances where it can be shown that the arbitrator is patently unfitted or otherwise unsuited to continue the conduct of the reference. This in turn provides at least some explanation for the apparent double-headed effect of setting aside awards.

8.11.5 But whatever may be the true position in relation to the non-appellate review of awards, the position under the 1979 Act is very different, for an appeal on a question of law is not of itself evidence of misconduct and does not without more reflect adversely on the qualities of the arbitrator or his competence to conduct the reference. The difference is potentially sufficiently great to suggest that the effect of a setting aside under the 1979 Act may not follow the reasoning adopted under the non-appellate reviewing jurisdiction. Whereas the award is wholly annulled, it may be doubted if the effect of an order is further to remove the arbitrator from his appointment and expunge his jurisdiction. In principle it would seem right that it should

---

3. Cf. *Lloyd del Pacifico* v. *Board of Trade* (1930) 37 Ll.L.Rep. 103, 110.

4. Contrast *Kemp* v. *Rose* (1858) 1 Giff. 258.

5. *Stockport Metropolitan Borough Council* v. *O'Reilly* [1983] 2 Lloyd's Rep. 70. Note also *Rooke, Sons & Co.* v. *Piper & May* (1927) 28 Ll.L.Rep. 49.

5a. This does not necessarily involve any change of identity or any change in the composition of the tribunal.

remain open to the parties to return the dispute to the appointed arbitrator, who, with the aid of the judgment given on the appeal, may again address and determine the dispute in issue.

8.11.6 There is also some doubt as to the precise legal position which prevails when it is the award of an arbitral appeal tribunal which is set aside. The particular question which arises is whether both the original and appeal awards survive, so that in the event of an appeal being entertained it is at least open for the appeal award to be set aside and the original award reinstated. In the hierarchy of court appeals such a result frequently occurs; and there is evidence in the decided cases that there exists a judicial partiality to adopt a similar stance in relation to contractual arbitral appeals.[6] But there is here again a fundamental theoretical difficulty. Where a contractual appeal is instigated it would seem that the appeal award replaces the original award, and in strictness this is even so when the appeal award simply affirms the original decision. There is only one award, the appeal award, which is the final and binding award and which represents the award made on an arbitration agreement within the meaning of section 1(2). Since the original award does not retain any independent existence and therefore is unable to emerge separately from the reference, there is in effect no element of choice and nothing capable of being reinstated. The only way the effect of the original award may be reinstated is by the exercise of the power to vary the appeal award.

---

6. Cf. *Hookway & Co. Ltd.* v. *Alfred Isaacs & Sons and Others* [1954] 1 Lloyd's Rep. 491; *London Export Corporation Ltd.* v. *Jubilee Coffee Roasting Company Ltd.* [1958] 1 Lloyd's Rep. 197, 204, per Diplock J., "I think that the award must be set aside. The effect of so doing, since the award was an appellate award, is to reinstate the award of the umpire from which the buyers appealed."

CHAPTER 9

PROCEDURE AND PRACTICE
APPERTAINING
TO FULL APPEALS

9.1 GENERAL POLICY

9.1.1 Subject to the particular Rules of Court that apply specifically to substantive appeals, the same considerations of procedure and policy apply to substantive appeals as are applicable to applications for leave to appeal. Procedurally, the application for leave to appeal and the preliminaries to a full appeal progress concurrently.[1]

Once leave to appeal is given it behoves the appellant to pursue the appeal expeditiously.[2] Such an obligation arises implicitly from the terms of the 1979 Act and is consonant with the policy and object of the legislation. In consequence, after obtaining leave to appeal the appellant must promptly apply for and obtain a hearing date for the motion.[2a] Although the conduct and prosecution of an appeal is with the appellant, it is equally the duty of the respondent not to be party to any conduct or agreement productive of unwarranted delay.[3] Delay is on occasions produced by the attempt to accommodate counsel, often with the agreement of the parties, with the object of securing that the appeal is argued by counsel who appeared in the arbitration. Although the desirability of this aim is readily appreciated, the court has nonetheless refused to consider such accommodation as justifying unreasonable delay, except in very special circumstances.[4] A party in breach of the duty of proper dispatch may be censured by the adverse exercise of judicial discretion, such as the refusal to permit the amendment of a notice of motion,[5] or the striking out of the entire proceedings.[5a]

9.1.2 Beyond the policy closely associated with the 1979 legislation there are other pragmatic and judicial considerations for encouraging the speedy dispatch of arbitral

---

1. R.S.C. Order 73, and Chapter 7.
2. *Rheinoel G.m.b.H.* v. *Huron Liberian Co. (The Concordia C)* [1985] 2 Lloyd's Rep. 55; *Leon Corporation* v. *Atlantic Lines and Navigation Co. Inc. (The Leon)* [1985] 2 Lloyd's Rep. 470; *Secretary of State for the Environment* v. *Euston Centre Investment Ltd.* [1994] 2 All E.R. 415.
2a. See *Guide to Commercial Court Practice* (1990), para 7.2. The *Guide* is set out in Appendix I.
3. *The Leon, Ibid.*
4. *The Concordia C, supra*, p. 58, per Bingham J., "In conclusion, I draw attention to the lamentable fact that it is now over 15 months since this award was made and over 11 months since leave to appeal was given. I am told that the delay over the past year has arisen from attempts to accommodate Counsel, one of whom did not in the event appear to argue the appeal. If the objects of the new Act are to be achieved, delays of this length are plainly unacceptable. I shall do my best to see that such delays do not recur. The Court naturally values the assistance of Counsel who have appeared before the arbitrators, but only exceptionally could this assistance justify delay. The engagements of Counsel will not in future be permitted to prevent the prompt disposal of appeals where leave is given in the absence of very special circumstances."
5. *The Leon, supra*, p. 476. See also note 2a, *supra*.
5a. *Secretary of State for the Environment* v. *Euston Centre Investment Ltd., supra*, note 2.

appeals. Delay may render the arbitration stale and prejudice future orders that may be considered, such as remission of the award or remission for further reasons. Where there is delay there is also the risk that the law relevant to the determination of the dispute may change between the making of the award and the hearing of the appeal.[6] Except for circumstances when the change only operates prospectively, such legal development invariably cultivates difficulty.[7]

9.2 FULL APPEAL DISTINCT FROM APPLICATION FOR LEAVE TO APPEAL

9.2.1 The procedure and practice relating to an application for leave to appeal has been considered previously.[1] There is a distinct and unambiguous difference between an application for leave and the full appeal. The application for leave is concerned with the question whether an appeal should be admitted into the judicature, and about this decision there has developed a significant fabric of policy.[2] Where leave to appeal is given the sole question before the court is whether the award manifests an error of law, and if it does, to respond to the error in any of the ways provided for in section 1(2) of the 1979 Act.[3] At this stage the history of the appeal and the policy associated with the initial question of leave to appeal play no part. The sole question is whether the appellant has established legal error in the award: the whole issue is one of right or wrong, there being no place for degrees of rightness or wrongness, which concepts are capable of playing a weighty role in the initial question of leave to appeal.[4]

9.2.2 The separateness of an application for leave to appeal and a full appeal is also emphasised in contemporary practice. The two stages are perceived as distinct and separate, taking place at separate moments in time and before different judges. Only in exceptional circumstances will a full appeal follow immediately after giving leave to appeal, with both stages heard by the same judge.[5]

When the decision to give leave to appeal is itself appealed to the Court of Appeal under section 1(6A),[6] it is open to the court to defer the hearing of the full appeal until the appeal on the question of leave has been determined by the Court of Appeal.[7]

9.3 THE APPEAL HEARING

9.3.1 The appeal is not in the form of a rehearing. Questions of fact remain throughout for the arbitrator. The appeal is confined to determining whether an error of law is

6. Cf. *Pancommerce S.A.* v. *Veecheema B.V.* [1982] 1 Lloyd's Rep. 645, 646 (a case under the former special case procedure).
7. See Chapter 6, para. 6.2.16. for the relevance of a change in the applicable law to the exercise of judicial discretion to give or refuse leave to appeal.
1. Chapter 7.
2. See Chapters 5 and 6.
3. See Chapter 8.
4. *Vinava Shipping Co. Ltd.* v. *Finelvet A.G. (The Chrysalis)* [1983] 1 Lloyd's Rep. 503, 506, per Mustill J. See also, generally, *London Borough of Islington* v. *P.G.M.* (1993, unreported).
5. *Italmare Shipping Co.* v. *Ocean Tanker Co. Inc. (The Rio Sun)* [1981] 2 Lloyd's Rep. 489, 495; *Tor Line A.B.* v. *Alltrans Group of Canada Ltd. (The TFL Prosperity)* [1982] 1 Lloyd's Rep. 617, 627. See, further, *infra*, para. 9.7.
6. Considered in Chapter 10, para. 10.2.
7. Cf. *Hiscox* v. *Outhwaite (No. 2)* [1991] 3 All E.R. 143.

disclosed in the award and takes the form of submissions and argument directed to the alleged legal error or errors, together with a consideration of such affidavit evidence as may have been served with the originating notice of motion.[1] It is also open to the court to take into account any reasons which may have been volunteered by the judge giving leave to appeal,[2] and also any dissenting arbitral opinions which may have been given.[3] The focus of the appeal is therefore directed to the legal correctness of the award or that part of the award alleged to be in error, including any extraneous documents and materials expressly or impliedly incorporated into the award.[4]

9.3.2 In legal argument on an appeal from an arbitration award, there is a doubt whether it is open to counsel to accept a proposition of law for the purpose of the appeal, but at the same time reserve the right to argue to the contrary in any subsequent on-appeal. This kind of strategy is quite common in litigation generally, but in the context of arbitral appeals it is at least arguable that the practice is opposed to the policy of the 1979 Act.[5]

9.3.3 Although it is usual for the respondent to appear and defend the award, or otherwise seek to uphold the award on grounds other than those relied on by the arbitrator,[6] this is not essential to enable an appeal to proceed. A respondent is not compelled to attend and may choose not to appear, in which case the appeal will proceed in his absence provided process has been properly served. The position is obviously less satisfactory when the respondent chooses not to appear, for the court is in danger of hearing only one side of the argument; but the absence of the respondent does nothing to dilute the evidentiary burden of proof on the appellant to establish on a balance of probabilities evidence of legal error. The balance is struck by highlighting the professional duty of counsel for the appellant who is obliged to bring all the relevant points before the court, including those militating against the appellant's position.[7]

9.4 PROVINCE OF THE APPEAL

9.4.1 In giving leave to appeal it is also the dominant prevailing practice to specify the question or questions of law in relation to which leave is given.[1] This establishes the

1. See *infra*.
2. *Bunge A.G.* v. *Sesostrad S.A. (The Alkeos C)* [1984] 1 Lloyd's Rep. 687.
3. See Chapter 8, para. 8.4.   4. *Ibid.*
5. In *L'Office Cherifien des Phosphates and Unitramp S.A.* v. *Yamashita-Shinnihon Steamship Co. Ltd. (The Boucraa)* [1993] 2 Lloyd's Rep. 149, 153, argument to this effect was advanced but the court did not rule on the matter.
6. *Infra*, para. 9.8.
7. *Canadian Pacific (Bermuda) Ltd.* v. *Lagon Maritime Overseas (The Fort Kipp)* [1985] 2 Lloyd's Rep. 168, 169. See also *Siporex Trade S.A.* v. *Comdel Commodities Ltd.* [1986] 2 Lloyd's Rep. 428; *Brinks Mat Ltd.* v. *Elcombe* [1988] 1 W.L.R. 1350; *Sumitomo Heavy Industries Ltd.* v. *Oil and Natural Gas Commission* [1994] 1 Lloyd's Rep. 45.
1. See Chapter 7, para. 7.2.7. For examples of the practice see *Heinrich Hanno & Co. B.V.* v. *Fairlight Shipping Co. (The Kostas K)* [1985] 1 Lloyd's Rep. 231, 236–237; *President of India* v. *Taygetos Shipping Co. S.A. (The Agenor)* [1985] 1 Lloyd's Rep. 155, 156. See further by way of illustration, *Showa Oil Tanker Co. Ltd. of Japan* v. *Maravan S.A. of Caracas, (The Larissa)* [1983] 2 Lloyd's Rep. 325, 326; *Stinnes Interoil G.m.b.H.* v. *A. Halcoussis & Co. (The Yanxilas) (No. 2)* [1984] 1 Lloyd's Rep. 676, 677; *The President of India* v. *Lips Maritime Corp. (The Lips)* [1985] 2 Lloyd's Rep. 180, 181 (first instance); *Valla Giovanni & Co. S.p.A.* v. *Gebr Van Weelde Scheepvaartkantoor B.V. (The Chanda)* [1985] 1 Lloyd's Rep. 563, 564; *Elpidoforos Shipping Corporation* v. *Furness Withy (Australia) Pty. Ltd. (The Oinoussian Friendship)* [1987] 1 Lloyd's Rep. 258, 259; *Nova Petroleum International Establishment* v. *Tricon Trading Ltd.* [1989] 1 Lloyd's Rep. 312, 316.

province of the substantive appeal and delineates the ambit of the submissions, argument and the ultimate role and responsibility of the appeal judge.[2] It follows that the appellate process may be as broad or as narrow as the order made on the application for leave to appeal chooses to render it. The appeal judge has no jurisdiction to decide questions of law which were in issue before the arbitrator but with regard to which no leave to appeal has been given. Given that the parameters of the appellate process are drawn as an incident of the judicial discretion to give or refuse leave to appeal, and also the necessity of certainty in the appellate process, it is highly desirable that the terms on which leave is granted should be clear and unambiguous. Although an appeal is confined to the specified questions of law, there is nothing to prevent the court of its own motion or in response to an application made by a party reformulating any specified question of law where this would be helpful to the disposal of the appeal, as where it presents the legal question in a more apposite and answerable form.[3] The court will be particularly less reluctant to reformulate the question of law when the original order has been made in general terms.[3a]

9.4.2 Where leave to appeal is given without limitation then the order giving leave will be construed in the light of the notice of originating motion.[4] In such a circumstance it is at least open for leave to be construed as having been given at large and consequently to embrace any question of law fairly arising out of the award.[5]

The question of leave to appeal is not a one-off phenomenon, and following the giving of leave on the initial application it is possible for subsequent applications to be made and acceded to, so increasing the range of appealable questions of law. Further, leave to appeal may even be given by the judge during the hearing of the substantive appeal.[6]

9.5 ORIGINATING NOTICE OF MOTION AND TIME LIMITS

9.5.1 An appeal to the High Court under section 1(2) of the 1979 Act is made by originating notice of motion issuing from the Admiralty and Commercial Registry to a single judge in court.[1] The notice of originating motion must be served and the appeal entered within 21 days after the award has been made and published to the parties: provided that, where reasons material to the appeal are given on a date subsequent to the publication of the award, the period of 21 days shall run from the date on which the reasons are given.[2] The issue of the originating notice initiates a pending action

---

2. See, for example, *Canadian Pacific (Bermuda) Ltd.* v. *Lagon Maritime Overseas (The Fort Kipp)* [1985] 2 Lloyd's Rep. 168. *New A Line* v. *Erechthion Shipping Co. S.A. (The Erechthion)* [1987] 2 Lloyd's Rep. 180. But bearing in mind contemporary practice, it will be rare for reasons to be volunteered on an application for leave to appeal, see Chapter 7, para. 7.3.3.

3. *Canadian Pacific (Bermuda) Ltd.* v. *Lagon Maritime Overseas (The Fort Kipp)*, *supra*.

3a. *Exmar B.V.* v. *National Iranian Tanker Co. (The Trade Fortitude)* [1992] 1 Lloyd's Rep. 169.

4. *Kurkjian (Commodity Brokers) Ltd.* v. *Marketing Exchange for Africa Ltd. etc. and Others (No. 1)* [1986] 2 Lloyd's Rep. 614, 617.

5. *Michael I. Warde* v. *Feedex International Inc.* [1985] 2 Lloyd's Rep. 289 (first instance).

6. *Socony Mobil Oil Co. Inc. and Others* v. *West of England Ship Owners Mutual Insurance Association Ltd. (The Padre Island) (No. 2)* [1987] 2 Lloyd's Rep. 529.

1. R.S.C. Order 73, rule 2(2).

2. R.S.C. Order 73, rule 5(2), considered in Chapter 7, para. 7.2.4.

and this has the consequence of invariably permitting the summons seeking leave to appeal to be a summons in the action.[3]

The same time limit therefore applies to both the application for leave and the full appeal. But unlike the application for leave which is to a judge in chambers, the full appeal is to a single judge in open court.[4] Leave being a necessary precondition, it is the practice to enter an appeal subject to any necessary leave being obtained.[5]

9.5.2 As to when an award is made and published to the parties, and also when reasons are given, these issues have been considered previously in the text in relation to applications for leave to appeal. That discussion is of equal application to the present context.[6]

9.5.3 The court enjoys a discretion to extend the period of time within which an appeal may be brought, and this discretion is present even when the application for an extension is made after the expiration of the time limit.[7] The 21-day time limit is likely to be most troublesome when a foreign respondent is involved, with the consequence that the applicant appellant must obtain leave to serve the notice of motion outside the jurisdiction.[8]

The notice of motion, together with any other documents required to be served with the notice of motion,[9] must be served at least two clear days before the date specified for the hearing.[10]

9.6 CONTENTS OF ORIGINATING MOTION

9.6.1 The appeal is made by originating motion which must state the grounds of the appeal and where an appeal is founded on evidence by affidavit or is made with the consent of the other parties, a copy of every affidavit intended to be used and of every consent given in writing must be served with the notice of originating motion.[1] Without prejudice to the generality of this requirement, the statement of the grounds of the appeal must specify the relevant parts of the award and reasons which are challenged, and a copy of the award and reasons, or the relevant parts thereof, must be lodged with the court and served with the notice of originating motion.[2]

9.6.2 A Practice Note which preceded a later amendment to the Rules of Court[3] provides to the extent to which it is relevant[4]:

1. Every notice of motion by way of appeal against an arbitration award under s. 1(2) of the Arbitration Act 1979 shall contain a succinct statement in numbered paragraphs of each ground upon which it is sought to contend that the arbitral tribunal erred in law. Reference shall be

---

3. R.S.C. Order 73, rule 3(3): also Chapter 7, para. 7.2.2.
4. *Infra*, para. 9.7.
5. See note to R.S.C. Order 73, rule 5 in *The Supreme Court Practice 1993*.
6. See Chapter 7, para. 7.2.4.
7. R.S.C. Order 3, rule 5.
8. R.S.C. Order 73 rule 7. The procedure governing service out of jurisdiction of the originating summons on an application for leave to appeal has previously been observed upon, see Chapter 7, para. 7.2.5.
9. *Infra*, para. 9.6.
10. R.S.C. Order 8, rule 2(2).
1. Order 73, rule 5(5).
2. Order 73, rule 5(6).
3. Effected by R.S.C. (Amendment) 1986 (S.I. 1986 No. 632 (L.2)).
4. Practice Direction (Arbitration Award: Appeal), para. 1, [1985] 1 W.L.R. 959; [1985] 2 All E.R. 383; [1985] 2 Lloyd's Rep. 300. See also Appendix H(5).

made to the paragraph or passage of the award and reasons where each alleged error it to be found. A copy of the award and reasons forming part of the award and any documents expressly incorporated in the award or such reasons shall accompany the notice of motion when the same is served and entered, unless the appeal arises from a minor part only of the award and reasons in which case the relevant extracts shall accompany the notice of motion.

3. Any statement provided under [para. 1] should contain specific reference to any authority relied on. A copy should be provided with the statement of any authority not contained in the *Law Reports*, the *Weekly Law Reports*, the *All England Law Reports*, *Lloyd's Law Reports* or the *English Reports*.

4. Where the applicant contends that any question of law arising out of an award concerns a term of contract or an event which is not a one-off clause or event, he shall serve on the respondent with his notice of motion and lodge with the Court an affidavit setting out the facts relied on in support of his contention. A respondent who challenges that contention shall provide to the applicant and to the Court, not later than two clear days before the application is listed for argument, an affidavit setting out the facts upon which he relies.

Many of the above directions are now incorporated in Order 73, rule 5, paragraphs (6) to (8), but not all. In particular, the directions in paragraph 3 of the Practice Note go beyond the present Rules of Court.

There is a discretion to permit an amendment of a notice of motion,[5] which may be exercised as late as the hearing of the substantive appeal. The favourable exercise of the discretion may be refused to an appellant who is in breach of the duty to prosecute the appeal expeditiously,[6] and even when exercised favourably, it may be rendered subject to terms when there is a risk of potential prejudice to the other party.[7]

9.7 APPELLATE JUDGE

9.7.1 The full appeal is to a single judge in open court.[1] The appeal is heard by a judge sitting in the Commercial Court, unless the appeal has been directed to be heard by a High Court judge not sitting in the Commercial Court.[2]

In the early practice following the enactment of the 1979 Act there were occasions when the same judge gave leave to appeal and heard the full appeal.[3] This arrangement was particularly convenient when the full appeal followed immediately upon giv-

---

5. *Kurkjian (Commodity Brokers) Ltd.* v. *Marketing Exchange for Africa Ltd. etc. and Others (No. 1)* [1986] 2 Lloyd's Rep. 614, 617.

6. *Leon Corporation* v. *Atlantic Lines and Navigation Co. Inc. (The Leon)* [1985] 2 Lloyd's Rep. 470, 476. See also *supra*, para 9.1.

7. *Astro Valiente Compania Naviera S.A.* v. *The Government of Pakistan Ministry of Food and Agriculture (The Emmanuel Colocotronis) (No. 1)* [1982] 1 Lloyd's Rep. 297, 301.

1. R.S.C. Order 73, rule 2(2). Note the adverse comment on this procedure by Boyd, "Innovation and Reform in the Law of Arbitration" (1983) 2 C.J.Q. 148, 162.

2. R.S.C. Order 73, rule 6(1). See also Chapter 7, para. 7.2.1.1.

3. See, for example, *Kodros Shipping Corpn.* v. *Empresa Cubana de Fletes (The Evia) (No. 2)* [1981] 2 Lloyd's Rep. 613; *The Evia* [1981] 2 Lloyd's Rep. 627; *Astro Valiente Compania Naviera S.A.* v. *The Government of Pakistan Ministry of Food and Agriculture (The Emmanuel Colocotronis) (No. 1)* [1982] 1 Lloyd's Rep. 297; *(No. 2)* [1982] 1 Lloyd's Rep. 286; *Stinnes Interoil G.m.b.H.* v. *A. Halcoussis & Co. (The Yanxilas) (No. 1)* [1983] 2 Lloyd's Rep. 445; *The Yanxilas (No. 2)* [1984] 1 Lloyd's Rep. 676; *Damon Compania Naviera* v. *E.A.L. Europe Afrika Line G.m.b.H. (The Nicki R)* [1984] 2 Lloyd's Rep. 186; *Pera Shipping Corpn.* v. *Petroship S.A. (The Pera)* [1984] 2 Lloyd's Rep. 363; *Arab Maritime Petroleum Transport Co.* v. *Luxor Trading Panama and Geogas Enterprise Geneva (The Al Bida)* [1986] 1 Lloyd's Rep. 142.

ing leave to appeal, although it was recognised that only in exceptional circumstances would such a mode of proceeding be allowed, as when the point of law in issue was very short and could be easily disposed of or in circumstances of great urgency.[4] But although there was no firm rule to the effect, the more general practice was for the judge hearing the full appeal to be different from the judge giving leave to appeal.[5] The virtue of the practice was that it avoided the risk of judicial impressions acquired in determining the application for leave being carried forward into the hearing of the full appeal, and so secured maximum potential judicial objectivity at the full appeal hearing.

9.7.2 The question of the identity relationship between the judge giving leave and the judge hearing the full appeal was reviewed by the Court of Appeal in *Hiscox* v. *Outhwaite (No. 2)*.[6] Lord Donaldson M.R.[7] affirmed the practice of separate identities, which was perceived as being consistent with the general policy of the 1979 legislation favouring the finality of awards, for "the judge granting leave will necessarily have formed and expressed his, albeit provisional, views on the merits".[8] It was nonetheless recognised that there would inevitably arise exceptional circumstances when it would be very right for the same judge to hear the full appeal. The Court of Appeal identified three possible exceptional circumstances: (1) urgency; (2) expediency, as when there was no other judge immediately available and it would save time to go straight on; and (3) where the matter had been fully deployed on the application for leave and the answer in the view of the judge was totally and unanswerably clear. In such a case it would be a considerable waste of costs to have a further substantive hearing.[9] On the facts of the case before it, the Court of Appeal concluded that there were no exceptional circumstances and accordingly ordered that the appeal be heard by a different judge from the judge who gave leave to appeal.[10]

9.8 RESPONDENT'S NOTICE

A respondent to an appeal who wishes to contend or at least reserve the right to contend that the award should be upheld on grounds not or not fully expressed in the award and reasons is not in the position of challenging the award and does not therefore require leave to appeal. His position is wholly defensive and he is not an

---

4. *International Sea Tankers Inc.* v. *Hemisphere Shipping Co. Ltd. (The Wenjiang)* [1982] 1 Lloyd's Rep. 128, 130; *Tor Line A.B.* v. *Alltrans Group of Canada Ltd. (The TFL Prosperity)* [1982] 1 Lloyd's Rep. 617, 626–627; *Bunge A.G.* v. *Sesostrad S.A. (The Alkeos C)* [1984] 1 Lloyd's Rep. 687, 691. See also *River Plate Products Netherlands B.V.* v. *Etablissement Coargrain* [1982] 1 Lloyd's Rep. 628.

5. See, for example, *Alfred C. Toepfer Schiffahrtsgesellschaft G.m.b.H.* v. *Tossa Marine Co. Ltd. etc. (The Derby)* [1985] 2 Lloyd's Rep. 325, 327; *Ngo Chew Hong Edible Oils Pte. Ltd.* v. *Scindia Steam Navigation Co. Ltd. (The Jalamohan)* [1988] 1 Lloyd's Rep. 443; *Palm Shipping Inc.* v. *Kuwait Petroleum Corpn. (The Sea Queen)* [1988] 1 Lloyd's Rep. 500; *Vitol B.V. (formerly T/A Vitol Trading B.V.)* v. *Compagnie Européenne des Pétroles* [1988] 1 Lloyd's Rep. 577.

6. [1991] 3 All E.R. 143.

7. McCowan and Leggatt L.JJ. agreeing.

8. *Ibid*. p. 145.

9. *Ibid*. p. 145.

10. *Ibid*. p. 146.

appellant.[1] But a respondent's notice, as required by the R.S.C., must be served on the applicant for leave and lodged with the court not later than two clear days before the hearing of the application for leave.[2] The detail of the procedure is also set out in a Practice Direction by Bingham J. on 3 May 1985, which provides to the extent to which it is material[3]:

2. Any respondent to such a motion by way of appeal who contends that the award should be upheld on grounds not or not fully expressed in the award and reasons should provide to the applicant and to the Court, not later than two clear days before the application for leave is listed for argument, a succinct statement of such grounds in numbered paragraphs, with reference where appropriate to any relevant paragraph or passage of the award and reasons.

3. Any statement provided under [para. 2] should contain specific reference to any authority relied on. A copy should be provided with the statement of any authority not contained in the *Law Reports*, the *Weekly Law Reports*, the *All England Law Reports*, *Lloyd's Law Reports* or the *English Reports*.

9.9 CROSS, CONTINGENT AND CONSOLIDATED APPEALS

9.9.1 There is nothing to preclude both parties to an award initiating appeals on a question of law arising out of an award. In such a circumstance cross-appeals will obtain.[1] Each appeal will continue to prevail within the procedural framework of the 1979 Act and, therefore, in the absence of consent, both parties will first require leave to appeal. In the situation where both parties wish to appeal it is just possible that a consensual appeal is a greater likelihood, with each party consenting to the appeal of the other party as a guarantee of their own appeal being allowed to progress to a full hearing.[2]

Where an appeal from an award is but one of several applications for relief, the hearing of the appeal may be deferred and agreed to be contingent on the application for non-appellate relief not being successful. Confronted with applications for appellate and non-appellate relief, the court may direct how the various applications will be heard.[2a]

9.9.2 The court enjoys a jurisdiction to direct that appeals from separate awards be

1. For judicial comment prior to the issue being expressly addressed in the R.S.C., see *Clea Shipping Corporation* v. *Bulk Oil International Ltd. (The Alaskan Trader)* [1983] 1 Lloyd's Rep. 315, 316; *Uni-Ocean Lines Pte. Ltd.* v. *C-Trade S.A. (The Lucille)* [1983] 1 Lloyd's Rep. 387, 394; *Stinnes Interoil G.m.b.H.* v. *A. Halcoussis & Co. (The Yanxilas) (No. 2)* [1984] 1 Lloyd's Rep. 676, 685; *President of India* v. *Taygetos Shipping Co. S.A. (The Agenor)* [1985] 1 Lloyd's Rep. 155, 160; *Heinrich Hanno & Co. B.V.* v. *Fairlight Shipping Co. Ltd. (The Kostas K)* [1985] 1 Lloyd's Rep. 231, 237.
2. R.S.C. Order 73, rule 5(9). See also Chapter 7, para. 7.2.3.
3. See also Appendix H(5), and [1985] 1 W.L.R. 959; [1985] 2 Lloyd's Rep. 300.
1. See, for example, *International Sea Tankers Inc.* v. *Hemisphere Shipping Co. Ltd. (The Wenjiang)* [1981] 2 Lloyd's Rep. 308; [1982] 1 Lloyd's Rep. 128 (C.A.); *The Wenjiang (No. 2)* [1983] 1 Lloyd's Rep. 400. *Uni-Ocean Pte. Ltd.* v. *C-Trade S.A. (The Lucille)* [1983] 1 Lloyd's Rep. 387; [1984] 1 Lloyd's Rep. 244 (C.A.). *Alfred C. Toepfer Schiffahrtsgesellschaft G.m.b.H.* v. *Tossa Marine Co. Ltd. etc. (The Derby)* [1984] 1 Lloyd's Rep. 635 (first instance); *Oriental Maritime Plc Ltd.* v. *Ministry of Food Government of the People's Republic of Bangladesh (The Silva Plana)* [1989] 2 Lloyd's Rep. 371; *Ellis Shipping Corporation* v. *Voest Alpine Intertrading (The Lefthero)* [1991] 2 Lloyd's Rep. 599.
2. See, for example, *Superfos Chartering A/S* v. *N.B.R. (London) Ltd. (The Saturnia)* [1984] 2 Lloyd's Rep. 366; *Société Anonyme Marocaine de L'Industrie du Raffinage* v. *Notos Maritime Corporation (The Notos)* [1985] 1 Lloyd's Rep. 149; *MSC Mediterranean Shipping Co. S.A.* v. *Alianca Bay Shipping Co. Ltd. (The Argonaut)* [1985] 2 Lloyd's Rep. 216.
2a. *Guide to Commercial Court Practice* (1990), para. 7.4. See Appendix I.

consolidated and heard together.[3] The jurisdiction is most likely to be exercised when the appeals are closely related, as when they raise similar questions of law arising from a common factual environment. Such a situation is likely to pertain in relation to separate awards resolving disputes arising under concurrent contracts between the same parties[4]; or in the case of separate awards resolving disputes under back-to-back contracts or other closely related contracts[5]; or in the case of separate awards determining disputes under separate contracts entered into on materially similar terms and raising common issues.[6]

9.10 CONCURRENT APPELLATE AND NON-APPELLATE RELIEF

There is nothing to preclude an appeal under the 1979 Act being pursued concurrently with other applications seeking relief under the arbitration or other legislation, or under the common law. Where there are concurrent applications seeking different modes of relief it may become necessary to manage the various applications to secure the efficient conduct of the litigation.[1] As previously observed, this may bring into existence the phenomenon of a contingent appeal.[2] To the contrary effect, the appeal may be established as the principal application, with the non-appellate applications held in reserve and only pursued in the event of the appeal failing.[3]

9.11 COSTS

9.11.1 The costs of an appeal are within the discretion of the court, and it follows that the way the discretion is exercised may vary from case to case.[1] Where the costs of the

---

3. See, for example, *Rederiaktiebolaget Gustav Erikson* v. *Dr Fawzi Ahmed Abou Ismail (The Herroe and Askoe)* [1986] 2 Lloyd's Rep. 281.
4. See, for example, *Comdel Commodities Ltd.* v. *Siporex Trade S.A. (No. 2)* [1988] 2 Lloyd's Rep. 590; *Esteve Trading Corpn.* v. *Agropec International (The Golden Rio)* [1990] 2 Lloyd's Rep. 273.
5. See, for example, *P & O Oil Trading Ltd.* v. *Scanoil A.B. (The Orient Prince)* [1985] 1 Lloyd's Rep. 389; *Heinrich Hanno & Co. B.V.* v. *Fairlight Shipping Co. Ltd. (The Kostas K)* [1985] 1 Lloyd's Rep. 231; *Ch. Daudruy Van Cauwenberghe & Fils S.A.* v. *Tropical Products Sales S.A. etc.* [1986] 1 Lloyd's Rep. 535; *C. Czarnikow Ltd.* v. *Bunge & Co. Ltd.* [1987] 1 Lloyd's Rep. 202; *President of India* v. *Jebsens (UK) Ltd. and Others (The General Capinpin)* [1987] 2 Lloyd's Rep. 354; [1989] 1 Lloyd's Rep. 232 (C.A.); *Kurt A. Becher G.m.b.H. & Co. K.G.* v. *Roplak Enterprises S.A. (The World Navigator)* [1991] 1 Lloyd's Rep. 277; [1991] 2 Lloyd's Rep. 23 (C.A.).
6. *Salen Rederierna A.B.* v. *Antaios Compania Naviera S.A. (The Antaios)* [1981] 2 Lloyd's Rep. 284 (first instance).
1. *Guide to Commercial Court Practice* (1990), para. 7.4. See Appendix I.
2. *Supra*, para. 9.9.
3. See, for example, *Comdel Commodities Ltd.* v. *Siporex Trade S.A. (No. 2)* [1988] 2 Lloyd's Rep. 590; *Oriental Maritime Pte. Ltd.* v. *Ministry of Food Government of the People's Republic of Bangladesh (The Silva Plana)* [1989] 2 Lloyd's Rep. 371; *Sociedad Iberica de Molturacion S.A.* v. *Nidera Handelscompagnie B.V.* [1990] 2 Lloyd's Rep. 240; *Cosmar S.A.* v. *Marimarna Shipping Co. Ltd. (The Mathew)* [1990] 2 Lloyd's Rep. 323.
1. Supreme Court Act 1981, section 51(1). See also *Tracomin S.A.* v. *Sudan Oil Seeds Co. Ltd.* [1983] 1 Lloyd's Rep. 560, 570.

application for leave to appeal have been held over, they will be disposed of at the same time as the costs of the full appeal.[2] Also, when there are concurrent applications, they may be treated as one set of costs.[3] It is even open to the court, in appropriate circumstances, not to make an outright order for costs but to declare that the costs of the appeal shall follow the final outcome in the arbitration.[4] This kind of order presumably is only possible when an interim award is being appealed or where the court is minded to order a remission.

9.11.2 Being a matter of discretion, the precise order which is appropriate in any case may pose an issue of great difficulty for the appellate judge.[5] The difficulty is avoided when there is an agreed order for costs.[6] The general rule is that costs follow the event, which means that the party victorious in the appeal will be awarded costs,[7] including the costs of the application for leave to appeal, when they remain in issue.[8] But precisely how "the event" is to be understood may itself give rise to a difficult question of definition. Success may come in different forms and be measured in different ways. So also there may be degrees of success. These and other nuances in the measurement of the precise extent a victorious party has been successful may find expression in the judicious determination of the appropriate order for costs. In particular, where an appeal has only been partially successful this is likely to be reflected in the order for costs.[9]

9.11.3 The general rule that costs follow the event is however only a rule of discretion and practice, and may be departed from where the circumstances justify such an approach. "The real question in all cases is whether in all the circumstances justice requires a departure from the ordinary principle."[10] Departure may be justified when the successful appellant had been guilty of gross delay in the prosecution of the appeal[11]; or where it can be shown that there existed some ulterior motive other than succeeding in the appeal[12]; or where bad as well as good points were argued.[13]

---

2. See, for example, *Pera Shipping Corporation* v. *Petroship S.A. (The Pera)* [1984] 2 Lloyd's Rep. 363, 366; *Greenmast Shipping Co. S.A.* v. *Jean Lion et Cie S.A. (The Saronikos)* [1986] 2 Lloyd's Rep. 277, 280; *Indian Oil Corp. Ltd.* v. *Greenstone Shipping S.A. (The Ypatianna)* [1987] 2 Lloyd's Rep. 286, 298.
3. *Cargill Inc.* v. *Marpro Ltd. (The Aegis Progress)* [1983] 2 Lloyd's Rep. 570, 579.
4. Cf. *Charles E. Ford Ltd.* v. *AFEC Inc.* [1986] 1 Lloyd's Rep. 307, 316.
5. Cf. *Tradax Export S.A.* v. *Italcarbo Societa di Navigazione S.p.A. (The Sandalion)* [1983] 1 Lloyd's Rep. 514, 520.
6. Cf. *Black King Shipping Corp. and Wayang (Panama) S.A.* v. *Mark Ronald Massie (The Litsion Pride)* [1985] 1 Lloyd's Rep. 437, 519.
7. *Tor Line A.B.* v. *Alltrans Group of Canada Ltd. (The TFL Prosperity)* [1982] 1 Lloyd's Rep. 617, 627–628; *D/S A/S Idaho* v. *Colossus Maritime S.A. (The Concordia Fjord)* [1984] 1 Lloyd's Rep. 385, 388; *Damon Compania Naviera* v. *E.A.L. Europe Afrika Line G.m.b.H. (The Nicki R)* [1984] 2 Lloyd's Rep. 186, 190.
8. *Pera Shipping Corporation* v. *Petroship S.A. (The Pera)* [1984] 2 Lloyd's Rep. 363, 366; *Action S.A.* v. *Britannic Shipping Corporation Ltd. (The Aegis Britannic)* [1985] 2 Lloyd's Rep. 481, 484.
9. *Transgrain Shipping B.V.* v. *Global Transporte Oceanico S.A. (The Mexico I)* [1988] 2 Lloyd's Rep. 149, 150 (appeal allowed in part and appellants awarded three-quarters of their costs).
10. *The Bedford Insurance Co. Ltd.* v. *Instituto de Ressaguros do Brasil and Others* [1984] 1 Lloyd's Rep. 218 (Note) per Parker J.
11. *Leon Corporation* v. *Atlantic Lines and Navigation Co. Inc. (The Leon)* [1985] 2 Lloyd's Rep. 470, 477.
12. Cf. *N.Z. Michalos* v. *The Food Corporation of India (The Apollon)* [1983] 1 Lloyd's Rep. 409, 416.
13. *Transworld Oil Ltd.* v. *North Bay Shipping Corporation (The Rio Claro)* [1987] 2 Lloyd's Rep. 173, 179.

Where the parties cannot agree on the taxation of costs and the matter is referred to the court, the general and usual rule is that taxation will be on a standard basis.[14] But in exceptional circumstances there is a discretion to direct taxation on an indemnity basis.[15]

14. R.S.C. Order 62, rule 12(11).
15. R.S.C. Order 62, rule 12(2). Cf. *The Food Corporation of India* v. *Carras Shipping Co. Ltd. (The Delian Leto)* [1983] 2 Lloyd's Rep. 496, 499; *Helmville Ltd.* v. *Astilleros Espanoles S.A. (The Jocelyne)* [1984] 2 Lloyd's Rep. 569, 576.

CHAPTER 10

ON-APPEALS ON QUESTIONS OF LEAVE AND LAW UNDER SECTION 1

10.1 INTRODUCTION

Under the appellate process relating to questions of law arising out of awards established by section 1 of the 1979 Act there exist two strata of judicial decision-making. The first, the preliminary determination whether to give or refuse leave to appeal; and the second, the substantive consideration of any appeal that is permitted.[1] In the first instance both decisions are made by a first tier judge, and on occasions it may be the same judge who determines both the question of leave to appeal and the substantive appeal.[2]

Section 1 also makes express and particular provision for on-appeals to the Court of Appeal from the decision of a first tier judge with regard both to a question of leave to appeal and the determination on a full substantive appeal. On-appeals on a question of leave are governed by section 1(6A); and with regard to substantive questions of law determined on appeal by section 1(7). Both are very restrictive provisions and give plain and unequivocal effect to the policy of the 1979 Act, which is that issues within the legislation should in the main terminate with a first tier judge and only in exceptional circumstances be allowed to proceed further to the Court of Appeal.[3]

10.2 ON-APPEAL FROM THE GRANT OR REFUSAL OF LEAVE TO APPEAL UNDER SECTION 1(3)(b)

10.2.1 Appeals only with leave of the High Court

10.2.1.1 From the grant or refusal of leave to appeal under section 1(3)(b) there exists an on-appeal to the Court of Appeal, subject to the terms of section 1(6A), wherein it is provided: "Unless the High Court gives leave, no appeal shall lie to the Court of Appeal from a decision of the High Court—(a) to grant or refuse leave under subsection (3)(b) . . . ."

Section 1(6A) was inserted into the 1979 Act by the Supreme Court Act 1981,

---

1. The position is outlined in Chapter 2.
2. See Chapters 7 and 9.
3. See also Chapter 1, para. 1.2.1.6.

section 148(3).[1] Prior to this insertion there existed no express constraint in the 1979 Act on the bringing of an on-appeal from the judicial decision to grant or refuse leave to appeal and this *casus omissus* meant that in the absence of any other constraint, of which there appeared to be none,[2] an appeal could be brought as of right.[3] This view of the situation appears to have been accepted by the Court of Appeal in *The Nema*[4] and *The Rio Sun*.[5] The fact that such a preliminary issue could penetrate so freely into the hierarchy of the courts, in stark contrast to the position in relation to substantive appeals under section 1(7),[6] was blatantly contrary to the policy of the 1979 Act, to the extent that it was a potential source of engineered delay, and it was for this reason that an early opportunity was taken to plug the initial legislative omission.[7] The effect of section 1(6A) is to override the decisions of the Court of Appeal in *The Nema* and *The Rio Sun* and to make a decision on the question of leave to appeal to the High Court appealable to the Court of Appeal, subject to the granting of leave to appeal by the High Court. Leave cannot be granted by the Court of Appeal, as is the case under section 1(7).[8]

10.2.1.2 The requirement of leave is a very familiar technique by which to restrict the otherwise general right of appeal. In broad terms its purpose is to operate as a check on hopeless, unnecessary or frivolous appeals.[9] In the case of section 1(6A), the general policy of the law is accentuated by the particular policy underlying the 1979 Act, which leads to an even more rigorous screening exercise. The broad and very precise policy of the 1979 Act is that the question of leave to appeal from an arbitration award is a preliminary and summary matter to be determined in the discretion of a first tier judge and only in the most exceptional circumstances should that decision be reviewed by the Court of Appeal.[10]

10.2.1.3 The question of leave to appeal to the Court of Appeal from the grant or refusal of leave to appeal from an arbitration award falls to be determined in the dis-

---

1. In consequence it only applies to decisions of the High Court pronounced after the commencement of the Supreme Court Act 1981: see s. 148(4) of the Act. For the commencement of the 1981 Act, see s. 153(2).

2. Contrast *Kaffeehandelsgesellschaft K.G.* v. *Plagefim Commercial S.A.* [1981] 2 Lloyd's Rep. 190, 193, where Mustill J. considered the application for leave an interlocutory matter, with an appeal therefore only possible with leave either of the High Court or the Court of Appeal.

3. Supreme Court Act 1981, sections 16 and 18.

4. *Pioneer Shipping Ltd.* v. *B.T.P. Tioxide Ltd. (The Nema)* [1980] 1 Q.B. 547, 564, per Lord Denning M.R.

5. *Italmare Shipping Co.* v. *Ocean Tanker Co. Inc. (The Rio Sun)* [1982] 1 W.L.R. 158. See also *Schiffahrtsagentur Hamburg Middle East Line G.m.b.H. Hamburg* v. *Virtue Shipping Corpn. Monrovia (The Oinoussian Virtue)* [1981] 1 Lloyd's Rep. 533; *International Sea Tankers Inc.* v. *Hemisphere Shipping Co. Ltd. (The Wenjiang)* [1982] 1 Lloyd's Rep. 128 (C.A.).

6. See *infra*, para. 10.3.

7. See *International Sea Tankers Inc.* v. *Hemisphere Shipping Co. Ltd. (The Wenjiang)* [1981] 2 Lloyd's Rep. 308, 315 per Robert Goff J. (first instance); *Aden Refinery Co. Ltd.* v. *Ugland Management Co. Ltd. (The Ugland Obo One)* [1987] 1 Q.B. 650, 666, per Mustill L.J. See also Sir John Donaldson, "Commercial Arbitration—1979 and After", in *Current Legal Problems* (1983) pp. 1–12, 5.

8. Considered *infra*, para. 10.3.4.

9. *Lane* v. *Esdaile* [1891] A.C. 210, 211–213, per Lord Halsbury L.C.

10. *Infra* and Chapter 1, para. 1.2.1.6. See also *Astro Valiente Compania Naviera S.A.* v. *The Government of Pakistan Ministry of Food and Agriculture (The Emmanuel Colocotronis) (No. 2)* [1982] 1 Lloyd's Rep. 286, 294, where Staughton J. in refusing leave to appeal to the Court of Appeal from his decision granting leave to appeal commented, "My reason for that is that in general I consider it undesirable that such leave should be granted other than in very rare cases".

cretion of the first tier judge to whom the application is made.[11] The general principle that is to govern the exercise of the discretion was very firmly and clearly laid down by the House of Lords in *The Antaios*.[12] Lord Diplock observed[13]:

This brings me to the "(6A) question" . . . when should a judge give leave to appeal to the Court of Appeal from his own grant or refusal of leave to appeal to the High Court from an arbitral award? I agree . . . that leave to appeal to the Court of Appeal should be granted by the judge under section 1(6A) only in cases where a decision whether to grant or to refuse leave to appeal to the High Court under section 1(3)(b) in the particular case in his view called for some amplification, elucidation or adaptation to changing practices of existing guidelines laid down by appellate courts; and that leave to appeal under section 1(6A) should *not* be granted in any other type of case. Judges should have the courage of their own convictions and decide for themselves whether, applying existing guidelines, leave to appeal to the High Court under section 1(3)(b) ought to be granted or not.

10.2.1.4 This dictum is unambiguous and robust. Leave to appeal under section 1(6A) must not be given unless the case falls within one of the categories of circumstances specified.[14] Where, for example, the judge takes the view that upon a substantial and arguable point of law arising in a "standard term" case the arbitrators so far from being probably wrong were on the contrary right, not only should leave to appeal under section 1(3)(b) be refused but also any application for leave to appeal to the Court of Appeal under section 1(6A).[15] It is only in the rare class of case where a question arises as to the guidelines themselves, of which *The Kerman*[16] is a classical illustration, that a judge will be justified in giving leave.[17] In *The Kerman*[18] Parker J. confronted and endeavoured to resolve the considerable difficulties involved in the abstract comprehension of the guidelines and in the application of the guidelines to contemporary practice. As such the amplification and/or elucidation of the then *Nema* guidelines was in issue and Parker J. was justified in giving leave to appeal from his dismissal of the application for leave under section 1(3)(b).[19]

10.2.1.5 It has previously been observed that *The Nema/Antaios* guidelines are not comprehensive and that situations may and do arise which are outside their scope.[20] It follows that a question touching on the proper exercise of the discretion under section 1(6)(A) will not invariably arise in the context of the enunciated guidelines, but may arise in association with applications outside the parameters of the guidelines. In the result a judge may equally be justified in giving leave under section 1(6A) when his decision relates to a question of law which in its nature or by virtue of the associated

---

11. *Aden Refinery Co. Ltd.* v. *Ugland Management Co. Ltd. (The Ugland Obo One)* [1987] 1 Q.B. 650.
12. *Antaios Compania Naviera S.A.* v. *Salen Rederierna A.B. (The Antaios)* [1985] A.C. 191.
13. *Ibid* p. 205. For the views expressed by Staughton J. on the initial application for leave under both s. 1(3)(b) and s. 1(6A), which are to the same general effect, see [1983] 2 Lloyd's Rep. 473, 476. Lord Diplock, while agreeing with the general approach adopted by Staughton J. to the s. 1(6A) question, nonetheless disapproved of his conclusion to give leave, see p. 202 *ibid*.
14. *Aden Refinery Co. Ltd.* v. *Ugland Management Co. Ltd. (The Ugland Obo One)*, *supra*.
15. *Antaios Compania Naviera S.A.* v. *Salen Rederierna A.B. (The Antaios)*, *supra*, p. 202.
16. *B.V.S. S.A. and Another* v. *Kerman Shipping Co. S.A. (The Kerman)* [1982] 1 W.L.R. 166.
17. *Petraco (Bermuda) Ltd.* v. *Petromed International S.A. and Beverli S.A.* [1988] 2 Lloyd's Rep. 357, 358–359.
18. *Supra*. See Chapter 5 for the contribution made by Parker J. in *The Kerman*, to an elaboration of *The Nema/Antaios* guidelines.
19. The earlier cases in which leave to appeal was granted under s. 1(6A) must now be considered in the light of the pronouncement of the House of Lords in *The Antaios*, *supra*.
20. See Chapter 6.

circumstances falls outside the ambit of the existing guidelines and with regard to which it is desirable that there should exist a definitive statement of the criteria that should be taken into account in considering such a case.[21]

10.2.1.6 The upshot of the preceding discussion is to strongly emphasise that the question of leave to appeal under section 1(3)(b) will be decided predominantly by the first tier judge who hears the application.[22] Rarely will an appeal from his decision be taken by the Court of Appeal. A first tier judge to whom an application for leave to appeal under section 1(6A) is made must appreciate that he is being invited to adopt an exceptional course of action.[23] The predisposition of the judge must be to refuse leave unless the case falls within the special circumstances discussed above. The resulting consequence must be that appeals under section 1(6A) will be exceptionally rare.

10.2.1.7 Appeals permitted under section 1(6A) are centrally concerned with the exercise of discretion under section 1(3)(b) and the relevant criteria. They assume the existence of a jurisdiction to determine the question whether to give or refuse leave to appeal. But the case of *Arab African Energy Corp. Ltd.* v. *Olieprodukten Nederland B.V.*[24] raises a conundrum as to whether an issue going to the question of jurisdiction may also be made subject to the appeal process established by section 1(6A). On the facts of the case an application for leave to appeal was accompanied by a dispute as to whether there existed a valid exclusion agreement. If a valid exclusion agreement existed the court had no jurisdiction to grant leave to appeal. The question was by agreement taken as a preliminary issue and ultimately the existence and validity of the exclusion agreement was upheld. The judge then gave leave to appeal, but without specifying the jurisdiction he was relying on. The question arises whether the judge was utilising section 1(6A), on the possible line of argument that leave to appeal was being refused because of the judge's decision on the disputed exclusion agreement. It is however difficult to see that section 1(6A) could be applicable in this kind of situation. As already indicated the subsection establishes an appeal on the question of the exercise of discretion, on the assumption that the jurisdiction to exercise the discretion exists. It is not applicable to jurisdictional disputes which represent a precondition to the existence of the discretion. To adopt section 1(6A) in this kind of situation would appear to extend the appellate process beyond its legitimate boundaries. A dispute concerning the existence and validity of an exclusion agreement is best resolved by reference to the jurisdiction of the High Court to grant declaratory relief[25]; but may alternatively be resolved by reference to the consultative case procedure established by section 2 of the 1979 Act,[26] or by an appeal from an interim award.[27]

---

21. *Bulk Oil (Zug) A.G.* v. *Sun International Ltd. and Sun Oil Trading Co.* [1983] 1 Lloyd's Rep. 655; [1983] 2 Lloyd's Rep. 587, 589, per Ackner L.J. On the facts of the case the question of law had an E.E.C. dimension. *Petraco (Bermuda) Ltd.* v. *Petromed International S.A. and Beverli S.A.* [1988] 2 Lloyd's Rep. 357, per Staughton L.J., where leave to appeal was sought on the basis of a point of law not argued before the arbitrator. See Chapter 6, paras. 6.2.10 and 6.2.13, respectively.

22. In exceptional instances the application for leave to appeal under s. 1(6A) may be heard by a different judge from the judge who heard the original application under s. 1(3)(b): see *Reardon Smith Line Ltd.* v. *Sanko Steamship Co. Ltd. (The Sanko Honour)* [1985] 1 Lloyd's Rep. 418, 421 *et seq.*

23. *Petraco (Bermuda) Ltd.* v. *Petromed International S.A. and Beverli S.A.*, *supra*, p. 358, Staughton L.J.

24. [1983] 2 Lloyd's Rep. 419, 423.

25. See Chapter 13, para. 13.5.6.

26. See Chapter 12.

27. See Chapter 12, para. 12.11.1.

10.2.2 Reasons to accompany the giving of leave to appeal

The practice to be adopted by a judge in considering an application for leave to appeal under section 1(3)(b) has previously been considered.[1] The general rule is that in granting or refusing leave to appeal the judge need not give reasons for his decision.[2] But when the judge also considers it appropriate to give leave to appeal under section 1(6A) from his decision to grant or refuse leave to appeal, he is obliged to give reasons for his decision to grant or refuse leave, so that the Court of Appeal may be informed of the perceived difficulty or question which warrants reconsideration of *The Nema/Antaios* guidelines by the Court of Appeal; or in the case of an application falling outside the ambit of the guidelines, of the new issue which demands fresh consideration by the Court of Appeal. In each circumstance the judge must not only explain why he has been persuaded to give leave to appeal to the Court of Appeal, but also why he has exercised his discretion in favour of granting or refusing leave to appeal from the arbitration award. In *The Antaios* Lord Diplock made the point in the following language[3]:

In the sole type of case in which leave to appeal to the Court of Appeal under section 1(6A) may properly be given the judge ought to give reasons for his decision to grant such appeal so that the Court of Appeal may be informed of the lacuna, uncertainty or unsuitability in the light of changing practices that the judge has perceived in the existing guidelines; moreover since the grant of leave entails also the necessity for the application of *Edwards* v. *Bairstow* [1956] A.C. 14 principles by the Court of Appeal in order to examine whether the judge had acted within the limits of his discretion, the judge should also give the reasons for the way in which he had exercised his discretion.[4]

The dictum is directed to cases falling within *The Nema/Antaios* guidelines, but the use of the phrase "the sole type of case" must now presumably be understood in the context of the subsequently developed law. As such the dictum sets the tone for all cases when leave to appeal under section 1(6A) may be properly given.

10.2.3 No appeal from a decision under section 1(6A)

10.2.3.1 Leave to appeal under section 1(6A) may only be granted by the High Court, and the grant of leave is a precondition to the jurisdiction of the Court of Appeal to entertain an appeal.[1] The Court of Appeal has no jurisdiction to give leave; nor is there an appeal to the Court of Appeal from the decision of a first tier appeal judge refusing leave to appeal under section 1(6A). In *Moran* v. *Lloyd's*[2] Sir John Donaldson M.R. considered that the decision of a first tier judge in refusing leave to appeal under section 1(3)(b) "cannot be questioned in this Court [i.e. Court of Appeal], since such an appeal does not lie without the leave of [the first tier judge] and he refused it".[3] This is in keeping with general principle and with the principle equally applicable

---

1. See Chapter 7, para. 7.3.
2. *Ibid*, para. 7.3.3.
3. *Supra* p. 205. See also *Petraco (Bermuda) Ltd.* v. *Petromed International S.A. and Beverli S.A.*, *supra* p. 359, Staughton L.J.
4. The role of the Court of Appeal when leave is granted is considered *infra*, para. 10.2.5.
1. *Aden Refinery Co. Ltd.* v. *Ugland Management Co. Ltd. (The Ugland Obo One)*, *supra*.
2. [1983] 1 Lloyd's Rep. 472 (C.A.).
3. *Ibid* p. 474.

to the giving and refusing of leave to appeal.[4] Moreover it is the clear design of the legislation that the question of leave under section 1(6A) is for the first tier judge and his decision is not to be undermined by an appeal or some other mode of review aimed at vacating his decision, provided the judge has arrived at what may be considered a "decision" in the eyes of the law.[5]

10.2.3.2 In *The Ugland Obo One*[6] the Court of Appeal was confronted with two novel arguments appertaining to the operation of section 1(6A), which, had they succeeded, would have had a profoundly adverse impact on the legislative policy associated with the 1979 Act. The first argument was to the effect that the ouster of the Court of Appeal's jurisdiction to determine appeals by virtue of section 1(6A), subject to the granting of leave by the judge determining the application, was of no application where it could be shown either that the judge had not in reality exercised any discretion whatsoever or had exercised his jurisdiction on the basis of inadmissible considerations. It was argued that where this could be established an appeal could be brought to the Court of Appeal, from the grant or refusal of leave to appeal under section 1(3)(b) without leave. The argument was advanced by way of analogy with the "Scherer principle" deriving from the decision of the Court of Appeal in *Scherer* v. *Counting Instruments Ltd.*[7] In its essence the effect of the "Scherer principle" is to render section 18(1)(f) of the Supreme Court Act 1981, which provides "No appeal shall lie to the Court of Appeal . . . (f) without the leave of the court or tribunal in question, from any order of the High Court or any other court or tribunal . . . relating only to costs which are by law left to the discretion of the court or tribunal . . . ", of no application where on the question of costs it can be shown that the judge has exercised his discretion without grounds or on the basis of extraneous grounds. The Court of Appeal rejected the argument because on the facts the judge at first instance had exercised a discretion and had also exercised it judicially. But the court also rejected the applicability of the principle to the 1979 Act. In *Re Racal Communications Ltd.*[8] the House of Lords had refused to apply the principle to section 441(3) of the Companies Act 1948. In the instant case the Court of Appeal also refused to extend the principle and considered that it was to be confined to the statutory provisions relating to costs. The "Scherer principle" was dismissed as being contrary to the plain and unambiguous language of section 1(6A) and also to the well-defined policy of the 1979 legislation.

10.2.3.3 The second line of argument was of a more general nature and addressed the question whether there could be an appeal to the Court of Appeal from the decision of a first tier judge refusing leave to appeal under section 1(6A). The Act itself does not expressly prohibit such an appeal and from this starting position it was again argued that an appeal lay if it could be shown that the first tier judge had not in reality exercised a discretion under section 1(6A) or had taken into consideration

---

4. *Kay* v. *Briggs* (1889) 22 Q.B.D. 343; *Lane* v. *Esdaile* [1891] A.C. 210. The latter decision was commented upon in *Rickards* v. *Rickards* [1990] Fam. 194, 201, per Lord Donaldson of Lymington M.R.: "In my judgment what *Lane* v. *Esdaile* decided, and all that it decided, was that where it is provided that an appeal shall lie *by leave* of a particular court or courts, neither the grant nor refusal of leave is an appealable decision." See also *Geogas S.A.* v. *Trammo Gas Ltd. (The Baleares)* [1991] 2 Lloyd's Rep. 318 (H.L.).
5. The point is further considered *infra*, para 10.2.3.4.
6. *Aden Refinery Co. Ltd.* v. *Ugland Management Co. Ltd. (The Ugland Obo One)*, *supra*.
7. [1986] 1 W.L.R. 615.
8. [1981] A.C. 374.

immaterial considerations. This, it was argued, represented a qualification to the decision of the House of Lords in *Lane* v. *Esdaile*,[9] which otherwise stood in firm opposition to the argument advanced and which decided that where it is provided that an appeal shall lie by leave of a particular court, neither the grant or refusal of leave is an appealable decision.[10] The argument again failed on the facts, for the Court of Appeal was satisfied that the judge had acted judicially in considering the question of leave to appeal. But the court was also of the opinion that no such appeal was possible in view of the decision in *Lane* v. *Esdaile*, which equally applied to section 1(6A) without qualification.[11]

10.2.3.4 In the result, where leave to appeal is not granted under section 1(6A), there is a total ouster of the jurisdiction of the Court of Appeal to review the decision of a judge granting or refusing leave to appeal to the High Court under section 1(3)(b). Without leave the section 1(3)(b) decision rests with the first tier judge and is final. The refusal of leave bars any right of appeal. However this is not to say that there is no remedy when a judge exercises the discretion so perversely that it cannot be said that he has made a decision within the meaning of section 1(3)(b). Without defining the remedy, Mustill L.J. has contemplated,[12]

I can envisage that if a judge had in truth never reached "a decision" at all on the grant or refusal of leave, but had reached his conclusion, not by any intellectual process, but through bias, chance, whimsy, or personal interest, an appellate or other court might find a way to intervene.

10.2.4 Leave to appeal subject to conditions

The giving of leave to appeal under section 1(6A) may be made conditional on the applicant satisfying such lawful conditions as may be specified by the judge giving leave.[1] In *Arab African Energy Corp. Ltd.* v. *Olieprodukten Nederland B.V.*,[2] Leggatt J. granted leave to appeal subject to the applicants agreeing to the Court of Appeal having jurisdiction to order security for the costs of the appeal and other identified surplus costs.

10.2.5 Role of Court of Appeal when leave granted

10.2.5.1 When leave to appeal is granted the jurisdiction of the Court of Appeal is invoked to review the discretionary decision granting or refusing leave to appeal under section 1(3)(b) by the first tier judge. The mode of review is a very different process from an orthodox appeal involving a rehearing, with the Court of Appeal following its long-established practice in relation to the review of discretionary powers.

In the first place the Court of Appeal will not interfere if its sole conclusion is that it would have exercised the discretion differently from the first tier judge. The possibility of differences of judicial opinion is inherent in the exercise of discretionary powers and it is in the nature of the process that different judges may come to differ-

---

9. [1891] A.C. 210.
10. For recent judicial consideration of the principle see *Bland* v. *Chief Supplementary Benefit Officer* [1983] 1 W.L.R. 262; *Bokhari* v. *Mahmood, The Times,* 18 April 1988; *Rickards* v. *Rickards, supra,* note 4.
11. See also Donaldson, "Commercial Arbitration—1979 and After" in *Current Legal Problems* (1983) pp. 1–12, 5.
12. *Aden Refinery Co. Ltd.* v. *Ugland Management Co. Ltd. (The Ugland Obo One), supra,* p.666.
1. Arbitration Act 1979, s. 7(1)(b).
2. [1983] 2 Lloyd's Rep. 419, 423.

ent conclusions.[1] So long as the first tier judge has come to a conclusion which it was open to a judge acting reasonably to arrive at, the Court of Appeal will not interfere, even though it would have been inclined to act differently in the circumstances.

10.2.5.2 The discretion however must be exercised judiciously and in keeping with general principle. In the present context this substantially means in accordance with the decisions of the House of Lords in *The Nema* and *The Antaios* and with the guidelines that derive from these two decisions and other associated developments.[2] If in the declared reasons of the first tier appeal judge it can be observed that the judge has gone wrong in principle, in that he has failed to apply the relevant considerations or has taken into account irrelevant considerations or that he has otherwise arrived at an unreasonable conclusion, such as to show that the judge must have misdirected himself, the Court of Appeal may intervene and substitute its own decision for that of the first tier judge.

10.2.5.3 The approach of the Court of Appeal under section 1(6A) follows general principle, by which is meant that the supervisory jurisdiction of the Court of Appeal is exercised in a manner consistent with the principles that have been developed generally in relation to the exercise of appellate supervisory powers over the discretionary jurisdiction of judges at first instance and subordinate tribunals.[3] This was recognised by Lord Diplock in *The Antaios*.[4] The governing principles are to be found in two leading decisions, one of the House of Lords in *Edwards* v. *Bairstow*[5] and the other of the Court of Appeal in *Associated Provincial Picture Houses Ltd.* v. *Wednesbury Corporation*.[6] In the former Lord Radcliffe, speaking in the context of an appeal on a case stated from the determination of General Commissioners for Income Tax, said[7]:

When the case comes before the court it is its duty to examine the determination having regard to its knowledge of the relevant law. If the case contains anything ex facie which is bad law and which bears upon the determination, it is, obviously, erroneous in point of law. But, without any such misconception appearing ex facie, it may be that the facts found are such that no person acting judicially and properly instructed as to the relevant law could have come to the determination under appeal. In those circumstances, too, the court must intervene. It has no option but to assume that there has been some misconception of the law and that this has been responsible for the determination. So there, too, there has been error in point of law.

10.2.5.4 In the latter, which is a case directed to the meaning of unreasonableness as a basis of challenging the activities of subordinate bodies in administrative law, and which has given birth to the so-called Wednesbury principle, Lord Greene M.R. observed[8]:

It is true the discretion must be exercised reasonably. Now what does that mean? Lawyers fami-

1. *Aden Refinery Co. Ltd.* v. *Ugland Management Co. Ltd. (The Ugland Obo One)*, *supra*, p. 341 per Sir John Donaldson M.R., p. 346 per Mustill L.J.
2. See Chapters 5 and 6.
3. Cf. *The Makefjell* [1976] 2 Lloyd's Rep. 29, 39; *Conry* v. *Simpson and Others* [1983] 3 All E.R. 369 (C.A.); *Cook Industries Inc.* v. *B.V. Handelsmaatschappij Jean Delvaux* [1985] 1 Lloyd's Rep. 120; *G* v. *G* [1985] 1 W.L.R. 647.
4. *Supra*, p. 205.
5. [1956] A.C. 14. See also *Antaios Compania Naviera S.A.* v. *Salen Rederierna A.B. (The Antaios)*, *supra*, p. 205, where Lord Diplock comments, "the grant of leave entails also the necessity for the application of *Edwards* v. *Bairstow* [1956] A.C. 14 principles by the Court of Appeal in order to examine whether the judge had acted within the limits of his discretion . . . ".
6. [1948] 1 K.B. 223.
7. *Supra*, p. 36.
8. *Supra*, p. 229.

liar with the phraseology commonly used in relation to exercise of statutory discretions often use the word "unreasonable" in a rather comprehensive sense. It has frequently been used and is frequently used as a general description of the things that must not be done. For instance, a person entrusted with a discretion must, so to speak, direct himself properly in law. He must call his own attention to the matters which he is bound to consider. He must exclude from his consideration matters which are irrelevant to what he has to consider. If he does not obey those rules, he may truly be said, and often is said, to be acting "unreasonably". Similarly, there may be something so absurd that no sensible person could ever dream that it lay within the powers of the authority. Warrington L.J. in *Short* v. *Poole Corporation*[9] gave the example of the red-haired teacher, dismissed because she had red hair. That is unreasonable in one sense. In another sense it is taking into consideration extraneous matters. It is so unreasonable that it might almost be described as being done in bad faith; and, in fact, all these things run into one another.

10.2.5.5 The role of the Court of Appeal is therefore very restricted and potential intervention is confined to circumstances when the first tier judge has gone wrong in principle or arrived at a determination which in the prevailing circumstances of the case is manifestly unsupportable. The nature of the appellate review renders it imperative that the first tier judge give reasons explaining his decision to grant or refuse leave to appeal.[10] But once the Court of Appeal is satisfied that the first tier judge has fallen into fundamental error it must approach the question of leave to appeal afresh and substitute its own decision for that of the first tier judge.[11]

10.2.5.6 The practice to be followed by the Court of Appeal mirrors that of the first tier judge. The appellate court should not give reasons for its decision unless it decides to refuse leave to appeal.[12] Presumably reasons will also be necessary if there is a prospect of an on-appeal to the House of Lords, as where the Court of Appeal itself gives leave to appeal or the Appeal Committee of the House of Lords is to be invited to give leave to appeal. But apart from the practice to be adopted in the narrow exercise of its supervisory role, it would appear clear from the manner in which the discretion associated with section 1(6A) is structured that the Court of Appeal also possesses an important enunciatory role in relation to the criteria relevant to the exercise of the discretion arising out of section 1(3)(b). In each case it will be for the Court of Appeal to endorse the existing guidelines; or to amplify or elucidate the existing guidelines; or to adapt them in the face of changing practices. And when novel and hitherto unconsidered situations arise, the Court of Appeal will have the responsibility of laying down new guidelines to meet the demands of these particular cases and which will be complementary to *The Nema/Antaios* guidelines.[13]

10.2.5.7 When inclined to grant leave to appeal, the Court of Appeal has the same jurisdiction to attach conditions as that possessed by the High Court under section 1(4) of the 1979 Act.[14]

---

9. [1926] Ch. 66.
10. *Supra*, para 10.2.2.
11. *Petraco (Bermuda) Ltd.* v. *Petromed International S.A. and Beverli S.A.*, *supra* p. 360, per Staughton L.J. See also *Atlas Maritime Co. S.A.* v. *Avalon Maritime Ltd. (The Coral Rose) (No. 3)* [1991] 2 Lloyd's Rep. 374 (C.A.).
12. *Ibid.*
13. *Petraco (Bermuda) Ltd.* v. *Petromed International S.A. and Beverli S.A.*, *supra*.
14. See Chapter 4 and Supreme Court Act 1981, s. 15(3).

10.3 ON-APPEAL FROM THE SUBSTANTIVE DECISION OF AN APPEAL JUDGE ON A QUESTION OF LAW

10.3.1 Introduction

10.3.1.1 An appeal to the Court of Appeal from the decision of a judge at first instance under section 1(2) on an appeal from an arbitration award is governed by section 1(7) of the 1979 Act. The subsection provides:

No appeal shall lie to the Court of Appeal from a decision of the High Court on an appeal under this section unless—
 (a) the High Court or the Court of Appeal gives leave; and
 (b) it is certified by the High Court that the question of law to which its decision relates either is one of general public importance or is one which for some other special reason should be considered by the Court of Appeal.

The subsection follows the format adopted in the Criminal Appeal Act 1968, with regard to appeals in criminal matters from the Court of Appeal, Criminal Division, to the House of Lords[1]; and is also identical with the provisions of section 2(3) of the 1979 Act.[2] It is expressly confined to an appeal "from a decision of the High Court on an appeal under this section". This clearly is a reference to substantive decisions on appeals from arbitration awards made under section 1(2) and excludes decisions of the High Court on preliminary applications for leave to appeal under section 1(3)(b), or for leave to apply for reasons or further reasons under section 1(5)(b), or the making or refusal of an order for reasons or further reasons under section 1(5). Appeals from these decisions are governed by section 1(6A).[3]

10.3.1.2 The restrictive preconditions specified in section 1(7) continue to apply even when the initial appeal from an arbitration award is made with the consent of all the parties and is brought under the terms of section 1(3)(a).[4] Consent to the initial appeal does not extend to an on-appeal. There are however circumstances when following the giving of leave to appeal under section 1(3)(b) it also becomes the obligation of the first tier judge who hears the substantive appeal, if requested, to fulfil the preconditions specified in section 1(7) and so facilitate an on-appeal.[5]

With regard to substantive appeals from the High Court to the Court of Appeal there arise two general issues. The first appertains to the procedural preconditions governing the appellate process and which is the dominant concern of section 1(7). The second relates to the role and powers of the Court of Appeal when an appeal is brought.

10.3.2 Procedural preconditions governing appeals

10.3.2.1 An appeal under section 1(7) cannot be brought as of right. The subsection is patently restrictive with the *prima facie* rule framed in the negative and to the effect

---

1. Criminal Appeal Act 1968, s. 33(2) and Administration of Justice Act 1960, s. 1(2). For an example of the legislation in operation, see, *R* v. *Kemp* [1988] 1 W.L.R. 846. See also *Gelberg* v. *Miller* [1961] 1 All E.R. 618; *National Westminster Bank* v. *Arthur Young & Co.* [1985] 1 W.L.R. 1123.
2. See Chapter 12, para. 12.9.3.
3. *Supra*, para. 10.2, and Chapter 11, para. 11.10.
4. Chapter 4, para. 4.2. See also *Babanaft International Co. S.A.* v. *Avant Petroleum Inc. (The Oltenia)* [1982] 2 Lloyd's Rep. 99, 106, per Donaldson L.J.
5. This point is considered *infra*, para. 10.3.4.18 *et seq.*

that there shall not be any on-appeal from the decision of the first tier judge unless the requisite certification and leave are obtained. The policy of the legislation is unambiguous. Whereas appeals from arbitration to the High Court under the 1979 Act will be rare, on-appeals from the High Court to the Court of Appeal will be still rarer. Kerr L.J. has summarised the policy of the legislation in the following terms[1]:

Since the 1979 Act has come into force and its effect has been laid down in a number of decisions, in particular [*The Nema*], only a few decisions by arbitrators have reached the Court of Appeal. This is in accordance with the policy of the Act to discourage appeals from arbitrators on issues of law and only to allow them to proceed beyond the court of first instance in exceptional circumstances.

10.3.2.2 The fundamental effect of section 1(7) is to render an on-appeal subject to two indispensable and essentially distinct preconditions. The first is a certificate given by the High Court that the question(s) of law in issue is one of general public importance or there exists some other special reason why the question of law should be considered by the Court of Appeal.[2] A certificate may only be given by the High Court (the judge at first instance) and from the decision to give or refuse a certificate there exists no appeal,[3] nor any mode of non-appellate review, provided the judge at first instance has arrived at what may be considered a "decision" in the eyes of the law.[4] If a certificate is refused, then that is the end of the matter and no appeal may be brought.[5] In effect the decision of the judge at first instance is rendered final.

10.3.2.3 If on the other hand a certificate is given, a party wishing to appeal must further obtain leave to appeal either from the High Court or the Court of Appeal. In the first instance application for leave will invariably be to the High Court[6] and only if this application is refused will it be necessary to apply to the Court of Appeal. There is however no appeal from the decision of the High Court on an application for leave. The application to the Court of Appeal exists as an alternative mode of application and not as an appeal from the refusal of the High Court to grant leave.[7] It is possible for the High Court to grant the necessary certificate and refuse leave,[8] in which case the applicant continues to have the right to apply to the Court of Appeal.[9] But the jur-

---

1. *Alfred C. Toepfer Schiffahrtsgesellschaft G.m.b.H.* v. *Tossa Marine Co. Ltd. etc. (The Derby)* [1985] 2 Lloyd's Rep. 325, 327. Also *The Antaios* [1981] 2 Lloyd's Rep. 284, 300, Robert Goff J. (first instance), "It seems to me that the whole scheme of the Act is basically that on the questions of law which fall within the Act the intention is that primarily there should be one appeal, and one appeal only, and that is to this Court".
2. Considered *infra*, para. 10.3.3.
3. *Compagnie Européene des Pétroles* v. *Vitol B.V. (formerly T/A Vitol Trading B.V.)* [1988] 1 Lloyd's Rep. 577, per Parker L.J. (Note).
4. Cf. *Aden Refinery Co. Ltd.* v. *Ugland Management Co. Ltd. (The Ugland Obo One)* [1987] 1 Q.B. 650, 666, Mustill L.J.
5. *Compagnie Européene des Pétroles* v. *Vitol B.V. (formerly T/A Vitol Trading B.V.)*, *supra*.
6. This is not an express requirement of the legislation but as a matter of practice it will be overwhelmingly convenient to the applicant to seek leave to appeal at the same time as the application for a certificate.
7. See *infra*, para. 10.2.4.
8. See, for example, *Obestain Inc.* v. *National Mineral Development Corpn. Ltd. (The Sanix Ace)* [1987] 1 Lloyd's Rep. 465, 471; *Transworld Oil Ltd.* v. *North Bay Shipping Corpn. (The Rio Claro)* [1987] 2 Lloyd's Rep. 173, 179; *Marc Rich & Co. Ltd.* v. *Tourlotti Compania Naviera S.A. (The Kalliopi A)* [1987] 2 Lloyd's Rep. 268 (Note); *Comdel Commodities Ltd.* v. *Siporex Trade S.A. (No. 2)* [1988] 2 Lloyd's Rep. 590, 599; *Sealace Shipping Co. Ltd.* v. *Oceanvoice Ltd. (The Alecos M)* [1990] 1 Lloyd's Rep. 82, 85.
9. See, for example, *Procter & Gamble Philippine Manufacturing Corpn.* v. *Kurt A. Becher G.m.b.H. & Co. K.G.* [1988] 2 Lloyd's Rep. 21, 27; *President of India* v. *Jebsens (UK) Ltd.* [1989] 1 Lloyd's Rep. 232, 234; *Geogas S.A.* v. *Trammo Gas Ltd. (The Baleares)* [1991] 2 All E.R. 110 (C.A.).

isdiction of the Court of Appeal to grant leave is dependent on the High Court giving a certificate.[10] Where there is an appeal and cross-appeal each requires a certificate and leave if they are both to proceed further.[11] From a decision of the Court of Appeal giving or refusing leave to appeal there exists no appeal to the House of Lords.[12]

10.3.2.4 An appeal under section 1(7) may be brought against the whole or part of a judgment at first instance. It follows that a certificate and leave may be given with regard to all questions of law in issue or only in relation to one or some of the issues. Where the leave granted is so restricted, it follows that the Court of Appeal is confined to a consideration of those issues of law in respect of which leave has been given.

Although not expressed in section 1(7), both the High Court and Court of Appeal may attach conditions to the granting of leave.[13]

10.3.3 Certification

The first logical step for a prospective appellant is to persuade the High Court to grant a certificate to the effect that the question of law to which its decision relates is either one of general public importance or one which for some other special reason should be considered by the Court of Appeal. Given the policy of the 1979 Act it is clear that certificates under section 1(7) should not be given too readily.[1]

10.3.3.1 General public importance

10.3.3.1.1 This phrase bears in part its ordinary meaning, conveying the notion of a question of law of importance to society at large, but it is not confined to this meaning. If it were it would be an unacceptably restrictive interpretation in the context of arbitration practice. In consequence the judiciary has adopted a more expansive approach and placed a reasonable and sensible interpretation on the phrase; as a result it has come to possess a "very specialised meaning".[2] The interpretation first put on the phrase by Robert Goff J., at first instance, in *The Nema* has attracted general approval[3]:

---

10. *Compagnie Européene des Pétroles* v. *Vitol B.V. (formerly T/A Vitol Trading B.V.)*, *supra*.

11. See, for example, *Arab Maritime Petroleum Transport Co.* v. *Luxor Trading Corpn. and Geogas Enterprise S.A. (The Al Bida)* [1987] 1 Lloyd's Rep. 124; *Motor Oil Hellas (Corinth) Refineries S.A.* v. *Shipping Corpn. of India (The Kanchenjunga)* [1989] 1 Lloyd's Rep. 354.

12. *Geogas S.A.* v. *Trammo Gas Ltd. (The Baleares)* [1991] 2 Lloyd's Rep. 318 (H.L.).

13. *Infra*, para. 10.3.5.

1. *Pera Shipping Corporation* v. *Petroship S.A. (The Pera)* [1985] 2 Lloyd's Rep. 103, 105, per Lloyd L.J., "it is important that certificates under that sub-section [i.e. section 1(7)] should not be given too readily. Otherwise, one of the main objects of the 1979 Act will be frustrated". See also *Seacrystal Shipping Ltd.* v. *Bulk Transport Group Shipping Co. Ltd. (The Kyzikos)* [1987] 1 Lloyd's Rep. 48, 59, per Webster J.

2. *Petroleo Brasileiro S/A etc.* v. *Elounda Shipping Co. (The Evanthia M)* [1985] 2 Lloyd's Rep. 154, 157, per Mustill J.

3. *B.T.P. Tioxide Ltd.* v. *Pioneer Shipping Ltd. and Armada Marine S.A. (The Nema)* [1980] 2 Lloyd's Rep. 83, 94. See also *Charles E. Ford Ltd.* v. *AFEC Inc.* [1986] 2 Lloyd's Rep. 307, 316, per Bingham J., "I think that the point is one of general public importance, by which I do not mean the whole commercial community but to such part of the commercial community as trade on this form;" *Maritime Transport Overseas G.m.b.H.* v. *Unitramp Salen Rederierne A.B. etc. (The Antaios)* [1981] 2 Lloyd's Rep. 284, 300, per Robert Goff J, "In *The Nema* I gave a certificate on the grounds that I came to the conclusion that the word 'public' did not refer to the man on the Clapham omnibus but to the man in the Baltic Exchange. Therefore, I said that 'public importance' was construed to mean as being of importance to that section of the trade which is affected by the decision, which I think must have been intended."

Now I entirely accept [counsel's] submission that the word "public" here must be given a sensible meaning in its context. It must refer not to the public at large but to a significant section, a relevant section, of the public. I am satisfied that, in the context of the kind of cases that come before this Court on appeal from arbitrators, a matter which, for example, affects the shipping community or maritime arbitration generally would be a matter which affects a significant section of the public. So if there is a question of general importance to such a section of the community, then it would be a question of general public importance within this sub-section.

It would seem therefore that a question of law may be of general public importance if it is of importance to the public at large or to any particular segment, group or established relationship within society manifesting what may be described as a community of interest. What would appear to be essential is that there exists a wider body of persons interested in the result beyond the immediate parties themselves,[4] and that this wider body possesses a sufficient cohesiveness to enjoy a collective identity.

10.3.3.1.2 In each case it is for the judge at first instance to determine whether the question of law is of general public importance. In so determining the judge must act independently and disregard any provisional views that may have been expressed by judges on earlier occasions when leave to appeal was being sought.[5] Such other judicial opinions may be taken into account but they are not conclusive. The test of general public importance would seem to be one of fact and degree. Each question of law must be assessed in the context of the case, taking into account the background of legal developments and the interests of the relevant section of the public. As a matter of practice, where there are several questions of law in issue, one or some of which clearly raise questions of general public importance, a judge may be inclined to assess the remaining legal questions with a less demanding eye and allow all or some to proceed forward to the Court of Appeal by association.[5a] But there is no established practice to this effect and ultimately the final judicial judgment will be governed by the prevailing facts and circumstances.

10.3.3.1.3 There is a discernible if imprecise association between the interpretation given to the phrase "general public importance" and the philosophy underlying *The Nema/Antaios* guidelines. The importance of the question of law in issue to a wider interest group has a significant role to play in the exercise of the discretion on the question whether or not to grant leave to appeal from an arbitration award. But it would be patently wrong to press this point so as to suggest that they are parallel concepts. It would result in a line of reasoning to the effect that whenever leave to appeal was granted under section 1(3)(b), that same question of law automatically satisfied the test of "general public importance" for the purpose of section 1(7)(b). This is clearly not the case and the argument is also contrary to the policy of the 1979 Act in relation to on-appeals.[6] Section 1(7) represents a second statutory filter, the general

4. *Geogas S.A.* v. *Trammo Gas Ltd.* *(The Baleares)* [1991] 2 All E.R. 110, 125, Leggatt L.J.

5. *Italmare Shipping Co.* v. *Ocean Tanker Co. Inc.* *(The Rio Sun)* [1982] 1 Lloyd's Rep. 404, 409.

5a. See, for example, *Sig Bergesen D.Y. A/S* v. *Mobil Shipping and Transportation Co.* *(The Berge Sund)* [1992] 1 Lloyd's Rep. 460, 469, Steyn J.

6. See, for example, *Maritime Transport Overseas G.m.b.H.* v. *Unitramp Salen Rederierna A.B. etc.* *(The Antaios)* [1981] 2 Lloyd's Rep. 284, 300, where Robert Goff J. refers to another case where he refused a certificate and explained that decision in the following terms, "In another case, concerned actually with the construction of the Standard Building Conditions of the British Steel Corporation, although those are widely used, I refused leave on the grounds that they were just the standard conditions of one particular company and that, of itself, was not enough to make it of general public importance to the building and construction industry." See, also *Italmare Shipping Co.* v. *Ocean Tanker Co. Inc.* *(The Rio Sun)* [1982] 1 Lloyd's Rep. 404, 409.

purpose of which is to secure that of the few appeals permitted to the High Court only a small proportion will succeed in moving upward to the Court of Appeal.[7] The legislation clearly contemplates that although a question of law may merit consideration by a first tier judge, nonetheless it may not merit further consideration by the Court of Appeal.[8]

10.3.3.1.4 But although the relationship between "general public importance" and *The Nema/Antaios* guidelines must not be overworked, nonetheless that some manner of relationship might exist was accepted in a majority decision of the Court of Appeal in *The Baleares*.[9] In the context of a wider discussion concerning the precise impact of *The Nema/Antaios* guidelines on the exercise of the discretion governing on-appeals,[10] the majority viewed the significance of *The Nema/Antaios* guidelines as being confined to an assessment of the general public importance of the question of law in issue. It was accepted that the kind of criteria which might be taken into account were in each case very similar. In the words of Leggatt L.J. the test of general public importance may involve a consideration by the court "whether the question of law is one-off, whether it raises a point of general legal principle, whether it is likely to arise fairly often, whether it involves the construction of a clause in common form or whether it is important, at any rate in the trade in which it is used".[11] In *The Ulyanovsk*[12] a similar approach was adopted by Steyn J. who considered it a relevant question to ask whether the question of law in issue had recurred or was likely to recur with a fair degree of frequency. On the facts it was held not and the learned judge refused a certificate.

10.3.3.1.5 It follows that a question of construction may give rise to a question of law of general public importance. This will particularly be the case when the contract is a standard form in current use in a particular market or line of trade, or the contractual words are of a kind widely adopted.[13] Only in exceptional circumstances is the construction of a one-off contract or clause likely to raise a question of general public

---

7. *Supra* and Chapter 1, para. 1.2.1.6.

8. In *Cargill Inc.* v. *Marpro Ltd. (The Aegis Progress)* [1983] 2 Lloyd's Rep. 570, 579, Hobhouse J., in refusing a certificate commented, "I consider [that the case] is within the spirit of the type of situation where the legislature has intended that the decision of the first instance Judge should stand and it should rest with the first instance Judge."

9. *Geogas S.A.* v. *Trammo Gas Ltd. (The Baleares)* [1991] 2 All E.R. 110 (Leggatt and Ralph Gibson L.JJ., Dillon L.J. dissenting).

10. Discussed *infra*, para. 10.3.4.12.

11. *Ibid* p. 124.

12. *Novorossisk Shipping Co.* v. *Neopetro Co. Ltd. (The Ulyanovsk)* [1990] 1 Lloyd's Rep. 425, 433–434.

13. *B.T.P. Tioxide Ltd.* v. *Pioneer Shipping Ltd. and Armada Marine S.A. (The Nema)* [1980] Q.B. 547, 565 per Lord Denning M.R.; *Bunge A.G.* v. *Sesostrad S.A. (The Alkeos C)* [1984] 1 Lloyd's Rep. 687, 691; *Petroleo Brasileiro S/A etc.* v. *Elounda Shipping Co. (The Evanthia M)* [1985] 2 Lloyd's Rep. 154, 157; *Charles E. Ford Ltd.* v. *AFEC Inc.* [1986] 2 Lloyd's Rep. 307, 316. See also *Motor Oil Hellas (Corinth) Refineries S.A.* v. *Shipping Corpn. of India (The Kanchenjunga)* [1987] 2 Lloyd's Rep. 509, 519; *Transgrain Shipping B.V.* v. *Global Transporte Oceanico S.A. (The Mexico I)* [1988] 2 Lloyd's Rep. 149, 158; *Transworld Oil Ltd.* v. *North Bay Shipping Corpn. (The Rio Claro)* [1987] 2 Lloyd's Rep. 173, 179; *Belgravia Navigation Co. S.A.* v. *Cannor Shipping Ltd. (The Troll Park)* [1988] 1 Lloyd's Rep. 55; [1988] 2 Lloyd's Rep. 423 (C.A.); *President of India* v. *Jebsens (UK) Ltd. and Others (The General Capinpin) etc.* [1989] 1 Lloyd's Rep. 232 (C.A.); *Comdel Commodities Ltd.* v. *Siporex Trade S.A. (No. 2)* [1989] 2 Lloyd's Rep. 13, 18; *Oriental Maritime Pte. Ltd.* v. *Ministry of Food, Govt. of the People's Republic of Bangladesh (The Silva Plana) etc.* [1989] 2 Lloyd's Rep. 371, 376; *Socap International Ltd.* v. *Marc Rich & Co. A.G.* [1990] 2 Lloyd's Rep. 175, 177; *Esteve Trading Corp.* v. *Agropec International (The Golden Rio)* [1990] 2 Lloyd's Rep. 273, 281; *Etablissements Soules et Cie* v. *Intertradax S.A.* [1991] 1 Lloyd's Rep. 378, 383.

importance.[14] The distinction here made was highlighted by Lord Diplock in *The Nema*, when commenting upon section 1(7) in the following terms,[15] "The subsection also draws a significant distinction between a question of law which arises in connection with a 'one-off' case and a question of law of general importance to a substantial section of the commercial community, such as may arise under standard term contracts". It will be recalled that *The Nema* was considered a one-off case and the first tier judge was criticised for giving a certificate and granting leave to appeal. The general importance to be attached to the construction of a standard form may be further heightened if the question arises in a standard type of situation,[16] or the point in issue has never previously come before a court,[17] or the point has prevailed for some time in its sphere and is of considerable and recurrent relevance.[18] Contrariwise, the more one-off the factual milieu the less important the question of construction may become.[19] But the simple fact that the construction of a contract has a wider significance beyond the interests of the immediate parties and therefore cannot be considered a wholly one-off case does not necessarily guarantee its characterisation as a question of general public importance.[20]

10.3.3.1.6 Where the issue is the construction of an additional clause, amendment or addendum grafted onto a standard form, the same general principles apply as to standard forms *per se* if the addition, amendment or addendum can be closely identified with the general character of the standard form.[21] Where in contrast they are shown to be unusual or not inevitable in the relevant sphere of practice, then the likelihood is that they will be characterised as one-off and in consequence the significance of the associated legal question in issue will be substantially lessened.[22] There may also be other relevant considerations. If the addendum to a standard form results in an ill-constructed document, this may be a factor which encourages the judge to conclude that the case ought not to go beyond a first tier consideration.[23] The same conclusion

---

14. *Geogas S.A.* v. *Trammo Gas Ltd. (The Baleares)* [1991] 2 All E.R. 110, 116, per Dillon L.J., "on a true construction of s. 1(7)(b) of the 1979 Act it must be very seldom, if ever, appropriate for the judge at first instance to grant a certificate under s. 1(7)(b) in a one-off case". Also Leggatt L.J. at p. 125.

15. *Pioneer Shipping Ltd. and Others* v. *B.T.P. Tioxide Ltd. (The Nema)* [1982] A.C. 724, 740.

16. *Empresa Cubana De Fletes* v. *Kissavos Shipping Co. S.A. (The Agathon) (No. 2)* [1984] 1 Lloyd's Rep. 183, 193.

17. *Filikos Shipping Corporation of Monrovia* v. *Shipmair B.V. (The Filikos)* [1981] 2 Lloyd's Rep. 555, [1983] 1 Lloyd's Rep. 9 (C.A.); *Superfos Chartering A/S* v. *N.B.R. (London) Ltd. (The Saturnia)* [1984] 2 Lloyd's Rep. 366, 372–373.

18. *Alfred C. Toepfer Schiffahrtsgesellschaft G.m.b.H.* v. *Tossa Marine Co. Ltd. etc. (The Derby)* [1984] 1 Lloyd's Rep. 635, 645; *Athens Cape Naviera S.A.* v. *Deutsche Dampfschiffahrtsgesellschaft "Hansa" Aktiengesellschaft and Another (The Barenbels)* [1984] 2 Lloyd's Rep. 388, 393; *Marc Rich & Co. Ltd.* v. *Tourlotti Compania Naviera S.A. (The Kalliopi A)* [1987] 2 Lloyd's Rep. 268 (Note).

19. *Rederiaktiebolaget Gustav Erikson* v. *Dr Fawzi Ahmed Abou Ismail (The Herroe and Askoe)* [1986] 2 Lloyd's Rep. 281, 285.

20. *Phoenix Shipping Co.* v. *Apex Shipping Corpn. (The Apex)* [1982] 2 Lloyd's Rep. 407, 416. See also *Maritime Transport Overseas G.m.b.H.* v. *Unitramp Salen Rederierna A.B. etc. (The Antaios)* [1981] 2 Lloyd's Rep. 284, 300.

21. *Tor Line A.B.* v. *Alltrans Group of Canada Ltd. (The TFL Prosperity)* [1982] 1 Lloyd's Rep. 617; *D/S A/S Idaho* v. *Colossus Maritime S.A. (The Concordia Fjord)* [1984] 1 Lloyd's Rep. 385, 388; *C.A. Venezolana de Navegacion* v. *Bank Line Ltd (The Roachbank)* [1988] 2 Lloyd's Rep. 337, 341.

22. *Schiffahrtsagentur Hamburg Middle East Line G.m.b.H.* v. *Virtue Shipping Corpn. (The Oinoussian Virtue) (No. 2)* [1981] 2 Lloyd's Rep. 300, 308.

23. *Petroleo Brasileiro S/A etc.* v. *Elounda Shipping Co. (The Evanthia M)* [1985] 2 Lloyd's Rep. 154, 157.

may be arrived at when an additional clause is so badly drafted in its structure and punctuation as to defy any conventional approach to the construction of contracts.[24]

The importance of a question of construction may be accentuated if it is shown to have provoked disagreement between experienced and respected arbitrators, or between judges or between arbitrators and judges.[25] So also if it questions accepted legal principle[26] or raises an implication as to the effect of a decision of an appellate court.[27] Where a question of law arises in the context of conflicting judicial decisions at first instance then it is almost by definition a question of law of general public interest.[28]

10.3.3.1.7 Although questions of construction tend to be dominant in the day-to-day functioning of the Commercial Court they are patently not exhaustive of the kinds of cases capable of falling within the statutory concept of questions of law of general public importance. Other questions of law may readily be so characterised, and this will be particularly the case when a profound question of law arises, or a question of principle is in issue, or a question of law arises in the character of a test case, or a disputed question of law arises in the context of conflicting judicial pronouncements.[29] The implied indemnity of a shipowner under a charterparty to recover for loss suffered by complying with the orders of charterers[30]; the principles governing the remuneration of a shipowner who performs services outside the terms of a charterparty at the request of the charterer[31]; and the legal basis of equitable set-offs in the context of time charterparties,[32] are examples of cases that have been considered as raising questions of general public importance to the shipping community. In contrast, the more a question of law embodies a material factual element the less the likelihood it will be perceived as a question of law of general public importance, and this will be particularly the case when the factual element is of a one-off nature.[33]

10.3.3.1.8 Although the question of general public importance will often be assessed against the backdrop of the broader judicial context, it is not necessarily the case that the concept is to be perceived as synonymous with, for example, an open question of law or a question of law in relation to which there exist conflicting judicial decisions or dicta. It is open for a question of general public importance to be recognised even against a settled legal backdrop. Thus in *The Leon*[34] Hobhouse J. was prepared to certify a question of law to be of general public importance notwithstanding

---

24. *Uni-Ocean Lines Pte. Ltd.* v. *C-Trade S.A. (The Lucille)* [1983] 1 Lloyd's Rep. 387, 399.
25. *Superfos Chartering A/S* v. *N.B.R. (London) Ltd. (The Saturnia)* [1984] 2 Lloyd's Rep. 366, 372–373.
26. *Empresa Cubana De Fletes* v. *Kissavos Shipping Co. S.A. (The Agathon) (No. 2)* [1984] 1 Lloyd's Rep. 183, 193.
27. *D/S A/S Idaho* v. *Colossus Maritime S.A. (The Concordia Fjord)* [1984] 1 Lloyd's Rep. 385, 388.
28. *Antaios Compania Naviera S.A.* v. *Salen Rederierna A.B. (The Antaios)* [1985] A.C. 191, 204. *Geogas S.A.* v. *Trammo Gas Ltd. (The Baleares)* [1991] 2 All E.R. 110 (C.A.). See also Chapter 5, para. 5.2.4.7.
29. Cf. *Filikos Shipping Corpn. of Monrovia* v. *Shipmair B.V. (The Filikos)* [1981] 2 Lloyd's Rep. 555, [1983] 1 Lloyd's Rep. 9 (C.A.); *Procter & Gamble Philippine Manufacturing Corpn.* v. *Kurt A. Becher G.m.b.H. & Co. K.G.* [1988] 2 Lloyd's Rep. 21.
30. *Uni-Ocean Lines Pte. Ltd.* v. *C-Trade S.A. (The Lucille)* [1983] 1 Lloyd's Rep. 387; [1984] 1 Lloyd's Rep. 244 (C.A.).
31. *Greenmast Shipping Co. S.A.* v. *Jean Lion et Cie S.A. (The Saronikos)* [1986] 2 Lloyd's Rep. 277.
32. *Leon Corporation* v. *Atlantic Lines and Navigation Co. Inc. (The Leon)* [1985] 2 Lloyd's Rep. 470, 477.
33. *Supra* n. 14.
34. *Supra* n. 32.

that there existed clear authority of the Court of Appeal and no case had been made out before the judge for disturbing the appellate decision.[35]

10.3.3.2 Other special reason

10.3.3.2.1 If it cannot be shown that the question of law to which the decision of the High Court relates is one of general public importance, a certificate may nonetheless be granted if alternatively it can be established that there exists "some other special reason" why the question of law should be considered by the Court of Appeal. The concept of "some other special reason" is not defined by the legislation, nor are any guidelines given. This renders it a "difficult and invidious"[1] issue. But it is clear that its meaning must extend upon the concept of "general public importance". Moreover given the policy of the 1979 Act, it is also probably true to assert that the judiciary should not come to the interpretation of "special reasons" with zeal and enterprise but should confine the concept within strict and limited boundaries.[2]

10.3.3.2.2 The courts have firmly come down against the notion that the fact a first tier judge is disagreeing with a respected and experienced arbitrator(s) constitutes a special reason.[3] Nor is the fact that the first tier appellate judicial decision has been made against the background of disparate arbitral awards likely to be perceived as a special reason.[4] Where, however, a first tier judge in determining an appeal is differing from the observations of another judge or the Court of Appeal uttered on the application for leave to appeal, this may constitute a special reason.[5] That this should be the case is however far from convincing, for observations made on an application for leave are necessarily provisional and of no binding authority. But given that the present practice is not to give reasons when granting leave to appeal,[6] the likelihood of such divergence is now increasingly rare. There is also judicial observation to the

---

35. On the facts of the case counsel had launched a radical attack on the law of equitable set-off which if justified would be of the greatest significance to the commercial community. But contrast *The Transcontinental Underwriting Agency S.R.L.* v. *Grand Union Insurance Co. Ltd. and P.T. Reasuransi Umum Indonesia* [1987] 2 Lloyd's Rep. 409, 415, where Hirst J. refused a certificate on the ground "that in my decision here I have done no more than apply fairly well established principles laid down by Courts of the highest authority".

1. *Damon Compania Naviera* v. *E.A.L. Europe Afrika Line G.m.b.H. (The Nicki R)* [1984] 2 Lloyd's Rep. 186, 190, per Bingham J.

2. The approach of Lloyd L.J. in *Pera Shipping Corpn.* v. *Petroship S.A. (The Pera)* [1985] 2 Lloyd's Rep. 103, 105, would appear to provide support for the statement in the text.

3. *Damon Cia Naviera* v. *E.A.L. Europe Afrika Line G.m.b.H. (The Nicki R)* [1984] 2 Lloyd's Rep. 186, 190; *Reardon Smith Line Ltd.* v. *Sanko Steamship Co. Ltd. (The Sanko Honour)* [1985] 1 Lloyd's Rep. 418, 422; *Pera Shipping Corpn.* v. *Petroship S.A. (The Pera)* [1985] 2 Lloyd's Rep. 103, 105, per Lloyd L.J., p. 108 per Griffiths L.J. *Geogas S.A.* v. *Trammo Gas Ltd. (The Baleares)* [1991] 2 All E.R. 110, 113, 115, per Dillon L.J., p. 123, per Leggatt L.J.

4. *International Sea Tankers Inc.* v. *Hemisphere Shipping Co. Ltd. (The Wenjiang) (No. 2)* [1983] 1 Lloyd's Rep. 400, 409.

5. *Bunge A.G.* v. *Sesostrad S.A. (The Alkeos C)* [1984] 1 Lloyd's Rep. 687, 691. On the facts of the case a certificate was given on the basis that the question of law was one of general public importance *and* that there were other special reasons. The latter were not further explained but on the facts the only possible special reason was a divergence of view between the judge determining the appeal and a different judge in giving leave to appeal. See also *International Sea Tankers Inc.* v. *Hemisphere Shipping Co. Ltd. (The Wenjiang) (No. 2)* [1983] 1 Lloyd's Rep. 400, 409, where a divergence of view between a judge and the Court of Appeal on the application for leave to appeal was not in principle dismissed as a possible special reason. But on the facts the effect of the divergence was countered by subsequent authority which had rendered the issue in question certain.

6. See Chapter 7, para. 7.3.3.

effect that the fact that the Court of Appeal on an application for leave to appeal expressed provisional views as to the importance of the question of law involved is not a special reason.[7]

10.3.3.2.3 It is not a special reason that a party or counsel disagrees with the view which the judge on appeal has come to and wishes to challenge that view, and is therefore anxious that the matter should be considered by the Court of Appeal.[8] Where there is both an appeal and cross-appeal, it is not a special reason that the question of law in issue is intimately linked with the legal question raised in the other party's appeal and with regard to which leave to appeal to the Court of Appeal has been granted.[9] It is also unlikely that the size of a claim may in itself amount to a special reason[10]; nor is it a special reason that the way in which the question of law has been determined by the High Court may have ramifications for the legal relations between the losing arbitrating party and his professional advisers.[11] In *The Lucille*[12] Bingham J. was of the opinion that where the conclusion which the judge has come to on appeal is of importance far transcending the particular case then this represents some other special reason why the legal issue in question should be considered by the Court of Appeal. The difficulty with this reasoning is that it tends to amalgamate the two limbs of section 1(7)(b), for if a question of law has this wider significance it is likely that it is equally capable of being perceived as a question of law of general public importance, in the sense considered earlier.

10.3.3.2.4 The approach adopted by Steyn J. in *The Alecos M*[13] suggests that a special reason may derive from the nature of the question of law in issue, even though the question is not one of general public importance. On the facts of the case the question of law in issue concerned the proper measure of damages for breach of contract. No question of principle was in issue and Steyn J. rejected a submission that the case raised a question of law of transcending importance to the mercantile community. On the contrary, the case concerned the application of first principles to a factual situation which was unlikely to recur. But Steyn J. proceeded to express the opinion that the application of first principles was always of great importance and of particular value in relation to the law governing damages. Although the point is not fully articulated, it seems that these latter considerations were analysed as establishing a special reason. Compared with earlier authorities and judicial dicta, this approach appears to represent a less restrictive approach to the concept of a special reason. It is also a debatable approach for it is at least arguable that the express legislative allusion to questions of law of general public importance excludes the possibility of any other category of question of law being a special reason and also encourages the view that a special reason is a reference to some contextual consideration distinct from the character of the question of law in issue.

---

7. *Italmare Shipping Co.* v. *Ocean Tanker Co. Inc. (The Rio Sun)* [1982] 1 Lloyd's Rep. 404, 409, per Parker J.
8. *Damon Compania Naviera* v. *E.A.L. Europe Afrika Line G.m.b.H. (The Nicki R)* [1984] 2 Lloyd's Rep. 186, 190.
9. *Superfos Chartering A/S* v. *N.B.R. (London) Ltd. (The Saturnia)* [1984] 2 Lloyd's Rep. 366, 373 (first instance).
10. *Babanaft International Co. S.A.* v. *Avant Petroleum Inc. (The Oltenia)* [1982] 2 Lloyd's Rep. 99, 105, per Donaldson L.J. (this was a case under s. 2(3) of the 1979 Act).
11. *Ibid.*
12. *Uni-Ocean Lines Pte. Ltd.* v. *C-Trade S.A. (The Lucille)* [1983] 1 Lloyd's Rep. 387, 399.
13. *Sealace Shipping Co. Ltd.* v. *Oceanvoice Ltd. (The Alecos M)* [1990] 1 Lloyd's Rep. 82, 83, 85.

10.3.3.2.5 It is difficult, if not impossible, to extract any general principle from the judicial deliberations to date. It may even be misguided to seek a governing principle, but to accept that the concept of a "special reason" is quintessentially a factual judgement made on the facts and circumstances of individual cases. The only point made clear by the language of section 1(7)(b) is that a "special reason" must relate to the question of law in issue and that it extends to the primary special reason relating to the general public importance of a question of law. Beyond these considerations there appears to exist no constraint and the authorities seem to suggest that a special reason may derive either from the nature and particular significance of the question of law in issue or from the factual matrix within which the question of law arises.

10.3.4 Leave of the High Court or Court of Appeal

10.3.4.1 In addition to a certificate, leave to appeal given by the High Court or Court of Appeal must also be obtained before an appeal may be brought. The fact that leave is necessary connotes a discretion. Neither court is obliged to give leave, but in any given circumstance may grant leave following the giving of a certificate. The drafting of section 1(7) makes it plain that paragraphs (a) and (b) are to be interpreted as distinct and cumulative provisions, with paragraph (a) extending upon the requirements of paragraph (b).[1] The fact that a certificate has been given under paragraph (b) will not result automatically in leave being granted under paragraph (a). Notwithstanding the granting of a certificate, leave may nonetheless validly be refused. But on the facts of any particular case it may of course be that once a certificate has been granted there also exist powerful reasons for giving leave.[2] The fact of the grant of a certificate offers at least some evidence that the question of law in issue merits consideration by the Court of Appeal.[3] Viewed in general terms, the object of the certificate is to characterise the question of law in issue as one worthy of consideration by the Court of Appeal; whereas the discretionary jurisdiction about the question of leave regulates the decision whether the particular and certified question of law should in the circumstances of the case be actually brought before the Court of Appeal. When leave is given, the appeal is confined to those questions of law specified in the order granting leave to appeal.

10.3.4.2 The existence of the discretion raises a question as to the factors to be taken into account in the exercise of the discretion to grant or refuse leave to appeal. In this connection there ought in principle to be no difference whether it is the High Court or the Court of Appeal which is being requested to grant leave. The Court of Appeal does however occupy a more distant and less involved position than the High Court and this in turn may have some influence on the respective referential frame-

---

1. *Supra.* See also *Uni-Ocean Lines Pte. Ltd.* v. *C-Trade S.A. (The Lucille)* [1983] 1 Lloyd's Rep. 387, 399, where the approach adopted by Bingham J. would appear to offer support for the statement in the text. Also *Empresa Cubana De Fletes* v. *Kissavos Shipping Co. S.A. (The Agathon) (No. 2)* [1984] 1 Lloyd's Rep. 183, 193, where Hobhouse J. considered certification and leave to be "two essential independent matters".

2. See, for example, *Athens Cape Naviera S.A.* v. *Deutsche Dampfschifffahrtsgesellschaft "Hansa" Aktiengesellschaft (The Barenbels)* [1984] 2 Lloyd's Rep. 388; *Greenmast Shipping Co. S.A.* v. *Jean Lion et Cie S.A. (The Saronikos)* [1986] 2 Lloyd's Rep. 277; *L'Office Cherifien des Phosphates and Unitramp S.A.* v. *Yamashita Shinnihon Steamship Co. Ltd. (The Boucraa)* [1993] 2 Lloyd's Rep. 149, 156.

3. *Geogas S.A.* v. *Trammo Gas Ltd. (The Baleares)* [1991] 2 All E.R. 110, 123, Leggatt L.J. See also *Charles E. Ford Ltd.* v. *AFEC Inc.* [1986] 2 Lloyd's Rep. 307, 316.

works of the two courts, particularly when the correctness of the decision of the first tier appellate judge is being assessed.[4] But the Act itself gives no express guidance on the exercise of the discretion and in consequence the governing criteria are to be extracted from the judicial development of the legislation, although even in this regard there is yet to emerge a comprehensive statement.[5]

10.3.4.3 The broad approach would appear to be clear and follows the general policy underlying the 1979 Act. The emphasis which the 1979 Act is interpreted as placing on the speedy finality of awards means that even when an appeal from an arbitration award to the High Court is allowed, the issue will customarily stop with the first tier judge and only in rare and exceptional circumstances will an on-appeal to the Court of Appeal be permitted. Even when an arbitration award therefore proves not to be final, the 1979 Act is nonetheless interpreted as manifesting a concern to see that the decision of the first tier appeal judge will in general be the final determination of the disputed question of law arising out of the award. Lord Diplock in *The Nema* established the basic tenet of policy in the following terms[6]:

Section 1(7) is another provision in favour of reaching finality as soon as possible; the stringent conditions imposed upon a further appeal from the judge to the Court of Appeal are clearly adopted from the provisions of the Criminal Appeal Act 1968 relating to appeals to the House of Lords in criminal matters—another field of law in which speedy finality is much to be desired.

This broad approach to the question of leave to appeal onward has been echoed consistently by later judges.[7] In particular Donaldson L.J. considered "[t]hat it is, and should be, more difficult to appeal to the Court of Appeal than to the High Court was confirmed by Lord Diplock in *The Nema*".[8] But it is equally clear that the general rule favouring finality is of a *prima facie* nature and may be displaced when circumstances prevail weighing in favour of permitting an on-appeal.

10.3.4.4 As for the question of appealability, or more mundanely which questions of law are fit and proper to bring before the Court of Appeal and which may be left to the final decision of a first tier judge, it would appear that the judicial discretion falls to be applied in the same manner and is based on similar criteria as are relevant to the exercise of discretion under section 1(3)(b), but subject to the overriding *prima facie* rule that the discretion of the first tier appeal judge should normally be final. In *The Agathon (No. 2)* Hobhouse J. summarised the approach to be adopted with particular and succinct clarity[9]:

---

4. Cf. *Marc Rich & Co. Ltd.* v. *Tourlotti Compania Naviera S.A. (The Kalliopi A)* [1987] 2 Lloyd's Rep. 268 (Note). The point is considered further *infra*.

5. Cf. *C.A. Venezolana de Navegacion* v. *Bank Line Ltd. (The Roachbank)* [1988] 2 Lloyd's Rep. 337, 341, where the comments of Mustill L.J., sitting as a single judge hearing the initial application for leave, are recorded in the judgment of Neill L.J.

6. *Pioneer Shipping Ltd. and Others* v. *B.T.P. Tioxide Ltd. (The Nema)* [1982] A.C. 724, 740.

7. *Aden Refinery Co. Ltd.* v. *Ugland Management Co. Ltd. (The Ugland Obo One)* [1987] 1 Q.B. 650, 667, per Mustill L.J., "the right of onward appeal has been greatly attenuated". See also *B.T.P. Tioxide Ltd.* v. *Pioneer Shipping Ltd. and Armada Marine S.A. (The Nema)* [1980] Q.B. 547, 560, where Lord Denning M.R. speaks of an appeal "[u]sually stopping at the judge, with no appeal to the Court of Appeal".

8. *Babanaft International Co. S.A.* v. *Avant Petroleum Inc. (The Oltenia)* [1982] 1 W.L.R. 871, 881–882.

9. *Empresa Cubana De Fletes* v. *Kissavos Shipping Co. S.A. (The Agathon) (No. 2)* [1984] 1 Lloyd's Rep. 183, 193. See also *Islamic Republic of Iran Shipping Lines* v. *P & O Bulk Shipping Ltd. etc.* [1985] 2 Lloyd's Rep. 494 (Note).

The second matter is the question of leave to appeal and I consider here I have to take into account the policy of finality in arbitration matters and I have to apply similar principles to those which were laid down in *The Nema* with regard to leave to appeal to the Judge.

10.3.4.5 The relevance of *The Nema/Antaios* guidelines to on-appeals under section 1(7) was subsequently implicitly accepted by Donaldson L.J. in *The Oltenia*[10] and explicitly by Neill L.J. in *The Roachbank*.[11] In the latter case, Neill L.J. observed,[12]

. . . it is important to bear in mind that in *The Nema* itself Lord Diplock, in the course of his speech, clearly indicated that when one is considering a further appeal to this Court under s. 1(7), the stringent conditions which apply to any application to the Court should be no less carefully observed at that stage than on the original application. That means that before it would be right for this Court to give leave, what one might call *The Nema* conditions would have to be satisfied and would have to be satisfied very fully.

In the upshot it would appear to be the case that the question of appealability must be determined against the backdrop of the statements of principle enunciated by the House of Lords in *The Nema* and *The Antaios*.[13]

10.3.4.6 The impact of the relevance of *The Nema/Antaios* guidelines is to introduce into the exercise of the discretion associated with the issue of leave to on-appeal considerations relating to the wider interest in the question of law in issue; the extent to which an appellate determination will contribute to the certainty and comprehensiveness of English law, particularly English commercial law; and an assessment of the correctness of the judgment of the first tier appeal judge, with the appropriate test of correctness varying with the character of the question of law. But in this regard it must again be emphasised that *The Nema/Antaios* guidelines are but guidelines and are applicable only in normal circumstances. Their adoption therefore does not preclude a regard to other and broader considerations in situations which cannot be considered ordinary.[14] Further, to incorporate the philosophy of *The Nema/Antaios* guidelines into the second appellate stage under the 1979 Act does not inevitably result in the associated discretion being exercised in the mirror image of the discretion associated with the first appellate link between arbitral awards and High Court. With the passage of time the context of the question of law may change and a different view taken of the importance and significance of the question of law, and of the benefits of a decision by a superior appellate court. Moreover, in relation to the issue of correctness, it is the decision of the first tier appeal judge which is under review and not the decision of the arbitrator or arbitral tribunal.[15]

10.3.4.7 An immediate consequence of the applicability of *The Nema/Antaios* guidelines is that the more the relevance of any question of law in issue is confined to the parties in dispute, as where the question of law concerns the construction of a one-off contract or contractual clause, or is otherwise a question of construction or other manner of legal question arising in one-off circumstances, or involves no point of substantial legal or practical significance and in which there exists no wider interest, the

---

10. *Supra*, note 8.
11. *C.A. Venezolana de Navegacion* v. *Bank Line Ltd. (The Roachbank)* [1988] 2 Lloyd's Rep. 337.
12. *Ibid* pp. 341–342.
13. *Islamic Republic of Iran Shipping Lines* v. *P & O Bulk Shipping Ltd.* [1985] 2 Lloyd's Rep. 494, per Mustill L.J.
14. *Geogas S.A.* v. *Trammo Gas Ltd. (The Baleares)* [1991] 2 All E.R. 110, 119, per Dillon L.J.
15. Considered further *infra*.

greater the reason for refusing leave.[16] On the other hand, the more likely it is that the question of law is of interest beyond the immediate arbitrating parties, as where the construction of a standard form contract or clause is in issue, or the question of law arises in the context of common and recurrent circumstances, or an important point of legal principle is raised by it, the more a first tier judge should consider granting leave,[17] while constantly bearing in mind that it is the policy of the legislation that normally most matters should not proceed beyond the first tier appeal judge.[18] In *The Nema*[19] Lord Diplock, reading beyond the express statutory language and signposting the general approach to be adopted, said of section 1(7) that it also "draws a significant distinction between a question of law which arises in connection with a 'one-off' case and a question of law of general importance to a substantial section of the commercial community such as may arise under standard term contracts".

10.3.4.8 So also leave will rarely be given when there is a substantial factual element or personal judgement entwined with the question of law. Questions of mixed fact and law and conclusions of law are now recognised to be matters largely for the decision of arbitrators and even when they enter the judicial system rarely will they progress beyond the first tier judge,[20] and the more particular the facts to the disputing parties, the firmer this approach is likely to be applied. In *The Nema*[21] the House of Lords was of the clear opinion that the first tier judge should not have certified and given leave to appeal under section 1(7). It will be recalled that the question of law in issue was the frustration of a divisible voyage charterparty in the context of factual circumstances unique to the particular contract and therefore an illustration of a question of law arising in the context of one-off circumstances. But whereas questions of contractual frustration may turn on the facts peculiar to individual situations, this is not universally the case. The Suez cases following the closure of the Suez Canal in

---

16. *Petroleo Brasileiro S/A etc.* v. *Elounda Shipping Co. (The Evanthia M)* [1985] 2 Lloyd's Rep. 154, 157; *Rederiaktiebolaget Gustav Erikson* v. *Dr Fawzi Ahmed Abou Ismail (The Herroe and Askoe)* [1986] 2 Lloyd's Rep. 281, 285, where the court treated as academic an application for leave to appeal based on facts which turned on the particular circumstances of the case and did not raise any point of general public importance.

17. *Tor Line A.B.* v. *Alltrans Group of Canada Ltd. (The TFL Prosperity)* [1982] 1 Lloyd's Rep. 617, 628; [1983] 2 Lloyd's Rep. 18 (C.A.); *Uni-Ocean Lines Pte Ltd.* v. *C-Trade S.A. (The Lucille)* [1983] 1 Lloyd's Rep. 387, 399; [1984] 1 Lloyd's Rep. 244 (C.A.); *D/S A/S Idaho* v. *Colossus Maritime S.A. (The Concordia Fjord)* [1984] 1 Lloyd's Rep. 385, 388; *Alfred C. Toepfer Schiffahrtsgesellschaft G.m.b.H* v. *Tossa Marine Co. Ltd.* [1984] 1 Lloyd's Rep. 635, 645; [1985] 2 Lloyd's Rep. 325 (C.A.); *Superfos Chartering A/S* v. *N.B.R. (London) Ltd. (The Saturnia)* [1984] 2 Lloyd's Rep. 366, 372–373; [1987] 2 Lloyd's Rep. 43 (C.A.); *Athens Cape Naviera S.A.* v. *Deutsche Dampfschiffahrtsgesellschaft "Hansa" Aktiengesellschaft and Another (The Barenbels)* [1984] 2 Lloyd's Rep. 388, 393; [1985] 1 Lloyd's Rep. 528 (C.A.); *Société Anonyme Marocaine de L'Industrie du Raffinage* v. *Notos Maritime Corpn. (The Notos)* [1985] 1 Lloyd's Rep. 149; [1985] 2 Lloyd's Rep. 334 (C.A.); *Charles E. Ford Ltd.* v. *AFEC Inc.* [1986] 2 Lloyd's Rep. 307, 316; *Transgrain Shipping B.V.* v. *Global Transporte Oceanico S.A. (The Mexico I)* [1988] 2 Lloyd's Rep. 149, 159.

18. *Phoenix Shipping Co.* v. *Apex Shipping Corpn. (The Apex)* [1982] 2 Lloyd's Rep. 407, 416; *Cargill Inc.* v. *Marpro Ltd. (The Aegis Progress)* [1983] 2 Lloyd's Rep. 570, 579.

19. *Pioneer Shipping Ltd. and Others* v. *B.T.P. Tioxide Ltd. (The Nema)* [1982] A.C. 724, 740. See also *Charles E. Ford Ltd.* v. *AFEC Inc.* [1986] 2 Lloyd's Rep. 307, 316.

20. *International Sea Tankers Inc.* v. *Hemisphere Shipping Co. Ltd. (The Wenjiang) (No. 2)* [1983] 1 Lloyd's Rep. 400, 409; *Pioneer Shipping Ltd. and Another* v. *B.T.P. Tioxide Ltd. (The Nema)* [1980] 1 Q.B. 547, 564–565, per Lord Denning M.R. (C.A.).

21. *Pioneer Shipping Ltd. and Others* v. *B.T.P. Tioxide Ltd. (The Nema)* [1982] A.C. 724, 740, per Lord Diplock, p. 746, per Lord Roskill.

1956 provide a clear illustration of this. The U.S. soya bean embargo of 1973 and the entrapment of shipping in the Shatt al Arab as a consequence of the Iran–Iraq conflict are more recent illustrations. Where there arise events of this kind, which have a wide potential impact and their effect on a large number of standard forms or similarly worded contracts is or is likely to be in issue, then different considerations may apply and in the circumstances there may be good reason, based on such considerations as the desirability of obtaining the guidance of a superior court and the need for legal certainty, for allowing the matter to proceed to the Court of Appeal. The same kind of considerations may assume a relevance when the precise question of law in issue relates to such matters as causation, remoteness, waiver, fundamental breach, or to concepts such as that of a safe port under a contract of affreightment.[22]

10.3.4.9 Beyond the nature of the question of law and the broad legal and factual environment in which the question is raised, the prospect of the likely success of an appeal will also be a relevant and important consideration. In many regards it may even be perceived as the central consideration. If the first tier judge or Court of Appeal is satisfied that the decision on the first appeal is right or it is highly probable that it is right, as, for example, when it is consistent with clear authority of an appellate court, there is little or no basis for inviting the Court of Appeal to reconsider the point, or it is at least primarily a question for the Court of Appeal itself to decide whether the matter is to go any further.[23] In such a circumstance the only likely justification for an appeal would be the desirability of a more contemporary decision of the Court of Appeal, as satisfying the demands for legal certainty or as representing an appropriate response to a current question of law of material importance.

10.3.4.10 The question of the correctness of the first appellate decision represents an invidious exercise for the first tier judge whose decision it is, for the judge is literally obliged to scrutinise the correctness of his own decision, in all probability immediately after making it, and for this purpose will be required to do so in a fresh and objective light. This might be thought of as demanding the impossible for hopefully no judge has anything but a firm belief in the correctness of his decisions, notwithstanding the familiar and engaging judicial humility suggesting the contrary.[24] But although the position may be awkward and unrealistic, it may not be quite impossible, for acting judiciously even a judge who is happily committed to the position he has adopted may nonetheless admit the force of argument which has been rejected and the possibility of an alternative final position being defensible. A judge who has decided in a particular way may continue to acknowledge the arguability of the contrary position and in making this concession admit to a degree varying with the precise circum-

---

22. Compare the discussion in Chapter 5, para. 5.2.6.

23. *Leon Corporation* v. *Atlantic Lines and Navigation Co. Inc. (The Leon)* [1985] 2 Lloyd's Rep. 470, 477; *Action S.A.* v. *Britannic Shipping Corpn. Ltd. (The Aegis Britannic)* [1985] 2 Lloyd's Rep. 481, 484, where Staughton J. on a question relating to the construction of a cesser clause in a voyage charterparty granted a certificate but refused to give leave because he considered himself to have applied the law laid down by the Court of Appeal over the last 94 years and if the matter was to go further it should be for the Court of Appeal to give leave. The application to the Court of Appeal was also refused, see [1987] 1 Lloyd's Rep. 119. See also *Marc Rich & Co. Ltd.* v. *Tourlotti Compania Naviera S.A. (The Kalliopi A)* [1987] 2 Lloyd's Rep. 268 (Note).

24. See the observations of Leggatt L.J. in *Geogas S.A.* v. *Trammo Gas Ltd. (The Baleares)* [1991] 2 All E.R. 110, 123.

stances of individual cases that his personal conclusion may be wrong.[25] But although the legislation in this regard creates a difficulty it also provides a mode of escape for all does not turn on the decision of the first tier appeal judge. Even if leave to appeal is refused by the first tier appeal judge following the first appeal, it remains open to the applicant to seek leave to appeal from the Court of Appeal.[26] The latter forum shares none of the difficulty of the first tier judge and stands in a detached and independent position. The Court of Appeal is appropriately positioned to arrive at a provisional and objective assessment of the correctness of the judgment of the first tier appeal judge.[27] An appeal judge who is happy with the correctness of the decision he has arrived at and therefore refuses leave to appeal, does so in the knowledge that the applicant for leave may approach the Court of Appeal directly, and may even consider this the right approach to adopt in the circumstances.[28] The fact that the appeal judge at first instance has no doubt about the correctness of his decision is not a conclusive reason for refusing leave to appeal if there are also present other valid considerations which emphasise the desirability of obtaining the decision of the Court of Appeal.[29] But even where the possibility of error is conceded and leave to appeal is given, it is not desirable that the basis of the doubt be articulated. The scrutiny of the judgment must be left to the appeal hearing.[30] The same principle applies to applications for leave to appeal made to the Court of Appeal.[31]

10.3.4.11 The relevance of the correctness of the decision of the first tier appeal judge begs the question as to the precise standard of scrutiny to be applied. Here again the philosophy of *The Nema/Antaios* guidelines exerts its influence, with the standard varying with the characterisation of the question of law in issue. In a one-off case the burden on the applicant is to show the first tier judge to be obviously wrong; and in a standard case, to adduce a strong *prima facie* case of error. It is this position that Neill L.J. in *The Roachbank*[32] appears to be endorsing in intimating that to succeed in obtaining leave to appeal from the Court of Appeal it is necessary for the applicant to show that the appeal judge was "either plainly wrong, or at any rate that there was a strong *prima facie* case for saying that he was in error". It would appear to

25. *Etablissements Soules et Cie* v. *Intertradax S.A.* [1991] 1 Lloyd's Rep. 378, 383, per Hobhouse J., "With regard to leave, I have formed a clear view about the right answer to this but I recognise that it is a point which is fairly arguable both ways, and on which the arbitrators, who are familiar with the trade in which they are arbitrating, have formed a view which is different from my own, both in the first instance and before the appeal board. Therefore I think it is appropriate that I should give leave to appeal." See also *Oriental Maritime Pte. Ltd.* v. *Ministry of Food, Government of the People's Republic of Bangladesh (The Silva Plana) etc.* [1989] 2 Lloyd's Rep. 371, 376, where Steyn J. refused leave to appeal because the opposing view was not realistically arguable. If it had been leave would have been given. *Alfred C. Toepfer Schiffahrtsgesellschaft G.m.b.H.* v. *Tossa Marine Co. Ltd. (The Derby)* [1984] 1 Lloyd's Rep. 635, 645, per Hobhouse J., "although I have arrived at my conclusion without doubt, it is a point which is fully arguable, in my view, on both sides . . . ".
26. *European Grain & Shipping Ltd.* v. *R. & H. Hall plc* [1990] 2 Lloyd's Rep. 139, 144, per Steyn J.
27. *Marc Rich & Co. Ltd.* v. *Tourlotti Compania Naviera S.A. (The Kalliopi A)* [1987] 2 Lloyd's Rep. 268 (Note); *Islamic Republic of Iran Shipping Lines* v. *P & O Bulk Shipping Ltd.* [1985] 2 Lloyd's Rep. 494 (Note).
28. Cf. *Comdel Commodities Ltd.* v. *Siporex Trade S.A. (No. 2)* [1988] 2 Lloyd's Rep. 590, 599; *Socap International Ltd.* v. *Marc Rich & Co. A.G.* [1990] 2 Lloyd's Rep. 175, 177.
29. *Alfred C. Toepfer Schiffahrtsgesellschaft G.m.b.H.* v. *Tossa Marine Co. Ltd. (The Derby)* [1984] 1 Lloyd's Rep. 635, 645.
30. *Marc Rich & Co. Ltd.* v. *Tourlotti Compania Naviera S.A. (The Kalliopi A)* [1987] 2 Lloyd's Rep. 268 (Note), 269, per Bingham L.J.
31. *Ibid.*
32. *Supra* pp. 342–343.

follow that where the question of law assumes the character of a conclusion of law or a question of mixed fact and law, leave to appeal will not be given unless it can be shown that the appeal judge has erred in principle or arrived at a determination which is plainly wrong or unreasonable.

10.3.4.12 The legitimacy of integrating the philosophy of *The Nema/Antaios* guidelines into the discretion arising under section 1(7)(a) was however rejected by a majority decision of the Court of Appeal in *The Baleares*.[33] The opinion of the majority was that *The Nema/Antaios* guidelines have no application to section 1(7)(a) and that the overriding test in each case is whether "the question of law is worthy of consideration by the Court of Appeal".[34] Incorporated into this test would be a consideration of such questions as whether there was sufficient doubt about the correctness of the judge's decision; whether the decision of the Court of Appeal would add significantly to the clarity and certainty of English commercial law; or whether there existed any other reason why the Court of Appeal should consider the question of law. While conceding that due regard must be had to the speedy finality of arbitration awards, the majority position was that section 1(7)(a) should not be construed in a special and restrictive way. It was wrong to set up section 1(3)(b) as a model or to use it as an analogy. Once an appeal from an award was allowed to enter the court system, there was thereafter no special restriction on on-appeals to the Court of Appeal, except for the terms of section 1(7), which were to be interpreted unrestrictively.[35] Dillon L.J.[36] was of the very opposite opinion and considered that in an ordinary case leave to appeal to the Court of Appeal ought not to be granted unless *The Nema/Antaios* guidelines were satisfied.

10.3.4.13 The majority view is not a wholly isolated approach and does appear to be in harmony with some aspects of earlier judicial behaviour and comment, although there must be caution not to overplay the significance of general judicial comment. In *The Chrysalis*[37] Mustill J. gave leave to appeal because he considered it appropriate that a higher court should have the opportunity to examine a question of law which bore on the general law of contract. In *Charles E. Ford Ltd.* v. *AFEC Inc.*[38] Bingham J. gave leave to appeal because "the point is one of substance and is one that the Court of Appeal might think is valuable to consider". Bingham L.J. in *The Kalliopi A*[39] gave leave to appeal not solely because he had real doubt about the correctness of the first tier judgment, but also because he considered there was advantage in having the authority of the Court of Appeal on the point in question, even if that ultimately supported the decision of the first tier judge. The difficulty however with the majority view in *The Baleares* is that it is difficult to reconcile with and may even be in conflict with the judgment of Lord Diplock in *The Nema* and the stream of restrictive jurisprudence which has followed on from it.[40] The dissenting opinion of Dillon L.J. appears to be more closely aligned with the policy of the 1979 Act and with authority, the

---

33. [1991] 2 All E.R. 110 (Leggatt and Ralph Gibson L.JJ., Dillon L.J. dissenting).
34. *Ibid*, Ralph Gibson L.J. p. 121; Leggatt L.J. p. 127.
35. The majority decision is fully stated in the judgment of Leggatt L.J.
36. *Ibid* p. 112 *et seq*.
37. [1983] 1 Lloyd's Rep. 503, 514.
38. [1986] 2 Lloyd's Rep. 307, 316.
39. [1987] 2 Lloyd's Rep. 268 (Note). See also *Esteve Trading Corporation* v. *Agropec International (The Golden Rio)* [1990] 2 Lloyd's Rep. 273, 281, per Evans J.
40. *Supra*. See also Chapter 1, para. 1.2.1.6.

combined effect of which is to adopt a very restrictive view of both appeals and on-appeals under the 1979 legislation.

10.3.4.14 Alongside the central considerations discussed above there are other more peripheral factors which may influence the exercise of the discretion to give or refuse leave to on-appeal. One such potential consideration is the impact the granting of leave may have on the arbitral process. This may be of particular relevance when the appeal is from an interim award, with the consequence that the arbitral process has yet to be concluded. The bringing of the initial appeal will have introduced delay and additional expense, and in the circumstances of any particular case the court may be unwilling to interrupt the arbitral process and compound matters further by granting leave to appeal to the Court of Appeal.[41] Arguments in favour of finality may assume greatest weight when there is evidence that the parties have by their conduct delayed the arbitral process beyond that necessarily incidental to an appeal.[42]

10.3.4.15 The sum of money involved in the dispute may also assume a significance, although the extent to which considerations of quantum may touch upon the exercise of judicial discretion is never easy to grasp with any sense of assurance. On a strict analysis quantum should be of little or no significance; it is not of itself an irresistible determinator of difficulty, importance and appealability. But it may nonetheless readily colour perceptions of gravity and importance, and channel judicial thought in the direction of the legitimate expectations of the parties and the demands of justice.[43] Quantum therefore can never be wholly ignored, although equally there always will exist uncertainty as to its precise potential impact. Ultimately all will turn on the facts and circumstances of individual cases. The fact however that the sum of money involved is relatively small is highly unlikely to preclude an otherwise appealable question of law being allowed to progress to the Court of Appeal.[44] On the other hand the fact that a substantial sum is in dispute may give emphasis to other factors inclining towards the giving of leave to appeal or help tilt the argument in a finely balanced situation. It would seem that only if *The Nema/Antaios* guidelines are ignored can quantum assume an independent force.[45]

10.3.4.16 The question also arises whether the wishes of the parties may have any role to play in the exercise of the discretion. Section 1(7) contains no express provision corresponding with section 1(3)(a) under which an appeal from an arbitration award to a first tier judge may be secured by the consent of all the parties to the reference. What therefore if both parties wish there to be a further appeal to the Court of Appeal: should the exercise of discretion uncritically follow the wishes of the parties or should there be retained a discretion to frustrate their mutual desire? The question

---

41. *Empresa Cubana de Fletes* v. *Kissavos Shipping Co. S.A. (The Agathon) (No. 2)* [1984] 1 Lloyd's Rep. 183, 193; *Leon Corporation* v. *Atlantic Lines and Navigation Co. Inc. (The Leon)* [1985] 2 Lloyd's Rep. 470, 477.

42. *Leon Corporation* v. *Atlantic Lines and Navigation Co. Inc. (The Leon)*, *ibid*.

43. Cf. *Geogas S.A.* v. *Trammo Gas Ltd. (The Baleares)* [1991] 2 All E.R. 110, 128, per Leggatt L.J., "The sum at stake is nearly £1.5m together with interest. Whichever party had lost before the judge would have wished to appeal."

44. *Charles E. Ford Ltd.* v. *AFEC Inc.* [1986] 2 Lloyd's Rep. 307, 316. See also *Empresa Cubana de Fletes* v. *Kissavos Shipping Co. S.A. The Agathon (No. 2)* [1984] 1 Lloyd's Rep. 183, 193; *Superfos Chartering A/S* v. *N.B.R. (London) Ltd. (The Saturnia)* [1984] 2 Lloyd's Rep. 366, 372–373.

45. Cf. *Geogas SA* v. *Trammo Gas Ltd. (The Baleares)*, *supra*, p. 114, where the reasons of Staughton L.J. in refusing leave on the initial application on the papers are incorporated into the judgment of Dillon L.J.

has not been squarely considered to date but there is a dictum of Donaldson L.J. expressing the opinion that "the wishes of the parties would no doubt be a very powerful factor".[46] Looking at the issue as one of first impression, it may be that when the parties are in agreement and desire an on-appeal a more generous approach may be adopted to the question of leave. Their mutual assent may operate to displace the policy of the legislation and with the primary concern shifting to a protection of the appellate process from misuse. Provided that the question of law is of a kind which it is proper and suitable for the Court of Appeal to consider there appears to be no obvious reason why the parties should be precluded from having their appeal. To apply the kind of test suggested by the majority in *The Baleares*[47] may even be appropriate in such a circumstance.

10.3.4.17 In *The Baleares*[48] the question also arose whether the discretion, when exercised by the Court of Appeal, should take into account the precise decision of the first tier appeal judge, whether it was one allowing or dismissing the appeal. The logic of the point is that a referral to the decision on the first appeal enables it to be ascertained whether the applicant for leave to on-appeal has before him a decision of the arbitral tribunal which he has expressly assented to or the substituted decision of an appeal judge which he did not expressly assent to. If on the first appeal the appeal was dismissed and the award affirmed it is the former: but if the first appeal succeeded and as a result the award was set aside or varied it is the latter. The reasoning then proceeds that there is greater cause for granting leave to appeal when the applicant is seeking to challenge the substituted decision of an appeal judge, rather than the original decision of an arbitral tribunal. The argument appears to have won over the majority in *The Baleares*, and in particular Leggatt L.J. was of the opinion that the position of the applicant was strengthened because "having won before the three experienced (and legally qualified) arbitrators, they have lost on appeal".[49] Dillon L.J.[50] however rejected the significance of the point and it may be that the legitimacy of the point is closely tied to the ultimate fate of the wider approach taken by the majority in the Court of Appeal. It may be added that the approach of the majority reposes uneasily with the firmly developed proposition that the fact that a first tier appeal judge is differing from an experienced arbitrator or tribunal does not represent a "special reason" for the purposes of section 1(7)(b).[51]

10.3.4.18 Although the giving or refusal of leave is a question of discretion, there would appear to exist a particular circumstance when the discretion is either materially constrained or even possibly overridden. The qualification exists when the disputed question of law arises in the context of conflicting judicial decisions at first instance, and in which circumstances there appears to be an obligation to give leave to on-appeal. This kind of situation may arise, for example, when a standard form contract has been construed differently by the courts on the various occasions it has come forward for consideration. Such a position is highly undesirable in itself and not conducive to the certainty which is so important in commercial transactions. In *The*

46. *Babanaft International Co. Ltd.* v. *Avant Petroleum Inc. (The Oltenia)* [1982] 1 W.L.R. 871, 881–882.
47. *Supra*, para. 10.3.4.12.
48. *Supra*, note 33.
49. *Supra*, p. 128.
50. *Supra*, p. 115.
51. *Supra*, para. 10.3.3.2.

Antaios[52] Lord Diplock laid down what appears to be a fairly firm rule to guide the lower courts whenever leave to appeal is sought with regard to a question of law that arises in such a context:

If there are conflicting decisions, the judge should give leave to appeal to the High Court, and whatever judge hears the appeal should in accordance with the decision that he favours give leave to appeal from his decision to the Court of Appeal with the appropriate certificate under section 1(7) as to the general public importance of the question to which it relates; for only thus can be attained that desirable degree of certainty in English commercial law which section 1(4) of the Act of 1979 was designed to preserve.

Whereas the primary rule was followed in cautious and qualified terms by the Court of Appeal in *The Ugland Obo One*, there was no similar reservation in relation to the secondary rule relating to on-appeals. Sir John Donaldson M.R. observed[53]:

Where there are conflicting decisions at first instance, a judge should give favourable consideration, in an appropriate case, to giving leave to appeal if, but only if, he is of the view that it was a proper case for the High Court not only to add another judicial decision, but, having done so, to grant a certificate and leave to appeal to [the Court of Appeal] under s. 1(7) of the 1979 Act. It is not in the interests of arbitrators or the commercial community that a situation should be allowed to continue in which there are conflicting decisions each of which binds all commercial arbitrators.

10.3.4.19 Lord Diplock in *The Antaios* made it plain that the rule applies only where there are conflicting decisions at first instance and that it does not extend to circumstances when there exist conflicting dicta.[54] The distinction between decisions (*ratio decidendi*) and dicta is well understood, although not always easy to make. But to draw such a firm distinction in the present context is far from being readily comprehensible for dicta frequently play a significant part in legal argument and are often incorporated into the reasoning of judges and arbitrators. Moreover experience suggests that conflicting dicta are as capable of producing uncertainty as conflicting decisions.[55] Nonetheless the distinction was accepted by the Court of Appeal in *The Roachbank*[56] and represented one of the reasons why on the facts of the case leave to appeal was refused. The negative aspect of the rule is however *prima facie* in nature and even when confronted with conflicting dicta there is a discretion to give leave in appropriate circumstances. Further, Lord Diplock said nothing of conflicting decisions or dicta of appellate courts and confronted with such a situation a strong argument in favour of granting leave is capable of being mustered, particularly where the effect of the conflict is to introduce uncertainty in any significant area of law.[57] Nor does the rule apply when there exist conflicting decisions of arbitrators.[58] But whether it is conflicting decisions or dicta which are in issue leave is only likely to be granted if the on-appeal will lead to the resolution of the conflict. If it would be possible for the Court of Appeal to decide the on-appeal without directly addressing the pre-existing

52. *Antaios Compania Naviera S.A.* v. *Salen Rederierna A.B. (The Antaios)* [1985] A.C. 191, 204.
53. *Aden Refinery Co. Ltd.* v. *Ugland Management Co. Ltd. (The Ugland Obo One)* [1987] 1 Q.B. 650, 661.
54. *Supra*, p. 204. See also Chapter 5, para. 5.2.4.7.
55. See Thomas, "*The Antaios: The Nema* Guidelines Reconsidered" [1985] J.B.L. 200–208.
56. [1988] 2 Lloyd's Rep. 337, 342.
57. Contrast *International Sea Tankers Inc.* v. *Hemisphere Shipping Co. Ltd. The Wenjiang (No. 2)* [1983] 1 Lloyd's Rep. 400, 409.
58. *Aden Refinery Co. Ltd.* v. *Ugland Management Co. Ltd. (The Ugland Obo One)*, *supra*, p. 661, per Sir John Donaldson M.R. See also Chapter 5, para. 5.2.4.9.

judicial conflict, this will represent a powerful reason for refusing leave, and the fact that if leave were granted the Court of Appeal would nevertheless be likely to express an opinion on the issue will of itself be insufficient to sway the deliberation towards giving leave to appeal.[59]

10.3.4.20 The factors identified above are obviously not necessarily exclusive and the weight to be given to any one or more of them will necessarily turn on the circumstances of individual cases. But as for the identification of other relevant factors it is possible, in view of the policy of the 1979 Act, that the courts may take a narrower view than might be taken on a question of leave arising outside the 1979 Act.[60] In considering the question of leave it would appear that the same approach is to be adopted by both the High Court and Court of Appeal,[61] but with regard to the assessment of certain criteria, such as the correctness of the decision of the first tier judge, it is clear that the Court of Appeal is in a happier position.[62] Judicial practice also supports the notion that some questions of leave are more appropriately decided by the Court of Appeal. A first tier judge may refuse leave not because it is without question the type of case that should not go forward but because if leave is to be given it is the type of case where leave should come from the Court of Appeal.[63] But the Court of Appeal should not grant leave merely because it provides an opportunity for developing an understanding of the proper practice to be followed under the 1979 Act, except when it is satisfied that the appeal is likely to succeed if brought.[64] In other words it is not open to the Court of Appeal to do what the House of Lords appears to have done in *The Nema* and *The Antaios*.

10.3.5 Leave subject to conditions

Although it is not expressed overtly in the language of section 1(7), in granting leave to appeal a court may attach conditions. The jurisdiction to make the giving of leave conditional was accepted by Robert Goff J., at first instance, in *The Nema*[1] and has never been questioned since. The precise source of the jurisdiction would seem not to have been closely considered. But in principle it would appear to arise either implicitly as a necessary adjunct to the discretion under section 1(7) or under the terms of section 28 of the Arbitration Act 1950, which is equally applicable to the 1979 Act.[2]

In each case the decision whether to give conditional or unconditional leave, and if the former, what manner of condition to attach, falls to be determined in the discretion of the court. In this the fundamental obligation is to act judiciously. In practice the most common conditions are likely to be a requirement that the applicant provide

59. *C.A. Venezolana de Navegacion* v. *Bank Line Ltd.* (*The Roachbank*) [1988] 2 Lloyd's Rep. 337.
60. *International Sea Tankers Inc.* v. *Hemisphere Shipping Co. Ltd. The Wenjiang (No. 2)*, *supra*.
61. For the approach to be adopted by a judge of the Court of Appeal, see, *Islamic Republic of Iran Shipping Lines* v. *P & O Bulk Shipping Ltd.* [1985] 2 Lloyd's Rep. 494 (Note).
62. *Empresa Cubana de Fletes* v. *Kissavos Shipping Co. S.A.* (*The Agathon*) (*No. 2*) [1984] 1 Lloyd's Rep. 183, 193.
63. *Empresa Cubana de Fletes* v. *Kissavos Shipping Co. S.A.* (*The Agathon*) (*No. 2*), *ibid*; *D/S A/S Idaho* v. *Colossus Maritime S.A.* (*The Concordia Fjord*) [1984] 1 Lloyd's Rep. 385, 388.
64. *Islamic Republic of Iran Shipping Lines* v. *P & O Bulk Shipping Ltd.* [1985] 2 Lloyd's Rep. 494 (Note).
1. *B.T.P. Tioxide Ltd.* v. *Pioneer Shipping Ltd. and Armada Marine S.A.* (*The Nema*) [1980] 2 Lloyd's Rep. 83, 94.
2. Section 7(1)(b). Section 28 of the 1950 Act is only applicable if the decision giving leave to appeal is perceived as "an order" of the court.

or arrange an acceptable personal or third party undertaking or security for the costs of the appeal[3] or for the amount of the claim.[4] But the jurisdiction extends more broadly and may touch upon the exercise of the appellate powers of the first tier appeal judge[5] or be utilised to ensure that the on-appeal process proceeds expeditiously and efficiently.[6]

10.3.6 Position of the Court of Appeal on substantive appeals

10.3.6.1 Once the procedural hurdles are negotiated, a certificate is given and leave granted the substantive question of law comes before the Court of Appeal. In reviewing the appealed question(s) of law the position of the Court of Appeal is analogous to that of a first tier appeal judge[1]. The appeal takes the form of argument on the question(s) of law in issue, with the Court of Appeal enjoying the same powers as are conferred on a first tier appellate judge under section 1(2).[2] The jurisdiction of the Court of Appeal is of course confined to those questions of law with regard to which a certificate and leave to appeal have been given, with the appellate court also bound by the facts found by the arbitral tribunal.[3]

Where an appeal is dismissed the effect is to affirm the decision and order of the first tier appellate judge.[4] The reasoning of the Court of Appeal may however be at variance from that of the first appeal judge,[5] and in affirming his decision the Court of Appeal may also choose to vary the precise order made.[6]

10.3.6.2 The primary effect of allowing an appeal is to set aside the judgment and order of the first tier appellate judge and to restore the decision of the arbitral tri-

---

3. In *Athens Cape Naviera S.A.* v. *Deutsche Dampfschiffahrtsgesellschaft "Hansa" Aktiengesellschaft and Another (The Barenbels)* [1984] 2 Lloyd's Rep. 388, 393, Sheen J. granted leave on condition that the applicant for leave provide security or give an undertaking from a reputable bank or other acceptable security for the costs of the appeal should it fail. See also *Portaria Shipping Co.* v. *Gulf Pacific Navigation Co. Ltd. (The Selene G)* [1981] 2 Lloyd's Rep. 180, 186, where Robert Goff J. gave leave to appeal subject to "the buyers' undertaking through their Counsel to provide security for costs of the appeal in a sum and a form reasonably acceptable to the sellers' solicitors . . .".

4. *B.T.P. Tioxide Ltd.* v. *Pioneer Shipping Ltd. and Armada Marine S.A. (The Nema)* [1980] 2 Lloyd's Rep. 83, 94, where Robert Goff J. accepted that a condition of this kind could be imposed but "that impecuniosity is not of itself a ground for imposing a condition of this kind".

5. *Indian Oil Corporation Ltd.* v. *Greenstone Shipping S.A. (The Ypatianna)* [1987] 2 Lloyd's Rep. 286, 299, where Staughton J. made an order of remission conditional on notice of appeal being given within the prescribed period of time.

6. *Etablissements Soules et Cie* v. *Intertradax S.A.* [1991] 1 Lloyd's Rep. 378, 383, per Hobhouse J., where a condition was attached requiring notice of appeal to be served within an abridged period of time and that any appeal be prosecuted with expedition.

1. See Chapter 9, para. 9.3.

2. Supreme Court Act 1981, s. 15(3). Considered in *Compagnie Européene des Pétroles* v. *Vitol B.V. (formerly T/A Vitol Trading B.V.)* [1988] 1 Lloyd's Rep. 577 (Note).

3. *Pagnan S.p.A.* v. *Tradax Ocean Transportation S.A.* [1987] 2 Lloyd's Rep. 342, 353, per Dillon L.J.

4. See, for example, *Pagnan S.p.A.* v. *Tradax Ocean Transportation S.A.* [1987] 2 Lloyd's Rep. 342; *Naviera Mogor S.A.* v. *Société Metallurgique de Normandie (The Nogar Marin)* [1988] 1 Lloyd's Rep. 412; *Motor Oil Hellas (Corinth) Refineries S.A.* v. *Shipping Corporation of India (The Kanchenjunga)* [1989] 1 Lloyd's Rep. 354; *Everglade Maritime Inc.* v. *Schiffahrtsgesellschaft Detlef von Appen m.b.H. (The Maria)* [1993] 2 Lloyd's Rep. 168.

5. See, for example, *Athens Cape Naviera S.A.* v. *Deutsche Dampfschiffahrtsgesellschaft "Hansa" Aktiengesellschaft etc. (The Barenbels)* [1985] 1 Lloyd's Rep. 528.

6. See, for example, *Eurico S.p.A.* v. *Philipp Brothers (The Epaphus)* [1987] 2 Lloyd's Rep. 215.

bunal.[7] But again the reasoning of the Court of Appeal may be different from that of the arbitration tribunal.[8] In allowing an appeal it is also open to the Court of Appeal to vary an arbitration award,[9] although this power is likely to be exercised restrictively and in the kind of circumstances previously considered in relation to the appellate powers of a first tier judge.[10] Section 1(8) continues to be applicable when a variation is directed following an appeal to the Court of Appeal, with the result that the varied award takes effect as if it were the award of the arbitration tribunal.

It is also within the power of the Court of Appeal to remit an award to the reconsideration of an arbitration tribunal, together with the opinion of the appellate court on the question of law which is the subject of the appeal. Remission is again a power likely to be utilised selectively and with the Court of Appeal having regard to the general considerations developed about the exercise of the power by first tier appellate judges.[11] Where an award is remitted the tribunal must make its reconsidered award within three months of the date of the order, unless the order directs otherwise.[12]

10.4 ON-APPEALS—CONSIDERATIONS OF PRACTICE

10.4.1 Certificate

10.4.1.1 The granting of a certificate under section 1(7)(b) is in the sole jurisdiction of the first tier appellate judge. From his decision there exists no appeal: nor may an alternative application be made to the Court of Appeal. Also, provided the judge has made a legitimate decision in the eyes of the law there does not exist any mode of non-appellate review of his decision.[1]

The object of the certificate is to define the basis and boundaries of any future appeal.[2] But the certificate does not of itself secure an appeal: for this to occur it must be accompanied by the granting of leave.[3] Given its purpose it is highly desirable for the certificate to identify with precision the question(s) of law certified.[4] Failure to do

---

7. See, for example, *Seacrystal Shipping Ltd.* v. *Bulk Transport Group Shipping Co. Ltd. (The Kyzikos)* [1987] 2 Lloyd's Rep. 122; *Marc Rich & Co. Ltd.* v. *Tourlotti Compania Naviera S.A. (The Kalliopi A)* [1988] 2 Lloyd's Rep. 101; *State Trading Corporation of India* v. *M. Golodetz Ltd. etc.* [1989] 2 Lloyd's Rep. 277; *Sealace Shipping Co. Ltd.* v. *Oceanvoice Ltd. (The Alecos M)* [1991] 1 Lloyd's Rep. 120; *Kurt A. Becher G.m.b.H. & Co. K.G.* v. *Roplak Enterprises S.A. (The World Navigator)* [1991] 2 Lloyd's Rep. 23; *Geogas S.A.* v. *Trammo Gas Ltd. (The Baleares)* [1993] 1 Lloyd's Rep. 215.
8. See, for example, *Colonial Bank* v. *European Grain & Shipping Ltd. (The Dominique)* [1988] 1 Lloyd's Rep. 215.
9. See, for example, *Vagres Compania Maritima S.A.* v. *Nissho-Iwai American Corpn. (The Karin Vatis)* [1988] 2 Lloyd's Rep. 330; *Sig. Bergesen D.Y. & Co.* v. *Mobil Shipping and Transportation Co. (The Berge Sund)* [1993] 2 Lloyd's Rep. 453, 463.
10. See Chapter 8, para. 8.9.
11. See Chapter 8, para. 8.10. See, also, *Vagres Compania Maritima S.A.* v. *Nissho-Iwai American Corpn. (The Karin Vatis), supra*, where the Court of Appeal remitted the issue of interest in default of agreement; *Ellis Shipping Corpn.* v. *Voest Alpine Intertrading (The Lefthero)* [1992] 2 Lloyd's Rep. 109, where case remitted for a fresh calculation of demurrage due.
12. Section 1(2).
1. Cf. *Aden Refinery Co. Ltd.* v. *Ugland Management Co. Ltd. (The Ugland Obo One)* [1987] 1 Q.B. 650, 666, per Mustill L.J.
2. *Cargill UK Ltd.* v. *Continental UK Ltd.* [1989] 2 Lloyd's Rep. 290, 295, per Parker L.J.
3. *Infra.*
4. See, for example, *Geogas S.A.* v. *Trammo Gas Ltd. (The Baleares)* [1991] 2 All E.R. 110, 113 (C.A.).

so will render the appeal process uncertain and may place the Court of Appeal in a position of difficulty in the event of a later application for leave to appeal being made to it.[5] In the final analysis it is the responsibility of counsel to invite the first tier judge to make it clear which question(s) of law is being certified.

A certificate may be particular or general. It may relate to a specific or specified questions of law[6] or it may relate to all the questions of law in issue. Where the latter approach is adopted care must be taken to ensure that all the questions of law are capable of being identified clearly from the judgment of the first tier judge.[7] The need for precision is such that it would be helpful if the judge was to indicate not only the questions of law which are certified but also the questions of law excluded from the certificate.[8]

10.4.1.2 Although the certificate defines the scope of the question(s) of law to be considered by the Court of Appeal it would appear that it does not necessarily place a corresponding constraint on the scope of the argument and exclude consideration of other aspects of the judgment appealed. Parker L.J., *obiter dictum*, has presented the general guideline in the following terms[9]:

I accept that the clear purpose of the section is to limit any appeal and if, for example, the point certified went to liability only it would not in my view be open to an appellant to seek to appeal on damages. It is, however, clear that argument on a certified point and any decision thereon may be so interlinked with, or have such consequences upon, other aspects of the decision appealed from that it would be wrong to conclude that the point or points certified are to be argued in strict isolation. It must be left to the Court of Appeal to decide in each case how far outside the certified point the parties may legitimately range.

A certificate is most likely to be sought immediately following the judgment of the first tier judge on the appeal from the arbitration award. Each of the parties may be granted a certificate. An application for a certificate may only be made once. If the application on this occasion is refused the court has no jurisdiction to entertain a renewed application, even if made within the relevant time period.[10]

10.4.2 Leave to appeal

10.4.2.1 Leave to appeal may be sought from the first tier appellate judge or the Court of Appeal. In practice it is highly likely that the application will be made in the first instance to the first tier judge concurrently with the application for a certificate. Only if leave is refused at this stage will it become necessary to make a renewed appli-

---

5. See, for example, *Islamic Republic of Iran Shipping Lines* v. *P & O Bulk Shipping Ltd.* [1985] 2 Lloyd's Rep. 494 (Note).

6. See, for example, *Indian Oil Corpn. Ltd.* v. *Greenstone Shipping S.A. (The Ypatianna)* [1987] 2 Lloyd's Rep. 286, 298–299. *C.A. Venezolana de Navegacion* v. *Bank Line Ltd. (The Roachbank)* [1988] 2 Lloyd's Rep. 337, 341.

7. *Vinava Shipping Co. Ltd.* v. *Finelvet A.G. (The Chrysalis)* [1983] 1 Lloyd's Rep. 503, 513–514; *Comdel Commodities Ltd.* v. *Siporex Trade S.A. (No. 2)* [1988] 2 Lloyd's Rep. 590, 599.

8. Cf. *Indian Oil Corporation Ltd.* v. *Greenstone Shipping S.A. (The Ypatianna)* [1987] 2 Lloyd's Rep. 286, 298–299, per Staughton J.

9. *Cargill UK Ltd.* v. *Continental UK Ltd.* [1989] 2 Lloyd's Rep. 290, 295.

10. *National Westminster Bank plc* v. *Arthur Young McClelland Moores & Co. (a firm) (No. 2)* [1991] 3 All E.R. 21.

cation to the Court of Appeal.[1] Where leave is given it is necessarily limited to the certified questions of law.[2]

Leave may be granted to each of the parties to an arbitration, so that cross-appeals from the decision of the first tier appeal judge may come before the Court of Appeal.[3] A party victorious before the first tier appeal judge and who wishes to protect his judgment by adducing alternative argument in its support in the event of the other party being given leave to appeal may do so through a respondent's notice.[4]

10.4.2.2 When leave to appeal is sought from the Court of Appeal the application will usually represent a distinct proceeding from the hearing of the substantive appeal.[5] Only very rarely will the two proceedings be merged with the Court of Appeal hearing full argument and thereafter determining the question of leave according to the view it takes of the merits of the substantive appeal.[6] The likelihood of merger is probably greatest when application for leave is made to a full Court of Appeal,[7] although even in this kind of situation it is not inevitable.

Application for leave will in the first place be considered *ex parte* and on documents only by a single judge of the Court of Appeal.[8] The appeal judge may determine the application himself and grant or refuse the application, or direct that the application be renewed in open court, either *ex parte* or *inter partes*,[9] or refer the application to a full Court of Appeal.[10] The latter course is only likely to be followed when an application raises important questions of principle, such as the proper criteria to be borne in mind by an appeal judge in considering an application for leave.[11] In referring the matter to a full Court of Appeal, the appeal judge may also give directions relating to the hearing of the substantive appeal in the event of leave to appeal being granted, in particular whether the full appeal will immediately follow the application for leave or be heard at a later date.[12] If the initial application made *ex parte* on documents to a single appeal judge is refused, the unsuccessful party has the right to renew the application in open court.[13] On the other hand, if the application is granted, any party

---

1. See further, *infra*. Note also R.S.C. Order 59, rule 14(4).
2. *Arab Maritime Petroleum Transport Co.* v. *Luxor Trading Corpn. and Geogas Enterprise S.A. (The Al Bida)* [1987] 1 Lloyd's Rep. 124, 125, per Parker L.J.
3. See, for example, *Pagnan S.p.A.* v. *Tradax Ocean Transportation S.A.* [1986] 2 Lloyd's Rep. 646; [1987] 2 Lloyd's Rep. 342 (C.A.); *Motor Oil Hellas (Corinth) Refineries S.A.* v. *Shipping Corpn. of India (The Kanchenjunga)* [1987] 2 Lloyd's Rep. 509, 519.
4. R.S.C. Order 59, rule 6.
5. *Action S.A.* v. *Britannic Shipping Corpn. Ltd. (The Aegis Britannic)* [1987] 1 Lloyd's Rep. 119, 120, per Dillon L.J.
6. *Ibid*.
7. See, for example, *Belgravia Navigation Co. S.A.* v. *Cannor Shipping Ltd. (The Troll Park)* [1988] 2 Lloyd's Rep. 423 (C.A.).
8. R.S.C. Order 59, rule 14(2).
9. *Ibid*.
10. R.S.C. Order 59, rule 14(10).
11. *C.A. Venezolana de Navegacion* v. *Bank Line Ltd. (The Roachbank)* [1988] 2 Lloyd's Rep. 337, 341; *Geogas S.A.* v. *Trammo Gas Ltd. (The Baleares)* [1991] 2 All E.R. 110, 114, per Dillon L.J. for an account of contemporary practice. Contrast *Compagnie Europeene des Petroles* v. *Vitol B.V. (formerly T/A Vitol Trading B.V.)* [1988] 1 Lloyd's Rep. 577 (C.A.).
12. See, for example, *Marc Rich & Co. Ltd.* v. *Tourlotte Compania Naviera S.A. (The Kalliopi A)* [1987] 2 Lloyd's Rep. 268 (Note); *Geogas S.A.* v. *Trammo Gas Ltd. (The Baleares), ibid.; C.A. Venezolana de Navegacion* v. *Bank Line Ltd. (The Roachbank), ibid.*
13. R.S.C. Order 59, rule 14(2a).

affected by the appeal has the right to have the grant of leave reconsidered *inter partes* in open court.[14]

A single judge of the Court of Appeal or the full court will determine the application on the basis of skeleton arguments presented in advance and read by the court before the hearing, together with relevant documents and oral argument at the hearing.[15] An application for leave may be heard *ex parte*.[16]

10.4.3 Time limits

It is highly advisable for an application for leave to appeal to be made not later than four weeks after the date on which the judgment of the court below was sealed or otherwise prefected.[1] An application for leave to appeal is made when it has been set down in the Civil Appeals Office.[2] The advantage of applying within the four week period is that in the event of leave to appeal being granted, the time for serving notice of appeal is automatically extended by seven days from the grant of leave to appeal, thereby making it unnecessary to apply for an extension of time.[3] The same position does not appertain when the application for leave to appeal is made outside the four week period.

10.4.4. Costs

10.4.4.1 In determining an appeal the Court of Appeal also has a discretionary jurisdiction to dispose of the costs of the on-appeal, and in the exercise of its discretion may also adjust any order of costs made by the first tier appellate judge.

When an appeal is successful the traditional order is for the appellant to be awarded costs "here and below", indicating the proceedings before the first tier appeal judge and the Court of Appeal.[1] In the event of an appeal being unsuccessful, the usual order is for the respondent to be given the costs of the on-appeal, with the order of costs made by the first tier appeal judge left undisturbed.

But the order for costs is in all instances discretionary and variations on the usual orders may be justified by the facts and circumstances of individual cases.[2]

10.4.4.2 When an application for leave to appeal is granted the question of costs is,

---

14. R.S.C. Order 59, rule 14(2b).
15. For the necessity and form of skeleton arguments see: *Practice Direction (Court of Appeal: Presentation of Argument)* [1989] 1 W.L.R. 281; *Practice Direction (Court of Appeal: Skeleton Argument Time Limits)* [1990] 1 W.L.R. 794. See also *The Supreme Court Practice 1993*, para. 59/9/15 *et seq.*; R.S.C. Order 59, rule 14(1A).
16. R.S.C. Order 59, rule 9.
1. R.S.C. Order 59, rule 4(1).
2. See *Supreme Court Practice 1993*, para. 59/4/6.
3. R.S.C. Order 59, rule 4(3).
1. See, for example, *State Trading Corporation of India Ltd.* v. *M. Golodetz Ltd.* (*Now Transcontinental Affiliates Ltd.*) [1989] 2 Lloyd's Rep. 277, 289 (C.A.); *Transgrain Shipping B.V.* v. *Global Transporte Oceanico S.A.* (*The Mexico I*) [1990] 1 Lloyd's Rep. 507, 516 (C.A.).
2. *Naviera Mogor S.A.* v. *Société Métallurgique de Normandie* (*The Nogar Marin*) [1988] 1 Lloyd's Rep. 412, 422 (appeal dismissed and order made that costs below to remain undisturbed, but respondents to have only two-thirds of their costs of the appeal).

in the absence of special circumstances, likely to be deferred and treated as part of the costs of the full appeal. Only when an application is rejected is it likely that a separate order for costs will be made and in ordinary circumstances the unsuccessful applicant will be compelled to bear the costs of the application.

PART III

MATTERS INCIDENTAL AND RELATING TO APPEALS FROM ARBITRATION AWARDS

CHAPTER 11

REASONED AWARDS
SECTION 1(5) AND (6)

11.1 INTRODUCTION

11.1.1 There has not been developed within the sphere of English jurisprudence any ubiquitous and unambiguous doctrine demanding that all judgments, awards and other determinations given within the province of the administration of justice must be reasoned. In the result the reach of doctrine is uncertain and the relationship between theory and practice ambiguous. In constitutional strictness the general rule is that a puisne judge need not give reasons for his judgment but only in exceptional circumstances would a judge find justification for not giving reasons.[1] The rule of judicial practice is that all judgments must be reasoned unless there exists compelling justification for not giving reasons. Nor is a duty to give reasons perceived as an inseverable facet of the doctrine of natural justice.[2] As a consequence the extent to which a public tribunal or office holder is obliged to give reasons is a troublesome and uncertain issue,[3] although on occasions the question may be governed by statute.[4]

11.1.2 Arbitration fora are private, domestic and consensual tribunals which have developed within a jurisprudential environment in which a positive duty to give reasoned awards has been absent. Although such a duty may and often is established by contract, and even though as a matter of practice reasons are frequently given voluntarily, neither the common law nor legislative developments to date have obliged the giving of reasoned awards.[5] At common law reasons are not perceived as an essential precondition to the substantive validity of an award and an arbitrator or umpire who fails to give reasons is not guilty of misconduct, for the omission does not transgress any implied duty. Although procedural fairness is a central concept in English arbitral law it has never extended to embrace a duty to give reasoned awards. The English position stands in sharp contrast to that which prevails in many foreign

---

1. See generally, Lord Justice Bingham, "Reasons and Reasons for Reasons: Difference Between a Court Judgment and an Arbitration Award" (1988) 4 Arb. Int. 141; Bridge, "The Duty to Give Reasons for Decisions as an Aspect of Natural Justice", in *Fundamental Duties*, Ed. Lasok *et al.*
2. *R* v. *Gaming Board for Great Britain, ex parte Benaim* [1972] Q.B. 417; *McInnes* v. *Onslow Fane* [1978] 3 All E.R. 211; *Payne* v. *Lord Harris* [1981] 1 W.L.R. 754; *Public Service Board of New South Wales* v. *Osmond* (1986) 60 A.L.J.R. 209; *R.* v. *Civil Service Appeal Board, ex parte Cunningham* [1991] 4 All E.R. 310 (C.A.); Wade, *Administrative Law* (6th edn.) p. 547.
3. Flick, "Administrative Adjudications and the Duty to Give Reasons: A Search for Criteria" [1978] P.L. 16; Lord Woolfe, *Protection of the Public—A New Challenge*, pp. 92–97 (Hamlyn Lectures: Forty-First Series). See also *R* v. *Secretary of State ex p. Harrison* [1988] 3 All E.R. 86.
4. For example, Tribunals and Inquiries Act 1992, s.10. For consideration of earlier legislation to the same effect, see *Mountview Court Properties Ltd.* v. *Devlin* (1970) 21 P. & C.R. 689.
5. *Infra.*

jurisdictions where "speaking" or "motivated" awards are obligatory and by virtue of the disparity there exists at least some attendant risk that any attempt to enforce an unreasoned English award in a foreign jurisdiction may fail or be resisted by reference to the doctrine of *ordre public*.[6]

11.1.3 To an extent, the absence of reasons is more consistent with private and consensual arbitration than with the public arm of the administration of justice. Arbitration is a manifold and various institution functioning in a variety of spheres and with regard to which the arbitrating parties may harbour a range of expectations. The sheer scope and variety of the institution probably renders it unwise to lay down an immutable and ubiquitous doctrine of whatever content in relation to reasons.[7] If the parties wish sudden death arbitration it is undesirable and without justification for the law to intervene and ordain a reasoned award and thereby also inflict delay and additional expense. On occasions the character of the dispute to be resolved is just not readily susceptible to reasoned explanation. Where the dispute is one of fact an arbitrator can often say no more than that he prefers the evidence of a particular witness to that of another. In a quality dispute, often characterised as look-sniff arbitration, a trade arbitrator draws on his expertise and judgement founded on long experience and which he would no doubt find difficult to articulate.[8] Psychological responses such as "hunch" and "feel" have equal roles to play in both litigation and arbitration and again come to the fore when adjudicatorial reactions and conclusions are incapable of being sustained by precise factual explanation.[9] There is therefore much to be found in the total arbitral experience that strongly supports the proposition that there should be no general and invariable rule obliging arbitrators to give reasons for their awards.

11.1.4 But equally this general approach must not be allowed to blinker the recognition of the potential value of reasons and also that there are circumstances when reasons may be both feasible and highly desirable. If the parties wish a reasoned award it is clearly right that they be able to translate their desire into a contractual mandate. If arbitrators are minded to volunteer reasons they should be encouraged in the practice except where the contractual mandate stipulates the contrary or there are present special considerations. In the so-called technical arbitrations the arbitral process follows judicial procedure closely with questions of law, documentary construction and fact brought forward for determination by professional arbitrators, often legally trained, but otherwise always very experienced in the practice of arbitration, following the presentation of parol and documentary evidence, and argument advanced by lawyers on behalf of the parties. Within this particular kind of arbitral environment the claim for reasoned awards is at its highest and may even be perceived as an integral facet of the arbitral process.

11.1.5 The precise practice that prevails with regard to the making of reasoned awards is impossible to gauge because of the absence of any kind of reliable record. In general terms it might be anticipated that the giving of reasons is probably a function of the status of the arbitrator, the nature of the dispute and the character of the arbi-

6. Report on Arbitration, *supra*, para. 7. See Appendix A.
7. Lord Diplock, "The Case Stated—Its Use and Abuse" (1978) 44 Arbitration 107, 111.
8. Bingham, "Reasons and Reasons for Reasons: Differences Between a Court Judgment and an Arbitration Award", *supra*, p. 145, "tapioca pellets either are, in the experienced judgment of a trade arbitrator, of fair average quality or they are not; whichever way his opinion goes there is probably not much that he can usefully add by exegesis".
9. Cf. *The Chrysalis* [1983] 1 Lloyd's Rep. 503, 513.

tration. Professional arbitrators and judge-arbitrators may view the making of reasoned awards as an aspect of their professionalism; whereas trade and lay arbitrators may be unenthusiastic and consider themselves ill-trained and unqualified for the task. The less a dispute is concerned with fact, questions of quality and commercial practice, and the more it is concerned with questions of law, mixed fact and law, and conclusions of law, the more likely, or, at least, the more justified, a reasoned award. The two factors here identified as increasing the likelihood of a reasoned award are in turn closely associated with technical arbitrations, which may be *ad hoc* or institutional in character. A feature of the latter is that provision is sometimes made for internal appeals and this phenomenon again emphasises the need for the first tier award to be reasoned. But whereas the reality of prevailing practice may be beyond precise definition and analysis there has nonetheless prevailed a general impression that the "general pattern is . . . that English awards are given without reasons"[10] and this impression has in turn led to the judgement that reasoned awards are not as prevalent as they ought to be. Some of the reasons for the reluctance to give reasoned awards may be deducible from the preceding discussion, but it is further generally agreed that a principal historical cause for the reluctance was the emergence at common law of a mode of judicial review based on error of law on the face of an award.[11]

11.1.6 The emergence of the common law jurisdiction sounded a clear warning that the more greatly the reasoning of arbitrators was revealed in the substance of awards the greater the risk that errors of law might be unearthed and the finality of awards disturbed by judicial review. The making of reasoned awards could with some justification be viewed as giving hostages to fortune.[12] But the risk was capable of circumvention by virtue of the absence of any statutory or common law duty to provide reasons. Quite simply, the arbitrator was mandated or of his own volition gave nothing more sophisticated than a bare award which contained no record of his reasoning, a form of award described as a *dispositif* in some jurisdictions. The practice avoided the risk of judicial review for error of law on the face of the award but was otherwise potentially unsatisfactory for it denied the parties any knowledge of the basis of the arbitrator's decision. The answer to this particular problem was in turn found in the practice of giving extra-award reasons. A statement of the reasons of the arbitrator was set out in a separate document issued at the same time or quickly following the publication of an award and with the document not intended to be part of the award, with the intention invariably buttressed by an express rubric to that effect. Such a practice was perfectly valid and lives on notwithstanding that the ground of judicial review that spawned it has been erased by the Arbitration Act 1979, and even though the practice may now be perceived as contrary to the policy of the 1979 Act. Prevailing arbitral practice has in fact developed yet a step further with extra-award reasons also invariably made subject to what may be described a "restricted reasons agreement", the effect of which is to preclude any allusion to the extra-award reasons for the purpose of any manner of legal proceeding on or connected with the award.[13]

---

10. Report on Arbitration, *supra*, para. 6. Note also *Glafki Shipping Co. S.A.* v. *Pinios Shipping Co. No. 1 (The Maira) (No. 2)* [1985] 1 Lloyd's Rep. 300, where the Court of Appeal considered the award before the court, which was fully reasoned and with relevant documents incorporated, unusual.

11. Lord Diplock, "The Case Stated—Its Use and Abuse", *supra*. See also Chapter 1, para. 1.4.1.

12. Cf. *Trave Schiffahrtsgesellschaft m.b.H. & Co. K.G.* v. *Ninemia Maritime Corporation (The Niedersachsen)* [1986] Q.B. 802, 808B, per Sir John Donaldson M.R.

13. See *infra*, para. 11.2.6.

In its Report on Arbitration the Commercial Court Committee summarised the position prevailing at the time of its Report in the following terms[14]:

Under English law the Courts have jurisdiction to set aside any arbitral award, if it appears from the award itself or from documents incorporated in the award that the arbitrator has reached some erroneous conclusion of fact or law. The Court cannot correct the error. It can only quash the award leaving the parties free to begin the arbitration again.

As a result of the existence of this power, English arbitrators customarily avoid giving any reasons for their awards, confining themselves to reciting that a dispute has arisen between the parties and that they award that A should pay B a specified sum. Where the parties wish to know the reasons for the award or the arbitrator wishes to give them, this is achieved by giving the reasons in a separate document which expressly states that it is not part of the award and by obtaining an undertaking from the parties that they will not seek to refer to or use the reasons for the purposes of any legal proceedings. The general pattern is, however, that English awards are given without reasons.

11.1.7 Whereas the emergence of the common law jurisdiction had a significantly negative impact on the making of reasoned awards, the same cannot be said of the statutory special case procedure, although the statutory procedure offered little compensation by virtue of its limited application and the form of practice which developed about the procedure. The stating of an award as a special case only arose when agreed to by an arbitrator or umpire, or at the direction of the High Court. It necessarily required some manner of written award, which came to assume a common stylistic format, by which a question of law or the provisional or alternative opinion of an arbitral tribunal on a question of law was communicated to the High Court for its determination. To this extent an award stated as a special case was quite distinct from a bare award. Yet it was not a reasoned award in the purest meaning of that term, for it did not in strictness set out the reasoning of an arbitral tribunal. In its essentials it confined itself to a statement of the emergence of the dispute and associated arbitration, the evidence and assertions of the parties, the factual findings of the tribunal and the question(s) of law to be considered by the court.[15]

11.1.8 Against this backdrop of historical development and practice it is widely predicted that the 1979 Act will effect change with reasoned awards being encouraged and consequently becoming more prevalent, even possibly the normal practice.[16] The impact the Act has actually had to date in this regard is again impossible to assess because of the absence of firm data. But if the Act does achieve this effect it will be as an indirect result of its provisions, for the Act does not establish a positive general duty to give reasons.[17] In repealing the common law reviewing jurisdiction based on error of law on the face of an award and replacing it by an appeal process founded on reasoned awards, the Act removes the foremost obstacle to reasoned awards. Under the post-1979 legal regime the former reluctance to give reasons has no place, for even if the reasoning of an arbitrator is set out in an award and is found to contain an error of law, the fact that an appeal can now only progress with leave means that an appeal will not automatically follow every revealed or alleged error of law, and it is indeed

14. *Supra*, paras. 5 and 6.
15. See Chapter 1, para. 1.4.2. Report on Arbitration, *supra*, paras. 10 and 11.
16. *Trave Schiffahrtsgesellschaft m.b.H. & Co. K.G.* v. *Ninemia Maritime Corporation (The Niedersachsen)* [1986] Q.B. 802, 808B, per Sir John Donaldson, M.R., "The giving of reasoned awards is to be encouraged . . ."
17. *Infra*, para. 11.4.1.

the policy of the legislation that it should not. Under the new legislation an award will frequently be final and binding notwithstanding that its reasoning reveals an error of law.[18] The only express powers to be found in the 1979 Act exist as a necessary adjunct to the new appeal process and arise under section 1(5) and (6), by virtue of which the court is vested with a discretionary power to remit an unreasoned or insufficiently reasoned award to an arbitrator for further consideration. Where an award is wholly unreasoned the jurisdiction of the court is dependent on the preconditions specified in section 1(6).[19] It is considered generally that the cumulative effect of section 1 of the 1979 Act is to work a tacit and significant change of policy supporting the making of reasoned awards in appropriate circumstances,[20] and there is emerging some evidence to suggest that the new policy is making an impact on arbitral practice.[21]

11.1.9 A significant consequence of the realignment of policy effected by the 1979 Act is to draw English arbitral law on the subject of reasoned awards closer to the legal position adopted in many foreign jurisdictions[22] and also to the prevailing principles of international jurisprudence as manifested in conventions,[23] the UNCITRAL Model Law[24] and the arbitral rules of international institutions.[25] In so doing the risk of English awards being unenforceable in foreign jurisdictions on grounds of national public policy is also materially reduced.[26]

11.1.10 No introduction to the subject of reasoned awards would be complete without at least some preliminary comment on two essential issues. What are reasons? And what are the potential benefits associated with the giving of reasons?

A well structured award probably incorporates to a greater or lesser degree the following categories of information, although not necessarily in the order of the textual presentation here adopted—an introduction to the background to the dispute, the establishment and procedure of the arbitration (or umpirage where appropriate), and the issues in question or dispute: an indication of the evidence produced and a summary of the arguments advanced by the parties; a statement of the findings and conclusions of fact and law, and of the ultimate determination(s) of the tribunal; an explanation, to the extent necessary, which must vary with the circumstances of each

---

18. See Chapter 5 for a discussion of the policy underlying the new appeal process.

19. *Infra*, para. 11.4.

20. *Schiffahrtsagentur Hamburg Middle East Line G.m.b.H.* v. *Virtue Shipping Corporation (The Oinoussian Virtue)* [1981] 1 Lloyd's Rep. 533, 537. See also *Trave Schiffahrtsgesellschaft m.b.H. & Co. K.G.* v. *Ninemia Maritime Corporation (The Niedersachsen)* [1986] Q.B. 802, 808B, per Sir John Donaldson M.R.

21. See, Chapman, "FOSFA Arbitration" [1986] 2 Arb. Int. 323; Stephenson, *Arbitration for Contractors*, p. 49; Steyn and Veeder, "England: National Report", in *International Handbook on Commercial Arbitration*.

22. For comparative surveys see, *Arbitration Law in Europe*, I.C.C. Publication; Carbonneau, "Rendering Arbitral Awards with Reasons: The Elaboration of a Common Law of International Transactions" (1985) 22 Co. Jn. Trans. Law 579.

23. For example, European Convention on International Commercial Arbitration 1961, Art. VIII.

24. Art. 31(2): "The award shall state the reasons upon which it is based, unless the parties have agreed that no reasons are to be given or the award is an award on agreed terms under Article 30."

25. LCIA Rules (1994) Art. 16.1; LMAA Terms (1994) r. 21. The ICC Rules contain no express requirement but the Internal Rules of the Court of Arbitration, r. 17, require the Court of Arbitration when scrutinising a draft arbitral award, to pay particular attention, *inter alia*, to the need for reasons for awards under the mandatory rules of the place of arbitration.

26. Where the Convention on the Recognition and Enforcement of Foreign Arbitral Awards 1958 (New York Convention) applies, the possible ground of challenge based on public policy would arise under Art. V(2)(b).

case, of the various findings, conclusions and ultimate determination(s). Adopting this approach an award may be analysed as embodying two general categories of information—the static and the dynamic. That which is descriptive or which is asserted as a finding, conclusion or ultimate determination belongs to the former category; whereas that which is presented by way of explanation for a finding, conclusion or ultimate determination may be regarded as the dynamic and intellectual element of an award. The explanations provided represent the reasoning of an arbitral tribunal. As such the reasoning represents but an aspect, albeit a vitally important aspect, of a global award. The reasoning charts the connection between evidence and argument on the one hand and findings and conclusions of fact and law on the other; and thereafter between findings and conclusions and the ultimate determinations.

11.1.11 In the above analysis "reasons" are viewed as being synonymous with "reasoning". It has to be admitted that this is to adopt a very puristic and narrow approach, for it draws a precise distinction between the reasoning process and the information ruminated and also the product of the process. Whereas this approach may have a clear attraction in the abstract, it does not follow that the word "reasons" when used in a statute will be interpreted in the same way. Much will no doubt turn on the context of the legislation and the perceived purpose of the legislation, and as it will be observed later, the judges, in interpreting the word "reasons" in the context of the 1979 Act, have adopted a very broad approach, with reasons interpreted to mean not only "reasoning" in the strict sense but also the findings, conclusions and determinations of arbitrators.[27]

11.1.12 What is the virtue of a reasoned award? It has already been observed that there are occasions when reasoned awards are inappropriate or difficult to provide. Whenever they are made they will always to varying degrees produce delay and additional costs, and are to this extent antithetical to some of the perceived advantages of arbitration.[28] Their existence may also render an award vulnerable whenever there exists a system of judicial review based on error in the award.[29] Where this kind of risk exists arbitrators will often wish to take legal advice before making a reasoned award.[30] This was a feature of the former special case procedure, although for different reasons. The stylistic pattern of special case awards resulted in lawyers being engaged to secure that awards were properly structured and presented.[31] There are nonetheless circumstances when reasoned awards are both feasible and desirable, and on these occasions there is much that may be advocated in their favour. They give arbitral decisions a transparency and are a guard against perverseness, arbitrariness, caprice, whim and corruption.[32] They satisfy the natural and understandable desire of the parties to know why they have won or, and probably of greater significance, why

27. *Infra*, para. 11.6.2.
28. Cf. *Kurkjian* v. *Marketing Exchange (No. 2)* [1986] 2 Lloyd's Rep. 618, 624, per Staughton J; Davies, "How the 1979 Act is working from an arbitrator's point of view" in *The Arbitration Act 1979 And Its Effect On Commercial Disputes*, Lloyd's of London Press Conference Papers (20 November 1980).
29. Lord Mansfield is reported to have advised the judges of the Court of King's Bench in the following terms, "Consider what you consider justice requires and decide accordingly. But never give your reasons, for your judgment will probably be right, but your reasons will certainly be wrong"; cited in Bingham, *op. cit*, *supra*, note 1, p. 147.
30. This an arbitrator will be authorised to do in the absence of an express or implied prohibition in his mandate: see Chapter 12, para. 12.11.3.2.
31. See Chapter 1, para. 1.4.2 and *infra*, para. 11.6.3.
32. Cf. Bingham, *op. cit.*, *supra*, note 1.

they have lost.[33] But even a party who has been less successful than he hoped may wish to know the reasons for only his partial success. As such the giving of reasons helps to remove speculation, provides reassurance and contributes towards establishing consumer contentment with the chosen dispute resolving process, even on the part of those adversely affected. The presence of reasons may therefore indirectly help to secure the finality of an award. The requirement of reasons may also serve to improve the quality of the decision-making process and the performance of the decision makers. Nothing concentrates and disciplines the mind and hones the intellect more than the knowledge that any decision arrived at must be explained to the parties.[34] Reasons are a prerequisite to any system of appeal,[35] and also further assist where there exists a wider non-appellate review jurisdiction.[36] To perform its function an appellate tribunal must be aware not only of the decision of the lower forum, whether judicial or arbitral, but also of the reasoning that underpins the decision. It is not exceptional for an appellate court to agree with the decision of a tribunal at first instance but to disapprove of the reasoning by which it arrived at the decision. In sum, reasons render arbitral awards and arbitration a more rational process. "The making of an award is, or should be, a rational process. Formulating and recording the reasons tends to accentuate its rationality."[37]

11.1.13 In association with institutional arbitration the publication of reasoned awards may also serve as a kind of non-binding precedent or at least provide guidelines to others who may in the future utilise that same scheme of institutional arbitration.[38] To those who advocate the existence of a *lex mercatoria* the practice of giving reasoned awards in international commercial arbitration represents an important source for the statement and development of the principles of this distinct and contentious strand of "law".[39]

11.2 REASONED AWARDS PRIOR TO AND APART FROM THE 1979 ACT—COMMON LAW

11.2.1 The general rule

11.2.1.1 Under the common law an arbitrator or umpire is not under any obligation to make a reasoned or speaking award.[1] An operative award[2] is valid: by which is

---

33. Cf. *Meek* v. *City of Birmingham District Council* [1987] 1 R.L.R. 250, 254 (C.A.).
34. Report on Arbitration, *supra*, paras. 26 and 31.
35. Report on Arbitration, *supra*, paras. 27 and 28.
36. For an example, see *Comdel Commodities Ltd.* v. *Siporex Trade S.A.* [1990] 2 All E.R. 552 (H.L.).
37. Report on Arbitration, *supra*, para. 26, cited in *Trave Schiffahrtsgesellschaft m.b.H. & Co. K.G.* v. *Ninemia Maritime Corporation (The Niedersachsen)* [1986] Q.B. 802, 808B, per Sir John Donaldson, M.R. See also *Kansa General Ins. Co. Ltd.* v. *Bishopsgate Insurance plc* [1988] 1 Lloyd's Rep. 503, 510, 511 per Hirst J.
38. An example is provided in the practice adopted by the New York Maritime Arbitrators of publishing awards, albeit in an anonymised format.
39. See Cremades, "The Impact of International Arbitration on the Development of Business Law" (1983) 31 Am. J. Comp. L. 526; Carbonneau, "Rendering Arbitral Awards with Reasons: The Elaboration of a Common Law of International Transactions" (1985) 23 Co. Jn. of Trans. L. 579.
1. *Re Keane's Award* (1847) 9 L.T. (O.S.) 59; *Heaven & Kesterton Ltd.* v. *Sven Widaeus A/B* [1958] 1 W.L.R. 248; *Tramountana Armadora S.A.* v. *Atlantic Shipping Co. S.A.* [1978] 1 Lloyd's Rep. 391, 399, per Donaldson J.; *Mutual Shipping Corporation* v. *Bayshore Shipping Co. (The Montan)* [1985] 1 Lloyd's Rep. 189, 191, Sir John Donaldson M.R. (C.A.).
2. Also variously described as an unmotivated or decisive award, or a *dispositif*.

meant an award with no greater content than formal recitals (if any) and a finding for the claimant together with a compensatory or other remedial order, or a finding for the respondent and a dismissal of the claim; together with an associated order for costs and interest (if any). In making an unreasoned award it cannot without more be alleged that an arbitrator or umpire has acted *ultra vires* or misconducted himself or the arbitral proceedings; nor in consequence is the award void or susceptible to be set aside or remitted under section 22 and 23(2) of the Arbitration Act 1950. Nor may the absence of reasons be raised as a defence in proceedings brought to enforce the award.

11.2.1.2 The general position at common law also serves to emphasise that no duty to make a reasoned award arises under the common law from the status of an arbitrator or umpire as a quasi-judicial person. In the historical development of arbitration law there has been a tendency to attribute the existence of duties and powers to the fact that an arbitrator occupies a position analogous to a judge.[3] This manner of analysis has now fallen into disfavour and in the contemporary law there is witnessed a clear movement away from status to contract, which is perceived as the all-embracing basis of arbitration.[4] Unless a duty, right or power emanates from express or implied contract, or alternatively is established by statute, it does not exist at all.

11.2.1.3 Notwithstanding the position at common law, but subject ultimately to the terms of his mandate,[5] an arbitrator or umpire is not precluded from gratuitously making a reasoned award, and an arbitrator or umpire who so acts is not guilty of misconduct. Following the 1979 legislation it has been judicially observed *obiter dictum*, that an arbitrator who is of a mind to volunteer reasons is obliged to give reasons in such sufficiency as to satisfy the requirements of section 1(5) of the 1979 Act.[6] Although to draw such a parallel may have the advantage of general convenience, it is in other regards a far from obvious proposition. Unsolicited reasons might be thought as having no wider purpose than informing the parties why they had won and lost.

11.2.1.4 As previously observed the existence of the common law jurisdiction to set aside awards for error of law on their face disinclined arbitrators and umpires from gratuitously making reasoned awards[7] but this disinclination did not necessarily reflect a wider policy antithetical to reasoned awards. There is no reason to believe that the post 1979 era favouring the making of reasoned awards is a newly emergent virtue, notwithstanding that the practice of making reasoned awards is in all probability now more widespread. If this is an accurate analysis then the true effect of the 1979 Act is to give greater momentum to an established policy and not necessarily to create a new policy.

11.2.2 Express and implied contract

11.2.2.1 Notwithstanding the general posture of the common law there is nothing to preclude parties stipulating for a reasoned award by express or implied contract. Such

---

3. See, for example, *Re Enoch and Zaretsky, Bock & Co.* [1910] 1 K.B. 327; *In re Crighton and Law Car and General Insurance Corpn. Ltd.* [1910] 2 K.B. 738.
4. *Bremer Vulkan Schiffbau und Maschinenfabrik* v. *South India Shipping Corporation* [1981] A.C. 909 per Lord Diplock.
5. See *infra*, para. 11.2.2.
6. *Trave Schiffahrtsgesellschaft m.b.H. & Co. K.G.* v. *Ninemia Maritime Corporation (The Niedersachsen)* [1986] 1 Q.B. 802, 807, Sir John Donaldson M.R.
7. *Supra*, para. 11.1.6.

an agreement may enjoy an independent existence or be incorporated into an arbitration agreement or arbitration rules. It may be specifically contracted for or it may arise by implication from established practice or the prevailing circumstances. But no contract to make a reasoned award arises by implication from the mere appointment of an arbitrator or umpire. It may be entered into prior to the commencement of an arbitration or subsequently. Once established an agreement demanding reasons is the basis of the mandate of the arbitrator or umpire in question. It is the duty of an arbitrator or umpire to conduct an arbitration in accordance with the terms of his mandate as agreed by the parties at the time of his appointment or as subsequently amended or extended by the parties. The effect of the mandate may go to the jurisdiction of an arbitrator or umpire or raise a question of misconduct. In consequence any unreasoned award made may in strictness be void, as being *ultra vires* the arbitrator, but will otherwise be an award capable of being set aside or remitted under the Arbitration Act 1950, sections 22 and 23(2).[1] In the absence of special circumstances the likely response of the court will be to remit the defective award.[2]

11.2.2.2 Where reasons are stipulated for by contract, it is also open for the agreement to further specify the meaning of reasons; the extent of the obligation to provide reasons; the form and language in which the reasons are to be made; whether they are to be confidential; and any question of authentication. In *The Niedersachsen* Sir John Donaldson M.R. suggested, *obiter dictum*, that a contractual obligation to provide reasons is to be construed as establishing an equivalent obligation to that arising under section 1(5) of the 1979 Act.[3] It is difficult to apprehend why the traditional freedom of contract associated with arbitration is now to be constrained by the 1979 legislation. Whereas parallel obligations may arise in any given instance, it would seem equally open to the parties to define their own requirements differently. At most the dictum of the Master of the Rolls may represent a presumption of construction to be applied whenever the express mandate of the parties is couched in general terms and does not suggest anything to the contrary.

11.2.2.3 In contemporary practice the increasing acceptance of the desirability of reasoned awards, both nationally and internationally, is reflected in the requirement of almost all institutional arbitral rules that awards shall be reasoned unless the parties agree otherwise.[4] Such rules when expressly or impliedly incorporated into arbitration agreements assume a contractual force.

But just as arbitrating parties may by contract depart from the common law rule, so also may they by express or implied contract adopt the common law rule. The terms of

---

1. Cf. *Christopher Brown Ltd.* v. *Genossenschaft Oesterreichischer etc.* [1954] 1 Q.B. 8.

2. The prevailing judicial attitude would appear to be to do all that is possible to save an award rather than strike it down wholly and render the arbitral process of no effect: see generally, Mustill and Boyd, *op. cit.*, *supra* pp. 563–564.

3. *Trave Schiffahrtsgesellschaft m.b.H. & Co. K.G.* v. *Ninemia Maritime Corporation (The Niedersachsen)* [1986] Q.B. 802, 807. Further considered *infra*.

4. See, for example, Chartered Institute of Arbitration Rules (1988) r. 14.1; Institute of Civil Engineering Arbitration Practice (1983) r. 18; London Court of International Arbitration Rules (1985) r. 16.1; UNCITRAL Arbitration Rules (1976) Art. 32.2. It is noteworthy that the International Chamber of Commerce Rules do not contain an express requirement, but the awards made are invariably reasoned and are anticipated to be so by r. 17 of the Internal Rules of the Court of Arbitration.

a mandate may oblige an arbitrator or umpire to make an unreasoned award[5] or to give extra-award reasons.[6]

11.2.3 Unilateral request

11.2.3.1 Whereas the common law yields its general rule to contract, it is less easy to divine the attitude of the common law in the face of a unilateral request for reasons, as where one or some of the parties to a reference request a reasoned award and in which request the other party or parties refuse to join or acquiesce, or may even oppose. The position is now non-contractual and would seem also to be free of conclusive authority.

11.2.3.2 The observation of Staughton J. in *Michael I. Warde* v. *Feedex International Inc.*,[1] suggesting that when confronted with an unilateral request for reasons an arbitrator should make a reasoned award, save in exceptional circumstances, is probably in strictness applicable only to the post-1979 law and practice. Its potential to influence any analysis of the common law position must however be recognised. The difficulties associated with a unilateral request is that of necessity it implies that there does not exist any clear mandate one way or the other. Equally the rights of the other party cannot be ignored. An express mandate to give or not to give reasons cannot be affected by a subsequent unilateral request. In the absence of such a clear mandate, a unilateral request to give reasons is to request a form of award which the other party has neither expressly agreed to nor rejected. A practical and safe practice for an arbitrator would be to give notice to the other party of the request. If the other party expressly or impliedly agrees to a reasoned award there is no difficulty and the issue may be translated into contract. A failure to respond might fairly be construed as tacit assent, or at least indifference. But where the request meets with opposition the arbitrator must tread more cautiously and probably only give reasons if satisfied that the making of a reasoned award is in the best interests of the arbitral process and entails no unfair prejudice to the protesting party. This comment is, however, speculative for the position at common law does not appear to have been firmly decided or even seriously considered.

11.2.3.3 Following the 1979 Act the position has been clarified and this issue is returned to later in the chapter. This being the case, it is unnecessary to consider what manner of reasons a party is entitled to following a positive response to a unilateral request for reasons at common law.

11.2.4 Orders for costs

11.2.4.1 Subject to the express terms of an arbitration agreement an arbitrator is obliged to dispose of the question of costs.[1] Subject again to the terms of an arbitration agreement the jurisdiction is discretionary and extends over both the costs of

---

5. Cf. *Michael I. Warde* v. *Feedex International Inc.* [1984] 1 Lloyd's Rep. 310, 315, per Staughton J.
6. Considered *infra*, para. 11.2.6. See London Maritime Arbitrators Association Terms (1994), r. 21.
1. [1984] 1 Lloyd's Rep. 310, 315. Further considered *infra*, para. 11.8.1.6.
1. Arbitration Act 1950, s. 18(1) and (4). See also *Fitzsimmons* v. *Mostyn (Lord)* [1904] A.C. 46; *Re Becker, Schillan & Co. and Barry Bros.* [1921] 1 K.B. 391; *Mansfield* v. *Robinson* [1928] 2 K.B. 353; *Nils Heime Akt* v. *G. Merel & Co. Ltd.* [1959] 2 Lloyd's Rep. 292; *Messers Ltd.* v. *Heidner & Co.* [1960] 1 Lloyd's Rep. 500.

the reference and of the award.[2] With regard to the latter an arbitrator enjoys under the common law a possessary lien over the award as security for payment of his remuneration and expenses.[3] Beyond determining by whom, to whom and in what manner costs or any part thereof shall be paid, an arbitrator may also tax or settle the amount of costs to be so paid.[4] The legislature has also directed itself to this branch of arbitration law and the relevant provisions are set out in the Arbitration Act 1950, sections 18 and 19. In terms of broad principle, relating to considerations such as jurisdiction and judicial review, there is no distinction to be drawn between that part of an award which disposes of the substantive dispute and another part of the same award which carries the order as to costs,[5] athough in sections 18 and 19 of the 1950 Act particular statutory regulatory and review powers are introduced which are applicable only to the question of costs and fees.[6] Under the pre-1979 Act law an arbitrator who erred in principle or made an unreasonable award when addressing a question of costs was guilty of technical misconduct and that part of the award embodying the order of costs might be set aside or remitted under sections 23(2) and 22 of the Arbitration Act 1950.[7] Following the 1979 Act that part of an award dealing with costs falls to be reviewed under the appellate process established by the 1979 Act.[8]

11.2.4.2 With regard to orders for costs, the general common law rule apropos reasoned awards applied In relation to an order for costs embodied in an *ordinary* award[9] an arbitrator was not obliged, in the absence of an express or implied contract to the contrary, to give reasons for his order.[10] The general rule prevailed even when an order was unusual, as where an order departed from a *prima facie* rule underlying the exercise of discretion, the most important of which was the rule that costs follow the event.[11]

The absence of reasons did not render an order for costs embodied in an award immune from review but it did present obvious difficulties to a party who wished to

2. Arbitration Act 1950, s. 18(1). As a matter of construction it would seem that an allusion to the costs of a reference alone includes the costs of an award: see *Re Walker and Brown* (1882) 9 Q.B.D. 434.

3. *Smeaton Hanscomb & Co. Ltd.* v. *Sassoon I. Setty, Son & Co. (No. 2)* [1953] 1 W.L.R. 1481, 1484, per Devlin J. The existence of the possessory lien is implicitly acknowledged by s. 19(1) of the Arbitration Act 1950.

4. Arbitration Act 1950, s. 18(1). In practice it is more probable that costs will be taxed otherwise; as for example by the High Court, which is the taxing authority in all cases except where the award otherwise directs: see s. 18(2). By agreement taxation may also be delegated to a costs arbitrator, as for example under the Costs Arbitration Service provided by the Chartered Institute of Arbitrators. This scheme is however confined to the costs of the reference and does not extend to the costs of the award. For details of the scheme see Bernstein, *Handbook of Arbitration Practice* (2nd ed., 1993), Appendix D.

5. *Heaven and Kesterton* v. *Sven Widaeus A/B* [1958] 1 W.L.R. 248, 255–256, per Diplock J.

6. See, in particular, section 18(3), (4) and (5), and section 19(1) and (3).

7. *Heaven and Kesterton* v. *Sven Widaeus A/B, supra; Tramountana Armadora S.A.* v. *Atlantic Shipping Co. S.A.* [1978] 1 Lloyd's Rep. 391. As an alternative to remission the parties could agree to accept the order of the court in substitution, see *Lewis* v. *Haverfordwest R.D.C.* [1953] 1 W.L.R. 1486; *Smeaton Hanscomb & Co. Ltd.* v. *Sassoon I. Setty, Son & Co. (No. 2)* [1953] 1 W.L.R. 1481; *The Erich Schroeder* [1974] 1 Lloyd's Rep. 192; *The Ios I* [1987] 1 Lloyd's Rep. 321.

8. *King* v. *Thomas McKenna Ltd.* [1991] 1 All E.R. 653 (C.A.). The point is further discussed in Chapter 6, para. 6.2.14.

9. For the position with regard to an order for costs in an award stated in the form of a special case, see *infra*, para. 11.3.3.

10. *Heaven and Kesterton* v. *Sven Widaeus A/B* [1958] 1 W.L.R. 248; *Perry* v. *Stopher* [1959] 1 W.L.R. 415; *Matheson & Co. Ltd.* v. *A. Tabah & Sons* [1963] 2 Lloyd's Rep. 270; *Patroclos Shipping Co.* v. *Société Secopa* [1980] 1 Lloyd's Rep. 405.

11. *Ibid.* See also *Rosen & Co. Ltd.* v. *Dowley & Selby* [1943] 2 All E.R. 172; *Leif Hoegh & Co. A/S* v. *Maritime Mineral Carriers Ltd. (The Marques De Bolarque)* [1983] 1 Lloyd's Rep. 660.

challenge the order.[12] Nor could the court assist in such circumstances by directing that the award be remitted so that reasons might be given.[13] To counter this difficulty, and to facilitate the dispensing of justice, various qualifications were developed to the established general principle.

11.2.4.3 The judiciary had for some time consistently emphasised that although reasons were not obligatory when an arbitrator was minded to make an unusual order of costs, they were nonetheless desirable and in such a circumstance it was advisable for an arbitrator to give reasons. Such reasons were obviously of enormous assistance to the parties and to the court and could save time and expense. As a matter of good practice therefore an arbitrator should explain his reasons for making an unusual order as to costs.[14] Also, where the court was satisfied that an arbitrator or umpire had misdirected himself or made an unreasonable order and was consequently of a mind to remit the award, it might further direct that in so far as the arbitrator or umpire wished on reconsideration to make an unusual order as to costs, the justification for such an order must be stated in the fresh order as to costs.[15]

11.2.4.4 Furthermore, when reasons were not given, the court was prepared to allow the parties to hazard opinions, deducible from the facts of the dispute and the award, as to the possible reasons which moved the arbitrator to act as he had. The parties and their representatives might also present affidavit evidence recounting their recollections of the arbitral proceedings. The process was inevitably slightly speculative, but even this potential danger could be avoided if, as came to be customary, the arbitrator also put in an affidavit explaining his reasons for making the order.[16]

11.2.4.5 The whole position under the pre-1979 Act law was summarised by Mocatta J. in the following terms[17]:

There is no need for an umpire or arbitrator, if he so exercises his discretion as to depart from the general rule,[18] to state the reason why he does so in his award. On the other hand, in all probability, in most cases where an umpire/arbitrator does so act, it would save costs if he were to state his reasons in his award. In that event the parties would not be put to the expense of trying to ascertain what his reasons were and possibly moving the Court to set aside the award. If the award does depart from the general rule as to costs but bears on its face no statement of the reasons supporting that departure, the party objecting to the award in that respect may

---

12. See, *Matheson & Co. Ltd.* v. *A. Tabah & Sons, ibid*, per Megaw J.; *Dineen* v. *Walpole* [1969] 1 Lloyd's Rep. 261, 265, per Davies L.J., "[t]he arbitrator does not, of course, have to state reasons for his award, but there must be shown to be reasons on which he could exercise his discretion in the way that he did"; also *Patroclos Shipping Co.* v. *Société Secopa* [1980] 1 Lloyd's Rep. 405.

13. *Matheson & Co. Ltd.* v. *A. Tabah & Sons, ibid*. Contrast *Heaven & Kesterton Ltd.* v. *Etablissements François Albiac et Cie* [1956] 2 Lloyd's Rep. 316. But where reasons were given which were ambiguous or uncertain the award could be remitted for reconsideration, see *infra* n. 19.

14. *L. Figueiredo Navegacas S.A.* v. *Reederei Richard Schroeder K.G. (The Erich Schroeder)* [1974] 1 Lloyd's Rep. 192; *Tramountana Armadora S.A.* v. *Atlantic Shipping Co. S.A.* [1978] 1 Lloyd's Rep. 391; *Blue Horizon Shipping Co. S.A.* v. *E. D. & F. Man Ltd. (The Aghios Nicolaos)* [1980] 1 Lloyd's Rep. 17 (C.A.).

15. *Patroclos Shipping Co.* v. *Société Secopa* [1980] 1 Lloyd's Rep. 405.

16. *Heaven and Kesterton* v. *Sven Widaeus A/B, supra. Tramountana Armadora S.A.* v. *Atlantic Shipping Co. S.A., supra*, pp. 393–394. See also the observations in *King* v. *Thomas McKenna Ltd.* [1991] 1 All E.R. 653, 663–664 (C.A.).

17. *L. Figueiredo Navegacas S.A.* v. *Reederei Richard Schroeder K.G. (The Erich Schroeder)* [1974] 1 Lloyd's Rep. 192, 193–194.

18. That is, that costs follow the event.

bring before the court such evidence as he can obtain as to the grounds, or lack of grounds, bearing upon the unusual exercise of discretion by the arbitrator or umpire.

Further, where reasons for an order of costs were given but were shown to be unintelligible and therefore innately incapable of justifying the order made, the court enjoyed a jurisdiction to remit that part of the award for reconsideration.[19] The order to remit might again be accompanied by a direction that in the event of the order of costs being unusual, the arbitrator was to state his reasons in support of the order.[20]

11.2.4A Interest awards

11.2.4A.1 The jurisdiction of an arbitrator to award interest may derive from legislation,[1] contract[2] or the general law.[3] The object of an award of interest is to compensate a successful party who has been kept out of his money[4] and this being the case an arbitrator, in the absence of special considerations, should always address the issue of interest.[5] It was, in the pre-1979 Act law, misconduct to fail to do so.[6] The *prima facie* rule is that a losing party should be ordered to pay interest at a reasonable rate running from the date the amount or amounts due should reasonably have been paid.[7] But in the final analysis the award of interest is to be decided in the discretion of the arbitrator and this may justify a departure from the *prima facie* rule or even a refusal to make any award. The pervasive obligation is that the discretion shall be exercised judicially.[8]

11.2.4A.2 There appears to have been much less direct judicial observation on the need or desirability of reasoned interest awards than was the case with regard to awards of costs.[9] Nonetheless there is reason for thinking that a parallel approach was at least tacitly advocated.[10] As a matter of law therefore reasons were not an essential precondition, but as a matter of practice they were to be greatly encouraged. And whenever an arbitrator was of a mind to make an unusual award or not to make any award at all he should in good practice provide reasons explaining the course adopted.

11.2.5 Reasons and the validity of an award

11.2.5.1 Although at common law reasons are not a necessary precondition of a valid award, nonetheless where reasons are given they may assume a relevance in relation to the substantive validity of an award.

19. *Leif Hoegh and Co. A/S* v. *Maritime Mineral Carriers Ltd. (The Marques De Bolarque)* [1982] 1 Lloyd's Rep. 68.
20. *Patroclos Shipping Co.* v. *Société Secopa* [1980] 1 Lloyd's Rep. 405.
1. Arbitration Act 1950, sections 19A and 20. The former was inserted by the Administration of Justice Act 1982, section 15(6) and Schedule 1, Part IV. Considered in *Food Corporation of India* v. *Marastro Compania Naviera S.A. (The Trade Fortitude)* [1987] 1 W.L.R. 134, [1986] 2 Lloyd's Rep. 209.
2. Cf. *Chandris* v. *Isbrandtsen-Moller Co. Inc.* [1951] 1 K.B. 240, (1950) 84 Ll. L. Rep. 347.
3. See the review of the law in *President of India* v. *La Pintada Compania Navigacion (The La Pintada)* [1985] A.C. 104, [1984] 2 Lloyd's Rep. 9.
4. *Kemp (A.B.) Ltd.* v. *Talland* [1956] 2 Lloyd's Rep. 681, 691, Devlin J.
5. *The Myron* [1970] 1 Q.B. 527, 536, Donaldson J.
6. *P. J. Van Der Zijden Wildhandel N.V.* v. *Tucker & Cross Ltd.* [1976] 1 Lloyd's Rep. 341.
7. *Panchaud Frères S.A.* v. *R. Pagnan & Fratelli* [1974] 1 Lloyd's Rep. 394, 409, Kerr J.
8. See Chapter 6, para. 6.2.14.2. See also *Attorney-General of the Republic of Ghana and Ghana National Petroleum Corpn.* v. *Texaco Overseas Tankships Ltd. (The Texaco Melbourne)* [1992] 1 Lloyd's Rep. 319 (Note).
9. See Chapter 6, para. 6.2.14.1.
10. Cf. *Panchaud Frères S.A.* v. *R. Pagnan & Fratelli, supra*, note 7.

Among other considerations an award must be certain to be valid.[1] At common law an uncertain award suffers from a material substantive defect and is invalid. When challenged an uncertain award may be set aside, and it was only with the statutory enlargement of the judicial reviewing powers of awards that a power to remit was introduced.[2] The test of the certainty of an award is not the understanding a third party would give to an award but that of the parties themselves taking into account the terms of the submission and the circumstances appertaining to the reference.[3] If reasons, in the broad sense of that term,[4] are given which are ambiguous, incomprehensible, confused or inconsistent this may have the broader effect of rendering the award uncertain and in consequence challengeable.[5] It is, however, probable that in this regard a distinction has to be drawn between the operative or decisive part of an award and the reasons, in the narrow sense of the term, which underlie an award. Provided the operative part of an award is certain the demand of the common law is satisfied and it matters not that the supporting reasoning recorded elsewhere in the award is otherwise confused, inconsistent or unintelligible. In this manner of situation the significance of any revealed deficiency in the reasoning may be of no further import than to disclose an error of fact, which is unreviewable, or an error of law which is subject to review.[6]

11.2.5.2 Depending on the degree of uncertainty and the circumstances appertaining to the reference, an award which in its operative part is tainted with uncertainty may either be set aside or remitted to the arbitrator for further consideration.[7] It is likely that in the contemporary law the court will be predisposed to do all that is possible to save an award and therefore where possible to order remission rather than strike down an award.[8] But any attempt to enforce an uncertain award is likely to be refused by the court.[9]

11.2.6 Extra-award reasons and "restricted reasons agreements"

11.2.6.1 The presence of the common law jurisdiction to set aside awards for error of law on their face led to the emergence of a practice of making an "operative" or

---

1. *Hopcraft* v. *Hickman* (1824) 2 Sim. & St. 130; *Re Tribe and Upperton* (1835) 3 Ad. & El. 295; *Re Marshall and Dresser* (1843) 3 Q.B. 878; *Smith* v. *Hartley* (1851) 20 L.J.C.P. 169; *Simpson* v. *IRC* [1914] 2 K.B. 842; *Margulies Bros. Ltd.* v. *Dafnis Thomaides & Co. (U.K.) Ltd. (No. 2)* [1958] 1 Lloyd's Rep. 250; *Cremer* v. *Samanta* [1968] 1 Lloyd's Rep. 156; *River Plate Products Netherlands B.V.* v. *Etablissement Coargrain* [1982] 1 Lloyd's Rep. 628.
2. The statutory jurisdiction is now established by the Arbitration Act 1950, s. 22.
3. *Wohlenberg* v. *Lageman* (1815) 6 Taunt. 251; *Plummer* v. *Lee* (1837) 2 M. & W. 495; *Wrightson* v. *Bywater* (1838) 3 M. & W. 199; *Hewitt* v. *Hewitt* (1841) 1 Q.B. 110; *Round* v. *Hatton* (1842) 10 M. & W. 660; *Nickels* v. *Hancock* (1855) 7 De G.M. & G. 300; *Fabrica Lombarda di Acido Tartarico* v. *Fuerst Bros. Ltd.* (1921) 8 Ll.L.Rep. 57.
4. For the definition of "reasons" under the 1979 Act, see *infra*, para. 11.6.2.
5. *Oleificio Zucchi S.p.A.* v. *Northern Sales Ltd.*, [1965] 2 Lloyd's Rep. 496; *Moran* v. *Lloyd's* [1983] 1 Lloyd's Rep. 472.
6. *Moran* v. *Lloyd's* [1983] 1 Lloyd's Rep. 472, 475–476, per Sir John Donaldson M.R.
7. Under the jurisdiction conferred by the Arbitration Act 1950, s. 22, and under the common law.
8. See, for example, *Oakland Metal Co. Ltd.* v. *D. Benaim & Co. Ltd.* [1953] 2 Lloyd's Rep. 192; *Oleificio Zucchi S.p.A.* v. *Northern Sales Ltd.* [1965] 2 Lloyd's Rep. 496; *Sunbeam Shipping Co. Ltd.* v. *President of India (The Atlantic Sunbeam)* [1973] 1 Lloyd's Rep. 482; *Mallozzi* v. *Carapelli S.p.A.* [1975] 1 Lloyd's Rep. 229.
9. *Moran* v. *Lloyd's* [1983] 1 Lloyd's Rep. 472, 475–476, per Sir John Donaldson M.R.

"decisive" award only, and publishing the reasons for an award in a separate document made available to the parties contemporaneously with or subsequent to the publication of an award.[1] The practice was particularly effective, for any error of law revealed in the separate reasons was not an error of law appearing on the face of an award and could not therefore be used as a basis for challenging an award.[2] It also had the effect of informing the parties of the reasoning of the arbitral tribunal and so they were duly informed why they had respectively won or lost. An extraneous document, however, is not necessarily independent of an award. It may be expressly or impliedly incorporated into an award.[3] In the case of an extraneous document setting out the reasons for an award the implication is very strong, if not irresistible.[4] The implication, however, could and invariably was effectively countered by publishing the reasons under an express rubric indicating that they do not form part of an award.[5] Such a practice is valid if within the express or implied mandate of an arbitral tribunal. But even in the absence of a pre-existing authority, if the parties voluntarily take up an award together with an extraneous document setting out the reasons for the award, which is provided subject to an express rubric of the kind here under consideration, their conduct may be construed as a ratification, or otherwise as giving rise to an estoppel or waiver.

11.2.6.2 The practice developed further so as to secure that extra-award reasons are not only totally divorced from the award to which they relate but also to preclude any reference to extra-award reasons in any legal proceedings directly or indirectly associated with the award. A typical rubric is in the following terms[6]: "These reasons do not form part of the award. They are issued after its publication and are given on the understanding that no use shall be made of them in any action on, or in connection with, the award." It is implicit in the practice and indeed in the authorities which have considered the practice[7] that without such a restriction extra-award reasons may be referred to in legal proceedings arising out of or connected with the reference of a dispute to arbitration or an award. This further manner of restriction is customarily described in terms of "confidential reasons" but this may be too sweeping an appellation, for the effect of the rubric is to restrict any allusion to the reasons for specific purposes

---

1. See para. 11.1.6, *supra*. Also Thomas, "Arbitration: the basis and validity of a restricted reasons agreement" [1986] L.M.C.L.Q. 235. For criticisms of the practice, see Schmitthoff, "The Reform of the English Law of Arbitration" [1977] J.B.L. 305; Schmitthoff, *"Commercial Law in a Changing Economic Climate"* (1977) p. 42.

2. *Intermare Transport G.m.b.H.* v. *International Copra Export Corporation (The Ross Isle and Ariel)* [1982] 2 Lloyd's Rep. 589, 593, per Staughton J.

3. *Champsey Bhara & Co.* v. *Jivraj Balloo Spinning & Weaving Co. Ltd.* [1923] A.C. 480 (P.C.); *Aktiebolaget Legis* v. *Berg & Sons Ltd.* [1964] 1 Lloyd's Rep. 203.

4. *Kent* v. *Elstob* (1802) 3 East. 18, 21; *Sharman* v. *Bell* (1816) M. & J. 504, 506; *Giacoma Costa fu Andrea* v. *British Italian Trading Co. Ltd.* [1961] 2 Lloyd's Rep. 392, 405; *Pearl Marin Shipping A/B* v. *Pietro Cingolani S.A.S. (The General Valdes)* [1982] 1 Lloyd's Rep. 17, 20–21 (C.A.).

5. For judicial observations on the development of the practice, see, *Compania de Naviera Nedelka S.A.* v. *Tradax Internacional S.A. (The Tres Flores)* [1972] 2 Lloyd's Rep. 384, 391, per Mocatta J.; *Montan Shipping Corporation.* v. *Bayshore Shipping Co. (The Montan)* [1985] 1 Lloyd's Rep. 189, 191, per Sir John Donaldson M.R. (C.A.).

6. Extracted from the facts in *Atlantic Lines and Navigation Co. Inc.* v. *Italmare S.p.A. (The Apollon)* [1985] 1 Lloyd's Rep. 597.

7. Considered *infra*.

and beyond this they may be freely alluded to.[8] For present purposes it is proposed to adopt the phrase "restricted reasons agreement" to describe the practice.

11.2.6.3 The authority of an arbitral tribunal to express its extra-award reasons in restricted form will again turn on the terms of its express or implied mandate, although, in the absence of pre-existing authority, parties who voluntarily take up an award together with restricted extra-award reasons may be held to have ratified the authority of the arbitral tribunal, or otherwise to have waived or to be estopped from exercising their right to challenge the authority of the arbitral tribunal. Where the question of authority is unproblematical an issue does survive as to the validity of a "restricted reasons agreement". Sir John Donaldson M.R. in *The Montan*[9] expressed the view that "[s]uch an agreement purports to oust the jurisdiction of the Court and is void as being contrary to public policy". This appears a somewhat extreme analysis, for "restricted reasons agreements" do not oust the courts of their jurisdiction; to the contrary they anticipate the possibility of judicial involvement. Their intended purpose is to shield the reasons from legal embroilment, with the unavoidable consequence that the involvement of the courts is made substantially more difficult. Most of the limited judicial opinion which exists on the subject is to this effect, although at the same time it is cautious not to give "restricted reasons agreements" an unqualified application. The weight of judicial opinion recognises the agreements to be *prima facie* valid but capable of being displaced by considerations of overriding public policy. In *The Ross Isle and Ariel*, Staughton J. expressed his analysis in the following terms[10]:

> . . . I accept that there are circumstances in which the public interest requires that notwithstanding the private contract of the parties that they will treat such reasons confidentially, still they may be disclosed to the court. On the other hand, there is, as it seems to me, a strong public interest that arbitrators, if they choose, should be free to publish reasons of a confidential nature and the parties should be free, if they choose, to accept reasons on that basis. Whether, in any particular case, the public interest in favour of disclosure to the court overrides the general public interest that confidential reasons may be published for the interest of the parties without endangering the rule that there must be an end to litigation, is a matter for decision in that case.

11.2.6.4 In *The Montan*, Hobhouse J., at first instance, was of the same view,[11] as also ostensibly was Sir Roger Ormrod in the Court of Appeal.[12] Subsequently in

---

8. *Mutual Shipping Corporation* v. *Bayshore Shipping Co. (The Montan)* [1985] 1 Lloyd's Rep. 189, 191, per Sir John Donaldson M.R., who there refers to the practice as the giving of "claused" or "restricted" reasons.

9. *Ibid* p. 192. In its totality the opinion of the Master of the Rolls was as follows:
   " . . . I agree that where restricted reasons are given and accepted by the parties, the parties must be deemed to have agreed that the reasons cannot be placed before the court. Such an agreement purports to oust the jurisdiction of the court and is void as being contrary to public police. Were it otherwise the court would be powerless in the face of misconduct or even fraud revealed by the restricted reasons. We can therefore look at the arbitrator's reasons, although I hasten to add that no question of misconduct and still less of fraud arises or has ever been suggested."

10. *Intermare Transport G.m.b.H.* v. *International Copra Export Corporation (The Ross Isle and Ariel)* [1982] 2 Lloyd's Rep. 589, 593. (The dictum was uttered without the benefit of full argument.)

11. [1984] 1 Lloyd's Rep. 389, 392.

12. *Supra*, p. 198, "Whichever way of looking at this problem is correct, it is clear to my mind that the

The Apollon Webster J. summarised the effect of the case law in the following language[13]:

I take the effect of these dicta to be that in the present case the parties cannot, without leave, use the reasons (which do not form part of the award and which are given on the understanding that no use shall be made of them in any action on, or in connection with, the award) for the purpose of supporting any grounds upon which they seek to rely on an application to remit the award, but that the court may look at the reasons primarily in order to satisfy itself that there has been no fraud or misconduct of such a kind that the court takes the view that it should act upon the evidence of those reasons in the absence of any other, or any other sufficient, evidence of such misconduct, and possibly also to resolve a doubt arising out of the evidence.

11.2.6.5 The concept of overriding public policy is probably not to be construed as synonymous with the "interests of justice". Merely to assert that a case of injustice to a party may be revealed by referring to the restricted reasons is not in itself reason enough to displace a restricted reasons agreement.[14] Public policy in the present context is likely to be viewed narrowly and only likely to arise in exceptional circumstances,[15] as where there exists an allegation or suspicion of fraud or gross misconduct. It is doubtful that the public policy regulator will be activated otherwise than when a court is confronted with an allegation or strong suspicion of opprobrious or turpitudinous conduct. Mere technical misconduct would appear insufficient.[16] In *The Apollon*[17] Webster J. appeared to be of this opinion but was also prepared to extend the considerations of public policy to include "admitted mistake". It is less easy to comprehend the justification for this enlarged view. An error of fact or law is not even considered as misconduct in the technical sense and the opposite opinion expressed by Hobhouse J. in *The Montan* that no error of law or fact can justify overriding a "restricted reasons agreement" appears preferable.[18]

11.2.6.6 To the extent a "restrictive reasons agreement" is valid it takes effect as a contract between the parties to a reference, and to which the arbitrator or umpire may also be a party where this is the prevailing intention.[19] There is clearly no obstacle to an express or implied contract being established prior to the making of an award and the publication of the extra-award and restricted reasons.[20] But even in the absence of

---

parties themselves cannot blindfold the court, only the court itself can do that and in the vast majority of cases it will do so. But in those rare cases where an error occurs of the kind which we are considering in this case, the court cannot decline to interfere without gravely prejudicing in the eyes of the lay world the machinery of justice."

13. *Atlantic Lines and Navigation Co. Inc.* v. *Italmare S.p.A. (The Apollon)*, *supra*, p. 601.
14. *Mutual Shipping Corporation* v. *Bayshore Shipping Co. (The Montan)* [1984] 1 Lloyd's Rep. 389, 393, per Hobhouse J. (first instance).
15. *Ibid.*
16. *Ibid*: also in the Court of Appeal [1985] 1 Lloyd's Rep. 189, 192, per Sir John Donaldson M.R.
17. *Atlantic Lines and Navigation Co. Inc.* v. *Italmare S.p.A. (The Apollon)*, *supra*, p. 601.
18. *Mutual Shipping Corporation* v. *Bayshore Shipping Co. (The Montan)* (first instance), *supra*, p. 393.
19. *Mutual Shipping Corporation* v. *Bayshore Shipping Co. (The Montan)* (first instance), *supra*, p. 392. Contrast *Mutual Shipping Corporation* v. *Bayshore Shipping Co. (The Montan)*, C.A., *supra*, p. 198, per Sir Roger Ormrod, who queries the contractual basis of a "restricted reasons agreements" and contemplates their recognition to be a matter of practice.
20. An implied contract would probably come into existence when parties referred a dispute to institutional arbitration with knowledge of the prevailing practice within the institutional arbitration of giving extra-award and restricted reasons, or where the prevailing practice is so notorious that the parties may be attributed with constructive knowledge of the practice.

such a contract, where the parties voluntarily take up restricted reasons without protest there is at that moment the potential for establishing an implied contract that the reasons are to be accepted as restricted.[21] The basis of a "restricted reasons agreement" being contractual, the ambit of the agreement will turn on the construction of the contract. There is in practice no standard rubric and the "restricted reasons agreements" which have to date come before the courts have manifested variations in their drafting.

Extra-award reasons and "restricted reasons agreements" in the context of the 1979 Act are considered later in this chapter.[22]

11.3 REASONED AWARDS PRIOR TO AND APART FROM THE 1979 ACT—LEGISLATION

11.3.0 Introduction

The arbitration legislation, excluding the 1979 Act, is wholly silent on the question of reasoned awards. There exists in the body of accumulated legislation no express duty to provide reasons. Where reasons are provided in pursuance of an arbitral mandate or gratuitously there is nothing in the legislation that governs the definition of reasons or provides a qualitative measure of the reasons to be provided, nor the format of a reasoned award. If the reasons provided are incomplete, inadequate or otherwise deficient there exists no specific power directed towards the provision of a cure, although the general remitting power arising under the Arbitration Act 1950, section 22, may offer some assistance in this kind of situation.

But although the arbitration legislation in its generality is notable for its disregard of the question of reasons and reasoned awards there are nonetheless aspects of the legislation which may assume a relevance when questions relating to the matter of reasons, in the broad sense of that term, come into issue.

11.3.1 Special case award—remission for further facts

11.3.1.1 The former procedure of stating an arbitral award as a special case under the Arbitration Act 1950, section 21, has previously been described.[1] Although it was not expressly provided for in the legislation it was a necessary inference of the procedure that a special case award must be in writing and that the arbitrator or umpire concerned must provide sufficient factual information to enable the court to answer the

---

21. *Intermare Transport G.m.b.H.* v. *International Copra Export Corporation (The Ross Isle and Ariel)*, *supra*, p. 593; *Mutual Shipping Corporation* v. *Bayshore Shipping Co. (The Montan)*, *supra*, pp. 392–393 (first instance); p. 192 (C.A.).
22. *Infra*, para. 11.6.5.1.3.
1. See Chapter 1, para. 1.4.2 .

question(s) of law in issue.[2] It is now well appreciated that in practice special case awards came to assume a formal and standardised format, with the arbitrator or umpire deciding questions of fact and the court deciding the question(s) of law put before the court on the basis of the facts found and stated in the award.[3]

11.3.1.2 Under the special case procedure an arbitrator or umpire was not obliged to provide a statement of his reasons in the precise meaning of that term.[4] His essential and irreducible obligation was to make material and relevant findings of fact, to state his conclusions of fact and his award.[5] The arbitrator was entitled to confine himself to findings of fact that were material to the question(s) of law argued before him and which were set down in the special case.[6] Unless it was otherwise essential in the circumstances of any particular case, an arbitrator or umpire was not obliged to provide a narrative of the evidence, or set out the particular evidence on which his findings and conclusions were founded, or the contentions of the parties, or annex any documentary evidence to the award.[7] In strictness an arbitrator or umpire was not even obliged to set out his own determination of the question of law in issue but in practice it was both desirable and helpful for him to do so[8]; and anticipating that the court might arrive at a different determination, the practice of making alternative awards was developed.[9] The general position was different where the question of law in issue concerned whether a finding of fact was supported by or was contrary to the evidence presented at the reference. In order to determine this kind of legal question the court required greater access to the evidence on which the arbitrator or umpire relied, although even in this regard it required no more than a summary of the effect of the evidence before the tribunal.[10]

11.3.1.3 If a special case award did not provide an adequate statement of fact to enable the court to determine the question(s) of law stated it had a discretionary power to remit. There was a doubt whether the power to remit arose as a necessary incident of the special case procedure or was an application of the jurisdiction arising under section 22 of the 1950 Act. The latter was probably the true source of the

2. See *Nello Simoni* v. *A/S M/S Straum* (1949) 83 Ll.L.Rep. 157, 161, per Devlin J., "But it is no part of the duty of an umpire to find every conceivable fact which the parties might want to rely on if they raise matters later which they do not raise before him. His duty is simply to set out those facts which are necessary in order that the question of law which he is invited to state for the Court may be answered."

3. See n. 1 *supra* and *infra*.

4. *Bergerco U.S.A.* v. *Vegoil Ltd.* [1984] 1 Lloyd's Rep. 440, 443, per Hobhouse J., "Under the case stated procedure an arbitrator is under no obligation to give reasons. He must merely find the facts and state his conclusions and award."

5. *Ibid.*

6. *Nello Simoni* v. *A/S M/S Straum*, *supra*. See also *Hudson's Bay Co.* v. *Domingo Mumbru Sociedad Anonima* (1922) 10 Ll.L.Rep. 476.

7. *Willesden Borough Corporation* v. *Municipal Mutual Insurance Ltd.* (1945) 78 Ll.L.Rep. 256, 259; *Universal Cargo Carriers Corporation* v. *Citati* [1957] 2 Q.B. 401, 453; *Oricon Waren-Handelsgesellschaft m.b.H.* v. *Intergraan N.V.* [1967] 2 Lloyd's Rep. 82, 98; *Thomas Borthwick (Glasgow) Ltd.* v. *Faure Fairclough Ltd.* [1968] 1 Lloyd's Rep. 16, 23; *Pagnan and Fratelli* v. *Corbisa Industrial Agropacuaria Ltd.* [1969] 2 Lloyd's Rep. 129, 143; *Port Sudan Cotton Co.* v. *Govindaswamy Chettiar & Sons* [1977] 1 Lloyd's Rep. 166, 179–180.

8. *Pilgrim Shipping Co. Ltd.* v. *State Trading Corporation of India Ltd. (The Hadjitsakos)* [1975] 1 Lloyd's Rep. 356; *P. J. Van der Zijden Wildhandel N.V.* v. *Tucker and Cross Ltd.* [1975] 2 Lloyd's Rep. 240; *Arta Shipping Co. Ltd.* v. *Thai Europe Tapioca Service Ltd. (The Johnny)* [1977] 2 Lloyd's Rep. 1; *Intertradex S.A.* v. *Lesieur-Tourteaux S.A.R.L.* [1978] 2 Lloyd's Rep. 509; *Bremer Handelsgesellschaft m.b.H.* v. *J. H. Rayner Co. Ltd.* [1978] 2 Lloyd's Rep. 73.

9. See, for example, *Government of Ceylon* v. *Chandris* [1965] 2 Lloyd's Rep. 204.

10. *Tersons Ltd.* v. *Stevenage Development Corporation* [1965] 1 Q.B. 37.

power.[11] But whatever its precise source, the discretionary jurisdiction was cautiously exercised.[12] Confronted with insufficient or ambiguous or irreconcilable factual findings the court might be most readily moved to order remission, for without remission it could not discharge its function.[13] The practice that developed of the parties presenting an arbitral tribunal with lists of desired findings of fact to a degree protected against the possibility of a special case award being so deficient, but otherwise the practice was not universally well received.[14] But the jurisdiction was not available for the purpose of reviewing or going behind the factual findings of an arbitral tribunal.[15] Although in each case remission was a question of discretion, it became settled practice that the court would not remit for further findings fact to support argument on a legal issue not argued before the arbitrator or umpire.[16] Nor, where the question of law was concerned with the sufficiency of evidence to support a finding or conclusion of fact, would the court order remission unless it could be shown that the arbitrator or umpire had been put on notice prior to making the award.[17]

11.3.2 Special case award—unusual order for costs

The general interrelationship between reasons and costs at common law has been considered previously.[1] A qualification is now necessary to that statement with regard to an unusual order for costs embodied in a special case award. When minded to make an unusual order the arbitrator or umpire was also obliged to set out in his award the

11. In *European Grain and Shipping Ltd.* v. *Peter Cremer* [1983] 1 Lloyd's Rep. 211, 218, Bingham J. in ordering remission of an award expressed himself to be exercising a power under s. 22 of the Arbitration Act 1950. See also *Universal Cargo Carriers Corp.* v. *Pedro Citati* [1957] 2 Lloyd's Rep. 191; *Gill & Duffus S.A.* v. *Berger & Co. Inc.* [1981] 2 Lloyd's Rep. 233, 236, [1982] 1 Lloyd's Rep. 101; *Vanden Avenne-Izegem P.V.B.A.* v. *Finagrain S.A.* [1985] 2 Lloyd's Rep. 99, 101; *Interbulk Ltd.* v. *Aiden Shipping Co. Ltd. (The Vimeira) (No. 1)* [1985] 2 Lloyd's Rep. 410 (C.A.) (Note). *Reinante Transoceanic Navegacion S.A.* v. *The President of India (The Apiliotis)* [1985] 1 Lloyd's Rep. 255.
12. *The White Rose* [1969] 2 Lloyd's Rep. 52; *Transamerican Shipping Corporation* v. *Tradax Export S.A.* [1980] 1 Lloyd's Rep. 107.
13. *Overseas Buyers Ltd.* v. *Granadex S.A.* [1980] 2 Lloyd's Rep. 608, 613. *Japan Lines Ltd.* v. *Mediolanum Shipping Co.* [1981] 1 Lloyd's Rep. 455; *Mitsubishi International G.m.b.H.* v. *Bremer Handelsgesellschaft m.b.H.* [1981] 1 Lloyd's Rep. 106; *Andre & Cie S.A.* v. *Tradax Export S.A.* [1983] 1 Lloyd's Rep. 254; *Gill and Duffus S.A.* v. *Berger & Co. Inc.* [1983] 1 Lloyd's Rep. 622 (C.A.); *Mediolanum Shipping Co.* v. *Japan Lines Ltd. (The Mediolanum)* [1984] 1 Lloyd's Rep. 136; *Gill & Duffus* v. *Berger* [1984] 1 Lloyd's Rep. 227 (H.L.); *La Pintada Compania Navegacion S.A.* v. *The President of India (The La Pintada) (No. 2)* [1984] 1 Lloyd's Rep. 305; *Steel Authority of India Ltd.* v. *Hind Metals Inc.* [1984] 1 Lloyd's Rep. 405.
14. *Vinava Shipping Co. Ltd.* v. *Finelvet A.G. (The Chrysalis)* [1983] 1 Lloyd's Rep. 503, 507–508.
15. *Overseas Buyers Ltd.* v. *Granadex S.A.* [1980] 2 Lloyd's Rep. 608, 613; *Bremer Handelsgesellschaft m.b.H.* v. *Westzucker G.m.b.H. (No. 2)* [1981] 2 Lloyd's Rep. 130, 207, 213–214 (C.A.); *Transoceanic Petroleum Carriers* v. *Cook Industries Inc. (The Mary Lou)* [1981] 2 Lloyd's Rep. 272, 283; *European Grain & Shipping Ltd.* v. *Peter Cremer* [1983] 1 Lloyd's Rep. 211, 217.
16. *Sinason-Teicher Inter-American Grain Corporation* v. *Oilcakes and Oilseeds Trading Co. Ltd.* [1954] 1 Lloyd's Rep. 376; *Universal Cargo Carriers Corporation* v. *Citati* [1957] 2 Q.B. 401; *Yamashita Shinnihon SS Co. Ltd* v. *Elios S.p.A. (The Lily Prima)* [1976] 2 Lloyd's Rep. 487; *Toepfer* v. *Schwarze* [1980] 1 Lloyd's Rep. 385 (C.A.); *Bremer Handelsgesellschaft m.b.H.* v. *Westzucker G.m.b.H. (No. 2)* [1981] 2 Lloyd's Rep. 130 (C.A.); *Cook Industries Inc.* v. *Meunerie Liégeois S.A.* [1981] 1 Lloyd's Rep. 359; *Tradax Export S.A.* v. *Cook Industries Inc.* [1982] 1 Lloyd's Rep. 385 (C.A.).
17. *Mondial Trading Co. G.m.b.H.* v. *Gill & Duffus Zuckerhandelsgesellschaft m.b.H.* [1980] 1 Lloyd's Rep. 376, 379. See also *Universal Petroleum Co. Ltd. (in liquidation)* v. *Handels- und Transport Gesellschaft m.b.H.* [1967] 1 Lloyd's Rep. 517, 523 (C.A.).
1. *Supra*, para. 11.2.4.

grounds that persuaded him to depart from the usual form of order.[2] A failure to discharge this obligation might have amounted to misconduct or to have rendered the special case award substantively defective. Whatever the precise analysis its effect was to render the award capable of being remitted under section 22 of the Arbitration Act 1950, which represented the usual form of relief.[3]

11.3.3 Correcting erroneous reasons

The extent to which the courts have jurisdiction to review awards for error in the adopted reasons, again using that term in its broadest sense, was and continues to be an uncertain topic. The early authorities in particular are frequently ambiguous and of uncertain import. Many of them now have to be understood in the context of subsequent legislative developments, particularly the emergence of the slip rule jurisdiction[1] and the discretionary jurisdiction to remit for admitted mistake.[2] The latter jurisdiction has now been rendered at least vulnerable by section 1(1) of the 1979 Act, in so far as it asserts that "the High Court shall not have jurisdiction to set aside or remit an award on an arbitration agreement on the grounds of error of fact . . . on the face of the award". By implication the same statutory statement suggests that there did exist some such jurisdiction prior to the 1979 legislation, although it does nothing to clarify the doubts existing as to the extent of the jurisdiction.

11.3.3.1 Slip rule jurisdiction

11.3.3.1.1 An arbitrator or umpire has no inherent jurisdiction to correct an award. Once an award is made in final form an arbitrator or umpire is *functus officio* and cannot in consequence reopen the award[3] unless the award is remitted by agreement of the parties[4] or by order of the court exercising the jurisdiction arising under section 22 of the Arbitration Act 1950.[5] An exception to this general rule is now provided by section 17 of the 1950 Act,[6] which is the present source of the so-called slip rule jurisdiction and provides:

Unless a contrary intention is expressed in the arbitration agreement the arbitrator or umpire shall have power to correct in an award any clerical mistake or error arising from any accidental slip or omission.

11.3.3.1.2 The jurisdiction is conferred on an "arbitrator or umpire"; it is contractual in nature and arises by way of an implied term in an arbitration agreement. It may be displaced by an express term to the contrary and establishes a discretionary

---

2. *Smeaton Hanscomb & Co. Ltd.* v. *Sassoon I. Setty, Son & Co. (No. 2)* [1953] 1 W.L.R. 1481, 1485, per Devlin J.
3. *Ibid.*
1. See *infra*, para. 11.3.3.1.
2. See *infra*, para. 11.3.3.2.
3. *Henfree* v. *Bromley* (1805) 6 East 309; *Irvine* v. *Elnon* (1806) 8 East 54; *Ward* v. *Dean* (1832) 3 B. & Ad. 234; *Mordue* v. *Palmer* (1870) 6 Ch. App. 22; *Sutherland & Co.* v. *Hannevig Bros. Ltd.* [1921] 1 K.B. 336.
4. *I.R.C.* v. *Hunter* [1914] 3 K.B. 423, 428, per Scrutton J., "A referee, having once issued his award, cannot issue another without the consent of both parties."
5. See *infra*, 11.3.3.2.
6. The section re-enacts the Arbitration Act 1889, s.7(c). See generally Thomas, "The power of arbitrators to cure accidental errors" [1985] L.M.C.L.Q. 263.

jurisdiction. It does not oblige an arbitrator or umpire to correct accidental errors, although an unreasonable refusal to exercise the jurisdiction may amount to misconduct.[7] The jurisdiction is confined to accidental errors "in an award", which includes the award and incorporated documents.[8] The error must appear on the face of an award, although it is not equally necessary that the particular accident of commission or omission from which the error derives also appear on the face of an award.[9]

11.3.3.1.3 The jurisdiction arising under section 17 has historically been construed narrowly. It is confined to clerical mistakes in the strict sense, as where a slip of commission or omission occurs in the "writing up" of an award,[10] or more generally when by virtue of an accidental slip or omission something is inadvertently included in or left out of an award.[11] A principal theme in the authorities is that the accidental error must be of the pen and not of the mind. Section 17 according to this thesis only applies to unintentional inclusions or omissions. If on the other hand an arbitrator or umpire has fallen into inadvertent error and incorporates into an award that which is intended, albeit mistakenly, section 17 has no application for this is solely a mistake of the mind.[12] This particular approach to the interpretation of section 17 limits greatly the applicability of the correcting jurisdiction and has been challenged in more recent times. Under the expansionist view, harmony between mind and pen does not preclude the applicability of section 17, if it can otherwise be shown that an arbitrator or umpire made an error derived from an accidental slip or omission in coming to a determination of the mind. It is sufficient if an accidental slip or omission is made which leads to an error in an award.[13] This wider approach would appear to be fully supportable by reference to the language of the section and also to give a desirable emphasis to the two distinct wings of the jurisdiction which derives from the section, namely, a power to correct (i) clerical mistakes, and (ii) errors arising from any accidental slip or omission.

11.3.3.1.4 But section 17 has no wider province. It cannot be used by an arbitrator or umpire who has second thoughts and as a means of correcting an award.[14] An

---

7. A possible alternative remedy open to an aggrieved party would be to seek declaratory relief and in association therewith a mandatory injunction may also be available.

8. *Pearl Marin Shipping A/B* v. *Pietro Cingolani S.A.S. (The General Valdes)* [1981] 1 Lloyd's Rep. 170; [1982] 1 Lloyd's Rep. 17 (C.A.).

9. *Mutual Shipping Corporation* v. *Bayshore Shipping Co. (The Montan)* [1984] 1 Lloyd's Rep. 389, 394–395, per Hobhouse J. (first instance).

10. *Sutherland and Co.* v. *Hannevig Bros. Ltd.* [1921] 1 K.B. 336, 341, per Rowlatt J., a clerical mistake was "something almost mechanical—a slip of the pen or something of that kind". An omission by a clerk in copying a draft award was also capable of amounting to a clerical mistake: see, *Mordue* v. *Palmer* (1870) 6 Ch. App. 22. See also *Ward* v. *Dean* (1832) 3 B. & Ad. 234 (names of the parties confused); *Benabu & Co.* v. *Produce Brokers Co.* (1921) 7 Ll.L.Rep. 45 (umpire signed award "as arbitrator" although he intended to sign "as umpire").

11. *Sutherland and Co.* v. *Hannevig Bros. Ltd.*, *ibid*, p. 341, per Rowlatt J., "an accidental slip occurs when something is wrongly put in by accident, and an accidental omission occurs when something is left out by accident." In *Mutual Shipping Corporation* v. *Bayshore Shipping Co. (The Montan)* [1985] 1 Lloyd's Rep. 189, 196, Robert Goff L.J. withheld from any attempt at a definition of the phrase "error arising from any accidental slip or omission" and was content with the thought that "the animal is, I suspect, usually recognisable when it appears on the scene".

12. *In re an Arbitration between Stringer and Riley Bros.* [1901] 1 Q.B. 105; *Pedler* v. *Hardy* (1902) 18 T.L.R. 591; *Sutherland and Co.* v. *Hannevig Bros. Ltd.*, *supra; Fuga A.G.* v. *Bunge A.G.* [1975] 2 Lloyd's Rep. 192.

13. *Mutual Shipping Corporation* v. *Bayshore Shipping Co. (The Montan)* [1984] 1 Lloyd's Rep. 389 (first instance); [1985] 1 Lloyd's Rep. 189 (C.A.).

14. *Ibid*, pp. 193–194, per Sir John Donaldson M.R.

"intended decision" cannot be corrected, even if its effect is different from that contemplated.[15] Nor does section 17 establish a jurisdiction which enables an arbitrator or umpire to expound, elaborate or amplify an ambiguous award.[16] Hobhouse J. has expressed the limitations of section 17 in the following language[17]:

> It in no way allows any change of mind by the arbitrator, nor does it allow the arbitrator to correct mistakes of reasoning or of evaluation or assessment or even of expression. If an arbitrator intended to use a certain form of words, then it is not open to an arbitrator, under s. 17, to alter the wording of the award when he discovers that its effect is different from that which he had expected.

11.3.3.2 Admitted mistake

11.3.3.2.1 Where a mistake is made in an award and the arbitrator or umpire whose award it is admits the error, the High Court enjoys a discretionary jurisdiction under section 22 to remit the award so that it may be reconsidered by the arbitrator or umpire who has fallen into confessed error.[1] This is the so called "admitted mistake" head of jurisdiction.[2] In addition to confessing the error, in contemporary practice the arbitrator or umpire will also invariably invite the court to remit the award. Although, doubtlessly this reinforces the affidavit of the arbitrator or umpire it is unlikely that it represents an indispensable precondition to the jurisdiction of the court.[3] A plain admission may even be construed as carrying by implication an invitation to remit. The admission must, however, be that of the arbitrator or umpire in question and it is in consequence insufficient if the admission is simply recorded in an affidavit sworn by one of the arbitrating parties.[4]

   11.3.3.2.2 In its historical context the jurisdiction exists as a significant exception to the general rule in favour of the finality of awards and its incident that an award is not to be set aside or remitted for mistake.[5] It is also clear that certain authorities associated with the early emergence of the jurisdiction are now to be regarded as illustrative of the slip rule jurisdiction, which was introduced subsequent to their determination and which jurisdiction now arises under section 17 of the 1950 Act.[6] The fact that the

15. *Allen* v. *Greenslade* (1875) 33 L.T. 567.
16. *Sutherland and Co.* v. *Hannevig Bros. Ltd.*, *supra*, p. 341 per Rowlatt J.
17. *Mutual Shipping Corporation* v. *Bayshore Shipping Co. (The Montan)*, *supra*, p. 394 (first instance). Contrast the observations of Robert Goff L.J. in the Court of Appeal, *supra*, pp. 195–197.
   1. *Walton* v. *Swanage Pier Co.* (1862) 10 W.R. 629; *Flynn* v. *Roberston* (1869) L.R. 4 C.P. 324; *Dinn* v. *Blake* (1875) L.R. 10 C.P. 388; *In re Baxters and Midland Rly Co.* (1906) 95 L.T. 20; *The Mello* (1948) 81 Ll.L.Rep. 230.
   2. See generally *Mills* v. *Bowyers' Society* (1856) 3 K. & J. 66, *Hodgkinson* v. *Fernie* (1857) 3 C.B.N.S. 189; *Hogge* v. *Burgess* (1858) 3 H. & N. 293; *Re Keighley Maxsted & Co. and Bryan Durant & Co.* [1893] 1 Q.B. 405; *Re Montgomery Jones & Co. and Liebenthal & Co.* (1898) 78 L.T. 406; *Re Baxters and Midland Railway Co.* (1906) L.T. 20.
   3. *Anglo-Saxon Petroleum Co.* v. *Adamastos Shipping Co. Ltd.* [1957] 2 Q.B. 233, per Devlin J.; *Mutual Shipping Corporation* v. *Bayshore Shipping Co. (The Montan)* [1985] 1 Lloyd's Rep. 189, 197 per Robert Goff L.J. (C.A.); [1984] 1 Lloyd's Rep. 389, 396, per Hobhouse J. (first instance).
   4. *Phillips* v. *Evans* (1843) 12 M. & W. 309; *Mills* v. *Bowyers' Society* (1856) 3 K. & J. 66; *Hogge* v. *Burgess* (1858) 3 H. & N. 293; *Re Keighley, Maxsted & Co. and Durrant & Co.* [1893] 1 Q.B. 405; *Anglo-Saxon Petroleum Co.* v. *Adamastos Shipping Co. Ltd.* [1957] 2 Q.B. 233.
   5. *Phillips* v. *Evans*, *ibid*; *Hutchinson* v. *Shepperton* (1849) 13 Q.B. 955.
   6. For example, *Re Hall and Hinds* (1841) 2 Man. & G. 847; The same is also probably the case with regard to *Hutchinson* v. *Shepperton* (1849) 13 Q.B. 955. The slip rule jurisdiction was first introduced by the Arbitration Act 1889, s. 7(c) and is discussed *supra*, para. 11.3.3.1.

"admitted mistake" jurisdiction has survived the introduction of the slip rule jurisdiction clearly indicates that the two heads of jurisdiction are not coterminous and that the "admitted mistake" jurisdiction is broader in scope. It may be that whereas the jurisdiction under section 17 of the 1950 Act is confined to accidental errors, the jurisdiction associated with "admitted mistake" is not so confined and enables an arbitral tribunal to reconsider, to have second thoughts, and to alter its original decision. Whereas certain authorities are consistent with this interpretation of the jurisdiction,[7] the point nonetheless remains uncertain, for there exist dicta to the contrary effect.[8] It is however clear that the jurisdiction extends to mistakes of commission and omission,[9] and to mistakes of fact and law,[10] although this latter statement must now be read in the context of the later discussion of the impact of the 1979 Act on the jurisdiction to remit for "admitted mistake".[11]

11.3.3.2.3 Recent judicial consideration of the jurisdiction of the court to remit for mistake has called into question the very basis of the jurisdiction. In *The Montan*[12] the Court of Appeal, *obiter dictum*, refused to consider that an admission of error was a prerequisite to the court's power to direct remission. Although as a general rule the mistake must be admitted, the Court of Appeal nonetheless considered that the court possesses a discretion to remit even in the absence of any admission of error. This perception of the court's jurisdiction appears controversial and to be inconsistent with a substantial line of authority[13]; and it was a view which Webster J. in *The Apollon*,[14] after a comprehensive review of the authorities, declined to follow. The only way, it is suggested, that the observations of the Court of Appeal in *The Montan* can be supported is by drawing a distinction between the scope of the remitting jurisdiction as defined by the open language of section 22 and the way in which the court, as a question of discretion, is prepared to exercise the jurisdiction.[15] The adoption of this approach theoretically extends the potential of the remitting jurisdiction beyond that suggested by authority, but as a question of discretion it may be doubtful that the

---

7. *The Mello* (1948) 81 Ll.L.Rep. 230; *Anglo-Saxon Petroleum Co. Ltd.* v. *Adamastos Shipping Co. Ltd.* [1957] 2 Q.B. 233 per Devlin J.

8. *In re Baxters and Midland Rly Co.* (1906) 95 L.T. 20; *Mutual Shipping Corporation* v. *Bayshore Shipping Co. (The Montan)* [1984] 1 Lloyd's Rep. 389, 396, per Hobhouse J. (first instance); [1985] 1 Lloyd's Rep. 189, 192–193, per Sir John Donaldson M.R. (C.A.).

9. *Caswell* v. *Groucutt* (1862) 31 L.J. Ex. 361; *Flynn* v. *Robertson* (1869) L.R. 4 C.P. 324; *In re Baxters and Midland Rly. Co.* (1906) 95 L.T. 20.

10. *Dinn* v. *Blake* (1875) L.R. 10 C.P. 388; *Re Keighley, Maxsted & Co. and Bryan Durant & Co.* [1893] 1 Q.B. 405; *In re Baxters and Midland Rly. Co.* (1906) 95 L.T. 20; *Kaffeehandelsgesellschaft K.G.* v. *Plagefim Commercial S.A.* [1981] 2 Lloyd's Rep. 190.

11. *Infra*, para. 11.3.3.2.5.

12. *Mutual Shipping Corporation* v. *Bayshore Shipping Co. (The Montan)* [1985] 1 Lloyd's Rep. 189, 193, per Sir John Donaldson M.R. and pp. 196–197 per Robert Goff L.J.

13. *Knox* v. *Symmonds* (1791) 1 Ves. Jun. 369; *Anderson* v. *Darcey* (1812) 18 Ves. Jun. 447; *In re Hall & Hinds* (1841) 2 M. & G. 847 (although it is not mentioned in the judgment of Chief Justice Tyndall, in giving the judgment of the Court of Common Pleas, two of the three-arbitrator tribunal admitted mistakes on affidavit, and the third verbally expressed his assent to the statement sworn by his co-arbitrators); *In Re Mills and The Society of the Mystery of Bowyers* (1865) 3 Kay & J. 66; *Flynn* v. *Robertson* (1869) L.R. 4 C.P. 324; *Dinn* v. *Blake* (1875) L.R. 10 C.P. 388; *Re Keighley Maxsted & Co. and Bryan Durant & Co.* [1893] 1 Q.B. 405; *Re Montgomery Jones & Co. and Liebenthal & Co.* (1898) 78 L.T. 406; *In re Baxters and Midland Rly. Co.* (1906) 95 L.T. 20.

14. *Atlantic Lines and Navigation Co. Inc.* v. *Italmare S.p.A. (The Apollon)* [1985] 1 Lloyd's Rep. 597.

15. As was done by the Court of Appeal in *King* v. *Thomas McKenna Ltd.* [1991] 1 All E.R. 653.

court would view this as desirable,[16] and in turn, this reluctance might take further support from the policy associated with the 1979 Act.

11.3.3.2.4 An issue of some uncertainty is to determine precisely the standing of the jurisdiction to remit for "admitted mistake" following the enactment of section 1(1) of the 1979 Act, which by its express terms states "the High Court shall not have jurisdiction to set aside or remit an award on an arbitration agreement on the grounds of errors of fact or law on the face of the award". The denial of jurisdiction is not all-embracing for the subsection is confined to awards made on an "arbitration agreement"[17] and to errors "on the face of the award".[18] With regard to awards made on parol arbitration agreements and to admitted errors of fact or law which do not appear on the face of an award the subsection would seem to have no application.[18a] But even in relation to these kinds of situations the policy associated with the 1979 Act may well influence the exercise of any associated judicial discretion.

11.3.3.2.5 First, to consider errors of law. In this regard the policy of the 1979 Act would appear clear. It is to establish a single review procedure based on appeals from reasoned awards. The overriding object appears to be that any preceding common law review jurisdiction is to be abrogated.[19] That a residue of this former review jurisdiction continues to survive where an arbitrator or umpire admits an error of law which does not appear on the face of an award would, in all probability, be an unintended result. But in the post-1979 Act phase it is highly unlikely that the courts will be willing to entertain argument to this effect. Parties who wish to challenge awards for error of law are likely to be constrained to use the new appeal procedure which applies to "any questions of law arising out of an award."[20] If a party cannot bring himself within the appeal process for error of law then it is arguable that he is without any remedy.

11.3.3.2.6 The surviving position with regard to errors of fact probably offers greater difficulty. In its express terms section 1(1) emphasises the general principle but equally does not in any way impinge upon the slip rule jurisdiction under section 17 of the 1950 Act, which is an exception to the general principle.[21] Many errors of fact which appear on the face of an award are likely to fall within the parameters of the slip jurisdiction. Any other category of factual error appearing on the face of an award would appear immune from review unless the error can be associated with a species of misconduct,[22] which would seem unlikely, for the weight of contemporary authority

16. But contrast the wide approach to section 22 taken in *Indian Oil Corporation Ltd.* v. *Coastal (Bermuda) Ltd.* [1990] 2 Lloyd's Rep. 407; the case was argued on appeal before the Court of Appeal in *King* v. *Thomas McKenna, ibid.*, but settled before judgment was given: and in *Breakbulk Marine Services Ltd.* v. *Dateline Navigation Co. Ltd.* (19 March 1992, unreported). The cases and their implication are discussed in Veeder, "Remedies against Arbitral Awards: Setting Aside, Remission and Rehearing", in *Yearbook of the Arbitration Institute of the Stockholm Chamber of Commerce 1993*.

17. See Chapter 1, para. 1.7.5.
18. See Chapter 1, para. 1.4.1.
18a. See Chapter 1, para. 1.4.
19. See Chapter 1, para. 1.3.
20. See Chapter 3.
21. Discussed *supra*, para. 11.3.3.1.
22. In *Re Hall & Hinds* (1841) 2 M. & G. 847 a gross error of fact on the face of an award was considered misconduct. (It is submitted that this aspect of the case must be viewed with great caution. The facts of the case would now fall within the slip rule jurisdiction and in contemporary authority it is repeatedly asserted that an error of fact is not misconduct.) There is some dicta that appears to suggest that an arbitrator who makes findings of fact which are not only not supported by the weight of evidence but which show that the

suggests that factual error, without more, is no misconduct.[23] But where does this leave the jurisdiction to remit for admitted mistake of fact? The question is difficult but it would appear that the jurisdiction is unaffected by the 1979 Act. What probably saves it is the special feature that the mistake is admitted by the arbitrator and with the arbitrator expressly or impliedly seeking the opportunity to correct the error. It is also of significance that the survival of the jurisdiction was assumed by the Court of Appeal in *King* v. *Thomas McKenna Ltd*,[24] although the issue here under discussion was not directly in question. If the 1979 Act is of any effect, it is probably as a constraining influence, securing that the future development of the admitted mistake jurisdiction will be closely scrutinised and cautiously utilised.

11.3.4 Uncertain reasons

11.3.4.1 Certainty is an essential prerequisite of a valid award. An uncertain award is neither valid nor enforceable,[1] but it is possible for the uncertainty to be cured by a remission under section 22 of the Arbitration Act 1950. An award must convey clearly the arbitrator's decision on the matters referred, so that the parties are able to ascertain their rights and obligations arising out of the award free of doubt. The precise cause of the uncertainty would seem immaterial: what matters is the consequence. The uncertainty must be that of the award itself and it follows that the enquiry must confine its attention to the award, save that regard may also be had to external documents incorporated into the award.[2] In all probability the certainty of an award is not to be assessed wholly objectively, but predominantly from the standpoint of the parties.[3] It is the parties who have the immediate experience of the reference and of the surrounding circumstances, and looked at from their standpoint an award may be clear and comprehensible, but yet unintelligible to an outsider. Regard must also be had to the precise terms of an arbitrator's mandate which would appear an essential benchmark to any qualitative assessment of an award.[4] Where an award itself provides a formula for unravelling an uncertainty which appears on its face, the courts have shown themselves willing to apply the maxim *id certum est quod certum reddi potest*.[5]

11.3.4.2 The precise ambit of the requirement that awards be certain is itself a little

arbitrator has wholly disregarded the evidence may be guilty of misconduct; see *Evanghelinos* v. *Leslie and Anderson* (1920) 4 Ll.L.Rep. 17; *Jordenson & Co.* v. *Stora Kopparbergs Bergslags Aktiebolag* (1931) 41 Ll.L.Rep. 201; *Temple SS Co. Ltd.* v. *V/O Sovfracht* (1943) 76 Ll.L.Rep. 35.

23. *Moran* v. *Lloyd's* [1983] 1 Lloyd's Rep. 472; *King* v. *Thomas McKenna Ltd.* [1991] 1 All E.R. 653; *Geogas S.A.* v. *Trammo Gas Ltd.* (*The Baleares*) [1993] 1 Lloyd's Rep. 215.

24. [1991] 1 All E.R. 653.

1. *Hopcraft* v. *Hickman* (1824) 2 Sim. & St. 130; *Re Tribe and Upperton* (1835) 3 Ad. El. 295; *Re Marshall and Dresser* (1843) 3 Q.B. 878; *Smith* v. *Hartley* (1851) 20 L.J.C.P. 169; *Margulies Bros. Ltd.* v. *Dafnis Thomaides & Co. (U.K.) Ltd.* [1958] 1 W.L.R. 398; *River Plate Products Netherlands B.V.* v. *Etablissement Coargrain* [1982] 1 Lloyd's Rep. 628; *Montrose Canned Foods Ltd.* v. *Eric Wells (Merchants) Ltd.* [1965] 1 Lloyd's Rep. 597.

2. *Margulies Bros. Ltd.* v. *Dafnis Thomaides & Co. (U.K.) Ltd.* [1956] 1 W.L.R. 398.

3. *Wohlenberg* v. *Lageman* (1815) 6 Taunt 251; *Plummer* v. *Lee* (1837) 2 M. & W. 495; *Wrightson* v. *Bywater* (1838) 3 M. & W. 199; *Round* v. *Hatton* (1842) 10 M. & W. 660; *Nickels* v. *Hancock* (1855) 7 De G.M. & G. 300; *Fabrica Lombarda di Acido Tartaries* v. *Fuerst Bros. Ltd.* (1921) 8 Ll.L.Rep. 57.

4. *Cargey* v. *Aitcheson* (1823) 2 B. & C. 170; *Waddle* v. *Downman* (1844) 12 M. & W. 562.

5. *Wohlenberg* v. *Lageman* (1815) 6 Taunt 251; *Higgins* v. *Willes* (1828) 3 Man. & Ry. K.B. 382. For the limitations of the maxim see *Margulies Bros. Ltd.* v. *Dafnis Thomaides & Co. (U.K.) Ltd.* [1958] 1 Lloyd's Rep. 250, 253, per Diplock J.

uncertain. It most clearly applies to the operative part of an award and it is in this regard that most of the issues have arisen. What is not clear is whether the concept extends to other parts of an award and also whether the certainty of the operative part of an award may be affected by the tenor of an award as a whole, with the consequence that the reasoning embodied in an award may be capable of assuming a relevance in relation to any question raised as to the certainty of the operative award. There are also suggestions in the authorities that the requirement of certainty and the mode by which the certainty of an award is to be assessed may extend beyond the strict boundaries of the operative part of an award. Diplock J. has spoken of "unintelligibility" in the same breath as "uncertainty".[6] In the early authorities there are also suggestions that an award is uncertain if it is inconsistent with the reasoning which underlies it,[7] or if it contains inconsistent adjudications,[8] or if it reveals an uncertainty as to how precisely the matters in dispute were decided.[9] But in more recent times it has been denied that inconsistency in the arbitrator's findings of fact may represent a ground for challenging an award.[10]

11.3.5 Reasons and the enforcement of awards

11.3.5.1 An award may be enforced by action at common law[1] or under the summary statutory procedure established by section 26 of the Arbitration Act 1950, which provides that an "award on an arbitration agreement may, by leave of the High Court or a judge thereof,[2] be enforced in the same manner as a judgment or order to the same effect, and where leave is so given, judgment may be entered in terms of the award".[3] The two forms of process are available with regard to both domestic and foreign awards[4] and are also adopted for the enforcement of foreign awards under international conventions.[5] Although the statutory process is discretionary, it has nonetheless come to be perceived as the principal mode of enforcement and is made fairly freely available. It is only denied to an applicant when there exists a real ground for doubting the validity of an award,[6] in which case the applicant is compelled to resort to the common law action, in the course of which the question of validity will be fully considered, and has to be established by the plaintiff in accordance with the civil burden of proof.[7]

11.3.5.2 A substantive defect in an award, rendering an award bad on its face, rep-

---

6. *Margulies Bros. Ltd.* v. *Dafnis Thomaides & Co. (U.K.) Ltd.* [1958] 1 W.L.R. 398.
7. *Ames* v. *Milward* (1818) 8 Taunt 637.
8. *Duke of Beaufort* v. *Welch* (1839) 10 Ad. & El. 527. *Seccombe* v. *Babb* (1840) 6 M. & W. 129; *Williams* v. *Moulsdale* (1840) 7 M. & W. 134; *Grenfell* v. *Edgecombe* (1845) 7 Q.B. 661.
9. *Martin* v. *Burge* (1836) 4 A. & E. 973.
10. *Geogas S.A.* v. *Trammo Gas Ltd.* (*The Baleares*) [1993] 1 Lloyd's Rep. 215, 232, Steyn L.J.
1. See generally *Russell on Arbitration*, *op. cit.*, *supra*, Chapter 20; Mustill and Boyd, *Commercial Arbitration*, *op. cit.*, *supra*, Chapter 28.
2. For the prevailing practice, see R.S.C. Order 73, r.3.
3. Section 26(1).
4. *Norske Atlas Insurance Co. Ltd.* v. *London General Insurance Co. Ltd.* (1927) 28 Ll.L.Rep. 104.
5. Arbitration Act 1950, Part II, s. 36(1); Arbitration Act 1975, s. 3(1)(a).
6. *Middlemiss* v. *Hartlepool Corpn.* [1972] 1 W.L.R. 1643, 1647, Lord Denning M.R. Contrast the earlier approach in *Re Boks and Co. and Peters, Rushton and Co. Ltd.* [1919] 1 K.B. 491, per Scrutton L.J.; *Margulies Bros. Ltd.* v. *Dafnis Thomaides Ltd.* [1958] 1 W.L.R. 398, 404, per Diplock J.; *Nationale des Coopératives Agricoles de Céréales* v. *Robert Catterall & Co. Ltd.* [1959] 1 All E.R. 721, 725 (C.A.).
7. Cf. *Smith* v. *Martin* [1925] 1 K.B. 745; *Oil Products Trading Co. Ltd.* v. *Société de Gestion d'Entreprises Coloniales* (1934) 150 L.T. 475.

resents a potential defence to any attempt to enforce an award by whatever mode of process.[8] Uncertainty on the face of an award, which has previously been considered,[8a] may in consequence represent a potential defence[9] but where such a defence is with justification pleaded, it is also open to the court to remit the award under the section 22 jurisdiction, with the object of resolving the uncertainty and rendering the award enforceable.[10] Further, in *Margulies Bros. Ltd.* v. *Dafnis Thomaides & Co. (U.K.) Ltd*,[11] Diplock J. considered that following the emergence of the summary statutory enforcement process, it was an implied term of every arbitration agreement, within the meaning of the arbitration legislation, that every money award (as contrasted with a declaratory award) must be in a form rendering it enforceable in the same manner as a judgment for the purposes of section 26. Where the implied term is broken the court again enjoys a jurisdiction under section 22 to remit the award so that it can be put into an enforceable form. If it is also the case that an arbitrator is guilty of misconduct if he infringes an express or implied term of his mandate,[12] then this may represent yet a further basis for the remission of an unenforceable award.

11.4 REASONED AWARDS UNDER THE 1979 ACT—INTRODUCTION

11.4.1 The 1979 Act is the first statutory measure to address directly the question of reasoned awards. The Act does not establish an all-pervasive duty on the part of arbitrators and umpires to make reasoned awards. Less ambitiously, it establishes a qualified and discretionary jurisdiction whereunder the High Court may, in response to an application properly brought within the terms of section 1(5), and subject to the jurisdictional preconditions specified in section 1(6), make an order directing that reasons or further reasons be given with regard to an award made. The 1979 Act does not displace the preceding common law and general statutory law, nor does it displace established arbitral practice. It exists as a new dimension extending upon and modifying the position as it existed under the preceding law and practice. The fact that legislation was considered necessary is also, to some extent, an implied acknowledgement of the limitations of the preceding law.

11.4.2 The new statutory provision is set out in section 1(5) and (6), wherein it is provided:

(5) Subject to subsection (6) below, if an award is made and, on an application made by any of the parties to the reference—
    (a) with the consent of all the other parties to the reference, or
    (b) subject to section 3 below, with the leave of the court,
it appears to the High Court that the award does not or does not sufficiently set out the reasons for the award, the court may order the arbitrator or umpire concerned to state the reasons for

---

8. Cf. *Love* v. *Honeybourne* (1824) 4 D & R. 814; *Re Tribe and Upperton* (1835) 3 A. & E. 295; *Hewitt* v. *Hewitt* (1841) 1 Q.B. 110; *Re Marshall and Dresser* (1843) 3 Q.B. 878; *Waddle* v. *Downman* (1844) 12 M. & W. 562; *Re Tidswell* (1863) 33 Beav. 213.

8a. *Supra*, para. 11.2.5.

9. *Supra*, note 8. Also *Margulies Bros. Ltd.* v. *Dafnis Thomaides & Co. (U.K.) Ltd.* [1958] 1 Lloyd's Rep 250 (C.A.).

10. *Montrose Canned Foods Ltd.* v. *Eric Wells (Merchants) Ltd.* [1965] 1 Lloyd's Rep. 597; *Oricon Waren-Handels G.m.b.H.* v. *Intergraan N.V.* [1967] 2 Lloyd's Rep. 82; *Cremer* v. *Samanta and Samanta* [1968] 1 Lloyd's Rep. 156.

11. [1958] 1 W.L.R. 398.

12. *London Export Corpn. Ltd.* v. *Jubilee Coffee Roasting Co. Ltd.* [1958] 1 Lloyd's Rep. 197.

his award in sufficient detail to enable the court, should an appeal be brought under this section, to consider any questions of law arising out of the award.

(6) In any case where an award is made without any reason being given, the High Court shall not make an order under subsection (5) above unless it is satisfied—

(a) that before the award was made one of the parties to the reference gave notice to the arbitrator or umpire concerned that a reasoned award would be required; or

(b) that there is some special reason why such a notice was not given.

11.4.3 The broad jurisprudential effect of section 1(5) is to extend the jurisdiction of the court to direct the remission of an award for reconsideration.[1] The legislation cannot be associated directly with any general move in policy aimed at improving the rationality of the arbitral process or subscribing to a right of arbitrating parties to know why they have won or lost. The new power exists as an indispensable incident to the new appeal procedure, for without such a power the appeal procedure might not function at all or otherwise imperfectly. The new appeal process is based on reasoned awards and it is consequently essential that there exists an ancillary judicial power to ensure that reasoned awards are made and that the reasons manifested in awards are adequate to enable the court to discharge its reviewing function. The power to direct the giving of reasons is therefore a power conferred in aid of the right of appeal.[2] It cannot be invoked for some other unrelated purpose, such as the informing of the parties *per se* or to assist the determination of a preliminary question of law under the machinery established by section 2 of the 1979 Act. Nor can the statutory power be invoked when the necessary preconditions to the appellate process are absent, so that an appeal could not be brought under section 1, as where a question of fact alone is in issue or where, notwithstanding that a question of law is in issue, it is in the context of the dispute an insubstantial question of law.[3] It would equally appear to follow that the jurisdiction is lost when there is present a valid exclusion agreement excluding the possibility of an appeal.[4] Not only does the appeal procedure provide the fundamental rationale of the new statutory power, it also defines the limits of the jurisdiction, for the High Court may only order reasons or further reasons "in sufficient detail to enable the court, should an appeal be brought under this section, to consider any question of law arising out of the award".[5] The association with the appeal procedure is further emphasised by the manner in which both the appeal procedure and the power to direct the giving of reasons are integrated into the same section of the 1979 Act. Notwithstanding this close structural association, it is further not the case that the institution of an appeal or even an immediate intent to appeal is an essential precondition to the making of an order for reasons.[6] It is, however, the case that the relevant subsections are to be construed in the context of section 1 as a whole and against the backdrop of the policy associated with the new appellate system.[7]

11.4.4 But the strict view of the proper province of the new power to direct the

---

1. The general jurisdiction arises under s. 22 of the Arbitration Act 1950.
2. Staughton, "The Arbitration Act 1979—a Pragmatic Compromise" [1979] N.L.J. 920, 922.
3. See Chapters 3 and 4.
4. See Chapter 13.
5. Section 1(5). See further, para. 11.6.4.
6. See *infra*, para. 11.8.1.3.
7. *Kansa General Insurance Co. Ltd.* v. *Bishopsgate Insurance plc* [1988] 1 Lloyd's Rep. 503, 507, per Hirst J.

giving of reasons does not preclude the 1979 Act from achieving a much wider potential impact. The new legislation implicitly recognises the desirability of reasons and encourages the making of reasoned awards.[8] As was discussed in the introduction to the present chapter, the grounds for advocating a system of arbitral law and practice founded on reasoned awards are many and manifold, and extend beyond the facilitation of appeals. Section 1(5) is itself a symbolic expression of this wider potential purpose, as also is the abolition of the common law jurisdiction to set aside an award for error of law on its face and its replacement by a limited right of appeal. By this development the root cause of the historical reluctance to give reasoned awards and the drift into giving extra-award reasons has been removed and the survival of such attitudes and practices in the post-1979 Act period has become much more difficult to support.[9] Following the enactment of the 1979 legislation a reasoned award is substantially less vulnerable than was formerly the case; this being so it may be speculated that under prevailing conditions arbitrators and umpires ought to be more inclined to make reasoned awards and parties also more ready to agree that they should do so. The more widely this spirit gains acceptance the less will be the need to resort to the statutory power introduced by the 1979 Act, with good arbitral practice becoming defined in terms which pre-empts the new statutory power.[10] The language of section 1(6) is also at least open to the interpretation that it creates by implication a quasi-duty on the part of an arbitrator or umpire to give a reasoned award when such an award is requested by any party to a reference.[11] Not only does the 1979 Act act as an impetus to the making of reasoned awards, there is also at least a suggestion in the contemporary law that it contributes towards the establishment of the prevailing standard, so that the notion of a reasoned award under the 1979 Act will, subject to the express terms of an arbitrator's mandate, also come to represent a norm of general application. There is a strong suggestion of this possibility in *The Niedersachsen* where Sir John Donaldson M.R. observed[12]:

The Arbitration Act 1979 nowhere defines what is meant by a "reasoned award", but it is clear from s.1(5) that what is meant is one which states the reasons for the award in sufficient detail for the court to consider any question of law arising therefrom, if, of course, it were to give leave to appeal. This is what a party is asking for, if he gives notice that a reasoned award is required. This is what, notwithstanding the absence of such a notice, he will be entitled to expect, if the relevant arbitral rules require the giving of a reasoned award. This, again, is what he will be entitled to expect if, notwithstanding the absence of such a notice, the arbitrator indicates that it is his intention to make a reasoned award.

Notwithstanding the contribution which the 1979 Act makes to changing the philoso-

---

8. *Schiffahrtsagentur Hamburg Middle East Line G.m.b.H.* v. *Virtue Shipping Corpn.* (*The Oinoussian Virtue*) [1981] 1 Lloyd's Rep. 533, 537, per Robert Goff. J.; *Trave Schiffahrtsgesellschaft m.b.H. & Co. K.G.* v. *Ninemia Maritime Corpn.* (*The Niedersachsen*) [1986] Q.B. 802, 807D, per Sir John Donaldson M.R.; *Universal Petroleum Co. Ltd.* v. *Handels- und Transport Gesellschaft m.b.H.* [1987] 1 Lloyd's Rep. 517, 528, per Kerr L.J. (C.A.).

9. The historical attitude to the question of reasoned awards and the practices it gave rise to have been considered *supra*, para. 11.2.6.

10. *Universal Petroleum Co. Ltd.* v. *Handels- und Transport Gesellschaft m.b.H.* [1987] 1 Lloyd's Rep. 517, 528, per Kerr L.J. (C.A.).

11. See *infra*, para. 11.7.3.1.7.

12. *Trave Schiffahrtsgesellschaft m.b.H. & Co. K.G.* v. *Ninemia Maritime Corpn.* (*The Niedersachsen*) [1986] Q.B. 802, 807.

phical environment with regard to reasoned awards, it otherwise does not impinge on pre-1979 practices developed with regard to the giving of reasons. Thus the parties continue to be entitled to regulate the giving of reasons by express or implied contract. Subject to the terms of their mandate, arbitrators may continue to volunteer reasoned awards and give extra-award reasons; and it remains open to a party to make a unilateral non-contractual request for reasons, although the significance of such a request has been materially affected by section 1(6)(a).

11.4.5 To the extent that section 1(5) establishes a jurisdiction to remit an award for further consideration it bears an obvious and close relationship with section 22 of the Arbitration Act 1950. There is also a potential overlap between the two statutory provisions, and the manner in which this is managed by the court will be considered later.[13] There are, however, significant points of contrast. Under section 1(5) an award may only be remitted to "the arbitrator or umpire" concerned. Given the underlying rationale of the jurisdiction this is of course compelling logic. In contrast, the jurisdiction arising under section 22, which is of a much more general nature, has been adapted by the courts to allow remission to a new arbitrator or umpire where the circumstances justify such an order.[14] In practice an order of this character is likely to be very rare, and it may also be doubted whether such an order is valid under section 22 as presently drafted. A further difference relates to the manner the two powers may be instigated. Under section 1(5) an application must be made by a party to a reference,[15] whereas under section 22 the court may remit of its own motion.

11.4.6 Beyond establishing the parameters of the new jurisdiction section 1(5) does not further specify the criteria to be taken into account by the court in exercising the discretion associated with the statutory jurisdiction. As with the case of the judicial discretion arising under section 1(3)(b),[16] this has been left to unfold in the course of the judicial development of the legislation and it is inevitable that the judicial approach has been significantly influenced by the perceived general policy underlying the 1979 Act.[17] In theory the judicial discretion comes into issue on two occasions. First, on an application for leave to apply, which on the face of the legislation is an essential preliminary when all the other parties to the reference do not consent to an application under section 1(5). Secondly, where leave is granted, on the substantive application. But in practice the two stages have been merged and in consequence so also have the discretionary questions.[18] By virtue of the close affinity between section 1 appeals and the power to direct the giving of reasons it would be difficult to apprehend that the applicable statutory provisions and issues of judicial discretion can develop otherwise than in a policy environment common to both.

11.4.7 Except where an application is made with the consent of all the other parties to a reference, the right to apply for an order directing reasons or further reasons is lost where the parties have executed a valid exclusion agreement.[19]

---

13. See *infra*, para. 11.11.
14. *Peterson* v. *Ayre* (1854) 14 C.B. 665; *Richard Clear & Co. Ltd.* v. *Bloch* (1922) 13 Ll.L.Rep. 462; *Re Fuerst Bros. & Co. Ltd. and R.S. Stephenson* [1951] 1 Lloyd's Rep. 429.
15. See *infra*, para. 11.5.2.
16. See Chapters 5 and 6.
17. See *infra*, para. 11.8.
18. See *infra*, para. 11.12.2.1.
19. See *infra*, para. 11.9; and Chapter 13.

11.5 APPLICATION FOR A SECTION 1(5) ORDER

11.5.1 When may an application be made

11.5.1.1 The High Court has no jurisdiction under section 1(5) unless an award has been made. The subsection opens with the phrase "if an award is made". It necessarily follows that it is redundant to seek leave to apply prior to the making of an award.

With regard to the pre-award phase subsection (5) offers no remedy and the parties must seek alternative remedies. Thus where an arbitrator or umpire is mandated from the moment of his appointment to make a reasoned award, or one or both parties request or direct an arbitrator or umpire during the course of a reference to give a reasoned award, but the arbitrator or umpire refuses to comply and insists that only an operative award will be made, there exists no immediate remedy under subsection (5). In this kind of situation it would seem that the parties have two alternative courses of action available to them. The first is to protest and seek an order under subsection (5) after an award has been made. Alternatively they may move for an immediate remedy and seek declaratory relief and also possibly a mandatory injunction; or they may seek to revoke the authority of or to remove the arbitrator or umpire under sections 1 and 23(1) of the Arbitration Act 1950. The conduct of the arbitrator or umpire might also amount to an anticipatory breach of contract and therefore in theory at least an action for damages might also be available, but it is unlikely that damages would represent an appropriate remedy.[1]

11.5.1.2 For the purposes of section 1(5) an award includes an interim, interim final and final award: a first tier award of a sole arbitrator, umpire or arbitral tribunal and the award of an appeal arbitration tribunal; a monetary, declarative or directative award. In the case of a multi-arbitrator tribunal an award alludes to any award which is capable of being a valid award of the arbitral tribunal.[2] This may be a majority award or the award of a designated arbitrator, such as the appointed chairman or president of the arbitral tribunal. All will turn on the precise contractual terms governing the decision-making powers of the multi-arbitrator tribunal.

There is in the legislation no specification as to the form of an award. It may in consequence apply to both formal and informal awards. A parol award is *prima facie* valid[3] and the concept of reasons and of a reasoned award may equally apply to an informal award albeit very awkwardly. But informal awards offer obvious and profound difficulties of proof,[4] which difficulties are compounded in the context of the provisions of section 1(5) and (6). They are exceptionally rare in practice[5] and it is

---

1. The availability of a remedy which seeks to compel an arbitrator or umpire to give reasons would appear to be untried and also to be an issue of uncertainty. But it is difficult to see that some kind of remedy is not available in principle. In indicating that no reasons will be given an arbitrator would in many instances be in breach of contract, but any question of damages would be difficult to quantify and also probably would not provide an adequate remedy for the aggrieved party.

2. See Chapter 3, para. 3.3. Also *Kansa General Insurance Co. Ltd.* v. *Bishopsgate Insurance plc* [1988] 1 Lloyd's Rep. 503.

3. *Roberts* v. *Watkins* (1863) 32 L.J.C.P. 291; *Thompson* v. *Miller* (1867) 15 W.R. 353. Contrast the now repealed Arbitration Act 1889, Sch. 1, para. (c).

4. An informal award must also be declared to the parties for it to be valid and enforceable; see *Thompson* v. *Miller, ibid.*

5. It may even be ventured that they are unknown in contemporary practice.

highly improbable that any manner of award other than a written award will come forward for consideration under section 1(5).

11.5.1.3 It is also to be noted that an award under section 1(5) is not expressly connected to an arbitration agreement within the meaning of the 1979 Act.[6] It is, however, doubtful if this will result in section 1(5) being interpreted as applicable to awards made on parol arbitration agreements. The contemporary judicial inclination is to associate the arbitration legislation with written arbitration agreements, within the meaning of section 32 of the Arbitration Act 1950, even when the particular parcel of legislation in issue does not make any express reference to an arbitration agreement.[7] Further, the close relationship between section 1(2) and section 1(5) must not be lost sight of. The former relates to appeals on any question of law arising out of "an award made on an arbitration agreement", with arbitration agreement defined as in section 32 of the Arbitration Act 1950.[8] It is also the case that subsection (5) is to be interpreted in the context of section 1 as a whole.[9] All appears to indicate that the subsection is tied to awards made on arbitration agreements as defined in the 1979 Act.

11.5.1.4 Subsection (5) requires that an award shall have been "made" but offers no definition of the term. There is much legal technicality surrounding the meaning of the making of an award.[10] But this learning appears to have little practical application to the operation of section 1(5). Before a party to a reference will be in a position to complain about the absence or insufficiency of reasons in an award, the party or his representatives will of necessity have had sight of the award. As such it will be an award which has not only been made in the technical sense,[11] but also actually delivered to at least one of the parties.

11.5.2 Who may make an application

An application may be made "by any of the parties to the reference".[1] In this regard section 1(5) corresponds with section 1(3) and the discussion of the phrase in the context of section 1(3) is of equal application to section 1(5).[2] The reference to "any" party means that an application may be made either by the claimant or respondent in an arbitration, or even by both.[3]

Section 1(5) confers no right to apply on arbitrators and umpires. The subsection therefore cannot be utilised by arbitrators and umpires as a means of reopening an award after it has been made and when the arbitrator or umpire is *functus officio*.

11.5.3 Preconditions to an application

An application for an order under section 1(5) is not a matter of absolute right but may only be made either with the consent of all the other parties to the reference or

---

6. See Chapter 1, para. 1.7.5.
7. See, for example, *Imperial Metal Industries (Kynoch) Ltd.* v. *Amalgamated Union of Engineering Workers* [1979] 1 All E.R. 847.
8. See Chapter 3, para. 3.4.
9. *Supra*, para. 11.4.
10. See Chapter 3, para. 3.3.9.
11. See *Hiscox* v. *Outhwaite (No. 1)* [1992] 1 A.C. 562, 594, Lord Oliver.
1. Section 1(5).
2. See Chapter 2, para. 2.2.
3. See *infra*, para. 11.12.

with leave of the High Court. These preconditions mirror those contained in section 1(3) with regard to appeals.[1]

11.5.3.1 Consent of all the other parties to the reference

11.5.3.1.1 The consent must be that of *all* the other parties to the reference and where unanimous consent exists it is unnecessary to seek leave of the court. Such consent also overrides any exclusion agreement that may have been executed previously.[1] In this regard the unanimous consent acts either as a waiver or as a displacing subsequent contract.[2]

A similar precondition is laid down in section 1(3)(a) with regard to an appeal on a question of law and the discussion in Chapter 4 of that particular precondition is of equal application to the same precondition set out in section 1(5)(a).[3]

There is in section 1(5)(a) no express stipulation as to the form of the consent. This may suggest that a parol consent communicated to the party wishing to make an application is sufficient. But R.S.C. Order 73, rule 5(5) requires that a copy of every consent given in writing must be served with the originating summons. This appears to contemplate that the consent must be in writing or that an initial parol consent must be subsequently acknowledged by writing.[4] But whatever be the strict legal requirement, as a matter of practice it is highly desirable that the consent be given in writing.

11.5.3.1.2 In practice the consent of all the other parties is unlikely to be readily volunteered. Such consent will predominantly be sought by a party who has lost in an arbitration and who wishes to set up an appeal. For the other party or parties to consent to an application will therefore be to engage in an act which has the potential to prejudice the victory. Where both or all the parties are contemplating an appeal the position may be different and in this circumstance an application with consent is a more likely possibility, for the parties may be happy to engage in a mutual accommodation. It would also seem possible for consent to be given conditionally, for example, without prejudice to the award made in the arbitration. The implication of a "without prejudice" consent would appear to be that notwithstanding the consent to a section 1(5) application and the possibility of an appeal there following, the parties, so far as their mutual obligations are concerned, agree to be bound by the terms of the original award. This kind of procedure might be followed where the award raises a question in the nature of a test case.

11.5.3.2 Leave of the High Court

11.5.3.2.1 Alternatively an application for an order under section 1(5) may be made with leave of the High Court,[1] with the jurisdiction of the court to entertain an appli-

---

1. See Chapter 4.
1. Section 1(5)(a) is not made "subject to section 3 below" as is section 1(5)(b). Further, section 3(1)(b) alludes to section 1(5)(b) only.
2. See, *infra*, para. 11.9.
3. See Chapter 4, para. 4.2.
4. See *infra*, para. 11.12.1.3.
1. Section 1(5)(b). For an example of leave being sought and granted, see *Vermala Shipping Enterprises Ltd.* v. *The Minerals and Metals Trading Corpn. of India Ltd. (The Gay Fidelity)* [1982] 1 Lloyd's Rep. 469.

cation for leave dependent on the absence of an exclusion agreement.[2] If leave is refused then the matter is closed and the award must stand as originally made, although there does exist a limited right of appeal under the provisions of section 1(6A), from the grant or refusal of leave to apply.[3]

Paragraphs (a) and (b) of section 1(5) are expressed disjunctively, thereby suggesting that an application to the High Court for leave to apply may be made as an alternative proceeding and is not preconditioned by a failed attempt to first obtain the consent of all the other parties to the reference. But given that the question of leave falls to be determined in the discretion of the court, the failure by a party first to seek to proceed by consent, when it is reasonable for him to make the attempt, may possibly be taken into account by the court in the exercise of its discretion.[4] An application with consent offers the advantage of expedition and savings in costs and in practice it is likely therefore to be the first method of advancing to be considered by a party.

11.5.3.2.2 As with appeals on questions of law under section 1(2) and (3)(b), in the absence of consent an application under section 1(5)(b) involves two separate stages. First, an application to the court for leave to apply for an order for reasons or further reasons. Secondly, if leave is granted, the hearing and determination of the application.[5] Whereas with regard to appeals from awards on questions of law the two stages are distinct and separate,[6] the same is not true of the developed practice under section 1(5). With regard to the latter the two stages have effectively been merged into one, with the consequence that the statutory requirement of preliminary leave has been rendered somewhat artificial.[7] Staughton J. has explained the prevailing practice in the following terms[8]:

Since the buyer does not have the consent of the sellers, it will be observed that he needs both the leave of the Court to make the application and, if he obtains that leave, an order of the Court that further reasons be stated. There is a similar two-stage process in s. 1(2) and (3), which deals with appeals from arbitrators on questions of law. There the two stages involve different considerations; often the application for leave is heard separately from the substantive appeal which follows if leave is given. But in the case of sub-s. (5), which deals with reasons or further reasons, it was not suggested to me that any different considerations apply to an application for leave, and the application for reasons or further reasons if leave is given. The two processes are in practice one and the same application.

The upshot is that if following an application the court decides to make an order, it equally gives leave to apply, either expressly or impliedly. It necessarily follows that the discretion associated with the question of leave to apply is based on the same considerations of policy and subject to the same criteria as have been developed in association with the discretion connected with the decision to make or refuse an order on a full application.[9] So also when an award is made without any reasons being given, the

---

2. Section 1(5)(b) is expressed to be "subject to section 3 below". See also s. 3(1)(b). Exclusion agreements are discussed *infra*, para. 11.9, and in Chapter 13.

3. See *infra*, para. 11.10.

4. See the consideration of the similar point under s. 1(3) in Chapter 4, para. 4.1.2.

5. The existence of the two stages is expressly recognised in the provisions of s. 1(6A), which is considered *infra*, para. 11.10.

6. See Chapter 4, para. 4.3.1.

7. See, for example, *Vermala Shipping Enterprises Ltd.* v. *The Minerals and Metals Trading Corpn. of India Ltd. (The Gay Fidelity), supra.*

8. *Michael I. Warde* v. *Feedex International Inc.* [1984] 1 Lloyd's Rep. 310, 311.

9. See *infra*, para. 11.8.

court has neither jurisdiction to give leave nor to make an order under subsection (5), unless the terms of subsection (6) are satisfied.[10]

11.5.4 Conditional applications

Where one party to a reference applies for an order for reasons or further reasons it is possible for the other or another party to the same reference to make a conditional or protective counter-application for reasons or further reasons in the same proceedings.[1] The effect of a conditional application is that it will be pursued only in the event of the court being of a mind to make an order in response to the initial application. If no order is made then the conditional application is not pursued.[2]

The conditional application is of strategic utility when the initial application for reasons or further reasons is associated with a concurrent or prospective application for leave to appeal on a question of law. If granted the order may reveal reasons which may be utilised by the applicant in the appeal and which the other party will be obliged to counter. In order to do so effectively he may require the thinking of the arbitrator or umpire to be revealed still further and the conditional application is a useful procedural technique for achieving this objective. It is in the result a mode of procedure that protects the position of the other party and enables him to advance his own application, if it proves necessary, in the same proceeding before the court.[3]

11.6 JURISDICTION OF THE HIGH COURT TO MAKE SECTION 1(5) ORDERS

11.6.1 The general basis of jurisdiction

When an application is properly made the High Court has jurisdiction to make an order for reasons if it is satisfied that the award in question does not or does not sufficiently set out the reasons for the award.[1] Where the complaint alleges the total absence of reasons the jurisdiction of the High Court is further preconditioned by the need to establish that the terms of section 1(6) have been satisfied.[2] But to establish jurisdiction does not automatically result in an order for reasons or further reasons being made, for beyond the question of jurisdiction the court enjoys a discretion whether or not to make an order.[3]

Under section 1(5) the jurisdiction of the court revolves about two distinct but associated criteria: the absence of reasons and the insufficiency of reasons, with each criterion posing a question which is confined to the award in issue. Each raises a question of fact or of fact and degree and, as it will be seen, neither is free of difficulty,

---

10. The limitations introduced by section 1(6) are considered *infra* at para. 11.7.3.
1. See, for example, *Universal Petroleum Co. Ltd.* v. *Handels- und Transport Gesellschaft m.b.H.* [1987] 1 Lloyd's Rep. 517, 522 (C.A.).
2. See, *Clea Shipping Corporation* v. *Bulk Oil International Ltd. (The Alaskan Trader)* [1983] 1 Lloyd's Rep. 315, 316, 319, per Bingham J.
3. See also *infra*, para. 11.12.2.3.
1. Section 1(5). See also *Universal Petroleum Co. Ltd.* v. *Handels- und Transport Gesellschaft m.b.H.* [1987] 1 Lloyd's Rep. 517.
2. See *infra*, para. 11.7.3.
3. See *infra*, para. 11.8.

although, in general terms, the question whether or not any reasons have been given might be expected to be a far less troublesome issue than a question directed to the sufficiency of reasons provided.

There is inherent in section 1(5) a number of fundamental issues which have to be addressed and understood before the test of jurisdiction can be applied. What is the proper perception of "reasons", and, more generally, that of a "reasoned award" for the purposes of section 1(5)? Also, by what criterion or criteria is the "sufficiency" of reasons to be assessed? In searching for an understanding of these concepts it is not necessarily helpful to seek philosophical explanations. It seems clear that analytical and qualitative issues will inevitably be at play, but equally it must be borne in mind that what is under scrutiny is the interpretation of a commercial statute which has as its principal aim the establishment of an appeal procedure based on reasoned awards. Questions of interpretation are therefore likely to be tainted with a strong flavouring of pragmatism. There are also associated questions of evidence. In determining a question related to jurisdiction, to what extent is the court confined to the four corners of the award in issue, or may the court also have regard to extraneous evidence? It is proposed to discuss these various questions and issues in the ensuing text.

11.6.2 Reasons

11.6.2.1 The Act provides no definition of reasons. Some attention has already been given to the concept of reasons in the abstract in the introduction to the present chapter, but that discussion is not necessarily conclusive for present purposes. The immediate issue here is somewhat different and is foremost an exercise aimed at determining the meaning of a particular word in a statutory context.

In the structural format of a typical award the concept of "reasons" is capable of being approached in either a narrow or broad fashion. In the narrow sense "reasons' may be confined to a record of the intellectual exercise engaged in by an arbitrator or umpire as he sojourns from the evidence and argument to the initial findings of fact and law and therefrom to his conclusions and ultimate award. On this analysis "reasons" represent the "how" and the "why" of the findings, conclusions and award and is perceived as bearing a meaning synonymous with the "reasoning" of an arbitrator or umpire. In this narrow sense reasons are to be distinguished from the narrative, operative and other structural aspects of a typical award, such as the recitals, actual findings, conclusions and ultimate award.

11.6.2.2 But bearing in mind the purpose and context of the 1979 Act such an understanding of "reasons" is far too narrow. The general object underpinning the section 1(5) power is to provide information on the basis of which it may be determined whether a question of law arises, and if so to enable the question of law to be reviewed. To achieve this it is often necessary to be informed not only of the "how" and the "why", but also of the "what" of an arbitrator's decision. What is required is a full statement of the decision arrived at and the "basis" or "grounds" of the decision; an entire statement of the thinking of the arbitrator and the information taken into account. On this view the concept of "reasons" comes forward as a broad and flexible notion, with the term potentially encapsulating any information within the cognition of an arbitrator or umpire relating to the reference in question, and which contributed to the thinking of the arbitrator and the finalising of the award. Adopting this broad approach, the reference to "reasons" in section 1(5) is capable of alluding not only to the reasoning of an arbitrator or umpire strictly perceived, but as extending to the entire factual and legal foundations on which the award is made including the decisions actually made.

11.6.2.3 It is the broad view of the concept of "reasons" which has been adopted in the interpretation of the 1979 Act, with the immediate and important consequence that "reasons" include findings of fact. In *The Oinoussian Virtue* Robert Goff J. commented[1]:

> . . . in my judgment the expression "reasons" in this sub-section [i.e. subsection (5)] cannot be limited to "reasoning", but must include the relevant facts upon which the arbitrator's conclusion is based. Of course, a reasoned award need not take any particular form; though a typical form of reasoned award which now comes before the court is one in which the arbitrator, having set the general scene and identified the dispute between the parties, then sets out the parties' respective contentions, makes any further findings of fact which may be desirable for the purpose of considering those contentions, and then sets out his conclusion and reasons for reaching that conclusion. In such an award, facts found by the arbitrator appear to me to form an inseparable part of the total reasons for his award.

In *J. H. Rayner (Mincing Lane) Ltd.* v. *Shaher Trading Co.*,[2] it was common ground between the parties that the power under section 1(5) covered both the giving of reasons and the factual findings necessary to support them. Again, in *The Yanxilas*,[3] Bingham J. drew a distinction between findings of fact and reasons and extended the section 1(5) order made to both.

11.6.2.4 If under the statute "reasons" include findings of fact it is hardly possible to resist the premise that they also include findings of secondary facts and conclusions of fact. Equally, it is difficult to apprehend that there should in this matter be any distinction between law and fact and that a statement or conclusion of law is equally an aspect of the "reasons". Support of this view may be derived from a dictum of Bingham J. in *J. H. Rayner (Mincing Lane) Ltd.* v. *Shaher Trading Co.*,[4] where the learned judge considered that the professional legal advisers of the parties, "should be quite clear what is the factual and in general terms the legal basis of the award". Taking the implications still further forward, it would seem even possible for the statement or declaration of the ultimate award to be considered as "reasons".

11.6.2.5 The concept of "reasons" for the purposes of the 1979 Act is not to be analysed wholly in qualitative terms. The object sought to be achieved can never be lost sight of and this will give the concept a "purposive" complexion and by reference to which the boundaries of the concept will be ultimately defined. Thus an explanation given by an arbitrator which is unconnected with the substantive dispute or potential appeal does not qualify as reasons for the purposes of the 1979 Act, notwithstanding that in the abstract the explanation is capable of analysis as a reasoned explanation. An example of what may be described as extraneous reasons is provided by the decision in *The Kostas Melas*.[5] Arbitrators whose conduct had been challenged pro-

---

1. *Schiffahrtsagentur Hamburg Middle East Line G.m.b.H. Hamburg* v. *Virtue Shipping Corpn. of Monrovia. (The Oinoussian Virtue)* [1981] 1 Lloyd's Rep. 533, 539.
2. [1982] 1 Lloyd's Rep. 632, 633.
3. *Stinnes Interoil G.m.b.H.* v. *A. Halcoussis & Co. (The Yanxilas)* [1982] 2 Lloyd's Rep. 445, 452.
4. *Supra,* p. 637.
5. *S. L. Sethia Liners Ltd.* v. *Naviagro Maritime Corporation (The Kostas Melas)* [1981] 1 Lloyd's Rep. 18, 30.

vided the court with a statement setting out the reasons why they had acted in a way which was later objected to, and on the basis of which attempts had been made to have the award set aside or remitted for misconduct. The statement was prefaced by the phrase, "since our conduct has been called in question". It was held that since the document had come into existence for an extraneous purpose, it had no relevance in contributing to the reasons for the award.

11.6.2.6 In summary, to understand the reference to "reasons" in section 1(5) it is important to keep in mind the purpose of the subsection, which is to render possible or provide qualitative support for the appellate procedure established under section 1(2). So viewed "reasons" come forth as a more expansive concept than pure reasoning and are capable of including findings and conclusions of fact and law, including the ultimate substantive expression of an interim or final award. All or any of such items of information may be necessary in order to enable the parties, their professional advisers and the court to assess what an arbitrator or umpire has decided and why it was so decided, the facts and law that were accepted and acted upon, and the way the various findings, conclusions and ultimate award have been arrived at.

11.6.3 Reasoned awards

11.6.3.1 Again the Act provides no definition of a reasoned award. Indeed the phrase as such only appears on a single occasion in section 1(6)(a), but it is otherwise quite clearly a central issue in section 1(5). Just as an understanding of "reasons" is essential, so also is the perception of a "reasoned award" within the new scheme of filtered appeals established under section 1 of the 1979 Act.

A "reasoned award" in its essential essence is defined by inference from the terms of section 1(5) and as such is an award which sets out the reasons of an arbitrator or umpire in sufficient detail to enable the court, should an appeal be brought under section 1(2), to review any question of law arising out of an award.[1] But this is wholly descriptive and of limited help. Beyond the inference suggested by the statutory language there arise questions of form, format, content and general judicial perception as to the approach to be adopted.

11.6.3.2 There is in section 1(5) no express stipulation as to the form of a reasoned award and in consequence it is at least possible that both a parol and written award may fall within the designation, although the idea of a reasoned parol award raises obvious and great difficulties of conception and proof. But the assumption here made is far from being incontrovertible and as a question of interpretation it is not impossible for the reference to award in subsections (5) and (6) to be confined to written awards. But whatever the proper interpretation of the statute, the likelihood of a parol award is largely academic for they are so exceptionally rare in practice as to be effectively extinct.

11.6.3.3 From the first the judges have been eager to disassociate their expectation of reasoned awards under the new law from the practice that prevailed in association with the special case procedure. That practice had resulted in formal and stylised

---

1. *Trave Schiffahrtsgesellschaft m.b.H. & Co. K.G.* v. *Ninemia Maritime Corpn. (The Niedersachsen)* [1986] Q.B. 802, 807; *Kansa General Insurance Co. Ltd.* v. *Bishopsgate Insurance plc* [1988] 1 Lloyd's Rep. 503, 509.

awards, which were described by the Commercial Court Committee in its Report on Arbitration in the following terms[2]:

> An award in the form of a special case is quite different from a simple final award. It is customarily somewhat formalized. Beginning with a recital of the agreement under which the arbitrator derives his jurisdiction, it then sets out the nature of the dispute and the rival contentions of the parties both on fact and law. This is followed by a series of findings of fact and a statement of the questions of law which are being submitted to the Court for decision. In conclusion, it will usually contain alternative awards to take effect according to how the Court answers the questions of law and may provide that if the award is not set down (entered in the list of cases for hearing in the High Court) within a specified time, one of the alternative awards shall take effect as a final award. In a few cases the possible permutations of answers are so numerous that it is impossible for the arbitrator to make alternative awards covering all contingencies. In such cases it is usual for the arbitrator to ask that the case be remitted to him so that he may make a final award in the light of the Court's judgment.

11.6.3.4 A salient feature of a special case award was that it was unreasoned in the narrow sense of the term for beyond stating the findings and conclusions of an arbitrator or umpire it gave no indication of how the findings, conclusions and award had been arrived at.[3] It was therefore wholly different from a reasoned award.[4] Such was their technicality that in drawing up special case awards arbitrators and umpires often felt the need to take professional advice and assistance, which in turn increased costs and also delayed the arbitral process.[5]

11.6.3.5 In discouraging the continuation of the practice associated with special case awards, the judicial antipathy has concentrated on such matters as their form, rigidity, technical demands and the absence of the "why". The discouragement does not however extend further and embrace the kind of information customarily associated with special case awards. Setting the scene to both the dispute and the establishment of the arbitration,[6] identifying the issues, reviewing the submissions and making findings and conclusions of fact and law, which were standard features of special case awards, are equally viewed as vital aspects of the new species of reasoned awards.[7]

11.6.3.6 But under the new law arbitrators must go a step further and provide a record of their reasoning. Moreover the mood and tone of the entire exercise is materially changed.[8] Arbitrators and umpires are encouraged to do no more than provide at the end of the hearing or soon afterwards nothing more sophisticated than a straightforward and unpretentious account of their findings and an explanation of their award, all of which they should be able to achieve without professional assistance. What is required is a personal, sincere and open statement of what they have decided and why they have so decided, with the "what" and "why" explained sufficiently so as to be free of any real doubt. The new emphasis is on substance and not form, with

---

2. *Supra*, para. 10.

3. For examples of the form and content of typical special case awards see *Bremer Handelsgesellschaft m.b.H.* v. *C. Mackprang Jr.* [1980] 1 Lloyd's Rep. 210; *Thomas P. Gonzalez Corpn.* v. *Muller's Mühle Muller G.m.b.H. & Co. K.G. (No. 2)* [1980] 1 Lloyd's Rep. 445; *Fratelli Moretti S.p.A.* v. *Nidera Handelscompagnie B.V.* [1980] 1 Lloyd's Rep. 534; *Pagnan and Fratelli* v. *Tradax Overseas S.A.* [1980] 1 Lloyd's Rep. 665.

4. Report *supra*, para. 11.

5. Report *supra*, para. 20.

6. This can be of particular relevance because of the way the discretion associated with the application for leave to appeal under section 1(3)(b) is exercised; see Chapter 5, para. 5.2.2.

7. As is revealed in the ensuing discussion.

8. *Vinava Shipping Co. Ltd.* v. *Finelvet A.G. (The Chrysalis)* [1983] 1 Lloyd's Rep. 503, 508.

allowance made for the range of backgrounds from which arbitrators are drawn. Excessive formality, comprehensiveness, meticulousness, technicality, legal jargon and the pursuit of historical lines of legal reasoning are all not only unnecessary but *prima facie* undesirable.[9] A reasoned award is not to be understood as something synonymous with a typical High Court judgment.

11.6.3.7 An early and general indication of the desired approach was offered by Robert Goff J. in *The Oinoussian Virtue*[10]:

. . . a reasoned award need not take any particular form: though a typical form of reasoned award which now comes before the court is one in which the arbitrator, having set the general scene and identified the dispute between the parties, then sets out the parties' respective contentions, makes any further findings of fact which may be desirable for the purpose of considering those contentions, and then sets out his conclusion and reasons for reaching that conclusion.

The approach to be adopted by trade arbitrators in making awards in the context of the new legislation was outlined by Donaldson L.J. in *Bremer Handelsgesellschaft m.b.H.* v. *Westzucker G.m.b.H. (No. 2)* in the following terms[11]:

It is of the greatest importance that trade arbitrators working under the 1979 Act should realize that their whole approach should now be different. At the end of the hearing they will be in a position to give a decision and the reasons for that decision. They should do so at the earliest possible moment. The parties will have made their submissions as to what actually happened and what is the result in terms of their respective rights and liabilities. All this will be fresh in the arbitrators' minds and there will be no need for further written submissions by the parties. No particular form of award is required. Certainly no one wants a formal "Special Case". All that is necessary is that the arbitrators should set out what, on their view of the evidence, did or did not happen and should explain succinctly why, in the light of what happened, they have reached their decision and what that decision is. This is all that is meant by a "reasoned award".

For example, it may be convenient to begin by explaining briefly how the arbitration came about—"X sold to Y 200 tons of soyabean meal on the terms of GAFTA Contract 100 at U.S.$Z per ton c.i.f. Bremen. X claimed damages for non-delivery and we were appointed arbitrators". The award could then briefly tell the factual story as the arbitrators saw it. Much would be common ground and would need no elaboration. But when the award comes to matters in controversy, it would be helpful if the arbitrators not only gave their view of what occurred, but also made it clear that they have considered any alternative version and have rejected it, e.g., "The shippers claimed that they shipped 100 tons at the end of June. We are not satisfied that this is so", or as the case may be, "We are satisfied that this was not the case". The arbitrators should end with their conclusion as to the resulting rights and liabilities of the parties. There is nothing about this which is remotely technical, difficult or time consuming.

It is sometimes said that this involves arbitrators in delivering judgments and that this is something which requires legal skills. This is something of a half truth. Much of the art of giving a judgment lies in telling a story logically, coherently and accurately. This is something which requires skill, but it is not a legal skill and it is not necessarily advanced by legal training. It is certainly a judicial skill, but arbitrators for this purpose are Judges and will have no difficulty in acquiring it. Where a 1979 Act award differs from a judgment is in the fact that the arbitrators will not be expected to analyse the law and the authorities. It will be quite sufficient that they should explain how they reached their conclusion, e.g., "We regarded the conduct of the buyers, as we have described it, as constituting a repudiation of their obligations under the contract and the subsequent conduct of the sellers, also as described, as amounting to an acceptance of that repudiatory conduct putting an end to the contract". It can be left to others to argue

---

9. See *Clea Shipping Corpn.* v. *Bulk Oil International Ltd. (The Alaskan Trader)* [1983] 1 Lloyd's Rep. 315, 318.

10. *Schiffahrtsagentur Hamburg Middle East Line G.m.b.H.* v. *Virtue Shipping Corporation (The Oinoussian Virtue)* [1981] 1 Lloyd's Rep. 533, 539.

11. [1981] 2 Lloyd's Rep. 130, 132–133.

that this is wrong in law and to a professional Judge, if leave to appeal is given, to analyse the authorities. This is not to say that where arbitrators are content to set out their reasoning on questions of law in the same way as Judges, this will be unwelcome to the Courts. Far from it. The point which I am seeking to make is that a reasoned award, in accordance with the 1979 Act, is wholly different from an award in the form of a special case. It is not technical, it is not difficult to draw and above all it is something which can and should be produced promptly and quickly at the conclusion of the hearing. That is the time when it is easiest to produce an award with all the issues in mind.

11.6.3.8 This statement of the judicial anticipation of what is demanded under the 1979 Act has been judicially endorsed on many occasions subsequently.[12] With each endorsement there has tended to be introduced additional nuances and qualifications, cumulatively contributing to a total statement of the idea of a reasoned award. In *J. H. Rayner (Mincing Lane)* v. *Shaher Trading Co.*, Bingham J. after adopting the dictum of Donaldson L.J., further observed[13]:

So far as principle is concerned, it seems to me plain that under the new Act awards of arbitral tribunals should not be scrutinised with an over critical or pedantic eye and the Court should not insist that every factual "t" is crossed and every argumentative "i" is dotted . . . What is necessary is that the arbitrators should set out what, on their view of the evidence did or did not happen, and should explain succinctly why, in the light of what happened, they reached their decision and what that decision is.

11.6.3.9 It is unnecessary for arbitrators to consider in meticulous detail every disputed issue and every argument and contention advanced by the parties or their advocates.[14] In keeping with the attitude adopted towards special case awards, a summary and review of the parol and documentary evidence is not only discouraged but considered ill-advised.[15] Nor are arbitrators expected to provide reasons for every conclusion they arrive at. But an explanation must be given of the basis of an award and of any material conclusions arrived at that contributed to the determination of the issue in dispute.[16] Arbitrators are very much concerned with the merits of the arguments presented and must openly state in their awards what view they have taken on the merits.

11.6.3.10 Any construction of a reasoned award cannot ignore the purpose underlying a reasoned award and the procedural environment in which an award will come forward for consideration. In the first place a reasoned award is demanded as a necessary aid to determining an application for leave to appeal and any substantive appeal which follows. As is clear from the language of section 1(5), a reasoned award is fundamentally an award which sets out the reasons in sufficient detail to enable the court,

---

12. In all the significant subsequent authorities in which the concept of a reasoned award has been considered the dictum of Donaldson L.J. has been acknowledged and endorsed. The authorities are variously cited in the text.

13. [1982] 1 Lloyd's Rep. 632, 636.

14. For the duty of a judge in this regard see *Eagle Trust Co. Ltd.* v. *Pigott-Brown* [1985] 3 All E.R. 119, 122, per Griffiths L.J. Considered in *Bradley* v. *Hanseatic Shipping Co. Ltd.* [1986] 2 Lloyd's Rep. 34, 37, per Lawton L.J.

15. *Wates Ltd.* v. *Greater London Council*, *The Times*, 25 March 1981; *Trave Schiffahrtsgesellschaft m.b.H. & Co. K.G.* v. *Ninemia Maritime Corpn.* (*The Niedersachsen*) [1986] 1 Q.B. 802.

16. *Clea Shipping Corpn.* v. *Bulk Oil International Ltd.* (*The Alaskan Trader*), *supra*, p. 318; *Hayn Roman & Co. S.A.* v. *Cominter (U.K.) Ltd.* [1982] 2 Lloyd's Rep. 458, 464; *Universal Petroleum Co. Ltd.* v. *Handels- und Transport Gesellschaft m.b.H.* [1987] 1 Lloyd's Rep. 517, 527. The point is further discussed *infra*.

in the event of an appeal, to consider any question of law arising out of the award.[17] With this point in mind it would seem patent that an award must cover the ground adequately and, in particular, give special attention to the contentions which assume a central importance in the context of the global dispute,[18] for it is from these regions of the global dispute that an attempt to launch an appeal is most likely to emanate. This fairly obvious but important point has received its due emphasis. In *Hayn Roman & Co. S.A.* v. *Cominter (U.K.) Ltd.*, Robert Goff J. observed[19]:

> . . . it is incumbent upon arbitrators, in giving their reasons, to explain on what basis they have rejected contentions that have been advanced before them. They are not being asked to go into great detail, they are simply being asked to deal with submissions which have been advanced before them because this is just the kind of matter on which the parties, if their contentions are rejected, may wish to pursue an appeal.

In *Universal Petroleum Co. Ltd.* v. *Handels- und Transport Gesellschaft m.b.H.*, Kerr L.J. commented[20]:

> A reasoned award is usually requested in order to lay the foundations for a possible application for leave to appeal. An arbitrator should therefore remember to deal in his reasoned awards with all issues which may be described as having a "conclusive" nature, in the sense that he should give reasons for his decisions on all issues which lead to conclusions on liability or other major matters in dispute on which leave to appeal may subsequently be brought. Such issues should not be difficult to identify, and the arbitrator should if necessary be reminded about them.

11.6.3.11 When a central or material issue is under consideration and on which the arbitrator has come to a conclusion, he should enunciate in his award not only the basis on which he has arrived at his conclusion but also any other basis which may have existed having regard to the evidence and argument in the arbitration. The existence of a possible alternative basis for any conclusion may have a material bearing on the issue of substantiality and on the exercise of discretion on an application for leave to appeal.

11.6.3.12 Although appeals are confined to questions of law, an arbitrator or umpire is not required to analyse the law and engage in a detailed scrutiny of the relevant authorities.[21] Arbitrators and umpires who have legal training and experience may well attempt such an analytical exposition and in the opinion of Sir John Donaldson M.R. any such attempt will not be unwelcome.[22] Arbitrators and umpires who come from a commercial or non-legal professional background may readily accept the judicial invitation not to enter the technical and conceptual maze of legal science. But even legally qualified arbitrators and umpires must refrain from the temptation to engage in the deep and comprehensive analysis typical of judgments, for otherwise the potential advantage of expedition will be lost. This was made clear by the House of Lords in *The Antaios*,[23] where the award was accompanied by reasons that ran to 96

---

17. *Supra*, n. 1. See also *infra*, para. 11.6.4.
18. *Supra*, n. 15.
19. [1982] 2 Lloyd's Rep. 458, 464.
20. [1987] 1 Lloyd's Rep. 517, 527.
21. *Bremer Handelsgesellschaft m.b.H.* v. *Westzucker G.m.b.H. (No. 2)*, *supra*, pp. 132–133; *J. H. Rayner (Mincing Lane) Ltd.* v. *Shaher Trading Co.* [1982] 1 Lloyd's Rep. 632, 637, per Bingham J., "I do not in any way mean that there should be any detailed consideration of the authorities or anything of that sort".
22. *Bremer Handelsgesellschaft m.b.H.* v. *Westzucker G.m.b.H. (No. 2)*, *supra*, pp. 132–133.
23. *Antaios Compania Naviera S.A.* v. *Salen Rederierna A.B. (The Antaios)* [1985] A.C. 191.

pages, of which 78 were devoted to a legal analysis of the central issue in dispute. Lord Diplock considered the reasons to be an "interesting, learned and detailed dissertation on the law", but to be "so lengthy as to be . . . inappropriate for inclusion in the reasons given by arbitrators for an award".

11.6.3.13 It is not to be forgotten that a reasoned award is the chief item of evidence before a judge in deciding whether or not to give leave to appeal. To this end arbitrators should bear in mind the kind of factors which the court may have regard to in considering a question of leave to appeal. In consequence the reasons should be sufficient to communicate the character of the legal dispute and to provide a picture of the emergence of the dispute, the establishment of the arbitration and what the parties were seeking from the reference.[24]

11.6.3.14 The picture of a reasoned award which has emerged from the preceding consideration appears to have come to dominate the general perception of reasoned awards in the post-1979 Act phase. In the result the same view of a reasoned award appears to prevail whether what is in contemplation is a possible appeal under the 1979 Act, or a contractual mandate to provide a reasoned award, or even an informal bilateral or unilateral request made to an arbitrator to provide a reasoned award.[25] But even if this represents the *prima facie* position, it remains open to the parties to vary the *prima facie* position by the express terms of the contractual mandate.

11.6.4 Reasons and reasoned awards as relative concepts

11.6.4.1 It would seem that any question enquiring after the making of "reasons" or "reasoned awards", or any associated question concerning the "sufficiency" of reasons, raises a relative and not an absolute issue. The answer fundamentally must turn on the purpose underlying the requirement that reasons be given. As previously outlined the demand for reasoned awards may be justified by reference to any one of three general grounds.[1] First, it may be claimed that they improve the quality and the rationality of the arbitral process. Secondly, the giving of reasons satisfies the natural desire of the parties to be informed why an arbitrator has decided in a particular way, and particularly the desire of the loser to know why he has lost. And finally they provide a basis for the judicial review of awards, whether by way of appeal or otherwise. It is at least arguable that the answer to any question which seeks a conceptual understanding of "reasons", "reasoned awards" and "sufficiency" is capable of varying according to the underlying purpose the reasons are expected to realise. The kind of explanation that might satisfy the parties' need to be informed would not necessarily be sufficient to enable a reviewing court to discharge its task properly. The kind of reasons that might be seen as securing a desirable qualitative standard for the arbitral process would not necessarily be adequate for an informing or reviewing function. But although in the abstract it may be possible to draw these distinctions, as a question of practice they may involve difficult and even unreal distinctions. The different purposes and the varying demands that may be associated with the giving of reasons do not necessarily exist in neat self-contained categories. Reasons which secure a basic

---

24. See Chapters 5 and 6.
25. *Trave Schiffahrtsgesellschaft m.b.H. & Co. K.G.* v. *Ninemia Maritime Corpn. (The Niedersachsen)*, *supra*, p. 396, per Donaldson L.J.
1. *Supra*, para. 11.1.

rationality for the arbitral process may also be sufficient to inform the parties and reasons which inform may also be adequate to enable a court to discharge a reviewing function. The possible permutations are many and may be further increased with variations in the circumstances of individual cases. The possibility of merger and overlap appears to have been accepted by Robert Goff J. in *The Oinoussian Virtue*[2] where the learned judge rejected a factual contention that where a reasoned award was volunteered by an arbitrator it was likely only to satisfy the object of informing the parties of the basis of the decision.

11.6.4.2 In the context of the 1979 Act there can be little doubt about the object. Reasons are required to facilitate an appellate reviewing function. The power established by section 1(5) is incidental to and in aid of the appeal process established by section 1(2). By the express terms of section 1(5), a reasoned award is an award which states an arbitrator's reasons for his award in sufficient detail to enable the High Court, should an appeal be brought under section 1, to consider any question of law arising out of an award. Further, the giving of reasons assists in the determination of the preliminary question whether or not leave to appeal should be given. If attention is confined to the essential essence of the legislation, reasons have no wider or alternative function such as information giving or securing a basic qualitative standard for the arbitral process, although these wider benefits may be incidentally achieved. The primary function of reasons under the 1979 Act was emphasised in the following language by Sir John Donaldson in *The Niedersachsen*[3]: "The Arbitration Act 1979 nowhere defines what is meant by a 'reasoned award', but it is clear from s. 1(5) that what is meant is one which states the reasons for the award in sufficient detail for the court to consider any question of law arising therefrom, if, of course, it were to give leave to appear."

11.6.4.3 Not all judicial dicta are so unambiguous in their identification of the primary objective. A particularly striking illustration is the dictum of Lloyd J. in *The Vimeira*, where the learned judge asserts,[4] "[t]he primary purpose of reasons for an award is to enable the parties to know why they have won or lost[5] . . . The secondary purpose is to enable the court to see whether leave to appeal should be granted on any question of law, in accordance with the guide-lines laid down in *The Nema*". Again, in *Hayn Roman & Co. S.A.* v. *Cominter (U.K.) Ltd.*, Robert Goff J. made the point, albeit by way of a secondary comment,[6] "[a]nyway, as a matter of commonsense, the [parties] are entitled to know why their contentions have been rejected". It would be excessively bold to attempt to marshal these dicta in support of a primary purpose at variance with that suggested above. They are outgunned by the express language of the statute and by the weight of authority. Yet they possibly reveal a residual judicial sympathy and also emphasise the imprudence of pressing a characterisation of purpose to unreal lengths. They also have an independent and supportable logic, for properly and cautiously construed they cannot be said to be erroneous. Even if

2. *Schiffahrtsagentur Hamburg Middle East Line G.m.b.H Hamburg* v. *Virtue Shipping Corpn. of Monrovia (The Oinoussian Virtue)* [1981] 1 Lloyd's Rep. 533, 536–537.
3. *Trave Schiffahrtsgesellschaft m.b.H. & Co. K.G* v. *Ninemia Maritime Corpn. (The Niedersachsen)* [1986] 1 Q.B. 802, 807.
4. *Interbulk Ltd.* v. *Aiden Shipping Co. Ltd. (The Vimeira)* [1983] 2 Lloyd's Rep. 424, 430–431.
5. Citing *Bremer Handelsgesellschaft m.b.H.* v. *Westzucker G.m.b.H. (No. 2)* [1981] 2 Lloyd's Rep. 130, which would not appear to expressly support the point made.
6. [1982] 2 Lloyd's Rep. 458, 464.

the primary purpose of reasons under the 1979 Act is to serve a reviewing function, in seeking to achieve this goal it is a necessary and inevitable incident that the parties will also be informed to a material degree. Appeals have to be instituted by the parties, who must contemplate not only the prospects of the full appeal but also the preliminary issue of leave to appeal. The parties must be possessed of sufficient information to assess the correctness of an award, to judge the possible outcome of any application for leave to appeal and of any full appeal hearing that may ultimately take place. As a practical matter the informing function of reasons under the 1979 Act is quite crucial and if having been informed the parties decide not to challenge the legal correctness of an award, the reasons will have served no wider function than that of informing the parties and placing them in a position to conduct their own review of the award. But even when this is the case, the wider and primary function of reasons under the 1979 Act will not have been without influence, for it will continue to govern the extent to which the parties are entitled to be informed, and to explain why they are being informed.

11.6.4.4 In the present context the definition of purpose is crucial, for it represents the indispensable benchmark by reference to which the central questions arising out of the 1979 legislation are to be answered. Only when there is a clarity of mind as to the object reasons are intended to achieve can there be intelligent and informed discussion of the issues relating to the basis of the court's jurisdiction under section 1(5).

11.6.5 Absence or insufficiency of reasons

The existence and sufficiency of reasons are central issues arising under section 1(5). The presence or absence of reasons is a question of fact; the sufficiency or insufficiency of any reasons given is a question of fact and degree. In each case it will be for an applicant to show on a balance of probabilities that an award is wholly unreasoned or that any reasons given are insufficient for the purpose of considering any question of law arising out of an award. The latter will necessarily entail a qualitative assessment of the award in question and all documents incorporated into the award by express or implied reference.[1] The extent to which the court may have regard to extraneous evidence is considered later in the text.[2]

Questions relating to the absence of reasons may raise many technical issues as to the precise understanding of the concept of reasons. On the other hand, questions addressing the sufficiency of reasons raise more judgmental issues, and for this reason will often represent the more difficult exercise.

11.6.5.1 Absence of reasons

11.6.5.1.1 An order may be made under section 1(5) when the award in question "does not . . . set out the reasons for the award". In the light of the preceding discussion this will be the case when an award simply finds for the claimant and stipulates the compensation payable or other remedy; or otherwise finds for the respondent and dismisses the claim. An award will no doubt continue to be an unreasoned award notwithstanding that it further contains narrative recitals identifying the parties, the dis-

1. *Michael I. Warde* v. *Feedex International Inc.* [1984] 1 Lloyd's Rep. 310, 311–312.
2. *Infra*, para. 11.6.5.3.

pute and the circumstances of the arbitrator's appointment; and equally if or in addition to a bare determination in favour of claimant or respondent, it also gives a bald direction with regard to the payment of costs and interest.[1] In these instances not only is there an absence of "reasons" in the narrow sense, but there is equally a total absence of any findings or conclusions of fact and/or law.

To the extent that reasons represent a qualitative concept it follows that mere content will not prevent an award from being characterised as an unreasoned award. The prevailing perception of reasons under the 1979 Act has already been discussed and all that was previously said is of significance to the present discussion.[1a] On that basis, if the arbitrator, beyond the formalities considered in the preceding paragraph, does no more than recite the argument of the parties or their professional representatives or summarise the evidence, it is again probable that the award is an unreasoned award.

11.6.5.1.2 In determining whether an award is reasoned or unreasoned it is probable that a global view must be taken of the award. A reference, for example, may give rise to two or more separate disputed issues for determination by an arbitrator. If the arbitrator gives reasons for one or more of the issues in dispute but only a bare determination with regard to the remaining issue or issues, it cannot be said, by virtue of that fact alone, that the award is unreasoned. For so long as reasons are given for the determination of at least one of the several issues referred, the award is definable as a reasoned award, albeit that the reasons given are, in the context of the reference in its totality insufficient.[2] The emphasis in the statute is on an award and not on the separate issues to be addressed in an award. The position is of course different when a separate interim or interim final award is made with regard to each of several issues in dispute, or where on its proper construction a single global award amounts to two or more distinct awards.

11.6.5.1.3 Subsections (5) and (6) contemplate the absence of reasons in an award. An award includes not only a formal award, but also external documentation which is expressly or impliedly incorporated by reference into an award.[3] Where the reasons are wholly set out in an external document that is not intended by the parties to be a part of an award, the award itself remains unreasoned. This is even more clearly the case if the external document appears under an express rubric stating that "these reasons do not form part of the award" or some such other phrase to like effect. The validity of a "separate reasons agreement" is well established, and has been considered earlier in this chapter.[4] Where there is also in existence a "restricted reasons agreement", whereunder extra-award reasons are to be treated as confidential, it would further appear that *prima facie* no allusion may be made to the extra-award

---

1. Cf. *Trave Schiffahrtsgesellschaft m.b.H. & Co. K. G.* v. *Ninemia Maritime Corporation (The Niedersachsen)* [1986] 1 Q.B. 802, 806, per Sir John Donaldson M.R., citing from the judgment of Staughton J. at first instance: "Those of us who practised before the passing of the 1979 Act will recall the typical unreasoned award which was simply in the form of the tribunal awarding such-and-such sum plus costs and interest or blandly dismissing the claim and no more."

1a. *Supra*, para. 11.6.2.

2. Cf. *Vermala Shipping Enterprises Ltd.* v. *The Minerals and Metals Trading Corpn. of India Ltd. (The Gay Fidelity)* [1982] 1 Lloyd's Rep. 469.

3. Cf. *Pearl Marin Shipping A/B* v. *Pietro Cingolani S.A.S. (The General Valdes)* [1982] 1 Lloyd's Rep. 17.

4. *Supra*, para.11.2.6.

reasons on the issue whether the award itself is unreasoned,[5] provided that on its proper construction the restricted reasons agreement extends to such an issue.[6]

11.6.5.1.4 In the present context reasons probably mean valid reasons, that is reasons which it is within the authority of an arbitrator to make. Reasons which are *ultra vires* are no reasons at all. Thus reasons given contrary to an express mandate prohibiting the making of a reasoned award, and which breach the parties are unwilling to ratify, are probably not to be perceived as valid reasons within the meaning of the 1979 Act and are therefore incapable of affecting the status of an award as an unreasoned award.

11.6.5.2 Insufficiency of the reasons

11.6.5.2.1 An order may again be made under section 1(5) when an award "does not sufficiently set out the reasons for the award".

This aspect of section 1(5) only applies when an arbitrator has given some valid, but nonetheless insufficient, reasons for his award; and for the purposes of the subsection it matters not whether the reasons were given under a contractual obligation, or at the request of a party, or gratuitously and in circumstances where there existed no special reason, within the meaning of section 1(6), why a notice requiring a reasoned award was not given.[1] Also, when some valid reasons have been made the restriction on the court's jurisdiction specified in section 1(6) is inapplicable, for the restriction only applies when an award is wholly unreasoned.[2]

11.6.5.2.2 The concept of the sufficiency of reasons is wholly tied to the associated appellate process on questions of law. Where an arbitrator or umpire is required, or of a mind, to make a reasoned award he must set out his reasons "in sufficient detail to enable the court . . . to consider any question of law arising out of the award."[3] The concept of a question of law for the purpose of section 1(5) is the same as under section 1(2) and again it is the case that the question of law must be one that arises out of an award and not out of an arbitration.[4] If the reasoning provided is sufficiently comprehensive and complete to achieve this objective, there is established a "reasoned award" within the contemplation of the Act and no question of an order for further reasons can arise.[5] If it is not, the possibility of an order under section 1(5) arises. A problem inherent in the stipulated test is that at the time of an application no particular question of law may have crystallised, indeed an application may be no more than a fishing exercise to determine whether it is possible for any question of law to be taken and an award appealed. But provided the court is satisfied that an application is bona fide, and notwithstanding the express language of the formulated test, section

5. *Gebr. van Weelde Scheepvartkantoor B.V.* v. *Société Industrielle d'Acide Phosphorique et d'Engrais etc. (The Dynashinky)* [1986] 1 Lloyd's Rep. 435, 437.
6. *Supra* n. 4.
1. *Trave Schiffahrtsgesellschaft m.b.H. & Co. K. G.* v. *Ninemia Maritime Corporation (The Niedersachsen)* [1986] 1 Q.B. 802.
2. See *infra*, para. 11.7.3.
3. *Michael I. Warde* v. *Feedex International Inc.* [1984] 1 Lloyd's Rep. 310, 312, per Staughton J.
4. *Universal Petroleum Co. Ltd.* v. *Handels- und Transport Gesellschaft m.b.H.* [1987] 1 Lloyd's Rep. 517, 524, per Kerr L.J.
5. *Trave Schiffahrtsgesellschaft m.b.H. & Co. K. G.* v. *Ninemia Maritime Corporation (The Niedersachsen)*, *supra*, p. 807, per Sir John Donaldson M.R.; *Universal Petroleum Co. Ltd.* v. *Handels- und Transport Gesellschaft m.b.H.* [1987] 1 Lloyd's Rep. 517, 524, per Kerr L.J.

1(5) would appear to contemplate the making of an order not only to facilitate the appellate role of the court with regard to an identified question of law, but also to assist the parties and indeed the court in determining whether any disputable question of law in fact arises out of an award.[6]

11.6.5.2.3 Insufficiency is both a quantitative and qualitative concept. What may be in issue is the existence of reasons and also the adequacy of reasons. There may be insufficiency because an arbitrator has failed to cover the ground with regard to a particular issue or in relation to some or all the issues raised before him. Reasons may have been provided for some determinations but not for others. But even when an arbitrator has covered the ground there may be insufficiency arising from the quality of the reasoning. The reasons may be excessively brief, insufficiently detailed, incomplete, disclosing gaps, or intrinsically obscure, ambiguous or inconsistent.[7] Not only must the reasoning be sufficiently full, but it must also be clear, coherent and of adequate assistance to explain the factual and legal basis of an award when carefully read by a reasonably intelligent person.[8] In *The Vimeira* Lloyd J. considered that "clarity is of the first importance in reasons for an award".[9] By implication reasons that are found to be obscure, ambiguous, general in the extreme, opaque, vague, unintelligible, contradictory or otherwise uncertain may be perceived as insufficient for the purposes of section 1(5).[10]

11.6.5.2.4 Reasoning that is innately insufficient is not necessarily saved by the fact that the court could probably guess at the full reasoning of an arbitrator. The point was emphasised in *Michael I. Warde* v. *Feedex International Inc.* by Staughton J., who observed[11]:

In the present case it seems to me that, if one looks only at the award of the Board of Appeal, there are not sufficient reasons to enable the Court to determine whether a question of law does arise, let alone to consider any such question of law. It does not reveal what the term of the contract was which the buyer was found or held to have broken, nor how he was found or held to have broken it. Certainly an intelligent guess could be made, which might well turn out to be right. But guessing, intelligent or otherwise, will not do. The Court must be informed with certainty, in sufficient detail to enable it to consider any questions of law arising out of the award.

11.6.5.2.5 Nor will the court readily be prepared to save the insufficiency of the reasons by incorporating by inference the submissions of one of the parties into the express reasons. For example, an arbitrator may be confronted by different arguments and submissions from the claimant and respondent. If the arbitrator subsequently makes an award in favour of one of the arbitrating parties without expressly stating his reasons, it could be argued that the arbitrator has impliedly accepted the argument

---

6. Cf. *Michael I. Warde* v. *Feedex International Inc.*, *supra*, p. 313.
7. *Universal Petroleum Co. Ltd.* v. *Handels- und Transport Gesellschaft m.b.H.* [1987] 1 Lloyd's Rep. 517; *Kansa General Insurance Co. Ltd.* v. *Bishopsgate Insurance plc* [1988] 1 Lloyd's Rep. 503.
8. Cf. *J. H. Rayner (Mincing Lane) Ltd.* v. *Shaher Trading Co.* [1982] 1 Lloyd's Rep. 632, 636–637, per Bingham J.
9. *Interbulk Ltd.* v. *Aiden Shipping Co. Ltd.* (*The Vimeira*) [1983] 2 Lloyd's Rep. 424, 431. See also *J. H. Rayner (Mincing Lane) Ltd.* v. *Shaher Trading Co.*, *ibid.*, pp. 636–637; *Clea Shipping Corporation* v. *Bulk Oil International Ltd.* [1983] 1 Lloyd's Rep. 315, 318; *Cefetra B.V.* v. *Alfred C. Toepfer International G.m.b.H.* [1994] 1 Lloyd's Rep. 93, 100–101.
10. *Universal Petroleum Co. Ltd.* v. *Handels- und Transport Gesellschaft m.b.H.*, *supra*; *Kansa General Insurance Co Ltd.* v. *Bishopsgate Insurance plc*, *supra*. See also by way of analogy *Elliot* v. *London Borough of Southwark* [1976] 1 W.L.R. 499; *The Marques de Bolarque* [1982] 1 Lloyd's Rep. 68.
11. [1984] 1 Lloyd's Rep. 310, 313.

and submissions of the victorious party and rejected the argument and submissions of the losing party; and that in consequence the argument and submissions of the victorious party are to be treated as part of the arbitrator's reasons. The implication has no strict logical basis and the court would appear to be justified in being reluctant to entertain such argument.

11.6.5.2.6 Brevity and succinctness in the reasons are not without more evidence of insufficiency.[12] It is clearly possible for the basis of an arbitrator's decision to be communicated adequately without verbosity. Equally, the legal basis of an award may be stated without deep and comprehensive analysis of the relevant legal authorities.[13]

Sufficiency is also quite distinct from all-embracing comprehensiveness and crystal clarity. The fact that the reasons are not fully stated or are not wholly free of obscuring does not preclude an award from being sufficiently reasoned.[14] It is not necessary for an arbitrator to cover every square millimetre of the ground with a microscope. It is open to an arbitrator to judge what is important and central to the resolution of a dispute and to emphasise his reasons in this regard to the exclusion of that which is peripheral. Bingham J. has made the point in the following terms[15]:

It is, of course, clear that arbitrators, when giving reasons, are not obliged to spell out every single reason for every single conclusion to which they come and are not obliged to deal in extenso with every contention advanced by advocates for the parties but it is necessary that the basis of important conclusions should be clear . . .

The sufficiency of reasons will always to a greater or lesser degree be associated with the construction of the award in question. The judicial approach to the construction of arbitral awards is now clearly established, with the judges intent on avoiding a strict and narrow approach.[16] The same approach is perpetuated under section 1(5) and in this regard Bingham J. has commented[17]: "So far as principle is concerned, it seems to be plain that under the new Act awards of arbitral tribunals should not be scrutinised with an over-critical or pedantic eye, and the court should not insist that every factual 't' is crossed and every argumentative 'i' is dotted." Moreover the sufficiency of the reasons is to be measured by reference to the award alone and not by reference to any wider contextual environment.[18] Reasons which are *prima facie* suf-

---

12. *L'Office National du Thé et du Sucre* v. *Philippine Sugar Trading (London) Ltd*. [1983] 1 Lloyd's Rep. 89, 91, per Lloyd J., "It is true they [i.e. the reasons] are succinct. But in my view they are adequate. I am unwilling to remit the award for further reasons." *Michael I. Warde* v. *Feedex International Inc*. [1984] 1 Lloyd's Rep. 310, 312, per Staughton J., "The whole reasoning of that award is contained in a single sentence, but it is none the worse for that. I do not doubt that it was clear enough for the parties and their representatives, and to the members of the Board of Appeal what was being decided. Some judgments in these Courts could with advantage be equally brief, as far as the parties and their representatives are concerned."

13. *Bremer Handelsgesellschaft m.b.H.* v. *Westzucker G.m.b.H. (No. 2)* [1981] 2 Lloyd's Rep. 130, 132–133. *J. H. Rayner (Mincing Lane) Ltd.* v. *Shaher Trading Co.* [1982] 1 Lloyd's Rep. 632, 637. See also *Antaios Compania Naviera S.A.* v. *Salen Rederierna A.B. (The Antaios)* [1985] AC 191, 200, per Lord Diplock.

14. *Cefetra B.V.* v. *Alfred C. Toepfer International G.m.b.H.* [1994] 1 Lloyd's Rep. 93, 100, Colman J.

15. *Clea Shipping Corporation* v. *Bulk Oil International Ltd. (The Alaskan Trader)* [1983] 1 Lloyd's Rep. 315, 318. See also *Granges Aluminium A.B.* v. *The Cleveland Bridge and Engineering Co. Ltd.*, *The Times*, 15 May 1990.

16. Chapter 8, para. 8.3.

17. *J. H. Rayner (Mincing Lane) Ltd.* v. *Shaher Trading Co.* [1982] 1 Lloyd's Rep. 632, 636.

18. See *infra*, para. 11.6.5.3.

ficient and adequate may not be diminished or detracted from by the introduction of evidence extrinsic to an award.[19]

11.6.5.2.7 The sufficiency of reasons will also to some degree be related to the ability of others to form an understanding of the factual and legal basis of an award. In so testing the sufficiency of the reasons the court will assume that an award, in the form made by an arbitrator or umpire, is to be read by a person of reasonable intelligence, who is capable of giving a careful reading to the reasons.[20]

11.6.5.3 Exclusion of extraneous evidence

11.6.5.3.1 The absence or insufficiency of reasons must be established in the award itself,[1] which includes any external material expressly or impliedly incorporated into the award.[1a] In determining an application for an order under section 1(5) the court, as a question of evidence, is confined to the four corners of the award. The absence or insufficiency of reasons must be established exclusively on the basis of an enquiry into the substance of the award. No extraneous evidence may be admitted in any form, including affidavit evidence or statements by counsel and solicitors.[2] This restrictive rule derives from the language of the legislation. The same rule appertains with regard to applications for leave to appeal under section 1(3)(b),[3] and one reason for the instant rule is to avoid the risk of the rule developed in relation to applications for leave to appeal being circumvented.[4] The general effect of the rule is to restrict the possibility of the necessary preconditions to the jurisdiction specified in section 1(5) being satisfied. To this extent the rule is in accord with the general policy of the 1979 Act, which is to minimise judicial detraction from the finality of awards.

11.6.5.3.2 To the general rule enunciated above there would appear to exist one clear exception. The court retains a discretion to receive evidence of the submissions made by the parties in an arbitration where they are not discernible in the award itself. The discretion had been exercised in this way by judges at first instance[5] prior to the decision of the Court of Appeal in *Universal Petroleum Co. Ltd.* v. *Handels- und Transport Gesellschaft m.b.H.*,[6] where the practice was before the court; and although the validity of the practice was not directly in issue, it is nonetheless of significance that it did not attract any adverse comment. The earlier authorities were not brought to the attention of the Court of Appeal but have subsequently been followed, again at first instance.[7] The principle is also one that makes ready sense. Knowledge

19. *Universal Petroleum Co. Ltd.* v. *Handels- und Transport Gesellschaft m.b.H.* [1987] 1 Lloyd's Rep. 517, 524.
20. *J. H. Rayner (Mincing Lane) Ltd.* v. *Shaher Trading Co.* [1982] 1 Lloyd's Rep. 632, 636.
1. This is made clear by the wording of section 1(5).
1a. *Supra*, para. 11.6.5.
2. *Universal Petroleum Co. Ltd.* v. *Handels- und Transport Gesellschaft m.b.H.* [1987] 1 Lloyd's Rep. 517.
3. See Chapter 7, para. 7.1.2.
4. *Universal Petroleum Co. Ltd.* v. *Handels- und Transport Gesellschaft m.b.H.* [1987] 1 Lloyd's Rep. 517, 521.
5. *Vermala Shipping Enterprises Ltd.* v. *The Minerals and Metals Trading Corporation of India Ltd.* (*The Gay Fidelity*) [1982] 1 Lloyd's Rep. 469, 470, per Staughton J.; *Hayn Roman & Co. S.A.* v. *Cominter (U.K.) Ltd.* [1982] 2 Lloyd's Rep. 458, where Robert Goff J. considered the submissions of the parties; *Michael I. Warde* v. *Feedex International Inc.* [1984] 1 Lloyd's Rep. 310, 312, per Staughton J.
6. *Supra*.
7. *Kansa General Insurance Co. Ltd.* v. *Bishopsgate Insurance plc* [1988] 1 Lloyd's Rep. 503, 510, 511, per Hirst J.

of the submissions made will often be crucial to a proper assessment of the adequacy and sufficiency of the reasons made in an award; as also will be a knowledge of the context in which the submissions were made, such as the pleadings (or equivalent) and evidence adduced.[8]

11.6.5.3.3 A further exception may exist where a multi-arbitrator tribunal fails to achieve unanimity and what is before the court is a majority award or the award of a single designated arbitrator. In this kind of circumstance it may be legitimate for the court to examine any opinion expressed by a dissenting arbitrator or arbitrators. In *Kansa General Insurance Co. Ltd.* v. *Bishopsgate Insurance plc*,[9] Hirst J., at first instance, had before him and consulted the minority opinion of a dissenting arbitrator. No objection was made, but equally the validity of the practice was not expressly considered. Dissenting opinions, it would seem, may be alluded to on an application for leave to appeal and on a full appeal.[10] This being so, and also having regard to the potential assistance they may give the court, it is difficult to apprehend why any different rule should apply in the present context.

11.6.5.4 Reasons and awards of costs

11.6.5.4.1 The general framework and principles of the 1979 Act apply equally to awards of costs. Just as arbitrators are encouraged under the 1979 Act to give reasons for their substantive decisions, so also they are encouraged to provide reasons for their awards of costs, particularly when minded to depart from normal principles.[1] When asked by a party to give reasons for any award of costs that may be made an arbitrator should respond positively and only in exceptional circumstances would an arbitrator be justified in refusing the request.[2] If a party desires reasons for the award of costs he would be advised to make the request in specific terms for it is uncertain whether a general request for a reasoned award will extend so as to include the award of costs.

11.6.5.4.2 With regard to an award of costs, the insufficiency of the reasons must be demonstrated by what appears on the face of an award. In contrast to the pre-1979 Act practice,[3] it would seem that an applicant will not be permitted to speculate as to the reasoning of an arbitrator, nor to introduce extraneous evidence.[4] Apart from the innate inadequacy of reasons that have already been given and appear on the face of an award, the main source of evidence of insufficiency will derive from a comparison of what the arbitrator has decided and his award of costs.[5] The more the award of costs departs from what might be considered the normal order in the context of the dispute and what has been decided, the more the award may call for further explanation and so provide the justification for perceiving the award to be insufficiently

---

8. *Gebr. van Weelde Scheepvartkantoor B.V.* v. *Société Industrielle D'Acide Phosphorique et D'Engrais etc. (The Dynashinky)* [1986] 1 Lloyd's Rep. 435, 437, per Hobhouse J.
9. *Supra.*
10. See Chapter 8, para. 8.4.
1. *King* v. *Thomas McKenna Ltd.* [1991] 1 All E.R. 653, 664, Lord Donaldson of Lymington M.R. (*obiter dictum*).
2. *Ibid.* Also *Smeaton Hanscomb & Co. Ltd.* v. *Sassoon I. Setty, Son & Co. (No. 2)* [1953] 1 W.L.R. 1481, 1485, Devlin J. See further, by way of example, *Everglade Maritime Inc.* v. *Schiffahrtsgesellschaft Detlef von Appen m.b.H. (The Maria)* [1992] 2 Lloyd's Rep. 167; [1993] 2 Lloyd's Rep. 168 (C.A.).
3. *Supra*, paras. 11.2.4. and 11.3.2.
4. *King* v. *Thomas McKenna Ltd.*, *supra*, note 1, pp. 663–664.
5. *Ibid.*

reasoned. But, on the other hand, the more an award of costs represents what might be considered the normal and predictable order, the more it may be regarded as speaking for itself and with the award consequently sufficiently reasoned.

11.6.5.5 Reasons and interest awards

11.6.5.5.1 All that has been said in relation to awards of costs would seem to be equally applicable to interest awards.[1]

11.6.5.5.2 Subject to the express terms of his mandate, an arbitrator is obliged to address the question of interest. An arbitrator who decides against making an award of interest is probably obliged to explain his decision. An explanation is also likely to be demanded if an arbitrator is minded to make an unusual order, relating to the rate of interest or the commencement, duration and continuity of the interest period.[2]

11.7 LIMITATIONS ON THE JURISDICTION OF THE HIGH COURT

11.7.1 Arbitrator or umpire concerned

An award may be remitted only to the arbitrator or umpire "concerned",[1] by which is meant the arbitrator or umpire responsible for making the award that has been brought before the court. The award cannot be remitted to a new arbitrator or umpire.[2] This is of course compelling logic, for it is only the arbitrator or umpire who heard the evidence and argument and who determined the dispute or disputes in issue who can provide a statement of the reasoning that prevailed in making the award.

Reference to "arbitrator" in section 1(5) includes an arbitration tribunal and arbitration appeal tribunal. In turn the existence of a multi-arbitrator tribunal raises certain issues and difficulties that do not arise when only a sole arbitrator is appointed. Where by the terms of an arbitration agreement it is provided that in the absence of unanimity the award shall be the decision of a majority of the arbitrators or the decision of a single designated arbitrator, then it would appear that it is the majority or the designated arbitrator who are the arbitrators or arbitrator "concerned" for the purpose of section 1(5).[3] The dissenting arbitrators would seem not to be within the statutory language and therefore are not party to the remitted award.

If it becomes impossible to remit an award to the arbitrator or umpire concerned because, for example, of death, disappearance or permanent incapacity, it would seem that the jurisdiction under section 1(5) is lost. Nor, it is suggested, can the jurisdiction be saved by the existence in such circumstances of a contractual power

---

1. *Supra*, para. 11.6.5.4.
2. *See*, Chapter 6, para. 6.2.14.2.
1. Section 1(5).
2. As is possible under s. 22 of the Arbitration Act 1950; although this interpretation placed on s. 22 is difficult to reconcile with the express language of the section: see *Rooke, Sons & Co.* v. *Piper and May* (1927) 28 Ll.L.Rep. 49; *London Export Corpn.* v. *Jubilee Coffee Roasting Co. Ltd.* [1958] 1 Lloyd's Rep. 197 (first instance).
3. See *Stinnes Interoil G.m.b.H.* v. *A. Halcoussis & Co.* (*The Yanxilas*)) [1982] 2 Lloyd's Rep. 445, 452, where Bingham J. remitted under s. 1(5)(b) for further findings and reasons underlying the decision of the majority of the arbitrators on a specified matter. See also *Kansa General Insurance Co. Ltd.* v. *Bishopsgate Insurance plc* [1988] 1 Lloyd's Rep. 503, where an order was sought directing a majority of arbitrators to give further reasons for their award.

enabling the parties or a statutory power enabling the court to appoint a substitute arbitrator or umpire. The remission, it is submitted, can only be to an arbitrator or umpire who was a party to the deliberations and decisions on the basis of which an award was made.

11.7.2 Jurisdiction limited in its scope to prospective appeals

By whatever criteria the concept of reasons is to be understood and the existence or sufficiency of reasons assessed, it is clear that once the court has resolved that is has jurisdiction, and determines in the exercise of its discretion to make an order, it cannot do more than order the arbitrator or umpire concerned "to state the reasons for his award in sufficient detail to enable the court, should an appeal be brought under [section 1(2)], to consider any question of law arising out of the award".[1]

To whatever extent it may be possible to conceive of different justifications for the giving of reasons, with each justification possibly having different quantitative and qualitative parameters, it is only the justification associated with the facilitation of appeals which assumes a relevance for the purpose of section 1(5). The jurisdiction of the court is constrained by the notion of prospective appeals on questions of law arising out of awards, which compounds in meaning with the same phraseology found in section 1(2).[2]

11.7.3 Unreasoned awards

Where what is in issue is not the insufficiency of reasons but the total absence of reasons, the jurisdiction of the court to make an order under section 1(5) is further constrained by section 1(6) which provides:

In any case where an award is made without any reason being given, the High Court shall not make an order under subsection (5) above unless it is satisfied—
   (a) that before the award was made one of the parties to the reference gave notice to the arbitrator or umpire concerned that a reasoned award would be required; or
   (b) that there is some special reason why such a notice was not given.

The subsection is peremptory. The High Court "shall not" make an order unless the terms of either paragraph (a) or (b) are satisfied. The subsection is a restriction on the jurisdiction of the court and not on the exercise of discretion. The court cannot make an order unless the terms of subsection (6) are satisfied[1]; but even where the terms of the subsection are satisfied, the court continues to enjoy a discretion under subsection (5) whether or not to make an order.[2]

---

1. Section 1(5). See also *Schiffahrtsagentur Hamburg Middle East Line G.m.b.H. Hamburg* v. *Virtue Shipping Corporation of Monrovia* (*The Oinoussian Virtue*) [1981] 1 Lloyd's Rep. 533, 539, per Robert Goff J., "under s. 1(5) of the 1979 Act . . . the Court may order an arbitrator to state the reasons for his award in sufficient detail to enable the Court, should an appeal be brought under s. 1 of the 1979 Act, to consider any question of law arising out of the award".
   2. See Chapter 3.
   1. *Schiffahrtsagentur Hamburg Middle East Line G.m.b.H. Hamburg* v. *Virtue Shipping Corporation of Monrovia (The Oinoussian Virtue)* [1981] 1 Lloyd's Rep. 533, 536; *Hayn Roman & Co. S.A.* v. *Cominter (U.K.) Ltd.* [1982] 1 Lloyd's Rep. 295, 296; *Michael I. Warde* v. *Feedex International Inc.* [1984] 1 Lloyd's Rep. 310, 312; *Trave Schiffahrtsgesellschaft m.b.H. & Co. K.G.* v. *Ninemia Maritime Corporation (The Niedersachsen)* [1986] 1 Q.B. 802, 807.
   2. *Hayn Roman & Co. S.A.* v. *Cominter (U.K.) Ltd.*, *ibid.* p. 297.

The consequence of section 1(6) is that where an award is made without reasons and neither of the parties requested that a reasoned award be made, and there exists no special reason to explain why such a request was not made, the court has no jurisdiction to make an order for reasons under section 1(5).[3] If the terms of section 1(6) are not satisfied the unreasoned award stands and thereafter it is literally impossible for the court to grant leave to appeal.[4]

11.7.3.1 Pre-award notice requesting reasoned award

11.7.3.1.1 In the first instance no order may be made under section 1(5) unless it is established that at least one of the parties gave notice to the arbitrator or umpire concerned before the award was made requiring a reasoned award.

The object underlying this restriction on the jurisdiction of the court is to preclude the risk of arbitrators and umpires being unfairly or oppressively burdened by court orders requiring them to provide reasons, when they were given no cause to believe that the parties wished to have a reasoned award and which with the passage of time following the making of the award it may be difficult or impracticable for them to provide.[5] Sir John Donaldson M.R. has said of section 1(6)(a)[6]:

The purpose of the sub-section is clear. It would be a considerable burden if an arbitrator, having given an award without any reasons and not having been asked to do otherwise by any of the parties, were subsequently to be ordered by the Court to give reasons for the award. Accordingly the court has no jurisdiction to make such an order, in the absence of special reasons why no such request was made.

11.7.3.1.2 Robert Goff J. pinpointed the potential burden on arbitrators more precisely[7]:

The purpose of the prior notice to the arbitrator, as it seems to me, is to prevent arbitrators from being required to give reasons after the award, by which time their memories have become dimmed and it may be difficult for them to recall the case in sufficient detail to give a reasoned award.

The essence of the position under the 1979 Act is that arbitrators are entitled to an advance warning that a reasoned award is required, and that in the absence of such a warning they have little to fear from the jurisdiction established by section 1(5). But if notice is given, the arbitrator must respond with the requisite sufficiency.

11.7.3.1.3 The Act says little about the legal requirements of a notice for the

---

3. *Schiffahrtsagentur Hamburg Middle East Line G.m.b.H. Hamburg* v. *Virtue Shipping Corporation of Monrovia (The Oinoussian Virtue), supra*, p. 536, where Robert Goff J. perceived the effect of s.1(6) "is to preclude an order for reasons, where none have been given and none have been asked for". *Michael I. Warde* v. *Feedex International Inc., supra*, p. 312, where Staughton J. comments, "s.1(6) excludes an order for reasons where (i) the award contains no reasons, (ii) neither party requested a reasoned award before it was made, and (iii) there is no special reason which would excuse the failure to make such a request in due time."

4. *Sethia Liners Ltd.* v. *Naviagro Maritime Corporation (The Kostas Melas)* [1981] 1 Lloyd's Rep. 18, 30.

5. See Kerr, "The Arbitration Act 1979" (1980) 43 M.L.R. 45, 50–51.

6. *Trave Schiffahrtsgesellschaft m.b.H. & Co. K.G.* v. *Ninemia Maritime Corporation (The Niedersachsen)* [1986] 1 Q.B. 802, 807.

7. *Hayn Roman & Co. S.A.* v. *Cominter (U.K.) Ltd.* [1982] 1 Lloyd's Rep. 295, 297. See also *Schiffahrtsagentur Hamburg Middle East Line G.m.b.H. Hamburg* v. *Virtue Shipping Corporation of Monrovia (The Oinoussian Virtue), supra*, pp. 536–537, per Robert Goff J.; *Gebr. van Weelde Scheepvartkantoor B.V.* v. *Société Industrielle D'Acide Phosphorique et D'Engrais etc. (The Dynashinky)* [1986] 1 Lloyd's Rep. 435, 436, per Hobhouse J.

purpose of section 1(6)(a). It may be presumed that the notice must be a valid and effective notice.[8] To amount to such a notice the language of the statute makes it clear that the notice must be communicated before an award is made, whether during the course of a reference or subsequently when the award is being considered[9] and continue unwithdrawn or unrevoked up to that time. When precisely an award is made has been considered elsewhere in the text.[10] There is no express requirement as to form and therefore it may be assumed that notice may be given orally or in writing although there is clear practical advantage in introducing an element of formality. In its purpose it may again be presumed that the notice must be clear and unambiguous.[11] In the event of doubt it is possible that the substantive adequacy of a notice is to be tested by reference to its impact on a reasonably experienced arbitrator or umpire. Would a reasonably experienced arbitrator or umpire understand the communication in question and in the circumstances of its making to be a request for a reasoned award? The notice must emanate from a party to the reference or an agent of such party acting with authority and be given to the arbitrator or umpire concerned. But although a notice must emanate from a party to the reference, it may be doubted that it is further necessary for the same party to actually communicate the notice. A notice communicated through or by a reliable third party may satisfy the statute.[12] What amounts to the giving of notice is open to both a positive and passive interpretation, so that notice may be given not only when a party to the reference does a positive act with the intention of communicating his state of mind, but also when the settled state of mind of a party to the reference comes to the attention of an arbitrator independently of any active act of transmission. Although both interpretations may be feasible, the interests of certainty would appear to be better served by the narrow interpretation insisting on some positive act on the part of the party to the reference intending to give notice.

11.7.3.1.4 The question of giving notice to an arbitrator or umpire raises a number of potential difficulties. The best form of notice is actual notice in the form of a personal communication with the arbitrator or umpire in question. But it is doubtful if the courts will insist on this as the only mode of satisfying the requirement of the statute. It is probable that any reasonable step taken by a party to a reference which would in the ordinary course of events be expected to bring the request for a reasoned award to the attention of the arbitrator or umpire in question prior to the making of an award will suffice. In other words considerations of commercial expediency may compel the courts in their interpretation of subsection (6)(a) to recognise the concept of constructive notice. If this is the case, then notice communicated to the place of business, professional address or home address of the arbitrator or umpire concerned may suffice, or indeed to any other address if there exists good and substantial reason for believing

8. The question as to what amounts to a valid and effective notice will in the final analysis turn on the interpretation of the 1979 Act. The judicial analysis of notice requirements in other legislation will at its highest only be of persuasive authority and often of little or no assistance. Equally the potential assistance offered by the Interpretation Act 1978 is likely to be very limited.
9. *Sethia Liners Ltd.* v. *Naviagro Maritime Corporation (The Kostas Melas)* [1981] 1 Lloyd's Rep 18, 29, per Robert Goff J.
10. Chapter 3, para. 3.3.9.
11. *Hayn Roman & Co. S.A.* v. *Cominter (U.K.) Ltd.*, *supra*, p. 296, per Robert Goff J., "I am not prepared to hold that a notice was given in sufficiently clear terms to constitute a notice [within] s.1(6)(a)."
12. Cf. *Dickinson* v. *Dodds* (1876) 2 Ch. D. 463.

that the arbitrator or umpire may be communicated with at that address.[13] The difficulty associated with the recognition of constructive notice is that it does not readily harmonise with the underlying policy of the legislation, but against this must be balanced the fair and reasonable expectations of the party or parties in question. But in the context of subsection 6(a) there would appear to be no case for incorporating the thinking underlying the postal rule in the law of contract.[14] Whether there has been a valid and effective notice would seem to turn on considerations relating to the actual or constructive delivery of the notice. The mere posting of a notice or otherwise placing of a notice in the hands of an intermediary for delivery to the arbitrator or umpire would appear insufficient. Equally it would seem that a misdirected notice is of no consequence,[15] except, possibly, when the misdirection can be attributed to the conduct of the arbitrator.

11.7.3.1.5 There also arises the question as to how notice is to be given to a multi-arbitrator tribunal. As a matter of general principle it might be anticipated that the common law would demand a separate notice communicated to each arbitrator,[16] while at the same time recognising the validity of a notice communicated to a single arbitrator which is thereafter transmitted onwards by the notified arbitrator to all the other arbitrators. The common law, however, surrenders to the express agreement of the parties and where, for example, one of the arbitrators is appointed chairman of the tribunal and is mandated to act on his own authority in matters relating to procedure,[17] such a mandate might well be construed as including an authority to receive a notice requiring reasons. It is, however, at least arguable that the language of subsection (6)(a) is drafted in personalised terms. It requires notice to be given to the "arbitrator or umpire" concerned, thus suggesting, admittedly with no compelling cogency, that it is sufficient if notice is given to any individual member of a multi-arbitrator tribunal. To contrary effect, the language of the subsection could equally translate into the "tribunal" concerned, in which case the subsection merely describes the problem without providing an answer. But whatever the difficulties of interpretation, it is suggested that the difficulty here confronted must be resolved in a practical and sensible manner and practical good sense appears to suggest that in the case of a multi-arbitrator tribunal it is sufficient if a notice requesting reasons is given to any member of the tribunal, subject to one qualification. If the rules of an arbitration expressly address the question and specify the way a reasoned award may be requested by any of the parties, then it is suggested that the requirement of the rules governs the question of what amounts to a valid notice.

11.7.3.1.6 In keeping with principle it may further be assumed that the communication of a notice to an agent of the arbitrator or umpire with actual or ostensible

---

13. Cf. R.S.C. Order 10 in relation to the service of writs and considered in *Barclays Bank of Swaziland* v. *Hahn*, *The Times*, 19 May 1989. Note also *Willowgreen Ltd.* v. *Smithers*, *The Times*, 14 December 1993.

14. The postal rule represents an exception to the general rule of contract that the acceptance of an offer is only effective upon communication to the offeror. The rule recognises that in specific circumstances an offer may be accepted on the posting of the acceptance: see *Holwell Securities Ltd.* v. *Hughes* [1974] 1 W.L.R. 155.

15. Cf. *Holwell Securities Ltd.* v. *Hughes*, *ibid.*

16. On the basis that each member of a multi-arbitrator tribunal makes a distinct personal contribution to a joint and common enterprise. For the contemporary judicial approach to this theoretical perception and its demands see, *European Grain & Shipping Ltd.* v. *Johnston* [1982] 2 Lloyd's Rep. 550.

17. As is the case under many of the formal rules promulgated by arbitral institutions; see, for example, London Court of International Arbitration Rules, Art. 5.3.

authority to receive such notice is equivalent to notice given to the arbitrator or umpire principal. Equally an arbitrator or umpire may ratify an unauthorised receipt of notice. Such issues may arise when an arbitrator, umpire or tribunal acts through or with the aid of a secretary or some other mode of administrative assistance. Also, where an arbitration agreement or arbitral rules define what shall amount to notice for the purposes of subsection (6), then it would appear desirable that there should exist a correspondence between the contract of the parties and the interpretation of the statute, with satisfaction of the former also satisfying the requirements of the statute. Thus if arbitral rules make provision for notice to be given to an institution administering the arbitration or to a named person or to a person occupying a specified position within the administering body, it is submitted that compliance with the rules ought also to amount to giving "notice to the arbitrator or umpire concerned" for the purpose of subsection (6)(a).[18]

11.7.3.1.7 Subsection (6)(a) is essentially directed to situations where there does not exist any contractual obligation to give a reasoned award. Where such an obligation exists, the failure to make a reasoned award probably amounts to both misconduct and breach of contract, and may be corrected by reference to any of the remedies available in respect of each of those branches of the law. The existence of a contractual obligation may also amount to notice for the purpose of subsection (6)(a) and therefore also render it possible for a remedy to be sought by reference to section 1(5).

11.7.3.1.7A The tenor of subsection (6)(a) suggests that even in the absence of contract, an arbitrator is under some manner of obligation to make a reasoned award following the receipt of a notice to that effect from one of the parties to the reference.[19] It probably would be too bold an interpretation of the legislation to suggest that it establishes an implied statutory duty. The duty, whatever its nature, does not assume an absolute character, for even when notice is given it would appear that an arbitrator retains a discretion, in appropriate circumstances, not to give reasons. It must be borne in mind that the notice is only necessary in the absence of a contractual mandate to give a reasoned award. But the giving of notice does have the legal force of heavily leaning the situation towards the giving of reasons. It serves to concentrate the mind of the arbitrator who must bear in mind the likely motive behind the notice requesting reasons and the general bias in the 1979 Act towards the giving of reasoned awards.[20] The circumstances are likely to be rare when an arbitrator will be justified in rejecting a request for reasons and therefore in practically all instances a notice requesting reasons will or ought to produce the desired result. In responding the arbitrator must also seek to satisfy the qualitative demands of section 1(5) and produce a reasoned award which is adequate to satisfy the requirements of the subsection and thereby avoid the need for a later application for an order under section 1(5). It may be justifiable to summarise the position by suggesting that the effect of giving notice under subsection (6) is to establish a quasi implied statutory duty to give reasons.[21]

18. Cf. *Hayn Roman & Co. S.A.* v. *Cominter (U.K.) Ltd.*, *supra*.
19. *Supra*, para. 11.4.4.
20. *Universal Petroleum Co. Ltd.* v. *Handels- und Transport Gesellschaft m.b.H.* [1987] 1 Lloyd's Rep. 517, 528, per Kerr L.J. (C.A.).
21. Cf. *Michael I. Warde* v. *Feedex International Inc.* [1984] 1 Lloyd's Rep. 310, 315, Staughton J.

11.7.3.1.8 There would appear to be nothing to preclude a notice under subsection (6)(a) from being conditional, with the obligation to give reasons depending on the precise decision of the arbitrator or umpire. For example, a party might request an award of costs or interest to be reasoned in the event of the arbitrator deciding to make an unusual order.

11.7.3.2 Special reasons

11.7.3.2.1 Notwithstanding the absence of notice, the court may continue to enjoy a jurisdiction to make an order for reasons if it is satisfied that there exists a "special reason" why notice was not given. This is the effect of section 1(6)(b).

The Act offers no definition of what amounts to a special reason. It is in each case question of fact whether or not a special reason exists to account for the failure to give notice. Regard must, however, be had to the precise statutory language. It is insufficient that there exists some explanation to account for the failure: it must be an explanation that warrants the epithet "special".[22] This suggests that carelessness or forgetfulness may in themselves and without more be insufficient to establish a special reason.[23] The onus of proof falls on the party who asserts the existence of a special reason to satisfy the court on a balance of probabilities that there exists a special reason to explain the failure to give notice.

11.7.3.2.2 In their approach to the interpretation of section 1(6)(b) it is unlikely that the judges will readily volunteer a precise definition of what amounts to a special reason, for such a strategy may achieve no more than unwittingly limit the scope for judicial intervention in future and unforeseen circumstances. The limited judicial consideration to date of paragraph (b) suggests that the concept of a special reason is potentially a broad and various notion, much in the manner of a lever by which it is open to the court to give effect to its perception of the demands of justice in individual cases.[24] In the words of Robert Goff J., "the sub-section must be construed sensibly in its context".[25] A special reason is most likely to be established when in the circumstances of any particular case and independent of notice an applicant can show reasonable justification for anticipating that a reasoned award would be made.[26] In such a circumstance the applicant will often have been misled by an express or implied representation. But the notion of a special reason is not confined to instances when an applicant has been misled. A special reason may also arise from a bona fide misunderstanding arising out of a procedural mishap. Robert Goff J. has speculated that a notice which went astray by accident could establish a special reason; as also might a bona fide misunderstanding between a solicitor acting for an applicant and the secretary of a trade association, as a result of which there arose a belief, in all good faith, that a request for a reasoned award had been made before the award was made.[27]

---

22. *Gebr. van Weelde Scheepvartkantoor B.V.* v. *Société Industrielle D'Acide Phosphorique et D'Engrais etc. (The Dynashinky)*, *supra*, p. 436, per Hobhouse J.
23. *Ibid.*
24. *Hayn Roman & Co. S.A.* v. *Cominter (U.K.) Ltd.*, *supra*, p. 297, per Robert Goff J.
25. *Ibid.*, p. 297.
26. *Ibid.*, p. 297.
27. *Ibid.*, p. 297.

11.7.3.3 *Special reasons—unreasoned awards of costs and interest*

The preceding discussion applies in its generality equally to awards of costs, but subject, possibly, to an important adaptation when an unreasoned and unusual award of costs is made. In this kind of situation, where no request for reasons has been made, there is a danger of the court's jurisdiction being defeated by virtue of section 1(6) unless a special reason exists for the failure to request reasons. The thought of the court not having jurisdiction to respond to this situation being unpalatable, Lord Donaldson of Lymington M.R. has speculated (*obiter dictum*)[1] that "parties cannot usually be expected to anticipate a departure from the normal principles as to costs and this might well be regarded as a 'special reason' for not having asked for reasons".

If this principle is adopted in relation to awards of costs, it would seem equally applicable to unreasoned and unusual awards of interest.

11.8 JUDICIAL DISCRETION UNDER SECTION 1(5)

11.8.1 Discretionary jurisdiction

Once the preconditions to the court's jurisdiction under section 1(5) and (6) are satisfied, it then falls to the exercise of judicial discretion to decide whether or not to make an order. Notwithstanding that judges on occasions suggest the contrary when generalising the effect of section 1(5),[1] there does not exist any right to an order under the subsection. The statutory language provides that the court *may* order the arbitrator or umpire concerned to state the reasons for his award. It follows that even when an applicant can establish that an award is unreasoned or insufficiently reasoned the court may nonetheless decide in the exercise of its discretion not to make an order.[2]

The Act does not further offer guidance as to how the discretion is to be exercised or indicate the criteria to be taken into account. On the face of the statute the discretion is unfettered and at large. In the ultimate the exercise of the discretion will turn on the facts and circumstances of individual cases, with the court having to decide in each instance whether or not it is a proper case to make an order.[3] In this regard the court is not confined to the award and its content, but may have regard to the wider circumstances.[4] There was an early judicial inclination to perceive the discretion as a broad and flexible phenomenon,[5] but that position has been recoiled from. It is now the view that the exercise of the discretion cannot be divorced from the general policy

1. *King* v. *Thomas McKenna Ltd*. [1991] 1 All E.R. 653, 664.
1. See, for example, *Kaffeehandelsgesellschaft K.G.* v. *Plagefim Commercial S.A.* [1981] 2 Lloyd's Rep. 190, 191, per Mustill J.; *Bremer Handelsgesellschaft m.b.H.* v. *Finagrain, Compagnie Commerciale Agricole et Financière S.A.* [1981] 2 Lloyd's Rep. 259, 265, per Lord Denning M.R.
2. *Michael I. Warde* v. *Feedex International Inc.* [1984] 1 Lloyd's Rep. 310, 312, per Staughton J.; *Kansa General Insurance Co. Ltd.* v. *Bishopsgate Insurance plc* [1988] 1 Lloyd's Rep. 503, 511, per Hirst J.
3. *Trave Schiffahrtsgesellschaft m.b.H. & Co. K.G.* v. *Ninemia Maritime Corporation (The Niedersachsen)* [1986] 1 Q.B. 802, 806, per Sir John Donaldson M.R., citing Staughton J. at first instance.
4. *Michael I. Warde* v. *Feedex International Inc.* [1984] 1 Lloyd's Rep. 310, 313, per Staughton J.
5. *Schiffahrtsagentur Hamburg Middle East Line G.m.b.H. Hamburg* v. *Virtue Shipping Corporation of Monrovia (The Oinoussian Virtue)* [1981] 1 Lloyd's Rep. 533, 540, per Robert Goff J.; *Vermala Shipping Enterprises Ltd.* v. *The Minerals and Metals Trading Corporation of India Ltd. (The Gay Fidelity)* [1982] 1 Lloyd's Rep. 469; *Hayn Roman & Co. S.A.* v. *Cominter (U.K.) Ltd.* [1982] 2 Lloyd's Rep. 458.

underlying the 1979 Act.[6] In the result the discretion has come to be cautiously perceived and to be exercised very sparingly.[7]

The question whether an award is unreasoned or insufficiently reasoned is to be determined wholly by reference to the award made, without the aid of extraneous evidence. In deciding in its discretion whether or not to make an order, the court may take into account evidence beyond the award itself.[8]

The nature and exercise of the discretion arising under section 1(5) has been the object of a measure of judicial consideration and the following discussion represents an attempt to isolate the criteria which have been taken into account and weighed in the exercise of the discretion. The identified criteria are of course not necessarily exclusive nor are they presented in any order of priority. It is one thing to identify the criteria which are relevant to the exercise of a particular head of judicial discretion, but quite another to order and relate them one against another. To even attempt to do so is possibly futile for the dynamic of judicial discretion is that it operates variously according to the factual context of individual cases.

11.8.1.1 Nature of the application

11.8.1.1.1 The preceding text will have shown that an application under section 1(5) may be made with the consent of all the other parties to the reference or with leave of the court, in which case the application will be unilateral and probably contested. The application may be for reasons or further reasons. It is suggested that the judicial response may well be influenced by and vary according to the precise nature of the application.

Where an application is made with consent there appears little justification for adopting the same cautious and restrictive approach that has evolved with regard to non-consensual applications.[1] By analogy with the position that prevails with regard to consensual appeals under section 1(3)(a),[2] the wider policy associated with the 1979 Act is wholly or at least substantially displaced when the parties have agreed a form of proceeding introduced by the 1979 Act, the natural effect of which is to detract from the finality of the award in question. In such a situation the reopening of the award and the costs and delay involved are brought about by the volition of the parties; and provided the jurisdiction of the court is properly established, it may be anticipated that only in the most exceptional circumstances would the court be inclined to reject the application and thereby frustrate the mutual desire of the parties.

11.8.1.1.2 An application under section 1(5) may be for an order for reasons or further reasons. In general terms it would appear that the criteria that have been identified as relevant to the exercise of the discretion apply whatever the precise nature of the application. Nonetheless, it is at least possible that in individual cases the

---

6. *Michael I. Warde* v. *Feedex International Inc.* [1984] 1 Lloyd's Rep. 310, 313, per Staughton J.; *Trave Schiffahrtsgesellschaft m.b.H. & Co. K.G.* v. *Niedersachsen Maritime Corporation (The Niedersachsen)* [1986] 1 Q.B. 802, 807–808, per Sir John Donaldson, M.R. (C.A.); *Gebr. van Weelde Scheepvartkantoor B.V.* v. *Société Industrielle D'Acide Phosphorique et D'Engrais etc.* [1986] 1 Lloyd's Rep. 435, 436, per Hobhouse J.

7. *Universal Petroleum Co. Ltd.* v. *Handels- und Transport Gesellschaft m.b.H.* [1987] 1 Lloyd's Rep. 517; *Kansa General Insurance Co. Ltd.* v. *Bishopsgate Insurance plc* [1988] 1 Lloyd's Rep. 503; *Granges Aluminium A.B.* v. *The Cleveland Bridge and Engineering Co. Ltd.*, *The Times*, 15 May 1990 (C.A.).

8. *Michael I. Warde* v. *Feedex International Inc.* [1984] 1 Lloyd's Rep. 310, 313, Staughton J.

1. See *infra*.

2. See Chapter 4, para. 4.2.

approach of the court and the manner in which it weighs particular criteria may differ according to whether the application is for reasons or further reasons. Where there are no reasons and the court retains a jurisdiction, then there may also possibly exist a breach of duty on the part of the arbitrator or otherwise some special consideration. In the result the applicant will not have received the kind of award he anticipated, or may have had a right to expect, or may otherwise find himself positioned somewhat unfortunately as a consequence of special circumstances. In this kind of situation there arise additional considerations touching on the rights and expectations of the applicant and the claims of justice, which have the potential to weigh significantly in favour of making an order for reasons. In contrast, where the application is for further reasons, the exercise is directed more to a strategic assessment of the applicant's case. In consequence the court may be inclined to adopt a more restrictive approach and in the absence of counterweighing factors be reluctant to intervene.

11.8.1.2 Finality

11.8.1.2.1. It is well established that the effect of the 1979 Act is to move arbitral jurisprudence significantly towards the recognition of the finality of awards. This central strand of policy continues to weigh critically in the exercise of the discretionary power under section 1(5).[1] On each occasion the discretionary power is exercised positively, the finality of an award is undermined; for the effect of an order is to remit and reopen an award to the extent specified in the order. The balance between the broad policy of the 1979 Act and the interventionist power arising under section 1(5) is struck by an initial judicial subscription to the finality of awards. Kerr L.J. has summarised the importance of finality in the following terms[2]:

The jurisdiction to order further or more detailed reasons under sub-s.(5)(b) should be exercised as sparingly as possible. Such orders involve a process of "to-ing and fro-ing" between the Court and the arbitrator, with consequential costs and delays before it is even known whether leave to appeal against the award will ultimately be granted. The effect of such orders is therefore greatly to postpone the effective finality of what was intended to be a final award. Any excessive or unnecessary resort to such orders runs counter to the purpose and policy of the 1979 Act, as explained—in particular—in *The Nema* and *The Antaios* and is liable to bring the Act into disrepute.

11.8.1.2.2 The emphasis on finality represents a significant facet of the operative framework of reference in addressing applications under section 1(5). Of itself it cannot dominate, for such an approach would effectively displace the subsection. The discretion must operate within and not remove the permissive statutory framework. The significance of the emphasis on finality is to declare that the judges will exercise their powers under section 1(5) with considerable circumspection, particularly when an application is made without the consent of all the other parties to the reference. The emphasis on the need to protect the finality of awards has with the continued judicial analysis and development of the discretion grown in significance, culminating in the

---

1. *Gebr. van Weelde Scheepvartkantoor B.V.* v. *Société Industrielle D'Acide Phosphorique et D'Engrais etc. (The Dynashinky)* [1986] 1 Lloyd's Rep. 435, 437, per Hobhouse J.; *Kansa General Insurance Co. Ltd.* v. *Bishopsgate Insurance plc* [1988] 1 Lloyd's Rep. 503, 513, per Hirst J.
2. *Universal Petroleum Co. Ltd.* v. *Handels- und Transport Gesellschaft m.b.H.* [1987] 1 Lloyd's Rep. 517, 528; cited in *Kansa General Insurance Co. Ltd.* v. *Bishopsgate Insurance plc* [1988] 1 Lloyd's Rep. 503, 509, per Hirst J.

decision of the Court of Appeal in *Universal Petroleum Co. Ltd.* v. *Handels- und Transport Gesellschaft m.b.H.*,[3] with the result that a cautious reading must now be given to the earlier authorities advocating a far less restrictive approach.[4]

11.8.1.2.3 It may however be questioned whether considerations of finality deserve to be pursued in this regard to the same degree as they are in relation to leave to appeal. To grant an order for reasons is admittedly a reopening of an award, but it does not of itself amount to a bridging of the divide between arbitration and the courts. It might quite reasonably be argued that a party has a greater right to an order for reasons than to the granting of an application for leave to appeal. The giving of reasons not only facilitates the judicial consideration of an application for leave to appeal and any full appeal that thereafter may follow, but also provides a platform for party scrutiny of an award. The reasons permit the parties to assess an award, to determine whether there exists any basis for seeking leave to appeal and to judge the prospects of success, on both the application for leave and full appeal. Only when so armed may a party contemplate the appellate process established by the 1979 Act. In the final analysis this appellate process may be denied to a party, but there is nothing in the Act to suggest that a party is to be equally denied the right to make an initial assessment of an award. The advantage of an order for reasons is that it will not inevitably encourage an application for leave. When fully apprised of the basis of an award an applicant may decide that there are no grounds for appeal, or, notwithstanding the presence of possible grounds, that on balance it is more prudent not to pursue an appeal. The making of a section 1(5) order may therefore even contribute to the policy of supporting the finality of awards associated with the 1979 Act: but at the same time the making of an order will not seriously prejudice that policy because there is no necessary association between the making of a section 1(5) order and the granting of leave to appeal.[5]

11.8.1.3 Appealability of award

11.8.1.3.1 The rationale of a section 1(5) order is that it is a necessary aid to the appellate process. The order is subsidiary: it is a preliminary to the overriding question whether leave to appeal should be granted.[1] This being the case, together with the natural disposition of courts not to act in vain, the discretion arising under section 1(5) has been fashioned in a purposive manner. Its exercise has come to be closely related to the contributive effect of any order which may be made. The court asks itself the question: if an order is made is there a real prospect of leave to appeal being granted? The greater the propensity to give an affirmative answer to this question the greater the likelihood that the court may be persuaded to make an order. In *The Niedersachsen*[2] the Court of Appeal articulated the criterion in the following terms:

---

3. [1987] 1 Lloyd's Rep. 517 (a two-judge Court of Appeal).
4. *Kansa General Insurance Co. Ltd.* v. *Bishopsgate Insurance plc* [1988] 1 Lloyd's Rep. 503, 511, per Hirst J.
5. See Chapter 6, para. 6.2.4.
1. *Universal Petroleum Co. Ltd.* v. *Handels- und Transport Gesellschaft m.b.H.* [1987] 1 Lloyd's Rep. 517, 526, per Kerr L.J.
2. *Trave Schiffahrtsgesellschaft m.b.H. & Co. K.G.* v. *Ninemia Maritime Corporation (The Niedersachsen)* [1986] 1 Q.B. 802, 808, citing Staughton J. at first instance.

"the degree of likelihood that if further reasons were given, the court would grant leave to appeal".

11.8.1.3.2 The issue of potential appealability being to the fore, it naturally follows that in the first instance the court must be satisfied that any order made would assist in revealing a question of law and not of fact.[3] In *The Dynashinky*,[4] Hobhouse J., at first instance, considered that the court must be, "satisfied at least on a *prima facie* basis, that there is some basis for making the reasons; in other words that there is probably some relevant point of law involved". Further, the question of law must be one that could substantially affect the rights of at least one of the parties, within the meaning of section 1(4). The concept of "substantiality" has been considered elsewhere in the text,[5] and its relevance to the discretion arising under section 1(5) has been emphasised by the Court of Appeal in *Universal Petroleum Co. Ltd.* v. *Handels- und Transport Gesellschaft m.b.H.*,[6] where Kerr L.J. gave one example of its potential relevance[7]:

. . . if there are several grounds for concluding that a claim succeeds or fails, there must be no remission under subsection 5(b) for more detailed reasons in support of the arbitrator's conclusion on one of those grounds if the existence of the other grounds would or should still lead to a refusal of leave to appeal. The reason is that an answer from the arbitrator which is favourable to an applicant for remission under subsection (5)(b) on that one ground could not "substantially affect the rights of the parties" if the existence of the other ground would still lead to a refusal of leave to appeal.

11.8.1.3.3 Beyond the basic prerequisite of establishing a substantial question of law, the issue of potential appealability must be measured by reference to *The Nema/ Antaios* guidelines and related considerations.[7a] The criteria that would be of relevance on an application for leave to appeal must be anticipated. In turn this means that the question of law in issue must be characterised and the appropriate test applied. Kerr L.J. has summarised the position in the following terms[8]:

Where a party applies for an order under sub-s. (5)(b), the decision whether or not to grant the application should never be taken without giving the fullest consideration possible at that stage to the question whether leave to appeal is likely to be granted by reference to the text of sub-s. (4) and *The Nema* and *The Antaios* decisions. Such orders should therefore never be made simply on a basis of "Let us wait and see what the arbitrator will say", but only if there appears to be a real prospect of leave to appeal being properly granted.

The approach has been endorsed by Hirst J., in accepting that the court must "pay very close regard to the eventual prospect of an application for leave to appeal, for which purpose the Court will necessarily have to decide what is the proper criterion to apply".[9]

11.8.1.3.4 Once the likely appealability of a particular question of law is estab-

---

3. *Michael I. Warde* v. *Feedex International Inc.* [1984] 1 Lloyd's Rep. 310, 313.
4. *Gebr. van Weelde Scheepvartkantoor B.V.* v. *Société Industrielle D'Acide Phosphorique et D'Engrais etc. (The Dynashinky)* [1986] 1 Lloyd's Rep. 435, 438.
5. Chapter 4, para. 4.3.3.
6. *Supra*, note 1.
7. *Supra*, p. 526.
7a. See Chapters 5 and 6.
8. *Universal Petroleum Co. Ltd.* v. *Handels- und Transport Gesellschaft m.b.H.*, *supra*, p. 528. See also *Michael I. Warde* v. *Feedex International Inc.* [1984] 1 Lloyd's Rep. 310, 313; *Trave Schiffahrtsgesellschaft m.b.H. & Co. K.G.* v. *Ninemia Maritime Corporation (The Niedersachsen)* [1986] 1 Q.B. 802, 808.
9. *Kansa General Insurance Co. Ltd.* v. *Bishopsgate Insurance plc* [1988] 1 Lloyd's Rep. 503, 511.

lished it matters not that there may also exist other questions of law that do not fall into the same characterisation. Where questions of law of differing characterisations are co-mingled, the court may be persuaded to make an order for reasons appertaining to all, notwithstanding that with regard to certain of the questions of law it would not have made an order had they stood in isolation. The likely appealability of one or some questions of law can have the effect of carrying with them other less significant questions of law.[10]

11.8.1.3.5 The criterion of appealability, can only be of relevance when a section 1(5) order is sought as a preliminary to an application for leave to appeal. It has no application when leave to appeal has previously been granted. In this situation the focus of concern is deflected away from the application for leave to appeal to the full appeal. The order is now sought to assist the judicial consideration of the identified question of law on the full appeal. It may be suggested that in such a situation the court will be inclined to make the order sought if satisfied that the making of the order would probably assist the court in disposing of the full appeal and there is nothing in the wider circumstances of the case, including the conduct of the applicant, to suggest that the assistance of the court should be withheld. As a general rule it is for an appellant to ensure that the factual and legal basis of an award is satisfactorily established before the hearing of a full appeal and an appellant who fails to do so may find the court unsympathetic to an application for a section 1(5) order made during the course of a full appeal.[11]

11.8.1.3.6 All that has been said so far assumes that the disputed question of law is identifiable or is at least to an acceptable degree of satisfaction capable of being identified. But this will not always be the case. In particular where the complaint is directed to the total absence of reasons, it will be impossible, or at least exceptionally difficult, to identify a disputed question of law. This being the case it is redundant to speculate on the likely success of a future application for leave to appeal. If the appealability criterion is applied uncompromisingly in this kind of circumstance the inevitable consequence is to exclude the availability of section 1(5), but this outcome would not necessarily be in harmony with the policy of the 1979 Act. Reasons may be sought under the 1979 Act not only to assist in appealing an identified question of law but also for the purpose of scrutinising an arbitral award and so determining whether there exists a disputable question of law. Appealability is not a universal criterion. Whereas unjustifiable "fishing expeditions" must be guarded against, there would appear nothing unprincipled about supporting bona fide scrutiny. In *Kansa General Insurance Co. Ltd.* v. *Bishopsgate Insurance plc*, Hirst J.[12] accepted the limitations of the appealability criterion in circumstances when no reasons had been given, but equally rejected any notion that the court was precluded from doing justice. On the facts of the case Hirst J. was prepared to make an order, notwithstanding the absence of reasons, because from an examination of the award as a whole and the reasons given in support of other conclusions, there was evidence that the arbitrator had fallen into error.

11.8.1.3.7 The emphasis on the criterion of appealability is clearly restrictive. It is

10. Cf. *J.H. Rayner (Mincing Lane) Ltd.* v. *Shaher Trading Co.* [1982] 1 Lloyd's Rep. 632.
11. *Cefetra B.V.* v. *Alfred C. Toepfer International G.m.b.H.* [1994] 1 Lloyd's Rep. 93, 100–101, Colman J.
12. [1988] 1 Lloyd's Rep. 503, 511.

increasingly observed that appeals from arbitration awards under the 1979 Act have been reduced to a trickle. If this is so, the same fact provides a strong indication of the limited availability of orders under section 1(5). The emergence of the importance of the potential appealability of an award in the exercise of the judicial discretion also serves to determine quite decisively the purpose underlying a section 1(5) order and to render hopeless the position of a party who seeks an order for reasons or further reasons so that he may be fully informed why he has won or lost, but with no further intention to invoke the appellate process. Even if the issue was at one time in a state of doubt, it now appears quite clear that section 1(5) cannot be used as an end in itself: it is ancillary to the appellate process. An applicant who declares that he seeks information *per se* and not to enable him to scrutinise an award for legal error or to assist in his application for leave to appeal is likely to receive short shrift.

11.8.1.4 Nature of the question of law

11.8.1.4.1 Where a question of law is identifiable, the precise nature of the question of law in issue is capable of representing a significant factor in the exercise of judicial discretion under section 1(5). So to assert without qualification is to do no more than effectively dress the criterion of "appealability" in different language.[1] But there exists within the general proposition a particular rule which merits separate consideration.

It was the case under the former special case procedure and it continues to be the case under the new appellate process that the court is exceptionally reluctant to allow appeals on questions of law relating to the existence or sufficiency of evidence in support of findings of fact.[2] To allow such appeals is to move dangerously close to trespassing on the traditional sanctity of arbitrators with regard to questions of fact. The same reluctance travels into the exercise of discretion under section 1(5). The court will resist an application for an order for reasons, the overt purpose of which is to reopen or "go behind" the primary findings of fact made by an arbitrator and set out in a reasoned award. The attitude of the judiciary has been expounded by Robert Goff L.J. in the following terms[3]:

The findings of the arbitrators now in question were findings as to the law of Qatar, and as such were findings of fact. We accept that a question whether there is any evidence to support a finding of fact may raise a question of law: see *Nello Simoni* v. *A/S M/S Stratum*, (1949) 83 Ll.L.Rep. 157 at p. 161, per Mr Justice Devlin (as he then was). It is conceivable that an appeal on such a question may lie under s. 1 of the 1979 Act; though appeals of this kind will be at least as much discouraged under that Act, as were special cases on similar points under the old procedure (see, for example, *Mondial Trading Co. G.m.b.H.* v. *Gill & Duffus Zuckerhandelsgesellschaft m.b.H.* [1980] 2 Lloyd's Rep. 376). But, if such an appeal is to be brought, it must in our judgment be based upon material which is contained in the award and reasons of the arbitration tribunal, and cannot be based on extraneous evidence as is done where, for example, it is sought to allege misconduct on the part of an arbitrator. If a party wishes to raise a point on an appeal to the High Court, he should invite the arbitration tribunal to make the necessary findings in the award; if no such findings are made, he can apply to the Court for an order,

1. *Supra*, para. 11.8.1.3.
2. See Chapter 6, para. 6.2.11.
3. *Athens Cape Naviera S.A.* v. *Deutsche Dampfschiffahrtsgesellschaft "Hansa" Aktiengesellschaft etc. (The Barenbels)* [1985] 1 Lloyd's Rep. 528, 532. See also Bingham, "Reasons and Reasons for Reasons: Difference between a Court Judgment and an Arbitration Award" (1988) 4 Arb. Int. 141, 152–153.

under s. 1(5) of the Act, for further reasons to be given, though he should not expect the Court to react enthusiastically to such an application in a case of this kind.

11.8.1.4.2 This principle was forcefully endorsed by the Court of Appeal in *Universal Petroleum Co. Ltd.* v. *Handels- und Transport Gesellschaft m.b.H.*[4] The view of the Court of Appeal was that *prima facie* unappealable awards are not by the use of section 1(5) to be converted into appealable awards. The jurisdiction arising under the subsection is not to be used for the purpose of conducting a cross-examination of an arbitrator or for the purpose of reopening arguments in the arbitration. The Court of Appeal expressed the view that provided an award is intrinsically consistent and not appealable by reference to *The Nema/Antaios* guidelines, the court will not order an arbitrator to give reasons for his primary findings with a view to establishing that the findings contain conclusions which no reasonable arbitrator could have reached. Although in strictness the court has jurisdiction to make such an order, nonetheless to exercise the discretion in favour of making an order contravenes principle.

11.8.1.4.3 In *Universal Petroleum* the Court of Appeal applied this principle to what may be described as an initial conclusion of law, that is a conclusion of law which represents a point of departure and on which the whole of the remainder of an arbitrator's reasoning is based. The particular conclusion of law in issue concerned the identity of the precise contractual documents and the terms of the contract. Being analogous to other primary findings, the Court of Appeal reasoned that the conclusion of law could not be challenged unless:

. . . either (i) the necessary foundation for a challenge to them has been laid, or (ii) the remainder of the award contains material which enables their correctness in law to be challenged, or (iii) there are gaps, inconsistencies or ambiguities in the arbitrator's reasons which cast sufficient doubt upon the correctness in law of these findings, *and* upon the consequent correctness of the award, to justify an order for more detailed reasons under sub-s. 5(b).[5]

Precondition (i) is of particular interest because it reveals that if parties wish to reserve to themselves the opportunity of challenging a primary finding or conclusion, they must take the necessary steps and specifically request an arbitrator to give reasons for his findings or conclusions.[6] The response of the arbitrator might include a summary of the evidence on which he based his findings or conclusions. Only in this kind of situation can it be said that the applicant has laid the necessary foundation which in turn appears to be an essential precondition to the court being prepared to consider an application under section 1(5).

11.8.1.5 Argument in the arbitration

An order for reasons or further reasons is unlikely to be granted with regard to a question or issue of law not canvassed before the arbitrator or umpire.[1] The general rule is that an arbitrator must resolve a dispute or difference referred on the basis of the

---

4. [1987] 1 Lloyd's Rep. 517.
5. *Ibid.*, p. 526.
6. Cf. *Mondial Trading Co. G.m.b.H.* v. *Gill & Duffus Zuckerhandelsgesellschaft m.b.H.* [1980] 2 Lloyd's Rep. 376, 379, Robert Goff J.
1. *Clea Shipping Corporation* v. *Bulk Oil International Ltd. (The Alaskan Trader)* [1983] 1 Lloyd's Rep. 315, 318, per Bingham J. For the manner the court may respond to an application for leave to appeal with regard to a question of law not argued in the arbitration, see Chapter 6, para. 6.2.13.

submissions, argument and evidence presented by the parties[2]; and the rationale of the power arising under section 1(5) is that it is a mechanism by which the decision of the arbitrator or umpire so arrived at may be further elucidated.

On an application for an order for reasons or further reasons it is in consequence relevant to enquire whether the issue in question was argued before the arbitrator. In so determining it is open to the court to examine the written submissions of the parties made in the arbitration[3] and presumably any other relevant documentary evidence that may exist. If the question or issue was not argued in the arbitration and the applicant is in truth seeking to establish fresh facts in order to take a new point or line of argument, then it is likely that only in exceptional circumstances will an order under section 1(5) be made.[4]

The relationship between the exercise of discretion and the argument before an arbitrator or umpire has been emphasised in several judgments at first instance.[5] The relationship is expressed with particular clarity by Robert Goff J. in *The Oinoussian Virtue*[6]:

But generally speaking if the further reasons sought form part of an argument fairly raised below, the court may be ready to make an order under s.1(5); but it may desist from making an order if, for example, the applicant requires new reasons in order to advance a point not taken below which, on established principles, the court may not in the interests of justice allow him to take . . .

11.8.1.6 Conduct of applicant

11.8.1.6.1 Whenever an order is sought that reposes in the discretion of the court the conduct of an applicant has the clear potential of assuming a relevance to the exercise of the discretion. That the conduct of an applicant may assume a relevance to the exercise of discretion under section 1(5) was recognised by Staughton J. in *Michael I. Warde* v. *Feedex International Inc.*,[1] where the learned judge posed the question[2]: "has there been anything in the conduct of the [applicant] in the proceedings thus far which should lead to the discretion being exercised against him?" In pursuing this enquiry the court is free to examine evidence beyond the award itself.[3]

Conduct in the present context may allude both to the conduct of an applicant in the course of a reference and to the motive of an applicant in making an application. As a minimum requirement the application must be made bona fide and the court is likely to respond with firm disfavour if it suspects that an application is made with the object of producing delay or of otherwise frustrating or baulking the arbitral process. It is

---

2. An arbitrator or umpire in appropriate circumstances may also draw on his own expertise and knowledge in resolving a dispute referred: see *Mediterranean and Eastern Export Co.* v. *Fortress Fabrics (Manchester) Ltd.* [1948] 2 All E.R. 186; *Interbulk Ltd.* v. *Aiden Shipping Co. Ltd. (The Vimeira)* [1983] 2 Lloyd's Rep. 424, 429.

3. *Vermala Shipping Enterprises Ltd.* v. *The Minerals and Metals Trading Corporation of India Ltd. (The Gay Fidelity)* [1982] 1 Lloyd's Rep. 469, 470, per Staughton J.

4. Cf. *Petraco (Bermuda) Ltd.* v. *Petromed International S.A.* [1988] 2 Lloyd's Rep. 357.

5. *Vermala Shipping Enterprises Ltd.* v. *The Minerals and Metals Trading Corporation of India Ltd. (The Gay Fidelity)*, *supra*; *Clea Shipping Corporation* v. *Bulk Oil International Ltd. (The Alaskan Trader)*, *supra*.

6. *Schiffahrtsagentur Hamburg Middle East Line G.m.b.H. Hamburg* v. *Virtue Shipping Corporation of Monrovia (The Oinoussian Virtue)* [1981] 1 Lloyd's Rep. 533, 540.

1. [1984] 1 Lloyd's Rep. 310.

2. *Ibid*, p. 313.

3. *Ibid*.

well to recall that a significant purpose underlying the 1979 Act is to overcome the abuses which developed about the former special case procedure.[4]

11.8.1.6.2 A facet of conduct relating to the course of a reference and which may assume a particular importance is whether or not the applicant requested a reasoned award. This question is probably only capable of assuming a significance when the arbitral mandate is silent on the issue of reasons, so there is an absence of express contractual obligation. Where an unreasoned award is made, the failure to have requested reasons will result, in the absence of special reasons, in the court having no jurisdiction to make an order by virtue of section 1(6). But the omission to request reasons will not automatically result in an unreasoned award, for the arbitrator or umpire may volunteer a reasoned award and in doing so the arbitrator may or may not be acting in accordance with the established practice of the arbitral process in question. Where such an award is also alleged to be insufficiently reasoned the court undoubtedly enjoys a jurisdiction to make an order under section 1(5), but as a question of discretion the absence of an express request for reasons may influence the court in the way it exercises the discretion.

11.8.1.6.3 The precise significance to be given to the absence of an express request for reasons gave rise to disagreement among Commercial judges at first instance.[5] The matter was however in due course addressed and probably settled by the Court of Appeal in *The Niedersachsen*, where Sir John Donaldson M.R. asserted[6]:

. . . a very important, and often decisive, factor in exercising this discretion must be the policy of the Act, which is that an arbitrator is generally under no obligation to give a reasoned award, unless asked to do so, and that, in the absence of such a request arbitrators should not be expected to give reasons for an award after the award has been published.

11.8.1.6.4 The absence of a request for reasons may be perceived in part as evidence that the applicant was at the time of the reference content with an unreasoned award or at least with such reasons as the arbitrator or umpire might be minded to give. It is also some evidence that the applicant was at the same moment in time prepared to receive the award as a final determination of the dispute. It may even in some circumstances suggest a breach of duty or more probably of a responsibility falling on the applicant. Kerr L.J. has suggested that where a disputed question of law is expressly and specifically referred to an arbitrator, and a future appeal is contemplated, the arbitrator should also be invited specifically to give reasons for his conclusions and so lay the foundation for any subsequent application for leave to appeal which may be made.[7] There seems little reason for the same principle not applying generally whenever a future appeal is contemplated. Contrariwise, when a request for reasons is made all the possible implications are inverted. Confronted with such a

---

4. See Chapter 1, para. 1.3.

5. In *Schiffahrtsagentur Hamburg Middle East Line G.m.b.H. Hamburg* v. *Virtue Shipping Corporation (The Oinoussian Virtue)* [1981] 1 Lloyd's Rep. 533, 537, Robert Goff J. considered the failure to ask for reasons to be irrelevant, although in strictness his comments were made on an application for leave to appeal and not on an application under section 1(5). Staughton J. adopted a contrary view in *Michael I. Warde* v. *Feedex International Inc.* [1984] 1 Lloyd's Rep. 310, 314, which opinion he again repeated at first instance in *The Niedersachsen, infra.*

6. *Trave Schiffahrtsgesellschaft m.b.H. & Co. K.G.* v. *Ninemia Maritime Corporation (The Niedersachsen)* [1986] 1 Q.B. 802, 808.

7. *Universal Petroleum Co. Ltd.* v. *Handels- und Transport Gesellschaft m.b.H* [1987] 1 Lloyd's Rep. 517, 526.

request there is also established a quasi-duty obliging an arbitrator or umpire to give reasons within the meaning of the 1979 Act, with any failure amounting to a breach of this duty.[8]

11.8.1.6.5 In contrast to the practice that developed in association with the special case procedure, the discretion under section 1(5) is not tied to evidence that the applicant has taken the necessary steps to ensure, as far as it was possible, that the relevant facts were found in the award. Provided reasons have been given or requested, or there exists a special reason why no request was made, it is unnecessary as a question of jurisdiction and discretion for the applicant to further show exertions to secure the giving of the "reasons" which are now sought under a remission of the award. In *The Oinoussian Virtue* Robert Goff J. made the point in the following terms[9]:

> . . . under the old procedure, it became established over the years that it was for the parties to ensure that so far as possible the relevant facts were found in the award: in the absence of evidence of this, the courts were reluctant to remit awards for further facts to be found. This approach has led to a most time-wasting and expensive practice under which, in many arbitrations, counsel draft long and complicated documents which are submitted to an arbitrator after the conclusion of the arbitration specifying every fact which his client wishes to be found. I cannot think that this undesirable consequence of the old procedure should be perpetuated under the new procedure.

But if the court is of the opinion that an applicant has in any way contributed to the absence of any relevant information in an award, it may in its discretion refuse to make an order under section 1(5), or make an order but with costs against the applicant.[10]

11.8.1.7 Ability to respond to an order

11.8.1.7.1 The ability of an arbitrator or umpire, in the circumstances of any case, to respond effectively to any order made under section 1(5) is a factor likely to be taken into consideration in the exercise of the discretion. An order may require an arbitrator or umpire to set out his reasons generally or to respond to a particular question or set of questions. There is little purpose in making an order if it is known or strongly suspected that the arbitrator or umpire will be unable to respond to the order, although rarely will such an extreme situation exist. A greater likelihood is that of finding an arbitrator or umpire who may experience difficulty in responding to the order in a way the parties and the court would consider satisfactory.

11.8.1.7.2 The extent to which it is reasonable to expect an arbitrator or umpire to be able to respond to the terms of an order, if made, is of course a question of fact to be assessed in the circumstances of individual cases. But it is nonetheless possible to identify factors that may be of significance. It may be considered that an arbitrator or umpire is best able to respond when an application for an order for reasons is made promptly following the publication of an award or where an arbitrator has set out some, but incomplete reasons, in his award or where the reasons have been incorporated in an external document, not part of the award, or when it is known the arbitrator has kept a private note of his reasons. But in the absence of special factors promptness

---

8. *Kansa General Insurance Co. Ltd.* v. *Bishopsgate Insurance plc* [1988] 1 Lloyd's Rep. 503, 511. See *supra*, para. 11.7.3.1.7A.
9. *Schiffahrtsagentur Hamburg Middle East Line G.m.b.H. Hamburg* v. *Virtue Shipping Corporation (The Oinoussian Virtue)* [1981] 1 Lloyd's Rep. 533, 540.   10. *Ibid.*

would appear the predominant consideration. A prompt application will ensure that any order made will be directed to an arbitrator or umpire at a time when his decision is still fresh in his mind and when he is in consequence well positioned to provide a reasoned award as defined by the 1979 Act.

11.8.1.7.3 The criterion under discussion, although potentially one of general application, is likely to be of greatest significance when an unreasoned award is made in the absence of any request for reasons but where there exists a special reason for the failure to request reasons. In these circumstances the terms of section 1(6) are satisfied and the court has jurisdiction to make an order. But in the exercise of its discretion the court has also recognised that it may be burdensome and unfair to require an arbitrator to give reasons in this kind of circumstance. In *The Dynashinky* Hobhouse J. saw it to be an aspect of the policy of the legislation that[1]: "arbitrators must not be oppressed by being asked, many months or weeks after they have prepared their award, to give reasons for that award. They ought to be asked to deal with it at the time when the matter is fresh in their memory."

11.8.1.7.4 Whereas the dictum provides an indication of the general judicial stance it does not and clearly cannot be interpreted to mean that there exists an overwhelming disinclination on the part of the court to make an order whenever the parties have failed to request a reasoned award. The "special reason" cases decided to date show otherwise. In *Hayn Roman & Co S.A.* v. *Cominter (U.K.) Ltd.*,[2] Robert Goff J. granted an order because, *inter alia*, as soon as the award was published the applicant's solicitor made known to the Committee of Appeal that a reasoned award had been expected. There had in consequence been no harmful delay and the appeal tribunal had in fact responded by preparing a statement of its reasons, although these had not been published pending the outcome of the application. In *The Dynashinky*[3] the arbitrators had given extra-award and restricted reasons. Notwithstanding that they might have to be refined or adapted for the purpose of any appeal, they nonetheless provided a basis for providing formal reasons in response to an order of the court. The arbitrators had again been given early notice of the application and in all likelihood still retained their notes and other records.

11.8.1.8 *Extra-award reasons*

The practice of giving extra-award reasons and the associated phenomenon of restricted reasons agreements have previously been considered.[1] They also give rise to many difficulties in the context of the 1979 Act.[2] Where the parties have expressly or impliedly mandated the making of extra-award reasons, or have otherwise acquiesced in the giving of extra-award reasons, this would appear to represent a particularly crucial factor and one strongly tending to influence against the making of an order under section 1(5). It may of course be that in such a situation the court has no jurisdiction by virtue of section 1(6), but even assuming the existence of jurisdiction, the conduct of the parties would appear to provide very strong evidence that they are content or

1. *Gebr. van Weelde Scheepvartkantoor B.V.* v. *Société Industrielle D'Acide Phosphorique et D'Engrais etc. (The Dynashinky)* [1986] 1 Lloyd's Rep. 435, 436.
2. [1982] 2 Lloyd's Rep. 458.
3. *Supra.*
1. See *supra*, para. 11.2.6.
2. *Ibid.*

even intend that the award be unreasoned and final. This perception appears to have been endorsed by Sir John Donaldson M.R., who in *The Niedersachsen* expressed the opinion that[3] "it is highly significant and relevant to the exercise of the discretion that the arbitrators had given privileged reasons. There is no point in arbitrators giving privileged reasons, and they would not be expected to do so, where they are intending to give, or think they have given, reasons in their award."

11.8.1.9 *The terms of the contractual mandate*

11.8.1.9.1 The making of a reasoned award is a matter which may be governed by the contractual mandate of the arbitrator or tribunal. This statement of principle is also implicitly recognised by section 3(4)(c) of the 1979 Act. Beyond demanding a reasoned award the mandate may further specify the range and quality of the reasons, although this is rare in practice. Contrariwise the mandate may direct that no reasons be given or that only extra-award reasons be given. The terms of the mandate may derive from the express or implied agreement of the parties and although in point of principle there is no difference between an express and implied agreement, nonetheless for present purposes the difference would appear capable of exerting an influence on the exercise of judicial discretion under section 1(5).

11.8.1.9.2 It may be anticipated that the precise terms of a mandate at least have the potential to assume a relevance in the exercise of the discretion under section 1(5). A positive mandate obliging the making of a reasoned award is a clear indication of the expectations of the parties and also provides at least some evidence that the parties do not necessarily perceive the award to be a final resolution of the dispute. Moreover, to the extent that no or at best inadequate reasons are given, the possibility of an arbitral breach of duty also exists. The presence of a positive mandate may therefore help to lean matters in favour of making an order, but in isolation it will not necessarily be conclusive, for otherwise there would be a danger of section 1(5) orders becoming a matter of course. The existence of a positive mandate is likely to be of greatest significance as an additional factor lending weight to the force of other considerations.

11.8.1.9.3 Where a mandate is expressed in negative terms and a reasoned award is proscribed, it is highly improbable that the court may be persuaded to make an order under section 1(5), even assuming the court to have jurisdiction. An arbitrator who disregards a negative mandate may also be presumed to be in breach of duty. The same reluctance may prevail where a mandate precisely defines and delineates the reasons to be provided and an arbitrator is found to have discharged the strict terms of his mandate. In this situation the parties have obtained precisely what they contracted for and in the absence of exceptional circumstances it is unlikely that the court will allow them to obtain further reasons by the affirmative exercise of the discretion under section 1(5). To put the point in general terms, where the parties have by express or implied agreement made known their expectations with regard to a reasoned or unreasoned award, it is likely that the court will be hesitant to exercise its discretion under section 1(5) so as to work what would in effect be a contractual variation. But the fact that the giving of reasons is regulated by the contractual mandate of

---

3. *Trave Schiffahrtsgesellschaft m.b.H & Co. K.B.* v. *Ninemia Maritime Corporation (The Niedersachsen)* [1986] 1 Q.B. 802, 809.

an arbitral tribunal does not of itself exclude the discretionary jurisdiction of the court under section 1(5).

11.8.1.10 Quantum of the award

The amount of money in issue is not of itself an overwhelming consideration but it is nonetheless probably true that the larger the sum of money in question, and the sums involved in arbitral disputes are often very large, the greater the potential influence it may have on the exercise of the judicial discretion. The influence may be direct, as where the quantum is exceptionally great and dominates thinking; or indirect, as where the sum in dispute adds weight to other criteria which the judge may legitimately have regard to. The scale of an award may well serve to pronounce its importance, both to the parties and in the general interest, and accentuate the importance of providing for the satisfaction of the parties, either by underscoring the correctness of the award or by affording the opportunity to pursue feasible grounds of challenge.[1]

11.8.1.11 Absence of arbitral unanimity

Whereas the absence of arbitral unanimity may provide some evidence of difficulty, importance and the need for judicial clarification, it is doubtful if without more it is capable of assuming a significant consideration in the exercise of the discretion. Majority awards and the awards of chairmen or presidents of arbitral tribunals are a common feature of contemporary practice and for the purposes of section 1(5) it is the valid and lawful award of the arbitral tribunal which is in issue, whatever be its precise character. The existence of dissent is in consequence unlikely to have a material influence, if any at all, on an application under section 1(5). Hirst J. has expressed the very firm opinion that "it would be quite wrong that the outcome of an application . . . should hinge in any way on non-unanimity among the arbitrators, which is a purely fortuitous actuation."[1]

11.8.1.12. Awards of costs and interest

11.8.1.12.1 Where the application is made in respect of an award of costs, the court will be disposed to make an order for reasons or further reasons whenever the applicant can show the order as to costs ostensibly to depart from normal principles and to be unusual. Lord Donaldson of Lymington M.R. has commented, *obiter dictum*[1]:

The fact that the order as to costs was not such as *prima facie* would have been expected to result from a judicial exercise of discretion, which used to be the foundation for the exercise of the court's powers under s.22 of the 1950 Act, would now I think be regarded as a justification for ordering reasons or further reasons to be given under s.1(5) of the 1979 Act.

By implication the court will in all ordinary circumstances refuse to make an order under section 1(5) when the order as to costs is usual or is otherwise an order the

---

1. *J. H. Rayner (Mincing Lane) Ltd.* v. *Shaher Trading Co.* [1982] 1 Lloyd's Rep. 632, 637, per Bingham J. "This is a very large award. The sellers are, I think, entitled to seek advice and be given advice as to whether the award is open to challenge."
1. *Kansa General Insurance Co. Ltd.* v. *Bishopsgate Insurance plc* [1988] 1 Lloyd's Rep. 503, 513.
1. *King* v. *Thomas McKenna Ltd*. [1991] 1 All E.R. 653, 664.

arbitrator could have made on the facts of the dispute. The fact that on the same facts the court would have exercised the discretion differently is of no significance.[2]

The same reasoning probably applies equally to interest awards.

11.8.1.13 *Time application made*

Under section 1(5) an application may be made at any time up to the final determination of an appeal. An application may be made not only as a preliminary step or in association with an application for leave to appeal, but also during the full appeal hearing. This follows from the general object of a section 1(5) order, which is to enable the court to determine any question of law arising out of an award. But although jurisdiction is retained until the appellate determination, as a matter of discretion, the more reluctant the court may be to make an order the more greatly the appeal process has progressed at the time of the application. It would be reasonable for the view to prevail that the question of the sufficiency of reasons should be resolved by the time of the application for leave to appeal, and in the event of leave being given, only rarely should it thereafter be necessary and justified to seek an order for reasons. On this view of the situation, an application made during the full appeal hearing is unlikely to be viewed with favour and will be closely scrutinised. In *Cefetra B.V.* v. *Alfred C. Toepfer International G.m.b.H.*,[1] an application for a section 1(5) order was made at the end of the appeal hearing, which Colman J. considered to be far too late.[2]

Where an application is made late in the appeal process, it will also be necessary for the applicant to obtain leave to apply out of time.[3]

11.8.2 Discretion to attach conditions

11.8.2.1 An order for reasons or further reasons may be made subject to such conditions as the court in its discretion considers necessary and just in the circumstances of any particular case. The power to attach conditions does not derive directly from section 1(5), which is silent on the point. Nor does there exist anything corresponding to the express provisions set out in section 1(4), whereby leave to appeal granted under section 1(3)(b) may be made subject to such conditions as the court considers appropriate.[1] The power derives from section 7(1) of the 1979 Act which renders section 28 of the Arbitration Act 1950 applicable to the 1979 Act.[2] Under section 28 an order may be made on such terms as to "costs or otherwise" as the authority making the order thinks just. In *Michael I. Warde* v. *Feedex International Inc.*[3] Staughton J.

---

2. Cf. *Ritter* v. *Godfrey* [1920] 2 K.B. 47, 52, Lord Sterndale; *Donald Campbell and Co. Ltd.* v. *Pollak* [1927] A.C. 732, 811, Viscount Cave.
   1. [1994] 1 Lloyd's Rep. 93.
   2. *Ibid.* pp. 100–101. Colman J. takes a different view of section 1(5) from that adopted in the text and considers that section 1(5) contemplates applications being made before an appeal is brought. From this Colman J. concludes: "There is therefore no jurisdiction to make an order under s.1(5) where the further reasons are sought for the purposes of an appeal which has not only been brought but also been given leave and substantially argued."
   3. See *infra*, para. 11.12.1.4.
   1. See Chapter 4, para. 4.3.4.
   2. See Chapter 1, para. 1.7.6.
   3. [1984] 1 Lloyd's Rep. 310, 316. Followed by Hirst J. in *Kansa General Insurance Co. Ltd.* v. *Bishopsgate Insurance plc* [1988] 1 Lloyd's Rep. 503, 514.

considered that the power arising under section 28 applied in its entirety to the 1979 Act, notwithstanding that section 7(1) in referring to section 28 described its effect in the restrictive phrase "terms as to costs of orders".

11.8.2.2 The kind of condition that may be attached is without constraint. In each case the power must be exercised judiciously, but subject to this basic tenet of principle, it is open to the court to attach any condition which can be shown to be just and necessary on the facts and circumstances of any particular case. Typical conditions would be an order requiring the amount of an award or a specified lesser sum to be paid into court or otherwise secured[4]; an order for security of costs[5]; or less typically an order that the applicant agree an issue as to the remaining jurisdiction of the arbitrator or umpire concerned[6]; or forbear from asserting a related claim.[7]

The discretion to attach conditions is vested directly in the court but it is unlikely that the court will be moved to attach a condition in the absence of an application to that effect by a party to the proceedings. A party who seeks the attachment of a condition is also likely to be encouraged to specify the condition(s) desired.

A refusal to attach a condition to an order made under section 1(5) will not preclude the possibility of a further application for the attachment of a condition on an application for leave to appeal, in the event of that stage being subsequently reached.[8]

11.8.3 The section 1(5)(b) discretion and leave to appeal under section 1(3)(b)

Although an order for reasons under section 1(5)(b) may be required to equip a party to seek leave to appeal under section 1(3)(b), it does not automatically follow from the fact the court is prepared to exercise its discretion in favour of making an order under section 1(5)(b) that it will also accede to an application for leave to appeal under section 1(3)(b).[1] The exercise of discretion under the two subsections is quite distinct and the manner the discretion is exercised with regard to the former statutory provision does not predetermine the exercise of discretion with regard to the latter. The making of an order for reasons may quite legitimately be followed by a refusal to give leave to appeal.[2]

But the failure to seek an order under section 1(5)(b) may offer a measure of disadvantage to an applicant who seeks leave to appeal from an award on the basis of the reasons as provided. In *Kaffeehandelsgesellschaft K.G.* v. *Plagefim Commercial S.A.*,[3] Mustill J. suggested that where the parties had not taken steps to secure a reasoned award, the court ought to be slow to scrutinise the award too closely with the

---

4. *Michael I. Warde* v. *Feedex International Inc.*, *supra*, p. 316. On the facts of the case the invitation to the court to attach a condition to this effect was refused. See also *Kansa General Insurance Co. Ltd.* v. *Bishopsgate Insurance plc, ibid.*; *Clea Shipping Corporation* v. *Bulk Oil International Ltd. (The Alaskan Trader)* [1982] 1 Lloyd's Rep. 315, 319.
5. *Vermala Shipping Enterprises Ltd.* v. *The Minerals and Metals Trading Corporation of India Ltd. (The Gay Fidelity)* [1982] 1 Lloyd's Rep. 469, 471–472.
6. *Ibid.*, p. 471.
7. *Clea Shipping Corporation* v. *Bulk Oil International Ltd. (The Alaskan Trader)*, *supra*, p. 319.
8. *Kansa General Insurance Co. Ltd.* v. *Bishopsgate Insurance plc, supra*, p. 514.
1. *Michael I. Warde* v. *Feedex International Inc.* [1984] 1 Lloyd's Rep. 310, 312, per Staughton J.
2. See Chapter 6, para. 6.2.4.
3. [1981] 2 Lloyd's Rep. 190, 191.

object of conjuring up a possible error of law not apparent on its face and hence a possible ground of appeal. Quite clearly this principle has potentially a much wider field of application than the present context.

11.9 EXCLUSION AGREEMENTS

11.9.1 Statutory exclusion agreements

The right to apply to the court, in the absence of the consent of all the other parties to the reference, for leave to apply for an order for reasons or further reasons is lost if there is in existence a valid and applicable exclusion agreement.[1] By the terms of section 1(5)(b) the jurisdiction of the court to give leave to apply is made "subject to section 3". By section 3(1)(b) it is provided that the High Court shall not under section 1(5)(b) grant leave to make an application with respect to an award if the parties have entered into an exclusion agreement. To achieve this effect the exclusion agreement must be valid and on its proper construction extend to an application for leave to apply for an order under section 1(5).

By section 3(1)(b) it is declared that the effect of an exclusion agreement is to preclude the court from granting leave to apply. The statutory drafting gives recognition to the procedural division within section 1(5), the initial application for leave and the full application, although the practice developed under the subsection has effectively erased the division.[2]

An exclusion agreement is of no effect when an application for leave to apply is made with the consent of all the other parties to the reference. Section 1(5)(a) is not expressed to be "subject to section 3" and it is probable that universal consent operates as a waiver of a pre-existing exclusion agreement.[3]

The subject of exclusion agreements is governed in its entirety by sections 3 and 4 of the 1979 Act and is discussed in detail in Chapter 13.

11.9.2 Quasi-exclusion agreements

If the parties wish to preclude the possibility of a future application for an order for reasons or further reasons a formal exclusion agreement clearly represents the best course. It is nonetheless possible for the same result to be achieved informally by the parties expressly demanding or otherwise being content with an unreasoned award. In this kind of situation there will exist no pre-award notice requesting a reasoned award, and also there will most clearly not exist any special reason why no notice was given. The award being unreasoned and the preconditions specified in section 1(6) being incapable of satisfaction, the jurisdiction of the court under section 1(5) does not arise.[1] In the result the parties will have obtained the benefit of finality by abstaining from asking for a reasoned award,[2] and without having entered into a formal exclusion agreement.[3]

---

1. *King* v. *Thomas McKenna Ltd.* [1991] 1 All E.R. 653, 664 (C.A.).
2. Considered *infra*, para. 11.12.2.1.
3. See Chapter 4, para. 4.1.3.

1. *Supra*, para. 11.7.3.
2. *Kaffeehandelsgesellschaft K.G.* v. *Plagefim Commercial S.A.* [1981] 2 Lloyd's Rep. 190, 191, per Mustill J.
3. See Chapter 13, para. 13.1.6.

11.10 ON-APPEALS FROM DECISIONS AND ORDERS UNDER SECTION 1(5)

11.10.1 Section 1(6A) provides, to the extent to which it is relevant:

Unless the High Court gives leave, no appeal shall lie to the Court of Appeal from a decision of the High Court—
(a) to grant or refuse leave under subsection . . . 5(b) above; or
(b) to make or not to make an order under subsection (5) above.

The subsection imposes a fetter on on-appeals from any decision of the High Court under section 1(5). In so doing it secures that the legislative regime surrounding section 1(5) is consistent with the policy of the 1979 Act, in so far as it attempts to ensure that an application for an order under section 1(5) shall generally be finally determined by the first tier judge who hears the application and only in exceptional circumstances will an on-appeal to the Court of Appeal be permitted.

11.10.2 The discussion in Chapter 10 of the same restriction on on-appeals to the Court of Appeal from the decision to grant or refuse leave to appeal under section 1(3)(b) is of equal application to the present context.[1] It must also be borne in mind that in practice an application for leave to apply under section 1(5)(b) and a full application are merged.[2] In essence therefore any question of an on-appeal will revolve about the decision to make or refuse an order for reasons or further reasons under subsection (5).

From the decision of the High Court on an application under section 1(5) there is no appeal to the Court of Appeal except with leave of the first tier judge. It is not open to the Court of Appeal to give leave, as is the case under sections 1(7) and 2(3). If the first tier judge refuses leave to appeal that is the end of the matter provided the refusal is a "decision" in the eyes of the law.[3] Nor does the *Scherer* principle[4] have any application.[5] In all ordinary circumstances the decision of the first tier judge will be final; and only in exceptional circumstances is leave to appeal likely to be given.

11.10.3 The requirement to first obtain leave is a restrictive provision which enables the court to control the on-appellate process. Given the policy of the 1979 Act it is clear that only rarely will the court be inclined to grant leave. In the vast majority of instances the decision of the first tier judge will be final.[6] Leave is only likely to be given when an important point of principle concerning the exercise of the discretion arising under section 1(5) is in question or when it is proposed to use the power arising under the subsection in an exceptional manner.[7] In *The Niedersachsen*[8] Staughton J.

---

1. Chapter 10, para. 10.2.
2. See *infra*, para. 11.12.2.1.
3. *Aden Refinery Co. Ltd.* v. *Ugland Management Co. Ltd. (The Ugland Obo One)* [1987] 1 Q.B. 650, 666, per Mustill L.J. See also Chapter 10, para. 10.2.3.4.
4. After the decision in *Scherer* v. *Counting Instruments Ltd.* [1986] 1 W.L.R. 615. Considered in Chapter 10, para. 10.2.3.2.
5. *Aden Refinery Co. Ltd.* v. *Ugland Management Co. Ltd. (The Ugland Obo One)*, *supra*.
6. *Universal Petroleum Co. Ltd.* v. *Handels- und Transport Gesellschaft m.b.H.* [1987] 1 Lloyd's Rep. 517, 522 (C.A.).
7. *Ibid.*
8. *Trave Schiffahrtsgesellschaft m.b.H. & Co. K.G.* v. *Ninemia Maritime Corporation (The Niedersachsen)* [1986] 1 Q.B. 802, 807.

(as he then was) was persuaded to grant leave to appeal because of what he perceived to be a disagreement between himself and Robert Goff J. (as he then was) over a question of principle concerning the relevance of the presence or absence of a request for reasons to the exercise of the judicial discretion in determining whether or not to make an order under section 1(5). In *Universal Petroleum Co. Ltd.* v. *Handels- und Transport Gesellschaft m.b.H.*[9] Webster J. gave leave to appeal because of the far-reaching consequences of the order he was reluctantly prepared to make, the effect of which was to sanction the use of the jurisdiction arising under section 1(5) as a means of "going-behind" the primary findings of an arbitrator. On appeal the approach was rejected as being contrary to fundamental principle.[10]

11.10.4 Although it will be rare for the Court of Appeal to have the opportunity to review the exercise of discretion by a first tier judge under section 1(5), when the occasion does arise its role is governed by the established position of appellate courts under English law in such matters. The Court of Appeal will only intervene if satisfied that the first tier judge has gone wrong in principle,[11] by which is meant that the judge has failed to take into account a relevant consideration or has taken into account an irrelevant consideration; or has otherwise arrived at a wholly unreasonable determination, in which case an error of principle is presumed.[12] The Court of Appeal is also likely to be sensitive to the fact that it is being invited to scrutinise the decision of the first tier judge in a much calmer, composed and reflective atmosphere than probably prevailed on the initial presentation of the application.[13]

11.11 RELATIONSHIP BETWEEN SECTION 1(5) AND ARBITRATION ACT 1950 SECTION 22

11.11.1 It would appear to be established that the court has a power under section 22 of the 1950 Act to remit an award for any defect appearing on the face of an award that renders it bad in law.[1] An award which is uncertain falls within this category, but the concept of uncertainty in the present context does not lend itself to ready definition. At common law the general theme seems to be that the decisions and directions of arbitrators and umpires, to the extent that they appear on the face of an award, must be comprehensible, certain and consistent.[2] In association with the former special case procedure the jurisdiction arising under section 22 was also utilised to remit special case awards for further findings of fact and for the purpose of elaborating

---

9. [1987] 1 Lloyd's Rep. 517, 519, 522.
10. *Ibid*. And see also, *supra*, para. 11.8.
11. *Universal Petroleum Co. Ltd.* v. *Handels- und Transport Gesellschaft m.b.H.*, *supra*.
12. Cf. Chapter 10, para. 10.2.5.
13. *Universal Petroleum Co. Ltd.* v. *Handels- und Transport Gesellschaft m.b.H.*, *supra*, p. 527.
1. See generally Mustill and Boyd, *Commercial Arbitration* (2nd edn.), Chapter 33; *Russell on Arbitration* (20th edn.), ed. Walton and Vitoria, Chapter 21.
2. *Ames* v. *Milward* (1818) 8 Taunt 637; *Martin* v. *Burge* (1836) 4 A. & E. 973; *Mischeff* v. *Smith* [1950] 2 K.B. 616; *Margulies Bros. Ltd.* v. *Dafnis Thomaides & Co. (U.K.) Ltd.* [1958] 1 W.L.R. 398; *Montrose Canned Foods Ltd.* v. *Eric Wells (Merchants) Ltd.* [1965] 1 Lloyd's Rep. 597; *Oricon Waren-Handels G.m.b.H.* v. *Intergraan N.V.* [1967] 2 Lloyd's Rep. 82; *Cremer* v. *Samanta and Samanta* [1968] 1 Lloyd's Rep. 156; *Moran* v. *Lloyd's* [1983] 1 Lloyd's Rep. 472 (C.A.).

and clarifying facts found in an award.[3] There is therefore an obvious potential parallel between the jurisdictions arising under section 1(5) of the 1979 Act and section 22 of the 1950 Act, although the latter otherwise confers a much broader jurisdiction.[4] It is also distinct for under section 22 it appears to be possible to remit to a new arbitrator or umpire,[5] and it is further the case that under section 22 the court may remit of its own volition.[6] There being this overlap between section 1(5) and section 22, the issue arises as to the precise relationship which exists between them.[7] The question was first addressed by Robert Goff J. in *The Oinoussian Virtue*[8] who considered that in cases arising under the 1979 Act, the specific jurisdiction established by section 1(5) should ordinarily be adopted in preference to the general jurisdiction arising under section 22. Robert Goff J. commented[9]:

A question therefore arises as to the relationship between applications to the Court for an order under s.22 of the 1950 Act to remit the award for further findings of fact, and applications under s.1(5) of the 1979 Act, where the applicant is asking for an order that the arbitrator should state further facts as part of his reasons. In my judgment, such an application should, in a case arising under the 1979 Act, ordinarily be made under s.1(5) of the 1979 Act and not under s.22 of the 1950 Act.

It is to be remembered that applications of this kind under s.22 of the 1950 Act were generally concerned with special cases, which are formal documents in which the arbitrator found certain facts and then stated a question of law for the opinion of the Court, and which have now been abolished. Furthermore, it appears to me that when a new procedure for the review of arbitration awards is contained in a statute, and that procedure embodies a process for obtaining further findings of fact, one should look rather to that process for that purpose than to the general power to remit contained in a previous statute.

11.11.2 No jurisdiction analogous to section 1(5) was established in association with the former special case procedure and therefore resort to the general jurisdiction to remit under section 22 of the 1950 Act was compelled upon the courts. That necessity no longer exists with regard to the new appeal procedure under the 1979 Act, for in association therewith the specific jurisdiction under section 1(5) has been created. Section 1(5) therefore represents the necessary and proper way of proceeding with

---

3. *Piccinini* v. *Partrederiet Trigon 11 (The Alfred Trigon)* [1981] 2 Lloyd's Rep. 333; *Bremer Handelsgesellschaft m.b.H.* v. *Archer Daniels Midland International S.A.* [1981] 2 Lloyd's Rep. 483; *Mediolanum Shipping Co.* v. *Japan Lines Ltd. (The Mediolanum)* [1982] 1 Lloyd's Rep. 47; *Leif Hoegh and Co. A/S* v. *Maritime Mineral Carriers Ltd. (The Marques de Bolarque)* [1982] 1 Lloyd's Rep. 68; *Gill & Duffus S.A.* v. *Berger & Co. Inc.* [1982] 1 Lloyd's Rep. 101. See also *supra*, para. 11.2.

4. The potential breadth of the jurisdiction arising under section 22 was considered by the Court of Appeal in *King* v. *Thomas McKenna Ltd.* [1991] 1 All E.R. 653.

5. *Peterson* v. *Ayre* (1854) 14 C.B. 665; *Richard Clear & Co. Ltd.* v. *Bloch* (1922) 13 Ll.L.Rep. 462; *Re Fuerst Bros. & Co. Ltd. and R. S. Stephenson* [1951] 1 Lloyd's Rep. 429. See also *Lord* v. *Hawkins* (1857) 2 H. & N. 55; *Vancouver (City of)* v. *Brandram-Henderson of B.C.* (1960) 23 D.L.R. (2d) 161. This particular interpretation given to section 22 is nonetheless contentious and would appear to be inconsistent with the rationale of the section.

6. *The Atlantic Sunbeam* [1973] 1 Lloyd's Rep. 482, 488–489; *Mallozzi* v. *Carapelli S.p.A.* [1975] 1 Lloyd's Rep. 229, 254–255; *Intertradax S.A.* v. *Lesieur-Torteaux S.A.R.L.* [1978] 2 Lloyd's Rep. 509, 514–515, 518; *Kaffeehandelsgesellschaft K.G.* v. *Plagefim Commercial S.A.* [1981] 2 Lloyd's Rep. 190, 193; *Gill & Duffus S.A.* v. *Berger & Co. Inc.* [1981] 2 Lloyd's Rep. 233, 236.

7. It is in some instances uncertain which section the court is proceeding under: see, for example, *Tor Line A.B.* v. *Alltrans Group of Canada Ltd. (The TFL Prosperity)* [1982] 1 Lloyd's Rep. 617; *Hayn Roman & Co. S.A.* v. *Cominter (U.K.) Ltd.* [1983] 1 Lloyd's Rep. 521, 529.

8. *Schiffahrtsagentur Hamburg Middle East Line G.m.b.H. Hamburg* v. *Virtue Shipping Corporation of Monrovia (The Oinoussian Virtue)* [1981] 1 Lloyd's Rep. 533.

9. *Ibid.*, pp. 539–540.

regard to a matter under the 1979 Act. In other matters the availability and ambit of section 22 are unaffected by the 1979 Act.

11.11.3 The approach adopted in *The Oinoussian Virtue* has received general judicial support.[10] But although section 1(5) represents the primary remedy, it does not otherwise wholly displace the jurisdiction arising under section 22.[11] The latter continues to enjoy a concurrent existence; and in appropriate circumstances, as for example where the applicant is seeking to overcome an unwarranted limitation revealed by section 1(5), the section may be resorted to. This residual right to resort to section 22 in appropriate circumstances has been recognised by Bingham J. in the following terms[12]: "The Court retains its power under s.22 of the 1950 Act to remit a matter referred to arbitration to the reconsideration of the arbitrator. This section may still be used where clarification of an award is sought, but its use for this purpose is largely superseded by s.1(5) of the 1979 Act."[13]

11.12 PRACTICE AND PROCEDURE APPERTAINING TO APPLICATIONS AND ORDERS UNDER SECTION 1(5)

11.12.1 Procedure on an application for leave and a full application

11.12.1.1 *Judge in chambers*

Order 73, rule 3(1) and (2) provides:

(1) Subject to the foregoing provisions of this Order and the provisions of this rule, the jurisdiction of the High Court or a judge thereof under . . . the Arbitration Act 1979 may be exercised by a judge in chambers, a master or the Admiralty Registrar.
(2) Any application . . .
   (b) under section 1(5) of the Arbitration Act 1979 (including any application for leave) . . . shall be made to a judge in chambers.

The terms "judge" and "chambers", in the context of the rule, have previously been considered in Chapter 7.[1]

This particular rule exists as an exception to the general rule laid down in Order 73, rule 2(1) that the jurisdiction of the High Court under the Arbitration Act 1979 is exercisable by a single judge in court.[2] The restriction of applications to a judge in chambers is probably explained by the potential difficulty and importance of applications under section 1(5), and the sensitive issues of policy which may be involved.

In point of principle there is no difference between proceedings in chambers and in

---

10. *J. H. Rayner (Mincing Lane) Ltd.* v. *Shaher Trading Co.* [1982] 1 Lloyd's Rep. 632, 633; *Stinnes Interoil G.m.b.H.* v. *A. Halcoussis & Co. (The Yanxilas)* [1982] 2 Lloyd's Rep. 445, 452, 453; *Evmar Shipping Corporation* v. *Japan Lines Ltd. (The Evmar)* [1984] 2 Lloyd's Rep. 581, 582–583.
11. Cf. *Stinnes Interoil G.m.b.H.* v. *A. Halcoussis & Co. (The Yanxilas)*, *ibid.*, pp. 452, 453.
12. *Bulk Oil (Zug) A.G.* v. *Sun International Ltd. and Sun Oil Trading Co. (No. 2)* [1984] 1 Lloyd's Rep. 531, 533. Cited in *Italmare S.p.A.* v. *Stellar Chartering and Brokerage Inc. (The Marina Di Cassano)* [1984] 2 Lloyd's Rep. 577, 579.
13. Note also *Sig Bergesen D.Y. A/S and Others* v. *Mobil Shipping and Transportation Co. (The Berge Sund)* [1992] 1 Lloyd's Rep. 460, 468; *Geogas S.A.* v. *Trammo Gas Ltd. (The Baleares)* [1993] 1 Lloyd's Rep. 215, 234, Steyn L.J.
1. Para. 7.2.1.
2. Order 73, r. 2(1) specifies the applications which must be made to a single judge in court.

open court.[3] Decisions made in chambers which raise questions of principle or are otherwise innately important are frequently given in open court at the request of or with the consent of the parties.[4] Only when a judge exercises a power in an exceptional manner might he be unwilling to give judgment in open court.[5]

When the award is that of a judge-arbitrator or a judge-umpire, application under section 1(5) is to the Court of Appeal.[6]

11.12.1.2 Form of application

An application under section 1(5), including an application for leave, shall, where an action is pending, be made by summons in the action, and in any other case by an originating summons which shall be in Form No. 10 in Appendix A of the *Supreme Court Practice*.[1]

The summons must be served on the arbitrator or umpire concerned and all the other parties to the reference.[2] With regard to proceedings before a judge-arbitrator or judge-umpire the summons must be served on the judge-arbitrator or judge-umpire and on all the other parties to the reference.[3]

The originating summons or the summons, as the case may be, must state the grounds of the application[4] and, where the application is founded on evidence by affidavit, or is made with the consent of the other parties, a copy of every affidavit intended to be used, or, as the case may be, of every consent given in writing, must be served with the originating summons or the summons.[5]

11.12.1.3 Applications with consent

Where an application is brought with the consent of all the other parties to the reference,[1] it is uncertain whether the consent must be in writing. As a matter of practice it is highly desirable that it should be in writing, but it is ambiguous whether the rules of court create a legal requirement to this effect. Order 73, rule 5(4), somewhat strangely applies only to rule 5(2)[2] and does not extend to rule 5(1)(c). Rule 5(5) could be construed as creating a requirement that consent be in writing, but equally it may allude only to any consent which the parties may have given in writing. Further, it may not require the consent to be in writing but only that the consent be subsequently evidenced by writing.

---

3. *Universal Petroleum Co. Ltd.* v. *Handels- und Transport Gesellschaft m.b.H.* [1987] 1 Lloyd's Rep. 517, 522, per Kerr L.J.
4. *Kansa General Insurance Co. Ltd.* v. *Bishopsgate Insurance plc* [1988] 1 Lloyd's Rep. 503, 504, per Hirst J.
5. *Universal Petroleum Co. Ltd.* v. *Handels- und Transport Gesellschaft m.b.H.*, *supra* p. 527, citing Webster J. at first instance.
6. Administration of Justice Act 1970, s. 4(5).
1. Order 73, r. 3(3).
2. Order 73, r. 3(4).
3. Order 59, r. 14(6).
4. See Appendix J(3) for a model precedent.
5. Order 73, r. 5(5).
1. Under section 1(5)(a) of the 1979 Act.
2. Order 73, r. 5(4) makes express reference to rule 5(2), but this may be a printing error, with the true legislative intention aimed at a reference to rule 5(3).

11.12.1.4 Time limit

An application to the court to direct an arbitrator or umpire to state reasons for an award under section 1(5) must be made, and the summons served, within 21 days after the award has been made and published to the parties.[1] This rule applies to an application made with the consent of all the other parties to the reference and to an application brought with leave of the court.

Time begins to run from the day following the publication of an award to the parties. The concept of the publication of an award to the parties has previously been considered.[2] The court enjoys a discretion to give leave to apply out of time.

11.12.2 Prevailing practice with regard to applications under section 1(5)

11.12.2.1 Merger of application for leave and full application

The significant feature of the practice relating to applications under section 1(5) is that the preliminary application for leave to apply and the full application are merged. In consequence the judge in chambers will hear full argument on the application and if minded to make an order will also go through the formality of giving leave to apply. On the other hand, when the judge is minded not to make an order, he has the option of effecting his purpose either by refusing leave to apply or by giving leave but rejecting the full application. The practice adopted under section 1(5) is therefore in sharp contrast to that applicable to section 1 appeals where the application for leave to appeal under section 1(3)(b) and the substantive appeal under section 1(2) are predominantly separate and distinct proceedings.[1]

11.12.2.2 Relationship between applications under section 1(5) and section 1(3)(b)

11.12.2.2.1 An applicant for an order under section 1(5) will predominantly have in mind the prospect of a future appeal and will consequently consider the application as a necessary preliminary or associated step. In this kind of circumstance an application under section 1(5) is a first step to be followed by an application for leave to appeal under section 1(3)(b).[1] The advantage of proceeding in this way is that the party is fully apprised of the findings and reasoning underlying an award before committing himself to an application for leave to appeal.

11.12.2.2.2 Nonetheless, it is possible for applications under section 1(5) and section 1(3)(b) to be brought concurrently or as alternatives.[2] How the court will respond to concurrent applications will patently depend on the circumstances of individual cases. Both may of course be rejected.[3] The fact that leave to appeal is granted does

---

1. Order 73, r. 5(1). See further, Chapter 7, para. 7.2.4.2.
2. See Chapter 7, para. 7.2.4.
1. See Chapter 9, para. 9.2.
1. For example, *Hayn Roman & Co. S.A.* v. *Cominter (U.K.) Ltd.* [1982] 1 Lloyd's Rep. 295; *J. H. Rayner (Mincing Lane) Ltd.* v. *Shaher Trading Co.* [1982] 1 Lloyd's Rep. 632; *Gebr. van Weelde Scheepvartkantoor B.V.* v. *Société Industrielle D'Acide Phosphorique et D'Engrais etc. (The Dynashinky)* [1986] 1 Lloyd's Rep. 435.
2. For example, *Universal Petroleum Co. Ltd.* v. *Handels- und Transport Gesellschaft m.b.H.* [1987] 1 Lloyd's Rep. 517. But note the comments in *Cefetra B.V.* v. *Alfred C. Toepfer International G.m.b.H.* [1994] 1 Lloyd's Rep. 93, 100–101, per Colman J.
3. For example, *Italmare Shipping Co.* v. *Tropwind A.G. (The Tropwind)* [1982] 2 Lloyd's Rep. 441.

not automatically mean an order under section 1(5) will also be made. It may with justification be refused.[4] Conversely, notwithstanding being prepared to make an order under section 1(5), the court may reject,[5] grant or adjourn the concurrent application under section 1(3)(b).[5a] Too ready a willingness to grant leave to appeal before the full reasons of the arbitrator are known may prove wasteful of judicial resources. Nevertheless, the granting of leave to appeal may be appropriate,[6] for example, where the section 1(5) application is for further reasons and it is clear from the reasons already provided that leave to appeal ought to be granted, but at the same time it is appreciated that the full substantive appeal cannot be heard until the further reasons are given.[7] On occasions the most appropriate course of action may be to adjourn the application for leave to appeal until the reasons or further reasons are known.[8] In many instances the court may have no choice but to make such an order because of the absence or paucity of stated reasons.

11.12.2.2.3 Where there are several questions or potential questions of law in issue it becomes possible for the court, in appropriate circumstances, to remit the award for further reasons with regard to certain of the issues of law and to give leave to appeal with regard to the other issues of law.[9] Again the hearing of the substantive appeal will invariably await the giving of the further reasons for it is only in exceptional circumstances that it is likely that the court may be persuaded to split the hearing of the substantive appeal into two or more distinct hearings with separate questions of law being taken in each.

11.12.2.3 Protective counter-applications

It has already been seen that an application under section 1(5) may be made by both or all the parties to a reference,[1] for it is quite possible for more than one of the parties to contemplate mounting an appeal. However, a not unusual circumstance is for the non-initiating party not to be of a mind to make a separate application, but to be concerned to safeguard his position in the event of the application made by the other party succeeding. In this kind of situation what may be described as a protective counter-application may be made. The hallmark of such an application is that it is contingent. There is no intention of pursuing the application unless the initial application of the other party is successful and an order for reasons made.[2]

4. For example, *Portaria Shipping Co.* v. *Gulf Pacific Navigation Co. Ltd. (The Selene G)* [1981] 2 Lloyd's Rep. 180.

5. For example, *Mondial Trading Co. G.m.b.H.* v. *Gill & Duffus Zuckerhandelsgesellschaft m.b.H.* [1980] 2 Lloyd's Rep. 376.

5a. See Chapter 6, para. 6.2.4.

6. For example, *Schiffahrtsagentur Hamburg Middle East Line G.m.b.H. Hamburg* v. *Virtue Shipping Corporation of Monrovia (The Oinoussian Virtue)* [1981] 1 Lloyd's Rep. 533; *Clea Shipping Corporation* v. *Bulk Oil International Ltd. (The Alaskan Trader)* [1983] 1 Lloyd's Rep. 315.

7. For example, *Clea Shipping Corporation* v. *Bulk Oil International Ltd. (The Alaskan Trader)*, *ibid.*

8. For example, *Vermala Shipping Enterprises Ltd.* v. *The Minerals and Metals Trading Corporation of India Ltd. (The Gay Fidelity)* [1982] 1 Lloyd's Rep. 469.

9. For example, *Stinnes Interoil G.m.b.H.* v. *A. Halcoussis & Co. (The Yanxilas)* [1982] 2 Lloyd's Rep. 445.

1. *Supra*, para. 11.5.2.

2. The practice is acknowledged in *Universal Petroleum Co. Ltd.* v. *Handels- und Transport Gesellschaft m.b.H.* [1987] 1 Lloyd's Rep. 517, 522. Compare Chapter 7, para. 7.2.3; Chapter 9, para. 9.8.

11.12.2.4 Respondents and extraneous evidence

An application made under section 1(5) is subject to the "four corners rule".[1] Subject to limited exceptions, no extraneous evidence may be introduced in support of the application. The application must be decided on the basis of the contents of the award. The Court of Appeal has nonetheless expressed the opinion, but without hearing argument on the issue, that the "four corners rule" has no application to a respondent opposing an application for a section 1(5) order and seeking to uphold the finality of the award.[2] Often a respondent may wish to resist an application by relying on matters raised in the arbitral hearing but not dealt with in the award. This the respondent is entitled to do and the court may be informed of such matters by affidavit or through counsel. The justification for the exception derives from the fact that the extrinsic evidence permitted in support of the respondent's opposition is not being used to challenge but to uphold the award. The essence of the respondent's position is that he wishes to bring to the attention of the court matters not expressly addressed on the face of the award and which arguably could induce the court to refuse to make an order under section 1(5), on the basis that such further information represents an alternative ground for refusing to interfere with the award.

11.12.3 Section 1(5) orders

11.12.3.1 Form of order

The precise form an order under section 1(5) may assume is within the discretion of the court and in this there is scope for substantial variety. Clearly an order may be tailored to elicit the desired response.

An order may be made in general or particular terms. Where there has been made an unreasoned or inadequately reasoned award the arbitrator or umpire may be the object of a general order to state his reasons.[1] Where it is the partiality or quality of the stated reasons that is in issue the court may pinpoint the particular issues that require elaboration or further elaboration and also give directions as to how the arbitrator should address or readdress each issue.[2]

A frequent practice is for the applicant to set out the particular question(s) he wishes to put to the arbitrator or umpire. If the application is successful the order made may reflect the character of the application and place a single or several questions before the arbitrator or umpire to be answered.[3] It is of course for the court to determine which questions should be put and how the questions are to be formu-

---

1. Considered *supra*, para. 11.6.5.3.
2. *Universal Petroleum Co. Ltd.* v. *Handels- und Transport Gesellschaft m.b.H.* [1987] 1 Lloyd's Rep. 517, 528, per Kerr L.J.
1. *Vermala Shipping Enterprises Ltd.* v. *The Minerals and Metals Trading Corporation of India Ltd. (The Gay Fidelity)* [1982] 1 Lloyd's Rep. 469, 472, per Staughton J., the arbitrator "need do no more than state, possibly on one side of one sheet of paper, what reasons he had in relation to this point".
2. Cf. *Kaffeehandelsgesellschaft K.G.* v. *Plagefim Commercial S.A.* [1981] 2 Lloyd's Rep. 190; *Clea Shipping Corporation* v. *Bulk Oil International Ltd. (The Alaskan Trader)* [1983] 1 Lloyd's Rep. 315.
3. *J. H. Rayner (Mincing Lane) Ltd.* v. *Shaher Trading Co.* [1982] 1 Lloyd's Rep. 632; *Kansa General Insurance Co. Ltd.* v. *Bishopsgate Insurance plc* [1988] 1 Lloyd's Rep. 503.

lated.[4] Where this practice is followed the order will assume the form of a "schedule of further reasons".[5]

The form an order is to take may be the object of agreement between the parties; and in deciding to make an order the court may in the first instance leave it to the parties to settle the form of the order subject to the approval of the court.

11.12.3.2 Conditional orders

In making an order the court may attach such conditions as it considers necessary and just in circumstances of individual cases.[1]

11.12.3.3 Successive orders

The exercise of judicial discretion in favour of making an order under section 1(5) does not exhaust the jurisdiction of the court. A second or further orders may be made if the first or earlier order fails to achieve its object or raises a new issue.[1]

A further remission may be necessary if the first response provides an inadequate or unsatisfactory statement of reasons or fails to provide a reasoned explanation of all the issues in question.[2] The need for a further order may also arise not from any inadequacy or incompleteness in the response but by virtue of what is revealed in the stated reasons. The response to the first order may reveal an arguable question of law, but before the court can place itself in a position to determine the question of law it may be necessary to obtain an answer to a further question or questions.[3]

11.13 COSTS

In relation to an application under section 1(5) the question of costs will fall to be determined in the discretion of the court in accordance with principle.

The question of costs may be disposed of immediately following the determination of the application or deferred and determined in association with the appeal process which may follow. Where the application is a preliminary to, or made in association with, a future or current appeal proceeding, the disposition may be to treat the application as an interlocutory matter, with the costs of the application treated as costs in the appeal.[1] It is probable that only rarely will a separate order for costs be made.

In keeping with general principle the costs of a section 1(5) application will *prima facie* follow the event. A successful applicant will normally be entitled to his costs, providing the making of the order has done him some good.[2] To be successful in the

---

4. *Ibid.*

5. See, for example, *Universal Petroleum Co. Ltd.* v. *Handels- und Transport Gesellschaft m.b.H.* [1987] 1 Lloyd's Rep. 517, 522.

1. *Supra*, para. 11.8.2.

1. Cf. *Vermala Shipping Enterprises Ltd.* v. *The Minerals and Metals Trading Corpn. of India Ltd. (The Gay Fidelity)* [1982] 1 Lloyd's Rep. 469.

2. Cf. *Hayn Roman & Co. S.A.* v. *Cominter (U.K.) Ltd.* [1982] 2 Lloyd's Rep. 458.

3. *J. H. Rayner (Mincing Lane) Ltd.* v. *Shaher Trading Co.* [1982] 1 Lloyd's Rep. 632, 637–638, per Bingham J.

1. For example, *Hayn Roman & Co.S.A.* v. *Cominter (U.K.) Ltd.* [1982] 1 Lloyd's Rep. 295, 297; *J. H. Rayner (Mincing Lane) Ltd.* v. *Shaher Trading Co.* [1982] 1 Lloyd's Rep. 632, 637.

2. *J. H. Rayner (Mincing Lane) Ltd.* v. *Shaher Trading Co.*, *ibid.*, p. 637.

present context it is not necessary for an applicant to succeed on every point argued, provided he has succeeded on all the central and dominant points.[3] All being a matter of discretion, it follows that even a successful applicant may be denied his costs, either in whole or in part, if his conduct justifies such a course. A successful applicant who can be shown to be responsible for the absence or insufficiency of reasons in the award runs a real risk of being penalised in costs.[4]

Where an application fails, the respondent will normally be entitled to costs.

3. *Kansa General Insurance Co. Ltd.* v. *Bishopsgate Insurance plc* [1988] 1 Lloyd's Rep. 503, 513.
4. *Schiffahrtsagentur Hamburg Middle East Line G.m.b.H. Hamburg* v. *Virtue Shipping Corporation (The Oinoussian Virtue)* [1981] 1 Lloyd's Rep. 533, 540.

CHAPTER 12

DETERMINATION OF PRELIMINARY POINTS OF LAW BY THE HIGH COURT AND ON–APPEALS THEREFROM THE CONSULTATIVE CASE SECTION 2

12.1 INTRODUCTION

12.1.1 Within a system of arbitration law which demands that arbitral decisions be made in accordance with the prevailing rules of law and also provides a channel of appeal, albeit of a restricted nature, from arbitration awards to the courts on questions of law, it is at least understandable, although not necessarily compelling, that there should also exist a procedure whereby questions of law that arise in the course of a reference may be brought as a preliminary issue before a court for determination by a judge and thereby provide guidance to an arbitrator or umpire in the future conduct of a reference. Such a procedure has existed in English law since the Arbitration Act 1889,[1] and although prior to the 1979 Act the process operated as a special case procedure, it became in practice widely alluded to as the consultative case procedure. The contemporary mode or procedure is established under section 2 of the 1979 Act,[2] with the purport of the section truncatedly described in the accompanying marginal subtitle as "Determination of preliminary point of law by court". This mode of representation, together with the substantive changes introduced by section 2,[3] may well influence a change in the manner in which the procedure is popularly perceived. But whatever professional usage and practice will ultimately ordain in this regard, the phrase "consultative case" continues to possess an aptness to describe even the much changed form of procedure introduced by section 2.[4]

12.1.2 It is possible to draw a rough and imperfect analogy between the arbitral consultative case procedure and the jurisdiction enjoyed by the High Court to determine a question of law arising in an action as a preliminary issue. The latter procedure is quite widely used and may be initiated by parties to litigation or imposed upon them

---

1. The history of the procedure is considered *infra*, para. 12.3. See also Chapter 1, para. 1.4.2. For judicial consideration of the pre-1979 mode of procedure see *Cogstad* v. *Newsum* [1921] 2 A.C. 528; *Freshwater* v. *Western Australian Insurance Co. Ltd.* (1933) 44 Ll.L.Rep. 282, 286; *Crane* v. *Hegeman-Harris Co. Inc.* [1939] 4 All E.R. 68; *Fidelitas Shipping Co. Ltd.* v. *V/O Exportchleb* [1965] 2 All E.R. 4 (C.A.); *Verheijdens Veevoeder Commissiehandel B.V.* v. *I.S. Joseph Co. Inc.* [1981] 1 Lloyd's Rep. 102.
2. Considered *infra*.
3. Considered *infra*.
4. *Babanaft International Co. S.A.* v. *Avant Petroleum Inc. (The Oltenia)* [1982] 2 Lloyd's Rep. 99, 106, per Donaldson L.J., "Section 2 is the successor in title to the old consultative case, which more aptly describes its nature."

by interlocutory order.[5] The distinction between the two procedures is, however, quite patent. Under the consultative case procedure a question of law is placed before an external body, the High Court, for an expression of its opinion as to the proper answer to the question of law raised, with the opinion of the High Court not *res judicata*.[6] In contrast, the judicatorial procedure involves the court itself isolating and determining a question of law as a preliminary issue, with its preliminary determination *res judicata*. The parties cannot subsequently in the same suit advance argument or adduce further evidence directed to showing that the issue was wrongly determined. Moreover the judicatorial procedure is not confined to questions of law but extends to disputed questions of fact. Further, it is a procedure governed by the Rules of Court which have no application to arbitration.

12.1.3 The jurisdiction vested in the High Court to determine preliminary points of law that arise in the course of a reference is yet another important witness to the widely held contemporary theoretical perspective that the courts and arbitration are not to be perceived as competitors but two complementary institutions acting in partnership.[7] It also amplifies that wing of the judicial jurisdiction which exists in aid of and to facilitate the arbitral process.[8] Although the power is interventionist, for its effect is to place before the court for its opinion a question of law originally referred to arbitration, and therefore yet another exception to the general rule that the courts do not intervene in the course of an arbitration, its ultimate purpose is to assist the arbitral process.[9] Sir John Donaldson M.R., resorting to the colloquial, has depicted the consultative case and the section 2 procedure in the following terms, "the parties nip down the road to pick the brains of one of Her Majesty's Judges and, thus enlightened, resume the arbitration".[10] The general rule against intervention is nonetheless reinforced by the policy framework of the 1979 Act,[11] which continues to exert an influence in matters of attendant procedure and discretion. Consequently the section 2 consultative case procedure is not available as of right. The consent of the other parties to the arbitration or of the arbitrator or umpire is first required.[11a] But even if the requisite consent is obtained, leave of the court is further required before a question of law may be placed before the court for its opinion.[11b] In this regard the nature and importance of the question of law and the potential impact of the judicial determi-

5. R.S.C. Order 18, r. 11; Order 33, rr. 3 and 4. For an example of parties consenting to questions of law being determined as preliminary issues, see, *Didymi Corpn.* v. *Atlantic Lines and Navigation Co. Inc.* [1987] 2 Lloyd's Rep. 166. And for examples of the determination of a preliminary question of law being ordered see *The Derbyshire* [1988] 1 Lloyd's Rep. 109; *Transpectrol Ltd.* v. *Transol Olieprodukten Nederland B.V.* [1989] 1 Lloyd's Rep. 309.

6. *Fidelitas Shipping Co. Ltd.* v. *V/O Exportchleb* [1966] 1 Q.B. 630, 642, 645, per Lord Diplock L.J. See also *infra*, para. 12.7.2.

7. *Halfdan, Greig & Co. A/S* v. *Sterling Coal and Navigation Corpn. (The Lysland)* [1973] 1 Lloyd's Rep. 293, 303, per Kerr J. (first instance), "There is now a close relationship and cooperation between specialist arbitration tribunals and the courts, in particular the Commercial Court." See also Kerr, "Arbitration and the Courts—The UNCITRAL Model Law" (1984) 50 J.C.I. Arb. 3, 5; Mustill, "Transnational Arbitration in English Law", pp. 15, 17 in *International Commercial and Maritime Arbitration*, ed. Rose.

8. As such the section may be associated with other statutory provisions such as the Arbitration Act 1979, s. 5 and the Arbitration Act 1950, s. 12(4), (5) and (6). See generally Kerr, "The English Courts and Arbitration", in Schmitthoff, *International Commercial Arbitration*, Vol. 1.

9. See Kerr, "The Arbitration Act 1979" (1980) 43 M.L.R. 45, 51–52.

10. *Babanaft International Co. S.A.* v. *Avant Petroleum Inc. (The Oltenia)* [1982] 2 Lloyd's Rep. 99, 106.

11. See Chapter 1, para. 1.5.

11a. See *infra*, para. 12.4.3.

11b. See *infra*, para. 12.6.

nation on the arbitral proceedings in question will inevitably loom large but are not necessarily exclusive considerations, for others may also legitimately influence the exercise of the judicial discretion.[12] But before it is open to the court to address the question of leave to apply, it must be satisfied, when the application is not made with the consent of all the other parties to the reference, that the determination of the question of law might produce substantial savings in costs and also that the question of law in issue is one in respect of which leave to appeal would be likely to be given under section 1(3)(b). These are preconditions which go to the jurisdiction of the court.[12a] Even when the court decides to admit and determine a question of law, it also perceives as a matter of practice that the process should be effected speedily and interrupt the arbitral proceedings to the minimum possible extent.[13]

12.1.4 The consultative case is a form of procedure that occupies a middle ground between the courts and arbitration, and provides yet another detraction from the purity of the role so frequently associated with each institution. It spotlights an exception to the general premise that in the field of commerce the principal role of the judicature is to determine disputes.[14] In their relationship to arbitration the courts have an established supportive jurisdiction, which derives predominantly from legislation.[15] The consultative case is an important component of this tradition and by contributing to legal accuracy, ultimately contributes to the proper discharge of the fundamental obligation of an arbitrator to determine disputes and differences referred by reference to the prevailing rules of law.[16] The existence of the consultative case procedure is also another detraction from the autonomy of the arbitration process. By virtue of its availability a question of law referred to the decision of an arbitrator may be withdrawn from the chosen arbitral procedure and determined otherwise than by the appointed arbitrator. The contribution of the outside institution, the court, is nonetheless perceived as a benign intervention; and although in strict theory the role of the court is advisory, in practice its opinion will almost invariably prevail and determine the question of law in issue.[17] But as with all procedures, the consultative case procedure is open to abuse and this is a possibility the court must constantly guard against.

12.1.5 The existence of the consultative case procedure means that with regard to a question of law arising in the course of a reference the parties have in many instances an election. They may either allow the disputed question of law to survive into an award and then consent to an appeal or seek leave to appeal under section 1(3).[18] Alternatively, they may forthwith seek to resolve the disputed question of law under the section 2 procedure. The potential advantage of the section 2 procedure is that it has the capacity to remove a cloud that otherwise might hang over the arbitration,

---

12. In general terms this is the cumulative effect of subsections (1) and (2) of section 2, which are considered in greater detail *infra*, paras. 12.5 and 12.6.

12a. Section 2(2): considered *infra*, para. 12.5.

13. *Babanaft International Co. S.A.* v. *Avant Petroleum Inc. (The Oltenia)* [1982] 2 Lloyd's Rep. 99, 106, per Donaldson L.J., "It is essentially a speedy procedure designed to interrupt the arbitration to the minimum possible extent . . . "

14. *A/B Gotaverken* v. *Westminster Corporation of Monrovia* [1971] 2 Lloyd's Rep. 505, 515, per Donaldson J.

15. See n. 8, *supra*.

16. The nature of the duty to determine disputes and differences by reference to the prevailing rules of law is discussed in Chapter 1, para. 1.2.2.2.

17. For the effect in law of the opinion of the court under a section 2 application, see *infra*, para. 12.7.2.

18. The appeal procedure from awards is considered in Part II of the text.

with the parties and tribunal aware throughout of the risk that any award made may become the subject of an application for leave to appeal. The early resolution of a disputed question of law may have the effect of clearing the way and speed up the arbitral process with consequential savings in effort, time and costs. It has the potential to give the remainder of the arbitral process a clear sense of direction and to help tailor issues of both fact and law. In so far as the early determination of a question of law may provide a bench-mark of relevance and materiality, it equally may provide a very useful service in eliminating questions of fact and law which previous to the determination were considered to be in issue. It is not impossible that the resolution at an early stage of a central question of law will effectively resolve the dispute between the arbitrating parties or at least encourage a settlement. Even when these circumstances do not prevail and the arbitration proceeds to an award, it is at least less likely that the award will be challenged when it is based on a judicial opinion as to the applicable law taken at a preliminary stage in the arbitral process.[19] But the fact that an award is based on a preceding judicial opinion on the relevant law does not give it an immunity from challenge.[20] Moreover the consultative case procedure is not confined to questions of law on the merits of the substantive dispute referred, but extends to any question of law arising in the course of a reference.[21] These wider legal questions may relate to considerations such as *vires* and procedure and which if sustained may threaten the validity of an award. Their early judicial determination again has the advantage of encouraging confidence in the arbitral process and protecting the validity of the future award.

12.1.6 The advantages offered by the consultative case procedure are, however, all potential and not assured. The facts and circumstances of individual cases must be weighed carefully before deciding to adopt the section 2 procedure, rather than any alternative procedure. Two considerations would appear to be crucial: the importance of the question of law in the context of the dispute and the availability of a sufficient platform of fact for the court to be able to offer a determination.[22] There is little purpose in putting forward a question of law for the opinion of the court unless there is clear evidence that the determination of the question will act as a stimulus to the resolution of the dispute at large. Also, the frequent close association between law and fact means that it is highly desirable that the factual milieu within which the court determines the question of law should mirror that likely to prevail in the arbitration proceedings. When imprudently adopted the consultative case procedure may achieve nothing other than delay and wasted costs. Something of a public caution was broadcasted by Donaldson J. in *The Caspian Sea*,[23] where the learned judge commented:

. . . the attractions of the consultative case or of an application under s. 2(1) of the Arbitration

19. See, generally, *A/B Gotaverken* v. *Westminster Corporation of Monrovia* [1971] 2 Lloyd's Rep. 505, 511, per Donaldson J; Kerr, "The English Courts and Arbitration", pp. 199–237, 215 in Schmitthoff, *International Commercial Arbitration*, Vol. 1.

20. See, *infra* para. 12.7.2.

21. For a consideration of the meaning of this phrase see *infra*, para. 12.4.4.

22. With regard to the jurisdiction of the courts to determine preliminary questions of law, it would appear to be the case that the jurisdiction is not to be used when either the relevant law or associated facts are uncertain, see *Attia* v. *British Gas plc* [1987] 3 W.L.R. 1101.

23. *Montedison S.p.A.* v. *Icroma S.p.A. (The Caspian Sea)* [1980] 1 Lloyd's Rep. 91, 94. See also *Seven Seas Transportation Ltd.* v. *Pacifico Union Marina Corp. (The Satya Kailash) etc.* [1982] 2 Lloyd's Rep. 465, 467, per Staughton J.

Act 1979 are often more apparent than real. Before resorting to either procedure, serious consideration should be given, in the words of s. 2(2) of the 1979 Act, to whether the determination of the application might produce substantial savings in costs to the parties.

12.1.7 The potential disadvantages and difficulties associated with the consultative case will be highlighted in the course of the later elaboration of the procedure established under section 2 of the 1979 Act. Their existence means that a party should not only adopt the section 2 procedure with caution but also give serious consideration to the alternative procedures available for determining a preliminary question of law arising in the course of a reference. There are two alternative procedures in particular that merit consideration. The first is to make a question of law the subject of an interim award and then to consent or seek leave to appeal with regard to the question of law arising out of the interim award under section 1.[24] The second is to seek declaratory relief. These alternative procedures and how they contrast with the section 2 consultative case procedure are considered in greater detail later in this chapter.[25]

12.1.8 The consultative case procedure received scant attention in the Report on Arbitration of the Commercial Court Committee.[26] In paragraph 36 there is, however, to be found an acceptance of the desirability of retaining a consultative case procedure equivalent to the special case under section 21(1)(a) of the Arbitration Act 1950.[27] The precise recommendation of the Committee was as follows:

There should be power in the High Court to require arbitrators to make a reasoned interim award—the equivalent of a special case under section 21(1)(a)—if, but only if, the Court was satisfied that a question of law had arisen in the course of the reference a decision on which might produce substantial savings in costs to the parties and that it was one in respect of which leave to appeal might be given.

12.1.9 Whereas the preconditions to jurisdiction recommended by the Committee have been given legislative effect by section 2(2),[28] the manner an application may be initiated under section 2(1) and the form in which the application is made, bears no semblance to that proposed by the Committee. In particular the court is given no power to direct that a preliminary question of law be framed for judicial determination. An application may be made only by a party to a reference and then only with the consent either of the arbitrator or umpire, or of all the other parties.[29] Nor does the process by which a preliminary question of law is brought before the court for determination bear any correspondence to a "reasoned interim award" as recommended by the Committee.[30]

The right to apply under section 2 of the 1979 Act for the determination of a preliminary question of law arising in the course of a reference may be excluded by a valid exclusion agreement, within the terms of sections 3 and 4 of the 1979 Act.[31]

---

24. The appeal procedure from awards is considered in Part II of the text and as there indicated applies equally to final and interim awards; see Chapter 3, para. 3.3.

25. See *infra*, para. 12.11.

26. Cmnd. 7284, 1978. The Report is considered in Chapter 1, para. 1.3, and set out in Appendix A.

27. The subsection was the immediate predecessor of section 2 of the 1979 Act and is considered *infra*, para. 12.3.

28. Considered *infra*, para. 12.5.

29. See *infra*, para. 12.4.2. In Boyd, "Innovation and Reform in the Law of Arbitration" (1983) 2 C.J.Q. 148, 165, advocates that an arbitrator ought to possess the power to direct the trial of a preliminary issue.

30. See *infra*, para. 12.10.

31. See *infra*, para. 12.8. The subject of exclusion agreements is considered separately in Chapter 13.

12.2 SECTION 2—AN INTRODUCTORY COMMENT

12.2.1 Section 2 of the Arbitration Act 1979, as amended by the Supreme Court Act 1981,[1] provides as follows:

(1) Subject to subsection (2) and section 3 below, on an application to the High Court made by any of the parties to a reference—

(a) with the consent of an arbitrator who has entered on the reference or, if an umpire has entered on the reference, with his consent, or

(b) with the consent of all the other parties,

the High Court shall have jurisdiction to determine any question of law arising in the course of the reference.

(2) The High Court shall not entertain an application under subsection (1)(a) above with respect to any question of law unless it is satisfied that—

(a) the determination of the application might produce substantial savings in costs to the parties; and

(b) the question of law is one in respect of which leave to appeal would be likely to be given under section 1(3)(b) above.

(2A) Unless the High Court gives leave, no appeal shall lie to the Court of Appeal from a decision of the High Court to entertain or not to entertain an application under subsection (1)(a) above.

(3) A decision of the High Court under subsection (1) above shall be deemed to be a judgment of the court within the meaning of section 16 of the Supreme Court Act 1981 (appeals to the Court of Appeal), but no appeal shall lie from such a decision unless—

(a) the High Court or the Court of Appeal gives leave; and

(b) it is certified by the High Court that the question of law to which its decision relates either is one of general public importance or is one which for some other special reason should be considered by the Court of Appeal.

12.2.2 In many regards sections 1(2) and 2 of the 1979 Act are complementary. Section 1(2) renders possible an appeal with regard to a question(s) of law arising out of an award made on an arbitration agreement[2]; whereas section 2 extends upon section 1(2) by making it possible for the court to determine any question of law arising in the course of a reference. Under section 2 a question of law may be identified for judicial determination at any time during the course of a reference, but once an award is made the jurisdiction is lost, with the appeal procedure under section 1(2) thereafter solely available.[3] The co-existence of the two sections also means that, except in those instances when a disputed question of law does not emerge until after an award is made, the parties have an election. A question of law in dispute during the course of a reference may either be determined without delay under section 2 or be allowed to travel into the ultimate award and then questioned on an appeal under section 1(2).

12.2.3 Although complementary in practice, the two procedures are otherwise materially distinct analytically. Under section 1(2) an award has been made; the arbitrator or umpire has declared his final mind as to fact and law and determined the dispute or an issue in the dispute in the case of an interim award. On the making of an award the arbitrator or umpire parts with his jurisdiction for good, or a part of his jurisdiction in the case of an interim award, subject to a limited statutory jurisdiction to

---

1. Section 148 and Sch. 5.
2. See Chapter 3.
3. Cf. *C. T. Cogstad & Co.* v. *H. Newsum, Sons & Co. Ltd.* [1921] 2 A.C. 528, 536, per Lord Parmoor, "Although a case may be stated under this section [Arbitration Act 1889, section 19] at any stage of the proceedings, it cannot be stated after an award has been made."

correct clerical mistakes and accidental errors,[4] and the power of the court to remit awards.[5] Appeals under section 1(2) test the correctness in law of the final opinion of an arbitrator or umpire as to the proper determination of the dispute in its entirety or in part. The position is very different under section 2. There is no award and so an arbitrator or umpire retains jurisdiction but takes the assistance of the opinion of the court as to the proper answer to a question of law that has arisen in the course of the reference. After the expression of the judicial opinion the dispute returns to the arbitrator or umpire who is then better positioned to discharge his continuing jurisdiction and express a final opinion on the determination of the dispute or difference referred.[6] Beyond not having expressed a final opinion in the form of a final or interim award, the arbitrator or umpire need not have expressed any opinion as to his view of the correct answer to the question of law in issue, notwithstanding that the court might on occasions find the expression of such a personal opinion useful. Nor indeed need the arbitrator or umpire have determined disputed questions of fact on which the question of law depends,[7] although such a failure may present serious difficulties to the consultative case procedure.[8]

12.2.4 Section 2 is also of note for it makes no express reference to an arbitration agreement. In general and unqualified terms it confers on the High Court a jurisdiction "to determine any question of law arising in the course of the reference".[9] This is in sharp contrast to section 1(2) where the appeal jurisdiction of the High Court is restricted to a question of law arising out of an award "made on an arbitration agreement",[10] and also to the default jurisdiction conferred under section 5 which alludes to "a reference under an arbitration agreement".[11] The drafting of section 2 in consequence raises the question whether the section is of general application and applies even when a reference arises under a parol arbitration agreement, or is it to be construed in common with the other sections in the 1979 Act and confined in its application to "written agreements", as defined by the Arbitration Act 1950, section 32, which applies equally to the 1979 Act?[12] The question itself is not of great practical importance, for predominantly arbitration agreements are in writing. Nevertheless it is not of such insignificance that it may be safely ignored. The issue has already been discussed in Chapter 1[13] and it is there suggested that notwithstanding the express words of section 2, it is likely that the courts will interpret the section as being applicable only to references arising under arbitration agreements as defined for the purposes of Part I of the Arbitration Act 1950.[13a]

12.2.5 But whatever the proper interpretation of section 2 and its precise relation-

4. Arbitration Act 1950, s. 17. The jurisdiction is considered in Chapter 11, para. 11.3.3.1.
5. The jurisdiction derives from the Arbitration Act 1950, s. 22. It is further possible for the parties to confer an express authority on an arbitrator or umpire to reopen an award in circumstances specified in the mandate. Such powers are often conferred under the rules of institutional arbitral organisations.
6. *C. T. Cogstad & Co.* v. *H. Newsum, Sons & Co. Ltd.* [1921] 2 A.C. 528, 536–537; *In re an Arbitration between Cogstad & Co. and H. Newsum, Sons & Co. Ltd.* [1921] 1 K.B. 87, 97 per Bankes L.J. (C.A.).
7. *Fidelitas Shipping Co. Ltd.* v. *V/O Exportchleb* [1966] 1 Q.B. 630, 645 per Diplock L.J.
8. The requirement of necessary findings of fact and the possible responses of the court when there exist insufficient findings of fact are considered *infra*, para. 12.6.
9. Section 2(1).
10. See Chapter 3, para. 3.4.
11. Section 5(1).
12. Arbitration Act 1979, s. 7(1)(e).
13. Para. 1.7.5.
13a. See Chapter 3, para. 3.4.

ship to section 1, it is nonetheless the case that section 2 is to be viewed in the context of the general policy underlying the 1979 Act, notwithstanding that Lord Diplock made no express reference to section 2 in his speech in *The Nema*[14] elucidating the legislative policy. Just as the cumulative effect of section 1, coupled with sections 3 and 4, is to reveal a legislative intention to promote the greater finality of arbitral awards,[15] so also the cumulative effect of section 2, coupled with sections 3 and 4, may be perceived as promoting the finality of the choice of arbitral forum.[16] A question of law referred to the decision of an arbitrator is to remain with the arbitrator unless there can be shown good cause for the court to intervene and interrupt the arbitration process. The essential prerequisites of good cause, it would seem, are that the question of law is of a kind such that it is proper for the court to consider it in the context of the general policy of the 1979 Act, and that the judicial intervention has at least the potential to be efficacious, in the sense that it might expedite the arbitral process and reduce the costs of the parties. This is the general effect of section 2(2)[17]; but beyond these prerequisites a general discretion exists and Lord Diplock in *The Antaios*[18] encouraged the judges to be vigilant in its exercise. Where all the parties consent to an application for leave to apply under section 2 the policy considerations are of course very different and the court need not be as demanding in its vigilance.[19]

12.3 HISTORICAL ANTECEDENTS OF SECTION 2

12.3.1 The Common Law Procedure Act 1854, section 5, made provision for an award, in whole or part, to be stated in the form of a special case for the opinion of the court.[1] This jurisdiction, subsequently reproduced in the Arbitration Act 1889, section 7(b), was of a restrictive character for it conferred no jurisdiction beyond the award. It was not until the enactment of the Arbitration Act 1889, section 19, that what became commonly alluded to as the "consultative case" procedure was introduced. The section provided:

Any referee, arbitrator or umpire may at any stage of the proceedings under a reference, and shall, if so directed by the court or a judge, state in the form of a special case for the opinion of the court any question of law arising in the course of the reference.

The section expanded the jurisdiction of the court, for it enabled a question of law arising in the course of a reference to be stated in the form of a special case for the opinion of the court. With the enactment of the 1889 statute there were established two special case procedures. The one related to an award under section 7(b) and the other to preliminary questions of law arising in the course of a reference, and prior to the making of an award, under section 19. But in practice the latter procedure was adopted far less than the former.

12.3.2 Although the special case on an award and consultative case procedures, as formulated by the 1889 Act, were complementary, they were nonetheless distinct in

---

14. [1982] A.C. 724. See Chapter 1, para. 1.5, for a discussion of the policy underpinning the 1979 Act.
15. *Ibid.*
16. See *infra.*
17. See *infra*, para. 12.5.1.
18. [1985] A.C. 191, 199.
19. See *infra*, para. 12.6.
1. For an outline history of the statement of an award as a special case, see Chapter 1, para. 1.4.2.

three fundamental regards. The court enjoyed a direct interventionist role only with regard to the consultative case. Under both section 7(b) and section 19 an arbitrator or umpire had a discretionary statutory power to state a special case. But only under section 19 did the court have jurisdiction to intervene and direct an arbitrator or umpire to state a consultative case. Although there existed an untrammelled right of appeal from the decision of the court on an award stated as a special case,[2] there existed no right of appeal whatsoever from the opinion of the court expressed on a consultative case.[3] This meant that the distinction between a consultative case and a special case on an award could be of crucial importance. It was, however, a distinction which was not always easy to draw and in instances of ambiguity all turned on the proper construction of the award.[4] If there existed an express declaration on the face of an award of the precise form of special case intended, this would in all but the most exceptional of circumstances be conclusive.[5] In the absence of any such express declaration, the distinction was governed by the implied intent of the arbitrator or umpire in making the award in question. Was it the intention to state the award in the form of a special case and relinquish seisin of the arbitration subject to the statutory jurisdiction to remit, or merely to seek the opinion of the court in a case stated.[6] The different appeal procedures also possibly accounted for the different practices adopted about the two procedures. A special case on an award was heard by a single judge, whereas a consultative case was heard by a Divisional Court, which came to be a court of three judges.

12.3.3 That these differences of law and practice existed was patently anomalous and capable of creating disadvantage.[7] They provoked considerable discussion and comment during the early decades of the present century and were eventually addressed by the Mackinnon Committee, which reported in 1927.[8] In a sympathetic report the Committee recommended that the two special case procedures be substantially unified in both law and practice.[9] In particular the Committee recommended that:

(1) the power of the court to direct a consultative case should be extended to an award as a special case under section 7(b);

(2) the right to appeal with regard to an award stated as a special case should be retained but that there should also be an appeal from the opinion of the court on a consultative case subject to the giving of leave either by the court giving the initial determination or the Court of Appeal;

---

2. *In re Kirkleathan Local Board and Stockton Water Board* [1893] 1 Q.B. 375.
3. *In re Knight and Tabernacle Permanent Building Society* [1892] 2 Q.B. 613, 618.
4. *In re Holland Steamship Co. and Bristol Steam Navigation Co.* (1906) 95 L.T. 769; *C. T. Cogstad & Co.* v. *H. Newsum, Sons & Co. Ltd.* [1921] 2 A.C. 528.
5. *C. T. Cogstad & Co.* v. *H. Newsum, Sons & Co. Ltd.*, *ibid.*, pp. 540–541, per Lord Parmoor; *In re an Arbitration between Cogstad & Co. and H. Newsum, Sons & Co. Ltd.* [1921] 1 K.B. 87, 97 per Bankes L.J. (C.A.). For a more recent illustration, see *Montedison S.p.A.* v. *Icroma S.p.A.* *(The Caspian Sea)* [1980] 1 Lloyd's Rep. 91.
6. *C. T. Cogstad & Co.* v. *H. Newsum, Sons & Co. Ltd.*, *ibid.*, per Lord Parmoor and Lord Carson.
7. See, for example, *British Westinghouse Electric and Manufacturing Co. Ltd.* v. *Underground Electric Rlys. Co. of London Ltd.* [1912] A.C. 673; *In re an Arbitration between The Olympia Oil and Cake Co. Ltd. and The Produce Brokers Co. Ltd.* [1915] 1 K.B. 233; [1916] 2 K.B. 321; [1917] 1 K.B. 320; [1916] 1 A.C. 314.
8. Report of Committee on The Law of Arbitration 1927, Cmd. 2817.
9. *Ibid.*, paras. 8–13.

(3) the practices adopted to each special case procedure should be unified so that in each instance the special case would be heard by a single judge.[10]

12.3.4 These recommendations were adopted and to the extent they required legislation to be made effective were given statutory force by section 9 of the Arbitration Act 1934, which was subsequently re-enacted in virtually identical terms by section 21 of the Arbitration act 1950.[11] In relation to the consultative case section 21(1) provided:

An arbitrator or umpire may, and shall if so directed by the High Court, state—
    (a) any question of law arising in the course of the reference, in the form of a special case for the decision of the High Court.

Subsection (3) made provision for an appeal to the Court of Appeal but only with the leave of the High Court or Court of Appeal. Section 21 of the 1950 Act continues in force for arbitrations to which the 1979 Act does not apply,[12] but is otherwise repealed by the 1979 Act,[13] and replaced by section 2 of the 1979 Act.

12.3.5 Like its statutory predecessors section 2 of the 1979 Act establishes a discretionary jurisdiction and is directed to questions of law arising in the course of a reference. But in other regards it is a radical departure from the historical pattern set by the earlier legislation and establishes the consultative case procedure on a fundamentally new basis. In sharp contrast to the preceding law the right to make application for a judicial determination is vested not in the arbitrator or umpire but in the parties to the reference. The High Court enjoys no intercessionary role. But even the right of the parties assumes a conditional nature, being dependent upon obtaining the consent either of the arbitrator or umpire who has entered on the reference or of all the other parties to the reference.[14] An arbitrator or umpire is not vested with any autonomous discretionary authority to make an application, but is otherwise capable of controlling the situation where the consent of all the other parties cannot be obtained, for in this circumstance the consent of the arbitrator or umpire must be obtained.[15] In the absence of party consent, the court enjoys jurisdiction to determine an application only if the conditions specified in section 2(2) are satisfied; and an appeal from its preliminary decision to give or refuse leave to apply is severely restricted by the terms of section 2(2A).[16] On-appeals to the Court of Appeal from the substantive determination of the first tier judge are subject to a certificate and the granting of leave, as specified in section 2(3).[17] But beyond matters of form, substance and jurisdiction, section 2 functions within a wholly different theoretical environment from its statutory predecessors and this will necessarily impinge on every aspect of discretion associated with the section.[18]

12.3.6 Throughout its historical existence the consultative case procedure has been

---

10. *Ibid.*, para. 11.
11. This section is identical with s. 9 of the Arbitration Act 1934 except that it makes reference to the "High Court", whereas s. 9 referred simply to the "Court".
12. See Chapter 1, para. 1.7.1. Also *D/S A/S Idaho* v. *Peninsular and Oriental Steam Navigation Co. (The Strathnewton)* [1982] 2 Lloyd's Rep. 296.
13. Sections 1(1) and 8(3)(b).
14. Section 2(1). The requirement is further discussed *infra*, para. 12.4.2.
15. *Ibid*.
16. *Infra*, para. 12.9.2.
17. *Infra*, para. 12.9.3.
18. *Infra*, para. 12.6.

little used.[19] Whereas the jurisdiction to state awards as special cases came to assume one of the dominant features of the arbitral landscape, the consultative case, in contrast, reposed somewhat inconspicuously. The emergence, with the enactment of the Arbitration Act 1934, of a general implied term in arbitration agreements (subject to a contrary intention expressed therein) empowering arbitrators and umpires to make interim awards,[20] which in turn might be stated in the form of a special case, probably contributed significantly to diminishing the relevance of the consultative case procedure.[21]

12.4 ANALYSIS OF SECTION 2—APPLICATIONS UNDER SECTION 2

12.4.1 Court to which application may be made

12.4.1.1 Applications under section 2 are to the High Court, which is the judicial organ vested with jurisdiction to entertain and determine any question of law arising in the course of a reference. It is to be noted that the jurisdiction is expressly vested in the "High Court" and not, more generally, in "the Court".[1] This has the effect of requiring the jurisdiction of the High Court to be exercised by a single judge of that court, except, *inter alia*, if by the Rules of Court it is made exercisable by a master, registrar or other officer of the court, or by any other person.[2] Under the prevailing Rules of Court the jurisdiction of the High Court under section 2 is exercised in open court by a single judge of the Commercial Court, unless any such judge otherwise directs.[3] County Courts have no jurisdiction under section 2.

12.4.1.2 Where a judge-arbitrator or judge-umpire is appointed,[4] it is uncertain whether an application is to be made to the High Court or Court of Appeal. The uncertainty arises from the language of section 4(5) of the Administration of Justice Act 1970, which is to the effect:

Any jurisdiction which is exercisable by the High Court in relation to arbitrators and umpires otherwise than under the Arbitration Act 1950 shall, in relation to a judge of the Commercial Court appointed as arbitrator or umpire, be exercisable instead by the Court of Appeal.

In strictness it would seem that an application under section 2 of the 1979 Act is not a jurisdiction exercisable by the High Court "in relation to arbitrators and umpires", but a jurisdiction exercisable in relation to questions of law arising in the course of a reference and brought before the court by a party to the reference.

---

19. See Kerr, "The English Courts and Arbitration" in *International Commercial Arbitration* (Vol. 1), ed. Schmitthoff.

20. Arbitration Act 1934, s. 7, which added a new para. (k) to Schedule 1 of the Arbitration Act 1889. The present law is set out in s. 14 of the Arbitration Act 1950. For the derivation of the statutory implied term see Report of Committee on The Law of Arbitration 1927, *supra*, para. 27. Prior to the Arbitration Act 1934 an arbitrator or umpire had no power to make an interim award unless authorised by the parties.

21. *Fidelitas Shipping Co. Ltd.* v. *V/O Exportchleb* [1966] 1 Q.B. 630, 647, per Diplock L.J.; p. 639 per Lord Denning M.R. See also *infra*, para. 12.11.1.

1. The phrase "the Court" replaced the former and familiar phrase "the Court or a Judge" and is now defined by R.S.C. Order 1, r .4(2).

2. Supreme Court Act 1981, s.19(3).

3. R.S.C. Order 73, r. 2(1)(c) and r. 6(1). See also *infra*, para. 12.10.

4. Under the terms of the Administration of Justice Act 1970, s. 4. See, further, Mustill and Boyd, *Commercial Arbitration* (2nd edn.), Chapter 20; *Russell on Arbitration* (20th edn.), ed. Walton and Victoria, pp. 108–109; Thomas, "Judge-Arbitrators" [1983] 1 L.M.C.L.Q. 120. See also Chapter 6, para. 6.2.6.4.

Adopting this narrow approach it is arguable that section 4(5) is inapplicable and that jurisdiction remains with the High Court. The difficulty with adopting this interpretation is that it flouts the clear policy of the Administration of Justice Act 1970, as particularly declared in section 4(4) and (5), to the effect that where a judge-arbitrator or judge-umpire is appointed the jurisdiction exercisable by the High Court in relation to the arbitral process shall be exercised instead by the Court of Appeal. This being the prevailing policy, and, ostensibly, there being no good reason for departing from it, it is probably desirable that the outwardly restrictive language of section 4(5) be given a generous interpretation so as to embrace applications made under section 2 of the 1979 Act.

12.4.1.3 Under section 2 the High Court has three distinct functions. The first is to satisfy itself that any application made is validly brought and that it has jurisdiction to determine the application. Secondly, to decide whether leave to apply should be granted; and thirdly to determine the question of law arising in the course of the reference and to which the application relates. These three functions are quite distinct and are discussed more fully in the immediately following text.

12.4.2 Who may initiate an application for leave to apply?

12.4.2.1 An application for leave to apply under section 2 may only be made by a party to a reference. The 1979 Act here again draws a distinction between a "reference" and an "arbitration agreement". The distinction and its possible effect have already been elaborated upon in Chapter 2[1] with regard to appeals from awards, and what was there said is of equal application to section 2. An arbitrator or umpire is not a party to a reference for the purpose of section 2 and the terms of section 2(1)(a) would appear to render any contrary view unarguable.

12.4.2.2 It is in the initiation of the procedure that a marked contrast is witnessed between section 2 and the former consultative case procedure. Under section 21 of the Arbitration Act 1950 the consultative case procedure could only be initiated by the arbitrator or umpire, either voluntarily or at the direction of the High Court. No doubt as a matter of good practice an arbitrator or umpire would not state a consultative special case without consulting the parties, and in stating a consultative special case the arbitrator or umpire would often be acting at the behest of one or both parties. If an arbitrator or umpire declined to comply with the wishes of the parties, an application could be made to the High Court for an order compelling a consultative case to be stated. But under section 21 of the 1950 Act it was at least possible for an arbitrator or umpire to state a consultative special case of his own volition and without the consent of the parties. It was also equally open to the court to direct a consultative case to be stated, notwithstanding that the arbitrator or umpire and all the other parties to the reference, apart from the applicant, were opposed to such a course of action.

12.4.2.3 The way the former consultative case was statutorily established also influenced the substance of judicial generalisations which addressed the *raison d'être* of the consultative case procedure. The procedure was seen dominantly as offering the prospect of judicial assistance to the arbitrator or umpire rather than to the parties. It

---

1. Para. 2.2.

offered the arbitrator or umpire the opportunity to seek the opinion of the court for his guidance and as an aid to arriving at an award. Typical of this perception is the dictum of Bowen L.J. in *In re an Arbitration between Knight and the Tabernacle Permanent Building Society*,[2] where the learned judge said of the consultative case procedure that it "contemplates a proceeding by the arbitrator for the purpose of guiding himself as to the course he should pursue in the reference". The same emphasis is found in the judgment of Lord Parmoor in *Cogstad (C.T.) & Co.* v. *H. Newsum, Sons & Co. Ltd.*,[3] where it is observed, "The purpose of a case stated under s. 19 [Arbitration Act 1989] is to enable the umpire to obtain guidance during the pendency of the reference, in order to assist him in arriving at his decision."

12.4.2.4 Under section 2 the emphasis appears to have changed, with the legislative assistance ostensibly offered to the parties rather than the arbitrator or umpire. Neither an arbitrator nor umpire may of his own volition directly initiate the section 2 procedure. Nor has the High Court jurisdiction to intervene and direct that an application under section 2 be made. The role of the arbitrator is not, however, wholly erased. It remains open to an arbitrator or umpire to attempt to persuade the parties or at least one of the parties of the desirability of an application under section 2. Further, where all the other parties to a reference refuse to consent to an application, the matter can only progress if the arbitrator or umpire who has entered on the reference consents. Such consent is likely to be readily forthcoming where the arbitrator has suggested to the parties that a section 2 application would be appropriate and may have assisted further by drafting or causing the relevant question(s) of law to be drafted.[4]

12.4.3 Consent a precondition to an application for leave to apply

A party to a reference may make an application under section 2 only with the consent of either: (a) an arbitrator or umpire who has entered on the reference; or (b) all the other parties to the reference.[1]

An application therefore cannot be made at will. The consent of the adjudicating person or tribunal, or of all the other parties to the reference must be obtained. In the latter case the effect of section 2(1)(b) is to require a prospective applicant to obtain the agreement of his adversary, or more neutrally, his co-arbitrating party,[2] which for obvious reasons may not be readily forthcoming. Even when there is an absence of antagonism, there may be genuine disagreement on the question whether an application should be made. But there will be occasions when there will exist a clear mutual advantage in obtaining a determination of the High Court on a question of law and with all the parties happy that an application be made. Where consent is given, it may be given subject to terms agreed between the parties.[3]

Consent is a question of fact and when in dispute the burden of proof will rest with

---

2. [1892] 2 Q.B. 613, 619 (C.A.).   3. [1921] 2 A.C. 528, 536.
   4. See, for example, *Lear and another* v. *Blizzard* [1983] 3 All E.R. 662.
   1. Section 2(1). See, for example, *Exercise Shipping Ltd.* v. *Bay Maritime Lines Ltd. (The Fantasy)* [1991] 2 Lloyd's Rep. 391, 392; [1992] 2 Lloyd's Rep. 235, 237 (C.A.).
   2. This manner of language is encouraged by the analysis of arbitration by the majority of the House of Lords in *Bremer Vulkan Schiffbau und Maschinenfabrik* v. *South India Shipping Corpn.* [1981] A.C. 909. But see *L'Office Cherifien des Phosphates and Unitramp S.A.* v. *Yamashita - Shinnihon Steamship Co. Ltd. (The Boucraa)* [1994] 1 Lloyd's Rep. 251.
   3. See, *infra*, para. 12.4.3.2.

the applicant to establish the existence of consent on a balance of probabilities. The notion of consent has previously been examined in relation to section 1(3)(a) and that commentary is of equal application to section 2(1).[4] Although section 2 is silent on the point, the effect of the Rules of Court would seem to require the consent to be given in writing.[5] This is a much stricter requirement than that the consent be evidenced by writing. The consent itself must be manifested in writing so that in substance and time the consent is at one with the writing.

12.4.3.1 Consent of arbitrator or umpire who has entered on the reference

It is probable that the consent of an arbitrator or umpire who has entered on a reference will only be sought when the consent of all the other parties cannot be obtained, although in strictness it is not necessary that the other parties be first approached. The terms of section 2(1)(a) however give rise to a number of quite central difficulties in association with the requirement that the consent of the adjudicator be obtained.

12.4.3.1.1 CONSENT OF AN ARBITRATOR

12.4.3.1.1.1 Under section 2(1)(a) an application may be made with the consent of "an arbitrator", which alludes, no doubt, to both a first tier and an appeal arbitrator. The phrase offers no difficulty where a sole arbitrator is appointed, but how is the phrase to be understood in the context of a multi-arbitrator arbitration tribunal. Is the consent of any one arbitrator sufficient or must the prospective applicant obtain the consent of the arbitration tribunal, in whatever way the decision of the tribunal may be validly expressed.

The adoption of the indefinite article, "*an* arbitrator", might be interpreted as suggesting any one arbitrator, even where a tribunal of two or more arbitrators is established.[1] It is true that the 1979 Act does elsewhere adopt the definite article, but to weigh on this distinction in order to suggest that a reference to arbitrator by the definite article produces an extended concept, so that "*the* arbitrator" also means "the arbitration tribunal", but that this result does not follow where the allusion is to "*an* arbitrator" is, it is suggested, far from convincing and also produces an incongruent conclusion. Reference to "arbitrator" in the 1979 Act, whether preceded by the definite or indefinite article, would seem no more than a convenient shorthand for "arbitration tribunal", thereby taking into account whatever manner of composition it may assume. Thus in section 1(5) the reference to "his award" is not to be personalised so as to mean the award of any arbitrator. It presumably refers to the award of the arbitration tribunal, in whatever way the award may be validly made. So also in section 1(8), where the statute refers to "the award of an arbitrator", it would appear to be clear that it is the valid award of the arbitration tribunal that is contemplated. And again the same would seem to be true of the phrase "an order made by the arbitrator" in section 5. By analogy, and as a matter of principle, it is submitted that the reference in section 2(1)(a) to "an arbitrator" is to be construed as a reference to an arbitration

4. See Chapter 4, para. 4.2.
5. R.S.C. Order 73, r. 5(4): the reference in r. 5(4) to paragraph (2) would appear to be a printing error, with the true intent being to refer to paragraph (3). See, *infra*, para. 12.10.
1. This is the interpretation favoured in Mustill and Boyd, *Commercial Arbitration* (2nd edn.), p. 622 and n. 12.

tribunal, when more than one arbitrator has been appointed. It is conceded that the contrary view is capable of taking support from the fact that section 2(1)(a) does not merely refer to "an arbitrator" but to "an arbitrator who has entered on the reference".[2] Outwardly this form of words does tend to accentuate the possibility of individual consent. But the phrase may be wholly fortuitous, with the draftsman of the legislation having nothing in mind beyond a simple sole arbitrator tribunal. And even if the circumstances are otherwise, the enlarged phrase is still not conclusive, for it is as logical to speak of an arbitration tribunal entering on a reference as it is a sole arbitrator, although the legal test will differ as between a sole and multi-arbitrator tribunal.[3]

12.4.3.1.1.2 The *prima facie* rule of the common law is that the awards and orders of an arbitration tribunal are valid if made with the unanimous agreement of all the members of the tribunal,[4] and this general rule probably applies equally to the giving of consent under section 2(1)(a). The general rule requiring unanimity is however capable of being displaced by the agreement of the arbitrating parties, and in practice it is often provided with regard to multi-arbitrator tribunals that the award of a majority or even a single specified arbitrator shall be valid and binding.[5] In the case of a reference to three arbitrators there is established by section 9 of the Arbitration Act 1950 an implied term in favour of majority awards.[6] The statutory implied term only arises in connection with a written arbitration agreement and may be displaced by a contrary intention expressed in the arbitration agreement. Section 9 is applicable to awards only, but the same principle may by contract be made applicable to orders. It is suggested therefore that the consent of a tribunal for the purpose of section 2 may be expressed in like manner as any order of the tribunal may be validly made; but where the parties have not made an express agreement to the contrary, consent requires the unanimous agreement of the tribunal.

12.4.3.1.1.3 Another feature encountered in practice is for the parties to mandate a named or otherwise specified arbitrator, very often the chairman of a three-arbitrator tribunal, to make in the name of the tribunal any procedural and interlocutory orders that may prove to be necessary in the course of the reference.[7] Such a practice may also have its advantages in a two-arbitrator tribunal. Where such a mandate exists, and provided on its proper construction it includes giving consent under section 2(1)(a), it is submitted that the question of consent is again governed by the express provisions in the arbitration agreement and may be given by the named or otherwise specified arbitrator.

12.4.3.1.1.4 The consent must however be that of the arbitration tribunal. Consent

---

2. See further, *infra*, para. 12.4.3.1.3.

3. *Ibid*.

4. *Little* v. *Newton* (1841) 2 M. & G. 351; 10 L.J.C.P. 88; *Stalworth* v. *Inns* (1844) 13 M. & W. 466; 14 L.J. Ex. 81; *United Kingdom Mutual S.S. Assurance Assoc.* v. *Houston & Co.* [1896] 1 Q.B. 567. Contrast *European Grain and Shipping Ltd.* v. *Johnston* [1982] 1 Lloyd's Rep. 414; [1982] 2 Lloyd's Rep. 550 (C.A.).

5. See, for example, The Chartered Institute of Arbitrators' Arbitration Rules (1988 edn.), Rule 14.2; The London Court of International Arbitration Rules (1985 edn.), Art. 16.3; Rules of the International Chamber of Commerce (1988), Art. 19.

6. Section 9 of the Arbitration Act 1950 as amended by s. 6(2) of the Arbitration Act 1979 is to the following effect: "Unless the contrary intention is expressed in the arbitration agreement, in any case where there is a reference to three arbitrators, the award of any two of the arbitrators shall be binding."

7. See, for example, The Chartered Institute of Arbitrators' Arbitration Rules (1988 edn.), Rule 5.3; The London Court of International Arbitration Rules (1985 edn.), Art. 5.3.

cannot be given by a third party, such as an organisation or an officer of an organisation by which the arbitration is administered. To the extent that the rules of an administered institutional arbitration may attempt to provide otherwise, they are exposed to the risk of being void, as being in direct conflict with section 2(1)(a).

12.4.3.1.2 CONSENT OF AN UMPIRE

Where an umpire has entered on a reference, an application for leave to apply under section 2(1) may be made with the consent of the umpire. The concept of "an umpire" does not produce the same difficulties of interpretation as does that of "an arbitrator". And the operation of section 2(1)(a) offers no problem in this regard when the application is made for the first time to an umpire. But what of the position where an earlier application for consent has been made to and refused by the arbitrators.[1] Is it open to a party to a reference to renew the application if and when an umpire enters on the reference in lieu of the arbitrators?

It is submitted that such a second application may be made. A reference to an umpire following a failure to agree by two arbitrators is not an appeal but a distinct and separate form of proceeding at which the dispute or difference is considered afresh.[2] This being the case, then in principle the application for consent is one made *de novo* and the earlier application does not raise any manner of estoppel, waiver or any other kind of obstacle. By the same reasoning the umpire must come to the application with a fresh and open mind, and the fact of the earlier application and refusal of consent ought not to be taken into account by the umpire in considering whether to give or refuse consent.

12.4.3.1.3 ENTERED ON THE REFERENCE

Consent is required of an arbitrator or umpire who has "entered on the reference"; the use of the definite article making it clear that it is the reference out of which the preliminary question of law arises and with regard to which the application is made that is the reference alluded to. The phrase is not defined by the 1979 Act, nor does it appear elsewhere in the arbitration legislation with regard to arbitrators. It does, however, appear in section 8 of the Arbitration Act 1950, in relation to umpires.[1] The phrase is patently ambiguous and its proper interpretation may give rise to difficulties.

12.4.3.1.3.1 *Arbitrator Entering On The Reference.* With regard to an arbitrator the question that arises is whether the phrase "entered on the reference" is synonymous with the acceptance by an arbitrator of his appointment as arbitrator, or in the case of an arbitration tribunal, the acceptance by all the individual arbitrators of their appointment; or whether some further step is demanded subsequent to a valid appointment. It is submitted that the phrase cannot be aligned with the "commencement of an arbitration" as defined by section 34 of the Limitation Act 1980, which would appear far too preliminary a step to be con-

---

1. In the context of the present discussion the arbitral tribunal will be one composed of two arbitrators: see Arbitration Act 1950, s. 8.
2. *Re Salkeld and Slater* (1840) 12 A. & E. 767; *Re Jenkins* (1841) 1 Dowl. (N.S.) 276; *Re Firth and Howlett* (1850) 1 L.N. & P. 63.
1. See *infra*, para. 12.4.3.1.3.4.

sidered as entering on a reference.[2] Nor is it sufficient merely to be named or designated as arbitrator in an arbitration agreement, or to have been invited to assume an appointment as arbitrator, or to be earmarked for nomination by a third party appointing authority.

12.4.3.1.3.2 A valid arbitral appointment, assuming all other procedural and substantive requirements are complied with, requires the consent to act of the designated person.[3] Without such consent there can be no valid appointment. Taking the guidance of decided authorities in the field of time limits,[4] it would appear that an arbitrator accepts his appointment when he communicates to the appointing arbitrating party, parties or third party his willingness to act as arbitrator and, where applicable, the consent to act is thereafter communicated to all the other parties to the dispute.[5] It may be that when an arbitrator consents to his appointment, in the sense considered above, he also "enters on the reference" for the purpose of section 2(1)(a). It is at least arguable that such an interpretation is consistent with the purpose of section 2 and also with the precise requirement of the section, which is not that an arbitrator shall have taken a step in the arbitral proceedings but that he shall have entered on the reference.

12.4.3.1.3.3 On the other hand, it is equally arguable that to enter on a reference connotes something beyond mere acceptance of appointment as an arbitrator. In pursuance of this line of argument, a reference is not entered on until some initial step has been taken to launch the arbitral process, as, for example by the arbitrator or the arbitration tribunal corresponding with the parties or convening a preliminary meeting with the parties. Where the tribunal is a multi-arbitrator tribunal, a preliminary meeting of the arbitrators or a preliminary communication between them may again be seen as sufficient to establish an entering on the reference. To adopt this interpretation of the phrase gives effect to the activist character of the adopted verb *to enter* and distinguishes it from the less active verb *to accept*. In practice it is unlikely that an arbitrator or tribunal will be asked to consent to an application to apply under section 2(1) before some act that is capable of representing the launch or an initial step in the conduct of the reference takes place. It may even be that to consider an application for consent to apply under section 2(1) will itself be construed as a step in the reference. But whatever the merits of this possibility, on the balance of argument it would seem

2. The Limitation Act 1980, s. 34(3) provides:
"For the purposes of this Act and of any other limitation enactment an arbitration shall be treated as being commenced—
    (a) when one party to the arbitration serves on the other party or parties a notice requiring him or them to appoint an arbitrator or to agree to the appointment of an arbitrator; or
    (b) where the arbitration agreement provides that the reference shall be to a person named or designated in the agreement, when one party to the arbitration serves on the other party or parties a notice requiring him or them to submit the dispute to the person so named or designated."
3. *Tradax Export S.A.* v. *Volkswagenwerk A.G.* [1970] 1 Q.B. 537.
4. Some forms of arbitration agreement contain contractual time limits which require the claimant's arbitrator to be appointed within a stipulated period of time. See, for example, *Ford* v. *Compagnie Furness* [1922] 2 K.B. 279; *Atlantic Shipping and Trading Co. Ltd.* v. *Louis Dreyfus & Co.* [1922] 2 A.C. 250; *Pinnock Bros.* v. *Lewis and Peat Ltd.* [1923] 1 K.B. 690; *Ayscough* v. *Sheed, Thompson & Co. Ltd.* (1924) 19 Ll.L.Rep. 104. For the power vested in the High Court to extend a time stipulation see Arbitration Act 1950, s. 27.
5. *Tew* v. *Harris* (1847) 11 Q.B. 7; *Ringland* v. *Lowndes* (1863) 15 C.B.N.S. 173, 196; *Tradax Export S.A.* v. *Volkswagenwerk A.G.* [1970] 1 Q.B. 537; [1970] 1 Lloyd's Rep. 62; *Edm. J. M. Mertens & Co. P.V.B.A.* v. *Veevoeder Import Export Vimex B.V.* [1979] 2 Lloyd's Rep. 372.

that before an arbitrator or tribunal enters on a reference some act must take place beyond mere valid acceptance of appointment. This submission also takes some support from authority. In *Iossifoglu* v. *Coumantaros*[6] Scott L.J. considered, in the context of a two-arbitrator tribunal, that the arbitrators did not enter on the reference until they had accepted their appointments and communicated with each other about the reference. It was not necessary for the arbitrators to have actually met and discussed the conduct of the reference.

12.4.3.1.3.4 Although unlikely in practice, as a matter of principle it would seem open to the parties to stipulate in an arbitration agreement precisely when an arbitrator or tribunal is to be considered as entering on the reference. When such an express term exists it would seem desirable and highly likely that the stipulation in the arbitration contract will govern the situation. This can be achieved quite simply by construing the legislation so as to embrace the express agreement of the parties.

12.4.3.1.3.4.1 *Umpire entering on reference.* The question when an umpire enters on a reference should possibly offer less difficulty for in many regards the statutory phrase has a more readily identifiable association with umpirage than arbitration, although, as it will be seen, any such expectation may be excessively optimistic. An umpire in essence steps into the arbitral process when a tribunal of two appointed arbitrators cannot agree.[7] By the terms of section 8(1) of the Arbitration Act 1950, in the absence of a contrary instruction, the two arbitrators may appoint an umpire at any time after they are themselves appointed, but are obliged to do so forthwith if they cannot agree. Whether arbitral disagreement exists is in each case a question of fact and is capable of being a troublesome issue.[8] Beyond the fact of disagreement, the parties may also stipulate for further procedural requirements, such as the giving of notice of failing to agree, as a necessary precondition to umpirage: and in the absence of an express agreement to this effect section 8(2) of the Arbitration Act 1950 will invariably be applicable.[9] Where, therefore, the parties have made contractual provision for umpirage, the umpire may be appointed prior or subsequent to the emergence of the disagreement.[10] In practice the former method frequently

---

6. [1941] 1 K.B. 396, 400 (C.A.).

7. It is usual to associate umpirage as a method of resolving a failure to agree among two appointed arbitrators. Section 8 of the Arbitration Act 1950 only applies in this circumstance. But in principle umpirage may be resorted to whenever an even-numbered arbitral tribunal is established, whatever the precise number of arbitrators in question. Umpirage, as with arbitration, is essentially a matter of contract.

8. *Hill* v. *Marshall* (1827) 5 L.J.O.S.C.P. 161; *Cudliff* v. *Walters* (1839) 2 Mood. & R. 232; *Winteringham* v. *Robertson* (1858) 27 L.J. Ex. 301; *Wicks* v. *Cox* (1847) 11 Jur. 542; *Lang* v. *Brown* (1855) 25 L.T.O.S. 297; *Iossifoglu* v. *Coumantaros* [1941] 1 K.B. 396; *Cerrito* v. *North Eastern Timber Importers Ltd.* [1952] 1 Lloyd's Rep. 330.

9. Section 8(2) provides: "Unless a contrary intention is expressed therein, every arbitration agreement shall, where such a provision is applicable to the reference, be deemed to include a provision that if the arbitrators have delivered to any party to the arbitration agreement, or to the umpire, a notice in writing stating that they cannot agree, the umpire may forthwith enter on the reference in lieu of the arbitrators." The subsection is ambiguous for it fails to make it clear whether it establishes an obligation to give written notice or whether it merely gives the arbitrators an election, so that they may give written notice if they wish. The ambiguity revolves around the phrase "if the arbitrators have delivered".

10. Cf. Arbitration Act 1950, s. 8(1).

prevails, in which case the appointment clearly pre-dates the activation of the umpire's authority. Indeed, in such a circumstance it is possible that the umpire's authority will never be activated, for the two arbitrators may find common ground and be in accord as to their award. This brief introductory statement of the concept of umpirage indicates that there are two essential preconditions to a valid umpirage. First, that the umpire shall have accepted his appointment, with acceptance in this context probably following the meaning given to the corresponding concept in the context of arbitration.[11] Secondly, that the two appointed arbitrators shall have failed to agree and also satisfied such procedural requirements as to notice and the like as may be prescribed, if any.[12] But again it is unlikely that the bare presence of these two preconditions will amount to an umpire entering on a reference for the purposes of section 2. It is likely that some further step is required, analogous to that considered in relation to arbitrators,[13] revealing that the umpire has at least begun to embark on the exercise of his authority, albeit in the most preliminary of ways. The terms of section 8(3) of the Arbitration Act 1950 also provide some support for this proposition.[14] In more general terms it is suggested that an umpire enters on a reference when he takes some step following his valid appointment which manifests an intention to act in lieu of the appointed arbitrators.[15] It is true that section 2(1) alludes only to an umpire who has "entered on the reference" but it is suggested that this phrase is to be construed as being equivalent to the more extended phrase "entered on a reference in lieu of the arbitrators", which appears in subsections (2) and (3) of section 8 of the 1950 Act. Again, merely to receive notice of disagreement, which is for example provided for by section 8(2) of the 1950 Act, would appear insufficient. Such a notice merely prepares the way for the umpire to take some step by way of entering on the reference.

12.4.3.1.3.5 It is often the case in practice, when umpirage is associated with the appointment of a two-arbitrator tribunal, for the umpire not only to be appointed in advance of any disagreement emerging between the appointed arbitrators but further to be invited to sit with the tribunal and sometimes also to act as chairman with procedural powers. The practice has potential advantages but also carries the risk of unnecessary expenditure. The advantage is that should the arbitrators fail to agree it is unnecessary to present for a second time the evidence and argument *in extenso* before the umpire, with consequential savings in time and costs. The disadvantage is that unnecessary costs will have been incurred in the event of the two arbitrators agreeing an award, in which case the umpire is rendered redundant.[16]

12.4.3.1.3.6 Where an umpire is invited merely to sit with the two arbitrators it would appear to be arguable that the umpire does not at that stage enter on the refer-

---

11. *Supra*, para. 12.4.3.1.3.1.
12. *Supra*.
13. *Supra*, para. 12.4.3.1.3.1.
14. Section 8(3) provides: "At any time after the appointment of an umpire, however appointed, the High Court may, on the application of any party to the reference and notwithstanding anything to the contrary in the arbitration agreement, order that the umpire shall enter upon the reference in lieu of the arbitrators and as if he were a sole arbitrator."
15. Cf. Arbitration Act 1950, s. 8(2) and (3).
16. See, *Termarea S.R.L.* v. *Rederiaktiebolaget Sally (The Dalny)* [1979] 2 Lloyd's Rep. 439, 441–442 per Mocatta J.

ence, notwithstanding his physical presence. It is only after the two arbitrators have failed to agree and become *functus officio*, and the umpire takes some step to act in lieu of the arbitrators, that the umpire enters on the reference. Again, the umpire does not enter on the reference automatically following the failure by the appointed arbitrators to agree. This would appear to be implicit in the language of section 8(2) of the Arbitration Act 1950. Some further step of a kind already considered would appear necessary. Up to this moment the physical presence of the umpire in his capacity as umpire carries no authority in matters of procedure, nor in relation to the substantive dispute. Further, the mere presence of the umpire, without more, does not divest the arbitrators of their authority and even if they allow the umpire to assume an advisory role, the arbitrators must be careful not to withdraw from their fundamental obligation to discharge their mandate collectively and individually.[17]

12.4.3.1.3.7 The position is less straightforward when an umpire is invited not only to sit with a two-arbitrator tribunal but also to act as chairman with procedural powers, which may include the authority to consent to an application that a question of law be determined by the High Court. The precise authority of an umpire-chairman will of course be governed by the terms of his mandate, which may be general or particular. The specific difficulty in this kind of circumstance is that the designated umpire is clothed with an authority exercisable in the primary arbitration and prior to the establishment of the umpirage. The necessary preconditions to a valid umpirage are obviously absent and it appears to be impossible to speak of the umpire exercising powers *qua* umpire and even of the umpire entering on the reference *qua* umpire. The answer to this particular conundrum may be to analyse the position of an umpire-chairman as being in reality a delegate of the arbitrators with authority to exercise prescribed powers. He would seem quite clearly not to be an umpire, notwithstanding the contemporary practice of describing him as an umpire, for the essential preconditions of umpirage are not present. He is no more than an umpire-elect. It is also impossible to describe the umpire-chairman as some manner of arbitrator with limited authority, for he has no part to play in resolving the actual dispute referred for decision. It would seem that the only way in which the umpire status of an umpire-chairman in the primary arbitration may be reserved is by giving the phrase "entered on a reference" a strict literal and non-technical meaning and refusing to interpret the phrase as alluding to an umpire who has entered on a reference "in lieu of the arbitrators". In this way it does at least become possible to characterise an umpire-chairman as an umpire who has entered on a reference and consequently with the jurisdiction to consent to a consultative case.

12.4.3.1.4 DUTY OF ARBITRATOR OR UMPIRE

12.4.3.1.4.1 It is clear that under section 2(1)(a) an arbitrator or umpire is not obliged to give consent. There is a discretion and in the exercise of the discretion an application for consent may be granted or legitimately declined. The 1979 Act, however, gives no assistance as to the matters that are to be weighed by an arbitrator or umpire

---

17. Contrast the London Maritime Arbitrators' Association Terms (1994), para. 16.

in considering a request for consent. Nor is it clear whether an arbitrator or umpire who refuses consent improperly is at risk of being condemned for misconduct.[1]

As a matter of general principle an arbitrator or umpire must exercise his discretion judiciously.[2] In the present context this probably requires that proper criteria must be taken into account and also that the arbitrator or umpire must come to a consideration of the relevant criteria in a manner that is fair to both parties.

12.4.3.1.4.2 It must be borne of mind that an arbitrator or umpire in giving consent is not determining that the court shall take an application under section 2. The consent merely makes it possible for a party to apply to the court.[3] It might therefore be considered that the role of an arbitrator or umpire should incline against the adoption of too demanding a scrutiny of any application and if in doubt to lean in favour of giving consent. But against this manner of approach the arbitrator or umpire must bear in mind that the court does not welcome futile applications and where the other party or parties are also objecting to a section 2 application, that there may be good cause for this objection.

12.4.3.1.4.3 In determining an application for consent it is difficult to see that an arbitrator or umpire can do much more than have a fundamental regard to those criteria specified in section 2(2).[4] Although in strictness these criteria are expressly stated as preconditions to the court's jurisdiction to entertain an application for leave to apply, they nonetheless touch in a more general manner on the two vital considerations underlying the rationale of section 2. If this is a right approach then an arbitrator or umpire must consider whether the determination of the preliminary question of law would expedite the arbitral process and in consequence produce a substantial saving in costs; and, further, whether the question of law is one in respect of which leave to appeal would be likely to be given under section 1(3)(b).[5] It cannot be expected that an arbitrator or umpire should address these questions with an inordinate refinement or precision. If he is satisfied that a question of law is in issue; that it is an arguable question of law and central to the dispute; that it is a question of law of importance and general interest and that it would be beneficial to have it determined by the court as a preliminary issue, then it is suggested that an arbitrator or umpire should give his consent and leave the final decision to the court on an application for leave. But ultimately the question of consent must be decided on the facts and circumstances of individual cases and in consequence any general rule or approach must have the capacity to yield to individual situations.

12.4.3.1.4.4 The motive behind an application must also be a relevant consider-

---

1. Arbitral misconduct although recognised by the arbitration legislation is not defined by it. The concept is very broad and may arise from the way an arbitrator or umpire conducts himself or the arbitration proceedings. It is customary to divide the concept into two wings. The first involves turpitude as where an arbitrator or umpire is dishonest, consciously prejudiced or otherwise perverse. The second wing connotes no suggestion of turpitude and is of a more technical character. In this latter sense there is misconduct if an arbitrator or umpire innocently makes a procedural error or omission. Where there exists misconduct the arbitrator or umpire may be removed by the High Court and the award may be set aside or remitted: see Arbitration Act 1950, ss. 22, 23(1) and (2). See also Report of Committee on The Law of Arbitration, Cmd. 2817 (1927), para. 22. Commercial Court Committee Report on Arbitration, Cmnd. 7284 (1978), para. 67. The latter is set out in Appendix A.
2. *Pioneer Shipping Ltd.* v. *B.T.P. Tioxide (The Nema)* [1982] A.C. 724, 739 per Lord Diplock.
3. See *infra*, para. 12.5.
4. See *infra*, para. 12.6.
5. See Chapters 5 and 6.

ation. If an arbitrator or umpire is satisfied that an application for consent is made not with the bona fide object of obtaining a judicial determination of a question of law as a preliminary issue but with the aim of frustrating or delaying the course of a reference, then this represents an overwhelming reason for refusing consent. To act otherwise would be fundamentally inconsistent with the policy underlying the 1979 Act.[6]

As indicated above, the fact that an application for consent is being made to an arbitrator or umpire will often mean that the other party or parties are opposing the application. In such a circumstance it would seem that there must also be a procedural duty on an arbitrator or umpire to hold a fair and even balance between the parties.[7] The precise requirement of this duty will no doubt fall to be decided on the facts and circumstances of individual cases. But, for example, where an arbitrator or umpire hears submissions and argument, then it would seem clear that they must take place in the presence and hearing of the other party, and with the opportunity given to respond.[8] If the submissions are made in writing then a copy must be made available to the other party and the opportunity given to comment thereon. The question of procedure may also be controlled by the express contract of the parties.

12.4.3.1.4.5 Under the former special case procedure, where an arbitrator or umpire refused to state a special case it was open to a party to seek an order of the court directing an arbitrator or umpire to state a special case, and it amounted to misconduct for an arbitrator or umpire to conduct a reference in such a way as to frustrate this alternative mode of proceeding vested in the parties.[9] No such procedure is possible under section 2(1) of the 1979 Act and, therefore, some alternative approach must be adopted. An arbitrator or umpire who without proper justification refuses consent, or who in hearing an application for consent fails to act fairly as between the parties, is probably guilty of misconduct. Under the law prior to the 1979 Act, it was misconduct for an arbitrator to make his consent to a consultative case conditional on the satisfaction by the applicant of an unjustifiable condition.[10] Provided, however, the arbitrator or umpire has acted honestly and in a manner which retains the confidence of the parties it is improbable that the court might be persuaded to exercise the power of removal under section 23(1) of the Arbitration Act 1950.[11] The more probable result is that the decision may be corrected by seeking declaratory and/or injunctive relief; and where the decision refusing consent is in the form of an interim award the jurisdiction to set aside or remit under the Arbitration Act 1950, sections 22 and 23(2) may be resorted to.

12.4.3.2 Consent of all the other parties

12.4.3.2.1 There is an analogy between section 1(3)(a) and section 2(1)(b) in that under each the divide between arbitration and the courts can be bridged with the con-

---

6. See Chapter 1, para. 1.5.
7. *Ian Keith Brown* v. *CBS (Contractors) Ltd.* [1987] 1 Lloyd's Rep. 279.
8. *Ibid*. On the facts of the case a procedural aberration was counterbalanced by the fact that the arbitrator had taken counsel's opinion.
9. See Chapter 1, para. 1.4.2.
10. *In re Enoch and Zaretzky, Bock & Co.'s Arbitration* [1910] 1 K.B. 327. The unjustifiable condition was to demand a cheque for £150 on account of legal and other expenses.
11. For authorities where the statutory power to remove is considered, see *Bremer Handelsgesellschaft m.b.H.* v. *Ets. Soules et Cie and Anthony G. Scott* [1985] 1 Lloyd's Rep. 160; *Tracomin S.A.* v. *Gibbs Nathaniel (Canada) Ltd. and George Jacob Bridge* [1985] 1 Lloyd's Rep. 586.

sent of all the other parties to a reference.[1] There is, however, also a significant point of difference between the two statutory provisions, for whereas under section 1(3)(a) consent secures an appeal the same is not necessarily the case with regard to an application under section 2(1)(b). Beyond consent there further exists a judicial discretion to give or refuse leave to apply.[2] The point must again be emphasised that the consent of *all* the other parties to a reference must be obtained, and the phrase "other parties" is an allusion to the parties to the reference in question who are not party to the application under section 2. Nor is an arbitrator or umpire who has entered on the reference a party to a reference for the purpose of section 2(1)(b).[3]

12.4.3.2.2 Where the consent of all the other parties is obtained the restrictions on the court's jurisdiction specified in section 2(2) do not apply.[4] The policy considerations that underlie the 1979 Act, and which influence the exercise of judicial discretion arising under the legislation, have a substantially reduced significance when all the parties to a reference are content for an application to be made to the court. But, as will be seen later in the text, the existence of the consent of all the other parties does not wholly erase the court's discretion with regard to the question whether or not to grant leave to apply.[5] Where such consent exists, however, it is highly probable that the court will only refuse leave to apply in the most exceptional circumstances.

12.4.3.2.3 As a question of practice it would seem logical for a party wishing to obtain consent for an application under section 2 to seek, in the first instance, the consent of all the other parties to the reference, and only if this consent is refused or is otherwise unobtainable, to then apply and seek the consent of an arbitrator or umpire who has entered on the reference. But beyond good practice, it may also be a principle relevant to the exercise of an arbitrator's or umpire's discretion under section 2(1)(a) and with the consequence that an arbitrator or umpire might be justified in refusing to consider an application for consent until the applicant had first sought the consent of all the other parties. But even if this is so, the point cannot be pressed too hard. It is always possible for exceptional circumstances to arise when it might be impossible or impracticable initially to seek the consent of the other parties, or when it may be appropriate for an arbitrator or umpire to consider an application for consent notwithstanding the failure first to seek the approval of all the other parties. In the final analysis all will turn on the facts and circumstances of individual cases.

12.4.4 Any question of law arising in the course of the reference

12.4.4.1 In section 2 there is found the same distinction between fact and law that is made in relation to appeals from awards under section 1(2).[1] The court enjoys no jurisdiction under section 2 to determine any disputed question of fact arising in the course of a reference. Questions of fact are for the arbitrator or arbitration tribunal alone. The jurisdiction is confined to questions of law, including questions of mixed

---

1. For example, *Babanaft International Co. S.A.* v. *Avant Petroleum Inc. (The Oltenia)* [1982] 1 Lloyd's Rep. 448; [1982] 2 Lloyd's Rep. 99 (C.A.), where disponent shipowners secured the consent of charterers to an application under section 2(1)(b).
2. See *infra*, para. 12.6.1.
3. See also Chapter 4, para. 4.2.3.
4. See *infra*, para. 12.5.1.
5. See *infra*, para. 12.6.1.
1. See Chapter 3, para. 3.2.

fact and law and conclusions of law. But although sections 1(2) and 2 share this common denominator they are otherwise significantly different. Under section 1(2) an appeal lies "on any question of law arising out of an award made on an arbitration agreement".[2] Whereas under section 2(1), the jurisdiction of the court is expressed as being "to determine any questions of law arising in the course of the reference", which would appear a much broader form of words and therefore to confer a more general jurisdiction.

12.4.4.2 The phrase "course of the reference" probably represents the arbitral phase running from the commencement of a reference to the making of an award. If this represents the correct approach the only likely difficulty is to determine precisely when a reference commences. It is suggested that for this purpose a distinction must be made between the commencement of a reference and the commencement of an arbitration for time limitation purposes under section 34 of the Limitation Act 1980 or any other limitation enactment,[3] or as that phrase is understood for the purposes of sections 3 and 4 of the 1979 Act.[4] It is suggested that for the purpose of section 2(1) a reference commences not with the mere service of a notice to appoint or to concur in the appointment of an arbitrator or tribunal, or to refer a dispute to a named or designated arbitrator, but with the valid appointment of an arbitrator or arbitration tribunal; and a valid appointment requires a communication by the arbitrator(s) of a consent to act and a notification of his (their) consent to the other parties.[5] In the case of an umpirage a reference probably commences when the umpire has accepted appointment and the preconditions to a valid umpirage are established.[6] The foregoing analysis also suggests that there is a distinction to be drawn between the commencement of a reference and the notion of entering on a reference which was considered earlier in the text.[7] Viewed logically, before an arbitrator or umpire can enter on a reference there must exist a pre-existing reference. There is less difficulty concerning the termination of the course of a reference. Once a final award is made and published the reference is at a close and the jurisdiction under section 2 extinguished.[8] But between the commencement and termination of a reference a consultative case may be initiated at any stage of the proceedings.[9]

12.4.4.3 The jurisdiction extends to *any* question of law arising in the course of a reference. It is quite clear that this includes any question of law relating to the substance of the dispute referred to arbitration. It is in this regard that section 2, as was its statutory predecessor, will be most frequently used. Thus, for example, in the case of a dispute arising out of a written contract, the opinion of the court on the proper construction of the contract may be sought as a preliminary step in the arbitration proceedings. So also may questions relating to the proper law of a contract; whether

2. See Chapter 3, para. 3.1.
3. See, for example, Arbitration Act 1950, s. 29, which is applicable to the Merchant Shipping Act 1894, s. 496, as amended.
4. Section 7(2) of the 1979 Act which applies s. 29(2) and (3) of the Arbitration Act 1950 to the concept of the "commencement of an arbitration" for the purposes of the 1979 Act. See Chapter 13, para. 13.4.2.2.
5. *Tradax Export S.A.* v. *Volkswagenwerk A.G.* [1970] 1 Q.B. 537; [1970] 1 Lloyd's Rep. 62; *Edm. J. M. Mertens & Co. P.V.B.A.* v. *Veevoeder Import Export Vimex B.V.* [1979] 2 Lloyd's Rep. 372.
6. *Supra*, para. 12.4.3.1.3.2.
7. *Supra*, para. 12.4.3.1.3.
8. *In re an Arbitration between Knight and The Tabernacle Permanent Building Society* [1891] 2 Q.B. 63, 70 per Fry L.J.
9. *Tabernacle Permanent Building Society* v. *Knight* [1892] A.C. 298, 302 per Lord Halsbury.

terms are incorporated by reference into a contract; whether a contract is frustrated by subsequent events, to take but a few of the possible legal questions that may arise.[10] To this extent there is a parallel between the kinds of questions of law capable of coming forward for preliminary determination under section 2 and the kinds of questions of law which may arise out of awards and which may be appealed under section 1(2). The same parallel exists with regard to questions of law appertaining to costs and the award of interest payments.[11]

12.4.4.4 But equally it would appear to be that the province of section 2 is not confined to questions of law that touch on the substance or merits of a dispute and associated questions relating to costs and interest. The statutory language is wide enough to embrace questions of law arising in relation to the arbitral process in general and as a result a preliminary question of law relating, for example, to the status, jurisdiction and powers of an arbitrator or umpire, or relating to the conduct of a reference, may be placed before the court for determination. To this extent the jurisdiction conferred by section 2 is significantly wider than that conferred under section 1(2).

12.4.4.5 That this broader jurisdiction exists under section 2 takes support from the natural and ordinary interpretation of the statutory language which alludes to "any question of law", and to such questions "arising in the course of the reference". The statute is cast in wide terms and there appears to be no justification for narrowing its horizons by adopting a restrictive interpretation. The decision in *The Vasso*[12] offers strong support for this broad and unrestrictive view of the proper province of the consultative case procedure. The questions of law placed before the court for determination concerned the question whether an arbitrator in a salvage arbitration had the power to make an order for inspection of property and whether such an order could be made in favour of cargo interests as distinct from salvors. The phrase "any question of law arising in the course of the reference" is also one found in the statutory predecessors of section 2,[13] and which in turn received a broad and unrestrictive construction. The authorities reveal a variety of interlocutory issues being raised under the consultative case procedure such as the power of arbitrators or umpires to amend points of defence[14]; order security for costs[15]; order discovery and further discovery[16]; order an affidavit of documents and interrogatories[17]; strike out a claim for want of prosecution[18]; and whether a remitted interim award stated as a special case raised an issue estoppel.[19] There is nothing associated with the 1979 Act to suggest that the historical precedents should now be departed from, although it must be conceded that

10. For examples under the pre-1979 consultative case procedure, see *Cogstad (C.T.) & Co.* v. *H. Newsum, Sons & Co.* [1921] 2 A.C. 528; *Verheijdens Veevoeder Commissiehandel B.V.* v. *Joseph Co. Inc.* [1981] 1 Lloyd's Rep. 102; *D/S A/S Idaho* v. *Peninsular and Oriental Steam Navigation Co. (The Strathnewton)* [1982] 2 Lloyd's Rep. 296; [1983] 1 Lloyd's Rep. 219; *Seven Seas Transportation Ltd.* v. *Pacifico Union Marina Corporation (The Satya Kailash and Oceanic Amity)* [1982] 2 Lloyd's Rep. 465; [1984] 1 Lloyd's Rep. 88 (C.A.).
11. Cf. *King* v. *Thomas McKenna Ltd.* [1991] 1 All E.R. 653.
12. [1983] 2 Lloyd's Rep. 346.
13. See *supra*, para. 12.3.
14. *In re an Arbitration between Crighton and The Law Car and General Insurance Corp. Ltd.* [1910] 2 K.B. 738.
15. *In re an Arbitration between Unione Stearinerie Lanza and Wiener* [1917] 2 K.B. 558.
16. *In re La Société Les Affréteurs Réunis and The Shipping Controller* [1921] 3 K.B. 1.
17. *Kursell* v. *Timber Operators and Contractors Ltd.* [1923] 2 K.B. 202.
18. *Crawford and Another* v. *A. E. A. Prowting Ltd.* [1973] 1 Q.B. 1.
19. *Fidelitas Shipping Co. Ltd.* v. *V/O Exportchleb* [1966] 1 Q.B. 630 (C.A.).

the jurisdictional preconditions stipulated in section 2(2) are difficult to reconcile with the kind of question of law that is likely to arise under the broader jurisdiction as here defined.[20]

12.4.4.6 In so far as questions of law relating to the conduct of a reference are capable of being brought forward under section 2 for determination by the High Court, the section provides an alternative remedy or approach not only to declaratory relief and an appeal from an interim award,[21] but also to applications under the Arbitration Act 1950, section 12(6), and under section 5 of the 1979 Act.[22]

12.4.4.7 By virtue of the general rule of English law that an arbitrator cannot determine his own jurisdiction, it was also the case under the former consultative case procedure that an arbitrator or umpire could not invoke the jurisdiction of the court to determine any question of law on which his jurisdiction depended, such as the validity of an arbitration agreement or of his appointment as arbitrator.[23] An arbitrator could only state a consultative case with regard to a question or issue over which he had jurisdiction. This technical limitation would appear no longer relevant to section 2, for thereunder the jurisdiction of the court may only be invoked by a party to a reference subject to the necessary consent, and it is suggested that a party to a reference may bring before the court a question of law relating to the jurisdiction of an arbitrator. The only constraint, so far as the parties are concerned, is that the question of law must be one that arises in the course of a reference and a question of jurisdiction would appear to fall quite clearly within this description.

12.4.4.8 Finally, the question of law must be one "arising" in the course of a reference. This presumably refers to a question of law that has arisen in the course of a reference and is current and in issue, as distinct from a hypothetical or academic question of law. Donaldson J. has considered that the statutory term excludes "questions of law which may or may not arise according to the view which the arbitrators thereafter take of the facts".[24] Also excluded, following the making of an award, is any question of law that "had arisen" in the course of a reference. But for a question of law to arise in the course of a reference it is doubtful that it is also necessary for the event or events out of which or in relation to which the question of law arises to have arisen in the course of a reference. It would seem possible for an event that pre-dates the commencement of a reference to give rise to a question of law that arises in the course of a reference.

12.5 JURISDICTION OF HIGH COURT TO ENTERTAIN APPLICATIONS UNDER SECTION 2

Confronted with a properly initiated application under section 2 the High Court has various distinct functions to discharge. First, it has to satisfy itself that it has jurisdic-

20. See *infra*, para. 12.5.1.
21. See *infra*, para. 12.11.
22. See Chapter 1, para. 1.2.1.7.1.
23. *Windsor R.D.C.* v. *Otterway and Fry* [1954] 1 W.L.R. 1494, 1497–1498 per Devlin J. Contrast *Den of Airlee S.S. Co. Ltd.* v. *Mitsui & Co. Ltd. and British Oil and Cake Mills Ltd.* (1912) 17 Com.C.S. 116, 132, per Farwell L.J.; *May* v. *Mills* (1914) 30 T.L.R. 287 (where the existence of a condition precedent to the jurisdiction of the arbitrator was in issue).
24. *A/B Gotaverken* v. *Westminster Corp. of Monrovia* [1971] 2 Lloyd's Rep. 505, 511.

tion to consider the application; secondly, if satisfied on the question of jurisdiction, it has next to consider whether to give leave to apply; and where leave is given, its final function is to determine the question of law submitted for its consideration.

12.5.1 Preconditions to the jurisdiction of the High Court

12.5.1.1 Section 2(2) provides:

The High Court shall not entertain an application under subsection (1)(a) above with respect to any question of law unless it is satisfied that—
    (a) the determination of the application might produce substantial savings in costs to the parties; and
    (b) the question of law is one in respect of which leave to appeal would be likely to be given under section 1(3)(b) above.

This limitation which is new and did not appear in the former legislation, might be interpreted as either a constraint on jurisdiction or on the exercise of discretion. As a question of practice, either interpretation would probably produce the same result. But given the language of the introductory phrase—"The High Court shall not entertain an application . . . "—the subsection is probably more accurately interpreted as a constraint on jurisdiction.[1] Notwithstanding this probability, the section might have operated less awkwardly if the subsection (2) stipulations had been presented as discretionary criteria; but as will be seen later in the text, they do nonetheless possess a patent relevance to the manner in which the judicial discretion is exercised under section 2(1).

12.5.1.2 The constraint on jurisdiction is not universal. It only applies where an application is initiated under section 2(1)(a) with the consent only of an arbitrator or umpire who has entered on a reference. Where the consent of all the other parties to the reference has been obtained and the application is initiated under section 2(1)(b), section 2(2) has no application. The essence of section 2(2) is that it applies when the consent of all the other parties is absent and not when the application is initiated with the consent of an arbitrator or umpire. In consequence, section 2(2) continues to be inapplicable where an application is initiated with the consent of all the other parties *and* of the arbitrator or umpire.[2]

12.5.1.3 Where an application is initiated with the consent of all the other parties under section 2(1)(b) there is much less need for any external judicial assessment of the wisdom or potential efficacy of the application. The matter is best left in the hands of the arbitrating parties. In *The Oltenia* Donaldson L.J. explained the governing policy in the following terms[3]: "no doubt . . . Parliament considered that prima facie it could be left to the parties to consider whether the determination of the question of law at that stage would be likely to lead to a substantial saving of costs (sub.s. 2(a)) and whether it could substantially affect their rights." But the fact that all the other parties consent to an application does not mean that the court is bound to give leave to

---

1. *The Vasso* [1983] 2 Lloyd's Rep. 346, 348, per Lloyd J.
2. *Gebr. Broere B.V.* v. *Saras Chimica S.p.A.* [1982] 2 Lloyd's Rep. 436, 440, per Parker J.
3. *Babanaft International Co. S.A.* v. *Avant Petroleum Inc. (The Oltenia)* [1982] 2 Lloyd's Rep. 99, 103 (C.A.).

apply. A discretion is retained[4] but it may be assumed that only in exceptional circumstances would the court elect to frustrate the common desire of the parties.

12.5.1.4 The jurisdictional preconditions specified in section 2(2) represent the most troublesome aspect of section 2. Not only can they give rise to difficult questions of fact, of relevance and of application to the range of legal questions that can come before the court under the section 2 procedure; but a fundamental question may be raised as to why they exist at all, at least in the form of jurisdictional preconditions. The answer, probably, is that section 2(2) manifests a legislative policy analogous to that underlying appeals under section 1(2).[5] Whereas under section 1 there is a clearly defined policy supporting the finality of awards, under section 2 there appears to exist a discernible policy which supports the finality of the choice of forum. If the parties choose to refer a question of law to an arbitration tribunal, then the policy of the 1979 Act is to tie them to their choice of tribunal unless it can be shown that there is good cause for referring the question of law to the court.[6] In broad terms section 2(2) suggests that good cause exists only when the involvement of the court is likely to expedite the arbitral process and the question of law in issue is of a kind that ought to be determined by the court. There is also an element of cross-fertilisation between good cause as defined in section 2(2) and the policy supporting the finality of awards associated with section 1, for to the extent that the court intervenes and determines as a preliminary issue a question of law under section 2, the greater must also be the likelihood that the ultimate award will be accepted as final by the parties.

12.5.1.5 It is also to be noted that the preconditions specified in paragraphs (a) and (b) of section 2(2) are not alternative but cumulative requirements. The conjunctive "and" would appear to make this interpretation incontrovertible. The court would also seem compelled to address the preconditions in alphabetical order. First, to consider whether the determination of the application might produce substantial savings in costs to the parties; and if so satisfied, to proceed to consider whether the question of law is one in respect of which leave to appeal would be likely to be given under section 1(3)(b).

12.5.1.6 Substantial savings in costs to the parties

12.5.1.6.1 The first precondition to jurisdiction is that the court must be satisfied that "the determination of the application might produce substantial savings in costs to the parties".

This precondition touches on a central rationale of the section 2 procedure, but it may equally give rise to very difficult questions of fact and degree. In addressing the question raised by the precondition it is clear that the judge will frequently be required to indulge in what may be described as a speculative prognostication. It will often be impossible to weigh the various considerations with scientific precision and come to an absolute conclusion. The most that can be reasonably expected is for the judge to come to the question in a general vein, taking into account the facts and circumstances of the case, the question of law in issue, the submissions of the parties and

---

4. See *infra*, para. 12.6.
5. See generally, Chapter 1, para. 1.5.
6. See *infra*, para. 12.6.2.

his own experience of the arbitration process, which in the case of a judge of the Commercial Court is likely to be considerable.

12.5.1.6.2 To an extent the judicial function is assisted by and its speculative character also endorsed by the precise statutory language of section 2(2)(a). In the first place the judge has only to be satisfied that there "might" be a saving in costs to the parties. He is not required to satisfy himself that there "will" be a saving in costs or that to determine the application will "probably" or is "likely" to produce such a saving. Further, the judge must be satisfied not that the determination of the application might produce savings, but that it might produce "substantial" savings in costs. What is "substantial" is in each case a question of fact and degree, but it would seem clear that a minor, trivial or inconsequential saving will not suffice. The object of the statute would appear to be that there shall be no judicial intervention in the arbitral process unless the potential saving is of real and material significance. The adopted statutory language also appears to encourage in this regard a general and broad approach, avoiding fine assessments and fatuous niceties.

12.5.1.6.3 There must be a possible substantial saving in costs "to the parties". Presumably this is to be construed as meaning "the parties to the reference".[1] The use of the plural appears to suggest that the judge must be satisfied that there is a potential saving in costs to all the parties and not merely to one or some of the parties. It would seem insufficient for an applicant to establish a potential saving only for himself. But again it is probable that a broad and commonsense approach has to be adopted and the parties to the reference viewed as a collectivity with a loose quasi-corporate character, rather than indulge in a close and precise examination of the position and circumstance of each individual party. As a matter of practice, a potential saving associated with the determination of a question of law as a preliminary issue will by virtue of the very nature of the benefit derived from a section 2 determination invariably represent a potential saving in costs to all the parties.

12.5.1.6.4 There is then the question, what precisely is meant by costs? The question is relevant for the precondition to jurisdiction necessarily requires the judge to draw a comparison between the costs that are likely to be incurred in the reference in the event of the question of law remaining undetermined by the court, and the costs likely to be incurred in the same reference with the advantage of the opinion of the court on the question of law in issue. In making this comparison the precise meaning of the phrase "costs to the parties" assumes an obvious significance. It would seem, in the first place, uncontentious to submit that "costs" is capable of alluding to all costs that come under the traditional labels of costs of the reference and costs of the award. But it is unlikely that more remote considerations may be taken into account, such as the benefits derived from obtaining an award that is more likely to be complied with by the parties and in consequence is less exposed to the risk of being challenged. Nor, probably, are the costs associated with the section 2 application to form part of the equation. Where the question of law in issue is the validity of an interlocutory order, the saving in costs which would result from a party not having to comply with the

1. This would appear to follow from the drafting of the introductory paragraph in section 2(1) where there is reference to "the parties to a reference"; and it would appear to follow that it is in the context of this phrase that all other references to "parties" or "other parties" in section 2 are to be understood.

order, should it have been wrongly made, is again not such a saving of cost that is within the meaning of section 2(2)(a).[2]

12.5.1.6.5 Savings in costs will predominantly be associated with and derive from savings in time. The determination of a preliminary point of law will in consequence *prima facie* produce a saving in costs if the determination will either effectively determine the result or alternatively materially shorten the reference. But often these benefits will only follow depending on the way the question of law is ultimately answered. If decided one way the reference may be materially foreshortened; if decided the other way no such benefit will result. But the fact the potential benefit to the parties revolves around the precise decision of the court will not deprive the court of jurisdiction because under section 2(1)(a) it is enough that the court is satisfied that to determine the application "might" result in a substantial saving in costs.[3]

12.5.1.6.6 The factual question raised by section 2(1)(a) will on occasions be quite readily answered, as where the question is whether a claim is time-barred.[4] On other occasions it will pose serious difficulties. A particular problem arises when the question associated with the precondition to jurisdiction is applied in the context of a question of law relating to the validity of an interlocutory order. In *The Vasso*[5] there were, *inter alia*, two preliminary questions of law. Did the arbitrator have power to make an order for inspection of property in salvage arbitration? And could such an order be made in favour of cargo interests, as distinct from salvors? Addressing the jurisdictional question in the context of the facts of the case Lloyd J. observed[6]:

Whichever way I may decide the question of law cannot determine the ultimate result or shorten the hearing. It may make it more difficult for the cargo-owners to prepare their case, or even obtain justice if I decide against them, but it will not, as far as I can see, save costs.

Nonetheless leave to apply was given, leaving it open whether it was right or wrong to do so. The case is, however, somewhat special for although in form it was an application under section 2, it seems in substance to have been treated by all the parties and the court as an appeal from an interim award.

12.5.1.7 Nature of the question of law

12.5.1.7.1 If the court is satisfied that to determine the question of law as a preliminary issue might produce substantial savings in costs to the parties, it must next and additionally consider whether the question of law in issue is one in respect of which leave to appeal would be likely to be given under section 1(3)(b).

This is the effect of section 2(2)(b) and its broad purpose would appear to be to bring sections 1 and 2 within a common policy framework. The principles governing the exercise of judicial discretion in determining whether to give or refuse leave to appeal under section 1(3)(b) have previously been considered and are generally embraced within *The Nema/Antaios* guidelines.[1] The pervading spirit and particular

2. *The Vasso* [1983] 2 Lloyd's Rep. 346, 348 per Lloyd J.
3. *Ibid.*
4. See, for example, *D/S A/S Idaho* v. *Peninsular and Oriental Steam Navigation Co. (The Strathnewton)* [1982] 2 Lloyd's Rep. 296; [1983] 1 Lloyd's Rep. 219 (C.A.).
5. *Supra.*
6. *Supra*, p. 348.
1. See Chapter 5.

premises underlying these guidelines are, by virtue of section 2(2)(b), of equal application to the jurisdictional basis of the court to entertain a section 2 application, where the consent of all the other parties is absent. One immediate consequence of this is that it becomes impossible to utilise section 2 so as to circumvent the restrictive policy associated with section 1(3)(b).

12.5.1.7.2 The court has only to satisfy itself that an appeal "would be likely to be given" and not that it "would be given" under section 1(3)(b). This suggests again that the court is not expected to do more than come to the question posed in a general and summary fashion, and to have regard not only to such brief submissions as may be permitted on the issue but also to draw on its own knowledge and experience of the giving of leave to appeal under section 1(3)(b). It would produce nothing but unnecessary delay if the court was required in each case to treat the question of jurisdiction as if it was an application under section 1(3)(b) and to give the issue the same consideration as is generally given to such applications.[2] It must not be lost sight of that the nature of the question of law is only of relevance under section 2(2)(b) to the question of the jurisdiction of the court to entertain an application for leave to apply under section 2(1).

12.5.1.7.3 There are, however, many difficulties associated with any attempt to bring section 1(2) appeals and section 2 applications within a common policy framework. One sphere of the discretion under section 1(3)(b) emphasises that leave to appeal is more likely to be given where the question of law is of importance because of its general interest to the public at large or to a segment of the public.[3] In contrast, the orthodox rationale of section 2 as a statutory measure assisting the efficiency of the arbitration process strongly suggests that the issue of the importance of a question of law may on occasions be a more polarised concept and closely tied to the interests of the parties to a reference. The fundamental object behind an application under section 2(1) is to expedite the resolution of a dispute by determining a question of law in issue in the arbitration at a preliminary stage. In such a situation what is crucial is the importance of the question of law in the context of the dispute between the parties and not the wider interests of society or any section of society. There is almost a conflict of philosophies between paragraphs (a) and (b) of subsection (2) which comes fully to the surface where a one-off question of law of importance to the parties arises in the course of a reference. The consultative case procedure prior to the 1979 Act would have accommodated such a question of law and the assistance of the court would have been proffered. Under section 2 the position is less certain and it may even be that the assistance of the court is not available, for by virtue of section 2(2)(b) it is at least arguable that the court lacks jurisdiction. Further, given that the determination of the court under section 2 is in the nature of an opinion and is not *res judicata* it is of substantially less value to the wider community than an appeal decided under section 1(2).[4]

12.5.1.7.4 Another difficulty arises from the fact that the discretion under section 1(3)(b) is also governed by a preliminary assessment of the rightness or wrongness of an arbitrator's decision.[5] There can be nothing comparable under section 2 for *ex*

2. For the practice relating to applications for leave to appeal under section 1(3)(b), see Chapter 7.
3. See Chapters 5 and 6.
4. See *infra*, para. 12.7.2.
5. See Chapter 5.

hypothesi there is no decision made by an arbitrator, although he may express an opinion as to what is the correct answer to the question of law in issue.[6] What is placed before the court for determination is a bare question of law, together with such factual findings as then exist,[7] or which may be agreed, which when answered will hopefully assist the arbitrator in arriving at his award.

There are still further practical difficulties in attempting to anticipate what would result on an application for leave to appeal under section 1(3)(b) if the question of law in issue were embodied in a reasoned award. There is, of course, no award and there never will be an award, so the court cannot operate on the basis of any precise analogy. When an application for leave to appeal is made the court is apprised of all the decided facts and any other determined questions of law. In other words the court is provided with a factual and legal context, which is quite vital to the feasibility of its reviewing role. If there is a contextual lacuna, it may make an order under section 1(5) and so obtain the necessary information.[8] But with regard to an application under section 2 there may be no or few accompanying decided facts or determined associated questions of law, and the position cannot be aided by an order under section 1(5) which has no application to section 2. The position may be compensated by the parties admitting facts or being prepared to assume the existence of facts for the purpose of the application. But the contextual bareness in which a question of law is often presented not only pinpoints a weakness in the section 2 procedure but represents yet another area of difficulty in endeavouring to apply the test laid down in section 2(2)(b). The court has to attempt to determine what would happen on an application for leave to appeal from an award without any knowledge of the factual and legal environment prevailing on the making of an award.

12.5.1.7.5 The range of legal questions that may arise for determination under section 2 is frequently wider than on an appeal under section 1(2).[9] Under section 2 any question of law arising in the course of a reference may be placed before the court for determination. Where a question of law is of a kind that it is outside the usual parameters of section 1(2) but within the terms of section 2, as in the case of the power of an arbitrator or umpire to make an interlocutory order, section 2(2)(b) becomes a difficult provision to apply.[10] But the position is not quite impossible for procedural decisions may be embodied in interim awards and this practice may provide the basis for any necessary analogy.

Section 2(2)(b) is something of a cuckoo in the nest. It involves a jurisdictional test that is in large measure unreal and speculative. The attempt to introduce into section 2 the particular strand of policy associated with section 1(2) appeals is also possibly flawed for the logic and ethos of the appellate policy does not necessarily fit into the rationale and practice associated with the determination of preliminary questions of law. It might have been better and served the policy of the legislation equally well had the statute required no more of the court than that it be satisfied that the question of law in issue was "substantial" in the sense the same term is used in section 1(4).[11] This

6. See, for example, *Seven Seas Transportation Ltd.* v. *Pacifico Union Marina Corpn. (The Satya Kailash and Oceanic Amity)* [1982] 2 Lloyd's Rep. 465, 467.
7. *Infra*, para. 12.5.1.7.5.
8. See Chapter 8, para. 8.5 and Chapter 11.
9. See *supra*, para. 12.4.4.
10. *The Vasso* [1983] 2 Lloyd's Rep. 346, 348, per Lloyd J.
11. See Chapter 4, para. 4.3.3.

in itself would appear to be a sufficient basis for the establishment of jurisdiction; with the question of discretion, whether to give leave to apply, arising subsequently.

12.5.1.7.6 Notwithstanding the problems, section 2(2)(b) exists and it cannot be ignored. The question therefore arises how precisely it is to be understood and applied. If it is given a literal interpretation it produces in many instances an impossible or impracticable situation. An alternative and more feasible approach is to interpret the statutory language in a manner consistent with the spirit of the central plank of policy associated with the exercise of discretion under section 1(3)(b), rather than by reference to the precise detail associated with *The Nema/Antaios* guidelines, always bearing in mind the precise status of the guidelines and the fact that they are neither absolute nor comprehensive in their application.[12] By adopting this manner of approach many of the anomalies may be avoided and it may even be possible to translate section 2(2)(b) into a workable concept.

12.6 DISCRETION WHETHER TO GIVE OR REFUSE LEAVE TO APPLY

12.6.1 Leave to apply a question of discretion

12.6.1.1 Once the court is satisfied that it has jurisdiction, it must then proceed to decide whether in its discretion it will give or refuse leave to apply for a judicial determination under section 2(1). That this preliminary discretion exists is now well established by authority[1] and it is also overtly recognised by the terms of section 2(2A).[2] In conferring a jurisdiction on the High Court, section 2(1) does not further proceed to compel the court to give a determination on every application properly made. Implicit in the terms of section 2(1) is a discretion whether or not to exercise the jurisdiction. The statutory phrase asserting that the High Court *shall have jurisdiction* is not construed as obliging the court to exercise its jurisdiction.

12.6.1.2 The preliminary discretion to give or refuse leave to apply is quite distinct from the determination of an application with regard to which leave has been given.[3] To the extent that section 2 has these two distinct and separate stages there exists an obvious analogy with the appellate procedure under section 1.[4] But there is otherwise an important difference between the two sections. Under section 1(3)(a), where all the parties consent they can have their appeal as of right.[5] But under section 2(1)(b) the consent of all the parties will not secure an application under section 2(1), for notwithstanding the presence of universal consent the discretion of the court to give or

---

12. See Chapter 5, para. 5.3.

1. *Babanaft International Co. S.A.* v. *Avant Petroleum Inc. (The Oltenia)* [1982] 2 Lloyd's Rep. 99, 103 per Donaldson L.J.; *The Vasso* [1983] 2 Lloyd's Rep. 346, 348–349, per Lloyd J. Contrast *Gebr. Broere B.V.* v. *Saras Chimica S.p.A.* [1982] 2 Lloyd's Rep. 436, 440 where Parker J. appears to suggest the contrary.

2. Considered *infra* at para. 12.9.2.

3. See *infra*, para. 12.10.4.

4. See Chapter 2, para. 2.1.

5. See Chapter 4, para. 4.2.

refuse leave to apply continues to exist.[6] The same is equally true when an application is made with the consent of an arbitrator or umpire who has entered on a reference.[7]

12.6.1.3 An application under section 2(1), therefore, cannot be made as of right. The discretion of the court functions in a manner similar to the exercise of discretion under section 1(3)(b) and may in consequence be perceived as a control mechanism by which the balance between the independence of the arbitral process and the interventionist jurisdiction of the court, albeit in aid of the arbitral process, is regulated. In each case the burden of proof will be with the applicant to satisfy the court on a balance of probabilities that it ought to give leave to apply.

12.6.2 The basis on which the discretion is exercised

12.6.2.1 The basis on which the discretion arising under section 2(1) is exercised has not to date been fully explored by the courts. It is on its face unfettered and unstructured for the statute does no more than recognise the existence of the discretion and does not specify the criteria that are to influence its exercise. But it would seem irresistible that the exercise of the discretion must be influenced and moulded by the same considerations of policy that are associated with the 1979 Act as a whole and which have been closely developed in association with the jurisdiction of the court to give leave to appeal from awards under section 1(3)(b).[1] This, it is submitted, is the case notwithstanding that section 2 did not receive any express recognition in the judgment of Lord Diplock in *The Nema*,[2] although it is possible that this omission is now compensated for by the admittedly brief allusion to the section by Lord Diplock in *The Antaios*[3] and where Lord Diplock exhorted judicial vigilance in the application of section 2.[4] If this is a right approach then section 2 is to be understood and applied in the context of a general policy the object of which is to move the posture of the law away from judicial interventionism towards arbitral autonomy. With regard to section 2 it is the autonomy of the arbitral process that is to the fore, and the impact of the embracing policy is to insist that a question of law referred to arbitration for determination shall be so determined unless there can be established good cause for the court to intervene and determine the question of law in issue. The terms of section 2(2), although primarily jurisdictional, also appear to have a relevance to the exercise of discretion,[5] and lend further support to the suggested general approach that is to govern the exercise of discretion.

12.6.2.2 From this statement of the likely general approach to the question of policy there would appear to arise several deductions, which also derive by analogy from the developed law with regard to the exercise of the discretion arising under section 1(3)(b).[6] The first is that the principles governing the exercise of discretion with regard to the consultative case, as that process existed prior to the 1979 Act, have no

---

6. *Babanaft International Co. S.A.* v. *Avant Petroleum Inc. (The Oltenia)* [1982] 2 Lloyd's Rep. 99, 106, per Donaldson L.J.
7. *Ibid.*
1. See Chapter 1, para. 1.5 and Chapter 5.
2. [1982] A.C. 724.
3. [1985] A.C. 191.
4. *Ibid* at p. 199.
5. See *infra*, para. 12.6.2.3.
6. See Chapters 5 and 6.

application to the exercise of the discretion under section 2. Although *The Lysland*[7] was not directly concerned with the consultative case, it may be presumed that the spirit of the principles there enunciated, were equally relevant to the consultative case. Secondly, the consultative case as it exists under section 2 is a more restricted process than that which existed under the former law. To this extent it may be said that not only is section 2 not available when the former consultative case would not have been available but also that section 2 may not be available in a situation where the former consultative case would have been available. Thirdly, the principles governing the exercise of the discretion under section 2 must be considered anew and formulated not only in the context of the rationale of the consultative case procedure but also in the context of the policy associated with the 1979 Act. This approach establishes a *prima facie* rule in favour of the autonomy of the arbitral process, and exhorts judicial vigilance in protection of the *prima facie* rule, but also recognises that the *prima facie* rule may be displaced on establishing good cause.

12.6.2.3 Questions of policy and discretion with regard to section 2 also appear to raise an issue which is absent in the case of appeals under section 1(2). Whereas the jurisdiction arising under section 2 is interventionist, it nonetheless has as its primary purpose the assistance of the arbitral process. The judicial role is not overtly supervisory, as is the jurisdiction to take appeals from awards under section 1(2), and this raises the question whether the policy identified with the 1979 Act and the emergent principles associated with the exercise of discretion under section 1(3)(b) are at all relevant to section 2. Given that the central purpose of section 2 is to establish a jurisdiction in aid of the arbitration process, it is at least arguable that the question of discretion should be governed solely by reference to circumstances peculiar to the particular application. This subjective slant is detectable in section 2(2)(a) and the upshot of this perspective would be to assert that leave to apply should be given, whatever the nature of the question of law in issue, whenever the court is satisfied that the judicial determination of the point of law as a preliminary issue would be beneficial to the reference, as where it could be shown effectively to resolve the dispute or materially foreshorten the arbitral process and thereby produce significant savings in costs.[8] In contrast the policy associated with the 1979 Act as applied to appeals under section 1(2) reveals a wider perspective, with the general importance of the question of law also being taken into account. Translated into a section 2 circumstance this wider perspective suggests that leave to apply should not be given, even when to determine the question of law would benefit the particular reference in the sense considered above, unless the question of law in issue is of a kind that its judicial determination might in some way be considered to be in the public interest. The precise legal effect of a judicial determination under section 2 does tend to detract from this approach,[9] but on the other hand the approach is clearly capable of taking support from the terms of section 2(2)(b), which would appear to establish a link between section 2 and the policy associated with appeals under section 1(2), at least to the extent that that policy

7. *Halfdan Greig & Co. A/S* v. *Sterling Coal and Navigation ei. and A.C. Neleman's Handel-en-Transportondernerning, (The Lysland)* [1973] 1 Q.B. 843, C.A., see para. 1.4.2.8 *et seq.*

8. Cf. Diplock, "The Case Stated—its Use and Abuse" (1978) 44 Arbitration 107, 110, where Lord Diplock expounds the opinion that the court ought not to order a consultative case, save in exceptional cases, and then proceeds to explain that "[t]he exceptional case that I have in mind is one where the decision of a point of law one way may make unnecessary the hearing of lengthy and costly evidence".

9. See *infra*, para. 12.7.2.

is capable of applying to section 2. Moreover, the stipulations specified in section 2(2) are cumulative and if it is right to assume that these cumulative considerations have a relevance, beyond the question of jurisdiction, to the exercise of discretion under section 2 then they strongly suggest that it is the latter and wider perspective which will dominate the judicial operation of section 2. In the result the question of discretion would appear to be dominated centrally by two considerations, namely, the potential efficacy of the intervention, which is to be assessed in the context of the particular reference, and the degree of interest in having the question of law judicially determined, which is to be assessed by reference to the nature of the question of law in issue and the wider environment of the reference. Is it the kind of question of law which in the context of the prevailing spirit of *The Nema/Antaios* guidelines, but not necessarily their precise detail, ought to be considered and determined by a judge of the High Court?[10] The concern within *The Nema/Antaios* guidelines with the correctness of the arbitral decision, which can have no application to the present context, nonetheless could translate itself into an enquiry into the appropriateness of the question of law in issue to arbitral or judicial resolution.

12.6.2.4 The limited judicial consideration of section 2 to date suggests that what has been characterised above as the wider perspective is the approach that will be pursued. In *The Vasso*[11] Lloyd J. indicated *obiter dictum* that he would be prepared to give leave to apply where the question of law was one of "general interest and importance".[12] Observations of the Court of Appeal in *The Oltenia*[13] also appear to place the operation of section 2 quite firmly within the wider policy associated with the 1979 Act. The appellate court was satisfied that the judge at first instance had been right to give leave to apply where the point of law in issue concerned the question whether a claim by disponent shipowners against voyage charterers was time-barred under the terms of the charterparty.

12.6.2.5 Beyond the central considerations of the potential efficacy of an intervention and the nature of the question of law, a number of further considerations may assume a relevance to the exercise of discretion. In keeping with the policy of the 1979 Act the motive underlying an application has a clear relevance. If the court is satisfied that the application for leave to apply is in reality being brought to delay, frustrate or otherwise baulk the arbitral process, this provides a clear basis for refusing leave to apply. The ability of the court to discharge the function expected of it would appear to be another relevant factor.[14] If it is unlikely, by virtue of the nature of the point of law in issue or because of the absence of sufficient findings of fact or the absence of any agreement or assumption as to fact, that the court will be able to provide a clear and decisive opinion on the question of law presented, this again may represent a good reason for refusing leave to apply. If the court cannot or is unlikely to be able to provide a determination, it is pointless to permit the section 2 procedure to be used in vain.

12.6.2.6 A further consideration may turn on whether the application is opposed by or is made with the consent of all the other parties to the reference. Where all the par-

---

10. Cf. *Verheijdens Veevoeder Commissiehandel B.V.* v. *I. S. Joseph Co. Inc.* [1981] 1 Lloyd's Rep. 102.
11. [1983] 2 Lloyd's Rep. 346.
12. *Ibid.* at p. 348.
13. *Babanaft International Co. S.A.* v. *Avant Petroleum Inc. (The Oltenia)* [1982] 2 Lloyd's Rep. 99.
14. *Ibid.*

ties support an application there would appear little purpose for the court to scrutinise the application as closely as it might otherwise be inclined to do when an application for leave to apply is made with the consent of an arbitrator or umpire only. In this kind of situation the jurisdictional preconditions specified in section 2(2) have no application and it may be left to the parties to judge whether obtaining a determination of the court is desirable and will assist in the speedy disposal of the reference to arbitration.[15] Moreover, in agreeing to an application the parties have also emphasised their preference for legal accuracy and also their implicit willingness to suffer interruption of the arbitral process in order to achieve it. It would seem therefore that when an application for leave is brought with the consent of all the parties to a reference, the court, in the absence of special considerations, may be strongly inclined to give leave to apply provided it can, in the circumstances of the case, provide a clear and decisive answer to the question of law in issue.

12.6.2.7 But even when the consent of all the other parties is absent, there will exist the consent of the arbitrator or umpire. This may be of some significance for it at least indicates that it is the view of the adjudicator, in the context of the reference, that the question of law is of relevance and importance and ought to be determined by the court. In a typical arbitration the consent of the arbitrator or umpire will also show that there is at least a majority view, that of the tribunal and one of the parties, in favour of obtaining the judicial determination of the question of law in issue. But the existence of such a majority opinion cannot nearly be as weighty as when the parties to the reference are unanimous on the question.

But the existence of consent, whether it be the unanimous consent of all the parties or the consent of the adjudicator alone, cannot of itself be conclusive for otherwise the question of discretion would be erased and every application entertained that satisfied the procedural and jurisdictional requirements of section 2. This is not the intention of the legislation. Nonetheless the fact that neither section 2(2) nor section 2(2A) apply when an application is brought under section 2(1)(b) does strongly suggest that where the consent of all the other parties to a reference is present an applicant is *prima facie* entitled to a judicial determination under section 2(1).

12.6.2.8 Where a judge of the Commercial Court has been appointed judge-arbitrator or judge-umpire[16] an applicant for a determination under section 2 would appear to bear a much greater burden of proof. Although giving leave to apply in such a circumstance is not precluded, it will nonetheless be very rare. The *raison d'être* of the judicial appointment is a recognition that the dispute referred to arbitration involves a weighty question of law and that it is desirable that it be determined by an arbitrator or umpire with substantial legal expertise and experience. Having entrusted a point of law to a Commercial Judge in an arbitral capacity, it may be presumed that only in exceptional circumstances will a party to a reference thereafter be given leave to seek the determination of a point of law by the court.[17] Where the judge-arbitrator or judge-umpire gives his consent to such an application this must represent weighty evidence of an exceptional circumstance, but without necessarily being conclusive. On

15. *Ibid*. p. 103 per Donaldson L.J.
16. Administration of Justice Act 1970, s. 4 and Sch. 3. See also Chapter 6, para. 6.2.6.4.
17. See *supra* para. 12.4.1.2 for a discussion as to whether the jurisdiction is exercisable by the High Court or Court of Appeal.

reflection, it may even be considered a little surprising that the consultative case procedure remains available when a judge-arbitrator or judge-umpire is appointed.

12.6.3 Giving leave subject to conditions

Although not expressly sanctioned by the language of section 2, it is probable that the court has a power to give leave to apply subject to conditions.[1] The jurisdiction may arise by implication from the express statutory terms or, alternatively, if the decision to give leave to apply amounts to an order of the court, by virtue of the applicability of the Arbitration Act 1950, section 28 to the 1979 Act.[2] In this regard the same analysis applies as was discussed in the context of orders for reasons or futher reasons under section 1(5).[3]

If this is a correct analysis it follows that it is open to the court to attach to the giving of leave to apply any condition which it considers just and appropriate in the circumstances of the particular case. Without prejudice to the generality of the power, a condition may be attached with regard to costs, security for costs, payment into court of the whole or part of the sum in dispute, or an undertaking extracted as to the future conduct of the reference. A point of interest and uncertainty is whether a condition may be made compelling the applicant to accept the determination of the court as final and precluding any attempt to appeal any future award made in the reference on the same legal issue.[4]

12.7 DETERMINATION OF PRELIMINARY QUESTIONS OF LAW BY THE HIGH COURT

12.7.1 Making the determination

12.7.1.1 Once leave to apply is given the court will proceed in open court to determine the question of law raised in the application. The practice surrounding applications under section 2 is considered later in this chapter.[1]

The determination of the court will be made following submissions and argument. The procedure requires that the question of law be clearly and precisely stated, and with the court concerned only with the specific question of law placed before it. Other questions of law are of no concern to the court, even if they are otherwise relevant to the merits of the dispute referred. In many instances the court will be able to determine the question of law by answering "Yes" or "No". But whether the court will in each and every case be able to provide such a terse and unambiguous answer will turn on such considerations as the nature of the question of law and the availability of necessary findings of fact. Where the necessary facts have not been found and cannot

---

1. The existence of such a jurisdiction appears to be accepted by Bowen L.J. in *In re an Arbitration between Knight and Tabernacle Permanent Building Society* [1892] 2 Q.B. 613, 620.
2. Section 7(1)(b).
3. Chapter 11, para. 11.8.2.
4. See *infra*, para. 12.7.2 as to the legal effect of a judicial determination under section 2.
1. See *infra*, para. 12.10.

be agreed they may have to be assumed in order to make it possible for the court to consider and determine the application,[2] although, as will be seen later in the text, this may influence the efficacy of the section 2 procedure. Where such an assumption is not possible the court may be able to provide only a conditional determination[3] or even decide that it cannot give a determination; although where there is a real risk that this will be the likely outcome it is unlikely that the court will give leave to apply in the first place.

12.7.1.2 The interrelationship between law and fact, and, in particular, the need for necessary findings of fact to be made in order to be able to provide an answer to many kinds of legal questions pinpoints yet another limitation on the efficacy of the section 2 procedure. Where all the facts have been found or at least all the facts pertinent to the particular question of law in issue, the court will be able to provide an unqualified answer which will retain its relevance throughout the reference. It is possible that the availability of apposite facts will bear some association to the precise moment in time, in relation to the reference, that the consultative case is sought. The optimum moment must be when the consultative case is sought at or towards the conclusion of a reference and when the arbitrator will be best positioned to make all the relevant findings of fact. Contrariwise, when the question of law is highlighted at the commencement or at an early stage in a reference, there is a danger that adequate findings of fact will not exist and consequently it may be necessary to agree or more probably assume the existence of facts for the purpose of the section 2 application. The inherent risk associated with this practice is that the facts as eventually found in the arbitration may not correspond with the agreed or assumed facts and thus render the determination given by the court valueless. There is also the risk that the actual factual findings subsequently made in the arbitration may give forth new and unanticipated questions of law that render the inital question of law otiose, with the associated section 2 procedure again rendered a wasteful investment. This manner of problem has always been associated with the consultative case procedure and at an early date it was articulated by Kay L.J. in the following terms[4]: "A case might be stated in the early part of an arbitration on a point of law which, on the facts as then appearing to the arbitrator, might seem material: but afterwards, when the facts were further ascertained, it might appear that the point was immaterial." There are, however, limits to the extent to which the court will admit assumed facts. In particular, the court will not permit itself to be placed in the examination room, giving answers on the basis of a variety of assumptions of fact which the court is invited to make.[5]

12.7.1.3 Under section 2 the court is obliged to determine the question of law brought before it. The court must actually decide the question of law in issue and not merely express an opinion on it.[6]

2. Cf. *Gebr. Broere B.V.* v. *Saras Chimica S.p.A.* [1982] 2 Lloyd's Rep. 436, 440; *Verheijdens Veevoeder Commissiehandel B.V.* v. *I. S. Joseph Co. Inc.* [1981] 1 Lloyd's Rep. 102; *Montedison S.p.A.* v. *Icroma S.p.A. (The Caspian Sea)* [1980] 1 Lloyd's Rep. 91.
3. *Babanaft International Co. S.A.* v. *Avant Petroleum Inc. (The Oltenia)* [1982] 1 Lloyd's Rep. 448, 455.
4. *In re an Arbitration between Knight and Tabernacle Permanent Building Society* [1892] 2 Q.B. 613, 621 (C.A.).
5. *A/B Gotaverken* v. *Westminster Corporation of Monrovia* [1971] 2 Lloyd's Rep. 505, 511, per Donaldson J.
6. *Ibid.*

12.7.2 Effect of the judicial determination

12.7.2.1 The precise effect of a consultative determination has long been a difficult and uncertain issue. There is no express provision made in the language of section 2; and the answer to the question is not concluded by section 2(3), which asserts a decision of the High Court under section 2 to be a judgment of the court within the meaning of the Supreme Court Act 1981, section 16. The object of this provision is to lay down a channel of appeal to the Court of Appeal from the determination of a first tier judge under section 2(1)[1] and beyond this it has no application or relevance. In the final analysis the answer to the question posed will turn on the proper interpretation of section 2(1).

12.7.2.2 The Arbitration Act 1889, section 19, expressly provided that a special case might be stated "for the opinion of the Court". In *In re an Arbitration between Knight and The Tabernacle Permanent Building Society*[2] the Court of Appeal held that the jurisdiction of the court under section 19 was consultative only and the opinion it expressed was not in the nature of a judgment or order. The object of the jurisdiction was to give guidance to an arbitrator but it did not divest an arbitrator of his authority as judge of both law and fact.[3] In the result there was no *res judicata*. A natural corollary to this interpretation given to section 19 was that an award might be stated in the form of a special case even when the award was based on the opinion of the court expressed in a consultative case. This somewhat surprising possibility was affirmed by the House of Lords in *British Westinghouse Electric and Machinery Co. Ltd.* v. *Underground Electric Railways Co. of London Ltd.*[4]

12.7.2.3 The subsequent legislative development of the consultative case procedure has witnessed a change of language and the question arises whether in turn this has worked a change in the legal analysis as to the effect of the judicial determination. In both section 9 of the Arbitration Act 1934 and section 21 of the Arbitration Act 1950, the special case was expressed to be stated for "the decision of the High Court". Under section 2 of the 1979 Act the High Court is expressed to have jurisdiction "to determine" any question of law arising in the course of the reference. There is in the change of statutory language at least the potential for a change of analysis, particularly under section 2, where the pronouncement of the court is at least capable of being perceived as a judicial "determination". In *In re an Arbitration between Knight and The Tabernacle Permanent Building Society*,[5] Lord Esher M.R. was of the opinion that there must be a determination or decision by the court before there can exist anything that may be described as equivalent to a judgment or order of the High Court.[6]

12.7.2.4 But notwithstanding this potential for analytical adjustment, there is evidence to suggest that the traditional analysis as to the effect of a consultative case sur-

---

1. See *infra*, para. 12.9.3.
2. [1892] 2 Q.B. 613 (C.A.).
3. *Ibid*. p. 619 per Bowen L.J.
4. [1912] A.C. 673. In *In re an Arbitration between Cogstad & Co. and H. Newsum, Sons and Co. Ltd.* [1921] 2 K.B. 87, 100, Scrutton L.J. observed, "when the arbitrator in his final award purports to act on the consultative opinion given by the Court that opinion can be questioned by legal proceedings up to the House of Lords on the ground of error of law appearing on the face of the award." See also *May* v. *Mills* (1914) 30 T.L.R. 287.
5. *Supra*.
6. *Supra*, p. 617. See also *Ex parte Dowes* (1886) 17 Q.B.D. 275; *Ex parte County Council of Kent* [1891] 1 Q.B. 725.

vives into the interpretation of section 2. In *The Constanza M* Lloyd J. observed in general and approving terms[7]: "ever since the decision of the Court of Appeal in *In re an Arbitration between Knight and The Tabernacle Permanent Building Society*, it has been held that the opinion of a court on a consultative case involves no order of any kind." In the *Oltenia*[8] Donaldson L.J. did not consider that a section 2 decision was *res judicata*. In the upshot it would appear that the decision of the Court of Appeal in *In re an Arbitration between Knight and The Tabernacle Permanent Building Society*[9] continues to hold sway. In consequence a "determination" under section 2 is not equivalent to a judgment or order, but more analogous to a declaratory judgment. There is no *res judicata* and the fact that an arbitrator has acted on the guidance provided under a section 2 application does not of itself preclude an appeal under section 1(2), but it may nonetheless be a fact relevant to the exercise of judicial discretion under section 1(3)(b).[10]

12.7.3 Duty of arbitrator or umpire to obey the judicial determination

12.7.3.1 This issue raises something of a problem because the 1979 Act is silent on the point and also because of the legal character of a determination of the High Court under section 2.[1] A determination under section 2 being probably only in the nature of a consultative opinion and therefore capable of being the subject of review on an appeal from an award, it might be considered that an arbitrator or umpire is free to follow or reject the judicial opinion expressed on an application. But considering the question in a pragmatic light there is something almost absurd in establishing a statutory consultative case procedure which may be adopted by the parties to a reference and yet with the arbitrator or umpire at the termination of the exercise free to disregard the opinion of the court.

12.7.3.2 The question here addressed has not come four square before the courts but the preponderance of judicial *dicta* appear to incline to the opinion that an arbitrator or umpire is under some manner of duty to follow a determination given by the court and that an arbitrator or umpire who departs from this duty may be guilty of misconduct. Lord Esher M.R. observed, "no doubt they [i.e. arbitrators] are bound to follow" the determination of the court.[2] Bowen L.J. considered that the opinion of the court "only binds the arbitrator in honesty and morals to act upon the law as the Court states it" and that "it might be a ground for impeaching his award on the ground of misconduct if he did not".[3] Cloveridge J. refused to venture beyond the opinion that the arbitrator "might" be bound by the opinion of the court.[4] In a dictum of more recent origin Diplock L.J. was of the opinion that the answer of the High Court to a question of law arising in the course of a reference and stated in a special case "is

7. [1980] 1 Lloyd's Rep. 505, 519.
8. *Babanaft International Co. S.A.* v. *Avant Petroleum Inc. (The Oltenia)* [1982] 2 Lloyd's Rep. 99, 106–107.
9. *Supra.*
10. See Chapter 6, para. 6.2.12.
1. Considered *supra*, para. 12.7.2.
2. *In re an Arbitration between Knight and The Tabernacle Permanent Building Society* [1891] 2 Q.B. 63, 68.
3. *Ibid.* [1893] 2 Q.B. 613, 619.
4. *May* v. *Mills* (1914) 30 T.L.R. 287.

binding upon the arbitrator, at any rate in the sense that it would be misconduct on his part to make an award which conflicted with it".[5]

12.7.3.3 These dicta are both individually and collectively uncertain and inconclusive. The general sense to be deduced from them appears to be that the responsible instinct of an arbitrator or umpire should be to accept and follow the judicial opinion laid down. To this extent it is probably possible to speak of an arbitrator being under a *prima facie* duty to adopt the opinion of the court. But beyond this there does not exist an absolute duty to do so. The recognition of an absolute duty would probably be inconsistent with the nature of the consultative case procedure and the factual basis on which that procedure often operates. If the judicial opinion is capable of being overturned on appeal, it is clearly difficult to demand blind allegiance to that opinion by the arbitrator. It is also possible, in the future course of a reference, for the determination of the court to become irrelevant or for the factual basis on which the judicial opinion was given to be disturbed by subsequent findings of fact. For these kinds of reasons it would seem desirable that an arbitrator possess a residual right to ignore the determination of the court, although in the nature of things this is a right which will be exercised only in exceptional circumstances. A possible summary of the position is to assert that an arbitrator is under a duty to follow the opinion expressed by the court on a consultative case unless on the facts and circumstances of any particular case there arise compelling reasons for not doing so. In the absence of any compelling reason, an arbitrator who refuses or fails to adopt the judicial opinion is probably guilty of misconduct.

12.8 EXCLUSION AGREEMENTS

No application may be made under section 2 for the determination of a preliminary question of law when there is in existence a valid exclusion agreement and all the parties to the reference refuse to consent to an application under section 2 being made.

Section 2(1) is expressly declared to be subject to section 3 which lays down the basis of a valid exclusion agreement. Section 3(1)(c) is to the effect that where the parties to a reference have entered into an exclusion agreement in relation to an award and with regard to which the determination of a question of law is material, no application may be made under section 2(1)(a) with respect to that question of law. Unfortunately the drafting of section 3(1) is particularly abstruse and raises difficulties concerning the precise way an exclusion agreement intending to apply to the right arising under section 2 should be drafted. The ambiguity also produces difficulties with regard to the proper construction of exclusion agreements.[1]

Notwithstanding the existence of a valid exclusion agreement it is open to all the parties to a reference to consent to an application for leave to apply under section 2(1)(b) and thereby waive the effect of an exclusion agreement. Exclusion agreements apply only to applications made under section 2(1)(a) and do not extend to applications made under section 2(1)(b).

Exclusion agreements are considered in greater detail in Chapter 13.

5. *Fidelitas Shipping Co. Ltd.* v. *V/O Exportchleb* [1966] 1 Q.B. 630, 645.
1. These issues are developed in Chapter 13.

12.9 ON-APPEALS UNDER SECTION 2

12.9.1 Introduction

It has been observed that there are two separate decisions which the High Court is obliged to make under section 2. There is the preliminary question whether to give or refuse leave to apply under the section: and if leave is granted, there follows the determination of the substantive question of law by the High Court. From each decision there is an appeal to the Court of Appeal, but in each case the terms on which an appeal may be pursued are strictly regulated by section 2.

On-appeals to the Court of Appeal from giving or refusing leave to apply are governed by section 2(2A); and on-appeals to the Court of Appeal from the determination by the High Court of a substantive question of law by section 2(3). It is again the clear policy of the 1979 Act that the two categories of decision that arise under section 2 shall repose substantially with the first tier judges and only in exceptional circumstances will on-appeals be permitted.[1]

There is the possiblity of a further appeal from the Court of Appeal to the House of Lords but this appellate link is not governed by the 1979 Act[2]. It will be exceptionally rare for a decision giving or refusing leave to apply to climb the hierarchy of courts to the House of Lords, and it is only likely to occur when a question of fundamental importance arises in connection with the principles governing the exercise of the discretion. Appeals from substantive determinations are more likely, although the occasions when they will ascend all the way to the House of Lords will again be rare.

12.9.2 On-appeals to the Court of Appeal from giving or refusing leave to apply

12.9.2.1 An appeal to the Court of Appeal from the decision of a first tier judge giving or refusing leave to make an application under section 2(1) is governed by the terms of section 2(2A), which provides: "Unless the High Court gives leave, no appeal shall lie to the Court of Appeal from a decision of the High Court to entertain or not to entertain an application under subsection 1(a) above." The subsection was inserted into section 2 by the Supreme Court Act 1981, section 148(3), and serves to infill a lacuna that existed in the 1979 Act as originally drafted. In its initial format the 1979 Act placed no express restriction on an appeal and in consequence an appeal probably could be brought as of right,[1] which represented a circumstance contrary to the policy of the 1979 Act. The new section 2(2A) is analogous in its origin and purpose to section 1(6A) and the earlier commentary in relation to section 1(6A) in Chapter 10 would seem to be equally applicable to section 2(2A).[2]

Under section 2(2A) there is no appeal to the Court of Appeal except with the leave of the first tier judge. The Court of Appeal has no jurisdiction to give leave to appeal, as is the case under section 2(3)(a). Nor is there, apart from section 2(2A), any appeal to the Court of Appeal from the grant or refusal of leave to apply by the High Court.

1. See Chapter 1, para. 1.2.1.6.   2. *Ibid.*
1. Cf. *Pioneer Shipping Ltd.* v. *B.T.P. Tioxide Ltd. (The Nema)* [1980] Q.B. 547 (C.A.); *Italmare Shipping Co.* v. *Ocean Tanker Co. Inc. (The Rio Sun)* [1982] 1 W.L.R. 158 (C.A.).
2. See Chapter 10, para. 10.2.

In the result where a first tier judge refuses leave to appeal then that is an end of the matter provided the refusal amounts to a "decision" in the eyes of the law.[3]

12.9.2.2 The decision whether to give or refuse leave to appeal to the Court of Appeal under section 2(2A) is one which falls within the discretion of the first tier judge who hears the application for leave to apply. The basis on which the discretion is to operate has not been so fully considered as the discretion associated with section 1(6A) of the 1979 Act and is for this reason more speculative. Nonetheless, section 2(2A) and section 1(6A) are analogous statutory provisions and the approach taken by Lord Diplock in *The Antaios*[4] to the exercise of the discretion under section 1(6A) probably provides a firm guideline to the likely judicial approach to the exercise of the discretion under section 2(2A). This approach, necessarily qualified to accommodate the less well developed body of judicial law relating to the exercise of the discretion on an application for leave to apply under section 2(1), would appear to suggest that a first tier judge should not give leave to appeal to the Court of Appeal under section 2(2A) unless there is in issue the proper basis for the exercise of the discretion on an application for leave to apply under section 2(1) or there is, in the opinion of the first tier judge, a need to amplify, elucidate or adapt to changing practices an adopted and existing criterion or criteria for the exercise of the discretion laid down by an appellate court.

12.9.2.3 It is to be noted that the restriction in section 2(2A) applies only to an application for leave to apply which comes within the terms of section 2(1)(a). In the result where an application for leave to apply is made with the consent of all the other parties and is therefore within section 2(1)(b) an appeal to the Court of Appeal from the giving or refusal of leave to apply may be made as of right. This is indeed curious and possibly unintentional. Section 2(2A) appears to be drafted on the assumption that no application for leave to apply is necessary when an application is made with the consent of all the other parties. As observed earlier this is not the case: the judicial discretion arises whether an application is within paragraph (a) or (b) of section 2(1).[4a] The drafting of section 2(2A) follows that of section 1(6A) but in the latter the specific reference to section 1(3)(b) is understandable for where the parties consent to an appeal within the terms of section 1(3)(a) they are entitled to their appeal and the court has no discretion in the matter.[5]

Beyond the points made above, the same kind of issues that have arisen in connection with section 1(6A) may equally arise with regard to section 2(2A), and the earlier commentary on section 1(6A) would appear equally relevant to section 2(2A).[6] So also the role of the Court of Appeal, when leave to appeal is given, in reviewing the exercise of discretion by a first tier judge in giving or refusing leave to apply under section 2(1) follows general principle and the earlier commentary is again equally relevant.[7]

---

3. *Aden Refinery Co. Ltd.* v. *Ugland Management Co. (The Ugland Obo One)* [1987] 1 Q.B. 650, 666, per Mustill L.J. The point made in the text is further considered in Chapter 10, para. 10.2.3.4.
4. [1985] A.C. 191, 205. See further Chapter 10, para. 10.2.
4a. *Supra*, para. 12.6.1.2.
5. See Chapter 4, para. 4.2.
6. *Supra* n. 2.
7. *Supra* n. 2.

12.9.3 On-appeals to the Court of Appeal from the determinations of preliminary points of law by the High Court

12.9.3.1 On-appeals to the Court of Appeal from the determinations of preliminary points of law by first tier judges under section 2(1) are governed by section 2(3),[1] which provides:

A decision of the High Court under sub-section (1) above shall be deemed to be a judgment of the court within the meaning of section 16 of the Supreme Court Act 1981 (appeals to the Court of Appeal), but no appeal shall lie from such a decision unless—

    (a) the High Court or the Court of Appeal gives leave; and

    (b) it is certified by the High Court that the question of law to which its decision relates either is one of general public importance or is one which for some other special reason should be considered by the Court of Appeal.

12.9.3.2 By virtue of the opening paragraph of subsection (3) a judicial determination under section 2(1) is deemed to be a judgment of the High Court within the meaning of section 16 of the Supreme Court Act 1981 and is therefore *prima facie* appealable to the Court of Appeal.[2] Statutory provision to this effect was first introduced by section 9 of the Arbitration Act 1934, giving effect to a recommendation of the Mackinnon Committee Report 1927.[3] Its effect was to counter the interpretation given by the Court of Appeal in *In re an Arbitration between Knight and Tabernacle Permanent Building Society*[4] to the initial statutory formulation of the consultative case procedure in section 19 of the Arbitration Act 1889, which was to the effect that a judicial opinion expressed thereunder was not a judgment or order within the meaning of the then relevant statutory provision, namely section 19 of the Judicature Act 1873, and in consequence there existed no on-appeal to the Court of Appeal from the opinion of a judge on a consultative case. Given the legal effect of a judicial opinion on a consultative case,[5] the Court of Appeal was also of the firm opinion that it was desirable that no right of appeal should exist.[6] The MacKinnon Committee saw the question of policy in a different light and notwithstanding the potential risks considered that a qualified right of appeal should exist.[7]

12.9.3.3 But although there is now established an appeal, the right of appeal is severely restricted. It is again the clear policy of the 1979 Act that as a general rule the section 2 procedure should come to a conclusion with the determination of the first tier judge. Only in exceptional circumstances is a preliminary question of law to be permitted to progress upward to the Court of Appeal, and even less rarely to progress further to the House of Lords. The arbitral process must not be exposed to unnecessary

---

1. As amended by the Supreme Court Act 1981, s. 148(3) and Sch. 5.
2. The Supreme Court Act 1981, s. 16(1), provides: "Subject as otherwise provided by this or any other Act (and in particular to the provision in section 13(2)(a) of the Administration of Justice Act 1969 excluding appeals to the Court of Appeal in cases where leave to appeal from the High Court directly to the House of Lords is granted under Part II of that Act), the Court of Appeal shall have jurisdiction to hear and determine appeals from any judgment or order of the High Court."
3. Cmd. 2817, paras. 8–11.
4. [1892] 2 Q.B. 613 (C.A.).
5. *Supra*, para. 12.7.2.
6. *Supra*, pp. 617–618 per Lord Esher M.R., "It seems to me that it would be most inexpedient that, where an opinion is given by the Court under this statute in the course of a reference for the guidance of arbitrators, there should be an appeal which might be carried up to the House of Lords."
7. *Supra*, n. 3.

interruptions. Sir John Donaldson M.R. has indicated the general policy to on-appeals in the following terms[8]:

It is [i.e. the section 2 procedure] a speedy procedure designed to interrupt the arbitration to the minimum possible extent and it is an exception to the general rule that the courts do not intervene in the course of an arbitration. If, other than in wholly exceptional cases, it were used to obtain definitive decisions from this court [i.e. the Court of Appeal] or even the House of Lords, it would create unaccceptable interruptions in the conduct of arbitrations.

12.9.3.4 By the terms of section 2(3) no appeal shall lie from the decision of the High Court under section 2 to the Court of Appeal unless (i) the High Court or Court of Appeal gives leave; and (ii) the High Court certifies that the preliminary point of law in issue is one of general public importance or there is some other special reason why the question of law should be considered by the Court of Appeal. From the decision of the High Court refusing leave or refusing to give a certificate there is no appeal to the Court of Appeal.[9] Provided the High Court has come to a valid "decision" there exists no jurisdiction to review the exercise of judicial discretion.[10] In laying down these cumulative preconditions section 2(3) mirrors the provisions set out in section 1(7) and the earlier commentary in the text on section 1(7) would appear to be of equal application to section 2(3),[11] subject to the particular observations that hereafter follow.[12]

12.9.3.5 The operation of section 2(3) has to date only arisen for consideration in a single case *The Oltenia*.[13] With the consent of the parties an application was made under section 2(1) to determine as a preliminary question of law whether the claim by disponent owners against charterers was on a proper construction of the charterparty time-barred. The charterparty was on the Asbatankvoy form and the time-bar requirement took the form of a typed special provision. After giving his opinion on the preliminary point of law Bingham J. gave a certificate under section 2(3)(b) but refused to give leave under section 2(3)(a). Leave was refused because the judge was in no doubt as to the answer to the question of law presented for determination. Bingham J. expressed his reasons for giving a certificate in the following terms[14]:

Although the clause is a one-off clause it is a variant of a clause that one sees not all that infrequently and I think that by analogy my decision on the clause could be relied on in the context of other clauses. Moreover, it could very well be that my decision on the clause would affect the use of such a clause. Those are both, in my judgment, reasons why it would be proper for the matter to be considered by the Court of Appeal, if they wish to do so. I further think that in

---

8. *Babanaft International Co. S.A.* v. *Avant Petroleum Inc. (The Oltenia)* [1982] 2 Lloyd's Rep. 99, 106 (C.A.).

9. See Chapter 10, para. 10.3 *et seq.*

10. Cf. *Aden Refinery Co. Ltd.* v. *Ugland Management Co. Ltd. (The Ugland Obo One)* [1987] 1 Q.B. 650, 666, per Mustill L.J. See also *Babanaft International Co. S.A.* v. *Avant Petroleum Inc. (The Oltenia)* [1982] 2 Lloyd's Rep. 99, 105, where Donaldson L.J. comments the "learned Judge's certificate cannot be questioned".

11. See Chapter 10, para. 10.3.

12. Contrast the former law in s. 21(3) of the Arbitration Act 1950 and whereunder an on-appeal was conditional on the giving of leave by either the High Court or the Court of Appeal, but with no further requirement of a certificate of the High Court. See also *Compania Comercial Y Naviera San Martin S.A.* v. *China National Foreign Trade Transportation Corp. (The Constanza M)* [1980] 1 Lloyd's Rep. 505.

13. *Babanaft International Co. S.A.* v. *Avant Petroleum Inc. (The Oltenia)* [1982] 1 Lloyd's Rep. 448. Considered by the Court of Appeal in *Geogas S.A.* v. *Trammo Gas Ltd. (The Baleares)* [1991] 2 All E.R. 110.

14. *Ibid.* p. 456.

respect of a large claim such as the present there could be ramifications as between the owners and their advisers and it would be unsatisfactory if that had to be resolved on the basis of any uncertainty as to what the correct law was. I shall accordingly certify in respect of the notice of motion under s.2(1)(b), according to s.2(3)(b), but I shall not, in respect of . . . the notice of motion . . . give leave. The effect therefore is that the owners are not shut out from going to the Court of Appeal but they are obliged to seek the leave of the Court of Appeal. My reason for refusing leave is that I would not wish it to be thought that there was any doubt in my mind as to the answer . . . on the motion . . .

12.9.3.6 The effect of Bingham J.'s decision was to compel the disponent owners, if they wished to take the matter further, to seek leave of the Court of Appeal. This they did and it was refused.[15] Although the Court of Appeal was of the opinion that it was a proper case for leave to be given to apply for a determination under section 2(1), the Court was equally of the opinion that it was not a proper case for leave to be given to appeal to the Court of Appeal under section 2(3). The Court of Appeal also commented on the certificate granted by Bingham J. and expressed suprise that the size of the claim and the possibility of future ramifications between the disponent owners and their advisers were considered as being capable of elevating the question to one of general public importance.[16] Of greater significance the Court of Appeal also took the opportunity to give an indication of the way the court should approach applications for leave to appeal under section 2(3)(a). From the leading judgment of Donaldson L.J.[17] (as he then was) the following principles would appear capable of being deduced.

12.9.3.7 In keeping with the policy of the 1979 Act, leave to appeal under section 2(3) should only be given in exceptional circumstances. Donaldson L.J. considered such an exceptional case to arise "where the preliminary question of law, if rightly decided, determines the whole dispute between the parties. In such a case, the application for leave to appeal should no doubt be considered as if it were one under s.1."[18] Donaldson L.J. also recognised that there might be other exceptional circumstances, but refrained from offering examples.

The fact that a judicial determination under section 2(1) is not *res judicata* represents an additional reason for refraining from allowing a section 2(1) determination to be appealed save in exceptional circumstances.[19]

12.9.3.8 With regard to substantive appeals from the High Court to the Court of Appeal the same preconditions apply to both sections 1 and 2, by virtue of section 1(7) and section 2(3). But this does not mean that the Court of Appeal takes the same attitude to applications for leave to appeal under both section 1(7) and section 2(3). By virtue of the manner in which the consent of the parties differs under sections 1 and 2 there is reason for saying that leave to appeal should be less readily given under section 2(3) than section 1(7). Under section 1(3)(a) where the parties consent they can have their appeal. In contrast, the consent of the parties under section 2(1)(b) does not mean that the court must decide to entertain an application. There remains the

---

15. [1982] 2 Lloyd's Rep. 99 (C.A.).
16. *Ibid.* p. 105. It was also mooted that Bingham J. may have considered these as "special reasons" why the legal question should be considered by the Court of Appeal. The Court of Appeal also conjectured that Bingham J. may have considered them to be make-weight factors.
17. Stephenson L.J. and Sir David Cairns concurring.
18. *Ibid.* p. 106.
19. *Ibid.* p. 107.

discretion of the court. From this comparison Donaldson L.J. deduced the following principle[20]:

But, in the light of the difference in the importance accorded to the agreement of the parties at the High Court stage, if there be any difference in the attitude of this court towards an application for leave to appeal under s.2 as compared with one to appeal under s.1, it must be that leave to appeal under the former is less readily given.

12.9.3.9 In determining whether to give leave to appeal the Court of Appeal's assessment of the correctness of the first tier judge's determination is of relevance. In this regard the Court of Appeal must ask itself similar questions (as distinct from the same questions) as the House of Lords has ruled a High Court judge must ask when considering an application for leave to appeal under section 1(3)(b).[21] In *The Oltenia* the point of law in question concerned the construction of a "one-off" clause in a contract and on the facts of the case it was far from apparent that the decision of the first tier judge was obviously wrong. To the contrary, it bore every indication of being right.[22]

The analogy with the *Nema/Antaios* guidelines further means that where it can be shown that the question put forward for determination under section 2 reveals a conflict or divergence of opinion between the High Court judges, then in the interest of uniformity and certainty leave to appeal should be given.[23]

The mere fact that the parties have consented to an application and which is therefore made under section 2(1)(b) is not in itself conclusive that leave to appeal to the Court of Appeal ought to be given. Donaldson L.J. expressed the view, "agreement to the High Court determining a question of law arising during the course of the reference is one thing. Agreeing to an appeal to the Court of Appeal from that determination is quite another . . . "[24] The distinction between the two is at its clearest when the application for leave to appeal to the Court of Appeal is contested by the other party to the arbitration.

12.9.3.10 The majority decision of the Court of Appeal in *The Baleares*[25] on the exercise of the discretion under section 1(7) has previously been considered.[26] That decision advocates a less restrictive approach to the question of on-appeals and suggests that leave to appeal should be given whenever the question of law in issue is worthy of consideration by the Court of Appeal. If this approach is in due course endorsed it seems very arguable, given the parallel between section 1(7) and section 2(3), that it will also represent the fundamental principle guiding the exercise of discretion under section 2(3). To this extent the approach of the Court of Appeal in *The Oltenia*[27] will be qualified. With regard to the latter, the majority in *The Baleares* considered Donaldson L.J. not to be laying down any statement of guiding principle, but merely to be expressing his reasons for deciding that case.[28]

20. *Ibid*. p. 106.
21. See Chapter 5.
22. *Ibid*. p. 106.
23. *Ibid*. p. 106.
24. *Ibid*. p. 106.
25. *Geogas S.A.* v. *Trammo Gas Ltd. (The Baleares)* [1991] 2 All E.R. 110 (C.A.).
26. Chapter 10, para. 10.3.4.12.
27. *Supra*.
28. Ralph Gibson L.J., p. 121; Leggatt L.J., p.127. Dillon L.J. dissenting.

12.9.3.11 Giving leave subject to conditions

Although not expressed in the language of section 2, it is probably the case that both the High Court and Court of Appeal may give leave to appeal subject to such conditions as the court in question considers appropriate and just in the circumstances of any particular case. The absence of any express power to impose conditions represents yet another parallel between section 2(3) and section 1(7), but under the latter the jurisdiction to impose conditions would appear to be accepted.[1] If this is the case, it would seem that a similar jurisdiction must arise under section 2(3) and that the kind of conditions that may be attached to leave granted under section 1(7) may equally be attached to leave granted under section 2(3).[2]

12.9.3.12 Role and jurisdiction of Court of Appeal

Following the giving of leave and a certificate, together with the satisfaction of any conditions imposed, the Court of Appeal proceeds to a consideration of the determination of the preliminary point of law by the first tier judge.

The appellate process will be in the nature of a review of the determination of the first tier judge, based on submissions, argument and documentary assessment.[1] The powers of the High Court on an appeal from an award as defined in section 1(2) are clearly not directly applicable to an appeal under section 2(3), but they are nonetheless indicative of the kind of appellate powers possessed by the Court of Appeal on an appeal under section 2(3). The Court of Appeal may confirm, vary or set aside the determination of the first tier judge and substitute its own determination of the question of law.[2]

The Court of Appeal will undoubtedly wish to review the determination of the first tier judge in the same factual context, taking into account not only the actual findings of fact of the arbitration tribunal but also any assumptions or agreements as to fact. On the appeal some variation of the assumptions or agreements as to fact may no doubt be allowed, but it may be anticipated that the Court of Appeal will be careful not to permit any variation that has the effect of causing a wholly new question of law to be placed before it and thereby work a change to its role, so that it ceases to be a body reviewing the determination of a first tier judge but an appellate body making a primary determination.

12.10 PRACTICE, PROCEDURE AND COSTS UNDER SECTION 2

12.10.1 General philosophy

The jurisdiction of the High Court under section 2(1) to determine preliminary questions of law arising in the course of a reference is an interventionist jurisdiction which

---

1. See Chapter 10, para. 10.3.5.
2. *Ibid.* See also *D/S A/S Idaho* v. *Peninsular and Oriental Steam Navigation Co. (The Strathnewton)* [1982] 2 Lloyd's Rep. 296, 303, for comment on the conditions capable of being imposed under the now repealed Arbitration Act 1950, section 21(3).
1. See, for example, *Exercise Shipping Co. Ltd.* v. *Bay Maritime Lines Ltd. (The Fantasy)* [1992] 1 Lloyd's Rep. 235 (C.A.).
2. See also the Supreme Court Act 1981, section 15(3).

interrupts the progress of the arbitration. As such it is an exception to the general rule that the courts will not intervene in the arbitral process. But when invoked it is a jurisdiction which must be implemented speedily and responded to expeditiously by the courts so that the interruption is limited to the minimum possible extent. The same philosophy prevails with regard to an appeal to the Court of Appeal from the determination of a first tier judge under section 2(3).[1]

12.10.2 Application for a section 2 determination

12.10.2.1 Originating motion to single judge

An application to the High Court under section 2(1) of the 1979 Act to determine a question of law arising in the course of a reference is made by originating motion to a single judge in court.[1] Judge in this context alludes to a Commercial Court judge, unless any such judge otherwise directs.[2] The application is made in open court and not in chambers.

12.10.2.2 Time limit

An application must be made, and notice thereof served, within 14 days after the arbitrator or umpire has consented to the application being made, or the other parties have so consented.[3] Any specified consent must probably be in writing[4] and the time at which consent is given being a question of fact. The 14-day period begins to run from the day next following the giving of consent[4a] and includes the whole of the fourteenth day.[4b]

12.10.2.3 Form and content of originating motion

12.10.2.3.1 The general provisions relating to originating motions are set out in R.S.C. Order 8 and the prevailing form of originating motion is to be found in the *Supreme Court Practice* (1993), Appendix A, Form 13, Vol. 2, Part. 2.[4c]

With regard to an application under section 2(1) the notice of originating motion must state the grounds of the application. Where an application is founded on evidence by affidavit or is made with the consent of an arbitrator or umpire or of the other parties, a copy of every affidavit intended to be used or, as the case may be, of every consent given in writing must be served with that notice.[5]

The Rules of the Supreme Court do not specify the precise manner in which a section 2 application is to be made. Under the former procedure the form of a consultative case became standardised and well understood, and when properly executed was

---

1. *Babanaft International Co. S.A.* v. *Avant Petroleum Inc. (The Oltenia)* [1982] 2 Lloyd's Rep. 99, 106, per Donaldson L.J.
   1. R.S.C. Order 73, r. 2(1)(e).
   2. R.S.C. Order 73, r. 6(1). See also Chapter 7, para. 7.2.1.1.
   3. R.S.C. Order 73, r. 5(3).
   4. R.S.C. Order 73, r. 5(4). This particular rule refers to preceding paragraph (2). This would seem an error, with the true intention being to refer to preceding paragraph (3).
   4a. R.S.C. Order 3, r. 2(2).
   4b. Cf. *Manorlike Ltd.* v. *Le Vitas Travel Agency and Consultative Services Ltd.* [1986] 1 All E.R. 573 (C.A.).
   4c. See Appendix J(4) for a suggested precedent.
   5. R.S.C. Order 73, r. 5(5).

an effective document for bringing the question of law and associated facts and contentions to the attention of the court.[6] The technical changes introduced by section 2 and the drift away from formalism which was witnessed in the discussion of reasoned awards in Chapter 11[7] probably mean that it is unlikely that the judges will insist that the former practice associated with the consultative case is to be perpetuated.

12.10.2.3.2 In the circumstances the most obvious form of procedure is for the applicant to swear an affidavit bringing the question of law and surrounding considerations, to the extent they are available, to the attention of the court. Acting within the same general philosophy as is applicable to reasoned awards, the affidavit should specify the question of law clearly and succinctly; the assertions and contentions of the parties, to the extent they are known; and the facts appertaining to the disputed legal question, again to the extent they are known and have been found by the arbitrator or umpire, or are otherwise agreed or to be assumed for the purpose of the application.

Where an application is made with the consent of an arbitrator or umpire who has entered on the reference then it is open for an affidavit in the same form as that considered above to be sworn by the arbitrator or umpire.

12.10.2.4 Service of originating motion out of jurisdiction

12.10.2.4.1 A notice of originating motion under the Arbitration Act 1979 and any order made on the motion may with leave of the court be served out of jurisdiction provided that the arbitration to which the motion or order relates is governed by English law or has been, is being, or is to be held, within the jurisdiction.[8] An application for the grant of leave must be supported by an affidavit stating the grounds on which the application is made and showing in what place or country the person to be served is or probably may be found; and no leave shall be granted unless it is made sufficiently to appear to the court that the case is a proper one for service out of the jurisdiction.[9]

The jurisdiction to give leave to serve a notice of originating motion out of jurisdiction extends on the general jurisdiction of the court under Order 11 to permit service out of jurisdiction. The practice is the same in all respects as under Order 11 and Order 11, rules 5, 6 and 8 are made expressly applicable by Order 73, rule 7(3).

12.10.2.4.2 The question of leave falls to be determined within the discretion of the court which must be satisfied that "the case is a proper one for service out of jurisdiction".[10] The jurisdiction is preconditioned, it would seem, by the need to establish that English law is the curial law of the arbitration. Order 73, rule 7(1) appears to assume that an arbitration with its seat within England and Wales is in matters of procedure always governed by English law and also that the curial law of an arbitration with a foreign seat may equally be English law. Neither assumption may be firmly subscribed to at the present time for the concept of the curial law of arbitration is in an uncertain and indeterminate state. The concept of the curial law of arbitration is considered

---

6. See, for example, the consultative case stated in *Montedison S.p.A.* v. *Icroma S.p.A. (The Caspian Sea)* [1980] 1 Lloyd's Rep. 91.
7. Para. 11.6.3.
8. R.S.C. Order 73, r. 7(1).
9. R.S.C. Order 73, r. 7(2).
10. R.S.C. order 73, r. 7(2).

elsewhere in the text and the language of Order 73, r. 7(1), must ultimately be considered in the context of that discussion.[11]

12.10.2.4.3 The approach of the judiciary to the exercise of the discretion under Order 73, r. 7, has been considered elsewhere in the text and that commentary is equally applicable to the present context.[12]

12.10.3 The question of jurisdiction under section 2(2)

Where an application is made under section 2(1)(a), with the consent solely of an arbitrator or umpire who has entered on the reference, the High Court shall not entertain an application unless it is satisfied that the conditions specified in paragraphs (a) and (b) of section 2(2) are satisfied. Where the application is made under section 2(1)(b), with the consent of all the other parties, section 2(2) has no application.[1]

The question remains how the court is to satisfy itself on the question of jurisdiction when an applicant has the consent of an arbitrator or umpire but lacks the consent of all the other parties. Both the 1979 Act and the Rules of Court are silent on the point. Yet it is clear that the court must satisfy itself at some stage as to the matters set out in section 2(2), for otherwise it has no jurisdiction to determine an application. In *Gebr. Broere B.V.* v. *Saras Chimica S.p.A.*[2] Parker J. considered that the question of jurisdiction should be included in the summons to fix a date for the hearing of argument on the main application and that no date will be fixed for such hearing unless and until the court is satisfied that the requirements of section 2(2) are fulfilled. Where, however, all the parties consent to an application, a date may be arranged without the necessity of any summons.

12.10.4 Application for leave to apply distinct from a determination of the question of law

12.10.4.1 There are two applications made under section 2. The first is for leave to apply and, if granted, the second is for a determination of the question of law that has arisen in the course of the reference.[1] The two are quite distinct and yet somewhat remarkably no recognition of the preliminary application for leave to apply is made in the Rules of Court. This suggests that as a matter of practice the two are merged, with the same time limits applying and with the application made subject to the necessary leave being obtained. The upshot of this practice is that the application for leave to apply is made to a judge in open court, which appears an excessively formal and not necessarily efficient way to determine what is a preliminary issue.[2]

12.10.4.2 The application for leave is in its nature a summary and expeditious proceeding, with the sole question before the court being whether or not to give leave to apply. It is not the occasion for full argument on the merits of the question of law, which is deferred to the hearing of the full application. The manner in which the dis-

---

11. See Chapter 1, para. 1.7.8.
12. See Chapter 7, para. 7.2.5.
1. *Supra*, paras. 12.4.3 and 12.5.1.2.
2. [1982] 2 Lloyd's Rep. 436, 440.
1. Considered *supra*, para. 12.6.1.
2. Contrast an application for leave to appeal under section 1(3)(b) which is now made to a judge in chambers: see Chapter 7, para. 7.2.1.

cretion is exercised has been considered earlier in the text.[3] Moreover the court has come to insist that in the absence of exceptional circumstances the application for leave to apply and the full application on the merits shall take place at two distinct hearings. In other words, as a general rule the court will not proceed immediately to determine the question of law following the giving of leave to apply. To this extent there is a correspondence with the practice followed under section 1 appeals.[4] Lloyd J. has explained the practice to be followed under section 2 in the following terms[5]:

At the conclusion of the application under s.2, it was obviously expected of me by the parties that I would go on to determine the questions of law there and then. I decided to do so having regard to the urgency of the matter. But I would echo in this case what was said by Mr. Justice Bingham in *The T.F.L. Prosperity*, [1982] 1 Lloyd's Rep. 617. Normally, the court will not determine questions of law under s.2(1)(a) immediately after a successful application, any more than it will hear an appeal under s.1. It is important that applications, whether under s.1 or s.2(1)(a), should be dealt with expeditiously, and should not become full dress hearings as they would if the application normally led straight on to the appeal.

12.10.4.3 As for the giving of reasons on an application for leave, the practice probably follows that which has evolved about appeals under section 1.[6] If this is the case, in the normal situation it will be sufficient for the judge to say that he gives or refuses leave to apply. No further reasons will be necessary unless warranted by the circumstances of any particular case. Reasons will only be obligatory when in giving or refusing leave to apply under section 2(1) the judge is also minded to give leave to appeal to the Court of Appeal under section 2(2A) from his decision.[7]

On an appeal under section 2(2A) the practice of the Court of Appeal, subject to its special role of reconsidering the criteria which are to appertain in determining an application for leave to apply, will in all probability mirror that developed by the High Court. In other words the Court of Appeal is likely to emphasise the summary character of the application and that the central object is not to determine the merits of the question of law in issue but to decide the narrower question whether leave to apply ought to be granted or refused. The Court of Appeal is also likely to insist, when leave to appeal is given under section 2(2A), that the appeal must be actively pursued.[8]

12.10.5 Application to Court of Appeal for leave to appeal under section 2(3)

12.10.5.1 Where a first tier judge certifies under section 2(3)(b) but refuses to give leave to appeal under section 2(3)(a) an applicant is not shut out. An appeal continues to be possible provided the Court of Appeal can be persuaded to give leave to appeal.[1]

In *The Oltenia*[2] the Court of Appeal considered the practice to be followed in seeking leave of the Court of Appeal under section 2(3)(a). The application for leave is quite separate from the appeal itself and will normally assume the form of a distinct preliminary hearing. Only in exceptional circumstances will it be justifiable for the full

3. *Supra*, para. 12.6.1.
4. Chapter 7, para. 7.3 and Chapter 9, para. 9.2.
5. *The Vasso* [1983] 2 Lloyd's Rep. 346, 348–349.
6. Chapter 7, para. 7.3.3.
7. *Ibid.*
8. Cf. *Babanaft International Co. S.A. v. Avant Petroleum Inc. (The Oltenia)* [1982] 2 Lloyd's Rep. 99.
1. Cf. *Geogas S.A. v. Trammo Gas Ltd. (The Baleares)* [1991] 2 All E.R. 110 (C.A.).
2. *Babanaft International Co. S.A. v. Avant Petroleum Inc. (The Oltenia)* [1982] 2 Lloyd's Rep. 99.

appeal to be listed to follow the application for leave. The application for leave is also to be heard expeditiously. On the facts of *The Oltenia* the application for leave to appeal was heard three months after the determination of the first tier judge and this was considered "much too long an interruption of a commercial arbitration".[3]

12.10.5.2 On an application for leave to appeal it is wholly inappropriate to allow prolonged adversarial argument. The Court of Appeal will read the judgment of the first tier judge and the skeleton arguments before hearing the application. The role of counsel for the applicant is to show good reason why leave to appeal to the Court of Appeal should be given and not to argue the merits of the appeal. To this end the Court of Appeal will permit preliminary argument on the correctness or wrongness of the determination of the first tier judge, or other argument directed to establishing that the case is one which should be taken on appeal by the Court of Appeal, irrespective of whether the first tier judge was right or wrong. Ultimately the Court of Appeal has to respond to the application by asking similar questions to those which the House of Lords has ruled should be asked by High Court judges in considering applications for leave to appeal under section 1(3)(b).[4]

12.10.5.3 An application for leave to appeal will in the first place be considered by a single judge of the Court of Appeal on the papers alone. If leave is refused the applicant has a right to initiate a renewed application before another judge of the Court of Appeal, which will be heard in open court and decided after hearing submissions and argument. Where the application raises a question of importance touching on the proper criteria to be borne in mind in considering an application for leave, it is probable that the application will be referred to a full Court of Appeal.[5]

12.10.6 Costs

The costs of an application are within the discretion of the judge who determines the preliminary point of law. The question of costs may be determined on the application, in which case the *prima facie* rule is that costs follow the event,[1] or they may be declared as costs of the arbitration and so left to be dealt with by the arbitration tribunal or umpire in an award.[2] Prior to making a final or interim award it is improbable that an arbitration tribunal or umpire can make any order as to costs for in its nature a consultative case under section 2 is not incorporated into or otherwise an aspect of an award.

12.11 ALTERNATIVE PROCEDURES TO SECTION 2

The section 2 procedure is but one mode of process by which a preliminary point of law may be determined during the course of a reference. The same or at least a similar

---

3. *Ibid.* p. 107 per Donaldson L.J.

4. *Ibid.* pp. 105–107 per Donaldson L.J. Contrast the majority view in *Geogas S.A.* v. *Trammo Gas Ltd. (The Baleares)*, [1991] 2 All E.R. 110 (C.A), considered *supra*, para. 12.9.3.10.

5. Cf. *Geogas S.A.* v. *Trammo Gas Ltd. (The Baleares)*, *ibid.* per Dillon L.J. See R.S.C. Ord. 59, r. 14.

1. Cf. *A/B Gotaverken* v. *Westminster Corporation of Monrovia* [1971] 2 Lloyd's Rep. 505, 515; *Montedison S.p.A.* v. *Icroma S.p.A. (The Caspian Sea)* [1980] 1 Lloyd's Rep. 91, 93; *D/S A/S Idaho* v. *Peninsular and Oriental Steam Navigation Co. (The Strathnewton)* [1982] 2 Lloyd's Rep. 296, 303.

2. *Ibid.*

result may be achieved by an appeal from an interim award, by seeking declaratory relief or by other procedures not involving any application to the courts of law. The variety of available procedures is fortuitous having regard to the potential shortcomings of the section 2 procedure, and their availability does mean that serious consideration may in each case be given to the precise mode of procedure best suited to serve individual circumstances. In practice it would appear that the section 2 procedure is little used, which was also the case under the former consultative case procedure, and this in itself is probably some evidence of the relative attractiveness of the available alternative procedures.

12.11.1 Appeals from interim awards

12.11.1.1 By the Arbitration Act 1950, section 14, in the absence of a contrary intention, every arbitration agreement is deemed to contain a provision empowering an arbitrator or umpire to make an interim award and that any reference in Part I of the 1950 Act to an award includes a reference to an interim award.[1] In consequence it was open for an interim award to be stated as a special case under section 21(1)(b) of the 1950 Act.[2] By virtue of section 7(1)(a) of the 1979 Act, section 14 of the 1950 Act is made equally applicable to the first six sections of the 1979 Act, with the consequence that any reference to an award in the 1979 Act again includes a reference to an interim award. An appeal under section 1(2) may therefore be brought with regard to any question of law arising out of a final or an interim award.[3]

12.11.1.2 Under the former special case procedure it was open for a preliminary question of law to be decided by an arbitrator in the form of an interim award and then stated as a special case under section 22(1)(b) of the Arbitration Act 1950. The procedure followed that generally applicable to special cases. The arbitrator found the relevant facts (if necessary) and then made his determination on the preliminary question of law. If appropriate an alternative award was made to meet the possible contingency of the court arriving at a different answer. Once the special case was answered by the court the arbitration was revived, and aided by the opinion of the court on the special case the arbitrator proceeded to consider and determine the outstanding issues.[4]

This alternative procedure for determining preliminary questions of law survives into the post-1979 Act law, although the procedural detail has changed. A preliminary question of law may be determined in the form of an interim award and then appealed under section 1(2).[5] But where all the other parties to the reference do not consent to

---

1. The section derives from ss. 7 and 21(3) of the Arbitration Act 1934.
2. See, for example, *Compagnie Tunisienne de Navigation S.A.* v. *Compagnie D'Armement Maritime S.A.* [1971] A.C. 573, 600.
3. See Chapter 3, para. 3.3.3.
4. *Supra*, n. 2.
5. For examples of this strategy being employed see *Pera Shipping Corpn.* v. *Petroship S.A. (The Pera)* [1984] 2 Lloyd's Rep. 363; *Minerals and Metals Trading Corpn. of India Ltd.* v. *Encounter Bay Shipping Co. Ltd. (The Samos Glory)* [1986] 2 Lloyd's Rep. 603; *The Transcontinental Underwriting Agency S.R.L.* v. *Grand Union Insurance Co. Ltd. and P.T. Reasuransi Umum Indonesia* [1987] 2 Lloyd's Rep. 409; *Dolphin Hellas Shipping S.A.* v. *Itemslot Ltd. (The Aegean Dolphin)* [1992] 2 Lloyd's Rep. 178.

an appeal, leave of the court must first be obtained under section 1(3)(b).[6] The exercise of judicial discretion on an application for leave to appeal in such a case will be governed by the same considerations of policy as apply generally and which were considered in detail in Chapters 5 and 6.[7]

12.11.1.3 The interim award procedure, although as a matter of practice it operates to produce a similar result as the section 2 procedure, is nonetheless a fundamentally different procedure. The differences are significant and may be enumerated as follows:

(a) Under the section 2 procedure an arbitrator does not decide a disputed question of law, although he may express an opinion as to the correct answer. A question of law is formulated by a party to the reference (sometimes with the assistance of the arbitrator or umpire) which is brought before the court so as to obtain the opinion of the court on the legal question in issue. In contrast, under the interim award procedure the arbitrator makes an actual determination of the question of law in issue which is then reviewed on an appeal to the High Court.

(b) It is probable that the opinion of the court under the section 2 procedure does not establish *res judicata* as to either fact or law. Nor is it in strictness absolutely binding on an arbitrator or umpire, although an arbitrator or umpire would have to show good reason for not following the opinion of the court and in the absence of such good reason the refusal to follow the judicial opinion would probably amount to misconduct.[8] In contrast the judgment of the High Court on an appeal from an interim award under section 1(2) is *res judicata*. Issues of fact and law cannot be reopened and the determination of the court is binding on the arbitrator or umpire.[9]

(c) The interim award procedure of necessity requires an award to be made. The section 2 procedure requires neither a decision from an arbitrator nor an award. All that is necessary is for a question of law to be formulated for determination by the High Court.[10] Further, whereas an interim award may attract an application for an order for reasons or further reasons under section 1(5) and (6), the concept of a reasoned award has no application to the section 2 procedure and equally section 1(5) and (6) has no application.[11]

(d) The interim award procedure is confined to a question of law arising out of an interim award made on an arbitration agreement in writing.[12] It is at least arguable that the section 2 procedure is not similarly restricted to questions of law arising out of a reference emanating from a written arbitration agree-

6. See, for example, *Filikos Shipping Corp. of Monrovia* v. *Shipmair B.V. (The Filikos)* [1981] 2 Lloyd's Rep. 555, where in the context of an indemnity claim by shipowners against charterers, the question whether the charterers could limit their liability on a proper construction of the charterparty was determined by the umpire as a preliminary issue in an interim award and then appealed with the consent of the parties. Contrast *Lief Hoegh & Co. A/S* v. *Petrolsea Inc. (The World Era) (No. 2)* [1993] 1 Lloyd's Rep. 363, where leave to appeal from an interim award was given, and where the question of law related to the right to withhold from inspection certain documents on the basis of "common interest privilege".

7. *The Vasso* [1983] 2 Lloyd's Rep. 346, 348. See, in particular, Chapter 6, para. 6.2.17.

8. See *supra*, paras. 12.7.2 and 12.7.3.

9. See, generally, Chapter 8.

10. See *supra*, paras. 12.4.4 and 12.10.2.3.

11. See Chapter 11 for an elaboration of "reasoned awards" and of section 1(5) and (6).

12. See, generally, Chapter 3.

ment. Section 2 makes no express reference to an arbitration agreement. It refers in the most general of terms to the High Court having jurisdiction to determine any question of law arising in the course of the reference. As such it is at least arguable that the section 2 procedure extends to oral arbitration agreements, although it has previously been suggested that this is an improbable interpretation.[13]

(e) An appeal from an interim award may be initiated by a party to a reference with the consent of all the other parties or with leave of the court.[14] The consent of an arbitrator or umpire is not required, nor the consent of the other parties, provided the court gives leave to appeal. Under the section 2 procedure the court has no direct involvement. An application for leave to apply may only be made with the consent of all the other parties or that of an arbitrator or umpire who has entered on the reference.[15]

(f) The interim award appeal procedure is not subject to any jurisdictional preconditions, save that leave to appeal is not to be given unless the question of law is substantial[15a] and the view the court takes of the basis on which it should exercise its discretion may substantially restrict the appellate process.[15b] In contrast, the jurisdiction of the court to determine an application for leave to apply under section 2(1)(a) is subject to the court being satisfied that the conditions specified in paragraphs (a) and (b) of section 2(2) appertain. Unless the court is so satisfied there is no jurisdiction.[16]

Notwithstanding these clear differences of substance and procedure between the interim award appeal procedure and the consultative case procedure under section 2, the two procedures in practice are capable of running in close parallel and are therefore not always easy to distinguish. As for the situation that prevailed pre-1979, this was due, at least in part, to the two procedures adopting similar documentary forms and to the emergence of what was styled an interim award in the form of a consultative case.[17]

12.11.1.4 Not only will the interim award appeal procedure produce the same result as the section 2 procedure but the foregoing discussion will have revealed that it will in many instances be a more effective and suitable procedure to adopt. In practice it appears to be adopted more frequently than the section 2 procedure. It has been suggested that the section 2 procedure is more appropriate "for use in a case where the question of law dominates the whole arbitration, not just a part of it, so that the arbitrator and the parties cannot sensibly approach the investigation of the facts without knowing, in the light of the answer to the question, what facts are really material."[18] And that the interim award procedure is more appropriate where "an

13. *Supra*, para. 12.2.4. See also Chapter 1, para. 1.7.5.
14. Section 1(3). See, generally, Chapter 4.
15. See *supra*, para. 12.4.2.
15a. See Chapter 4, para. 4.3.3.
15b. See Chapters 5 and 6.
16. See *supra*, para. 12.5.
17. See *supra*, para. 12.3.
18. Mustill and Boyd, *Commercial Arbitration* (2nd edn.), p. 621. See also, by way of example, *Exercise Shipping Co. Ltd.* v. *Bay Maritime Lines Ltd. (The Fantasy)* [1991] 2 Lloyd's Rep. 391, [1992] 1 Lloyd's Rep. 235 (C.A.); *Kuwait Maritime Transport Co.* v. *Rickmers Linie K.G. (The Danah)* [1993] 1 Lloyd's Rep. 351.

issue can be separated completely from the remainder of the dispute; where the facts can satisfactorily be investigated and decided without advance knowledge of the answer to the question of law; and where the decision of the Court has at least a reasonable prospect of concluding the dispute in favour of one party or the other".[18a]

The decision in *The Vasso*, considered earlier in the text,[19] also illustrates that where a preliminary question of law concerns the validity of an interlocutory order made by an arbitrator, the section 2 procedure may be particularly inappropriate and with the preconditions to jurisdiction specified in section 2(2) either impossible to assess or irrelevant. Such questions of law may therefore be better brought forward for judicial consideration as interim awards.

12.11.2 Declaratory relief

12.11.2.1 Another alternative mode of procedure is to seek a declaratory judgment with regard to a preliminary question of law.[1] Declaratory relief is a very flexible and widely available remedy in the realm of arbitration. It can be a particularly useful form of procedure by which to test *inter alia* the existence, validity, parties to, terms, construction and termination of an arbitration agreement[2]; or to address any question relating to the establishment and jurisdiction of an arbitration tribunal[3]; or the conduct of a reference, such as the procedural powers of an arbitrator[4]; or to test the validity or construction of an award.[5] The jurisdiction tends to be closely allied to the injunctive jurisdiction of the courts, for in practice it is common to seek declaratory and injunctive relief concurrently, with the injunction reinforcing the declaration.[6] Nonetheless the two kinds of jurisdiction are not coterminous, with the injunctive jurisdiction probably more limited.[7] Nor would it appear to be the case that a concurrent application for an injunction is necessarily prejudicial to the obtaining of declaratory relief.[8]

18a. *Ibid.* p. 620.

19. *Supra*, para. 12.5.1.4.

1. It is possible for declaratory relief to be sought and granted concurrently with a successful application under a process provided for by the 1979 Act; see, for example, *The Transcontinental Underwriting Agency S.R.L.* v. *Grant Union Insurance Co. Ltd. etc.* [1987] 2 Lloyd's Rep. 409.

2. See, for example, *Pagnan S.p.A.* v. *Granaria B.V. and Others* [1985] 2 Lloyd's Rep. 256; [1986] 2 Lloyd's Rep. 547 (C.A.); *Pine Top Insurance Co. Ltd.* v. *Unione Italiana Anglo Saxon Reinsurance Co. Ltd.* [1987] 1 Lloyd's Rep. 476; *Excomm Ltd.* v. *Guan Guan Shipping (Pte.) Ltd. (The Golden Bear)* [1987] 1 Lloyd's Rep. 330; *Federal Bulk Carriers Inc.* v. *C. Itoh & Co. Ltd. and Others (The Federal Bulker)* [1989] 1 Lloyd's Rep. 103 (C.A.).

3. See, for example, *Casili Grani* v. *Napier Shipping Co. (The World Ares)* [1984] 2 Lloyd's Rep. 481; *Asty Maritime Co. Ltd. and Panagiotis Stravelakis* v. *Rocco Giuseppe & Figli, S.N.C. and Others* [1984] 2 Lloyd's Rep. 459; *Rederij Lalemant* v. *Transportes Generales Navigacion S.A. (The Maria Lemos)* [1986] 1 Lloyd's Rep. 45; *Ashville Investments Ltd.* v. *Elmer Contractors Ltd.* [1988] 2 All E.R. 577.

4. See, for example, *Government of Gibraltar* v. *Kenney* [1956] 2 Q.B. 410. But note the observations of Steyn J. in *K/S A/S Bill Biakh and K/S A/S Bill Biali* v. *Hyundai Corporation* [1988] 1 Lloyd's Rep. 187.

5. See, for example, *Kaukomarkkinat O/Y* v. *Elbe Transporte-Union G.m.b.H. (The Kelo)* [1985] 2 Lloyd's Rep. 85; *Cook International Inc.* v. *B.V. Handelsmaatschappij Jean Delvaux and Braat, Scott and Meadows* [1985] 2 Lloyd's Rep. 225; *Ministry of Food Government of Bangladesh* v. *Bengal Lines Ltd. (The Bengal Pride)* [1986] 1 Lloyd's Rep. 167; *Baytur S.A.* v. *Finagro Holdings S.A.* [1992] 1 Lloyd's Rep. 134.

6. For example, see *Compagnie Européenne de Céréales S.A.* v. *Tradax Export S.A.* [1986] 2 Lloyd's Rep. 301 (declaration obtained that claim time-barred and an injunction granted restraining the claimants from proceeding with the arbitration).

7. See, generally, Thomas [1981] L.M.C.L.Q. 389.

8. Cf. *Government of Gibraltar* v. *Kenney* [1956] 2 Q.B. 410.

12.11.2.2 Declaratory relief derives from the inherent jurisdiction of the High Court, which jurisdiction is now also acknowledged by legislation.[9] It is a discretionary remedy which simply declares the legal rights, obligations or powers of the applicant and as with the section 2 procedure no *res judicata* is established with regard to either fact and law.[10] The relief may be sought by either claimant or respondent in an arbitration[11] and with the process initiated by writ or originating summons.[12] Respondents will in all probability seek to use the jurisdiction positively with a view to mounting a challenge, whereas claimants will probably view the jurisdiction as permissive and as a source of potential support.[13] The giving of negative declaratory relief is however a mode of relief not encouraged by the courts.[14] The discretion of the court may come into play at two distinct stages. First, at the preliminary stage, in determining whether or not to entertain an application for relief; and if the preliminary question is answered affirmatively, there then arises the second question of discretion, in deciding whether or not to grant the relief sought following a hearing.

In principle it would seem that declaratory relief may be sought to determine a preliminary question of law relating to the substantive dispute and arising in the course of a reference; and also to determine a question of law arising in the course of a reference and relating to the conduct of the reference itself. As a matter of practice, prevailing experience appears to suggest that the jurisdiction is little resorted to with regard to substantive questions of law, but is most frequently utilised in connection with procedural questions arising in the course of a reference, in relation to which it would appear a particularly appropriate form of procedure.

12.11.2.3 In deciding whether to give declaratory relief a central consideration will be the availability of alternative remedies, for where there exists an effective alternative remedy which is available to the applicant, the application for declaratory relief may be denied. In the context of the 1979 Act this may assume a material significance for the Act provides a specific mode of procedure and remedy. It is arguable that the section 2 procedure and also the possibility of appealing an interim award under section 1(2) represent tailor-made and effective procedures whereunder a judicial determination of a preliminary question of law arising in the course of a reference may be obtained. On the other hand, it may be doubted that these procedures are effective in all instances and this in turn may be of significance, for it would seem to be the case that the existence of an alternative remedy is not of itself sufficient to render declaratory relief unavailable unless the court also considers the alternative remedy more appropriate in the circumstances.[15] Taking a large and general view of the develop-

---

9. R.S.C. Order 15, r. 16. Also *F.* v. *West Berkshire Health Authority and Another* [1989] 2 All E.R. 545, 557, per Lord Brandon (H.L.).

10. *Supra.*, para. 12.7.2.

11. The *locus standi* of arbitrating parties would seem unambiguous. On the general principle governing *locus standi* see *Guaranty Trust Co. of New York* v. *Hannay* [1915] 2 K.B. 526; *Boulting* v. *Association of Cinematography, Television and Allied Technicians* [1963] 2 Q.B. 606; *Eastham* v. *Newcastle United Football Club* [1964] 1 Ch. 413; *Gouriet* v. *Union of Post Office Workers* [1978] A.C. 435.

12. *Punton* v. *Ministry of Pensions and National Insurance* [1963] 1 W.L.R. 186 (C.A.).

13. As where a claimant in arbitration seeks declarative relief to establish the jurisdiction of an arbitrator to decide a dispute or difference referred.

14. *Saipem S.p.A.* v. *Dredging V02 B.V. and Geosite Surveys Ltd. (The Volvox Hollandia)* [1987] 2 Lloyd's Rep. 520, 528; *S. B. Booker* v. *R. A. Bell* [1989] 1 Lloyd's Rep. 516, 517; *Sohio Supply Co.* v. *Gatoil (U.S.A.) Inc.* [1989] 1 Lloyd's Rep. 588, 593.

15. *Pyx Granite Co.* v. *Ministry of Housing and Local Government* [1966] A.C. 260.

ment of modern arbitration law, it would appear that the courts have taken a generous view of the availability of declaratory relief and have not always denied relief because of the existence of a statutory remedy in the arbitration or associated legislation. Nonetheless, each case must be judged on its own particular merits and the courts will doubtlessly also be careful not to permit the policy of the 1979 Act to be circumvented by the continued availability of the jurisdiction to seek declaratory relief.[16]

12.11.2.4 Where there exists a valid exclusion agreement under sections 3 and 4 of the 1979 Act excluding any application under section 2(1), there are also strong grounds for thinking that the jurisdiction to grant declaratory relief is also excluded as a question either of jurisdiction or discretion. Section 3(1)(a) does not purport to extend the impact of an exclusion agreement beyond section 2 but the existence of an exclusion agreement is likely to have a material influence on the exercise of judicial discretion. The fact of the exclusion agreement clearly shows that the parties wish and are content for all questions of law arising in the course of the reference to be determined solely by the arbitrator. It is unlikely that the courts will exercise the discretion associated with the jurisdiction to grant declaratory relief in such a way as to undermine the agreement of the parties and the policy of the 1979 Act. To do so would also be at variance with the declared policy of the courts to refuse to develop their wider jurisdiction in arbitral matters in a manner that would defeat the policy underlying the 1979 Act.[17]

12.11.3 Alternative procedures not involving the courts of law

12.11.3.1 An appeal from an interim award and declaratory relief are both alternatives to the section 2 procedure which involve an application to the courts. It is, however, possible to obtain an opinion on a preliminary question of law without the formality and cost of an application to the courts.

It is open to the parties to agree to put a question of law to a third party, such as an eminent Queen's Counsel, and that the arbitrator thereafter be bound or guided by the opinion given.[1] In this manner of procedure the opinion of counsel is substituted for that of the court. The procedure clearly has less authority than an application to the High Court, and, as with the section 2 procedure, an arbitrator is not in strictness compelled to follow the opinion given, except where the terms of the reference agreed by the parties provide otherwise. Nor is the opinion *res judicata*. Further, the opinion cannot be considered to have been given in a judicial capacity and therefore there exists the risk of legal liability if the opinion proves to be erroneous.[2] Where a third party opinion is taken in the fashion here described it clearly does not preclude the possibility of a subsequent application for leave to apply under section 2, but it might otherwise influence the exercise of judicial discretion in determining whether to give or refuse leave to apply under the section.

12.11.3.2 Another alternative is for the arbitrator simply to take legal advice on the question of law in issue, which is a power always open to an arbitrator unless the arbi-

---

16. Cf. *K/S A/S Bill Biakh and K/S A/S Bill Biali* v. *Hyundai Corporation* [1988] 1 Lloyd's Rep. 187.
17. See Chapter 1, para. 1.5.
1. Cf. *Wulff* v. *Dreyfus* (1917) L.J.K.B. 1368 (C.A.).
2. Under the principle enunciated in *Hedley Byrne & Co. Ltd.* v. *Heller & Partners Ltd.* [1964] A.C. 465, as subsequently developed.

tration agreement expressly or impliedly provides otherwise.[3] Where the parties have specifically appointed a non-legal arbitrator this is at least open to the possible construction of being an implied agreement to the contrary.[4] In taking legal advice on a point of law an arbitrator is free to accept or reject the advice proffered and he must be careful throughout to retain an independent judgment, so that the decision on the question of law is truly his and not that of the advising lawyer.[5] The professional fees incurred in taking legal advice will amount to costs of the award and in consequence it is, as a matter of practice, advisable for an arbitrator contemplating taking legal advice first to seek the express consent of the parties.[6] The fact that an arbitrator has sought and taken legal advice will not as a matter of jurisdiction preclude an application under section 2, but it may again represent a factor capable of being taken into account in the exercise of the associated discretion, although this would appear unlikely.

The right of an arbitrator to seek expert assistance appears to be accepted policy in the sphere of international arbitration and is enshrined in the UNCITRAL Model Law[7] and in the the Rules of various international arbitral organisations.[8]

3. *Proctor* v. *Williamson* (1860) 29 L.J.C.P. 157; *Ellison* v. *Bray* (1864) 9 L.T. 730; *Louis Dreyfus & Co.* v. *Arunachala Ayya* (1930) L.R. 58 Ind. App. 381. It is long established that an arbitrator may retain a lawyer to draw up an award; see *Behren* v. *Bremer* (1854) 3 C.L.R. 40; *Threlfall* v. *Fanshawe* (1850) 19 L.J.Q.B. 334; *Rolland* v. *Cassidy* (1888) 13 App.Cas. 770, 776–777. Following the introduction of new rules on direct professional access to the Bar of England and Wales, which came into force on 3 April 1989, it is open to an arbitrator to seek the advice of a barrister directly. See Bartlett (1989) 55.
4. *Proctor* v. *Williams or Williamson* (1859) 8 C.B. (N.S.) 386.
5. *Baker* v. *Cotterill* (1849) 18 L.J.Q.B. 345; *Ellison* v. *Bray* (1864) 9 L.T. 730; *Giacomo Costa fu Andrea* v. *British Italian Trading Co. Ltd.* [1961] 2 Lloyd's Rep. 392; affd. [1962] 1 Lloyd's Rep. 151.
6. In practice some arbitrators will only consent to their appointment on the condition that they are entitled to take legal advice if they judge it necessary. When the parties agree to the condition, then the power is an aspect of the express mandate of the arbitrator.
7. Article 26.
8. See, for example, London Court of International Arbitration Rules (1985), Art. 12; American Arbitration Association International Arbitration Rules (1991), Art. 23; Netherlands Arbitration Institute Arbitration Rules (1986), Art. 31.

CHAPTER 13

EXCLUSION AGREEMENTS
SECTIONS 3 AND 4

13.1 INTRODUCTION

13.1.1 The most radical aspect of the 1979 Act is its reversal of the policy enunciated by the Court of Appeal in *Czarnikow* v. *Roth, Schmidt & Co.*[1] with regard to the interrelationship between the courts and arbitration on questions of law. In *Czarnikow* it was decided that an agreement purporting to oust the jurisdiction of the High Court under the special case procedure was contrary to public policy and void. The emergence and substance of the public policy considerations have been previously considered in Chapter 1.[2] That important historical strand of arbitration jurisprudence is now displaced and for the first time the 1979 Act admits, subject to the stipulations set out in sections 3 and 4 of the Act, the validity of what is termed in the statute an "exclusion agreement". By this, in general terms, is meant an agreement which excludes all or any of the rights of appeal and application established under sections 1 and 2 of the 1979 Act.[3] In *The Nema*, Lord Diplock commented upon this aspect of the new legislation in the following terms[4]:

Section 3 gives effect to a reversal of public policy in relation to arbitration as it had been expounded more than half a century before in *Czarnikow* v. *Roth, Schmidt & Co.* [1922] 2 K.B. 478. Exclusion agreements, which oust the statutory jurisdiction of the High Court to supervise the way in which arbitrators apply the law in reaching their decisions in individual cases, are recognised as being no longer contrary to public policy. In principle they are enforceable, subject only to the special limitations imposed . . .

13.1.2 The emergence of valid exclusion agreements has accompanied the abolition of the special case procedure and its replacement by the new supervisory regime set out in sections 1 and 2 of the 1979 Act.[5] The new policy is confined to agreements which exclude the whole or any part of the scheme of judicial review established in these two sections.[6] It has, with one exception,[7] no wider application, and agreements which attempt to exclude the wider spheres of judicial supervision continue to be void, except where it can be shown that the statutory provision which creates the jurisdiction also provides for the displacement of that same jurisdiction by the agreement of

1. [1922] 2 K.B. 478.
2. See Chapter 1, para. 1.4.3.
3. See section 3(1), which is discussed *infra*, para. 13.2.
4. *Pioneer Shipping Ltd. and Others* v. *B.T.P. Tioxide Ltd. (The Nema)* [1982] A.C. 724, 740.
5. See Chapter 1, generally. The new appellate procedure established by section 1 is considered in Part II of the text; and the new consultative case procedure under section 2 in Chapter 12.
6. Section 3(1).
7. See s.3(3), considered *infra*, para. 13.3.2.3.

the parties. It is widely assumed that an agreement which purports to exclude the supervisory jurisdiction over awards conferred on the High Court by sections 22 and 23(2) of the Arbitration Act 1950 is contrary to public policy and void.[8]

13.1.3 Although the effect of the 1979 Act is to overturn the precise decision in *Czarnikow*, nonetheless many of the arguments which were accepted by the Court of Appeal in that case continue to receive recognition in sections 3 and 4 of the 1979 Act and account for the restrictive terms in which aspects of the legislation is expressed.[9] Thus there continues to be regard given to the need to protect the commercially weak from domination by those with greater commercial muscle. The concern for the need to continue the development of English commercial law as a comprehensive and coherent body of law, and as a system of law attractive to the international commercial community survives. These concerns are woven into the legislation and account for the requirement that in certain circumstances the validity of an exclusion agreement depends on it having been entered into after the commencement of the arbitration in relation to which the exclusion agreement appertains.[10] But, nonetheless, providing the terms of sections 3 and 4 are complied with, it remains possible to enter into a comprehensive and unchallengeable exclusion agreement and thereby, it is hoped, provide a stimulus to the further development of London as an international arbitration centre. There is witnessed in the approach adopted by the 1979 Act to the question of the validity of exclusion agreements an important example of the "pragmatic compromise" which the legislation as a whole manifests.[11]

13.1.4 The fundamental effect of an exclusion agreement is that it renders an arbitrator or umpire the final adjudicator of all questions of law touching upon the substance of a dispute referred to his jurisdiction. On questions of fact the arbitrator has long been the final voice and, as it has been observed upon earlier in the text, this principle is reinforced by section 1(1) of the 1979 Act.[12] But it has also long been the practice of the commercial community and others to refer both questions of fact and law to the decision of arbitrators and umpires, although not always prudent to do so, and when this is now done in association with an exclusion agreement all issues of fact and law rest with the arbitrator or umpire, and the traditional link between arbitration and the courts with regard to questions of law is severed. In a phrase the courts are shut out. An exclusion agreement introduces into English arbitral law a finality which previously it was impossible to achieve, but which is wholly consistent with the new policy underlying the 1979 Act. It makes possible what has become alluded to as sudden death arbitration.[13] With this finality also come associated advantages which have been identified by Ackner L.J. in the following terms[14]:

The reasons for foregoing the rights of appeal may be all or one of the following. Firstly, that

---

8. Contrast *Tullis* v. *Jacson* [1892] 3 Ch. 441, where it was held that a stipulation in a submission that neither party would attempt to set aside an award for alleged fraud of the arbitrator was valid. But in *Czarnikow* v. *Roth, Schmidt & Co.* [1922] 2 K.B. 478, 488, Scrutton L.J. reserved the right to reconsider the case. Note also *Union of India* v. *McDonnell Douglas Corporation* [1993] 2 Lloyd's Rep. 48.
9. For a full statement of the considerations of policy adopted by the Court of Appeal in *Czarnikow*, see Chapter 1, para. 1.4.3.
10. See section 3(6) and section 4(1), considered *infra*, para. 13.4.2.
11. See Chapter 1, para. 1.1.
12. See Chapter 1, para. 1.2.2.1.
13. See *Michael I. Warde* v. *Feedex International Inc.* [1984] 1 Lloyd's Rep. 310, 315, per Staughton J.
14. *Marine Contractors Inc.* v. *Shell Petroleum Co. of Nigeria Ltd.* [1984] 2 Lloyd's Rep. 77, 82.

the dispute is to be decided by the tribunal of the parties' choice. Secondly, that a decision which is final will be achieved as soon as possible, and this is made possible by excluding appeals, and thirdly, that the dispute is dealt with in privacy.

13.1.5 The existence of a valid exclusion agreement does not affect, in any way, the obligation of an arbitrator under English law to determine disputes and differences referred according to the prevailing rules of law, although not necessarily the rules of English law.[15] It is not a licence to decide a dispute by reference to extra-legal criteria: to act, for example, as *aimiable compositeur* or with authority to decide *ex aequo et bono*.[16] An exclusion agreement protects an arbitrator who falls into inadvertent error and not an arbitrator who turns a blind eye to or wilfully disregards the rules of law. It is an agreement that regulates the relationship between the courts and arbitration, not the law and arbitration. The wilful rejection or neglect of legal criteria probably amounts to misconduct, with the arbitrator or umpire in question and any award made subject to the supervisory jurisdiction of the court.[17]

13.1.6 Apart from entering into a formal exclusion agreement, it is possible to ensure the finality of an award by another procedure. Where the parties agree that an award shall be made without any reasons being given, it is thereafter effectively impossible to challenge the award. The existence of the agreement renders it probable that by virtue of section 1(6) the court has no jurisdiction to make an order for reasons under section 1(5). Even if the court does possess a jurisdiction, the existence of the agreement is likely to have a dominant impact on the exercise of the discretion under section 1(5).[18] The award being unreasoned it will also be impossible to detect any error of law arising out of the award. The ultimate effect is the same as if the parties had contracted for a reasoned award and also entered into a valid exclusion agreement. This has been recognised by Staughton J., who observed[19]:

If the parties wish to have sudden-death arbitration, they should be free to do so. They can of course achieve that by an exclusion agreement under ss. 3 and 4 of the 1979 Act, at all events if they do so after the commencement of the arbitration. I do not see why they should not reach much the same result by the simpler method of not asking for reasons.

13.1.7 Yet a further way of establishing finality is suggested by the decision of the House of Lords in *Hiscox* v. *Outhwaite*.[20] The House of Lords reasoned that an award signed by an arbitrator in Paris was also made in Paris and therefore a Convention award for the purposes of the Arbitration Act 1975,[21] notwithstanding that the entire arbitral process was otherwise wholly associated with London. Since the 1979 Act applies only to awards made in England and Wales,[22] the reasoning of the House of

---

15. See Chapter 1, para. 1.2.2.2.
16. See, generally, Thomas, "Commercial Arbitration—Justice According to Law" (1983) 2 C.J.Q. 166. For a contrary opinion see Rokison, "Arbitration—Advantages and Disadvantages", in The *Settlement of International Commercial Disputes*, Chartered Institute of Arbitrators (1982). See also Mann, "Private Arbitration and Public Policy" (1985) 4 C.J.Q. 257.
17. An arbitrator or umpire guilty of misconduct may be removed under s. 23(1) of the Arbitration Act 1950; and any award made may be set aside or remitted under ss. 23(2) and 22 of the same Act. The authority of an arbitrator may also be revoked under s. 1 of the 1950 Act.
18. See Chapter 11 for a discussion of the various issues raised in the text.
19. *Michael I. Warde* v. *Feedex International Inc.* [1984] 1 Lloyd's Rep. 310, 315.
20. [1992] 1 A.C. 562.
21. The 1975 Act gives legislative effect to the New York Convention on the Recognition and Enforcement of Foreign Arbitral Awards 1958. See Appendix F(4).
22. See Chapter 1, para. 1.7.8.

Lords appears to lay the ground for the development of a cynical stratagem by which to avoid the appeal process established by the 1979 Act. Quite simply, at the end of the reference the arbitrator is dispatched to a convenient location beyond the borders of England and Wales and instructed there to determine what his award should be and also to sign the award. The arbitrator then duly returns, releases the award in the usual way and with the award unappealable, being a foreign award for the purposes of the 1979 Act. The effectiveness of the stratagem will however depend on the reasoning of the House of Lords being given general application beyond the precise boundaries of the issue in question and also on the parties avoiding the existence of an estoppel, whereby they are denied the right to assert the award to be outside the ambit of the 1979 Act.

13.2 PREREQUISITES OF A VALID EXCLUSION AGREEMENT

13.2.1 Introduction

13.2.1.1 The essential facets of a valid exclusion agreement are set out in section 3(1) of the 1979 Act, which provides:

Subject to the following provisions of this section and section 4 below—
    (a) the High Court shall not, under section 1(3)(b) above, grant leave to appeal with respect to a question of law arising out of an award, and
    (b) the High Court shall not, under section 1(5)(b) above, grant leave to make an application with respect to an award, and
    (c) no application may be made under section 2(1)(a) above with respect to a question of law,
if the parties to the reference in question have entered into an agreement in writing (in this section referred to as an "exclusion agreement") which excludes the right of appeal under section 1 above in relation to that award or, in a case falling within paragraph (c) above, in relation to an award to which the determination of the question of law is material.

This definition and the stipulated effects of an exclusion agreement apply equally for the purpose of both sections 3 and 4 of the 1979 Act.[1]

13.2.1.2 From the terms of the subsection it is seen that an exclusion agreement is (i) an agreement in writing, (ii) entered into by the parties to the reference and (iii) which excludes any right of appeal or application established under sections 1 and 2 of the Act. Once the prerequisites of the subsection are satisfied the court is obliged to recognise and give effect to an exclusion agreement, unless the agreement is subsequently abandoned or it can be shown that a party has waived his rights under the agreement or is otherwise estopped from asserting any such right. The language of the subsection is peremptory. The High Court "shall not" grant leave under section 1(3)(b) and (5)(b); and "no application may be made" under section 2(1)(a). The word "may" in the latter context, it is submitted, has the same peremptory force as if "shall" had been the adopted word. The matter, therefore, is clearly not one of discretion and the enforcement of an exclusion agreement is wholly independent of such considerations as the reasonableness, fairness or justness of the agreement in the circumstances of individual cases.[2]

---

1. Section 4(5).
2. The Unfair Contract Terms Act 1977 has no application to exclusion agreements under the 1979 Act.

Consideration is now given to the fundamental features and necessary preconditions to a valid exclusion agreement. Where there exists a dispute as to the existence,
validity or applicability of an exclusion agreement the appropriate procedure is to
resolve the issue as a preliminary question.[3] An alternative form of procedure would
be to seek declaratory relief.

13.2.2 Agreement in writing

13.2.2.1 Agreement

13.2.2.1.1 Agreement is a contractual concept and connotes *consensus ad idem*. The
parties to a reference must be unambiguously of one mind—in perfect harmony—on
the question of the exclusion of all or any one of the rights specified in sections 1 and 2
of the 1979 Act. In more technical terms there must exist mutual promises to one
accord. In the ultimate the test of consensus is objective and not subjective.[1] In *Arab
African Energy Corpn. Ltd.* v. *Olieprodukten Nederland B.V.*[2] Leggatt J. summarised, without dissenting from, the argument of counsel in the following terms[3]: "to
constitute a valid exclusion agreement a provision must constitute a consensus
between the parties agreeing to forego their right. Only so can the parties be said to
have 'entered into' an exclusion agreement". Just as the obligation to arbitrate is
founded on agreement (the arbitration agreement), so also is the right to exclude the
supervisory role of the High Court with regard to questions of law and the associated
issue of reasoned awards. Frequently, each will emanate from a common agreement,
as where an arbitration agreement also embodies an exclusion agreement; but this
clearly is not necessarily the case, and on occasions it cannot be the case because of
the requirement that prevails in specified circumstances that an exclusion agreement
can only be validly entered into after the commencement of the arbitration proceedings in question.[4] In section 3(2) it is expressly recognised that an agreement may
amount to an exclusion agreement whether or not it forms part of an arbitration
agreement.[5]

13.2.2.1.2 Where an exclusion agreement is embodied in or incorporated into an
arbitration agreement, it would seem that it must stand as one with the arbitration
agreement in relation to questions appertaining to the initial and continuing existence
and validity of the agreement. So also, where in such a case the arbitration agreement
exists as a clause in a wider contract, it would seem that the exclusion agreement must
stand in the same relationship to the wider contract as would the arbitration agreement existing in isolation. Thus, although in general the initial existence and validity
of the arbitration agreement and exclusion agreement are inseverably associated with

3. R.S.C. Order 33, rr. 3 and 4(2). This procedure was adopted in *Arab African Energy Corpn. Ltd.* v.
Olieprodukten Nederland B.V. [1983] 2 Lloyd's Rep. 419.
1. Cf. *Smith* v. *Hughes* (1871) L.R. 6 Q.B. 597, 607; *Pearl Mill Co. Ltd.* v. *Ivy Tannery Co. Ltd.* [1919] 1
K.B. 78; *André et Compagnie S.A.* v. *Marine Transocean Ltd. (The Splendid Sun)* [1981] Q.B. 694 (C.A.);
Paal Wilson Co. A/S v. *Partrenreederi Hannah Blumenthal (The Hannah Blumenthal)* [1983] 1 A.C. 854;
Allied Marine Transport Ltd. v. *Vale do Rio Doce Navegação S.A. (The Leonidas D.)* [1985] 1 W.L.R. 925;
Food Corporation of India v. *Antclizo Shipping Corporation (The Antclizo)* [1987] 2 Lloyd's Rep. 130
(C.A.); [1988] 2 Lloyd's Rep. 93 (H.L.).
2. [1983] 2 Lloyd's Rep. 419.
3. *Ibid.* p. 420.
4. See *infra*, para. 13.4.2.
5. See *infra*, para. 13.5.2.

the factual establishment and initial validity of the wider contract,[5a] thereafter the arbitration agreement and exclusion agreement would seem to co-exist as a separate contract within the wider contract, with questions appertaining to their continuing existence and validity capable of determination independently of the wider contract.[6]

13.2.2.1.3 Where the exclusion agreement is in space and time separate from the arbitration agreement, as on occasions it must be to be a valid exclusion agreement, then it would seem that the exclusion agreement is conceptually quite distinct from the arbitration agreement that is at the root of the arbitral proceedings, and questions relating to the initial and continuing existence and validity of the exclusion agreement fall to be determined wholly independently of the arbitration agreement. But with regard to questions of construction it is probable that the position is different, with the two agreements considered as one.[7]

13.2.2.1.4 Although the concept of contractual agreement is one readily comprehended and capable of clear expression, there is nonetheless in any given situation uncertainty as to the weight and quality of evidence required to establish consensus to the satisfaction of the court. Herein often lies the element of policy. Whenever a question of the existence of an agreement is in issue a court cannot wholly divorce itself from the consequences of its decision. For this reason, it is submitted, the phenomenon of contractual agreement cannot be considered solely in terms of the orthodoxy of the component parts of consensus, but consideration must also be given to the status and relative positions of the parties, the substance of the agreement, the impact of any alternative findings open to the court, and the broad contractual environment of the situation. Bearing these considerations in mind, the wider reality of an exclusion agreement in the context of the 1979 Act is that it will predominantly be an incident of a commercial, construction, civil engineering or like agreement, in the vast majority of cases entered into by mature and experienced parties fully capable, if they conduct their affairs prudently, of looking after their own interests and invariably employing professional people to do just that. To this extent, and in keeping with established principle, the court ought to act as a vehicle for the facilitation of the intention of the parties and not as a destroyer of agreements. Exclusion agreements, it is submitted, are therefore not to be viewed with suspicion and distrust, and responded to narrowly and technically. In providing for exclusion agreements and the arbitral finality which they achieve the legislature has set the tone of the prevailing policy and it would be unjustified for the courts to attempt to restrictively harness that policy. Even when the *personae dramatis* and the context of the transaction are otherwise than as described above, as will infrequently be the case, it must be borne in mind that the 1979 Act has its own inbuilt protective regulator. This is the stipulation, in specified situations, that an exclusion agreement is only valid if entered into *after* the commencement of arbi-

---

5a. But see now *Harbour Assurance Co. (U.K.) Ltd.* v. *Kansa General International Assurance Co. Ltd. and others* [1993] 3 All E.R. 897 (C.A.) which appears to represent a step away from this general principle and to confine the general principle to instances where the initial defect also impeaches the arbitration agreement.

6. For the relationship between an arbitration agreement which exists as a contractual clause and the wider contract within which it is contained, see, *Heyman* v. *Darwins Ltd.* [1942] A.C. 356; *Mackender* v. *Feldia A.G.* [1967] 2 Q.B. 590; *Prodexport State Co. for Foreign Trade* v. *E.D. & F. Man Ltd.* [1973] Q.B. 389; *Dalmia Dairy Industries Ltd.* v. *National Bank of Pakistan* [1978] 2 Lloyd's Rep. 223.

7. Cf. *Sarma Navigation S.A.* v. *Sidermar S.p.A. (The Sea Pioneer)* [1979] 2 Lloyd's Rep. 408 (where two charterparties entered into by the same parties and in relation to the one ship were construed together).

tration proceedings.[8] The avowed object of this restriction, at least in part, is to protect weaker parties from the danger of an abuse of dominant position on the part of mightier parties. The statute having introduced a specific protective mechanism it would seem unsupportable for a court, in assessing argument directed to the existence or validity of a post-commencement exclusion agreement, to turn an excessively quizzical eye to the relative position of the parties.

13.2.2.1.5 It has been contended that the notion of an agreement for the purpose of section 3(1) is narrower than that sustained under the general principles of contract law. In particular, it has been argued that the intention to affect rights arising under sections 1 and 2 must be made manifest in an express provision *in extenso* in the corpus of an agreement directly entered into by the parties to the reference. The implications of the argument, if accepted, are that it is not open to the court to infer an exclusion agreement; nor to construe an ambiguous agreement as amounting to an exclusion agreement; and to negate the possibility of an exclusion agreement being incorporated by reference into any agreement between the parties. The argument and the last implication were however rejected by Leggatt J. in *Arab African Energy Corpn. Ltd. v. Olieprodukten Nederland B.V.*,[9] where it was held that an oral agreement confirmed in writing, which expressly incorporated the arbitral rules of the International Chamber of Commerce, containing an exclusion agreement (article 24),[10] was an effective vehicle for establishing an exclusion agreement within the meaning of section 3(1). Leggatt J. expressed the opinion,[11] "[s]ection 3(1) of the 1979 Act does not require the overt demonstration of an intention to exclude the right of appeal . . . In my judgement, the phrase 'an agreement in writing . . . which excludes the right of appeal' is apt to apply to an exclusion agreement incorporated by reference." The same reasoning was adopted by Staughton J. in *Marine Contractors Inc. v. Shell Petroleum Co. of Nigeria Ltd.*,[12] where the factual issue before the court was precisely the same as that in the *Arab African Energy* case.

13.2.2.1.6 English law, in general, adopts a generous and unrestrictive attitude towards the incorporation by reference of contractual terms. Provided the words of reference are apposite for their purpose such clauses can operate as widely or narrowly as the contracting parties desire.[13] Nor has English law attempted to distinguish between the range of stipulations that may be sought to be incorporated and insist, for example, that stipulations that particularly touch upon the substantive rights of the parties, such as exclusion and limitation terms, or the procedural rights of the parties, such as arbitration agreements and exclusion agreements, may only be capable of incorporation if they are expressly specified or identified in the words of reference. Within certain European jurisdictions a different principle applies. In, for example, the Swiss and Italian legal systems an external provision such as an arbitration

---

8. See *infra*, para. 13.4.2.

9. [1983] 2 Lloyd's Rep. 419.

10. See *infra* for a discussion of the issues of "form" and "construction" which this case also raises.

11. *Ibid*, p. 423.

12. [1984] 2 Lloyd's Rep. 77 (first instance). Although the case went to appeal this particular aspect of Staughton J.'s judgment was not within the appeal.

13. See, generally, *J. B. & S. Batchelor & Co. Ltd.* v. *SS Merak (Owners); (The Merak)* [1965] P. 223; *Smith* v. *South Wales Switchgear Ltd.* [1978] 1 W.L.R. 165; *Skips A/S Nordheim and others* v. *Syrian Petroleum Co. Ltd. and another (The Varenna)* [1983] 3 All E.R. 645, [1983] 2 Lloyd's Rep. 592 (C.A.).

agreement can only be incorporated by reference if it is directly alluded to.[14] The same principle has been followed by the European Court of Justice in its interpretation of exclusive jurisdiction agreements within the meaning of Article 17 of the Brussels Convention on Jurisdiction.[15] The reasoning underlying the European approach appears to be that only by adopting such a narrow rule can there be any reasonable assurance that there exists a true consensus between the parties. The same restrictions do not apply in English law wherein it is now clearly established that a general reference to an external document which contains an arbitration clause is sufficient to incorporate all the clauses, including the arbitration clause, providing the words of incorporation are capable on their proper construction of alluding to the arbitration agreement.[16] The recent authorities make it plain that this same broad principle is equally to be adopted with regard to exclusion agreements. Whatever the merits of the European principle, and notwithstanding the prevailing movement towards the harmonisation of the commercial laws of the member states of the E.E.C., the English Commercial Court has determined, in the absence of legislative dictat, that to maintain a consistency of approach with its resultant certainty is the policy which will best serve the commercial community.[17]

13.2.2.2 In writing

13.2.2.2.1 An exclusion agreement has an important formal element. It must be an agreement in writing. Doubtless, the object is to ensure that exclusion agreements are only recognised when their existence and terms are capable of being established with certainty. An oral exclusion agreement is in consequence void although such an agreement may otherwise have the capacity to influence the exercise of judicial discretion under section 1(3)(b) of the 1979 Act.[1]

In specifying the requirement of writing it is clear that no greater formality is required, as, for example, in the manner of a deed or the signature of one or all of the parties to the exclusion agreement.[2] Equally it may be assumed that writing includes printing, typography, computerised printouts, handwriting, and any other method of representing words in a visible and communicable form.[3]

13.2.2.2.2 The precise scope of the phrase "in writing" is a question of statutory interpretation. The formal requirement of writing often appears in legislation but the interpretation given to similar or corresponding phrases in other statutes is not necessarily conclusive.[4] Although these may provide useful guidelines, in the final analysis

---

14. See the discussion in *Tracomin S.A.* v. *Sudan Oil Seeds Co. Ltd.* [1983] 1 Lloyd's Rep. 560. Also *Marine Contractors Inc.* v. *Shell Petroleum Development Co. of Nigeria Ltd.*, *supra*, p. 79.

15. *Estasis Salotti* v. *RUWA* [1976] E.C.R. 1831; *Segoura* v. *Bonakdarian* [1976] E.C.R. 1861.

16. *T. W. Thomas & Co. Ltd.* v. *Portsea Steamship Co. Ltd.* [1912] A.C. 1; *Hogarth Shipping Co. Ltd.* v. *Blythe Greene Jourdan & Co. Ltd.* [1917] 2 K.B. 534; *Annefield (owners)* v. *Annefield (cargo owners), (The Annefield)* [1971] P. 168 (C.A.); *Federal Bulk Carriers Inc.* v. *C. Itoh & Co. Ltd. and others (The Federal Bulker)* [1989] 1 Lloyd's Rep. 103 (C.A.).

17. *Arab African Energy Corpn. Ltd.* v. *Olieprodukten Nederland B.V.*, *supra*, p. 423; *Marine Contractors Inc.* v. *Shell Petroleum Co. of Nigeria Ltd.*, *supra*, p. 79.

1. See Chapter 6, para. 6.2.20.

2. Contrast *Frank Fehr & Co.* v. *Kassam Jivraj & Co. Ltd.* (1949) 82 Ll.L.Rep. 673, 676 per Lord Greene M.R. See further Chapter 3, para. 3.4.

3. See Interpretation Act 1978, s. 5 and Schedule 1.

4. See, for example, Bills of Exchange Act 1882, s. 2; The Unsolicited Goods and Services Act 1971, s. 1(3).

statutory language has to be interpreted in its own statutory setting and this may lead to similar words and phrases in different statutes being interpreted differently. Nonetheless, according to the context, certain statutes may prove of greater relevance than others. In the present instance this is probably true of the Arbitration Act 1950, section 32, which provides the definition of an arbitration agreement for the purpose of Part I of the 1950 Act and which defines an arbitration agreement as being *inter alia* a "written agreement"; and also of the Arbitration Act 1975, section 7(1), which defines an arbitration agreement for the purposes of the 1975 Act as being *inter alia* "an agreement in writing (including an agreement contained in an exchange of letters or telegrams)".

13.2.2.2.3 Although the precise formulations in the two definition sections differ it is submitted that there is no difference of substance and that each definition conveys a common meaning. Within the arbitration legislation a reference to a "written agreement" is to the same effect as a reference to an "agreement in writing". The meaning of a "written agreement", as adopted in section 32 of the 1950 Act, has previously been considered[5] and that discussion showed that the phrase is given a wide meaning and alludes not only to an agreement *in* writing, in the narrow and pure sense, but also to any agreement which is recorded, authenticated, recognised, incorporated, or confirmed, in or by a written document. The section also embraces as a written agreement the particular example of an agreement in writing provided by section 7(1) of the 1975 Act, namely an agreement contained in an exchange of letters or telegrams.[6]

13.2.2.2.4 It would be more than strange if the courts were to construe the formal requirement attaching to an exclusion agreement under section 3(1) of the 1979 Act differently from the same formal requirement attaching to arbitration agreements under the arbitration legislation, and they have refused to do so. In *Arab African Energy Corpn. Ltd.* v. *Olieprodukten Nederland B.V.*[7] Leggatt J. considered that the phrase "agreement in writing" in section 3(1) of the 1979 Act has the same meaning as the phrase "written agreement" as adopted in section 32 of the Arbitration Act 1950. Although in strictness the form of words is different, and notwithstanding the canon of statutory interpretation that different words in associated legislation are *prima facie* to be given different meanings, the learned judge considered the intention of the legislature to be that both phrases are to carry a common meaning. In the result Leggatt J. concluded that what is demanded by the phrase adopted in section 3(1) of the 1979 Act is "a written expression adopted by both parties of an agreement reached between them or their agents".[8]

13.2.2.2.5 In *Arab African Energy Corpn. Ltd.* v. *Olieprodukten Nederland B.V.*,[9] sellers and purchasers, acting through brokers located in Paris, agreed orally to the sale and purchase of 25,000/30,000 tonnes of gas oil f.o.b. Constantza. The agreement was subsequently confirmed by two telex messages sent by the brokers acting for the purchasers to each of the principal parties. The telex messages began: "Ref. various to-day's telecoms, are pleased to confirm the following business . . . " The essential terms of the contract were then set out and there were included as "general terms" the

5. Chapter 1, para. 1.7.5; Chapter 3, para. 3.4.
6. *Ibid.*
7. [1983] 2 Lloyd's Rep. 419, 423.
8. *Ibid.*
9. *Ibid.* See further Kerr (1980) 43 M.L.R. 45, 53–54.

following provisions: "Inco terms 1980: English law—arbitration, if any, London according I.C.C. rules." Article 24 of the I.C.C. rules provided:

1. The arbitral award shall be final. 2. By submitting the dispute to arbitration by the International Chamber of Commerce, the parties shall be deemed to have undertaken to carry out the resulting award without delay and to have waived their right to any form of appeal insofar as such waiver can validly be made.

13.2.2.2.6 The question before the High Court was whether there existed a valid exclusion agreement such as to exclude the High Court granting leave to appeal under section 1(3)(b). The initial contract was oral in form. The terms of the contract were evidenced by the telex messages sent to the parties. They showed that by their oral agreement the parties had incorporated by express reference the Arbitration Rules of the I.C.C., which are a printed code of rules, and which in turn embodied a printed exclusion agreement.[10] The court held that in the circumstances an effective exclusion agreement had been entered into, and in effect determined that an oral agreement which incorporated by express reference an extraneous printed exclusion agreement was for the purposes of section 3(1) of the 1979 Act an agreement in writing entered into by the parties to the reference. In strict theory it would appear that the effect of the incorporation was to establish a contract which was in part oral and in part in writing. An alternative way of interpreting the facts is to see the reference to the I.C.C. Arbitration Rules in the confirmatory telexes as in effect incorporating these Rules into the telexes. As such the telexes were written confirmation of the existence of a parol exclusion agreement and in such form again satisfied the requirements of section 3(1). Although it was open to the court to arrive at its decision by either route of reasoning, the tenor of the judgment faintly suggests that the court may have been content to adopt that described above as the alternative approach.

13.2.2.2.7 If on the facts in the case there had been no attempt to incorporate the I.C.C. Arbitration Rules, but the confirmatory telex messages had each set out the terms of an exclusion agreement, as evidence of what the principal parties had agreed in their oral agreement, the formal requirements of section 3(1) would again have been satisfied.

13.2.2.2.8 To summarise: there would seem to be an agreement in writing for the purposes of section 3(1) when an exclusion agreement is:

(i) embodied as an express term in a written agreement;

(ii) embodied in a written offer and acceptance; whether in the form of an exchange of correspondence, telexes, or facsimile documents, or any other mode of formal exchange;

(iii) embodied in an external document which is incorporated by reference into a written agreement;

(iv) embodied as a term in a parol agreement which is subsequently recorded, authenticated, recognised, incorporated or confirmed in or by a written document or some other form of writing[11];

---

10. See *infra*, para. 13.3.
11. For an authority which may suggest the contrary, see *E. Turner and Sons Ltd.* v. *Mathind Ltd.* (1989) 5 Const. L.J. 273, which is considered in Chapter 3, para. 3.4.

(v) embodied in an external document which is incorporated by reference into a
parol agreement.[12]

13.2.3 Entered into by the parties to the reference

13.2.3.1 Entered into

An exclusion agreement must be a contract which the parties have actually entered
into and assumed immediately binding mutual promises. There is no exclusion agreement if the parties have only concurred that one or both parties shall have the option
of introducing a specified exclusion agreement at a future time, or have merely agreed
to agree to enter into an exclusion agreement at some future time. In the latter case it
is unlikely that there even exists an agreement in the eyes of the law.[1]

13.2.3.2 Parties to the reference

13.2.3.2.1 This phrase appears on several occasions in the 1979 Act and the discussion
of the potential meaning and import of the phrase found elsewhere in the text would
appear to be of equal application to the present context.[2] There are, however, certain
observations that may be made concerning the phrase that have a particular application to its adoption in the context of exclusion agreements.

In many instances an exclusion agreement is only valid if entered into after the commencement of an arbitration.[3] In such a case the parties to an exclusion agreement are
necessarily parties to the reference, whatever may be their precise relationship to the
initial arbitration agreement. But where an exclusion agreement may be validly
entered into prior to the commencement of an arbitration, it would seem that the rule
requiring an exclusion agreement to be entered into by parties to a reference does not
go so far as also to require that they be of that status when they first entered into an
exclusion agreement. It is sufficient for the purpose of section 3(1) that they subsequently become parties to a reference and are of that status when the effect of the
exclusion agreement is asserted. A valid pre-commencement exclusion agreement
may be entered into before the appointment of an arbitral tribunal and therefore
before the establishment of a reference; or even following the appointment of a tribunal, an agreement may be entered into prior to any act which may represent the
commencement of the reference. It is theoretically possible for parties to enter into an
exclusion agreement even before they enter into an arbitration agreement. It is submitted that the requirement of section 3(1) is met, in these kinds of situations, if the
parties to a pre-commencement exclusion agreement subsequently become parties to
the related reference and assert the exclusion agreement in that status. Any other construction, it is suggested, would seriously militate against the reasonable operation of
sections 3 and 4.

13.2.3.2.2 A query arises as to whether a valid exclusion agreement can only exist if

---

12. *Ibid.*
1. *Courtney Fairbairn Ltd.* v. *Tolaini Bros. (Hotels) Ltd.* [1975] 1 W.L.R. 297; *Scandinavian Trading
Tanker Co. A.B.* v. *Flota Petrolera Ecuatoriana (The Scaptrade)* [1981] 2 Lloyd's Rep. 425, 432; *Nile Co. for
the Export of Agricultural Crops* v. *H. & J. M. Bennett (Commodities) Ltd.* [1986] 1 Lloyd's Rep. 555, 587;
Star Steamship Society v. *Beogradska Plovidba (The Junior K)* [1988] 2 Lloyd's Rep. 583, 588.
2. See Chapter 2, para. 2.2; Chapter 12, para. 12.4.3.2. See also section 5.
3. See *infra*, para. 13.4.2.

all the parties to a reference are party to it; or whether it is possible for two or more, but not all, of the parties to enter into such an agreement, with the consequence that only those who are party to an exclusion agreement are bound by its terms and with the other parties free of contractual constraint. It is submitted that it is the former interpretation that prevails. The reference to "parties" in section 3(1) is probably a reference to *all* the parties, and without the unanimous assent of all the parties there cannot exist a valid exclusion agreement. But it does not follow that the effect of an exclusion agreement must impinge on the rights of all the parties to a reference. Just as an arbitration agreement may be unilateral in effect,[4] so also it is possible to conceive of an exclusion agreement which excludes the rights of one or some of the parties, but not all.

13.2.4 Affecting rights under sections 1 and 2

An exclusion agreement is one that affects all or some of the qualified rights of appeal and application that are established by sections 1 and 2 of the Act. These are the right to apply for leave to appeal under section 1(3)(b); the right to apply for leave to apply for a reasoned award under section 1(5)(b); and the right, with the necessary consent of an arbitrator or umpire who has entered on a reference, to apply for the judicial determination of a preliminary question of law under section 2(1)(a).

Under an exclusion agreement rights can only be affected by their exclusion. An exclusion agreement is one "which excludes the right".[1] It cannot otherwise qualify, amend, limit or render conditional the rights in question. The right either exists as established by the statute or it is abrogated by an exclusion agreement: there can exist no intermediate position.

An exclusion agreement, with one exception,[2] cannot have any wider effect beyond affecting rights under sections 1 and 2. It cannot in consequence extend so as to exclude the whole or any part of the jurisdiction of the High Court arising under the arbitration legislation and the common law to review arbitration agreements, arbitrators, the arbitral process and awards. An exclusion agreement, for example, that attempted to extend its reach so as to exclude the reviewing jurisdiction of the courts over awards, established under the Arbitration Act 1950, sections 22 and 23(2), would be void to that extent.

13.3 QUESTIONS OF CONSTRUCTION

Assuming there to be in existence an agreement in the appropriate form, which is a question of fact, there then follow two further possible questions, one a question of characterisation and the other a question of pure construction, both of which raise questions of law. The first concerns the question whether any particular agreement in writing amounts to an exclusion agreement within the meaning of section 3(1). When an affirmative answer is given to this initial question, there may then arise a second

4. *Tote Bookmakers Ltd.* v. *Development and Property Holding Co. Ltd.* [1985] Ch. 261; *Pittalis and others* v. *Sherefettin* [1986] 2 All E.R. 227 (C.A.).
1. Section 3(1).
2. See *infra*, para. 13.3.2.3.

question of construction relating to the precise ambit and scope of the exclusion agreement.

13.3.1 Whether an agreement in writing amounts to an exclusion agreement

13.3.1.1 Whether in any particular case an agreement in writing may be characterised as an exclusion agreement is a question of construction inseverably associated with the intention of the parties. Presumably the court will in each case attempt to ascertain whether the written agreement in issue manifests an intention to exclude all or any of the qualified rights arising under sections 1 and 2 of the 1979 Act.

The greater the degree of precision and specificity in the language of a written agreement the less contentious will be the question of its proper characterisation. Thus an agreement which expressly refers to the 1979 Act and to the exclusion of rights arising under sections 1 and/or 2, or which expressly declares itself to be an exclusion agreement within the meaning of section 3(1) of the Act, offers little scope for challenge and consequently merits adoption by those responsible for drafting exclusion agreements. Early commentaries on this aspect of the 1979 Act also favoured the certainty to be derived from the cautious practice of direct reference to the statute.[1] Nonetheless, it would seem to be clear that overt reference to the 1979 Act or to the relevant section(s) and subsection(s) is not an indispensable precondition. Nor could it be given that by virtue of section 3(2) an agreement entered into before the passing of the 1979 Act may be construed as an exclusion agreement.[2] It is open to the court to construe any form of words as being an exclusion agreement, notwithstanding that they do not expressly make any allusion to the 1979 Act, provided that on their proper construction they amount to an exclusion agreement within the contemplation of the section 3(1).[3]

13.3.1.2 In *Arab African Energy Corpn. Ltd.* v. *Olieprodukten Nederland B.V.*[4] the agreement in question was to the following effect: "By submitting the dispute to arbitration by the International Chamber of Commerce, the parties shall be deemed . . . to have waived their right to any form of appeal insofar as such waiver can validly be made." Did this amount to a valid exclusion agreement? The agreement had an obvious generality. It was founded on a provision (Article 24) contained in an international code of arbitral procedure (the I.C.C. Rules) which was formulated to operate in a range of different municipal jurisdictions. The ability to exclude judicial review would plainly vary from jurisdiction to jurisdiction. This was recognised by the Article and was the reason for the insertion of the concluding phrase "insofar as such waiver can validly be made". The phrase ensured that the Article only went so far as it was lawfully permissible in any domestic jurisdiction. The agreement was challenged on the ground that as a matter of construction it did not fulfil the requirements of section 3(1) of the 1979 Act. First, it was argued that the right of appeal was not stated to

---

1. See, *Supreme Court Practice* (1982), Vol. II, para. 3864; for the current edition see (1993), Vol. II, para. 5885. Mustill and Boyd, *supra, op. cit.*, pp. 634–635.
2. See *infra*, para. 13.5.1.
3. See, Donaldson, "Commercial Arbitration—1979 and After", in *Current Legal Problems* (1983), pp. 1–12, 7, "No special form of agreement is required, but it must, when properly construed, amount to an agreement in writing to exclude the right of appeal under section 1 or, as the case may be, section 2 or both." The lecture is reproduced in *International Commercial and Maritime Arbitration*, ed. Rose (1988).
4. [1983] 2 Lloyd's Rep. 419.

be excluded but merely deemed to be excluded: secondly, it was argued, that in order for the agreement to achieve its purpose more specific and precise language was necessary. Both contentions failed. The court refused to indulge the subtlety of the first argument and considered that parties who are deemed to have waived their right of appeal will be treated as having actually done so. In rejecting the second argument Leggatt J. observed,[5] "[i]t also seems to me that the exclusion (in effect) of every right of appeal which can lawfully be excluded, not only achieves the result but achieves it in a way which is harmonious with the 1979 Act and allows for those particular matters in which the right of appeal cannot be excluded." In *Marine Contractors Inc.* v. *Shell Petroleum Co. of Nigeria Ltd.*,[6] Staughton J. took the same view of the effect of Article 24 of the I.C.C. Arbitral Rules. As for the proper approach to the issue of construction the learned judge indicated,[7] "The question of whether there has been an exclusion agreement in a business contract should be decided on ordinary principles of construction of contracts without any predispositions one way or the other. By this test there is, in my judgment, plainly an exclusion agreement in art. 24 of the rules of the I.C.C."[8]

13.3.1.3 But clearly there are limits to the extent it is possible for a court to divine the requisite intent from general words or obtuse language. In *The Rio Sun*[9] Lord Denning M.R. considered *obiter dictum* that where parties agreed to accept an award as "final" this also amounted to an effective exclusion agreement.[10] This must, with respect, be very doubtful, if not a wholly unacceptable construction. The requirement of finality is a necessary precondition to the validity of an award and even when the parties do not expressly agree to accept an award as a final determination of the dispute or difference, such an undertaking is implied by statute.[11] This being the case, it is difficult to see how parties who expressly adopt in their arbitration agreements the often used formula that the award shall be final and binding are also to be attributed with the further intention of excluding rights of appeal and application under sections 1 and 2 of the 1979 Act. Without more, it is submitted that merely to agree that an award shall be final does not at the same time automatically establish an exclusion agreement.[12] Similarly, it would be hard to attribute an intention to enter into an exclusion agreement where the parties have done no more than make provision for a contractual appeal within the arbitral process. The establishment of a contractual arbitral appeal, without more, does not by necessary inference also exclude an appeal to the courts.

13.3.1.4 Although, with regard to the question of characterisation, the Act does not lay down guidelines to assist in ascertaining the intention of the parties, there is nonetheless set out in section 3(4) a statement of three categories of agreement that

5. *Ibid.* p. 423.
6. [1984] 2 Lloyd's Rep. 77.
7. *Ibid.* p. 79.
8. See, for example, the arbitration agreement in *Home Insurance Co. and St. Paul Fire and Marine Insurance Co.* v. *Administratia Assigurarilor De Stat* [1983] 2 Lloyd's Rep. 674, which reads, "The award of the Arbitrators or the Umpire . . . shall be final and binding upon all parties without appeal." This probably amounts to a valid exclusion agreement, although the question was not in issue in the case.
9. *Italmare Shipping Co.* v. *Ocean Tanker Co. Inc. (The Rio Sun)* [1982] 1 W.L.R. 158.
10. *Ibid.* p. 162.
11. Arbitration Act 1950, s. 16.
12. See also Donaldson, "Commercial Arbitration—1979 and After", in *International Commercial and Maritime Arbitration*, ed. Rose.

are not to be taken, without more, as establishing exclusion agreements. Section 3(4) provides:

Except as provided by subsection (1) above, sections 1 and 2 above shall have effect notwithstanding anything in any agreement purporting—
    (a) to prohibit or restrict access to the High Court; or
    (b) to restrict the jurisdiction of that court; or
    (c) to prohibit or restrict the making of a reasoned award.

13.3.1.5 Subsection (4) appears to impress the point that although general words are capable of being construed as an exclusion agreement within the meaning of section 3(1) there are nonetheless limits, and, in particular, that agreements which purport directly or indirectly to obstruct the path between the parties to a reference and the High Court do not, without more, amount to exclusion agreements. The difficulty with the subsection is that many of the kinds of agreement falling within paragraphs (a) and (b) would in general be void as being contrary to public policy.[13] But the subsection otherwise makes it clear that agreements restricting the remedial rights of the parties, such as arbitration agreements, *Scott* v. *Avery* clauses and jurisdictional agreements, which may in their various ways be considered agreements which restrict access to or the jurisdiction of the High Court, are not without more to be construed as also amounting to exclusion agreements. On the other hand agreements prohibiting or restricting the making of reasoned awards are lawful.[14] The existence of such an agreement is again not to be construed as also amounting to an exclusion agreement, although it may otherwise influence the exercise of judicial discretion under the 1979 Act.[15]

13.3.1.6 It has also been speculated[16] that a choice of a foreign curial law, which may be of only limited effect in English law,[17] may nonetheless amount to an exclusion agreement and so avoid the danger of parallel court proceedings. It is submitted that this is too bold a speculation. Such a construction may not be justified by reference to the ordinary principles of the construction of contracts and may even offend against the protective provisions of section 3(4).[18] But if it is correct law that a choice of a foreign curial law does not impinge upon the relationship between arbitration with its seat in England and Wales and the domestic courts,[19] then the reason which provoked the speculation would seem an improbable danger. There is, further, something unsatisfactory and even contradictory in viewing the one agreement as not excluding the domestic jurisdiction of the High Court, but yet capable of amounting to an exclusion agreement and so exclude access to the High Court.

13.3.2 Determining the scope of an established exclusion agreement

Once it is established that an exclusion agreement exists, there may then arise a second question of construction concerning the scope and ambit of an exclusion agree-

---

13. See, for example, *Anctil* v. *Manufacturers' Life Insurance Co.* [1899] A.C. 604; *Hyman* v. *Hyman* [1929] A.C. 601; *Lee* v. *The Showmen's Guild of Great Britain* [1952] 2 Q.B. 329, 342.
14. See, generally, Chapter 11.
15. See Chapter 6, para. 6.2.3.
16. *Union of India* v. *McDonnell Douglas Corporation* [1993] 2 Lloyd's Rep. 48, 51, per Saville J.
17. See Chapter 1, para. 1.7.8.2.
18. *Supra*, para. 13.3.1.4.
19. *Supra*, n. 17.

ment. In this regard two distinct issues may come into contention. The first to determine which award or awards an exclusion agreement applies to. The second to determine which of the qualified rights under sections 1 and 2 are excluded by an exclusion agreement.

13.3.2.1 The award or awards to which an exclusion agreement applies

13.3.2.1.1 The rights that are capable of being affected by an exclusion agreement are all tied in different ways to an award. The right of appeal appertains to "any question of law arising out of *an award*".[1] The jurisdiction of the court to order the giving of reasons or further reasons is dependent on the court being satisfied "that *the award* does not or does not sufficiently set out the reasons for *the award*".[2] Less directly, the consultative case procedure contemplates a *prospective award* to which the determination of the question of law is material.[3] The language of section 3(1) again clearly associates the abrogation of rights under sections 1 and 2 with an award or awards in connection with which the right or rights arise. Thus the court shall not give leave to appeal or to make application for reasons or further reasons where there has been entered into an exclusion agreement which "excludes the right of appeal under section 1 . . . in relation to *that award*".[4] And in relation to the consultative case procedure, no application may be made to an arbitrator or umpire who has entered on a reference when an exclusion agreement is entered into "in relation to *an award to which the determination of the question of law is material*".[5] Under section 3(1) the drafting technique is adopted of using the apposite award as a means of identifying the precise right or rights abrogated by an exclusion agreement.

 13.3.2.1.2 The range of awards which may be made and which will be binding on the parties to a reference who have also entered into an exclusion agreement may be very great. Within a single reference there may arise a number of interim awards and a single final award, or even a number of interim or partial final awards. Nor need the scenario be confined to a single reference. At a particular point in time there may exist concurrent references, and over a period of time there may also arise a number of consecutive references. It is clear from section 3(2) that an exclusion agreement may be drafted so as to relate to all or any of the various awards which may be binding on the parties, including awards that derive from separate references. To the extent to which it is relevant, section 3(2) provides: "An exclusion agreement may be expressed so as to relate to a particular award, to awards under a particular reference or to any other description of awards, whether arising out of the same reference or not;". The subsection is permissive and facultative. It indicates the scope of the contractual freedom open to parties in entering into and determining the province of an exclusion agreement. It is hard to imagine a more wide ranging provision for its general effect would appear to be that it is open to the parties to render the ambit of an exclusion agreement as wide or as narrow as they wish. The last of the three specific circumstances recognised in section 3(2) would appear to give the provision great potential breadth

---

1. Section 1(2).
2. Section 1(5).
3. Section 3(1).
4. Section 3(1).
5. Section 3(1).

and permit what may be described as master or umbrella exclusion agreements, applicable to all references which may arise and involve the parties in the future.

13.3.2.1.3 The upshot of section 3(2) is that the parties may restrict the application of an exclusion agreement to a particular award of whatever character, or they may render an exclusion agreement applicable to some or all of the various kinds of awards that may be made in the course of a particular reference. It is frequently the case that a final award is preceded by one or more interim awards, in the precise sense of that term, or that the final determination of the various issues and questions in dispute is split into several awards, and with those preceding the ultimate final award in point of time alluded to as interim or partial final awards. The ultimate final award is frequently an award of costs. Further, where two or more references are consolidated or otherwise conducted concurrently by agreement, it is possible for separate awards to be made with regard to the different sets of arbitrating parties. In these kinds of situations the parties may direct an exclusion agreement as they choose, so as to relate to all, or some or only a specified award. In this regard it will avoid possible later difficulties if an exclusion agreement is clear in its terms and communicates unambiguously the intention of the parties. The more general and vague the adopted language the more difficult it may be to discern the precise intention of the parties. Ultimately the issue is one of construction. In *Marine Contractors Inc.* v. *Shell Petroleum Co. of Nigeria Ltd.*[6] Staughton J., at first instance, was of the opinion that on the proper construction of the I.C.C. Arbitration Rules, the exclusion agreement constituted by Article 24 was not confined to final awards but extended also to interim awards.

13.3.2.1.4 Section 3(2) also makes it plain that an exclusion agreement may apply further to any other description of award whether arising out of the same reference or not. This would seem to indicate that a single exclusion agreement may be made applicable to any description of award made in two or more references taking place concurrently or consecutively. It would also appear to suggest that an exclusion agreement may be made applicable to any description of award made in a future reference or references of certain or uncertain event. Thus, for example, where parties are engaged in a regular course of business and consistently adopt the practice of referring disputes and differences to arbitration, it would appear to be open to them to execute what may be described as an umbrella exclusion agreement applicable to all or specified awards that are made in any future reference(s) that may come into being. In association with such an exclusion agreement there may exist restrictions, such as limiting the agreement to a fixed period of time. It follows that an umbrella exclusion agreement may pre-date an arbitration agreement out of which a reference arises.

But although section 3(2) by its terms establishes a broad contractual freedom, it is nonetheless a freedom which is in turn curtailed by the statutory restriction to the effect that in some instances an exclusion agreement is only valid if entered into after the commencement of the relevant arbitration.[7]

13.3.2.2 Rights abrogated by an exclusion agreement

13.3.2.2.1 With one exception,[1] an exclusion agreement may only affect those quali-

---

6. [1984] 2 Lloyd's Rep. 77, 80. *Supra*, para. 13.3.1.2.
7. See *infra*, para. 13.4.2
1. See *infra*, para. 13.3.2.3.

fied rights arising under sections 1 and 2 of the 1979 Act. But subject to this limitation, it is for the parties to determine whether an agreement is to extend to each of the three rights specified therein or is to be confined to a particular right or rights. In each case the precise effect of an exclusion agreement is a question of construction.

13.3.2.2.2 Where the parties desire an all-embracing exclusion they must be cautious to use language appropriate to achieve that purpose. The safest approach is to exclude the rights *per nominatim* and make express reference to the substance of the three rights or their statutory sources. Those wishing to be doubly sure might be tempted to do both. In the uncertainty that followed the enactment of the 1979 Act some commentaries were disposed to caution and suggested that the *per nominatim* approach was not only advisable but also necessary.[2] Not only would this be an encouragement of prolixious and technical drafting, it is almost certain that this is not the case. It is probable that the same result may be achieved by a succinct and well chosen form of words. Such a phrase might be: "all rights of appeal and application arising under the Arbitration Act 1979". There is sense in separately identifying the right of appeal and rights of application for they are technically different concepts and governed by different procedures. It is also far from certain that the court would construe an allusion solely to an appeal or to an application as impliedly incorporating the other. In *Arab African Energy Corpn. Ltd.* v. *Olieprodukten Nederland B.V.*[3] the phrase "any form of appeal" was predictably held to apply to an appeal under section 1(2), but the wider question whether this format was also capable of applying to applications under sections 1(5)(b) and 2(1)(a) was not in issue and not considered. The manner in which section 3(1) is drafted offers at least the suggestion that a form of words that excludes the right to apply for leave to appeal under section 1(3)(b) also operates to exclude an application under section 1(5)(b).[4] There is a possible logic in this if reasons are perceived as being solely associated with appeals. By adopting such a view it is readily arguable that if there can be no appeal it is of no possible benefit or purpose to grant leave to apply for reasons or further reasons. But subject to this possible qualification, the question of construction will in each case turn on the precise words adopted by the parties and the broad context within which the exclusion agreement was entered into. It must not however be forgotten that exclusion agreements will frequently be adopted by the commercial community where the subtlety of legal procedural distinctions and fine points of construction are not always appreciated. To business people a phrase such as "all rights of appeal" has a clear comprehensiveness and it is suggested that a court ought to be slow to adopt a construction which frustrates the intentions of the parties.

13.3.2.2.3 Another form of words that might be effective to achieve a complete exclusion of all rights is "all rights of judicial review under the Arbitration Act 1979". Judicial review is a broad and imprecise phrase but it is one that has been widely used with regard to the jurisdiction of the High Court under sections 1 and 2. It is also used in the statutory marginal note to section 1. The one source of danger to the draftsman

---

2. See, *Supreme Court Practice* (1982), Vol. II, para. 3864; for the current edition, see (1993), Vol. II, para. 5885. Mustill and Boyd, *Commercial Arbitration, supra, op. cit.*, pp. 634–635.

3. [1983] 2 Lloyd's Rep. 419.

4. This possibility derives from the way the final paragraph in section 3(1) is drafted, and deriving from which it would at least appear to be arguable that the reference to "right of appeal under section 1" is a global reference to the rights referred to in paragraphs (a) and (b) of section 3(1).

would be a failure to appreciate that section 1 is concerned with the judicial review of awards and section 2 with the judicial review of a reference. But if, as in the phrase considered above, no words of delimitation are introduced, it may be that the court will be prepared to give the adopted language its fullest import.

13.3.2.2.4 When an exclusion agreement is expressed to exclude a particular right only, it is unlikely that the court might be persuaded to attribute to the parties a wider intention than that specifically expressed. In this kind of circumstance the maxim *expressio unius est exclusio alterius* may prevail,[5] although it must be borne in mind that the maxim is no more than an aid to construction.[6] In the result it is probable that an express reference to section 1 is unlikely to be construed as extending to include section 2; and that an express reference to a right of appeal is unlikely to extend to include a right to seek a judicial determination of a preliminary question of law, although, as suggested earlier, it might include the right to seek an order for reasons or further reasons. So also an express reference to judicial review of awards is unlikely to be construed as embracing judicial assistance in the course of a reference.

13.3.2.3 Fraud

13.3.2.3.1 In section 3(3) there is set out a statutory rule of construction to the following effect.

In any case where—
    (a) an arbitration agreement, other than a domestic arbitration agreement, provides for disputes between the parties to be referred to arbitration, and
    (b) a dispute to which the agreement relates involves the question whether a party has been guilty of fraud, and
    (c) the parties have entered into an exclusion agreement which is applicable to any award made on the reference of that dispute,
then, except in so far as the exclusion agreement otherwise provides, the High Court shall not exercise its powers under section 24(2) of the principal Act (to take steps necessary to enable the question to be determined by the High Court) in relation to that dispute.

Section 24(2) of the Arbitration Act 1950 provides[1]:

Where an agreement between any parties provides that disputes which may arise in the future between them shall be referred to arbitration, and a dispute which so arises involves the question whether any such party has been guilty of fraud, the High Court shall, so far as may be necessary to enable that question to be determined by the High Court, have power to order that the agreement shall cease to have effect and power to give leave to revoke the authority of any arbitrator or umpire appointed by or by virtue of the agreement.

13.3.2.3.2 The subsection confers a discretionary jurisdiction on the High Court, which may be exercised with a view to transferring a dispute agreed to be referred and involving an allegation of fraud from arbitration to the High Court.[2] The jurisdiction only arises in the case of a submission under a non-domestic agreement to refer future disputes and the High Court is empowered, to the extent it is necessary to achieve its purpose, to order that the arbitration agreement shall cease to have effect and to give

5. The maxim in translation is to the effect—"that which is expressed puts an end to that which is silent".
6. *Dean* v. *Wiesengrund* [1955] 2 Q.B. 120, 130, per Jenkins L.J.
1. Section 24(2) has no application when a judge-arbitrator or judge-umpire is appointed: see Administration of Justice Act 1970, s. 4(4) and Schedule 3, art. 10.
2. For a recent judicial consideration of section 24(2), see, *Ashville Investments Ltd.* v. *Elmer Contractors Ltd.* [1988] 2 All E.R. 577.

leave to revoke the authority of any arbitrator or umpire appointed by or by virtue of the arbitration agreement.[3] Where the arbitration agreement which is to cease to have effect is a *Scott* v. *Avery* agreement, the court may further order, by virtue of section 25(4) of the 1950 Act, that the provision making an award a condition precedent to the bringing of an action shall also cease to have effect as regards the dispute in issue.

13.3.2.3.3 The consequential effect of section 3(3) is that where the parties have entered into an agreement to refer future disputes to arbitration, other than under a domestic arbitration agreement,[4] and a dispute which arises thereunder involves a question of fraud, if the parties have also entered into an exclusion agreement which is applicable to any award made on the reference of that dispute, the exclusion agreement, except in so far as it may otherwise provide, shall be construed as extending so as to exclude the jurisdiction of the High Court under section 24(2) of the 1950 Act. It is to be noted that this extended application of an exclusion agreement is only applicable in relation to non-domestic (or international) arbitration agreements, and applies to this category of arbitration agreement even when a special category dispute is referred thereunder.[5] Also, it is to be noted, section 3(3) does not introduce an absolute rule of construction. The effect of section 24(2) may be retained, in whole or in part, by express provision in an exclusion agreement.

13.3.2.3.4 A general theme within English law is that although fraud is arbitrable and an allegation of fraud may therefore be referred to the decision of an arbitrator,[6] nonetheless the very nature and potential consequences of an allegation of fraud strongly suggest that such allegations may be more appropriately considered by a court of law than an arbitral tribunal.[7] An allegation of fraud is a grave issue and in consequence any allegation must be specified with particularity and supported by compelling evidence before the allegation will be found to have been validly made.[8] In the English experience allegations of fraud tend to be rare and when made are the object of close and careful scrutiny. Section 24(2) of the 1950 Act establishes a mechanism by which this object may be achieved.[9] Throughout the present context fraud

---

3. See, Arbitration Act 1950, s. 1, for a general statement of the jurisdiction of the High Court to give leave to revoke the authority of an arbitrator or umpire.

4. See *infra*, para. 13.4.3.

5. See *infra*, para. 13.4.4.

6. It will in each case be a question of construction to determine whether the parties have by their arbitration agreement conferred a jurisdiction to determine disputes alleging fraud against a party; see, for example, *Cook* v. *Catchpole* (1864) 11 L.T. 264; *Stevens & Sons* v. *Timber and General Mutual Accident Insurance Association Ltd.* (1933) 45 Ll.L.Rep. 43. The problem of construction is erased when the parties expressly stipulate for the reference of a dispute involving fraud, see *Heyman* v. *Darwins Ltd.* [1942] A.C. 356, 392.

7. *Wallis* v. *Hirsch* (1856) 1 C.B.N.S. 316; *Russell* v. *Russell* (1880) 14 Ch. D. 471; *Minifie* v. *Railway Passengers Assurance Co.* (1881) 44 L.T. 552; *Vowdrey* v. *Simpson* [1896] 1 Ch. 166; *Barnes* v. *Youngs* [1898] 1 Ch. 414; *Green* v. *Howell* [1910] 1 Ch. 495; *Radford* v. *Hair* [1971] Ch. 758; *Camilla Cotton Oil Co.* v. *Granadex S.A. and Tracomin S.A.* [1976] 2 Lloyd's Rep. 10, 16 (H.L.); *Ashville Investments Ltd.* v. *Elmer Contractors Ltd.* [1988] 2 All E.R. 577.

8. *Camilla Cotton Oil Co.* v. *Granadex S.A. and Tracomin S.A.*, *supra*, p. 10, per Lord Wilberforce.

9. Where there is an allegation of fraud a court may also refuse an application for a stay of legal proceedings commenced in breach of an arbitration agreement. The refusal may arise out of the discretion enjoyed under s. 4(1) of the 1950 Act; and in the circumstances when s. 24(2) of the 1950 Act would be applicable, a discretion to refuse a stay also arises under s. 24(3); see, *Permavox Ltd.* v. *Royal Exchange Assurance* (1939) 64 Ll.L.Rep. 145. Where s. 1(1) of the Arbitration Act 1975 is applicable (legal proceedings brought in breach of a non-domestic arbitration agreement) the grant of a stay is mandatory, even when an allegation of fraud is made, except where the circumstances specified in section 1(1) prevail.

bears its narrow meaning as understood under the common law, alluding to fraudulent misrepresentation (deceit)[10] and other forms of dishonest conduct.

13.3.2.3.5 The purpose underlying section 3(3) is to protect against the policy of the 1979 Act and the effectiveness of exclusion agreements in the case of international arbitration agreements being undermined by the circumventory tactic of invoking the discretionary jurisdiction under section 24(2) of the 1950 Act. At the time of the passing of the 1979 Act the impression prevailed that fraud was more lightly entertained in many foreign jurisdictions than was the case in England, and that foreign lawyers acting under different codes of practice might in consequence be far readier to advance an accusation of fraud than would their English counterparts. Against this background, the jurisdiction vested in the High Court under section 24(2) of the 1950 Act represented a threat to the policy of the 1979 Act in its application to international arbitration held in London for it provided a potential stratagem for circumventing exclusion agreements otherwise validly executed under the 1979 Act.[11] The terms of section 3(3) make it plain that if the parties to international arbitration agreements wish to retain the jurisdiction established under section 24(2) of the 1950 Act, an express term to this effect must be incorporated into the exclusion agreement.

Section 3(3) has no application to domestic arbitration agreements. With regard to this category of arbitration agreement the pre-1979 policy prevails and any attempt to exclude the jurisdiction of the High Court under section 24(2) of the 1950 Act is void.

13.4 LIMITATIONS ON THE VALIDITY OF EXCLUSION AGREEMENTS

13.4.1 Statutory arbitrations

13.4.1.1 Exclusion agreements can only validly affect rights arising under sections 1 and 2 of the 1979 Act in relation to consensual arbitrations. They have no application to awards made and references arising under statutory arbitrations. In the result, rights of judicial review arising under sections 1 and 2, which are equally applicable to consensual and statutory arbitrations,[1] are in the case of statutory arbitrations entrenched and incapable of exclusion. This is the effect of section 3(5) which in peremptory and unqualified terms provides:

An exclusion agreement shall be of no effect in relation to an award made on, or a question of law arising in the course of a reference under, a statutory arbitration, that is to say, such an arbitration as is referred to in subsection (1) of section 31 of the principal Act.

13.4.1.2 A statute may provide that all or a particular class of disputes arising under the statute shall in each and every case or subject to conditions specified in the statute be exclusively determined by a scheme of arbitration established under the statute. It is customary for the statute also to prescribe the constitution of the arbitral tribunal and to lay down rules governing arbitral procedure, or to make provision for the making of procedural rules. This, in general terms, is what is meant by statutory arbi-

---

10. *Ashville Investments Ltd.* v. *Elmer Contractors Ltd.* [1988] 2 All E.R. 577, 599, per Bingham L.J.
11. *Hansard* (H.L.) Vol. 397, p. 1215.
1. Section 7(1)(d) of the Arbitration Act 1979 and s. 31 of the Arbitration Act 1950, considered *infra*. See also Chapter 1, para. 1.7.4.

tration and such schemes of statutory arbitration are established under a miscellany of statutes.[2] That this is also the perception of statutory arbitration for the purposes of section 3(5) is made clear by the allusion in the subsection itself that a statutory arbitration means, "such an arbitration as is referred to in subsection (1) of section 31 of the principal Act". Under section 31(1) of the Arbitration Act 1950 a statutory arbitration is described as, "every arbitration under any other Act (whether passed before or after the commencement of this Act)". The phrase "any other Act" refers to any statute other than the Arbitration Act 1950. In general terms, therefore, statutory arbitration refers to any scheme of arbitration established by statute other than the arbitration legislation.[3]

13.4.1.3 The mere fact that a statute establishes an alternative procedure to the courts of law for the determination of disputes arising under it does not automatically mean that the alternative scheme is to be characterised as statutory arbitration. In each case it is a question of statutory interpretation. Where a statute expressly describes the procedure established as arbitral this in most cases will be compelling, if not conclusive, evidence of the intention of the legislature. In other cases the legislative intention is to be extracted from an examination of the statute as a whole.[4]

13.4.1.4 Statutory arbitrations differ significantly from consensual arbitrations. In the first place they are invariably mandatory. The parties to a dispute or difference have no alternative but to resort to the statutory machinery. Secondly, they are public tribunals and therefore very different from the private and domestic character of arbitration tribunals established by the agreement of the parties. Generically statutory arbitrations are closer to administrative tribunals that proliferate within the English system of public law and in common with these public tribunals are subject to review by the prerogative orders which have no application to consensual arbitrations.[5] Thus statutory tribunals are subject to the judicial review procedure now governed by R.S.C. Order 51 and may additionally come within the province of various public statutory measures, such as the Tribunals and Inquiries Act 1992, section 10, which requires specified tribunals to give reasons for their decisions. But although innately public in character, they additionally continue, with certain exceptions, to be subject to the arbitration legislation unless expressly or impliedly excluded by the statutory provisions under which the arbitration is established.[6] This is the effect of section 31(1) of the 1950 Act which, subject to the provisions specified in subsection (2),[7] applies Part I of the 1950 Act "to every arbitration under any other Act (whether passed before or after the commencement of this Act) as if the arbitration were pursuant to an arbitration agreement and as if that other Act were an arbitration agreement, except in so far as this Act is inconsistent with that other Act or with any rules or procedure authorised or recognised thereby". In consequence the scheme of

---

2. See, generally, *Russell on Arbitration* (20th edn.), Chapter 2.

3. It does not, however, extend to arbitrations under s. 64 of the County Courts Act 1984: see s. 7(3) of the 1979 Act.

4. *Racecourse Betting Control Board* v. *Secretary for Air* [1944] Ch. 114.

5. *Racecourse Betting Control Board* v. *Secretary for Air, ibid.*; *Bremer Vulkan Schiffbau und Maschinenfabrik* v. *South India Shipping Corporation Ltd.* [1981] A.C. 909, 978, per Lord Diplock; *K/S A/S Bill Biakh and V/S A/S Bill Biali* v. *Hyundai Corporation* [1988] 1 Lloyd's Rep. 187, 190, per Steyn J.

6. See, for example, *Potato Marketing Board* v. *Merricks* [1958] 2 Q.B. 316.

7. By virtue of s. 31(2) of the 1950 Act the following provisions in Part I of the Act are inapplicable to statutory arbitrations: ss. 2(1), 3, 5, 18(3), 24, 25, 27 and 29.

judicial review established under the 1979 Act is equally applicable to statutory arbitration unless the statute under which the statutory arbitration is established expressly or impliedly excludes all or any of the rights arising under the 1979 Act.[8] When and to the extent the arbitration legislation is applicable statutory arbitrations assume a hybrid character, for they are subject to both public and private systems of law.

13.4.2 Moment exclusion agreement entered into

13.4.2.1 Introduction

13.4.2.1.1 The general rule is that an exclusion agreement is valid at whatever moment in time in relation to the arbitral process it is entered into. There are, however, two very important exceptions to this general rule. In the case of (i) domestic arbitration agreements and (ii) arbitrations that relate to special category disputes governed by the law of England and Wales, an exclusion agreement is of legal effect only if entered into *after the commencement of the arbitration* in which the award is made or in which the question of law arises. In these instances a pre-commencement exclusion agreement is in the language of sections 3(6) and 4(1) of "no effect". This is an ambiguous phrase and could mean that the exclusion agreement is either void or unenforceable. Taking into account the underlying policy of the legislation it is highly probable that the former interpretation will prevail, although for practical purposes it is doubtful if any significant consequence turns on the distinction. The ineffectiveness of an exclusion agreement would appear to be an issue not confined to the pleadings, but a point capable of being taken by the court of its own volition.

13.4.2.1.2 The two exceptions, as was discussed in Chapter 1,[1] are influenced by different policy considerations. The fact of their existence does however mean that there is introduced into the law yet a further mode of characterising arbitration agreements. For purposes associated with the validity of exclusion agreements under the 1979 Act arbitration agreements may be characterised as (i) domestic arbitration agreements; (ii) arbitration agreements under which special category disputes are referred; and (iii) international arbitration agreements, a residual category not expressly recognised in the 1979 Act. In practice arbitration agreements within the second category would invariably also be international arbitration agreements but for the particular character of the dispute referred. This scheme of characterisation will be adopted later in the text for the purpose of developing a statement of the relevant law. But before moving forward to that discussion, the crucial test of a valid exclusion agreement introduced by the 1979 Act makes it necessary to confront as an initial issue the question of when an arbitration is commenced. The question is far from novel and frequently arises in the context of contractual and statutory time limits.

13.4.2.2 Commencement of an arbitration

13.4.2.2.1 By virtue of section 7(2) of the 1979 Act, subsections (2) and (3) of section 29 of the Arbitration Act 1950 are made applicable to determine when an arbitration

---

8. This would appear to be the combined effect of the Arbitration Act 1979, s. 7(1)(d) and the Arbitration Act 1950, s. 31(1).
1. See para. 1.3.

is deemed to be commenced for the purposes of the 1979 Act. To the extent to which it is relevant, section 29 of the principal Act provides[1]:

(2) . . . an arbitration shall be deemed to be commenced when one party to the arbitration agreement serves on the other party or parties a notice requiring him or them to appoint or concur in appointing an arbitrator, or, where the arbitration agreement provides that the reference shall be to a person named or designated in the agreement, requiring him or them to submit the dispute to the person so named or designated.

(3) Any such notice as is mentioned in subsection (2) of this section may be served either—
  (a) by delivering it to the person on whom it is to be served; or
  (b) by leaving it at the usual or last known place of abode in England of that person; or
  (c) by sending it by post in a registered letter addressed to that person at his usual or last known place of abode in England;

as well as in any other manner provided in the arbitration agreement; and where a notice is sent by post in manner prescribed by paragraph (c) of this subsection, service thereof shall, unless the contrary is proved, be deemed to have been effected at the time at which the letter would have been delivered in the ordinary course of post.

13.4.2.2.2 In subsection (2) two distinct situations would appear to be contemplated. The first is the case of an arbitration agreement which neither names nor otherwise designates an arbitrator. In this kind of situation an arbitration is commenced when one party to the arbitration agreement serves a notice on the other party or parties requiring him or them to appoint or concur in appointing an arbitrator. The first alternative is relevant to a two or three-arbitrator tribunal, with each party appointing an arbitrator. In such a case an arbitration is commenced when one party serves a notice requiring the other party to appoint his arbitrator. The second alternative is applicable to a sole-arbitrator tribunal. In such a case an arbitration is commenced when one party serves a notice on the other party requiring him to concur in the appointment of an arbitrator.[2]

The second situation contemplated by subsection (2) is where an arbitration agree-

---

1. The statutory definition of the "commencement of an arbitration" in s. 29(2) and (3) of the 1950 Act is followed closely by the statutory definition of the same concept in s. 34(3) and (4) of the Limitation Act 1980, which is applicable to the 1980 Act and any other limitation enactment. This latter statutory definition is however structured differently and not expressed in precisely the same language. It is to the following effect:

  "(3) For the purposes of this Act and of any other limitation enactment an arbitration shall be treated as being commenced—
    (a) when one party to the arbitration serves on the other party or parties a notice requiring him or them to appoint an arbitrator or to agree to the appointment of an arbitrator; or
    (b) where the arbitration agreement provides that the reference shall be to a person named or designated in the agreement, when one party to the arbitration serves on the other party or parties a notice requiring him or them to submit the dispute to the person so named or designated.
  (4) Any such notice may be served either—
    (a) by delivering it to the person on whom it is to be served; or
    (b) by leaving it at the usual or last-known place of abode in England and Wales of that person; or
    (c) by sending it by post in a registered letter addressed to that person at his usual or last-known place of abode in England and Wales:
  as well as in any other manner provided in the arbitration agreement."

2. See *Nea Agrex S.A.* v. *Baltic Shipping Co. Ltd. and Intershipping Charter Co. (The Agios Lazaros)* [1976] 2 Lloyd's Rep. 47; [1976] Q.B. 933 (a case concerned with the interpretation of the Limitation Act 1939, s. 27(2)); *Court Line Ltd.* v. *Aktiebolaget Gøtaverken (The Halcyon The Great)* [1984] 1 Lloyd's Rep. 283.

ment names or designates an arbitrator. In this kind of situation the arbitration is commenced when one party to the arbitration agreement serves a notice on the other party or parties requiring him or them to submit the dispute to the person(s) so named or designated.[3]

13.4.2.2.3 An uncertainty associated with section 29(2) is whether it provides an exclusive statutory definition of the moment an arbitration is commenced, or whether it is capable of being superseded by the express agreement of the parties. In other words, is it open to the parties as a question of contract to define the moment their arbitration is to be considered as having commenced, and in so doing specify an event not identified in section 29(2). With regard to the service of notice subsection (3) recognises that the matter may be governed by the agreement of the parties. Subsection (2) is also expressed as a "deeming" provision and this may at least suggest that it is not mandatory, but is to be interpreted as establishing an implied term or as otherwise operating in a manner analogous to an implied term. On its proper interpretation subsection (2) would appear to be subordinate to the will of the parties and to entertain the possibility of the parties defining as a matter of contract the precise moment the arbitration is to commence. Such an interpretation would also be consistent with principle. The decision of the Court of Appeal in *The Agios Lazaros*[4] also appears to offer a certain support for the conclusion here suggested.

13.4.2.2.4 Whether there is a valid notice claiming arbitration within any of the above situations will in each case turn on the proper construction of the document in question. In this regard it is highly improbable that the court will adopt an excessively technical approach and it would seem to be the case that a valid notice may be inferred from general language. In *The Agios Lazaros* Lord Denning M.R. was prepared to conclude that[5] "in any case a simple notice in writing requiring the difference to be submitted to arbitration is deemed to be a commencement of the arbitration". Such a notice carries by implication a request to the other party to appoint or concur in appointing an arbitrator, or to submit the dispute or difference to a named or designated arbitrator. The drawing of such an inference is not prejudiced by the fact that a communication is couched in polite and courteous terms, or because it also expresses a willingness to come to an amicable settlement. On the facts in *The Agios Lazaros* a letter in the terms, "Please advise your proposals in order to settle this matter or name your arbitrators", was held sufficient to effect a commencement of the arbitration and with the consequence that a contractual time limit ceased to run.[6]

13.4.2.2.5 The notice must be in writing and may be effectively served by any mode specified in subsection (3), or in any manner provided for in the arbitration agreement.[7] It must also intimate some information as to the dispute or disputes to be

---

3. Section 29(2) of the Arbitration Act 1950 is in this regard more ambiguous than s. 34(3) of the Limitation Act 1980. It is submitted that both statutory provisions enjoy a common meaning and that the construction to be given to s. 29(2) follows the much clearer structural presentation adopted in s. 34(3).

4. *Supra*, note 2. Considered in *Peter Cremer G.m.b.H. & Co.* v. *Sugat Food Industries Ltd. (The Rimon)* [1981] 2 Lloyd's Rep. 640.

5. *Supra*, note 2, p. 51.

6. See also *Surrendra Overseas Ltd.* v. *Government of Sri Lanka* [1977] 1 Lloyd's Rep. 653.

7. Cf. *N.V. Stoom Maats "De Maas"* v. *Nippon Yusen Kaisha (The Pendrecht)* [1980] 2 Lloyd's Rep. 56, 64; *Nea Agrex S.A.* v. *Baltic Shipping Co. Ltd. (The Agios Lazaros)*, *supra*, per Goff L.J. at p. 55, Shaw L.J. at p. 58.

referred to arbitration.[8] Where the commencement of an arbitration is wholly governed by the express agreement of the parties it is presumably possible for the requirement of written notice to be dispensed with, although this is an unlikely prospect in practice.

13.4.2.2.6 The commencement of an arbitration is a separate concept from the question as to when an arbitrator is validly appointed. As the law presently stands an arbitration may be commenced before the necessary preconditions to the appointment of an arbitrator, as a question of law, have been satisfied.[9]

13.4.3 Domestic arbitration agreements

The limitation on the effectiveness of an exclusion agreement in relation to an award made on or a question of law arising in the course of a reference under a domestic arbitration agreement is expressed in section 3(6) in the following terms:

An exclusion agreement shall be of no effect in relation to an award made on, or a question of law arising in the course of a reference under, an arbitration agreement which is a domestic arbitration agreement unless the exclusion agreement is entered into after the commencement of the arbitration in which the award is made or, as the case may be, in which the question of law arises.

The predominant policy underlying section 3(6) is to protect against the abuse of dominant position when there exists an imbalance in the commercial and negotiating strengths of the contracting parties.[1] There is a danger that parties such as consumers and small retailers, who enjoy little bargaining muscle, would, without some statutory protection, be compelled by the superior might of powerful commercial interests with whom they conduct business, often on the basis of standard form contracts, to surrender their legal rights under the 1979 Act against their true wishes. In such circumstances exclusion agreements would be the product of imposition rather than voluntary agreement. The Act provides protection against this danger by rendering ineffective any exclusion agreement entered into before the commencement of a relevant arbitration. It is at this stage that the effect of any power imbalance is most acute and the need for protection greatest. Although the weaker party may have no real choice but to accept an arbitration agreement,[2] he is not also compelled to yield to an exclusion agreement that may be embodied in an arbitration agreement or otherwise associated with it. Equally the Act assumes that after a dispute or difference has arisen and been referred to arbitration the position of the parties is likely to be more fairly balanced and in consequence an exclusion agreement entered into at this stage is likely to be the product of a genuine consensus, so excluding the justification for any legislative protection. This presumably may take the form of affirming, after the commencement of an arbitration, an earlier and ineffective exclusion agreement.

---

8. *Court Line Ltd.* v. *Aktiebolaget Gøtaverken (The Halcyon The Great)*, *supra*.
9. For an elucidation of the preconditions to a valid arbitral appointment, see *Tradax Export S.A.* v. *Volkswagenwerk A.G.* [1970] 1 Lloyd's Rep. 62.
1. See Chapter 1, para. 1.3.10.
2. For statutory protection now offered to consumers, see the Consumer Arbitration Agreements Act 1988.

13.4.3.1 Concept of a domestic arbitration agreement

13.4.3.1.1 For the purpose of the 1979 Act a domestic arbitration agreement is defined by section 3(7) in the following terms[1]:

In this section "domestic arbitration agreement" means an arbitration agreement which does not provide, expressly or by implication, for arbitration in a State other than the United Kingdom and to which neither—

(a) an individual who is a national of, or habitually resident in, any State other than the United Kingdom, nor

(b) a body corporate which is incorporated in, or whose central management and control is exercised in, any State other than the United Kingdom,

is a party at the time the arbitration agreement is entered into.

For the purposes of section 3(7) an arbitration agreement bears the same meaning as under section 32 of the 1950 Act.[2] That is, it is a written agreement to submit present or future differences to arbitration, whether an arbitrator is named therein or not.

To qualify as "domestic" an arbitration agreement must satisfy two general requirements. The one as to the seat of the arbitration specified in the arbitration agreement; and the other as to the nationality and territorial ties of the parties to the arbitration agreement, both natural and juristic, at the time the agreement is entered into.

13.4.3.1.2 In defining a domestic arbitration agreement the legislation adopts a negative approach indicating what it is not rather than what it is, with the concept thereafter emerging by necessary inference from the negative stipulations. The approach is cumbersome, complex, and unnecessarily confusing. When the definition is turned on its head and given a positive orientation, which is an exercise not without its dangers and difficulties, a domestic arbitration agreement comes forth as an arbitration agreement that (i) provides, expressly or impliedly, for arbitration in the United Kingdom and (ii) at the time the arbitration agreement is entered into, every party thereto is either (a) an individual who is a national of and habitually resident in the United Kingdom, or (b) a body corporate which is incorporated in and whose central management and control is exercised in the United Kingdom. In the generality of matters it is doubtful if the statutory concept loses anything by this inversion. To prove any of the positive stipulations is also by necessary inference to establish the corresponding negative stipulations in the statutory definition. It would be very exceptional for a natural person to be *habitually* resident in more than one State, or for a company to have its *central management and control* in more than one State. Again it may be presumed that a company can only have one place of incorporation, in the strict sense of that term, although a company operating in a foreign State may be required to register under the municipal law of that State. It is on the other hand possible for a natural person to have dual nationality, but this does not appear to pose a difficulty for within the concept of a domestic arbitration agreement the nationality of a natural person is tied to habitual residence.

The central thrust of the statutory definition is to confine the notion of a domestic arbitration agreement to agreements which provide, expressly or impliedly, for arbitration within the United Kingdom and which are entered into by natural and corporate persons with United Kingdom nationality and who also retain a very close

1. The definition follows closely the definition of the same concept in s. 1(4) of the Arbitration Act 1975. There is, however, one signficant difference which is considered later in the text at para. 13.4.3.2.4.
2. Section 7(1)(c). See also Chapter 1, para. 1.7.5 and Chapter 3, para. 3.4.

territorial association with the United Kingdom. From this general proposition there arise a number of clear deductions. If an arbitration agreement provides, expressly or impliedly, for arbitration in a state other than the United Kingdom, it cannot be a domestic arbitration agreement, even if the parties are nationals of and have a close territorial tie with the United Kingdom. So also an arbitration agreement which provides, expressly or impliedly, for arbitration in the United Kingdom cannot be a domestic arbitration agreement if, at the time the agreement was entered into, all, some or one of the parties was a national of or habitually resident in a state other than the United Kingdom; or, in the case of corporate parties, all, some or one was incorporated in or had its central management and control in a state other than the United Kingdom.

13.4.3.1.3 Beyond the criteria specified in section 3(7), other factors that might be thought of as diluting the link between an arbitration agreement and the United Kingdom are irrelevant. Thus considerations touching on the negotiation and making of an arbitration agreement, the location of the dispute and the governing law have no part to play. The fact that an arbitration agreement was negotiated and entered into in a foreign state is immaterial. As also is the fact that the dispute or difference to which an arbitration agreement relates emanates from an act, incident or circumstance which took place in a foreign state. The fact that the governing law of the dispute or arbitration agreement is a system of law other than English law is again of no significance. Thus if two nationals of the United Kingdom who are also habitually resident in the United Kingdom contract abroad on terms contemplating a foreign performance and on the basis of a foreign governing law, and subsequently refer to arbitration a dispute arising thereunder in pursuance of a London arbitration clause contained in the contract, the arbitration agreement continues to be characterised as a domestic arbitration agreement.

13.4.3.2 Facets of the statutory definition

Within the definition of a domestic arbitration agreement provided in section 3(7) there exist a number of concepts that require a measure of amplification. There also exist a number of ambiguities and uncertainties that merit identification and consideration. Many of the issues raised will turn on the proper interpretation of section 3(7) and this will raise the broader question of whether the subsection is to be interpreted strictly and narrowly or whether it is to be given a generous and embracing interpretation. It is suggested that since the effect of characterising an arbitration agreement as domestic is to place a restriction on the validity of a pre-commencement exclusion agreement, the courts ought to be slow to artificially designate as "domestic" arbitration agreements with an associated foreign element. But in the ultimate all will turn on the proper interpretation of section 3(7). It has previously been observed that the presence of a foreign element will not necessarily preclude an arbitration agreement from being characterised as domestic.

13.4.3.2.1 UNITED KINGDOM

To amount to a domestic arbitration agreement there must be an express or implied provision for arbitration in the United Kingdom and the parties must enjoy a defined relationship with the United Kingdom. At least this becomes the case when the statutory definition is reformulated to express positive criteria.

In the absence of a contrary intention in the 1979 Act, of which there would appear to be no sign, the term "United Kingdom" means Great Britain and Northern Ireland.[1] In turn, Great Britain embraces England, Wales and Scotland.[2] In the absence of express statutory provision to the contrary, and again no such provision is to be found in the 1979 Act, the term "United Kingdom" does not extend so as to include the Channel Islands and Isle of Man.[3]

But although the concept of a domestic arbitration agreement is in its positive formulation defined *inter alia* by reference to its association with the United Kingdom, the 1979 Act does not otherwise extend to all the constituent parts of the United Kingdom. It is confined to England and Wales, and does not extend to Scotland and Northern Ireland.[4] In the result an arbitration agreement which provides for arbitration in Scotland or Northern Ireland and which is entered into by parties who satisfy the provisions of section 3(7), is a domestic arbitration agreement, notwithstanding that the 1979 Act has no application if the arbitration is actually held in Scotland or Northern Ireland, for in that case the curial law is *prima facie* Scots law or the law of Northern Ireland, of which the 1979 Act is not a part.[5]

13.4.3.2.2 SITUS OF THE ARBITRATION

13.4.3.2.2.1 A domestic arbitration agreement is an agreement that does not provide, expressly or impliedly, for arbitration in any state other than the United Kingdom; or substantially to the same effect, it is an agreement which does provide, expressly or impliedly, for arbitration within the United Kingdom.

The statutory definition appears to assume that every arbitration agreement either makes an express provision as to the *situs* of an arbitration, or where it does not, that the intention of the parties as to the question of *situs* is capable of being identified by implication. Very often the *situs* of an arbitration will be agreed by the parties and expressed in the arbitration agreement or in incorporated Rules. When this is the case the position is unproblematical. But in the absence of an express agreement, the proper implication to be drawn from an arbitration agreement may give rise to difficulties. In each case it will be a question of fact to be decided on the facts, circumstances and context of individual cases. Where two resident nationals refer to arbitration a wholly domestic dispute, the inference that they intend the arbitration to be held within their home state would appear incontrovertible. But where there is present an international element, the question of the proper inference to be drawn becomes more problematical. An appropriate implication may be suggested by the previous practice of the parties, if any exists; or, where relevant, in association with the choice of institutional arbitration. Thus, for example, where a dispute is referred to an arbitrator who is a member of the London Maritime Arbitrators' Association or who is appointed to act under the scheme of Lloyd's Salvage Arbitration, which are

---

1. Interpretation Act 1978, s. 5, Sch. 1. The Act came into force on 1 January 1979.
2. Union with Scotland Act 1706, preamble, Art. 1, as read with the Interpretation Act 1978, s. 22(1), Sch. 2, para. 5(a).
3. *Supra*, n. 1. Contrast the British Nationality Act 1981, s. 50, wherein it is stipulated that the "United Kingdom" means Great Britain, Northern Ireland and the Islands, taken together. The "Islands" mean the Channel Islands and the Isle of Man.
4. See Chapter 1, para. 1.7.2.
5. See Chapter 1, para. 1.7.8.

organisations with strong London connections and which only function in London, it would appear a strong, if not irresistible, inference that the parties intend the *situs* of their arbitration to be London. The same principle may equally apply in relation to London commodity arbitrations. But where there exists no pre-existing arbitral relationship between the parties and the parties have not adopted a mode of arbitration with a strong geographical association, the question of an implied choice of *situs* becomes a very difficult one and may reduce itself to a speculative exercise.

13.4.3.2.2.2 A particular difficulty arises when the parties expressly defer the question of the *situs* of an arbitration until a dispute arises. In this situation there exists no express provision in the arbitration agreement as to the *situs* of the arbitration and the conduct of the parties would also appear to preclude the recognition of any implied provision as to the *situs*. A variant of this kind of circumstance is when the choice of *situs* is delegated by the parties to the arbitration tribunal or to an institution. In these situations there is in strictness no express or implied provision as to *situs* to be found in the arbitration agreement. The parties are coming to the choice by an alternative method. A possible solution to the problem may be found by aligning the intention of the parties with their later decision or the decision of the arbitration tribunal or third party, so that the parties are taken to have intended the *situs* ultimately chosen. This kind of approach is of course only possible so long as section 3(7) is not interpreted as requiring the actual *situs* to be identified at the time the agreement is entered into. It is sufficient that the arbitration agreement makes provision for the means by which the *situs* is to be established. But it is far from certain that this line of argument would succeed for the express language of section 3(7) is clear and may prove very difficult to circumvent. Moreover it may be that the test of intention, express or implied, is to be applied at the time the arbitration agreement is entered into, thus placing the question of *situs* and the *status* of the parties on a common footing.

13.4.3.2.2.3 It may however be the case that the problems contemplated above do not arise, for it is possible to take a radically different approach to the interpretation of section 3(7). In its express language what the subsection requires is that there should be absent an implied choice of *situs* in a State other than the United Kingdom and not that there should be capable of being identified an implied choice of *situs* within the United Kingdom. It is at least arguable that there is no obligation under section 3(7) beyond establishing the absence of an implied choice of a foreign *situs*: the absence of an implied choice of *situs* in a State other than the United Kingdom satisfies without more the particular provision of section 3(7) in question. The advantage of this approach is that the many problems which arise as an incident of modern arbitral practice are avoided, as also are the factual difficulties in establishing an implied intention to arbitrate within the United Kingdom. If this proves an accurate approach to the problem it also reveals a danger associated with the earlier approach adopted in the text of expounding the concept of a domestic arbitration agreement by inverting the negative language of section 3(7) into positive assertions.

13.4.3.2.2.4 A further question which arises from the definition is whether the question of characterisation depends wholly on the express or implied intent of the parties in relation to the *situs* of the arbitration or whether it is additionally necessary for the arbitration to actually take place at the intended *situs*. Doubtlessly in the great majority of instances there will be no variance between the two and the actual arbitral process will be established according to the intentions of the parties as declared in the arbitration agreement. But this is not inevitably the case and the potential difficulty may be amplified through a straightforward example. A and B, both nationals of and habitually resident in the United Kingdom, enter into a contract containing an arbitration agreement which designates Brussels as the place of any future arbitration. An exclusion agreement is included in the arbitration agreement. Later, after a dispute arises out of the contract, not being a special category dispute, the parties agree in writing to refer the dispute to London arbitration. The validity of the exclusion agreement will depend on the characterisation of the arbitration agreement, which in turn will depend on the proper interpretation of section 3(7). At the time the arbitration agreement is first entered into it is clearly not a domestic arbitration agreement for it provides for a foreign *situs*, and if the test applies at this point in time the exclusion agreement is valid. But the later variation agreed by the parties results in the arbitration actually being held in the United Kingdom, with the consequence that all the elements of a domestic arbitration agreement are present, although they did not exist from the start and have been built up over time and through a contractual variation. If the test may be deferred to take into account the subsequent developments, the arbitration agreement is domestic and the exclusion agreement is ineffective. The language of section 3(7) does not provide a clear answer to this kind of issue and in particular there is ambiguity concerning the precise interpretation to be given to the phrase "arbitration agreement". Is the phrase confined to the initial arbitration agreement entered into by the parties, or does the phrase also embrace any subsequent amendments that may be agreed? Also, the reference in section 3(7) to "at the time the arbitration agreement is entered into" would appear to relate specifically to the status of the parties and not to the *situs* of the arbitration, but it may nonetheless be of assistance in divining the intention of the legislature. The answer to the problem may ultimately be found in the fundamental object underpinning section 3(7) which is to provide a test for determining the effectiveness of exclusion agreements. In this matter those contemplating arbitration require a certain and reliable test so that they can manage their affairs with assurance; and they require to occupy this position at the moment they are committing themselves to arbitration. The language of section 3(7) appears to be in sympathy with this objective by focusing on the provision as to *situs* made in the arbitration agreement, to the exclusion of all else. Considerations of policy and statutory interpretation therefore appear to suggest that the allusion to arbitration agreement in section 3(7) is a reference to the arbitration agreement first entered into by the parties, and that the question of *situs* turns wholly on its provisions. In the result, if an arbitration agreement provides for a foreign *situs* the agreement is a non-domestic arbitration agreement and the characterisation cannot thereafter be affected by the later conduct of the parties, even if the result of that conduct is to agree a *situs* in the United Kingdom.

13.4.3.2.3 ARBITRATING PARTIES

Section 3(7) recognises two general categories of arbitrating parties, namely natural and juristic persons.

13.4.3.2.3.1 Natural persons. When a natural person is an arbitrating party it must be shown that the party is not "an individual who is a national of, or habitually resident in, any State other than the United Kingdom".

Nationality will be a concept defined by municipal law. The relevant domestic law is found in the British Nationality Act 1981. The Act, however, refers not to United Kingdom nationality but to British nationality, which is a corresponding concept.

Habitually resident is qualitatively a significantly different relationship to a state than nationality, domicile or presence. Residence is not however a uniform concept, for it is possible to conceive of degrees of residency, with the phrase habitually resident suggesting a more enduring physical presence than secondary, temporary or occasional residence. The contemporary tendency is to equate the meaning of habitual residence with ordinary residence.[1] The latter has been judicially defined as referring "to a man's abode in a particular place or country which he has adopted voluntarily and for settled purposes as part of the regular order of his life for the time being, whether of short or long duration".[2] According to this approach habitual residence is a function of the quality of the residence and not its precise duration. Nor is the designation necessarily disturbed by periods of absence. Habitual residence does not demand continuous residence.[3] The residence must, however, be lawful.[4] Although the point is probably not yet fiirmly concluded, as a matter of English law it seems possible for a person to have more than one habitual residence.[5]

Residence is a question of fact and habitual residence a question of fact and degree.[6]

The allusion in section 3(7)(a) to "individual" probably includes partnerships and all manner of other unincorporated bodies and organisations. Where the "individual" party to an arbitration agreement is such an entity it is the nationality or habitual residence of the unincorporated entity that is in issue and not that of the party mandated to act on behalf of the entity. So also the reference to "individual" would seem not to exclude agency, in which case it is the nationality or habitual residence of the principal and not the agent that is in issue.

13.4.3.2.3.2 Juristic persons. In the contemporary commercial climate the greater likelihood is that an arbitrating party will be a company or other incorporated entity. When this is the case it is a requirement of section 3(7)(b) that the body corporate is one which is not incorporated in, or whose central management and control is not exercised in, any State other than the United Kingdom.

The place of incorporation of a body corporate is a question of record and unlikely to cause difficulty. In the domestic context company incorporation is achieved principally by registration under the Companies Act 1985. A potentially much more difficult question is to determine the place at which a company's central management and control is exercised. In each case this is a question of fact and degree. It may correspond with the place of incorporation or it may be a distinct and different place. In general terms the place of a company's central management and control will be the place where the actual directing power of the corporate affairs is located.[7]

---

1. *Kapur* v. *Kapur* [1984] F.L.R. 920, 926, Bush J. Contrast *Cruse* v. *Chittum* [1974] 2 All E.R. 940, 943.
2. *R.* v. *Barnet London Borough Council, ex p. Shah* [1983] 2 A.C. 309, 343, Lord Scarman.
3. *Cruse* v. *Chittum* [1974] 2 All E.R. 940. See also *Levene* v. *I.R.C.* [1928] A.C. 234; *Stransky* v. *Stransky* [1954] P. 428; *Oundijian* v. *Oundijian* [1979] 1 F.L.R. 198.
4. *R.* v. *Barnet London Borough Council, ex p. Shah* [1983] 2 A.C. 309.
5. *Lysaght* v. *I.R.C.* [1928] A.C. 234; *Hopkins* v. *Hopkins* [1951] P. 116.
6. *Lysaght* v. *I.R.C.* [1928] A.C. 234.
7. *Swedish Central Rail Co.* v. *Thompson* [1925] A.C. 495; *Egyptian Delta Land and Investment Co.* v. *Todd* [1929] A.C. 1; *Unit Construction Co. Ltd.* v. *Bullock (Inspector of Taxes)* [1960] A.C. 351.

Although the question is only likely to arise exceptionally rarely, it would seem that a company's central management and control is not necessarily confined to a single location. Where the corporate directing power is equally divided between two or more locations, so also the company's central management and control is divided to the same extent.[8]

13.4.3.2.4 AT THE TIME THE ARBITRATION AGREEMENT IS ENTERED INTO

13.4.3.2.4.1 The attributes that must attach to natural and juristic arbitrating parties, which are specified in paragraphs (a) and (b) of section 3(7), must prevail "at the time the arbitration agreement is entered into".

The moment an arbitration agreement is entered into is a question of fact to be decided in the circumstances of each case. An arbitration agreement being a special contract, the question is analogous to the general enquiry as to when a contract is entered into, which is a question to the same effect as a question enquiring when a contract first came into existence. The issue is not when an arbitration agreement is asserted, or the arbitral process commenced, but when the arbitration agreement is first entered into, which is necessarily of earlier occurrence, although subsequent to the negotiation of an arbitration agreement. Where an arbitration agreement is embodied in an offer, the arbitration agreement is entered into when the offer is accepted and the acceptance communicated to the offeror. In circumstances when the need for communication is unnecessary or otherwise expressly or impliedly waived, the agreement is complete once the offeree accepts the offer. It is however not every situation that lends itself to analysis in terms of offer and acceptance; and when this is the case a court will be compelled to adopt a more general and possibly instinctive approach to the question whether an arbitration agreement exists and, if so, the moment it came into existence. But whatever approach is adopted, the fundamental issue in each case is to determine the precise moment a contractual arbitral nexus was established between the parties.

13.4.3.2.4.2 The concept of a domestic arbitration agreement also arises under section 1 of the Arbitration Act 1975, whereunder the distinction between a domestic and non-domestic arbitration agreement is made in connection with the court's jurisdiction to stay legal proceedings brought in disregard of an arbitration agreement. For the purpose of the 1975 Act a domestic arbitration agreement is defined by section 1(4) of that Act. The definition is identical to that set out in the Arbitration Act 1979, section 3(7), save in one important regard. Under the 1975 Act the attributes of the parties as to nationality, habitual residence etc., must prevail at "the time the proceedings are commenced," alluding to court proceedings brought in disregard of the arbitration agreement. In contrast, under the 1979 Act, the attributes of the parties must prevail "at the time the arbitration agreement is entered into". Although it may appear strange for the concept of a domestic arbitration agreement to be differently defined in the two statutes, the difference is nonetheless the product of a conscious decision influenced by a desire to give the fullest support to the policy underlying the 1979 Act. The variation from the definition adopted in the 1975 Act was introduced during the passage of the Bill in the House of Lords with the object of avoiding preju-

---

8. *Swedish Central Rail Co.* v. *Thompson* [1925] A.C. 495.

dice to those who were initially parties to international arbitration agreements[1] but who subsequently changed their nationality, residence, etc, before the commencement of arbitral proceedings thereunder. Without the introduced amendment, such a change of circumstance might have operated under the formula of the 1975 Act to change the characterisation of an arbitration agreement and thereby frustrate the attempt by the parties to contract out of judicial review. If allowed this would have frustrated the policy of the 1979 Act which is to give the international community a general freedom to exclude judicial review on questions of law. The definition in the 1975 Act was a potential danger to the achievement of this policy. Under section 3(7) of the 1979 Act it is therefore provided that the attributes specified in paragraphs (a) and (b) must be satisfied at the time an arbitration agreement is entered into. Any subsequent changes are of no consequence and cannot affect the effectiveness of any pre-commencement exclusion agreement.[2]

13.4.4 Special category disputes

Where an award or question of law arising in the course of a reference relates, in whole or in part, to a special category dispute, an exclusion agreement is ineffective unless it is entered into after the commencement of the arbitration in question, except where the award or question of law in issue relates to a contract which is expressed to be governed by a system of law other than that of England and Wales, in which case an exclusion agreement is valid whenever entered into. This is the effect of section 4(1) of the Act and although the phrase "special category disputes" is not one that appears in the statute, it is nonetheless a phrase that has acquired a certain currency and provides a useful shorthand for the range of awards and questions falling within section 4(1). The section provides:

Subject to subsection (3) below, if an arbitration award or a question of law arising in the course of a reference relates, in whole or in part, to—
    (a) a question or claim falling within the Admiralty jurisdiction of the High Court, or
    (b) a dispute arising out of a contract of insurance, or
    (c) a dispute arising out of a commodity contract,
an exclusion agreement shall have no effect in relation to the award or question unless either—
    (i) the exclusion agreement is entered into after the commencement of the arbitration in which the award is made or, as the case may be, in which the question of law arises, or
    (ii) the award or question relates to a contract which is expressed to be governed by a law other than the law of England and Wales.

In contrast to a domestic arbitration agreement, which is defined by reference to the intended *situs* of the arbitration and the relationship of the arbitrating parties to a State other than the United Kingdom,[1] a special category dispute arbitration is defined solely by reference to the nature of the dispute or difference referred. It is, of course, possible for a special category dispute as defined in section 4(1) to be referred under a domestic arbitration agreement as defined in section 3(7). Where this occurs the question arises whether it is section 3(6) or section 4(1) that takes pre-

---

1. See *infra*, para. 13.4.5.
2. See, generally, Kerr (1980) 43 M.L.R. 45, 56.
1. *Supra*, para. 13.4.3.1.

cedence. The question only assumes a significance when the merits of a special category contractual dispute are governed by a system of law other than that of England and Wales. When the law of England and Wales prevails (which will often be the case) then the limitation on the validity of an exclusion agreement is the same under both section 3(6) and section 4(1). Where, on the other hand, a foreign system of law governs (which includes Scots law and the law of Northern Ireland), then section 3(6) and section 4(1) are at variance and the question of precedence must be confronted. The Act does not expressly address the issue; but there are otherwise strong reasons for suggesting that section 4(1) takes precedence over section 3(6). Section 4(1) is the more specific provision, and where the legislature enacts both a general and specific provision it would appear a reasonable inference of statutory interpretation that it is the intention of the legislature, in the absence of any expressly stated intention to the contrary, that the particular is to take precedence over the general. To take as an example the following illustration. Two nationals of the United Kingdom, who are also habitually resident in the United Kingdom, enter into a contract of insurance in Germany, with the contract adopting German law as the proper law of the contract and including a London arbitration clause incorporating an exclusion agreement. In this situation the arbitration agreement is a domestic arbitration agreement within section 3(7) and the reference relates to a special category dispute within the meaning of section 4(1). Under section 3(6) the exclusion agreement is ineffective because it was entered into before the commencement of an arbitration. Under section 4(1) it is effective whenever entered into, by virtue of the foreign governing law. In this situation, it is submitted, section 4(1) prevails over section 3(6) with the consequence that the exclusion agreement is effective.[2]

13.4.4.1 *Preconditions to the effectiveness of an exclusion agreement in relation to special category disputes*

An exclusion agreement is ineffective with regard to an award or question of law arising in the course of a reference relating to a special category dispute unless either it is a post-commencement agreement or the award or question relates to a contract expressed to be governed by a law other than the law of England and Wales.[1]

13.4.4.1.1 POST-COMMENCEMENT AGREEMENT

In the first place an exclusion agreement is ineffective unless entered into after the commencement of the arbitration in which the award is made or, as the case may be, in which the question of law arises.[2]

This is a parallel provision to that applicable to domestic arbitration agreements under section 3(6) and the earlier discussion in the text relating to the commencement of arbitration[3] is of equal application to the present limitation which derives from section 4(1)(i).

---

2. The discussion in the text is highly academic for the reasons set out *infra* in para. 13.4.4.1.2.5.
1. Section 4(1)(i) and (ii).
2. Section 4(1)(i).
3. *Supra*, para. 13.4.2.

13.4.4.1.2 CONTRACT GOVERNED BY A FOREIGN SYSTEM OF LAW

13.4.4.1.2.1 Further, an exclusion agreement is ineffective unless the award or question of law arising in the course of a reference relates to a contract which is expressed to be governed by a law other than the law of England and Wales.[4] In this circumstance even a pre-commencement exclusion agreement is valid. But the provision is confined to contractual legal questions and further to contractual legal questions that are governed by a foreign system of law. No corresponding provision exists with regard to domestic arbitration agreements.

Under the terms of section 4(1)(ii) there is required to exist a contract "which is expressed to be governed by" a foreign law. This form of words offers no difficulty where the proper law is expressly stipulated for and on a narrow interpretation it is at least arguable that the statute is confined to this kind of circumstance.[5] The precise reference in section 4(1)(ii) is to a governing law expressed in the singular, but it would be unrealistic to interpret the statute literally and thereby fail to accommodate the situation where different parts of a contract are expressly governed by different systems of foreign law,[6] and also the possibility of alternative governing laws, as when the governing law is contingent.[7]

13.4.4.1.2.2 On occasions the parties delegate the choice of proper law to an arbitrator or tribunal, usually in the form of a contingent right.[8] How this practice fits into the provisions of section 4(1)(ii) is far from easy to resolve. Whereas the parties are expressly specifying the means by which the proper law is to be selected, it is difficult to perceive it further as an express provision as to the governing law, although it is open to argument that the parties may identify the governing law either directly and personally or through the agency of others. But there is yet a further difficulty, for the precise system of law an arbitrator or tribunal will select is a matter of discretion and therefore uncertain. It may or may not be a foreign system of law. Nonetheless by the time the award is made or the question of law arises, the choice of governing law will be known and if a system of law other than the law of England and Wales has been chosen then it is at least arguable that that choice may be attributed to the parties through the agency of the arbitrator or tribunal. The argument is of course speculative

4. Section 4(1)(ii).

5. Under the English common law there existed a general freedom to choose the proper law of a contract, subject to an exceptionally peripheral limitation which was unlikely to come into issue provided the parties exercised their power to choose realistically: see *Vita Food Products Inc.* v. *Unus Shipping* [1939] A.C. 277, 289–290, Lord Wright; *Tzortzis* v. *Monark Line* [1968] 1 All E.R. 949, 951–952, Lord Denning M.R. For the contemporary law see, generally, the Contracts (Applicable Law) Act 1990, Schedule 1, Art. 3. There may on occasions exist a statutory restriction on the freedom to choose, see, for example, Unfair Contract Terms Act, section 27(2); Contracts (Applicable Law) Act 1990, Schedule 1, Art. 3(3).

6. *Quaere*: how is the Act to be applied if the proper law is split between English law and a foreign law. Possibly the answer might turn on which system of law the resolution of the dispute depended on.

7. See, for example, the bill of lading clause considered by the Court of Appeal in *Astro Venturosa Compania Naviera* v. *Hellenic Shipyards S.A. (The Mariannina)* [1983] 1 Lloyd's Rep. 12 (C.A.).

8. See, for example, Rules for the I.C.C. Court of Arbitration (1988), Art. 13.3, "The parties shall be free to determine the law to be applied by the arbitrator to the merits of the dispute. In the absence of any indication by the parties as to the applicable law, the arbitrator shall apply the law designated as the proper law by the rule of conflict which he deems appropriate"; London Court of International Arbitration Rules (1985), Art. 13.1, "Unless the parties at any time agree otherwise, and subject to mandatory limitations of any applicable law, the Tribunal shall have the power, on the application of any party or of its own motion, but in either case only after giving the parties a proper opportunity to state their views, to: (a) determine what are the rules of law governing or applicable to any contract, or arbitration agreement or issue between the parties;".

but it would achieve the desirable goal of keeping the legislation in step with contemporary arbitral practice. A narrower interpretation would produce the contrary conclusion and although it produces an unattractive outcome it is clearly arguable that the language of section 4(1)(ii) on its plain reading requires the parties' expression of the proper law to be expressly embodied directly in the contract itself.

13.4.4.1.2.3 Under the general principles of conflict of laws the choice of the proper law of a contract may be express or implied.[9] A question again arises whether this general principle carries forward into the interpretation of section 4(1)(ii), so that the expression of the parties may also be capable of being implied from the nature and general terms of the contract, and the circumstances surrounding the making of the contract. On its natural and ordinary interpretation the language of the legislation appears to give a negative answer. The requirement is that the contract must be expressed to be governed by a foreign system of law and this would appear to leave no scope for implication. The policy appears to be that only in the case of an express choice of a foreign system of law is a pre-commencement exclusion agreement effective.

13.4.4.1.2.4 There is provided by section 4(1)(ii) an ingenious means by which the restriction in section 4(1)(i) may be circumvented without losing the advantage, if it be so perceived, of having English law govern the merits of the dispute. Section 4(1)(ii) requires the expression of a law other than the law of England and Wales, but it imposes no condition as to the character or tradition to which the foreign law must belong. There is in consequence nothing to prevent the foreign law being in all regards but for its national identity the same as or substantially the same as the law of England and Wales. The law of Bermuda and Hong Kong provide examples of such foreign systems of law. In the upshot parties to a contract with a special category subject matter who, for example, express the law of Bermuda to be the governing law of the contract and also stipulate for London arbitration, may effectively enter into a pre-commencement exclusion agreement, notwithstanding that any special category dispute which might later arise will, in all but name, be governed by the law of England and Wales. This stratagem is widely appreciated and has become alluded to as "the Bermuda hole".[10]

13.4.4.1.2.5 In strictness it would appear that section 4(1)(ii) is an unnecessary provision for in the English conflict of laws process questions of foreign law are characterised as questions of fact and therefore are not subject to review under the 1979 Act.[11] Nonetheless the statutory provision probably serves a useful purpose in communicating to the international commercial community the clear signal that it is possible to adopt London arbitration and at the same time, through the device of a choice of foreign law agreement, avoid the review procedures of the 1979 Act.

13.4.4.2 Special category disputes

The special category disputes are defined in section 4(1)(a)(b) and (c). The lettered paragraphs identify three broad and distinct categories, namely:

9. See the Contracts (Applicable Law) Act 1990, Schedule 1, Art. 4; also *Amin Rasheed Shipping Corporation* v. *Kuwait Insurance Co. (The Al Wahab)* [1984] A.C. 50.
10. See further Kerr (1980) 43 M.L.R. 45, 55; Steyn and Veeder, "National Reports—England" in *Yearbook Commercial Arbitration*, Vol. XIV (1989).
11. See Chapter 3, para. 3.2.

> (a) a question or claim falling within the Admiralty jurisdiction of the High Court;
>
> (b) a dispute arising out of a contract of insurance;
>
> (c) a dispute arising out of a commodity contract.

If an award or question of law arising in the course of a reference relates, in whole or in part, to any claim, question or dispute falling within any of the above categories it is a special category dispute and within section 4(1).

13.4.4.2.1 A QUESTION OR CLAIM FALLING WITHIN THE ADMIRALTY JURISDICTION OF THE HIGH COURT[1]

13.4.4.2.1.1 Jurisdiction is a term which alludes to the power of a court to hear and determine claims and questions. The Admiralty jurisdiction of the High Court is exercised by the Admiralty Court, which is a specialist sub-organ within the Queen's Bench Division of the High Court.[2] In the present context, jurisdiction is confined to subject matter jurisdiction and has no application to jurisdiction over persons and property.

The scope and substance of the Admiralty jurisdiction has been the subject of gradual legislative codification and expansion since the early nineteenth century. The process was a domestic phenomenon until the definition of a maritime claim in the Brussels Arrest Convention 1952[3] was adopted as the essential, but not quite entire, basis of English Admiralty jurisdiction by the Administration of Justice Act 1956. This particular development did not however wholly fracture the historical continuity of the process, for the Brussels Convention appears to have been significantly influenced by the English experience and reproduced much that was familiar. The significant change was in the language adopted to define aspects of the jurisdiction and this inevitably gave and continues to give rise to problems of interpretation. In particular the question frequently arises whether the contemporary language defining the Admiralty jurisdiction is to be interpreted from an historical perspective or whether it is to be given its ordinary and natural meaning, irrespective of the results that approach produces.[4]

13.4.4.2.1.2 Compared with earlier times the contemporary Admiralty jurisdiction is extensive, but it remains finite and difficulties continue to arise concerning the boundaries of the jurisdiction.[5] The Supreme Court Act 1981, sections 20 to 24, is the principal source of the contemporary Admiralty jurisdiction and procedure. Section

---

1. See generally McGuffie *et al.*, *Admiralty Practice* (*British Shipping Laws*, Vol. 1); Meeson, *The Practice and Procedure of the Admiralty Court*; Jackson, *Enforcement of Maritime Claims*; Thomas, *Maritime Liens* (*British Shipping Laws*, Vol. 14). See also Appendix L.
2. Supreme Court Act 1981, ss. 6(1)(b) and 62(2).
3. International Convention Relating to the Arrest of Seagoing Ships, signed at Brussels on 10 May 1952.
4. For recent examples see *Gatoil International Inc.* v. *Arkwright Boston Manufacturers Mutual Ins. Co.* [1985] A.C. 255; *The River Rima* [1988] 2 Lloyd's Rep. 193; *Petrofina S.A.* v. *AOT Ltd. (The Maersk Nimrod)* [1991] 3 All E.R. 161; *Brian Clarkson Ltd.* v. *The Owners of the Ship "Sea Friends"* [1991] 2 Lloyd's Rep. 333.
5. *Ibid.*

20(1), in particular, defines the sources of subject-matter jurisdiction and effectively asserts the jurisdiction to be drawn from three main derivations. First, the various claims, questions and proceedings specified in section 20(2) and (3) of the Supreme Court Act 1981.[6] This represents the principal source of subject matter jurisdiction. Secondly, any other Admiralty jurisdiction possessed by the High Court immediately before the commencement of the Supreme Court Act 1981. This particular head of jurisdiction connects with the "sweeping up" provision to section 1(1) of the Administration of Justice Act 1956 and retains to the Admiralty Court two specific sources of jurisdiction. First, the jurisdiction vested in the High Court of Admiralty before 1 November 1875. This alludes to the inherent jurisdiction of the original High Court of Admiralty and to the statutory jurisdiction conferred by the Admiralty Court Acts of 1840 and 1861, notwithstanding that these statutes have been repealed. Also retained is any other jurisdiction conferred by or under any statute which came into force on or after 1 November 1875 and before the coming into force of the Administration of Justice Act 1956, even though the legislation has since been repealed.[7] This second source of jurisdiction is of secondary importance but is capable of assuming a particular significance whenever jurisdiction cannot be established by reference to section 20(2) and (3) of the Supreme Court Act 1981. Thirdly, the Admiralty jurisdiction extends to any jurisdiction connected with ships or aircraft which is vested in the High Court otherwise than under section 20 of the Supreme Court Act 1981 and which is by Rules of Court made or coming into force after the commencement of the 1981 Act assigned to the Queen's Bench Division and directed by the Rules to be exercised by the Admiralty Court.[8]

13.4.4.2.1.3 The Admiralty Court has no jurisdiction to determine any claim or question certified by the Secretary of State to be a claim or question which falls to be determined in accordance with the Rhine Navigation Convention.[9]

For the purposes of section 4(1)(a) of the 1979 Act the primary question is whether any dispute referred to arbitration would if litigated be a matter within the Admiralty jurisdiction of the High Court. If an affirmative answer is given it thereafter matters not that there might have existed some limitation on the assumption of jurisdiction over persons[10] or that in the circumstances of the claim the Admiralty Court might have been obliged[11] or capable of being persuaded to surrender jurisdiction.[12] A dispute referred to arbitration is capable of falling within the Admiralty jurisdiction even if it is but one aspect of a composite legal nexus involving non-Admiralty aspects, providing the Admiralty aspect is capable of severance and being treated as an independent and separate issue.[13]

---

6. See Appendix L.

7. See *The Queen of the South* [1968] 1 Lloyd's Rep. 182; Wiswall, *The Development of Admiralty Jurisdiction and Practice since 1800*.

8. Admiralty Practice is governed by R.S.C. Order 75.

9. Supreme Court Act 1981, s. 23. The Rhine Navigation Convention is defined in s. 24(1) to mean "the Convention of the 7th October 1868 as revised by any subsequent Convention".

10. As under the Supreme Court Act 1981, s. 22.

11. By virtue, for example, of the Civil Jurisdiction and Judgments Acts 1982 and 1991.

12. On the grounds of *lis alibi pendens*, an exclusive jurisdiction clause or the doctrine of *forum non conveniens*.

13. *Petrofina S.A.* v. *AOT Ltd. (The Maersk Nimrod)* [1991] 3 All E.R. 161; [1991] 1 Lloyd's Rep. 269.

13.4.4.2.2 A DISPUTE ARISING OUT OF A CONTRACT OF INSURANCE

13.4.4.2.2.1 *Contract of insurance*

13.4.4.2.2.1.1 A contract of insurance is a very familiar phenomenon but it is a far from straightforward matter to define a contract of insurance. Apart from the definition provided by the Marine Insurance Act 1906, section 1,[1] which is of course of relevance only to that statute, no definition of general application has been provided by the legislature or developed by the judges. The problem of characterisation is further exacerbated by the absence of agreed criteria and by the possibility that the definition may represent a shifting concept, varying with the context in which the question arises.[2]

13.4.4.2.2.1.2 Although the problem of definition raises many fundamental and difficult issues, these issues are only likely to arise rarely. In practice the concept of a contract of insurance is likely to be treated as raising a commercial question to be answered substantially by reference to the perceptions of the commercial community. It is suggested that what is defined as an insurance contract within the commercial community will generally be treated as a contract of insurance for the purposes of the 1979 Act. Thus a contract which emanates from within the insurance industry; which asserts itself to be an insurance contract or is widely assumed to be an insurance contract; is accompanied by a policy; adopts the terminology of the insurance world, for example, insurer and insured/assured; makes reference to the payment of a premium and otherwise manifests the customary incidents of insurance, will invariably be considered a contract of insurance.

13.4.4.2.2.1.3 A contract which fails this test is not necessarily outside the characterisation. On the application of a stricter and more technical approach a contract may be defined as a contract of insurance notwithstanding that it would not be readily recognised as such by the commercial community. Various definitions of a contract of insurance are provided in the leading texts,[3] thereby suggesting that there continue to exist differences of opinion as to the principal and indispensable features of a contract of insurance.[4] Nonetheless a contract of insurance is predominantly a contract of indemnity[5] but it is also clear that not all contracts of indemnity are contracts of insurance. In general terms, to amount to a contract of insurance it would appear that the contract must exhibit the following criteria:

(1) there must exist a right to compensation as distinct from a discretion to make compensation[6];

---

1. Which defines a contract of marine insurance as "a contract whereby the insurer undertakes to indemnify the assured in manner and to the extent thereby agreed, against marine losses, that is to say, the losses incident to the marine adventure". See, generally, Arnould, *The Law of Marine Insurance*, (16th edn.) *(British Shipping Laws)*; Hardy Ivamy, *Marine Insurance* (4th edn.).

2. Birds, *Modern Insurance Law* (3rd edn.), Chapter 1.

3. See *MacGillivray and Parkington on Insurance Law* (9th edn.), Chapter 1; Merkin and McGee, *Insurance Contract Law*, Chapter A1; Colinvaux, *The Law of Insurance* (5th edn.), Chapter 1; Hardy Ivamy, *General Principles of Insurance Law* (5th edn.), Chapter 1; Clarke, *The Law of Insurance Contracts* (2nd edn.), Chapter 1.

4. Cf. *Travel & General Insurance Co.* v. *Barron, The Times*, 25 November 1988, where a contract for the issue of a bond in favour of a third party was considered not to be a contract of insurance.

5. See, for example, Marine Insurance Act 1906, s. 1, *supra*, n. 1.

6. *Medical Defence Union* v. *Department of Trade* [1979] 2 All E.R. 420.

   (2) the compensation must be payable in money or in money's worth[7];

   (3) the compensation must be dependent on an uncertain event, and probably also an event outside the control of the party assuming the risk[8];

   (4) in the case of indemnity insurance, the risk, if it materialises, must be prejudicial to the indemnified party and thereby also emphasise that party's insurable interest in the subject matter of the insurance.[9]

Beyond these criteria it is undecided whether the issue of a policy of insurance is an essential element, but it is difficult to see that it should be.[10]

The 1979 Act makes reference to a contract of insurance without any further limitation. This would suggest that the statute applies to all forms of insurance, including indemnity and non-indemnity insurance, first and third party insurance, marine and non-marine insurance, mutual and non-mutual insurance, and also to reinsurance.

13.4.4.2.2.2 Dispute

13.4.4.2.2.2.1 Whether there exists a dispute will in each case be a question of fact, but the precise interpretation to be placed on the statutory word has yet to be considered judicially.

There are judicial dicta which suggest that a distinction is to be drawn between a "dispute" and a "difference".[1] The associated reasoning suggests that whereas a mere failure to agree amounts to a "difference", it does not inevitably and without more amount to a "dispute". By implication it would seem that for a failure to agree to amount to a "dispute" it must be accompanied by some degree of hostility, assertiveness or contest. This judicial approach has however been associated with the construction of the word "dispute" when used in an arbitration agreement, although the approach has not been regarded as appropriate to all contexts.[2] It does not follow that the same refined distinction will be imported into the 1979 Act.

13.4.4.2.2.2.2 The question of what amounts to a dispute is one that particularly arises in the context of section 1(1) of the Arbitration Act 1975 and was also associated with the statutory predecessors of the section.[3] It is of course trite that the same word may be construed differently in different statutes, but both the Arbitration Acts of 1975 and 1979 are integral parts of English arbitration legislation and this may result in a common approach or at least the exercise of a powerful influence.[3a] The interpretation given to section 1(1) of the 1975 Act suggests that for there to be a

---

   7. *Department of Trade and Industry* v. *St. Christopher's Motorists' Association Ltd.* [1974] 1 All E.R. 395; *Medical Defence Union* v. *Department of Trade, ibid.*

   8. *Prudential Insurance Co.* v. *I.R.C.* [1904] 2 K.B. 658; *Gould* v. *Curties* [1913] 3 K.B. 84.

   9. *Ibid.*

   10. Contrast *Hampton* v. *Toxteth Co-operative Society* [1915] 1 Ch. 721; *Hall D'Ath* v. *British Provident Association* (1932) 48 L.T.R. 240.

   1. *May and Butcher Ltd.* v. *The King* [1934] 2 K.B. 17n, per Viscount Dunedin, "a failure to agree . . . is a very different thing from a dispute"; *F. & G. Sykes (Wessex) Ltd.* v. *Fine Fare Ltd.* [1967] 1 Lloyd's Rep. 53, 60 per Danckwerts L.J., "the word 'differences' seems to me to be particularly apt for a case where the parties have not agreed." See also *Hayter* v. *Nelson and Home Insurance Co.* [1990] 2 Lloyd's Rep. 265.

   2. *Didymi Corporation* v. *Atlantic Lines and Navigation Co. Inc.* [1987] 2 Lloyd's Rep 166, 169, per Hobhouse J.

   3. Arbitration Clauses (Protocol) Act 1924, s. 1, as amended by Arbitration (Foreign Awards) Act 1930, s. 8; Arbitration Act 1950, s. 4(2).

   3a. See Chapter 1, para. 1.7.6.

dispute there must exist a contention as to liability, quantum of damages or remedy. Where a claim is admitted there is no dispute. So also where there exists no valid defence to a claim for a liquidated sum there is no dispute[4]; as also there would appear to be no dispute when a question of liability is irresistible.[5] The same approach may apply with regard to part of a claim. Where a claim consists of separate identifiable and quantifiable items, and with regard to certain items of claim liability is admitted, it is open to the court to conclude that there exists no dispute with regard to the admitted item or items of claim, but only in respect of the remaining items.[6] Where liability alone is admitted the parties may continue to be in dispute if the quantum of damages remains in issue.[7] In this situation, provided the claim is not capable of fragmentation, the circumstances are likely to be very rare when the court will be able to identify a certain measure of damages as indisputably due and to hold that there exists no dispute between the parties to that extent. The fact that the quantum of damages is in issue will generally render such a "minimum assessment" unacceptable.[8]

13.4.4.2.2.3 Arising out of

13.4.4.2.2.3.1 The dispute must "arise out of" a contract of insurance. This form of phrase is often adopted in the drafting of arbitration agreements and although the interpretation of the statutory phrase will not necessarily follow the judicial construction of the same phrase used contractually, the latter nonetheless probably provides a signpost of the possible judicial approach to the interpretation of the statute.

In its contractual adoption the phrase has been construed very widely.[1] The only significant restriction arises from the inherent logic of the phrase—disputes arising out of a contract—suggesting the existence in fact and law of a contract, the terms of which the parties are agreed on. In the result the phrase when construed contractually has been held not to extend to disputes with regard to the factual existence of a contract, or concerning the question whether an agreement is in law void *ab initio*, or in relation to the terms of the contract and with regard to which a party might seek rectification.[2] But otherwise, if the existence of a valid contract is accepted, any dispute which can only be decided by recourse to the contract in question is a dispute "arising

---

4. *Nova (Jersey) Knit Ltd.* v. *Kammgarn Spinnerei G.m.b.H.* [1977] 1 W.L.R. 713.
5. Cf. *Channel Tunnel Group Ltd. and Another* v. *Balfour Beatty Construction Ltd. and Others* [1993] A.C. 334, 355–357, Lord Mustill.
6. *Ellis Mechanical Services* v. *Wates Construction* [1978] 1 Lloyd's Rep. 33 (note); [1976] B.L.R. 60.
7. *Associated Bulk Carriers Ltd.* v. *Koch Shipping Inc. (The Fuohsan Maru)* [1978] 1 Lloyd's Rep. 24 (C.A.).
8. *Ibid.* Contrast the dissenting judgment of Lord Denning M.R.
1. There is some controversy as to whether the phrase "arising out of a contract" is wider than "arising under a contract". In *Heyman* v. *Darwins Ltd.* [1942] A.C. 356, 399, Lord Porter considered "arising out of a contract" to be wider than "arising under a contract". In *Government of Gibraltar* v. *Kenney* [1956] 2 Q.B. 410, Sellers L.J. was of the same opinion. But in *Union of India* v. *Aaby's (E.B.) Rederi A/S* [1975] A.C. 797, 814–815, Viscount Dilhorne considered there to be no difference of meaning between the two phrases. On this issue see also *Henck (Gunter)* v. *André & Cie S.A.* [1970] 1 Lloyd's Rep. 235; *Ethiopian Oilseeds & Pulses Export Corporation* v. *Rio Del Mar Foods Inc.* [1990] 1 Lloyd's Rep. 86.
2. Cf. *Ashville Investments Ltd.* v. *Elmer Contractors Ltd.* [1988] 2 All E.R. 577 where an arbitral jurisdiction to determine disputes arising "in connection" with a contract was held to confer a jurisdiction to order rectification of the contract. See also *Printing Machinery Co. Ltd.* v. *Linotype and Machinery Ltd.* [1912] 1 Ch. 566; *Crane* v. *Hegeman-Harris Co. Inc.* [1939] 4 All E.R. 68.

out of" that contract.[3] It must be also emphasised that the dispute must arise out of "the contract" and not any other source, such as an arbitration award.[4]

13.4.4.2.2.3.2 If the above approach is correct it would mean that any dispute relating to, for example, the construction of a contract[5]; an alleged breach of an express[6] or implied term, whatever the source of the implied term,[7] and even when the term in question is an arbitration clause[8]; whether a breach entitles a party to accept it as repudiatory[9]; damages, including any question of causation, remoteness and quantification[10]; injunctive or declaratory relief; frustration[11]; voidability, whether for mistake, fraud, non-disclosure, misrepresentation, duress at common law or equity[12]—are disputes arising out of a contract. Provided the contract lies at the heart of the issue a dispute concerning a related statutory or restitutionary entitlement may also be perceived as a dispute arising out of the contract,[13] as also may a related claim in tort brought by one party against the other.[14] The phrase is also broad enough to embrace disputes as to whether a contract has subsequently been varied or replaced by a new contract.[15] But in the final analysis the context is all important and in interpreting the statutory words the court may choose not to be influenced by precedent and logic, but give to the words a broader province, such as might be supported by commercial good sense.[16]

13.4.4.2.3 A DISPUTE ARISING OUT OF A COMMODITY CONTRACT

13.4.4.2.3.1 The concept of a "dispute" and the meaning of the phrase "arising out of" in this context will doubtlessly carry the same understanding and meaning as previously discussed in relation to contracts of insurance.[1]

By section 4(2) of the 1979 Act a "commodity contract" is defined as a contract (a) for the sale of goods regularly dealt with on a commodity market or exchange in England or Wales which is specified for the purposes of this section by an order made by the Secretary of State; and (b) of a description so specified.

13.4.4.2.3.2 The requisite specifications are made in the Arbitration (Commodity Contracts) Order 1979.[2] The markets and exchanges specified fall into two groups.[3]

3. *Heyman* v. *Darwins Ltd.* [1942] A.C. 356. See also *H. E. Daniel Ltd.* v. *Carmel Exporters and Importers Ltd.* [1953] 2 Q.B. 242; *Government of Gibraltar* v. *Kenney* [1956] 2 Q.B. 410, 421.
4. *Getreide-Import G.m.b.H.* v. *Contimar S.A. Compania Industrial Comercial y Maritima* [1953] 1 W.L.R. 793.
5. *Thorburn* v. *Barnes* (1867) L.R. 2 C.P. 384; *North British Rly.* v. *Newburgh etc. Co.* 1911 S.C. 710.
6. *Aaby's (E.B.) Rederi A/S* v. *Union of India (The Evje)* [1975] A.C. 797.
7. *Produce Brokers Co.* v. *Olympia Oil & Cake Co.* [1916] 1 A.C. 314.
8. *Mantovani* v. *Carapelli S.p.A.* [1980] 1 Lloyd's Rep. 375.
9. *Heyman* v. *Darwins Ltd.*, *supra*.
10. *Heyman* v. *Darwins Ltd.*, *supra* p. 385, per Lord Wright. Contrast *Lawson* v. *Wallasey Local Board* (1882) 11 Q.B.D. 229 where the phrase "any difference . . . concerning anything in connection with the contract" was held not to extend to a dispute as to damages for breach of implied term.
11. *Heyman* v. *Darwins Ltd.*, *supra*; *Kruse* v. *Questier & Co.* [1953] 1 Q.B. 669; *Government of Gibraltar* v. *Kenney*, supra; *Henck (Gunter)* v. *André Cie S.A.* [1970] 1 Lloyd's Rep. 235.
12. *Stebbing* v. *Liverpool and London and Globe Insurance Co. Ltd.* [1917] 2 K.B. 433; *Heyman* v. *Darwins Ltd.*, *supra*.
13. *Government of Gibraltar* v. *Kenney* [1956] 2 Q.B. 410; *Pilgrim Shipping Co.* v. *State Trading Corporation of India (The Hadjitsakos)* [1975] 1 Lloyd's Rep. 356.
14. *The Eschersheim* [1976] 1 W.L.R. 430.
15. *Faghirzadeh* v. *Rudolf Woolf S.A. (Pty.) Ltd.* [1977] 1 Lloyd's Rep. 630.
16. Cf. *Samick Lines Co. Ltd.* v. *Owners of the Ship Antonis P. Lemos* (*Th Antonis P. Lemos*) [1985] A.C. 711.
1. *Supra.*   2. S.I. 1979 No. 754. See also Appendix E.   3. Article 2.

The first are markets set out in Part I of the Schedule to the 1979 Order—

    The London Cocoa Terminal Market
    The London Coffee Terminal Market
    The London Grain Futures Market
    The London Metal Exchange
    The London Rubber Terminal Market
    The Gafta Soya Bean Meal Futures Market
    The London Sugar Terminal Market
    The London Vegetable Oil Terminal Market
    The London Wool Terminal Market

13.4.4.2.3.3. The second group applies to any market in which contracts of sale are subject to the rules and regulations of one or other of the associations set out in Part II of the Schedule of the 1979 Order, whether or not the market is a market on which commodities are bought and sold at a particular place. The associations enumerated are:

    The Cocoa Association of London Limited
    The Coffee Trade Federation
    The Combined Edible Nut Trade Association
    Federation of Oils, Seeds and Fats Associations Limited
    The General Produce Brokers' Association of London
    The Grain and Feed Trade Association Limited
    The Hull Seed, Oil and Cake Association
    The Liverpool Cotton Association Limited
    London Jute Association
    London Rice Brokers' Association
    The National Federation of Fruit and Potato Trades Limited
    The Rubber Trade Association of London
    Skin, Hide and Leather Traders' Association Limited
    The Sugar Association of London
    The Refined Sugar Association
    The Tea Brokers' Association of London
    The British Wool Confederation

13.4.4.2.3.4 The descriptions of contract specified by the 1979 Order again fall into two general groups.[4] First, contracts for the sale of goods on any market specified in Parts I and II of the Schedule to the Order. Secondly, contracts for the sale of goods which are subject to the arbitration rules of the London Metal Exchange or of an association set out in Part II of the Schedule to the 1979 Order.

For the purpose of the 1979 Order "market" means a commodity market or exchange.[5] The Order makes no attempt to define a "contract for the sale of goods", which characterisation probably has the same meaning as that expressed in section 1 of the Sale of Goods Act 1979, being a contract by which the seller transfers or agrees to transfer the property in goods to the buyer for a money consideration, called the price.

The general effect of section 4(2) and the 1979 Order is to render section 4(1)(c)

---

4. Article 3.
5. Article 1(2).

applicable to all the main commodity markets, exchanges and trade associations, and to trading on their standard form contracts.

13.4.4.3 *Underlying policy and survival of the special categories*

13.4.4.3.1 In terms of policy the restricted right to exclude judicial review of awards and questions relating to special category disputes has represented one of the most difficult issues arising under the legislation. Disputes that fall within the special categories traditionally represent the mainstream of disputes referred to London arbitration and are predominantly international and governed by English law. The historic role of the courts in supervising London arbitration has made a major contribution to the consistent evolution of English commercial law, and secured its comprehensiveness and relevance. In turn these qualities have resulted in English commercial law being widely adopted by the international commercial community. If the established link between the courts and this branch of arbitration was to be severed there is at least the danger that the continued development and appeal of English commercial law would be threatened. There was also at the time of enacting the new legislation no evidence of any great demand for an unfettered right to contract out of judicial review by the consumers of London institutional arbitration. But there were of course some who wished for such a right, and given that the parties to special category disputes are predominantly foreign nationals and corporations, usually equally positioned in terms of bargaining power, the Commercial Court Committee saw no good reason to refuse them the right, notwithstanding its potential impact on the development of English commercial law.[1] But the Committee also perceived that there were dangers in introducing an unqualified right to exclude judicial review too quickly and without giving the new appellate regime introduced by the 1979 Act a fair trial period. Without some manner of protective restriction, there was a risk that exclusion agreements might speedily become a normal trading term in standard form contracts. There was also a danger that the prevailing discontent with the pre-1979 special case procedure might result in an exaggerated and ill-judged rush to adopt contracting-out clauses. Consequently the Committee recommended that the right to contract out of judicial review before a dispute had arisen and been referred to arbitration should be restricted, and the restriction ultimately adopted by the legislature is set out in section 4(1)(i) and (ii).[2] But the restriction was intended by the Committee to be no more than transitional. It was to survive for a period of two to three years during which time the international commercial community would have the opportunity to assess the new system of appeals from reasoned awards and hopefully recognise its virtues and advantages. But if this proved not the case and the desire for an unqualified right of contracting out continued to be sought, then it was contemplated that the protective restrictions should be removed.

13.4.4.3.2 Section 4(3) sets out an express power by which the restrictive provisions in section 4(1) may, by order made by the Secretary of State, either be extinguished or continued in a modified restricted form. There is no power in section 4(3) to extend the categories of special disputes. This could only be achieved by fresh legislation. Section 4(3) is to the following effect:

1. See Chapter 1, para. 1.3.11.
2. *Supra*, para. 13.4.4.1.

The Secretary of State may by order provide that subsection (1) above—
  (a) shall cease to have effect; or
  (b) subject to such conditions as may be specified in the order, shall not apply to any exclusion agreement made in relation to an arbitration award of a description so specified;
and an order under this subsection may contain such supplementary, incidental and transitional provisions as appear to the Secretary of State to be necessary or expedient.

The power to make an order under subsection (3) is exercisable by statutory instrument, subject to annulment in pursuance of a resolution of either House of Parliament.[3]

13.4.4.3.3 Many years have now passed since the coming into force of the 1979 Act and no order has been made under section 4(3). There was early agreement that the trial period should be extended and there presently appears to exist no immediate prospect of any reassessment. This would seem to suggest a general acceptance of section 4 by the commercial and legal worlds. In 1985 the Commercial Court Committee's Sub-Committee on Arbitration Law favoured the retention of the status quo, and on the available evidence also considered this conclusion to be the favoured approach of a substantial majority within the commercial world.[4] This view was in due course endorsed in 1990 in the Second Report of the Departmental Advisory Committee on Arbitration Law.[5] The emerging indications appear to be that section 4(1) is yet another temporary measure which is going to enjoy a full and long life. But there are still dissenting voices[6] and the question of the special categories is currently being reconsidered by the Departmental Advisory Committee on Arbitration Law.[6a]

13.4.5 International arbitration agreements

13.4.5.1 The phrase "international arbitration agreement" does not appear in the 1979 Act. It is nonetheless a useful way of alluding to the residuary category of arbitration agreements which are neither domestic nor relate to special category disputes. An international arbitration agreement is an arbitration agreement which does not fall within the definition of a domestic arbitration agreement as set out in section 3(7)[1]; nor is it an arbitration agreement, whether domestic or otherwise, that relates to a special category dispute as defined in section 4(1).[2] Without the special provisions made by section 4(1), the vast majority of arbitration agreements relating to special category disputes would fall within the category here designated as international, for in practice they tend to share a number of common features. Under each category it is frequently the case that one or both parties will be of a foreign nationality or otherwise have strong foreign connections and that the contract or event out of which the dispute arises will have little or no connection with the United Kingdom. But where

---

3. Section 4(4).
4. See Appendix B.
5. See Appendix C.
6. See, for example, Cohen, "Excluding Appeals to the Courts in Maritime Arbitration" [1992] L.M.C.L.Q. 1; Veeder, "Remedies against Arbitral Awards: Setting Aside, Remission and Rehearing" in [1993] *Yearbook of the Arbitration Institute of the Stockholm Chamber of Commerce*, 125–140.
6a. See Steyn (1993) 9 Arb. Int. 405 (Note).
1. *Supra*, para. 13.4.3.1.
2. *Supra*, para. 13.4.4.

an international arbitration agreement relates to a special category dispute, it would appear clear that the specific provisions of section 4(1) prevail.

13.4.5.2 The significance of identifying the residual category of international arbitration agreements is that when an award is made on or a question of law arises in the course of a reference under an international arbitration agreement there exists no procedural fetter on the validity of an exclusion agreement. An exclusion agreement may validly be executed either before or after the commencement of an arbitration and the identity of the governing law assumes no significance. In other words, in relation to international arbitration agreements the general rule is that an exclusion agreement is valid whenever entered into applies.[3] In the result an exclusion agreement may be incorporated into an international arbitration agreement or otherwise agreed to in association with such an agreement.

13.4.5.3 As observed upon in Chapter 1 the accommodation of international arbitration agreements is a major concern of the 1979 Act. That this class of arbitration should be free from constraint and the parties at liberty to exclude the rights of judicial review established under sections 1 and 2 is a fundamental goal of the legislation. The hallmark of international arbitration agreements is that they are untouched by the restrictions which for various considerations of policy the Act otherwise imposes and it is consequently open to the parties to freely establish an arbitration tribunal as the final arbiter of both fact and law.[4]

13.5 MISCELLANEOUS CONSIDERATIONS APPLICABLE TO EXCLUSION AGREEMENTS

13.5.1 Pre- and post-1979 Act agreements

Section 3(2) expressly provides that "an agreement may be an exclusion agreement for the purposes of this section [i.e. section 3] whether it is entered into before or after the passing of this Act . . . " It would appear to matter not whether the pre-Act agreement was entered into in contemplation of the pending legislation or in total ignorance of it and wholly fortuitously. So long as the parties have entered into an agreement which is capable of being construed as an exclusion agreement within the meaning of section 3, that it would seem is sufficient.

To this extent the 1979 Act possesses a retroactive effect, for it would appear that by virtue of section 3(2) an agreement which at the time it was entered into was invalid, or at best of dubious validity, has with the passing of the new legislation been rendered valid, providing, of course, it otherwise satisfies the criteria as to what amounts to a valid exclusion agreement. But section 3(2) does not otherwise override the restrictive provisions found elsewhere in the Act and by virtue of which, in specified circumstances, an exclusion agreement is only valid if entered into after the commencement of the arbitration to which it relates.[1]

In the nature of things this aspect of section 3(2) is a transitional provision and will with the passage of time become redundant, if it is not already so.

---

3. *Supra*, para. 13.4.2.1.
4. See Chapter 1, para. 1.3.
1. *Supra*, para. 13.4.2.

13.5.2 Exclusion agreements and arbitration agreements

By section 3(2) it is again provided that "an agreement may be an exclusion agreement for the purposes of this section [i.e. section 3] . . . whether or not it forms part of an arbitration agreement". This presumably is a reference to the physical location of an exclusion agreement and not to its theoretical impact. The subsection emphasises that the validity of an exclusion agreement is not dependent upon it having any particular physical relationship to the arbitration agreement with which it is associated. It follows that an exclusion agreement may be expressly embodied in an arbitration agreement, or incorporated into an arbitration agreement by reference to an external document or other source, or it may exist independently of the arbitration agreement with which it is associated. In the latter case the exclusion agreement may exist as a separate clause in a contract that also contains the arbitration clause, or in a wholly distinct agreement, as where the exclusion agreement is a separate agreement entered into subsequently to the arbitration agreement or the contract containing the arbitration clause. Given that in specified instances an exclusion agreement is only valid if entered into after the commencement of an arbitration, it is inevitable that in these instances an exclusion agreement will exist apart from the arbitration agreement out of which the relevant award or reference arises.

But although an arbitration agreement and associated exclusion agreement may be physically independent, it is unlikely that they are equally theoretically independent. It would seem that each represents a vital component in the factual and legal matrix of the other; and therefore when a question of construction arises the two agreements are likely to be addressed as effectively representing a single agreement.

13.5.3 Exclusion agreements and the general law of contract

13.5.3.1 It is probable that an exclusion agreement is to be perceived as a special category of contract and subject to the general law of contract. To this extent there is an analogy between an exclusion agreement and an arbitration agreement. The establishment, construction, termination, validity and voidability of an exclusion agreement and of rights thereunder are in consequence subject to the general principles of the law of contract, save to the extent they are modified by the 1979 Act. As previously observed, the Act makes particular requirements with regard to the form of an exclusion agreement,[1] and, in particular circumstances, as to the moment in time in relation to a reference it may be validly entered into.[2]

13.5.3.2 An arbitration agreement which exists as a clause in a contract is analysed as a self-contained contract, collateral or ancillary to the main contract.[2a] In turn this mode of analysis has given birth to the doctrine of separability; the principal object of which is to protect the jurisdiction of arbitrators and give full effect to the intention of the arbitrating parties. Although the initial factual existence and legal validity of the two contracts are inextricably associated,[2b] the same is not necessarily the case in relation to their termination. An arbitration clause in a contract may on its proper con-

---

1. *Supra*, para. 13.2.2.2.
2. *Supra*, para. 13.4.2.
2a. *Heyman* v. *Darwins Ltd.* [1942] A.C. 356; *Bremer Vulkan Schiffbau und Maschinenfabrik* v. *South India Shipping Corpn.* [1981] A.C. 909, 980.
2b. *Heyman* v. *Darwins Ltd.*, *ibid.* See also *Joe Lee Ltd.* v. *Lord Dalmeny and Others* [1927] 1 Ch. 300.

struction survive the premature termination of the embracing contract. This may be the case when the wider contract is avoided for misrepresentation, mistake or duress, or where the wider contract is frustrated or otherwise terminated by the acceptance of a repudiatory breach or by the operation of an express term.[3] But in other circumstances, for example, illegality rendering a contract void *ab initio*, both the wider contract and the arbitration agreement are concurrently void.[4] Where an exclusion agreement also exists within the corpus of an arbitration clause or even as a separate clause in the same contract it is at least arguable that it falls to be analysed as being as one with the arbitration agreement and in consequence survives or falls alongside the arbitration agreement. To the extent that the arbitration agreement survives the premature termination of the wider contract so also does the exclusion agreement. If the arbitration clause is rescinded or extinguished with the wider contract, so also is the exclusion agreement. But even if the theoretical analysis is to the contrary, with the extinction of the arbitration clause the exclusion agreement is rendered redundant.

13.5.3.3 Where an exclusion agreement exists as a separate and independent contract the same considerations do not apply. The autonomy of the agreement means that all questions of law and fact raised in relation to it are to be answered without reference to any contract or arbitration agreement associated with the exclusion agreement.

13.5.3.4 An exclusion agreement may be subsequently varied or abandoned by the mutual agreement of the parties. It is uncertain whether the later agreement need also be in writing,[5] but in keeping with principle it may be express or implied. Equally rights arising under an exclusion agreement may be waived or a party estopped from asserting them. The possibility of waiver was accepted in principle by Staughton J. and the Court of Appeal in *Marine Contractors Inc.* v. *Shell Petroleum Co. of Nigeria Ltd.*[6] Staughton J. emphasised that waiver required proof of a "clear and unequivocal representation by each party that neither would rely on the exclusion agreement".[7] This would appear to be the language of mutual waiver, but there would appear to be nothing to preclude a party unilaterally waiving an entitlement under an exclusion agreement. In most cases waiver is a unilateral phenomenon. Merely to ask for reasons does not amount to a waiver of an exclusion agreement.[8]

---

3. *Stebbing* v. *Liverpool and London and Globe Insurance Co. Ltd.* [1917] 2 K.B. 433; *Woodall* v. *Pearl Assurance Co.* [1919] 1 K.B. 593; *Sanderson & Son* v. *Armour & Co.*, 1922 Sess. Cas. (H.L.) 117, 121, per Lord Finlay; *Champsey Bhara & Co.* v. *Jivraj Balloo Spinning and Weaving Co. Ltd.* [1923] A.C. 480; *Scott & Sons* v. *Del Sel*, 1923 Sess. Cas. (H.L.) 37; *Macaura* v. *Northern Assurance Co. Ltd.* [1925] A.C. 619; *Toller* v. *Law Accident Insurance Society Ltd.* (1936) 55 Ll.L.Rep. 258; *Heyman* v. *Darwins Ltd.* ibid; *Crestar Ltd.* v. *Carr and Another, The Times*, 6 May 1987.

4. *David Taylor & Son Ltd.* v. *Barnett Trading Co.* [1953] 1 W.L.R. 562; *Dalmia Dairy Industries* v. *National Bank of Pakistan* [1978] 2 Lloyd's Rep. 223, 285–293. But see the qualification to this general principle introduced in *Harbour Assurance Co. (U.K.) Ltd.* v. *Kansa General International Insurance Co. Ltd.* [1993] 3 All E.R. 897 (C.A.).

5. See the discussion in Chapter 3, para. 3.4.9.

6. [1984] 2 Lloyd's Rep. 77.

7. *Ibid.* p. 81.

8. *Ibid.* Contrast *Italmare Shipping Co.* v. *Ocean Tanker Co. Inc.* [1981] 2 Lloyd's Rep. 489, 494, per Lord Denning M.R. The judgment of Lord Denning is criticised in Donaldson, "Commercial Arbitration— 1979 and After", in *International Commercial and Maritime Arbitration*, ed. Rose.

13.5.4 Bilateral and unilateral exclusion agreements

It is settled law that bilateralism is not a necessary precondition to the validity of an arbitration agreement.[1] An arbitration agreement which obliges one party to arbitrate but leaving the other party free to litigate is a valid arbitration agreement. In practice such unilateral agreements are exceptionally rare. The vast preponderance of arbitration agreements commit all the parties thereto to arbitration.

As a matter of principle it would seem that an exclusion agreement is capable of following the legal pattern of an arbitration agreement and therefore may be bilateral or unilateral in effect. One party may be excluded from the right to seek judicial review, while the other party or parties are free to seek to activate the rights of review established by the 1979 Act. Where the arbitration agreement is unilateral it would appear to follow quite logically that any associated exclusion agreement must also operate unilaterally.

The 1979 Act does not expressly endorse the above line of reasoning but neither does it expressly negate the possibility. The notion of a unilateral exclusion agreement would appear to be consistent with the terms of section 3(1) and is further unlikely to be perceived as repugnant on grounds of public policy. It is true that section 3(1) demands that all the parties to the reference enter into an exclusion agreement,[2] but it does not further demand that the benefit of an exclusion agreement be received by all the parties.

13.5.5 The governing law of exclusion agreements

Although an exclusion agreement is a substantive agreement and is capable of subsisting as a distinct and separate contract,[1] in the context of the conflict of laws it is probably to be characterised as procedural and in consequence the innate validity and scope of an exclusion agreement is to be determined by the *lex fori*, that is English law. A right of appeal and the right to seek a judicial determination of a preliminary question of law are each procedural in character[2] and it is probably equally the case that any agreement excluding either right is also to be characterised as procedural. To so assert is also to accept that a different conflict rule may apply to exclusion agreements than to arbitration agreements and this will continue to be the case when an exclusion agreement is embodied in an arbitration agreement.

13.5.6 Disputed exclusion agreements and arbitrators

13.5.6.1 There is no indication given in the 1979 Act as to how an arbitrator or umpire is to conduct himself when the validity or applicability of an exclusion agreement is challenged. The potential difficulty may arise in connection with an application under

---

1. *Pittalis and Others* v. *Sherefettin* [1986] 2 All E.R. 227. Overruling *Tote Bookmakers Ltd. and Development and Property Holding Co. Ltd.* [1985] Ch. 261. See also *Woolf* v. *Collis Removal Service* [1948] 1 K.B. 11, 17, per Asquith L.J. (C.A.); *Westfal-Larsen and Co. A/S* v. *Ikerigi Compania Naviera S.A. (The Messiniaki Bergen)* [1983] 1 Lloyd's Rep. 424, 425–426, per Bingham J. Contrast *Baron* v. *Sunderland Corpn.* [1966] 2 Q.B. 56, 64, per Davies L.J. (C.A.).
2. *Supra*, para. 13.2.1.
1. *Supra*, para. 13.5.2.
2. See further Chapter 1, para. 1.7.8.

section 2.[1] An application for the determination of a preliminary point of law by the court can only be instituted either with the consent of all the other parties or with the consent of the arbitrator or umpire who has entered on the reference.[2] Where the consent of the other parties cannot be obtained, the right of application to the court is lost if there exists a valid and applicable exclusion agreement.[3] The circumstance may be contemplated of a party, having failed to obtain the consent of all the other parties, and notwithstanding the existence of an ostensible exclusion agreement, pressing an arbitrator or umpire to consent to an application on the basis that there exists no exclusion agreement as a question of fact, or that any agreement that does exist is invalid as a question of law or is inapplicable as a question of construction. In the face of these arguments the other party or parties to the reference are likely to urge the contrary contention and suggest to the arbitrator or umpire that a valid and applicable exclusion agreement exists. Confronted with this kind of issue, how is an arbitrator or umpire to act? In particular, to what extent should the disputed issue weigh on the exercise of the discretion whether or not to give consent.

13.5.6.2 It is a general principle of English arbitral law that an arbitrator cannot determine his own jurisdiction[4]; nor can an arbitrator decide any question on which the existence of his jurisdiction depends.[5] It is equally likely to be the case, albeit for different reasons, that an arbitrator has no authority to decide a question relating to the existence, validity and proper construction of an exclusion agreement, and even if the parties are content for an arbitrator to make an initial determination or express an opinion on the question, that determination or opinion is not binding on the court. All questions and disputes relating to an exclusion agreement would appear to be for the final decision of the court.

13.5.6.3 If this is a correct analysis then the only question that arises is whether an arbitrator in the exercise of his discretion arising under section 2 should take into account the fact of the disputed exclusion agreement or ignore it wholly. In favour of the latter course it is at least arguable that the presence or otherwise of an exclusion agreement is of no concern to an arbitrator, for the effect of an exclusion agreement is to preclude an application to the High Court and not to the arbitrator. The assertion of or challenge to an exclusion agreement is consequently an issue to be taken solely on the application to the High Court for leave to apply. But even if this argument fails

---

1. See Chapter 12.
2. Section 2(1)(a) and (b).
3. Section 3(1)(c).
4. *Produce Brokers Co. Ltd.* v. *Olympic Oil & Cake Co. Ltd.* [1916] A.C. 314, 327, per Lord Parker; *Champsey Bhara & Co.* v. *Jivraj Balloo Spinning and Weaving Co.* [1923] A.C. 480, 488, per Lord Dunedin; *Heyman* v. *Darwins Ltd.* [1942] A.C. 356.
5. *Munro* v. *Bognor U.D.C.* [1915] 3 K.B. 167; *Golodetz* v. *Schrier* (1947) 80 Ll.L.Rep. 647; *Christopher Brown Ltd.* v. *Genossenschaft Oesterreichischer Waldbesitzer R. G.m.b.H.* [1954] 1 Q.B. 8; *Luanda Exportadora and Others* v. *Wahbe Tamari & Sons and Others* [1967] 2 Lloyd's Rep. 353; *Willock* v. *Pickfords Removals Ltd.* [1979] 1 Lloyd's Rep. 244; *Blue Circle Industries plc* v. *Holland Dredging Co. (U.K.) Ltd., The Times,* 23 March 1987; *Ashville Investments Ltd.* v. *Elmer Contractors* [1988] 2 All E.R. 577. The general rule that an arbitrator whose jurisdiction depends on an arbitration clause in a contract cannot conclusively determine the factual existence and legal validity of the contract may be circumvented by conferring an appropriate jurisdiction under a distinct and separate *ad hoc* submission: see, for example, *Astro Valiente Compania Naviera S.A.* v. *The Government of Pakistan Ministry of Food and Agriculture (The Emmanuel Colocotronis) (No. 1)* [1982] 1 Lloyd's Rep. 297 (specific submission agreed by the parties recorded in the headnote); *Saleh Farid* v. *Mackinnon Mackenzie & Co. Ltd. (The Sheba and Shamsan)* [1983] 2 Lloyd's Rep. 500, 504–505, per Bingham J.

to prevail, it would otherwise appear the advisable course for an arbitrator to take if he considers there to exist a good arguable case that the exclusion agreement is defective in fact or law. If, however, the existence of the challenged exclusion agreement may legitimately be taken into account, an arbitrator would be prudent not to admit the exclusion agreement as a consideration influencing the exercise of his discretion so as to refuse to consent to the consultative case unless clearly satisfied on the basis of the evidence and the representations of the parties that a valid and applicable exclusion agreement existed. A refusal to give consent in such circumstances could have the beneficial effect of avoiding a futile application being made to the court, while leaving it open for the aggrieved party to seek judicial review of the arbitral decision by reference to the concept of arbitral misconduct or by seeking declaratory relief. When on an application for consent a party also indicates an intention to test the validity of an exclusion agreement, it might be judicious for an arbitrator to adjourn consideration of the application until the opinion of the court is known, and this would be particularly so if the arbitrator also considered the existence, validity or applicability of the exclusion agreement to be an arguable issue.[6]

6. Compare the approach adopted when the jurisdiction of an arbitrator is in question: *Golodetz* v. *Schrier* (1947) 80 Ll.L.Rep. 647, 650, *Christopher Brown Ltd.* v. *Genossenschaft Oesterreichischer Waldbesitzer R. G.m.b.H.* [1954] 1 Q.B. 8, 12–13; *Luanda Exportadora and others* v. *Wahbe Tamari & Sons and Others* [1967] 2 Lloyd's Rep. 353, 364.

APPENDICES

COMMERCIAL COURT COMMITTEE REPORT ON ARBITRATION 1978, Cmnd 7284

Introductory

1. The Commercial Court Committee was established in order to provide a direct link between the commercial users of the Court and the Court itself, thus improving the service which the Court is able to offer. The Judges of the Commercial Court are *ex officio* members and the other members represent the main categories of user. These are bankers, shipowners, charterers, shippers, underwriters, commodity merchants and dealers, brokers, professional arbitrators, solicitors and barristers. In addition, the Committee has members who give it links with national maritime law associations throughout the world, with North America and the European Economic Community and with the United Kingdom Department of Trade.

2. The Committee's terms of reference are to consider and keep under review the working of the Commercial Court and the Arbitration Special Case procedure and to make recommendations to the Lord Chancellor as may be necessary from time to time. This report concerns arbitration and, in particular, the Special Case procedure.

JUDICIAL SUPERVISION AND REVIEW OF ARBITRATION PROCEEDINGS

Supervisory powers

3. All systems of law provide for some degree of judicial supervision of arbitral proceedings and awards. These powers enable the Courts to intervene in cases of fraud or bias by the arbitrators, contravention of the rules of natural justice or action in excess of jurisdiction. In the case of the English Courts these powers are conferred by sections 22, 23 and 24 of the Arbitration Act 1950.[1]

Powers of review

4. Most systems of law adopt the philosophy that the parties, having chosen their own tribunal, must accept its decisions "with all faults". Accordingly, they make no, or very little, provision for a review by the Courts of arbitral decisions which may be based upon erroneous conclusions of fact or law. Until recently the law of Scotland was based upon this philosophy. However this has never been the approach of the law of England or of some systems derived from that law. English law provides for two different forms of review, namely by motion to set aside the award for error on its face and by a reference to the High Court of an award in the form of a special case.

(a) Setting aside an award for error on its face

5. Under English law the Courts have jurisdiction to set aside any arbitral award, if it appears from the award itself or from documents incorporated in the award that the arbitrator has

---

1. See Appendix 1 [Appendix 1 to the Report is not reproduced in this Appendix.]

reached some erroneous conclusion of fact or law. The Court cannot correct the error. It can only quash the award leaving the parties free to begin the arbitration again.

6. As a result of the existence of this power, English arbitrators customarily avoid giving any reasons for their awards, confining themselves to reciting that a dispute has arisen between the parties and that they award that A should pay B a specified sum. Where the parties wish to know the reasons for the award or the arbitrator wishes to give them, this is achieved by giving the reasons in a separate document which expressly states that it is not part of the award and by obtaining an undertaking from the parties that they will not seek to refer to or use the reasons for the purposes of any legal proceedings. The general pattern is, however, that English awards are given without reasons.

7. In this important respect English arbitral awards differ from those of most other countries. In the case of arbitrations held under the laws of Belgium, the Federal Republic of Germany, France, Italy and the Netherlands, the giving of reasons is normally obligatory. When it comes to enforcing an English arbitral award in a foreign country, there is always some doubt whether objection may not be taken to it on the ground that it is "unmotivated", to use the continental term, although the Committee knows of no case in which this objection has yet been upheld.

(b) Appeal by way of special case

8. Under Section 21 of the Arbitration Act 1950[2], which re-enacts earlier provisions to the like effect, an arbitrator may and, if so directed by the High Court, must state his award or part of that award or any question of law arising in the course of the reference in the form of a special case for the opinion of the High Court. A somewhat similar provision was introduced into Scots law by the Administration of Justice (Scotland) Act 1972.

9. The section applies to all arbitrations conducted within England or Wales. Although the question submitted to the Court must concern English law, it is not impossible for such a question to be raised where the dispute arises out of a contract governed by foreign law. Thus English law may be relevant by *renvoi* or as being the *lex fori*.

10. An award in the form of a special case is quite different from a simple final award. It is customarily somewhat formalized. Beginning with a recital of the agreement under which the arbitrator derives his jurisdiction, it then sets out the nature of the dispute and the rival contentions of the parties both on fact and law. This is followed by a series of findings of fact and a statement of the questions of law which are being submitted to the Court for decision. In conclusion, it will usually contain alternative awards to take effect according to how the Court answers the questions of law and may provide that if the award is not set down (entered in the list of cases for hearing in the High Court) within a specified time, one of the alternative awards shall take effect as a final award. In a few cases the possible permutations of answers are so numerous that it is impossible for the arbitrator to make alternative awards covering all contingencies. In such cases it is usual for the arbitrator to ask that the case be remitted to him so that he may make a final award in the light of the Court's judgment.

11. An award in the form of a special case rarely gives any reason for the arbitrator's conclusions of fact or for any tentative decision on questions of law. It is thus wholly different from a reasoned award.

12. The section in terms gives the arbitrator a discretion whether or not to state his award in the form of a special case, and gives the High Court a discretion whether or not to order him to do so. However, case law[3] has or is widely thought to have, established that if any real point of law arises the arbitrator should adopt the special case procedure even if there is no great sum in dispute, no point of general importance is involved or the answer is reasonably clear.

Entrenchment of the special case procedure

13. The law of England does not permit parties to an arbitration agreement to contract out of their statutory right to obtain an order that the arbitrator state his award in the form of a special

2. See Appendix 1.
3. See *Halfdan, Grieg & Co. A.S.* v. *Sterling Coal & Navigation Corp. anr.* (*The Lysland*) [1973] 1 Q.B. 843.

case. That this is the law was established in *Czarnikow* v. *Roth, Schmidt and Company* [1922] 2 K.B. 478 by a decision of a Court of Appeal consisting of Bankes, Scrutton and Atkin L.JJ., whose combined authority in matters of commercial law is probably unequalled. It is a decision of such importance that relevant extracts from the judgments are reproduced at Appendix 2. As will be seen, it was based upon the considerations of public policy that there should, in principle, be no sphere of national activity in which the King's writ did not run, that there should be but one system of law and that those who were commercially weak should be protected by law from those who were commercially strong.

14. The law of Scotland is different. This is not because different considerations of public policy apply north of the Border, but because the procedure was unknown to Scots law before 1972. What was then introduced was a limited right to resort to the Courts, i.e., a right in all cases other than those in which the parties had expressly agreed to exclude the right. The Scots have moved some way towards the English legal position. For reasons which will appear, the Committee consider that the time has come when the English must move some way towards the Scottish legal position.

Advantages and disadvantages of judicial review

15. The advantages and disadvantages of a right to judicial review, whether entrenched or unentrenched, fall to be considered separately from the merits of the particular procedure by which this review is achieved.

16. The value of some right to judicial review, and of one which is entrenched, has proved itself over the years. In other jurisdictions the law administered by arbitrators has been able to diverge from that administered by the Courts and the fact that individual arbitrators are not bound by the decision of other arbitrators exacerbates the problem. Certainty of rights and duties is of cardinal importance in a commercial relationship and the absence of an entrenched right of judicial review leads inevitably to uncertainty. A further advantage of this entrenched right has been the opportunity which it has afforded to the Courts of developing English commercial law in line with the changing needs of the times. It is an opportunity which has not been neglected by the Courts and English law has become the popular choice for commercial interests throughout the world.

17. The most obvious disadvantage of any such right is that it conflicts with one of the prime objects of arbitration as a means of resolving commercial disputes, namely the achievement of a speedy and final decision. Whilst the Commercial Court can and does on occasion provide an even speedier service than do arbitrators and whilst it is almost always able to review an award as soon as the parties are ready to appear, a judicial review introduces an additional stage in the proceedings and inevitably causes some delay.

18. A less obvious, but very real, disadvantage of an entrenched right has emerged during the last decade with the advent of vast new supranational development contracts. The parties are often consortia which directly or indirectly include foreign governments and their agencies. They would like to adopt English law as the proper law of the contract and to have their disputes resolved in England by English professional arbitrators, whose reputation is second to none. But, for reasons which are quite understandable, they are reluctant to submit to the jurisdiction of *any* national Court. As a result of the existence of the entrenched right of judicial review which exists in England these arbitrations are held elsewhere. Whilst it is impossible to compute the resulting loss to the national economy, it is not inconsiderable and has indeed been put as high as £500 million a year.[4] Some or all of this loss would be avoided if the parties to such contracts were free to contract out of the right of judicial review.

Defects of the special case as a method of judicial review

19. In the Alexander Lecture on the "Use and Abuse of the Case Stated"[5] Lord Diplock drew attention to the fact that the special case procedure was a nineteenth century adaptation of a similar procedure used by the criminal courts of Quarter Sessions. It was originally applied to

4. See speech by Lord Cullen of Ashbourne, House of Lords Official Report, 15 May 1978, Col 99.
5. "Arbitration", 1978 Vol. 44, p. 107.

arbitration by the Common Law Procedure Act 1854. The purpose in each case was to produce a decision which could not only be reviewed but also be corrected by the reviewing court instead of being merely upheld or quashed. The time has now come when it is necessary to consider whether there may not be another way of achieving this object which has fewer disadvantages.

20. As has been mentioned, an award in the form of a special case is a somewhat formalized document. This may be a reflection of its origins. But in practice arbitrators who are confronted with the need to make an award in this form often feel the need for legal advice. This increases the cost of arbitration and inevitably involves some delay.

21. A much more serious objection is that the procedure is capable of being used by undeserving parties for the sole purpose of postponing the day when they have to meet their commitments. This is a relatively new phenomenon, bred no doubt of the current inflationary world economic situation in which cash flow has assumed a new importance and unstable rates of exchange may greatly vary the value of an award to the successful party and its burden on the unsuccessful party, according to the time when it becomes enforceable.

22. It is no part of the purpose of this report to provide a detailed guide on how to achieve these delays. Suffice it to say that a successful application for an award to be stated in the form of a special case involves the arbitrator in additional work, which must inevitably create some delay. Thereafter a date for a hearing by the Court must be obtained and full argument has to take place. This involves further delay. An unsuccessful applicant can appeal to the High Court or even to the Court of Appeal against the refusal of the arbitrator to state his award in this form. This too will create considerable delay.

23. It may be thought that the Court should be in a position to recognise and to prevent or at least discourage unmeritorious applications. Unfortunately, this is not the case. At the stage at which a decision has to be made whether or not an arbitrator shall be ordered to state his award in the form of a special case, the arbitrator has not yet made any findings of fact upon the basis of which a decision can be made. Faced with hypothetical findings of fact, it is very difficult for a Court to be certain that no serious questions of law can arise for decision. All doubts must be resolved in favour of the applicant for an award in the form of a special case and, as a result, such applications are rarely refused.

24. Last, but by no means least, an award in the form of a special case is not enforceable as a final award until the Court has answered the questions of law and either upheld one of the arbitrator's alternative awards or remitted the matter to the arbitrator to enable him to make a final award.

The alternative of judicial review based on reasoned awards

25. The existing obstacle to a judicial review based upon reasoned awards is the power and the duty of the Court to set aside awards for error on their face. This obstacle could easily be removed and this system would then have considerable attractions.

26. In every case an arbitrator would be free to give reasons for his award. This would in itself be an improvement, if arbitrators took advantage of the facility. The making of an award is, or should be, a rational process. Formulating and recording the reasons tends to accentuate its rationality. Furthermore, unsuccessful parties will often, and not unreasonably, wish to know why they have been unsuccessful. This change in the law would make this possible.

27. Given a reasoned award, an unsuccessful party could know whether he had a just cause for complaint. Where no reasons were given initially and he thought that an error had been made, he could ask for reasons to be supplied. If the arbitrator refused to supply them, the Court could, in appropriate cases, order him to do so. This would be no great burden on the arbitrator provided that the application was made promptly. He would have had some reasons for making the award and all that he would need to do would be to summarize them in ordinary language. Nothing formal would be required.

28. Armed with the reasons for an award, the unsuccessful party could apply to the Court for leave to appeal. The right to appeal could be restricted to questions of law arising out of the decision, leaving all questions of fact to be decided finally by the arbitrator. Furthermore, unlike the position when the Court is being asked to order an arbitrator to state an award in the form of a special case, the Court would know whether any particular question of law really

arose for decision since both it and the parties would have access to the facts as found by the arbitrator. Additional restrictions could be imposed on the circumstances in which leave to appeal would be given and in which a further appeal to the Court of Appeal would be permitted.

29. An additional advantage of a change to reasoned awards lies in the fact that this would tend to assimilate English awards to those made in other countries, thus making English awards more acceptable and readily enforceable abroad.

30. Finally, there would be the great advantage that every award would be a final award and immediately enforceable as such, subject only to the right of the Court in appropriate cases to impose a stay of execution pending an appeal. Such a stay could, of course, be granted subject to conditions, such as that the amount awarded be brought into Court.

31. In a word, a system of judicial review based upon reasoned awards would place very grave obstacles in the way of those seeking unmeritoriously to avoid meeting their just obligations, would improve the standard of awards and would render them more easily and speedily enforceable. The same system is used for the review of decisions of the industrial tribunals and of the Restrictive Practices Court and has worked well.

Recommendations on judicial review

32. In the light of these considerations the Committee makes the recommendations set out below.

33. The system of judicial review based upon the special case procedure should be replaced by one based upon reasoned awards. This would involve comparatively minor amendments to the 1950 Act. Section 21 would be repealed and the Court would be deprived of the power and duty to set an award aside because of errors of fact or law on the face of the award. Arbitrators would be encouraged to give reasons for their awards, but would only be obliged to do so if it was necessary for the purposes of the new review procedure. A new section 21 would define the right of appeal to the High Court.

34. The new right of appeal would be confined to questions of law, all decisions on questions of fact being for the arbitrator alone.

35. This right of appeal should be restricted to cases in which either the High Court gives leave to appeal or all parties so agree. Leave to appeal should only be given if the High Court is satisfied that the question of law in issue might be determined on appeal in a way which would affect the rights of the parties under the award. The High Court should be free to impose conditions upon the parties seeking leave, such a requirement that the minimum sum due to the successful party should be paid over to him or that the sum in dispute should be secured.

36. There should be power in the High Court to require arbitrators to make a reasoned interim award—the equivalent of a special case under section 21(1)(*a*)—if, but only if, the Court was satisfied that a question of law had arisen in the course of the reference a decision on which might produce substantial savings in costs to the parties and that it was one in respect of which leave to appeal might be given.

37. The right of further appeal from the High Court to the Court of Appeal should be strictly limited. It would arise only on a certificate of the Judge of the High Court that the question of law was one of general importance to other persons engaged in some branch of industry, commerce or other activities or for some other special reason and then only with the leave of that Judge or of the Court of Appeal.

38. The Committee considers that these reforms would provide English law with a modern and efficient system of judicial review which would meet the legitimate needs of those who submit their disputes to arbitration. Successful parties would be able to obtain speedy enforcement of awards. Unsuccessful parties would be able to obtain relief in the comparatively rare cases in which an arbitrator misapplied the law in a material respect, but would be deprived of the opportunity of avoiding their commitments by procedural devices.

Entrenchment of the right to judicial review

39. The Committee has next had to consider the extent to which the right to judicial review should remain entrenched as it is at present or whether it should be a right which parties are free to give up by agreement. The same considerations do not necessarily apply to all types of arbitration.

40. Under the Arbitration Act 1975, arbitration agreements are divided into "domestic arbitration agreements" and other (non-domestic) agreements. In substance, the former are defined by section 1(4) of the Act[6] as being agreements which do not provide for arbitration abroad and to which no foreign national or resident or foreign company is a party. Non-domestic arbitration agreements are not defined, but are necessarily foreign or international in character.

41. For present purposes these foreign and international arbitration agreements can be divided into the "supranational contract" group and the "special category disputes" group. The supranational group comprises arbitration agreements relating to disputes under the large new development contracts to which reference was made in paragraph 18 of this report. They are often recognizable as such, but have so far defied definition. The special category disputes group comprises arbitration agreements relating to the types of commercial dispute which traditionally are resolved by the London international arbitration service. In general they arise out of contracts which can be roughly categorized as maritime, insurance and contracts relating to commodities of types which are dealt with on established United Kingdom markets.

42. The Committee is greatly impressed by the public policy considerations set out in the judgments in *Czarnikow* v. *Roth, Schmidt and Co.*,[7] but it must be remembered that the context was an attempt by the Refined Sugar Association to oust the jurisdiction of the Courts by a blanket agreement reached when the contract was made and *before* any dispute had arisen. Furthermore, it was being applied to all agreements concluded on the terms of the Association's rules. Such contracts were governed by English law. Different considerations may apply when the parties reach an agreement *after* a particular dispute has arisen and in relation to that dispute or when the contract is governed by a law other than that of the United Kingdom.

43. There are undoubtedly situations, rare though they may be, in which speed and finality of decision are of the utmost importance. In such cases we think that the parties would be prepared to accept some risk that the arbitrator's decision might not be correct. Whether such a situation has arisen can only be determined *after* a particular dispute has arisen and in relation to that dispute. The element of consumer protection will no longer be needed, since the main sanction compelling a party with limited bargaining power to agree to forgo any rights of appeal is a refusal to enter into a contract with him unless he does so. At the stage at which disputes have arisen, the contract has already been made. Furthermore, in practice one party's interest in obtaining an agreement to oust the jurisdiction of the Courts will, at this stage, almost always be counterbalanced by the other party's interest in refusing to enter into such an agreement. In the view of the Committee, agreements to forgo the right to review by the Court will be extremely rare and will only be made when they are justified in the interests of all parties. The Committee therefore recommends that in the case of all types of arbitration agreement, there shall be no entrenched right of appeal in relation to particular disputes once those disputes have arisen and have been referred to arbitration. At that stage the parties should be able, if they wish, to contract out of the right to appeal to the High Court.

44. The case of an agreement which is governed by foreign law but provides for English arbitration presents even less justification for an entrenched right. Any basis for a review by the English Courts would be most unusual. The Committee therefore recommends that where the dispute arises out of a contract whose proper law is expressly stated to be a system of law other than that of the United Kingdom or any part thereof, there shall be no right of review by the English Courts unless the parties expressly agree that there shall be such a right.

45. The supranational agreement raises a particular problem. As we have already stated, the parties to such a contract may reasonably object to arbitral awards concerning their disputes being referred to *any* national court. They are always fully advised by experts and need no protection. Their disputes are not usually of a nature which would contribute much to the development of English commercial law. They want to use English arbitration and English professional arbitrators, but are deterred by an entrenched right to review from doing so. The Committee is

6. See Appendix 1.
7. See Appendix 2.

in no doubt that it is in the national interest that this deterrent be removed, provided always that the position of the special category disputes is not thereby prejudiced. The Committee believes that this can be achieved, but if it were faced with making a choice between competing interests, the members would unhesitatingly favour the interests of the special category disputes group both on economic grounds and in recognition of the contribution which that group has made, is making and can continue to make to the development of English commercial law.

46. This leaves only the problem of what should be done about entrenching a right of review in relation to domestic arbitration agreements and special category disputes up to the moment when disputes have arisen and been referred to arbitration.

47. So far as domestic arbitration agreements are concerned, the Committee recommends that the right should remain entrenched for the public policy reasons set out in the judgment in *Czarnikow* v. *Roth, Schmidt and Co.*[8] In particular the Committee wishes to draw attention to the fact that parties to domestic arbitration agreements are often of very unequal bargaining power and that the weaker party needs the protection of an entrenched right of judicial review.

48. In the case of the special category disputes group the parties are usually of more equal bargaining power and the majority are foreign nationals or companies. The major public policy considerations are that there is no evidence of any very widespread desire to be able to contract out of a right of judicial review and that such a right is very important to the maintenance of English law as the first choice of law in international commerce.

49. It may reasonably be said that if few of those concerned wish to contract out, there is no reason to entrench the right. This is correct, subject to two qualifications. The first is that whilst few would reach such a decision if they gave the matter careful consideration in relation to a particular contract, there is a risk that a contracting-out clause might imperceptibly become a normal trading term. The second is that at the present time there is without doubt considerable and justified dissatisfaction at the abuse of the existing special case procedure and a temporary and abnormal increase in the number of parties wishing to contract out. Once a change has been made to judicial review based upon reasoned awards and sufficient time has elapsed for the superiority of the new system to be appreciated, an entirely different attitude should emerge. If it does not, and the parties, having applied their minds to the problem in the context of a particular contract, wish to contract out of the right of judicial review, we think that they should be allowed to do so.

50. In the light of these considerations the Committee considers that for a period of two to three years after a change to judicial review based upon reasoned awards, the right to that review should be entrenched for the special category disputes group of arbitration agreements. Any amending statute should, however, contain power to vary this provision at the end of this period in the light of the then existing circumstances. The variation which the Committee contemplates as a possibility is that parties to special category disputes agreements would then be free to contract out of the right to judicial review *before* disputes arose provided that (a) the contracting out agreement was in writing and was separate from the arbitration agreement and (b) was formally registered with the High Court.

51. The Committee has given much thought to whether the general rule for non-domestic arbitration agreements should be that which it proposes for the special disputes category, with the supranational contracts having the exceptional right to contract out or whether the general rule should be a right to contract out with the special disputes category remaining subject to exceptional entrenchment. They would have preferred the former approach, but fear that the difficulty of defining supranational contracts will dictate the adoption of the latter. Provided that the special category disputes group is adequately defined, this should not matter.

Recommendations on entrenchment

52. To summarize the Committee's conclusions in relation to the entrenchment of a right to judicial review, we recommend that:

---

8. See Appendix 2.

(a) *Contracts governed by foreign law.* There should in general be no right to judicial review where the dispute arises out of a contract whose proper law is expressly stated to be a system of law other than that of the United Kingdom or any part thereof. Nevertheless, in such cases the parties should be free at any time and on any terms to agree that there should be such a right in relation to any particular or to all disputes between them and the Courts should thereupon have jurisdiction to enter upon a review in accordance with that agreement.

(b) *Contracting out after a dispute has arisen.* After a dispute has arisen and been referred to arbitration all parties should be free to agree to exclude any right to judicial review in relation to that dispute. This would apply to all types of arbitration agreement whether domestic or non-domestic, including special category disputes.

(c) *Contracting out before a dispute has arisen.*

   (i) *Domestic arbitration agreements.* The right to judicial review should be entrenched and the parties should not be able to agree to exclude it.

   (ii) *Special category disputes.* For a period of two or three years from the introduction of the new right to a judicial review based upon a reasoned award, this right should be entrenched to the same extent as in relation to domestic arbitration agreements. Thereafter the entrenchment could, if necessary, be modified to permit contracting out if the agreement to do so was in writing, was in an agreement separate from the agreement to refer disputes to arbitration and was registered with the High Court.

   (iii) *Other non-domestic arbitration agreements including supranational agreements.* There should be no entrenched right to judicial review in relation to these types of arbitration agreement, thus allowing the parties, and in particular the parties to supranational agreements, to contract out and to use the services of English arbitration and English professional arbitrators without the slightest fear that they might end up before the High Court.

53. In the view of the Committee the need for these simple, but far-reaching, reforms is extremely urgent. This country can retain its position as the international leader in commercial law and arbitration only so long as it provides the service which its customers need. The existing customers, many of whom are of long standing, need an appeals system which is speedy and efficient, yet cannot be abused. Our future customers, the parties to supranational contracts, need to be able to contract out of the appeals system if so advised. Only when this becomes possible will they consider England as a possible venue for arbitration. Time is short, for if they once establish arbitral links with other countries, it will become very much more difficult to attract them to this country.

OTHER REFORMS IN THE LAW OF ARBITRATION

54. The Arbitration Act 1950, like its predecessors, has proved a most successful statute and the only major reform which is required is that in relation to the powers of judicial review. However, after a quarter of a century of operation, it would be surprising if it was not capable of improvement. The Committee has been able to identify certain weaknesses and would like to see these remedied. These are the subject of this part of the report.

55. The Committee is acutely aware that Parliamentary time is at a premium and that unless an amendment of the law of arbitration has great legal and economic importance, as is without doubt the case in relation to the powers of judicial review, it is difficult to obtain such time. However, the making of minor improvements in arbitration procedure is not the most controversial field of human endeavour and the Committee hope that it will prove possible to remedy these minor defects in addition to dealing with the powers of judicial review. In this context we think that consideration should be given to establishing an Arbitration Rules Committee with powers similar to those of the Supreme Court Rules Committee. This would relieve Parliament of the need to consider detailed amendments to the Act both now and in the future.

Consolidation of arbitrations

56. The High Court has power under the Rules of the Supreme Court, Order 4, rule 10 to order actions to be consolidated and tried together or one such action to be stayed until another has been determined, this power being exercisable where there are common factors in all the actions. This is a most useful power, the exercise of which can produce significant savings in costs. There is a real need for the High Court to have an analogous power in relation to arbitrations. The Committee consider that this would be a suitable subject for the attention of an Arbitration Rules Committee.

Sanctions in case of delay or failure to comply with the arbitrator's directions

57. A favourite ploy by those who seek delay is to ignore the time table fixed by the arbitrator or to fail to comply with directions for the delivery of a defence or for discovery. Parties to an action in the Commercial Court who adopted similar tactics would receive short shrift, since the Court would strike out the claim or counterclaim or debar the defendant from defending. In cases which fall within section 12(6) of the 1950 Act,[9] it is possible for parties to obtain an order from the High Court and for that Court to apply sanctions in the event of default. However this is not widely known, does not cover all forms of foot-dragging and involves at least two attendances on the High Court—the first to obtain an order and further attendances to invoke sanctions. What is required is a power for the High Court to apply sanctions for disobedience of orders made by the arbitrator. This too is a suitable subject for the attention of an Arbitration Rules Committee.

Appointment of arbitrators by the Court

58. Section 10 of the 1950 Act[10] empowers the High Court to appoint an arbitrator or umpire in various circumstances. Due no doubt to an oversight, there is no power to make the appointment if the arbitration agreement provides that it shall be made by a stranger, e.g., the President of a professional body, and he fails or refuses to make the appointment (see *National Enterprises Ltd.* v. *Racal Communications Ltd.* [1974] 2 Lloyd's Rep. 21). This is a gap which should be filled.

Appointment of third arbitrator

59. Where an arbitration agreement provides that the reference should be to three arbitrators, one to be appointed by each of the parties and the third by those arbitrators, section 9(1) of the 1950 Act[11] converts the third arbitrator into an umpire. As such he has no jurisdiction unless and until the two other arbitrators disagree. This is unpopular with those sections of the commercial community which favour three-arbitrator agreements. They point out, not unreasonably, that if they had wanted an umpire, they would have so provided in their agreement. Instead they wanted a third arbitrator who would be seized of their dispute *ab initio*. Parliament, for reasons which are wholly unexplained, has frustrated their intentions. This complaint is unanswerable and should be remedied by amending the section.

Costs

60. Section 18(1) of the 1950 Act[12] gives arbitrators power to tax or settle the amount of the costs of the reference, but it is widely believed that section 23 of the Solicitors Act 1957[13] prevents them taxing or settling the costs of a foreign lawyer on the grounds that they are unqualified persons acting as solicitors. It is probable that this is a misconception of the law, since a foreign lawyer acting for a client in an arbitration is not doing anything which is reserved to the

9. See Appendix 1.
10. See Appendix 1.
11. See Appendix 1.
12. See Appendix 1.
13 See Appendix 1.

solicitors' profession. However it is desirable that this point be clarified and once again it is a matter which could, perhaps, be dealt with by an Arbitration Rules Committee.

61. Section 18(2) of the 1950 Act[14] provides that costs shall be taxable in the High Court unless the award otherwise directs. Thus an arbitrator has a choice whether to tax the costs personally or to leave it to the High Court. What he cannot do is to refer the taxation to an expert such as a retired taxing master or an experienced costs clerk. The High Court Taxing Office is overburdened with work and arbitrators rarely have the expertise to tax costs themselves. A power to refer a taxation to an expert would therefore be valuable. This too could be looked at by an Arbitration Rules Committee armed with suitable powers.

Offers to settle and payment into Court

62. In an action, the defendant can pay into Court a sum which he considers to be sufficient to meet the amount which the plaintiff will eventually be awarded. Within a limited period the plaintiff can, if he wishes, take this sum out of Court in full satisfaction of his claims and will thereupon be entitled to the costs of the action. Alternatively he can go on with the action in the hope he will recover more than the sum in Court. If his hopes are realized, he will *prima facie* be entitled to all the costs of the action. If they are not realized, he will be entitled to the costs up to the date of payment into Court, but will have to pay the defendant's costs incurred after that date. It is a very strict rule of Court that the Judge cannot be told that money has been paid into Court and, still more, how much has been paid in until he has given judgment. He is then told and makes the appropriate order as to costs.

63. There is difficulty in adapting this procedure to arbitrations since the award usually deals with liability, damages, interest and costs all in the same document and the parties have no opportunity of making submissions about costs after the other issues have been determined. A somewhat imperfect solution has been adopted whereby the respondent in the arbitration makes a "sealed offer" of settlement. The claimant can accept it or reject it. If he rejects it, the offer is placed in a sealed envelope and handed to the arbitrator on terms that it shall not be opened until after he has decided upon all issues other than costs. The system is open to the objection that the arbitrator, unlike a Judge, will know that some offer of settlement has been made, although he will not know how much. There is the further objection that the arbitrator must be subject to a great temptation to open the envelope before deciding how much to award.

64. The Committee recommends that an arbitrator should make his award on all issues including costs without being told that any offer of settlement has been made, but that he should be empowered to re-open so much of the award as relates to costs upon subsequent proof that an offer of settlement was made before or during the hearing of the arbitration.

65. There is a further objection to the system in that it is one thing to make an offer in settlement, but quite another to produce the necessary money to back that offer. Under the Court system, the offer is of no effect unless accompanied by the money. Under the arbitration system, there is no guarantee that the party making the offer has the money to back it if the offer is accepted. The Committee recommends that the respondents in arbitration proceedings who wish to make an offer of settlement which may affect the arbitrator's decision as to costs should be obliged to pay the amount offered into Court.

66. The points mentioned in paragraphs 63–65 could well be considered and dealt with by an Arbitration Rules Committee.

"Misconduct"

67. Section 23 of the 1950 Act[15] provides certain remedies if the arbitrator or umpire has "misconducted himself or the proceedings". Few would object to this terminology if what was referred to was dishonesty or a breach of business morality upon the part of the arbitrator or umpire. But the section has been held to apply to procedural errors or omissions by arbitrators

14. See Appendix 1.
15. See Appendix 1.

who are doing their best to uphold the highest standards of their profession. In this context the terminology causes considerable offence, even in a permissive society. The Committee would like to see some other term substituted for "misconducted" which reflects the idea of irregularity rather than misconduct. It may be said that this point is merely cosmetic, but arbitrators are not to be criticised for their sensitivity and the Courts should not be required to use opprobrious terminology about arbitrators and be obliged to take time explaining that when they have found that the arbitrator has misconducted himself, they were not using the words in any ordinary sense.

ACKNOWLEDGMENTS AND APOLOGIES

68. The Committee would like to acknowledge the great assistance which it has received from Lord Diplock's Alexander Lecture, the Joint Committee of the London Court of Arbitration, the Institute of Arbitrators and the London Maritime Arbitrators Association under the chairmanship of Mr. Clifford Clark, the London Arbitration Group under the chairmanship of Mr. Mark Littman Q.C. and the many individuals who have been consulted both directly and indirectly.

69. In some parts of this report the words "England" and "English" have been used as abbreviations for "England and Wales" and "English and Welsh" respectively. Similarly the word "London" has been used as an abbreviation for "London and the other commercial centres of England and Wales". The Committee tenders its apologies to any and all who regard this approach as cavalier.

70. By agreement of the other members of the Committee, this report is signed on their behalf by the Chairman and the Secretary.

6 June 1978

JOHN F. DONALDSON
Chairman

J. L. POWELL
Secretary

. . .

APPENDIX 2. EXTRACTS FROM THE JUDGMENTS IN CZARNIKOW v. ROTH, SCHMIDT AND COMPANY [1922] 2 K.B. 478

BANKES L.J. . . . The ground of objection to the rule is that as an agreement it ousts the jurisdiction of the Courts of law, and is consequently against public policy and void. The importance of maintaining in its integrity the rule of law in reference to public policy is in my opinion a matter of considerable importance at the present time. Powerful trade organizations are encouraging, if not compelling, their members and persons who enter into contracts with their members to agree, as far as they can lawfully do so, to abstain from submitting their disputes to the decision of a Court of law. The present case is a case in point. There have been others before the Courts. Among commercial men what are commonly called commercial arbitrations are undoubtedly and deservedly popular. That they will continue their present popularity I entertain no doubt, so long as the law retains sufficient hold over them to prevent and redress any injustice on the part of the arbitrator, and to secure that the law that is administered by an arbitrator is in substance the law of the land and not some homemade law of the particular arbitrator or the particular association. To release real and effective control over commercial arbitrations is to allow the arbitrator, or the Arbitration Tribunal, to be a law unto himself, or themselves, to give him or them a free hand to decide accordingly to law or not according to law as he or they think fit, in other words to be outside the law. At present no individual or association is, so far as I am aware, outside the law except a trade union. To put such associations as

483

the Refined Sugar Association in a similar position would in my opinion be against public policy. Unlimited power does not conduce to reasonableness of view or conduct. . . .

SCRUTTON L.J. . . . In countless cases parties agree to submit their disputes to arbitrators whose decision shall be final and conclusive. But the Courts, if one of these parties brings an action, never treat this agreement as conclusively preventing the Courts from hearing the dispute. They consider the merits of the case, including the fact of the agreement of the parties, and either stay the action or allow it to proceed according to the view they form of the best method of procedure; and they have always in my experience declined to fetter their discretion by laying down any fixed rules on which they will exercise it. If they allow the action to proceed they pay no further attention, and give no legal effect, to any further proceedings in the arbitration: *Doleman Sons* v. *Ossett Corporation* [1912] 3 K.B. 257, 269. They do not allow the agreement of private parties to oust the jurisdiction of the King's Courts. Arbitrators, unless expressly otherwise authorized, have to apply the laws of England. When they are persons untrained, in law and especially when as in this case they allow persons trained in law to address them on legal points, there is every probability of their going wrong, and for that reason Parliament has provided in the Arbitration Act that, not only may they ask the Courts for guidance and the solution of their legal problems in special cases stated at their own instance, but that the Courts may require them, even if unwilling, to state cases for the opinion of the Court on the application of a party to the arbitration if the Courts think it proper. This is done in order that the Courts may insure the proper administration of the law by inferior tribunals. In my view to allow English citizens to agree to exclude this safeguard for the administration of the law is contrary to public policy. There must be no Alsatia in England where the King's writ does not run. It seems quite clear that no British Court would recognize or enforce an agreement of British citizens not to raise a defence of illegality by British law. But for the decision of *Tullis* v. *Jacson* [1892] 3 Ch. 441. I should have thought it equally clear that no agreement not to raise a defence of fraud was enforceable. Fraud usually involves a criminal offence, and if there were in fact fraud an agreement not to bring it before the King's Courts was, I should have thought, clearly contrary to public policy. I reserve my right to consider *Tullis* v. *Jacson* if a similar clause should come before me. Without attempting precisely to define the limits within which an agreement not to take proceedings in the King's Courts is unenforceable, I think an agreement to shut out the power of the King's Courts to guide the proceedings of inferior tribunals without legal training in matters of law before them is calculated to lead to erroneous administration of law, and therefore injustice, and should therefore not be recognized by the Courts. I am ready to go very far in ignoring technicalities and irregularities on the part of arbitrators, unless there is some real substance of error behind them, but I think commercial men will be making a great mistake if they ignore the importance of administering settled principles of law in commercial disputes, and trust to the judgment of business men, however experienced in business, based only on the facts of each particular case, and with no knowledge of or guidance in the principles of law which must control the facts and which arbitrators must administer. . . .

ATKIN L.J. . . . I think that it is still a principle of English law that an agreement to oust the jurisdiction of the Courts is invalid. It is so stated or assumed in all the judgments of the judges who advised the House of Lords in *Scott* v. *Avery* 3 H.L.C. 811, and the principle is affirmed by Lord Chelmsford. The effect of the decision is to establish that an agreement that the rights of the parties shall be determined by arbitration as a condition precedent to an action is not an agreement ousting the jurisdiction of the Court. There is no cause of action and therefore no jurisdiction until an award is made, and when made the Courts have complete jurisdiction. The jurisdiction that is ousted in this case is not the common law jurisdiction of the Courts to give a remedy for breaches of contract, but the special statutory jurisdiction of the Court to intervene to compel arbitrators to submit a point of law for determination by the Courts. This appears to me to be a provision of paramount importance in the interests of the public. If it did not exist arbitration clauses making an award a condition precedent would leave lay arbitrators at liberty to adopt any principles of law they pleased, in the case of powerful associations such as the present, able to impose their own arbitration clauses upon their members, and, by their uniform contract, conditions upon all non-members contracting with members, the result might be that in time codes of law would come to be administered in various trades differing substantially from the English mercantile law. The policy of the law has given to the High Court large powers over inferior Courts for the very purpose of maintaining a uniform standard of justice and one uniform system of law. Analogous powers have been possessed by the Court over arbitrators, and have been extended by the provisions of s. 19. If an agreement to oust the common law jurisdiction of the Court is invalid every reason appears to me to exist for holding that an agreement to oust the Court of this statutory jurisdiction is invalid. . . .

COMMERCIAL COURT COMMITTEE SUB-COMMITTEE ON ARBITRATION LAW, FINAL REPORT, 22 OCTOBER 1985[1]

JUDICIAL CONTROL ON QUESTIONS OF LAW

12. The 1979 legislation made two alterations to the existing regime for appeals on questions of law:

(i) Except in the case of domestic contracts and certain categories of international commercial contracts, the parties were given the liberty, in advance of any dispute, to contract out of the right of appeal.

(ii) Even where the right is not excluded by agreement, the Court has a discretion whether or not to entertain an appeal. This discretion has, by judicial decision, been very narrowly confined.

13. The system introduced by the 1979 Act was acknowledged to be a compromise between the demands of finality and the need to maintain some control over the determination of disputes according to law. The general opinion appears to be that the balance has been struck in a satisfactory manner. We have not detected any body of opinion which favours the restoration of the unfettered right of appeal, and there is little support for the view that the right of appeal should be completely abolished, at least in the absence of a fundamental appraisal of English arbitral procedure.

14. One aspect of the 1979 Act requires special consideration: namely, the singling out of certain specified categories of transaction in respect of which the parties cannot bind themselves in advance to exclude the right of appeal. When the 1979 legislation was under debate it was contemplated that these categories would be reviewed after a few years, in order to see whether experience showed that contracting out could properly be extended to all non-domestic arbitrations. We have therefore done our best to see whether opinions on this point have changed during the past few years. The problem here is that the users of English arbitration are numerous and are scattered world-wide. It is therefore impossible to make a direct canvass of their opinions, and we have had to obtain their views at second hand through the medium of the lawyers and arbitrators who conduct their disputes, and the trade associations and similar bodies who represent their interests and provide an institutional framework for their arbitrations. Against this rather limited perspective, it does seem to us clear that not only is there no pressure from users for the extension of the right to contract out of appeals to all international contracts, but that there is a substantial majority in favour of leaving matters as they are at present.

15. At the time when we prepared the Working Paper[2] it had seemed to us that there was one exception to this general opinion: namely, the special category of insurance transactions. Subsequently, however, we have had the benefit of opinions expressed by persons directly concerned in the insurance industry. These favour the retention of insurance contracts in the special categories. In these circumstances, we are no longer disposed to recommend the exercise of the Secretary of State's powers under section 4(3) of the 1979 Act to delete these contracts from the scope of section 4(1)(a).

---

1. Under the Chairmanship of the Rt. Hon. Lord Justice Mustill (as he then was).
2. Dated 1 February 1985.

APPENDIX C

THE DEPARTMENTAL ADVISORY COMMITTEE ON ARBITRATION LAW, SECOND REPORT, MAY 1990[1]

COURT SUPERVISION—THE SPECIAL CATEGORIES

13. Although Section 3 of the Arbitration Act 1979 gives the parties the power to exclude the right of appeal (given by Section 1) on questions of law to the High Court, Section 3 restricts the ability to enter into an exclusion agreement in the case of certain specified categories of dispute; shipping, insurance and commodity contracts. The 1985 Report concluded that these special categories should be maintained. The Committee considered whether the retention of special categories, in particular insurance contracts, was justified. The Committee noted that the law appeared to work well in practice. No representations for a change were received. The Committee endorse the conclusion of the 1985 Report that the special categories should at present be maintained.

---

1. Under the Chairmanship of The Hon. Mr Justice Steyn (as he then was). The Report is available from the Department of Trade and Industry.

ARBITRATION ACT 1979

Judicial review of arbitration awards

1.—(1) In the Arbitration Act 1950 (in this Act referred to as "the principal Act") section 21 (statement of case for a decision of the High Court) shall cease to have effect and, without prejudice to the right of appeal conferred by subsection (2) below, the High Court shall not have jurisdiction to set aside or remit an award on an arbitration agreement on the ground of errors of fact or law on the face of the award.

(2) Subject to subsection (3) below, an appeal shall lie to the High Court on any question of law arising out of an award made on an arbitration agreement; and on the determination of such an appeal the High Court may by order—

(a) confirm, vary or set aside the award; or
(b) remit the award to the reconsideration of the arbitrator or umpire together with the court's opinion on the question of law which was the subject of the appeal;

and where the award is remitted under paragraph (b) above the arbitrator or umpire shall, unless the order otherwise directs, make his award within three months after the date of the order.

(3) An appeal under this section may be brought by any of the parties to the reference—

(a) with the consent of all the other parties to the reference; or
(b) subject to section 3 below, with the leave of the court.

(4) The High Court shall not grant leave under subsection (3)(b) above unless it considers that, having regard to all the circumstances, the determination of the question of law concerned could substantially affect the rights of one or more of the parties to the arbitration agreement; and the court may make any leave which it gives conditional upon the applicant complying with such conditions as it considers appropriate.

(5) Subject to subsection (6) below, if an award is made and, on an application made by any of the parties to the reference—

(a) with the consent of all the other parties to the reference, or
(b) subject to section 3 below, with the leave of the court,

it appears to the High Court that the award does not or does not sufficiently set out the reasons for the award, the court may order the arbitrator or umpire concerned to state the reasons for his award in sufficient detail to enable the court, should an appeal be brought under this section, to consider any question of law arising out of the award.

(6) In any case where an award is made without any reason being given, the High Court shall not make an order under subsection (5) above unless it is satisfied—

(a) that before the award was made one of the parties to the reference gave notice to the arbitrator or umpire concerned that a reasoned award would be required; or
(b) that there is some special reason why such a notice was not given.

(6A) Unless the High Court gives leave, no appeal shall lie to the Court of Appeal from a decision of the High Court—

(a) to grant or refuse leave under subsection 3(b) or 5(b) above; or
(b) to make or not to make an order under subsection (5) above.

(7) No appeal shall lie to the Court of Appeal from a decision of the High Court on an appeal under this section unless—

(a) the High Court or the Court of Appeal gives leave; and
(b) it is certified by the High Court that the question of law to which its decision relates either is one of general public importance or is one which for some other special reason should be considered by the Court of Appeal.

(8) Where the award of an arbitrator or umpire is varied on appeal, the award as varied shall have effect (except for the purposes of this section) as if it were the award of the arbitrator or umpire.

Note: Sub-s. (6A) was added by s. 148(2) of the Supreme Court Act 1981.

Determination of preliminary point of law by court

2.—(1) Subject to subsection (2) and section 3 below, on an application to the High Court made by any of the parties to a reference—

(a) with the consent of an arbitrator who has entered on the reference or, if an umpire has entered on the reference, with his consent, or
(b) with the consent of all the other parties,

the High Court shall have jurisdiction to determine any question of law arising in the course of the reference.

(2) The High Court shall not entertain an application under subsection (1)(a) above with respect to any question of law unless it is satisfied that—

(a) the determination of the application might produce substantial savings in costs to the parties; and
(b) the question of law is one in respect of which leave to appeal would be likely to be given under section 1(3)(b) above.

(2A) Unless the High Court gives leave, no appeal shall lie to the Court of Appeal from a decision of the High Court to entertain or not to entertain an application under subsection (1)(a) above.

(3) A decision of the High Court under [sub-section (1) above] shall be deemed to be a judgment of the court within the meaning of section [16 of the Supreme Court Act 1981] (appeals to the Court of Appeal), but no appeal shall lie from such a decision unless—

(a) the High Court or the Court of Appeal gives leave; and
(b) it is certified by the High Court that the question of law to which its decision relates either is one of general public importance or is one which for some other special reason should be considered by the Court of Appeal.

Note: The words in square brackets were substituted by the Supreme Court Act 1981, s. 148(3) and Sch. 5. Section 148 of that Act added sub-s. (2A).

Exclusion agreements affecting rights under sections 1 and 2

3.—(1) Subject to the following provisions of this section and section 4 below—

(a) the High Court shall not, under section 1(3)(b) above, grant leave to appeal with respect to a question of law arising out of an award, and
(b) the High Court shall not, under section 1(5)(b) above, grant leave to make an application with respect to an award, and

(c) no application may be made under section 2(1)(a) above with respect to a question of law,

if the parties to the reference in question have entered into an agreement in writing (in this section referred to as an "exclusion agreement") which excludes the right of appeal under section 1 above in relation to that award or, in a case falling within paragraph (c) above, in relation to an award to which the determination of the question of law is material.

(2) An exclusion agreement may be expressed so as to relate to a particular award, to awards under a particular reference or to any other description of awards, whether arising out of the same reference or not; and an agreement may be an exclusion agreement for the purposes of this section whether it is entered into before or after the passing of this Act and whether or not it forms part of an arbitration agreement.

(3) In any case where—

(a) an arbitration agreement, other than a domestic arbitration agreement, provides for disputes between the parties to be referred to arbitration, and

(b) a dispute to which the agreement relates involves the question whether a party has been guilty of fraud, and

(c) the parties have entered into an exclusion agreement which is applicable to any award made on the reference to that dispute,

then, except in so far as the exclusion agreement otherwise provides, the High Court shall not exercise its powers under section 24(2) of the principal Act (to take steps necessary to enable the question to be determined by the High Court) in relation to that dispute.

(4) Except as provided by subsection (1) above, sections 1 and 2 above shall have effect notwithstanding anything in any agreement purporting—

(a) to prohibit or restrict access to the High Court; or

(b) to restrict the jurisdiction of that court; or

(c) to prohibit or restrict the making of a reasoned award.

(5) An exclusion agreement shall be of no effect in relation to an award made on, or a question of law arising in the course of a reference under, a statutory arbitration, that is to say, such an arbitration as is referred to in subsection (1) of section 31 of the principal Act.

(6) An exclusion agreement shall be of no effect in relation to an award made on, or a question of law arising in the course of a reference under, an arbitration agreement which is a domestic arbitration agreement unless the exclusion agreement is entered into after the commencement of the arbitration in which the award is made or, as the case may be, in which the question of law arises.

(7) In this section "domestic arbitration agreement" means an arbitration agreement which does not provide, expressly or by implication, for arbitration in a State other than the United Kingdom and to which neither—

(a) an individual who is a national of, or habitually resident in, any State other than the United Kingdom, nor

(b) a body corporate which is incorporated in, or whose central management and control is exercised in, any State other than the United Kingdom,

is a party at the time the arbitration agreement is entered into.

Exclusion agreements not to apply in certain cases

4.—(1) Subject to subsection (3) below, if an arbitration award or a question of law arising in the course of a reference relates, in whole or in part, to—

(a) a question or claim falling within the Admiralty jurisdiction of the High Court, or

493

(b) a dispute arising out of a contract of insurance, or

(c) a dispute arising out of a commodity contract,

an exclusion agreement shall have no effect in relation to the award or question unless either—

    (i) the exclusion agreement is entered into after the commencement of the arbitration in which the award is made or, as the case may be, in which the question of law arises, or

    (ii) the award or question relates to a contract which is expressed to be governed by a law other than the law of England and Wales.

(2) In subsection (1)(c) above "commodity contract" means a contract—

    (a) for the sale of goods regularly dealt with on a commodity market or exchange in England or Wales which is specified for the purposes of this section by an order made by the Secretary of State; and

    (b) of a description so specified.

(3) The Secretary of State may by order provide that subsection (1) above—

    (a) shall cease to have effect; or

    (b) subject to such conditions as may be specified in the order, shall not apply to any exclusion agreement made in relation to an arbitration award of a description so specified;

and an order under this subsection may contain such supplementary, incidental and transitional provisions as appear to the Secretary of State to be necessary or expedient.

(4) The power to make an order under subsection (2) or subsection (3) above shall be exercisable by statutory instrument which shall be subject to annulment in pursuance of a resolution of either House of Parliament.

(5) In this section "exclusion agreement" has the same meaning as in section 3 above.

Interlocutory orders

5.—(1) If any party to a reference under an arbitration agreement fails within the time specified in the order or, if no time is so specified, within a reasonable time to comply with an order made by the arbitrator or umpire in the course of the reference, then, on the application of the arbitrator or umpire or of any party to the reference, the High Court may make an order extending the powers of the arbitrator or umpire as mentioned in subsection (2) below.

(2) If an order is made by the High Court under this section, the arbitrator or umpire shall have power, to the extent and subject to any conditions specified in that order, to continue with the reference in default of appearance or of any other act by one of the parties in like manner as a judge of the High Court might continue with proceedings in that court where a party fails to comply with an order of that court or a requirement of rules of court.

(3) Section 4(5) of the Administration of Justice Act 1970 (jurisdiction of the High Court to be exercisable by the Court of Appeal in relation to judge-arbitrators and judge-umpires) shall not apply in relation to the power of the High Court to make an order under this section, but in the case of a reference to a judge-arbitrator or judge-umpire that power shall be exercisable as in the case of any other reference to arbitration and also by the judge-arbitrator or judge-umpire himself.

(4) Anything done by a judge-arbitrator or judge-umpire in the exercise of the power conferred by subsection (3) above shall be done by him in his capacity as judge of the High Court and have effect as if done by that court.

(5) The preceding provisions of this section have effect notwithstanding anything in any agreement but do not derogate from any powers conferred on an arbitrator or umpire, whether by an arbitration agreement or otherwise.

(6) In this section "judge-arbitrator" and "judge-umpire" have the same meaning as in Schedule 3 to the Administration of Justice Act 1970.

Minor amendments relating to awards and appointments of arbitrators and umpires

6.—(1) In subsection (1) of section 8 of the principal Act (agreements where reference is to two arbitrators deemed to include provision that the arbitrators shall appoint an umpire immediately after their own appointment)—

(a) for the words "shall appoint an umpire immediately" there shall be substituted the words "may appoint an umpire at any time"; and

(b) at the end there shall be added the words "and shall do so forthwith if they cannot agree".

(2) For section 9 of the principal Act (agreements for reference to three arbitrators) there shall be substituted the following section—

"Majority award of three arbitrators

9. Unless the contrary intention is expressed in the arbitration agreement, in any case where there is a reference to three arbitrators, the award of any two of the arbitrators shall be binding."

(3) In section 10 of the principal Act (power of court in certain cases to appoint an arbitrator or umpire) in paragraph (c) after the word "are", in the first place where it occurs, there shall be inserted the words "required or are" and the words from "or where" to the end of the paragraph shall be omitted.

(4) At the end of section 10 of the principal Act there shall be added the following subsection—

"(2) In any case where—

(a) an arbitration agreement provides for the appointment of an arbitration or umpire by a person who is neither one of the parties nor an existing arbitrator (whether the provision applies directly or in default of agreement by the parties or otherwise), and

(b) that person refuses to make the appointment or does not make it within the time specified in the agreement or, if no time is so specified, within a reasonable time,

any party to the agreement may serve the person in question with a written notice to appoint an arbitrator or umpire and, if the appointment is not made within seven clear days after the service of the notice, the High Court or a judge thereof may, on the application of the party who gave the notice, appoint an arbitrator or umpire who shall have the like powers to act in the reference and make an award as if he had been appointed in accordance with the terms of the agreement."

Application and interpretation of certain provisions of Part I of principal Act

7.—(1) References in the following provisions of Part I of the principal Act to that Part of that Act shall have effect as if the preceding provisions of this Act were included in that Part, namely,—

(a) section 14 (interim awards);

(b) section 28 (terms as to costs of orders);

(c) section 30 (Crown to be bound);

(d) section 31 (application to statutory arbitration); and

(e) section 32 (meaning of "arbitration agreement").

(2) Subsections (2) and (3) of section 29 of the principal Act shall apply to determine when an arbitration is deemed to be commenced for the purposes of this Act.

(3) For the avoidance of doubts, it is hereby declared that the reference in subsection (1) of section 31 of the principal Act (statutory arbitrations) to arbitration under any other Act does not extend to arbitration under section 92 of the County Courts Act [1984] (cases in which proceedings are to be or may be referred to arbitration) and accordingly nothing in this Act or in Part I of the principal Act applies to arbitration under the said section 92.

Short title, commencement, repeals and extent

8.—(1) This Act may be cited as the Arbitration Act 1979.

(2) This Act shall come into operation on such day as the Secretary of State may appoint by order made by statutory instrument; and such an order—

    (a) may appoint different days for different provisions of this Act and for the purposes of the operation of the same provision in relation to different descriptions of arbitration agreement; and

    (b) may contain such supplementary, incidental and transitional provisions as appear to the Secretary of State to be necessary or expedient.

(3) In consequence of the preceding provisions of this Act, the following provisions are hereby repealed, namely—

    (a) in paragraph (c) of section 10 of the principal Act the words from "or where" to the end of the paragraph;

    (b) section 21 of the principal Act;

    (c) in paragraph 9 of Schedule 3 to the Administration of Justice Act 1970, in sub-paragraph (1) the words "21(1) and (2)" and sub-paragraph (2).

(4) This Act forms part of the law of England and Wales only.

STATUTORY INSTRUMENTS MADE UNDER THE ARBITRATION ACT 1979

E(1) ARBITRATION ACT 1979 (COMMENCEMENT) ORDER 1979
(SI 1979 No 750)

Article 1: Citation and interpretation

1.—(1) This Order may be cited as the Arbitration Act 1979 (Commencement) Order 1979.

(2) In this Order "the Act" means the Arbitration Act 1979.

Article 2: Appointed day

2. The Act shall come into operation on 1st August 1979 (hereinafter referred to as "the appointed day"), but, except as provided in Article 3 of this Order, shall not apply to arbitrations commenced before that date.

Article 3: Commencement

3. If all the parties to a reference to arbitration commenced before the appointed day have agreed in writing that the Act should apply to that arbitration, the Act shall so apply from the appointed day or the date of the agreement whichever is the later.

Note: "Commenced" has the meaning assigned to it by section 7(2) of the Act: see Interpretation Act 1978, s.11.

E(2) ARBITRATION (COMMODITY CONTRACTS) ORDER 1979
(SI 1979 No 754)

1.—(1) This Order may be cited as the Arbitration (Commodity Contracts) Order 1979 and shall come into operation on 1st August 1979.

(2) In this Order—

"the Act" means the Arbitration Act 1979;

"market" means a commodity market or exchange.

2. The following markets are hereby specified for the purpose of section 4 of the Act—

(a) the markets set out in Part I of the Schedule hereto;

(b) any market in which contracts for sale are subject to the rules or regulations of one or other of the associations set out in Part II of the Schedule, whether or not the market is a market on which commodities are bought and sold at a particular place.

3. The following descriptions of contract are hereby specified for the purpose of section 4 of the Act—

(a) contracts for the sale of goods on any market specified in Article 2 of this Order;

(b) contracts for the sale of goods which are subject to arbitration rules of the London Metal Exchange or of an association set out in Part II of the Schedule hereto.

SCHEDULE

Part I—Markets

The London Cocoa Terminal Market
The London Coffee Terminal Market
The London Grain Futures Market
The London Metal Exchange
The London Rubber Terminal Market
The Gafta Soya Bean Meal Futures Market
The London Sugar Terminal Market
The London Vegetable Oil Terminal Market
The London Wool Terminal Market

Part II—Markets in which contracts are subject to rules and regulations of the following Associations

The Cocoa Association of London Limited
The Coffee Trade Federation
The Combined Edible Nut Trade Association
Federation of Oils, Seeds and Fats Associations Limited
The General Produce Brokers' Association of London
The Grain and Feed Trade Association Limited
The Hull Seed, Oil and Cake Association
The Liverpool Cotton Association Limited
London Jute Association
London Rice Brokers' Association
The National Federation of Fruit and Potato Trades Limited
The Rubber Trade Association of London
Skin, Hide and Leather Traders' Association Limited
The Sugar Association of London
The Refined Sugar Association
The Tea Brokers' Association of London
The British Wool Confederation

APPENDIX F

OTHER LEGISLATION RELATING TO ARBITRATION

F(1) ARBITRATION ACT 1950

An Act to consolidate the Arbitration Acts 1889 to 1934.

PART I. GENERAL PROVISIONS AS TO ARBITRATION

Effect of arbitration agreements, &c.

Authority of arbitrators and umpires to be irrevocable

1. The authority of an arbitrator or umpire appointed by or by virtue of an arbitration agreement shall, unless a contrary intention is expressed in the agreement, be irrevocable except by leave of the High Court or a judge thereof.

Death of party

2.—(1) An arbitration agreement shall not be discharged by the death of any party thereto, either as respects the deceased or any other party, but shall in such an event be enforceable by or against the personal representative of the deceased.

(2) The authority of an arbitrator shall not be revoked by the death of any party by whom he was appointed.

(3) Nothing in this section shall be taken to affect the operation of any enactment or rule of law by virtue of which any right of action is extinguished by the death of a person.

Bankruptcy

3.—(1) Where it is provided by a term in a contract to which a bankrupt is a party that any differences arising thereout or in connection therewith shall be referred to arbitration, the said term shall, if the trustee in bankruptcy adopts the contract, be enforceable by or against him so far as relates to any such differences.

(2) Where a person who has been adjudged bankrupt had, before the commencement of the bankruptcy, become a party to an arbitration agreement, and any matter to which the agreement applies requires to be determined in connection with or for the purposes of the bankruptcy proceedings, then, if the case is one to which subsection (1) of this section does not apply, any other party to the agreement or, with the consent of the committee of inspection, the trustee in bankruptcy, may apply to the court having jurisdiction in the bankruptcy proceedings for an order directing that the matter in question shall be referred to arbitration in accordance with the agreement, and that court may, if it is of opinion that, having regard to all the circumstances of the case, the matter ought to be determined by arbitration, make an order accordingly.

Staying court proceedings where there is submission to arbitration

4.—(1) If any party to an arbitration agreement, or any person claiming through or under him, commences any legal proceedings in any court against any other party to the agreement, or

499

any person claiming through or under him, in respect of any matter agreed to be referred, any party to those legal proceedings may at any time after appearance, and before delivering any pleadings or taking any other steps in the proceedings, apply to that court to stay the proceedings, and that court or a judge thereof, if satisfied that there is no sufficient reason why the matter should not be referred in accordance with the agreement, and that the applicant was, at the time when the proceedings were commenced, and still remains, ready and willing to do all things necessary to the proper conduct of the arbitration, may make an order staying the proceedings.

[(2) Notwithstanding anything in this Part of this Act, if any party to a submission to arbitration made in pursuance of an agreement to which the protocol set out in the First Schedule to this Act applies, or any person claiming through or under him, commences any legal proceedings in any court against any other party to the submission, or any person claiming through or under him, in respect of any matter agreed to be referred, any party to those legal proceedings may at any time after appearance, and before delivering any pleadings or taking any other steps in the proceedings, apply to that court to stay the proceedings, and that court or a judge thereof, unless satisfied that the agreement or arbitration has become inoperative or cannot proceed or that there is not in fact any dispute between the parties with regard to the matter agreed to be referred, shall make an order staying the proceedings.]

Note: The words in square brackets were repealed by s. 8(2)(a) of the Arbitration Act 1975.

Reference of interpleader issues to arbitration

5. Where relief by way of interpleader is granted and it appears to the High Court that the claims in question are matters to which an arbitration agreement, to which the claimants are parties, applies, the High Court may direct the issue between the claimants to be determined in accordance with the agreement.

Arbitrators and umpires

When reference is to a single arbitrator

6. Unless a contrary intention is expressed therein, every arbitration agreement shall, if no other mode of reference is provided, be deemed to include a provision that the reference shall be to a single arbitrator.

Power parties in certain cases to supply vacancy

7. Where an arbitration agreement provides that the reference shall be to two arbitrators, one to be appointed by each party then, unless a contrary intention is expressed therein—

    (a) if either of the appointed arbitrators refuses to act, or is incapable of acting, or dies, the party who appointed him may appoint a new arbitrator in his place;

    (b) if, on such a reference, one party fails to appoint an arbitrator, either originally, or by way of substitution as aforesaid, for seven clear days after the other party having appointed his arbitrator, has served the party making default with notice to make the appointment, the party who has appointed an arbitrator may appoint that arbitrator to act as sole arbitrator in the reference and his award shall be binding on both parties as if he had been appointed by consent:

Provided that the High Court or a judge thereof may set aside any appointment made in pursuance of this section.

Umpires

8.—(1) Unless a contrary intention is expressed therein, every arbitration agreement shall, where the reference is to two arbitrators, be deemed to include a provision that the two arbitrators may appoint an umpire at any time after they are themselves appointed, and shall do so forthwith if they cannot agree.

(2) Unless a contrary intention is expressed therein, every arbitration agreement shall, where such a provision is applicable to the reference, be deemed to include a provision that if the arbitrators have delivered to any party to the arbitration agreement, or to the umpire, a notice in writing stating that they cannot agree, the umpire may forthwith enter on the reference in lieu of the arbitrators.

(3) At any time after the appointment of an umpire, however appointed, the High Court may, on the application of any party to the reference and notwithstanding anything to the contrary in the arbitration agreement, order that the umpire shall enter upon the reference in lieu of the arbitrators and as if he were a sole arbitrator.

Note: Sub-s. (1) is printed as amended by s. 6(1) of the Arbitration Act 1979. In relation to arbitrations to which the Arbitration Act 1979 does not apply, sub-s. (1) applies in its unamended form, as follows—
"Unless a contrary intention is expressed therein, every arbitration agreement shall, where the reference is to two arbitrators be deemed to include a provision that the two arbitrators shall appoint an umpire at any time after they are themselves appointed."

Majority award of three arbitrators

9. Unless the contrary intention is expressed in the arbitration agreement, in any case where there is a reference to three arbitrators, the award of any two of the arbitrators shall be binding.

Note: This section is printed as amended by s. 6(2) of the Arbitration Act 1979. In relation to arbitrations to which the Arbitration Act 1979 does not apply, the section applies in its unamended form which reads as follows:
"**9**—(1) Where an arbitration agreement provides that the reference shall be to three arbitrators, one to be appointed by each party and the third to be appointed by the two appointed by the parties, the agreement shall have effect as if it provided for the appointment of an umpire, and not for the appointment of a third arbitrator, by the two arbitrators appointed by the parties.
(2) Where an arbitration agreement provides that the reference shall be to three arbitrators to be appointed otherwise than as mentioned in subsection (1) of this section, the award of any two of the arbitrators shall be binding."

Power of court in certain cases to appoint an arbitrator or umpire

10.—(1) In any of the following cases—

(a) where an arbitration agreement provides that the reference shall be to a single arbitrator, and all the parties do not, after differences have arisen, concur in the appointment of an arbitrator;

(b) if an appointed arbitrator refuses to act, or is incapable of acting, or dies, and the arbitration agreement does not show that it was intended that the vacancy should not be supplied and the parties do not supply the vacancy;

(c) where the parties or two arbitrators are required or are at liberty to appoint an umpire or third arbitrator and do not appoint him;

(d) where an appointed umpire or third arbitrator refuses to act, or is incapable of acting, or dies, and the arbitration agreement does not show that it was intended that the vacancy should not be supplied, and the parties or arbitrators do not supply the vacancy;

any party may serve the other parties or the arbitrators, as the case may be, with a written notice to appoint or, as the case may be, concur in appointing, an arbitrator, umpire or third arbitrator, and if the appointment is not made within seven clear days after the service of the notice, the High Court or a judge thereof may, on application by the party who gave the notice, appoint an arbitrator, umpire or third arbitrator who shall have the like powers to act in the reference and make an award as if he had been appointed by consent of all parties.

(2) In any case where—

(a) an arbitration agreement provides for the appointment of an arbitrator or umpire by a person who is neither one of the parties nor an existing arbitrator (whether the provision applies directly or in default of agreement by the parties or otherwise), and

(b) that person refuses to make the appointment or does not make it within the time specified in the agreement or, if no time is so specified, within a reasonable time

any party to the agreement may serve the person in question with a written notice to appoint an arbitrator or umpire and, if the appointment is not made within seven clear days after the service of the notice, the High Court or a judge thereof may, on the application of the party who gave the notice, appoint an arbitrator or umpire who shall have the like powers to act in the reference and make an award as if he had been appointed in accordance with the terms of the agreement.

(3) In any case where—

(a) an arbitration agreement provides that the reference shall be to three arbitrators, one to be appointed by each party and the third to be appointed by the two appointed by the parties or in some other manner specified in the agreement; and

(b) one of the parties ("the party in default") refuses to appoint an arbitrator or does not do so within the time specified in the agreement or, if no time is specified, within a reasonable time,

the other party to the agreement, having appointed his arbitrator, may serve the party in default with a written notice to appoint an arbitrator.

[(3A) A notice under subsection (3) must indicate whether it is served for the purposes of subsection (3B) or for the purposes of subsection (3C).

(3B) Where a notice is served for the purposes of this subsection, then unless a contrary intention is expressed in the agreement, if the appointment is not made within seven clear days after the service of the notice—

(a) the party who gave the notice may appoint his arbitrator to act as sole arbitrator in the reference; and

(b) his award shall be binding on both parties as if he had been appointed by consent.

(3C) Where a notice is served for the purposes of this subsection, then if the required appointment is not made within seven clear days after the service of the notice, the High Court or a judge thereof may, on the application of the party who gave the notice, appoint an arbitrator on behalf of the party in default who shall have the like powers to act in the reference and make an award (and, if the case so requires, the like duty in relation to the appointment of a third arbitrator) as if he had been appointed in accordance with the terms of the agreement.

(3D) The High Court or a judge thereof may set aside any appointment made by virtue of subsection (3B).]

(4) Except in a case where the arbitration agreement shows that it was intended that the vacancy should not be supplied, paragraph (b) of each of subsections (2) and (3) shall be construed as extending to any such refusal or failure by a person as is there mentioned arising in connection with the replacement of an arbitrator who was appointed by that person (or, in default of being so appointed, was appointed under that subsection) but who refuses to act, or is incapable of acting or has died.

Note: This section is printed as amended in sub-s. (1) by s. 6(3) of the Arbitration Act 1979, the addition of sub-s. (2) by s. 6(4) of the Arbitration Act 1979 and the addition of sub-s. (3) by s. 58 of the Administration of Justice Act 1985. In relation to arbitrations to which the Arbitration Act 1979 does not apply the section reads as if the words "required or are" were omitted from para. (c) of sub-s. (1), and sub-s. (2) were omitted altogether. Sub-s. (3) has been prospectively replaced and new sub-ss. (3A)–(3D) prospectively inserted by s. 101 of the Courts and Legal Services Act 1990, see below. Section 101(2)(3) of the Courts and Legal Services Act 1990 also prospectively apply to s. 10.

Power of official referee to take arbitrations

[**11.**—(1) An official referee may, if in all the circumstances he thinks fit, accept appointment as sole arbitrator, or as umpire, by or by virtue of an arbitration agreement.

(2) An official referee shall not accept appointment as arbitrator or umpire unless the Lord Chief Justice has informed him that, having regard to the state of official referees' business, he can be made available to do so.

(3) The fees payable for the services of an official referee as arbitrator or umpire shall be taken in the High Court.

(4) Schedule 3 to the Administration of Justice Act 1970 (which modifies this Act in relation to arbitration by judges, in particular by substituting the Court of Appeal for the High Court in provisions whereby arbitrators and umpires, their proceedings and awards are subject to control and review by the court) shall have effect in relation to official referees appointed as arbitrators or umpires as it has effect in relation to judge-arbitrators and judge-umpires (within the meaning of that Schedule).

(5) Any jurisdiction which is exercisable by the High Court in relation to arbitrators and umpires otherwise than under this Act shall, in relation to an official referee appointed as arbitrator or umpire, be exercisable instead by the Court of Appeal.

(6) In this section "official referee" means any person nominated under section 68(1)(a) of the Supreme Court Act 1981 to deal with official referees' business.

(7) Rules of the Supreme Court may make provision for—

(a) cases in which it is necessary to allocate references made under or by virtue of arbitration agreements to official referees;

(b) the transfer of references from one official referee to another.]

Note: This section has been prospectively replaced by a new section 11 contained in s. 99 of the Courts and Legal Services Act 1990, see below.

Conduct of proceedings, witnesses, &c.

Conduct of proceedings, witnesses, &c.

12.—(1) Unless a contrary intention is expressed therein, every arbitration agreement shall, where such a provision is applicable to the reference, be deemed to contain a provision that the parties to the reference, and all persons claiming through them respectively, shall, subject to any legal objection, submit to be examined by the arbitrator or umpire, on oath or affirmation, in relation to the matters in dispute, and shall, subject as aforesaid, produce before the arbitrator or umpire all documents within their possession or power respectively which may be required or called for, and do all other things which during the proceedings on the reference the arbitrator or umpire may require.

(2) Unless a contrary intention is expressed therein, every arbitration agreement shall, where such a provision is applicable to the reference, be deemed to contain a provision that the witnesses on the reference shall, if the arbitrator or umpire thinks fit, be examined on oath or affirmation.

(3) An arbitrator or umpire shall, unless a contrary intention is expressed in the arbitration agreement, have power to administer oaths to, or take the affirmations of, the parties to and witnesses on a reference under the agreement.

(4) Any party to a reference under an arbitration agreement may sue out a writ of subpoena ad testificandum or a writ of subpoena duces tecum, but no person shall be compelled under any such writ to produce any document which he could not be compelled to produce on the trial of an action, and the High Court or a judge thereof may order that a writ of subpoena ad testificandum or of subpoena duces tecum shall issue to compel the attendance before an arbitrator or umpire of a witness wherever he may be within the United Kingdom.

(5) The High Court or a judge thereof may also order that a writ of habeas corpus ad testificandum shall issue to bring up a prisoner for examination before an arbitrator or umpire.

(6) The High Court shall have, for the purpose of and in relation to a reference, the same power of making orders in respect of—

503

(a) security for costs;

(b) . . .

(c) the giving of evidence by affidavit;

(d) examination on oath of any witness before an officer of the High Court or any other person, and the issue of a commission or request for the examination of a witness out of the jurisdiction;

(e) the preservation, interim custody or sale of any goods which are the subject matter of the reference;

(f) securing the amount in dispute in the reference;

(g) the detention, preservation or inspection of any property or thing which is the subject of the reference or as to which any question may arise therein, and authorising for any of the purposes aforesaid any persons to enter upon or into any land or building in the possession of any party to the reference, or authorising any samples to be taken or any observation to be made or experiment to be tried which may be necessary or expedient for the purpose of obtaining full information or evidence; and

(h) interim injunctions or the appointment of a receiver;

as it has for the purpose of and in relation to an action or matter in the High Court:

Provided that nothing in this subsection shall be taken to prejudice any power which may be vested in an arbitrator or umpire of making orders with respect to any of the matters aforesaid.

Note: Sub-s. (6)(b) has been prospectively repealed by the Courts and Legal Services Act 1990, s. 103, see below.

Provisions as to awards

Time for making award

13.—(1) Subject to the provisions of subsection (2) of section twenty-two of this Act, and anything to the contrary in the arbitration agreement, an arbitrator or umpire shall have power to make an award at any time.

(2) The time, if any, limited for making an award, whether under this Act or otherwise, may from time to time be enlarged by order of the High Court or a judge thereof, whether that time has expired or not.

(3) The High Court may, on the application of any party to a reference, remove an arbitrator or umpire who fails to use all reasonable dispatch in entering on and proceeding with the reference and making an award, and an arbitrator or umpire who is removed by the High Court under this subsection shall not be entitled to receive any remuneration in respect of his services.

For the purposes of this subsection, the expression "proceeding with a reference" includes, in a case where two arbitrators are unable to agree, giving notice of that fact to the parties and to the umpire.

Want of prosecution

[**13A.**—(1) Unless a contrary intention is expressed in the arbitration agreement, the arbitrator or umpire shall have power to make an award dismissing any claim in a dispute referred to him if it appears to him that the conditions mentioned in subsection (2) are satisfied.

(2) The conditions are—

(a) that there has been inordinate and inexcusable delay on the part of the claimant in pursuing the claim; and

(b) that the delay—

(i) will give rise to a substantial risk that it is not possible to have a fair resolution of the issues in that claim; or

(ii) has caused, or is likely to cause or to have caused, serious prejudice to the respondent.

(3) For the purpose of keeping the provision made by this section and the corresponding pro-

vision which applies in relation to proceedings in the High Court in step, the Secretary of State may by order made by statutory instrument amend subsection (2) above.

(4) Before making any such order the Secretary of State shall consult the Lord Chancellor and such other persons as he considers appropriate.

(5) No such order shall be made unless a draft of the order has been laid before, and approved by resolution of, each House of Parliament.]

Note: This section was inserted by the Courts and Legal Services Act 1990, section 102.

Interim awards

14. Unless a contrary intention is expressed therein, every arbitration agreement shall, where such a provision is applicable to the reference, be deemed to contain a provision that the arbitrator or umpire may, if he thinks fit, make an interim award, and any reference in this Part of this Act to an award includes a reference to an interim award.

Specific performance

15. Unless a contrary intention is expressed therein, every arbitration agreement shall, where such a provision is applicable to the reference, be deemed to contain a provision that the arbitrator or umpire shall have the same power as the High Court to order specific performance of any contract other than a contract relating to land or any interest in land.

Awards to be final

16. Unless a contrary intention is expressed therein, every arbitration agreement shall, where such a provision is applicable to the reference, be deemed to contain a provision that the award to be made by the arbitrator or umpire shall be final and binding on the parties and the persons claiming under them respectively.

Power to correct slips

17. Unless a contrary intention is expressed in the arbitration agreement, the arbitrator or umpire shall have power to correct in an award any clerical mistake or error arising from any accidental slip or omission.

Costs, fees and interest

Costs

18.—(1) Unless a contrary intention is expressed therein, every arbitration agreement shall be deemed to include a provision that the costs of the reference and award shall be in the discretion of the arbitrator or umpire, who may direct to and by whom and in what manner those costs or any part thereof shall be paid, and may tax or settle the amount of costs to be so paid or any part thereof, and may award costs to be paid as between solicitor and client.

(2) Any costs directed by an award to be paid shall, unless the award otherwise directs, be taxable in the High Court.

(3) Any provision in an arbitration agreement to the effect that the parties or any party thereto shall in any event pay their or his own costs of the reference or award or any part thereof shall be void, and this Part of this Act shall, in the case of an arbitration agreement containing any such provision, have effect as if that provision were not contained therein:

Provided that nothing in this subsection shall invalidate such a provision when it is a part of an agreement to submit to arbitration a dispute which has arisen before the making of that agreement.

(4) If no provision is made by an award with respect to the costs of the reference, any party to the reference may, within fourteen days of the publication of the award or such further time as the High Court or a judge thereof may direct, apply to the arbitrator for an order directing by

and to whom those costs shall be paid, and thereupon the arbitrator shall, after hearing any party who may desire to be heard, amend his award by adding thereto such directions as he may think proper with respect to the payment of the costs of the reference.

(5) Section sixty-nine of the Solicitors Act 1932 (which empowers a court before which any proceeding is being heard or is pending to charge property recovered or preserved in the proceeding with the payment of solicitors' costs) shall apply as if an arbitration were a proceeding in the High Court, and the High Court may make declarations and orders accordingly.

Taxation of arbitrator's or umpire's fees

19.—(1) If in any case an arbitrator or umpire refuses to deliver his award except on payment of the fees demanded by him, the High Court may, on an application for the purpose, order that the arbitrator or umpire shall deliver the award to the applicant on payment into court by the applicant of the fees demanded, and further that the fees demanded shall be taxed by the taxing officer and that out of the money paid into court there shall be paid out to the arbitrator or umpire by way of fees such sum as may be found reasonable on taxation and that the balance of the money, if any, shall be paid out to the applicant.

(2) An application for the purposes of this section may be made by any party to the reference unless the fees demanded have been fixed by a written agreement between him and the arbitrator or umpire.

(3) A taxation of fees under this section may be reviewed in the same manner as a taxation of costs.

(4) The arbitrator or umpire shall be entitled to appear and be heard on any taxation or review of taxation under this section.

Power of arbitrator to award interest

[**19A.**—(1) Unless a contrary intention is expressed therein, every arbitration agreement shall, where such a provision is applicable to the reference, be deemed to contain a provision that the arbitrator or umpire may, if he thinks fit, award simple interest at such rate as he thinks fit:

    (a) on any sum which is the subject of the reference but which is paid before the award, for such period ending not later than the date of the payment as he thinks fit; and

    (b) on any sum which he awards, for such period ending no later than the date of the award as he thinks fit.

(2) The power to award interest conferred on an arbitrator or umpire by subsection (1) above is without prejudice to any other power of an arbitrator or umpire to award interest.]

Note: This section was added by the Administration of Justice Act 1982, section 15(6) and Part IV of Schedule 1. It came into force on 1 April 1983 by virtue of the Administration of Justice Act 1982 (Commencement No 1) Order 1983, SI 1983 No 236.

Interest on awards

20. A sum directed to be paid by an award shall, unless the award otherwise directs, carry interest as from the date of the award and at the same rate as a judgment debt.

Special cases, remission and setting aside of awards, &c.

Statement of case

21. [Repealed.]

Note: The repeal of this section was effected by s. 8(3)(b) of the Arbitration Act 1979. In relation to arbitrations to which the Arbitration Act 1979 does not apply, the section applies in its unrepealed form, as follows:

"(1) An arbitrator or umpire may, and shall if so directed by the High Court, state—
    (a) any question of law arising in the course of the reference; or
    (b) an award or any part of an award,
in the form of a special case for the decision of the High Court.
(2) A special case with respect to an interim award or with respect to a question of law arising in the course of a reference may be stated, or may be directed by the High Court to be stated, notwithstanding that proceedings under the reference are still pending.
(3) A decision of the High Court under this section shall be deemed to be a judgment of the Court within the meaning of section twenty-seven of the Supreme Court of Judicature (Consolidation) Act 1925 (which relates to the jurisdiction of the Court of Appeal to hear and determine appeals from any judgment of the High Court), but no appeal shall lie from the decision of the High Court on any case stated under paragraph (a) of subsection (1) of this section without the leave of the High Court or of the Court of Appeal."

Power to remit award

22.—(1) In all cases of reference to arbitration the High Court or a judge thereof may from time to time remit the matters referred, or any of them, to the reconsideration of the arbitrator or umpire.
(2) Where an award is remitted, the arbitrator or umpire shall, unless the order otherwise directs, make his award within three months after the date of the order.

Removal of arbitrator and setting aside of award

23.—(1) Where an arbitrator or umpire has misconducted himself or the proceedings, the High Court may remove him.
(2) Where an arbitrator or umpire has misconducted himself or the proceedings, or an arbitration or award has been improperly procured, the High Court may set the award aside.
(3) Where an application is made to set aside an award, the High Court may order that any money made payable by the award shall be brought into court or otherwise secured pending the determination of the application.

Power of court to give relief where arbitrator is not impartial or the dispute involves question of fraud

24.—(1) Where an agreement between any parties provides that disputes which may arise in the future between them shall be referred to an arbitrator named or designated in the agreement, and after a dispute has arisen any party applies, on the ground that the arbitrator so named or designated is not or may not be impartial, for leave to revoke the authority of the arbitrator or for an injunction to restrain any other party or the arbitrator from proceeding with the arbitration, it shall not be a ground for refusing the application that the said party at the time when he made the agreement knew, or ought to have known, that the arbitrator, by reason of his relation towards any other party to the agreement or of his connection with the subject referred, might not be capable of impartiality.
(2) Where an agreement between any parties provides that disputes which may arise in the future between them shall be referred to arbitration, and a dispute which so arises involves the question whether any such party has been guilty of fraud, the High Court shall, so far as may be necessary to enable that question to be determined by the High Court, have power to order that the agreement shall cease to have effect and power to give leave to revoke the authority of any arbitrator or umpire appointed by or by virtue of the agreement.
(3) In any case where by virtue of this section the High Court has power to order that an arbitration agreement shall cease to have effect or to give leave to revoke the authority of an arbitrator or umpire, the High Court may refuse to stay any action brought in breach of the agreement.

Power of court where arbitrator is removed or authority of arbitrator is revoked

25.—(1) Where an arbitrator (not being a sole arbitrator), or two or more arbitrators (not being all the arbitrators) or an umpire who has not entered on the reference is or are removed

507

by the High Court or the Court of Appeal, the High Court may, on the application of any party to the arbitration agreement, appoint a person or persons to act as arbitrator or arbitrators or umpire in place of the person or persons so removed.

(2) Where the authority of an arbitrator or arbitrators or umpire is revoked by leave of the High Court or the Court of Appeal, or a sole arbitrator or all the arbitrators or an umpire who has entered on the reference is or are removed by the High Court or the Court of Appeal, the High Court may, on the application of any party to the arbitration agreement, either—

(a) appoint a person to act as sole arbitrator in place of the person or persons removed; or
(b) order that the arbitration agreement shall cease to have effect with respect to the dispute referred.

(3) A person appointed under this section by the High Court or the Court of Appeal, as an arbitrator or umpire, shall have the like power to act in the reference and to make an award as if he had been appointed in accordance with the terms of the arbitration agreement.

(4) Where it is provided (whether by means of a provision in the arbitration agreement or otherwise) that an award under an arbitration agreement shall be a condition precedent to the bringing of an action with respect to any matter to which the agreement applies, the High Court or the Court of Appeal, if it orders (whether under this section or under any other enactment) that the agreement shall cease to have effect as regards any particular dispute, may further order that the provision making an award a condition precedent to the bringing of an action shall also cease to have effect as regards that dispute.

Enforcement of award

Enforcement of award

26.—(1) An award on an arbitration agreement may, by leave of the High Court or a judge thereof, be enforced in the same manner as a judgment or order to the same effect, and where leave is so given, judgment may be entered in terms of the award.

(2) If—

(a) the amount sought to be recovered does not exceed the current limit on jurisdiction in section 40 of the County Courts Act [1984], and
(b) a county court so orders,

it shall be recoverable (by execution issued from the county court or otherwise) as if payable under an order of that court and shall not be enforceable under subsection (1) above.

(3) An application to the High Court under this section shall preclude an application to a county court, and an application to a county court under this section shall preclude an application to the High Court.

Miscellaneous

Power of court to extend time for commencing arbitration proceedings

27. Where the terms of an agreement to refer future disputes to arbitration provide that any claims to which the agreement applies shall be barred unless notice to appoint an arbitrator is given or an arbitrator is appointed or some other step to commence arbitration proceedings is taken within a time fixed by the agreement, and a dispute arises to which the agreement applies, the High Court, if it is of opinion that in the circumstances of the case undue hardship would otherwise be caused, and notwithstanding that the time so fixed has expired, may, on such terms, if any, as the justice of the case may require, but without prejudice to the provisions of any enactment limiting the time for the commencement of arbitration proceedings, extend the time for such period as it thinks proper.

Terms as to costs, &c.

28. Any order made under this Part of this Act may be made on such terms as to costs or otherwise as the authority making the order thinks just:

[Provided that this section shall not apply to any order made under subsection (2) of section four of this Act.]

Note: The words in square brackets were repealed by section 8(2)(b) of the Arbitration Act 1975.

Extension of section 496 of the Merchant Shipping Act 1894

29.—(1) In subsection (3) of section four hundred and ninety-six of the Merchant Shipping Act 1894 (which requires a sum deposited with a wharfinger by an owner of goods to be repaid unless legal proceedings are instituted by the shipowner), the expression "legal proceedings" shall be deemed to include arbitration.

(2) For the purposes of the said section four hundred and ninety-six, as amended by this section, an arbitration shall be deemed to be commenced when one party to the arbitration agreement serves on the other party or parties a notice requiring him or them to appoint or concur in appointing an arbitrator, or, where the arbitration agreement provides that the reference shall be to a person named or designated in the agreement, requiring him or them to submit the dispute to the person so named or designated.

(3) Any such notice as is mentioned in subsection (2) of this section may be served either—

(a) by delivering it to the person on whom it is to be served; or
(b) by leaving it at the usual or last known place of abode in England of that person; or
(c) by sending it by post in a registered letter addressed to that person at his usual or last known place of abode in England;

as well as in any other manner provided in the arbitration agreement; where a notice is sent by post in manner prescribed by paragraph (c) of this subsection, service thereof shall, unless the contrary is proved, be deemed to have been effected at the time at which the letter would have been delivered in the ordinary course of post.

Crown to be bound

30. This Part of this Act [(except the provisions of subsection (2) of section four thereof)] shall apply to any arbitration to which His Majesty, either in right of the Crown or of the Duchy of Lancaster or otherwise, or the Duke of Cornwall, is a party.

Note: The words in square brackets were repealed by s. 8(2)(c) of the Arbitration Act 1975.

Application of Part I to statutory arbitrations

31.—(1) Subject to the provisions of section thirty-three of this Act, this Part of this Act, except the provisions thereof specified in subsection (2) of this section, shall apply to every arbitration under any other Act (whether passed before or after the commencement of this Act) as if the arbitration were pursuant to an arbitration agreement and as if that other Act were an arbitration agreement, except in so far as this Act is inconsistent with that other Act or with any rules or procedure authorised or recognised thereby.

(2) The provisions referred to in subsection (1) of this section are subsection (1) of section two, section three, [subsection (2) of section four,] section five, subsection (3) of section eighteen and sections twenty-four, twenty-five, twenty-seven and twenty-nine.

Note: The words in square brackets were repealed by s. 8(2)(d) of the Arbitration Act 1975.

Meaning of "arbitration agreement"

32. In this Part of this Act, unless the context otherwise requires, the expression "arbitration agreement" means a written agreement to submit present or future differences to arbitration, whether an arbitrator is named therein or not.

Operation of Part I

33. This Part of this Act shall not affect any arbitration commenced (within the meaning of subsection (2) of section twenty-nine of this Act) before the commencement of this Act, but shall apply to an arbitration so commenced after the commencement of this Act under an agreement made before the commencement of this Act.

Extent of Part I

34. [Subsection (2) of section four of this Act shall—

   (a) extend to Scotland, with the omission of the words "Notwithstanding anything in this Part of this Act" and with the substitution, for references to staying proceedings, of references to sisting proceedings; and
   (b) extend to Northern Ireland, with the omission of the words "Notwithstanding anything in this Part of this Act";

but,] save as aforesaid, none of the provisions of this Part of this Act shall extend to Scotland or Northern Ireland.

Note: The words in square brackets were repealed by s. 8(2)(e) of the Arbitration Act 1975.

PART II. ENFORCEMENT OF CERTAIN FOREIGN AWARDS

Note: Part II re-enacts Part I of the Arbitration (Foreign Awards) Act 1930.

Awards to which Part II applies

35.—(1) This Part of this Act applies to any award made after the twenty-eighth day of July, nineteen hundred and twenty-four—

   (a) in pursuance of an agreement for arbitration to which the protocol set out in the First Schedule to this Act applies; and
   (b) between persons of whom one is subject to the jurisdiction of some one of such Powers as His Majesty, being satisfied that reciprocal provisions have been made, may by Order in Council declare to be parties to the convention set out in the Second Schedule to this Act, and of whom the other is subject to the jurisdiction of some other of the Powers aforesaid; and
   (c) in one of such territories as His Majesty, being satisfied that reciprocal provisions have been made, may by Order in Council declare to be territories to which the said convention applies;

and an award to which this Part of this Act applies is in this Part of this Act referred to as "a foreign award".

(2) His Majesty may by a subsequent Order in Council vary or revoke any Order previously made under this section.

(3) Any Order in Council under section one of the Arbitration (Foreign Awards) Act 1930, which is in force at the commencement of this Act shall have effect as if it had been made under this section.

Note: The following states became Contracting States for the purposes of the protocol in the First Schedule:

Albania (T.S. 56/1925 Cmd. 2577).
Austria (T.S. 29/1928 Cmd. 3266).
Bahamas (T.S. 43/1931 Cmd. 4015).
Belgium (T.S. 56/1925 Cmd. 2577).
Brazil (T.S. 38/1932 Cmd. 4249).
British Guiana (T.S. 32/1926 Cmd. 2804).
British Honduras (T.S. 32/1926 Cmd. 2804).

Burma (excluding Karenni States) (T.S. 75/1938 Cmd. 5930).
Ceylon (T.S. 75/1926 Cmd. 2804).
Czechoslovakia (T.S. 43/1931 Cmd. 4015).
Danzig (T.S. 75/1938 Cmd. 5930).
Denmark (T.S. 56/1925 Cmd. 2577).
Estonia (T.S. 33/1929 Cmd. 3491).
Falkland Islands and Dependencies (T.S. 32/1926 Cmd. 2804 & T.S. 39/1934 Cmd. 4809).
Finland (T.S. 56/1925 Cmd. 2577).
France (T.S. 29/1928 Cmd. 3266).
Gambia (Colony and Protectorate) (T.S. 32/1926 Cmd. 2804 & T.S. 39/1934 Cmd. 4809).
Germany (T.S. 56/1925 Cmd. 2577).
Gibraltar (T.S. 32/1926 Cmd. 2804).
Gold Coast (including Ashanti, Northern Territories and Togoland under British Mandate) (T.S. 32/1926 Cmd. 2804 & T.S. 43/1931 Cmd. 4015).
Greece (T.S. 32/1926 Cmd. 2804).
India (T.S. 56/1937 Cmd. 5654).
Iraq (T.S. 32/1926 Cmd. 2804).
Italy (T.S. 56/1925 Cmd. 2577).
Jamaica (including Turks and Caicos Islands and the Cayman Islands) (T.S. 32/1926 Cmd. 2804 & T.S. 43/1931 Cmd. 4015).
Japan (including Chosen, Taiwan, Karafuto, leased territory of Kwangtung and Japanese Mandated Territories) (T.S. 28/1928 Cmd. 3266 & T.S. 33/1929 Cmd. 3491).
Kenya (Colony & Protectorate) (T.S. 32/1926 Cmd. 2804 & T.S. 39/1934 Cmd. 4809).
Leeward Islands (T.S. 32/1926 Cmd. 2804).
Luxemburg (T.S. 52/1930 Cmd. 3816).
Malta (T.S. 32/1926 Cmd. 2804).
Mauritius (T.S. 32/1926 Cmd. 2804).
Monaco (T.S. 29/1927 Cmd. 3022).
Netherlands (including Netherlands Indies, Surinam and Curaçao) (T.S. 56/1925 Cmd. 2577; T.S. 75/1938 Cmd. 5930 & T.S. 31/1940 Cmd. 6253).
Newfoundland (T.S. 56/1925 Cmd. 2577).
New Zealand (T.S. 32/1926 Cmd. 2804).
Northern Rhodesia (T.S. 32/1926 Cmd. 2804).
Norway (T.S. 29/1927 Cmd. 3022).
Palestine (excluding Trans-Jordan) (T.S. 32/1926 Cmd. 2804 & T.S. 39/1934 Cmd. 4809).
Poland (T.S. 43/1931 Cmd. 4015).
Portugal (T.S. 52/1930 Cmd. 3816).
Roumania (T.S. 56/1925 Cmd. 2577).
St. Helena (T.S. 32/1926 Cmd. 2804).
Siam (T.S. 52/1930 Cmd. 3816).
Southern Rhodesia (T.S. 56/1925 Cmd. 2577).
Spain (T.S. 32/1926 Cmd. 2804).
Sweden (T.S. 33/1929 Cmd. 3491).
Switzerland (T.S. 29/1928 Cmd. 3266).
Tanganyika Territory (T.S. 32/1926 Cmd. 2804).
Trans-Jordan (T.S. 39/1934 Cmd. 4809).
Uganda (T.S. 33/1929 Cmd. 3491).
United Kingdom of Great Britain and Northern Ireland (T.S. 4/1925 Cmd. 2312).
Windward Islands (Granada, St. Lucia, St. Vincent) (T.S. 32/1926 Cmd. 2804).
Zanzibar (T.S. 32/1926 Cmd. 2804).

Orders in Council made under the Act of 1930 are still in force for the following territories whose sovereigns are parties to the convention in the Second Schedule:

Antigua (S.R. & O. 1933 No. 42).
Bahamas (S.R. & O. 1931 No. 669).
Belgium (S.R. & O. 1930 No. 674), with Congo and Ruanda-Urundi (S.R. & O. 1930 No. 1096).
British Guiana (S.R. & O. 1931 No. 669).
British Honduras (S.R. & O. 1931 No. 669).
Burma (S.R. & O. 1939 No. 152).
Danzig (S.R. & O. 1938 No. 1360).
Denmark (S.R. & O. 1930 No. 674).
Dominica (S.R. & O. 1933 No. 42).

Estonia (S.R. & O. 1930 No. 674).
Falkland Is. (S.R. & O. 1931 No. 669).
France (S.R. & O. 1931 No. 669).
Germany (S.R. & O. 1930 No. 1096).
Gibraltar (S.R. & O. 1931 No. 669).
Gold Coast ((a) Colony; (b) Ashanti; (c) Northern Territories; (d) Togoland under British Mandate) (S.R. & O. 1931 No. 669).
Italy (S.R. & O. 1931 No. 166).
Jamaica (including Turks and Caicos Islands and Cayman Islands) (S.R. & O. 1931 No. 669).
Kenya (S.R. & O. 1931 No. 669).
Leeward Islands (S.R. & O. 1933 No. 42).
Luxemburg (S.R. & O. 1930 No. 1096).
Malta (S.R. & O. 1935 No. 133).
Mauritius (S.R. & O. 1931 No. 898).
Newfoundland (S.R. & O. 1931 No. 166).
New Zealand (with Western Samoa) (S.R. & O. 1930 No. 674).
Northern Rhodesia (S.R. & O. 1931 No. 898).
Palestine (excluding Trans-Jordan) (S.R. & O. 1931 No. 669).
Portugal (S.R. & O. 1931 No. 166).
Roumania (S.R. & O. 1931 No. 898).
Siam (S.R. & O. 1931 No. 898).
Spain (S.R. & O. 1930 No. 674).
Sweden (S.R. & O. 1930 No. 674).
Switzerland (S.R. & O. 1930 No. 1096).
Tanganyika Territory (S.R. & O. 1931 No. 669).
Uganda Protectorate (S.R. & O. 1931 No. 669).
United Kingdom (S.R. & O. 1930 No. 674).
Windward Islands (S.R. & O. 1931 No. 669).
Zanzibar (S.R. & O. 1939 No. 669).

Orders in Council under the 1950 Act have been made in respect of the following territories whose sovereigns are parties to the convention in the Second Schedule (see S.I. 1978 No. 186, and (for Grenada) S.I. 1979 No. 304):

The United Kingdom of Great Britain and Northern Ireland	Greece
	Grenada
Belize	India
British Virgin Islands	The Republic of Ireland
Cayman Islands	Israel
Falkland Islands and Dependencies	Italy
Gibraltar	Japan
Hong Kong	Kenya
Montserrat	Luxembourg
Turks and Caicos Islands	Mauritius
West Indies, Associated States (Antigua, Dominica, St. Lucia, St. Vincent, St. Christopher, Nevis and Anguilla)	Netherlands (including the Netherlands Antilles)
	New Zealand
Austria	Pakistan
Belgium	Portugal
Czechoslovakia	Romania
Denmark	Spain
Finland	Sweden
France	Switzerland
Federal Republic of Germany	United Republic of Tanzania
German Democratic Republic	Thailand
	Yugoslavia

Effect of foreign awards

36.—(1) A foreign award shall, subject to the provisions of this Part of this Act, be enforceable in England either by action or in the same manner as the award of an arbitrator is enforceable by virtue of section twenty-six of this Act.

(2) Any foreign award which would be enforceable under this Part of this Act shall be treated as binding for all purposes on the persons as between whom it was made, and may accordingly

be relied on by any of those persons by way of defence, set off or otherwise in any legal proceedings in England, and any references in this Part of this Act to enforcing a foreign award shall be construed as including references to relying on an award.

Conditions for enforcement of foreign awards

37.—(1) In order that a foreign award may be enforceable under this Part of this Act it must have—

(a) been made in pursuance of an agreement for arbitration which was valid under the law by which it was governed;
(b) been made by the tribunal provided for in the agreement or constituted in manner agreed upon by the parties;
(c) been made in conformity with the law governing the arbitration procedure;
(d) become final in the country in which it was made;
(e) been in respect of a matter which may lawfully be referred to arbitration under the law of England;

and the enforcement thereof must not be contrary to the public policy or the law of England.

(2) Subject to the provisions of this subsection, a foreign award shall not be enforceable under this Part of this Act if the court dealing with the case is satisfied that—

(a) the award has been annulled in the country in which it was made; or
(b) the party against whom it is sought to enforce the award was not given notice of the arbitration proceedings in sufficient time to enable him to present his case, or was under some legal incapacity and was not properly represented; or
(c) the award does not deal with all the questions referred or contains decisions on matters beyond the scope of the agreement for arbitration.

Provided that, if the award does not deal with all the questions referred, the court may, if it thinks fit, either postpone the enforcement of the award or order its enforcement subject to the giving of such security by the person seeking to enforce it as the court may think fit.

(3) If a party seeking to resist the enforcement of a foreign award proves that there is any ground other than the non-existence of the conditions specified in paragraphs (a), (b) and (c) of subsection (1) of this section, or the existence of the conditions specified in paragraphs (b) and (c) of subsection (2) of this section, entitling him to contest the validity of the award, the court may, if it thinks fit, either refuse to enforce the award or adjourn the hearing until after the expiration of such period as appears to the court to be reasonably sufficient to enable that party to take the necessary steps to have the award annulled by the competent tribunal.

Evidence

38.—(1) The party seeking to enforce a foreign award must produce—

(a) the original award or a copy thereof duly authenticated in manner required by the law of the country in which it was made; and
(b) evidence proving that the award has become final; and
(c) such evidence as may be necessary to prove that the award is a foreign award and that the conditions mentioned in paragraphs (a), (b) and (c) of subsection (1) of the last foregoing section are satisfied.

(2) In any case where any document required to be produced under subsection (1) of this section is in a foreign language, it shall be the duty of the party seeking to enforce the award to produce a translation certified as correct by a diplomatic or consular agent of the country to which that party belongs, or certified as correct in such other manner as may be sufficient according to the law of England.

(3) Subject to the provisions of this section, rules of court may be made under section [84 of

the Supreme Court Act 1981], with respect to the evidence which must be furnished by a party seeking to enforce an award under this Part of this Act.

Note: The words in square brackets were substituted by the Supreme Court Act 1981, Sch. 5.

Meaning of "final award"

39. For the purposes of this Part of this Act, an award shall not be deemed final if any proceedings for the purpose of contesting the validity of the award are pending in the country in which it was made.

Saving for other rights, &c.

40. Nothing in this Part of this Act shall—

(a) prejudice any rights which any person would have had of enforcing in England any award or of availing himself in England of any award if neither this Part of this Act nor Part I of the Arbitration (Foreign Awards) Act 1930, had been enacted; or

(b) apply to any award made on an arbitration agreement governed by the law of England.

Application of Part II to Scotland

41.—(1) The following provisions of this section shall have effect for the purpose of the application of this Part of this Act to Scotland.

(2) For the references to England there shall be substituted references to Scotland.

(3) For subsection (1) of section thirty-six there shall be substituted the following subsection:—

"(1) A foreign award shall, subject to the provisions of this Part of this Act, be enforceable by action, or, if the agreement for arbitration contains consent to the registration of the award in the Books of Council and Session for execution and the award is so registered, it shall, subject as aforesaid, be enforceable by summary diligence."

(4) For subsection (3) of section thirty-eight there shall be substituted the following subsection:—

"(3) The Court of Session shall, subject to the provision of this section, have power, exercisable by statutory instrument, to make provision by Act of Sederunt with respect to the evidence which must be furnished by a party seeking to enforce in Scotland an award under this Part of this Act."

Note: This section is printed as amended by the Statutory Instruments Act 1946 and the Law Reform (Miscellaneous Provisions) (Scotland) Act 1966.

Application of Part II to Northern Ireland

42.—(1) The following provisions of this section shall have effect for the purpose of the application of this Part of this Act to Northern Ireland.

(2) For the references to England there shall be substituted references to Northern Ireland.

(3) For subsection (1) of section thirty-six there shall be substituted the following subsection:—

"(1) A foreign award shall, subject to the provisions of this Part of this Act, be enforceable either by action or in the same manner as the award of an arbitrator under the provisions of the Common Law Procedure Amendment Act (Ireland) 1856 was enforceable at the date of the passing of the Arbitration (Foreign Awards) Act 1930."

[(4) For the reference, in subsection (3) of section thirty-eight, to section ninety-nine of the Supreme Court of Judicature (Consolidation) Act 1925, there shall be substituted a reference to section sixty-one of the Supreme Court of Judicature (Ireland) Act 1877, as amended by any subsequent enactment.]

Note: The words in square brackets, as amended by Sch. 1 to the Northern Ireland Act 1962, were repealed by s. 122(2) of and Sch. 7 to the Judicature (Northern Ireland) Act 1978.

[Saving for pending proceedings

43. Any proceedings instituted under Part I of the Arbitration (Foreign Awards) Act 1930 which are uncompleted at the commencement of this Act may be carried on and completed under this Part of this Act as if they had been instituted thereunder.]

Note: This section was repealed by the Statute Law (Revision) Act 1978.

PART III. GENERAL

Short title, commencement and repeal

44.—(1) This Act may be cited as the Arbitration Act 1950.

(2) This Act shall come into operation on the first day of September, nineteen hundred and fifty.

(3) The Arbitration Act 1889, the Arbitration Clauses (Protocol) Act 1924, and the Arbitration Act 1934 are hereby repealed except in relation to arbitrations commenced (within the meaning of subsection (2) of section twenty-nine of this Act) before the commencement of this Act, and the Arbitration (Foreign Awards) Act 1930 is hereby repealed; and any reference in any Act or other document to any enactment hereby repealed shall be construed as including a reference to the corresponding provision of this Act.

FIRST SCHEDULE. PROTOCOL ON ARBITRATION CLAUSES SIGNED ON BEHALF OF HIS MAJESTY AT A MEETING OF THE ASSEMBLY OF THE LEAGUE OF NATIONS HELD ON THE TWENTY-FOURTH DAY OF SEPTEMBER, NINETEEN HUNDRED AND TWENTY-THREE

The undersigned, being duly authorised, declare that they accept, on behalf of the countries which they represent, the following provisions:—

1. Each of the Contracting States recognises the validity of an agreement whether relating to existing or future differences between parties, subject respectively to the jurisdiction of different Contracting States by which the parties to a contract agree to submit to arbitration all or any differences that may arise in connection with such contract relating to commercial matters or to any other matter capable of settlement by arbitration, whether or not the arbitration is to take place in a country to whose jurisdiction none of the parties is subject.

Each Contracting State reserves the right to limit the obligation mentioned above to contracts which are considered as commercial under its national law. Any Contracting State which avails itself of this right will notify the Secretary-General of the League of Nations, in order that the other Contracting States may be so informed.

2. The arbitral procedure, including the constitution of the arbitral tribunal, shall be governed by the will of the parties and by the law of the country in whose territory the arbitration takes place.

The Contracting States agree to facilitate all steps in the procedure which require to be taken in their own territories, in accordance with the provisions of their law governing arbitral procedure applicable to existing differences.

3. Each Contracting State undertakes to ensure the execution by its authorities and in accordance with the provisions of its national laws of arbitral awards made in its own territory under the preceding articles.

4. The tribunals of the Contracting Parties, on being seized of a dispute regarding a contract made between persons to whom Article 1 applies and including an arbitration agreement whether referring to present or future differences which is valid in virtue of the said article and capable of being carried into effect, shall refer the parties on the application of either of them to the decision of the arbitrators.

Such reference shall not prejudice the competence of the judicial tribunals in case the agreement or the arbitration cannot proceed or becomes inoperative.

5. The present Protocol, which shall remain open for signature by all States, shall be ratified. The ratifications shall be deposited as soon as possible with the Secretary-General of the League of Nations, who shall notify such deposit to all the signatory States.

6. The present Protocol shall come into force as soon as two ratifications have been deposited. Thereafter it will take effect, in the case of each Contracting State, one month after the notification by the Secretary-General of the deposit of its ratification.

7. The present Protocol may be denounced by any Contracting State on giving one year's notice. Denunciation shall be effected by a notification addressed to the Secretary-General of the League, who will immediately transmit copies of such notification to all the other signatory States and inform them of the date of which it was received. The denunciation shall take effect one year after the date on which it was notified to the Secretary-General, and shall operate only in respect of the notifying State.

8. The Contracting States may declare that their acceptance of the present Protocol does not include any or all of the under-mentioned territories: that is to say, their colonies, overseas possessions or territories, protectorates or the territories over which they exercise a mandate.

The said States may subsequently adhere separately on behalf of any territory thus excluded. The Secretary-General of the League of Nations shall be informed as soon as possible of such adhesions. He shall notify such adhesions to all signatory States. They will take effect one month after the notification by the Secretary-General to all signatory States.

The Contracting States may also denounce the Protocol separately on behalf of any of the territories referred to above. Article 7 applies to such denunciation.

SECOND SCHEDULE. CONVENTION   Section 35
ON THE EXECUTION OF FOREIGN ARBITRAL AWARDS
SIGNED AT GENEVA ON BEHALF OF HIS MAJESTY ON THE
TWENTY-SIXTH DAY OF SEPTEMBER,
NINETEEN HUNDRED AND TWENTY-SEVEN

Article 1

In the territories of any High Contracting Party to which the present Convention applies, an arbitral award made in pursuance of an agreement, whether relating to existing or future differences (herein-after called "a submission to arbitration") covered by the Protocol on Arbitration Clauses, opened at Geneva on September 24th 1923, shall be recognised as binding and shall be enforced in accordance with the rules of the procedure of the territory where the award is relied upon, provided that the said award has been made in a territory of one of the High Contracting Parties to which the present Convention applies and between persons who are subject to the jurisdiction of one of the High Contracting Parties.

To obtain such recognition or enforcement, it shall, further, be necessary:—

  (a) That the award has been made in pursuance of a submission to arbitration which is valid under the law applicable thereto;

  (b) That the subject-matter of the award is capable of settlement by arbitration under the law of the country in which the award is sought to be relied upon;

  (c) That the award has been made by the Arbitral Tribunal provided for in the submission to arbitration or constituted in the manner agreed upon by the parties and in conformity with the law governing the arbitration procedure;

  (d) That the award has become final in the country in which it has been made, in the sense that it will not be considered as such if it is open to *opposition, appel* or *pourvoi en cassation* (in the countries where such forms of procedure exist) or if it is proved that any proceedings for the purpose of contesting the validity of the award are pending;

  (e) That the recognition or enforcement of the award is not contrary to the public policy or to the principles of the law of the country in which it is sought to be relied upon.

Article 2

Even if the conditions laid down in Article 1 hereof are fulfilled, recognition and enforcement of the award shall be refused if the Court is satisfied:—

(a) That the award has been annulled in the country in which it was made;
(b) That the party against whom it is sought to use the award was not given notice of the arbitration proceedings in sufficient time to enable him to present his case; or that being under a legal incapacity, he was not properly represented;
(c) That the award does not deal with the differences contemplated by or falling within the terms of the submission to arbitration or that it contains decisions on matters beyond the scope of the submission to arbitration.

If the award has not covered all the questions submitted to the arbitral tribunal, the competent authority of the country where recognition or enforcement of the award is sought can, if it thinks fit, postpone such recognition or enforcement or grant it subject to such guarantee as that authority may decide.

Article 3

If the party against whom the award has been made proves that under the law governing the arbitration procedure, there is a ground, other than the grounds referred to in Article 1(a) and (c), and Article 2(b) and (c), entitling him to contest the validity of the award in a Court of Law, the Court may, if it thinks fit, either refuse recognition or enforcement of the award or adjourn the consideration thereof, giving such party a reasonable time within which to have the award annulled by the competent tribunal.

Article 4

The party relying upon an award or claiming its enforcement must supply, in particular:—

(1) The original award or a copy thereof duly authenticated, according to the requirements of the law of the country in which it was made;
(2) Documentary or other evidence to prove that the award has become final, in the sense defined in Article 1(d), in the country in which it was made;
(3) When necessary, documentary or other evidence to prove that the conditions laid down in Article 1, paragraph 1 and paragraph 2(a) and (c), have been fulfilled.

A translation of the award and of the other documents mentioned in this Article into the official language of the country where the award is sought to be relied upon may be demanded. Such translation must be certified correct by a diplomatic or consular agent of the country to which the party who seeks to rely upon the award belongs or by a sworn translator of the country where the award is sought to be relied upon.

Article 5

The provisions of the above Articles shall not deprive any interested party of the right of availing himself of an arbitral award in the manner and to the extent allowed by the law or the treaties of the country where such award is sought to be relied upon.

Article 6

The present Convention applies only to arbitral awards made after the coming into force of the Protocol on Arbitration Clauses, opened at Geneva on September 24th 1923.

517

Article 7

The present Convention, which will remain open to the signature of all the signatories of the Protocol of 1923 on Arbitration Clauses, shall be ratified.

It may be ratified only on behalf of those Members of the League of Nations and non-Member States on whose behalf the Protocol of 1923 shall have been ratified.

Ratifications shall be deposited as soon as possible with the Secretary-General of the League of Nations, who will notify such deposit to all the signatories.

Article 8

The present Convention shall come into force three months after it shall have been ratified on behalf of two High Contracting Parties. Thereafter, it shall take effect, in the case of each High Contracting Party, three months after the deposit of the ratification on its behalf with the Secretary-General of the League of Nations.

Article 9

The present Convention may be denounced on behalf of any Member of the League or non-Member State. Denunciation shall be notified in writing to the Secretary-General of the League of Nations, who will immediately send a copy thereof, certified to be in conformity with the notification, to all the other Contracting Parties, at the same time informing them of the date on which he received it.

The denunciation shall come into force only in respect of the High Contracting Party which shall have notified it and one year after such notification shall have reached the Secretary-General of the League of Nations.

The denunciation of the Protocol on Arbitration Clauses shall entail, ipso facto, the denunciation of the present Convention.

Article 10

The present Convention does not apply to the Colonies, Protectorates or territories under suzerainty or mandate of any High Contracting Party unless they are specially mentioned.

The application of this Convention to one or more of such Colonies, Protectorates or territories to which the Protocol on Arbitration Clauses, opened at Geneva at September 24th 1923, applies, can be effected at any time by means of a declaration addressed to the Secretary-General of the League of Nations by one of the High Contracting Parties.

Such declaration shall take effect three months after the deposit thereof.

The High Contracting Parties can at any time denounce the Convention for all or any of the Colonies, Protectorates or territories referred to above. Article 9 hereof applies to such denunciation.

Article 11

A certified copy of the present Convention shall be transmitted by the Secretary-General of the League of Nations to every Member of the League of Nations and to every non-Member State which signs the same.

F(2) ARBITRATION (INTERNATIONAL INVESTMENT DISPUTES) ACT 1966

Enforcement of Convention awards

Registration of Convention awards

1.—(1) This section has effect as respects awards rendered pursuant to the Convention on the settlement of investment disputes between States and nationals of other States which was opened for signature in Washington on 18th March 1965.

That Convention is in this Act called "the Convention", and its text is set out in the Schedule to this Act.

(2) A person seeking recognition or enforcement of such an award shall be entitled to have the award registered in the High Court subject to proof of the prescribed matters and to the other provisions of this Act.

(3) Where any pecuniary obligation imposed by the award is expressed in a currency other than the currency of the United Kingdom, the award shall be registered as if that obligation were expressed in the currency of the United Kingdom converted on the basis of the rate of exchange prevailing at the date when the award was rendered pursuant to the Convention.

(4) In addition to the pecuniary obligations imposed by the award, the award shall be registered for the reasonable costs of and incidental to registration.

(5) If at the date of the application for registration the pecuniary obligations imposed by the award have been partly satisfied, the award shall be registered only in respect of the balance, and accordingly if those obligations have then been wholly satisfied, the award shall not be registered.

(6) The power to make rules of court under section 99 of the Supreme Court of Judicature (Consolidation) Act 1925 shall include power—

(a) to prescribe the procedure for applying for registration under this section, and to require an applicant to give prior notice of his intention to other parties,

(b) to prescribe the matters to be proved on the application and the manner of proof, and in particular to require the applicant to furnish a copy of the award certified pursuant to the Convention,

(c) to provide for the service of notice of registration of the award by the applicant on other parties,

and in this and the next following section "prescribed" means prescribed by rules of court.

(7) For the purposes of this and the next following section—

(a) "award" shall include any decision interpreting, revising or annulling an award, being a decision pursuant to the Convention, and any decision as to costs which under the Convention is to form part of the award,

(b) an award shall be deemed to have been rendered pursuant to the Convention on the date on which certified copies of the award were pursuant to the Convention dispatched to the parties.

(8) This and the next following section shall bind the Crown (but not so as to make an award enforceable against the Crown in a manner in which a judgment would not be enforceable against the Crown).

Effect of registration

2.—(1) Subject to the provisions of this Act, an award registered under section 1 above shall, as respects the pecuniary obligations which it imposes, be of the same force and effect for the purposes of execution as if it had been a judgment of the High Court given when the award was rendered pursuant to the Convention and entered on the date of registration under this Act, and, so far as relates to such pecuniary obligations—

(a) proceedings may be taken on the award,

(b) the sum for which the award is registered shall carry interest,

(c) the High Court shall have the same control over the execution of the award,

as if the award had been such a judgment of the High Court.

(2) Rules of court under section 99 of the Supreme Court of Judicature (Consolidation) Act 1925 may contain provisions requiring the court on proof of the prescribed matters to stay execution of any award registered under this Act so as to take account of cases where enforcement of the award has been stayed (whether provisionally or otherwise) pursuant to the Convention, and may provide for the provisional stay of execution of the award where an application is made pursuant to the Convention which, if granted, might result in a stay of enforcement of the award.

Procedural provisions

Application of Arbitration Act 1950 and other enactments

3.—(1) The Lord Chancellor may by order direct that any of the provisions contained in—

(a) section 12 of the Arbitration Act 1950 (attendance of witnesses, production of documents, etc.) or any corresponding enactments forming part of the law of Northern Ireland, and

(b) the Foreign Tribunals Evidence Act 1856 (which relates to the taking of evidence in the United Kingdom for the purpose of proceedings before a foreign tribunal),

shall apply to such proceedings pursuant to the Convention as are specified in the order, with or without any modifications or exceptions specified in the order.

(2) Subject to subsection (1) above, neither the Arbitration Act 1950 nor the Arbitration Act (Northern Ireland) 1937 shall apply to proceedings pursuant to the Convention, but this subsection shall not be taken as affecting section 4(1) of the Arbitration Act 1950 (stay of court proceedings where there is submission to arbitration) or section 4 of the said Act of Northern Ireland.

(3) An order made under this section—

(a) may be varied or revoked by a subsequent order so made, and

(b) shall be contained in a statutory instrument.

Immunities and privileges

Status, immunities and privileges conferred by the Convention

4.—(1) In Section 6 of Chapter I of the Convention (which governs the status, immunities and privileges of the International Centre for Settlements of Investment Disputes established by the Convention, of members of its Council and Secretariat and of persons concerned with conciliation or arbitration under the Convention) Articles 18 to 20, Article 21(a) (with Article 22 as it applies Article 21(a)), Article 23(1) and Article 24 shall have the force of law.

(2) Nothing in Article 24(1) of the Convention as given the force of law by this section shall be construed as—

(a) entitling the said Centre to import goods free of customs duty without any restriction on their subsequent sale in the country to which they were imported, or

(b) conferring on that Centre any exemption from duties or taxes which form part of the price of goods sold, or

(c) conferring on that Centre any exemption from duties or taxes which are no more than charges for services rendered.

(3) For the purposes of Article 20 and Article 21(a) of the Convention as given the force of law by this section, a statement to the effect that the said Centre has waived an immunity in the circumstances specified in the statement, being a statement certified by the Secretary-General of the said Centre (or by the person acting as Secretary-General), shall be conclusive evidence.

Supplemental

Government contribution to expenses under the Convention

5. The Treasury may discharge any obligations of Her Majesty's Government in the United Kingdom arising under Article 17 of the Convention (which obliges the Contracting States to meet any deficit of the International Centre for Settlement of Investment Disputes established under the Convention), and any sums required for that purpose shall be met out of money provided by Parliament.

Application to British possessions, etc.

6.—(1) Her Majesty may by Order in Council direct that the provisions of this Act shall extend, with such exceptions, adaptations and modifications as may be specified in the Order, to—

(a) the Isle of Man,

(b) any of the Channel Islands,

(c) any colony, or any country or place outside Her Majesty's dominions in which for the time being Her Majesty has jurisdiction, or any territory consisting partly of one or more colonies and partly of one or more such countries or places.

(2) An Order in Council under this section—

(a) may contain such transitional and other supplemental provisions as appear to Her Majesty to be expedient;

(b) may be varied or revoked by a subsequent Order in Council under this section.

Application to Scotland

7. In the application of this Act to Scotland—

(a) for any reference to the High Court there shall be substituted a reference to the Court of Session;

(b) the Court of Session shall have power by Act of Sederunt to make rules for the purposes specified in section 1(6) and section 2(2) of this Act;

(c) registration under section 1 of this Act shall be effected by registering in the Books of Council and Session, or in such manner as the Court of Session may by Act of Sederunt prescribe;

(d) for any reference to the entering of a judgment there shall be substituted a reference to the signing of the interlocutor embodying the judgment;

(e) for section 3 of this Act there shall be substituted the following section:—

Proceedings in Scotland

"**3.**—(1) The Secretary of State may by order make provision, in relation to such proceedings pursuant to the Convention as are specified in the court, being proceedings taking place in Scotland, for the attendance of witnesses, the taking of evidence and the production of documents.

(2) The Secretary of State may by order direct that the Foreign Tribunals Evidence Act 1856 (which relates to the taking of evidence in the United Kingdom for the purpose of proceedings before a foreign tribunal) shall apply to such proceedings pursuant to the Convention as are specified in the order, with or without any modifications or exceptions specified in the order.

(3) An order made under this section—

(a) may be varied or revoked by a subsequent order so made, and

(b) shall be contained in a statutory instrument.";

and in any reference in this Act, or in the Convention as given the force of law in Scotland by this Act, to the staying of execution or enforcement of an award registered under this Act the expression "stay" shall be construed as meaning sist.

Application to Northern Ireland

8. In the application of this Act to Northern Ireland—

(a) references to the High Court shall, unless the context otherwise requires, be construed as references to the High Court in Northern Ireland,

(b) for the references to section 99 of the Supreme Court of Judicature (Consolidation) Act 1925 there shall be substituted references to section 7 of the Northern Ireland Act 1962.

521

Short title and commencement

9.—(1) This Act may be cited as the Arbitration (International Investment Disputes) Act 1966.

(2) This Act shall come into force on such day as Her Majesty may by Order in Council certify to be the day on which the Convention comes into force as regards the United Kingdom.

Section 1   SCHEDULE. TEXT OF CONVENTION

CONVENTION ON THE SETTLEMENT OF INVESTMENT DISPUTES BETWEEN STATES
AND NATIONALS OF OTHER STATES

Preamble

The Contracting States

Considering the need for international co-operation for economic development, and the role of private international investment therein;

Bearing in mind the possibility that from time to time disputes may arise in connection with such investment between Contracting States and nationals of other Contracting States;

Recognizing that while such disputes would usually be subject to national legal processes, international methods of settlement may be appropriate in certain cases;

Attaching particular importance to the availability of facilities for international conciliation or arbitration to which Contracting States and nationals of other Contracting States may submit such disputes if they so desire;

Desiring to establish such facilities under the auspices of the International Bank for Reconstruction and Development;

Recognizing that mutual consent by the parties to submit such disputes to conciliation or to arbitration through such facilities constitutes a binding agreement which requires in particular that due consideration be given to any recommendation of conciliators, and that any arbitral award be complied with; and

Declaring that no Contracting State shall by the mere fact of its ratification, acceptance or approval of this Convention and without its consent be deemed to be under any obligation to submit any particular dispute to conciliation or arbitration,

Have agreed as follows:

CHAPTER I. INTERNATIONAL CENTRE FOR SETTLEMENT OF
INVESTMENT DISPUTES

Section 1. Establishment and Organization

Article 1

(1) There is hereby established the International Centre for Settlement of Investment Disputes (hereinafter called the Centre).

(2) The purpose of the Centre shall be to provide facilities for conciliation and arbitration of investment disputes between Contracting States and nationals of other Contracting States in accordance with the provisions of this Convention.

Article 2

The seat of the Centre shall be at the principal office of the International Bank for Reconstruction and Development (hereinafter called the Bank). The seat may be moved to another place by decision of the Administrative Council adopted by a majority of two-thirds of its members.

Article 3

The Centre shall have an Administrative Council and a Secretariat and shall maintain a Panel of Conciliators and a Panel of Arbitrators.

Section 2. The Administrative Council

Article 4

(1) The Administrative Council shall be composed of one representative of each Contracting State. An alternate may act as representative in case of his principal's absence from a meeting or inability to act.

(2) In the absence of a contrary designation, each governor and alternate governor of the Bank appointed by a Contracting State shall be *ex officio* its representative and its alternate respectively.

Article 5

The President of the Bank shall be *ex officio* Chairman of the Administrative Council (hereinafter called the Chairman) but shall have no vote. During his absence or inability to act and during any vacancy in the office of President of the Bank, the person for the time being acting as President shall act as Chairman of the Administrative Council.

Article 6

(1) Without prejudice to the powers and functions vested in it by other provisions of this Convention, the Administrative Council shall

(a) adopt the administrative and financial regulations of the Centre;
(b) adopt the rules of procedure for the institution of conciliation and arbitration proceedings;
(c) adopt the rules of procedure for conciliation and arbitration proceedings (hereafter called the Conciliation Rules and the Arbitration Rules);
(d) approve arrangements with the Bank for the use of the Bank's administrative facilities and services;
(e) determine the conditions of service of the Secretary-General and of any Deputy Secretary-General;
(f) adopt the annual budget of revenues and expenditures of the Centre;
(g) approve the annual report on the operation of the Centre.

The decision referred to in sub-paragraphs (a), (b), (c) and (f) above shall be adopted by a majority of two-thirds of the members of the Administrative Council.

(2) The Administrative Council may appoint such committees as it considers necessary.

(3) The Administrative Council shall also exercise such other powers and perform such other functions as it shall determine to be necessary for the implementation of the provisions of this Convention.

Article 7

(1) The Administrative Council shall hold an annual meeting and such other meetings as may be determined by the Council, or convened by the Chairman, or convened by the Secretary-General at the request of not less than five members of the Council.

(2) Each member of the Administrative Council shall have one vote and, except as otherwise herein provided, all matters before the Council shall be decided by a majority of the votes cast.

(3) A quorum for any meeting of the Administrative Council shall be a majority of its members.

(4) The Administrative Council may establish, by a majority of two-thirds of its members, a procedure whereby the Chairman may seek a vote of the Council without convening a meeting of the Council. The vote shall be considered valid only if the majority of the members of the Council cast their votes within the time limit fixed by the said procedure.

Article 8

Members of the Administrative Council and the Chairman shall serve without remuneration from the Centre.

Section 3. The Secretariat

Article 9

The Secretariat shall consist of a Secretary-General, one or more Deputy Secretaries-General and staff.

Article 10

(1) The Secretary-General and any Deputy Secretary-General shall be elected by the Administrative Council by a majority of two-thirds of its members upon the nomination of the Chairman for a term of service not exceeding six years and shall be eligible for re-election. After consulting the members of the Administrative Council, the Chairman shall propose one or more candidates for each such office.

(2) The offices of Secretary-General and Deputy Secretary-General shall be incompatible with the exercise of any political function. Neither the Secretary-General nor any Deputy Secretary-General may hold any other employment or engage in any other occupation except with the approval of the Administrative Council.

(3) During the Secretary-General's absence or inability to act, and during any vacancy of the office of Secretary-General, the Deputy Secretary-General shall act as Secretary-General. If there shall be more than one Deputy Secretary-General, the Administrative Council shall determine in advance the order in which they shall act as Secretary-General.

Article 11

The Secretary-General shall be the legal representative and the principal officer of the Centre and shall be responsible for its administration, including the appointment of staff, in accordance with the provisions of this Convention and the rules adopted by the Administrative Council. He shall perform the function of registrar and shall have the power to authenticate arbitral awards rendered pursuant to this Convention, and to certify copies thereof.

Section 4. The Panels

Article 12

The Panel of Conciliators and the Panel of Arbitrators shall each consist of qualified persons, designated as hereinafter provided, who are willing to serve thereon.

Article 13

(1) Each Contracting State may designate to each Panel four persons who may but need not be its nationals.

(2) The Chairman may designate ten persons to each Panel. The persons so designated to a Panel shall each have a different nationality.

Article 14

(1) Persons designated to serve on the Panels shall be persons of high moral character and recognized competence in the fields of law, commerce, industry or finance, who may be relied upon to exercise independent judgment. Competence in the field of law shall be of particular importance in the case of persons on the Panel of Arbitrators.

(2) The Chairman, in designating persons to serve on the Panels, shall in addition pay due

regard to the importance of assuring representation on the Panels of the principal legal systems of the world and of the main forms of economic activity.

Article 15

(1) Panel members shall serve for renewable periods of six years.

(2) In case of death or resignation of a member of a Panel, the authority which designated the member shall have the right to designate another person to serve for the remainder of that member's term.

(3) Panel members shall continue in office until their successors have been designated.

Article 16

(1) A person may serve on both Panels.

(2) If a person shall have been designated to serve on the same Panel by more than one Contracting State, or by one or more Contracting States and the Chairman, he shall be deemed to have been designated by the authority which first designated him or, if one such authority is the State of which he is a national by that State.

(3) All designations shall be notified to the Secretary-General and shall take effect from the date on which the notification is received.

Section 5. Financing the Centre

Article 17

If the expenditure of the Centre cannot be met out of charges for the use of its facilities, or out of other receipts, the excess shall be borne by Contracting States which are members of the Bank in proportion to their respective subscriptions to the capital stock of the Bank, and by Contracting States which are not members of the Bank in accordance with rules adopted by the Administrative Council.

Section 6. Status, Immunities and Privileges

Article 18

The Centre shall have full international legal personality. The legal capacity of the Centre shall include the capacity

(a) to contract;
(b) to acquire and dispose of movable and immovable property;
(c) to institute legal proceedings.

Article 19

To enable the Centre to fulfil its functions, it shall enjoy in the territories of each Contracting State the immunities and privileges set forth in this Section.

Article 20

The Centre, its property and assets shall enjoy immunity from all legal process, except when the Centre waives this immunity.

Article 21

The Chairman, the members of the Administrative Council, persons acting as conciliators or arbitrators or members of a Committee appointed pursuant to paragraph (3) of Article 52, and the officers and employees of the Secretariat.

(a) shall enjoy immunity from legal process with respect to acts performed by them in the exercise of their functions, except when the Centre waives this immunity;

525

(b) not being local nationals, shall enjoy the same immunities from immigration restrictions, alien registration requirements and national service obligations, the same facilities as regards exchange restrictions and the same treatment in respect of travelling facilities as are accorded by Contracting States to the representatives, officials and employees of comparable rank of other Contracting States.

Article 22

The provisions of Article 21 shall apply to persons appearing in proceedings under this Convention as parties, agents, counsel, advocates, witnesses or experts; provided, however, that sub-paragraph (b) thereof shall apply only in connection with their travel to and from, and their stay at, the place where the proceedings are held.

Article 23

(1) The archives of the Centre shall be inviolable, wherever they may be.

(2) With regard to its official communications, the Centre shall be accorded by each Contracting State treatment not less favourable than that accorded to other international organizations.

Article 24

(1) The Centre, its assets, property and income, and its operations and transactions authorized by this Convention shall be exempt from all taxation and customs duties. The Centre shall also be exempt from liability for the collection or payment of any taxes or customs duties.

(2) Except in the case of local nationals, no tax shall be levied on or in respect of expense allowances paid by the Centre to the Chairman or members of the Administrative Council, or on or in respect of salaries, expense allowances or other emoluments paid by the Centre to officials or employees of the Secretariat.

(3) No tax shall be levied on or in respect of fees or expense allowances received by persons acting as conciliators, or arbitrators, or members of a Committee appointed pursuant to paragraph (3) of Article 52, in proceedings under this Convention, if the sole jurisdictional basis for such tax is the location of the Centre or the place where such proceedings are conducted or the place where such fees or allowances are paid.

CHAPTER II. JURISDICTION OF THE CENTRE

Article 25

(1) The jurisdiction of the Centre shall extend to any legal dispute arising directly out of an investment, between a Contracting State (or any constituent subdivision or agency of a Contracting State designated to the Centre by that State) and a national of another Contracting State, which the parties to the dispute consent in writing to submit to the Centre. When the parties have given their consent, no party may withdraw its consent unilaterally.

(2) "National of another Contracting State" means:

(a) any natural person who had the nationality of a Contracting State other than the State party to the dispute on the date on which the parties consented to submit such dispute to conciliation or arbitration as well as on the date on which the request was registered pursuant to paragraph (3) of Article 28 or paragraph (3) of Article 36, but does not include any person who on either date also had the nationality of the Contracting State party to the dispute; and

(b) any juridical person which had the nationality of a Contracting State other than the State party to the dispute on the date on which the parties consented to submit such dispute to conciliation or arbitration and any juridical person which had the nationality of the Contracting State party to the dispute on that date and which, because of foreign control, the parties have agreed should be treated as a national of another Contracting State for the purposes of this Convention.

(3) Consent by a constituent subdivision or agency of a Contracting State shall require the approval of that State unless that State notifies the Centre that no such approval is required.

(4) Any Contracting State may, at the time of ratification, acceptance or approval of this Convention or at any time thereafter, notify the Centre of the class or classes of disputes which it would or would not consider submitting to the jurisdiction of the Centre. The Secretary-General shall forthwith transmit such notification to all Contracting States. Such notification shall not constitute the consent required by paragraph (1).

Article 26

Consent of the parties to arbitration under this Convention shall, unless otherwise stated, be deemed consent to such arbitration to the exclusion of any other remedy. A Contracting State may require the exhaustion of local administrative or judicial remedies as a condition of its consent to arbitration under this Convention.

Article 27

(1) No Contracting State shall give diplomatic protection, or bring an international claim, in respect of a dispute which one of its nationals and another Contracting State shall have consented to submit or shall have submitted to arbitration under this Convention, unless such other Contracting State shall have failed to abide by and comply with the award rendered in such dispute.

(2) Diplomatic protection, for the purposes of paragraph (1), shall not include informal diplomatic exchanges for the sole purpose of facilitating a settlement of the dispute.

CHAPTER III. CONCILIATION

Section 1. Request for Conciliation

Article 28

(1) Any Contracting State or any national of a Contracting State wishing to institute conciliation proceedings shall address a request to that effect in writing to the Secretary-General who shall send a copy of the request to the other party.

(2) The request shall contain information concerning the issues in dispute, the identity of the parties and their consent to conciliation in accordance with the rules of procedure for the institution of conciliation and arbitration proceedings.

(3) The Secretary-General shall register the request unless he finds, on the basis of the information contained in the request, that the dispute is manifestly outside the jurisdiction of the Centre. He shall forthwith notify the parties of registration or refusal to register.

Section 2. Constitution of the Conciliation Commission

Article 29

(1) The Conciliation Commission (hereinafter called the Commission) shall be constituted as soon as possible after registration of a request pursuant to Article 28.

(2)(a) The Commission shall consist of a sole conciliator or any uneven number of conciliators appointed as the parties shall agree.

(b) Where the parties do not agree upon the number of conciliators and the method of their appointment, the Commission shall consist of three conciliators, one conciliator appointed by each party and the third, who shall be the president of the Commission, appointed by agreement of the parties.

Article 30

If the Commission shall not have been constituted within 90 days after notice of registration of the request has been dispatched by the Secretary-General in accordance with paragraph (3) of Article 28, or such other period as the parties may agree, the Chairman shall, at the request of either party and after consulting both parties as far as possible, appoint the conciliator or conciliators not yet appointed.

Article 31

(1) Conciliators may be appointed from outside the Panel of Conciliators, except in the case of appointments by the Chairman pursuant to Article 30.

(2) Conciliators appointed from outside the Panel of Conciliators shall possess the qualities stated in paragraph (1) of Article 14.

Section 3. Conciliation Proceedings

Article 32

(1) The Commission shall be the judge of its own competence.

(2) Any objection by a party to the dispute that that dispute is not within the jurisdiction of the Centre, or for other reasons is not within the competence of the Commission, shall be considered by the Commission which shall determine whether to deal with it as a preliminary question or to join it to the merits of the dispute.

Article 33

Any conciliation proceeding shall be conducted in accordance with the provisions of this Section and, except as the parties otherwise agree, in accordance with the Conciliation Rules in effect on the date on which the parties consented to conciliation. If any question of procedure arises which is not covered by this Section or the Conciliation Rules or any rules agreed by the parties, the Commission shall decide the question.

Article 34

(1) It shall be the duty of the Commission to clarify the issues in dispute between the parties and to endeavour to bring about agreement between them upon mutually acceptable terms. To that end, the Commission may at any stage of the proceedings and from time to time recommend terms of settlement to the parties. The parties shall cooperate in good faith with the Commission in order to enable the Commission to carry out its functions, and shall give their most serious consideration to its recommendations.

(2) If the parties reach agreement, the Commission shall draw up a report noting the issues in dispute and recording that the parties have reached agreement. If, at any stage of the proceedings, it appears to the Commission that there is no likelihood of agreement between the parties, it shall close the proceedings and shall draw up a report noting the submission of the dispute and recording the failure of the parties to reach agreement. If one party fails to appear or participate in the proceedings, the Commission shall close the proceedings and shall draw up a report noting that party's failure to appear or participate.

Article 35

Except as the parties to the dispute shall otherwise agree, neither party to a conciliation proceeding shall be entitled in any other proceeding, whether before arbitrators or in a court of law or otherwise, to invoke or rely on any views expressed or statements or admissions or offers of settlement made by the other party in the conciliation proceedings, or the report or any recommendations made by the Commission.

Section 1. Request for Arbitration

Article 36

(1) Any Contracting State or any national of a Contracting State wishing to institute arbitration proceedings shall address a request to that effect in writing to the Secretary-General who shall send a copy of the request to the other party.

(2) The request shall contain information concerning the issues in dispute, the identity of the parties and their consent to arbitration in accordance with the rules of procedure for the institution of conciliation and arbitration proceedings.

(3) The Secretary-General shall register the request unless he finds, on the basis of the information contained in the request, that the dispute is manifestly outside the jurisdiction of the Centre. He shall forthwith notify the parties of registration or refusal to register.

Section 2. Constitution of the Tribunal

Article 37

(1) The Arbitral Tribunal (hereinafter called the Tribunal) shall be constituted as soon as possible after registration of a request pursuant to Article 36.

(2)(a) The Tribunal shall consist of a sole arbitrator or any uneven number of arbitrators appointed as the parties shall agree.

(b) Where the parties do not agree upon the number of arbitrators and the method of their appointment, the Tribunal shall consist of three arbitrators, one arbitrator appointed by each party and the third, who shall be the president of the Tribunal, appointed by agreement of the parties.

Article 38

If the Tribunal shall not have been constituted within 90 days after notice of registration of the request has been dispatched by the Secretary-General in accordance with paragraph (3) of Article 36, or such other period as the parties may agree, the Chairman shall, at the request of either party and after consulting both parties as far as possible, appoint the arbitrator or arbitrators not yet appointed. Arbitrators appointed by the Chairman pursuant to this Article shall not be nationals of the Contracting State party to the dispute or of the Contracting State whose national is a party to the dispute.

Article 39

The majority of the arbitrators shall be nationals of States other than the Contracting State party to the dispute and the Contracting State whose national is a party to the dispute; provided, however, that the foregoing provisions of this Article shall not apply if the sole arbitrator or each individual member of the Tribunal has been appointed by agreement of the parties.

Article 40

(1) Arbitrators may be appointed from outside the Panel of Arbitrators, except in the case of appointments by the Chairman pursuant to Article 38.

(2) Arbitrators appointed from outside the Panel of Arbitrators shall possess the qualities stated in paragraph (1) of Article 14.

Section 3. Powers and Functions of the Tribunal

Article 41

(1) The Tribunal shall be the judge of its own competence.

(2) Any objection by a party to the dispute that that dispute is not within the jurisdiction of the Centre, or for other reasons is not within the competence of the Tribunal, shall be considered by the Tribunal which shall determine whether to deal with it as a preliminary question or to join it to the merits of the dispute.

Article 42

(1) The Tribunal shall decide a dispute in accordance with such rules of law as may be agreed by the parties. In the absence of such agreement, the Tribunal shall apply the law of the Contracting State party to the dispute (including its rules on the conflict of laws) and such rules of international law as may be applicable.

(2) The Tribunal may not bring in a finding of *non liquet* on the ground of silence or obscurity of the law.

(3) The provisions of paragraphs (1) and (2) shall not prejudice the power of the Tribunal to decide a dispute *ex aequo et bono* if the parties so agree.

Article 43

Except as the parties otherwise agree, the Tribunal may, if it deems it necessary at any stage of the proceedings,

- (a) call upon the parties to produce documents or other evidence, and
- (b) visit the scene connected with the dispute, and conduct such enquiries there as it may deem appropriate.

Article 44

Any arbitration proceeding shall be conducted in accordance with the provisions of this Section and, except as the parties otherwise agree, in accordance with the Arbitration Rules in effect on the date on which the parties consented to arbitration. If any question of procedure arises which is not covered by this Section or the Arbitration Rules or any rules agreed by the parties, the Tribunal shall decide the question.

Article 45

(1) Failure of a party to appear or to present his case shall not be deemed an admission of the other party's assertions.

(2) If a party fails to appear or to present his case at any stage of the proceedings the other party may request the Tribunal to deal with the questions submitted to it and to render an award. Before rendering an award, the Tribunal shall notify, and grant a period of grace to, the party failing to appear or to present its case, unless it is satisfied that that party does not intend to do so.

Article 46

Except as the parties otherwise agree, the Tribunal shall, if requested by a party, determine any incidental or additional claims or counter-claims arising directly out of the subject-matter of the dispute provided that they are within the scope of the consent of the parties and are otherwise within the jurisdiction of the Centre.

Article 47

Except as the parties otherwise agree, the Tribunal may, if it considers that the circumstances so require, recommend any provisional measures which should be taken to preserve the respective rights of either party.

Section 4. The Award

Article 48

(1) The Tribunal shall decide questions by a majority of the votes of all its members.

(2) The award of the Tribunal shall be in writing and shall be signed by the members of the Tribunal who voted for it.

(3) The award shall deal with every question submitted to the Tribunal, and shall state the reasons upon which it is based.

(4) Any member of the Tribunal may attach his individual opinion to the award, whether he dissents from the majority or not, or a statement of his dissent.

(5) The Centre shall not publish the award without the consent of the parties.

Article 49

(1) The Secretary-General shall promptly dispatch certified copies of the award to the parties. The award shall be deemed to have been rendered on the date on which the certified copies were dispatched.

(2) The Tribunal upon the request of a party made within 45 days after the date on which the award was rendered may after notice to the other party decide any question which it had omitted to decide in the award, and shall rectify any clerical, arithmetical or similar error in the award. Its decision shall become part of the award and shall be notified to the parties in the same manner as the award. The periods of time provided for under paragraph (2) of Article 51 and paragraph (2) of Article 52 shall run from the date on which the decision was rendered.

Section 5. Interpretation, Revision and Annulment of the Award

Article 50

(1) If any dispute shall arise between the parties as to the meaning or scope of an award, either party may request interpretation of the award by an application in writing addressed to the Secretary-General.

(2) The request shall, if possible, be submitted to the Tribunal which rendered the award. If this shall not be possible, a new Tribunal shall be constituted in accordance with Section 2 of this Chapter. The Tribunal may, if it considers that the circumstances so require, stay enforcement of the award pending its decision.

Article 51

(1) Either party may request revision of the award by an application in writing addressed to the Secretary-General on the ground of discovery of some fact of such a nature as decisively to affect the award, provided that when the award was rendered that fact was unknown to the Tribunal and to the applicant and that the applicant's ignorance of that fact was not due to negligence.

(2) The application shall be made within 90 days after the discovery of such fact and in any event within three years after the date on which the award was rendered.

(3) The request shall, if possible, be submitted to the Tribunal which rendered the award. If this shall not be possible, a new Tribunal shall be constituted in accordance with Section 2 of this Chapter.

(4) The Tribunal may, if it considers that the circumstances so require, stay enforcement of the award pending its decision. If the applicant requests stay of enforcement of the award in his application, enforcement shall be stayed provisionally until the Tribunal rules on such request.

Article 52

(1) Either party may request annulment of the award by an application in writing addressed to the Secretary-General on one or more of the following grounds:

(a) that the Tribunal was not properly constituted;

(b) that the Tribunal has manifestly exceeded its powers;

(c) that there was corruption on the part of a member of the Tribunal;

(d) that there has been a serious departure from a fundamental rule of procedure; or

(e) that the award has failed to state the reasons on which it is based.

(2) The application shall be made within 120 days after the date on which the award was rendered except that when annulment is requested on the ground of corruption such application shall be made within 120 days after discovery of the corruption and in any event within three years after the date on which the award was rendered.

(3) On receipt of the request the Chairman shall forthwith appoint from the Panel of Arbitrators an *ad hoc* Committee of three persons. None of the members of the Committee shall have been a member of the Tribunal which rendered the award, shall be of the same nationality as any such member, shall be a national of the State party to the dispute or of the State whose national is a party to the dispute, shall have been designated to the Panel of Arbitrators by either of those States, or shall have acted as a conciliator in the same dispute. The Committee shall have the authority to annul the award or any part thereof on any of the grounds set forth in paragraph (1).

(4) The provisions of Articles 41–45, 48, 49, 53 and 54, and of Chapters VI and VII shall apply *mutatis mutandis* to proceedings before the Committee.

(5) The Committee may, if it considers that circumstances so require, stay enforcement of the award pending its decision. If the applicant requests a stay of enforcement of the award in his application, enforcement shall be stayed provisionally until the Committee rules on such request.

(6) If the award is annulled the dispute shall, at the request of either party, be submitted to a new Tribunal constituted in accordance with Section 2 of this Chapter.

Section 6. Recognition and Enforcement of the Award

Article 53

(1) The award shall be binding on the parties and shall not be subject to any appeal or to any other remedy except those provided for in this Convention. Each party shall abide by and comply with the terms of the award except to the extent that enforcement shall have been stayed pursuant to the relevant provisions of this Convention.

(2) For the purposes of this Section, "award" shall include any decision interpreting, revising or annulling such award pursuant to Articles 50, 51 and 52.

Article 54

(1) Each Contracting State shall recognize an award rendered pursuant to this Convention as binding and enforce the pecuniary obligations imposed by that award within its territories as if it were a final judgment of a court in that State. A Contracting State with a federal constitution may enforce such an award in or through its federal courts and may provide that such courts shall treat the award as if it were a final judgment of the courts of a constituent state.

(2) A party seeking recognition or enforcement in the territories of a Contracting State shall furnish to a competent court or other authority which such State shall have designated for this purpose a copy of the award certified by the Secretary-General. Each Contracting State shall notify the Secretary-General of the designation of the competent court or other authority for this purpose and of any subsequent change in such designation.

(3) Execution of the award shall be governed by the laws concerning the execution of judgments in force in the State in whose territories such execution is sought.

Article 55

Nothing in Article 54 shall be construed as derogating from the law in force in any Contracting State relating to immunity of that State or of any foreign State from execution.

CHAPTER V. REPLACEMENT AND DISQUALIFICATION OF CONCILIATORS
AND ARBITRATORS

Article 56

(1) After a Commission or a Tribunal has been constituted and proceedings have begun, its composition shall remain unchanged; provided, however, that if a conciliator or an arbitrator should die, become incapacitated, or resign, the resulting vacancy shall be filled in accordance with the provisions of Section 2 of Chapter III or Section 2 of Chapter IV.

(2) A member of the Commission or Tribunal shall continue to serve in that capacity notwithstanding that he shall have ceased to be a member of the Panel.

(3) If a conciliator or arbitrator appointed by a party shall have resigned without the consent of the Commission or Tribunal of which he was a member, the Chairman shall appoint a person from the appropriate Panel to fill the resulting vacancy.

Article 57

A party may propose to a Commission or Tribunal the disqualification of any of its members on account of any fact indicating a manifest lack of the qualities required by paragraph (1) of Article 14. A party to arbitration proceedings may, in addition, propose the disqualification of an arbitrator on the ground that he was ineligible for appointment to the Tribunal under Section 2 of Chapter IV.

Article 58

The decision on any proposal to disqualify a conciliator or arbitrator shall be taken by the other members of the Commission or Tribunal as the case may be, provided that where those members are equally divided, or in the case of a proposal to disqualify a sole conciliator or arbitrator, or a majority of the conciliators or arbitrators, the Chairman shall take that decision. If it is decided that the proposal is well-founded the conciliator or arbitrator to whom the decision relates shall be replaced in accordance with the provisions of Section 2 of Chapter III or Section 2 of Chapter IV.

CHAPTER VI. COST OF PROCEEDINGS

Article 59

The charges payable by the parties for the use of the facilities of the Centre shall be determined by the Secretary-General in accordance with the regulations adopted by the Administrative Council.

Article 60

(1) Each Commission and each Tribunal shall determine the fees and expenses of its members within limits established from time to time by the Administrative Council and after consultation with the Secretary-General.

(2) Nothing in paragraph (1) of this Article shall preclude the parties from agreeing in advance with the Commission or Tribunal concerned upon the fees and expenses of its members.

Article 61

(1) In the case of conciliation proceedings the fees and expenses of members of the Commission as well as the charges for the use of the facilities of the Centre, shall be borne equally by the parties. Each party shall bear any other expenses it incurs in connection with the proceedings.

(2) In the case of arbitration proceedings the Tribunal shall, except as the parties otherwise

agree, assess the expenses incurred by the parties in connection with the proceedings, and shall decide how and by whom those expenses, the fees and expenses of the members of the Tribunal and the charges for the use of the facilities of the Centre shall be paid. Such decision shall form part of the award.

CHAPTER VII. PLACE OF PROCEEDINGS

Article 62

Conciliation and arbitration proceedings shall be held at the seat of the Centre except as hereinafter provided.

Article 63

Conciliation and arbitration proceedings may be held, if the parties so agree,

- (a) at the seat of the Permanent Court of Arbitration or of any other appropriate institution, whether private or public, with which the Centre may make arrangements for that purpose; or
- (b) at any other place approved by the Commission or Tribunal after consultation with the Secretary-General.

CHAPTER VIII. DISPUTES BETWEEN CONTRACTING STATES

Article 64

Any dispute arising between Contracting States concerning the interpretation or application of this Convention which is not settled by negotiation shall be referred to the International Court of Justice by the application of any party to such dispute, unless the States concerned agree to another method of settlement.

CHAPTER IX. AMENDMENT

Article 65

Any Contracting State may propose amendment of this Convention. The text of a proposed amendment shall be communicated to the Secretary-General not less than 90 days prior to the meeting of the Administrative Council at which such amendment is to be considered and shall forthwith be transmitted by him to all the members of the Administrative Council.

Article 66

(1) If the Administrative Council shall so decide by a majority of two-thirds of its members, the proposed amendment shall be circulated to all Contracting States for ratification, acceptance or approval. Each amendment shall enter into force 30 days after dispatch by the depositary of this Convention of a notification to Contracting States that all Contracting States have ratified, accepted or approved the amendment.

(2) No amendment shall affect the rights and obligations under this Convention of any Contracting State or of any of its constituent subdivisions or agencies, or of any national of such State arising out of consent to the jurisdiction of the Centre given before the date of entry into force of the amendment.

CHAPTER X. FINAL PROVISIONS

Article 67

This Convention shall be open for signature on behalf of States members of the Bank. It shall also be open for signature on behalf of any other State which is a party to the Statute of the

International Court of Justice and which the Administrative Council, by a vote of two-thirds of its members, shall have invited to sign the Convention.

Article 68

(1) This Convention shall be subject to ratification, acceptance or approval by the signatory States in accordance with their respective constitutional procedures.

(2) This Convention shall enter into force 30 days after the date of deposit of the twentieth instrument of ratification, acceptance or approval. It shall enter into force for each State which subsequently deposits its instrument of ratification, acceptance or approval 30 days after the date of such deposit.

Article 69

Each Contracting State shall take such legislative or other measures as may be necessary for making the provisions of this Convention effective in its territories.

Article 70

This Convention shall apply to all territories for whose international relations a Contracting State is responsible, except those which are excluded by such State by written notice to the depositary of this Convention either at the time of ratification, acceptance or approval or subsequently.

Article 71

Any Contracting State may denounce this Convention by written notice to the depositary of this Convention. The denunciation shall take effect six months after receipt of such notice.

Article 72

Notice by a Contracting State pursuant to Article 70 or 71 shall not affect the rights or obligations under this Convention of that State or of any of its constituent subdivisions or agencies or of any national of that State arising out of consent to the jurisdiction of the Centre given by one of them before such notice was received by the depositary.

Article 73

Instruments of ratification, acceptance or approval of this Convention and of amendments thereto shall be deposited with the Bank which shall act as the depositary of this Convention to States members of the Bank to any other State invited to sign the Convention.

Article 74

The depositary shall register this Convention with the Secretariat of the United Nations in accordance with Article 102 of the Charter of the United Nations and the Regulations thereunder adopted by the General Assembly.

Article 75

The depositary shall notify all signatory States of the following:

  (a) signatures in accordance with Article 67;
  (b) deposits of instruments of ratification, acceptance and approval in accordance with Article 73;
  (c) the date on which this Convention enters into force in accordance with Article 68;
  (d) exclusions from territorial application pursuant to Article 70;

(e) the date on which any amendment of this Convention enters into force in accordance with Article 66; and

(f) denunciations in accordance with Article 71.

DONE at Washington in the English, French and Spanish languages, all three texts being equally authentic, in a single copy which shall remain deposited in the archives of the International Bank for Reconstruction and Development, which has indicated by its signature below its agreement to fulfil the functions with which it is charged under this Convention.

(Here follow the signatures)

F(3) ADMINISTRATION OF JUSTICE ACT 1970

Section 4: Power of judges of Commercial Court to take arbitrations

4.—(1) A judge of the Commercial Court may, if in all circumstances he thinks fit, accept appointment as sole arbitrator, or as umpire, by or by virtue of an arbitration agreement within the meaning of Arbitration Act 1950, where the dispute appears to him to be of a commercial character.

(2) A judge of the Commercial Court shall not accept appointment as arbitrator or umpire unless the Lord Chief Justice has informed him that, having regard to the state of business in the High Court and at assizes, he can be made available to do so.

(3) The fees payable for the services of a judge as arbitrator or umpire shall be taken in the High Court.

(4) Schedule 3 to this Act shall have effect for modifying, and in certain cases replacing, provisions of the Arbitration Act 1950, in relation to arbitration by judges and, in particular, for substituting the Court of Appeal for the High Court in provisions of that Act whereby arbitrators and umpires, their proceedings and awards, are subject to control and review by the court.

(5) Any jurisdiction which is exercisable by the High Court in relation to arbitrators and umpires otherwise than under the Arbitration Act 1950 shall, in relation to a judge of the Commercial Court appointed as arbitrator or umpire, be exercisable instead by the Court of Appeal.

Schedule 3: Application of Arbitration Act 1950 to Judge-Arbitrators

1. In this Schedule—

(a) "the Act" means the Arbitration Act 1950;

(b) "arbitration agreement" has the same meaning as in the Act; and

(c) "judge-arbitrator" and "judge-umpire" mean a judge of the Commercial Court appointed as arbitrator or, as the case may be, as umpire by or by virtue of an arbitration agreement.

2. In section 1 of the Act (authority of arbitrator to be irrevocable except by leave of the court), in its application to a judge-arbitrator or judge-umpire, the Court of Appeal shall be substituted for the High Court.

3. The power of the High Court under section 7 of the Act (vacancy among arbitrators supplied by parties) to set aside the appointment of an arbitrator shall not be exercisable in the case of the appointment of a judge-arbitrator.

4. Section 8(3) of the Act (power of the High Court to order umpire to enter immediately on reference as sole arbitrator) shall not apply to a judge-umpire; but a judge-umpire may, on the application of any party to the reference and notwithstanding anything to the contrary in the arbitration agreement, enter on the reference in lieu of the arbitrators and as if he were the sole arbitrator.

5.—(1) The powers conferred on the High Court or a judge thereof by section 12(4), (5) and (6) of the Act (summoning of witnesses, interlocutory orders, etc.) shall be exercisable in the case of a reference to a judge-arbitrator or judge-umpire as in the case of any other reference to arbitration, but shall in any such case be exercisable also by the judge-arbitrator or judge-umpire himself.

(2) Anything done by an arbitrator or umpire in the exercise of powers conferred by this paragraph shall be done by him in his capacity as judge of the High Court and have effect as if done by that court, but nothing in this paragraph prejudices any power vested in the arbitrator or umpire in his capacity as such.

6. Section 13(2) and (3) of the Act (extension of time for making award; provision for ensuring that reference is conducted with reasonable dispatch) shall not apply to a reference to a judge-arbitrator or judge-umpire; but a judge-arbitrator or judge-umpire may enlarge any time limited for making his award (whether under the Act or otherwise), whether that time has expired or not.

7.—(1) Section 18(4) of the Act (provision enabling a party in an arbitration to obtain an order for costs) shall apply, in the case of a reference to a judge-arbitrator, with the omission of the words from "within fourteen days" to "may direct."

(2) The power of the High Court to make declarations and orders for the purposes of section 18(5) of the Act (charging order for solicitor's costs) shall be exercisable in the case of an arbitration by a judge-arbitrator or judge-umpire as in the case of any other arbitration, but shall in any such case be exercisable also by the judge-arbitrator or judge-umpire himself.

(3) A declaration or order made by an arbitrator or umpire in the exercise of the power conferred by the last foregoing sub-paragraph shall be made by him in his capacity as judge of the High Court and have effect as if made by that court.

8.—(1) Section 19 of the Act (power of High Court to order delivery of award on payment of arbitrator's fees into court) shall not apply with respect to the award of a judge-arbitrator or judge-umpire.

(2) A judge-umpire may withhold his award until the fees payable to the arbitrators have been paid into the High Court.

(3) Arbitrator's fees paid into court under this paragraph shall be paid out in accordance with rules of court, subject to the right of any party to the reference to apply (in accordance with the rules) for any fee to be taxed, not being a fee which has been fixed by written agreement between him and the arbitrator.

(4) A taxation under this paragraph may be reviewed in the same manner as a taxation of the costs of an award.

(5) On a taxation under this paragraph, or on a review thereof, an arbitrator shall be entitled to appear and be heard.

9.—(1) In sections [. . .], 22 and 23 of the Act (special case, remission and setting aside of awards, etc.), in their application to a judge-arbitrator or judge-umpire, and to a reference to him and to his award thereon, the Court of Appeal shall be substituted for the High Court.

. . .

10.—(1) Section 24(2) of the Act (removal of issue of fraud for trial in the High Court) shall not apply to an agreement under or by virtue of which a judge-arbitrator or judge-umpire has been appointed; nor shall leave be given by the High Court under that subsection to revoke the authority of a judge-arbitrator or judge-umpire.

(2) Where, on a reference of a dispute to a judge-arbitrator or judge-umpire, it appears to the judge that the dispute involves the question whether a party to the dispute has been guilty of fraud, he may, so far as may be necessary to enable that question to be determined by the High Court, order that the agreement by or by virtue of which he was appointed shall cease to have effect and revoke his authority as arbitrator or umpire.

(3) An order made by a judge-arbitrator or judge-umpire under this paragraph shall have effect as if made by the High Court.

11. Section 25 of the Act (powers of court on removal of arbitrator or revocation of arbitration agreement) shall be amended as follows:—

(a) after the words "the High Court" where they first occur in subsection (1), where they occur for the first and second time in subsection (2), and in subsections (3) and (4), there shall be inserted the words "or the Court of Appeal"; and

(b) after those words where they occur for the second time in subsection (1) and for the third time in subsection (2) there shall be inserted the words "or the Court of Appeal, as the case may be."

12. The leave required by section 26 of the Act (enforcement in High Court) for an award on an arbitration agreement to be enforced as mentioned in that section may, in the case of an award by a judge-arbitrator or a judge-umpire, be given by the judge-arbitrator or judge-umpire himself.

Note: Paragraph 9 was amended by the Arbitration Act 1979, s. 8(3).

F(4) ARBITRATION ACT 1975

An Act to give effect to the New York Convention on the Recognition and Enforcement of Foreign Arbitral Awards.

Effect of arbitration agreement on court proceedings

Staying court proceedings where party proves arbitration agreement

1.—(1) If any party to an arbitration agreement to which this section applies, or any person claiming through or under him, commences any legal proceedings in any court against any other party to the agreement, or any person claiming through or under him, in respect of any matter agreed to be referred, any party to the proceedings may at any time after appearance, and before delivering any pleadings or taking any other steps in the proceedings, apply to the court to stay the proceedings; and the court, unless satisfied that the arbitration agreement is null and void, inoperative or incapable of being performed or that there is not in fact any dispute between the parties with regard to the matter agreed to be referred, shall make an order staying the proceedings.

(2) This section applies to any arbitration agreement which is not a domestic arbitration agreement; and neither section 4(1) of the Arbitration Act 1950 nor section 4 of the Arbitration Act (Northern Ireland) 1937 shall apply to an arbitration agreement to which this section applies.

(3) In the application of this section to Scotland, for the references to staying proceedings there shall be substituted references to sisting proceedings.

(4) In this section "domestic arbitration agreement" means an arbitration agreement which does not provide, expressly or by implication, for arbitration in a State other than the United Kingdom and to which neither—

(a) an individual who is a national of, or habitually resident in, any State other than the United Kingdom; nor
(b) a body corporate which is incorporated in, or whose central management and control is exercised in, any State other than the United Kingdom;

is a party at the time the proceedings are commenced.

Enforcement of Convention awards

Replacement of former provisions

2. Sections 3 to 6 of this Act shall have effect with respect to the enforcement of Convention awards; and where a Convention award would, but for this section, be also a foreign award within the meaning of Part II of the Arbitration Act 1950, that Part shall not apply to it.

Effect of Convention awards

3.—(1) A Convention award shall, subject to the following provisions of this Act, be enforceable—

(a) in England and Wales, either by action or in the same manner as the award of an arbitrator is enforceable by virtue of section 26 of the Arbitration Act 1950;

(b) in Scotland, either by action or, in a case where the arbitration agreement contains consent to the registration of the award in the Books of Council and Session for execution and the award is so registered, by summary diligence;

(c) in Northern Ireland, either by action or in the same manner as the award of an arbitrator is enforceable by virtue of section 16 of the Arbitration Act (Northern Ireland) 1937.

(2) Any Convention award which would be enforceable under this Act shall be treated as binding for all purposes on the persons as between whom it was made, and may accordingly be relied on by any of those persons by way of defence, set off or otherwise in any legal proceedings in the United Kingdom; and any reference in this Act to enforcing a Convention award shall be construed as including references to relying on such an award.

Evidence

4. The party seeking to enforce a Convention award must produce—

(a) the duly authenticated original award or a duly certified copy of it; and

(b) the original arbitration agreement or a duly certified copy of it; and

(c) where the award or agreement is in a foreign language, a translation of it certified by an official or sworn translator or by a diplomatic or consular agent.

Refusal of enforcement

5.—(1) Enforcement of a Convention award shall not be refused except in the cases mentioned in this section.

(2) Enforcement of a Convention award may be refused if the person against whom it is invoked proves—

(a) that a party to the arbitration agreement was (under the law applicable to him) under some incapacity; or

(b) that the arbitration agreement was not valid under the law to which the parties subjected it or, failing any indication thereon, under the law of the country where the award was made; or

(c) that he was not given proper notice of the appointment of the arbitrator or of the arbitration proceedings or was otherwise unable to present his case; or

(d) (subject to subsection (4) of this section) that the award deals with a difference not contemplated by or not falling within the terms of the submission to arbitration or contains decisions on matters beyond the scope of the submission to arbitration; or

(e) that the composition of the arbitral authority or the arbitral procedure was not in accordance with the agreement of the parties or, failing such agreement, with the law of the country where the arbitration took place; or

(f) that the award has not yet become binding on the parties, or has been set aside or suspended by a competent authority of the country in which, or under the law of which, it was made.

(3) Enforcement of a Convention award may also be refused if the award is in respect of a matter which is not capable of settlement by arbitration, or if it would be contrary to public policy to enforce the award.

(4) A Convention award which contains decisions on matters not submitted to arbitration may be enforced to the extent that it contains decisions on matters submitted to arbitration which can be separated from those on matters not so submitted.

(5) Where an application for the setting aside or suspension of a Convention award has been made to such a competent authority as is mentioned in subsection (2)(f) of this section, the court before which enforcement of the award is sought may, if it thinks fit, adjourn the proceed-

ings and may, on the application of the party seeking to enforce the award, order the other party to give security.

Saving

6. Nothing in this Act shall prejudice any right to enforce or rely on an award otherwise than under this Act or Part II of the Arbitration Act 1950.

General

Interpretation

7.—(1) In this Act—

"arbitration agreement" means an agreement in writing (including an agreement contained in an exchange of letters or telegrams) to submit to arbitration present or future differences capable of settlement by arbitration;

"Convention award" means an award made in pursuance of an arbitration agreement in the territory of a State, other than the United Kingdom, which is a party to the New York Convention; and

"the New York Convention" means the Convention on the Recognition and Enforcement of Foreign Arbitral Awards adopted by the United Nations Conference on International Commercial Arbitration on 10th June 1958.

(2) If Her Majesty by Order in Council declares that any State specified in the Order is a party to the New York Convention the Order shall, while in force, be conclusive evidence that that State is a party to that Convention.

(3) An Order in Council under this section may be varied or revoked by a subsequent Order in Council.

Note: The following States have been declared by Order in Council S.I. 1979 No. 304 to be parties to the Convention:

Australia (including all the external territories for the international relations of which Australia is responsible)	Democratic Kampuchea
	Republic of Korea
	Kuwait
Austria	Madagascar
Belgium	Mexico
Benin	Morocco
Botswana	Netherlands (including the Netherlands Antilles)
Bulgaria	Niger
Central African Empire	Nigeria
Chile	Norway
Cuba	Philippines
Czechoslovakia	Poland
Denmark	Romania
Ecuador	South Africa
Egypt	Spain
Finland	Sri Lanka
France (including territories of the French Republic)	Sweden
	Switzerland
Federal Republic of Germany and Berlin (West)	Syrian Arab Republic
German Democratic Republic	Thailand
Ghana	Trinidad and Tobago
Greece	Tunisia
Holy See	Union of Soviet Socialist Republics
Hungary	United Republic of Tanzania
India	United States of America (including all the
Israel	territories for the international relations of
Italy	which the United States of America is
Japan	responsible)

Short title, repeals, commencement and extent

8.—(1) This Act may be cited as the Arbitration Act 1975.

(2) The following provisions of the Arbitration Act 1950 are hereby repealed, that is to say—

(a) section 4(2);
(b) in section 28 the proviso;
(c) in section 30 the words "(except the provisions of subsection (2) of section 4 thereof)";
(d) in section 31(2) the words "subsection (2) of section 4"; and
(e) in section 34 the words from the beginning to "save as aforesaid".

(3) This Act shall come into operation on such a date as the Secretary of State may by order made by statutory instrument appoint.

(4) This Act extends to Northern Ireland.

F(5) STATE IMMUNITY ACT 1978

An Act to make new provisions with respect to proceedings in the United Kingdom by or against other States; to provide for the effect of judgments given against the United Kingdom in the courts of States parties to the European Convention on State Immunity; to make new provision with respect to the immunities and privileges of heads of State; and for connected purposes.

PART I. PROCEEDINGS IN THE UNITED KINGDOM BY OR AGAINST OTHER STATES

Immunity from jurisdiction

General immunity from jurisdiction

1.—(1) A State is immune from the jurisdiction of the courts of the United Kingdom except as provided in the following provisions of this Part of this Act.

(2) A court shall give effect to the immunity conferred by this section even though the State does not appear in the proceedings in question.

Submission to jurisdiction

2.—(1) A State is not immune as respects proceedings in respect of which it has submitted to the jurisdiction of the courts of the United Kingdom.

(2) A State may submit after the dispute giving rise to the proceedings has arisen or by a prior written agreement; but a provision in any agreement that it is to be governed by the law of the United Kingdom is not to be regarded as a submission.

(3) A State is deemed to have submitted—

(a) if it has instituted the proceedings; or
(b) subject to subsections (4) and (5) below, if it has intervened or taken any step in the proceedings.

(4) Subsection 3(b) above does not apply to intervention or any step taken for the purpose only of—

(a) claiming immunity; or
(b) asserting an interest in property in circumstances such that the State would have been entitled to immunity if the proceedings had been brought against it.

(5) Subsection 3(b) above does not apply to any step taken by the State in ignorance of facts entitling it to immunity if those facts could not reasonably have been ascertained and immunity is claimed as soon as reasonably practicable.

(6) A submission in respect of any proceedings extends to any appeal but not to any counter-claim unless it arises out of the same legal relationship or facts as the claim.

(7) The head of a State's diplomatic mission in the United Kingdom, or the person for the time being performing his functions, shall be deemed to have authority to submit on behalf of the State in respect of any proceedings; and any person who has entered into a contract on behalf of and with the authority of a State shall be deemed to have authority to submit on its behalf in respect of proceedings arising out of the contract.

Commercial transactions and contracts to be performed in the United Kingdom

3.—(1) A State is not immune as respects proceedings relating to—

(a) a commercial transaction entered into by the State; or

(b) an obligation of the State which by virtue of a contract (whether a commercial transaction or not) falls to be performed wholly or partly in the United Kingdom.

(2) This section does not apply if the parties to the dispute are States or have otherwise agreed in writing; and subsection (1)(b) above does not apply if the contract (not being a commercial transaction) was made in the territory of the State concerned and the obligation in question is governed by its administrative law.

(3) In this section "commercial transaction" means—

(a) any contract for the supply of goods or services;

(b) any loan or other transaction for the provision of finance and any guarantee or indemnity in respect of any such transaction or of any other financial obligation; and

(c) any other transaction or activity (whether of a commercial, industrial, financial, professional or other similar character) into which a State enters or in which it engages otherwise than in the exercise of sovereign authority;

but neither paragraph of subsection (1) above applies to a contract of employment between a State and an individual.

Arbitrations

9.—(1) Where a State has agreed in writing to submit a dispute which has arisen, or may arise, to arbitration, the State is not immune as respects proceedings in the courts of the United Kingdom which relate to the arbitration.

(2) This section has effect subject to any contrary provision in the arbitration agreement and does not apply to any arbitration agreement between States.

F(6) LIMITATION ACT 1980

Application of Act and other limitation enactments to arbitrations

34.—(1) This Act and any other limitation enactment shall apply to arbitrations as they apply to actions in the High Court.

(2) Notwithstanding any term in an arbitration agreement to the effect that no cause of action shall accrue in respect of any matter required by the agreement to be referred until an award is made under the agreement, the cause of action shall, for the purposes of this Act and any other limitation enactment (whether in their application to arbitrations or to other proceedings), be deemed to have accrued in respect of any such matter at the time when it would have accrued but for that term in the agreement.

(3) For the purposes of this Act and of any other limitation enactment an arbitration shall be treated as being commenced—

(a) when one party to the arbitration serves on the other party or parties a notice requiring him or them to appoint an arbitrator or to agree to the appointment of an arbitrator; or

(b) where the arbitration agreement provides that the reference shall be to a person named or designated in the agreement, when one party to the arbitration serves on the other party or parties a notice requiring him or them to submit the dispute to the person so named or designated.

(4) Any such notice may be served either—

(a) by delivering it to the person on whom it is to be served; or

(b) by leaving it at the usual or last-known place of abode in England and Wales of that person; or

(c) by sending it by post in a registered letter addressed to that person at his usual or last-known place of abode in England and Wales:

as well as in any other manner provided in the arbitration agreement.

(5) Where the High Court—

(a) orders that an award be set aside; or

(b) orders, after the commencement of an arbitration, that the arbitration agreement shall cease to have effect with respect to the dispute referred;

the court may further order that the period between the commencement of the arbitration and the date of the order of the court shall be excluded in computing the time prescribed by this Act or by any other limitation enactment for the commencement of proceedings (including arbitration) with respect to the dispute referred.

(6) This section shall apply to an arbitration under an Act of Parliament as well as to an arbitration pursuant to an arbitration agreement.

Subsections (3) and (4) above shall have effect, in relation to an arbitration under an Act, as if for the references to the arbitration agreement there were substituted references to such of the provisions of the Act or of any order scheme, rules, regulations or byelaws made under the Act as relate to the arbitration.

(7) In this section—

(a) "arbitration", "arbitration agreement" and "award" have the same meanings as in Part I of the Arbitration Act 1950; and

(b) references to any other limitation enactment are references to any other enactment relating to the limitation of actions, whether passed before or after the passing of this Act.

F(7) SUPREME COURT ACT 1981

Restrictions on appeals to Court of Appeal

18.—(1) No appeal shall lie to the Court of Appeal— . . .

(g) except as provided by the Arbitration Act 1979, from any decision of the High Court—

(i) on an appeal under section 1 of that Act on a question of law arising out of an arbitration award; or

(ii) under section 2 of that Act on a question of law arising in the course of the reference; . . .

F(8) CIVIL JURISDICTION AND JUDGMENTS ACT 1982

Interim relief in England and Wales and Northern Ireland in the absence of substantive proceedings

25.—(1) The High Court in England and Wales or Northern Ireland shall have power to grant interim relief where—

(a) proceedings have been or are to be commenced in a Contracting State other than the United Kingdom or in a part of the United Kingdom other than that in which the High Court in question exercises jurisdiction; and

(b) they are or will be proceedings whose subject-matter is within the scope of the 1968 Convention as determined by Article 1 (whether or not the Convention has effect in relation to the proceedings).

(2) On an application for any interim relief under subsection (1) the court may refuse to grant that relief if, in the opinion of the court, the fact that the court has no jurisdiction apart from this section in relation to the subject-matter of the proceedings in question makes it inexpedient for the court to grant it.

(3) Her Majesty may by Order in Council extend the power to grant interim relief conferred by subsection (1) so as to make it exercisable in relation to proceedings of any of the following descriptions, namely—

(a) proceedings commenced or to be commenced otherwise than in a Contracting State;

(b) proceedings whose subject-matter is not within the scope of the 1968 Convention as determined by Article 1;

(c) arbitration proceedings.

(4) An Order in Council under subsection (3)—

(a) may confer power to grant only specified descriptions of interim relief;

(b) may make different provision for different classes of proceedings, for proceedings pending in different countries or courts outside the United Kingdom or in different parts of the United Kingdom, and for other different circumstances; and

(c) may impose conditions or restrictions on the exercise of any power conferred by the Order.

(5) An Order in Council under subsection (3) which confers power to grant interim relief in relation to arbitration proceedings may provide for the repeal of any provision of section 12(6) of the Arbitration Act 1950 or section 21(1) of the Arbitration Act (Northern Ireland) 1937 to the extent that it is superseded by the provisions of the Order.

(6) Any Order in Council under subsection (3) shall be subject to annulment in pursuance of a resolution of either House of Parliament.

(7) In this section "interim relief", in relation to the High Court in England and Wales or Northern Ireland, means interim relief of any kind which that court has power to grant in proceedings relating to matters within its jurisdiction, other than—

(a) a warrant for the arrest of property; or

(b) provision for obtaining evidence.

Security in Admiralty proceedings in England and Wales or Northern Ireland in case of stay, &c

26.—(1) Where in England and Wales or Northern Ireland a court stays or dismisses Admiralty proceedings on the ground that the dispute in question should be submitted to arbitration or to the determination of the courts of another part of the United Kingdom or of an overseas country, the court may if in those proceedings property has been arrested or bail or other security has been given to prevent or obtain release from arrest—

(a) order that the property arrested be retained as security for the satisfaction of any award or judgment which—

(i) is given in respect of the dispute in the arbitration or legal proceedings in favour of which those proceedings are stayed or dismissed; and

(ii) is enforceable in England and Wales or, as the case may be, in Northern Ireland; or

(b) order that the stay or dismissal of those proceedings be conditional on the provision of equivalent security for the satisfaction of any such award or judgment.

(2) Where a court makes an order under subsection (1), it may attach such conditions to the order as it thinks fit, in particular conditions with respect to the institution or prosecution of the relevant arbitration or legal proceedings.

(3) Subject to any provisions made by rules of court and to any necessary modifications, the same law and practice shall apply in relation to property retained in pursuance of an order made by a court under subsection (1) as would apply if it were held for the purposes of proceedings in that court.

Overseas judgments given in breach of agreement for settlement of disputes

32.—(1) Subject to the following provisions of this section, a judgment given by a court of an overseas country in any proceedings shall not be recognised or enforced by the United Kingdom if—

(a) the bringing of those proceedings in that court was contrary to an agreement under which the dispute in question was to be settled otherwise than by proceedings in the courts of that country; and

(b) those proceedings were not brought in that court by, or with the agreement of, the person against whom the judgment was given; and

(c) that person did not counterclaim in the proceedings or otherwise submit to the jurisdiction of that court.

(2) Subsection (1) does not apply where the agreement referred to in paragraph (a) of that subsection was illegal, void or unenforceable or was incapable of being performed for reasons not attributable to the fault of the party bringing the proceedings in which the judgment was given.

(3) In determining whether a judgment given by a court of an overseas country should be recognised or enforced in the United Kingdom, a court in the United Kingdom shall not be bound by any decision of the overseas court relating to any of the matters mentioned in subsection (1) or (2).

(4) Nothing in subsection (1) shall affect the recognition or enforcement in the United Kingdom of—

(a) a judgment which is required to be recognised or enforced there under the 1968 Convention;

(b) a judgment to which Part I of the Foreign Judgments (Reciprocal Enforcement) Act 1933 applies by virtue of section 4 of the Carriage of Goods by Road Act 1965, section 17(4) of the Nuclear Installations Act 1965, section 13(3) of the Merchant Shipping (Oil Pollution) Act 1971, section 5 of the Carriage by Railway Act 1972, section 5 of the Carriage of Passengers by Road Act 1974 or section 6(4) of the Merchant Shipping Act 1974.

Note: This section came into force on 24 August 1982. Also note the provision of paragraph 8(1) of Part II of Schedule 13 to the same Act:

"**Section 32 and associated repeal**
  8—(1) Section 32 shall not apply to any judgment—
  (a) which has been registered under Part II of the Administration of Justice Act 1920, Part I of the Foreign Judgments (Reciprocal Enforcement) Act 1933 or Part I of the Maintenance Orders (Reciprocal Enforcement) Act 1972 before the time when that section comes into force; or
  (b) in respect of which proceedings at common law for its enforcement have been finally determined before that time."

Certain steps not to amount to submission to jurisdiction of overseas court

33.—(1) For the purposes of determining whether a judgment given by a court of an overseas country should be recognised or enforced in England and Wales or Northern Ireland, the person against whom the judgment was given shall not be treated as having submitted to the jurisdiction of the court by reason only of the fact that he appeared (conditionally or otherwise) in the proceedings for all or any one or more of the following purposes, namely—

(a) to contest the jurisdiction of the court;

(b) to ask the court to dismiss or stay the proceedings on the ground that the dispute in question should be submitted to arbitration or to the determination of the courts of another country;

(c) to protect, or obtain the release of, property seized or threatened with seizure in the proceedings.

(2) Nothing in this section shall affect the recognition or enforcement in England and Wales or Northern Ireland of a judgment which is required to be recognised or enforced there under the 1968 Convention.

Note: This section came into force on 24 August 1982. Also note the provision of paragraph 9(1) of Part II of Schedule 13 to the same Act:

"Section 33 and associated repeal

9—(1) Section 33 shall not apply to any judgment—

(a) which has been registered under Part II of the Administration of Justice Act 1920, or Part I of the Foreign Judgments (Reciprocal Enforcement) Act 1933 before the time when that section comes into force; or

(b) in respect of which proceedings at common law for its enforcement have been finally determined before that time."

F(9) COURTS AND LEGAL SERVICES ACT 1990

Note: Part V of this Act prospectively amends ss. 10, 11, prospectively repeals s. 12(6)(b) and inserts a new s. 13A into the Arbitration Act 1950. Part V also prospectively inserts a new s. 43A into the Supreme Court Act 1981.

PART V. ARBITRATION

Arbitration by official referee

99. For section 11 of the Arbitration Act 1950 (reference to official referee) there shall be substituted—

"Power of official referee to take arbitrations

11.—(1) An official referee may, if in all the circumstances he thinks fit, accept appointment as sole arbitrator, or as umpire, by or by virtue of an arbitration agreement.

(2) An official referee shall not accept appointment as arbitrator or umpire unless the Lord Chief Justice has informed him that, having regard to the state of official referees' business, he can be made available to do so.

(3) The fees payable for the services of an official referee as arbitrator or umpire shall be taken in the High Court.

(4) Schedule 3 to the Administration of Justice Act 1970 (which modifies this Act in relation to arbitration by judges, in particular by substituting the Court of Appeal for the High Court in provisions whereby arbitrators and umpires, their proceedings and awards are subject to control and review by the court) shall have effect in relation to official referees appointed as arbitrators or umpires as it has effect in relation to judge-arbitrators and judge-umpires (within the meaning of that Schedule).

(5) Any jurisdiction which is exercisable by the High Court in relation to arbitrators and

umpires otherwise than under this Act shall, in relation to an official referee appointed as arbitrator or umpire, be exercisable instead by the Court of Appeal.

(6) In this section 'official referee' means any person nominated under section 68(1)(a) of the Supreme Court Act 1981 to deal with official referees' business.

(7) Rules of the Supreme Court may make provision for—

(a) cases in which it is necessary to allocate references made under or by virtue of arbitration agreements to official referees;

(b) the transfer of references from one official referee to another."

Specific powers of arbitrator exercisable by High Court

100. After section 43 of the Supreme Court Act 1981 there shall be inserted the following section—

"Specific powers of arbitrator exercisable by High Court

43A. In any cause or matter proceeding in the High Court in connection with any contract incorporating an arbitration agreement which confers specific powers upon the arbitrator, the High Court may, if all parties to the agreement agree, exercise any such powers."

Power of parties in certain cases to fill vacancy

101.—(1) In section 10 of the Arbitration Act 1950 (power of court in certain cases to appoint an arbitrator or umpire), the following shall be substituted for subsection (3)—

"(3) In any case where—

(a) an arbitration agreement provides that the reference shall be to three arbitrators, one to be appointed by each party and the third to be appointed by the two appointed by the parties or in some other manner specified in the agreement; and

(b) one of the parties ('the party in default') refuses to appoint an arbitrator or does not do so within the time specified in the agreement or, if no time is specified, within a reasonable time,

the other party to the agreement, having appointed his arbitrator, may serve the party in default with a written notice to appoint an arbitrator.

(3A) A notice under subsection (3) must indicate whether it is served for the purposes of subsection (3B) or for the purposes of subsection (3C).

(3B) Where a notice is served for the purposes of this subsection, then unless a contrary intention is expressed in the agreement, if the required appointment is not made within seven clear days after the service of the notice—

(a) the party who gave the notice may appoint his arbitrator to act as sole arbitrator in the reference; and

(b) his award shall be binding on both parties as if he had been appointed by consent.

(3C) Where a notice is served for the purposes of this subsection, then, if the required appointment is not made within seven clear days after the service of the notice, the High Court or a judge thereof may, on the application of the party who gave the notice, appoint an arbitrator on behalf of the party in default who shall have the like powers to act in the reference and make an award (and, if the case so requires, the like duty in relation to the appointment of a third arbitrator) as if he had been appointed in accordance with the terms of the agreement.

(3D) The High Court or a judge thereof may set aside any appointment made by virtue of subsection (3B)."

(2) Section 10 of the Act of 1950 shall continue to apply in relation to any arbitration agreement entered into before the commencement of this section as if this section had not been enacted.

(3) Subsection (2) does not apply if a contrary intention is expressed in the arbitration agreement, whether or not as the result of a variation made after the commencement of this section.

Want of prosecution

102. After section 13 of the Arbitration Act 1950 (time for making an award) there shall be inserted—

> **"Want of prosecution**
> **13A.**—(1) Unless a contrary intention is expressed in the arbitration agreement, the arbitrator or umpire shall have power to make an award dismissing any claim in a dispute referred to him if it appears to him that the conditions mentioned in subsection (2) are satisfied.
> (2) The conditions are—
>> (a) that there has been inordinate and inexcusable delay on the part of the claimant in pursuing the claim; and
>> (b) that the delay—
>>> (i) will give rise to a substantial risk that it is not possible to have a fair resolution of the issues in that claim; or
>>> (ii) has caused, or is likely to cause or to have caused, serious prejudice to the respondent.
> (3) For the purpose of keeping the provision made by this section and the corresponding provision which applies in relation to proceedings in the High Court in step, the Secretary of State may by order made by statutory instrument amend subsection (2) above.
> (4) Before making any such order the Secretary of State shall consult the Lord Chancellor and such other persons as he considers appropriate.
> (5) No such order shall be made unless a draft of the order has been laid before, and approved by resolution of, each House of Parliament."

Repeal of High Court's power to order discovery etc.

103. Section 12(6)(b) of the Arbitration Act 1950 (power of High Court to order discovery of documents and interrogatories) shall cease to have effect.

RULES OF THE SUPREME COURT 1965 (AS AMENDED)

G(1) ORDER 73 (ARBITRATION PROCEEDINGS)

Arbitration proceedings not to be assigned to the Chancery Division (O. 73, r. 1)

1. [*Revoked.*]

Matters for a judge in court (O. 73, r. 2)

2.—(1) Every application to the Court—

(a) to remit an award under section 22 of the Arbitration Act 1950, or
(b) to remove an arbitrator or umpire under section 23(1) of that Act, or
(c) to set aside an award under section 23(2) thereof, or
(d) [*Revoked.*]
(e) to determine, under section 2(1) of that Act, any question of law arising in the course of a reference,

must be made by originating motion to a single judge in court.

(2) Any appeal to the High Court under section 1(2) of the Arbitration Act 1979 shall be made by originating motion to a single judge in court.

(3) An application for a declaration that an award made by an arbitrator or umpire is not binding on a party to the award on the ground that it was made without jurisdiction may be made by originating motion to a single judge in court, but the foregoing provision shall not be taken as affecting the judge's power to refuse to make such a declaration in proceedings begun by motion.

Matters for judge in chambers or master (O. 73, r. 3)

3.—(1) Subject to the foregoing provisions of this Order and the provisions of this rule, the jurisdiction of the High Court under the Arbitration Act 1950 and the jurisdiction of the High Court under the Arbitration Act 1975 and the Arbitration Act 1979 may be exercised by a judge in chambers, a master or the Admiralty Registrar.

(2) Any application

(a) for leave to appeal under section 1(2) of the Arbitration Act 1979, or
(b) under section 1(5) of that Act (including any application for leave), or
(c) under section 5 of that Act,

shall be made to a judge in chambers.

(3) Any application to which this rule applies shall, where an action is pending, be made by summons in the action, and in any other case by an originating summons which shall be in Form No. 10 in Appendix A.

(4) Where an application is made under section 1(5) of the Arbitration Act 1979 (including any application for leave), the summons must be served on the arbitrator or umpire and on any other party to the reference.

Applications in district registries (O. 73, r. 4)

4. An application under section 12(4) of the Arbitration Act 1950 for an order that a writ of subpoena ad testificandum or of subpoena duces tecum shall issue to compel the attendance before an arbitrator or umpire of a witness may, if the attendance of the witness is required within the district of any district registry, be made at that registry, instead of at the Admiralty and Commercial Registry, at the option of the applicant.

Time-limits and other special provisions as to appeals and application under the Arbitration Acts (O. 73, r. 5)

5.—(1) An application to the Court—

(a) to remit an award under section 22 of the Arbitration Act 1950, or
(b) set aside an award under section 23(2) of that Act or otherwise, or
(c) to direct an arbitrator or umpire to state the reasons for an award under section 1(5) of the Arbitration Act 1979,

must be made, and the summons or notice must be served, within 21 days after the award has been made and published to the parties.

(2) In the case of an appeal to the Court under section 1(2) of the Arbitration Act 1979, the notice must be served, and the appeal entered, within 21 days after the award has been made and published to the parties:

Provided that, where reasons material to the appeal are given on a date subsequent to the publication of the award, the period of 21 days shall run from the date on which the reasons are given.

(3) An application, under section 2(1) of the Arbitration Act 1979, to determine any question of law arising in the course of a reference, must be made and notice thereof served within 14 days after the arbitrator or umpire has consented to the application being made, or the other parties have so consented.

(4) For the purpose of paragraph (2) the consent must be given in writing.

(5) In the case of every appeal or application to which this rule applies, the notice of originating motion, the originating summons or the summons, as the case may be, must state the grounds of the appeal or application and, where the appeal or application is founded on evidence by affidavit, or is made with the consent of the arbitrator or umpire or of the other parties, a copy of every affidavit intended to be used, or, as the case may be, of every consent given in writing, must be served with that notice.

(6) Without prejudice to paragraph (5), in an appeal under section 1(2) of the Arbitration Act 1979 the statement of the grounds of the appeal shall specify the relevant parts of the award and reasons, and a copy of the award and reasons, or the relevant parts thereof, shall be lodged with the court and served with the notice of originating motion.

(7) Without prejudice to paragraph (5), in an application for leave to appeal under section 1(2) of the Arbitration Act 1979, any affidavit verifying the facts in support of a contention that the question of law concerns a term of a contract or an event which is not a one-off term or event must be lodged with the court and served with the notice of originating motion.

(8) Any affidavit in reply to an affidavit under paragraph (7) shall be lodged with the court and served on the applicant not less than two clear days before the hearing of the application.

(9) A respondent to an application for leave to appeal under section 1(2) of the Arbitration Act 1979 who desires to contend that the award should be upheld on grounds not expressed or not fully expressed in the award or reasons shall not less than two clear days before the hearing of the application lodge with the court and serve on the applicant a notice specifying the grounds of his contention.

Applications and appeals to be heard by Commercial Judges (O. 73, r. 6)

6.—(1) Any matter which is required, by rule 2 or 3, to be heard by a judge, shall be heard by a Commercial Judge, unless any such judge otherwise directs.

(2) Nothing in the foregoing paragraph shall be construed as preventing the powers of a Commercial Judge from being exercised by any judge of the High Court.

Service out of the jurisdiction of summons, notice, etc. (O. 73, r. 7)

7.—(1) Subject to paragraph (1A) service out of the jurisdiction of—

(a) any originating summons or notice of originating motion under the Arbitration Act 1950 or the Arbitration Act 1979, or

(b) any order made on such a summons or motion as aforesaid,

is permissible with the leave of the Court provided that the arbitration to which the summons, motion or order related is governed by English law or has been, is being, or is to be held, within the jurisdiction.

(1A) Service out of the jurisdiction of an originating summons for leave to enforce an award is permissible with the leave of the Court whether or not the arbitration is governed by English law.

(2) An application for the grant of leave under this rule must be supported by an affidavit stating the grounds on which the application is made and showing in what place or country the person to be served is, or probably may be found; and no such leave shall be granted unless it shall be made sufficiently to appear to the Court that the case is a proper one for service out of the jurisdiction under this rule.

(3) Order 11, rules 5, 6 and 8, shall apply in relation to any such summons, notice or order as is referred to in paragraph (1) as they apply in relation to notice of a writ.

Registration in High Court of foreign awards (O. 73, r. 8)

8. Where an award is made in proceedings on an arbitration in any part of Her Majesty's dominions or other territory to which Part I of the Foreign Judgments (Reciprocal Enforcement) Act 1933 extends, being a part to which Part II of the Administration of Justice Act 1920 extended immediately before the said Part I was extended thereto, then, if the award has, in pursuance of the law in force in the place where it was made, become enforceable in the same manner as a judgment given by a court in that place, Order 71 shall apply in relation to the award as it applies in relation to a judgment given by that court, subject, however, to the following modifications:—

(a) for references to the country of the original court there shall be substituted references to the place where the award was made; and

(b) the affidavit required by rule 3 of the said Order must state (in addition to the other matters required by that rule) that to the best of the information or belief of the deponent the award has, in pursuance of the law in force in the place where it was made, become enforceable in the same manner as a judgment given by a court in that place.

Registration of awards under Arbitration (International Investment Disputes) Act 1966 (O. 73, r. 9)

9.—(1) In this rule and in any provision of these rules as applied by this rule—

"the Act of 1966" means the Arbitration (International Investment Disputes) Act 1966;

"award" means an award rendered pursuant to the Convention;

"the Convention" means the Convention referred to in section 1(1) of the Act of 1966;

"judgment creditor" and "judgment debtor" means respectively the person seeking recognition or enforcement of an award and the other party to the award.

(2) Subject to the provisions of this rule, the following provisions of Order 71, namely, rules 1, 3(1) (except sub-paragraphs (c)(iv) and (d) thereof) 7 (except paragraph (3)(c) and (d) thereof), 8 and 10(3), shall apply with the necessary modifications in relation to an award as they apply in relation to a judgment to which Part II of the Foreign Judgments (Reciprocal Enforcement) Act 1933 applies.

(3) An application to have an award registered in the High Court under section 1 of the Act of 1966 shall be made by originating summons which shall be in Form No. 10 in Appendix A.

(4) The affidavit required by Order 71, rule 3, in support of an application for registration shall—

(a) in lieu of exhibiting the judgment or a copy thereof, exhibit a copy of the award certified pursuant to the Convention, and

(b) in addition to stating the matters mentioned in paragraph 3(1)(c)(i) and (ii) of the said rule 3, state whether at the date of the application the enforcement of the award has been stayed (provisionally or otherwise) pursuant to the Convention and whether any, and if so what, application has been made pursuant to the Convention which, if granted, might result in a stay of the enforcement of the award.

(5) There shall be kept in the Central Office under the direction of the senior master a register of the awards ordered to be registered under the Act of 1966 and particulars shall be entered in the register of any execution issued on such an award.

(6) Where it appears to the court on granting leave to register an award or on an application made by the judgment debtor after an award has been registered—

(a) that the enforcement of the award has been stayed (whether provisionally or otherwise) pursuant to the Convention, or

(b) that an application has been made pursuant to the Convention which, if granted, might result in a stay of the enforcement of the award,

the court shall, or, in the case referred to in sub-paragraph (b), may, stay execution of the award for such time as it considers appropriate in the circumstances.

(7) An application by the judgment debtor under paragraph (6) shall be made by summons and supported by affidavit.

Enforcement of arbitration awards (O. 73, r. 10)

10.—(1) An application for leave under section 26 of the Arbitration Act 1950 or under section 3(1)(a) of the Arbitration Act 1975 to enforce an award on an arbitration agreement in the same manner as a judgment or order may be made ex parte but the Court hearing the application may direct a summons to be issued.

(2) If the Court directs a summons to be issued, the summons shall be an originating summons which shall be in Form No. 10 in Appendix A.

(3) An application for leave must be supported by affidavit—

(a) exhibiting
   (i) where the application is under section 26 of the Arbitration Act 1950, the arbitration agreement and the original award or, in either case, a copy thereof;
   (ii) where the application is under section 3(1)(a) of the Arbitration Act 1975, the documents required to be produced by section 4 of that Act,

(b) stating the name and the usual or last known place of abode or business of the applicant (hereinafter referred to as "the creditor") and the person against whom it is sought to enforce the award (hereinafter referred to as "the debtor") respectively,

(c) as the case may require, either that the award has not been complied with or the extent to which it has not been complied with at the date of the application.

(4) An order giving leave must be drawn up by or on behalf of the creditor and must be served on the debtor by delivering a copy to him personally or by sending a copy to him at his usual or last known place of abode or business or in such other manner as the Court may direct.

(5) Service of the order out of the jurisdiction is permissible without leave, and Order 11, rules 5, 6 and 8, shall apply in relation to such an order as they apply in relation to a writ.

(6) Within 14 days after service of the order or, if the order is to be served out of the jurisdiction, within such other period as the Court may fix, the debtor may apply to set aside the order, and the award shall not be enforced until after the expiration of that period or, if the debtor applies within that period to set aside the order, until after the application is finally disposed of.

(7) The copy of that order served on the debtor shall state the effect of paragraph (6).

(8) In relation to a body corporate this rule shall have effect as if for any reference to the place of abode or business of the creditor or the debtor there were substituted a reference to the registered or principal address of the body corporate; so, however, that nothing in this rule shall

affect any enactment which provides for the manner in which a document may be served on a body corporate.

G(2) ORDER 59, RULES 1A AND 7

1A. For all purposes connected with appeals to the Court of Appeal, a judgment or order shall be treated as final or interlocutory in accordance with the following provisions of this rule.

. . .

7. Notwithstanding anything in paragraph (3)—

    (a) orders made on an appeal to the High Court under section 1(2) of the Arbitration Act 1979 shall be treated as final orders;

    (b) all other orders made in connection with or arising out of an arbitration or arbitral award shall be treated as interlocutory orders; without prejudice to the generality of the foregoing, such orders shall include—

        (i) orders made in connection with the appointment or removal of an arbitrator or umpire;

        (ii) orders made on or in connection with applications for an extension of time for commencing arbitration proceedings;

        (iii) orders setting aside an arbitral award or remitting the matter to an arbitrator or umpire (other than orders setting aside the award or remitting the matter made on an appeal in pursuance of the said section 1(2)); and

        (iv) orders made on or in connection with applications for leave to enforce an award.

PRACTICE DIRECTIONS AND STATEMENTS

H(1) PRACTICE DIRECTION BY MR JUSTICE KERR AS TO HEARINGS IN SEPTEMBER (MARCH 1977)

As part of the present scheme to provide an extended service to the public during the month of September one of the judges of the Commercial Court will be available to hear commercial actions and summonses covered by R.S.C., O.72 throughout September 1977. Applications for hearings in September will be dealt with in the same manner as fixtures during term time. As at present, dates for actions and Special Cases will be fixed by the judge in charge of the Commercial List (on a "not before" basis) and dates for summonses by his clerk. The scheme will apply equally to proceedings issued in the Commercial Court and to proceedings transferred to the court. Summonses will generally be heard on Tuesdays and Fridays, but there will be flexibility. To obtain a date for a hearing in September it will not be necessary to establish that the matter is "Long Vacation Business" within R.S.C., O.64, r.4, but the judge in charge of the list will exercise a discretion whether or not to accept fixtures for September. In exercising this discretion preference will be given to urgent matters (including in particular commercial matters which would otherwise come before one of the vacation judges), Special Cases and short cases. In cases of urgency and if time permits, the scheme will also apply to the judge sitting as sole arbitrator or umpire in short arbitrations pursuant to s.4 of the Administration of Justice Act 1970.

Applications for dates for hearings in September can in principle be made at any time from now. In practice, however, September fixtures are unlikely to be granted before Easter, but then increasingly as the summer progresses. The reason is to maintain flexibility and to keep dates available for urgent matters nearer the time. But an exception will be made for Special and Consultative Cases stated by arbitration tribunals which are only expected to take one to two days and which cannot be fitted in before the end of July. These are ready for trial, rarely settle, and should in principle be dealt with as soon as possible.

H(2) DIRECTIONS FOR LONDON GIVEN BY LORD LANE C.J. ON 31 JULY 1981

All proceedings in the Queen's Bench Division for hearing in London shall be set down in the appropriate list and administered as follows:

1. The Crown Office List

(a) Proceedings required to be heard by or applications required to be made to a Divisional Court of the Queen's Bench Division;

(b) Proceedings pursuant to R.S.C., O.53, O.54 and O.56 which may be heard by a single Judge;

(c) Actions directed to be set down in the Crown Office List;

(d) Proceedings pursuant to R.S.C., O.55, O.94 and O.111;

(e) Save as is otherwise expressly provided, any other special case or case stated under any statute or order.

2. Administrative Provisions in respect of the Crown Office List

Without prejudice to any party's right to apply for directions to a Judge for the time being hearing matters in the Crown Office List and the right of the Master of the Crown Office to refer such a matter to a Judge, the Crown Office List shall be administered by the Crown Office under the direction of the Master of the Crown Office.

3. The Jury List

Actions ordered to be tried by a Judge and jury.

4. The Non-Jury List

(a) Actions other than jury actions or short causes set down under the provisions of R.S.C., O.34, r.3;
(b) Preliminary questions or issues ordered to be tried under R.S.C., O.33, rr.3 and 4(2);
(c) Motions to commit other than those required to be heard by a Divisional Court of the Queen's Bench Division;
(d) Motions for judgment.

5. The Short Cause List

Actions ordered to be tried by a Judge alone where the time estimated for the trial does not exceed four hours.

12. The Commercial List

(a) Actions for trial in the Commercial Court.
(b) Any matter in paragraph 4 hereof which appertains to a matter in the Commercial Court.

13. The Arbitration Case List

Proceedings under R.S.C., O.73, r.2

14. Administrative Provisions—Commercial and Arbitration Case Lists

Actions or other proceedings in the Commercial Court will be dealt with as follows:

(a) Any party to an action to be tried in the Commercial Court may at any stage in the proceedings apply to the Commercial Judge by summons to fix a date for the trial or to vary or vacate such a date.
(b) An order made by the Court fixing the date of hearing will normally also provide for a date by which the cause must be set down for trial in the Commercial List.
(c) When a party to an action who has set it down for trial notifies the other parties to the action that he has done so, he should also inform the Commercial Court Listing Officer to the same effect.
(d) If any action which has been set down for trial in the Commercial Court is settled or withdrawn, or if the estimate of length of trial is revised, it shall be the duty of all parties to notify the Court of the fact without delay.
(e) (i) Any proceeding in the Arbitration Case List shall in the first instance be referred to the Judge in charge of the Commercial List for his consideration as to its suitability for retention in that list.
   (ii) Where the Judge directs that such a matter shall be heard by a Commercial Judge any party may thereafter apply to fix a date for trial.

H(3) PRACTICE DIRECTION BY MR JUSTICE PARKER GIVEN ON 9 NOVEMBER 1981

Statement on revised practice

As is stated in the Annual Practice the Commercial Court has always sought to adapt its procedure to the continually changing needs of the commercial community and there has for some time existed, as a means of communication between the Court and that community, the Commercial Court Committee.

One of the principal functions of the Court has been and still is to deal swiftly with urgent matters. This it has done by bringing on for trial swiftly, cases in which for one reason or another, justice requires such a course to be taken, and by disposing as quickly as possible of other urgent matters such as applications for summary judgment, for orders continuing or discharging interlocutory injunctions for interlocutory orders of various kinds, for orders to arbitrators to state a special case under the Arbitration Act, 1950, or, now, motions for leave to appeal under the Arbitration Act, 1979, and so on.

Recently the volume of such urgent matters requiring early disposal has very considerably increased. In 1978 for example, 1180 summonses occupying 115 judge days were heard while in the year to July, 1981, the comparative figures were 2106 summonses and 277 judge days.

The result has been that return dates for such urgent matters have had to be put further and further ahead. In order that earlier return dates may be given for such matters which are likely to occupy less than one day, it has been decided, after discussion in the Commercial Court Committee to introduce, initially for an experimental period only, a new system.

As from Friday Nov. 20 all five Commercial Judges will normally sit on Fridays solely for the purpose of dealing with summonses and other short but urgent matters, and Tuesdays will cease to be summons days.

I say normally for it is recognized:

(1) that such a practice might involve the parties to a case part heard on a Thursday in unjustifiable extra expense if the case were adjourned to Monday in order to enable the Judge to deal with short matters on Friday.

(2) that there may be short matters which for one reason or another cannot be heard on a Friday and must be heard on a Tuesday or some other day.

(3) that if all Judges are taking short matters on Fridays there may be insurmountable difficulties for both sides of the profession in having more than one matter in which they are involved coming on the same day.

The new system will therefore be operated on a flexible basis so as to obviate, or at least to reduce to a minimum, the foregoing difficulties and any others which may be found to arise when it is in operation.

In order that the new system can operate efficiently two essential requirements must be fulfilled. They are:

(1) Parties must notify the Commercial Court Office of any change in the estimated lengths of their summonses or other matters immediately such changes become known.

(2) Where Counsel are involved in more than one summons listed for a particular date, notification of that fact may be made to such office by Counsel's Clerks not later than 9.30 a.m. on the day prior to the return date.

In anticipation of the possible introduction of this system, the number of matters listed for Tuesdays has recently been kept down to a minimum but there are some which are still so listed. The parties involved should, if they possibly can, apply for the matter to be refixed for a Friday. This need not involve any delay.

The new system will make it possible for some at least of matters which are presently fixed for dates more than two months in the future to be refixed for earlier dates. Parties with such late return dates, who wish their matters to be heard earlier, should make application to Mr. Bird for earlier dates.

In conclusion I should stress two points:

(1) The purpose of the system is to accelerate urgent matters. Applications for leave to

appeal under the 1979 Act are normally regarded as being in this category. I should, however, mention that there are several hundred applications for leave to appeal or other matters arising out of arbitration awards which were issued more than a year ago but for which no return date has yet been sought. Such, and other, dormant applications, although coming within a category normally regarded as urgent, will, if hereafter proceeded with, not be regarded as urgent in the absence of some convincing argument for sudden urgency being shown. It may be that many of them are in fact dead. If they are it would be of the greatest assistance to the Court if that fact could be notified as soon as possible.

(2) It may be that the benefit to litigants which the new system is designed to produce will produce difficulties not presently envisaged.

It will be of the greatest assistance if the existence of, and any suggestions for dealing with, any such difficulties are promptly communicated to the Commercial Court Committee in accordance with the open invitation which appears at par. 72/8/3 of the Annual Practice.[1]

H(4) STATEMENT BY MR JUSTICE PARKER GIVEN ON 15 MARCH 1982

There has for some time been exhibited in the Commercial Court Office a notice stating that all documents relevant to a chambers application should be lodged by noon on the day before the hearing date and warning that a failure to comply may result in the application not being heard.

Despite this, there are very many cases in which, for no good reason, the documents are not lodged by the time indicated and in some cases documents are not handed in until the application is called on.

This places a severe and unnecessary burden on Mr Bird and his staff who have to spend time trying to chase up documents by telephone. It also leads to hearing times being unnecessarily prolonged because the Court has been unable to read the documents in advance.

With the steadily increasing numbers of applications and the concentration of applications into Friday's list it has become necessary for documents to be lodged two days instead of one day before the hearing and for cases in which there is a failure to comply with this requirement to be stood out at the expense of the party in default unless good cause for the failure is shown and the failure will not unduly prolong the hearing time for the application.

In addition, in order that the Court should have an early opportunity to consider whether a case is suitable for retention in the commercial list the main pleadings should always be lodged at the time of the first inter partes application in any action. Many cases are launched in the commercial list for no better reason than that one or other or both parties are banks, or shipping companies, or insurers, or commodity traders, or that the action is for breach of contract for sale of goods. If the issues in the case are not commercial issues at all but, for example a quality dispute in a sale of goods case, or a conversion or fraud, the resolution of which involves no commercial expertise, the case will normally be transferred to the Q.B. List.

Accordingly, the existing notice will be replaced as from 22nd March 1982 by the following notice[2]:

It is the responsibility of both parties to an application to the Commercial Judge-in-Chambers to lodge all documents relevant to the application in Room 198 [now Room 61] by noon two days before the date fixed for the hearing. Any affidavits already filed should be bespoken and the exhibits, if any, lodged. On the first occasion when any inter-partes application is made in an action the documents should always include the main pleadings and the parties should be prepared, if necessary, to justify the retention of the action in the Commercial List.

Failure to comply with this direction will normally result in the application not being heard on the date fixed at the expense of the party in default.

A copy of this notice should be attached to the copy application served on the parties.

1. Suggestions concerning the Commercial Court.
2. For the current format of the notice, see Chapter 7, para. 7.2.1.2.

Copies will be available in the office and it is the responsibility of the applicant to attach a copy to the summons served on the opposite party.

In order that this change may be as widely known as possible, Mr Bird will be sending copies of the new notice to those firms of solicitors who most frequently use the Court with a request that it be drawn to the attention of all concerned.

The co-operation which will enable the Court to deal with its business without unnecessary delays will, I hope, make it unnecessary to make frequent use of the sanction of standing cases out.

H(5) PRACTICE DIRECTION BY MR JUSTICE BINGHAM GIVEN ON 3 MAY 1985

Application for leave to appeal against arbitration awards

1. Every notice of motion by way of appeal against an arbitration award under s.1(2) of the Arbitration Act 1979 shall contain a succinct statement in numbered paragraphs of each ground upon which it is sought to contend that the arbitral tribunal erred in law. References shall be made to the paragraph or passage of the award and reasons where each alleged error is to be found. A copy of the award and reasons forming part of the award and any documents expressly incorporated in the award or such reasons shall accompany the notice of motion when the same is served and entered, unless the appeal arises from a minor part only of the award and reasons in which case the relevant extracts shall accompany the notice of motion.

2. Any respondent to such a motion by way of appeal who contends that the award should be upheld on grounds not or not fully expressed in the award and reasons should provide to the applicant and to the Court, not later than two clear days before the application for leave is listed for argument, a succinct statement of such grounds in numbered paragraphs, with reference where appropriate to any relevant paragraph or passage of the award and reasons.

3. Any statement provided under pars. 1 and 2 should contain specific reference to any authority relied on. A copy should be provided with the statement of any authority not contained in the *Law Reports*, the *Weekly Law Reports*, the *All England Law Reports*, *Lloyd's Law Reports* or the *English Reports*.

4. Where the applicant contends that any question of law arising out of an award concerns a term of contract or an event which is not a one-off clause or event, he shall serve on the respondent with his notice of motion and lodge with the Court an affidavit setting out the facts relied on in support of his contention. A respondent who challenges that contention shall provide to the applicant and to the Court, not later than two clear days before the application is listed for argument, an affidavit setting out the facts upon which he relies.

Submission of papers for Commercial Court summonses

Every summons issued for hearing in the Commercial Court has attached to it a note beginning in this way:

> It is the responsibility of both parties to an application to the Commercial Judge-in-Chambers to lodge all documents to the application in Room 198 [now Room 61] by noon two days before the date fixed for the hearing. Any affidavit already filed should be bespoken and the exhibits, if any, be lodged. On the first occasion when any *inter-partes* application is made in an action the documents should always include the main pleadings . . .
>
> Failure to comply with this direction will normally result in the application not being heard on the date fixed at the expense of the party in default.

The object of this direction is to enable the Clerk to the Commercial Court to prepare the papers for delivery to the Judge who will hear the summons, and to enable that Judge to read and assimilate the papers before the hearing so as to avoid unnecessary and time-consuming reading aloud.

Unhappily, this practice has been widely disregarded. It is not uncommon for the Clerk to the Commercial Court to find that no papers at all have been lodged at the appointed time, even though the parties expect and intend the summons to be effective. Even more commonly it turns out at the hearing that, although some documents have been lodged, others have not, and nothing has been done to bespeak significant affidavits or to provide copies with the Court papers. Much time is often wasted, and inconvenience caused, as a result.

The purpose of this statement is to make plain that in future compliance with this practice will be rigorously insisted upon. In particular I wish to emphasize.

(1) that the Clerk to the Commercial Court has been instructed not to list any summons for hearing if no papers have been lodged with him by the appointed time.

(2) that if it turns out at the hearing that documents have not been lodged which should have been lodged, the course which will ordinarily be followed will depend on which party is in default: if it is the plaintiff or applicant, the summons will ordinarily be adjourned at his expense; if it is the defendant or respondent, the summons may proceed but he will ordinarily be ordered to pay the costs.

It is to the advantage of all users of the Court that this practice should be scrupulously observed.

H(6) PRACTICE DIRECTION BY MR JUSTICE HIRST GIVEN ON 23 OCTOBER 1987

Last Term Staughton J. consulted the City of London Law Society and the London Common Law and Commercial Bar Association concerning proposals for limitation of time for interlocutory hearings, which form such an important part of the Commercial Court's work.

This was supported by the Solicitors, but the Bar expressed misgivings. After further consideration the Commercial Court Judges have decided to prescribe stricter control of time limits for a trial period of 12 months encompassing the Legal Year 1987 to 1988.

Progress will be monitored meantime and any representations will be carefully considered when it comes under review in the Summer of 1988.

The efficient working of the system depends on accurate estimates of the time needed for a summons. It is therefore incumbent upon counsel and solicitors to take special care in this respect. In future any summons which over-runs its estimate will probably be adjourned.

Subject only to the exception specified below, the Clerk to the Commercial Court will not accept estimates exceeding the following:

1. Summons to set aside etc.   4 hours
2. Order XIV   4 hours
3. Set aside judgment in default   2 hours
4. Set aside or vary injunction   2 hours
5. Amendments of pleadings   1 hour
6. Further discovery (including interrogatories)   1 hour
7. Further and Better Particulars $\frac{1}{2}$ hour
8. Security for cost $\frac{1}{2}$ hour

These are *maxima*, not guidelines. Proper estimates in each category will often be much shorter, and over-estimating is wasteful, not only of the Court time, but also of the opportunity of other litigants to get their summonses heard.

A longer time will only be allocated upon application in writing by Counsel to the Judge in charge of the Commercial List, or such other Judge as he may nominate, specifying the extra time required and the reasons why.

In all cases, whatever their duration, written outlines of submissions (which can be in note form), should be submitted by both parties in advance. In cases estimated for 2 hours or more, the additional documents specified in the Guide to Commercial Court Practice will also be required.

All estimates should be made on the assumption that the Judge will have read in advance the affidavits and all written submissions, but not the exhibits.

Although a departure from previous practice, this is only a further small step towards reducing the present unacceptable delays in the Commercial Court. However, it signifies a determination to continue to enhance our efficiency, though the scope for improvement, particularly in cutting waiting time for the longer trials, is limited by our present resources.

Other recent measures to improve efficiency are set out in the Guide, and particular attention is drawn to Section X and Annexe B, dealing with the requirements for the Summons for Directions. Their purpose is to focus the attention both of practitioners and of the Court at an early stage of the proceedings on steps designed to curtail the duration and expense of the trial especially through mutual exchanges in advance of information between the parties. This also tends to promote settlements. In future the Court will be unwilling to hear Summonses for Directions which do not comply with these requirements, and may also impose costs' penalties.

It is not always appreciated that this new regime requires not only the exchange of experts' reports, but also, in the normal run of case, the exchange of written statements of the oral evidence of intended witnesses of fact, subject of course to all proper objections, such as in fraud cases. With this innovation, made possible under the recent enactment of Order 38 Rule 2A, the Commercial Court, together with the Chancery Division and the Official Referees Court are breaking new ground in a procedure which should curtail the amount of oral evidence (particularly evidence-in-chief), and also reduce the number of witnesses who eventually need to be called.

Dated October 23, 1987.

H(7) PRACTICE DIRECTION GIVEN BY LORD LANE C.J. WITH THE CONCURRENCE OF THE ADMIRALTY JUDGE AND THE JUDGE IN CHARGE OF THE COMMERCIAL LIST ON 2 NOVEMBER 1987

1. The rules of the Supreme Court (Amendment) 1987 (S.I. 1987 No. 1423), the relevant provisions of which come into force on November 2 1987 provide for the creation of an Admiralty and Commercial Court Registry. This Direction gives details of the new administrative arrangements.

2. Administrative Structure

The new Registry will combine the Admiralty Registry and the Commercial Court Listing Office and, in addition, will take over all work on Commercial Court cases previously carried out in the Central Office. While all process will need to show whether the case is proceeding in the Admiralty Court or the Commercial Court, there will be a continuous run of numbers for all originating process, one cause book and a common court file and filing system.

3. The Court File

A court file will be maintained for each case. The documents relevant to a particular case will be kept on the file, including the originating process, acknowledgement of service, notices of change of solicitors, summonses, affidavits, pleadings and orders. The Admiralty Registry and, in some cases, the Judge may make their notes of any interlocutory matter on the file. The file will normally be kept in the Registry, but it will be sent to a Judge or the Registrar when required by him. It will be available in court on the trial of any action or interlocutory application.

4. Issue of Process

All originating process in the Admiralty Court and Commercial Court, that is writs, originating summonses and originating motions will be issued in the Registry. Fees will continue to be paid to the Supreme Court Accounts Office.

5. Filing of Documents

Documents in Commercial Court proceedings will not be accepted for filing in Room 81 after October 30 1987. All affidavits filed in Room 81 up to and including October 30 1987 will be retained there.

On the first interlocutory application made in any Commercial Court case on or after November 2 1987 a full set of such pleadings as have been served must be lodged in the Registry together with all affidavits in the proceedings previously filed in Room 81. These will be retained on the court file. Exhibits to affidavits will normally be returned to the parties.

6. Interlocutory Applications in Commercial Court Proceedings

There will be no change in the current procedure. Parties will continue to draw any order from the Judge's endorsement. The order should be presented to the Registry for issue and entry.

7. Interlocutory Applications in Admiralty Proceedings

Orders will be drawn by the parties and should be presented to the Registry for checking against the Registrar's or Judge's note and for issue and entry.

8. Orders, Decrees and Judgments in Admiralty and Commercial Proceedings

A certificate under Order 35 Rule 10 will be issued by the Court in appropriate cases and entered on the file.

9. Judgment by Default in Commercial Actions

All applications for judgment by default should be presented to the Registry together with the appropriate supporting documents. It is not necessary to produce a certificate of non-acknowledgement of service.

10. Applications to masters in Commercial Court Matters

Applications in Commercial Court matters which are at present dealt with by Queen's Bench masters, *e.g.* applications for charging orders, should be made in the Registry and dealt with where possible by the Queen's Bench Master disposing of Admiralty matters or as the Senior Master may direct.

11. Listing

Listing of Admiralty and Commercial cases will be co-ordinated in the Registry.

12. Setting Down for Trial

All Admiralty and Commercial Court matters will be set down in the Registry.

H(8) PRACTICE DIRECTION BY MR JUSTICE HIRST GIVEN ON 5 FEBRUARY 1988

As a result of a previous Practice Direction issued in November 1967, there was instituted in the Commercial Court a Waiting List under provisions prescribed in detail on page 1101 of the Supreme Court Practice 1988. The scheme ran alongside the normal procedure, still in force, for all cases in the Commercial Court to be allocated, in effect, fixed dates, which is generally accepted to be essential, particularly in view of the number of foreign litigants and witnesses involved.

Owing to the acute congestion in the list of fixed cases during the 1970s, which resulted in waiting cases only very rarely being called into the list, the scheme fell into disuse, and this Practice Direction supersedes the previous one.

Following recent discussions in the Commercial Court Committee, it became apparent that there is strong support, both from barrister and solicitor practitioners in the Court, and from lay users, for the re-institution of a similar scheme. The purpose is to make sure that the Courts' resources are used with the maximum efficiency at times when, as a result of an unexpected volume of settlements, court time is available at short notice.

In future the following provisions will apply:

(1) There will be established a Waiting List for cases with an estimated duration of not more than 4 days (it is not feasible to fit longer cases into the scheme).

(2) It will be open to parties from today onwards to apply by consent for their case to be placed in the list, either on the Summons for Directions, or at the time of the application to fix a trial date.

(3) In cases in which the Summons for Directions has already been heard, and/or where the trial date has already been fixed, consent applications may be made from now onwards to the Commercial Court Listing Offices for the case to be placed in the Waiting List.

(4) The Waiting List will be published in the Commercial Court Listing Room.

(5) All cases in the Waiting List will also be granted a trial date (if not already granted) in accordance with present practice.

(6) While there can be no guarantee that the placing in the Waiting List will ensure a hearing at an earlier date, there is a reasonable chance that it will do so, since such cases will be given priority when any vacancies occur.

(7) Cases on the Waiting List may be listed for hearing at short notice, though every effort will be made to give as long notice as possible. Inevitably, however, some inconvenience to solicitors and counsel will result.

(8) The smooth working of the scheme will be greatly enhanced if practitioners give early warning to the Commercial Court Listing Offices of likely compromises (which will of course be treated in complete confidence) and prompt and immediate notification of actual settlements. There have unfortunately recently been instances of the Commercial Court Listing Offices having no inkling of an impending or actual settlement until the eve of the fixed date, and sometimes only on the morning of the day on which the case has been listed for trial. This is extremely unjust to other litigants whose cases are still pending. In order to discourage repetition, the Court may in future in such cases call for an explanation in Open Court from solicitors and counsel.

(9) In view of the frequent and well justified complaints as to the long delay in obtaining fixed trial dates in the Commercial Court, it is to be hoped that there will be a strong positive response to this opportunity to obtain speedier trials.

(10) The working of the scheme will be reviewed after it has run for approximately a year, and any representations or comments will be carefully considered.

Dated February 5, 1988.

H(9) PRACTICE DIRECTION BY MR JUSTICE HIRST GIVEN ON 22 APRIL 1988

On 5th February last I announced the establishment of a Waiting List for Commercial Court Cases of an estimated duration of 4 days or less in which cases could be entered by consent with a view to their being listed for hearing at short notice.

I have since received representations from a number of solicitors practising regularly in the Commercial Court that the requirement of consent from all parties is a serious drawback to the working of the scheme, since it is often very difficult to obtain agreement.

To meet this criticism, and to secure other improvements, the following changes, which have been approved by all the Judges of the Commercial Court, will apply from now onwards:

1. For cases awaiting trial, any party who wishes to enter his case in the Waiting List, but is unable to secure the party's consent, may apply on 2 clear days' notice to the Judge in charge of the Commercial List for an Order that the case should be so entered. Such applications, on

which of course all parties will be entitled to be heard, will normally be heard on Fridays. Furthermore the Waiting List will be no longer restricted to cases of 4 days estimated duration or less, though of course a longer case is always more difficult to fit in at short notice, and therefore less likely to be listed for early hearing.

2. Under existing practice, short summonses, though usually heard on Fridays, have been treated as available for listing on other days at short notice. In future all summonses, whatever their estimated duration, and also any applications for leave to appeal against arbitration awards, will be liable to be listed at short notice at any time. The same will apply to Arbitration Appeals.

In both classes of case every effort will be made to give as long notice as possible, but inevitably some inconvenience to solicitors and counsel will result; this is unavoidable if we are to achieve the main objectives to cut the excessive waiting times for Commercial Court cases, and to ensure full use of the Court's resources.

In addition I wish to draw attention to problems which have arisen in relation to the submission of papers for Commercial Court summonses.

The requirements are clearly set out in Section V of the Guide to Commercial Court Practice. These were based on the Practice Direction issued on 3rd May 1985 (1985 2 Lloyd's Reports 301); they were further clarified and extended in the Statement made by me on 16th October 1987, particularly with reference to the limitation of time estimates and the submission of skeleton arguments.

It has been the experience of Commercial Court Judges and of the Clerk to the Commercial Court that these directions are frequently not being followed.

Compliance will in future be rigorously enforced, and, without in any way qualifying or modifying any of the previous Directions, which are expressly reiterated, I wish to stress and to some extent refine the more important requirements:

(i) Copies (not originals) of the relevant documents should be lodged in the Commercial Court Listing Office by noon 2 days before the date fixed for the hearing. These should include the main pleadings, and the affidavits and exhibits, which should all be bound in a convenient loose-leaf file or files.

(ii) Whatever the estimated duration of the summons, counsel's skeleton arguments must be lodged not later than 4 p.m. on the day before the hearing, and preferably with the documents. Unless otherwise arranged, these should be lodged in the Commercial Court Listing Office, and not delivered to the Judge or to the Court in which the summons will be heard. These can be in note form, and need do no more than outline the main submissions, so that the Judge knows what are the points in issue.

The purpose of these requirements is to ensure that all relevant documents and submissions are available for the Judge to read and assimilate them in advance, thus saving time at the hearing itself. Where no papers are lodged at the appointed time, the Clerk to the Commercial Court already has instructions not to list the summons for hearing. In addition, in future he will report to the Judge any instance of partial non-compliance, and parties in default may expect to incur penalties in costs.

Dated April 22, 1988.

H(10) PRACTICE DIRECTION BY LORD LANE C.J. GIVEN ON 5 MARCH 1990

Commercial Court

1. This Practice Direction shall come into force with effect from 19th March 1990.

2. The first edition of the *Guide to Commercial Court Practice* was published in 1986. With the approval of the Judges of the Commercial Court a revised edition has been prepared and adopted by the Commercial Court Committee. The Practice of the Court as set out in the revised edition of the Guide should now be followed, subject to the Rules of the Supreme Court and any orders that may be made in individual cases. The forms appended to the Guide may be revised by the Court from time to time.

3. *The Summons for Directions:* As more fully set out in section XII of the Guide, for the

Court to be able to give satisfactory directions for the trial of an action it is necessary that the parties fulfil their duty under Order 25 rule 6 to give the relevant information to the Court. In order to assist parties to identify the information which the Court requires and to give it in an economical and efficient fashion, the parties will be required to give the information on a sheet in the form set out in Appendix IV to the Guide.

Unless the Commercial Judge gives leave to dispense with the use of the sheet, a copy of the form shall be attached to every summons for directions that is issued and every copy summons served and it shall be the duty of the solicitor to complete and lodge with the Court (with copies to the other parties) not later than two clear days before the return date a signed information sheet. More than one party may join in the completion of a single information sheet but in that case it must be signed by each of the Solicitors on the record for those parties. If a party fails to comply with this direction, the Court may adjourn the summons with an appropriate order for costs against the party or person in default.

In third party proceedings the parties need not lodge an information sheet on the first formal hearing of the summons for third party directions. But an information sheet must be completed and lodged for the hearing on which full third party directions are to be given; this hearing should if possible take place at the same time as the hearing of the summons for directions in the main action.

4. After a date for trial has been given by the Listing Officer, any summons, application or notice should prominently state the trial date on the face of the document above or below the title of the action.

5. *Pre-Trial Check-Lists:* Costs are too often wasted because solicitors do not comply with the direction to lodge these lists; solicitors must lodge them without waiting to be reminded. If they wish to be excused lodging check-lists they must obtain an express order to that effect.

H(11) DIRECTION UNDER ORDER 72, RULE 2(3), BY MR JUSTICE HOBHOUSE GIVEN ON 12 MARCH 1990

The question has been raised whether, when a judgment in default is entered in a Commercial Action for damages and/or interest to be assessed, the assessment can be carried out by a Queen's Bench Master under O.37, r.1, without a further order of the Commercial Judge under O.72, r.2. For the avoidance of doubt it is directed under O.72, r.2(3), that, unless, on the application of any party to the action or on the reference of the Master, the Judge otherwise orders, any assessment of damages or interest under a default judgment entered in a Commercial Action shall be heard and determined by a Master of the Queen's Bench Division.

GUIDE TO COMMERCIAL COURT PRACTICE*

INTRODUCTION

The Commercial Court was brought into existence in 1895 for the purpose of providing a court in which there was a greater familiarity with the subject matter of commercial and mercantile disputes and to provide procedures which would enable those disputes to be justly determined expeditiously and efficiently and without unnecessary formality.

These remain the objectives of the Commercial Court and the Judges of the Court and the practitioners seek to use their expertise and experience to further these ends. The Commercial Court Committee on which the "users" as well as Judges and practitioners are represented is designed to assist the Court to remain responsive to the needs of litigants and the efficient administration of justice.

The work of the Court is highly diverse. At one extreme, it includes heavy and complex litigation involving very large sums of money in which the trials can occupy in excess of half a year. At the other, it includes actions or arbitration matters where the dispute is confined and may be only a single issue of fact or law. Sometimes an urgent remedy or response is required; in other cases lengthy preparation is necessary before the dispute can be ready for trial. The procedure of the Court has to take account of the whole range of the Court's work. It is the policy of the Court that in principle the trial or other hearing should take place at the earliest date that the parties can be ready; the Court will do its best, within the resources made available to it, to achieve this end.

From its inception, a feature of the procedure of the Court has been that interlocutory matters have been dealt with by the Judges of the Court. In commercial litigation, particularly where there is an international element, interlocutory hearings frequently involve matters of great importance to the parties. Further, if the Court is to fulfil its role in providing an effective pre-trial procedure, it is in practice necessary to involve those who have the responsibility for the conduct of such trials.

The practitioners, both solicitors and barristers, are mainly specialists in commercial litigation and consequently bring to the work of the Court a high degree of expertise and efficiency. At its best, litigation before the Court is notable for the co-operation, and realism, of the parties' representatives. However, as in all litigation, the procedure of the Court has to take account of the fact that not all litigants are disinterestedly seeking justice. Similarly there are cases where the legal representatives do not progress the litigation in the manner or with the expedition that the proper administration of justice requires. Where appropriate, the Court does not hesitate to use its powers to order that costs thrown away should be borne by the individual responsible.

Skeleton arguments are extensively used. They are an essential part of the efficient conduct of contested hearings both at the interlocutory and at the trial stage. They are an effective means of saving costs. They are not a substitute for oral argument. Often skeleton arguments are over-elaborate or too lengthy; their purpose is to identify, as concisely as possible, issues and propositions of fact and law (with references) and, where relevant, the grounds of relief relied upon.

*© Crown copyright. Issued on a Practice Note by Lord Lane C.J. on 25 July 1986 and a revised edition issued on a Practice Note by Lord Lane C.J. on 5 March 1990.

The provision of a skeleton argument does not relieve counsel of the duty to provide a list of authorities to the usher of the relevant court, though counsel may, if it is convenient, also supply the Court with photocopies of the passages to be relied on from the authorities.

A high percentage of Commercial Court actions are settled before trial. The procedures of the Court must assist this process, particularly by assisting each party to be informed of the real strength of the other's case well in advance of the trial date. However, a balance has to be struck between this objective and the avoidance of disproportionate expenditure at the pre-trial stage.

This Guide does not seek to provide a litigation handbook nor a blue-print to which all litigation must unthinkingly conform. It rather seeks to provide the framework within which litigation in the Commercial Court can continue to be conducted in accordance with the objectives of the Court.

Under section 4 of the Administration of Justice Act 1970 a Judge of the Commercial Court may, if in all the circumstances he thinks fit and the state of business in the High and Crown Courts permits, accept appointment as a sole arbitrator or as an umpire. This option has been little used and the state of business has usually precluded acceptance of such appointments; however, if further information is required enquiry can be made of the Clerk of the Commercial Court or the Judge in charge of the Commercial Court List.

The Commercial Court office at Room 61 in the Royal Courts of Justice is staffed by the Clerk to the Commercial Court, Mr David Bird, and his assistant(s). Any enquiries may be addressed to—

> The Clerk to the Commercial Court,
> Royal Courts of Justice,
> The Strand, London WC2A 2LL.
> Telephone: 071 936 6826
> Telex: 296983 COMM-G

I. COMMERCIAL ACTIONS

1.1 Order 72 of the Rules of The Supreme Court makes special provision for Commercial Actions and their trial in the Commercial Court. Commercial Actions are entered in the Admiralty and Commercial Registry; listing for the Commercial Court is in the hands of the Clerk of the Commercial Court. The Judge for the time being in charge of the List is referred to as the Commercial Judge. Arbitration proceedings are governed by Order 73.

1.2 "Commercial action" is defined in O. 72, r. 1(2) to include "any cause arising out of the ordinary transactions of merchants and traders and, without prejudice to the generality of the foregoing words, any cause relating to the construction of a mercantile document, the export or import of merchandise, affreightment, insurance, banking, mercantile agency and mercantile usage". This definition dates from 1895 and has long been regarded as unnecessarily archaic. The Commercial Court Committee in its submission to the Civil Justice Review urged a definition which was expressed in more appropriate language and conformed more closely to the practice of this Court as stated in the first edition of this Guide.

1.3 In exercising the discretion given to him by O. 72, rr. 5 and 6, the Commercial Judge is likely to consider whether the subject matter of the action and the issues of fact and law likely to arise and the procedures to be followed make the action suitable for the Commercial Court; the matters suitable for determination by the Court include:

(a) contracts relating to ships and shipping,
(b) insurance and reinsurance,
(c) banking, negotiable instruments, and international credit,
(d) the international carriage of goods,
(e) contracts relating to aircraft,
(f) the purchase and sale of commodities,
(g) the operation of international markets and exchanges,
(h) the construction and performance of mercantile contracts,
(i) the law and practice of arbitration and questions connected with or arising from commercial arbitration,

(j) any other matter or any question of fact or law which is particularly suitable for decision by a Judge of the Commercial Court.

1.4 Applications relating to arbitration under O. 73, r. 2 and r. 3 are required by O. 73, r. 6 to be heard by a Judge of the Court unless any such Judge otherwise directs. Such directions are ordinarily made, if no significant point of arbitration law or practice is raised, in rent-review arbitrations for transfer to a Judge of the Chancery Division, and in building and civil engineering arbitrations to an Official Referee.

II. STARTING A COMMERCIAL ACTION

2.1 The same forms of originating process are available in the Commercial Court as for non-commercial actions: writ, notice of motion and originating summons. In each case the document must be marked "Queen's Bench Division, Commercial Court" and issued out of the Admiralty and Commercial Registry (O. 6, r. 7; O. 7, r. 5; O. 8, r. 3). Where the originating process is an originating summons attention must be paid to different procedures to be followed thereafter under O. 28 and O. 73.

2.2 Even if not started as a Commercial Action, an application may be made to the Commercial Judge for the action to be transferred to the Commercial Court. Whether or not transfer is ordered is in the discretion of the Judge. Such an order may be made at any stage of the action and for limited purposes only, though normally the order is made at an early stage and the transferred action will remain in the Court until its conclusion.

2.3 An action started in the Commercial Court may be transferred out on the order of the Judge made at any stage of the action and whether or not applied for by either party. Such an order will not be made after directions have been given for the trial of the action in the Commercial Court save where some exceptional factor arises.

2.4 Where leave is required to issue the proceedings (or to serve them out of the jurisdiction), leave is normally applied for and granted on a paper application to the Judge.

2.5 Leave to renew a writ or otherwise to extend time within which the originating process may validly be served is applied for on affidavit. The application will not be granted unless a good reason for doing so is shown and the criteria stated in the relevant authorities are satisfied. (See *The Myrto* [1987] A.C. 597; *Waddon* v. *Whitecroft-Scovill* [1988] 1 W.L.R. 309.) Service of process in some foreign countries normally takes a very long time to complete; it is therefore incumbent upon solicitors to take prompt steps to effect service. The shorter periods of validity for writs, which will come into effect 4th June 1990, will make prompt service even more important. (See also the new O. 6, r. 8(2A).)

III. EX PARTE APPLICATIONS

3.1 Save where the application involves the giving of undertakings by the applicant to the Court, *ex parte* applications are normally made on affidavit without the need for an attendance before the Judge. Any application for an interlocutory injunction will require an attendance.

3.2 Applications should only be made *ex parte* where the applicant is not required to issue a summons. A summons must normally be issued where the respondent is already a party to the action. Where the applicant relies on O. 29, r. 1(2), he must be prepared to show that the urgency is such as to make the issue and service of a summons impractical; even in such cases he may be required to give notice of his application to the person to be affected by the application.

3.3 On all *ex parte* applications it is the duty of the applicant and those acting for him to make full disclosure to the Court of all matters relevant to the application and whether the Court should grant the relief asked: this includes disclosure to the Court of matters which are or may be adverse to the applicant. Failure to make such disclosure is a breach of a duty owed to the Court and, besides the other remedies available to aggrieved parties, may lead to the setting aside of the Order made on the ground of non-disclosure alone. The disclosure should be made on affidavit.

3.4 Save in exceptional circumstances where time does not permit, all the evidence relied upon in support of the application and other relevant documents must be lodged in advance with the Clerk of the Commercial Court. See further the Practice Direction of 30th March 1983 (Appendix I). The papers should include on a separate sheet or sheets a draft of the order sought (and any document(s) referred to in the draft order). Where the application is for leave to issue a Third Party or similar notice, the papers lodged should include copies of the writ and any pleadings already served in the action.

IV. SERVICE OUT OF THE JURISDICTION

4.1 Before issuing a writ or seeking leave to serve out of the jurisdiction, it is necessary to consider whether the jurisdiction of the English Courts is affected by the Civil Jurisdiction and Judgments Act 1982. Where each claim in the writ is a claim which the Court has by virtue of the Civil Jurisdiction and Judgments Act 1982 power to hear and determine, service of the writ out of the jurisdiction is permissible without leave provided that the requirements of O. 11, r. 1(2) are satisfied and the writ is endorsed with a statement complying with O. 6, r. 7(1)(b); care must be taken to see that that statement is endorsed only when the statement is correct.

4.2 On applications for leave under O. 11, r. 1(1) and O. 72, r. 4, the affidavit required by O. 11, r. 4 must, *inter alia*:

    (1) identify the paragraph or paragraphs of O. 11, r. 1(1) relied on as giving the Court jurisdiction to order service out, together with a summary of the facts relied on as bringing the case within each such paragraph;

    (2) state the belief of the deponent that there is a good cause of action and state in what place or country the defendant is or probably may be found;

    (3) summarise the considerations relied upon as showing that the case is a proper one in which to subject a party outside the jurisdiction to proceedings within it;

    (4) draw attention to any features which might reasonably be thought to weigh against the making of the order sought;

    (5) state the deponent's grounds of belief and sources of information;

    (6) exhibit copies of the documents referred to and any other significant documents.

4.3 The documents submitted with the application must include a draft of the order sought, which should also state the time for acknowledgement of service which is applicable in accordance with O. 11, r. 1(3) and the Extra Jurisdiction Tables set out in Part III C of the Supreme Court Practice.

4.4 A copy or draft of the writ or other process which it is sought to issue and serve must be provided for the Judge to initial. It should be remembered that if the endorsement to the writ includes causes of action or claims not covered by the grounds on which leave to serve out of the jurisdiction can properly be granted, leave will be refused unless the draft is amended to restrict it to proper claims. Where the application is for the issue of a concurrent writ, the documents submitted must also include a copy of the original writ.

4.5 Service out of the jurisdiction in arbitration matters is governed by O. 73, r. 7. The 1968 Convention on Jurisdiction does not apply to arbitration: see Article 1(4).

V. MAREVA AND ANTON PILLER INJUNCTIONS

5.1 Applications are made *ex parte* because of the need not to disclose the making of the application to the party affected. However, save in cases where the urgency is such that there has not been any opportunity to do so, the applicant must nevertheless issue his writ and swear his affidavit first, before making the application, and should give as much notice to the Clerk of the Commercial Court of the intention to make the application as the circumstances permit and lodge with him the documents to be used on the application.

5.2 On such applications, the duty to make full disclosure to the Court (see paragraph 3.3 above) is particularly important.

5.3 Attention is drawn to the Practice Direction dated 30th March 1983, [1983] 1 W.L.R. 434

(see Appendix I); it is equally appropriate when applications are made to the Commercial Judge.

5.4 Examples of Orders which may be made by way of *Mareva* and Anton Piller injunctions are included in Parts A and B of Appendix II. The specimen orders there set out are intended to give guidance on the main undertakings and orders which a party should consider when preparing a draft order.

5.5 The usual *Mareva* injunction in the Commercial Court is one which applies until trial or further order, giving the defendant or any other interested party liberty to apply; a provision for the defendant to give notice of any application to discharge or vary the injunction is usually included as a matter of convenience but it is not proper to attempt to fetter the right of the defendant to apply *ex parte* if need be. However applications to discharge or vary injunctions are properly made by summons in the ordinary course. The usual form of order has the advantage that unnecessary interlocutory hearings are avoided; but in some cases it may be appropriate to order that the injunction should have only a limited duration so that the parties will come back before the Court at an early date on an *inter-partes* hearing. The phrase "until trial or further order" is normally understood to cover the period up to the completion of the trial by the delivery of a final judgment; if an injunction continuing after judgment is required, say until the judgment has been satisfied, an application to that effect must be made.

5.6 It is good practice to draft an injunction so that it includes a proviso which permits acts, which would otherwise be a breach of the injunction, to be done with the written consent of the plaintiff's solicitors; this enables the parties to agree in effect to the variations (or exhaustion) of the injunction without the necessity of coming back to the Court.

5.7 Where a plaintiff is not able to show assets within the jurisdiction of the Court to provide substance to the undertakings given, particularly the undertakings in damages, the plaintiff may be required as a condition of the grant of the injunction to back his undertakings by providing some readily available security within the jurisdiction. Applicants should be prepared to deal with this point; failure to anticipate a need to back the undertaking can be a cause of unsatisfactory delay.

VI. SUMMONSES INTER PARTES

6.1 Attention is drawn to the requirements of the Practice Direction dated 3rd May 1985, [1985] 2 Lloyd's Rep. 301 set out in Appendix I: an appropriate notice is attached to every summons issued in the Commercial Court. Failure to comply with the Practice Direction is the most common reason why summonses have to be stood out or not listed. Any summons issued after a trial date has been given should prominently state on its face above or below the title of the action the date for which the trial has been fixed.

6.2 Most summonses are listed for hearing on Fridays on which day all the Judges sitting in the Court will normally be taking summonses; they may however be listed on any day of the week. (See the Practice Statement, 9th November 1981, Appendix I.) Non-counsel summonses are normally listed before the Commercial Judge.

6.3 On 23rd October 1987, a Practice Direction was given, [1987] 3 All E.R. 799 (see Appendix I), which provided the Clerk of the Commercial Court and practitioners with maximum estimates of hearing time which would be acceptable for various categories of summonses. These maxima have proved more than adequate and should not be exceeded save in special circumstances and with the consent of the Commercial Judge. They do not relieve practitioners of the responsibility to give accurate estimates to the Clerk of the Commercial Court. Estimates are particularly important where more than one summons is to be heard at the same time or where there is a multiplicity of parties.

6.4 For summonses to be disposed of efficiently it is essential that the practitioners should co-operate in preparing the relevant documents, even for short contested summonses and even though the primary responsibility for preparing documents for the Court lies with the applicant; this duty to co-operate is particularly important where more than one summons in the same action is to be heard at the same time. Documents should be bundled in paginated bundles which are the same for everyone; the copies must be legible; indices should be included wherever appropriate; affidavits and exhibits must be marked on their first page in accordance with O. 41, r. 9(5) and the Practice Direction of 21st July 1983 (see Appendix I); where a deponent has sworn more than one affidavit, the exhibits should be numbered sequentially to the exhibits to the previous affidavit (ibid); where there are a number of exhibits with selections from the correspondence, it is usually best that they should all be put in a single chronological (paginated) sequence; the preparation of the bundles should not be left to the last moment; they should be prepared in time for counsel to prepare for the hearing and incorporate the references in their skeleton arguments. See further Section XVI below. It is the duty of any party lodging documents with the Court to see that all other parties are informed of that fact and the contents and pagination and that copies are where necessary supplied to the other parties.

6.5 The level of preparation that is appropriate depends on the circumstances. For all contested summonses estimated to last for at least 20 minutes, some form of concise skeleton argument, however short, is useful; it indicates to the parties and to the Court what points are and are not in issue and enables the Court to read the relevant documents in advance. They enable the hearing to concentrate from the start on the actual points that need to be argued and decided. For most types of summons it is of assistance for the applicant to provide a chronology and such documents (like indices and *dramatis personae* which are also useful) once prepared can be easily updated and are of continuing usefulness throughout the life of the action.

6.6 Summonses which are expected to last more than half a day normally involve a greater volume of evidence and other documents and more extensive issues of fact and/or law. They accordingly require a longer lead-time for preparation and exchange of evidence; if the parties have difficulty in agreeing a time-table for such preparation, they should ask the Court for directions. Similarly, if it comes to the notice of the Court that the summons is not being brought on as expeditiously as it should, the Court may of its own motion list it for directions. A specimen of the type of time-table that should be followed for the heavier summonses was given in the first edition of this Guide and is reproduced, in a revised form, in Appendix III. The last-minute exchange of affidavits must wherever possible be avoided. Attention is also drawn to Section XVI below.

6.7 On the hearing of any summons every effort must be made to avoid the reading aloud of documents or authorities. The Court will expect simply to be referred to the actual passages relied on by the relevant party.

6.8 Very many summonses are disposed of by consent. Consent orders may be submitted to the Court for initialling without the need for an attendance; in such cases care must be taken to ensure that a copy of the actual consent order requested is included together with written evidence of the consent of every party affected or potentially affected by the order. For consent orders on the summons for directions see Section XII below. Where the consent order includes an undertaking, the Court may require the attendance of the party giving the undertaking, but will in any case require the lodging of an original document signed by the party's solicitor.

VII. ARBITRATION MATTERS

7.1 These matters are governed by O. 73. They ordinarily arise on proceedings commenced by a Notice of Motion (rule 2) or an Originating Summons (rule 3) or *ex parte* (rule 10). A Notice of Motion should not be used save where authorised by O. 73, r. 2; thus it should not be used where a declaration is being sought unless the application is for a declaration that an award is not binding on the ground that it was made without jurisdiction. Service out of the jurisdiction is covered by rule 7.

7.2 In arbitration matters it is the particular duty of the Court to see that court proceedings are not a cause of delay. A hearing date must be applied for promptly after the issue of the relevant process or after obtaining leave to appeal under the Arbitration Act 1979. Delay will prejudice any application for relief. Where it comes to the notice of the Court that improper delay is occurring, it may itself direct that the matter be listed.

7.3 Applications for leave to appeal under the 1979 Act are made by a summons issued under the relevant Notice of Motion. The Practice Direction dated 3rd May 1985 (see [1985] 2 Lloyd's Rep. 300 and Appendix I) sets out various requirements which must be complied with. The application for leave to appeal is considered in accordance with the criteria laid down in *The Nema* [1982] A.C. 724 and *The Antaios* [1985] A.C. 191; accordingly the hearing will not be expected to last more than half an hour. Any leave to appeal may be given on terms; these may restrict the points on which leave to appeal is given or require the provision of security etc. For the hearing of the substantive motion of appeal the parties are expected to lodge skeleton arguments in the same way as for other contested hearings.

7.4 Where both an application is being made by motion to set aside or remit under the 1950 Act and by summons for leave to appeal under the 1979 Act the Court may direct that one application be heard before the other or that they be heard together if that is appropriate.

7.5 Applications under O. 73, r. 10 for leave to enforce an award are made on written application by affidavit. Care must be taken to see that the affidavit and the draft order meet the requirements of the rule.

7.6 Applications under section 12(6) of the Arbitration Act 1950 for an order that a claimant give security for costs are made by originating summons and the matters stated in Section VIII are applicable.

VIII. SECURITY FOR COSTS

8.1 Applicants for security for costs should take into account the decision of the Court of Appeal in *De Bry* v. *Fitzgerald* (1st November 1988): their affidavit should deal with not only the residence of the plaintiff (or other respondent to the application) and the location of his assets but also with the actual practical difficulties (if any) or enforcing an order for costs against him.

8.2 Successive applications for security can be granted where the circumstances warrant. If a plaintiff wishes to seek to preclude any further application it is incumbent upon him to make that clear.

8.3 First applications for security should not be made later than the summons for directions and in any event any application should not be left until close to the trial (or other relevant hearing) date. Delay to the prejudice of the other party or the administration of justice will probably cause the application to fail, as will any use of the application to harass the other party.

8.4 It is not usually convenient or appropriate to order an automatic stay of the proceedings pending the provision of the security. It leads to delay and may disrupt the preparation of the action for trial, or other hearing. Experience shows that it is usually better to give the plaintiff (or other relevant party) a reasonable time within which to provide the security and the other party a liberty to apply in the event of default. This enables the Court to put the plaintiff to his election and then, if appropriate, to dismiss the action.

8.5 Where the dispute on an application for security for costs relates to the correct evaluation of the amount of costs likely to be allowed to a successful defendant on taxation, parties should consider whether it could be advantageous for the Judge hearing the summons to sit with a Taxing Master as an informal assessor and the Judge himself may take such an initiative. Such summonses will be comparatively rare as disputes on *quantum* more usually depend upon such matters as predicting the likely length of the trial or what expert evidence will be required; in deciding such matters the Judge will not need the assistance of an assessor. When a summons is believed to be suitable for the involvement of an assessor, it is important that the parties communicate that fact to the Court as soon as possible after the issue of the summons and in any event well before any return date.

IX. PLEADINGS

9.1 Commercial actions can be ordered to be tried without pleadings (O. 72, r. 7(3)). Where the issues have already been adequately defined by affidavits, or the parties have agreed the facts or the issue is solely a defined question of law it may be suitable to make such an order. However pleadings are normally an essential part of the preparation of the case for trial and judgment; they identify and define the issues; they inform the opposite party of the case he has to meet. In the Commercial Court pleaders are expected to draft their pleadings with proper regard to these objectives.

9.2 O. 72, r. 7(1) requires commercial pleadings to be "as brief as possible" and they are accordingly called "Points of Claim", "Points of Defence" etc. The complexity of the subject matter and the issues involved in many commercial actions and the number of parties will often make pleadings running to many paragraphs and pages inevitable. It is nonetheless desirable that pleaders should in all cases be on their guard to avoid prolixity and avoid pleading evidence; they should—

(1) where possible, give references to documents instead of incorporating long quotations from the documents in the pleading;
(2) where lengthy citations from documents are called for, annex these in a schedule to the pleading;
(3) plead particulars as particulars not as primary allegations;
(4) where lengthy particulars are called for, annex these in a schedule to the pleading;
(5) where possible, plead to scheduled particulars by a corresponding schedule.

9.3 When pleading a defence or reply to an earlier pleading it should be remembered that a simple denial does not allow that party to advance a positive case on the relevant issue; failure to plead a positive case may lead to that party being penalised in costs at a later stage (particularly if an adjournment of the trial is necessary) or, if costs are not an adequate remedy, to his losing the opportunity to advance the positive case.

9.4 Under O. 72, r. 7(2) particulars are only to be applied for where they are necessary to enable a party to be informed of the case he has to meet or otherwise for the just, expeditious, and economical disposal of the case. Particulars may be an economical way of avoiding the need for interrogatories. Particulars may be rendered unnecessary where an order can be made under O. 38, rr. 2A or 38 requiring the party to serve documents which identify the evidence relied upon in support of an allegation. Particulars should always be first requested by a letter enclosing the request and should only be made the subject of an application to the Court in the absence of a prompt and acceptable response; on such application the Court will rule on the request as well as the time within which it must be responded to.

9.5 A pleadings bundle is normally required for the use of the Court on any interlocutory hearing as well as at the trial. It is therefore good practice for solicitors to keep a flagged running bundle of the pleadings together with a running index. The index should give the date upon which any document was served and it is very helpful if the date of service is also annotated on the front of the pleading itself (in a similar way to an affidavit). The Points of Claim should state on its face the date of the issue of the writ (O. 18, r. 15(3)). Where the pleadings are very bulky they should be subdivided and it may, in any event, be advantageous to put the particulars in a separate bundle.

X. AMENDMENT OF PLEADINGS

10.1 Order 20 governs the amendment of pleadings in the Commercial Court as elsewhere in the High Court. The requirements of that Order, however, may result in delay, expense and a degree of formality inappropriate to Commercial Court litigation.

10.2 In the interest of avoiding unnecessary costs and formality questions of amendment should wherever possible be dealt with by consent. Attention is drawn to O. 20, r. 12(1) which now extends to all Divisions of the High Court and allows amendments to be made by agreement; greater use should be made of this rule. Consequential amendments should be made under this rule as well. A party should consent to a proposed amendment unless he has substantial grounds for objecting to it.

10.3 Late amendments should be avoided and may be disallowed if other parties are prejudiced in a way that a costs order will not adequately compensate.

10.4 The use of coloured inks to indicate amendments represents the normal practice and is usually the most convenient way of identifying what amendments have been made and in what sequence. However, such identification may not always be necessary and, having regard to the fact that documents are most commonly copied in black and white, may involve unnecessary expense. Therefore parties should in appropriate cases remember that other methods can be adopted (such as the use of marginal notes) and that where there are extensive amendments it may be better to make a fair copy of the relevant pleading(s) as authorised (or required) by O. 20, r. 10(1).

XI. DISCOVERY AND INTERROGATORIES

11.1 In commercial litigation the discovery and inspection of documents are usually a major, and costly, exercise but are an important part of the process by which a just resolution of the parties' dispute is achieved. It is the normal practice, and the Court expects, that the parties' representatives adopt a high level of co-operation and avoid disputes wherever possible; it is very rare that there needs to be a contested summons in relation to discovery.

11.2 The fact that a party is resident overseas or, by reason of subrogation, is not personally interested in the outcome of the litigation is no excuse for failing, having been given a reasonable period of time, to provide full discovery in accordance with the Rules of Court and any specific orders made.

11.3 Informal methods of giving discovery are encouraged provided they do not leave in doubt what discovery has and has not been given. Affidavits are only ordered if it is clear that they are necessary or will save costs.

11.4 Under O. 27, r. 4, it is incumbent upon a party who does not admit the authenticity of a document listed in another party's list to serve a notice within the time limit laid down by r. 4(2), otherwise he is to be taken as having admitted the authenticity of the documents listed in accordance with r. 4(1).

11.5 Parties should always have in mind that costs and time may be saved if certain issues in the action can be postponed together with the discovery that relates to such issues. It may also be possible for certain issues to be decided without substantial discovery.

11.6 *Interrogatories*: In the past interrogatories have not often been ordered in the Commercial Court as there are usually other less formal ways of procuring the appropriate disclosure or admissions. Under the new Order 26 which came into force on 5th February 1990 interrogatories may be served without the necessity for a court order beforehand. It is to be noted that interrogatories are still only to be asked for where they are necessary for disposing fairly of the cause or matter or for saving costs (O. 26, r. 1(1)) and the Court in making any order shall take into account any offer to give particulars, make admissions or produce documents. It thus appears likely that the practice of the Commercial Court will remain similar to that at present. However, information about any interrogatories will be expected on the hearing of the summons for directions (see Appendix IV) and references are included in the standard directions and the pre-trial check-list (Appendices V and VI). Oppressive interrogatories will be strongly discouraged and attempts to interrogate at a late stage before the trial will be unlikely to receive judicial support unless clearly justified. Suitable times to interrogate (if at all) will probably be after discovery and after exchange of witness statements.

XII. THE SUMMONS FOR DIRECTIONS

12.1 The summons for directions in the Commercial Court is governed by Order 25. The summons may under O. 25, r. 1(7) and O. 72, r. 8(1) be issued by any party at any time after any defendant has given notice of intention to defend and whether or not pleadings are closed. In the ordinary way, however, the appropriate time to issue the summons in a commercial action is after the inspection of documents has been completed. The reason is that the main purpose of the summons is to give directions for the trial and, usually, at any earlier stage insufficient is known of the actual issues which will have to be tried and the witnesses to be called and an adequate estimate of the length of trial cannot be given. A summons which is issued before the action is ready for the giving of directions for trial will be adjourned.

12.2 Cases in which it is appropriate to issue the summons at an earlier stage include actions where the issues to be tried are already sufficiently known, or discovery is to be a formality, or where an expedited trial is being asked for, or where a very long trial is to be anticipated so that, although there will be a long lead-time, it is desirable that a date for the trial be ear-marked and a time-table settled.

12.3 Order 25 imposes various duties upon the Court which the Court is required to have regard to on the hearing of the summons. These are summarised in rule 1(1): it is the

"occasion for the consideration by the Court of the preparations for the trial of the action so that—
(a) all matters which must or can be dealt with on interlocutory applications and have not already been dealt with may so far as possible be dealt with, and
(b) such directions may be given as to the future course of the action as appear best adapted to secure the just expeditious and economical disposal thereof."

Rule 4 specifically requires the Court to "endeavour to secure that the parties make all admissions and all agreements as to the conduct of the proceedings which ought reasonably to be made by them . . .".

12.4 Rule 6 imposes a corresponding duty on the parties to the action and their advisers "to give all such information and produce all such documents on any hearing of the summons as the Court may reasonably require for the purposes of enabling it properly to deal with the summons". Rule 6(3) provides that failure to discharge this duty can lead to adverse costs orders and/or to a party's pleadings being struck out or its claim dismissed.

12.5 Accordingly, the summons involves both the parties and the Court in a review of the action; this exercise needs to be carried out effectively but economically. Even if the parties are agreed upon the directions they would like, the Court still has to make its own assessment; therefore in all cases it is required that at least one of the parties shall be represented at the hearing and that that representative shall have an actual knowledge of the action and the issues in it. As an aid to providing the Court with the requisite information in an economical fashion, each party shall complete and lodge with the Court (with copies to the other parties) not later than 2 clear days before the hearing of the summons a signed information sheet in the form set out in Appendix IV. (Where an agreed information sheet is lodged jointly on behalf of more than one party, it should still be signed by each of the solicitors involved.) If, as for example where the summons is issued exceptionally before the completion of discovery and inspection, it is not thought useful to complete an information sheet at that stage, a dispensation should be asked for by letter to the Commercial Judge at the time of issuing the summons.

12.6 The parties should not regard it as their duty for the purposes of the summons to prepare a full list of the issues technically remaining open on the pleadings but should simply identify those issues which the party believes are likely to be critical at the trial.

12.7 Among the matters which should be considered on the summons are, besides the making of admissions, the possibility of having an agreed statement of facts, trying some issues before others, ordering the trial of a preliminary issue, directing that the evidence be given on affidavit (with or without cross-examination) etc.

12.8 A crucial matter on the summons is to estimate when the trial can take place. This in turn depends on being able to assess how many days the trial is likely to occupy and how long it will take the parties to complete their preparations for trial. In principle the trial should take place at the earliest date that the parties can be ready and the Court will do its best, within the resources made available to it, to assist in achieving this end. The directions should normally be drafted so as to provide a specified series of dates by which the various steps are to be taken, leading forward from the date of the hearing of the summons; working backwards from the trial date is not usually so satisfactory and often delays the settlement of those actions which are likely to be settled before trial. Where an expedited trial is being asked for the parties will normally be expected to show a high degree of co-operation with each other and with the Court in preparing the action for trial expeditiously and efficiently and in shortening the length of trial asked for.

12.9 Standard Directions are set out in Appendix V. Parties should have these directions in mind in drafting their summons or proposed order and should follow their scheme save where they are prepared to submit to the Court that it is inappropriate. Other matters relevant to the summons for directions are contained in Sections XIII to XVIII.

12.10 Where directions are required in third party or contribution proceedings, the summons when first issued usually only needs to deal with formal matters such as pleadings and discovery, the remainder of the directions being ordered to stand over; at that stage the summons can be dealt with informally and there will normally be no need for an information sheet or an attendance. But if the directions asked for will affect the main action or concern the trial or evidence, then the summons should be handled in the same way as the summons in the main action and should, if possible, be heard at the same time.

12.11 Where the proceedings were begun by originating summons the procedure for obtaining directions and other orders is laid down in O. 28.

12.12 Summonses for directions are normally listed on Friday before the Commercial Judge. On the hearing of any summons for directions or any restored summons, the party having the conduct of the summons must ensure that the papers supplied to the Court include the full bundle of pleadings together with copies of all the interlocutory orders that have been made and of the information sheets. After a trial date has been given, any summons, application (including an application for a consent order or judgment) or notice should prominently state the trial date on the face of the document above or below the title of the action.

XIII. PRELIMINARY ISSUES

13.1 Under O. 33, rr. 3 and 4, the Court has a wide discretion whether to make orders for some issues to be tried before others and for the mode of trial. It is the experience of the Court that this power could with advantage be more widely invoked. Costs can often be saved by identifying decisive issues, or potentially decisive issues, and ordering that they be tried first. The decision of one issue may enable the parties to settle the remainder of the dispute.

13.2 At the stage of the summons for directions consideration should always be given to the possibility of a preliminary issue the resolution of which is likely to shorten the proceedings as, for example, a relatively short question of law which can be tried without significant delay (though the implications of a possible appeal for the remainder of the action must not be lost sight of). The Court may suggest the trial of a preliminary issue but it will rarely make an order without the concurrence of at least one of the parties.

13.3 At the stage of the final preparation for the trial, or even at the commencement of the trial itself, it may be advantageous to separate issues and take them consecutively.

13.4 It will often be advantageous to try liability first. Damages questions can if necessary be referred to an Official or Special Referee (O. 36, r. 10) or a Master or Registrar, or the parties may choose to ask an arbitrator to decide them. The same logic can be applied to other factual questions.

XIV. EXCHANGE OF EVIDENCE: FACTUAL WITNESSES

14.1 Orders are normally made under O. 38, r. 2A and parties are usually required to follow the same time-table for serving Civil Evidence Act Notices as for exchanging witness statements. The experience of the Court is that such orders are very effective in saving time and costs at the trial and in enabling the parties to evaluate the dispute between them with a view to settlement. They involve the parties in interlocutory expense but it is cost-effective and assists to serve the interests of justice.

14.2 The standard direction is that the statements shall be signed by the witnesses; this has the advantage that each witness is required to lend his personal credit to the statement. It is also possible for the Court to order that the statement be put in the form of an affidavit. The party's representatives should be aware of the impropriety of serving a statement known to be false or of allowing a witness to sign a statement which the witness does not in all respects actually believe to be true. Quite apart from matters of propriety, service of such a statement will merely lead to that witness, and even that party's case, being discredited.

14.3 The statement should, in the words of the rule, be "the oral evidence which the party intends to lead" from that witness at the trial. It should not include inadmissible or irrelevant evidence. It should represent the whole truth of the witness's evidence on the points covered. It should, save for informal matters, be expressed in the witness's own words not those of the lawyer. Where the witness is not fluent enough in English to give his evidence in English, the signed statement should be in the witness's own language and a translation provided. The rules of any relevant professional body regarding the drafting of statements should be observed.

14.4 The standard directions include a direction that *unless otherwise ordered* the statement shall stand as the evidence in chief of the witness. This does not fetter in any way the discretion open to the Judge at the trial as to the amount of oral evidence that he permits to be led from the witness. What is then appropriate will depend upon the circumstances in each case. The main object is to avoid time-consuming oral examinations in chief where they are not strictly necessary in the interests of justice. In many cases there will be matters arising from other statements or other evidence which, subject to O. 38, r. 2A(5)(a), have to be covered; the witness may between the time of signing his statement and being called as a witness at the trial have a different recollection of matters included in his statement. Where there is a contested conversation, meeting or series of events, it may be better for the relevant witnesses to give their evidence in chief on those points orally in the traditional way; but even in such cases it may be better to let the witness's unaided recollection be tested in cross-examination. The fact that a witness's credit is challenged is not normally a reason for not putting his statement in chief (and still less a reason for not making an order under r. 2A in the first place). See also paragraph 19.4 below.

14.5 Parties are reminded that under r. 2A(7) any party failing to comply with a direction given under r. 2A(2) is not to be entitled to adduce evidence to which the direction related without the leave of the Court.

14.6 The exchange of statements can facilitate the making of an order under O. 38, r. 3 for evidence of particular facts to be given in a particular way.

14.7 Unlike expert's reports, witness statements are not normally read by the Judge in advance without an express invitation to do so. There may be an objection to admissibility or the witness may never be called. Accordingly, if parties wish the Judge to read witness statements in advance, they should make that clear at the time of providing the trial documents to the Court. Where there is to be an objection to admissibility or relevance, the objection should if possible be communicated to the other party before the time that the trial documents are prepared so that it may be resolved by agreement and/or taken into account in the preparation of the bundles. However it should be remembered that it will rarely be necessary to remove the parts objected to physically from the bundle; some annotation of the objection will normally suffice. Where a party has decided not to call a witness whose statement has been exchanged, that fact should be taken into account in making up the trial bundles and referred to in the pre-trial check-list.

14.8 Exceptionally, there are cases where relevant matters about which evidence can properly be given continue to occur after the time of the exchange of statements; such matters should if possible be dealt with by agreement and if necessary the summons for directions must be restored. The existence of the need for such additional evidence must be disclosed on the pre-trial check-list. There may be other exceptional cases where issues of credit arise from the exchanged statements which may either involve the calling of additional evidence or, very exceptionally, the non-disclosure of such additional evidence. How such situations are best dealt with must depend upon the circumstances but it must be remembered that at some stage the party adducing the additional evidence will require the leave of the Court.

XV. EXCHANGE OF EVIDENCE: EXPERT WITNESSES

15.1 Order 38, r. 4 allows the Court to limit the expert to be called at the trial. O. 38, r. 36 imposes further restrictions upon adducing expert evidence. The reasons underlying these rules are that expert evidence nearly always involves the expenditure of substantial sums of costs and is often wrongly thought to be necessary, thus wasting costs; also, expert evidence needs to be prepared in a structured manner under the supervision of the Court.

15.2 Whether or not there are issues requiring expert evidence should be apparent from the pleadings; in particular, any allegation of foreign law should be pleaded. The standard directions provide for the exchange of experts' reports and will identify the topics to be covered unless this is clear beyond doubt. It is normally best that this exchange take place a reasonable time after the statements of factual witnesses have been exchanged. This allows the expert reports to take into account the contents of those statements.

15.3 Good practice requires that the parties attempt to eliminate or reduce the expert issues if possible in advance of the trial. To this end the Court will not on the summons for directions authorise the calling of expert witnesses at the trial unless the need for such oral evidence appears inevitable. In some cases it may be appropriate to order a meeting between experts under O. 38, r. 38(3). In most cases it is appropriate to require the parties to make a further application after the exchange of the reports; different provision may be made for different expert topics.

15.4 At the trial the evidence of the experts (or of the experts on a particular topic) is usually taken together at the same time and after the factual evidence has been given; this should if possible be agreed by the parties before the trial and should at the latest be raised with the Judge at the start of the trial (or at the pre-trial review if there is one). Expert evidence is as far as possible given by reference to the reports exchanged, both as a matter of evidence in chief and cross-examination. (See also O. 38, rr. 42 and 43.)

15.5 Where the expert evidence refers to photographs, plans, analyses, measurements, survey reports or other similar documents and these have not already been disclosed on discovery, these must be provided to the opposite party at the same time as the exchange of reports. (See also O. 38, r. 5.) Prior to the trial it may become necessary for the parties to exchange supplementary reports; this can be done by agreement. Any supplementary reports should be exchanged not later than 3 weeks before the trial date in accordance with the standard directions; but such exchange should normally take place earlier before the time that the pre-trial check-lists have to be lodged. Similarly, well in advance of the hearing, paginated legible bundles of any authoritative sources (together with translations where necessary) should be prepared so that they can be provided to counsel and lodged with the Court with the other trial documents.

15.6 In cases with a high scientific content consideration should be given to saving time and cost by means of assessors (O. 33, r. 2(c)) or the appointment of a Court expert (O. 40).

XVI. DOCUMENTS

16.1 The efficient preparation of documents for the use on any hearing is a very important part of commercial litigation. This applies both to summonses and to trials. To this end:

(a) Bundles should be paginated, fully legible and of a convenient size.

(b) Bundles should have an identification and be labelled on their exterior with the short title of the action and a description of their contents.

(c) Bundles of correspondence and similar documents should be arranged chronologically; for bundles not being arranged chronologically, indices and dividers (or flags) are normally appropriate and documents should always bear their date on the first page.

(d) Where a bundle is made up from documents originating from more than one source, as for example a sequence from the exhibits to more than one affidavit or from the discovery of more than one party, the individual copy documents used should, unless this is clearly unnecessary, have on them an indication of their origin.

(e) Where a document needs to be transcribed to make it fully legible or to be translated, the transcription or translation should be clearly marked and identified and adjacent to the original document.

(f) All bundles should be suitably secured having regard to the use that will have to be made of them. Bundles for use for counsel and the Court at a trial are usually best placed in lever-arch files so that additions and rearrangements can be made as the need arises; but such bundles are less easy for witnesses to use than ordinary ring binders.

(g) For the trial a handy sized core bundle should (unless clearly unnecessary) also be provided containing the really important documents upon which the case will turn or to which repeated reference will have to be made. The documents in this bundle should normally be paginated but should also bear the reference to where they may be found in the main bundles. The bundles supplied to the Court should be contained in a loose-leaf file which can easily have further documents added to it if wished.

(h) Bundles and their pagination should be agreed in sufficient time before any hearing for counsel to be able to prepare for the hearing by reference to that pagination and to include it in their skeleton arguments. For summonses this should be at the latest 2 clear days before the hearing. For trials the latest time should ordinarily be about 3 weeks before the fixed date and the standard direction reflects this. Where oral witnesses are to be called at the trial, an appropriate set of bundles must also be provided for use in the witness-box.

16.2 A common error is to copy for the trial or other hearing far more documents than can reasonably be thought to be relevant or necessary. Copying costs are often a considerable cause of expense to the litigants. Accordingly, consideration must always be given to what documents are and are not relevant and necessary and only those that are included. It is recognised that a balance has to be struck between the cost of selecting documents for exclusion and the savings in having only the relevant documents but, in cases where the Court is of the opinion that costs have been wasted by the copying of unnecessary documents, the Court will have no hesitation in making a special order for costs against the relevant person.

16.3 The preparation of bundles of documents for trials and other hearings requires a high level of co-operation between the practitioners concerned. It is their duty to give this co-operation, and this is what ordinarily occurs. The unnecessary copying or duplication of documents or bundles, as will occur if there is a lack of co-operation, must be avoided. Where a party fails to co-operate and costs are thrown away the person responsible must expect to have to bear them.

16.4 In the ordinary course it is the responsibility of the plaintiff or applicant to prepare the bundles for the trial or other hearing. Where documents are required from other parties as well for inclusion in the bundles (e.g., composite bundles prepared in accordance with paragraph 16.1 (c) or (d) above), legible copies of those documents must ordinarily be supplied to the applicant at the latest 4 clear days before the return date of the summons, or to the plaintiff at the latest 5 weeks before the trial date. Where documents from the defendant or respondent are to be separately bundled, that party must prepare its own bundles unless it has, not later than the times previously stated, supplied legible copies to the plaintiff or applicant. The party preparing the bundles should, as a matter of course, provide the other parties in the trial or hearing with a set of the bundles within the timescale set out in paragraph 16.1(h) above and any additional copies may be provided on request. The cost of any bundles supplied should be paid for by the party receiving them.

16.5 Doubt sometimes arises concerning the status of documents in an agreed bundle. When bundles are agreed, the parties should also settle—

(a) whether they are doing no more than agree the composition and pagination of the bundles,

(b) whether they are also agreeing the authenticity of the documents even if any of them were not disclosed on discovery,

(c) whether they are also agreeing that any documents may be treated as evidence of the facts stated in them even though not covered by any Civil Evidence Act notice.

As a matter of good practice a party should always expressly make it clear if he disputes the authenticity of a document (see paragraph 11.4 above) or if he is expecting an agreement to waive the strict requirements of the Civil Evidence Acts.

16.6 Subject to the foregoing and the other provisions of this Guide, reference should also be made to the general Practice Direction dated 21st July 1983 (The Supreme Court Practice (1988) p.655).

XVII. PREPARATION FOR LONG TRIALS

17.1 Cases which will require exceptionally long trials can usually be identified at an early stage. They may involve a multiplicity of parties and a number of related proceedings, maybe third party proceedings, maybe proceedings started by other writs but having a related subject matter. Having been identified they should be the subject of appropriate planning and co-operation. They may be suitable for the early issue of the summons for directions.

17.2 It may be appropriate to ask the Court to allocate a single Judge, possibly with an alternate, to hear any interlocutory applications and/or to supervise the preparations for trial. (The allocation of a single Judge may limit the choice of dates for interlocutory hearings.) The Judge would normally be the Judge expected to take the trial. It will probably be desirable to direct that a pre-trial review should be held before the trial Judge between 8 and 4 weeks before the fixed date.

17.3 The pre-trial review should be attended by the counsel who are to represent the parties at the trial and has the purpose of enabling an informed discussion and assessment to take place of what will be involved in the trial, agreement about the best way for it to be conducted, and for any appropriate directions to be given by the Court. The possible advantages of preliminary issues should again be considered as should the organisation of the trial with some issues or topics being dealt with together or before others. Agreement can be reached or, if necessary, directions given to cover the order in which witnesses are going to be called and the manner in which they should give their evidence, the organisation of the documents, and generally the programming of the trial.

17.4 Because of the complexity of such cases it may be necessary to produce summaries of the pleadings which identify the issues, or main issues, that are raised by them. Similarly, other documents may have to be prepared beyond those normally required. At the trial there will be a greater need for documentary aids to advocacy. Both for opening statements and final speeches documents are required which set out the findings of fact asked for and the references to the evidence said to support them. The difference from an ordinary case is one of degree but the practitioners need to be provided with a time-table which takes account of the need to produce such documents. Precisely how much is done in writing and how much orally will depend on the circumstances of each case but the Court will expect counsel to make efficient use of documentary aids.

17.5 The volume of documents necessitates special consideration being given to the preparation of bundles and the segregation and, wherever possible, the exclusion of the marginally relevant. The volume of the documents can itself be an obstacle to the conduct of the trial. The technology available for the recording or presentation of documents is constantly improving and the Court is always willing to consider the use of technology by the parties to render the handling of documents and transcripts more efficient and less costly.

17.6 In view of the amount of Court time that is committed to providing fixed dates for long trials it is particularly important that parties observe the time-tables that have been laid down and keep the Clerk of the Commercial Court informed, in confidence, of any prospects of settlement.

XVIII. PRE-TRIAL CHECK-LIST

18.1 Unless an express order has been made to the contrary, the solicitors must not later than 2 months before the fixed date and without further reminder, lodge with the Clerk to the Commercial Court a completed pre-trial check-list in the form set out in Appendix VI (serving copies on the other parties at the same time). The completion of the check-list assists the parties themselves to check their readiness for the trial and lodging it with the Court at the time stated is an important aspect of the efficient organisation of the Commercial Court list.

18.2 If any party fails to lodge a check-list at the time stated, the case will ordinarily be then listed in chambers before the Commercial Judge so that the party in default can give his explanation and the Court can consider whether the trial date should be vacated. The costs of this hearing will ordinarily have to be borne by the solicitor(s) at fault. It is no excuse for the failure to lodge a check-list that some of the answers will be unsatisfactory.

18.3 Where the answers in the check-list indicate that the directions previously given have not been complied with or there is other indication that the case will not be ready for trial on the fixed date, the case will likewise be listed in chambers before the Commercial Judge so that he can consider whether the trial date should be vacated. If any party has been in default an adverse costs order may be made.

18.4 The check-list procedure in no way relieves the parties from complying with the directions that have been given or applying for any variation of those directions or for further directions in the ordinary way. The Commercial Judge may or may not give further directions when the case is listed before him under either of the preceding paragraphs.

XIX. THE TRIAL

19.1 The over-riding consideration in the conduct of the trial is to do, and be seen to do, justice between the parties with efficiency and without wasting costs. The trial is usually the most expensive part of the litigation. The Court will always co-operate with the parties in the saving of costs as, for example, by agreeing to the submission of documentary material and reading documents out of court. It will positively discourage oral procedures which are wasteful of time and costs without compensating advantage. Throughout the hearing every effort must be made to avoid prolonged reading aloud of documents and authorities.

19.2 *Preparation*: The bundles for the use of the Court, including in particular the pleadings bundle (together with all directions given in the action and any other relevant orders made at an earlier stage) and the core bundle, must be prepared in accordance with the preceding sections of this Guide and lodged with the Clerk of the Commercial Court (Room 61) not later than 3 clear days before the fixed date. Counsel for the plaintiffs, or other party to start at the trial, should not later than 2 clear days before the start of the trial lodge (with copies at the same time to their opponents)—

   (a) a chronology of the relevant events with references to the documents;
   (b) a *"dramatis personae"* where the number of companies and individuals and/or their inter-relationship warrants it and a list of the witnesses that each of the parties have indicated an intention to call;
   (c) a skeleton argument which should concisely list the issues which remain for trial with cross-references as appropriate to the pleadings, summarise the plaintiffs' case in relation to each of them with references to the key documents relied upon, and summarise the propositions of law to be advanced with references to the main authorities to be relied on.

The other counsel should each similarly not later than one clear day before the start of the trial provide to the Court (with copies at the same time to their opponents) a skeleton argument concisely stating the nature of their case on each of the issues to be tried; the character and length of this document will depend on the circumstances and whether there is any counterclaim or third party proceedings.

19.3 *The Opening*: Counsel's opening should be no longer than the circumstances require and should not, save at the request of the Judge, develop the submissions. It should be possible for the plaintiff's case and the issues to be tried to be explained to the Court fairly shortly by reference to the plaintiff's skeleton and the other documents provided. How various documents are dealt with during the opening will very much depend upon the circumstances: the Judge may be invited to rise and read documents to himself; the reading of documents may be left until the oral witnesses are in the witness box; counsel can take the Judge through documents providing him with cross-references, identifying the passages particularly relied upon, giving him an overview of the documentary side of the case and answering any questions he has about them. Whether the second of these courses is advantageous depends upon how the oral witnesses are going to give their evidence in chief; if it is in substance to be by production of their signed statements, it will usually be better for the Judge to have read the documents before-hand. What is to be avoided is the unnecessary reading out of documents aloud and duplication. The other counsel will usually each be invited to make a short statement based upon their own skeleton arguments at the end of the plaintiff's opening.

19.4 *The Evidence*: As previously indicated, the Judge may give directions about the order in which various topics and witnesses are taken. Oral witnesses should in any event give the uncontroversial or routine parts of their evidence by reference to their statements and in most cases can, subject to new matters which have arisen, simply adopt their signed statements (or reports) leaving their evidence to be probed and amplified in unrestricted cross-examination (and if appropriate in re-examination). There is rarely anything to be gained by simply taking a witness in chief through matters on which he has already set out his evidence in a signed statement or report; the effect of the standard direction (see paragraph 14.3) is that any party wishing to lead evidence orally from a witness in chief must be prepared to satisfy the Judge that such a course is justified. Where an interpreter is required, care must be taken by the solicitor for the party calling the relevant witness to see that the interpreter has sufficient ability to interpret the taking of evidence in court and is familiar with the commercial and technical words that will be used.

19.5 *Final Speeches*: Unless otherwise ordered or agreed, the first speech shall be by the plaintiff and the second by the defendant, with the plaintiff having a right of reply. The extent to which submissions are made in writing or aided by written material must depend upon the circumstances in each case. There is a right to make oral submissions and written submissions are usually only used with the agreement of the Court and counsel as a means of restricting the scope and length of the oral submissions. In heavy cases their use can save time and costs, particularly where there are a large number of matters to be covered; in other cases they would merely be productive of delay and can involve the parties in additional costs in their preparation. However, as on other hearings, it is advantageous and economical for counsel to submit a skeleton argument on matters of law together with references to legal authorities and to identify the findings of fact asked for in the light of the evidence given during the trial, together with the references to the evidence where necessary. What such documents need to consist of depends on the nature of the issues in the action and their complexity. Transcript references should be dealt with entirely in writing unless the Judge otherwise requests or the circumstances of the case demand.

19.6 *The Judgment*: Where judgment is reserved the Judge will often deliver his judgment by handing down the written text of his judgment without reading it out in court. In such cases he will ordinarily supply to counsel, the day before judgment is to be delivered, a copy of the draft text. The purpose of supplying this text is so that counsel may be ready to deal with any points arising when the judgment is delivered; any requirement to treat the text as confidential must be complied with. The judgment does not take effect until formally delivered in open court; copies will then be made available to the parties and law-reporters and to any other person requesting to see the text of the judgment. The Judge may direct that the written judgment may be used for all purposes as the text of the judgment and that no transcript need be made.

XX. PROCEDURES AFTER THE TRIAL

20.1 Unless, on the application of any party to the action, the Judge otherwise orders, all proceedings for the enforcement of any judgment or order for the payment of money in actions in the Commercial List are automatically referred to the Masters of the Queen's Bench Division. (See the direction of Mr Justice Lloyd, 1982, Appendix I.) Any applications in connection with such enforcement should accordingly be made, not to the Commercial Judge, but to the designated Queen's Bench Master.

20.2 Where judgment is entered in default for damages or interest to be assessed, such assessment will, in the absence of some different direction or order, be heard and determined by a Queen's Bench Master. (See O. 37, r. 1 and the Direction of Hobhouse J., 12th March 1990, Appendix I.)

20.3 Applications to continue, vary or discharge injunctions or undertakings should still be made to the Judge. If a party wishes to continue a *Mareva* injunction after trial or judgment, the application should be made to a Judge before the previous injunction has expired.

APPENDIX J

PRECEDENTS[1]

J(1) SUMMONS FOR LEAVE TO APPEAL

IN THE HIGH COURT OF JUSTICE
QUEEN'S BENCH DIVISION
COMMERCIAL COURT

IN THE MATTER OF THE ARBITRATION ACTS 1950–79
AND
IN THE MATTER OF AN ARBITRATION

BETWEEN:

BLACK SHIPPING COMPANY LIMITED

Plaintiffs
(Owners)

and

BROWN SUGAR COMPANY LIMITED

Defendants
(Charterers)

LET the BROWN SUGAR COMPANY LIMITED of 69 Treacle Street, London, SE1, attend before the Judge in the Commercial Court, Royal Courts of Justice, Strand, London, WC2A 2LL on   day the   day of   19   at   in the   noon on the hearing of an application by the above named Plaintiffs (hereinafter referred to as "the Owners") pursuant to s. 1(3)(b) of the Arbitration Act 1979 for an Order that the Owners have leave to appeal to the High Court on the questions of law arising out of an Award dated 3rd September 1993 made by Frederick Ackroyd Haphazard as a sole arbitrator in an arbitration between the Owners and the Defendants (hereinafter referred to as "the Charterers") namely:

(i) whether on the facts found the Charterparty between the Owners and the Charterers dated November 24th 1990 terminated at midnight on February 21st 1991 by reason of the Charterers' repudiation thereof.

(ii) whether the Owners were obliged to accept the Charterers repudiation of the said contract if the Charterers established that the Owners had "no legitimate interest" in keeping the contract in existence and

(iii) if the answer to (i) is "yes", whether on the facts found the Owners had "no legitimate interest" in keeping the contract in existence.

on the grounds set out in the Notice of Motion herein (and in the affidavit of Percival Feeble-Tryon served herewith);

---

1. The precedents included in this Appendix are taken from *The Practice and Procedure of the Commercial Court* (3rd edn., 1990), with the generous agreement of the author, The Hon, Mr Justice Colman.

AND for an order that the costs of and incidental to this application be paid by the Charterers

Dated the   day of   19
To: [Defendants' Solicitors]
This Summons was taken out by Messrs   of   Solicitors for the Plaintiffs.

J(2) ORIGINATING NOTICE OF MOTION FOR APPEAL

IN THE HIGH COURT OF JUSTICE
QUEEN'S BENCH DIVISION
COMMERCIAL COURT

IN THE MATTER OF THE ARBITRATION ACTS 1950 TO 1979
AND
IN THE MATTER OF AN ARBITRATION

BETWEEN:

BLACK SHIPPING COMPANY LIMITED

Applicants
Owners

and

BROWN SUGAR COMPANY LIMITED

Respondents
Charterers

ORIGINATING NOTICE OF MOTION FOR APPEAL

TAKE NOTICE that the High Court of Justice Queen's Bench Division Commercial Court at the Royal Courts of Justice, Strand, London, WC2A 2LL will be moved on the expiration of   clear days after the service of this notice or as soon thereafter as Counsel can be heard, by Counsel on behalf of the above named Applicants (hereinafter referred to as "Owners") FOR AN ORDER that the Arbitration Award dated 3rd September 1993 made by Frederick Ackroyd Haphazard as a sole arbitrator in an arbitration between the Owners and the Respondents (hereinafter referred to as "the Charterers") be varied to the effect that

(1) the declaration made in the award declaring that the Charterparty dated November 24th 1990 terminated at midnight on February 21st 1991 be set aside and/or reversed
(2) the Owners are awarded
    (i) $1,000,000, this being the unpaid hire due under the Charterparty 1st February –31st December 1991
    (ii) Interest on the above sum at a rate of 17% per annum.
(3) the Charterers bear and pay their own and the Owners costs of the arbitration and the costs of the Award, such costs to be taxed if not agreed.

AND FOR AN Order that the costs of and incidental to this appeal be paid by the Charterers such costs to be taxed if not agreed.

AND FURTHER TAKE NOTICE that the grounds of this appeal are as follows:

(1) That on the facts found and as a matter of law the conclusions of the Arbitrator (as set out in the Award) are clearly wrong and/or are such that could not have been reached by a reasonable Arbitrator.

(2) That the Arbitrator having held that the Charterers repudiated the Charterparty by intimating their intention not to pay any further hire for the vessel erred in law in some or all of the following respects.

    (i) In concluding that the Charterers were entitled to a declaration that the Charterparty terminated automatically by reason of their own repudiation thereof: see Award, para.—.

    (ii) In holding that the Owners should have accepted the Charterers' repudiation by midnight on February 21st 1991: see Reasons, para.—.

    (iii) In failing to apply the principles of law, established by the *ratio decidendi* of *White and Carter (Councils) Limited* v. *McGregor* [1962] A.C. 413, that an injured party is entitled to elect whether or not to accept repudiation by the other party or hold him to the contract: see Reasons, para.—.

    (iv) In failing to apply the principle of law that an unaccepted repudiation/renunciation of a contract is a "thing writ in water".

    (v) In holding that, notwithstanding that the Owners had no obligation to accept the Charterers' repudiation in February 1991, the Owners had no legitimate interest in pursuing their claim for hire rather than a claim for damages: see Reasons, para.—.

    (vi) Having held that the vessel remained at Charterers' disposal at an anchorage off London until the expiry of the time charter period on 31st December 1991, in failing to hold that the Owners were entitled to a declaration that the Charterparty remained in force and that the vessel was on hire until the said date: see Award, para.—.

(3) That, in the premises, the Arbitrator should not have awarded the Charterers the declaration referred to in (2)(i) herein and their costs of the arbitration, but should have awarded the Owners:

    (i) $1,000,000, this being the unpaid hire due 1st February–31st December 1991

    (ii) Interest on the above sum at a rate of 17% per annum,

and the Arbitrator should have further ordered that the Charterers bear and pay their own and the Owners' costs of the arbitration and the costs of the Award.

DATED the   day of   19

J(3) ORIGINATING SUMMONS FOR AN ORDER DIRECTING THE ARBITRATOR TO STATE FURTHER REASONS[1]

IN THE HIGH COURT OF JUSTICE   19   B No.
QUEEN'S BENCH DIVISION
COMMERCIAL COURT

IN THE MATTER OF THE ARBITRATION ACTS 1950 TO 1979
AND
IN THE MATTER OF AN ARBITRATION

---

1. The form prescribed by R.S.C. Order 73, rule 3.

BETWEEN:

BLACK SHIPPING COMPANY LIMITED

Plaintiff

and

BROWN SUGAR COMPANY LIMITED

First Defendants

and

FREDERICK ACKROYD HAPHAZARD[2]

Second Defendant

LET ALL PARTIES attend the Judge in the Commercial Court, Royal Courts of Justice, Strand, London, on   day the   day of   19   , at   o'clock in the forenoon, on the hearing of an application by the above named Plaintiff pursuant to s. 1(5) of the Arbitration Act 1979 that the arbitrator should state further reasons for his holding that "the Owners had no legitimate interest in pursuing their claim for hire rather than a claim for damages" and that the said reasons should include:

(1) The reason why the owners did not have a "legitimate interest" in continuing the charterparty at midnight on 21st February 1991, and

(2) The submissions advanced at the hearing on the question of the Owners' legitimate interest by (a) the Plaintiff and (b) the First Defendants, indicating which submissions he rejected and which he accepted.

AND let the Defendants etc. . . . .[3]

J(4) ORIGINATING MOTION FOR THE DECISION OF A PRELIMINARY POINT OF LAW[1]

IN THE HIGH COURT OF JUSTICE   19   B No.
QUEEN'S BENCH DIVISION
COMMERCIAL COURT

IN THE MATTER OF THE ARBITRATION ACTS 1950 TO 1979
AND
IN THE MATTER OF AN ARBITRATION

BETWEEN:

BLACK SHIPPING COMPANY LIMITED

Applicants
Owners

and

BROWN SUGAR COMPANY LIMITED

Respondents
Charterers

NOTICE OF ORIGINATING MOTION

2. The arbitrator must be served with the summons under R.S.C. Order 73, rule 3(4).
3. Thereafter as per the formal parts of Form No. 10 in R.S.C., Vol. 2, Appendix A.
1. The form prescribed by R.S.C. Order 73, rule 2(1)(e).

TAKE NOTICE that the High Court of Justice Queen's Bench Division Commercial Court at the Royal Courts of Justice, Strand, London, WC2A 2LL, will be moved on the expiration of   clear days after the service of this notice or as soon thereafter as Counsel can be heard, by Counsel on behalf of the above named Applicants for the determination by the High Court pursuant to s. 2(1)(a)[2] of the Arbitration Act 1979 of the following question of law which has arisen in the course of an arbitration between the Applicants and the Respondents before Frederick Ackroyd Haphazard, namely:

Whether an agent acting within his actual or ostensible authority, made a statement which was untrue in circumstances where he had no reasonable grounds to believe that it was true, could be held liable for that statement under the Misrepresentation Act 1967 s. 2(1)?

AND for an Order that the Respondents pay the costs of and incidental to this application.

DATED the   day of   19

2. If the application is made with the consent of the arbitrator or umpire: section 2(1)(b) if it is made with the consent of the parties.

APPENDIX K

MODEL EXCLUSION CLAUSES

K(1) EXCLUSION CLAUSE IN SHORT FORM FOR FUTURE DISPUTES TO TAKE EFFECT BEFORE THE COMMENCEMENT OF THE ARBITRATION

Exclusion clause in short form for inclusion in a contract or arbitration clause for the purposes of the Arbitration Act 1979 relating to future disputes and to take effect before the commencement of the arbitration.

The parties agree to exclude any right of application under section 2 or appeal to the High Court under section 1(2) of the Arbitration Act 1979 with respect to any question of law arising in the course of the reference or out of any award.

K(2) EXCLUSION AGREEMENT FOR FUTURE DISPUTES TO TAKE EFFECT BEFORE THE COMMENCEMENT OF THE ARBITRATION

Exclusion agreement for the purposes of the Arbitration Act 1979 relating to future disputes and to take effect before the commencement of the arbitration.

THIS EXCLUSION AGREEMENT is made the   day of   BETWEEN   [names and addresses etc of the parties]

WHEREAS
(1) The parties entered into an agreement dated   (date) [character of the agreement for example, for the sale of certain goods]
(2) The agreement contains an arbitration clause under which all disputes and differences arising between the parties should be determined by arbitration
(3) The parties wish that any such future disputes shall be determined finally by the Arbitrator

IT IS AGREED in accordance with the Arbitration Act 1979 Section 3 that the right of appeal by either party to the High Court under section 1 of that Act shall be excluded in relation to the award of the Arbitrator and that neither party shall have the right to apply to the High Court under Section 2(1)(a) of that Act for the determination of any question of law arising in the course of the reference to arbitration.

AS WITNESS etc

[signatures of the parties]

K(3) EXCLUSION AGREEMENT FOR EXISTING DISPUTES ENTERED INTO AFTER THE COMMENCEMENT OF THE ARBITRATION

Exclusion agreement for the purposes of the Arbitration Act 1979 relating to existing disputes and entered into after the commencement of the arbitration

I

THIS EXCLUSION AGREEMENT is made the   day of   BETWEEN   [*names and addresses etc of parties*]

WHEREAS
(1) The parties are the parties to a contract dated   [*date*]
(2) A dispute has arisen between them as to   [*nature of dispute*]
(3) In accordance with clause   of the contract   [*arbitrator(s)*] ("the Arbitrator[s]") [has *or* have] been appointed arbitrator[s] to determine that dispute
(4) The parties desire that the dispute shall be determined finally by the Arbitrator[s]

NOW IT IS AGREED in accordance with the Arbitration Act 1979 Section 3 that the right of appeal by either party to the High Court under Section 1 of that Act shall be excluded in relation to the award of the Arbitrator[s] on the above-recited dispute and that neither party shall have the right to apply to the High Court under Section 2(1)(a) of that Act for the determination of any question of law arising in the course of the reference to arbitration.

AS WITNESS etc

[*signatures of all parties*]

II

IN THE MATTER OF THE ARBITRATION ACTS 1950–1979
AND
IN THE MATTER OF AN ARBITRATION BETWEEN

Claimant

and

Respondent

EXCLUSION AGREEMENT

We the undersigned having referred to arbitration the dispute that has arisen under the contract between us dated the   day of   and having appointed   to be Arbitrator in the reference HEREBY AGREE pursuant to Section 3 of the Arbitration Act 1979 that the jurisdiction of the High Court under Sections 1 and 2 of the said Act in respect of this Arbitration shall be excluded.

Signed by or on behalf of the Claimant by:
Dated this   day of   19

Signed by or on behalf of the Respondent by:
Dated this   day of   19

ADMIRALTY JURISDICTION OF THE HIGH COURT

SUPREME COURT ACT 1981, SECTION 20

Admiralty jurisdiction

Admiralty jurisdiction of High Court

20.—(1) The Admiralty jurisdiction of the High Court shall be as follows, that is to say—

(a) jurisdiction to hear and determine any of the questions and claims mentioned in subsection (2);

(b) jurisdiction in relation to any of the proceedings mentioned in subsection (3);

(c) any other Admiralty jurisdiction which it had immediately before the commencement of this Act; and

(d) any jurisdiction connected with ships or aircraft which is vested in the High Court apart from this section and is for the time being by rules of court made or coming into force after the commencement of this Act assigned to the Queen's Bench Division and directed by the rules to be exercised by the Admiralty Court.

(2) The questions and claims referred to in subsection (1)(a) are—

(a) any claim to the possession or ownership of a ship or to the ownership of any share therein;

(b) any question arising between the co-owners of a ship as to possession, employment or earnings of that ship;

(c) any claim in respect of a mortgage of or charge on a ship or any share therein;

(d) any claim for damage received by a ship;

(e) any claim for damage done by a ship;

(f) any claim for loss of life or personal injury sustained in consequence of any defect in a ship or in her apparel or equipment, or in consequence of the wrongful act, neglect or default of—

    (i) the owners, charterers or persons in possession or control of a ship; or

    (ii) the master or crew of a ship, or any other person for whose wrongful acts, neglects or defaults the owners, charterers or persons in possession or control of a ship are responsible,

being an act, neglect or default in the navigation or management of the ship, in the loading, carriage or discharge of goods on, in or from the ship, or in the embarkation, carriage or disembarkation of persons on, in or from the ship;

(g) any claim for loss of or damage to goods carried in a ship;

(h) any claim arising out of any agreement relating to the carriage of goods in a ship or to the use or hire of a ship;

(j) any claim in the nature of salvage (including any claim arising by virtue of the application, by or under [section 87 of the Civil Aviation Act 1982], of the law relating to salvage to aircraft and their apparel and cargo);

(k) any claim in the nature of towage in respect of a ship or an aircraft;

(l) any claim in the nature of pilotage in respect of a ship or an aircraft;

(m) any claim in respect of goods or materials supplied to a ship for her operation or maintenance;

(n) any claim in respect of the construction, repair or equipment of a ship or in respect of dock charges or dues;

(o) any claim by a master or member of the crew of a ship for wages (including any sum allotted out of wages or adjudged by a superintendent to be due by way of wages);

(p) any claim by a master, shipper, charterer or agent in respect of disbursements made on account of a ship;

(q) any claim arising out of an act which is or is claimed to be a general average act;

(r) any claim arising out of bottomry;

(s) any claim for the forfeiture or condemnation of ship or of goods which are being or have been carried, or have been attempted to be carried, in a ship, or for the restoration of a ship or any such goods after seizure, or for droits of Admiralty.

(3) The proceedings referred to in subsection (1)(b) are—

(a) any application to the High Court under the Merchant Shipping Acts 1894 to 1979 other than an application under section 55 of the Merchant Shipping Act 1894 for the appointment of a person to act as a substitute for a person incapable of acting;

(b) any action to enforce a claim for damage, loss of life or personal injury arising out of—
    (i) a collision between ships; or
    (ii) the carrying out of or omission to carry out a manoeuvre in the case of one or more of two or more ships; or
    (iii) non-compliance, on the part of one or more of two or more ships, with the collision regulations;

(c) any action by shipowners or other persons under the Merchant Shipping Acts 1894 to 1979 for the limitation of the amount of their liability in connection with a ship or other property.

(4) The jurisdiction of the High Court under subsection (2)(b) includes power to settle any account outstanding and unsettled between the parties in relation to the ship, and to direct that the ship, or any share thereof, shall be sold, and to make such other order as the court thinks fit.

(5) Subsection (2)(e) extends to—

(a) any claim in respect of a liability incurred under the Merchant Shipping (Oil Pollution) Act 1971; and

(b) any claim in respect of a liability falling on the International Oil Pollution Compensation Fund under Part I of the Merchant Shippping Act 1974.

(6) The reference in subsection (2)(j) to claims in the nature of salvage includes a reference to such claims for services rendered in saving life from a ship or an aircraft or in preserving cargo, apparel or wreck as, under sections 544 to 546 of the Merchant Shipping Act 1894, or any Order in Council made under [section 87 of the Civil Aviation Act 1982], are authorised to be made in connection with a ship or an aircraft.

(7) The preceding provisions of this section apply—

(a) in relation to all ships or aircraft, whether British or not and whether registered or not and wherever the residence or domicile of their owners may be;

(b) in relation to all claims, wherever arising (including, in the case of cargo or wreck salvage, claims in respect of cargo or wreck found on land); and

(c) so far as they relate to mortgages and charges, to all mortgages or charges, whether registered or not and whether legal or equitable, including mortgages and charges created under foreign law:

Provided that nothing in this subsection shall be construed as extending the cases in which money or property is recoverable under any of the provisions of the Merchant Shipping Acts 1894 to 1979.

INDEX